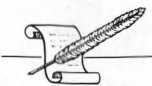

# HISTORIC
# DOCUMENTS
# OF
# 1981

Cumulative Index 1977-81

Congressional Quarterly Inc.

Printed in the United States of America

Congressional Quarterly Inc.
1414 22nd St. N.W., Washington, D.C. 20037

The Library of Congress cataloged the first issue of this title as follows:

Historic documents. 1972—
    Washington. Congressional Quarterly Inc.

1. United States—Politics and government—1945— —Yearbooks.
2. World politics—1945— —Yearbooks. I.Congressional Quarterly Inc.

E839.5.H57                    917.3'03'9205                    72-97888
ISBN 0-87187-229-3

# FOREWORD

Publication of *Historic Documents of 1981* carries through a tenth year the project launched by Congressional Quarterly with *Historic Documents 1972*. The purpose of this continuing series of volumes is to give students, scholars, librarians, journalists and citizens convenient access to documents of basic importance in the broad range of public affairs.

To place the documents in perspective, each entry is preceded by a brief introduction containing background materials, in some cases a short summary of the document itself and, where necessary, relevant subsequent developments. We believe these introductions will prove increasingly useful in future years when the events and questions now covered are less fresh in one's memory and the documents may be difficult to find or unobtainable.

Among the events chronicled in 1981 were the inauguration of President Ronald Reagan and the simultaneous release of Americans held hostage in Iran for 444 days. But the euphoria was dimmed by continuing economic problems, which the new administration promptly tackled with an unconventional program of budget and tax cuts coupled with increased defense spending. By August, against heavy odds, most of the president's program was in place and a new word, "Reaganomics," had been added to the language.

The year also saw a rash of violence directed against public figures, including Egyptian President Anwar al-Sadat, who was killed, and President Reagan and Pope John Paul II, who survived assassination attempts.

For women the year was a mixed success, with Sandra Day O'Connor becoming the first female justice of the Supreme Court, but with setbacks experienced in the efforts to win more time for state approval of the Equal Rights Amendment and to eliminate all-male draft registration.

These and other developments added substantially to the usual outpouring of presidential statements, court decisions, committee reports, special studies and speeches of national or international importance. We have selected for inclusion in this book as many as possible of the documents that in our judgment will be of more than transitory interest. Where space limitations prevented reproduction of the full texts, the excerpts used were chosen to set forth the essential and, at the same time, to preserve the flavor of the materials.

Carolyn Goldinger
Editor

Washington, D.C.
March 1982

174919

# Historic Documents of 1981

*Editor:* Carolyn Goldinger
*Contributing Editors:* John L. Moore, Martha V. Gottron
*Contributors:* Nancy A. Blanpied, Prentice Bowsher,
        Suzanne de Lesseps, James R. Ingram, Nancy
        Lammers, Mary McNeil, Elizabeth H. Summers,
        Margaret C. Thompson
*Cumulative Index:* Nancy A. Blanpeid

## Book Department

David R. Tarr   *Director*
Joanne D. Daniels   *Director, CQ Press*
John L. Moore   *Associate Editor*
Michael D. Wormser   *Associate Editor*
Martha V. Gottron   *Senior Editor*
Barbara R. de Boinville   *Senior Editor, CQ Press*
Susan Sullivan   *Developmental Editor, CQ Press*
Margaret C. Thompson   *Assistant Editor*
Diane C. Hill   *Editor/Writer*
Sari Horwitz   *Editor/Writer*
Nancy Lammers   *Editor/Writer*
Mary McNeil   *Editor/Writer*
Janet Hoffman   *Indexer*
Carolyn Goldinger   *Researcher/Editorial Assistant*
Patricia M. Russotto   *Researcher*
Esther D. Wyss   *Researcher*
Patricia Ann O'Connor   *Contributing Editor*
Elder Witt   *Contributing Editor*

## Congressional Quarterly Inc.

Eugene Patterson   *Editor and President*
Wayne P. Kelley   *Publisher*
Peter A. Harkness   *Executive Editor*
Robert C. Hur   *General Manager*
I.D. Fuller   *Production Manager*
Maceo Mayo   *Assistant Production Manager*
Sydney E. Garriss   *Computer Services*

# How to Use This Book

The documents are arranged in chronological order. If you know the approximate date of the report, speech, statement, court decision or other document you are looking for, glance through the titles for that month in the Table of Contents below.

If the Table of Contents does not lead you directly to the document you want, make a double check by turning to the Index at the end of the book. There you may find references not only to the particular document you seek but also to other entries on the same or a related subject. The Index in this volume is a **five-year cumulative index** of Historic Documents covering the years 1977-1981.

The introduction to each document is printed in italic type. The document itself, printed in roman type, follows the spelling, capitalization and punctuation of the original or official copy. In some cases, boldface headings in brackets have been added to highlight the organization of the text. Where the full text is not given, omissions of material are indicated by the customary ellipsis points.

# TABLE OF CONTENTS

## January

# February

# March

# April

### Pardon of Miller and Felt

### Maxim Shostakovich Defection

### Commemoration of the Holocaust

# May

### Freedom of Information

### Death of IRA Hunger Striker

# June

# July

# August

# September

# October

# November

# December

# HISTORIC
# DOCUMENTS
# OF
# 1981

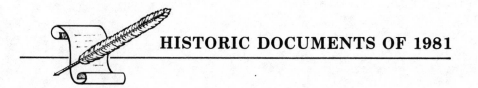 HISTORIC DOCUMENTS OF 1981

# January

# SURGEON GENERAL'S REPORT
# ON 'THE CHANGING CIGARETTE'
## January 12, 1981

*The report of the U.S. surgeon general on the health consequences of smoking, issued January 12, said that the new lower-tar, lower-nicotine cigarettes appeared to provide "some small protection" to smokers from the risk of lung cancer. The report warned, however, that there was little reason to believe that the cigarettes reduced the risk of cardiovascular diseases or a number of other ailments implicated in smoking.*

*Entitled "The Changing Cigarette," the report also raised a new specter for cigarette smokers. Health risks could well be present, it indicated, in the artificial additives used by the manufacturers to bolster flavor diminished by the cigarettes' lower tar and nicotine content. The nature of the additives was unknown both to the public and to the federal government, the report asserted. Moreover, it continued, there were no published data on the additives' "biological effects" or their "combustion products."*

## Background

*In a preface, Dr. Julius B. Richmond, the Carter administration's surgeon general and assistant secretary for health of the Department of Health and Human Services, stated that since 1964, when the surgeon general's first report on smoking was issued, smoking had declined from 40.3 percent of the population to 32.5 percent. Moreover, per capita consumption of cigarettes, he wrote, was at the lowest level since 1957.*

3

Kenneth E. Warner, an associate professor at the University of Michigan's School of Public Health, wrote in the February 1981 issue of Science that up until 1964 cigarette consumption in the country had risen throughout the century. "Continued increases would have been expected in the absence of an antismoking campaign, especially with more women smoking . . . and decreases in the nicotine content of cigarettes," Warner wrote.

The issue of increased numbers of women smoking had been the subject of the 1980 surgeon general's report. In it Richmond had warned that lung cancer would overtake breast cancer as the leading cancer-related cause of death among women. (Historic Documents of 1980, p. 17)

## Lower-Nicotine Cigarettes

The 1981 report indicated that while the newer lower-tar, lower-nicotine cigarettes appeared to reduce slightly the risk of lung cancer, there was little evidence that they had any favorable effect on the incidence of cardiovascular disease, coronary heart disease, other coronary diseases, emphysema, bronchitis or the complications of pregnancy.

The changes in the manufacture of cigarettes had not produced "a clearly demonstrated effect" on cardiovascular disease, the report said, adding that "some studies suggest that a decreased risk of CHD [coronary heart disease] may not have occurred." Indeed, the report said that carbon monoxide gas might be the main link to heart disease in the smoking of cigarettes. If that were true, the reduction in tar and nicotine would have virtually no effect on the risk to smokers of heart disease.

## Artificial Additives

Cigarette advertisements in recent years, the report said, had focused on the flavor of reduced tar and nicotine cigarettes "enhanced presumably by the addition of tobacco constituents or by the addition of new flavoring materials, such as natural or synthetic chemicals." In an article in The New York Times, Robert Reinhold wrote that the additives included "shellac, caramel, eugenol and other chemicals, some of which produce carcinogens when burned."

Speaking at a news conference the day the report was issued, Dr. Richmond said he had been negotiating with the tobacco industry to learn more about the additives. The industry considered such information to be trade secrets and thus protected by law.

A spokesman for the Tobacco Institute, William D. Toohey, called the 1981 report "markedly candid" and more moderate in tone than earlier surgeon general's reports on smoking. Newspaper accounts quoted

*Toohey as saying that the industry was cooperating with the surgeon general in trying to reach an arrangement for the release of information on the additives.*

> *Following are excerpts from "The Changing Cigarette," a report by the surgeon general on the health consequences of smoking, issued January 12, 1981.* (Boldface headings in brackets have been added by Congressional Quarterly to highlight the organization of the text.):

# Introduction

Great changes have taken place in the cigarette product in recent decades. In 1954, the average "tar" yield of the sales-weighted average cigarette was 37 mg and average nicotine yield was 2 mg. In 1980, the comparable figures are expected to be less than 14 mg of "tar" and less than 1 mg of nicotine. No cigarette marketed in the United States in 1979 yielded more than 30 mg of "tar."[1]

Smokers have turned to these new products because of health concerns. In the 1950s, cigarette manufacturers introduced cigarette filters as "health protection" and advertised them widely. The 1964 Report of the Surgeon General's Advisory Committee on Smoking and Health did not discuss cigarette smoke filtration, but in 1966 the Public Health Service reviewed the issue of smoke constituents. That report stated, "The preponderance of scientific evidence strongly suggests that the lower the 'tar' and nicotine content of cigarette smoke, the less harmful would be the effect." Thereafter, Government and tobacco industry scientists conducted studies of cigarette engineering and tobacco cultivation that could lead to lower "tar" and nicotine yields. Later, when new products appeared, cigarette manufacturers aggressively promoted them through advertising.

The request by Congress for an assessment of the "relative health risks associated with smoking cigarettes of varying levels of 'tar,' nicotine, and carbon monoxide," and "the health risks associated with smoking cigarettes containing any substances commonly added to commercially manufactured cigarettes" has come at an appropriate time. In the 2 years since Congress called for the present study, manufacturers have marketed cigarettes that yield as little as 0.01 mg of "tar" when measured by present Federal Trade Commission technology.

The technology of producing lower "tar" cigarettes has progressed well beyond a simple reduction in the amount of tobacco in the cigarette or the removal of a portion of the "tar" by filtration. Present technology has achieved "tar" reduction by alterations in plant genetics, changes in the

---

[1] "Tar" is the term given to the particulate matter of cigarette smoke that is retained by a Cambridge filter pad after extraction of nicotine and water. In this Report, the term "tar" is placed in quotation marks to emphasize that "tar" is not a single constituent but consists of many different chemical constituents and classes of constituents.

cultivation and processing of the tobacco leaf, and changes in cigarette paper and filtration of the cigarette.

The methods used in testing cigarettes by machine may not correspond to the way persons actually smoke. There is evidence to suggest that the cigarette yields measured by machine are very different from the yields that the consumer actually obtains by smoking the cigarette, due in part to the difference in patterns of smoking between testing machines and individual smokers. Therefore, tar measurements of current cigarettes may not reflect the same estimate of risk provided by the "tar" measurement of cigarettes manufactured at the time of the 1966 Public Health Service Review.

Another closely related concern about lower "tar" and nicotine cigarettes is the use of flavorings and other chemical additives. In order to enhance consumer acceptability, flavoring substances are added to cigarettes; it may be that the lower the "tar" yield, the more flavoring additives are used. It is impossible to make an assessment of the risks of these additives, as cigarette manufacturers are not required to reveal what additives they use. No agency of the Federal Government currently exercises oversight or regulatory authority in the manufacture of cigarette products. Further, no agency is empowered to require public or confidential disclosure of the additives actually in use by the cigarette manufacturers.

At the same time that changes have occurred in the cigarette, marked changes have occurred in the smoking patterns of the U.S. population that may have substantially altered the risk of smoking lower "tar" cigarettes. Over recent years, smokers have been taking up regular smoking at younger ages, and the number of women who smoke currently far exceeds the number from several decades previously. The multiplicative risks of smoking and oral contraceptive use is an example of how changes in the population of smokers can make both quantitative and qualitative changes in the nature of the risk. The proportion of the population that smokes has declined, but the average number of cigarettes smoked by each smoker appears to have increased over several decades. Changes have occurred in the environment, dietary habits, and behavioral patterns of the population, which may alter the interaction between cigarette smoking and other risk factors for disease. Thus, we have a continually changing population of smokers who smoke a continually changing cigarette in a continually changing manner....

## [LUNG CANCER AND HEART DISEASE]

... Lung cancer is the disease process in which the relative risk of lower "tar" and nicotine cigarettes has been most clearly evaluated. Approximately 85 percent of the incident cases of lung cancer can be directly attributed to cigarette smoking; there are relatively few problems with changing criteria for classification of cause of death, and there is a clear, linear dose-response relationship. Moreover, the "tar" portion of the smoke probably contains most of the carcinogenic activity of the whole smoke. If the reduction in machine-measured "tar" yield is accompanied by an actual reduction in smoker exposure dose, then there should be a relatively proportionate reduction in lung cancer risk. Lower "tar" cigarettes are associated with a reduction in the risk of developing lung cancer, although the proportionate reduction in risk is substantially less than that of "tar" yield.

A smaller percent reduction in lung cancer risk versus that of measured cigarette "tar" yield could result from several factors, including compensation (such as an increased depth of inhalation or a greater number of cigarettes smoked per day), or from a lack of comparable reductions in other carcinogens.

For several reasons, it is difficult to extrapolate these risk reduction data to the current very low "tar" cigarettes. Because the lower "tar" yield of the cigarettes evaluated in the published studies probably was accomplished predominantly by reducing the weight of tobacco in the cigarette and by removing "tar" through filtration, use of these cigarettes might reasonably be expected to result in a lower smoke exposure if compensation did not occur. It is not clear, however, that the alterations in the techniques of tobacco processing and cigarette manufacture that have produced the very low machine-measured "tar" yields can be expected to result in similar reductions in actual smoker exposure to toxic smoke constituents. In addition, the potential carcinogenic effect of the substances added to these cigarettes has not been evaluated. The demonstrated reduction in mouse skin tumorigenicity of "tar" has not, however, been accompanied by a reduction in the incidence or mortality rates due to lung cancer among humans.

Cigarette smoking is an independent risk factor for coronary heart disease, one that interacts synergistically with other risk factors such as hypertension and hypercholesterolemia. The effect of cigarette smoking in coronary heart disease risk is clearly dose related, and cessation of smoking reduces the risk. Estimation of the impact of varying cigarettes on coronary heart disease risk is difficult, because the exact etiologic agent(s) have not been identified. A number of agents have been suggested to be active in the development of coronary heart disease, including nicotine and carbon monoxide. Any change in risk that might occur because of switching to lower "tar" and nicotine cigarettes might be expected to become evident more rapidly for coronary heart disease risk than for cancer risk, due to the acute effects of cigarette smoke in causing adverse coronary heart disease events such as sudden death.

As in the case of cancer, the expectation that a risk reduction for coronary heart disease would accompany the use of lower "tar" and nicotine cigarettes is based on the premise that the use of lower "tar" cigarettes results in a reduction of exposure to the responsible smoke constituents. This assumption is reasonable if nicotine is a major etiologic agent, because there is a close relationship between the "tar" and nicotine yields for individual cigarettes. That is, among the cigarettes currently available in the United States, a lower "tar" cigarette is also a lower nicotine cigarette.

The variations of the other constituents in the particulate phase of the smoke in relation to "tar" yield is largely unknown, especially in those cigarettes specially formulated to produce very low machine measurements of "tar" yields.


## [CARBON MONOXIDE GAS]


Carbon monoxide is one gas in cigarette smoke that may be closely associated with coronary heart disease risk, perhaps through interference with myocardial oxygenation, enhancement of platelet adhesiveness, or promotion of atherosclerosis. The relationship between carbon monoxide yield and "tar" yield, however, has not been as thoroughly examined as that between "tar" and nicotine. The factors that influence the carbon monoxide yield are closely related to the manufacturing process (e.g., porosity of the paper, filter ventilation, etc.), and therefore may vary somewhat independently of "tar" yield. In addition, the absorption of carbon monoxide is more dependent on depth of inhalation than is the absorption of nicotine and, if the use of lower "tar" products results in a compensatory increase in depth of inhalation, smoker exposure to carbon monoxide may remain unchanged or actually increase. The reality of this concern is borne out by those studies that show no lowering of carboxyhemoglobin levels in smokers who switch to lower "tar" cigarettes. If carbon monoxide is an active etiologic agent for cigarette-related coronary heart disease, and if significant compensatory changes in the style of smoking occur with use of lower "tar" cigarettes, then the risk of coronary heart disease with lower "tar" cigarettes may be similar to, or possibly greater than, the risk of smoking higher "tar" cigarettes.

Some other agents in the gas phase of cigarette smoke have also been suggested as possible contributors to the development of coronary heart disease. Little is known about the relationship between the yield of the gas phase of the smoke and the "tar" yield. The change in formulation that allows the reduction in "tar" yield of the new lower "tar" cigarettes has not been examined for its effect on the yield of individual gas phase constituents. The potential for creating new substances and for increasing the yields of existing gas phase constituents by changes in formulation cannot be assessed from existing data, but may well impact on the risk of coronary heart disease produced by smoking lower "tar" cigarettes.

It is not surprising that the studies looking at the relative risk of lower "tar" cigarettes reviewed in the cardiovascular section have not produced a clear estimate of relative risk, given the difficulty in relating a difference in "tar" yield to a difference in coronary heart disease risk and the existence of gaps in our understanding of the etiologic agents in smoke that cause coronary heart disease. Thus, the impact of a reduction in the "tar" yield of cigarettes on the coronary heart disease risk produced by smoking cannot be estimated at this time.

Approximately 70 percent of chronic obstructive lung disease deaths are attributable to cigarette smoking. The number of deaths attributed to chronic obstructive lung disease is much smaller than the number of lung cancer deaths. This fact, and the relatively long interval of time between the onset of symptomatic chronic airflow limitation and death from respiratory failure, reduce the usefulness of mortality data from chronic lung disease in assessing the relative risks of lower "tar" cigarettes. Therefore, attention has focused on the level of symptoms and measured reductions in air flow for evaluating relative risk of chronic obstructive lung disease.

## [LUNG INJURIES]

As reviewed in the section on chronic obstructive lung disease, there are three major aspects of cigarette-induced lung injury: chronic mucous hypersecretion, airway inflammation and narrowing, and alveolar septal destruction. The causal agents for each type of lung injury may be different, and therefore each type may be affected quite differently by a reduction in the "tar" yield of the cigarette.

The mucous hypersecretion and cough are a response of the lung to the chronic irritant effects of cigarette smoke. To the extent that a reduction in "tar" yield reflects a reduction in smoke exposure, smoking lower "tar" cigarettes should result in reduced cough and sputum production. In the studies that have looked at this question, the expected decrease in cough and sputum production has indeed accompanied the use of lower "tar" cigarettes.

Airflow limitation is not produced by mucous hypersecretion *per se* but rather by airway narrowing and loss of parenchymal lung units. The same studies that showed a reduction in symptoms with the use of lower "tar" cigarettes failed to show a similarly reduced effect on air flow limitation. This finding may indicate that tests of air flow limitation are not sufficiently sensitive to measure the differences in extent of disease. It could also result from a failure to produce lower exposure to the causative agent(s) with the use of lower "tar" cigarettes, either due to a lack of reduction in concentration of the agent(s) or to compensatory changes in smoking behavior....

The relative risks for both the mother and the fetus of smoking lower "tar" and nicotine cigarettes during pregnancy are of great concern, both because of the numbers of young women who smoke and because of younger women's more frequent use of lower "tar" cigarettes. The increased use of cigarettes with lower "tar" yields has not been investigated for its effect on changes in risk of adverse effects of smoking on pregnancy. Accordingly, no reduction in risk relative to higher "tar" and nicotine cigarettes has been demonstrated.

Of particular concern is the potential teratogenic effect of additives and their combustion products. Thus, it is not possible to assume that switching to a lower "tar" cigarette would have an effect in reducing risk during or after pregnancy. It is clear that the only recommendation that can be made to reduce risk in the smoking mother is for her to quit smoking . . . .

## [LOWER 'TAR' CIGARETTES]

In the past few years, cigarettes delivering less than 10 mg of "tar" by FTC test have been placed on the market. These cigarettes apparently employ efficient filters together with various degrees of smoke dilution. The extreme reduction of "tar" and nicotine delivery by these cigarettes suggests significant differences in combustion processes. Substantial differences in the chemical nature of both mainstream and sidestream smoke might result from such changes.

Some or all of the new lower "tar" and nicotine cigarettes are manufactured by processes that involve the use of chemicals or flavor additives to improve consumer acceptability. The nature of these additives, and their combustion products, that are currently used in marketed cigarettes is not available to the public or to the Government. Likewise, there are no published data on the biologic effects of these additives or their combustion products.

Very low yield cigarettes may add to present concerns with respect to sidestream smoke. While these cigarettes may deliver such low levels of "tar," nicotine, and gas phase constituents that smokers cannot compensate completely, the delivery of sidestream smoke may not be reduced. Indeed, the sidestream smoke might contain more of some substances (e.g., pyrolytic products of flavor additives) than does the sidestream smoke of higher yield cigarettes. For very low yield cigarettes, the risk of the sidestream smoke may equal that of the mainstream smoke. The chemical and physical nature of sidestream smoke should be determined on new cigarettes . . . .

## FLAVOR ADDITIVES

The development of lower "tar" and nicotine cigarettes has tended to yield products that lacked the taste components to which the smoker had become accustomed. In order to keep such products acceptable to the consumer, the manufacturers reconstitute aroma or flavor. There are several ways in which this can be achieved. Flavor extracts of tobacco can be added to the lower-yield blends. Other plant extracts can be used to supplement the flavor spectrum, synthetic flavors can be added, or a combination of techniques can be applied. Powdered cocoa, one flavoring additive that is probably used in U.S. cigarettes, has been found to increase mouse skin tumorigenicity of the "tar" from a standard experimental cigarette at each of two dose levels.

The burning of cigarettes with flavor additives produced increased and perhaps novel types of semivolatile agents, including traces of mutagenic compounds. The mutagenic agents were found in the basic fraction of the semivolatile portion obtained from heating the tobacco mixtures. Chemically, the agents thus far identified were substituted pyrazines and other aza-arenes with and without amino groups.

The exact delineation of the chemical structure of additives, their pyrolytic products, the possible carcinogenic properties, and the quantities found in smoke of lower "tar" cigarettes is urgently needed in order to assure the consumer that the filter, lower "tar" and nicotine cigarette does not carry additional or new health risks.

## [HEART DISEASE]

There is evidence from four studies of the association between cardiovascular disease and the use of lower "tar" and nicotine cigarettes. Hammond et al., in their prospective study of volunteers of the American Cancer Society, have shown reductions of 10 to 20 percent in observed coronary deaths among persons smoking lower "tar" and nicotine cigarettes when compared with those who reported smoking similar numbers of regular cigarettes per day. Hawthorne and Fry, in three prospective surveys of over 18,000 persons in west-central Scotland, showed a slightly increased relative coronary mortality in persons who smoked filtered cigarettes compared with persons who smoked unfiltered cigarettes. Dean et al., in a retrospective mortality study in northeast England published by the Tobacco Research Council, showed relative risks of about 0.6 for coronary heart disease and 0.4 for cerebrovascular disease in filter cigarette users versus smokers of unfiltered cigarettes. Unfortunately, smoking habits of cases and controls were obtained from different sources and at different times, confounding the study design. Recent unpublished data from Framingham have failed to show a lower CHD risk among smokers of filter cigarettes, and in younger men there was actually a slightly higher rate of coronary disease among smokers of filtered cigarettes.

This study took into account the other major CHD risk factors (cholesterol, blood pressure, and age); the increased risk in filter smokers is independent of effects attributed to these other factors. Overall, use of lower "tar" and nicotine cigarettes has not produced a consistent decrease in risk for cardiovascular disease; indeed, in some studies a slight increase in risk has been seen. Additional studies will be needed to assess the actual impact of any changes in the composition of cigarettes on subsequent CHD rates. Terms like "lower yield" may describe only part of the change; other additives and the overall use of the cigarette might actually increase risk. Wald has shown that, in the United Kingdom, while lung cancer mortality fell in men from 1956-60 to 1969-73, with the change to filter cigarettes, CHD mortality increased. The author wondered whether the decrease in "tar" accounted for the lower lung cancer death rates, and whether unchanged levels of carbon monoxide might have contributed to the observed continuing rise in CHD death rates . . . .

## SUMMARY

1. Nicotine appears to be the primary pharmacological reinforcer in tobacco, but other pharmacological and psychosocial factors may also contribute a reinforcing effect.
2. It appears that some smokers make compensatory adjustments in their smoking behavior with cigarettes of different yields that might increase the amounts of harmful substances entering the body. The frequency and amount of spontaneous compensatory changes in smoking style with different cigarettes require further investigation.
3. Additional information is needed on the role of lower "tar" and nicotine cigarettes in the initiation, maintenance, and cessation of smoking.
4. Rigorous comparative behavioral studies involving animals are needed to provide comprehensive, experimentally valid results on behavioral aspects of smoking.
5. Laboratory techniques developed for study of opioids and alcohol should be adapted for studies of tolerance and dependence on nicotine.
6. Improved laboratory facilities are necessary for more tightly controlled behavioral research. A particular need exists for clinically acceptable cigarettes with standardized ingredients.
7. Smoking-machine measurements that more closely simulate the practices of human smokers must be developed.

# GLOBAL FUTURE REPORT
## January 14, 1981

*The Carter administration January 14 issued a major set of proposals for dealing with global resource, environment and population problems that earlier had been outlined in* The Global 2000 Report, *issued July 24, 1980.* (Historic Documents of 1980, p. 665.)

*The new proposals, contained in a 250-page report,* Global Future: Time To Act, *called for the United States in concert with other nations to double international resources available for family planning, to increase world food aid and to develop global plans for reversing the depletion of world forests and the spread of deserts.*

*Further, the report acknowledged in the United States a lack of adequate data sources and policy coordination on global issues, and it recommended establishment of a government center charged with such responsibility. The report also urged creation of a public-private group for encouraging private-sector responses to global problems.*

*The report was prepared by the State Department and the Council on Environmental Quality (CEQ) at the request of the president after the earlier report had been published. At a news conference when releasing the report, CEQ Chairman Gus Speth said that "This report basically is a plea for action. Our basic conclusion is that the United States must respond to these global challenges with concerted and vigorous action because our longer-term political and economic security, as well as that of other nations, is at stake."*

## Population and Food

*If family planning resources were doubled and contraceptive methods improved, the report said, it might be possible to reduce world population projections for the year 2000 by 500 million people, from 6.3 billion to 5.8 billion.*

*In addition, the report said, a 30 to 50 percent increase in U.S. food and agricultural assistance over the next few years could stimulate production of three times as much from other sources, and the result would be adequate diets for an additional 25-30 million people in the world.*

## Fuel and Water

*To offset the projected consumption of fuelwood, used by half of humankind for cooking and heating, current rates of tree planting must be increased five-fold, the report said. It said the United States should support increased World Bank fuelwood-forestry lending, a major expansion of Agency for International Development and Peace Corps fuelwood assistance and adoption of a global fuelwood program at the 1981 United Nations Conference on New and Renewable Sources of Energy.*

*With 148 of the world's major river basins shared by two or more countries, and water needs certain to increase greatly, the potential for conflict is high, and the need for improved resource management is acute, the report said. It urged the United States to join other countries in determining water needs by region, improving water management and sharing expertise and knowledge.*

*Energy conservation should continue to be a major global concern, the report said, and it should be encouraged through increasingly efficient consumption and reliance on market rate pricing.*

*In the report's preface, Speth and Secretary of State Edmund S. Muskie said, "This report is only the beginning of a process the United States and other countries across the globe must engage in over the next few years. We must change the way in which we address and resolve long-range global problems, issues of critical importance to our common future. The Global 200 Report has been described as a reconnaissance of the future. It describes what might be, if action is not taken. It is within the power of this country, working with other countries to alter the future. The resources exist. The solutions can be found. The will to act must be summoned."*

*Following are excerpts from the introductory chapter of* Global Future: Time to Act, *issued January 14, 1981. (Boldface headings in brackets have been added by Congressional Quarterly to highlight the organization of the text.):*

## SHAPING U.S. RESPONSE

... In July 1980, with the release of *The Global 2000 Report,* President Carter asked for a review of U.S. government programs related to the most serious issues identified in the study and for recommendations for needed changes. This report was prepared with the assistance of a score of government agencies, many institutions outside the government, and hundreds of intensely concerned individuals. Its recommendations are presented in the spirit not of a fixed or final program but as a body of good ideas for the first round of an effective response to the immensely challenging problems before us. Based on the thoughtful efforts of a great many experienced, knowledgeable people within and outside the U.S. government, the report is intended to suggest answers and options — to open a fruitful discussion involving both the public and the government leaders who will develop and execute U.S. policy in the coming years.

The recommendations are for both fresh starts and continuing efforts in the areas identified as needing priority attention. They emphasize our special strengths — especially scientific and technical — and they look to others for leadership in *their* areas of special strength.

The report stresses that international cooperation is imperative in maintaining a productive and habitable earth. No one nation can tackle the problems alone....

### [Sustainable Economic Development]

In thinking about ways to meet the global challenge, those working on this effort kept in mind several basic guiding ideas. One of them is the urgent need for sustainable economic development.... It is not realistic to expect people living at the margin of existence, struggling for their day-to-day survival, to think about the long-term survival of the planet. Economic development of a sustainable nature, far from being antagonistic to protection of global resources and the environment, is absolutely necessary to its success.

This report concludes: "Only a concerted attack on the socioeconomic roots of extreme poverty, one that provides people with the opportunity to earn a decent livelihood in a nondestructive manner, will permit protection of the world's natural systems. Nor will development and economic reforms have lasting success unless they are suffused with concern for ecological stability and wise management of resources." The key concept here is *sustainable* development. Economic development, if it is to be successful over the long term, must proceed in a way that protects the natural resource base of the developing nations.

There are many opportunities to shape development in ways that protect renewable resources for long-term productivity — opportunities that are open to both rich and poor countries. For example, dams or new industries can be better planned to avoid adverse impacts on croplands or fisheries. Transportation systems may be developed that, unlike the auto highway system, do not encourage sprawl and are not solely dependent on petroleum. Agricultural systems can be built on a more sustainable resource-conserving basis, which makes use of organic as well as chemical fertilizer, interplanting of legumes or development of new nitrogen-fixing crops, use of farm machinery that is the right size to fit the job, and pest control methods that use natural predators and selective pesticides rather than broad-scale application of persistent, destructive chemicals.

### [Third World Development]

There are many ways in which the United States, other developed countries, and international organizations can contribute to sustainable economic development in the Third World. One of them is international development assistance. Foreign aid is only a part of the complex of trade and monetary issues, domestic policies, and availability of investment capital from many sources that influence economic growth in developing countries. Nonetheless, it is a vital element in the mix. A sustained commitment to development assistance by the richer nations, including the oil-rich nations, is critical to breaking this cycle of hunger, misery, and resource degradation in the Third World.

Several industrialized countries contribute to development assistance the amount proposed as reasonable and necessary by the United Nations — 0.7 percent of annual gross national product. Contrary to a widely shared public impression, the United States no longer leads in giving aid for development. Although we do make the largest contributions in absolute amounts, in terms of share of GNP contributed we are 15th out of 17 industrialized nations — just ahead of Austria and Italy.

This report recommends a substantially increased U.S. commitment to development assistance programs. Far from simply "throwing money at problems," this report's proposals would single out programs that are strategically well-planned where the U.S. contribution is meshed with those of other countries and international organizations and where recipient countries both need the assistance and are able to use it effectively....

### [Technical Assistance]

Direct financial assistance for development projects is just one way to encourage sustainable economic growth. Another is the provision of technical assistance, not only to the neediest countries that are recipients of foreign aid but also to middle or higher income developing countries.

Many of the recommendations in this report emphasize tapping U.S. scientific and technical know-how, using our experience in inventory and assessment of natural resources, resource management, and institution-building and training — as well as our scientific research skills....

Many of the federal agencies contributing ideas to this report noted the frustration felt by highly competent technical people — U.S. government foresters, land use planners, wildlife managers, pollution control engineers — who cannot easily respond to foreign countries' requests for technical assistance in resource management and environmental protection. Several institutional impediments stand in the way. Chapter 10, Institutional Changes, discusses possible remedies, including a special budget process by which technical assistance programs of many agencies would be considered together and a total budget allocation parceled out among them. . . .

## [Institutional Changes]

Among the dozens of suggestions for developing institutions and laws that will assure steadfast, adequate attention to global issues, two stand out. One is to centralize authority for fostering the development of an integrated U.S. strategy on global resources, environment, and population in one single government institution. The other is to establish a hybrid public-private institute to supplement the government effort, to stimulate independent analysis, and to involve private groups — industry, labor, environmental, population, academic, and others — in a creative dialogue with the government.

This central government body would cope with a gamut of needs from data collection and analysis to policy development. As this report repeatedly points out, some of the critical information needed for analysis of global resource and environment problems simply does not exist. A central coordinating body should stimulate global data collection and provide for easy access. It should also project trends and analyze the probable results of different responses to global problems. The weaknesses in the government's modeling abilities, described in *The Global 2000 Report,* can be cured only by a more holistic approach, achieved through better coordination.

Finally, coordinated development of policy is absolutely essential. All the pieces must be evaluated and brought together in a coherent whole — a job attempted in this report for the first round, but one that must be continued, expanded, and made a permanent, high priority part of government operations. . . .

In general, the recommendations in the report are initial steps, the first increments in what needs to be done, efforts which must be duplicated, enhanced, repeated, and expanded upon many times over by other nations and international organizations, by private institutions, by business, and by industries. A guiding hand at the center of the U.S. government's share of the response is critical — not only for coordination but for staying power.

Americans — and citizens of other nations throughout the world — must make a commitment and stick with it. . . .

With each year of inaction, the problems become harder to cure. The opportunity to stabilize the world's population below 10 billion, for example, is slipping away; the longer it takes the world to reach replacement fertility levels, the greater the ultimately stabilized world population will probably be.

Provided we manage the earth's resources wisely, future generations will not be faced with a crisis in which our planet will cease to support the number of people living on it. But that specter is now visible. To restore and protect the earth as an ecologically and politically stable habitat for the human race may be the most serious task of the last 20 years of this century.

## SUMMARY OF RECOMMENDATIONS

### Population

#### Problem

Between now and the year 2000, almost 2 billion more people will be added to the present world population of 4.5 billion. Ninety percent of the growth will occur in low income countries, where populations are predominantly young and have their childbearing years ahead of them. At the very least, explosive population growth makes the provision of decent conditions for the world's people more difficult. In some areas, it is already overwhelming efforts to educate, house, and employ the population. And the attempts of growing numbers of people to wrest a living from the land is undermining the very soil, water, and forest resources on which long-term stability and improvements in standard of living depend....

#### U.S. Interests

Unless population growth can be brought under control, the world's efforts to solve a broad range of environmental, resource, and economic problems will be undercut. Thus, the many important interests the United States has in solving these problems — reducing the potential for social unrest, political instability, international conflict over control of land and resources, massive migration of "ecological refugees," and deterioration of world prosperity and trade — are at stake.

#### U.S. Strategy

The United States is by far the world's leader in international population assistance, providing more than one-half of total governmental aid. However, overall international population assistance (including U.S. assistance) has declined in real terms during this decade. At the same time, there is mounting evidence that population programs work; demands for family planning are growing. U.S. strategy should be based on cooperation with other nations and international organizations to raise population assistance substantially, encouraging others to increase their contributions, elevating international awareness of population problems, improving understanding of relationships between population growth and national security, and strengthening research into more effective population control measures....

## *Recommendations*

The United States should:

● Together with other donors and international organizations, launch a program aimed at significantly increasing family planning over the next decade by doubling resources available and improving maternal and child health care.

● Expand government assistance for research in more effective contraception methods suited to the needs of recipient countries.

● Develop a U.S. national population policy that includes attention to issues such as population stabilization; availability of family planning programs; just, consistent, and workable immigration laws; improved information needs; and institutions to ensure continued attention to domestic population issues.

## Food and Agriculture

### *Problem*

Population increases will place great stress on world food supply. Although food production may expand 90 percent (under optimistic assumptions) by the year 2000, the increase will be less than 15 percent on a per capita basis. And this global estimate disguises regional disparities; food availability and nutrition levels may scarcely improve in South Asia and the Middle East and may actually decline in the poorer parts of Africa. Of particular concern is the ability to improve world agricultural yields in the face of pressures leading to degradation of agricultural soil and water resources and the conversion of some of the best cropland to other uses.

### *U.S. Interests*

The potential for political and social instability in a world with large numbers of hungry and starving people is well known. Under such conditions, the demand for food assistance from the United States, the world's largest bread basket, is likely to grow. This means difficult policy and economic decisions about expansion of U.S. food aid to poor nations on concessional terms. Further, protection of the agricultural resource base is one of the global problems the United States directly shares with other countries. . . .

### *U.S. Strategy*

The U.S. approach in recent years has been to assist other nations to expand food production through giving high priority to agriculture in the U.S. development assistance program. The United States has also tried to strengthen international bodies (e.g., the Food and the Agriculture Organization) in this area and has maintained the world's largest food relief program. The proposed U.S. strategy calls for a continuation of these efforts, but also for special attention to a new dimension of the world food problem: the deterioration of the productive capacity of the world's agricultural resource base. . . .

### Recommendations

The United States should:

● Expand significantly U.S. development assistance to the crucial food sector in low income countries.

● Establish an Interagency Task Force on World Agricultural Lands (on the model of the Interagency Task Force on Tropical Forests) to assess world agricultural lands and trends affecting their productivity, review current national and international responses, recommend a coordinated U.S. strategy as part of international efforts to address the problem, and provide the foundation for proposals for an international plan of action.

● Lead by example in protection and wise management of U.S. agricultural lands; elements in the program should include:

— Federal technical and financial assistance to state and local governments wishing to develop land preservation policies and soil and water conservation programs.

— An Agricultural Land Conservation Fund to help finance state and local conservation programs.

— Financial incentives to help preserve farmland.

— Examination by federal agencies of programs affecting agricultural lands . . . to ensure that their actions do not unnecessarily encourage farmland conversion.

— Examination and use by state and local governments of growth management tools to discourage farmland conversions.

— New initiatives to improve soil conservation.

● Propose an international technical conference on conversion of agricultural lands.

● Strengthen national and international programs to preserve crop germ plasm.

● Through assistance, cooperation, and research programs, domestic and international, encourage the use of sustainable agricultural management techniques, including integrated pest management, more efficient use of commercial fertilizer, and biological fixation of nitrogen.

● Work activity toward a better international food reserve system.

### [Renewable Energy and Conservation]

### Problem

While most of the world, rich and poor, is having to adjust to soaring oil prices, the developing countries without their own oil resources are hardest hit. They are now spending $50 billion per year to buy oil — almost twice the amount they receive collectively from all outside sources for development assistance. At the same time, the world's poorest half, most of whom rely mainly on traditional fuels such as firewood and agricultural waste, face another energy crisis: dwindling supplies of firewood. This combination is aggravating already severe economic and ecological problems and adding to the difficulties of achieving economic growth.

### U.S. Interests

The link between U.S. national interests and those of other countries — especially the developing countries — is nowhere more obvious than in energy. Greater use of energy conservation and development of renewable energy resources can benefit rich and poor nations alike. Success in these areas would ease pressures on the world oil market and give the world a longer time to make the transition from overdependence on oil. Greater use of conservation and renewable energy in developing countries can contribute greatly to sustainable economic growth of the Third World, in which the United States has broad foreign policy and national security interests. . . .

### U.S. Strategy

A broad effort, including energy conservation and increased efficiency; accelerated production from nonrenewable commercial sources, such as oil, gas, coal, and hydropower; and expanded and sustained production of energy from renewable sources is needed to meet developing country — and indeed global — energy needs. A U.S. strategy to promote energy conservation and renewable energy sources both at home and abroad is just one element in that broad program, but a key element. Long-term environmental and natural resource constraints point to the need for sustained priority attention to renewable sources and conservation. The strategy proposed here includes a boost in U.S. development assistance for energy, principally for a share in a coordinated international program to plant trees for fuelwood. It also includes strengthened technical assistance to a broad range of developing countries — rising middle income nations, as well as the low income developing countries in which the Agency for International Development (AID) efforts are concentrated.

### Recommendations

The United States should:

● Support recent World Bank proposals for a major increase in assistance for fuelwood growing and conservation. . . .

● Encourage the World Bank to accelerate lending for renewable energy and conservation activities and support the idea of a new World Bank energy facility.

● Develop mechanisms for easier access by developing countries to new energy technologies developed by the U.S. government and also, so far as possible, to privately owned technologies.

● Study ways to make U.S. government technical experts in renewable energy and conservation more readily available to a broad range of developing countries, including a voluntary program of short-term technical assistance that would tap the abilities of the private sector.

● Participate actively in the 1981 UN Conference on New and Renewable Sources of Energy.

● Establish an interagency task force to develop a realistic strategy for achieving the goal of 20 percent of U.S. energy from renewable sources by 2000.

## Tropical Forests

### Problem

The conversion of forested land to agricultural use and the demand for fuelwood and forest products are depleting the world's forests at an alarming rate — as much as 18-20 million hectares annually, an area one-half the size of California. Most of the loss is in the tropical regions of developing nations where some 40 percent of the remaining forests may disappear by 2000....

### U.S. Interests

The loss of wood products and forest-derived drugs and pharmaceuticals, the unprecedented extinction of plant and animal species with loss of tropical forest habitat, and the potential risk of large-scale climate change argue strongly for U.S. concern and involvement. In addition, accelerated erosion and siltation from deforested watersheds are undercutting development assistance investments in agriculture and water supply projects, many financed by the United States....

### U.S. Strategy

The United States has taken the lead in the past 2 years to bring the deforestation problem to international attention in the United Nations and elsewhere. World awareness of the problem and commitments to action are increasing, and the first steps toward a coordinated global plan of action (based on a U.S. initiative) have been taken. Domestically, U.S. government and private institutions are beginning to mount new efforts. The U.S. Interagency Task Force on Tropical Forests reported to the President in July on a comprehensive "Policy, Strategy, and Program for the United States." The proposed near-term strategy for the United States is to continue to promote international awareness and action; selectively to support key international organizations that would play lead roles in a worldwide attack on the problem; to strengthen the capabilities of U.S. public and private sector institutions to contribute; and to insure that the limited tropical forests of the United States are properly managed.

## Recommendations

The United States should:

• Press for adoption by the international community of a "global plan of action" on tropical deforestation.

• Provide financial and technical assistance to enable the FAO [Food and Agriculture Organization] to fulfill the international leadership role.

• Coordinate U.S. programs closely with the FAO and World Bank to optimize use of resources.

• Designate and support the Forest Service's Institute of Tropical Forestry (Puerto Rico) and Institute of Pacific Islands Forestry (Hawaii) as "national centers" for tropical forest research, education, and training.

• Call upon the World Bank to design and support an international cooperative program on reforestation of large watersheds.

• Expand the tropical forest management capabilities of AID and the Peace Corps.

• Pursue, through the Interagency Task Force, a new partnership of government and private industry to broaden the base of U.S. planning and to improve U.S. technical contributions to international programs.

## Biological Diversity

### Problem

The accelerating destruction and pollution of habitat for wild animals and plants threaten extinction of species in the next 20 years on an unprecedented scale. As much as 15-20 percent of all species on earth could be lost in the next 20 years, about one-half because of the loss and degradation of tropical forests and the rest principally in fresh water, coastal, and reef ecosystems. . . .

### U.S. Interests

The U.S. interest in preserving biological diversity is truly global and long term. A great many of the species under threat have not even been classified or given scientific names, much less studied for their possible benefits. The potential for new pharmaceuticals is extremely significant; about one-half the commercial drugs now on the world market were originally derived from living organisms. Wild plants and animals provide a wealth of materials and chemicals, such as woods, fibers, oils, resins, and dyes. The locally cultivated varieties and wild relatives of the world's major food crops are sources of genetic traits essential to improving crop yields and resistance to pests and diseases. Wild plants and local cultivars and wild animals may also prove invaluable sources of new foods.

### U.S. Strategy

The United States has long been a leader, domestically and internationally, in the conservation of wild living resources and biological diversity.... The proposed strategy would continue these efforts and add to them an emphasis on cooperative international action toward selection of priority areas worldwide for conservation of ecosystems and habitat of wild plants and animals; and toward multiple use of natural ecosystems to serve human purposes, to conserve the fauna and flora of the ecosystems, and to maintain their continued functioning as well.

### Recommendations

The United States should:

• Establish a federal Interagency Task Force on Conservation of Biological Diversity to develop a comprehensive long-term strategy to maintain biological diversity, integrating national and international programs.

• Examine and select for increased U.S. support existing international programs to identify priority areas for protection of biological diversity.

• Consider proposing the establishment of an international fund to help developing countries protect and manage critical ecological reserves and habitat, especially in tropical forests.

• Increase support of national and international efforts to inventory the world's flora and fauna and to collect species and germ plasm.

• Increase U.S. assistance for training wildlife management and conservation professionals of developing countries, especially at selected institutions in those countries.

• Expand our ability to offer U.S. technical expertise in conservation of biological diversity to other countries.

## Coastal and Marine Resources

### Problem

Growing threats to coastal and marine ecosystems come from urban and industrial development and destruction of productive coastal wetlands and reefs; pollutants washed from the land, dumped or discharged into the ocean, or deposited from the atmosphere; and uncontrolled exploitation of world fisheries. The worldwide harvest of fish — a major component of the world's food supply — has leveled off and by the year 2000 may contribute less to the world's nutrition, on a per capita basis, than it does today....

### U.S. Interests

Increased pressure on traditional fisheries may lead to collapse of major sources of protein. Conversion and pollution of coastal wetlands in the United States and throughout the world undermine the resource base of fisheries and wildlife....

### U.S. Strategy

The United States should improve management of its own fisheries on an ecologically sound basis and share this expertise with other countries.

Similarly, U.S. programs to inventory, monitor and protect coastal resources should be improved and the results shared internationally....

### Recommendations

The United States should:

● Prepare for a U.S. technical conference to review and improve ecologically sound fisheries management.

● Expand support of fisheries management in developing countries bilaterally and by means of increased funding to the FAO.

● Inventory and map coastal resources and assess the inputs and impacts of major pollutants into coastal and marine areas from land-based sources; cooperate with other countries to do likewise.

● Expand efforts to establish marine sanctuaries and seek international agreement on the protection of habitat of migrating species.

● Continue to support a moratorium on all commercial whaling until the continued survival of whales can be assured.

● Undertake research needed to implement the Antarctic Living Resources Treaty; continue efforts to assure that exploitation of Antarctic mineral resources will not take place until a decision has been made — on the basis of sufficient information — that such development is acceptable.

## Water Resources

### Problem

Human needs for water will greatly increase over the next 20 years; in one-half the countries of the world, population growth alone will cause demands to double. Data on water availability and quality are exceptionally poor, but it is clear that problems of water supply will be serious in many regions....

### U.S. Interests

Unless water supplies are managed successfully, U.S. development assistance efforts will be undercut, need for drought relief will increase, and pressures for mass migration will mount. With 148 of the world's major river basins shared by two or more countries, the United States must anticipate an increasing number of conflicts among countries over competing uses of water....

### U.S. Strategy

A major U.S. goal is to heighten awareness of water management issues. This goal in turn requires the development of an adequate data base — now simply unavailable — and subsequently a coherent strategy on world water needs by region....

### Recommendations

The United States should:

- Establish an Interagency Committee on Global Water Supply and Management to assess data and monitoring of world water availability and needs, identify potential areas of conflict over water resources, and propose ways for the United States to cooperate with other nations in this area by sharing expertise and knowledge.

- Improve U.S. bilateral technical assistance in water resource management and increase financial support of the FAO for training in water management.

- Increase research efforts to reduce water needs for irrigation.

- Participate actively in international efforts to assure safe drinking water as a major development goal.

- Encourage the creation of conflict resolution arrangements to anticipate and help resolve international disputes over water supply or quality.

## Global Pollution

### Problem

The earth's life support systems are threatened by certain byproducts of economic development and industrial growth. Contamination from hazardous substances and nuclear waste, man-induced climate modification from the buildup of $CO_2$, damage to the stratospheric ozone layer, and acid precipitation could adversely affect virtually every aspect of the earth's ecosystems and resource base and, ultimately, mankind.

### U.S. Interests

As one of the world's most industrialized countries, the United States has already felt the effects of contamination from domestic sources of hazardous substances and from acid precipitation. With increasing trade and industrialization in other countries, contamination is increasingly global in nature. The U.S. interest in protecting and maintaining the health of agricultural systems, natural ecosystems, and human populations in our own country and globally dictates increasing cooperation on the international front. . . .

### U.S. Strategy

The United States has worked actively over the past several years to build an international consensus on the seriousness of certain global pollution problems. This effort should continue as well as efforts to involve and support international organizations, to work toward bilateral agreements, and to institute domestic controls as appropriate.

### Recommendations

The United States should:

● Work toward improving international agreements to control hazardous substances and waste.

● Improve the U.S. system for notifying recipient countries of the export of hazardous substances that are banned for all or most uses in the United States, and, in exceptional cases of extremely hazardous banned substances, provide for control over their export.

● Improve U.S. ability to handle hazardous wastes.

● Develop procedures for regulating the export of hazardous wastes.

● Take national and international measures to reduce amounts of nuclear waste and control their disposal and to protect the global commons from radioactive material.

● Analyze alternative global energy futures with special emphasis on $CO_2$ buildup and work toward an international consensus on action to reduce $Co_2$ buildup.

● Support further research on acid precipitation, continue bilateral work with Canada on transboundary air pollution, and intensify legal efforts to control acid deposition.

● Support more research on ozone depletion, encourage action by international organizations, and move toward more effective action to protect the stratospheric ozone layer.

● Improve national and international climate programs.

## Sustainable Development

### Problem

Many of the world's most severe environmental problems are in part a consequence of extreme poverty: deprived people are forced to undermine the productivity of the land on which they live in their necessary quest for food, fuel, and shelter. People who have no other choice for getting their living plant crops on poor, erodible soils, graze their stock on marginal land that turns to desert from overuse, cut trees that are needed to stabilize soils and water supplies, burn dung needed to fertilize and condition agricultural soils.

### U.S. Interests

The U.S. government has long recognized the importance to U.S. national interests of global economic progress and protection of the global environment. Increasing poverty and misery in large parts of the world add to the potential for political instability, depress trade (one-third of U.S. exports are now bought by developing countries), and increase pressures for mass migration. Moreover, if degradation of the earth's renewable resource base continues, the United States, like the rest of the world, will be faced with higher prices for food, building materials, and a host of other materials natural systems provide.

### U.S. Strategy

The United States is committed to measures that will improve prospects for economic growth in developing countries, including an open international trading system, international financial assistance for poorer countries hard hit by oil price rises, and international development assistance.... The proposed U.S. strategy is, first, to increase considerably our present level of development assistance, targeting the increase to the key needs of food, energy, and population and health and carefully coordinating the whole program with programs of international organizations and other countries. A second strategic element is to concentrate our technical assistance in areas where we are strongest: scientific and technical know-how, resource management, and institution building. Private sector as well as government talents should be put to better use....

### Recommendations

The United States should:

• Make up its overdue obligations to the World Bank and other development funds and contribute its share to the World Bank's general capital increase.

• Provide a major expansion in U.S. development assistance targeted to food, energy, population and health and coordinated with programs of other countries and international organizations.

• Urge the World Bank and other international organizations to integrate resource and environmental considerations more fully into their planning.

• Increase resource management expertise in AID programs and encourage all U.S. agencies with significant activities abroad to integrate resource and environmental considerations further into their decisionmaking.

• Develop ways to use the scientific, technical, resource management, and environmental expertise of U.S. government agencies more effectively, both in AID programs and in other international cooperation programs.

### [Improving our Capacity to Respond]

### Problem

The U.S. government currently lacks the capacity adequately to project and evaluate future trends; take global population, resource, and environmental considerations into account in its programs and decisionmaking; and work with other countries to develop transnational solutions to these problems.

### U.S. Interests

... [G]lobal population, resource, and environment problems have the potential for serious adverse impacts on the domestic and international interests of the United States. As a large consumer of world resources and, at the same time, repository of scientific know-how, the United States should act in concert with other countries to resolve future problems. To do so effectively, the U.S. government must have the capacity to project long-term global problems and to act on them.

### U.S. Strategy

To date, U.S. strategy on long-term global population, resources, and environment problems has been formulated largely on an ad hoc basis. The proposed U.S. strategy is to create a stronger capability in the federal government to: project and analyze global trends, coordinate policymaking on long-term global issues, put into place action-forcing mechanisms such as budget review procedures, encourage involvement of the private sector, and increase public awareness.

### Recommendations

The United States should:

• Establish a government center as coordinator to insure adequate data collection and modeling capability as the basis for policy analysis on long-term global population, resource, and environment issues.

• Improve the quality of data collection and modeling for global issues and promote wider access to data and models.

• Establish a Federal Coordinating Unit, preferably in the Executive Office of the President, to develop federal policy and coordinate ongoing federal programs concerning global population, resource, and environment issues. Activities should include coordinating data and modeling efforts described above; issuing biennial reports; assessing global population, resource, and environment problems; and serving as a focal point for development of policy on long-term global issues.

• Adopt action-forcing devices, such as budget review procedures, a Presidential message, creation of a blue-ribbon commission, establishing an office in each federal agency to deal with long-term global issues, or passage of legislation formalizing a mandate to federal agencies to address long-term global issues. . . .

• Create the Global Population, Resources, and Environment Analysis Institute, a hybrid public-private institution, to strengthen and supplement federal government efforts on long-term global analyses.

• Improve the budget process to make technical expertise of U.S. agencies more readily available to other countries.

• Assure environmental review of major U.S. government actions significantly affecting natural or ecological resources of global importance; designate tropical forests, croplands, and coastal wetland-estuarine and reef ecosystems as globally important resources.

• Continue to raise global population, resource, and environment issues in appropriate international organizations and other countries in formulating solutions.

• Enlist the business community in formulating responses to long-term global problems.

• Increase public awareness of global population, resource, and environment issues.

# CARTER'S FAREWELL ADDRESS
## January 14, 1981

*In delivering his farewell address to the nation January 14, President Carter put aside the combative rhetoric of his unsuccessful re-election campaign and returned to earlier themes of nuclear arms control, human rights, environmental protection and the threat of single-issue groups. His tone was reflective, his mood relaxed. He appeared to have recovered from the depression and humiliation of his defeat.*

*Two issues that had dominated his losing race against Ronald Reagan — the economy and the Americans held hostage in Iran — were nearly absent from the speech. The economy was not discussed, and Iran was mentioned only in passing. Carter said he would continue to pray for the hostages, who were released six days later, minutes after Carter left the presidency. (Hostage release, p. 145)*

*The themes Carter stressed in his farewell were evocative of his campaign style in 1976, when he crisscrossed the country as a rather obscure candidate and former one-term governor of Georgia.*

## Special Interests and Nuclear Arms

*The president's first concern was the proliferation of single-interest groups, which he said was "a disturbing factor" that "tends to distort our purposes, because the national interest is not always the sum of all our single or special interests." He said the fragmented pressures of single-interest groups required a strong presidency. "In the moments of decision, after the different and conflicting views have all been aired," he said, "it's the President who then must speak to the nation and for the nation."*

*Carter seemed gloomiest in talking about the need for arms control. The danger of a nuclear conflagration was becoming greater, he said, as existing arsenals were expanded and new nations developed their own weapons. "[I]t may only be a matter of time, before madness, desperation, greed, or miscalculation lets loose this terrible force," he said.*

## Environment and Human Rights

*Carter warned that unless action was taken soon to protect the planet's resources and environment, "[T]he world of the year 2000 will be much less able to sustain life than it is now. . . . There are real and growing dangers to our simple and our precious possessions: the air we breath, the water we drink, and the land which sustains us."*

*The protection of human rights, Carter said, was central to the American vision. "America did not invent human rights," he said. "In a very real sense, it's the other way around. Human rights invented America. Ours was the first nation in the history of the world to be founded explicitly on such an idea."*

*Citing the Declaration of Independence's call for the right to life, liberty and the pursuit of happiness, Carter said that "For this generation, ours, life is nuclear survival; liberty is human rights; the pursuit of happiness is a planet whose resources are devoted to the physical and spiritual nourishment of its inhabitants."*

*Following is the text of President Carter's nationally televised farewell address, delivered January 14, 1981. (Boldface headings in brackets have been added by Congressional Quarterly to highlight the organization of the text.):*

In a few days I will lay down my official responsibilities in this office, to take up once more the only title in our democracy superior to that of President, the title of citizen.

Of Vice President Mondale, my Cabinet, and the hundreds of others who have served with me during the last 4 years, I wish to say publicly what I have said in private: I thank them for the dedication and competence they've brought to the service of our country. But I owe my deepest thanks to you, the American people, because you gave me this extraordinary opportunity to serve.

We've faced great challenges together, and we know that future problems will also be difficult. But I'm now more convinced than ever that the United States, better than any other country, can meet successfully whatever the future might bring. These last 4 years have made me more certain than ever of the inner strength of our country, the unchanging value of our principles and ideals, the stability of our political system, the ingenuity and the decency of our people.

Tonight I would like first to say a few words about this most special office, the Presidency of the United States. This is at once the most powerful office in the world and among the most severely constrained by law and custom. The President is given a broad responsibility to lead but cannot do so without the support and consent of the people, expressed formally through the Congress and informally in many ways through a whole range of public and private institutions. This is as it should be.

Within our system of government every American has a right and a duty to help shape the future course of the United States. Thoughtful criticism and close scrutiny of all government officials by the press and the public are an important part of our democratic society. Now, as in the past, only the understanding and involvement of the people through full and open debate can help to avoid serious mistakes and assure the continued dignity and safety of the Nation.

Today we are asking our political system to do things of which the Founding Fathers never dreamed. The government they designed for a few hundred thousand people now serves a nation of almost 230 million people. Their small coastal republic now spans beyond a continent, and we also now have the responsibility to help lead much of the world through difficult times to a secure and prosperous future.

## [Single-issue Groups]

Today, as people have become ever more doubtful of the ability of the Government to deal with our problems, we are increasingly drawn to single-issue groups and special interest organizations to ensure that whatever else happens, our own personal views and our private interests are protected. This is a disturbing factor in American political life. It tends to distort our purposes, because the national interest is not always the sum of all our single or special interests. We are all Americans together, and we must not forget that the common good is our common interest and our individual responsibility.

Because of the fragmented pressures of these special interests, it's very important that the office of the President be a strong one and that its constitutional authority be preserved. The President is the only elected official charged with the primary responsibility of representing all the people. In the moments of decision, after the different and conflicting views have been aired, it's the President who then must speak to the Nation and for the Nation.

I understand after 4 years in this office, as few others can, how formidable is the task the new President-elect is about to undertake, and to the very limits of conscience and conviction, I pledge to support him in that task. I wish him success, and Godspeed.

I know from experience that Presidents have to face major issues that are controversial, broad in scope, and which do not arouse the natural support of a political majority. For a few minutes now, I want to lay aside my role as leader of one nation, and speak to you as a fellow citizen of the world about three issues, three difficult issues: The threat of nuclear destruction, our stewardship of the physical resources of the planet, and the preeminence of the basic rights of human beings.

## [Nuclear Threat]

It's now been 35 years since the first atomic bomb fell on Hiroshima. The great majority of the world's people cannot remember a time when the nuclear shadow did not hang over the Earth. Our minds have adjusted to it, as after a time our eyes adjust to the dark. Yet the risk of a nuclear conflagration has not lessened. It has not happened yet, thank God, but that gives us little comfort, for it only has to happen once.

The danger is becoming greater. As the arsenals of the superpowers grow in size and sophistication and as other governments, perhaps even in the future dozens of governments, acquire these weapons, it may only be a matter of time before madness, desperation, greed or miscalculation lets loose this terrible force.

In an all-out nuclear war, more destructive power than in all of World War II would be unleashed every second during the long afternoon it would take for all the missiles and bombs to fall. A World War II every second — more people killed in the first few hours than all of the wars of history put together. The survivors, if any, would live in despair amid the poisoned ruins of a civilization that had committed suicide.

National weakness, real or perceived, can tempt aggression, and thus cause war. That's why the United States can never neglect its military strength. We must and we will remain strong. But with equal determination, the United States and all countries must find ways to control and to reduce the horrifying danger that is posed by the enormous world stockpiles of nuclear arms.

This has been a concern of every American President since the moment we first saw what these weapons could do. Our leaders will require our understanding and our support as they grapple with this difficult but crucial challenge. There is no disagreement on the goals or the basic approach to controlling this enormous destructive force. The answer lies not just in the attitudes or actions of world leaders but in the concern and the demands of all of us as we continue our struggle to preserve the peace.

Nuclear weapons are an expression of one side of our human character. But there's another side. The same rocket technology that delivers nuclear warheads has also taken us peacefully into space. From that perspective, we see our Earth as it really is — a small and fragile and beautiful blue globe, the only home we have. We see no barriers of race or religion or country. We see the essential unity of our species and our planet; and with faith and common sense, that bright vision will ultimately prevail.

# [Stewardship of Planet]

Another major challenge, therefore, is to protect the quality of this world within which we live. The shadows that fall across the future are cast not only by the kinds of weapons we've built, but by the kind of world we will either nourish or neglect. There are real and growing dangers to our simple and our most precious possessions: The air we breathe, the water we drink, and the land which sustains us. The rapid depletion of irreplaceable minerals, the erosion of topsoil, the destruction of beauty, the blight of pollution, the demands of increasing billions of people, all combine to create problems which are easy to observe and predict, but difficult to resolve. If we do not act, the world of the year 2000 will be much less able to sustain life than it is now.

But there is no reason for despair. Acknowledging the physical realities of our planet does not mean a dismal future of endless sacrifice. In fact, acknowledging these realities is the first step in dealing with them. We can meet the resource problems of the world — water, food, minerals, farmlands, forests, overpopulation, pollution — if we tackle them with courage and foresight.

# [Human Freedoms]

I've just been talking about forces of potential destruction that mankind has developed and how we might control them. It's equally important that we remember the beneficial forces that we have evolved over the ages and how to hold fast to them. One of those constructive forces is the enhancement of individual human freedoms throughout the strengthening of democracy and the fight against deprivation, torture, terrorism and the persecution of people through the world. The struggle for human rights overrides all differences of color or nation or language. Those who hunger for freedom, who thirst for human dignity, and who suffer for the sake of justice, they are the patriots of this cause.

I believe with all my heart that America must always stand for these basic human rights at home and abroad. That is both our history and our destiny.

America did not invent human rights. In a very real sense, it is the other way around. Human rights invented America. Ours was the first nation in the history of the world to be founded explicitly on such an idea. Our social and political progress has been based on one fundamental principle: the value and importance of the individual. The fundamental force that unites us is not kinship or place of origin or religious preference. The love of liberty is the common blood that flows in American veins.

The battle for human rights, at home and abroad, is far from over. We should never be surprised nor discouraged, because the impact of our efforts has had and will always have varied results. Rather, we should take pride that the ideals which gave birth to our Nation still inspire the hopes of oppressed people around the world. We have no cause for self-righteousness or complacency, but we have every reason to persevere, both within our own country and beyond our borders.

## [American Values]

If we are to serve as a beacon for human rights, we must continue to perfect here at home the rights and the values which we espouse around the world: a decent education for our children, adequate medical care for all Americans, an end to discrimination against minorities and women, a job for all those able to work, and freedom from injustice and religious intolerance.

We live in a time of transition, an uneasy era which is likely to endure for the rest of the century. It will be a period of tensions, both within nations and between nations, of competition for scarce resources, of social, political, and economic stresses and strains. During this period we may be tempted to abandon some of the time-honored principles and commitments which have been proven during the difficult times of past generations. We must never yield to this temptation. Our American values are not luxuries, but necessities — not the salt in our bread, but the bread itself. Our common vision of a free and just society is our greatest source of cohesion at home and strength abroad, greater even than the bounty of our material blessings.

Remember these words: "We hold these truths to be self-evident, that all men are created equal, that they are endowed by their Creator with certain inalienable Rights; that among these are Life, Liberty and the pursuit of Happiness."

This vision still grips the imagination of the world. But we know that democracy is always an unfinished creation. Each generation must renew its foundations. Each generation must rediscover the meaning of this hallowed vision in the light of its own modern challenges. For this generation, ours, life is nuclear survival; liberty is human rights; the pursuit of happiness is a planet whose resources are devoted to the physical and spiritual nourishment of its inhabitants.

## [Hostages]

During the next few days I will work hard to make sure that the transition from myself to the next President is a good one, that the American people are served well. And I will continue, as I have the last 14 months, to work hard and to pray for the lives and the well-being of the American hostages held in Iran. I can't predict yet what will happen, but I hope you will join me in my constant prayer for their freedom.

As I return home to the South, where I was born and raised, I look forward to the opportunity to reflect and further to assess, I hope with accuracy, the circumstances of our times. I intend to give our new

President my support, and I intend to work as a citizen, as I've worked here in this office as President, for the values this Nation was founded to secure.

Again, from the bottom of my heart, I want to express to you the gratitude I feel. Thank you, fellow citizens, and farewell.

# NATIONAL AGENDA FOR THE 1980s
## January 16, 1981

*Recommending an "agenda" for the nation in the 1980s, a presidential commission presented its report at the White House January 16, less than four days before Jimmy Carter left office. Accepting the report, Carter said that its recommendations for the most part were "compatible with what I myself would advocate." But the report also was viewed as consistent with many of the major goals of the incoming Reagan administration.*

*The report, A National Agenda for the Eighties, had stirred controversy even before its formal release, after one of its proposals was leaked to the press. That recommendation called for a new urban policy that would encourage citizens to follow job opportunities from the older cities of the North to the growing "Sun Belt" areas of the South and Southwest.*

*Compiled by the President's Commission for a National Agenda for the Eighties, the report was 14 months in preparation. Carter said he had named the commission in response to his concern that there had emerged "a number of factors — such as a changing economy, increasing global interdependence, the shortage of energy supplies, and the splintering of the political system — that will affect the nation dramatically. . . ."*

*On presenting the 213-page report, William J. McGill, commission chairman and former president of Columbia University, told Carter that "There are no simple nostrums." But McGill said the commission had come up with a "mix of politics" that had a good prospect of "seeing us through the eighties safely."*

*When he appointed the commission in 1979, Carter had described its role as a "direct outgrowth" of six days of intensive consultations that he had held at Camp David, the presidential retreat in the Maryland mountains, in July of that year. (Historic Documents of 1979, p. 559)*

## Shift to Sun Belt

*Provoking the most heated response was the recommendation suggesting that ". . . as the major long-term goal of federal urban policy" the federal government should encourage the migration of citizens to fresh opportunities in the Sun Belt. "Assisting people to follow jobs rather than concentrating solely on attempting to steer jobs to where people are," the report said, "is a major goal in any adjustment strategy."*

*Two members of the agenda commission, Benjamin L. Hooks, the executive director of the National Association for the Advancement of Colored People, and Carl Holman, president of the National Urban Coalition, said that they dissented from the migration notion. The recommendation also drew strong criticism from political leaders in the Northeast and Midwest.*

*Carter, in a statement January 16, said he disagreed "with the implication" that the government should facilitate "the population trend from the Frostbelt to the Sunbelt." The president added, "We cannot abandon our older urban areas."*

## Other Recommendations

*A number of the report's recommendations seemed "liberal" in tone. In social and economic policy, the report recommended the complete federalization of the welfare system, a comprehensive national health insurance program and a guaranteed minimum "security" income to replace food stamps and other federal assistance programs. It also called for ratification of the Equal Rights Amendment and said the federal government should expand its role in the area of civil rights.*

*On the other hand, the report took generally "conservative" positions in recommending more flexible environmental regulations, increased deregulation of business and an economic policy aimed at stimulating productivity through tax incentives. The report urged caution in the nation's synthetic fuels program. Subsidies should be limited, it said, to "standby assistance, such as price-support guarantees designed to protect developers against a drop in world oil prices."*

> *Following are excerpts from the report of the President's Commission for a National Agenda for the Eighties, recommending policies for the federal government during the*

*decade.* (Boldface headings in brackets have been added by Congressional Quarterly to highlight the organization of the text.):

# Chapter 3

## Restoring Growth of Output and Employment

... The economic outlook for the Eighties is brighter than recent experience would suggest. Some of the factors that retarded growth in the Seventies will probably be less important in the Eighties. Yet there is no room for complacency. Over the long run, the growth of income and consumption per person cannot exceed the growth of productivity. To avoid a sharp slowdown in the growth of income per person in the Eighties, we must restore substantial growth in productivity.

Essentially, there are two alternatives. The first is to accept the slower growth rates that have characterized the past few years. The advantage of this alternative is that it would not require short-run deferrals of consumption in order to expand our productive capacity. The disadvantage is that it would require a substantial readjustment of expectations. Americans could no longer reasonably expect the substantial improvements in the standard of living that were such a prominent feature of the post-World War II decades.

A second alternative — the one we endorse — is to place a higher priority on achieving economic growth. It is important to realize that economic growth, like any other national goal, has a price tag. More rapid economic growth would require more investment of capital in plant and equipment, and that would require deferring other expenditures. But we believe this is the more desirable course.

Economic growth is important because it is the best means of attaining many other objectives. Growth is desirable to the extent that it improves the quality of life for Americans when the noneconomic side effects of growth are properly taken into account. Appropriate environmental, health, safety, and land-use policies can succeed in directing growth in a manner that minimizes the negative side effects that have accompanied some economic activities in the past.

Only a sustained increase in real output will enable the United States to achieve a broad range of national and international goals — from a general rise in the standard of living to improved social benefits for the needy; from retraining and providing jobs for the unemployed to improving the nation's competitiveness in exports and enhancing its leadership role in the world community. . . .

Even goals not customarily associated with economic growth, such as increased longevity, an improved environment, and increased safety, are more easily afforded in an expanding rather than a stagnating economy. Economic growth would ease the difficulties that individuals and communities will face in making adjustments to economic and technological change. It would, finally, enhance the prospects for recreating the national consensus that is so sorely needed.

### [Expectations and Reality]

No matter how successful we are in restoring economic growth, there will be a gap between expectations and reality, perhaps especially for the baby boom generation whose expectations were formed in the Fifties and Sixties, a gap which could well result in significant social and political problems. We will therefore need to develop strategies to respond to this gap and to prepare the public for the new resource and entitlement realities of the Eighties. How painful a process this will be depends largely on the degree to which we are able to achieve substantial economic growth.

Restoring growth will, as noted, entail costs and some difficult short-term trade-offs. Both technological innovations and capital investment require real resources, and if they are to claim an increased share of GNP, other things — personal consumption and government expenditures — must receive a declining share. Moreover, the private sector will make most of the decisions to adopt new technologies and to expand investment. It will do so only if government restores a stable, growth-promoting economic environment. Public policies to restore growth must, therefore, affect government tax revenues and/or expenditures. For example, tax reductions to induce savings and investment would, in the short run at least, diminish the amount of revenue available for the expansion of government programs. Higher direct subsidies or tax incentives for research and development would have a similar effect. Thus, without new revenue sources that do not themselves discourage growth, government expenditures will have to grow less rapidly than we have become accustomed to since the mid-Sixties. Calls for substantial real increases in specific components of federal expenditures — defense, energy, entitlement programs, or anything else — cannot all be accommodated simultaneously if growth is to be restored.

### [Effect on the Poor]

One source of objections to the policy changes that are necessary to restore economic growth is a fear that they will be undertaken at the expense of the needy. We are well aware of the potential asymmetries of economic growth, but it need not follow that the poor will be selectively harmed. The lot of the disadvantaged can be improved both by policies directed at stimulating the growth of the economy and by programs that directly transfer income or services to them. Both kinds of policies have an important role, and ... this report suggests improvements in our current transfer programs. Nevertheless, in choosing a policy mix for the Eighties, it is true that growth-promoting policies will entail a reduction in the growth of government expenditures, which could take the form of slower growth of direct transfer programs. The immediate impact would be to do less for the disadvantaged than might otherwise have been done.

An expanding economy will ameliorate and reverse this effect in two ways. Increased job opportunities will raise the income of the poor and reduce the number who need government assistance, thereby permitting more generous assistance to those remaining in poverty. Moreover, growth creates a larger "pie" from which transfers can be made, allowing for further expansion of transfer programs in the future. And, of course, even in the short run, transfer programs need not be the only — or even a primary — source of funds for promoting growth. Choosing an appropriate mix of policies — to assist the needy, to invigorate the economy, and to pursue many other objectives while fairly distributing necessary sacrifices — will be a principal item on our agenda during the Eighties.

## [Policies for Growth and Employment]

### A More Stable Economic Environment

To achieve our objective of increased economic growth will require change and improvements in a number of government policies. The most important contribution of government would be the provision of a more stable economic environment. Wide swings in credit availability, in interest rates, and in the rate of economic expansion increase the difficulty that both households and firms have in making rational long-term plans. The effect is greater timidity in making investments — and therefore slower growth. A more stable economic environment would also permit management in the private sector to concentrate less on short-term financial results and more on the long-range goal of increasing real output. Indeed, it can be argued that a *consistent* economic policy which accomplishes a steady acceptable rate of growth over the full decade would be preferable to a policy that temporarily achieved a higher but difficult to sustain growth rate.

### Increased Savings and Investment

Increased capital formation is necessary if we are to achieve higher growth, and the Commission believes that at the present time a greater fraction of GNP should be devoted to savings and investment. Increased savings will mean a smaller share of the GNP for current public and private consumption. Although, by definition, saving is deferred consumption, to denominate it as a "sacrifice" is to misname it. Given an adequate return on savings and investment and substantially lower rates of inflation, many Americans would voluntarily choose to defer a larger fraction of their consumption to the future.

A number of broad approaches have been suggested to stimulate savings and investment. We can enhance the incentives for investment by increasing the after-tax return on investment in any of several ways, such as by expanding the investment tax credit, by further accelerating depreciation schedules, by eliminating the double taxation of dividends, or by integrating the personal and corporate income taxes. We can also increase private saving by shifting incentives in the tax system away from consumption. A third approach is to reduce the federal budget deficit. To finance a deficit, either the government must compete with private investment for available savings, or the Federal Reserve must cover the government's deficit by creating money, leading to higher inflation, which also discourages private capital formation.

The difficulty arises in attempting to translate the general prescription for an increase in savings and investment into a specific mixture of the above policies. There is first the question of which policies will achieve a given increase in capital formation most efficiently. How much, for example, will investment be stimulated by a particular tax policy? What are the relative merits of general tax reduction vs. more narrowly targeted investment incentives?

Then there is the broader question of how much stimulus to capital formation should be provided, given competing claims on government resources. If the federal deficit is not to increase, for reasons noted just above, then tax incentives for capital formation must be accompanied by increases in other taxes or by slower growth in government spending. The need for additional investment must, therefore, be balanced against the competing needs of other programs, such as welfare, housing, or defense. In making these adjustments, it is not a question of going entirely in one direction or another, but of choosing the point on the spectrum where the balance seems most appropriate.

### Restore Productivity Growth

Productivity — defined as output per hour of labor input — is the heart of any agenda for sustained growth in income per person. Over the last decade, the rate of increase of productivity slowed substantially, although the aggregate data may have somewhat overestimated the magnitude of the slowdown actually experienced, as productivity is especially difficult to measure when the economy undergoes rapid change as it did in the Seventies. Nevertheless, slower productivity growth is the primary factor underlying the serious slowdown in the expansion of real GNP in this country.

The productivity slowdown resulted from a number of factors, including the slower growth of capital relative to labor, diminishing transfers of labor out of low productivity agricultural employment, adjustments to higher energy prices, and shifts in individual attitudes and motivations toward work. The costs imposed by regulation may also have retarded productivity growth, but the magnitude of the effect is uncertain. Some of the slowdown cannot be explained by *any measurable* factors and is therefore attributed to reduced innovation in the broadest sense of that term. Innovation results in part from scientific and technological discoveries, applications, and refinements, permitting many improvements in the efficiency of machinery and equipment. Also important over the long term are increases in the ingenuity, skill, and training of the work force and improvements in the general organization and management of production.

To combat the slowdown in productivity growth, the Commission advocates (in addition to the above incentives for capital formation) increased tax incentives for private spending on research and development; increased government support of basic research; and a renewed emphasis on improving productivity in the public sector. Issues regarding the specific mix of policies and the appropriate balance with other objectives arise here, just as they did with respect to capital formation.

Moreover, there is a limit to what public policy can do to increase productivity. Technological, managerial, and organizational improvement is ultimately the province of both management and labor within the individual firm. A more stable economic environment would encourage management to take a longer range view of investment and of research and development and to place more emphasis on productivity — better use of human, capital, and natural resources. At the firm level, this might mean greater emphasis on productivity and "quality of work life" programs, from top management on down to first-line supervisors and employees. Such programs are most effective when undertaken with cooperation between labor and management. If the dignity of the employee is respected and the connotation of "work faster!" is avoided, productivity programs can be more successful in gaining the cooperation of workers and obtaining the benefits of their knowledge about how productivity might be improved. Prevalent values among members of the baby boom generation suggest that opportunities to help shape their individual work environments will significantly affect their work attitudes and performance. Pay incentive programs tied to improved productivity performance and wider use of employee stock ownership plans and other employee ownership models may contribute to this end.

### Structural Employment Policies

A rapidly growing and changing economy does not automatically eliminate unemployment. In part this problem is caused by the imbalances that inevitably occur between occupational and industrial sectors, geographic regions, and skill requirements. In addition, other barriers to employment, such as discrimination, make the linkage between growth and reduced unemployment less than perfect. Therefore, even with higher economic growth in the Eighties, specific employment policies will still be needed to reduce structural unemployment.

Without such programs, the potential abilities and energies of our labor force will not be fully utilized. Unemployment affects minority groups most seriously because they are over-represented among less skilled workers with little seniority. To reduce the severity of these problems, employment programs should give greater emphasis to training in marketable skills. The programs should be more heavily targeted toward hard-to-employ workers than they are at present. For the educationally and economically disadvantaged, incentives should be created to encourage career-related skill development. Wherever possible, these incentives should be structured to foster private sector provision of job training and employment. Special attention should be given to the concern that governmentally mandated high labor costs may retard both employment and skill training for these workers. At the same time, policies that facilitate labor mobility so that workers can better adapt to geographic shifts in employment opportunities should be emphasized over attempts to induce industries to locate in high unemployment areas....

The flow of illegal immigration into this country increases the number of unskilled and disadvantaged workers. The status of these immigrants makes them highly vulnerable to exploitation, and their presence distorts the labor market in localized areas. During the decade we should consider whether the adoption of a formal "temporary worker" program would rationalize this immigration, protecting such workers from exploitation, while at the same time protecting our own low-income and minority workers from unfair competition. This issue must, of course, be considered within the larger framework of our relations with neighboring countries, with attention to such areas as trade, energy, and technical and economic assistance.

### Economic Regulation

Controls over prices, profits, and entry into numerous utility, transportation, and service industries are traditional forms of economic regulation that have often been shown to have a stifling effect on economic initiative and development. Increasingly, we have come to recognize the benefits of substantially reducing most forms of economic regulation. Not only are such programs difficult to administer fairly, but economic regulation often retards innovation, productivity, and competition that would normally lead to better service at lower prices. Previous experiments with deregulation — notably in the airlines and brokerage industries — have proven largely successful. The Commission endorses the trend toward economic deregulation and joins those who call for fewer economic controls on the transportation, communications, finance, energy, health, and insurance industries. Instead of economic regulation, government should rely on a competitive marketplace, policed by antitrust laws, to achieve efficient and rational services and prices. For health, safety, and environmental objectives, regulation will continue to be necessary, and improved regulatory techniques can be employed to achieve these objectives more efficiently and effectively....

The removal of economic controls on an industry frequently will cause transition problems — problems which should neither be ignored nor allowed to impede deregulation. Regulation normally affects the pattern of prices and availability of services. Removal of economic controls, while benefiting many, will leave some people worse off, at least temporarily. In the case of airline deregulation, shortly after controls were lifted, several small communities lost their regularly scheduled airline service. The Commission is concerned that legislators recognize this kind of problem and deal with it in a way that minimizes disruption while allowing deregulation to proceed. A failure to do so may seriously interfere with the political acceptability of economic deregulation. . . .

## ENERGY AND ECONOMIC GROWTH

A common reading of recent history holds that OPEC's upward ratcheting of world oil prices during the 1970s — with a fourfold increase in the cost of crude oil in 1974, followed by a doubling in 1979 — trapped the United States in the "energy crisis," a term that has secured itself in the American political vocabulary. This interpretation misconstrues the nature of the energy problem, perhaps in order to draw attention to, and galvanize support for, particular responses to it — many of which have been overwrought and ill advised.

The adequacy of the nation's energy supplies over the coming decades is a serious matter that needs no exaggeration, nor does it admit of instant resolution. The causes of the energy predicament confronting the United States lie in a convergence of this nation's soaring demand for energy, notably petroleum, and the inescapable diminution of our own — and, ultimately, the world's — known reserves of conventional crude oil.

By the middle of the 1970s, the United States found itself sliding into the unwanted role of the world's leading oil buyer, reaching for imports to meet nearly half our demand, to compensate for the depletion of its own oil fields. This nation thus helped to inflate world oil demand, enabling OPEC's members to assert greater power over prices and supplies. As a result, prices suddenly soared, and the availability of oil became a dominant concern in global economic and political strategies.

Having gone through the wrenching experiences of the past decade, with two recessions and unprecedented inflation among the consequences attributable, at least in part, to the escalating costs of energy, what has this nation learned? These sharp increases at least forced the United States toward a recognition that the age of cheap and plentiful oil has come to a close, and that a transition to other energy supplies must be devised. OPEC has, by its actions, underscored this requirement, for we are continuously threatened by the possibility that a handful of countries could shut off our imports and thereby cause a severe shock to our society. The challenge to be addressed is how the process of transition from oil to alternate sources of fuel and power should be carried out, and how we can protect ourselves from interruptions in supplies in the interim. . . .

## [Limits of Coal]

Coal already dominates its major U.S. market — the electric utility sector, where it supplies the energy for nearly half the total power generation, providing about three times more power than oil or gas and about four times more than hydroelectric or nuclear plants. Moreover, coal is likely to be by far the leading energy source for new power plants.

However, coal's ability to penetrate other energy-consuming sectors of the U.S. economy is limited, given the current state of deployment of coal-processing technology and the comparative advantages of oil and gas. For example, the use of coal by the industrial sector has fallen steadily since the embargo, from 4.4 Quads in 1973 to 3.6 Quads in 1979, while coal long ago lost its markets in the railroad and home-heating sectors. Despite the abundance of U.S. coal reserves, coal simply cannot be put into widespread use quickly, especially in meeting the demand for liquid fuel. And despite coal's relative advantage over oil in market price, there are high environmental costs associated with expanded consumption of coal that also must be taken into account. . . . Thus, while coal's prospects may look brighter than those of oil and gas, it cannot by itself redress the U.S. energy supply deficit.

Development of synthetic fuels — oil from shale, and oil from gas and coal — at last may be getting under way, but it remains to be seen whether these fuels can compete on their own without substantial government subsidies, and whether the serious environmental issues associated with these technologies can be resolved.

## [Setbacks for Nuclear Power]

Nuclear power, now beset with a multitude of afflictions, clearly will not deliver as much energy as once was expected, nor at the low price that once was projected. Indeed, because of the cutbacks in power reactor output that followed the latest setback to nuclear power development, the accident at Three Mile Island, nuclear power in 1979 dropped to the number five ranking among sources of electric power, trailing coal, gas, oil and hydroelectric power, which is undergoing a dramatic resurgence.

As of mid-1980, nuclear energy was providing about 10 percent of the nation's electricity. Seventy-four power reactors were listed in operation. The total number of units in service, under construction, or planned was 176 in mid-1980, down from a peak of 236 in 1975. Construction of nuclear power plants has leveled off after registering sharp increases in the early 1970s, while orders for new units have virtually halted.

Given the present constraints against the expansion of nuclear power — which include rising construction costs, slower than expected demand for electric power, regulatory impediments, and public concern over reactor siting, operating safety, and waste disposal — the nuclear option cannot be counted upon to contribute extra power during this decade beyond what is already available or coming on line. . . .

## Chapter 4

## [NEW PERSPECTIVES ON URBAN AMERICA]

...Over the past several decades, demographic and economic forces have transformed urban America dramatically. Understanding the scale, direction, and pace of these forces is essential before making coherent policy recommendations. Also, prior to recommending what government should or should not do, there is a need to consider carefully what government is and is not capable of accomplishing in such a complex policy area.

In general, we recommend that the nation respond to urban change by promoting strategies of adjustment, rather than attempt to reverse the changes experienced by communities across the land. In large measure, these changes — including the transformation of local economies, the lower density settlement patterns, and the growth in locations beyond metropolitan areas — are often beneficial to the nation as a whole, even though they may have undesirable short-term effects on specific communities. The pace, if not the direction, of larger scale trends can occasionally be influenced by wise public policy; adjusting to the direction of change, as well as moderating its pace, then, should be our primary objective.

From a long-range perspective, we urge the federal government to assign priority to the development of a blend of social and economic policies that encourages the health and vitality of the nation as a whole and of all its citizens regardless of where in the nation they might live. The urban consequences of essentially nonurban policies will continue to outweigh those of narrow and explicitly urban policies. The general implication is that, in the long run, the fates and fortunes of specific places be allowed to fluctuate. Throughout the process of economic change, people — more so than places — should be insulated from the multiple hardships that accompany the transformation of the nation — in its communities, its economy, and the larger society.

## [Role of Federal Government]

Earlier we urged the government to adopt economic policies that promote steady economic growth, encourage investment, create jobs, and inhibit inflation. We must retain the capability to create wealth even as we continue to develop more equitable means of distributing it. Here we urge the government to adopt social policies that have as their collective aim ensuring that those who can work are able to and those who cannot work are able to lead a life of dignity while their welfare is provided through alternative means. The government should aim principally to remove barriers between people and economic opportunity. We believe that a people-to-jobs strategy based on vigorous government programs of assisted migration and skill acquisition should receive the emphasis that has been reserved in recent years for job-to-people strategies dependent upon local economic development. Efforts must be redoubled to train the unskilled, to retrain the displaced, and to assist those who wish to relocate to areas where employment opportunities abound.

In the interim — until such a major policy reorientation can be accomplished — the federal government can take important steps toward easing the plight of beleaguered urban areas, without foreclosing its long-range policy. There is a recognized need for reorganizing and coordinating its major community and economic development programs. A number of grant-in-aid programs should be consolidated and their resources more carefully targeted to localities most in need. Grants to localities should be accompanied by sufficient transfer of authority so that local officials have the flexibility to address diverse local needs with external funds. Responsibilities should not be mandated to localities without the assurance of the availability of the resources needed to execute them. In general, federal urban policy efforts should be evaluated by their collective capacity to ease the burdens on Governors, mayors, and others of local and state governance.

## The Transformation of Cities

Contrary to conventional wisdom, cities are not permanent; their strength is related to their ability to reflect change rather than to fend it off. Their imposing physical features — the vast interwoven networks of factories, homes, commercial establishments, and the transportation routes linking them — belie cities' underlying susceptibility to historical trends. Standing at the intersection of virtually all the important shaping forces of an era — demographic, economic, political, cultural — cities articulate, and continuously rearticulate, our changing national circumstances. Although they are the settings for all manner of abiding cultural institutions, cities serve us better as mirrors than as museums. They must be permitted to reflect changing technological capabilities and social circumstances, rather than be constrained by an attempt to preserve under glass any particular historical combination of them. To attempt to restrict or reverse the processes of change — for whatever noble intentions — is to deny the benefits that the future may hold for us as a nation.

Whatever else they are, cities are economic entities; first and foremost they are the settings where great wealth is produced and distributed. A city's physical arrangements and material life are largely determined by the technological state of the art that existed as the city grew and by its role in a local and regional economy for which it serves as a linchpin. Much evidence exists to suggest that the economy of the United States, like that of many of the older industrial societies, has for years now been undergoing a critical transition from being geographically concentrated, centralized, and manufacturing-based to being increasingly deconcentrated, decentralized, and service-based. In the process, many cities of the old industrial heartland — for example, in the states of New York, Pennsylvania, Ohio, Michigan and Illinois — are losing their status as thriving industrial capitals, a position they have held through the first half of the century.

These cities are not dying. Rather, they are transforming, and in the future they will likely perform a narrower range of vital and specialized tasks for the larger urban society. Central location and compactness will continue to be essential to many urban enterprises and attractive to many urban dwellers. These older cities are gradually evolving; their physical appearance and economic function are becoming increasingly reflective of the newer social roles that history is assigning them. This transformation of older cities from centers of manufacturing and production to centers of services and consumption will require that their "health" be defined at new, and often lower, levels of population and employment.

## [White-collar Cities]

The central city in the future will likely experience great increases in the number of white-collar office jobs in managerial, professional, financial, and "knowledge" occupations. Also nurtured will be the allied services that these workers, their families, and employing institutions will require during and after the working day. The proportion of manufacturing jobs will decline, and the blue-collar labor force will be much reduced from previous levels as a result of the loss of manufacturing and allied jobs from central cities.

Cities can no longer be expected to perform alone the traditional role of providing employment for the unskilled, unemployed, poor, and dependent urban underclass.

The general decline in rural migration to cities may well remove from a municipality's shoulders the traditional burden of acculturating newcomers to urban life and assimilating them into urban society. (The rising tide of foreign immigrants — particularly from the Caribbean — may in fact restore some of these functions to a few cities.) The older industrial cities will continue to be national and regional centers performing important commercial, service, financial, governmental, and cultural functions. But they will share many of those tasks with smaller communities far removed from central locations. They will become scaled-down residential centers for households defined by a narrower range of age, composition, and income differences.

Geographically, population shifts and economic trends within cities will create an urban landscape characterized by lower density industrial and residential settlements oriented around multiple smaller and more specialized centers of concentration (e.g., large suburban shopping malls, office and industrial parks). The historical dominance of core central cities will be diminished as certain production, residential, commercial, and cultural functions disperse to places beyond them. In demographic terms, continuing suburbanization within metropolitan areas will be accompanied by both a broader dispersion of people to the periphery of metropolitan areas and a reconcentration of population in the countryside. For the foreseeable future, the rate of growth in nonurban areas will continue to exceed that in metropolitan areas, and the South and West will grow at rates exceeding those in the North and East.

### [No Urban Renaissance]

An often-noted "urban renaissance" within cities — while enriching and laudable — seems not to be taking place on anything like the scale suggested in popular commentary. On the contrary, we have no evidence of a return *en masse* of the upper middle class to the cities nor any accompanying large-scale residential and civic rejuvenation. To be sure, certain inner-city neighborhoods are unmistakably enjoying forms of real estate upgrading and restoration, but statistically such changes amount only to a thin patina across the urban landscape. Thus, between 1968 and 1979, only one-half of one percent of the nearly 20 million housing units in cities has been affected by revitalization or restoration efforts. Moreover, in excess of 70 percent of the people residing in revitalized central city units were already central city dwellers, not returning suburban immigrants. What the statistical indices do reveal, however, is the ongoing, relentless deterioration of living conditions and income levels, relative to suburban locations, as old central cities progress toward economic transformation.

Change, however, while inevitable, is often as unwelcome in public matters as it is in our private lives. It is seldom more unwelcome than when it threatens arrangements to whose preservation we may be deeply committed. Often, in revering the cities where we are born, live, or work, we unconsciously cling to a certain image of what that city *is* — an image inextricably tied to a specific timeframe — and we forget that cities, like all living things, change. Change invariably entails a mix of advantages and disadvantages; yet the disadvantages are usually perceived to be clear and unmistakable, while the current advantages may be less easily recognized and long-range advantages may be imperceptible. The special challenge for policymakers confronting change, therefore, is to weather the disillusionments and deprivations occasioned by major change and to try to discern the underlying trends, and, if possible, to adjust to them.

### [Understanding Change]

This, of course, is an ideal scenario. In fact, few of us are so philosophical and visionary in the face of profound change. Government, however — as an important locus of authority, planning, and guidance in a society — has a greater responsibility than its citizens to understand change and to facilitate those changes that it can or should not try to prevent. Admittedly, that is not always an easy task in a system such as ours where government is continuously responsible to the people, many of whom are suffering from the accompaniments of change.

Indeed, we do not need scholarly treatises to remind us of the lamentable byproducts of urban deconcentration for the older industrial cities; the erosion of the tax base, hence of fiscal solvency; the increased ghettoization of the poor and minorities; the enduring high rates of unemployment and chronic economic depression in poverty neighborhoods; the deterioration of municipal services and their delivery systems; the "excessive" use of resources per capita; the fear of crime — all of which are associated with the dispersion of urban America into lower density social and economic arrangements.

The burden for people left in central cities is heavy. For many — the young and old, racial or ethnic minorities, and women — access to the traditional avenues to success has been blocked by discrimination and the dispersal of economic opportunity to places outside central cities. Whereas the city's process of upgrading had enabled earlier generations of migrants and their offspring to use the city as a launching pad, a growing proportion of urban residents are now left behind, consigned to become a nearly permanent urban underclass.

The relative decline of the older urban centers in the North-Central and Northeast regions has been accompanied by a corresponding growth of newer cities in the Sunbelt regions of the South and Southwest. These changes are the predictable results of economic change, but they are no less traumatic. Understandably, pressures have built up rapidly for special programs of compensatory aid, in some instances bailouts to avoid bankruptcy. We cannot confront these problems with disinterest and detachment, yet we cannot avoid the fact that growth and decline are integral parts of the same dynamic process in urban life. When the federal government steps in to try to alter these dynamics, it generates a flood of demands that may sap the initiative of urban governments because of the expectation of continuing support. There must be a better way.

### Federal Urban Policy in the Eighties

In instances of deep-seated and inexorable historical transformation, there is a fundamental problem in attempting to halt the shrinking of a metropolitan area or to revitalize obsolete industries that in the past have been expected to adapt themselves to changing circumstances. In our view, the moral and material resources of government would be better expended in planning for the future and helping people to adjust to new imperatives in ways that derive from an understanding and acceptance of change.

Because the negative consequences of change visit people first and foremost, we should try to help people bear their often painful burdens, and, as quickly as possible, facilitate transition to new locations and jobs.

This is not, we recognize, the customary or popular view. Traditionally, the government has focused much of its resources on localities, in part because of the growing political demands of jurisdictions undergoing traumatic change and in part because it is politically safer to aid places (and their political leadership) than people directly. Thus, we have allocated billions of public dollars in recent years to develop selected localities in the hope that the endeavor will help people, albeit indirectly. Much evidence seems to indicate, however, that such strategies achieve very little in upgrading those localities, let alone in helping the unemployed, underemployed, and dependent whose fortunes are not directly tied to the functioning of local economies. Localities have proved to be very difficult to shore up or "revitalize," despite all our place-oriented redevelopment programs. Federal assistance to local government has often been ineffective in eliminating the multiple distresses of "pockets of poverty" within "pockets of plenty."

It is time, then, despite all the difficulties entailed, to alter the pattern of place-oriented, spatially sensitive, national urban policies, and to ask, instead, what more people-oriented, spatially neutral, national social and economic policies might accomplish, if not in the immediate future, then certainly in the long run. In return, federal programs must be employed to assist the transformation of local communities to achieve health and vitality at lower population levels, and with a transformed economic base, and to ameliorate the undesirable impacts of these transitions.

### [Retraining and Relocating]

Thus, as the major long-term goal of federal urban policy, the Commission urges government to place greater emphasis on retraining and relocation assistance efforts designed to link people with economic opportunity, wherever that opportunity might be. Specific measures to emphasize would include job creation, skill acquisition and assisted relocation programs targeted to the employable, cash assistance plans for those who cannot work and for the "working poor," and, finally, subsidies to private employers to ensure that jobs created by government are only temporary and supplemental bridges to eventual employment in the private sector. The principal purpose of such programs would be to increase people's mobility by helping them acquire the necessary skills to ensure their continuing relevance to a changing economy. In short, much greater attention should be given to developing strategies that allow people to adjust to shifts in the location of economic opportunity. Assisting people to follow jobs, rather than concentrating solely on attempting to steer jobs to where people are, is a major goal in any adjustment strategy. Without the prospect of acquiring necessary retraining to participate in the rapidly changing economy, large segments of the urban lower classes face nearly permanent exclusion from an increasingly specialized economy that has less and less use for unskilled labor....

# Chapter 5

## [Strengthening Political Parties]

... We are particularly interested in strengthening the parties in the selection of Presidential and Congressional candidates. For the former, primary elections and the national media have tended to replace the decisions of party leaders, an event which has in turn worked to the disadvantage of candidates with experience in Washington and stature in the party, and in favor of candidates who run against Washington and are new to the national political scene. Working alliances along party lines between Congressional party majorities and the White House have become steadily more difficult, while competition between the Hill and the President has become almost a tradition of government.

In Congressional elections, the clout and effectiveness which the major parties once held have been quickly seized by interest groups that can mobilize portions of the public. The number of groups organized to lobby the federal government has risen, and their influence has grown correspondingly. Members of Congress are aware that interest groups often control a large number of votes and that many people are thought to cast their ballots on the basis of a candidate's stand on a single issue. Accordingly, key single-issue groups receive more attention from members of the House and Senate than they might have hoped to receive in an era of stronger political parties and coalitions.

The following recommendations are intended to strengthen the electoral process and to strengthen the political parties as stabilizing entities in the democracy:

1. Public funding for Congressional elections should be adopted, and a portion of these funds should be granted to the national committees of the parties to allocate to individual candidates. Public funding would decrease the influence of single-issue groups over decisionmaking in Congress, and giving some of these funds to the national committees of the parties would enable the party leadership to influence members of Congress through the granting of contributions to election campaigns.

2. Presidential primary elections should continue, as before, to play a major role in the selection of Presidential nominees, but instead of the current multiplicity of primaries, there should only be four, organized roughly by time zone and schedule on set dates separated by one month. It is our hope that such a system will diminish the excessive emphasis currently given the earliest state primaries.

3. A certain proportion of the delegate positions at a party's Presidential nominating convention — perhaps one-fifth to one-third of the whole — should be reserved for the party's elected officeholders,

major recent candidates, and its own officers. This measure is not aimed at replacing the primaries, but merely at altering the current balance which prevents party leaders from playing an important role in the nominating process. . . .

# STATE OF THE UNION MESSAGE
## January 16, 1981

*In one of his last actions as president, Jimmy Carter on January 16 sent Congress a State of the Union message that described the nation as basically sound but acknowledged that serious problems remained.*

*Instead of delivering a State of the Union address to a joint session of Congress, Carter sent a 76-page written statement to the Capitol. Personal appearances before Congress had been a tradition in the 20th century. The last outgoing president to send Congress only a written message had been Dwight D. Eisenhower in 1961.*

*News coverage of Carter's message was almost totally eclipsed by fast-moving events in Tehran, Iran, and Algiers, Algeria, leading to the freeing on January 20 of 52 American hostages held captive by Iran for 444 days.* (Hostages, p. 145)

*"Our economy is recovering from a recession," Carter wrote. "A national energy plan is in place and our dependence on foreign oil is decreasing. We have been at peace for four uninterrupted years." But Carter warned that the United States faced inflation, unemployment, an uncertain world market and trouble spots ahead.*

*Carter listed dozens of accomplishments as seen by his administration. They included enactment of a comprehensive energy policy, a sharp rise in defense spending, the revamping of the Civil Service System and a strong commitment to human rights.*

*Calling his budget proposals prudent and restrained, Carter said that "The rate of growth in federal spending has been held to a minimum."*

*And he noted that "high inflation cannot be attributed solely to govern-
ment spending." He credited his administration with adding 9 million
new jobs to the economy, including large increases for women and
members of minority groups.*

*He claimed credit for decontrolling oil and natural gas prices. But he
did not mention that he initially opposed those measures and supported
them only after Congress had made it clear that his backing was a
condition for passage of his energy policy.*

*The departing president urged Congress to pass several measures.
They included proposals to establish national health insurance, increase
training programs for jobless youths, improve medical care for children
and revise the welfare system.*

> *Following are excerpts from the text of President Jimmy
> Carter's State of the Union message sent to Congress
> January 16, 1981.* (Boldface headings in brackets have been
> added by Congressional Quarterly to highlight the organiza-
> tion of the text.)

*To the Congress of the United States:*

The State of the Union is sound. Our economy is recovering from a
recession. A national energy plan is in place and our dependence on foreign
oil is decreasing. We have been at peace for four uninterrupted years.

But, our Nation has serious problems. Inflation and unemployment are
unacceptably high. The world oil market is increasingly tight. There are
trouble spots throughout the world, and 52 American hostages are being
held in Iran against international law and against every precept of human
affairs.

However, I firmly believe that, as a result of the progress made in so
many domestic and international areas over the past four years, our
Nation is stronger, wealthier, more compassionate and freer than it was
four years ago. I am proud of that fact. And I believe the Congress should
be proud as well, for so much of what has been accomplished over the past
four years had been due to the hard work, insights and cooperation of
Congress. I applaud the Congress for its efforts and its achievements.

In this State of the Union Message I want to recount the achievements
and progress of the last four years and to offer recommendations to the
Congress for this year. While my term as President will end before the 97th
Congress begins its work in earnest, I hope that my recommendations will
serve as a guide for the direction this country should take so we build on
the record of the past four years.

## RECORD OF PROGRESS

When I took office, our Nation faced a number of serious domestic and
international problems:

● no national energy policy existed, and our dependence on foreign oil was rapidly increasing;

● public trust in the integrity and openness of the government was low:

● the Federal government was operating inefficiently in administering essential programs and policies;

● major social problems were being ignored or poorly addressed by the Federal government;

● our defense posture was declining as a result of a defense budget which was continuously shrinking in real terms;

● the strength of the NATO Alliance needed to be bolstered;

● tensions between Israel and Egypt threatened another Middle East war; and

● America's resolve to oppose human rights violations was under serious question.

Over the past 48 months, clear progress has been made in solving the challenges we found in January of 1977:

● almost all of our comprehensive energy program have [sic] been enacted, and the Department of Energy has been established to administer the program;

● confidence in the government's integrity has been restored, and respect for the government's openness and fairness has been renewed;

● the government has been made more effective and efficient: the Civil Service system was completely reformed for the first time this century; 14 reorganization initiatives have been proposed to the Congress, approved, and implemented; two new Cabinet departments have been created to consolidate and streamline the government's handling of energy and education problems; inspectors general have been placed in each Cabinet department to combat fraud, waste and other abuses; the regulatory process had been reformed through creation of the Regulatory Council, implementation of Executive Order 12044 and its requirement for cost-impact analyses, elimination of the unnecessary regulation, and passage of the Regulatory Flexibility Act; procedures have been established to assure citizen participation in government; and the airline, trucking, rail and communications industries are being deregulated;

● critical social problems, many long ignored by the Federal government, have been addressed directly; an urban policy was developed and implemented to reverse the decline in our urban areas; the Social Security System was refinanced to put it on a sound financial basis; the Humphrey-Hawkins Full Employment Act was enacted; Federal assistance for education was expanded by more than 75 percent; the minimum wage was increased to levels needed to ease the effects of inflation; affirmative action has been pursued aggressively — more blacks, Hispanics and women have been appointed to senior government positions and to judgeships than at any other time in our history; the ERA ratification deadline was extended to aid the ratification effort; and minority business procurement by the Federal government has more than doubled;

● the Nation's first sectoral policies were put in place, for the auto and steel industries, with my Administration demonstrating the value of cooperation between the government, business and labor;

● reversing previous trends, real defense spending has increased every year since 1977; the real increase in FY 1980 defense spending is well above 3 percent and I expect FY 1981 defense spending to be even higher; looking ahead, the defense program I am proposing is premised on a real increase in defense spending over the next five years of 20 percent or more;

● the NATO Alliance has proven its unity in responding to the situations in Eastern Europe and Southwest Asia and in agreeing on the issues to be addressed in the review of the Helsinki Final Act currently underway in Madrid;

● the peace process in the Middle East established at Camp David and by the Peace Treaty between Egypt and Israel is being buttressed on two fronts: steady progress in the normalization of Egyptian-Israeli relations in many fields, and the commitment of both Egypt and Israel, with United States' assistance, to see through to successful conclusion the autonomy negotiations for the West Bank and Gaza;

● the Panama Canal Treaties have been put into effect, which has helped to improve relations with Latin America.

● we have continued this Nation's strong commitment to the pursuit of human rights throughout the world, evenhandedly and objectively; our commitment to a worldwide human rights policy has remained firm; and many other countries have given high priority to it;

● our resolve to oppose aggression, such as the illegal invasion by the Soviet Union into Afghanistan, has been supported by tough action.

## I. Ensuring Economic Strength

### Economy

During the last decade our Nation has withstood a series of economic shocks unprecedented in peacetime. The most dramatic of these has been the explosive increases of OPEC oil prices. But we have also faced world commodity shortages, natural disasters, agricultural shortages and major challenges to world peace and security. Our ability to deal with these shocks has been impaired because of a decrease in the growth of productivity and the persistence of underlying inflationary forces built up over the past 15 years.

Nevertheless, the economy has proved to be remarkably resilient. Real output has grown at an average rate of 3 percent per year since I took office, and employment has grown by 10 percent. We have added about 8 million productive private sector jobs to the economy. However, unacceptably high inflation — the most difficult economic problem I have faced — persists.

This inflation — which threatens the growth, productivity, and stability of our economy — requires that we restrain the growth of the budget to the maximum extent consistent with national security and human compassion. I have done so in my earlier budgets, and in my FY '82 budget. However, while restraint is essential to any appropriate economic policy, high inflation cannot be attributed solely to government spending. The growth in budget outlays has been more the result of economic factors than the cause of them. . . .

## The 1982 Budget

The FY 1982 budget I have sent to the Congress continues our four-year policy of prudence and restraint. While the budget deficits during my term are higher than I would have liked, their size is determined for the most part by economic conditions. And in spite of these conditions, the relative size of the deficit continues to decline. In 1976, before I took office, the budget deficit equalled 4 percent of gross national product. It had been cut to 2.3 percent in the 1980 fiscal year just ended. My 1982 budget contains a deficit estimated to be less than 1 percent of our gross national product.

The rate of growth in Federal spending has been held to a minimum. Nevertheless, outlays are still rising more rapidly than many had anticipated, the result of many powerful forces in our society:

We face a threat to our security, as events in Afghanistan, the Middle East, and Eastern Europe make clear. We have a steadily aging population and, as a result, the biggest single increase in the Federal budget is the rising cost of retirement programs, particularly social security. We face other important domestic needs: to continue responsibility for the disadvantaged; to provide the capital needed by our cities and our transportation systems; to protect our environment; to revitalize American industry; and to increase the export of American goods and services so essential to the creation of jobs and a trade surplus.

Yet the Federal Government itself may not always be the proper source of such assistance. For example, it must not usurp functions if they can be more appropriately decided upon, managed, and financed by the private sector or by State and local governments. My Administration has always sought to consider the proper focus of responsibility for the most efficient resolution of problems.

We have also recognized the need to simplify the system of grants to State and local governments. I have again proposed several grant consolidations in the 1982 budget, including a new proposal that would consolidate several highway programs. . . .

Fiscal restraint must be continued in the years ahead. Budgets must be tight enough to convince those who set wages and prices that the Federal Government is serious about fighting inflation but not so tight as to choke off all growth.

Careful budget policy should be supplemented by other measures designed to reduce inflation at lower cost in lost output and employment.

These other steps include measures to increase investment — such as the tax proposals included in my 1982 budget — and measures to increase competition and productivity in our economy. Voluntary incomes policies can also directly influence wages and prices in the direction of moderation and thereby bring inflation down faster and at lower cost to the economy. Through a tax-based incomes policy (TIP) we could provide tax incentives for firms and workers to moderate their wage and price increases. In the coming years, control of Federal expenditures can make possible periodic tax reductions. The Congress should therefore begin now to evaluate the potentialities of a TIP program so that when the next round of tax reductions is appropriate a TIP program will be seriously considered.

## Employment

During the last four years we have given top priority to meeting the needs of workers and providing additional job opportunities to those who seek work. Since the end of 1976:

• almost 9 million new jobs have been added to the nation's economy

• total employment has reached 97 million. More jobs than ever before are held by women, minorities and young people. Employment over the past four years has increased by:

—17% for adult women

—11% for blacks, and

—30% for Hispanics

• employment of black teenagers increased by more than 5%, reversing the decline that occurred in the previous eight years.

Major initiatives launched by this Administration helped bring about these accomplishments and have provided a solid foundation for employment and training policy in the 1980's.

In 1977, as part of the comprehensive economic stimulus program:

• 425,000 public service jobs were created

• A $1 billion youth employment initiative funded 200,000 jobs

• the doubling of the Job Corps to 44,000 slots began and 1 million summer youth jobs were approved — a 25 percent increase.

In 1978:

• the Humphrey-Hawkins Full Employment Act became law

• the $400 million Private Sector Initiatives Program was begun

• a targeted jobs tax credit for disadvantaged youth and others with special employment barriers was enacted

• the Comprehensive Employment and Training Act was reauthorized for four years.

In 1979:

• a $6 billion welfare reform proposal was introduced with funding for 400,000 public service jobs

• welfare reform demonstration projects were launched in communities around the country

● the Vice President initiated a nationwide review of youth unemployment in this country.

In 1980:

● the findings of the Vice President's Task Force revealed the major education and employment deficits that exist for poor and minority youngsters. As a result a $2 billion youth education and jobs initiative was introduced to provide unemployed youth with the basic education and work experience they need to compete in the labor market of the 1980's.

● As part of the economic revitalization program several steps were proposed to aid workers in high unemployment communities:

—an additional 13 weeks of unemployment benefits for the long term unemployed.

—$600 million to train the disadvantaged and unemployed for new private sector jobs.

—positive adjustment demonstrations to aid workers in declining industries.

● The important Title VII Private Sector Initiatives Program was reauthorized for an additional two years.

In addition to making significant progress in helping the disadvantaged and unemployed, important gains were realized for all workers:

● an historic national accord with organized labor made it possible for the views of working men and women to be heard as the nation's economic and domestic policies were formulated.

● the Mine Safety and Health Act brought about improved working conditions for the nation's 500,000 miners.

● substantial reforms of the Occupational Safety and Health Administration were accomplished to help reduce unnecessary burdens on business and to focus on major health and safety problems.

● the minimum wage was increased over a four year period from $2.30 to $3.35 an hour.

● the Black Lung Benefit Reform Act was signed ito law.

● attempts to weaken the Davis-Bacon Act were defeated.

While substantial gains have been made in the last four years, continued efforts are required to ensure that this progress is continued:

● government must continue to make labor a full partner in the policy decisions that affect the interests of working men and women

● a broad, bipartisan effort to combat youth unemployment must be sustained

● compassionate reform of the nation's welfare system should be continued with employment opportunities provided for those able to work

● workers in declining industries should be provided new skills and help in finding employment

### Trade

Over the past year, the U.S. trade picture improved as a result of solid export gains in both manufactured and agricultural products. Agricultural exports reached a new record of over $40 billion, while manufactured exports have grown by 24 percent to a record $144 billion. In these areas the United States recorded significant surpluses of $24 billion and $19 billion respectively. While our oil imports remained a major drain on our foreign exchange earnings, that drain was somewhat moderated by a 19 percent decline in the volume of oil imports.

U.S. trade negotiators made significant progress over the past year in assuring effective implementation of the agreements negotiated during the Tokyo Round of Multilateral Trade Negotiations. Agreements reached with the Japanese government, for example, will assure that the United States will be able to expand its exports to the Japanese market in such key areas as telecommunications equipment, tobacco, and lumber. Efforts by U.S. trade negotiators also helped to persuade a number of key developing countries to accept many of the non-tariff codes negotiated during the Multilateral Trade Negotiations. This will assure that these countries will increasingly assume obligations under the international trading system. . . .

## II. Creating Energy Security

Since I took office, my highest legislative priorities have involved the reorientation and redirection of U.S. energy activities and for the first time, to establish a coordinated national energy policy. The struggle to achieve that policy has been long and difficult, but the accomplishments of the past four years make clear that our country is finally serious about the problems caused by our overdependence on foreign oil. Our progress should not be lost. We must rely on and encourage multiple forms of energy production — coal, crude oil, natural gas, solar, nuclear, synthetics — and energy conservation. The framework put in place over the last four years will enable us to do this.

### National Energy Policy

As a result of actions my Administration and the Congress have taken over the past four years, our country finally has a national energy policy:

• Under my program of phased decontrol, domestic crude oil price controls will end September 30, 1981. As a result exploratory drilling activities have reached an all-time high;

• Prices for new natural gas are being decontrolled under the Natural Gas Policy Act — and natural gas production is now at an all time high; the supply shortages of several years ago have been eliminated;

• The windfall profits tax on crude oil has been enacted providing $227 billion over ten years for assistance to low-income households, increased mass transit funding, and a massive investment in the production and development of alternative energy sources;

• The Synthetic Fuels Corporation has been established to help private companies build the facilities to produce energy from synthetic fuels;

● Solar energy funding has been quadrupled, solar energy tax credits enacted, and a Solar Energy and Energy Conservation Bank has been established;

● A route has been chosen to bring natural gas from the North Slope of Alaska to the lower 48 states;

● Coal production and consumption incentives have been increased, and coal production is now at its highest level in history;

● A gasoline rationing plan has been approved by Congress for possible use in the event of a severe energy supply shortage or interruption;

● Gasohol production has been dramatically increased, with a program being put in place to produce 500 million gallons of alcohol fuel by the end of this year — an amount that could enable gasohol to meet the demand for 10 percent of all unleaded gasoline;

● New energy conservation incentives have been provided for individuals, businesses and communities and conservation has increased dramatically. The U.S. has reduced oil imports by 25 percent — or 2 million barrels per day — over the past four years.

## [Development of Domestic Energy Sources]

Although it is essential that the Nation reduce its dependence on imported fossil fuels and complete the transition to reliance on domestic renewable sources of energy, it is also important that this transition be accomplished in an orderly, economic, and environmentally sound manner. To this end, the Administration has launched several initiatives.

Leasing of oil and natural gas on federal lands, particularly the outer continental shelf, has been accelerated at the same time as the Administration has reformed leasing procedures through the 1978 amendments to the Outer Continental Shelf Lands Act. In 1979 the Interior Department held six OCS lease sales, the greatest number ever, which resulted in federal receipts of $6.5 billion, another record. The five-year OCS Leasing schedule was completed, requiring 36 sales over the next five years.

Since 1971 no general federal coal lease sales were suspended. Over the past four years the Administration has completely revised the federal coal leasing program to bring it into compliance with the requirements of [the] 1976 Federal Land Planning and Management Act and other statutory provisions. The program is designed to balance the competing interests that affect resource development on public lands and to ensure that adequate supplies of coal will be available to meet national needs. As a result, the first general competitive federal coal lease sale in ten years will be held this month.

In July 1980, I signed into law the Energy Security Act of 1980 which established the Synthetic Fuels Corporation. The Corporation is designed to spur the development of commercial technologies for production of synthetic fuels, such as liquid and gaseous fuels from coal and the production of oil from oil shale. The Act provides the Corporation with an initial $22 billion to accomplish these objectives. The principal purpose of the legislation is to ensure that the nation will have available in the late 1980's the option to undertake commercial development of synthetic fuels if that becomes necessary. The Energy Security Act also provides significant incentives for the development of gasohol and biomass fuels, thereby enhancing the nation's supply of alternative energy sources.

### [Sustainable Energy Future]

The Administration's 1977 National Energy Plan marked an historic departure from the policies of previous Administrations. The plan stressed the importance of both energy *production* and *conservation* to achieving our ultimate national goal of relying primarily on secure sources of energy. The National Energy Plan made energy conservation a cornerstone of our national energy policy.

In 1978, I initiated the Administration's Solar Domestic Policy Review. This represented the first step towards widespread introduction of renewable energy sources into the Nation's economy. As a result of the Review, I issued the 1979 Solar Message to Congress, the first such message in the Nation's history. The Message outlined the Administration's solar program and established an ambitious national goal for the year 2000 of obtaining 20 percent of this Nation's energy from solar and renewable sources. The thrust of the federal solar program is to help industry develop solar energy sources by emphasizing basic research and development of solar technologies which are not currently economic, such as photovoltaics, which generate energy directly from the sun. At the same time, through tax incentives, education, and the Solar Energy and Energy Conservation Bank, the solar program seeks to encourage state and local governments, industry, and our citizens to expand their use of solar and renewable resource technologies currently available.

As a result of these policies and programs, the energy efficiency of the American economy has improved markedly and investments in renewable energy sources have grown significantly. It now takes 3½ percent less energy to produce a constant dollar of GNP than it did in January 1977. This increase in efficiency represents a savings of over 1.3 million barrels a day of oil equivalent, about the level of total oil production now occurring in Alaska. Over the same period, Federal support for conservation and solar energy has increased by more than 3000 percent, to $3.3 billion in FY 1981, including the tax credits for solar energy and energy conservation investments — these credits are expected to amount to $1.2 billion in FY 1981 and $1.5 billion in FY 1982.

### [Nuclear Safety and Security]

Since January 1977, significant progress has been achieved in resolving three critical problems resulting from the use of nuclear energy: radioactive waste management, nuclear safety and weapons proliferation.

In 1977, the Administration announced its nuclear nonproliferation policy and initiated the International Fuel Cycle Evaluation. In 1978, Congress passed the Nuclear Nonproliferation Act, an historic piece of legislation.

In February 1980, the Administration transmitted its nuclear waste management policy to the Congress. This policy was a major advance over all previous efforts. . . .

The accident at Three Mile Island made the nation acutely aware of the safety risks posed by nuclear power plants. In response, the President established the Kemeny Commission to review the accident and make recommendations. Virtually all of the Commission's substantive recommendations were adopted by the Administration and are now being implemented by the Nuclear Regulatory Commission. The Congress adopted the President's proposed plan for the Nuclear Regulatory Commission and the Nuclear Safety Oversight Committee was established to ensure that the Administration's decisions were implemented.

Nuclear safety will remain a vital concern in the years ahead. We must continue to press ahead for the safe, secure disposal of radioactive wastes, and prevention of nuclear proliferation.

While significant growth in foreign demand for U.S. steam coal is foreseen, congestion must be removed at major U.S. coal exporting ports such as Hampton Roads, Virginia, and Baltimore, Maryland. My Administration has worked through the Interagency Coal Task Force Study to promote cooperation and coordination of resources between shippers, railroads, vessel broker/operators and port operators, and to determine the most appropriate Federal role in expanding and modernizing coal export facilities, including dredging deeper channels at selected ports. . . .

## III. Enhancing Basic Human and Social Needs

For too long prior to my Administration, many of our Nation's basic human and social needs were being ignored or handled insensitively by the Federal government. Over the last four years, we have significantly increased funding for many of the vital programs in these areas; developed new programs where needs were unaddressed; targeted Federal support to those individuals and areas most in need of our assistance; and removed barriers that have unnecessarily kept many disadvantaged citizens from obtaining aid for their most basic needs.

Our record has produced clear progress in the effort to solve some of the country's fundamental human and social problems. My Administration and the Congress, working together, have demonstrated that government must and can meet our citizens' basic human and social needs in a responsible and compassionate way.

But there is an unfinished agenda still before the Congress. If we are to meet our obligations to help all Americans realize the dreams of sound health care, decent housing, effective social services, a good education, and a meaningful job, important legislation still must be enacted. National Health Insurance, Welfare Reform, Child Health Assessment Programs, are before the Congress and I urge their passage.

## HEALTH

### National Health Plan

During my Administration, I proposed to Congress a National Health Plan which will enable the country to reach the goal of comprehensive, universal health care coverage. The legislation I submitted lays the foundation for this comprehensive plan and addresses the most serious problems of health financing and delivery. It is realistic and enactable. It does not overpromise or overspend, and, as a result, can be the solution to the thirty years of Congressional battles on national health insurance....

### [Services to the Poor and Underserved]

During my Administration, health services to the poor and underserved have been dramatically increased. The number of National Health Service Corps (NHSC) assignees providing services in medically underserved communities has grown from 500 in 1977 to nearly 3,000 in 1981. The population served by the NHSC has more than tripled since 1977. The number of Community Health Centers providing services in high priority underserved areas has doubled during my Administration, and will serve an estimated six million people in 1981. I strongly urge the new Congress to support these highly successful programs.

### Mental Health

One of the most significant health achievements during my Administration was the recent passage of the Mental Health Systems Act, which grew out of recommendations of my Commission on Mental Health. I join many others in my gratitude to the First Lady for her tireless and effective contribution to the passage of this important legislation.

The Act is designed to inaugurate a new era of Federal and State partnership in the planning and provision of mental health services. In addition, the Act specifically provides for prevention and support services to the chronically mentally ill to prevent unnecessary institutionalization and for the development of community-based mental health services. I urge the new Congress to provide adequate support for the full and timely implementation of this Act....

### Food and Nutrition

Building on the comprehensive reform of the Food Stamp Program that I proposed and Congress passed in 1977, my Administration and the

Congress worked together in 1979 and 1980 to enact several other important changes in the Program. These changes will further simplify administration and reduce fraud and error, will make the program more responsive to the needs of the elderly and disabled, and will increase the cap on allowable program expenditures. The Food Stamp Act will expire at the end of fiscal 1981. It is essential that the new Administration and the Congress continue this program to ensure complete eradication of the debilitating malnutrition witnessed and documented among thousands of children in the 1960's.

### Drug Abuse Prevention

At the beginning of my Administration there were over a half million heroin addicts in the United States. Our continued emphasis on reducing the supply of heroin, as well as providing treatment and rehabilitation to its victims, has reduced the heroin addict population, reduced the number of heroin overdose deaths by 80%, and reduced the number of heroin related injuries by 50%. We have also seen and encouraged a national movement of parents and citizens committed to reversing the very serious and disturbing trends of adolescent drug abuse.

Drug abuse in many forms will continue to detract, however, from the quality of life of many Americans. To prevent that, I see four great challenges in the years ahead. First, we must deal aggressively with the supplies of illegal drugs at their source, through joint crop destruction programs with foreign nations and increased law enforcement and border interdiction. Second, we must look to citizens and parents across the country to help educate the increasing numbers of American youth who are experimenting with drugs to the dangers of drug abuse. Education is a key factor in reducing drug abuse. Third, we must focus our efforts on drug and alcohol abuse in the workplace for not only does this abuse contribute to low productivity but it also destroys the satisfaction and sense of purpose all Americans can gain from the work experience. Fourth, we need a change in attitude, from an attitude which condones the casual use of drugs to one that recognizes the appropriate use of drugs for medical purposes and condemns the inappropriate and harmful abuse of drugs. I hope the Congress and the new Administration will take action to meet each of these challenges.

## EDUCATION

The American people have always recognized that education is one of the soundest investments they can make. The dividends are reflected in every dimension of our national life — from the strength of our economy and national security to the vitality of our music, art, and literature. Among the accomplishments that have given me the most satisfaction over the last four years are the contributions that my Administration has been able to make to the well-being of students and educators throughout the country.

This Administration has collaborated successfully with the Congress on landmark education legislation. Working with the Congressional leadership, my Administration spotlighted the importance of education by creating a new Department of Education. The Department has given education a stronger voice at the Federal level, while at the same time reserving the actual control and operation of education to states, localities, and private institutions. The Department has successfully combined nearly 150 Federal education programs into a cohesive, streamlined organization that is more responsive to the needs of educators and students. The Department has made strides to cut red tape and paperwork and thereby to make the flow of Federal dollars to school districts and institutions of higher education more efficient. It is crucial that the Department be kept intact and strengthened.

Our collaboration with the Congress has resulted in numerous other important legislative accomplishments for education. A little over two years ago, I signed into law on the same day two major bills — one benefiting elementary and secondary education and the other, postsecondary education. The Education Amendments of 1978 embodied nearly all of my Administration's proposals for improvements in the Elementary and Secondary Education Act, including important new programs to improve students' achievement in the basic skills and to aid school districts with exceptionally high concentrations of children from low-income families. The Middle Income Student Assistance Act, legislation jointly sponsored by this Administration and the Congressional leadership, expanded eligibility for need-based Basic Educational Opportunity Grants to approximately one-third of the students enrolled in postsecondary education and made many more students eligible for the first time for other types of grants, work-study, and loans. . . .

Last year, I proposed to the Congress a major legislative initiative that would direct $2 billion into education and job training programs designed to alleviate youth unemployment through improved linkages between the schools and the work place. This legislation generated bipartisan support; but unfortunately, action on it was not completed in the final, rushed days of the 96th Congress. I urge the new Congress — as it undertakes broad efforts to strengthen the economy as well as more specific tasks like reauthorizing the Vocational Education Act — to make the needs of our nation's unemployed youth a top priority for action. Only by combining a basic skills education program together with work training and employment incentives can we make substantial progress in eliminating one of the most severe social problems in our nation — youth unemployment, particularly among minorities. I am proud of the progress already made through passage of the Youth Employment and Demonstration Project Act of 1977 and the substantial increase in our investment in youth employment programs. The new legislation would cap these efforts.

## INCOME SECURITY

### Social Security

One of the highest priorities of my Administration has been to continue the tradition of effectiveness and efficiency widely associated with the social security program, and to assure present and future beneficiaries that they will receive their benefits as expected. The earned benefits that are paid monthly to retired and disabled American workers and their families provide a significant measure of economic protection to millions of people who might otherwise face retirement or possible disability with fear. I have enacted changes to improve the benefits of many social security beneficiaries during my years as President.

The last four years have presented a special set of concerns over the financial stability of the social security system. Shortly after taking office I proposed and Congress enacted legislation to protect the stability of the old age and survivors trust fund and prevent the imminent exhaustion of the disability insurance trust fund, and to correct a flaw in the benefit formula that was threatening the long run health of the entire social security system. The actions taken by the Congress at my request helped stabilize the system. That legislation was later complemented by the Disability Insurance Amendments of 1980 which further bolstered the disability insurance program, and reduced certain inequities among beneficiaries.

My commitment to the essential retirement and disability protection provided to 35 million people each month has been demonstrated by the fact that without interruption those beneficiaries have continued to receive their social security benefits, including annual cost of living increases. Changing and unpredictable economic circumstances require that we continue to monitor the financial stability of the social security system. To correct anticipated short-term strains on the system, I proposed last year that the three funds be allowed to borrow from one another, and I urge the Congress again this year to adopt such interfund borrowing. To further strengthen the social security system and provide a greater degree of assurance to beneficiaries, given projected future economic uncertainties, additional action should be taken. Among the additional financing options available are borrowing from the general fund, financing half of the hospital insurance fund with general revenues, and increasing the payroll tax rate. The latter option is particularly unpalatable given the significant increase in the tax rate already mandated in law....

### Welfare Reform

In 1979 I proposed a welfare reform package which offers solutions to some of the most urgent problems in our welfare system. This proposal is embodied in two bills — The Work and Training Opportunities Act and

The Social Welfare Reform Amendments Act. The House passed the second of these two proposals. Within the framework of our present welfare system, my reform proposals offer achievable means to increase self-sufficiency through work rather than welfare, more adequate assistance to people unable to work, the removal of inequities in coverage under current programs, and fiscal relief needed by States and localities.

Our current welfare system is long overdue for serious reform; the system is wasteful and not fully effective. The legislation I have proposed will help eliminate inequities by establishing a national minimum benefit, and by directly relating benefit levels to the poverty threshold. It will reduce program complexity, which leads to inefficiency and waste, by simplifying and coordinating administration among different programs.

I urge the Congress to take action in this area along the lines I have recommended.

### Child Welfare

My Administration has worked closely with the Congress on legislation which is designed to improve greatly the child welfare services and foster care programs and to create a Federal system of adoption assistance. These improvements will be achieved with the recent enactment of H.R. 3434, the Adoption Assistance and Child Welfare Act of 1980. The well-being of children in need of homes and their permanent placement have been a primary concern of my Administration. This legislation will ensure that children are not lost in the foster care system, but instead will be returned to their families where possible or placed in permanent adoptive homes. . . .

### HOUSING

For the past 14 months, high interest rates have had a severe impact on the nation's housing market. Yet the current pressures and uncertainties should not obscure the achievements of the past four years.

Working with the Congress, the regulatory agencies, and the financial community, my Administration has brought about an expanded and steadier flow of funds into home mortgages. Deregulation of the interest rates payable by depository institutions, the evolution of variable and renegotiated rate mortgages, development of high yielding savings certificates, and expansion of the secondary mortgage market have all increased housing's ability to attract capital and have assured that mortgage money would not be cut off when interest rates rose. These actions will diminish the cyclicality of the housing industry. Further, we have secured legislation updating the Federal Government's emergency authority to provide support for the housing industry through the Brooke-Cranston program, and creating a new Section 235 housing stimulus program. These tools will enable the Federal Government to deal quickly and effectively with serious distress in this critical industry. . . .

We have devoted particular effort to meeting the housing needs of low and moderate income families. In the past four years, more than 1 million subsidized units have been made available for occupancy by lower income Americans and more than 600,000 assisted units have gone into construction. In addition, we have undertaken a series of measures to revitalize and preserve the nation's 2 million units of public and assisted housing. . . .

## Highways

Our vast network of highways, which account for 90 percent of travel and 80 percent by value of freight traffic goods movement, is deteriorating. If current trends continue, a major proportion of the Interstate pavement will have deteriorated by the end of the 1980's.

Arresting the deterioration of the nation's system of highways is a high priority objective for the 1980's. We must reorient the Federal mission from major new construction projects to the stewardship of the existing Interstate Highway System. Interstate gaps should be judged on the connections they make and on their compatibility with community needs.

During this decade, highway investments will be needed to increase productivity, particularly in the elimination of bottlenecks, provide more efficient connections to ports and seek low-cost solutions to traffic demand.

My Administration has therefore recommended redefining completion of the Interstate system, consolidating over 27 categorical assistance programs into nine, and initiating a major repair and rehabilitation program for segments of the Interstate system. This effort should help maintain the condition and performance of the Nation's highways, particularly the Interstate and primary system; provide a realistic means to complete the Interstate system by 1990; ensure better program delivery through consolidation, and assist urban revitalization. In addition, the Congress must address the urgent funding problems of the highway trust fund, and the need to generate greater revenues.

## Mass Transit

In the past decade the nation's public transit systems' ridership increased at an annual average of 1.1% each year in the 1970's (6.9% in 1979). Continued increases in the cost of fuel are expected to make transit a growing part of the nation's transportation system.

As a result, my Administration projected a ten year, $43 billion program to increase mass transit capacity by 50 percent, and promote more energy efficient vehicle uses in the next decade. The first part of this proposal was the five year, $24.7 billion Urban Mass Transportation Administration reauthorization legislation I sent to the Congress in March, 1980. I urge the 97th Congress to quickly enact this or similar legislation in 1981.

73

My Administration was also the first to have proposed and signed into law a non-urban formula grant program to assist rural areas and small communities with public transportation programs to end their dependence on the automobile, promote energy conservation and efficiency, and provide transportation services to impoverished rural communities.

A principal need of the 1980's will be maintaining mobility for all segments of the population in the face of severely increasing transportation costs and uncertainty of fuel supplies. We must improve the flexibility of our transportation system and offer greater choice and diversity in transportation services. While the private automobile will continue to be the principal means of transportation for many Americans, public transportation can become an increasingly attractive alternative. We, therefore, want to explore a variety of paratransit modes, various types of buses, modern rapid transit, regional rail systems and light rail systems....

## Railroads

In addition, the Federal government must reassess the appropriate Federal role of support for passenger and freight rail services such as Amtrak and Conrail. Our goal through federal assistance should be to maintain and enhance adequate rail service, where it is not otherwise available to needy communities. But Federal subsidies must be closely scrutinized to be sure that they are a stimulus to, and not a replacement for, private investment and initiative. Federal assistance cannot mean permanent subsidies for unprofitable operations....

## Maritime Policy

During my Administration I have sought to ensure that the U.S. maritime industry will not have to function at an unfair competitive disadvantage in the international market. As I indicated in my maritime policy statement to the Congress in July, 1979, the American merchant marine is vital to our Nation's welfare, and Federal actions should promote rather than harm it. In pursuit of this objective, I signed into law the Controlled Carrier Act of 1978, authorizing the Federal Maritime Commission to regulate certain rate cutting practices of some state-controlled carriers, and recently signed a bilateral maritime agreement with the People's Republic of China that will expand the access of American ships to 20 specified Chinese ports, and set aside for American-flag ships a substantial share (at least one-third) of the cargo between our countries. This agreement should officially foster expanded U.S. and Chinese shipping services linking the two countries, and will provide further momentum to the growth of Sino-American trade.

There is also a need to modernize and expand the dry bulk segment of our fleet. Our heavy dependence on foreign carriage of U.S.-bulk cargoes deprives the U.S. economy of seafaring and shipbuilding jobs, adds to the balance-of-payments deficit, deprives the Government of substantial tax revenues, and leaves the United States dependent on foreign-flag shipping for a continued supply of raw materials to support the civil economy and war production in time of war.

I therefore sent to the Congress proposed legislation to strengthen this woefully weak segment of the U.S.-flag fleet by removing certain disincentives to U.S. construction of dry bulkers and their operation under U.S. registry....

## SPECIAL NEEDS

### Women

The past four years have been years of rapid advancement for women. Our focus has been two-fold: to provide American women with a full range of opportunities and to make them a part of the mainstream of every aspect of our national life and leadership.

I have appointed a record number of women to judgeships and to top government posts. Fully 22 percent of all my appointees are women, and I nominated 41 of the 46 women who sit on the Federal bench today. For the first time in our history, women occupy policymaking positions at the highest level of every Federal agency and department and have demonstrated their ability to serve our citizens well.

We have strengthened the rights of employed women by consolidating and strengthening enforcement of sex discrimination laws under the EEOC, by expanding employment rights of pregnant women through the Pregnancy Disability Bill, and by increasing federal employment opportunities for women through civil service reform, and flexi-time and part-time employment.

By executive order, I created the first national program to provide women businessowners with technical assistance, grants, loans, and improved access to federal contracts.

We have been sensitive to the needs of women who are homemakers. I established an Office of Families within HHS and sponsored the White House Conference on Families. We initiated a program targeting CETA funds to help displaced homemakers. The Social Security system was amended to eliminate the widow's penalty and a comprehensive study of discriminatory provisions and possible changes was presented to Congress. Legislation was passed to give divorced spouses of foreign service officers rights to share in pension benefits.

We created an office on domestic violence within HHS to coordinate the 12 agencies that now have domestic violence relief programs, and to distribute information on the problem and the services available to victims....

## Older Americans

My Administration has taken great strides toward solving the difficult problems faced by older Americans. Early in my term we worked successfully with the Congress to assure adequate revenues for the Social Security Trust Funds. And last year the strength of the Social Security System was strengthened by legislation I proposed to permit borrowing among the separate trust funds. I have also signed into law legislation prohibiting employers from requiring retirement prior to age 70, and removing mandatory retirement for most Federal employees. In addition, my Administration worked very closely with Congress to amend the Older Americans Act in a way that has already improved administration of its housing, social services, food delivery, and employment programs.

This year, I will be submitting to Congress a budget which again demonstrates my commitment to programs for the elderly. It will include, as my previous budgets have, increased funding for nutrition, senior centers and home health care, and will focus added resources on the needs of older Americans.

With the 1981 White House Conference on Aging approaching, I hope the new Administration will make every effort to assure an effective and useful conference. This Conference should enable older Americans to voice their concerns and give us guidance in our continued efforts to ensure the quality of life so richly deserved by our senior citizens.

## Refugees

We cannot hope to build a just and humane society at home if we ignore the humanitarian claims of refugees, their lives at stake, who have nowhere else to turn. Our country can be proud that hundreds of thousands of people around the world would risk everything they have — including their own lives — to come to our country.

This Administration initiated and implemented the first comprehensive reform of our refugee and immigration policies in over 25 years. We also established the first refugee coordination office in the Department of State under the leadership of a special ambassador and coordinator for refugee affairs and programs. The new legislation and the coordinator's office will bring common sense and consolidation to our Nation's previously fragmented, inconsistent, and in many ways, outdated, refugee and immigration policies.

With the unexpected arrival of thousands of Cubans and Haitians who sought refuge in our country last year, outside of our regular immigration and refugee admissions process, our country and its government were tested in being compassionate and responsive to a major human emergency. Because we had taken steps to reorganize our refugee programs, we met that test successfully. I am proud that the American people responded to this crisis with their traditional good will and hospitality. . . .

While we must remain committed to aiding and assisting those who come to our shores, at the same time we must uphold our immigration and refugee policies and provide adequate enforcement resources. As a result of our enforcement policy, the illegal flow from Cuba has been halted and an orderly process has been initiated to make certain that our refugee and immigration laws are honored.

This year the Select Commission on Immigration and Refugee Policy will complete its work and forward its advice and recommendations. I hope that the recommendations will be carefully considered by the new Administration and the Congress, for it is clear that we must take additional action to keep our immigration policy responsive to emergencies and ever changing times.

## Veterans

This country and its leadership has a continuing and unique obligation to the men and women who served their nation in the armed forces and help maintain or restore peace in the world.

My commitment to veterans — as evidenced by my record — is characterized by a conscientious and consistent emphasis in these general areas:

First, we have worked to honor the Vietnam veteran. During my Administration, and under the leadership of VA Administrator Max Cleland, I was proud to lead our country in an overdue acknowledgement of our Nation's gratitude to the men and women who served their country during the bitter war in Southeast Asia. . . .

My Administration was able to launch a long sought after psychological readjustment and outreach program, unprecedented in its popularity, sensitivity and success. This program must be continued. The Administration has also grappled with the difficult questions posed by some veterans who served in Southeast Asia and were exposed to potentially harmful substances, including the herbicide known as Agent Orange. We have launched scientific inquiries that should answer many veterans' questions about their health and should provide the basis for establishing sound compensation policy. We cannot rest until their concerns are dealt with in a sensitive, expeditious and compassionate fashion.

Second, we have focused the VA health care system on the needs of the service-connected disabled veteran. We initiated and are implementing the first reform of the VA vocational rehabilitation system since its inception in 1943. Also, my Administration was the first to seek a cost-of-living increase for the recipients of VA compensation every year. My last budget also makes such a request. The Administration also launched the Disabled Veterans Outreach Program in the Department of Labor which has successfully placed disabled veterans in jobs. Services provided by the VA health care system will be further targeted to the special needs of disabled veterans during the coming year. . . .

## GOVERNMENT ASSISTANCE

### [Aid To State and Local Governments]

Since taking office, I have been strongly committed to strengthening the fiscal and economic condition of our Nation's State and local governments. I have accomplished this goal by encouraging economic development of local communities, and by supporting the General Revenue Sharing and other essential grant-in-aid programs....

During my Administration, total grants-in-aid to State and local governments have increased by more than 40 percent — from $68 billion in Fiscal Year 1977 to $96 billion in Fiscal Year 1981. This significant increase in aid has allowed States and localities to maintain services that are essential to their citizens without imposing onerous tax burdens. It also has allowed us to establish an unprecedented partnership between the leaders of the Federal government and State and local government elected officials.

### General Revenue Sharing

Last year Congress enacted legislation that extends the General Revenue Sharing program for three more years. This program is the cornerstone of our efforts to maintain the fiscal health of our Nation's local government. It will provide $4.6 billion in each of the next three years to cities, counties and towns. This program is essential to the continued ability of our local governments to provide essential police, fire and sanitation services....

## SCIENCE AND TECHNOLOGY

Science and technology contribute immeasurably to the lives of all Americans. Our high standard of living is largely the product of the technology that surrounds us in the home or factory. Our good health is due in large part to our ever increasing scientific understanding. Our national security is assured by the application of technology. And our environment is protected by the use of science and technology. Indeed, our vision of the future is often largely defined by the bounty that we anticipate science and technology will bring.

The Federal government has a special role to play in science and technology. Although the fruits of scientific achievements surround us, it is often difficult to predict the benefits that will arise from a given scientific venture. And these benefits, even if predictable, do not usually lead to ownership rights. Accordingly, the Government has a special obligation to support science as an investment in our future.

My Administration has sought to reverse a decade-long decline in funding. Despite the need for fiscal restraint, real support of basic research has grown nearly 11% during my term in office. And, my Administration has sought to increase the support of long-term research in the variety of mission agencies. In this way, we can harness the American genius for innovation to meet the economic, energy, health, and security challenges that confront our nation.

● *International Relations and National Security.* Science and technology are becoming increasingly important elements of our national security and foreign policies. This is especially so in the current age of sophisticated defense systems and of growing dependence among all countries on modern technology for all aspects of their economic strength. For these reasons, scientific and technological considerations have been integral elements of the Administration's decisionmaking on such national security and foreign policy issues as the modernization of our strategic weaponry, arms control, technology transfer, the growing bilateral relationship with China, and our relations with the developing world. . . .

● *Space Policy.* The Administration has established a framework for a strong and evolving space program for the 1980's.

The Administration's space policy reaffirmed the separation of military space systems and the open civil space program, and at the same time, provided new guidance on technology transfer between the civil and military programs. The civil space program centers on three basic tenets: First, our space policy will reflect a balanced strategy of applications, science, and technology development. Second, activities will be pursued when they can be uniquely or more efficiently accomplished in space. Third, a premature commitment to a high challenge, space-engineering initiative of the complexity of Apollo is inappropriate. As the Shuttle development phases down, however, there will be added flexibility to consider new space applications, space science and new space exploration activities.

● Technology Development. The Shuttle dominates our technology development effort and correctly so. It represents one of the most sophisticated technological challenges ever undertaken, and as a result, has encountered technical problems. Nonetheless, the first manned orbital flight is now scheduled for March, 1981. I have been pleased to support strongly the necessary funds for the Shuttle throughout my Administration.

● Space Applications. Since 1972, the U.S. has conducted experimental civil remote sensing through Landsat satellites, thereby realizing many successful applications. Recognizing this fact, I directed the implementation of an operational civil land satellite remote sensing system, with the operational management responsibility in Commerce's National Oceanic and Atmospheric Administration. In addition, because ocean observations from space can meet common civil and military data requirements, a National Oceanic Satellite System has been proposed as a major FY 1981 new start.

● Space Science Exploration. The goals of this Administration's policy in space science have been to: (1) continue a vigorous program of planetary exploration to understand the origin and evolution of the solar system; (2)

utilize the space telescope and free-flying satellites to usher in a new era of astronomy; (3) develop a better understanding of the sun and its interaction with the terrestrial environment; and (4) utilize the Shuttle and Spacelab to conduct basic research that complements earth-based life science investigations.

## THE ARTS

The arts are a precious national resource.

Federal support for the arts has been enhanced during my Administration by expanding government funding and services to arts institutions, individual artists, scholars, and teachers through the National Endowment for the Arts. We have broadened its scope and reach to a more diverse population. We have also reactivated the Federal Council on the Arts and Humanities. . . .

## THE HUMANITIES

In recently reauthorizing Federal appropriations for the National Endowment for the Humanities, the Congress has once again reaffirmed that "the encouragement and support of national progress and scholarship in the humanities . . . while primarily a matter for private and local initiative, is also an appropriate matter of concern to the Federal Government" and that "a high civilization must not limit its efforts to science and technology alone but must give full value and support to the other great branches of man's scholarly and cultural activity in order to achieve a better understanding of the past, a better analysis of the present, and a better view of the future.". . .

I will be proposing an increase in funding this year sufficient to enable the Endowment to maintain the same level of support offered our citizens in Fiscal Year 1981. . . .

## INSULAR AREAS

I have been firmly committed to self-determination for Puerto Rico, the Virgin Islands, Guam, American Samoa and the Northern Mariana Islands, and have vigorously supported the realization of whatever political status aspirations are democratically chosen by their peoples. This principle was the keystone of the comprehensive territorial policy I sent the Congress last year. I am pleased that most of the legislative elements of that policy were endorsed by the 96th Congress. . . .

## [IV. Removing Governmental Waste]

One of my major commitments has been to restore public faith in our Federal government by cutting out waste and inefficiency. In the past four years, we have made dramatic advances toward this goal, many of them previously considered impossible to achieve. Where government rules and operations were unnecessary, they have been eliminated, as with airline, rail, trucking and financial deregulation. Where government functions are needed, they have been streamlined, through such landmark measures as the Civil Service Reform Act of 1978. I hope that the new administration and the Congress will keep up the momentum we have established for effective and responsible change in this area of crucial public concern.

## Civil Service Reform

In March 1978, I submitted the Civil Service Reform Act to Congress. I called it the centerpiece of my efforts to reform and reorganize the government. With bipartisan support from Congress, the bill passed, and I am pleased to say that implementation is running well ahead of the statutory schedule. Throughout the service, we are putting into place the means to assure that reward and retention are based on performance and not simply on length of time on the job. In the first real test of the Reform Act, 98 percent of the eligible top-level managers joined the Senior Executive Service, choosing to relinquish job protections for the challenge and potential reward of this new corps of top executives. Though the Act does not require several of its key elements to be in operation for another year, some Federal agencies already have established merit pay systems for GS-13-15 managers, and most agencies are well on their way to establishing new performance standards for all their employees. All have paid out, or are now in the process of paying out, performance bonuses earned by outstanding members of the Senior Executive Service. Dismissals have increased by 10 percent, and dismissals specifically for inadequate job performance have risen 1500 percent, since the Act was adopted. Finally, we have established a fully independent Merit Systems Protection Board and Special Counsel to protect the rights of whistle-blowers and other Federal employees faced with threats to their rights. . . .

## Regulatory Reform

During the past four years we have made tremendous progress in regulatory reform. We have discarded old economic regulations that prevented competition and raised consumer costs, and we have imposed strong management principles on the regulatory programs the country needs, cutting paperwork and other wasteful burdens. The challenge for the future is to continue the progress in both areas without crippling vital health and safety programs.

Our economic deregulation program has achieved major successes in five areas:

*Airlines:* The Airline Deregulation Act is generating healthy competition, saving billions in fares, and making the airlines more efficient. The Act provides that in 1985 the CAB [Civil Aeronautics Board] itself will go out of existence.

*Trucking:* The trucking deregulation bill opens the industry to competition and allows truckers wide latitude on the routes they drive and the goods they haul. The bill also phases out some of the old law's immunity for setting rates. The Congressional Budget Office estimates these reforms will save as much as $8 billion per year and cut as much as half a percentage point from the inflation rate.

*Railroads:* Overregulation has stifled railroad management initiatives, service, and competitive pricing. The new legislation gives the railroads the freedom they need to rebuild a strong, efficient railroad industry.

*Financial Institutions:* With the help of the Congress, over the past four years we have achieved two major pieces of financial reform legislation — legislation which has provided the basis for the most far-reaching changes in the financial services industry since the 1930's. The International Banking Act of 1978 was designed to reduce the advantages that foreign banks operating in the United States possessed in comparison to domestic banks. The Depository Institutions Deregulation and Monetary Control Act, adopted last March, provides for the phased elimination of a variety of anti-competitive barriers to financial institutions and freedom to offer services to and attract the savings of consumers, especially small savers.

Recently, I submitted to the Congress my Administration's recommendations for the phased liberalization of restrictions on geographic expansion by commercial banks. . . .

*Telecommunications:* While Congress did not pass legislation in this area, the Federal Communications Commission has taken dramatic action to open all aspects of communications to competition and to eliminate regulations in the areas where competition made them obsolete. The public is benefitting from an explosion of competition and new services. . . .

These steps have already saved billions of dollars in regulatory costs and slashed thousands of outmoded regulations. We are moving steadily toward a regulatory system that provides needed protections fairly, predictably, and at minimum cost.

I urge Congress to continue on this steady path and resist the simplistic solutions that have been proposed as alternatives. Proposals like legislative veto and increased judicial review will add another layer to the regulatory process, making it more cumbersome and inefficient. The right approach to reform is to improve the individual statutes — where they need change — and to ensure that the regulatory agencies implement those statutes sensibly.

## Paperwork Reduction

The Federal Government imposes a huge paperwork burden on business, local government, and the private sector. Many of these forms are needed for vital government functions, but others are duplicative, overly complex or obsolete.

During my Administration we cut the paperwork burden by 15 percent, and we created procedures to continue this progress. . . .

## [V. Protecting Basic Rights]

I am extremely proud of the advances we have made in ensuring equality and protecting the basic freedoms of all Americans.

● The Equal Employment Opportunity Commission (EEOC) and the Office of Federal Contract Compliance (OFCCP) have been reorganized and strengthened and a permanent civil rights unit has been established in OMB [Office of Management and Budget].

● To avoid fragmented, inconsistent and duplicative enforcement of civil rights laws, three agencies have been given coordinative and standard-setting responsibilities in discrete areas: EEOC for all employment-related activities, HUD [Department of Housing and Urban Development] for all those relating to housing, and the Department of Justice for all other areas.

● With the enactment of the Right to Financial Privacy Act and a bill limiting police search of newsrooms, we have begun to establish a sound, comprehensive, privacy program.

Ratification of the Equal Rights Amendment must be aggressively pursued. Only one year remains in which to obtain ratification by three additional states.

The Congress must give early attention to a number of important bills which remain. These bills would:

● strengthen the laws against discrimination in housing. Until it is enacted, the 1968 Civil Rights Act's promise of equal access to housing will remain unfulfilled;

● establish a charter for the FBI [Federal Bureau of Investigation] and the intelligence agencies. The failure to define in law the duties and responsibilities of these agencies has made possible some of the abuses which have occurred in recent years;

● establish privacy safeguards for medical research, bank, insurance, and credit records; and provide special protection for election fund transfer systems. . . .

### Fair Housing

The Fair Housing Act Amendments of 1980 passed the House of Representatives by an overwhelming bipartisan majority only to die in the Senate at the close of the 96th Congress. The leaders of both parties have pledged to make the enactment of fair housing legislation a top priority of the incoming Congress. The need is pressing and a strengthened federal enforcement effort must be the primary method of resolution. . . .

## [VI. Natural Resources]

Two of our Nation's most precious natural resources are our environment and our vast agricultural capacity. From the beginning of my Administration, I have worked with the Congress to enhance and protect, as well as develop our natural resources. In the environmental areas, I have been especially concerned about the importance of balancing the need for resource development with preserving a clean environment, and have taken numerous actions to foster this goal. In the agricultural area, I have taken the steps needed to improve farm incomes and to increase our agricultural production to record levels. That progress must be continued in the 1980's....

## Protection of Alaska Lands

Passage of the Alaska National Interest Lands Conservation Act was one of the most important conservation actions of this century. At stake was the fate of millions of acres of beautiful land, outstanding and unique wildlife populations, native cultures, and the opportunity to ensure that future generations of Americans would be able to enjoy the benefits of these nationally significant resources. As a result of the leadership, commitment, and persistence of my Administration and the Congressional leadership, the Alaska Lands Bill was signed into law last December.

The Act adds 97 million acres of new parks and refuges, more than doubling the size of our National Park and National Wildlife Refuge Systems. The bill triples the size of our national wilderness system, increasing its size by 56 million acres....

## [Pollution and Hazardous Chemicals]

Over the past four years, there has been steady progress towards cleaner air and water, sustained by the commitment of Congress and the Administration to these important national objectives. In addition, the Administration has developed several new pollution compliance approaches such as alternative and innovative waste water treatment projects, the "bubble" concept, the "offset" policy, and permit consolidation, all of which are designed to reduce regulatory burdens on the private sector.

One of the most pressing problems to come to light in the past four years has been improper hazardous waste disposal. The Administration has moved on three fronts. First, we proposed the Oil Hazardous Substances and Hazardous Waste Response, Liability and Compensation Act (the "Superfund" bill) to provide comprehensive authority and $1.6 billion in funds to clean up abandoned hazardous waste disposal sites. In November 1980 the Congress passed a Superfund bill which I signed into law.

Second, the administration established a hazardous waste enforcement strike force to ensure that when available, responsible parties are required to clean up sites posing dangers to public health and to the environment. To date, 50 lawsuits have been brought by the strike force.

Third, regulations implementing subtitle C of the Resource Conservation and Recovery Act were issued. The regulations establish comprehensive controls for hazardous waste and, together with vigorous enforcement, will help to ensure that Love Canal will not be repeated.

### The Future

For the future, we cannot — and we must not — forget that we are charged with the stewardship of an irreplaceable environment and natural heritage. Our children, and our children's children, are dependent upon our maintaining our commitment to preserving and enhancing the quality of our environment. . . .

### The Farm Economy

The farm economy is sound and its future is bright. Agriculture remains a major bulwark of the nation's economy and an even more important factor in the world food system. The demand for America's agricultural abundance, here and abroad, continues to grow. In the near-term, the strength of this demand is expected to press hard against supplies, resulting in continued price strength.

The health and vitality of current-day agriculture represents a significant departure from the situation that existed when I came to office four years ago. In January 1977, the farm economy was in serious trouble. Farm prices and farm income were falling rapidly. Grain prices were at their lowest levels in years and steadily falling. Livestock producers, in their fourth straight year of record losses, were liquidating breeding herds at an unparalleled rate. Dairy farmers were losing money on every hundredweight of milk they produced. Sugar prices were in a nosedive.

Through a combination of improvements in old, established programs and the adoption of new approaches where innovation and change were needed, my Administration turned this situation around. Commodity prices have steadily risen. Farm income turned upward. U.S. farm exports set new records each year, increasing over 80 percent for the four year period. Livestock producers began rebuilding their herds. Dairy farmers began to earn a profit again. . . .

## VII. Foreign Policy

From the time I assumed office four years ago this month, I have stressed the need for this country to assert a leading role in a world undergoing the most extensive and intensive change in human history.

My policies have been directed in particular at three areas of change:

• the steady growth and increased projection abroad of Soviet military power — power that has grown faster than our own over the past two decades.

• the overwhelming dependence of Western nations, which now increasingly includes the United States, on vital oil supplies from the Middle East.

• the pressures of change in many nations of the developing world, in Iran and uncertainty about the future stability of many developing countries.

As a result of those fundamental facts, we face some of the most serious challenges in the history of this nation. The Soviet invasion of Afghanistan is a threat to global peace, to East-West relations, and to regional stability and to the flow of oil. As the unprecedented and overwhelming vote in the General Assembly demonstrated, countries across the world — and particularly the non-aligned — regard the Soviet invasion as a threat to their independence and security. Turmoil within the region adjacent to the Persian Gulf poses risks for the security and prosperity of every oil importing nation and thus for the entire global economy. The continuing holding of American hostages in Iran is both an affront to civilized people everywhere, and a serious impediment to meeting the self-evident threat to widely-shared common interests — including those of Iran.

But as we focus our most urgent efforts on pressing problems, we will continue to pursue the benefits that only change can bring. For it always has been the essence of America that we want to move on — we understand that prosperity, progress and most of all peace cannot be had by standing still. A world of nations striving to preserve their independence, and of peoples aspiring for economic development and political freedom, is not a world hostile to the ideals and interests of the United States. We face powerful adversaries, but we have strong friends and dependable allies. We have common interests with the vast majority of the world's nations and peoples.

There have been encouraging developments in recent years, as well as matters requiring continued vigilance and concern:

● Our alliances with the world's most advanced and democratic states from Western Europe through Japan are stronger than ever.

● We have helped to bring about a dramatic improvement in relations between Egypt and Israel and an historic step towards a comprehensive Arab-Israeli settlement.

● Our relations with China are growing closer, providing a major new dimension in our policy in Asia and the world.

● Across southern Africa from Rhodesia to Namibia we are helping with the peaceful transition to majority rule in the context of respect for minority as well as majority rights.

● We have worked domestically and with our allies to respond to an uncertain energy situation by conservation and diversification of energy supplies based on internationally agreed targets.

● We have unambiguously demonstrated our commitment to defend Western interests in Southwest Asia, and we have significantly increased our ability to do so.

● And over the past four years the U.S. has developed an energy program which is comprehensive and ambitious. New institutions have been established such as the Synthetic Fuels Corporation and Solar Bank. Price decontrol for oil and gas is proceeding. American consumers have risen to the challenge, and we have experienced real improvements in consumption patterns. . . .

One very immediate and pressing objective that is uppermost on our minds and those of the American people is the release of our hostages in Iran.

We have no basic quarrel with the nation, the revolution or the people of Iran. The threat to them comes not from American policy but from Soviet actions in the region. We are prepared to work with the government of Iran to develop a new and mutually beneficial relationship.

But that will not be possible so long as Iran continues to hold Americans hostages, in defiance of the world community and civilized behavior. They must be released unharmed. We have thus far pursued a measured program of peaceful diplomatic and economic steps in an attempt to resolve this issue without resorting to other remedies available to us under international law. This reflects the deep respect of our nation for the rule of law and for the safety of our people being held, and our belief that a great power bears a responsibility to use its strength in a measured and judicious manner. But our patience is not unlimited and our concern for the well-being of our fellow citizens grows each day.

## [AMERICAN MILITARY STRENGTH]

The maintenance of national security is my first concern, as it has been for every president before me.

We must have both the military power and the political will to deter our adversaries and to support our friends and allies.

We must pay whatever price is required to remain the strongest nation in the world. That price has increased as the military power of our major adversary has grown and its readiness to use that power been made all too evident in Afghanistan. The real increases in defense spending, therefore probably will be higher than previously projected; protecting our security may require a larger share of our national wealth in the future.

### The U.S.-Soviet Relationship

We are demonstrating to the Soviet Union across a broad front that it will pay a heavy price for its aggression in terms of our relationship. Throughout the last decades U.S.-Soviet relations have been a mixture of cooperation and competition. The Soviet invasion of Afghanistan and the imposition of a puppet government have highlighted in the starkest terms the darker side of their policies — going well beyond competition and the legitimate pursuit of national interest, and violating all norms of international law and practice.

This attempt to subjugate an independent, non-aligned Islamic people is a callous violation of international law and the United Nations Charter, two fundamentals of international order. Hence, it is also a dangerous threat to world peace. For the first time since the communization of Eastern Europe after World War II, the Soviets have sent combat forces into an area that was not previously under their control, into a non-aligned and sovereign state.

The destruction of the independence of the Afghanistan government and the occupation by the Soviet Union have altered the strategic situation in that part of the world in a very ominous fashion. It has significantly shortened the striking distance to the Indian Ocean and the Persian Gulf for the Soviet Union.

It has also eliminated a buffer between the Soviet Union and Pakistan and presented a new threat to Iran. These two countries are now far more vulnerable to Soviet political intimidation. If that intimidation were to prove effective, the Soviet Union could control an area of vital strategic and economic significance to the survival of Western Europe, the Far East, and ultimately the United States.

It has now been over a year since the Soviet invasion of Afghanistan dealt a major blow to U.S.-Soviet relations and the entire international system. The U.S. response has proven to be serious and far-reaching. It has been increasingly effective, imposing real and sustained costs on the USSR's economy and international image.

Meanwhile, we have encouraged and supported efforts to reach a political settlement in Afghanistan which would lead to a withdrawal of Soviet forces from that country and meet the interests of all concerned. It is Soviet intransigence that has kept those efforts from bearing fruit.

Meanwhile, an overwhelming November resolution of the United Nations General Assembly on Afghanistan has again made clear that the world has not and will not forget Afghanistan. And our response continues to make it clear that Soviet use of force in pursuit of its international objectives is incompatible with the notion of business-as-usual.

## Bilateral Communication

U.S.-Soviet relations remain strained by the continued Soviet presence in Afghanistan, by growing Soviet military capabilities, and by the Soviets' apparent willingness to use those capabilities without respect for the most basic norms of international behavior.

But the U.S.-Soviet relationship remains the single most important element in determining whether there will be war or peace. And so, despite serious strains in our relations, we have maintained a dialogue with the Soviet Union over the past year. Through this dialogue, we have ensured against bilateral misunderstndings and miscalculations which might escalate out of control, and have managed to avoid the injection of superpower rivalries into areas of tension like the Iran-Iraq conflict.

## Poland

Now, as was the case a year ago, the prospect of Soviet use of force threatens the international order. The Soviet Union has completed preparations for a possible military intervention against Poland. Although the situation in Poland has shown signs of stabilizing recently, Soviet forces remain in a high state of readiness and they could move into Poland on short notice. We continue to believe that the Polish people should be allowed to work out their internal problems themselves, without outside interference, and we have made clear to the Soviet leadership that any intervention in Poland would have severe and prolonged consequences for East-West detente, and U.S.-Soviet relations in particular.

## Defense Budget

For many years the Soviets have steadily increased their real defense spending, expanding their strategic forces, strengthened their forces in Europe and Asia, and enhanced their capability for projecting military force around the world directly or through the use of proxies. Afghanistan dramatizes the vastly increased military power of the Soviet Union.

The Soviet Union has built a war machine far beyond any reasonable requirements for their own defense and security. In contrast, our own defense spending declined in real terms every year from 1968 through 1976.

We have reversed this decline in our own effort. Every year since 1976 there has been a real increase in our defense spending — and our lead has encouraged increase by our allies. With the support of the Congress, we must and will make an even greater effort in the years ahead.

The Fiscal Year 1982 budget would increase funding authority for defense to more than $196 billion. This amount, together with a supplemental request for FY 1981 of about $6 billion, will more than meet my Administration's pledge for a sustained growth of 3 percent in real expenditures, and provides for 5 percent in program growth in FY 1982 and beyond.

The trends we mean to correct cannot be remedied overnight; we must be willing to see this program through. To ensure that we do so I am setting a growth rate for defense that we can sustain over the long haul.

The defense program I have proposed for the next five years will require some sacrifice — but sacrifice we can well afford.

The defense program emphasizes four areas:

● It ensures that our strategic nuclear forces will be equivalent to those of the Soviet Union and that deterrence against nuclear war will be maintained;

● It upgrades our forces so that the military balance between NATO and the Warsaw Pact will continue to deter the outbreak of war — conventional or nuclear — in Europe;

● It provides us the ability to come quickly to the aid of friends and allies around the globe;

● And it ensures that our Navy will continue to be the most powerful on the seas.

## Strategic Forces

We are strengthening each of the three legs of our strategic forces. The cruise missile production which will begin next year will modernize our strategic air deterrent. B-52 capabilities will also be improved. These steps will maintain and enhance the B-52 fleet by improving its ability to deliver weapons against increasingly heavily defended targets.

We are also modernizing our strategic submarine force. Four more Poseidon submarines backfitted with new, 4,000 mile Trident I missiles began deployments in 1980. Nine Trident submarines have been authorized through 1981, and we propose one more each year.

The new M-X missile program to enhance our land-based intercontinental ballistic missile force continues to make progress. Technical refinements in the basing design over the last year will result in operational benefits, lower costs, and reduced environmental impact. The M-X program continues to be an essential ingredient in our strategic posture — providing survivability, endurance, secure command and control and the capability to threaten targets the Soviets hold dear.

Our new systems will enable U.S. strategic forces to maintain equivalence in the face of the mounting Soviet challenge. We would however need an even greater investment in strategic systems to meet the likely Soviet buildup without SALT....

## Forces for NATO

We are greatly accelerating our ability to reinforce Western Europe with massive ground and air forces in a crisis. We are undertaking a major modernization program for the Army's weapons and equipment, adding armor, firepower, and tactical mobility.

We are prepositioning more heavy equipment in Europe to help us cope with attacks with little warning, and greatly strengthening our airlift and sealift capabilities.

We are also improving our tactical air forces — buying about 1700 new fighter and attack aircraft over the next five years — and increasing the number of Air Force fighter wings by over 10 percent.

We are working closely with our European allies to secure the Host Nation Support necessary to enable us to deploy more quickly a greater ratio of combat forces to the European theater at a lower cost to the United States.

## Security Assistance

As we move to enhance U.S. defense capabilities, we must not lose sight of the need to assist others in maintaining their own security and independence. Events since World War II, most recently in Southwest Asia, have amply demonstrated that U.S. security cannot exist in a vacuum, and that our own prospects for peace are closely tied to those of our friends. The security assistance programs which I am proposing for the coming fiscal year thus directly promote vital U.S. foreign policy and national security aims — and are integral parts of our efforts to improve and upgrade our own military forces. . . .

### Rapid Deployment Forces

We are systematically enhancing our ability to respond rapidly to non-NATO contingencies wherever required by our commitments or when our vital interests are threatened.

The rapid deployment forces we are assembling will be extraordinarily flexible: They could range in size from a few ships or air squadrons to formations as large as 100,000 men, together with their support. Our forces will be prepared for rapid deployment to any region of strategic significance. . . .

### Naval Forces

Seapower is indispensable to our global position — in peace and also in war. Our shipbuilding program will sustain a 550-ship Navy in the 1990's and we will continue to build the most capable ships afloat.

The program I have proposed will assure the ability of our Navy to operate in high threat areas, to maintain control of the seas and protect vital lines of communication — both military and economic — and to provide the strong maritime components of our rapid deployment forces. This is essential for operations in remote areas of the world, where we cannot predict far in advance the precise location of trouble, or preposition equipment on land.

### Military Personnel

No matter how capable or advanced our weapons systems, our military security depends on the abilities, the training and the dedication of the people who serve in our armed forces. I am determined to recruit and to retain under any foreseeable circumstances an ample level of such skilled and experienced military personnel. This Administration has supported for FY 1981 the largest peacetime increase ever in military pay and allowances.

We have enhanced our readiness and combat endurance by improving the Reserve Components. All reservists are assigned to units structured to complement and provide needed depth to our active forces. Some reserve personnel have also now been equipped with new equipment.

### Mobilization Planning

We have completed our first phase of mobilization planning — the first such Presidentially-directed effort since World War II. The government-wide exercise of our mobilization plans at the end of 1980 showed, first, that planning pays off and, second, that much more needs to be done.

## Our Intelligence Posture

Our national interests are critically dependent on a strong and effective intelligence capability. We will maintain and strengthen the intelligence capabilities needed to assure our national security. Maintenance of and continued improvements in our multi-faceted intelligence effort are essential if we are to cope successfully with the turbulence and uncertainties of today's world.

The intelligence budget I have submitted to the Congress responds to our needs in a responsible way, providing for significant growth over the Fiscal Year 1981 budget. This growth will enable us to develop new technical means of intelligence collection while also assuring that the more traditional methods of intelligence work are also given proper stress. We must continue to integrate both modes of collection in our analyses.

## REGIONAL POLICIES

Every President for over three decades has recognized that America's interests are global and that we must pursue a global foreign policy.

Two world wars have made clear our stake in Western Europe and the North Atlantic area. We are also inextricably linked with the Far East — politically, economically, and militarily. In both of these, the United States has a permanent presence and security commitments which would be automatically triggered. We have become increasingly conscious of our growing interests in a third area — the Middle East and the Persian Gulf area.

We have vital stakes in other major regions of the world as well. We have long recognized that in an era of interdependence, our own security and prosperity depend upon a larger common effort with friends and allies throughout the world.

## The Atlantic Alliance

At the outset of this Administration, I emphasized the primacy of our Atlantic relationship in this country's national security agenda. We have made important progress toward making the Atlantic Alliance still more effective in a changing security environment.

In recognition of the threat which the Soviet invasion of Afghanistan posed to Western interests in both Europe and Southwest Asia, NATO foreign and defense ministers have expressed full support for U.S. efforts to develop a capability to respond to a contingency in Southwest Asia and have approved an extensive program to help fill the gap which could be created by the diversion of U.S. forces to that region.

The U.S. has not been alone in seeking to maintain stability in the Southwest Asian area and insure access to the needed resources there. The

European nations with the capability to do so are improving their own forces in the region and providing greater economic and political support to the residents of the area. In the face of the potential danger posed by the Iran-Iraq conflict, we have developed coordination among the Western forces in the area of the Persian Gulf in order to be able to safeguard passage in that essential waterway.

Concerning developments in and around Poland, the allies have achieved the highest level of cohesion and unity of purpose in making clear the effects on future East-West relations of a precipitous Soviet act there. . . .

### The U.S. and the Pacific Nations

The United States is a Pacific nation, as much as it is an Atlantic nation. Our interests in Asia are as important to us as our interests in Europe. Our trade with Asia is as great as our trade with Europe. During the past four years we have regained a strong, dynamic and flexible posture for the United States in this vital region.

Our major alliances with Japan, Australia and New Zealand are now stronger than they ever have been, and together with the nations of western Europe, we have begun to form the basic political structure for dealing with international crises that affect us all. Japan, Australia and New Zealand have given us strong support in developing a strategy for responding to instability in the Persian Gulf.

Normalization of U.S. relations with China has facilitated China's full entry into the international community and encouraged a constructive Chinese role in the Asia-Pacific region. Our relations with China have been rapidly consolidated over the past year through the conclusion of a series of bilateral agreements. We have established a pattern of frequent and frank consultations between our two governments, exemplified by a series of high-level visits and by regular exchanges at the working level, through which we have been able to identify increasingly broad areas of common interest on which we can cooperate.

United States relations with the Association of Southeast Asian Nations (ASEAN) have also expanded dramatically in the past four years. ASEAN is now the focus for U.S. policy in Southeast Asia, and its cohesion and strength are essential to stability in this critical area and beyond.

Soviet-supported Vietnamese aggression in Indochina has posed a major challenge to regional stability. In response, we have reiterated our security commitment to Thailand and have provided emergency security assistance for Thai forces facing a Vietnamese military threat along the Thai-Cambodian border. We have worked closely with ASEAN and the UN to press for withdrawal of Vietnamese forces from Cambodia and to encourage a political settlement in Cambodia which permits that nation to be governed by leaders of its own choice. We still look forward to the day when Cambodia peacefully can begin the process of rebuilding it [sic] social, economic and political institutions, after years of devastation and occupation. And, on humanitarian grounds and in support of our friends in the region, we have worked vigorously with international organizations to arrange relief and resettlement for the exodus of Indochinese refugees which threatened to overwhelm these nations.

We have maintained our alliance with Korea and helped assure Korea's security during a difficult period of political transition.

We have amended our military base agreement with the Philippines, ensuring stable access to these bases through 1991. The importance of our Philippine bases to the strategic flexibility of U.S. forces and our access to the Indian Ocean is self-evident.

Finally, we are in the process of concluding a long negotiation establishing Micronesia's status as a freely associated state.

We enter the 1980's with a firm strategic footing in East Asia and the Pacific, based on stable and productive U.S. relations with the majority of countries of the region. We have established a stable level of U.S. involvement in the region, appropriate to our own interests and to the interests of our friends and allies there.

### The Middle East and Southwest Asia

The continuing Soviet occupation of Afghanistan and the dislocations caused by the Iraq-Iran war serve as constant reminders of the critical importance for us, and our allies, of a third strategic zone stretching across the Middle East, the Persian Gulf, and much of the Indian subcontinent. This Southwest Asian region has served as a key strategic and commercial link between East and West over the centuries. Today it produces two-thirds of the world's oil exports, providing most of the energy needs of our European allies and Japan. It has experienced almost continuous conflict between nations, internal instabilities in many countries, and regional rivalries, combined with very rapid economic and social change. And now the Soviet Union remains in occupation of one of these nations, ignoring world opinion which has called on it to get out.

We have taken several measures to meet these challenges.

### Middle East

In the Middle East, our determination to consolidate what has already been achieved in the peace process — and to buttress that accomplishment with further progress toward a comprehensive peace settlement — must remain a central goal of our foreign policy. Pursuant to their peace treaty, Egypt and Israel have made steady progress in the normalization of their relations in a variety of fields, bringing the benefits of peace directly to their people. The new relationship between Egypt and Israel stands as an example of peaceful cooperation in an increasingly fragmented and turbulent region.

Both President Sadat and Prime Minister Begin remain committed to the current negotiations to provide full autonomy to the inhabitants of the

West Bank and Gaza. These negotiations have been complex and difficult, but they have already made significant progress, and it is vital that the two sides, with our assistance, see the process through to a successful conclusion. We also recognize the need to broaden the peace process to include other parties to the conflict and believe that a successful autonomy agreement is an essential first step toward this objective.

We have also taken a number of steps to strengthen our bilateral relations with both Israel and Egypt. We share important strategic interests with both of these countries.

We remain committed to Israel's security and are prepared to take concrete steps to support Israel whenever that security is threatened.

## Persian Gulf

The Persian Gulf has been a vital crossroads for trade between Europe and Asia at many key moments in history. It has become essential in recent years for its supply of oil to the United States, our allies, and our friends. We have taken effective measures to control our own consumption of imported fuel, working in cooperation with the other key industrial nations of the world. However, there is little doubt that the healthy growth of our American and world economies will depend for many years on continued safe access to the Persian Gulf's oil production. The denial of these oil supplies would threaten not only our own but world security.

The potent new threat from an advancing Soviet Union, against the background of regional instability of which it can take advantage, requires that we reinforce our ability to defend our regional friends and to protect the flow of oil. We are continuing to build on the strong political, economic, social and humanitarian ties which bind this government and the American people to friendly governments and peoples of the Persian Gulf.

We have also embarked on a course to reinforce the trust and confidence our regional friends have in our ability to come to their assistance rapidly with American military force if needed. We have increased our naval presence in the Indian Ocean. We have created a Rapid Deployment Force which can move quickly to the Gulf — or indeed any other area of the world where outside aggression threatens. We have concluded several agreements with countries which are prepared to let us use their airports and naval facilities in an emergency. We have met requests for reasonable amounts of American weaponry from regional countries which are anxious to defend themselves. And we are discussing with a number of our area friends further ways we can help to improve their security and ours, both for the short and the longer run.

## South Asia

We seek a South Asia comprising sovereign and stable states, free of outside interference, which can strengthen their political institutions according to their own national genius and can develop their economies for the betterment of their people.

The Soviet invasion of Afghanistan has posed a new challenge to this region, and particularly to neighboring Pakistan. We are engaged in a continuing dialogue with the Pakistan government concerning its development and security requirements and the economic burden imposed by Afghan refugees who have fled to Pakistan. We are participating with other aid consortium members in debt rescheduling and will continue to cooperate through the UNHCR in providing refugee assistance. We remain committed to Pakistan's territorial integrity and independence.

Developments in the broad South/Southwest Asian region have also lent a new importance to our relations with India, the largest and strongest power in the area. We share India's interest in a more constructive relationship. Indian policies and perceptions at times differ from our own, and we have established a candid dialogue with this sister democracy which seeks to avoid the misunderstandings which have sometimes complicated our ties. . . .

## Africa

The United States has achieved a new level of trust and cooperation with Africa. Our efforts, together with our allies, to achieve peace in southern Africa, our increased efforts to help the poorest countries in Africa to combat poverty, and our expanded efforts to promote trade and investment have led to growing respect for the U.S. and to cooperation in areas of vital interest to the United States.

Africa is a continent of poor nations for the most part. It also contains many of the mineral resources vital for our economy. We have worked with Africa in a spirit of mutual cooperation to help the African nations solve their problems of poverty and to develop stronger ties between our private sector and African economies. Our assistance to Africa has more than doubled in the last four years. Equally important, we set in motion new mechanisms for private investment and trade. . . .

In southern Africa the United States continues to pursue a policy of encouraging peaceful development toward majority rule. In 1980, Southern Rhodesia became independent as Zimbabwe, a multiracial nation under a system of majority rule. Zimbabwean independence last April was the culmination of a long struggle within the country and diplomatic efforts involving Great Britain, African states neighboring Zimbabwe, and the United States.

The focus of our efforts in pursuit of majority rule in southern Africa has now turned to Namibia. Negotiations are proceeding among concerned parties under the leadership of UN Secretary General Waldheim. This should lead to implementation of the UN plan for self-determination and independence for Namibia during 1981. If these negotiations are successfully concluded, sixty-five years of uncertainty over the status of the territory, including a seven-year-long war, will be ended.

Common efforts to resolve the Zimbabwean and Namibian issues have brought the United States closer both to its Western allies — Great Britain, France, the Federal Republic of Germany, and Canada — and to African states such as Tanzania, Zambia, Mozambique, Angola, and Botswana, with whom relations have at some times in the past been difficult. The success of these common undertakings demonstrates that complex problems with sometimes bitter and bloody histories can be resolved peacefully through negotiation. . . .

### North Africa

In early 1979, following a Libyan-inspired commando attack on a Tunisian provincial city, the U.S. responded promptly to Tunisia's urgent request for assistance, both by airlifting needed military equipment and by making clear our longstanding interest in the security and integrity of this friendly country. The U.S. remains determined to oppose other irresponsible Libyan aspirations. Despairing of a productive dialogue with the Libyan authorities, the U.S. closed down its embassy in Libya and later expelled six Libyan diplomats in Washington in order to deter an intimidation campaign against Libyan citizens in the U.S.

U.S. relations with Algeria have improved, and Algeria has played an indispensable and effective role as intermediary between Iran and the U.S. over the hostage issue. . . .

### Latin America and the Caribbean

The principles of our policies in this hemisphere have been clear and constant over the last four years. We support democracy and respect for human rights. We have struggled with many to help free the region of both repression and terrorism. We have respected ideological diversity and opposed outside intervention in purely internal affairs. We will act, though, in response to a request for assistance by a country threatened by external aggression. We support social and economic development within a democratic framework. We support the peaceful settlement of disputes. We strongly encourage regional cooperation and shared responsibilities within the hemisphere to all these ends, and we have eagerly and regularly sought the advice of the leaders of the region on a wide range of issues.

Last November, I spoke to the General Assembly of the Organization of American States of a cause that has been closest to my heart — human rights. It is an issue that has found its time in the hemisphere. The cause is not mine alone, but an historic movement that will endure.

At Riobamba, Ecuador, last September four Andean Pact countries, Costa Rica, and Panama broke new ground by adopting a "Code of Conduct," stating that joint action in defense of human rights does not violate the principles of nonintervention in the internal affairs of states in this hemisphere. The Organization of American States has twice condemned the coup that overturned the democratic process in Bolivia and the widespread abuse of human rights by the regime which seized power. The Inter-American Commission on Human Rights has gained world acclaim for its dispassionate reports. It completed two major country studies this year in addition to its annual report. In a resolution adopted without opposition, the OAS General Assembly in November strongly supported the work of the Commission. The American Convention on Human Rights is in force and an Inter-American Court has been created to judge human rights violations. This convention has been pending before the Senate for two years; I hope the United States this year will join the other nations of the hemisphere in ratifying a convention which embodies principles that are our tradition.

The trend in favor of democracy has continued. During this past year, Peru inaugurated a democratically elected government. Brazil continues its process of liberalization. In Central America, Hondurans voted in record numbers in their first national elections in over eight years. In the Caribbean seven elections have returned governments firmly committed to the democratic traditions of the Commonwealth.

Another major contribution to peace in the hemisphere is Latin America's own Treaty for the Prohibition of Nuclear Weapons. On behalf of the United States, I signed Protocol I of this Treaty in May of 1977 and sent it to the Senate for ratification. I urge that it be acted upon promptly by the Senate in order that it be brought into the widest possible effect in the Latin American region. . . .

The Panama treaties have been in force for over a year. A new partnership has been created with Panama; it is a model for large and small nations. A longstanding issue that divided us from our neighbors has been resolved. The security of the canal has been enhanced. The canal is operating as well as ever, with traffic through it reaching record levels this year. Canal employees, American and Panamanian alike, have remained on the job and have found their living and working conditions virtually unchanged.

In 1980, relations with Mexico continued to improve due in large measure to the effectiveness of the Coordinator for Mexican Affairs and the expanded use of the U.S.-Mexico Consultative Mechanism. By holding periodic meetings of its various working groups, we have been able to prevent mutual concerns from becoming political issues. The Secretary of State visited Mexico City in November, and, along with the Mexican Secretary of Foreign Relations, reviewed the performance of the Consultative Mechanism. The office of the Coordinator has ensured the implementation of my directive to all agencies to accord high priority to Mexican concerns. Trade with Mexico rose by almost 60 percent to nearly $30 billion, making that country our third largest trading partner.

These are all encouraging developments. Other problems remain, however.

The impact of large-scale migration is affecting many countries in the hemisphere. The most serious manifestation was the massive, illegal exodus from Cuba last summer. The Cuban government unilaterally encouraged the disorderly and even deadly migration of 125,000 of its citizens in complete disregard for international law or the immigration laws of its neighbors. Migrations of this nature clearly require concerted action, and we have asked the OAS to explore means of dealing with similar situations which may occur in the future. . . .

In Central America, the future of Nicaragua is unclear. Recent tensions, the restrictions on the press and political activity, an inordinate Cuban presence in the country and the tragic killing by the security forces of a businessman well known for his democratic orientation, cause us considerable concern. These are not encouraging developments. But those who seek a free society remain in the contest for their nation's destiny. They have asked us to help rebuild their country, and by our assistance, to demonstrate that the democratic nations do not intend to abandon Nicaragua to the Cubans. As long as those who intend to pursue their pluralistic goals play important roles in Nicaragua, it deserves our continuing support.

In El Salvador, we have supported the efforts of the Junta to change the fundamental basis of an inequitable system and to give a stake in a new nation to those millions of people, who for so long, lived without hope or dignity. As the government struggles against whose who would restore an old tyranny or impose a new one, the United States will continue to stand behind them.

We have increased our aid to the Caribbean, an area vital to our national security, and we should continue to build close relations based on mutual respect and understanding, and common interests. . . .

## The International Economy

A growing defense effort and a vigorous foreign policy rest upon a strong economy here in the United States. And the strength of our own economy depends upon our ability to lead and compete in the international marketplace.

## Energy

Last year, the war between Iraq and Iran led to the loss of nearly 4 million barrels of oil to world markets, the third major oil market disruption in the past seven years. This crisis has vividly demonstrated once again both the value of lessened dependence on oil imports and the continuing instability of the Persian Gulf area.

Under the leadership of the United States, the 21 members of the International Energy Agency took collective action to ensure that the oil shortfall stemming from the Iran-Iraq war would not be aggravated by competition for scarce spot market supplies. We are also working together to see that those nations most seriously affected by the oil disruption — including our key NATO allies Turkey and Portugal — can get the oil they need. At the most recent IEA Ministerial meeting we joined the other members in pledging to take those policy measures necessary to slice our joint oil imports in the first quarter of 1981 by 2.2 million barrels.

Our international cooperation efforts in the energy field are not limited to crisis management. At the Economic Summit meetings in Tokyo and Venice, the heads of government of the seven major industrial democracies agreed to a series of tough energy conservation and production goals. We are working together with all our allies and friends in this effort.

Construction has begun on a commercial scale coal liquefaction plant in West Virginia co-financed by the United States, Japan and West Germany. An interagency task force has just reported to me on a series of measures we need to take to increase coal production and exports. This report builds on the work of the International Energy Agency's Coal Industry Advisory Board. With the assurances of a reliable United States steam coal supply at reasonable prices, many of the electric power plants to be built in the 1980's and 1990's can be coal-fired rather than oil burning....

## International Monetary Policy

Despite the rapid increase in oil costs, the policy measures we have taken to improve domestic economic performance have had a continued powerful effect on our external accounts and on the strength of the dollar. A strong dollar helps in the fight against inflation.

There has also been considerable forward movement in efforts to improve the functioning of the international monetary system. The stability of the international system of payments and trade is important to the stability and good health of our own economy. We have given strong support to the innovative steps being taken by the International Monetary Fund and World Bank to help promote early adjustment to the difficult international economic problems. Recent agreement to increase quotas by fifty percent will ensure the IMF has sufficient resources to perform its central role in promoting adjustment and financing payments imbalances. The World Bank's new structural adjustment lending program will also make an important contribution to international efforts to help countries achieve a sustainable level of growth and development....

## Food — The War On Hunger

The War on Hunger must be a continuous urgent priority. Major portions of the world's population continue to be threatened by the specter of hunger and malnutrition. During the past year, some 150 million people in 36 African countries were faced with near disaster as the result of serious drought-induced food shortages. Our government, working in concert with the UN's Food and Agricultural Organization (FAO), helped to respond to that need. But the problems of hunger cannot be solved by short-term measures. We must continue to support those activities, bilateral and multilateral, which aim at improving food production especially in developing countries and assuring global food security. These measures are necessary to the maintenance of a stable and healthy world economy.

I am pleased that negotiation of a new Food Aid Convention, which guarantees a minimum annual level of food assistance, was successfully concluded in March. The establishment of the International Emergency Wheat Reserve will enable the U.S. to meet its commitment under the new Convention to feed hungry people, even in times of short supply.

Of immediate concern is the prospect of millions of Africans threatened by famine because of drought and civil disturbances. The U.S. plea for increased food aid resulted in the organization of an international pledging conference and we are hopeful that widespread starvation will be avoided.

Good progress has been made since the Venice Economic Summit called for increased effort on this front. We and other donor countries have begun to assist poor countries develop long-term strategies to improve their food production. The World Bank will invest up to $4 billion in the next few years in improving the grain storage and food-handling capacity of countries prone to food shortages.

Good progress has been made since the Tokyo Economic Summit called for increased effort on this front. The World Bank is giving this problem top priority, as are some other donor countries. The resources of the consultative Group on International Agricultural Research will be doubled over a five-year period. The work of our own Institute of Scientific and Technological Cooperation will further strengthen the search for relevant new agricultural technologies.

The goal of freeing the world from hunger by the year 2000 should command the full support of all countries.

## THE HUMAN DIMENSION OF FOREIGN POLICY

### Human Rights

The human rights policy of the United States has been an integral part of our overall foreign policy for the past several years. This policy serves the national interest of the United States in several important ways: by encouraging respect by governments for the basic rights of human beings, it promotes peaceful, constructive change, reduces the likelihood of internal pressures for violent change and for the exploitation of these by our adversaries, and thus directly serves our long-term interest in peace and stability; by matching espousal of fundamental American principles of freedom with specific foreign policy actions, we stand out in vivid contrast to our ideological adversaries; by our efforts to expand freedom elsewhere, we render our own freedom, and our own nation, more secure. Countries that respect human rights make stronger allies and better friends.

Rather than attempt to dictate what system of government or institutions other countries should have, the U.S. supports, throughout the world, the internationally recognized human rights which all members of the United Nations have pledged themselves to respect. . . .

Those who see a contradiction between our security and our humanitarian interests forget that the basis for a secure and stable society is the bond of trust between a government and its people. I profoundly believe that the future of our world is not to be found in authoritarianism: that wears the mask of order, or totalitarianism that wears the mask of justice. Instead, let us find our future in the human face of democracy, the human voice of individual liberty, the human hand of economic development.

## Humanitarian Aid

The United States has continued to play its traditional role of safehaven for those who flee or are forced to flee their homes because of persecution or war. During 1980, the United States provided resettlement opportunities for 216,000 refugees from countries around the globe. In addition, the United States joined with other nations to provide relief to refugees in country of first asylum in Africa, the Middle East, and Asia.

The great majority of refugee admissions continued to be from Indochina. During 1980, 168,000 Indochinese were resettled in the United States. Although refugee populations persist in camps in Southeast Asia, and refugees continue to flee Vietnam, Laos and Kampuchea, the flow is not as great as in the past. One factor in reducing the flow from Vietnam has been the successful negotiation and commencement of an Orderly Departure Program which permits us to process Vietnamese for resettlement in the United States with direct departure from Ho Chi Minh Ville in an orderly fashion. The first group of 250 departed Vietnam for the United States in December, 1980.

In addition to the refugees admitted last year, the United States accepted for entry into the United States 125,000 Cubans who were expelled by Fidel Castro. Federal and state authorities, as well as private voluntary agencies, responded with unprecedented vigor to coping with the unexpected influx of Cubans.

Major relief efforts to aid refugees in countries of first asylum continued in several areas of the world. In December, 1980, thirty-two nations, meeting in New York City, agreed to contribute $65 million to the continuing famine relief program in Kampuchea. Due in great part to the generosity of the American people and the leadership exercised in the international arena by the United States, we have played the pivotal role in ameliorating massive suffering in Kampuchea.

The United States has taken the lead among a group of donor countries who are providing relief to some two million refugees in the Horn of Africa who have been displaced by fighting in Ethiopia. U.S. assistance, primarily to Somalia, consists of $35 million worth of food and $18 million in cash and kind. Here again, United States efforts can in large part be credited with keeping hundreds of thousands of people alive. . . .

## THE CONTROL OF NUCLEAR WEAPONS

Together with our friends and allies, we are striving to build a world in which peoples with diverse interests can live freely and prosper. But all that humankind has achieved to date, all that we are seeking to accomplish, and human existence itself can be undone in an instant — in the catastrophe of a nuclear war.

Thus one of the central objectives of my Administration has been to control the proliferation of nuclear weapons to those nations which do not have them, and their further development by the existing nuclear powers — notably the Soviet Union and the United States.

### Non-proliferation

My Administration has been committed to stemming the spread of nuclear weapons. Nuclear proliferation would raise the spectre of the use of nuclear explosives in crucial, unstable regions of the world endangering not only our security and that of our Allies, but that of the whole world. Non-proliferation is not and can not be a unilateral U.S. policy, nor should it be an issue of contention between the industrialized and developing states. The international non-proliferation effort requires the support of suppliers as well as importers of nuclear technology and materials.

We have been proceeding on a number of fronts:

• First, we have been seeking to encourage nations to accede to the Non-Proliferation Treaty. The U.S. is also actively encouraging other nations to accept full-scope safeguards on all of their nuclear activities and is asking other nuclear suppliers to adopt a full-scope safeguards requirement as a condition for future supply.

• Second, the International Nuclear Fuel Cycle Evaluation (INFCE), which was completed in 1980, demonstrated that suppliers and recipients can work together on these technically complex and sensitive issues. While differences remain, the INFCE effort provides a broader international basis for national decisions which must balance energy needs with non-proliferation concerns.

• Finally, we are working to encourage regional cooperation and restraint. Protocol I of the Treaty of Tlatelolco which will contribute to the lessening of nuclear dangers for our Latin American neighbors ought now to be ratified by the United States Senate.

### Limitations on Strategic Arms

I remain convinced that the SALT II Treaty is in our Nation's security interest and that it would add significantly to the control of nuclear weapons. I strongly support continuation of the SALT process and the negotiation of more far-reaching mutual restraints on nuclear weaponry.

## Conclusion

We have new support in the world for our purposes of national independence and individual human dignity. We have a new will at home to do what is required to keep us the strongest nation on earth.

We must move together into this decade with the strength which comes from realization of the dangers before us and from the confidence that together we can overcome them.

JIMMY CARTER

The White House,
January 16, 1981.

# PRESIDENT'S ECONOMIC REPORT; ECONOMIC ADVISERS' REPORT

## January 17, 1981

*In his valedictory Economic Report, released January 17, President Carter listed what he said were the economic achievements of his administration and issued a warning on "supply-side" tax cuts advocated by President-elect Reagan and many of his advisers.*

*Carter's Council of Economic Advisers, in an accompanying 336-page report to Congress, forecast a modest recovery in 1981 from a recession in the previous year, but it also predicted that inflation would continue at a double-digit rate. To provide incentives to slow inflation by influencing the setting of wages and prices, the president's economists recommended a tax-based incomes policy (TIP).*

*Carter claimed several accomplishments in the economic sphere — the growth of employment by 11 percent, an 8 percent rise in real per capita income since 1976, a stronger U.S. dollar and an improved balance of payments. But he cautioned, "I do not believe that we should now commit budgetary resources to large-scale personal tax cuts which will stimulate consumption far more than investment and thereby foreclose the possibility of meeting the nation's critical investment requirements."*

### 'Supply-Side' Tax Cuts

*The Council of Economic Advisers sounded its own cautionary note on the efficacy of supply-side tax cuts — those designed to increase the supply of goods through increased savings and investment, as opposed to*

105

*those intended to stimulate the economy through increased demand and consumer spending. "Most empirical studies have concluded," the council said, "that changes in personal income tax rates would have only a small effect on saving." The council also said:*

*● Specific investment-oriented tax cuts for business were likely to increase savings, investment and productivity by a much more significant degree than cuts in personal income taxes.*

*● Productivity-oriented tax reductions would yield improvements in the inflation rate that were "helpful and significant" yet modest in the face of a 10 percent underlying inflation rate.*

*● The supply response, although an important element of any tax reduction, would be substantially less than the demand response, especially in the short term.*

*● Since reductions in business and personal taxes would hike demand faster than supply, they must be designed to restrain demand sufficiently to reduce inflation.*

*While noting that there were "no costless ways to reduce inflation," President Carter's economists suggested that a tax-based incomes policy would reduce inflation and lower unemployment. The specific TIP approach the council believed would work best, called a "temporary hurdle TIP," would provide a tax credit to groups of workers whose average pay increase did not exceed a specified standard. The council said that TIP would be "part of a broad campaign for voluntary restraint in wage and price increases."*

## Economic Outlook

*Carter's Council of Economic Advisers, headed by Charles L. Schultze, predicted that in 1981 the real growth rate would be about 1.75 percent, with almost all of that coming in the last half of the year. The council also projected real growth in 1982 at 3.5 percent, and it said that the unemployment rate would gradually decline and that inflation would slow by about 1.5 percent.*

*Other economic forecasts:*
*● Consumer spending would be sluggish in 1981 but would pick up in 1982 as a result of gains in disposable income from personal tax cuts.*
*● Business capital spending would pick up during the second half of 1981 due to proposed business tax breaks, and real business capital spending was expected to increase substantially faster in 1982 than real GNP.*
*● The dollar would remain strong, and the U.S. current account would remain in surplus through 1982.*
*● Growth in the labor force would average about 1.75 percent over the ensuing two years. The unemployment rate would be between 7.5 and 7.75*

*percent at the end of 1981 and decline to between 7.25 and 7.5 percent during 1982.*

- *Private wages were expected to increase 10-10.5 percent in 1981, with the rate slowing noticeably in 1982.*
- *The Consumer Price Index (CPI) was expected to increase 12.6 percent over 1981. During 1982, the CPI increase was expected to drop to about 9.6 percent.*

*Two negatives were foreseen that could alter this outlook: a clash between the demand for funds and the monetary targets of the Federal Reserve, and the possibility of much higher oil prices as a result of continued unrest in the Middle East. Conversely, if there were higher productivity, more moderate wage gains or favorable crop developments, the outlook, and especially the rate of inflation, was likely to improve.*

*Following are excerpts from the final economic message of President Jimmy Carter, and from Chapter One,* Inflation and Growth in the 1980s, *of the* Annual Report of the Council of Economic Advisers, *issued in the same volume January 17, 1981.* (Boldface headings in brackets have been added by Congressional Quarterly to highlight the organization of the text.):

# ECONOMIC REPORT OF THE PRESIDENT

*To the Congress of the United States:*
Over the next few years our country faces several economic challenges that will test the will of our people and the capability of our government. We must find ways to bring down a stubborn inflation without choking off economic growth; we must channel a much larger share of our national output to investment and reverse a decade-long decline in productivity growth; and we must continue to reduce the Nation's dangerous vulnerability to disruptive changes in the world supply and price of oil....

## Strengths and Accomplishments

During the economic turmoil that characterized the decade of the 1970s, and especially during the past 4 years, the American economy succeeded in providing additional jobs for its people on a scale unsurpassed in our history. Employment grew by almost 25 percent over the decade, and by more than 11 percent in the past 4 years alone. Not only were jobs provided for a sharply rising population reaching working age, but job opportunities were opened up by the millions for new second earners, principally women. Neither Europe nor Japan came even close to the job performance of the American economy.

Along with employment, real per capita incomes grew during the past 4 years, despite the losses forced on the Nation by the huge increases in world oil prices and the effects of a slowing growth in productivity. As the year 1980 ended, per capita income, after taxes and adjusted for inflation, was some 8 percent higher than it was in 1976.

We have heard much about American industry losing its competitive edge in international markets and about the "deindustrialization" of America. In fact, during the 3 years prior to the onset of the 1980 recession — and the effects of that recession will be transient — the growth of industrial production in the United States was larger than it was in Germany, France, or the United Kingdom. The volume of American nonfarm exports rose by 35 percent between 1977 and the middle of 1980, and the share of U.S. exports among the total exports of the industrial countries rose by about 1¼ percentage points, reversing a declining trend that had been underway since the 1950s.

America's balance of payments is strong in large part because of its superior export performance. Despite a massive $40-billion annual drain of funds to pay for the oil-price increases of 1979 and 1980, our exports of goods and services now exceed our imports. Unlike the situation in most other oil-importing nations, our country's external balance is in surplus.

The dollar is also strong. After a period of weakness in its value abroad, we took decisive action 2 years ago to stabilize the dollar. Since then, in a world of sharply changing circumstances and disruptions of oil supply, the dollar has remained strong, and has risen in value compared to most major currencies.

While it is imperative that our country increase the share of its national output devoted to investment, the reason is not that investment has been weak in recent years. Between 1976 and 1980, real business investment grew almost 6 percent a year, substantially faster than GNP as a whole. Because of that rapid growth the share of business investment in GNP during the past 3 years exceeded that of any other 3-year period in the last three decades.

There are other areas where the Nation has made more progress than we sometimes realize. While we are properly concerned to limit the growth in Federal spending and voice our impatience with the waste and inefficiency that often exist in government programs, we should not forget the good that has been accomplished with these programs. Examples abound. In the early 1960s, for instance, infant mortality in the United States was scandalously high compared to other countries, and most of that high mortality was concentrated among the poor. Due in large part to programs like Medicaid, infant mortality has fallen sharply. More generally, we have dramatically improved access to medical care for the poor and the aged. Through Federal grants we have strengthened the mass transit systems of our major cities and helped our municipalities install critically needed waste treatment plants. We have helped millions of young people, who could not otherwise have afforded it, get a college education, and we have provided job training for workers who needed new skills.

Much attention is now focused on how to reduce the costs and ease the burden of Federal regulation to protect the environment, health, and safety. Concern about excessive regulatory costs is surely warranted, and my Administration has taken a number of specific steps to deal with the problem. In focusing attention on the burden of regulation, however, we should not lose sight of the substantial progress that has been made in enriching our lives, improving our health, and beautifying our country.

## Tackling Difficult Issues

During the past 4 years the Nation has taken a series of important and in some cases painful steps to deal with its energy problems. Starting almost 2 years ago, we began to phase out controls on domestic oil and natural gas prices. We thus moved to end the dangerous practice of holding U.S. energy prices below the world market price, a practice which tended to subsidize wasteful consumption and perpetuate our excessive dependence on oil imports.

Working with the Congress we also put in place the other principal elements of a comprehensive program to increase energy production and conserve energy use. We levied a windfall profits tax to divert the inevitable windfalls from oil decontrol to pay for the National Energy Program initiatives and to reduce the impact of decontrol on the poor.

Partly as a result of these policies we have begun to see dramatic results in both the supply and conservation of energy. There are now 70 percent more drilling rigs in operation than when my Administration took office, and the number of oil and gas wells being drilled has reached a new record. By late 1980 the United States was importing almost 30 percent less oil than it did 2 years ago and our gasoline use had dropped by more than 10 percent over the same period. While some of the reduction in energy use was due to the recession, most of it reflects real energy conservation. . . .

Because of the slowdown in birth rates in the past 15 years, the 1980s will see about half as fast a growth in the labor force as in the 1970s. The proportion of experienced workers will rise, contributing to an increase in productivity, while the proportion of young people will fall, leading to a drop in unemployment.

There are a number of reasons, therefore, to confront with hope the economic challenges that face us. We have a solid record of achievement. In the fields of energy and deregulation we have already laid the foundations on which the future can build. And there are some favorable trends underway that should help raise productivity and reduce unemployment in the years ahead.

## Unresolved Problems

Despite much progress in recent years, we are faced with some serious problems. An inflation that was already bad became worse after the 1979 oil-price increase. Productivity growth, which had been declining sporadically for a decade, virtually ceased in the last several years. And although we have made substantial progress in adapting our economy to a world of higher oil prices, we remain dangerously vulnerable to serious supply disruptions originating abroad.

These problems are closely related to each other. Our inflation stems in part from our oil vulnerability and our slowing productivity growth. High and rising inflation, in turn, tends to cause economic reactions that depress productivity. As we make progress in one of these areas, we will also make progress in the others.

None of the problems is so intractable that we cannot overcome it. But all are so deep-seated that progress will come slowly, only with persistence, and at the cost of some sacrifice on the part of us all.

## Inflation

In the first half of the 1960s inflation averaged about 1 percent a year, so low as to be virtually unnoticeable. In the past 15 years, however, the underlying rate of inflation has risen sporadically but inexorably and it is now running at about 10 percent a year.

During those 15 years there have been three major episodes in which the rate of inflation surged upward. The first came in the late 1960s, when the Vietnam war and the Great Society programs were financed for a number of years without a tax increase. The consequent high budget deficits during a period of economic prosperity generated strong inflationary pressures as total spending became excessive relative to the Nation's productive capacity. The second inflationary surge, which came in the early 1970s, was associated with the first massive oil-price increase, a worldwide crop shortage which drove up food prices, and an economy which again became somewhat overheated in 1972 and 1973. The third inflationary episode came in 1979 and 1980. It was principally triggered by another massive oil-price increase, but part of the rise in inflation may also have been due to overall demand in the economy pressing on available supply. Throughout the past decade, the slowing growth in productivity has pushed up the increase in business costs, adding its bit to the rise of inflation.

Late in each of the three inflationary episodes monetary and fiscal restraints were applied, and at the end of each a recession took place, with rising unemployment and idle capacity. Inflation did fall back somewhat, but at the end of each recession it had not declined to the level from which it started. And so the inflationary process has been characterized by ratchet-like behavior. A set of inflationary causes raises the rate of inflation; when the initiating factors disappear, inflation does not recede to its starting position despite the occurrence of recession; the wage-price spiral then tends to perpetuate itself at a new and higher level. Instead of an occasional 3 percentage point rise in inflation, which disappeared when the initial causes of the inflation were gone, our basic inflation rate rose first from 1 to 4 percent, then from 4 to 7 percent, and in this latest episode from 7 to 10 percent. It is this downward insensitivity of inflation in the face of economic slack that has given the last 15 years their inflationary bias. . . .

## Budget and Tax Policies

It is now estimated that the Federal budget for the current fiscal year 1981 will be in deficit by $55 billion, substantially more than I had hoped or planned. In part the size of that deficit reflects the loss of revenues induced by the recession from which our economy is now beginning to recover. Had the unemployment rate remained at the 6 percent level where it stood when I first submitted the 1981 budget last year, the deficit would now be less than $20 billion. . . .

Although my 1982 budget emphasizes the need for fiscal restraint, and for reduction of the deficit, it also takes the first major step in a long-term program of tax reductions aimed at increasing capital formation.

The causes of the longer-term slowdown in productivity growth are many — and some of them are still unknown. But a major depressing factor has been the failure of the Nation's capital stock to increase relative to its rapidly growing labor force in the past 5 or 6 years. Unlike earlier periods, American workers have not been working with increasing amounts of capital. Improving the trend of productivity growth will require restoring the growth of capital per worker.

Higher investment will also be critically required throughout America's energy-using industries to speed up the replacement of older energy-inefficient plant and machinery with newer energy-saving capital. In addition, a large expansion of energy-producing industries — both conventional and nonconventional — will add further to investment needs. . . .

The central feature of the tax policies I am proposing is their emphasis on increasing investment. By 1985, an unusually high 45 percent of the tax reductions will be directed toward spurring investment. But even this will not itself be sufficient to raise investment to the levels our country will need in the decade ahead in order to improve its productivity growth and deal with its energy problems. Careful control of Federal spending, however, will create the leeway for additional investment-oriented tax reductions in later years, within the framework of the overall budgetary restraint required to fight inflation. I do not believe that we should now commit budgetary resources to large-scale personal tax cuts which will stimulate consumption far more than investment and thereby foreclose the possibility of meeting the Nation's critical investment requirements.

## Monetary Policy

Monetary policy is the responsibility of the Federal Reserve System, which is independent of the Executive. I respect that independence. But there are several broad aspects of monetary policy having to do with public perceptions that do fall within the purview of the President in his role as national leader.

Sustained restraint in monetary policy is a prerequisite to lowering inflation. The Federal Reserve exercises this restraint principally by keeping a strict limit on the growth of the Nation's money supply. In October 1979 the Federal Reserve modified its earlier policies and operating procedures to increase sharply the emphasis it gives to controlling the money supply. The Federal Reserve each year sets targets for monetary growth and seeks to hold the growth of the money supply within the targets. Increasingly the public in general and the financial community in particular have come to associate the credibility of the Federal Reserve and its determination to fight inflation with its success in keeping money growth continuously within the preannounced targets. It is very important, however, that public opinion not hold the Federal Reserve to such a rigid form of monetary targeting as to deprive it of the flexibility it needs to conduct a responsible monetary policy. . . .

Only if the public understands the realities, and the complexities, of carrying out an anti-inflationary monetary policy can the Federal Reserve successfully apply the measured restraint necessary to wring out inflation at minimum cost in production and jobs. On the one hand, the country must face the fact that in a world with a stubborn 10 percent inflation rate, keeping a tight rein on the growth of the money supply inevitably leads to interest rates that average significantly higher than those we were accustomed to in earlier periods of lower inflation. On the other hand, the public and the financial community must not become so obsessed with the mechanics of monetary targeting that any change in targets or any short-run deviation of money growth from those targets is taken as a sign that monetary restraint has been weakened.

Without reasoned and persistent monetary restraint, inflation cannot be licked. Perhaps more than in any other area of economic policy, however, achieving success in monetary policy depends on an informed public opinion.

## Incomes Policies

For the past 2 years my Administration has urged business and labor to comply with a set of voluntary pay and price standards. Even though it was introduced at a very difficult time — just before the oil-price explosion of 1979 — this voluntary program of wage and price restraint did moderate the pace of inflation. It significantly reduced — although it could not eliminate — the effect of the oil-price rise on the underlying inflation rate.

After 2 years of operation there is general agreement that the current pay and price standards would not continue to be effective in their present form and without additional support. For this reason we have carefully examined the possibility of strengthening a voluntary incomes policy by using the tax system to provide incentives to firms and workers to slow the rate of inflation. This approach has been labeled a tax-based incomes policy (TIP). The detailed results of our review are contained in the accompanying *Annual Report of the Council of Economic Advisers....*

## Energy

I am once again proposing that the Congress increase the Federal excise tax on gasoline by 10 cents per gallon as an additional incentive to cut petroleum consumption. The need for this tax is, if anything, even greater than it was 7 months ago when the Congress overturned my action to impose a gasoline conservation fee administratively.

We have once more seen a tightening of world oil supplies. The massive inventories built up in late 1979 and early 1980 have been drawn upon to make up for the loss of exports from Iran and Iraq. If that conflict should continue or if exports do not return to normal, the buffer which those record high inventories provided will be exhausted. Even in the last 2 months, we have seen significant escalation in prices charged by some OPEC members. National security requires us to put additional downward pressure on consumption of gasoline and other petroleum products. If we do not, OPEC may do it for us.

Paradoxically, one of the reasons given earlier for rejecting my proposed tax was that it was too small — some would have preferred a tax of 50 cents or even a dollar per gallon. Whether, over time, this Nation should move toward gasoline taxes that are comparable with those of our Western European allies is not a question that has to be answered now. In any event, to do so overnight would shock the economy excessively. At current gasoline consumption levels, a 50-cent per gallon tax would draw approximately $50 billion per year out of consumers' pockets and require excessive adjustments by consumers and industry. It is much more sensible to start with the level I have proposed....

## Summing Up: The Need for Balance

In the years immediately ahead, our country will be wrestling with two central domestic issues. The first is economic in nature: How can we reduce inflation while maintaining the economic growth that keeps our people employed? The second is even broader: What is the proper role of government in our society as spender of tax revenues and regulator of industry?

I am confident we can successfully come to grips with both of these issues. We would make a costly mistake, however, if we approached these problems with the view that there is some single answer to the economic problem and a single criterion for determining the role of government. The resolution of both of these great issues demands a balancing of many approaches and many considerations. Indeed, the only helpful simple proposition is the one which states that any simple and quick answer is automatically the wrong one.

The approach I have set forth in this *Report* will successfully meet the economic challenge. But it relies on not one but a number of essential elements. To reduce inflation we must be prepared for a period of sustained budgetary and monetary restraint. But since we know that this also tends to depress the growth of output and employment, we must not conclude that the greater the restraint the better. We want a degree of restraint that takes into account society's interest in employment and production as well as its concern to lower inflation. We can improve our prospects significantly by introducing investment-oriented tax cuts that increase supply and productivity. But the supply response will not be so quick or so great as to constitute an answer in and of itself. And, in particular, it would be very dangerous to make budgetary policy in the belief that the supply response can be so large as to wipe out the need for fiscal prudence and budgetary restraint. We can improve our prospects still further by the use of voluntary incomes policies, strengthened when budgetary resources become available by tax incentives for wage moderation. But, again, incomes policies alone will not do the job. If we try to rely on them excessively, we will do more harm than good. Only with a balance among the various elements, and only with persistence in the realization that sure progress will come gradually, can we have both lower inflation and better growth.

Sorting out the proper role of government also requires us to strike a balance. At times Federal spending has grown too rapidly. But in recent years its growth did not result from the introduction of a host of new government programs by spendthrift politicians or a surge of profligacy by wasteful bureaucrats. It stemmed mainly from two sources: *first,* increased military spending to meet national security goals that are overwhelmingly supported by the American people; and *second,* the growth of long established and broadly accepted social security and social insurance programs that are directly or indirectly indexed against inflation or automatically responsive to an increase in unemployment.

There is some waste. There is some abuse. I have instituted a number of reforms to cut it back. I am sure my successors will continue this important effort. But waste and abuse are not the fundamental issues. The essence of the challenge that faces us is how to balance the various benefits that government programs confer on us against their costs in terms of higher taxes, higher deficits, and sometimes higher inflation.

It is my view that we must strike the balance so as to restrict for some time the overall growth of Federal spending to less than the growth of our economy, despite the faster increase of the military component of the budget. As a consequence, in my 1982 budget I have proposed a series of program reductions. I have suggested a delay in the effective date of new programs I believe important. I have recommended improvements in the index we use to adjust Federal programs for inflation.

I think we will do a better job in striking the right balance over the years ahead if we keep two principles in mind: The first is to recognize *reality*. The choices are in fact difficult, and we should not pretend that all we have to do is find wasteful programs with zero benefits. The second is to act with *compassion*. Some government programs provide special benefits for the poor and the disadvantaged; while these programs must not be immune from review and reform, they should not bear the brunt of the reductions.

The same general viewpoint is appropriate when we approach the problem of government as regulator, especially in protecting the environment, health, and safety. When we first awoke to the fact of generations of environmental neglect, we rushed to compensate for our mistake and paid too little attention to problems of cost and effectiveness. Sometimes the laws we passed and the deadlines we set took too little account of their economic impact. For 4 years my Administration has been engaged in a major program of finding ways to make regulations more cost-effective and to strike a reasonable balance between environmental concerns and economic costs. A strong foundation has been laid. Much remains to be done. But lasting progress will not come unless we realize that there is a balance to be struck. Those who believe that virtually all regulation is bad and that the best regulation is a dead regulation will come to grips with the real problem no more successfully than the enthusiasts who believe that concern with regulatory costs is synonymous with lack of concern for the environment.

I believe that the government has indeed overregulated and that regulatory reform must continue to be a major objective of the Federal Government, as it has been during my Administration. But I also believe that true reform involves finding better ways to identify and to give proper consideration to gains as well as costs.

My reading of the distant and the nearby past gives me confidence that the American people can meet the challenges ahead. There are no simple formulas. There will be no quick victories. But an understanding of the diverse concerns we have, a pragmatic willingness to bring to bear a varied array of weapons, and persistence in the effort will bring success.

# THE ANNUAL REPORT OF THE COUNCIL OF ECONOMIC ADVISERS

In the 1980s the United States will confront a variety of stubborn problems that have developed during the past 15 years. Chief among these problems is one that is shared by most other industrial countries — the persistence of large wage and price increases, even in the face of high unemployment and slack production. This problem poses the single most important challenge to U.S. economic policy — reducing inflation while maintaining a reasonably prosperous and growing economy.

Many other problems are themselves closely related to inflation, either as cause or as consequence. Our Nation's productivity growth has virtually halted in recent years. The era of cheap energy has ended, the world has grown vulnerable to supply disruptions, and the course of domestic inflation and unemployment has become closely dependent on economic and political developments in the oil-rich but politically unstable Middle East. Meanwhile, the struggle to find a proper balance between a clean, healthy, and safe environment, on the one hand, and satisfactory economic growth with lower inflation, on the other, will continue. All of these developments, together with the growing interdependence of the world economy, have set in motion major changes in economic structure, occupational skill requirements, and industrial location that will continue to pose sizable adjustment problems to many industries, communities, and workers.

While the magnitude of these economic challenges is cause for serious concern, it does not warrant pessimism. During the 1970s the U.S. economy performed quite well in many important respects. Over that decade our country outperformed most other major countries in providing jobs for its people.... Employment grew almost 25 percent as the American economy created jobs not only for millions of youths entering the labor market for the first time but also for millions of women, who found job opportunities in growing numbers. This performance continued through the last years of the decade at an increased pace. While the growth in the number of employed persons was temporarily interrupted by the recession of 1980, the basic performance was virtually unparalleled....

In recent years the United States has successfully begun to tackle some of its most difficult problems. After years of inaction followed by several years of vigorous debate, and with some painful sacrifices, we have put into place the major elements of an energy program which is already paying dividends in the form of greater energy conservation and improved supply prospects. After decades in which the documented evidence about the greater productivity and efficiency to be gained from economic deregulation had been ignored, this Nation finally acted during the past 4 years to deregulate its airline, trucking, and railroad industries, and major elements of its financial industry. And during the 1980 recession the executive branch and the Congress showed their willingness to maintain the restraint and discipline needed to control inflation by resisting strong pressures for a hasty and potentially inflationary fiscal stimulus.

As this *Report* will have several occasions to point out, there are no simple and clear-cut answers to the complex economic problems confronting our country. Many of them will yield only gradually to persistent efforts pursued on many fronts. In some cases where our knowledge is particularly uncertain, we may have to try several approaches before finding an effective solution. Nevertheless, the willingness to tackle difficult problems which this country has shown in the last several years provides a reason to temper concern about the seriousness of our economic problems with a belief that they can be met successfully....

## Inflation

The Nation has for some time now experienced inflation that would have been unimaginable in earlier days. Although people's lives and the course of business may not, at first glance, appear radically different from what they were in 1960 before the recent inflation began, inflation has taken a very real toll. The uncertainty it has brought with it cannot be measured, but the consequent anxiety has torn at the fabric of our society. People feel less able to mark their progress and fear that the next round of inflation will leave them poorer. In a number of ways — such as introducing cost-of-living adjustments into wage contracts and indexing the benefits of social welfare programs — institutions have evolved to compensate for some of the uncertainty. But these institutions may sometimes only heighten the arbitrary redistribution of income brought on by inflation — redistribution that society often finds undesirable and unfair. In addition to these painful effects, moreover, inflation reduces the Nation's prospects for growth. The reduction may not appear dramatic, but it impairs the efficiency of the free-enterprise system and discourages capital investment, innovation, and risk-taking.

Rising prices, it should be remembered, are not in the aggregate synonymous with a reduction in real income. When prices rise, someone receives the additional revenues. And for the economy as a whole, rising prices have gone together with rising money incomes. But a wage or salary increase comes infrequently and in a large lump, while prices tend to increase all the time. Furthermore, a pay increase may be viewed as uncertain and as a reward for effort, but price increases seem entirely beyond a consumer's control. As a result, a recent wage increase may be forgotten when the grocery bill rises. Thus rising prices are often treated as something that directly lower real incomes, even when in fact for the Nation as a whole they do not. Of course, the resulting anxiety is no less real.

But when the country pays sharply higher prices to foreign oil producers, that does indeed lower its real income. We are poorer because we receive less oil than we did previously for the same amount of money. That would be true whether or not general inflation followed increases in the price of oil. The induced inflation, in the form of generally higher wages, salaries, and prices, is not the cause of the real income decline — the Nation's higher oil bill is.

A similar phenomenon occurs when growth in productivity slows. Slower productivity growth leads to a slower rise in real incomes. A decline in productivity growth may be accompanied by an unchanged pace of wage and salary increases, in which case inflation will rise. But a slackening of productivity growth may also result in lower wage increases and an unchanged inflation rate. In either case the same slowdown in the growth of real income would have occurred. It was not caused by inflation. . . .

The uncertainty created by inflation also obstructs the conduct of economic policy. To the extent that high and rising inflation unhinges expectations from reality, the connection between economic policies and their results is attenuated, and the difficulties of policymaking are increased. Inflation itself is then more difficult to control. There is a temptation for macroeconomic policy to make announcements and take measures to impress the markets, but the intangible gains so purchased tend to evaporate rapidly. . . .

## [UNDERLYING RATE]

Over the past 15 years the underlying rate of inflation has risen from about 1 percent in the first half of the 1960s to 9 or 10 percent now. The increase has not been steady. Instead, there have been three major episodes. Each period began with a sharp increase in the underlying rate and ended with the rate falling only part way to its original level. Thus, each new inflationary period has started from a higher underlying level than its predecessor.

The first jump in the underlying inflation rate came during the Vietnam war, when a large rise in both military expenditures and outlays for Great Society programs was financed for several years without a tax increase. This led to a very large Federal budget deficit superimposed on an economy already operating at a high level. The result was a classic example of an excess of demand over supply. The underlying inflation rate rose from about 1 percent in the 1961-65 period to 4 or 5 percent by 1969. By the end of the decade the forces pushing up the inflation rate receded as taxes were belatedly raised and Vietnam war outlays declined. Although the economy entered a recession in 1970, the underlying rate of inflation continued at about 4 to 5 percent until wage and price controls were introduced in August 1971. For a short period the controls held down inflation in prices but did not reduce the growth in costs.

Another inflationary episode began in late 1973 as the result of two major developments. A poor crop year worldwide caused a sharp surge in food prices, and the Arab oil embargo at the end of 1973 was followed by a threefold increase in world oil prices. Although the full impact of the increase in world oil prices was muted in the United States by price controls on domestically produced oil, energy prices and the prices of energy-using products increased sharply. Aggregate demand grew sharply in 1972 and early in 1973. A worldwide boom led to a major inventory buildup and a widely based acceleration of raw materials prices in 1973-74. Finally, the distortions and inequities brought on by wage and price controls created irresistible pressures for easing the controls in 1973 and eliminating them in 1974. When this occurred, there was a burst of price and wage increases.

When this burst receded, the U.S. economy entered its worst recession in 40 years. While the underlying rate of inflation fell back from its late 1974 peak, it did not fall to its starting point. Aside from brief fluctuations, it settled down in the 6 to 7 percent range from 1976 through 1978.

The most recent inflationary episode was triggered when the Organization of Petroleum Exporting Countries (OPEC) raised oil prices in 1979 and early 1980. Relative to the size of the U.S. economy, the recent price increase was larger than the 1973-74 increase. By the end of 1974 the world price of oil had tripled from about $4 to about $12 per barrel, thereby adding about $18 billion to our bill for imported oil, or roughly 1.4 percent of gross national product (GNP). Since the price of domestically produced petroleum (which at that time accounted for about two-thirds of the petroleum used in the United States) was restrained by controls, the average U.S. price remained lower than prices throughout the rest of the world. Still, domestic oil prices almost doubled, so that the total increase in consumer costs was almost 3 percent of GNP.

During the most recent shock the price of imported oil rose from about $15 per barrel at the end of 1978 to $35 at the close of 1980. This added about $50 billion to the cost of the oil we now import into the United States, or about 2 percent of GNP. Since domestic crude oil prices were in the process of being decontrolled during this period, the price of domestic oil increased by about $15 per barrel, adding another $60 billion to the oil costs paid by consumers.

The forces of inflation during this period were also strengthened to some extent by the behavior of aggregate demand. There was some acceleration of wages in 1978 as unemployment fell sharply. And for a time in late 1978 and early 1979, there appeared to be some excess demand in product markets.

Spurred by these developments, inflation surged in 1979 and early 1980. As measured by the CPI [Consumer Price Index] — which was also heavily influenced by sharp increases in mortgage interest rates — inflation reached annual rates of 15 to 20 percent in the first quarter of 1980. By the spring of 1980 the forces that had given rise to this inflationary episode subsided, and the economy entered a brief recession. The measured inflation rate receded from its peak, but the underlying rate appears to have leveled off in the 9 to 10 percent range, up several notches from the 6 to 7 percent level at which the period had started.

## THE SOURCES OF INFLATION

The chief problem with respect to inflation is not the sporadic developments that generate inflationary impulses. Instead, it is the ratchet-like nature of the inflationary process which makes it resistant to downward pressures. . . . The size of the inflationary bursts of recent years has not been out of line with those which occurred earlier in the century, but recent inflation has had an upward bias and has fluctuated around a rising trend line. An understanding of the "causes" of inflation must therefore encompass not only the various factors that give rise to particular inflationary episodes but also the reasons why inflation has developed a ratchet-like character.

## [Role of Aggregate Demand]

The inflation rate which occurs in any given year is a composite of the individual wage and price decisions made by millions of businesses, unions, and workers. Those decisions are influenced by the strength of demand relative to supply. As demand (or spending) — on the part of consumers, business, and government — declines relative to supply, there is pressure on workers to moderate their wage demands lest employment fall, and on producers to restrain prices for fear of losing sales. The converse also holds true: the smaller the number of unemployed people and the lower the amount of unused industrial capacity, the greater the upward pressure on wages and prices. Some evidence also suggests that a rapid rise in demand can generate upward pressure on both wages and prices, even if the level of demand is not excessive. In general, if demand is in rough balance with supply, the underlying rate of inflation for the economy as a whole will remain basically unchanged, even though prices and wages in individual sectors may fluctuate in response to conditions in particular markets. If excess demand exists, or if the rate of increase in demand is very large, the underlying rate of inflation will tend to rise. If aggregate demand falls below supply, some downward pressure will be exerted on inflation.

Expectations about the future state of aggregate demand are also an important determinant of inflation. Wage decisions and many price decisions cannot easily be reversed. Wages are often set for at least a year, and under most major union contracts they are set for 3 years. There are also many advantages to both buyers and sellers in avoiding frequent product price changes. As a consequence, decisionmakers have to think not only about market conditions at present but also about what they are likely to be in the future. Thus, both current and *expected* aggregate demand influence the rate of inflation. Moreover, a firm's decisions today about what wages to offer or what prices to set for any future period will be conditioned by its expectations about the wages its competitors will pay and the prices its competitors will charge, and by the incomes that will be earned by its customers. In short, today's inflation rate is strongly influenced by what people expect it to be tomorrow.

It was excess aggregate demand during the Vietnam war that drove up the underlying rate of inflation from 1 percent to 4 or 5 percent by the end of the 1960s. Although increases in oil and food prices were the principal causes of the next two inflationary surges, pressures from aggregate demand again played an identifiable role. The most troublesome feature of the inflation of the past 15 years, however, has been the fact that after each of the three inflationary episodes the underlying rate of inflation did not fall back to its earlier level. To what extent was this outcome a demand-related phenomenon?

At the end of each inflationary episode the economy entered a recession — in 1970-71, in 1974-75, and in 1980. Unemployment rose steeply, and substantial amounts of idle capacity appeared.... The failure of inflation to fall back to earlier levels is therefore not attributable to excess demand.

On the other hand, there clearly would have been some level of demand low enough to have caused business and labor to moderate the increase in wages and prices substantially so as to return to the earlier level of inflation. But for reasons discussed later, the rate of wage and price increase has become relatively insensitive to a moderate degree of economic slack. As a consequence, the cost of the necessary restraint — in terms of additional unemployment, idle capacity, and lost income, production, and investment — would have been extremely high.

### [Federal Budget Deficits]

The Federal budget balance at any given time is an important factor in determining the level of current aggregate demand in the economy. If the Federal budget is in deficit, total spending — private and public — will be higher than it would be if taxes had been raised or spending had been cut to produce a balanced Federal budget. Any tax or spending measure that turned a budget deficit into a balanced budget would tend to reduce demand relative to supply and put downward pressure on the inflation rate. Furthermore, since businesses made wage and price decisions at least partly in the light of what they expect market conditions to be, announcements of future budget policies have a strong effect on current economic conditions and on the rate of inflation. Thus budget deficits can contribute to inflation both by being a part of current aggregate demand and by contributing to expectations about future aggregate demand. . . .

If government budget deficits are the cause of inflation, it should make no difference whether the deficit occurs at the Federal, State, or local level. For example, the Federal revenue-sharing program, which grants Federal tax revenues to State and local governments, has the effect of reducing State and local deficits (or increasing their surpluses) by increasing the Federal deficit. If the program were eliminated, but both levels of government continued to tax the same amount and maintain the same level of services, the Federal deficit would be reduced — but the total deficit, and its inflationary consequences, would be unchanged. In fact, principally because the State and local governments accumulate funds to pay employee pension costs, their budgets usually show a surplus. . . .

The notion that budget deficits are the chief cause of inflation also founders on a comparison of budget deficits and inflation among different countries. Japan and Germany in recent years have had much better success in combating inflation than the United States. Yet their budget deficits, especially those of Japan, have been much higher relative to the size of their economies than has been the case in the United States. . . .

### [Supply Shocks]

Sharply higher prices in one sector of the economy can lead to surges in inflation even when excess aggregate demand is absent. These sudden and massive changes generally spring from conditions that cannot be controlled. The most important of these have been increases in food prices resulting from shortages and increases in oil prices mandated by OPEC. These events are no different from such common supply disruptions as strikes, accidents, and natural disasters, but they are much larger, and it is their size which makes their effects exceptional.

Price shocks have both direct and indirect effects. Consumers feel the price increases directly, and these direct effects may be magnified by the brevity of the time in which they occur, resulting in extraordinary jumps in reported inflation rates. In addition, price increases in agricultural or energy raw materials translate indirectly into price increases in the final products that utilize those materials, although the degree and timing of the pass-through depend on market conditions. This secondary impact is quite important in the case of petroleum, half of which is used by businesses in production and transportation.

As an abrupt increase in the price of an important commodity translates into an increase in the cost of living, pressure builds for wage gains to match the new inflation. Some gains take place automatically where wages are linked to prices through cost-of-living clauses in union contracts. Additional acceleration occurs as new contracts are negotiated. As businesses observe the rising wage-price spiral, they are likely to expect a higher future level of inflation. They are then somewhat more likely to grant larger wage increases, both in the belief that rising inflation will make it possible to pass through increases in higher prices and in order to avoid losing workers. Through this process, a sharp increase in food or oil prices can lead to a rise in the underlying inflation rate.

The magnitude of the inflationary process set in motion by an oil-price increase or some other supply shock depends on the state of the economy. The more prosperous the economy and the lower the unemployment level, the more likely it is that the initial increase in prices will lead to higher wage increases and a higher underlying inflation rate.

In addition to their inflationary consequences, supply shocks also create recessionary forces. The very large increases in oil prices in 1974 and 1979 not only spurred inflation but simultaneously depressed aggregate demand. They were therefore largely responsible for the recessions of 1974-75 and 1980. After paying sharply higher prices for petroleum products, consumers had less to spend on other goods and services. But those who received the revenues from higher oil prices — foreign and domestic oil producers — increased their demands for U.S. exports and investment goods only gradually. On balance, therefore, aggregate demand and spending fell, leading to lower output and reduced employment.

Such a simultaneous increase in inflation and unemployment brought on by supply shocks creates a dilemma for economic policy. If monetary and fiscal policies produce additional aggregate demand to "compensate" for the recessionary forces set in motion by a supply shock, there is likely to be a large induced rise in inflation. If, on the other hand, no effort is made to compensate, aggregate demand will fall. But given the relative insensitivity of wage and price decisions to moderate slack in the economy, some increase in the underlying inflation rate is nonetheless likely. Only sharply restrictive monetary and fiscal policies, which strengthen the forces leading to recession, can prevent an increase in the underlying inflation rate. While recessionary forces came into play in 1974 and 1980, the slackening of aggregate demand was not sufficient to avoid another upward ratcheting of the inflation rate.

### [Declining Productivity Growth]

Over the past decade — and perhaps since the mid-1960s — the rate of productivity growth in the United States has slackened.... This slackening has been an unwelcome development, since productivity growth can offset the effects of rising wages on business costs and prices. When productivity growth slows but increases in wages continue, the rate of increase in costs and prices rises. While short-term variations in productivity growth may not be recognized in setting prices, a longer-lasting slowdown in productivity will be reflected in higher prices. Once prices begin to rise in response to this pressure, another round of wage demands is stimulated as workers try to offset the increased cost of living. This raises the underlying inflation rate yet again.

### [Wages and Prices]

If wages and prices were sensitive to a moderate degree of slack in the economy, careful control of aggregate demand through monetary and fiscal policy could bring rising inflation to a halt quickly and at a modest cost. True, mistakes in policy might occur from time to time, and supply shocks over which the government has no control would still take place. But inflation could be brought down relatively quickly and easily if it did not have — as it has now — a large degree of inertia.

Before World War II, and perhaps in the immediate postwar years, wages and prices were more sensitive in a downward direction.... Several careful economic studies show that in that earlier period a moderate or short-lived slackening of aggregate demand tended to reduce the rate of inflation significantly. Those who have compared that earlier era with more recent times differ in their views as to precisely why things have changed, but the basic causes are clear.

During the past several decades the vast majority of firms, labor unions, and workers have come to expect that expansionary government policies will be applied sooner or later to reverse recessionary tendencies in the economy. Since current wage and price decisions are strongly influenced by what workers and firms think the future will hold, the expectation of stimulus removes much of the motivation for moderating wage and price behavior. Businesses and unions have also developed a growing tendency to turn to government for relief, often with some success, when their high prices and wages lead them into competitive difficulties. All of these factors have weakened the incentive for businesses and workers to restrain their wage and price demands, even in the face of softening markets. These actions do not depend on specific knowledge about future government policies but are based on the widespread view that "the government won't allow things to get too bad."

Prior to World War II, however, popular expectations were different. The Federal Government had historically played little role in smoothing the economic cycles, and substantial depressions as well as mild recessions occurred periodically. Up until the 1930s there was no unemployment insurance, social security, or deposit insurance to ameliorate the consequences of economic downturns. When markets started to weaken, there was no reason to believe that any support — in the aggregate or for individuals — would be forthcoming from the government. As a consequence, wages and prices quickly subsided as businesses and workers scrambled to survive. The cycle, furthermore, was self-reinforcing. Because inflation often led to a slump, followed by a speedy reduction in inflation, businessmen and others came to expect that inflation would not last long; this expectation itself moderated their behavior with respect to wages and prices.

After World War II, however, the United States and other industrial countries decided that the costs of this kind of painful adjustment were too high. Thus, countercyclical policy was founded. The success of that policy, and the existence of various programs of income support to protect individuals in case of unemployment, have changed the character of expectations. In the new environment the appearance of slack markets, idle capacity, and higher unemployment leads to far less moderation in wage and price increases. Downward flexibility has not disappeared, but it has diminished.

Current wage and price behavior has deep-seated structural origins and is not based solely on current expectations about governmental behavior. Since most large wage contracts run for 2 or 3 years, the rate of wage increase in any particular year will have been determined in part by negotiations in earlier years under different conditions. In addition, the expiration dates of multiyear wage contracts for different industries are staggered, and the wage increases negotiated in any industry will be influenced to some extent by the size of earlier increases won by unions in other industries. Moreover, the prospect of further inflation over the life of these contracts has led to the inclusion of cost-of-living clauses, which provide wage increases even when markets are slack. Although union contracts cover less than one-quarter of the civilian labor force, the partial insulation of these contracts from current economic events has some effect on the wages that nonunion firms must pay.

Quite apart from the existence of written contracts, there are mutual advantages to both firms and workers from wage-setting practices that are relatively insensitive to economic slack. In complicated modern societies the costs of acquiring information about alternative job opportunities are very high for workers, and the costs of training a skilled work force are very large for businesses. Both workers and firms see benefits in establishing long-term relationships. One way for a firm to attract and hold a skilled work force is an implicit agreement not to engage in extensive wage-cutting during periods of weak markets. As a consequence, many firms are unwilling to take a chance of losing out in the labor market by being among the first to reduce wage increases.

Other institutions besides those of wage-contracting contribute to the downward insensitivities of prices and wages. In the case of prices, the downward pressure that would normally be exerted by competitive forces in slack markets is significantly muted in large oligopolistic industries by market strategy considerations and various forms of administered prices. Finally, government intervention in individual markets through regulation, which may fix wages, the price or quality of the product, or the conditions under which production takes place, adds further rigidity.

Some of the economic institutions and practices that contribute to wage and price rigidity themselves evolved in response to expectations that government economic policy would continue to be supportive. Although the persistent application of demand restraint is likely to reduce them, they should not be expected to disappear easily or quickly.

Downward wage and price rigidity makes the costs of reducing inflation through monetary and fiscal restraint quite large. It is difficult to estimate the costs with precision, but representative econometric studies suggest that reducing inflation by 1 percentage point would require a sacrifice of $100 billion in lost output (in 1980 prices) and a one-half percentage point rise in the unemployment rate over a period of about 3 years. Most of the costs would be incurred in the first half of the period. These statistical estimates, however, are based on historical relationships. There has never been a period of sustained economic restraint in recent times from which direct evidence of the costs could be drawn. The possibility that they would grow significantly smaller if restraint persisted is discussed later in this chapter.

In sum, it is the costs imposed on society when demand restraint clashes with the downward insensitivity of wages and prices that makes it so difficult to reduce inflation by applying monetary and fiscal restraint. Viewed in this perspective, the central problem of economic policy is not how to reduce inflation. If that were the only objective, a sufficiently draconian level of demand restraint could be found to do the job. The real issue is twofold: How large are the costs society is willing to bear to realize the benefits of lower inflation, and can policies be designed to lower those costs so that inflation can be reduced faster with smaller losses in output and employment? . . .

## MONETARY POLICY

The Federal Reserve bears a substantial share of the responsibility for carrying out aggregate demand management. . . . [T]he monetary authorities must first confront the question of the appropriate degree of economic restraint. The problem is to achieve a proper balance in order to reduce inflationary pressures at a minimum cost in lost jobs and production. Formulating and implementing policies to achieve this balance in a period characterized by wide fluctuations in economic and financial conditions confronts the monetary authorities with a number of serious additional challenges. While these problems are generally technical in nature, the manner in which they are resolved can have a significant impact on the degree of monetary restraint.

Monetary policy can exert no direct control over aggregate demand. It must exert its influence indirectly, that is, by affecting actual and expected conditions in the money and credit markets. The linkages between what it can control (the cost and availability of bank reserves), its intermediate indicators of conditions in the money and credit markets (the monetary aggregates and interest rates), and its ultimate goals (the impact on real growth and prices) are imperfect and often are not directly observable, even after the fact. In evaluating these linkages, the monetary authorities must rely on predicted relationships based on economic theory and historical experience, and there is plenty of room for slippage. These technical problems create considerable uncertainty for the makers of monetary policy.

A related issue is that the effectiveness of the monetary authorities in bringing down inflation depends on how firms and individuals perceive monetary policy. Private sector expectations of the likely success of monetary policy influence its actual success. Consequently, it is important that the monetary authorities demonstrate that they have chosen a strategy that will achieve their anti-inflation objectives. Moreover, their actions must indicate that they have the technical capability to meet these objectives while responding forcefully to new situations and to any divergence between desired and actual developments.

In recent years the debate on these issues has focused on the Federal Reserve's target growth ranges for monetary aggregates and on the process of setting and implementing these targets. The targets are defined in terms of the narrow measures of the money stock (formerly $M-1$ and now $M-1A$ and $M-1B$, which include currency and various types of checkable deposits), the broader measures of the money stock (M2 and M3, which include currency and checkable deposits as well as time and savings deposits and other deposit-like instruments), and bank credit. The Federal Reserve has used monetary growth targets internally since the early 1970s, and since 1975 it has announced them publicly in testimony before the Congress.

In October 1979 the Federal Reserve modified its procedures for implementing monetary policy in order to give greater emphasis to keeping the growth of the aggregates within the target ranges, even if that meant more variation in interest rates. By this change, the Federal Reserve was widely perceived as having established the realization of its targets as a benchmark for measuring the performance of monetary policy.

While the notion of monetary targeting may appear quite straightforward, in practice there are a number of questions that must be resolved in carrying out a targeting strategy. Among these, three in particular deserve attention here:

- How should the Federal Reserve set its monetary growth targets, both in terms of choosing particular measures of money and choosing numerical targets?
- What is the appropriate monetary policy response when the relationships among economic variables, on which the initial targets were set, appear to shift?
- How rigidly should the Federal Reserve adhere to its longer-run growth ranges over the short run?

## [Appropriate Measure of Money]

Debate over selection of the appropriate measure by which to guide monetary policy must take into account the tradeoff between the ability of the Federal Reserve to control any monetary aggregate and the influence of that aggregate on overall demand. For example, the monetary base, composed of currency held by the public plus bank reserves, is probably the easiest for the Federal Reserve to control. But studies have shown that the relationship between the monetary base and aggregate demand is not very close. The narrow measures of the money stock (M−1A and M−1B) are somewhat harder to control but in general have been more closely tied to aggregate demand. Some economists argue that a broader measure of the money stock, such as M−2, has the most stable relationship with aggregate demand, but the very breadth of this measure — including as it does a mixture of the liabilities of several types of financial institutions — makes it rather difficult to control.

A related issue is how the various measures of the money stock should be defined. The rapid evolution of the financial markets in recent years ... has blurred the historical distinctions between the types of financial instruments and rendered somewhat ambiguous what should be treated as "money." These developments have been partly responsible for the recent instabilities in the relationship among the narrow monetary measures, economic activity, and interest rates — instabilities commonly referred to as shifts in money demand.

In light of these considerations, the Federal Reserve has chosen to consider a family of monetary aggregates to impart a needed degree of flexibility. Thus, while a narrow aggregate like M−1B has been accorded primary emphasis, there may be periods when it provides an uncertain guide for monetary policy. At such times the Federal Reserve may put more emphasis on the broader measures of the money stock, such as M−2.

## [Numerical Targets]

Once the Federal Reserve determines which monetary aggregates to target, numerical target ranges must be set to achieve the appropriate degree of aggregate demand restraint. The targeting procedure could, for example, begin by determining the appropriate path for nominal GNP that would be consistent with a gradual decline in inflation. Abstracting from cyclical variations in real economic expansion, a steady reduction of inflation would imply a gradual decline in nominal GNP growth.

Given this objective, the monetary authorities would need to estimate growth rates for the monetary aggregates that would satisfy the needs of an economy moving along the presumed declining path of nominal GNP. These would then become the basis for choosing the target growth ranges. Over the past two decades a given growth rate of the narrow measures of money has, on average, financed a 2 to 3 percentage point faster rate of expansion of nominal GNP, although the pattern has varied from year to year. This relationship suggests that the goal of a gradual decline in the growth of nominal GNP would be consistent with a gradual lowering in the target ranges, although not necessarily every year.

Starting with its 1975 targets as a base, the Federal Reserve has, in fact, adhered to a policy of lowering the target range by a small amount in each year.... What has been the result? In some years (1977, 1978 and 1980) the targets were exceeded. In the others there were apparent shifts in money demand such that actual money growth was much lower than would be predicted on the basis of historical relationships.

... [T]hose years when actual money growth was in the target ranges (1976 and 1979) were periods in which there were the largest downward shifts in money demand. In effect, actual money growth during these periods supported a greater-than-expected growth of nominal GNP. In the remaining years money growth was nearer the rate expected from historical money-demand relationships, but that growth was above the target range. These two factors — money demand shifts and missing the targets — help to explain how such low values for the monetary growth targets could have persisted in a period of high nominal GNP growth. Over the entire period more nominal growth was accommodated than is implied by the monetary targets and the historical relationships.

Although the continuing application of monetary restraint could call for reductions of the monetary growth ranges over time, there are a number of problems which have to be faced. In particular, the question arises about the extent to which adjustments in monetary targets ought to be made when structural changes occur in the economy.

In the last decade there have been several abrupt shifts in the relationships among important economic factors — disruptions related to jumps in oil and food prices as well as to shifts in money demand. The problem for the Federal Reserve is how, if at all, to adjust monetary growth targets in response to these changes. This requires an evaluation of the likely direct impact of monetary and credit conditions on economic activity, as well as an assessment of how altering the monetary targets would affect wages and prices....

## Conclusions

One of the major lessons that emerges repeatedly in the preceding discussion is the need for understanding, by the public generally and the financial community in particular, of the complexities of monetary policy. Monetary targeting provides an invaluable tool to increase monetary discipline, to communicate Federal Reserve intentions, and to evaluate performance. But the advantages of a semi-automatic rule to guide the monetary authorities are not absolute. In a world where economic and financial markets are subject to major and unpredictable changes, deviations from the Federal Reserve's announced intention to reduce steadily the annual target ranges may sometimes be necessary. Targets, once set, may occasionally have to be modified. And allowing short-run deviations of actual from targeted money growth may be called for if care is taken not to let them persist. But if the public interprets occasional necessary changes in the longer-run monetary target ranges, or short-run deviations of actual money growth from those targets, as evidence that the Federal Reserve has lessened its determination to fight inflation, the monetary authorities will be put in an untenable position. If they fail to make the adjustment in the monetary targets that is called for by a major change in economic circumstances, or if they attempt to avoid all short-run deviations of actual from targeted money growth, monetary policy may produce unwanted results. If, on the other hand, they do change the targets or allow temporary deviations, their actions may be misunderstood by the public and their credibility consequently impaired. The monetary authorities will face this problem once again in 1981. . . .

# Incomes Policies

Even if they are followed with persistence and acquire a credibility that favorably affects expectations, monetary and fiscal restraints are likely to reduce inflation only slowly and at significant cost in lost output and employment. Incomes policies attempt to lower these costs. By directly influencing the setting of wages and prices, incomes policies seek to decrease the inflation and increase the growth of output and employment that result from any given degree of demand restraint. A tight monetary target, for example, is compatible either with a small reduction in inflation and zero economic growth or a larger reduction in inflation and positive economic growth. By persuading workers and employers to accept lower pay and price increases, an incomes policy tries to make the second combination possible.

Incomes policies range from the informal pressure on a few large corporations and unions exerted by the Kennedy Administration to the formal review of price and wage increases by the Council on Wage and Price Stability (CWPS) to even more formal schemes based on the tax system, examined in detail below. While mandatory wage and price controls are the extreme form of an incomes policy, the discussion in this chapter is confined to voluntary forms, that is, forms which do not involve legal prohibition of excessive wage and price increases.

An effective incomes policy encourages various groups in society to accept lower wages and prices for the goods and services they supply in the expectation that the wages and prices they pay will also be lower. An incomes policy that gains widespread support can meet these expectations. Workers agree to lower their wage demands, and thus unit labor costs rise more slowly. Firms moderate their price increases, and therefore workers' costs of living rise more slowly. The implicit agreement made among government, workers, and firms to take simultaneous actions to slow the wage-price spiral through the mechanism of the incomes policy is thus successful principally to the extent that people believe it will be successful.

To have a lasting influence on inflation, an incomes policy must do more than lower the current rate of increase in wages and prices. It must also lower expectations about the *future* rate of inflation. Workers must believe that they can achieve their real wage demands with lower nominal wage gains, and firms must believe that large nominal wage gains or other cost increases will be hard to pass on into prices. While our knowledge about the formation of expectations leaves much to be desired, it does suggest that a short-lived reduction in inflation may be insufficient to change expectations sharply. To be successful in lowering inflationary expectations, therefore, an incomes policy probably has to be in effect for more than a single year.

Even more important, an incomes policy will have no hope of a lasting effect unless it is accompanied by monetary and fiscal restraint. If there is excess demand in labor and product markets, or if monetary and fiscal policies create expectations of excess demand, the basic tenet of an incomes policy is destroyed. Individual employers or groups of workers cannot then assume that their own moderation will be matched by moderation from others.

Although incomes policies can help to reduce inflation, they also tend to create losses of economic efficiency. Ideally, economic policy seeks to lower the *average* rate of wage and price increase while leaving individual wages and prices to adjust freely around that average in response to circumstances in particular markets. In reality, of course, an incomes policy cannot operate on a statistical average but must deal with the wages and prices of individual firms. Therefore, incomes policies inevitably discourage to some extent movements in prices and wages relative to each other. Over time, the failure of relative prices to adjust in response to changing conditions leads to mounting losses of economic efficiency. The more rigid and mandatory in character the incomes policy, and the longer it is kept in place, the greater will be the efficiency costs.

This Administration has judged the benefits of a relatively flexible and voluntary incomes policy to be significantly greater than its costs. In late 1978 the Administration set forth voluntary standards for pay and price increases as the centerpiece of an incomes policy. This section of Chapter 1 briefly reviews that program, and then evaluates a wide range of measures known as tax-based incomes policies (TIPs) under which tax penalties or rewards are employed as a means of inducing moderation in wage and price increases.

## [PAY AND PRICE STANDARDS]

For the past 2 years the Administration's incomes policy has centered on the voluntary pay and price standards. Administered by CWPS, this program applied to firms of all sizes, but only large firms were asked to submit data on pay and either prices or margins. The standards set by CWPS were designed to reflect the structures of different industries. Compliance was encouraged by appealing to firms and workers to restrain price and pay increases in the public interest. CWPS also used public opinion and the threatened loss of government contracts to encourage compliance.

Although the standards were voluntary and were in place during the difficult period of the 1979 OPEC oil price explosion, they appear to have played a role in moderating inflation. Studies by CWPS and the Council of Economic Advisers have estimated that annual wage increases were 1 to 1½ percentage points lower during 1979 than they would have been without the standards. The consequent reductions in labor costs also appear to have been passed on to consumers through lower price increases. A more recent evaluation of the pay and price standards by CWPS suggests that the program continued to have a moderating effect in the second year.

After 2 years of operation there seems to be general agreement that the current pay and price standards could not continue to be effective if simply extended in their present form. Workers and firms no longer appear to be willing to moderate wage and price rises in the expectation that the standards will restrain inflation.

## TAX-BASED INCOMES POLICIES

One way of strengthening a voluntary standards program would be to supplement it with a tax-based incomes policy, or a TIP. Such a policy would use the tax system to provide tangible incentives to firms and workers to slow the rate of inflation.

As the discussion in this section later concludes, the most effective kind of TIP would be one that rewarded employees of firms whose rate of wage increase was below the standard. Such a program would significantly reinforce the spirit of cooperation used in other voluntary forms of incomes policies without creating as many distortions as a mandatory program. Firms and workers that agreed to moderate their price and wage increases would be making less of a sacrifice under a TIP than under other voluntary programs. And in sectors of the economy in which relative prices and wages were too low, a TIP would allow adjustments. The most serious distortions in relative prices and wages that develop under mandatory controls would be avoided under a TIP.

Several years ago the Carter Administration proposed to the Congress one particular version of a TIP — the "real wage insurance" program — but the proposal was not acted upon by the Congress, and in fact was not subjected to widespread public discussion and debate. TIPs continue to represent an important untried innovation in the area of anti-inflation policy. While TIPs may impose administrative and efficiency costs, those costs appear to be far less than would be incurred by reducing inflation solely through restraining aggregate demand.

Various kinds of TIPs have been suggested. Under a pay TIP, for example, the government would set a standard for pay increases over the coming year. Groups of workers whose average pay increase did not exceed the standard would be in compliance. In one version of the pay TIP, firms whose wage increases exceeded the standard would be assessed a tax penalty. In another version, all workers in a complying group would receive a tax credit, including individuals within the group whose pay raises were above the standard. Similarly, a price TIP would provide penalties or rewards to firms on the basis of their average price increases relative to a set of standards.

In virtually all versions of the TIP it is the *average* rate of wage or price increase within the firm that is compared with the standard for purposes of determining tax penalties or rewards. With this approach, firms are able to change the relative pay and prices of subgroups of workers and products. Merit pay plans and promotions that give individual pay raises in excess of the standard can still be used to encourage productivity.

Although the flexibility of TIPs makes them attractive, using the tax system to reduce inflation poses serious administrative problems. These problems present the major obstacles to designing an effective TIP program....

On balance ... a temporary hurdle TIP — a tax credit to groups of workers whose average pay increase does not exceed a specified standard — seems superior to the other variants. Because keeping records and complying with the standard would be voluntary in this type of TIP, firms that found the administrative costs too high could choose not to participate. As with all forms of TIPs, relative wage changes could still occur in response to economic and other developments, although increases in excess of the standard would "cost" workers the TIP tax credit. The efficiency costs would be small at first, but over time the distortions of the TIP would rise and its effectiveness would fall.

Together with a "jawboning" campaign aimed at producing widespread compliance with the standard by lowering expectations of inflation, such a TIP could lower the rate of inflation. Without jawboning, the cost of inducing compliance among workers with anticipated pay raises far above the standard would be prohibitive. Even workers who expected pay raises near the standard might be reluctant to sacrifice part of a pay raise that might be built into future wages in exchange for a small tax credit that only lasted for 1 or 2 years. The major appeal of wage moderation is that if everyone cooperates by accepting a smaller wage increase, the lower nominal wage gains will be matched by lower price increases. Real wages will not fall, but inflation will. A TIP alone cannot provide sufficient economic incentives to make a low wage increase more attractive than a large one. However, with public appeals to moderation and clear evidence of fiscal and monetary restraint, a TIP can contribute to slowing the inflationary spiral. . . .

There are no costless ways to reduce inflation. Using demand restraint alone imposes very large costs of forgone output and unemployment for modest reductions in inflation. A successful TIP can shift more of the effect of demand restraint from output to prices and thus can cut substantially the costs of reducing inflation. Although a TIP would itself impose administrative and efficiency costs on the economy, the costs for a short period of time would be small. They would surely be outweighed by the benefits in reduced inflation and lower unemployment that a TIP would bring. . . .

TIPs are novel, and most people are unfamiliar with either the opportunities they present or the difficulties they pose. It is therefore highly unlikely that a TIP could take effect in 1981. But it would be useful for the public in general, and the Congress in particular, to begin evaluating the pros and cons of TIPs so that when the time comes for the next round of Federal tax cuts a TIP program will be seriously considered. . . .

## [RESPONSES TO TAX CUTS]

Tax reductions have two principal effects. On the one hand, individuals and firms will buy more goods and services. As a tax cut is spent and respent throughout the economy, the resulting increase in nominal GNP will exceed the original tax cut. As a result of this multiplier process, aggregate demand will rise by more than the tax cut. But tax cuts also increase the supply of goods and services. Since lower tax rates allow individuals and firms to keep a larger fraction of their income after taxes, the lower rates affect incentives to work, to save, and to invest the savings, increasing potential GNP.

Although the magnitude of the multiplier varies according to the nature of the tax cut, aggregate demand typically rises by about twice the size of a reduction in taxes. Thus, a tax cut equal to 1 percent of GNP will increase aggregate demand by about 2 percent. To match the increase in demand, a 2 percent increase in supply would also be required. To the extent that its supply response is less than the additional demand it creates, any tax reduction adds to the pressures of demand on the rate of inflation.

But there are two ways in which such tax cuts can be made while still restraining demand. First, tax reductions may offset increases in other taxes. As discussed earlier, inflation pushes taxpayers into higher tax brackets, so that the average effective tax rate — the ratio of tax revenues to GNP — rises. Consumption is depressed and economic growth reduced. In the years ahead, periodic tax reductions will therefore be both possible and necessary to keep aggregate demand from falling. Second, a tax reduction accompanied by Federal spending reductions of roughly the same magnitude will not change aggregate demand; hence, even if the supply response to a tax cut is smaller than the demand response, inflationary pressures will not be generated.

Thus, it is clear that the design and timing of supply-oriented tax cuts depend importantly on the specific relationship between the demand-side and supply-side responses. If such tax reductions fail to generate enough supply to offset the additional demand they create — and the evidence discussed below suggests this to be the case, particularly for personal tax reductions — they must then be integrated like any tax cut into policies of demand management.

## [SUPPLY-SIDE RESPONSE]

A 10 percent reduction in marginal tax rates on individuals (approximately a $30-billion personal tax cut in 1981) would increase the total demand for goods and services by $60 billion, or 2 percent of GNP. It could also lead to increases in individual work and saving in response to the lower tax rates and thereby increase potential GNP. How much of the increase in demand would be matched by such increases in supply? . . .

A reduction in personal income tax rates increases both the income out of which an individual worker can save and the after-tax return to saving. It would also tend to discourage borrowing by reducing the value of the income tax deduction for interest payments. If the increases in personal saving find their way into additional business investment, productivity will rise.

Most empirical studies have concluded that changes in personal income tax rates would have only a small effect on personal saving. At best, a 10 percent reduction in tax rates would increase personal saving less than 3 percent. This means that the saving rate — the average share of personal saving in disposable income, which over the last 5 years has averaged 5.7 percent — would rise by no more than 0.2 percentage point. The additional saving would at most be equivalent to only about 0.2 percent of GNP.

Even if every dollar of personal saving that resulted from a 10 percent tax cut were invested in business plant and equipment — and some, in fact, would flow into housing — the effects on output and on productivity would be small. If the tax cut and the higher saving continued for 5 years, the additional saving and investment would increase potential GNP by less than 0.3 percent and lead to a negligible increase in the annual rate of productivity growth.

This examination of likely responses thus suggests that even under the most optimistic circumstances, a 10 percent reduction in tax rates would not induce enough additional work, saving, or investment to offset more than a fraction of the 2 percent increase in aggregate demand that would accompany the tax cut.

## BUSINESS TAX CUTS

It was pointed out earlier that a tax cut that liberalized the business depreciation allowance or increased the investment tax credit could, after a time, have a fairly substantial effect on the Nation's productive potential. Such a tax cut, amounting to 1 percent of GNP, could raise potential output by perhaps 1½ percent over a 5-year period.

This would still be less than the 2 percent rise in aggregate demand that would also be generated, however. More important, the increase in demand would come relatively quickly, most of it within 1½ to 2 years. The increase in supply, on the other hand, would occur very gradually. As a consequence, the tax cut would tend to increase demand pressures, especially in the years immediately following it. While tax reductions that are effective in raising investment are essential in a long-term strategy to promote economic growth, business tax cuts, like personal tax cuts, must be designed to fit into an overall framework of fiscal restraint.

## CONCLUSIONS

This analysis of the macroeconomic effects of Federal tax reductions suggests several conclusions for the development of fiscal policy:

*First,* specific investment-oriented tax reductions for business are likely to increase saving, investment, and productivity by a much more significant degree than cuts in personal income taxes.

*Second,* productivity-oriented tax reductions will yield improvements in the inflation rate that are helpful and significant, but still relatively modest in the context of a 10 percent underlying inflation rate.

*Third,* the supply response, while a critically important feature of any tax reduction, will be substantially less than the demand response, particularly in the short run.

*Fourth,* since reductions in both business and personal taxes will increase demand faster than supply, they must be designed and carried out in ways that are consistent with the demand restraint needed to reduce inflation.

It is sometimes alleged that the potentially inflationary effects of a large tax cut can be avoided if the Federal Reserve steadfastly pursues its goal of keeping the growth of the monetary aggregates within tight targets. But if taxes are reduced while the Federal Reserve pursues an unchanged monetary policy, aggregate demand will nevertheless increase, especially in the short run. The increase in demand would lead to a rise in interest rates that would dampen the increase in aggregate demand but not eliminate it. Additional inflationary pressure would then result.

A very large tax cut unaccompanied by the necessary spending cuts would lead to both an increase in inflation and a sharp rise in interest rates. . . .

# REAGAN'S INAUGURAL ADDRESS
## January 20, 1981

Former California governor and screen actor Ronald Wilson Reagan was sworn in as the country's 40th president at 11:57 a.m. on January 20, amid concluding events in the Iranian hostage crisis as melodramatic as the most gripping Hollywood thriller.

Reagan stood hatless under a warm and sunny sky on the West Front of the Capitol and took the oath of office from Chief Justice Warren E. Burger. Then he turned to face the nation's monuments on the Mall and thousands of spectators on the Capitol grounds and delivered a 20-minute inaugural address that stressed his recurrent campaign themes of antagonism to continued big government and faith in the American people.

### Hostages Released

Nearly half a world away in Iran, two planes carrying American hostages stood poised for takeoff at Tehran's airport, their departure delayed in a race with the clock that ticked off the final moments of the Carter administration. Negotiations for the hostages' release after 444 days in captivity had been concluded at 8:31 a.m. on Inauguration Day, and President Carter had hoped to announce their release before leaving office.

Instead, as Reagan finished his address, Press Secretary James S. Brady tapped the new president on the shoulder and whispered that the first plane had at last left the ground. The hostages' delayed departure

137

*was widely interpreted as a personal slap against Carter by Iranian hardliners. As a conciliatory gesture, Reagan appointed Carter his personal representative to greet the released hostages January 21 at an Air Force hospital in Wiesbaden, West Germany. (Hostages' release, p. 145)*

## Address

*In his remarks, Reagan said, "We are a nation that has a government — not the other way around. . . . It is my intention to curb the size and influence of the federal establishment. . . ."*

*Picking up another campaign theme, the president said that "We have every right to dream heroic dreams. Those who say we're in a time when there are no heroes, they just don't know where to look."*

*Observers classified the speech as vintage Reagan, stressing familiar themes and drawing on a familiar style laced with praise for America's heroes, both famous and obscure. Breaking with recent practice, Reagan became the first president to be inaugurated on the Capitol's West Front; and, only days short of his 70th birthday on February 6, he became the oldest person to take the office.*

*After the ceremony, Reagan's first act as president was to order a freeze on the hiring of civilian employees by all executive departments and agencies. He signed the order in the President's Room of the Capitol before joining congressional leaders for lunch in Statuary Hall.*

*Following is the text of President Ronald Reagan's inaugural address, delivered January 20, 1981. (Boldface headings in brackets have been added by Congressional Quarterly to highlight the organization of the text.):*

To a few of us here today this is a solemn and most momentous occasion. And, yet, in the history of our Nation it is a commonplace occurrence. The orderly transfer of authority as called for in the Constitution routinely takes place, as it has for almost two centuries, and few of us stop to think how unique we really are. In the eyes of many in the world, this every-4-year ceremony we accept as normal is nothing less than a miracle.

Mr. President, I want our fellow citizens to know how much you did to carry on this tradition. By your gracious cooperation in the transition process you have shown a watching world that we are a united people pledged to maintaining a political system which guarantees individual liberty to a greater degree than any other, and I thank you and your people for all your help in maintaining the continuity which is the hallmark of our Republic.

The business of our Nation goes forward. These United States are confronted with an economic affliction of great proportions. We suffer from the longest and one of the worst sustained inflations in our national history. It distorts our economic decisions, penalizes thrift and crushes the struggling young and the fixed-income elderly alike. It threatens to shatter the lives of millions of our people.

Idle industries have cast workers into unemployment, human misery, and personal indignity. Those who do work are denied a fair return for their labor by a tax system which penalizes successful achievement and keeps us from maintaining full productivity.

## [Burden of Public Spending]

But great as our tax burden is, it has not kept pace with public spending. For decades we have piled deficit upon deficit, mortgaging our future and our children's future for the temporary convenience of the present. To continue this long trend is to guarantee tremendous social, cultural, political, and economic upheavals.

You and I, as individuals, can, by borrowing, live beyond our means, but for only a limited period of time. Why, then, should we think that collectively, as a nation, we're not bound by that same limitation? We must act today in order to preserve tomorrow. And let there be no misunderstanding — we are going to begin to act, beginning today.

The economic ills we suffer have come upon us over several decades. They will not go away in days, weeks, or months, but they will go away. They will go away because we as Americans have the capacity now, as we've had in the past, to do whatever needs to be done to preserve this last and greatest bastion of freedom.

In this present crisis, government is not the solution to our problem; government is the problem. From time to time we've been tempted to believe that society has become too complex to be managed by self-rule, that government by an elite group is superior to government for, by, and of the people. Well, if no one among us is capable of governing himself, then who among us has the capacity to govern someone else? All of us together — in and out of government — must bear the burden. The solutions we seek must be equitable with no one group singled out to pay a higher price.

We hear much of special interest groups. Well, our concern must be for a special interest group that has been too long neglected. It knows no sectional boundaries or ethnic and racial divisions, and it crosses political party lines. It is made up of men and women who raise our food, patrol our streets, man our mines and factories, teach our children, keep our homes, and heal us when we're sick — professionals, industrialists, shopkeepers, clerks, cabbies, and truck drivers. They are, in short, "We the people," this breed called Americans.

## [Healthy, Growing Economy]

Well, this administration's objective will be a healthy, vigorous, growing economy that provides equal opportunities for all Americans with no barriers born of bigotry or discrimination. Putting America back to work means putting all Americans back to work. Ending inflation means freeing all Americans from the terror of runaway living costs. All must share in the productive work of this "new beginning," and all must share in the bounty of a revived economy. With the idealism and fair play which are the core of our system and our strength, we can have a strong and prosperous America at peace with itself and the world.

So, as we begin, let us take inventory. We are a nation that has a government — not the other way around. And this makes us special among the nations of the Earth. Our government has no power except that granted it by the people. It is time to check and reverse the growth of government which shows signs of having grown beyond the consent of the governed.

It is my intention to curb the size and influence of the Federal establishment and to demand recognition of the distinction between the powers granted to the Federal Government and those reserved to the States or to the people. All of us need to be reminded that the Federal Government did not create the States; the States created the Federal Government.

Now so there will be no misunderstanding, it's not my intention to do away with government. It is rather to make it work — work with us, not over us; to stand by our side, not ride on our back. Government can and must provide opportunity, not smother it; foster productivity, not stifle it.

## [Freedom of Individual]

If we look to the answer as to why for so many years we achieved so much, prospered as no other people on Earth, it was because here in this land we unleashed the energy and individual genius of man to a greater extent than has ever been done before. Freedom and the dignity of the individual have been more available and assured here than in any other place on Earth. The price for this freedom at times has been high. But we have never been unwilling to pay that price.

It is no coincidence that our present troubles parallel and are proportionate to the intervention and intrusion in our lives that result from unnecessary and excessive growth of government. It is time for us to realize that we're too great a nation to limit ourselves to small dreams. We're not, as some would have us believe, doomed to an inevitable decline. I do not believe in a fate that will fall on us no matter what we do. I do believe in a fate that will fall on us if we do nothing. So, with all the creative energy at our command, let us begin an era of national renewal. Let us renew our determination, our courage, and our strength. And let us renew our faith and our hope.

## [Citizens Are Heroes]

We have every right to dream heroic dreams. Those who say we're in a time when there are no heroes, they just don't know where to look. You can see heroes every day going in and out of factory gates. Others, a handful in number, produce food enough to feed all of us and much of the world beyond. You meet heroes across a counter. And they're on both sides of that counter. There are entrepreneurs with faith in themselves and faith in an idea who create new jobs, new wealth and opportunity. They're individuals and families whose taxes support the government and whose voluntary gifts support church, charity, culture, art, and education. Their patriotism is quiet but deep. Their values sustain our national life.

Now, I have used the words "they" and "their" in speaking of these heroes. I could say "you" and "your," because I'm addressing the heroes of whom I speak — you, the citizens of this blessed land. Your dreams, your hopes, your goals are going to be the dreams, the hopes, and the goals of this administration, so help me God.

We shall reflect the compassion that is so much a part of your makeup. How can we love our country and not love our countrymen; and loving them, reach out a hand when they fall, heal them when they're sick, and provide opportunity to make them self-sufficient so they will be equal in fact and not just in theory?

Can we solve the problems confronting us? Well, the answer is an unequivocal and emphatic "yes." To paraphrase Winston Churchill, I did not take the oath I've just taken with the intention of presiding over the dissolution of the world's strongest economy.

In the days ahead I will propose removing the roadblocks that have slowed our economy and reduced productivity. Steps will be taken aimed at restoring the balance between the various levels of government. Progress may be slow, measured in inches and feet, not miles, but we will progress. It is time to reawaken this industrial giant, to get government back within its means, and to lighten our punitive tax burden. And these will be our first priorities, and on these principles, there will be no compromise.

On the eve of our struggle for independence a man who might have been one of the greatest among the Founding Fathers, Dr. Joseph Warren, president of the Massachusetts Congress, said to his fellow Americans, "Our country is in danger, but not to be despaired of.... On you depend the fortunes of America. You are to decide the important question on which rests the happiness and liberty of millions yet unborn. Act worthy of yourselves."

## [Happiness and Liberty]

Well, I believe we, the Americans of today, are ready to act worthy of ourselves, ready to do what must be done to ensure happiness and liberty for ourselves, our children, and our children's children. And as we renew ourselves here in our own land, we will be seen as having greater strength throughout the world. We will again be the exemplar of freedom and a beacon of hope for those who do not now have freedom.

To those neighbors and allies who share our ideal of freedom, we will strengthen our historic ties and assure them of our support and firm commitment. We will match loyalty with loyalty. We will strive for mutually beneficial relations. We will not use our friendship to impose on their sovereignty, for our own sovereignty is not for sale.

As for the enemies of freedom, those who are potential adversaries, they will be reminded that peace is the highest aspiration of the American people. We will negotiate for it, sacrifice for it; we will not surrender for it now or ever.

Our forbearance should never be misunderstood. Our reluctance for conflict should not be misjudged as a failure of will. When action is required to preserve our national security, we will act. We will maintain sufficient strength to prevail if need be, knowing that if we do so we have the best chance of never having to use that strength.

Above all we must realize that no arsenal or no weapon in the arsenals of the world is so formidable as the will and moral courage of free men and women. It is a weapon our adversaries in today's world do not have. It is a weapon that we as Americans do have. Let that be understood by those who practice terrorism and prey upon their neighbors.

I'm told that tens of thousands of prayer meetings are being held on this day, and for that I'm deeply grateful. We are a nation under God, and I believe God intended for us to be free. It would be fitting and good, I think, if each Inaugural Day in future years it should be declared a day of prayer.

This is the first time in our history that this ceremony has been held, as you've been told, on this West Front of the Capitol. Standing here, one faces a magnificent vista, opening up on this city's special beauty and history. At the end of this open mall are those shrines to the giants on whose shoulders we stand.

Directly in front of me, the monument to a monumental man. George Washington, father of our country. A man of humility who came to greatness reluctantly. He led America out of revolutionary victory into infant nationhood. Off to one side, the stately memorial to Thomas Jefferson. The Declaration of Independence flames with his eloquence. And then, beyond the Reflecting Pool, the dignified columns of the Lincoln Memorial. Whoever would understand in his heart the meaning of America will find it in the life of Abraham Lincoln.

Beyond these monuments to heroism is the Potomac River, and on the far shore the sloping hills of Arlington National Cemetery, with its row upon row of simple white markers bearing crosses or Stars of David. They add up to only a tiny fraction of the price that has been paid for our freedom.

Each one of those markers is a monument to the kind of hero I spoke of earlier. Their lives ended in places called Belleau Wood, The Argonne,

Omaha Beach, Salerno, and halfway around the world on Guadalcanal, Tarawa, Pork Chop Hill, the Chosin Reservoir, and in a hundred rice paddies and jungles of a place called Vietnam.

Under one such marker lies a young man, Martin Treptow, who left his job in a small town barbershop in 1917 to go to France with the famed Rainbow Division. There, on the western front, he was killed trying to carry a message between battalions under heavy artillery fire.

We're told that on his body was found a diary. On the flyleaf under the heading, "My Pledge," he had written these words: "America must win this war. Therefore I will work, I will save, I will sacrifice, I will endure, I will fight cheerfully and do my utmost, as if the issue of the whole struggle depended on me alone."

The crisis we are facing today does not require of us the kind of sacrifice that Martin Treptow and so many thousands of others were called upon to make. It does require, however, our best effort, and our willingness to believe in ourselves and to believe in our capacity to perform great deeds, to believe that together and with God's help we can and will resolve the problems which confront us.

And after all, why shouldn't we believe that? We are Americans.

God bless you, and thank you.

# IRANIAN RELEASE OF U.S. HOSTAGES
## January 20, 1981

*As power in the United States shifted on Inauguration Day from the Carter to the Reagan administration, 52 American hostages in Tehran were freed by the Iranian government, ending 444 days of highly publicized and politically volatile captivity that began November 4, 1979, with terrorists' seizure of the U.S. Embassy.*

*Many U.S. political observers felt that the hostage issue — including an unsuccessful rescue attempt in April 1980 in which eight servicemen died — was a major factor contributing to the election defeat of Jimmy Carter by Ronald Reagan.* (Iran rescue attempt, Historic Documents of 1980, p. 351)

*After months of sometimes frustrating negotiations, final agreement was reached on the hostages' release in the waning minutes of the Carter administration. But the hostages' planes did not leave the airport in Tehran until 12:25 p.m. (EST) in the early minutes of the Reagan presidency.*

*Former President Jimmy Carter flew home to Georgia, then left the next day to greet the hostages in Germany at Reagan's request. After an emotional meeting with the hostages, Carter reported that there had been many incidents of cruel treatment by the Iranians during the 444 days of captivity. Originally more than 60 Americans were held hostage, but five women and eight blacks were released in November 1979. One white male hostage, Richard Queen, was released after becoming ill.*

## Conditions for Release

*The complex agreements were based on four conditions announced September 12, 1980, by Ayatollah Ruhollah Khomeini: return of the late*

*Shah Muhammed Reza Pahlavi's wealth, cancellation of American claims against Iran, unfreezing of Iranian assets in American banks and a promise not to intervene in Iran's affairs. Negotiation of the agreements was carried out through the Algerian government, which served as an intermediary.*

*Under the agreements, release of the hostages triggered three payments totaling $7.977 billion from the $11-$12 billion in Iranian assets frozen November 14, 1979, by President Carter. Of the total, $2.9 billion was paid directly to Iran, $3.7 billion was paid to U.S. and foreign banks on Iranian loans from the banks and $1.4 billion was held in escrow, pending settlement of further bank loans and interest disputes. Other transfers were to follow. (Court on claims settlement, p. 559)*

*Also under the agreements, the United States was to provide information on U.S. assets of the late shah for subsequent action by the Iranians; and the United States agreed to void all private claims against Iran then pending in U.S. courts and to prohibit future litigation based on existing claims.*

*Further, the United States and Iran agreed to submit disputed claims to an international arbitration tribunal, comprised of three members each appointed by the two countries and three additional members chosen by the appointed members.*

## Return of Hostages

*When the hostages' planes finally did take off, they flew first to Algiers, with a refueling stop in Athens, and then to Rhein-Main Air Base in West Germany where the former hostages rested and received tests and therapy at an Air Force hospital at Wiesbaden. The 52 arrived back in the United States on January 25 at Stewart Airport near West Point, N.Y., where two days were provided for further relaxation and family reunions.*

*On January 27, the former captives held a news conference at West Point before flying to Washington for a tumultuous motorcade through the city and an official greeting from President Reagan at the White House. "Welcome home," the president told the former hostages; and of other threats of terrorism he said, "Let terrorists be aware that ... our policy will be one of swift and effective retribution."*

> *Following are the texts of President Carter's announcement January 19 that an agreement to release the hostages had been reached; the agreement to release and the settlement of claims between Iran and the United States, initialed by Deputy Secretary of State Warren M. Christopher in Algiers January 19; excerpts from Carter's statement in Plains, Ga., January 20 that the hostages had cleared*

*Iranian air space; excerpts from Carter's remarks at Rhein-Main Air Base near Frankfurt, West Germany, January 21; the denial of mistreatment of the hostages issued by the Iranian Foreign Ministry January 27; President Reagan's welcoming speech at the White House January 27; and White House remarks of Bruce Laingen, deputy chief of mission in Tehran, January 27:*

# CARTER ANNOUNCEMENT OF AGREEMENT

I know you've been up all night with me and I appreciate that very much.

We have now reached an agreement with Iran which will result, I believe, in the freedom of our American hostages. The last documents have now been signed in Algiers, following the signing of the documents in Iran which will result in this agreement. We still have a few documents to sign before the money is actually transferred and the hostages are released.

The essence of the agreement is that following the release of our hostages, then we will unfreeze and transfer to the Iranians a major part of the assets which were frozen by me when the Iranians seized our embassy compound and took our hostages. We have also reached complete agreement on the arbitration procedures between ourselves and Iran with the help of the Algerians which will resolve the claims that exist between residents of our Nation and Iran and vice-versa.

I particularly want to express my public thanks, as I have already done privately, to the Algerians, to their President, their Foreign Minister, Ben Yahia, and to the three-man negotiating teams who have done such a superb job in fair and equitable arbitration between ourselves and the officials of Iran. We don't yet know exactly how fast this procedure will go. We are prepared to move as rapidly as possible. All the preparations have been completed pending the final documents being signed.

I will have more to say to you when our American hostages are actually free. In the meantime, Jody Powell will stay in close touch with developments, working with the Secretary of State, the Secretary of Treasury, my legal counsel, Lloyd Cutler. I'm talking frequently with Warren Christopher in Algiers and Jody Powell will keep you informed about developments.

Thank you very much.

# AGREEMENT TO RELEASE HOSTAGES

The Government of the Democratic and Popular Republic of Algeria, having been requested by the Governments of the Islamic Republic of Iran and the United States of America to serve as an intermediary in seeking a mutually acceptable resolution of the crisis in their relations arising out of the detention of the 52 United States nationals in Iran, has consulted extensively with the two governments as to the commitments which each is willing to make in order to resolve the crisis within the framework of the four points stated in the resolution of November 2, 1980, of the Islamic Consultative Assembly of Iran.

On the basis of formal adherences received from Iran and the United States, the Government of Algeria now declares that the following interdependent commitments have been made by the two governments:

## General Principles

The undertakings reflected in this Declaration are based on the following general principles:

A. Within the framework of and pursuant to the provisions of the two Declarations of the Government of the Democratic and Popular Republic of Algeria, the United States will restore the financial position of Iran, in so far as possible, to that which existed prior to November 14, 1979. In this context, the United States commits itself to ensure the mobility and free transfer of all Iranian assets within its jurisdiction, as set forth in Paragraphs 4-9.

B. It is the purpose of both parties, within the framework of and pursuant to the provisions of the two Declarations of the Government of the Democratic and Popular Republic of Algeria, to terminate all litigation as between the Government of each party and the nationals of the other, and to bring about the settlement and termination of all such claims through binding arbitration. Through the procedures provided in the Declaration, relating to the Claims Settlement Agreement, the United States agrees to terminate all legal proceedings in United States courts involving claims of United States persons and institutions against Iran and its state enterprises, to nullify all attachments and judgments obtained therein, to prohibit all further litigation based on such claims, and to bring about the termination of such claims through binding arbitration.

### Point I: Non-Intervention in Iranian Affairs

1. The United States pledges that it is and from now on will be the policy of the United States not to intervene, directly or indirectly, politically or militarily, in Iran's internal affairs.

### Points II and III:
### Return of Iranian Assets
### And Settlement of U.S. Claims

2. Iran and the United States (hereinafter "the parties") will immediately select a mutually agreeable central bank (hereinafter "the Central Bank") to act, under the instructions of the Government of Algeria and the Central Bank of Algeria (hereinafter "The Algerian Central Bank") as

depositary of the escrow and security funds hereinafter prescribed and will promptly enter into depositary arrangements with the Central Bank in accordance with the terms of this declaration. All funds placed in escrow with the Central Bank pursuant to this declaration shall be held in an account in the name of the Algerian Central Bank. Certain procedures for implementing the obligations set forth in this Declaration and in the Declaration of the Democratic and Popular Republic of Algeria concerning the settlement of claims by the government of the United States and the government of the Islamic Republic of Iran (hereinafter "the Claims Settlement Agreement") are separately set forth in certain Undertakings of the Government of the United States of America and the Government of the Islamic Republic of Iran with respect to the Declaration of the Democratic and Popular Republic of Algeria.

3. The depositary arrangement shall provide that, in the event that the Government of Algeria certifies to the Algerian Central Bank that the 52 U.S. nationals have safely departed from Iran, the Algerian Central Bank will thereupon instruct the Central Bank to transfer immediately all monies or other assets in escrow with the Central Bank pursuant to this declaration, provided that at any time prior to the making of such certification by the Government of Algeria, each of the two parties, Iran and the United States, shall have the right on seventy-two hours notice to terminate its commitments under this declaration.

If such notice is given by the United States and the foregoing certification is made by the Government of Algeria within the seventy-two hour period of notice, the Algerian Central Bank will thereupon instruct the Central Bank to transfer such monies and assets. If the seventy-two hour period of notice by the United States expires without such a certification having been made, or if the notice of termination is delivered by Iran, the Algerian Central Bank will thereupon instruct the Central Bank to return all such monies and assets to the United States, and thereafter the commitments reflected in this declaration shall be of no further force and effect.

## Assets in the Federal Reserve Bank

4. Commencing upon completion of the requisite escrow arrangements with the Central Bank, the United States will bring about the transfer to the Central Bank of all gold bullion which is owned by Iran and which is in the custody of the Federal Reserve Bank of New York, together with all other Iranian assets (or the cash equivalent thereof) in the custody of the Federal Reserve Bank of New York, to be held by the Central Bank in escrow until such time as their transfer or return is required by Paragraph 3 above.

## Assets in Foreign Branches
## Of U.S. Banks

5. Commencing upon the completion of the requisite escrow arrangements with the Central Bank, the United States will bring about the transfer to the Central Bank, to the account of the Algerian Central Bank, of all Iranian deposits and securities which on or after November 14, 1979, stood upon the books of overseas banking offices of U.S. banks, together with interest thereon through December 31, 1980, to be held by the Central Bank, to the account of the Algerian Central Bank, in escrow until such time as their transfer or return is required in accordance with Paragraph 3 of this Declaration.

## Assets in U.S. Branches
## Of U.S. Banks

6. Commencing with the adherence by Iran and the United States to this declaration and the claims settlement agreement attached hereto, and following the conclusion of arrangements with the Central Bank for the establishment of the interest-bearing security account specified in that agreement and Paragraph 7 below, which arrangements will be concluded within 30 days from the date of this Declaration, the United States will act to bring about the transfer to the Central Bank, within six months from such date, of all Iranian deposits and securities in U.S. banking institutions in the United States, together with interest thereon, to be held by the Central Bank in escrow until such time as their transfer or return is required by Paragraph 3.

7. As funds are received by the Central Bank pursuant to Paragraph 6 above, the Algerian Central Bank shall direct the Central Bank to (1) transfer one-half of each such receipt to Iran and (2) place the other half in a special interest-bearing security account in the Central Bank, until the balance in the security account has reached the level of $1 billion. After the $1 billion balance has been achieved, the Algerian Central Bank shall direct all funds received pursuant to Paragraph 6 to be transferred to Iran. All funds in the security account are to be used for the sole purpose of securing the payment of, and paying, claims against Iran in accordance with the claims settlement agreement. Whenever the Central Bank shall thereafter notify Iran that the balance in the security account has fallen below $500 million, Iran shall promptly make new deposits sufficient to maintain a minimum balance of $500 million in the account. The account shall be so maintained until the President of the Arbitral Tribunal established pursuant to the claims settlement agreement has certified to the Central Bank of Algeria that all arbitral awards against Iran have been satisfied in accordance with the claims settlement agreement, at which point any amount remaining in the security account shall be transferred to Iran.

## Other Assets in the U.S. and Abroad

8. Commencing with the adherence of Iran and the United States to this declaration and the attached claims settlement agreement and the conclusion of arrangements for the establishment of the security account, which arrangements will be concluded within 30 days from the date of this Declaration, the United States will act to bring about the transfer to the Central Bank of all Iranian financial assets (meaning funds or securities) which are located in the United States and abroad, apart from those assets referred to in Paragraph 5 and 6 above, to be held by the Central Bank in escrow until their transfer or return is required by Paragraph 3 above.

9. Commencing with the adherence by Iran and the United States to this declaration and the attached claims settlement agreement and the making by the Government of Algeria of the certification described in Paragraph 3 above, the United States will arrange, subject to the provisions of U.S. law applicable prior to November 14, 1979, for the transfer to Iran of all Iranian properties which are located in the United States and abroad and which are not within the scope of the preceding paragraphs.

## Nullification of Sanctions and Claims

10. Upon the making by the Government of Algeria of the certification described in Paragraph 3 above, the United States will revoke all trade sanctions which were directed against Iran in the period November 4, 1979, to date.

11. Upon the making by the Government of Algeria of the certification described in Paragraph 3 above, the United States will promptly withdraw all claims now pending against Iran before the International Court of Justice and will thereafter bar and preclude the prosecution against Iran of any pending or future claim of the United States or a United States national arising out of events occurring before the date of this declaration related to (A) the seizure of the 52 United States nationals on November 4, 1979, (B) their subsequent detention, (C) injury to United States property or property of the United States nationals within the United States Embassy compound in Tehran after November 3, 1979, and (D) injury to the United States nationals or their property as a result of popular movements in the course of the Islamic Revolution in Iran which were not an act of the Government of Iran. The United States will also bar and preclude the prosecution against Iran in the courts of the United States of any pending or future claim asserted by persons other than the United States nationals arising out of the events specified in the preceding sentence.

### Point IV: Return of the Assets of
### The Family of the Former Shah

12. Upon the making by the Government of Algeria of the certification described in Paragraph 3 above, the United States will freeze, and prohibit

151

any transfer of, property and assets in the United States within the control of the estate of the former Shah or of any close relative of the former Shah served as a defendant in U.S. litigation brought by Iran to recover such property and assets as belonging to Iran. As to any such defendant, including the estate of the former Shah, the freeze order will remain in effect until such litigation is finally terminated. Violation of the freeze order shall be subject to the civil and criminal penalties prescribed by U.S. law.

13. Upon the making by the Government of Algeria of the certification described in Paragraph 3 above, the United States will order all persons within U.S. jurisdiction to report to the U.S. Treasury within 30 days, for transmission to Iran, all information known to them, as of November 3, 1979, and as of the date of the order, with respect to the property and assets referred to in Paragraph 12. Violation of the requirement will be subject to the civil and criminal penalties prescribed by U.S. law.

14. Upon the making by the Government of Algeria of the certification described in Paragraph 3 above, the United States will make known, to all appropriate U.S. courts, that in any litigation of the kind described in Paragraph 12 above the claims of Iran should not be considered legally barred either by sovereign immunity principles or by the act of state doctrine and that Iranian decrees and judgments relating to such assets should be enforced by such courts in accordance with United States law.

15. As to any judgment of a U.S. court which calls for the transfer of any property or assets to Iran, the United States hereby guarantees the enforcement of the final judgment to the extent that the property or assets exist within the United States.

16. If any dispute arises between the parties as to whether the United States has fulfilled any obligation imposed upon it by Paragraphs 12-15, inclusive, Iran may submit the dispute to binding arbitration by the tribunal established by, and in accordance with the provisions of, the claims settlement agreement. If the tribunal determines that Iran has suffered a loss as a result of a failure by the United States to fulfill such obligation, it shall make an appropriate award in favor of Iran which may be enforced by Iran in the courts of any nation in accordance with its laws.

## Settlement of Disputes

17. If any other dispute arises between the parties as to the interpretation of performance of any provision of this declaration, either party may submit the dispute to binding arbitration by the tribunal established by, and in accordance with the provisions of, the claims settlement agreement. Any decision of the tribunal with respect to such dispute, including any award of damages to compensate for a loss resulting from a breach of this declaration or the claims settlement agreement, may be enforced by the prevailing party in the courts of any nation in accordance with its laws.

Initialed on January 19, 1981

by Warren M. Christopher
Deputy Secretary of State
of the Government of the United States
By virtue of the powers vested in him by his
Government as deposited with the government of Algeria

# SETTLEMENT OF CLAIMS

The Government of the Democratic and Popular Republic of Algeria, on the basis of formal notice of adherence received from the Government of the Islamic Republic of Iran and the Government of the United States of America, now declares that Iran and the United States have agreed as follows:

## Article I

Iran and the United States will promote the settlement of the claims described in Article II by the parties directly concerned. Any such claims not settled within six months from the date of entry into force of this agreement shall be submitted to binding third-party arbitration in accordance with the terms of this agreement. The aforementioned six months' period may be extended once by three months at the request of either party.

## Article II

1. An International Arbitral Tribunal (the Iran-United States Claims Tribunal) is hereby established for the purpose of deciding claims of nationals of the United States against Iran and claims of nationals of Iran against the United States, and any counterclaim which arises out of the same contract, transaction or occurrence that constitutes the subject matter of that national's claim, if such claims and counterclaims are outstanding on the date of this agreement, whether or not filed with any court, and arise out of debts, contracts (including transactions which are the subject of letters of credit or bank guarantees), expropriations or other measures affecting property rights, excluding claims described in Paragraph 11 of the Declaration of the Government of Algeria of January 19, 1981, and claims arising out of the actions of the United States in response to the conduct described in such paragraph, and excluding claims arising under a binding contract between the parties specifically providing that any disputes thereunder shall be within the sole jurisdiction of the competent Iranian courts in response to the Majlis position.

2. The Tribunal shall also have jurisdiction over official claims of the United States and Iran against each other arising out of contractual

arrangements between them for the purchase and sale of goods and services.

3. The Tribunal shall have jurisdiction, as specified in Paragraphs 16-17 of the Declaration of the Government of Algeria of January 19, 1981, over any dispute as to the interpretation or performance of any provision of that declaration.

## Article III

1. The Tribunal shall consist of nine members or such larger multiple of three as Iran and the United States may agree are necessary to conduct its business expeditiously. Within ninety days after the entry into force of this agreement, each government shall appoint one-third of the members. Within thirty days after their appointment, the members so appointed shall by mutual agreement select the remaining third of the members and appoint one of the remaining third President of the Tribunal. Claims may be decided by the full Tribunal or by a panel of three members of the Tribunal as the President shall determine. Each such panel shall be composed by the President and shall consist of one member appointed by each of the three methods set forth above.

2. Members of the Tribunal shall be appointed and the Tribunal shall conduct its business in accordance with the arbitration rules of the United Nations Commission on International Trade Law (UNCITRAL) except to the extent modified by the parties or by the Tribunal to ensure that this agreement can be carried out. The UNCITRAL rules for appointing members of three-member Tribunals shall apply *mutatis mutandis* to the appointment of the Tribunal.

3. Claims of nationals of the United States and Iran that are within the scope of this agreement shall be presented to the Tribunal either by claimants themselves, or, in the case of claims of less than $250,000, by the Government of such national.

4. No claim may be filed with the Tribunal more than one year after the entry into force of this agreement or six months after the date the President is appointed, whichever is later. These deadlines do not apply to the procedures contemplated by Paragraphs 16 and 17 of the Declaration of the Government of Algeria of January 19, 1981.

## Article IV

1. All decisions and awards of the Tribunal shall be final and binding.

2. The President of the Tribunal shall certify, as prescribed in Paragraph 7 of the Declaration of the Government of Algeria of January 19, 1981, when all arbitral awards under this agreement have been satisfied.

3. Any award which the Tribunal may render against either government shall be enforceable against such government in the courts of any nation in accordance with its laws.

## Article V

The Tribunal shall decide all cases on the basis of respect for law, applying such choice of law rules and principles of commercial and international law as the Tribunal determines to be applicable, taking into account relevant usages of the trade, contract provisions and changed circumstances.

## Article VI

1. The seat of the Tribunal shall be The Hague, The Netherlands, or any other place agreed by Iran and the United States.

2. Each government shall designate an agent at the seat of the Tribunal to represent the Tribunal and to receive notices or other communications directed to it or to its nationals, agencies, instrumentalities, or entities in connection with proceedings before the Tribunal.

3. The expenses of the Tribunal shall be borne equally by the two governments.

4. Any question concerning the interpretation or application of this agreement shall be decided by the Tribunal upon the request of either Iran or the United States.

## Article VII

For the purposes of this agreement:

1. A "national" of Iran or of the United States, as the case may be, means (a) a natural person who is a citizen of Iran or the United States; and (b) a corporation or other legal entity which is organized under the laws of Iran or the United States or any of its states or territories, the District of Columbia or the Commonwealth of Puerto Rico, if, collectively, natural persons who are citizens of such country hold, directly or indirectly, an interest in such corporation or entity equivalent to fifty per cent or more of its capital stock.

2. "Claims of nationals" of Iran or the United States, as the case may be, means claims owned continuously, from the date on which the claim arose to the date on which this agreement enters into force, by nationals of that state, including claims that are owned indirectly by such nationals through ownership of capital stock or other proprietary interests in juridical persons, provided that the ownership interests of such nationals, collectively, were sufficient at the time the claim arose to control the corporation or other entity, and provided, further, that the corporation or other entity is not itself entitled to bring a claim under the terms of this agreement. Claims referred to the Arbitral Tribunal shall, as of the date of filing of such claims with the Tribunal, be considered excluded from the jurisdiction of the courts of Iran, or of the United States, or of any other court.

3. "Iran" means the Government of Iran, any political subdivision of

Iran, and any agency, instrumentality, or entity controlled by the Government of Iran or any political subdivision thereof.

4. The "United States" means the Government of the United States, any political subdivision of the United States, any agency, instrumentality or entity controlled by the Government of the United States or any political subdivision thereof.

## Article VIII

This agreement shall enter into force when the Government of Algeria has received from both Iran and the United States a notification of adherence to the agreement.

Initialed on January 19, 1981

by Warren M. Christopher
Deputy Secretary of State
of the Government of the United States
By virtue of the powers vested in him by his
Government as deposited with the Government of Algeria

# CARTER STATEMENT IN PLAINS

...Just a few moments ago, on Air Force One before we landed at Warner Robins, I had received word, officially, for the first time, that the aircraft carrying the 52 American hostages had cleared Iranian airspace on the first leg of the journey home and that every one of the 52 hostages was alive, was well and free.

It's impossible for me to realize — or any of us — how they feel on that plane because they recognize that they are hostages no more, they are prisoners no more, and they are coming back to this land that we all love.

Our diplomats will be arriving sometime in the near future — I can't yet tell you exactly when — in Algiers. The Algerians, the last few weeks, have been real heroes. They have literally worked day and night — from their President, their Foreign Minister, the president of their national bank and others — to try to gain the freedom of the American hostages.

And I want to express my personal, and also my political, official and public thanks to the people of Algeria.

They'll be flying on two Algerian planes — they are now. They'll refuel in Athens, Greece; after they land in Algiers, they will transfer to an American plane and they will fly from there to Germany, land near Frankfurt in a military air base, and go from there about 30 miles away to the hospitals in Wiesbaden, Germany, where American doctors and others will be waiting for them.

Former Secretary Cyrus Vance will be there to shake their hands and to put his arms around them when they come down from the airplane. I had the plane standing by in Washington, with Secretary Vance in charge. And I directed that the plane take off the moment the hostage planes' wheels cleared the ground.

After a brief rest in Germany — three or four days, probably — then the hostages will come back home to be reunited with their families.

As suggested yesterday morning by our new President Reagan, early tomorrow morning I will leave for Germany to welcome our hostages to freedom. And I know I will take with me the joy and the relief of our entire nation.

Throughout this time of trial, we Americans have stood as one, united in our prayers, steadfast in our concern for fellow Americans in peril.

I doubt that at any time in our history more prayers have reached heaven for any Americans than have those given to God in the last 14 months.

We've achieved, at the end of this crisis, the two objectives that I set for this nation, and for myself, when they were first seized: to secure their safety and their ultimate release, and to do so on terms that would always preserve the honor and the dignity and the best interests of our nation.

As I said a few hours ago in a brief press announcement, the essence of this agreement is that as our people are freed, we're releasing a part of the assets belonging to Iran, which I froze by Presidential order after our embassy was seized and the hostages were taken.

There will also be established a firm, established procedure, involving binding arbitration completely in accordance with American law, and international law, to resolve any remaining claims that might exist by American people against Iran, or vice versa.

Our people held captive, and their families here at home, have borne this ordeal with courage and with honor.

Our nation acted as a great nation ought to act: not only with justified outrage at a despicable and illegal act, but with purpose and constant restraint in the face of severe provocation; working always to uphold the law in the face of lawlessness in Iran. We've kept faith with our principles and our people and as a result, we've reached this day of joy and thanksgiving. . . .

# CARTER REMARKS IN WEST GERMANY

I've just completed, on behalf of all the American people, one of the acts in my life which has been the most moving and gratifying, in meeting with and discussing the future and the past with the now-liberated Americans who were held hostage in Iran for so long.

I pointed out to them that since their capture by the Iranian terrorists and their being held in this despicable act of savagery, that the American peoples' hearts have gone out to them; that our nation has been united as perhaps never before in history, and that the prayers that have gone up from the people around the world to God, for their safety, have finally been answered.

I pointed out that the Iranian Working Group within the State Department, set up the very day they were captured, has functioned 24 hours a day and will still be in existence until they're all safely at home with their own families.

This dedication has been mirrored by the hundreds of millions of people in our country whose hearts have gone out to these heroes. . . .

One very serious fact is becoming evident. And that is that our Americans in Iran were mistreated much worse than has been previously revealed.

The acts of barbarism which were perpetrated on our people by Iran can never be condoned.

Iran, in my judgment, and the people responsible in Iran for this criminal act, ought to be condemned by all law-loving, decent people of the world.

It's been an abominable circumstance. It's been an abominable circumstance that will never be forgotten. . . .

This has been a very moving experience for me and one I appreciate.

Shortly before I landed in Germany, I talked with President Reagan. He asked me to relate to the liberated Americans his deep thanks for their freedom and his best wishes to every one of them. And to express to them on behalf of the American people, through the President — President Reagan — our care for them; our hope for a speedy return to our country.

I'm very grateful that President Reagan suggested that I come over here. I expressed to the newly freed Americans in some small way, at least, the hope that the American people have shared in a remarkable demonstration of unity for their ultimate freedom, and our thanks that God has finally answered the millions of prayers that have gone to heaven for their lives and for their safety. . . .

# IRANIAN NOTE DENYING ABUSE

In the name of the Most High.

In connection with the baseless rumors and biased propaganda about the disturbing and torturing of the 52 Americans in Iran, it is essential to inform the people of the world, particularly the American nation, of the following points:

1. Torture in Islam is not only forbidden but a great sin. For this reason, with the information the Government of the Islamic Republic of Iran has about the way of thinking and behavior of the Moslem students following the line of the Imam, it confidently and explicitly declares that the rumors of torture or harm to the Americans are mere lies, and are categorically denied.

2. Such rumors and propaganda, whose main objective are to damage the credibility of the Islamic Republic of Iran in the international community, are in fact another part of the measures and stands of the U.S. against our Islamic revolution.

3. The statements of some of the released hostages on alleged torture and maltreatment are the result of malicious suggestions and brainwashing which they were subjected to during the days they were hospitalized in spite of being healthy, and thus imprisoned, in Germany without being allowed to meet their families.

4. Six Algerian doctors had examined all the 52 Americans before the latter's departure from Iran, and had confirmed their health.

5. Representatives of the Algerian Government had previously met and held talks with the 52 former hostages. During these talks none of the Americans had said anything indicative of torture or maltreatment.

6. The Algerian Ambassador to Iran had met with them and has given written confirmation on their health.

7. Before boarding the airplane, each of the former hostages was escorted by two guards to the loading ramp among the shouts of "God is great!" and "Death to America!" Thus any claims of insulting or injuring them are flatly denied.

8. The interviews held with the 52 Americans during two days of their stay in Iran have been broadcast through telecommunication satellites and television networks for the enlightenment of the open-minded people of the world, and will be distributed throughout the world in videotapes by representatives of the Islamic Republic of Iran.

In conclusion, the Government of the Islamic Republic of Iran is confident that the free people of the world will not be influenced by the ill will of the enemies of freedom and freedom-seeking.

# REAGAN'S GREETING TO HOSTAGES

Cardinal Cooke, thank you, I think, for delivering this weather. We had been promised showers. We're most grateful.

Welcome to the Ambassadors of our friends in neighboring countries who are here today. And I can think of no better way to let you know how Nancy and I feel about your presence here today than to say on behalf of us, of the Vice President and Barbara, the Senators, the Members of Congress, the members of the Cabinet, and all of our fellow citizens, these simple words: Welcome home.

You are home, and believe me, you're welcome. If my remarks were a sermon, my text would be lines from the 126th Psalm, "We were like those who dreamed. Now our mouth is filled with laughter and our tongue with shouts of joy. The Lord has done great things for us. We are glad." You've come home to a people who for 444 days suffered the pain of your imprisonment, prayed for your safety, and most importantly, shared your determination that the spirit of free men and women is not a fit subject for barter.

You've represented under great stress the highest traditions of public service. Your conduct is symbolic of the millions of professional diplomats, military personnel, and others who have rendered service to their country.

We're now aware of the conditions under which you were imprisoned. Though now is not the time to review every abhorrent detail of your cruel confinement, believe me, we know what happened. Truth may be a rare commodity today in Iran; it's alive and well in America.

By no choice of your own, you've entered the ranks of those who throughout our history have undergone the ordeal of imprisonment: the crew of the *Pueblo*, the prisoners in two World Wars and in Korea and Vietnam. And like those others, you are special to us. You fulfilled your duty as you saw it, and now like the others, thank God you're home, and our hearts are full of gratitude.

I'm told that Sergeant Lopez here put up a sign in his cell, a sign that normally would have been torn down by those guards. But this one was written in Spanish, and his guards didn't know that *"Viva la roja, blanco, y azul"* means "Long live the red, white, and blue." They may not understand what that means in Iran, but we do, Sergeant Lopez, and you've filled our hearts with pride. *Muchas gracias.*

Two days ago, Nancy and I met with your families here at the White House. We know that you were lonely during that dreadful period of captivity, but you were never alone. Your wives and children, your mothers and dads, your brothers and sisters were so full of prayers and love for you that whether you were conscious of it or not, it must have sustained you during some of the worst times. No power on Earth could prevent them from doing that. Their courage, endurance, and strength were of heroic measure, and they're admired by all of us.

But to get down now to more mundane things, in case you have a question about your personal futures, you'll probably have less time to rest than you'd like. While you were on your way to Germany, I signed a hiring freeze in the Federal Government. In other words, we need you, your country needs you, and your bosses are panting to have you back on the job.

Now, I'll not be so foolish as to say forget what you've been through; you never will. But turn the page and look ahead, and do so knowing that for all who served their country, whether in the Foreign Service, the military, or as private citizens, freedom is indivisible. Your freedom and your individual dignity are much cherished. Those henceforth in the representation of this Nation will be accorded every means of protection that America can offer.

Let terrorists be aware that when the rules of international behavior are violated, our policy will be one of swift and effective retribution. We hear it said that we live in an era of limit to our powers. Well, let it also be understood, there are limits to our patience.

Now, I'm sure that you'll want to know that with us here today are families of the eight heroic men who gave their lives in the attempt to effect your rescue. "Greater glory hath no man than that he lay down his life for another." And with us also are Colonel Beckwith and some of the men who did return from that mission. We ask God's special healing for those who suffered wounds and His comfort to those who lost loved ones. To them, to you, and to your families, again, welcome from all America and thank you for making us proud to be Americans.

And now, ladies and gentlemen, I call on, to speak for this wonderful group of returnees, Bruce Laingen, Deputy Chief of Mission in Tehran. Mr. Laingen.

# LAINGEN REMARKS AT WHITE HOUSE

*Mr. President, Mrs. Reagan, members of the Cabinet, Vice President and Mrs. Bush — I think I've got that out of order of priority in protocol terms — members of the Diplomatic Corps who are here, and all you beautiful people out there:*

I'm not sure I'm capable of this after that emotionally draining, but beautiful experience that all of us have just had on the streets of this magnificent city, Mr. President. I hope you were watching TV, because I don't think any of us Americans have ever seen anything quite like it, quite so spontaneous, quite so beautiful in terms of the best qualities of our people. And we are deeply grateful for it.

Mr. President, our flight to freedom is now complete: thanks to the prayers and good will of countless millions of people, not just in this country but all around the world; the assistance of those many countries and governments who understood the values and principles that were at stake in this crisis; and the love and affection of our countrymen from all those tens of thousands out there on the streets today, to that lady that we saw standing on a hillside as we came in from Andrews, all alone, with no sign, no one around her, holding her hand to her heart — the enveloping love and affection of smalltown America of the kind we witnessed in that wonderful 2-day stop in New York State, West Point and its environs, and last, but not least, on this flight to freedom, the United States Air Force on Freedom I.

Mr. President, I give you now 52 Americans, supplemented by a 53d, today, Richard Queen sitting over here, overjoyed in reunion with our families, the real heroes in this crisis; 53 Americans, proud to rejoin their professional colleagues who had made their flight to freedom earlier — our 6 colleagues who came here with the great cooperation and friendship of our Canadian friends, and our 13 who came earlier. I give you now 53 Americans, proud, as I said earlier today, to record their undying respect and affection for the families of those brave eight men who gave their lives so that we might be free, 53 of us proud today, this afternoon, and also to see and to meet with some of those families and Colonel Beckwith and some of those who came back. Fifty-three Americans who will always have a love affair with this country and who join with you in a prayer of thanksgiving for the way in which this crisis has strengthened the spirit and resilience and strength that is the mark of a truly free society.

Mr. President, we've seen a lot of signs along the road, here and up in New York. They are marvelous signs, as is the spirit and enthusiasm that accompanies this what we've been calling "a celebration of freedom." They are signs that have not been ordered. They are spontaneous, sincere signs that reflect the true feelings of the hearts of those who hold them, even those, I suppose, like "IRS welcomes you" — [*laughter*] — which we saw today as we came into town, and another one that said, "Government workers welcome you back to work." Well, we're ready.

There was another sign that said, and I think that says it as well as any as far as we're concerned: "The best things in life are free." But even better than that was a sign that we saw as we left West Point today along a super-highway up there that someone had hastily put out: "And the world will be better for this." We pray, Mr. President, that this will be so.

Mr. President, in very simple words that come from the hearts of all of us, it is good to be back. Thank you, America, and God bless all of you. Thank you very much.

# COURT ON TELEVISED TRIALS
## January 26, 1981

*Nothing in the U.S. Constitution forbids states to experiment with television coverage of criminal trials, a unanimous Supreme Court ruled January 26. However, Chief Justice Warren E. Burger, delivering the court's opinion, said that television coverage might threaten the fairness of a particular trial and thus be constitutionally improper.*

*"Dangers lurk in this, as in most, experiments," Burger said, "but unless we were to conclude that television coverage under all conditions is prohibited by the Constitution, the states must be free to experiment."*

*The vote, in the case of* Chandler v. Florida, *was 8-0. Justice John Paul Stevens did not participate. A number of observers said that the decision removed the debate over courtroom television from the strict realm of constitutionality to a broader area of social and political policy.*

*The case centered on a breaking-and-entering at a well-known Miami, Fla., restaurant. Two men convicted of burglary argued that the mere presence of cameras in the courtroom had so affected the behavior of the participants that it denied them their constitutional right to a fair trial.*

## Background

*Cameras were barred from all federal courtrooms in reaction to the "circus-like" atmosphere created at the 1930s trial of Bruno Richard Hauptmann, convicted of the kidnapping death of the small son of aviator Charles A. Lindbergh and his wife Anne Morrow Lindbergh.*

*States generally followed that pattern until the 1970s, with the single exception of Colorado, which had allowed television into courtrooms since 1956. In the years since 1975, however, more than half the states had adopted permanent or experimental rules allowing television coverage of trials or other court proceedings.*

*But the Supreme Court in 1965 had ruled, in Estes v. Texas, that televising the trial of financier Bille Sol Estes over his objection denied him a fair trial. Of the nine justices taking part in Estes, three — William J. Brennan Jr., Potter Stewart and Byron R. White — were still on the court and participated in the 1981 Chandler case. All three in 1965 had dissented from the Estes ruling.*

## The Opinion

*In Chandler, the court rejected the defendants' argument that the Estes decision flatly banned televised trials. That ruling, wrote Chief Justice Burger, was not "an absolute ban on state experimentation with an evolving technology which ... was in its relative infancy in 1964, and is, even now, in a state of continuing change."*

*Nor did the current members of the court see any reason to impose such a ban, Burger continued. Publicity could jeopardize the fairness of any trial, he wrote, but courts had a number of means of preventing that threat from becoming a reality.*

*The chief justice said that opponents of televised trials had not shown that the presence of broadcasting equipment and the knowledge that a trial was being broadcast always affected participants in such a way as to deny the defendant a fair trial.*

## State Experimentation

*Burger quoted Justice Louis D. Brandeis on the value of experimentation by the states. Brandeis wrote in 1932 that "[i]t is one of the happy incidents of the federal system that a single courageous state may, if its citizens choose, serve as a laboratory; and try novel social and economic experiments without risk to the rest of the country."*

*The chief justice noted that the court had only a limited role in reviewing such experimentation. "We are not empowered by the Constitution," he wrote, "to oversee or harness state procedural experimentation; only when the state action infringes fundamental guarantees are we authorized to intervene."*

*Justices Stewart and White agreed with the outcome of the court's ruling, but argued that Estes did flatly ban television from courtrooms and should be explicitly overruled.*

*Following are excerpts from the Supreme Court's majority
opinion, delivered January 26, 1981, that television coverage
of courtroom trials did not automatically violate a defendant's right to a fair trial:*

No. 79-1260

| | |
|---|---|
| Noel Chandler and Robert<br>Granger, Appellants,<br>*v.*<br>State of Florida. | On Appeal from the Supreme<br>Court of Florida. |

[January 26, 1981]

CHIEF JUSTICE BURGER delivered the opinion of the Court. [JUS-
TICE STEVENS took no part in the decision of this case.]

The question presented on this appeal is whether, consistent with
constitutional guarantees, a state may provide for radio, television, and
still photographic coverage of a criminal trial for public broadcast,
notwithstanding the objection of the accused.

## I

### A

*Background.* Over the past 50 years, some criminal cases characterized
as "sensational" have been subjected to extensive coverage by news media,
sometimes seriously interfering with the conduct of the proceedings and
creating a setting wholly inappropriate for the administration of justice.
Judges, lawyers, and others soon became concerned, and in 1937, after
study, the American Bar Association House of Delegates adopted Judicial
Canon 35, declaring that all photographic and broadcast coverage of
courtroom proceedings should be prohibited. In 1952, the House of
Delegates amended Canon 35 to proscribe television coverage as well. The
Canon's proscription was reaffirmed in 1972 when the Code of Judicial
Conduct replaced the Canons of Judicial Ethics and Canon 3A (7) super-
seded Canon 35....

In February 1978, the American Bar Association Committee on Fair
Trial-Free Press proposed revised standards. These included a provision
permitting courtroom coverage by the electronic media under conditions to
be established by local rule and under the control of the trial judge, but
only if such coverage was carried out unobtrusively and without affecting
the conduct of the trial. The revision was endorsed by the ABA's Standing
Committee on Standards for Criminal Justice and by its Committee on
Criminal Justice and the Media, but it was rejected by the House of
Delegates on February 12, 1979.

In 1978, based upon its study of the matter, the Conference of State Chief Justices, led by a vote of 44 to 1, approved a resolution to allow the highest court of each state to promulgate standards and guidelines regulating radio, television, and other photographic coverage of court proceedings.

*The Florida Program.* In January 1975, while these developments were unfolding, the Post-Newsweek Stations of Florida petitioned the Supreme Court of Florida urging a change in Florida's Canon 3A (7). In April 1975, the court invited presentations in the nature of a rulemaking proceeding, and, in May of that year, it announced an experimental program for televising one civil and one criminal trial under specific guidelines. These initial guidelines required the consent of all parties. It developed, however, that in practice such consent could not be obtained. The Florida Supreme Court then supplemented its order and established a new one-year pilot program during which the electronic media were permitted to cover all judicial proceedings in Florida without reference to the consent of partici- pants, subject to detailed standards with respect to technology and the conduct of operators. The experiment began in July 1977 and continued through June 1978.

When the pilot program ended, the Florida Supreme Court received and reviewed briefs, reports, letters of comment, and studies. It conducted its own survey of attorneys, witnesses, jurors, and court personnel through the Office of the State Court Coordinator. A separate survey was taken of judges by the Florida Conference of Circuit Judges. The court also studied the experience of six states that had, by 1979, adopted rules relating to electronic coverage of trials, as well as that of the 10 other states that, like Florida, were experimenting with such coverage.

Following its review of this material, the Florida Supreme Court concluded "that on balance there [was] more to be gained than lost by permitting electronic media coverage of judicial proceedings subject to standards for such coverage." The Florida court was of the view that because of the significant effect of the courts on the day-to-day lives of the citizenry, it was essential that the people have confidence in the process. It felt that broadcast coverage of trials would contribute to wider public acceptance and understanding of decisions. Consequently, after revising the 1977 guidelines to reflect its evaluation of the pilot program, the Florida Supreme Court promulgated a revised Canon 3A (7)....

The implementing guidelines specify in detail the kind of electronic equipment to be used and the manner of its use. For example, no more than one television camera and only one camera technician are allowed. Existing recording systems used by court reporters are used by broadcast- ers for audio pickup. Where more than one broadcast news organization seeks to cover a trial, the media must pool coverage. No artificial lighting is allowed. The equipment is positioned in a fixed location, and it may not be moved during trial. Videotaping equipment must be remote from the courtroom. Film, videotape, and lenses may not be changed while the court is in session. No audio recording of conferences between lawyers, between parties and counsel, or at the bench is permitted. The judge has sole and plenary discretion to exclude coverage of certain witnesses, and the jury may not be filmed. The judge has discretionary power to forbid coverage whenever satisfied that coverage may have a deleterious effect on the paramount right of the defendant to a fair trial. The Florida Supreme Court has the right to revise these rules as experience dictates, or indeed to bar all broadcast coverage of photography in courtrooms.

**B**

In July 1977, appellants were charged with conspiracy to commit burglary, grand larceny, and possession of burglary tools. The counts covered breaking and entering a well-known Miami Beach restaurant.

The details of the alleged criminal conduct are not relevant to the issue before us, but several aspects of the case distinguish it from a routine burglary. At the time of their arrest, appellants were Miami Beach policemen. The State's principal witness was John Sion, an amateur radio operator who, by sheer chance, had overheard and recorded conversations between the appellants over their police walkie-talkie radios during the burglary. Not surprisingly, these novel factors attracted the attention of the media.

By pretrial motion, counsel for the appellants sought to have Experimental Canon 3A (7) declared unconstitutional on its face and as applied. The trial court denied relief but certified the issue to the Florida Supreme Court. However, the Supreme Court declined to rule on the question, on the ground that it was not directly relevant to the criminal charges against the appellants. *State* v. *Granger* (Fla. 1977).

After several additional fruitless attempts by the appellants to prevent electronic coverage of the trial, the jury was selected. At *voir dire,* the appellants' counsel asked each prospective juror whether he or she would be able to be "fair and impartial" despite the presence of a television camera during some, or all, of the trial. Each juror selected responded that such coverage would not affect his or her consideration in any way. A television camera recorded the *voir dire.*

A defense motion to sequester the jury because of the television coverage was denied by the trial judge. However, the court instructed the jury not to watch or read anything about the case in the media and suggested that jurors "avoid the local news and watch only the national news on television." Subsequently, defense counsel requested that the witnesses be instructed not to watch any television accounts of testimony presented at trial. The trial court declined to give such an instruction, for "no witness' testimony was [being] reported or televised [on the evening news] in any way."

A television camera was in place for one entire afternoon, during which the state presented the testimony of Sion, its chief witness. No camera was present for the presentation of any part of the case for the defense. The camera returned to cover closing arguments. Only two minutes and fifty-five seconds of the trial below were broadcast — and those depicted only the prosecution's side of the case.

The jury returned a guilty verdict on all counts. Appellants moved for a new trial, claiming that because of the television coverage, they had been denied a fair and impartial trial. No evidence of specific prejudice was tendered.

The Florida District Court of Appeal affirmed the convictions. It declined to discuss the facial validity of Canon 3A (7); it reasoned that the Florida Supreme Court, having decided to permit television coverage of criminal trials on an experimental basis, had implicitly determined that such coverage did not violate the federal or state constitutions. Nonetheless, the District Court of Appeal did agree to certify the question of the facial constitutionality of Canon 3A (7) to the Florida Supreme Court. The District Court of Appeal found no evidence in the trial record to indicate that the presence of a television camera had hampered appellants in presenting their case or had deprived them of an impartial jury.

The Florida Supreme Court denied review, holding that the appeal, which was limited to a challenge to Canon 3A (7), was moot by reason of its decision in *Petition of the Post Newsweek Stations, Florida, Inc.* (Fla. 1979), rendered shortly after the decision of the District Court of Appeal.

## II

At the outset, it is important to note that in promulgating the revised Canon 3A (7), the Florida Supreme Court pointedly rejected any state or federal constitutional right of access on the part of photographers or the broadcast media to televise or electronically record and thereafter disseminate court proceedings....

The Florida court relied on our holding in *Nixon* v. *Warner Communications, Inc.* (1977), where we said:

"In the first place,... there is no constitutional right to have [live witness] testimony recorded and broadcast. Second, while the guarantee of a public trial, in the words of Mr. Justice Black, is "a safeguard against any attempt to employ our courts as instruments of persecution," it confers no special benefit on the press. Nor does the Sixth Amendment require that the trial — or any part of it — be broadcast live or on tape to the public. The requirement of a public trial is satisfied by the opportunity of members of the public and the press to attend the trial and report what they have observed."

The Florida Supreme Court predicated the revised Canon 3A (7) upon its supervisory authority over the Florida courts, and not upon any constitutional imperative. Hence, we have before us only the limited question of the Florida Supreme Court's authority to promulgate the canon for the trial of cases in Florida courts.

This Court has no supervisory jurisdiction over state courts, and, in reviewing a state court judgment, we are confined to evaluating it in relation to the Federal Constitution.

## III

Appellants rely chiefly on *Estes* v. *Texas* (1964), and Chief Justice Warren's separate concurring opinion in that case. They argue that the televising of criminal trials is inherently a denial of due process, and they read *Estes* as announcing a *per se* constitutional rule to that effect.

Chief Justice Warren's concurring opinion, in which he was joined by Justices Douglas and Goldberg, indeed provides some support for the appellants' position:

"While I join the Court's opinion and agree that the televising of criminal trials is inherently a denial of due process, I desire to express additional views on why this is so. In doing this, I wish to emphasize that our condemnation of televised criminal trials is not based upon generalities or abstract fears. The record in this case presents a vivid illustration of the inherent prejudice of televised criminal trials and supports our conclusion that this is the appropriate time to make a definitive appraisal of television in the courtroom."

If appellants' reading of *Estes* were correct, we would be obliged to apply that holding and reverse the judgment under review.

The six separate opinions in *Estes* must be examined carefully to evaluate the claim that it represents a *per se* constitutional rule fobidding all electronic coverage. Chief Justice Warren and Justices Douglas and Goldberg joined Justice Clark's opinion announcing the judgment, thereby creating only a plurality. Justice Harlan provided the fifth vote necessary in support of the judgment. In a separate opinion, he pointedly limited his concurrence:

"I concur in the opinion of the Court, subject, however, to the reservations and only to the extent indicated in this opinion."

A careful analysis of Justice Harlan's opinion is therefore fundamental to an understanding of the ultimate holding of *Estes*.

Justice Harlan began by observing that the question of the constitutional permissibility of televised trials was one fraught with unusual difficulty:

"Permitting television in the courtroom undeniably has mischievous potentialities for intruding upon the detached atmosphere which should always surround the judicial process. Forbidding this innovation, however, would doubtless impinge upon one of the valued attributes of our federalism by preventing the states from pursuing a novel course of procedural experimentation. My conclusion is that there is no constitutional requirement that television be allowed in the courtroom, *and, at least as to a notorious criminal trial such as this one, the considerations against allowing television in the courtroom so far outweigh the countervailing factors advanced in its support as to require a holding that what was done in this case infringed the fundamental right to a fair trial* assured by the due Process Clause of the Fourteenth Amendment." (emphasis added).

He then proceeded to catalogue what he perceived as the inherent dangers of televised trials.

"In the context of a trial of intense public interest, there is certainly a strong possibility that the timid or reluctant witness, for whom a court appearance even at its traditional best is a harrowing affair, will become more timid or reluctant when he finds that he will also be appearing before a 'hidden audience' of unknown but large dimensions. There is certainly a strong possibility that the 'cocky' witness having a thirst for the limelight will become more 'cocky' under the influence of television. And who can say that the juror who is gratified by having been chosen for a front-line case, an ambitious prosecutor, a publicity-minded defense attorney, and even a conscientious judge will not stray, albeit unconsciously, from doing what 'comes naturally' into pluming themselves for a satisfactory television 'performance'?''

Justice Harlan faced squarely the reality that these possibilities carry "grave potentialities for distorting the integrity of the judicial process," and that, although such distortions may produce no telltale signs, "their effects may be far more pervasive and deleterious than the physical disruptions which all would concede would vitiate a conviction." The "countervailing factors" alluded to by Justice Harlan were, as here, the educational and informational value to the public.

JUSTICE STEWART, joined by JUSTICES BLACK, BRENNAN, and WHITE in dissent, concluded that no prejudice had been shown and that Estes' Fourteenth Amendment rights had not been violated. While expressing reservations not unlike those of Justice Harlan and those of Chief Justice Warren, the dissent expressed unwillingness to "escalate this personal view into a *per se* constitutional rule." The four dissenters disagreed both with the *per se* rule embodied in the plurality opinion of Justice Clark and with the judgment of the Court that "the *circumstances of [that]* trial led to a denial of [Estes'] Fourteenth Amendment rights." (emphasis added).

Parsing the six opinions in *Estes,* one is left with a sense of doubt as to precisely how much of Justice Clark's opinion was joined in, and supported by, Justice Harlan. In an area charged with constitutional nuances, perhaps more should not be expected. Nonetheless, it is fair to say that Justice Harlan viewed the holding as limited to the proposition that *"what was done in this case* infringed the fundamental right to a fair trial assured by the Due Process Clause of the Fourteenth Amendment," (emphasis added), he went on:

"*At the present juncture,* I can only conclude that televised trials, *at least in cases like this one,* possess such capabilities for interfering with the even course of the judicial process that they are constitutionally banned." (emphasis added).

Justice Harlan's opinion, upon which analysis of the constitutional holding of *Estes* turns, must be read as defining the scope of that holding; we conclude that *Estes* is not to be read as announcing a constitutional rule barring still photographic, radio and television coverage in all cases and under all circumstances. It does not stand as an absolute ban on state experimentation with an evolving technology, which, in terms of modes of mass communication, was in its relative infancy in 1964, and is, even now, in a state of continuing change.

## IV

Since we are satisfied that *Estes* did not announce a constitutional rule that all photographic or broadcast coverage of criminal trials is inherently a denial of due process, we turn to consideration, as a matter of first impression, of the petitioner's suggestion that we now promulgate such a *per se* rule.

### A

Any criminal case that generates a great deal of publicity presents some risks that the publicity may compromise the right of the defendant to a fair trial. Trial courts must be especially vigilant to guard against any impairment of the defendant's right to a verdict based solely upon the evidence and the relevant law. Over the years, courts have developed a range of curative devices to prevent publicity about a trial from infecting jury deliberations. See, *e.g., Nebraska Free Press Association* v. *Stuart* (1975).

An absolute constitutional ban on broadcast coverage of trials cannot be justified simply because there is a danger that, in some cases, prejudicial broadcast accounts of pretrial and trial events may impair the ability of jurors to decide the issue of guilt or innocence uninfluenced by extraneous matter. The risk of juror prejudice in some cases does not justify an absolute ban on news coverage of trials by the printed media; so also the risk of such prejudice does not warrant an absolute constitutional ban on all broadcast coverage. A case attracts a high level of public attention because of its intrinsic interest to the public and the manner of reporting the event. The risk of juror prejudice is present in any publication of a trial, but the appropriate safeguard against such prejudice is the defendant's right to demonstrate that the media's coverage of his case — be it printed or broadcast — compromised the ability of the particular jury that heard the case to adjudicate fairly.

### B

As we noted earlier, the concurring opinion in *Estes* expressed concern that the very presence of media cameras and recording devices at a trial inescapably gives rise to an adverse psychological impact on the participants in the trial. This kind of general psychological prejudice, allegedly present whenever there is broadcast coverage of a trial, is different from the more particularized problem of prejudicial impact discussed earlier. If it could be demonstrated that the mere presence of photographic and recording equipment and the knowledge that the event would be broadcast invariably and uniformly affected the conduct of participants so as to impair fundamental fairness, our task would be simple; prohibition of broadcast coverage of trials would be required.

In confronting the difficult and sensitive question of the potential psychological prejudice associated with broadcast coverage of trials, we have been aided by *amicus* briefs submitted by various state officers involved in law enforcement, the Conference of Chief Justices, and the Attorneys General of 17 states in support of continuing experimentation such as that embarked upon by Florida, and by the American Bar Association, the American College of Trial Lawyers, and various members of the defense bar representing essentially the views expressed by the concurring Justices in *Estes.*

Not unimportant to the position asserted by Florida and other states is the change in television technology since 1962, when Estes was tried. It is urged, and some empirical data are presented, that many of the negative factors found in *Estes* — cumbersome equipment, cables, distracting lighting, numerous camera technicians — are less substantial factors today than they were at that time.

It is also significant that safeguards have been built into the experimental programs in state courts, and into the Florida program, to avoid some of the most egregious problems envisioned by the six opinions in the *Estes* case. Florida admonishes its courts to take special pains to protect certain witnesses — for example, children, victims of sex crimes, some informants, and even the very timid witness or party — from the glare of publicity and the tensions of being "on camera."

The Florida guidelines place on trial judges positive obligations to be on guard to protect the fundamental right of the accused to a fair trial. The Florida statute, being one of the few permitting broadcast coverage of criminal trials over the objection of the accused, raises problems not present in the statutes of other states. Inherent in electronic coverage of a trial is the risk that the very awareness by the accused of the coverage and the contemplated broadcast may adversely affect the conduct of the participants and the fairness of the trial, yet leave no evidence of how the conduct or the trial's fairness was affected. Given this danger, it is significant that Florida requires that objections of the accused to coverage be heard and considered on the record by the trial court. See, *e.g., Green* v. *State* (Fla. Dist. Ct. App. 1979). In addition to providing a record for appellate review, a pretrial hearing enables a defendant to advance the basis of his objection to broadcast coverage and allows the trial court to define the steps necessary to minimize or eliminate the risks of prejudice to the accused. Experiments such as the one presented here may well increase the number of appeals by adding a new basis for claims to reverse, but this is a risk Florida has chosen to take after preliminary experimentation. Here, the record does not indicate that appellants requested an evidentiary hearing to show adverse impact or injury. Nor does the record reveal anything more than generalized allegations of prejudice.

Nonetheless, it is clear that the general issue of the psychological impact of broadcast coverage upon the participants in a trial, and particularly upon the defendant, is still a subject of sharp debate — as the *Amicus* Briefs of the American Bar Association, the American College of Trial Lawyers, and others of the trial bar in opposition to Florida's experiment demonstrate. These *amici* state the view that the concerns expressed by the concurring opinions in *Estes,* see Part III, *supra,* have been borne out by actual experience. Comprehensive empirical data is still not available — at least on some aspects of the problem. For example, the *Amici* Brief of the Attorneys General concedes:

"The defendant's interest in not being harassed and in being able to concentrate on the proceedings and confer effectively with his attorney are crucial aspects of a fair trial. There is not much data on defendant's reactions to televised trials available now, but what there is indicates that it is possible to regulate the media so that their presence does not weigh heavily on the defendant. *Particular attention should be paid to this area of concern as study of televised trials continues."* (emphasis added).

The experimental status of electronic coverage of trials is also emphasized by the *Amicus* Brief of the Conference of Chief Justices:

"Examination and reexamination by state courts of the in-court presence of the electronic news media, *vel non,* is an exercise of the authority reserved to the states under our federalism."

Whatever may be the "mischievous potentialities [of broadcast coverage] for intruding upon the detached atmosphere which should always surround the judicial process," *Estes* v. *Texas,* at present no one has been able to present empirical data sufficient to establish that the mere presence of the broadcast media inherently has an adverse effect on that process. The appellants have offered nothing to demonstrate that their trial was subtly tainted by broadcast coverage — let alone that all broadcast trials would be so tainted.

Where, as here, we cannot say that a denial of due process automatically results from activity authorized by a state, the admonition of Justice Brandeis, dissenting in *New State Ice Co.* v. *Liebmann* (1932), is relevant:

"To stay experimentation in things social and economic is a grave responsibility. Denial of the right to experiment may be fraught with serious consequences to the Nation. It is one of the happy incidents of the federal system that a single courageous state may, if its citizens choose, serve as a laboratory; and try novel social and economic experiments without risk to the rest of the country. This Court has the power to prevent an experiment. We may strike down the statute which embodies it on the ground that, in our opinion, the measure is arbitrary, capricious, or unreasonable.... But in the exercise of this high power, we must be ever on our guard, lest we erect our prejudices into legal principles. If we would guide by the light of reason, we must let our minds be bold."

This concept of federalism, echoed by the states favoring Florida's experiment, must guide our decision.

## C

*Amici* members of the defense bar vigorously contend that displaying the accused on television is in itself a denial of due process. This was a source of concern to Chief Justice Warren and Justice Harlan in *Estes:* that coverage of select cases "singles out certain defendants and subjects them to trials under prejudicial conditions not experienced by others." (Warren, C.J., concurring). Selection of which trials, or parts of trials, to broadcast will inevitably be made not by judges but by the media, and will be governed by such factors as the nature of the crime and the status and position of the accused — or of the victim; the effect may be to titillate rather than to educate and inform. The unanswered question is whether electronic coverage will bring public humiliation upon the accused with such randomness that it will evoke due process concerns by being "unusual in the same way that being struck by lightning" is "unusual." *Furman* v. *Georgia* (1972) (STEWART, J., concurring). Societies and political systems, that, from time to time, have put on "Yankee Stadium" "show trials" tell more about the power of the state than about its concern for the decent administration of justice — with every citizen receiving the same kind of justice.

The concurring opinion of Chief Justice Warren joined by Justices Douglas and Goldberg in *Estes* can fairly be read as viewing the very broadcast of some trials as potentially a form of punishment in itself — a punishment before guilt. This concern is far from trivial. But, whether coverage of a few trials will, in practice, be the equivalent of a "Yankee Stadium" setting — which Justice Harlan likened to the public pillory long abandoned as a barbaric perversion of decent justice — must also await the continuing experimentation.

## D

To say that the appellants have not demonstrated that broadcast coverage is inherently a denial of due process is not to say that the appellants were in fact accorded all of the protections of due process in their trial. As noted earlier, a defendant has the right on review to show that the media's coverage of his case — printed or broadcast — compromised the ability of the jury to judge them fairly. Alternatively, a defendant might show that broadcast coverage of his particular case had an adverse impact on the trial participants sufficient to constitute a denial of due process. Neither showing was made in this case.

To demonstrate prejudice in a specific case a defendant must show something more than juror awareness that the trial is such as to attract the attention of broadcasters. *Murphy* v. *Florida* (1975). No doubt the very presence of a camera in the courtroom made the jurors aware that the trial was thought to be of sufficient interest to the public to warrant coverage. Jurors, forbidden to watch all broadcasts, would have had no way of knowing that only fleeting seconds of the proceeding would be reproduced. But the appellants have not attempted to show with any specificity that the presence of cameras impaired the ability of the jurors to decide the case on only the evidence before them or that their trial was affected adversely by the impact on any of the participants of the presence of cameras and the prospect of broadcast. . . .

## V

It is not necessary either to ignore or to discount the potential danger to the fairness of a trial in a particular case in order to conclude that Florida may permit the electronic media to cover trials in its state courts. Dangers lurk in this, as in most, experiments, but unless we were to conclude that television coverage under all conditions is prohibited by the Constitution, the states must be free to experiment. We are not empowered by the Constitution to oversee or harness state procedural experimentation; only when the state action infringes fundamental guarantees are we authorized to intervene. We must assume state courts will be alert to any factors that impair the fundamental rights of the accused.

The Florida program is inherently evolutional in nature; the initial project has provided guidance for the new canons which can be changed at will, and application of which is subject to control by the trial judge. The risk of prejudice to particular defendants is ever present and must be examined carefully as cases arise. Nothing of the "Roman circus" or "Yankee Stadium" atmosphere, as in *Estes,* prevailed here, however, nor have appellants attempted to show that the unsequestered jury was exposed to "sensational" coverage, in the sense of *Estes* or of *Sheppard* v. *Maxwell* (1966). Absent a showing of prejudice of constitutional dimensions to these defendants, there is no reason for this Court either to endorse or to invalidate Florida's experiment.

In this setting, because this Court has no supervisory authority over state courts, our review is confined to whether there is a constitutional violation. We hold that the Constitution does not prohibit a state from experimenting with the program authorized by revised Canon 3A (7).

*Affirmed.*

JUSTICE STEWART, concurring in the result.
Although concurring in the judgment, I cannot join the opinion of the

Court because I do not think the convictions in this case can be affirmed without overruling *Estes* v. *Texas* [1965].

I believe now, as I believed in dissent then, that *Estes* announced a *per se* rule that the Fourteenth Amendment "prohibits all telvision cameras from a state courtroom whenever a criminal trial is in progress." (White, J., dissenting). Accordingly, rather than join what seems to be a wholly unsuccessful effort to distinguish that decision, I would now flatly overrule it. . . .

The Court in *Estes* found the admittedly unobtrusive presence of television cameras in a criminal trial to be inherently prejudicial, and thus violative of Due Process of Law. Today the Court reaches precisely the opposite conclusion. I have no great trouble in agreeing with the Court today, but I would acknowledge our square departure from precedent.

JUSTICE WHITE, concurring in the judgment.

The Florida rule, which permits the televising of criminal trials under controlled conditions, is challenged here on its face and as applied. Appellants contend that the rule is facially invalid because the televising of *any* criminal trial over the objection of the defendant inherently results in a constitutionally unfair trial; they contend that the rule is unconstitutional as applied to them because their case attracted substantial publicity and, therefore, falls within the rule established in *Estes* v. *United States* (1965). The Florida court rejected both of these claims.

For the reasons stated by JUSTICE STEWART in his concurrence today, I think *Estes* is fairly read as establishing a *per se* constitutional rule against televising any criminal trial if the defendant objects. So understood, *Estes* must be overruled to affirm the judgment below. . . .

Whether the decision in *Estes* is read broadly or narrowly, I agree with JUSTICE STEWART that it should be overruled. I was in dissent in that case, and I remain unwilling to assume or conclude without more proof than has been marshalled to date that televising criminal trials is inherently prejudicial even when carried out under properly controlled conditions. A defendant should, of course, have ample opportunity to convince a judge that televising his trial would be unfair to him, and the judge should have the authority to exclude cameras from all or part of the criminal trial. But absent some showing of prejudice to the defense, I remain convinced that a conviction obtained in a state court should not be overturned simply because a trial judge refused to exclude television cameras and all or part of the trial was televised to the public. The experience of those States which have, since *Estes,* permitted televised trials supports this position, and I believe that the accumulated experience of those States has further undermined the assumptions on which the majority rested its judgement in *Estes*.

Although the Court's opinion today contends that it is consistent with *Estes,* I believe that it effectively eviscerates *Estes.* . . .

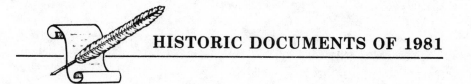

# February

# STATE DEPARTMENT REPORT
# ON HUMAN RIGHTS
### February 2, 1981

*Human rights conditions improved somewhat in the world in 1980 despite major increases in the world refugee population, according to the State Department's annual* Country Reports on Human Rights Practices. *Congressional release of the 1,140-page report, dated February 2, was delayed a week at the Reagan administration's request, to avoid embarrassment for South Korea's President Chun Doo Hwan, who was visiting Washington in early February. The report was critical of South Korea's handling of student demonstrations against the government in May 1980.*

*Surveying the human rights records of 153 countries, the report was prepared under the Carter administration, which placed heavy emphasis on international observance of human rights. The Reagan administration substituted international terrorism control as its most serious human rights issue.*

*The greatest gains were made against torture, disappearances and inhuman treatment of prisoners, the report said. Inflation and oil price increases undercut efforts of less developed countries to provide basic social needs, it said. And the status of civil and political freedoms was unchanged.* (Historic Documents of 1980, p. 189)

*Wars, persecution and natural disasters have generated more than 15 million refugees across the world in recent years, the report said. It called the burgeoning refugee population "a major area of human rights concern." Principal centers of refugee activity were in Indochina, Afghanistan and Ethiopia. In 1980 alone, the report said, more than 1.2 million Afghans and 1.5 million Somalis fled their homes.*

*The report was critical of the Soviet Union because of its continuing intervention in Afghanistan and its repression of internal dissidents, such as academician Andrei D. Sakharov, who was forced from Moscow in 1980 to virtual house arrest in Gorky.* (Historic Documents of 1980, p. 103)

*The report was also critical of Vietnam for persistent human rights violations, including the use of labor camps for more than 50,000 political prisoners, the forced departure of nearly one million Vietnamese and 500,000 ethnic Chinese and repression of the Khmer people in Kampuchea.*

*Among Latin American countries, the report cited human rights violations in Nicaragua, Guatamala and El Salvador by rival political factions; and in Bolivia by a military regime that seized power in July 1980. Argentina was seen as improving its record, despite "virulent" unofficial anti-Semitism and some evidence of official repression as reported by former Buenos Aires publisher Jacobo Timerman.*

*The report said that in South Africa, notwithstanding both domestic and international criticism, "the basic structures of apartheid continue to operate much as before," disenfranchising the black majority. Further, defiant South African administration of Namibia and guerrilla opposition by the South West African People's Organization have produced human rights violations by both sides.*

*Following are excerpts from the State Department* Country Reports on Human Rights Practices, *dated February 2 and released February 9, 1981, by the House Committee on Foreign Affairs and the Senate Committee on Foreign Relations. (Boldface headings in brackets have been added by Congressional Quarterly to highlight the organization of the text.):*

## Overview

1980 saw a continuing decrease in violations of the integrity of the person — especially disappeared persons, torture, and cruel and inhuman treatment or punishment — in countries whose human rights records have been subject of intense international scrutiny and criticism in recent years. Millions of citizens in countries where free elections, due process of law, an independent judiciary, and a free press are firmly established continued to expect and enjoy full legal guarantees and protections of the integrity of the person. By contrast, there were major violations of human rights, especially those of politically engaged persons and non-combatants, in countries caught up in civil strife and armed conflict.

Reliable reports and credible allegations from many countries not normally in the spotlight of international attention indicate that torture and cruel punishment continued to be practiced in 1980, whether proscribed by law or not. In many countries, prison conditions were harsh, competent legal counsel was not available, preventive detention was imposed for long periods of time under martial law and other states of emergency, trials were closed, and the right of appeal was qualified or denied. These rights often were denied to persons suspected of or charged with various political offenses and crimes against the security of the state.

Oil price increases and inflation seriously undercut the already limited capability of most less-developed countries to fulfill the basic human needs of their populations in 1980. The social welfare programs of many other countries were similarly, if less drastically, affected. Economic rights continued to rank higher than political and civil liberties on the agenda of many countries, especially in the Third World.

These commitments notwithstanding, major obstacles to the achievement of economic rights remained. They included: limited natural resources; high population growth rates; unequal distribution of income and land; inefficient management of human and natural resources; insufficient trained manpower; civil strife and armed conflicts; and, in some countries, corruption.

1980 saw little overall change in the status of political and civil freedoms in the world. Governments continued wholly or partly to deny these rights to the great majority of people through the imposition of dominant or single party systems which eliminated or restricted political choice and activity; harassment, repression and proscription of opposition parties; government by decree under martial law regimes and other states of exception; restrictions on freedom of expression, inquiry, association, assembly and the media. Exceptions to this prevailing pattern were the return of several countries to elected, civilian government.

A major area of human rights concern is the burgeoning world refugee population. Over 15 million refugees have been generated in recent years by war, civil strife, national disasters and persecution. In 1980, alone, over 1.2 million Afghans and 1.5 million Somalis fled their homes. Although international and non-governmental organizations and the governments of most first asylum countries are attempting to find and strengthen measures for dealing with these issues, much work remains to be done.

Four other areas of human rights concern deserve mention because they adversely affect the welfare and rights of people in many parts of the world. These are the practice of child labor, the continuing existence of various forms of slavery and forced labor, the genital mutilation of young females, and the discrimination which migrant and guest workers from the less-developed world experience in some of the industrialized countries.

## [Institutions for Human Rights]

1980 saw continuing advances in the building of regional and international institutions for the protection of basic human rights. The creation of new bodies and the strengthening of existing ones reflect the growing recognition that human rights abuses are a legitimate subject of international concern. Over the long run, such institutions can make a vital contribution to the advancement of human freedoms.

Human rights issues remain prominently on the international agenda. The United Nations General Assembly's Third Committee on Human Rights adopted some 35 resolutions on human rights in 1980, several of which consolidated earlier advances on issues such as disappeared persons, mass exoduses, summary executions, United Nations fact-finding missions, and the upgrading of the Human Rights Division to a Center. The United Nations Human Rights Commission and Subcommission continued to make progress in developing and refining complaint and investigation procedures.

At a symposium in Baghdad in 1979, the Union of Arab Jurists addressed major human rights issues and, in its final communique, recommended that the Arab states ratify a draft Arab Covenant of Human Rights which would be submitted to Arab groups for comments and observations. In December 1980, a conference on "Human Rights in Islam" held in Kuwait brought together representatives from throughout the Islamic world. The conference was hosted by the Government of Kuwait and was sponsored by the International Commission of Jurists, the Union of Arab Lawyers, Kuwait University, and the Rockefeller Foundation.

In 1980, the European Commission on Human Rights and the European Court of Human Rights continued to hear and decide on cases involving violations of human rights in the twenty-two countries which are members of the Council of Europe. The Commission accepted for investigation approximately 350 individual complaints. In November, the Conference on Security and Cooperation in Europe (CSCE) review meeting got underway in Madrid to review compliance with the Helsinki Final Act and to consider new proposals to enhance cooperation in Europe in human rights, security and other areas. The Final Act commits signatory countries to provide their citizens with, among other things, basic civil and political liberties. During the pre-Christmas session of the CSCE meeting, participants repeatedly pointed out that the Soviet Union and some East European states had failed to live up to their obligation under the Final Act to assure these human rights. In addition, the Soviet Union was criticized for the banishment of Andrei Sakharov at a meeting on scientific cooperation in Hamburg which was attended by scientists from the 35 signatory countries of the Helsinki Final Act.

The Inter-American Human Rights Commission (IAHRC), under the auspices of the Organization of American States (OAS), continued its efforts to develop institutional and enforcement mechanisms for seeking compliance with human rights standards. In its annual report submitted to the OAS General Assembly in November, the IAHRC concluded that, while there have been positive developments in the observance of human rights in individual member states in 1980, there was no appreciable improvement in the overall human rights situation in Latin America. Specific reports on human rights developments in Chile, Paraguay, Uruguay and El Salvador were included. During 1980 the Commission issued special reports on Argentina and Haiti, based upon on-site observation missions made in 1979 and 1978, respectively. A third special report on political prisoners in Cuba was issued, based on information available to the Commission. During 1980, on-site observations were conducted in Colombia in April, and Nicaragua in October. In Colombia, the visit was conducted at the urgent invitation of the government and contributed to the satisfactory settlement of the occupation of the Dominican Republic Embassy in Bogota. The IAHRC also was requested by the Permanent Council of the OAS to examine the human rights situation in Bolivia following the military coup there in July which disrupted the democratic process then underway. The Bolivian government did not permit the IAHRC visit to take place.

Progress continued in 1980 toward strengthening basic human rights under the Organization of African Unity (OAU) framework. A committee of experts presented a draft Charter on Human Rights to an OAU Ministerial Conference in June. Review of the draft Charter continues and a second meeting to reach consensus is planned in 1981.

## [U.S. Human Rights Policy]

Mindful of both the progress achieved and the challenges that remain, this administration has implemented the Congressional directive of Section 502B of the Foreign Assistance Act, that "a principal goal of the foreign policy of the United States is to promote the increased observance of internationally recognized human rights. . . ." The body of United States human rights legislation created the framework upon which our policy is based.

Decisions on foreign assistance provided by the United States take human rights conditions into account. The transfer of police and military equipment is carefully reviewed in order to avoid identifying the United States with repressive practices. In addition, the human rights policy employs a varied mix of diplomatic tools: frank discussions with foreign officials; meetings with victims of human rights abuses; and, where private diplomacy is unavailing or unavailable, public statements of concern.

These instruments are applied in a manner that takes into account a country's history, culture, and current political environment and recognizes that human rights concerns must be balanced with other fundamental interests. Whatever the precise measure chosen in a particular situation, human rights issues are brought to the center stage of international relations where they must be addressed. In his 1980 State of the Union address, President Carter re-affirmed both America's commitment to the human rights policy and the contribution of this policy to world peace:

"We will continue to support the growth of democracy and human rights. When peoples and governments can approach their problems together — through open and democratic methods — the basis for stability and peace is far more solid and enduring.

"That is why our support for human rights in other countries is in our national interest as well as part of our national character."

## Argentina

... The human rights situation in Argentina improved in 1980, although serious problems remained. Most seriously, fundamental, internationally-recognized rights of the integrity of the person have been violated through the continued application by the security forces of the practice of disappearances, although at a level much lower than occurred in the first two years of the present military regime. In 1980, there were 28 or more reported disappearances; at least 12 have been credibly documented. Most observers believe torture and summary execution continue to be practiced in these cases.

The most carefully recorded and documented list of unexplained disappearances, compiled by the Permanent Assembly for Human Rights in Buenos Aires, contains about 5,600 cases for the period 1976 to 1979. Some estimates, however, run considerably higher. There is substantial evidence that most of those persons were abducted by the security forces and interrogated under torture. Many observers believe these persons have been summarily executed. There has been no accounting for past disappearances. . . .

The authorities have not yet accounted for the people who disappeared in the past. Government spokesmen have suggested that the bulk of the disappeared are dead. Noting the statements of former detainees who report that most of their fellows were executed, as well as lack of evidence to the contrary, most observers also believe that the great bulk of the disappeared are dead. . . .

The Argentine constitution requires that the president be a member of the Catholic Church, and the majority of Argentines profess this faith. Other religions are required to register with the government; all but the Jehovah's Witnesses are permitted to function, and there are substantial minority religious groups, including a 300,000-450,000 member Jewish community. The government publicly condemns religious prejudice.

Argentine Jews have well-developed community organizations, exercise their religion without restraints and participate fully in Argentine economic and cultural life. The government maintains correct relations with the Jewish community and there is no evidence of official anti-Semitic policy, although incidents of anti-Semitism occur. During the height of the "dirty war" there were credible reports of anti-Semitic behavior by the security forces and persecution of Jewish prisoners. Virulent anti-Semitic literature remains on sale in the country and openly anti-Semitic attitudes have been tolerated in state-controlled television. Several Jewish schools were bombed in July and August and more received anonymous threats. Though the culprits were never found, the government sought to reassure Argentine Jews. . . .

## Bolivia

...Since 1978, the frequency of changes of government has increased. Between July, 1978 and July 1980, there were three general national elections and four military coups. The latest such coup, led by army General Luis Garcia Meza Tejada on July 17, 1980, ousted the civilian government of interim President Lydia Gueiler. The coup also ended the progress that had been made in restoring constitutional democracy and destroyed the favorable human rights climate that characterized the transition from military to civilian government begun in 1977 by President Hugo Banzer.

Immediately upon seizing power, the Garcia Meza regime began a systematic campaign of oppression designed to gain control of the country and eliminate opposition. Hundreds of people were arrested and many were beaten and tortured. Some were killed. Pockets of resistance in the mines were eliminated by military force....

The government of President Lydia Gueiler respected Article 12 of the 1967 constitution which prohibits physical and mental torture. This is not true of the de facto regime headed by General Garcia Meza.

There are reliable reports by eyewitnesses of repeated and methodical beating of blindfolded prisoners by masked officials at the ministry of interior and at offices of the armed forces intelligence branch....

The Garcia Meza regime ... has systematically engaged in mental and physical abuse of political prisoners. There are reliable reports that persons were made to lie down in manure at the armed forces headquarters in La Paz after their arrests. American journalist Mary Helen Spooner was kept in a closet at the interior ministry in La Paz for several days without lights or windows and threatened with death unless she cooperated with her captors....

## El Salvador

El Salvador has long been dominated by powerful elites who ruled through the security forces. The elites' power rested in large landholdings and in the control of banking and the export of staple crops for their benefit. Faced with increasing demands for social change in the 1970s, traditional ruling groups continued their dominance by employing electoral fraud and repression. In the 1970's some political forces which were previously moderate, joined the radical left. The late 70's witnessed the emergence of an armed radical left. On October 15, 1979, a group of progressive military officers overthrew the regime of General Humberto Romero and created a civilian-military governing coalition called the Revolutionary Governing Junta (JRG). That Junta faced a highly polarized society in which the political process was discredited and a sizeable minority on both left and right employed violence to achieve their political ends....

The result of these contending forces has been a vicious cycle of provocation, outrage, and revenge which leaves a daily toll of murdered and often mutilated bodies on El Salvador's streets and highways. The Church has condemned the violence of left, right, and the security forces, affirming that the nation has reached the point where respect for human life no longer exists. Church institutions have been attacked and several clergy murdered, including the Archbishop of El Salvador, Oscar Romero, who many suspect to be a victim of the extreme right. . . .

## Nicaragua

During its first full year in power, the Government of National Reconstruction (GRN) has undertaken a number of ambitious policies to rebuild Nicaragua from the destruction left by the civil war of 1979 which overthrew the Somoza regime and to distribute economic wealth more evenly. The Nicaraguan government has publicly committed itself to respect human rights and has cooperated with visits by human rights organizations. However, the continued imprisonment without trial of over 5,000 political prisoners, the dubious standards of justice followed by special tribunals established to try the political prisoners, occasional reports of abuse of prisoners, and restrictions on freedom of the press and political assembly raise questions about the GRN's commitment to respect the human rights of all its citizens. . . .

There have been reports of physical abuse of prisoners during interrogation. The pro-FSLN newspaper *El Nuevo Diario* asserted on October 27, 1980, that there were reliable reports that torture was being used by police at the Palo Alto state security investigation center; other sources also allege that abuse of prisoners may take place at this center. There are credible reports of persons being seriously abused while held by the Department of State Security. Reportedly abused persons are obliged to sign statements that they have not been tortured and are threatened with severe retaliation if they should later claim to have been abused. . . .

There have been a few cases of prisoners "shot while attempting to escape" during 1980. Each of these cases occurred under circumstances which cast doubt on the veracity of the official version of the incidents. In one case, three victims reportedly died of single gunshot wounds to the head.

In November 1980, private sector leader Jorge Salazar was killed by Nicaraguan security forces, allegedly for gun-running and plots against the government. Salazar, by the government'a admission, was unarmed. Eyewitness accounts indicate that Salazar was shot in cold blood, differing with the government's account of an accidental shoot-out with his armed companion during an attempted arrest. . . .

The GRN established an entirely new judicial system when it came to power in July 1979, and created a body of laws which guarantees to all Nicaraguans an internationally-recognized standard of justice. The regular criminal and civil courts appear to function well.

The special tribunals, however, which try the political prisoners, are outside the normal judicial system. The GRN established these tribunals to deal with the over 7000 prisoners originally jailed for their association with the previous regime.

The special tribunals began functioning December 1979 and, by December 1980, they had initiated action on 4243 cases. Action has been completed on 2332 cases of which 152 resulted in acquittals. Of the 2180 persons convicted, two-thirds have been given prison sentences in excess of ten years. Thirty years is the maximum sentence under Nicaraguan law, and that sentence was given to approximately one-quarter of the persons convicted. Approximately one-third of the persons subject to the special tribunals have been freed prior to trial by the government prosecutor. In December, the government decreed pardons for 500 persons who had been convicted by the special tribunals. The pardons were recommended by the GRN-sponsored human rights commission and were intended to benefit persons under 18 and over 50, the infirm and women....

## Kampuchea

The central features of human rights in Kampuchea are the continuing violation by Vietnam of the Khmer nation's and people's right to national integrity and sovereignty, the repressive policies of both the Heng Samrin and Pol Pot contenders for power, and the thin margin of survival for most Khmer. Two hundred thousand Vietnamese troops continue to occupy and administer Kampuchea, two years after the invasion and overthrow of the brutally oppressive Pol Pot Democratic Kampuchea (DK) regime. Vietnamese forces and administrators stand above the law with respect to any and all human rights for the Khmer people. The Hanoi-controlled Heng Samrin administration has facilitated some resuscitation of normal Kampuchean life, but has been callous in providing basic food and medical needs to all but those Khmer who work directly within or around the administration Heng Samrin and his Vietnamese sponsors are attempting to construct.

Ordinary Khmer are left out, despite large-scale international relief donated to Kampuchea for their benefit. The Khmer people are caught between their fears of a restoration to power by the Pol Pot regime, of the dangers of associating or not associating with the fledgling Heng Samrin administration, and of the political and police network they see the Vietnamese erecting in Kampuchea....

## Philippines

Since declaring martial law in 1972, President Ferdinand E. Marcos has exercised virtually complete executive authority. He is both president and prime minister under the 1973 constitution, which calls for a transition to a parliamentary form of government. The Interim Legislative Assembly, elected in 1978, provides a forum for public debate on national issues. Its role, however, has been very limited, and major laws usually are enacted by presidential decree. . . . As the year ended, the government was preparing to lift martial law during January 1981. It was not clear how this would affect the exercise of civil and political liberties.

Civil and political rights are curtailed under martial law, although some restrictions have eased. In 1980, opposition activity increased among politicians, labor and students. Opposition candidates won a few posts in January provincial and municipal elections, the first held since 1971. Stimulated by the campaign and later by complaints of extensive vote fraud, opposition groups stepped up their public criticism, organized rallies and, in August, joined forces to issue a joint anti-martial-law statement. Labor and students held periodic demonstrations on economic and other issues as the year progressed. While these activities usually proceeded without interference, the government also sought to curb the momentum of unrest by selective arrests and detentions. . . .

The Philippines historically has had a highly skewed income distribution, with nearly 80 percent of the poor living in rural areas. Beneficiaries of development projects and land reform are raising their living standards. Landless laborers and farmers in the unirrigated highlands are the most disadvantaged groups. In recent years, inflation has eroded the purchasing power of low-income and middle-class families throughout the country. Largely because of low incomes, undernutrition is a common problem. In addition, there is a hardcore of first- and second-degree malnutrition. The percentages of children shown to have first- or second-degree malnutrition, while disturbing, may be overstated due to high growth standards chosen by the government. . . .

## Vietnam

Following the unification of North and South Vietnam under a Hanoi-based communist government in 1975, policies generating extensive human rights violations have been common in the Socialist Republic of Vietnam (SRV). In its effort to consolidate power the SRV meted out harsh sentences in prison-like conditions in "reeducation camps" to thousands of persons affiliated with the fallen regime of South Vietnam. By 1980 many lower-ranking officials of the former regime had been released, but probably at least 50,000 remain imprisoned in the labor camps. During the past five years the SRV government encouraged and at times coerced the departure of nearly one million Vietnamese, at least half of that number ethnic Chinese. At the Geneva conference on refugees in July 1979 Hanoi undertook to halt this flow of refugees and to cooperate with the United Nations Commissioner for Refugees (UNHCR) to organize a program for orderly legal departure. Progress has been slow in setting up the Orderly Departure Program and, although Hanoi generally has honored its pledge to stop the refugee flow, an average of 6,000 Vietnamese per month left the country clandestinely in 1980. Refugees have cited deteriorating economic conditions, repressive government controls, discrimination against Chinese, Catholics, and former officials of the South Vietnam regime, and stepped up military conscription as reasons for leaving. The increased conscription and the worsening social and economic conditions are in part the consequence of Vietnam's diversion of manpower and resources to its invasion and occupation of Kampuchea, an operation which has debilitated the already limited industrial and agricultural capability of the SRV. Corruption had an increasing impact upon life in Vietnam during the past year and affected the distribution of government services, ethnic discrimination, internal freedom of movement and emigration. Refugee accounts of government practices, although at times inconsistent, provide a reasonable pool of information about human rights trends in Vietnam....

## Afghanistan

Afghanistan, a poor and underdeveloped nation, has been torn by dissension and civil unrest since the April 1978 coup which overthrew President Daoud. In 1980, however, it suffered massive violations of its sovereignty and of the human rights of its citizens. In late December, 1979, the Soviet army entered Afghanistan in force and overthrew President Hafizullah Amin. In his place, the Soviets installed a regime headed by Babrak Karmal, who had followed the Soviet army into Afghanistan from his previous exile in Eastern Europe and the Soviet Union.

Today Afghanistan is a country torn by warfare. Some 85,000 Soviet troops and remnants of the Afghan army fight against spontaneous and nationwide resistance. The Afghan nationalists arrayed against them represent many different ethnic groups and beliefs. Afghan society as a whole remains highly conservative, Islamic, and traditional. The Babrek regime's base of support is limited to the Parchamist faction of the small People's Democratic Party of Afghanistan. It survives only under the protection of the Soviet occupiers....

Torture in prisons continues to be widely employed by Afghan authorities; evidence is furnished by surviving victims and other eyewitnesses. There are credible reports that Soviet advisors have been present during interrogation of prisoners where torture is alleged to have occurred. Other maltreatment is widespread, including beatings and sexual violations as well as incarcerations in jam-packed cells without heat, sanitary facilities or adequate food.

In the military conflict, torture appears to be used by all parties. Prisoners rarely are left alive on either side but frequently are subjected to torture and mutilation before being killed....

Summary execution of political prisoners continues under the Babrak regime, although much less frequently than under the Taraki and Amin governments. During these previous regimes, as many as 15,000 political prisoners were reported incarcerated in Kabul's Pol-i-Charki prison at one time, and executions numbered in the thousands.

Current estimates from reliable sources, including released foreign prisoners, puts the number of political prisoners somewhere between 3,000 and 9,000. . . .

Disappearance of citizens from their homes or from the streets continues under the current regime as it has in the past. When a citizen is arrested, he is frequently not heard from for months or longer, if ever. In addition to the disappearance of nationalists engaged in armed resistance to the current regime, people are presumed to disappear for political, economic, and religious reasons. Several cabinet ministers from the Amin government, businessmen and religious leaders are missing and widely believed either dead or in Pol-i-Charki prison. . . .

Legal emigration is more strictly controlled than under previous governments; for all intents and purposes, it is rendered impossible. Through December 1, 1980, however, a total of more than 1,300,000 Afghans escaped overland into Pakistan where they are now registered in refugee camps. Many thousands more (no reliable statistics exist) are in Iran and elsewhere. . . .

## South Korea

After some improvement in the earlier part of the year, the observance of civil and political rights in 1980 was marked by deterioration. The new government installed in September promised an easing of political restrictions it initiated but so far has placed considerable initial stress on "law and order." At the end of 1980, Korea remained under martial law with many basic political freedoms and rights suspended.

During the first four and one-half months of 1980 there was a marked improvement in the human rights climate. . . . By May, however, impatience of some groups with the political reform process, coupled with fears of the rising power of the military, led to massive student demonstrations in Seoul. The government responded on May 17 by declaring full martial law, dissolving the National Assembly, detaining some major political leaders, imposing strict press censorship, and banning all political activity. A student demonstration in Kwangju on May 18, and the heavy-handed military response to it, led to a virtual insurrection in that city that cost almost two hundred lives. . . .

# CHIEF JUSTICE ON CRIME
## February 8, 1981

*Chief Justice Warren E. Burger addressed the problems of crime and punishment in a speech to the American Bar Association (ABA) convention February 8 in Houston, Texas. Changing course from his earlier ABA appearances, where he customarily reported on the state of the judiciary, Burger warned that crime had created a "reign of terror in American cities" and that the judicial system had failed to deal with it.*

*Burger asked whether the judicial system afforded balanced protection for the rights of the accused and the rest of society. Statistics showed the system to be weighted heavily in favor of the offender, he said. The solution lay not in curing the ills of society but rather in deterrence — "swift arrest, prompt trial, certain penalty and — at some point — finality of judgment."*

*A true miscarriage of justice, he said, should always be open to review, "but the judicial process becomes a mockery of justice if it is forever open to appeals and retrials for errors in the arrest, the search or the trial. . . . Our search for true justice must not be twisted into an endless quest for technical errors unrelated to guilt or innocence."*

*In the United States, he continued, the criminal process can go on for years before the accused runs out of options. Even after sentence and confinement, the prisoner continues to file petitions and to bring suits against parole boards, wardens and judges. Burger said it was difficult to rehabilitate prisoners who were encouraged by the system to wage this continuing warfare with society.*

*Response to the chief justice's remarks was generally favorable. But a* New York Times *editorial February 11 pointed out that even the existing rate of arrests in the cities already was swamping the courts, delaying trials, crowding the prisons and frustrating the hope of deterrence. The* Times *stated that the main obstacle to effective change was the public's unwillingness to bear the costs, despite Burger's assertion that the war on crime was "as much a part of our national defense as the Pentagon budget."*

*Although Burger called for the "generous use of probation for first non-violent offenders," his proposals would send more people to prisons, where overcrowding already was a problem. (See court on double-celling, p. 477)*

*He called for extensive rehabilitation of penal institutions to provide a decent setting for expanded educational and vocational training, which would be mandatory for prisoners. Burger said he had spent his vacations for 25 years visiting prisons in other countries, as well as prisons in the United States. Some of the latter he said, were built 100 years ago for 800 prisoners but currently had "two thousand crowded ... inside their ancient walls."*

*Following are excerpts from Chief Justice Warren E. Burger's address to the American Bar Association, delivered February 8 in Houston, Texas.* (Boldface headings in brackets have been added by Congressional Quarterly to highlight the organization of the text.):

...I pondered long before deciding to concentrate today on this sensitive subject of crime, and I begin by reminding ourselves that under our enlightened Constitution and Bill of Rights, whose bicentennials we will soon celebrate, we have established a system of criminal justice that provides more protection, more safeguards, more guarantees for those accused of crime than any other nation in all history....

I put to you this question: Is a society redeemed if it provides massive safeguards for accused persons including pretrial freedom for most crimes, defense lawyers at public expense, trials, and appeals, retrials and more appeals — almost without end — and yet fails to provide elementary protection for its law-abiding citizens...?

For at least ten years many of our national leaders and those of other countries, have spoken of international terrorism, but our rate of routine, day-by-day terrorism in almost any large city exceeds the casualties of all the reported "international terrorists" in any given year.

Why do we show such indignation over alien terrorists and such tolerance for the domestic variety...?

What the American people want is that crime and criminals be brought under control so that we can be safe on the streets and in our homes and for our children to be safe in schools and at play. Today that safety is fragile.

It needs no more recital of the frightening facts and statistics to focus attention on the problem — a problem easier to define than to correct. We talk of having criminals make restitution or have the State compensate the victims. The first is largely unrealistic, the second is unlikely. Neither meets the central problem. Nothing will bring about swift changes in the terror that stalks our streets and endangers our homes, but I will make a few suggestions.

To do this I must go back over some history which may help explain our dilemma.

For a quarter of a century I regularly spent my vacations visiting courts and prisons in other countries, chiefly Western Europe. My mentors in this educational process were two of the outstanding penologists of our time: the late James V. Bennett, Director of the United States Bureau of Prisons and the late Torsten Ericksson, his counterpart in Sweden, where crime rates were once low, poverty was non-existent, correctional systems enlightened and humane. Each was a vigorous advocate of using prisons for educational and vocational training.

## [Poverty and Crime]

I shared and still share with them the belief that poverty and unemployment are reflected in crime rates — chiefly crimes against property. But if poverty were the principal cause of crime as was the easy explanation given for so many years, crime would have been almost non-existent in affluent Sweden and very high in Spain and Portugal. But the hard facts simply did not and do not support the easy claims that poverty is the controlling factor; it is just one factor. America's crime rate today exceeds our crime rate during the great depression.

We must not be misled by cliches and slogans that if we but abolish poverty crime will also disappear. There is more to it than that. A far greater factor is the deterrent effect of swift and certain consequences: swift arrest, prompt trial, certain penalty, and — at some point — finality of judgment.

To speak of crime in America and not mention the drugs and drug-related crime would be an oversight of large dimension. The destruction of lives by drugs is more frightening than all the homicides we suffer. . . .

Deterrence is the primary core of any effective response to the reign of terror in American cities. Deterrence means speedy action by society, but that process runs up against the reality that many large cities have either reduced their police forces or failed to keep them in balance with double-digit crime inflation. . . .

## ['True Justice']

To change this melancholy picture will call for spending more money than we have ever before devoted to law enforcement, and even this will be for naught if we do not re-examine our judicial process and philosophy with respect to finality of judgments. The search for "perfect" justice has led us on a course found nowhere else in the world. A true miscarriage of justice, whether 20-, 30- or 40-years old, should always be open to review, but the judicial process becomes a mockery of justice if it is forever open to appeals and retrials for errors in the arrest, the search or the trial. Traditional appellate review is the cure for errors, but we have forgotten that simple truth.

Our search for true justice must not be twisted into an endless quest for technical errors unrelated to guilt or innocence. . . .

I am not advocating a new idea but merely restating an old one that we have ignored. At this point, judicial discretion and judicial restraint require me to stop and simply to repeat that governments were instituted and exist chiefly to protect people. If governments fail in this basic duty they are not excused, they are not redeemed by showing that they have established the most perfect systems to protect the claims of defendants in criminal cases. A government that fails to protect both the rights of accused persons and also all other people has failed in its mission. I leave it to you whether the balance has been fairly struck.

Let me now try to place this in perspective: first, the bail reform statutes of recent years, especially as to non-violent crimes, were desirable and overdue; second, the provisions for a lawyer for every defendant were desirable and overdue; third, statutes to insure speedy trials are desirable but only if the same legislation provides the means to accomplish the objective.

Many enlightened countries succeed in holding criminal trials within four to eight weeks after arrest. First non-violent offenders are generally placed on probation, free to return to a gainful occupation under close supervision. But I hardly need remind this audience that our criminal process often goes on two, three, four or more years before the accused runs out all the options. Even after sentence and confinement, the warfare continues with endless streams of petitions for writs, suits against parole boards, wardens and judges.

## [Rehabilitation of Prisoners]

So we see a paradox — even while we struggle toward correction, education and rehabilitation of the offender, our system encourages prisoners to continue warfare with society. The result is that whatever may have been the defendant's hostility toward the police, the witnesses, the prosecutors, the judge and jurors — and the public defender who failed to win his case — those hostilities are kept alive. How much chance do you think there is of changing or rehabilitating a person who is encouraged to keep up years of constant warfare with society?

The dismal failure of our system to stem the flood of crime repeaters is reflected in part in the massive number of those who go in and out of prisons. In a Nation that has been thought to be the world leader in so many areas of human activity our system of justice — not simply the prisons — produces the world's highest rate of "recall" for those who are processed through it. How long can we tolerate this rate of recall and the devastation it produces?

What I suggest now . . . is a "damage control program." It will be long; it will be controversial; it will be costly — but less costly than the billions in dollars and thousands of blighted lives now hostage to crime.

To do this is as much a part of our national defense as the Pentagon budget.

Sometimes we speak glibly of a "war on crime." A war is indeed being waged but it is a war by a small segment of society against the whole of society. Now a word of caution: That "war" will not be won simply by harsher sentences; not by harsh mandatory minimum sentence statutes; not by abandoning the historic guarantees of the Bill of Rights. And perhaps, above all, it will not be accomplished by self-appointed armed citizen police patrols. At age 200, this country has outgrown the idea of private law and vigilantes. . . .

Now let me present the ultimate paradox: After society has spent years and often a modest fortune to put just one person behind bars, we become bored. The media loses interest and the individual is forgotten. Our humanitarian concern evaporates. In all but a minority of the States we confine the person in an overcrowded, understaffed institution with little or no library facilities, little if any educational program or vocational training. I have visited American prisons built more than 100 years ago for 800 prisoners, but with two thousand crowded today inside their ancient walls.

Should you look at the records you will find that the 300,000 persons now confined in penal institutions are heavily weighted with offenders under age 30. A majority of them cannot meet minimum standards of reading, writing and arithmetic. . . .

Now turn with me to a few steps which ought to be considered:

(1) Restore to all pretrial release laws the crucial element of dangerousness to the community based on a combination of the evidence then available and the defendant's past record, to deter crime-while-on-bail;

(2) Provide for trial within weeks of arrest for most cases, except for extraordinary cause shown;

(3) Priority for review on appeal within eight weeks of a judgment of guilt;

(4) Following exhaustion of appellate review, confine all subsequent judicial review to claims of miscarriage of justice;

and finally:

A. We must accept the reality that to confine offenders behind walls without trying to change them is an expensive folly with short term benefits — a "winning of battles while losing the war";

B. Provide for generous use of probation for first non-violent offenders, with intensive supervision and counseling and swift revocation if probation terms are violated;

C. A broad scale program of physical rehabilitation of the penal institutions to provide a decent setting for expanded educational and vocational training;

D. Make all vocational and educational programs mandatory with credit against the sentence for educational progress — literally a program to "learn the way out of prison," so that no prisoner leaves without at least being able to read, write, do basic arithmetic and have a marketable skill;

E. Generous family visitation in decent surroundings to maintain family ties, with rigid security to exclude drugs or weapons;

F. Counseling services after release.... All this should be aimed at developing the prisoner's respect for self, respect for others, accountability for conduct and appreciation of the value of work, of thrift and of family.

G. Encourage religious groups to give counsel on ethical behavior and occupational adjustment during and after confinement.

...A good many responsible qualified observers are reaching the stage that we must now accept the harsh truth that there may be some incorrigible human beings who cannot be changed except by God's own mercy to that one person. But we cannot yet be certain and in our own interest — in the interest of billions in dollars lost to crime and blighted if not destroyed lives — we must try to deter and try to cure.

This will be costly in the short run and the short run will not be brief. This illness our society suffers has been generations in developing, but we should begin at once to divert the next generation from the dismal paths of the past, to inculcate a sense of personal accountability in each schoolchild to the end that our homes, schools and streets will be safe for all.

# CONVICTION OF GARWOOD
# AS COLLABORATOR WITH ENEMY
## February 5-16, 1981

*Marine Corps Pfc. Robert R. Garwood, 34, was found guilty of collaborating with the enemy and of assaulting a fellow soldier while a prisoner of war in Vietnam. He thus became the only Vietnam prisoner of war to be tried by court-martial on collaboration charges and the first to be convicted on such charges since the Korean War.*

*Garwood, a native of Indiana, was a 19-year-old jeep driver when he disappeared near Danang, South Vietnam, in September 1965. He was not seen again by Americans until 1967 when other prisoners of war were taken to the camp where Garwood was being held. He surfaced in a Hanoi hotel early in 1979, when he passed a note to Ossi J. Rahkonen, a Finnish official of the World Bank. The note said: "I am an American in Vietnam. Are you interested?" In a short conversation, Garwood told Rahkonen that he had escaped from a forced labor camp about 100 miles northwest of Hanoi and had made his way to the hotel while the Vietnamese celebrated Tet. Rahkonen turned the note over to the State Department, and Garwood was returned to the United States in March 1979.*

*After a two-and-a-half-months-long trial, Garwood was convicted February 5 by a jury of five Marine Corps officers. On February 16 the same jury passed sentence, reducing his rank to private, depriving him of some back pay and giving him a dishonorable discharge. He had faced a possible life term.*

## Testimony

*Nine fellow former prisoners of war testified that Garwood dressed like a North Vietnamese soldier, lived with the enemy guards and carried a*

*Soviet-made rifle. They alleged that he interrogated and guarded prisoners, informed on them and urged them to collaborate with the enemy.*

*Defense attorneys did not deny that Garwood had lived with his captors, but said that coercive persuasion (brainwashing), torture and deprivation had left Garwood unable to understand the criminality of his acts. Defense psychiatrist Dr. Robert Rollins testified that Garwood was driven insane by watching the execution of South Vietnamese prisoners, some of whom had been forced to play Russian roulette. "He was not an emotionally strong person to begin with," Rollins said. "He was isolated. He was wounded. He saw people tortured and executed, and he was powerless physically."*

## Code of Conduct

*The case was viewed by legal experts as a test of the Code of Military Conduct, rules adopted by the armed services in 1955 to encourage high standards of conduct by American prisoners of war. Under the code American prisoners were required to resist cooperation with the enemy and to provide only name, rank, serial number and date of birth.*

*Some argued that prisoners subjected to extreme conditions of captivity could not be expected to distinguish between proper and improper conduct. Others pointed out that teen-aged soldiers are not trained to deal with torture and imprisonment.*

*Following are the texts of the charges brought against Pfc. Robert R. Garwood at his court-martial and a statement read by Capt. Lewis Olshin February 13, 1981, as it appeared in* The New York Times:

# CHARGES AGAINST GARWOOD

### Charge I: Violation of the Uniform Code Of Military Justice, Article 82

Specification: In that Private First Class Robert R. GARWOOD, U.S. Marine Corps, Sub Unit #2, Headquarters Company, Headquarters Battalion, Marine Corps Base, Camp Lejeune, North Carolina, on active duty, did, in the Republic of Vietnam, an area outside the territorial jurisdiction of the United States, on several occasions during the period from about March 1968 until about October 1969, by approaching the perimeter of front lines near American fire support bases in an area then known as the "I" Corps Area, and speaking through a bullhorn/megaphone requesting United States combat forces to throw down their weapons and to refuse to fight during combat operations against a hostile enemy force, and by appealing to United States troops in the field urging them to defect; solicit those forces to commit an act of misbehavior before the enemy in violation of Article 99, Uniform Code of Military Justice.

## Charge II: Violation of the Uniform Code Of Military Justice, Article 85

Specification: In that Private First Class Robert R. GARWOOD, U.S. Marine Corps, Sub Unit #2, Headquarters Company, Headquarters Battalion, Marine Corps Base, Camp Lejeune, North Carolina, on active duty, did, on or about 28 September 1965, in time of war, without authority and with intent to remain away therefrom permanently, absent himself from his unit, to wit: Service Company, Headquarters Battalion, 3d Marine Division, located in the Republic of Vietnam, and did remain so absent in desertion until on or about 22 March 1979.

## Charge III: Violation of the Uniform Code Of Military Justice, Article 104

Specification: In that Private First Class Robert R. GARWOOD, U.S. Marine Corps, Sub Unit #2, Headquarters Company, Headquarters Battalion, Marine Corps Base, Camp Lejeune, North Carolina, on active duty, did, in the Republic of Vietnam, an area outside the territorial jurisdiction of the United States, during the period from about April 1967, until on or about 27 January 1973, without proper authority, knowingly communicate and hold intercourse with the enemy by wearing the uniform of the enemy, carrying arms, and accepting a position in the armed forces of an enemy of the United States, to wit: the Democratic Republic of Vietnam; and by acting: (1) as an interpreter or assistant interpreter during political indoctrination classes conducted in the prisoner of war camps; (2) as an informer to the enemy captors regarding: complaints of prisoners of war about work details, feelings of prisoners of war toward their enemy guards; and the activities and attitudes of prisoners of war; (3) as an interrogator of prisoners of war upon their initial entry into camp, and on other occasions, by questioning them about their former units; the location of military units and types of weaponry; general attitudes of prisoners of war; any potential dissenters among the prisoners of war; and escape plans of any prisoners of war; (4) as an indoctrinator during classes and small-group indoctrination as a part of the camp political course which included extolling the virtues of Communist dogma and the National Liberation Front, by acting therein as a group discussion leader, a speechmaker, and an assistant indoctrinator to camp cadre; by personally conducting indoctrination sessions of prisoners of war, teaching them Vietnamese terminology and language, posing to them the opportunity to "cross over" and its benefits and the possibility of pardon and early release in exchange for strict obedience to camp rules and regulations, and ascribing to them the terms mercenaries and criminals of war; (5) as a guard while posted in a

199

guard hut; by escorting prisoners of war to and inside prisoner of war camps; by escorting prisoners of war outside said camps on wood and food runs; armed on each of these occasions; for said enemy forces during the interrogation, indoctrination, and internment of members of United States armed forces held by the said enemy as prisoners of war.

### Charge IV: Violation of the Uniform Code
### Of Military Justice, Article 105.

Specification 1: In that Private First Class Robert R. GARWOOD, U.S. Marine Corps, Sub Unit #2, Headquarters Company, Headquarters Battalion, Marine Corps Base, Camp Lejeune, North Carolina, on active duty, did, in the Republic of Vietnam, an area outside the territorial jurisdiction of the United States, during the period from about June 1968 until about December 1968, while in the hands of the enemy and in a position of authority over all other prisoners of war at detention camp number two, as a member of the enemy force maintaining and controlling the detention camp, maltreat Private First Class David N. HARKER, U.S. Army, a prisoner of war, by striking him in the ribs with his hand, without justifiable cause.

Specification 2: In that Private First Class Robert R. GARWOOD, U.S. Marine Corps, Sub Unit #2, Headquarters Company, Headquarters Battalion, Marine Corps Base, Camp Lejeune, North Carolina, on active duty, in the Republic of Vietnam, an area outside the territorial jurisdiction of the United States, during the period from about September 1968 until November 1968, while in the hands of the enemy and in a position of authority over other prisoners of war at detention camp number two, as a member of the enemy force maintaining and controlling the detention camp, did maltreat First Sergeant Richard F. WILLIAMS, U.S. Army, a prisoner of war, by saying to him, "I spit on you and all people like you disgust me," and "You're in the military only for the retirement, blood money made off Vietnamese people," or words to that effect, without justifiable cause.

# OLSHIN STATEMENT

Pfc. Garwood has heard the testimony of the American P.O.W.'s concerning what occurred from 1967 to 1969, and he accepts that as their honest and sincere rendition of what occurred. He has also heard the explanation of the psychiatrists and he accepts their explanation as to what occurred there, for he himself cannot explain to himself what occurred in Vietnam 12 years ago and believes he would never knowingly violate the law in the ways charged.

As best as Pfc. Garwood can reconstruct his past, he assures the court that he maintains his loyalty to his country. Pfc. Garwood began his 14-

year odyssey in Vietnam in September 1965 with his belief in both his loyalty to the Marine Corps and his loyalty to his country; he assures the court that the judicial process has strengthened his loyalty in both the Marine Corps and his country. Pfc. Garwood had hoped to be acquitted of these charges and to be allowed to continue to serve his country; however, he realizes that with this conviction his ability to stay in the Marine Corps has ended. He recognizes from talking to all the psychiatrists, both for the defense and the Government, that he is presently ill from causes which he does not understand and for which he will need and will seek psychiatric care.

Pfc. Garwood would like to assure the members that he is loyal to the Marine Corps, and has tried, throughout this trial, to conduct himself with dignity and in a manner which would not bring discredit upon the Marine Corps. To this end, he has specifically instructed his lawyers not to say anything which anyone would construe as being derogatory toward the United States Marine Corps.

As the members have learned during his trial, he has virtually no formal education and no skills. He will start at the bottom of the heap when he leaves the Marine Corps, and with the help of his doctors, lawyers and family, he hopes he will get well, get work, settle down and make everyone, especially Donna [Garwood's fiancée] and their two boys, proud of him.

He does not know how to explain what occurred in Vietnam 14 years ago; and, he does not know what anyone can say to explain the 14 years he erased from his life in Vietnam. He knows the experience he had in Vietnam will live with him forever and, together with his conviction, will leave marks upon him for the rest of his life.

In many ways, the two years since his freedom from Vietnam have been a punishment due to the attention and notoriety; the ridicule suffered by his family; and the fact that he and his family will have to live with this conviction and the mark upon their name that this conviction and the media attention has caused.

He asks the court to take into consideration after his many years of this trial, his need for the continued support from people other than his doctors and lawyers. He has found this support through Donna and her two sons, Butch and D. J. They need each other at this time in their lives. Naturally, Pfc. Garwood did not know them until he arrived in Jacksonville, N.C. But perhaps if there has been any good come from this trial, he asks this court to allow him to maintain this relationship and to permit their shattered lives the chance to heal by working together as one family.

Pfc. Garwood hopes that through the evidence the court has heard in sentencing, the court has found the humanity within him which will allow the court to return him to the people he loves.

# POPE'S JOURNEY TO THE FAR EAST
## February 15-26, 1981

*Pope John Paul II, leader of the Roman Catholic Church, made his first journey to the Far East in February, covering 20,500 miles in 12 days. Starting with a brief stopover in Karachi, Pakistan, February 16, the pope spent six days in the Philippines, the only predominantly Catholic country in Asia, and three days in Japan. Ten years earlier Pope Paul VI, the first pontiff to visit the Philippines, was wounded by a knife-wielding Bolivian.* (Shooting of John Paul II, p. 427)

*By visiting the Philippines, John Paul II stepped into a long-standing controversy between the authoritarian government of President Ferdinand E. Marcos and the church, symbolized by the opposition of Cardinal Jaime Sin, the archbishop of Manila. Eight of the 99 bishops of the Philippines had opposed the pope's visit, fearing that it would be seen as an endorsement of Marcos' regime.*

*Sin had opposed construction of a basilica that Imelda Marcos, the president's wife, had ordered for the pope's visit. The $100 million church, which would have held 40,000 people, was to feature a 48-foot statue of the infant Jesus. In a letter to Mrs. Marcos, Sin said he could not endorse so costly a project while most Filipinos live in poverty. President Marcos then halted the project.*

*In the Philippines the church itself was sharply divided between those who wanted it to devote itself to a purely spiritual mission and those who wanted it to be a force for social justice. The pope managed to walk a fine line between the factions. Reminding the priests and nuns that their duty is to God, he insisted that human institutions must serve man.*

## Human Rights and Poverty

*The pope was not reticent in speaking out against human rights abuses and poverty in the country. In his address at the presidential palace, Malacanang, with President and Mrs. Marcos by his side, the pope said that ". . .one can never justify any violation of the fundamental dignity of the human person or of the basic rights that safeguard this dignity."*

*Marcos, perhaps in preparation for the papal visit, ended eight years of martial law January 17. Re-elected to a six-year term June 16, 1981, he had been president since 1965.*

*Speaking at Tondo, a Manila slum, the pope chose as his theme the first Beatitude, "Blessed are the poor in spirit." The human rights of the poor must be cherished and protected, he said, and the poor must not turn to violence, class struggle or hate to bring about true liberation.*

*At Bacolod, where tensions between sugar plantation owners and workers had been high, the pope urged the owners and workers to unite in their common love for the land. He told the owners that they should not be guided by "the selfish accumulation of goods, but by the demands of justice and by the moral imperative of contributing to a decent standard of living" for the workers. The pope later made some of the same points in an encyclical on work. (Encyclical, p. 695)*

## Messages to China and Japan

*In a February 18 speech to Chinese Catholics living in the Philippines, the pope called upon China to re-establish friendly relations with the church. Diplomatic relations were broken after the communist takeover in 1949, and Peking had refused to resume them unless the Vatican broke its ties to Taiwan. In his talk, broadcast to the Asian mainland, the pope said that there was no conflict in being at the same time "truly Christian and authentically Chinese."*

*In the first papal visit to Japan, John Paul II chose to speak at Hiroshima, where the first atomic bomb was dropped in combat on August 6, 1945, destroying the city and killing more than 100,000 people. At the Hiroshima Peace Memorial February 25 the pope made a strong plea for world peace. "To remember the past is to commit oneself to the future," he said, asking the heads of state to forsake war and to work untiringly for disarmament.*

*The same day the pope spoke at the United Nations University in Hiroshima on the responsibility of modern science. Our future on this planet depends on a single factor, he said. "Humanity must make a moral about-face . . . and take a major step forward in civilization and wisdom." He urged his audience to avoid pursuing technological development for its own sake, subjecting it only to the test of economic usefulness and using it to pursue or maintain power. Science and technology find their justification in service to mankind, he said.*

*The pope ended his trip February 26 with the celebration of mass and the ordination of 15 priests in Nagasaki.*

*Following are excerpts from Pope John Paul II's address to Philippine government officials at Malacanang Palace, February 17; from his speech to the people of Tondo, Manila, February 18; from his address to plantation owners and workers at Bacolod, Philippines, February 20; from his speech at Peace Memorial Park, Hiroshima, Japan, February 25; and from his address at United Nations University, Hiroshima, Japan, February 25:*

# ADDRESS AT MALACANANG PALACE

2. ... The Philippine nation is deserving of particular honor since, from the beginning of its Christianization, from the moment that Magellan planted the cross in Cebu 460 years ago, on April 15, 1521, all through the centuries its people have remained true to the Christian faith. In an achievement that remains unparalleled in history, the message of Christ took root in the hearts of the people within a very brief span of time and the church was thus strongly implanted in this nation of 7,000 islands and numerous tribal and ethnic communities. ...

3. Due homage must be paid to this achievement of the Filipino people, but what you are also creates an obligation and it confers upon the nation a specific mission. A country that has kept the Catholic faith strong and vibrant through the vicissitudes of its history, the sole nation in Asia that is approximately 90 percent Christian, assumes by this very fact the obligation not only to preserve its Christian heritage but to bear witness to the values of its Christian culture before the whole world. ...

5. ... It is the joint effort of all the citizens that builds a truly sovereign nation, where not only the legitimate material interests of the citizens are promoted and protected, but also their spiritual aspirations that may at times arise; one can never justify any violation of the fundamental dignity of the human person or of the basic rights that safeguard this dignity. Legitimate concern for the security of a nation, as demanded by the common good, could lead to the temptation of subjugating to the state the human being and his or her dignity and rights. Any apparent conflict between the exigencies of security and of the citizens' basic rights must be resolved according to the fundamental principle — upheld always by the church — that social organization exists only for the service of man and for the protection of his dignity, and that it cannot claim to serve the common good when human rights are not safeguarded. People will have faith in the safeguarding of their security and the promotion of their well-being only to

the extent that they feel truly involved and supported in their very humanity....

# ADDRESS AT TONDO

... 4. Blessed are the poor in spirit. This is the opening statement of the Sermon on the Mount, in which Jesus proclaimed the Beatitudes as the program for all who want to follow him. The Beatitudes were meant not only for the people of his own day but for all generations throughout the ages; they are an invitation to everyone who accepts the name of Christian.... This is the message that I present to rich and poor alike, the message that the church in the Philippines, as elsewhere, must make her own and put into practice. Any church that wants to be a church of the poor must heed this challenge, discover its full depth and implement its full truth.

Here in Tondo, and in other parts of this land, there are many poor people and in them I also see the poor in spirit whom Jesus called blessed....

5. Being poor in spirit does not mean being unconcerned with the problems that beset the community, and nobody has a keener sense of justice than the poor people who suffer the injustices that circumstances and human selfishness heap upon them. Finding strength in human solidarity, the poor by their very existence indicate the obligation of justice that confronts society and all who have power, whether economic, cultural or political. And so it is the same truth of the first Beatitude that indicates a path that every person must walk. It tells those that live in material poverty that their dignity, their human dignity, must be preserved, that their inviolable human rights must be cherished and protected. It also tells them that they themselves can achieve much if they pool their skills and talents and especially their determination to be the artisans of their own progress and development.

The first Beatitude tells the rich, who enjoy material well-being or who accumulate a disproportionate share of material goods, that man is great not by reason of what he possesses but by what he is — not by what he has but by what he shares with others....

6. The church herself, the church in Asia, in the Philippines and in Tondo, will heed the call of the Beatitudes and be the church of the poor because she must do what Jesus did and proclaim the Gospel to the poor (cf. Lk. 4:18). But the preference that the church shows for the poor and underprivileged does not mean that she directs her concern only to one group or class or category. She preaches the same message to all: that God loves man and sent his Son for the salvation of all, that Jesus Christ is the savior, "the way, and the truth, and the life" (Jn. 14:6). Being the church of the poor means that she will speak the language of the Beatitudes to all people, to all groups or professions, to all ideologies, to all political and

economic systems. She does so not to serve political interests, nor to acquire power, nor to offer pretexts for violence, but to save man in his humanity and in this supernatural destiny....

7. My dear friends of Tondo, be faithful to Christ and joyfully embrace his Gospel of salvation. Do not be tempted by ideologies that preach only material values or purely temporal ideals, which separate political, social and economic development from the things of the spirit and in which happiness is sought apart from Christ. The road toward your total liberation is not the way of violence, class struggle or hate; ...

# ADDRESS AT BACOLOD

...5. I have been told that many of you here present are connected with the agricultural sector and more specificaly with the sugar cane cultivation, either as landowners, planters or laborers. You all live close to the land and the land provides your livelihood. To all of you I would address some special words in order to apply to you and your particular situation the social message of the church.

You love the land, you cherish the fertile plains. You belong to this land and this land belongs to you. I myself have always been close to nature and I understand your attachment to your rural setting.... In his gratuitous love, God did not only create man and woman, but he gave them the earth so that human life could be sustained through their efforts. From the beginning, and for the benefit of all, God has willed the interaction of land and labor so that the full dignity of man may always be protected and promoted....

...6. A truly Christian challenge is therefore presented to those that own or control the land. I know that many of you who are plantation owners or who are planters are truly concerned with the welfare of your workers, but the church, aware of her responsibilities, feels impelled to hold up before you again and again the ideal of love and justice and to encourage you to compare constantly your actions and attitudes with the ethical principles regarding the priority of the common good and regarding the social purpose of economic activity. The right of ownership is legitimate in itself but it cannot be separated from its wider social dimension....

The landowners and the planters should therefore not let themselves be guided in the first place by the economic laws of growth and gain, nor by the demands of competition or the selfish accumulation of goods, but by the demands of justice and by the moral imperative of contributing to a decent standard of living and to working conditions which make it possible for the workers and for the rural society to live a life that is truly human and to see all their fundamental rights respected....

...7. To all the sugar cane workers I say, as I say to all workers everywhere: Never forget the great dignity that God has granted you, never let your work degrade you but remember always the mission that God has entrusted to you: to be, by the work of your hands, his collaborators in the continuation of the work of creation. See in your work a labor of love, for your daily work expresses love for your dear ones and your commitment to the well-being of your family. Be proud to be workers of the land.

At the same time, know that the church supports you in your endeavors to have your rights as workers respected. Ninety years ago already, the great social encyclical *Rerum Novarum* spelled out very clearly that the worker is entitled to wages that give him a just share in the wealth he helps to produce, and that working conditions should be geared not to the ever increasing economic profit of the enterprise but to the inviolable dignity of man as an individual, as a provider for his family and as a builder of the society to which he belongs. It has been the constant teaching of the church that workers have a right to unite in free associations for the purpose of defending their interest and contributing as responsible partners to the common good. Such associations should be protected by appropriate laws which, rather that [sic] restrict their activities, should guarantee the free pursuit of the social welfare of all their members and of the workers in general. . . .

# ADDRESS AT HIROSHIMA

War is the work of man. War is destruction of human life. War is death.

Nowhere do these truths impose themselves upon us more forcefully than in this city of Hiroshima, at this peace memorial. Two cities will forever have their names linked together, two Japanese cities, Hiroshima and Nagasaki, as the only cities in the world that have had the ill fortune to be a reminder that man is capable of destruction beyond belief. Their names will forever stand out as the names of the only cities in our time that have been singled out as a warning to future generations that war can destroy human efforts to build a world of peace. . . .

4. To remember the past is to commit oneself to the future. To remember Hiroshima is to abhor nuclear war. To remember Hiroshima is to commit oneself to peace. To remember what the people of this city suffered is to renew our faith in man, in his capacity to do what is good, in his freedom to choose what is right, in his determination to turn disaster into a new beginning. In the face of the man-made calamity that every war is, one must affirm and reaffirm, again and again, that the waging of war is not inevitable or unchangeable. Humanity is not destined to self-destruction.

Clashes of ideologies, aspirations and needs can and must be settled and resolved by means other than war and violence. Humanity owes it to itself to settle differences and conflicts by peaceful means. The great spectrum of problems facing the many peoples in varying stages of cultural, social, economic and political development gives rise to international tension and conflict. It is vital for humanity that these problems should be solved in accordance with ethical principles of equity and justice enshrined in meaningful agreements and institutions. The international community should thus give itself a system of law that will regulate international relations and maintain peace, just as the rule of law protects national order.

5. Those who cherish life on earth must encourage governments and decision makers in the economic and social fields to act in harmony with the demands of peace rather than out of narrow self-interest. Peace must always be the aim: peace pursued and protected in all circumstances. Let us not repeat the past, a past of violence and destruction. Let us embark upon the steep and difficult path of peace, the only path that befits human dignity, the only path that leads to the true fulfillment of the human destiny, the only path to a future in which equity, justice and solidarity are realities and not just distant dreams.

6. And so, on this very spot where 35 years ago the life of so many people was snuffed out in one fiery moment, I wish to appeal to the whole world on behalf of life, on behalf of humanity, on behalf of the future.

To the heads of state and of government, to those who hold political and economic power, I say: Let us pledge ourselves to peace through justice; let us take a solemn decision, now, that war will never be tolerated or sought as a means of resolving differences; let us promise our fellow human beings that we will work untiringly for disarmament and the banishing of all nuclear weapons; let us replace violence and hate with confidence and caring.

To every man and woman in this land and in the world I say: Let us assume responsibility for each other and for the future without being limited by frontiers and social distinctions; let us educate ourselves and educate others in the ways of peace; let humanity never become the victim of a struggle between competing systems; let there never be another war.

To young people everywhere I say: Let us together create a new future of fraternity and solidarity; let us reach out toward our brothers and sisters in need, feed the hungry, shelter the homeless, free the downtrodden, bring justice where injustice reigns and peace where only weapons speak. Your young hearts have an extraordinary capacity for goodness and love. Put them at the service of your fellow human beings.

To everyone I repeat the words of the prophet: "They shall beat their swords into plowshares and their spears into pruning hooks. Nation shall not lift up sword against nation, neither shall they learn war any more" (Is. 2:4). . . .

# ADDRESS AT U.N. UNIVERSITY

. . . 3. Ladies and gentlemen, you who devote your lives to the modern sciences, you are the first to be able to evaluate the disaster that a nuclear war would inflict on the human family. And I know that ever since the explosion of the first atomic bomb many of you have been anxiously wondering about the responsibility of modern science and of the technology that is the fruit of that science. In a number of countries, associations of scholars and research workers express the anxiety of the scientific world in the face of an irresponsible use of science, which too often does grievous damage to the balance of nature or brings with it the ruin and oppression of man by man. One thinks in the first place of physics, chemistry, biology and the genetical sciences, of which you rightly condemn those applications or experimentations which are detrimental to humanity.

But one also has in mind the social sciences and the human behavioral sciences when they are utilized to manipulate people, to crush their minds, souls, dignity and freedom. Criticism of science and technology is sometimes so severe that it comes close to condemning science itself. On the contrary, science and technology are a wonderful product of a God-given human creativity, since they have provided us with wonderful possibilities and we all gratefully benefit from them. But we know that this potential is not a neutral one: It can be used either for man's progress or for his degradation. . . .

6. Our future on this planet, exposed as it is to nuclear annihilation, depends upon one single factor: Humanity must make a moral about-face. At the present moment of history there must be a general mobilization of all men and women of good will. Humanity is being called upon to take a major step forward in civilization and wisdom. A lack of civilization, an ignorance of man's true values, brings the risk that humanity will be destroyed. We must become wiser. . . .

9. Science and technology have always formed part of man's culture, but today we are witnessing the speedily increasing growth of a technology which seems to have destroyed its equilibrium with the dimensions of culture by acting as an element of division. Such is the great problem facing modern society. Science and technology are the most dynamic factors of the development of society today, but their intrinsic limitations do not make them capable, by themselves, of providing a power that will bind culture together. How then can a culture absorb science and technology, with their dynamism, without losing its own identity?

There are three temptations to be avoided in this regard. The first is the temptation to pursue technological development for its own sake, the sort of development that has for its only norm that of its own growth and affirmation, as if it were a matter of an independent reality in between nature and a reality that is properly human, imposing on man the inevitable realization of his ever new possibilities, as if one should always do what is technically possible. The second temptation is that of subjecting technological development to economic usefulness in accordance with the logic of profit or non-step economic expansion, thus creating advantages for some while leaving others in poverty, with no care for the true common good of humanity, making technology into an instrument at the service of the ideology of "having." Third, there is also the temptation to subject technological development to the pursuit or maintenance of power, as happens when it is used for military purposes and whenever people are manipulated in order that they may be dominated.

10. As men and women dedicated to culture, you enjoy immense moral credibility for acting upon all the centers of decision making, whether private or public, that are capable of influencing the politics of tomorrow. Using all honest and effective means, make sure that a total vision of man and a generous idea of culture prevail. Work out persuasive arguments so that everyone will be brought to understand that peace or the survival of the human race is henceforth linked indissolubly with progress, development and dignity for all people.

You will succeed in your task if you restate with conviction that "science and technology find their justification in the service that they render to man and to humanity"; and that rational science must be linked with a series of spheres of knowledge open wide to spiritual values....

# REAGAN ON ECONOMIC PLAN
## February 18, 1981

*Less than a month after he entered office, President Ronald Reagan on February 18 went before a joint session of Congress and a nationwide television audience to propose a massive program of tax and spending reductions.*

*The president on February 5, in a television speech from the White House, had put Americans on notice that they must accept deep cuts in federal programs. But his February 18 appearance in the chamber of the House of Representatives was the first time that he had laid out the details of his "program for economic recovery."*

*Reagan asked for budget cuts totaling $41.4 billion in 83 major federal programs, and he announced a plan to cut personal income rates 10 percent a year for three years. The size and sweep of the budget cuts the president proposed were sufficient to change the very nature of the federal government. The planned tax cuts were designed to set the economy on a course that some, but by no means all, economists believed would enhance economic growth and reduce inflation.*

### Four-Point Program

*Reagan's address was well received by his audience of legislators. The president said that his "comprehensive four-point program was aimed not only at reducing spending and taxing but also at reversing a "virtual explosion" in government regulation and at "encouraging" a consistent monetary policy. Only the independent Federal Reserve Board was empowered to make and carry out monetary policy.*

*President Reagan's tax- and budget-cutting proposals, however, were at the heart of his program. The administration's hope was that the economic package would produce a psychological impact strong enough to change the expectations of Americans. Economists for several years had characterized the nation's economy as in a state of "stagflation," with high rates of inflation, high unemployment and sluggish business activity.*

## Tax Cuts

*The reductions in the personal income tax rate proposed by the president would, if enacted, provide a broad trial for "supply-side economics." Most of Reagan's economists and many others in the academic and business worlds believed that large cuts would increase savings and investment and, over a period of time, increase productivity. Instead of reducing tax revenues, these economists thought, such cuts would generate increased revenues.*

*The validity of the supply-side argument was challenged by other economic experts. Indeed, the final Economic Report of President Jimmy Carter's Council of Economic Advisers, issued January 17, concluded that it would take tax cuts even larger than those recommended by President Reagan to have any more than a negligible effect on inflation and productivity. (Economic Report, p. 105)*

## Budget Reductions

*The many reductions that Reagan proposed in federal programs were spelled out in his administration's initial budget, released March 10. (For Reagan budget, see p. 325)*

*Most observers believed that a number of the cutbacks attacked long-standing abuses. The budget cutters tended to make the reductions in social and other programs whose origins were recent. Older programs, such as Social Security and Medicare, were spared. Only the Defense Department was to receive increased funds under Reagan's proposal.*

*Critics immediately said that the cuts appeared to be regressive, hitting social and other programs benefiting lower- and middle-class groups. But the president in his address promised that the government would "continue to fulfill the obligations that spring from our national conscience." And he spoke of a "social safety net" for those "who through no fault of their own must depend on the rest of us, the poverty stricken, the disabled, the elderly, all those with true need. . . ."*

*Following is the text of President Reagan's February 18, 1981, address on a "program for economic recovery," deliv-*

*ered to a nationally televised joint session of Congress.*
(Boldface headings in brackets have been added by Congressional Quarterly to highlight the organization of the text.):

Mr. Speaker, Mr. President, distinguished Members of Congress, honored guests, and fellow citizens:

Only a month ago I was your guest in this historic building, and I pledged to you my cooperation in doing what is right for this nation that we all love so much. I'm here tonight to reaffirm that pledge and to ask that we share in restoring the promise that is offered to every citizen by this, the last, best hope of man on Earth.

All of us are aware of the punishing inflation which has for the first time in 60 years held to double-digit figures for 2 years in a row. Interest rates have reached absurd levels of more than 20 percent and over 15 percent for those who would borrow to buy a home. All across this land one can see newly built homes standing vacant, unsold because of mortgage interest rates.

Almost 8 million Americans are out of work. These are people who want to be productive. But as the months go by, despair dominates their lives. The threats of layoffs and unemployment hang over other millions, and all who work are frustrated by their inability to keep up with inflation.

One worker in a Midwest city put it to me this way: He said, "I'm bringing home more dollars than I ever believed I could possibly earn, but I seem to be getting worse off." And he is. Not only have hourly earnings of the American worker, after adjusting for inflation, declined 5 percent over the past 5 years, but in these 5 years, Federal personal taxes for the average family increased 67 percent. We can no longer procrastinate and hope that things will get better. They will not. Unless we act forcefully — and now — the economy will get worse.

## [National Debt]

Can we, who man the ship of state, deny it is somewhat out of control? Our national debt is approaching $1 trillion. A few weeks ago I called such a figure, a trillion dollars, incomprehensible, and I've been trying ever since to think of a way to illustrate how big a trillion really is. And the best I could come up with is that if you had a stack of $1,000 bills in your hand only four inches high you would be a millionaire. A trillion dollars would be a stack of $1,000 bills 67 miles high. The interest on the public debt this year we know will be over $90 billion, and unless we change the proposed spending for the fiscal year beginning October 1st, we'll add another almost $80 billion to the debt.

Adding to our troubles is a mass of regulations imposed on the shopkeeper, the farmer, the craftsman, professionals, and major industry that is estimated to add $100 billion to the price of the things we buy, and it reduces our ability to produce. The rate of increase in American productivity, once one of the highest in the world, is among the lowest of all major industrial nations. Indeed, it has actually declined in the last 3 years.

Now, I've painted a pretty grim picture, but I think I've painted it accurately. It is within our power to change his [*sic*] picture, and we can act with hope. There's nothing wrong with our internal strengths. There has been no breakdown in the human, technological, and natural resources upon which the economy is built.

## [Four-point Proposal]

Based on this confidence in a system which has never failed us, but which we have failed through a lack of confidence and sometimes through a belief that we could fine-tune the economy and get it tuned to our liking, I am proposing a comprehensive four-point program. Now, let me outline in detail some of the principal parts of this program. You'll each be provided with a completely detailed copy of the entire program.

This plan is aimed at reducing the growth in government spending and taxing, reforming and eliminating regulations which are unnecessary and unproductive or counterproductive, and encouraging a consistent monetary policy aimed at maintaining the value of the currency. If enacted in full, this program can help America create 13 million new jobs, nearly 3 million more than we would have without these measures. It will also help us gain control of inflation.

It's important to note that we're only reducing the rate of increase in taxing and spending. We're not attempting to cut either spending or taxing levels below that which we presently have. This plan will get our economy moving again, [create] productivity growth, and thus create the jobs our people must have.

And I'm asking that you join me in reducing direct Federal spending by $41.4 billion in fiscal year 1982, and this goes along with another $7.7 billion in user fees and off-budget savings for a total of $49.1 billion. And this will still allow an increase of $40.8 billion over 1981 spending.

## [Full Funding for Truly Needy]

Now, I know that exaggerated and inaccurate stories about these cuts have disturbed many people, particularly those dependent on grant and benefit programs for their basic needs. Some of you have heard from constituents, I know, afraid that social security checks, for example, were going to be taken away from them. Well, I regret the fear that these unfounded stories have caused, and I welcome this opportunity to set things straight.

We will continue to fulfill the obligations that spring from our national conscience. Those who, through no fault of their own, must depend on the rest of us — the poverty stricken, the disabled, the elderly, all those with true need — can rest assured that the social safety net of programs they depend on are exempt from any cuts.

The full retirement benefits of the more than 31 million social security recipients will be continued, along with an annual cost-of-living increase. Medicare will not be cut, nor will supplemental income for the blind, aged, and disabled. And funding will continue for veterans pensions. School breakfasts and lunches for the children of low-income families will continue, as will nutrition and other special services for the aging. There will be no cut in Project Head Start or summer youth jobs.

All in all, nearly $216 billion worth of programs providing help for tens of millions of Americans will be fully funded. But government will not continue to subsidize individuals or particular business interests where real need cannot be demonstrated. And while we will reduce some subsidies to regional and local governments, we will at the same time convert a number of categorical grant programs into block grants to reduce wasteful administrative overhead and to give local governments and States more flexibility and control. We call for an end in duplication to Federal programs and reform of those which are not cost effective.

Now, already some have protested that there must be no reduction in aid to schools. Well, let me point out that Federal aid to education amounts to only 8 percent of the total educational funding, and for this 8 percent, the Federal Government has insisted on tremendously disproportionate share of control over our schools. Whatever reductions we've proposed in that 8 percent will amount to very little in the total cost of education. They will, however, restore more authority to States and local school districts.

Historically, the American people have supported by voluntary contributions more artistic and cultural activities than all the other countries in the world put together. I wholeheartedly support this approach and believe that Americans will continue their generosity. Therefore, I'm proposing a savings of $85 million in the Federal subsidies now going to the arts and humanities.

There are a number of subsidies to business and industry that I believe are unnecessary, not because the activities being subsidized aren't of value, but because the marketplace contains incentives enough to warrant continuing these activities without a government subsidy. One such subsidy is the Department of Energy's synthetic fuels program. We will continue support of research leading to development of new technologies and more independence from foreign oil, but we can save at least $3.2 billion by leaving to private industry the building of plants to make liquid or gas fuels from coal.

We're asking that another major industry — business subsidy I should say, the Export-Import Bank loan authority, be reduced by one-third in 1982. We're doing this because the primary beneficiaries of taxpayer funds in this case are the exporting companies themselves — most of them profitable corporations.

## [Cost of Government Borrowing]

This brings me to a number of other lending programs in which government makes low-interest loans, some of them at an interest rate as low as 2 percent. What has not been very well understood is that the Treasury Department has no money of its own to lend; it has to go into the private capital market and borrow the money. So, in this time of excessive interest rates, the Government finds itself borrowing at an interest rate several times as high as the interest rate it gets back from those it lends the money to. And this difference, of course, is paid by your constituents — the taxpayers. They get hit again if they try to borrow, because Government borrowing contributes to raising all interest rates.

By terminating the Economic Development Administration, we can save hundreds of millions of dollars in 1982 and billions more over the next few years. There's a lack of consistent and convincing evidence that EDA and its Regional Commissions have been effective in creating new jobs. They have been effective in creating an array of planners, grantsmen, and professional middlemen. We believe we can do better just by the expansion of the economy and the job creation which will come from our economic program.

The Food Stamp program will be restored to its original purpose, to assist those without resources to purchase sufficient nutritional food. We will, however, save $1.8 billion in fiscal year 1982 by removing from eligibility those who are not in real need or who are abusing the program. Even with this reduction, the program will be budgeted for more than $10 billion.

We will tighten welfare and give more attention to outside sources of income when determining the amount of welfare an individual is allowed. This, plus strong and effective work requirements, will save $520 million in the next year.

I stated a moment ago our intention to keep the school breakfast and lunch programs for those in true need. But by cutting back on meals for children of families who can afford to pay, the savings will be $1.6 billion in fiscal year 1982.

Now, let me just touch on a few other areas which are typical of the kinds of reductions we've included in this economic package. The Trade Adjustment Assistance program provides benefits for workers who are unemployed when foreign imports reduce the market for various American products, causing shutdown of plants and layoff of workers. The purpose is to help these workers find jobs in growing sectors of our economy. There's nothing wrong with that, but because these benefits are paid out on top of normal unemployment benefits, we wind up paying greater benefits to those who lose their jobs because of foreign competition than we do to their friends and neighbors who are laid off due to domestic competition. Anyone must agree that this is unfair. Putting these two programs on the same footing will save $1.15 billion in just 1 year.

## [Federal Regulation Burden]

Earlier I made mention of changing categorical grants to States and local governments into block grants. Now, we know of course that the categorical grant programs burden local and State governments with a mass of Federal regulations and Federal paperwork. Ineffective targeting, wasteful administrative overhead — all can be eliminated by shifting the resources and decisionmaking authority to local and State government. This will also consolidate programs which are scattered throughout the Federal bureaucracy, bringing government closer to the people and saving $23.9 billion over the next 5 years.

Our program for economic renewal deals with a number of programs which at present are not cost-effective. An example is Medicaid. Right now Washington provides the States with unlimited matching payments for their expenditures; at the same time, we here in Washington pretty much dictate how the States are going to manage those programs. We want to put a cap on how much the Federal Government will contribute, but at the same time allow the States much more flexibility in managing and structuring the programs. I know from our experience in California that such flexibility could have led to far more cost-effective reforms. Now, this will bring a savings of $1 billion next year.

The space program has been and is important to America, and we plan to continue it. We believe, however, that a reordering of priorities to focus on the most important and cost-effective NASA programs can result in a savings of a quarter of a million [sic] dollars.

Now, coming down from space to the mailbox, the Postal Service has been consistently unable to live within its operating budget. It is still dependent on large Federal subsidies. We propose reducing those subsidies by $632 million in 1982 to press the Postal Service into becoming more effective. In subsequent years, the savings will continue to add up.

The Economic Regulatory Administration in the Department of Energy has programs to force companies to convert to specific fuels. It has the authority to administer a gas rationing plan, and prior to decontrol it ran the oil price control program. With these and other regulations gone we can save several hundreds of millions of dollars over the next few years.

## [Defense Spending]

I'm sure there is one department you've been waiting for me to mention, the Department of Defense. It's the only department in our entire program that will actually be increased over the present budgeted figure. But even here there was no exemption. The Department of Defense came up with a number of cuts which reduce the budget increase needed to restore our military balance. These measures will save $2.9 billion in 1982 outlays, and by 1986 a total of $28.2 billion will have been saved — or perhaps I should say, will have been made available for the necessary things that we must do. The aim will be to provide the most effective defense for the lowest possible cost.

I believe that my duty as President requires that I recommend increases in defense spending over the coming years. I know that you're all aware — but I think it bears saying again — that since 1970 the Soviet Union has invested $300 billion more in its military forces than we have. As a result of its massive military buildup, the Soviets have made a significant numerical advantage in strategic nuclear delivery systems, tactical aircraft, submarines, artillery and anti-aircraft defense. To allow this imbalance to continue is a threat to our national security. Notwithstanding our economic straits, making the financial changes beginning now is far less costly than waiting and having to attempt a crash program several years from now.

We remain committed to the goal of arms limitation through negotiation. I hope we can persuade our adversaries to come to realistic balanced and verifiable agreements. But, as we negotiate, our security must be fully protected by a balanced and realistic defense program.

Now, let me say a word here about the general problem of waste and fraud in the Federal Government. One Government estimate indicated that fraud alone may account for anywhere from 1 to 10 percent — as much as $25 billion of Federal expenditures for social programs. If the tax dollars that are wasted or mismanaged are added to this fraud total, the staggering dimensions of this problem begin to emerge.

The Office of Management and Budget is now putting together an interagency task force to attack waste and fraud. We're also planning to appoint as Inspectors General highly trained professionals who will spare no effort to do this job. No administration can promise to immediately stop a trend that has grown in recent years as quickly as Government expenditures themselves, but let me say this: Waste and fraud in the Federal Government is exactly what I've called it before — an unrelenting national scandal, a scandal we're bound and determined to do something about.

## [Tax Proposals]

Marching in lockstep with the whole program of reductions in spending is the equally important program of reduced tax rates. Both are essential if we're to have economic recovery. It's time to create new jobs, to build and rebuild industry, and to give the American people room to do what they do best. And that can only be done with a tax program which provides incentive to increase productivity for both workers and industry.

Our proposal is for a 10-percent across-the-board cut every year for 3 years in the tax rates for all individual income taxpayers, making a total cut in tax-cut rates of 30 percent. This 3-year reduction will also apply to the tax on unearned income, leading toward an eventual elimination of the present differential between the tax on earned and unearned income.

Now, I would have hoped that we could be retroactive with this. But as it stands, the effective starting date for these 10-percent personal income tax rate reductions will call for as of July 1st of this year.

Again, let me remind you that while this 30-percent reduction will leave the taxpayers with $500 billion more in their pockets over the next 5 years, it's actually only a reduction in the tax increase already built into the system. Unlike some past "tax reforms," this is not merely a shift of wealth between different sets of taxpayers. This proposal for an equal reduction in everyone's tax rates will expand our national prosperity, enlarge national incomes, and increase opportunities for all Americans.

Some will argue, I know, that reducing tax rates now will be inflationary. A solid body of economic experts does not agree. And tax cuts adopted over the past three-fourths of a century indicate these economic experts are right. They will not be inflationary. I've had advice that in 1985 our real production of goods and services will grow by 20 percent and be $300 billion higher than it is today. The average worker's wage will rise in real purchasing power 8 percent, and this is in after-tax dollars. And this, of course, is predicated on a complete program of tax cuts and spending reductions being implemented.

The other part of the tax package is aimed directly at providing business and industry with the capital needed to modernize and engage in more research and development. This will involve an increase in depreciation allowances, and this part of our tax proposal will be retroactive to January 1st.

The present depreciation system is obsolete, needlessly complex, and is economically counterproductive. Very simply, it bases the depreciation of plant machinery and vehicles and tools on their original cost, with no recognition of how inflation has increased their replacement cost. We're proposing a much shorter write-off time than is presently allowed — a 5-year write-off for machinery, 3 years for vehicles and trucks, and a 10-year write-off for plant. In fiscal year 1982 under this plan, business would acquire nearly $10 billion for investment; by 1985, the figure would be nearly 45 billion.

These changes are essential to provide the new investment which is needed to create millions of new jobs between now and 1985 [1986], and to make America competitive once again in the world market. These won't be make-work jobs. They are productive jobs, jobs with a future.

I'm well aware that there are many other desirable and needed tax changes, such as indexing the income tax brackets to protect taxpayers against inflation; the unjust discrimination against married couples if both are working and earning; tuition tax credits; the unfairness of the inheritance tax, especially to the family-owned farm and the family-owned business; and a number of others. But our program for economic recovery is so urgently needed to begin to bring down inflation that I'm asking you to act on this plan first and with great urgency. And then, I pledge I will join with you in seeking these additional tax changes at the earliest date possible.

## [Overregulation]

American society experienced a virtual explosion in government regulation during the past decade. Between 1970 and 1979, expenditures for the major regulatory agencies quadrupled. The number of pages published annually in the *Federal Register* nearly tripled, and the number of pages in the *Code of Federal Regulations* increased by nearly two-thirds. The result has been higher prices, higher unemployment, and lower productivity growth. Overregulation causes small and independent business men and women, as well as large businesses, to defer or terminate plans for expansion. And since they're responsible for most of the new jobs, those new jobs just aren't created.

Now, we have no intention of dismantling the regulatory agencies, especially those necessary to protect environment and assure the public health and safety. However, we must come to grips with inefficient and burdensome regulations, eliminate those we can and reform the others.

I have asked Vice President Bush to head a Cabinet-level Task Force on Regulatory Relief. Second, I asked each member of my Cabinet to postpone the effective dates of the hundreds of new regulations which have not yet been implemented. Third, in coordination with the Task Force, many of the agency heads have already taken prompt action to review and rescind existing burdensome regulations. And finally, just yesterday I signed an Executive order that for the first time provides for effective and coordinated management of the regulatory process.

Much has been accomplished, but it's only a beginning. We will eliminate those regulations that are unproductive and unnecessary by Executive order where possible and cooperate fully with you on those that require legislation.

The final aspect of our plan requires a national monetary policy which does not allow money growth to increase consistently faster than the growth of goods and services. In order to curb inflation we need to slow the growth in our money supply.

Now, we fully recognize the independence of the Federal Reserve System and will do nothing to interfere with or undermine that independence. We will consult regularly with the Federal Reserve Board on all aspects of our economic program and will vigorously pursue budget policies that will make their job easier in reducing monetary growth. A successful program to achieve stable and moderate growth patterns in the money supply will keep both inflation and interest rates down and restore vigor to our financial institutions and markets.

## [Economic Recovery]

This, then, is our proposal — America's new beginning: a program for economic recovery. I don't want it to be simply the plan of my administration. I'm here tonight to ask you to join me in making it our plan. Together we can embark on this road — [*applause*] —

Thank you very much. I should have arranged to quit right there.

Well, together we can embark on this road not to make things easy, but to make things better. Our social, political, and cultural as well as our economic institutions, can no longer absorb the repeated shocks that have been dealt them over the past decades. Can we do the job? The answer is yes. But we must begin now.

We're in control here. There's nothing wrong with America that together we can't fix. I'm sure there will be some who will raise the familiar old cry, "Don't touch my program; cut somewhere else." I hope I've made it plain that our approach has been evenhanded, that only the programs for the truly deserving needy remain untouched. The question is, are we simply going to go down the same path we've gone down before, carving out one special program here, another special program there? I don't think that's what the American people expect of us. More important, I don't think that is what they want. They're ready to return to the source of our strength.

The substance and prosperity of our Nation is built by wages brought home from the factories and the mills, the farms, and the shops. They are the services provided in 10,000 corners of America; the interest on the thrift of our people and the returns for their risk-taking. The production of America is the possession of those who build, serve, create and produce.

For too long now, we've removed from our people the decisions on how to dispose of what they created. We have strayed from first principles. We must alter our course.

The taxing power of government must be used to provide revenues for legitimate government purposes. It must not be used to regulate the economy or bring about social change. We've tried that, and surely we must be able to see it doesn't work.

Spending by government must be limited to those functions which are the proper province of government. We can no longer afford things simply because we think of them. Next year we can reduce the budget by $41.4 billion, without harm to government's legitimate purposes or to our responsibility to all who need our benevolence. This, plus the reduction in tax rates, will help bring an end to inflation.

In the health and social services area alone, the plan we're proposing will substantially reduce the need for 465 pages of law, 1,400 pages of regulations, 5,000 Federal employees who presently administer 7,600 separate grants in about 25,000 separate locations. Over 7 million man and woman hours of work by State and local officials are required to fill out government forms.

I would direct a question to those who have indicated already an unwillingness to accept such a plan: Have they an alternative which offers a greater chance of balancing the budget, reducing and eliminating inflation, stimulating the creation of jobs, and reducing the tax burden? And, if they haven't, are they suggesting we can continue on the present course without coming to a day of reckoning? If we don't do this, inflation and the growing tax burden will put an end to everything we believe in and our dreams for the future.

We don't have an option of living with inflation and its attendant tragedy, millions of productive people willing and able to work but unable to find a buyer for their work in the job market. We have an alternative, and that is the program for economic recovery.

True, it'll take time for the favorable effects of our proposal to be felt. So, we must begin now. The people are watching and waiting. They don't demand miracles. They do expect us to act. Let us act together.

Thank you and good night.

# BREZHNEV AT 26TH PARTY CONGRESS
## February 23, 1981

*The Soviet Union's 26th Communist Party Congress, opened February 23 with a speech by party leader Leonid I. Brezhnev, was characterized by Kremlin watchers as one that kept the status quo firmly in place. For the first time in Soviet history, the congress did not produce a change in the Secretariat or Politburo, the party's chief policy-making body. Past congresses have shed light on events and thought in the Soviet Union, and, more importantly, have introduced new Russian leadership.*

*Coming only five weeks after the inauguration of U.S. President Ronald Reagan, the congress gave Brezhnev an opportunity to communicate his foreign policy line to the new administration. He stated that the international situation depended on the policies of both the U.S.S.R. and the United States and that solutions to international problems required a dialogue. "Experience shows that the crucial factor here is meetings at the summit level. This was true yesterday, and is still true today," he said.*

*Brezhnev also suggested a peace conference on the Middle East with the participation of the Palestine Liberation Organization. He urged an end to the Iran-Iraq war which, he said, "is of great advantage to imperialism." On Poland he said that "[W]e will not abandon fraternal, socialist Poland in its hour of need." He warned China that her military and political ties with the United States, Japan and a number of NATO (North Atlantic Treaty Organizaton) countries were a "hazardous game." On Afghanistan, which the Soviet Union invaded in December 1979, he said that the troops would be withdrawn when "the infiltration of counter-revolutionary gangs" was stopped. (Historic Documents of 1979, p. 965)*

*Almost 5,000 delegates, representing 17 million party members, attended the 26th Party Congress, held in the glass and stone Palace of Congresses in the Kremlin. More than 80 percent of the Central Committee membership elected at the 25th Congress was retained; a significant portion of the remainder had died or become ill. The size of the Central Committee was increased by 11 percent, to 319 from 287, to allow for new membership while retaining the existing roles.*

## Purposes of Party Congress

*The party congress, according to the rules of the Communist Party of the Soviet Union, was the "supreme organ" of the party because it was to be the most broadly representative. A congress was convened every five years to coincide with the transition to a new economic plan. It had four functions: to hear and approve the reports of the Central Committee, Central Auditing Commission and other central organizations; to review, amend and endorse the progam and rules of the party; to determine the party line on questions of domestic and foreign policy; and to elect the Central Committee and Central Auditing Commission. But these functions were in fact a pro forma exercise because all the decisions usually were made in private meetings of the Central Committee and the Politburo. There was no discussion or debate; instead the congress functioned as a stage to publicize Soviet policies.*

## Aging Soviet Leadership

*The Soviet leadership was aging; the average age of those serving on the Politburo was over 70, and on the Central Committee, over 60. Brezhnev turned 75 in December and was rumored to be in poor health. Television and radio broadcasts of Brezhnev's three-hour, 40-minute speech were interrupted after the first few minutes, and most of the speech was read over the air by an announcer. The broadcast switched back to the Palace of Congresses for the end of the address. A Soviet spokesman explained that the congress had decided on this format, but it lent credence to the doubts about Brezhnev's health. The congress closed March 3 with a short address by Brezhnev, pledging "absolute fulfillment of the Eleventh Five-Year Plan."*

*Specialists on the Soviet Union expected a power struggle when Brezhnev died or became too ill to serve. The Soviet Union had no formal, codified procedure for determining leadership succession.*

*Following are excerpts from the Report of the Central Committee of the CPSU (Communist Party of the Soviet Union) to the XXVI Congress of the Communist Party of the Soviet Union and the Immediate Tasks of the Party in Home and Foreign Policy delivered by L.I. Brezhnev, general secretary of the CPSU Central Committee, on February 23, 1981.* (Boldface headings in brackets have been added by Congressional Quarterly to highlight the organization of the text.)

... On the international plane, the period under review has been rough and complicated. It has been marked above all by an intensive struggle of two lines in world affairs: the line of bridling the arms race, strengthening peace and detente, and defending the sovereign rights and freedom of nations, on the one hand, and, on the other, the line of disrupting detente, escalating the arms race, of threats and interference in other countries' affairs, and of suppressing the liberation struggle....

The sphere of imperialist domination has narrowed. The internal contradictions in capitalist countries and the rivalry between them have grown sharper. The aggressiveness of imperialist policy, notably that of U.S. imperialism, has increased acutely.

When thunderclouds gathered on the international horizon by the beginning of the eighties, the Soviet Union continued to persevere in efforts to remove the threat of war and to preserve and deepen detente, and acted to expand mutually beneficial cooperation with most countries of the world....

## The International Policy of the CPSU

Our struggle to strengthen peace and deepen detente is, above all, designed to secure the requisite external conditions for the Soviet people to carry out its constructive tasks. Thereby we are also solving a problem of a truly global nature. For at present nothing is more essential and more important for any nation than to preserve peace and ensure the paramount right of every human being — the right to life....

There are special cases, too, when friends need urgent aid. This was the case with Vietnam, which became the target of a barbarian aggression by Peking in 1979. The Soviet Union and other countries of the socialist community promptly sent it shipments of food, medical supplies, building materials, and arms. This was also the case with Kampuchea, which had been devastated by the Pol Pot clique of Peking henchmen.

That, comrades, is socialist internationalism in action. Soviet people understand and approve of such action....

It should be noted in general that in recent years our countries have had to deal with their constructive tasks in more complicated conditions. The deterioration of the world economy and spiralling prices have played their part. The slowing of the process of detente and the arms race imposed by the imperialist powers are no small a burden for us as well.

Another thing is the visible sharpening of the ideological struggle. For the West it is not confined to the battle of ideas. It employs a whole system of means designed to subvert or soften up the socialist world.

## [Imperialist Hostility to Socialist States]

The imperialists and their accomplices are systematically conducting hostile campaigns against the socialist countries. They malign and distort everything that goes on in them. For them the main thing is to turn people against socialism.

Recent events have shown again and again that our class opponents are learning from their defeats. Their actions against the socialist countries are increasingly refined and treacherous.

And wherever imperialist subversive activity is combined with mistakes and miscalculations in home policy, there arise conditions that stimulate elements hostile to socialism. This is what has happened in fraternal Poland, where opponents of socialism supported by outside forces are, by stirring up anarchy, seeking to channel events into a counter-revolutionary course. As was noted at the latest plenary meeting of the Polish United Workers' Party Central Committee, the pillars of the socialist state in Poland are in jeopardy.

At present, the Polish comrades are engaged in redressing the critical situation. They are striving to enhance the Party's capacity for action and to tighten links with the working class and other working people, and are preparing a concrete programme to restore a sound Polish economy.

Last December's meeting of leaders of the Warsaw Treaty countries in Moscow has rendered Poland important political support. It showed clearly that the Polish Communists, the Polish working class, and the working people of that country can firmly rely on their friends and allies; we will not abandon fraternal, socialist Poland in its hour of need, we will stand by it.

The events in Poland show once again how important it is for the Party, for the strengthening of its leading role, to pay close heed to the voice of the masses, resolutely to combat all signs of bureaucracy and voluntarism, actively to develop socialist democracy, and to conduct a well-considered and realistic policy in foreign economic relations. . . .

## [China's Foreign Policy]

Special mention must be made of China. The experience of the social and economic development of the PRC over the past twenty years is a painful lesson showing what any distortion of the principles and essence of socialism in home and foreign policy leads to.

The present Chinese leaders themselves describe what happened in the period of the so-called cultural revolution in their country as "a most cruel feudal-fascist dictatorship". We have nothing to add to this assessment.

At present, changes are under way in China's internal policy. Time will show what they actually mean. It will show to what extent the present Chinese leadership will manage to overcome the Maoist legacy. But, unfortunately, there are no grounds yet to speak of any changes for the better in Peking's foreign policy. As before, it is aimed at aggravating the international situation, and is aligned with the policy of the imperialist powers. That, of course, will not bring China back to the sound road of development. Imperialists will never be friends of socialism.

The simple reason behind the readiness of the United States, Japan, and a number of NATO countries to expand their military and political ties with China is to use its hostility to the Soviet Union and the socialist community in their own, imperialist interests. That is a hazardous game.

As far as the people of China are concerned, we are deeply convinced that their true interests would be best served by a policy of peace and nothing but a policy of peace and normal relations with other countries.

If Soviet-Chinese relations are still frozen, the reason for this has nothing to do with our position. The Soviet Union has never sought, nor does it now seek any confrontation with the People's Republic of China. We follow the course set by the 24th and 25th Congresses of the CPSU, and would like to build our ties with that country on a good-neighbour basis. Our proposals for normalizing relations with China remain open, and our feelings of friendship and respect for the Chinese people have not changed....

## DEVELOPMENT OF RELATIONS WITH THE NEWLY-FREE COUNTRIES

Comrades, among the important results of the Party's international activity in the period under review we can list the visible expansion of cooperation with countries that have liberated themselves from colonial oppression.

These countries are very different. After liberation, some of them have been following the revolutionary-democratic path. In others capitalist relations have taken root. Some of them are following a truly independent policy, while others are today taking their lead from imperialist policy. In a nutshell, the picture is a fairly motley one.

Let me first deal with the socialist-oriented states, that is, states that have opted for socialist development. Their number has increased. Development along the progressive road is not, of course, the same from country to country, and proceeds in difficult conditions. But the main lines are *similar*. These include gradual elimination of the positions of imperialist monopoly, of the local big bourgeoisie and the feudal elements, and restriction of foreign capital. They include the securing by the people's state of commanding heights in the economy and transition to planned development of the productive forces, and encouragement of the cooperative movement in the countryside. They include enhancing the role of the working masses in social life, and gradually reinforcing the state apparatus with national personnel faithful to the people. They include anti-imperialist foreign policy. Revolutionary parties expressing the interests of the broad mass of the working people are growing stronger there.

In the period under review, the Soviet Union has concluded treaties of friendship and cooperation with Angola, Ethiopia, Mozambique, Afghanistan, and the People's Democratic Republic of Yemen. Recently, a treaty of friendship and cooperation was signed with Syria. I am sure that it will serve well to further the Soviet-Syrian friendship and the achievement of a just peace in the Middle East. . . .

Our country does everything it can to help many of the newly-free countries in training personnel — engineers, technicians, skilled workers, doctors, and teachers.

Tens of thousands of Soviet specialists are doing dedicated work on building sites in Asian and African countries, in industry and agriculture, and in hospitals and educational institutions. They are worthy representatives of their great socialist Motherland. We are proud of them, and send them heartfelt wishes of success.

Together with the other socialist countries, we are also helping to strengthen the defence capability of newly-free states if they request such aid. This was the case with, say, Angola and Ethiopia. Attempts were made to crush the people's revolutions in these countries by encouraging domestic counter-revolution or by outside aggression. We are against the export of revolution, and we cannot agree to any export of counter-revolution either.

## [Afghanistan and Iran]

Imperialism launched a real undeclared war against the Afghan revolution. This also created a direct threat to the security of our southern frontier. In the circumstances, we were compelled to render the military aid asked for by that friendly country.

The plans of Afghanistan's enemies have collapsed. The well-considered policy of the People's Democratic Party and the government of Afghanistan headed by Comrade Babrak Karmal, which is faithful to the national interests, has strengthened the people's power.

As for the Soviet military contingent, we will be prepared to withdraw it with the agreement of the Afghan government. Before this is done, the infiltration of counter-revolutionary gangs into Afghanistan must be completely stopped. This must be secured in accords between Afghanistan and its neighbours. Dependable guarantees are required that there will be no new intervention. Such is the fundamental position of the Soviet Union, and we keep to it firmly.

The revolution in Iran, which was a major event on the international scene in recent years, is of a specific nature. However complex and contradictory, it is essentially an anti-imperialist revolution, though reaction at home and abroad is seeking to change this feature.

The people of Iran are looking for their own road to freedom and prosperity. We sincerely wish them success in this, and are prepared to develop good relations with Iran on the principles of equality and, of course, reciprocity.

Of late, Islamic slogans are being actively put forward in some countries of the East. We Communists have every respect for the religious convictions of people professing Islam or any other religion. The main thing is what aims are pursued by the forces proclaiming various slogans. The banner of Islam may lead into struggle for liberation. This is borne out by history, including very recent history. But it also shows that reaction, too, manipulates with Islamic slogans to incite counter-revolutionary mutinies. Consequently, the whole thing hinges on the actual content of any movement. . . .

## [Recognition of New States]

In Africa, the Caribbean, and Oceania ten new states gained independence in the past five years, and were instantly recognized by the Soviet Union. The birth of the Republic of Zimbabwe, the mounting intensity of the liberation struggle in Namibia, and now also in the Republic of South Africa, are graphic evidence that the rule of "classic" colonialists and racists is approaching its end.

The imperialists are displeased with the fact that the newly-free countries are consolidating their independence. In a thousand ways they are trying to bind these countries to themselves in order to deal more freely with their natural riches, and to use their territory for their strategic designs. In so doing, they make extensive use of the old colonialist method of divide and rule.

Indeed, that is also the Western approach to the Irano-Iraqi war, which has been going on for five months — an absolutely senseless war from the viewpoint of the two countries' interests. But it is of great advantage to imperialism, which is anxious and eager in some way or other to restore its position in that region. We would like to hope that both Iraq and Iran draw the due conclusions from this.

The Soviet Union firmly calls for an early end to that fratricidal war, and a political settlement of the conflict. In practice, too, we are striving to facilitate this.

## [Middle East]

Now about the Middle East problem. In its bid for dominance in the Middle East, the United States has taken the path of the Camp David policy, dividing the Arab world and organizing a separate deal between Israel and Egypt. U.S. diplomacy has failed to turn this separate anti-Arab deal into a broader agreement of a capitulationist type. But it has succeeded in another way: a new deterioration of the situation has occurred in the region. A Middle East settlement was cast back.

What now? As we see it, it is high time to get matters off the ground. It is time to go back to honest collective search of an all-embracing just and realistic settlement. In the circumstances, this could be done, say, in the framework of a specially convened international conference.

The Soviet Union is prepared to participate in such work in a constructive spirit and with good will. We are prepared to do so jointly with the other interested parties — the Arabs (naturally including the Palestine Liberation Organization) and Israel. We are prepared for such search jointly with the United States — and I may remind you that we had some experience in this regard some years ago. We are prepared to cooperate with the European countries and with all those who are showing a sincere striving to secure a just and durable peace in the Middle East.

The U.N., too, could evidently continue to play a useful role in all this.

As for the substance of the matter, we are still convinced that if there is to be real peace in the Middle East, the Israeli occupation of all Arab territories captured in 1967 must be ended. The inalienable rights of the Arab people of Palestine must be secured, up to and including the establishment of their own state. It is essential to ensure the security and sovereignty of all the states of the region, including those of Israel. Those are the basic principles. As for the details, they could naturally be considered at the negotiations. . . .

## [RELATIONS WITH THE CAPITALIST STATES]

Comrades, in the period under review the USSR continued to pursue Lenin's policy of peaceful coexistence and mutually beneficial cooperation with capitalist states, while firmly repulsing the aggressive designs of imperialism.

A further aggravation of the general crisis of capitalism was witnessed during these years. To be sure, capitalism has not stopped developing. But it is immersed in what is already the third economic recession in the past ten years.

Inflation has grown to unheard-of dimensions. Since 1970 prices in the developed capitalist countries have risen on average by 130 percent and since 1975 by 50 percent. The inflation curve is getting steeper. Not for nothing did the new President of the United States admit in his inaugural address that the United States is suffering from "one of the worst sustained inflations in . . . national history", and that "it threatens to shatter the lives of millions" of Americans.

It is more than obvious that state regulation of the capitalist economy is ineffective. The measures that bourgeois governments take against inflation foster stagnation of production and growth of unemployment; what they do to contain the critical drop in production lends still greater momentum to inflation.

The social contradictions have grown visibly more acute. In capitalist society use of the latest scientific and technical achievements in production turns against the working people, and throws millions of factory workers into the streets. In the past ten years the army of unemployed in the developed capitalist states has doubled. In 1980 it totalled 19 million.

Attempts to dampen the intensity of the class struggle by social reforms of some kind are having no success either. The number of strikers has risen by more than one-third in these ten years, and is even officially admitted to have reached the 250 million mark.

The inter-imperialist contradictions are growing more acute, the scramble for markets and for sources of raw materials and energy is more frantic. Japanese and West European monopolies compete ever more successfully with US capital, and this even in the US domestic market too. In the seventies, the share of the United States in world exports has declined by nearly 20 percent.

The difficulties experienced by capitalism also affect its policy, including foreign policy. The struggle over basic foreign policy issues in the capitalist countries has grown more bitter. Visibly more active of late are the opponents of detente, of limiting armaments, and of improving relations with the Soviet Union and other socialist countries.

Adventurism and a readiness to gamble with the vital interests of humanity for narrow and selfish ends — this is what has emerged in a particularly barefaced form in the policy of the more aggressive imperialist circles. With utter contempt for the rights and aspirations of nations, they are trying to portray the liberation struggle of the masses as "terrorism." Indeed, they have set out to achieve the unachievable — to set up a barrier to the progressive changes in the world, and to again become the rulers of the peoples' destiny.

## [Military Expenditures in Capitalist Countries]

Military expenditures are rising unprecedentedly. In the United States they have climbed to an annual 150,000 million dollars. But even these astronomical figures are not high enough for the U.S. military-industrial complex. It is clamouring for more. The NATO allies of the United States, too, yielding to Washington's demands, have undertaken — though some with great reluctance — to increase military allocations automatically until almost the end of the present century.

A considerable portion of these tremendous sums is being spent on crash development of new types of strategic nuclear arms. Their appearance is accompanied by the advancing of military doctrines dangerous to peace, like the notorious Carter directive. They want people to believe that nuclear war can be limited, they want to reconcile them with the idea that such war is tolerable.

But that is sheer deception of the peoples! A "limited" nuclear war as conceived by the Americans in, say, Europe would from the outset mean the certain destruction of European civilization. And of course the United States, too, would not be able to escape the flames of war. Clearly, such plans and "doctrines" are a grave threat to all nations, including the people of the USA. They are being condemned all over the world. The peoples say an emphatic "No" to them.

Imperialist circles think in terms of domination and compulsion in relation to other states and peoples.

The monopolies need the oil, uranium and non-ferrous metals of other countries, and so the Middle East, Africa and the Indian Ocean are proclaimed spheres of US "vital interests". The US military machine is actively thrusting into these regions, and intends to entrench itself there for a long time to come. Diego Garcia in the Indian Ocean, Oman, Kenya, Somalia, Egypt — where next?

To split the expenses with others and at the same time to tie its NATO partners closer to itself, the United States is seeking to extend the functions of NATO. Washington strategists are obviously eager to involve dozens of other countries in their military preparations, and to enmesh the world in a web of US bases, airfields, and arms depots.

To justify this, Washington is spreading the story of a "Soviet threat" to the oil riches of the Middle East or the oil supply lines. That is a deliberate falsehood, because its authors know perfectly well that the Soviet Union has no intention of impinging on either the one or the other. And in general, it is absurd to think that the oil interests of the West can be "defended" by turning that region into a powder keg.

### [Proposals for Persian Gulf]

No, we have completely different views on how peace can really be secured in and around the Persian Gulf. Instead of deploying more and more naval and air armadas, troops and arms there, we propose that the military threat should be removed by concluding an international agreement. A state of stability and calm can be created in that region by joint effort, with due account for the legitimate interests of all sides. The sovereign rights of the countries there, and the security of maritime and other communications connecting the region with the rest of the world, can be guaranteed. That is the meaning of the proposals made recently by the Soviet Union.

This initiative gained broad support in the world, including a number of Persian Gulf countries. To be sure, there were also opponents of the Soviet proposal, and it is easy to guess in what camp. We would like to express our hope that the governments of the United States and other NATO countries will consider the whole issue calmly and without prejudice, so that we could jointly look for a solution acceptable to all.

Reaching an agreement on this issue could, moreover, give a start to the very important process of reducing the military presence in various regions of the World Ocean.

In our relations with the United States during all these years we have, as before, followed a principled and constructive line. It is only to be regretted that the former administration in Washington put its stakes on something other than developing relations or on mutual understanding. Trying to exert pressure on us, it set to destroying the positive achievements that had been made with no small effort in Soviet-American relations over the preceding years. As a result, our bilateral ties suffered a setback in a number of fields. The entry into force of the SALT-2 treaty was deferred. And negotiations with us on a number of arms limitation issues, such as reducing arms deliveries to third countries, were broken off unilaterally by the United States.

### [Military Equilibrium]

Unfortunately, also since the change of leadership in the White House openly bellicose calls and statements have resounded from Washington, as if specially designed to poison the atmosphere of relations between our countries. We would like to hope, however, that those who shape United States policy today will ultimately manage to see things in a more realistic light. The military and strategic equilibrium prevailing between the USSR and the USA, between the Warsaw Treaty and NATO, objectively serves to safeguard world peace. We have not sought, and do not now seek, military superiority over the other side. That is not our policy. But neither will we permit the building up of any such superiority over us. Attempts of that kind and talking to us from a position of strength are absolutely futile.

Not to try and upset the existing balance and not to impose a new, still more costly and dangerous round of the arms race — that would be to display truly wise statesmanship. And for this it is really high time to throw the threadbare scarecrow of a "Soviet threat" out of the door of serious politics.

Let's look at the true state of affairs.

Whether we take strategic nuclear arms or medium-range nuclear weapons in Europe, in both instances there is approximate parity between the sides. In respect of some weapons the West has a certain advantage, and we have an advantage in respect of others. This parity could be more stable if pertinent treaties and agreements were concluded.

There is also talk about tanks. It is true that the Soviet Union has more of them. But the NATO countries, too, have a large number. Besides, they have considerably more anti-tank weapons.

The tale of Soviet superiority in troops strength does not match the facts either. Combined with the other NATO countries, the United States has even slightly more troops than the Soviet Union and the other Warsaw Treaty countries.

So, what talk can there be of any Soviet military superiority?

### [Arms Race]

A war danger does exist for the United States, as it does for all the other countries of the world. But the source of the danger is not the Soviet

Union, nor any mythical Soviet superiority, but is the arms race and the tension that still prevails in the world. We are prepared to combat this true, and not imaginary, danger hand in hand with the United States, with the countries of Europe, with all countries in the world. To try and outstrip each other in the arms race or to expect to win a nuclear war, is dangerous madness.

It is universally recognized that in many ways the international situation depends on the policy of both the USSR and the USA. As we see it, the state of relations between them at present and the acuteness of the international problems requiring a solution necessitate a dialogue, and an active dialogue, at all levels. We are prepared to engage in this dialogue.

Experience shows that the crucial factor here is meetings at summit level. This was true yesterday, and is still true today.

The USSR wants normal relations with the USA. There is simply no other sensible way from the point of view of the interests of our two nations, and of humanity as a whole....

Speaking of European affairs, we must not ignore the new and serious dangers that have arisen to European peace. This refers first of all to the NATO decision of deploying new U.S. nuclear missiles in Western Europe. This decision is no "response" to any imagined Soviet challenge. Neither is it an ordinary "modernization" of the arsenal, as the West would have us believe. It speaks of an obvious intention to tilt the existing military balance in Europe in NATO's favour.

It must be clearly understood: the deployment in the FRG [Federal Republic of Germany], Italy, Britain, the Netherlands or Belgium of new US missiles, targeted against the USSR and its allies, is bound to affect our relations with these countries, to say nothing of how this will prejudice their own security. So, their governments and parliaments have reason to weigh the whole thing again and again.

The vital interests of the European nations require that Europe should follow a different path — the path blazed in Helsinki....

## TO STRENGTHEN PEACE, DEEPEN DETENTE, AND CURB THE ARMS RACE

... Let me begin with the problem of limiting nuclear armaments, which are the most dangerous to humanity. All these years, the Soviet Union has worked perseveringly to put an end to the race in such armaments, and to stop their further spread across the world. A tremendous amount of work was done, as you know, in preparing a treaty with the United States on limiting strategic arms. Much was done during the negotiations with the United States and Britain on the complete prohibition of nuclear weapons tests. We made an important move by declaring and reaffirming that we will not use nuclear weapons against non-nuclear countries which do not permit the deployment of such weapons on their territory. But we have also gone further in our proposals: that the manufacture of nuclear weapons be stopped and their stockpiles be reduced until they are completely eliminated.

The Soviet Union has also actively sought the prohibition of all other types of mass destruction weapons. And we have managed to achieve a few things in this field during the period under review. Already operative is a convention banning modification of the environment for military purposes. The basic provisions of a treaty prohibiting radiological weapons have been tentatively agreed upon. Negotiations on removing chemical weapons from the arsenals of states are under way, though at an intolerably slow pace. Action taken by the peace forces secured the suspension of plans for deploying neutron arms in Western Europe. All the greater is the outrage of nations over the new Pentagon attempts to hang the neutron Sword of Damocles over the countries of Europe. For our part, we declare once more that we will not begin manufacturing it if it does not appear in other countries, and that we are prepared to conclude an agreement banning the weapon once and for all. . . .

### [Afghanistan]

. . . It is sometimes said about our Persian Gulf proposals that they should not be divorced from the question of the Soviet military contingent in Afghanistan. What could be said on this score? The Soviet Union is prepared to negotiate the Persian Gulf as an independent problem. It is also prepared, of course, as I have already said, to participate in a separate settlement of the situation around Afghanistan. *But also we do not object to the questions connected with Afghanistan being discussed together with the questions of Persian Gulf security.* Naturally, this applies solely to the international aspects of the Afghan problem, and not to internal Afghan affairs. Afghanistan's sovereignty, like its non-aligned status, must be fully protected.

### [Negotiations on Strategic Arms]

Once again, we insistently call for restraint in the field of strategic armaments. It should not be tolerated that the nations of the world live in the shadow of a nuclear war threat.

Limitation and reduction of strategic armaments is a paramount problem. *For our part, we are prepared to continue the relevant negotiations with the United States without delay, preserving all the positive elements that have so far been achieved in this area.* It goes without saying that the negotiations can be conducted only on the basis of equality and equal security. We will not consent to any agreement that gives a unilateral advantage to the USA. There must be no illusions on this score. In our opinion, all the other nuclear powers should join these negotiations at the appropriate time.

The USSR is prepared to negotiate limitation of weapons of all types. At one time we offered to ban the development of the naval Trident missile system in the United States and of a corresponding system in our country. The proposal was not accepted. As a result, the United States has built the new Ohio submarine armed with Trident-1 missiles, while an analogous system, the Typhoon, was built in our country. So, who has stood to gain?

*We are prepared to come to terms on limiting the deployment of the new submarines — the Ohio type by the USA, and similar ones by the USSR. We could also agree to banning modernization of existing and development of new ballistic missiles for these submarines.*

Now about the nuclear-missile weapons in Europe. An ever more dangerous stockpiling of them is in train. A kind of vicious circle has arisen, with the actions of one side precipitating counter-measures by the other. How to break this chain?

*We suggest coming to terms that already now a moratorium should be set on the deployment in Europe of new medium-range nuclear-missile weapons of the NATO countries and the Soviet Union, that is, to freeze the existing quantitative and qualitative level of these weapons, natu- rally including the U.S. forward-based nuclear weapons in this region.* The moratorium could enter into force at once, the moment negotiations begin on this score, and could operate until a permanent treaty is concluded on limiting or, still better, reducing such nuclear weapons in Europe. In making this proposal, we expect the two sides to stop all preparations for the deployment of respective additional weapons, includ- ing U.S. Pershing-2 missiles and land-based strategic cruise missiles.

The peoples must know the truth about the destructive consequences for humankind of a nuclear war. *We suggest that a competent international committee should be set up, which would demonstrate the vital necessity of preventing a nuclear catastrophe.* The committee could be composed of the most eminent scientists of different countries. The whole world should be informed of the conclusions they draw.

There are, of course, many other pressing international problems in the world today. Their sensible solution would enable us to slacken the intensity of the international situation, and let the nations breathe with relief. But what is needed here is a far-sighted approach, political will and courage, prestige and influence. That is why it seems to us that it would be *useful to call a special session of the Security Council with the participa- tion of the top leaders of its member-states in order to look for keys to im- proving the international situation, and preventing war. If they so wish, leaders of other states could evidently also take part in the session.* Certainly, thorough preparations would be needed for such a session to achieve positive results.

In sum, comrades, the new measures we are proposing embrace a wide range of issues. They concern conventional as well as nuclear-missile armaments, land forces, and naval and air forces. They touch on the situation in Europe, in the Near East, the Middle East, and the Far East. They deal with measures of a military as well as a political nature. All of them pursue a single aim, our one common aspiration — to do everything possible to relieve the peoples of the danger of a nuclear war, to preserve world peace.

This, if you like, is an organic continuation and development of our Peace Programme in reference to the most burning, topical problems of present-day international life.

*To safeguard peace — no task is more important now on the international plane for our Party, for our people and, for that matter, for all the peoples of the world.*

By safeguarding peace we are working not only for people who are living today, and not only for our children and grandchildren; we are working for the happiness of dozens of future generations.

If there is peace, the creative energy of the peoples backed by the achievements of science and technology is certain to solve the problems that are now troubling people. To be sure, new, still loftier tasks will then arise before our descendants. But that is the dialectic of progress, the dialectic of life.

*Not war preparations that doom the peoples to a senseless squandering of their material and spiritual wealth, but consolidation of peace — that is the clue to the future. . . .*

# WHITE PAPER ON EL SALVADOR

## February 23, 1981

*The State Department February 23 issued a controversial white paper on the arms buildup by left-wing insurgents in the Central American nation of El Salvador. Entitled "Communist Interference in El Salvador," the report purported to offer "definitive evidence" that the Soviet Union and Cuba shipped arms to the rebels in El Salvador through Nicaragua from several Soviet-bloc nations.*

*The white paper was based on documents allegedly captured from leftist locations in El Salvador, and it outlined a shopping trip for weapons undertaken by Shafik Handal, the secretary general of the Salvadoran Communist Party. The report stated that Handal purchased used American weapons that were left behind in Vietnam and Ethiopia.*

*In June several American newspapers challenged the authenticity of the captured documents and the accuracy of the conclusions drawn by the State Department. The department defended the report in a point by point rebuttal.*

*In the days before he released the white paper, Secretary of State Alexander M. Haig Jr. sent copies to the embassies of American allies in Western Europe and Latin America. He also used the report and accompanying documents to brief members of Congress, lobbying for increased military aid for the government of President José Napoleón Duarte of El Salvador. The Reagan administration made clear that it wanted the Soviet Union and Cuba to know the administration was concerned about what Haig, in a January 28 news conference, had called the "risk-taking mode on the part of the Soviet Union" in the Western Hemisphere and "the exploitation of the Cuban proxy."*

*Thomas O. Enders, assistant secretary of state for inter-American affairs, became the administration's spokesman for a political approach to the civil war in El Salvador. In a July 16 speech to the World Affairs Council, Enders said that "only a genuinely pluralistic approach can enable a profoundly divided society to live with itself without violent convulsions, gradually overcoming its differences." Enders offered the help of the United States in bringing about elections in El Salvador, but he concluded his remarks by stressing the need for both economic and military aid to the Duarte government.*

*President Duarte visited the United States in September to confer with President Reagan and members of Congress and to address the United Nations. In a September 20 appearance on CBS's Face the Nation, Duarte said that his purpose was "to have the opportunity to talk to the people of the United States and to explain the real situation directly...." He said that he had not come to ask for military aid but for economic aid and technical assistance to prevent the flow of arms into El Salvador. He rejected the possibility that American troops or advisers would be needed. And he offered to negotiate with the left-wing insurgents if they would stop fighting and agree to peaceful elections.*

## Military Aid to El Salvador

*In the waning days of his administration, President Jimmy Carter had begun to restore aid that was cut off following the December 2, 1980, slaying of four American women missionaries. Carter released $5 million in non-lethal aid and added $5 million in military hardware when the left-wing insurgents began a concerted assault in January 1981. Carter had held up the aid to pressure the Salvadoran government to investigate the women's murders and to crack down on violence by the military. It was suspected that the women had been attacked by members of the Guarda Nacional; six members of the Guarda were later arrested, but by the end of 1981 no one had been brought to trial for the offense.*

*Haig succeeded in convincing some members of Congress to support additional military aid. But Robert E. White, Carter's ambassador to El Salvador, and other witnesses testified that right-wing extremists were chiefly responsible for the violence there. Increased military aid could lead to further repression, they argued, and even to the overthrow of the U.S.-backed junta. Some congressmen expressed the fear that El Salvador could become "another Vietnam," especially if the United States continued to send advisers. To allay these fears, a few advisers were withdrawn, but the number remained about the same.*

## Background

In 1981 President Duarte's government was caught between two warring factions. On one side were the old wealthy families, landowners and the military extremists who supported them; on the other was a left-wing coalition consisting of four groups, including the communists. The landowners opposed Duarte because he had attempted to institute reforms: he expropriated most large estates, giving the land to peasants in cooperatives, and he nationalized banks and export firms. Many of the wealthy families left El Salvador and reportedly were financing right-wing death squads that killed agrarian reformers and political moderates. The leftists nonetheless saw Duarte as the leader of a repressive military government. Duarte, once the exiled leader of the Christian Democratic Party, became president after the overthrow of Carlos Huberto Romero October 15, 1979. His return to El Salvador was marked by violence by the left.

Even before publication, the white paper was controversial. Shafik Handal, its primary subject, denied the authenticity of the documents cited as evidence. His February 9 statement came in reply to a February 6 New York Times article based on leaked information. "There is no doubt," Handal said, "that this is a maneuver to justify the growing supply of U.S. arms and military personnel to the genocidal Christian Democrat-military junta...." He called on the United States to establish "friendly and constructive relations" with the rebels who "will triumph today or tomorrow."

The controversy continued in the American press. On June 6 The Wall Street Journal published a lengthy article that alleged there were mistakes in the white paper. The Journal stated that guerrilla documents were attributed to people who did not write them and that statistics on the arms buildup were extrapolated in questionable ways. The white paper drew conclusions that were not based on the documents, the Journal said. While conceding some errors in the white paper, the State Department nonetheless stood by its conclusion and on June 17 issued its rebuttal to the criticisms of the Journal and The Washington Post.

Following are the texts of the State Department white paper, Communist Interference in El Salvador, issued February 23, 1981; of the statement of Shafik Handal, head of the Salvadoran Communist Party, issued February 9 and published by The New York Times February 26; excerpts from the State Department defense of the white paper, issued June 17; and excerpts from a speech by Assistant Secretary of State Thomas O. Enders, delivered July 16:

243

# STATE DEPARTMENT WHITE PAPER

## Summary

This special report presents definitive evidence of the clandestine military support given by the Soviet Union, Cuba, and their Communist allies to Marxist-Leninist guerrillas now fighting to overthrow the established Government of El Salvador. The evidence, drawn from captured guerrilla documents and war materiel and corroborated by intelligence reports, underscores the central role played by Cuba and other Communist countries beginning in 1979 in the political unification, military direction, and arming of insurgent forces in El Salvador.

From the documents it is possible to reconstruct chronologically the key stages in the growth of the Communist involvement:

• The direct tutelary role played by Fidel Castro and the Cuban Government in late 1979 and early 1980 in bringing the diverse Salvadoran guerrilla factions into a unified front;

• The assistance and advice given the guerrillas in planning their military operations;

• The series of contacts between Salvadoran Communist leaders and key officials of several Communist states that resulted in commitments to supply the insurgents nearly 800 tons of the most modern weapons and equipment;

• The covert delivery to El Salvador of nearly 200 tons of those arms, mostly through Cuba and Nicaragua, in preparation for the guerrillas' failed "general offensive" of January 1981;

• The major Communist effort to "cover" their involvement by providing mostly arms of Western manufacture.

It is clear that over the past year the insurgency in El Salvador has been progressively transformed into another case of indirect armed aggression against a small Third World country by Communist powers acting through Cuba.

The United States considers it of great importance that the American people and the world community be aware of the gravity of the actions of Cuba, the Soviet Union, and other Communist states who are carrying out what is clearly shown to be a well-coordinated, covert effort to bring about the overthrow of El Salvador's established government and to impose in its place a communist regime with no popular support.

## I. A Case of Communist Military Involvement in the Third World

The situation in El Salvador presents a strikingly familiar case of Soviet, Cuban, and other Communist military involvement in a politically troubled Third World country. By providing arms, training, and direction to a local insurgency and by supporting it with a global propaganda campaign, the Communists have intensified and widened the conflict, greatly increased the suffering of the Salvadoran people, and deceived much of the world about the true nature of the revolution. Their objective in El Salvador as elsewhere is to bring about — at little cost to themselves — the overthrow of the established government and the imposition of a Communist regime in defiance of the will of the Salvadoran people.

## THE GUERRILLAS: THEIR TACTICS AND PROPAGANDA

El Salvador's extreme left, which includes the long-established Communist Party of El Salvador (PCES) and several armed groups of more recent origin, has become increasingly committed since 1976 to a military solution. A campaign of terrorism — bombings, assassinations, kidnappings, and seizures of embassies — has disrupted national life and claimed the lives of many innocent people.

During 1980, previously fragmented factions of the extreme left agreed to coordinate their actions in support of a joint military battle plan developed with Cuban assistance. As a precondition for large-scale Cuban aid, Salvadoran guerrilla leaders, meeting in Havana in May, formed first the Unified Revolutionary Directorate (DRU) as their central executive arm for political and military planning and, in late 1980, the Farabundo Marti People's Liberation Front (FMLN), as the coordinating body of the guerrilla organizations. A front organization, the Revolutionary Democratic Front (FDR), was also created to disseminate propaganda abroad. For appearances sake, three small non-Marxist-Leninist political parties were brought into the front, though they have no representation in the DRU.

The Salvadoran guerrillas, speaking through the FDR, have managed to deceive many about what is happening in El Salvador. They have been aided by Nicaragua and by the worldwide propaganda networks of Cuba, the Soviet Union, and other Communist countries.

The guerrillas' propaganda aims at legitimizing their violence and concealing the Communist aid that makes it possible. Other key aims are to discredit the Salvadoran Government to misrepresent U.S. policies and actions, and to foster the impression of overwhelming popular support for the revolutionary movement.

Examples of the more extreme claims of their propaganda apparatus — echoed by Cuban, Soviet, and Nicaraguan media — are:

• That the United States has military bases and several hundred troops in El Salvador (in fact, the United States has no bases and fewer than 50 military personnel there);

• That the government's security forces were responsible for most of the 10,000 killings that occurred in 1980 (in their own reports in 1980, the guerrillas themselves claimed the killings of nearly 6,000 persons, including noncombatant "informers" as well as government authorities and military).

In addition to media propaganda, Cuba and the Soviet Union promote the insurgent cause at international forums, with individual governments, and among foreign opinion leaders. Cuba has an efficient network for introducing and promoting representatives of the Salvadoran left all over the world. Havana and Moscow also bring indirect pressure on some governments to support the Salvadoran revolutionaries by mobilizing local Communist groups.

## II. Communist Military Intervention
## A Chronology

Before September 1980 the diverse guerrilla groups in El Salvador were ill-coordinated and ill-equipped, armed with pistols and a varied assortment of hunting rifles and shotguns. At that time the insurgents acquired weapons predominantly through purchases on the international market and from dealers who participated in the supply of arms to the Sandinistas in Nicaragua.

By January 1981 when the guerrillas launched their "general offensive," they had acquired an impressive array of modern weapons and supporting equipment never before used in El Salvador by either the insurgents or the military. Belgian FAL rifles, German G-3 rifles, U.S. M-1, M-16, and AR-15 semiautomatic and automatic rifles, and the Israeli UZI submachinegun and Galil assault rifle have all been confirmed in the guerrilla inventory. In addition, they are known to possess .30 to .50 caliber machineguns, the U.S. M-60 machinegun, U.S. and Russian hand grenades, the U.S. M-79 and Chinese RPG grenade launchers, and the U.S. M-72 light antitank weapon and 81mm mortars. Captured ammunition indicates the guerrillas probably possess 60mm and 82mm mortars and 57mm and 75mm recoilless rifles.

Recently acquired evidence has enabled us to reconstruct the central role played by Cuba, other Communist countries, and several radical states in the political unification and military direction of insurgent forces in El Salvador and in equipping them in less than 6 months with a panoply of modern weapons that enabled the guerrillas to launch a well-armed offensive.

This information, which we consider incontrovertible, has been acquired over the past year. Many key details, however, have fallen into place as the result of the guerrillas' own records. Two particularly important document caches were recovered from the Communist Party of El Salvador in November 1980 and from the Peoples' Revolutionary Army (ERP) in January 1981. This mass of captured documents includes battle plans, letters, and reports of meetings and travels, some written in cryptic language and using code words.

When deciphered and verified against evidence from other intelligence sources, the documents bring to light the chain of events leading to the guerrillas' January 1981 offensive. What emerges is a highly disturbing pattern of parallel and coordinated action by a number of Communist and some radical countries bent on imposing a military solution.

The Cuban and Communist role in preparing for and helping to organize the abortive "general offensive" early this year is spelled out in the following chronology based on the contents of captured documents and other sources.

## INITIAL STEPS

The chronology of external support begins at the end of 1979. With salutations of "brotherly and revolutionary greetings" on December 16, 1979, members of the Communist Party of El Salvador (PCES), National Resistance (FARN), and Popular Liberation Forces (FPL) thank Fidel Castro in a letter for his help and "the help of your party comrades . . . by signing an agreement which establishes very solid bases upon which we begin building coordination and unity of our organizations." The letter, written in Havana, was signed by leaders of these three revolutionary organizations.

At an April 1980 meeting at the Hungarian Embassy in Mexico City, guerrilla leaders made certain "requests" (possibly for arms). Present at this meeting were representatives of the German Democratic Republic, Bulgaria, Poland, Vietnam, Hungary, Cuba, and the Soviet Union.

In notes taken during an April 28, 1980 meeting of the Salvadoran Communist Party, party leader Shafik Handal mentions the need to "speed up reorganization and put the Party on a war footing." He added, "I'm in agreement with taking advantage of the possibilities of assistance from the socialist camp. I think that their attitude is magnificent. We are not yet taking advantage of it." In reference to a unification of the armed movement, he asserts that "the idea of involving everyone in the area has already been suggested to Fidel himself." Handal alludes to the concept of unification and notes, "Fidel thought well of the idea."

## GUERRILLA CONTACTS IN HAVANA

From May 5 to June 8, 1980, Salvadoran guerrilla leaders report on meetings in Honduras, Guatemala, Costa Rica, and Nicaragua. They proceed to Havana and meet several times with Fidel Castro; the documents also note an interview with the German Democratic Republic (G.D.R.) Chairman Erich Honecker in Havana. During the Havana portion of their travels, the Salvadoran guerrilla leadership meets twice with the Cuban Directorate of Special Operations (DOE, the clandestine operations/special forces unit of the Cuban Ministry of Interior) to discuss guerrilla military plans. In addition, they meet with the Cuban "Chief of Communications."

During this period (late May 1980), the Popular Revolutionary Army (ERP) is admitted into the guerrilla coalition after negotiations in Havana.

The coalition then assumes the name of the Unified Revolutionary Directorate (DRU) and meets with Fidel Castro on three occasions.

After the Havana meetings, Shafik Handal leaves Havana on May 30, 1980 for Moscow. The other Salvadoran guerrilla leaders in Havana leave for Managua. During the visit of early June, the DRU leaders meet with Nicaraguan revolutionary leaders (Sandinistas) and discuss: (1) a headquarters with "all measures of security"; (2) an "international field of operations, which they (Sandinistas) control"; and (3) the willingness of the Sandinistas to "contribute in material terms" and to adopt "the cause of El Salvador as its own." The meeting culminated with "dinner at Humberto's house" (presumably Sandinista leader Humberto Ortega).

## SALVADORAN COMMUNIST PARTY LEADER'S
## TRAVELS IN THE EAST

From June 2 to July 22, 1980, Shafik Handal visits the U.S.S.R., Vietnam, the German Democratic Republic, Czechoslovakia, Bulgaria, Hungary, and Ethiopia to procure arms and seek support for the movement.

On June 2, 1980, Handal meets in Moscow with Mikhail Kudachkin, Deputy Chief of the Latin American Section of the Foreign Relations Department of the CPSU Central Committee. Kudachkin suggests that Handal travel to Vietnam to seek arms and offers to pay for Handal's trip.

Continuing his travels between June 9 and 15, Handal visits Vietnam where he is received by Le Duan, Secretary General of the Vietnamese Communist Party; Xuan Thuy, member of the Communist Party Central Committee Secretariat; and Vice Minister of National Defense Tran Van Quang. The Vietnamese, as a "first contribution," agree to provide 60 tons of arms. Handal adds that "the comrade requested air transport from the USSR."

From June 19 to June 24, 1980, Handal visits the German Democratic Republic (G.D.R.), where he is received by Hermann Axen, member of the G.D.R. Politburo. Axen states that the G.D.R. has already sent 1.9 tons of supplies to Managua. On July 21, G.D.R. leader Honecker writes the G.D.R. Embassy in Moscow that additional supplies will be sent and that the German Democratic Republic will provide military training, particularly in clandestine operations. The G.D.R. telegram adds that although Berlin possesses no Western-manufactured weapons — which the Salvadoran guerrillas are seeking — efforts will be undertaken to find a "solution to this problem." (NOTE: The emphasis on Western arms reflects the desire to maintain plausible denial.)

From June 24-27, 1980, Handal visits Czechoslovakia where he is received by Vasil Bilak, Second Secretary of the Czech Communist Party. Bilak says that some Czech arms circulating in the world market will be provided so that these arms will not be traced back to Czechoslovakia as the donor country. Transportation will be coordinated with the German Democratic Republic.

Handal proceeds to Bulgaria from June 27 to June 30, 1980. He is received by Dimitir Stanichev, member of the Central Committee Secretariat. The Bulgarians agreed to supply German-origin weapons and other supplies, again in an apparent effort to conceal their sources.

In Hungary, from June 30 to July 3, 1980, Handal is received by Communist Party General Secretary Janos Kadar and "Guesel" (probably Central Committee Secretary for Foreign Affairs Andras Gyenes). The latter offers radios and other supplies and indicates Hungarian willingness to trade arms with Ethiopia or Angola in order to obtain Western-origin arms for the Salvadoran guerrillas. "Guesel" promises to resolve the trade with the Ethiopians and Angolans himself, "since we want to be a part of providing this aid." Additionally, Handal secures the promise of 10,000 uniforms to be made by the Hungarians according to Handal's specifications.

Handal then travels to Ethiopia, July 3 to July 6. He meets Chairman Mengistu and receives "a warm reception." Mengistu offers "several thousand weapons," including: 150 Thompson submachineguns with 300 cartridge clips, 1,500 M-1 rifles, 1,000 M-14 rifles, and ammunition for these weapons. In addition, the Ethiopians agree to supply all necessary spare parts for these arms.

Handal returns to Moscow on July 22, 1980 and is received again by Mikhail Kudachkin. The Soviet official asks if 30 Communist youth currently studying in the U.S.S.R. could take part in the war in El Salvador. Before leaving Moscow, Handal receives assurances that the Soviets agree in principle to transport the Vietnamese arms.

## FURTHER CONTACTS IN NICARAGUA

On July 13, representatives of the DRU arrive in Managua amidst preparations for the first anniversary celebration of Somoza's overthrow. The DRU leaders wait until July 23 to meet with "Comrade Bayardo" (presumably Bayardo Arce, member of the Sandinista Directorate). They complain that the Sandinistas appear to be restricting their access to visiting world dignitaries and demanding that all contacts be cleared through them. During the meeting, Arce promises ammunition to the guerrillas and arranges a meeting for them with the Sandinista "Military Commission." Arce indicates that, since the guerrillas will receive some arms manufactured by the Communist countries, the Sandinista Army (EPS) will consider absorbing some of these weapons and providing to the Salvadorans Western-manufactured arms held by the EPS in exchange. (In January 1981 the Popular Sandinista Army indeed switched from using U.S.-made weapons to those of Soviet and East European origin.)

The DRU representatives also meet with visiting Palestine Liberation Organization (PLO) leader Yasir Arafat in Managua on July 22, 1980.

Arafat promises military equipment, including arms and aircraft. (A Salvadoran guerrilla leader met with FATAH leaders in Beirut in August and November, and the PLO has trained selected Salvadorans in the Near East and in Nicaragua.)

On July 27, the guerrilla General Staff delegation departs from Managua for Havana, where Cuban "specialists" add final touches to the military plans formulated during the May meetings in Havana.

## ARMS DELIVERIES BEGIN

In mid-August 1980, Shafik Handal's arms-shopping expedition begins to bear fruit. On August 15, 1980, Ethiopian arms depart for Cuba. Three weeks later the 60 tons of captured U.S. arms sent from Vietnam are scheduled to arrive in Cuba.

As a result of a Salvadoran delegation's trip to Iraq earlier in the year, the guerrillas receive a $500,000 logistics donation. The funds are distributed to the Sandinistas in Nicaragua and within El Salvador.

By mid-September, substantial quantities of the arms promised to Handal are well on the way to Cuba and Nicaragua. The guerrilla logistics coordinator in Nicaragua informs his Joint General Staff on September 26 that 130 tons of arms and other military material supplied by the Communist countries have arrived in Nicaragua for shipment to El Salvador. According to the captured documents, this represents one-sixth of the commitments to guerrillas by the Communist countries. (NOTE: To get an idea of the magnitude of this commitment, the Vietnamese offer of only 60 tons included 2 million rifle and machinegun bullets, 14,500 mortar shells, 1,620 rifles, 210 machineguns, 48 mortars, 12 rocket launchers, and 192 pistols.)

In September and October, the number of flights to Nicaragua from Cuba increased sharply. These flights had the capacity to transport several hundred tons of cargo.

At the end of September, despite appeals from the guerrillas, the Sandinistas suspend their weapons deliveries to El Salvador for 1 month, after the U.S. Government lodges a protest to Nicaragua on the arms trafficking.

When the shipments resume in October, as much as 120 tons of weapons and materiel are still in Nicaragua and some 300-400 tons are in Cuba. Because of the difficulty of moving such large quantities overland, Nicaragua — with Cuban support — begins airlifting arms from Nicaragua into El Salvador. In November, about 2.5 tons of arms are delivered by air before accidents force a brief halt in the airlift.

In December, Salvadoran guerrillas, encouraged by Cuba, begin plans for a general offensive in early 1981. To provide the increased support necessary, the Sandinistas revive the airlift into El Salvador. Salvadoran insurgents protest that they cannot absorb the increased flow of arms, but guerrilla liaison members in Managua urge them to increase their efforts as several East European nations are providing unprecedented assistance.

A revolutionary radio station — *Radio Liberacion* — operating in Nicaragua begins broadcasting to El Salvador on December 15, 1980. It exhorts the populace to mount a massive insurrection against the government. (References to the Sandinistas sharing the expenses of a revolutionary radio station appear in the captured documents.)

On January 24, 1981, a Cessna from Nicaragua crashes on takeoff in El Salvador after unloading passengers and possibly weapons. A second plane is strafed by the Salvadoran Air Force, and the pilot and numerous weapons are captured. The pilot admits to being an employee of the Nicaraguan national airline and concedes that the flight originated from Sandino International Airport in Managua. He further admits to flying two earlier arms deliveries.

Air supply is playing a key role, but infiltration by land and sea also continues. Small launches operating out of several Nicaraguan Pacific ports traverse the Gulf of Fonseca at night, carrying arms, ammunition, and personnel. During the general offensive on January 13, several dozen well-armed guerrillas landed on El Salvador's southeastern coast on the Gulf of Fonseca, adjacent to Nicaragua.

Overland arms shipments also continue through Honduras from Nicaragua and Costa Rica. In late January, Honduran security forces uncover an arms infiltration operation run by Salvadorans working through Nicaragua and directed by Cubans. In this operation, a trailer truck is discovered carrying weapons and ammunition destined for Salvadoran guerrillas. Weapons include 100 U.S. M-16 rifles and 81mm mortar ammunition. These arms are a portion of the Vietnamese shipment: A trace of the M-16s reveals that several of them were shipped to U.S. units in Vietnam where they were captured or left behind. Using this network, perhaps five truckloads of arms may have reached the Salvadoran guerrillas.

The availability of weapons and materiel significantly increases the military capabilities of the Salvadoran insurgents. While attacks raged throughout the country during the "general offensive" that began on January 10, it soon became clear that the DRU could not sustain the level of violence without suffering costly losses in personnel. By the end of January, DRU leaders apparently decided to avoid direct confrontation with government forces and reverted to sporadic guerrilla terrorist tactics that would reduce the possibility of suffering heavy casualties.

## III. The Government: The Search for Order and Democracy

Central America's smallest and most densely populated country is El Salvador. Since its independence in 1821, the country has experienced chronic political instability and repression, widespread poverty, and concentration of wealth and power in the hands of a few families. Although considerable economic progress took place in the 1960s, the political system remained in the hands of a traditional economic elite backed by the military. During the 1970s, both the legitimate grievances of the poor and landless and the growing aspirations of the expanding middle classes met increasingly with repression. El Salvador has long been a violent country with political, economic, and personal disputes often resulting in murders.

## THE PRESENT GOVERNMENT

Aware of the need for change and alarmed by the prospect of Nicaragua-like chaos, progressive Salvadoran military officers and civilians overthrew the authoritarian regime of General Carlos Humberto Romero in October 1979 and ousted nearly 100 conservative senior officers.

After an initial period of instability, the new government stabilized around a coalition that includes military participants in the October 1979 coup, the Christian Democratic Party, and independent civilians. Since March 1980, this coalition has begun broad social changes: conversion of large estates into peasant cooperatives, distribution of land to tenant farmers, and nationalization of foreign trade and banking.

Four Marxist-Leninist guerrilla groups are using violence and terrorism against the Salvadoran Government and its reforms. Three small non-Marxist-Leninist political parties — including a Social Democratic Party — work with guerrilla organizations and their political fronts through the Democratic Revolutionary Front (FDR), most of whose activities take place outside El Salvador.

The Government of El Salvador — headed since last December by Jose Napoleon Duarte, the respected Christian Democrat denied office by the military in the Presidential elections of 1972 — faces armed opposition from the extreme right as well as from the left. Exploiting their traditional ties to the security forces and the tendency of some members of the security forces to abuse their authority, some wealthy Salvadorans affected by the Duarte government's reforms have sponsored terrorist activities against supporters of the agrarian and banking reforms and against the government itself.

A symbiotic relationship has developed between the terrorism practiced by extremists of both left and right. Thousands have died without regard to class, creed, nationality, or politics. Brutal and still unexplained murders in December of four American churchwomen — and in January of two American trade unionists — added U.S. citizens to the toll of this tragic violence. The United States has made clear its interest in a complete investigation of these killings and the punishment of those responsible.

Despite bitter resistance from right and left, the Duarte government has stuck to its reform programs and has adopted emergency measures to ease the lot of the poor through public works, housing projects, and aid to marginal communities. On the political front, it has offered amnesty to its opponents, scheduled elections for a constituent assembly in 1982, and pledged to hand power over to a popularly elected government no later than mid-1983.

The government's pursuit of progress with order has been further hampered by the virtual breakdown of the law enforcement and judicial system and by the lack of an effective civil service.

The introduction of the reforms — some of which are now clearly irreversible — has reduced popular support for those who argue that change can only come about through violence. Few Salvadorans participate in antigovernment demonstrations. Repeated calls by the guerrillas for general strikes in mid- and late 1980 went unheeded. The Duarte government, moreover, has made clear its willingness to negotiate the terms of future political processes with democratic members of all opposition forces — most notably, by accepting the offer of El Salvador's Council of Bishops to mediate between the government and the Democratic Revolutionary Front.

In sum, the Duarte government is working hard and with some success to deal with the serious political, social, and economic problems that most concern the people of El Salvador.

## U.S. SUPPORT

In its commitment to reform and democracy, the Government of El Salvador has had the political support of the United States ever since the October 1979 revolution. Because we give primary emphasis to helping the people of El Salvador, most of our assistance has been economic. In 1980, the United States provided nearly $56 million in aid, aimed at easing the conditions that underlie unrest and extremism. This assistance has helped create jobs, feed the hungry, improve health and housing and education, and support the reforms that are opening and modernizing El Salvador's economy. The United States will continue to work with the Salvadoran Government toward economic betterment, social justice, and peace.

Because the solution in El Salvador should be of the Salvadorans' own making and nonviolent, the United States has carefully limited its military support. In January, mounting evidence of Communist involvement compelled President Carter to authorize a resupply of weapons and ammunition to El Salvador — the first provision of lethal items since 1977.

## IV. Some Conclusions

The foregoing record leaves little doubt that the Salvadoran insurgency has become the object of a large-scale commitment by Communist states outside Latin America.

● The political direction, organization, and arming of the insurgency is coordinated and heavily influenced by Cuba — with active support of the Soviet Union, East Germany, Vietnam, and other Communist States.

● The massing and delivery of arms to the Salvadoran guerrillas by those states must be judged against the fact that from 1977 until January 1981 the United States provided no weapons or ammunition to the Salvadoran Armed Forces.

● A major effort has been made to provide "cover" for this operation by supplying arms of Western manufacture and by supporting a front organization known as the Democratic Revolutionary Front to seek non-Communist political support through propaganda.

● Although some non-Communist states have also provided material support, the organization and delivery of this assistance, like the overwhelming mass of arms, are in the hands of Communist-controlled networks.

In short, over the past year, the insurgency in El Salvador has been progressively transformed into a textbook case of indirect armed aggression by Communist powers through Cuba.

# STATEMENT BY HANDAL

On Feb. 6, The New York Times published on its front page a commentary mentioning documents supposedly captured from Salvadoran guerrillas which suggest that leaders of Vietnam, Ethiopia, the Soviet Union, the German Democratic Republic, Bulgaria, Czechoslovakia and Hungary reached an agreement with me, in my position as secretary general of the Salvadoran Communist Party, to send armament to the revolutionary movement in my country. In this context, I make the following statement:

## [1]

I categorically reject as false the published claims about the above-mentioned agreement. There is no doubt that this is a maneuver to justify the growing supply of U.S. arms and military personnel to the genocidal Christian Democratic military junta and prepare the ground for an eventual military aggression in Central America.

## [2]

The Salvadoran people have been fighting for democratic freedom and, time and again, the reactionary military tyranny, invariably aided by successive U.S. Governments, has responded with massacres and repression. The military dictatorship, the oligarchy and the Government of the United States have thus pushed the Salvadoran people toward the armed struggle. It is a struggle legitimized and justified by history. No one can honestly be surprised that these people have now taken up arms to exercise their right to self-determination. Nevertheless, other explanations are now being found in supposed conspiracies of the Soviet Union and other Socialist countries with the Salvadoran Communist Party.

### [3]

I demand that the Government of the United States explain: With what moral right does it question the right of the Salvadoran people to arm themselves and carry out a war of survival, a just war of national liberation, against their executioners? What is the legal and moral authority of the U.S. Government to question this right, being, as everyone knows, the largest supplier of arms to the bloody dictatorships of Latin America and other continents?

### [4]

After so many experiences around the world, the U.S. Government should know by now that revolution is a historical law of social development which, despite the primitive desires of those who continue being our geographic neighbors, will triumph today or tomorrow in El Salvador. We should therefore think of our future relations. In our case, in no way do we want a future of hostile relations with the United States, with whose people we feel much sympathy and among whom so many of our compatriots live and work. On the contrary, we favor friendly and constructive relations based on mutual respect and coexistence. But the U.S. Government, it seems, prefers to work today to poison those future relations.

### [5]

Finally, the U.S. Government should clarify for U.S. and world public opinion: How did its intelligence services and the State Department obtain documents "captured" from Salvadoran guerrillas? Why were these supposed documents published first in New York and not in El Salvador? And why has the State Department rather than the fascist Christian Democratic junta assumed responsibility for their publication? Whatever the circumstances of the "denunciation" that appeared in The New York Times, with its repeated references to the State Department and U.S. intelligence services, it provides further evidence of the blatant way that the U.S. Government is intervening in the internal affairs of El Salvador, siding with the worst cause in favor of the rabid slaughterers, torturers and corrupt executioners of the Salvadoran people.

Is this the way that the United States defends its national security?

# STATE DEPARTMENT DEFENSE OF REPORT

The Department of State on February 23, 1981, issued a Special Report on Communist Interference in El Salvador. The Report was based on captured guerrilla documents, independent intelligence sources, and captured war materiel.

While much evidence of covert Communist arms supply activities was gathered by sensitive intelligence means, several key pieces of information from non-sensitive sources became available in late 1980 and early 1981:

— Two particularly important guerrilla document caches were recovered from the Communist Party of El Salvador in November 1980 and from the Peoples' Revolutionary Army (ERP) in January 1981. These documents were examined and found to be authentic and corroborated by other intelligence sources.

— In December 1980, the insurgents began to employ weapons never before used in El Salvador. Among them were US-made M-16 and M-14 rifles, M-79 grenade launchers, and Chinese-made 75mm recoilless rifles.

— In their mid-January offensive, the guerrillas expended large amounts of ammunition and lost many weapons. Aircraft flying arms from Nicaragua to El Salvador were destroyed; one pilot involved in this traffic was captured.

— In late January, the Government of Honduras captured a truck carrying M-16s and other weapons and ammunition destined for the guerrillas and arrested persons responsible. Most of the M-16s on the truck were traced directly to Vietnam.

This information was cited in the Special Report. In addition, sensitive intelligence corroborated and supplemented these sources, but only a few details in the Special Report were based on sensitive intelligence alone.

To provide the public with direct access to some of this information, 19 guerrilla documents were also released in whole or part with accompanying translations and the notation that they represented "only a very small portion of the total documents recovered." Captured documents are one of the few forms of raw intelligence that can be released without endangering sources or methods of intelligence collection important to our national security.

The State Department has addressed and will continue to address this matter in a spirit of openness, working with the press to make as much information as possible available to the public. State Department officials gave on-the-record statements and interviews on the Report and its contents, including the origin of the captured documents and the problems of analysis involved. Unpublished documents were made available for review on request by journalists.

On June 8, the *Wall Street Journal* and, on June 9, the *Washington Post,* published articles questioning the validity of the Special Report, focussing particularly on the captured documents. We have carefully reviewed the points raised in these articles. Our detailed comments are contained in the attachment. In brief, our findings are that:

— Most of the criticisms of the Special Report are either based on incorrect assumptions or are inaccurate;

— The few points of misstated detail or ambiguous formulations that have been correctly identified do not in any way change the conclusions of the Report; and

— The analysis and conclusions of the Special Report are soundly based and fully valid.

The conclusion is inescapable that Cuba and other Communist and radical states have interfered directly in El Salvador. In the words of the Special Report, "by providing arms, training, and direction to a local insurgency and by supporting it with a global propaganda campaign, the Communists have intensified and widened the conflict, greatly increased the suffering of the Salvadoran people, and deceived much of the world about the true nature of the revolution."

While outside forces are exploiting it, the Salvadoran conflict will not be ended until the local causes are addressed. The Department of State reaffirms the need, again in the words of the Special Report, "to deal with the serious political, social, and economic problems that most concern the people of El Salvador" — problems which the Duarte Government is seeking to confront with our support.

In sum, the conclusions, evidence and analysis of the Special Report are valid.

# ENDERS JULY 16 SPEECH

This winter one of our neighbors — El Salvador — was the target of a deadly challenge. On January 10, insurgent groups that had developed in El Salvador — but had united with Cuban help, had trained many of their people in Cuba, had just obtained infusions of modern arms through Cuba — launched a "final offensive" to overthrow the Salvadoran government.

Timing was critical to the guerrillas. On January 9, the insurgents' Radio Liberation boasted from Nicaragua that the offensive to be launched the next day meant that the new president of the United States would come to office too late to stop the guerrilla victory. But an unspoken internal factor was probably more important. In 1980 the new Salvadoran government — after its predecessors had for years ignored pressing socio-economic problems — had started a program of land reform to benefit the poor. The reform addressed key issues that the insurgents had hoped to exploit as their own. Every passing day was demonstrating that the guerrillas' premises — that they were dealing from strength at home and abroad — were wrong. . . .

Contrary to the insurgents' expectations, the Salvadorans contained the immediate January offensive on their own. Our assistance since has enabled the Duarte government to prevent the insurgents from turning their continuing outside support to new military advantage. Even more importantly, our assistance gives the Salvadoran people a chance to defend their right to self-determination by developing a political solution to the conflict.

And that is what I would like to talk about today: a political solution. For just as the conflict was Salvadoran in its origins, so its ultimate resolution must be Salvadoran.

For more than 18 months, El Salvador has had a government with a consistent and stable policy, one that emphasizes domestic reform, closer trade and diplomatic relations with neighboring nations, and firm resistance to outside intervention.

El Salvador, however, remains a divided country. It is divided between the insurgents and a great majority that opposes the extreme left's violent methods and foreign ties. It is divided between an equally violent minority on the extreme right that seeks to return El Salvador to the domination of a small elite and a great majority that has welcomed the political and social changes of the past 18 months.

The insurgents are divided within their own coalition — between those who want to prolong their ill-starred guerrilla campaign, and those who are disillusioned by their failure to win the quick military victory their leaders had proclaimed inevitable — between those who despise democracy as an obstacle to their ambitions to seize power, and those who might be willing to engage in democratic elections.

Finally, the vast majority of Salvadorans in the middle are also divided — over whether to emphasize the restoration of the country's economic health or the extension of the country's social reforms — between those who honor the army as one of the country's most stable and coherent institutions, and those who criticize it for failing to prevent right-wing violence — between those who see the need to develop participatory institutions, and those who maintain that there is no alternative to the old personalistic politics.

Only Salvadorans can resolve these divisions. Neither we nor any other foreign country can do so. It is therefore critical that the Salvadoran Government itself is attempting to overcome these divisions by establishing a more democratic system.

We wholeheartedly support this objective. Not out of blind sentiment, not out of a desire to reproduce everywhere a political system that has served Americans so extraordinarily well, and certainly not because we underestimate the difficulties involved.

Rather we believe that the solution must be democratic because only a genuinely pluralistic approach can enable a profoundly divided society to live with itself without violent convulsions, gradually overcoming its differences.

How can a country beset by so many troubles get from here to there? The first thing to say is that *promises must be kept.*

One can debate endlessly about El Salvador's land reform — whether the takeover of the big farms might have a high penalty in lost production for export, whether one can really give clear titles to over 200,000 individual peasant workers, and so forth. But the changes that have already taken place are real....

This understood, the compensation promised should also be provided, and on a just and effective basis. This is not only a matter of right, it is a practical necessity. El Salvador is known for the vigor and skill of its modern entrepreneurs, but entrepreneurs will not stay and work in El Salvador or anywhere else if they cannot expect fair treatment....

Second, *there must be demonstrable progress in controlling and eliminating violence from all sources.*

Violence of the left and violence of the right are inextricably linked. Since the failure of the January offensive, the tragic cycle of violence and counter violence has been most evident in Chalatenango and Morazan, the remote areas where guerrilla forces are concentrated, and where most of the violent incidents recently attributed to the far right and to government forces have taken place....

Cuban and Nicaraguan supplies to the guerrillas must stop. There is no doubt that Cuba was largely behind the arms trafficking that fueled the guerrilla offensive this winter. In April, when Socialist International representative Wischnewski confronted Castro with our evidence of Cuban interference, Castro admitted to him that Cuba had shipped arms to the guerrillas — just as we had said....

The other side of the coin is that more Salvadoran Army leadership is needed, both to fight rightist death squads and to control security force violence. This is a primary objective of our training effort. There must be improvement.

The basic reality, however, is that violence will likely be countered by violence until a rational and legitimate political process is devised to break this vicious circle.

This brings me to my third point, that *all parties that renounce violence should be encouraged to participate in the design of new political institutions and the process of choosing representatives for them.*

The government of El Salvador has announced that it will hold presidential elections in 1983. Prior to that a Constituent Assembly to be elected in 1982 will develop a new constitution. Four months ago, in March, President Duarte appointed an electoral commission to develop the necessary procedures. Last week, the government officially approved measures recognizing the legal status of registered parties and setting the procedures whereby these parties, and any new parties that come legally into existence, can participate in the election.

The parties already legally registered include two groups associated with the insurgent political front: the National Revolutionary Movement led by Guillermo Ungo, and the Democratic National Union, the electoral vehicle of the traditional Communist party. These parties, and any others that may wish to do so legally, now have before them the opportunity to test their strength against reformist and conservative parties according to the ultimate test of democracy: ballots, not bullets. . . .

As basic expressions of self-determination and national sovereignty, elections involve many delicate questions. They include technical matters (such as steps to ensure an accurate tally), confidence-building measures (such as providing witness of fairness and absence of coercion or intimidation from any source), and a host of fundamental matters such as the design of institutions, security for participants, and assurances that the results will be respected. . . .

If elections are held, would the results be respected? The government's intentions are clear. El Salvador's new military leaders have made the reform process possible. An army confident that its integrity will be respected, and that elections will be fair, can also be effective in curbing violence from the right as well as from the left. But it is only realistic to recognize that extremists on both left and right still oppose elections, and that an army suspicious that its institutional integrity might not be respected could itself become a destabilizing element. In this regard, we should recognize that El Salvador's leaders will not — and should not — grant the insurgents through negotiations the share of power the rebels have not been able to win on the battlefield. But they should be — and are — willing to compete with the insurgents at the polls.

To develop a serious, reliable electoral process in El Salvador, all non-violent political groups, whatever their relationship to the current government, will have to make their views known to each other and to the Electoral Commission. This will doubtless require careful discussion and quite possibly negotiation among the parties.

Elections are quintessentially matters of internal policy. But there may be ways other nations can assist. If requested by the government of El Salvador — and desired by those involved — other countries might be invited to facilitate such contacts and discussions or negotiations *on electoral issues* among eligible political parties. The United States is prepared, if asked, to join others in providing good offices to assist the Salvadorans in this task, which could prove critical to the search for a political solution to the conflict.

We have no preconceived formulas. We know that elections have failed in the past. We have no illusions that the task now will be anything but difficult. But we believe that elections open to all who are willing to renounce violence and abide by the procedures of democracy can help end El Salvador's long agony.

I have one more thing to say.

That is that *the search for a political solution will not succeed unless the United States sustains its assistance to El Salvador.*

This spring, after their offensive revealed their lack of popular support, the Democratic Revolutionary Front thought — we know from their own documents — that negotiations should be used as a delaying tactic while the insurgents attempted to regroup militarily.

Should members of the guerrilla command believe that they can make gains by military means, no participation in elections, no meaningful negotiations, no political solutions are likely to be forthcoming. The point is not that sustained U.S. assistance might lead to a government military victory. It is that a political solution can only be achieved if the guerrillas realize they cannot win by force of arms.

To ensure a climate in which a political solution can take place, the limited military programs we now have should be sustained. Our economic assistance, already more than three times our military aid, must continue to offset the guerrillas' efforts to prolong the war by sabotaging the economy. . . .

Our concern for El Salvador is not unique. The United States has met challenges like this before. Since World War II, under Democratic and Republican Presidents alike, the United States has used all appropriate instruments — political, economic, and military — to help friends and allies secure their vital interests as well as our own.

Our help for El Salvador is really very small — but it is vital. With it, El Salvador is making progress. The government, the Church, the trade unions, agrarian organizations, professional bodies, and organizations of businessmen are now all increasingly engaged in seeking a peaceful outcome to the conflict. Last March, the guerrillas' use of violence led the Apostolic Administrator to comment that "most of the public has turned its back on them." Elections now offer to those among them who want to end the violence a chance to work for peace.

The culmination of the search for peace is necessarily the responsibility of Salvadorans. But Salvadorans look to us for understanding and assistance. We can help by:

    — extending economic and military assistance to counter the disaster visited upon El Salvador by enemies of democracy;

    — standing by our friends while they work out a democratic solution; and

    — identifying and seizing opportunities to help such a solution actually take shape.

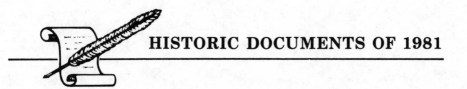

# March

# March

# REPORT ON IMMIGRATION

## March 1, 1981

*The Select Commission on Immigration and Refugee Policy issued a report March 1, U.S. Immigration Policy and the National Interest, that placed first priority on "bringing undocumented/illegal immigration under control, while setting up a rational system for legal immigration," according to its chairman, the Rev. Theodore M. Hesburgh, president of the University of Notre Dame.*

*The 453-page report, ordered by Congress in 1978, proposed several major initiatives: better border and interior law enforcement; legalization of qualified undocumented/illegal aliens; and a new immigrant admissions system. In addition, the report endorsed the Refugee Act of 1980, that set a 50,000 annual ceiling on refugees, subject to presidential adjustment, and recommended improved techniques for handling mass asylum emergencies such as the Cuban and Haitian boatlifts in 1980 and 1981. (Historic Documents of 1980, p. 337)*

*Most of the report's recommendations required action by Congress. The commission suggested that its recommendations be implemented in stages, beginning with strengthened efforts to halt illegal immigration and the employment of illegal aliens. The commission recommended substantial improvement of border patrols, with new equipment, more personnel and better training; and outlawing the employment of illegal aliens, with civil and perhaps criminal penalties for convicted employers.*

### Amnesty Proposed

*The commission suggested moving to legalize a substantial number of the 3.5-6 million illegal immigrants thought to be living in the United*

*States. It proposed amnesty for those who entered prior to January 1, 1980, and who continuously resided in the United States for some minimum time prescribed by Congress.*

*With the borders more secure and amnesty provided for many illegal immigrants, it would be appropriate to implement a new immigrant admissions system designed to stress family reunification and to clear up application backlogs, the commission said. It recommended retaining a numerical ceiling on annual immigration, while raising it from the current 270,000 to 350,000, and providing an additional 100,000 places a year for each of the next five years to reduce waiting lists.*

*Reviewing pressures for international migration, the commission said the problem had passed the point of effective control through nations' domestic policies, and, instead, had become "a major, rapidly growing world problem which requires a multinational solution."*

> *Following is the text of the introduction to* U.S. Immigration Policy and the National Interest, *the final report of the Select Commission on Immigration and Refugee Policy, issued March 1, 1981:*

> *If I am not for myself, who will be for me? But if I am for myself only, what am I? And if not now, when?*
>
> Hillel
> *Sayings of the Fathers* 1:14

Our history is largely the story of immigration. Even the Indians were immigrants. The ancestors of all other Americans — when measured in terms of world history — came here only yesterday.

As a refuge and a land of opportunity, the United States remains the world's number one magnet. This fact reaffirms the faith of our founding fathers and the central values we have adopted as a nation — freedom, equality under the law, opportunity and respect for diversity. Throughout our history, our leaders have seen in immigration the articulation of these deeply held and religiously based values. President Ronald W. Reagan, in his speech accepting the Republican nomination for the presidency, reminded us of that fact when he said:

> I ask you to trust that American spirit which knows no ethnic, religious, social, political, regional or economic boundaries: the spirit that burned with zeal in the hearts of millions of immigrants from every corner of the earth who came here in search of freedom....

Then, examining the events of the recent past, the President asked:

> Can we doubt that only a divine Providence placed this land — this island of freedom here as a refuge for all those people in the world who yearn to breath free? Jews and Christians enduring persecution

behind the Iron Curtain, the boat people of Southeast Asia, Cuba, and Haiti, the victims of drought and famine in Africa, the freedom fighters in Afghanistan and our own countrymen held in savage captivity.

Letters and oral testimony to the Select Commission affirm the continuing vitality of President Reagan's characterization of the United States as a land of opportunity and as a beacon of liberty for immigrants. We have listened carefully to these moving voices, but we have also been faced with the reality of limitations on immigration. If it is a truism to say that the United States is a nation of immigrants, it is also a truism that it is one no longer, nor can it become a land of unlimited immigration. As important as immigration has been and remains to our country, it is no longer possible to say as George Washington did that we welcome all of the oppressed of the world, or as did the poet, Emma Lazarus, that we should take all of the huddled masses yearning to be free.

The United States of America — no matter how powerful and idealistic — cannot by itself solve the problems of world migration. This nation must continue to have some limits on immigration. Our policy — while providing opportunity to a portion of the world's population — must be guided by the basic national interests of the people of the United States.

The emphasis in the Commission's recommendations, which are themselves complex, can be summed up quite simply: We recommend closing the back door to undocumented/illegal migration, opening the front door a little more to accommodate legal migration in the interests of this country, defining our immigration goals clearly and providing a structure to implement them effectively, and setting forth procedures which will lead to fair and efficient adjudication and administration of U.S. immigration laws.

## The United States and the World

In emphasizing that our recommendations must be consistent with U.S. national interests, we are aware of the fact that we live in a shrinking, interdependent world and that world economic and political forces result in the migration of peoples. We also are aware of how inadequately the world is organized to deal with the dislocations that occur as a result of such migrations. None of the great international issues of our time — arms control, energy, food or migration — can be solved entirely within the framework of a nation-state world. Certainly, there is no unilateral U.S. solution to any of these problems; we must work with a world organized along nation-state lines and with existing international organizations. As a nation responsible for the destiny of its people and their descendants, we can better deal with these problems by working with other nations to build more effective international mechanisms. That is why we begin our recommendations with a call for a new emphasis on internationalizing world migration issues. Since many, large-scale, international migrations are caused by war, poverty and persecution within sending nations, it is in the national interests of the United States to work with other nations to prevent or ameliorate those conditions.

## Immigration and the National Interest

That immigration serves humanitarian ends is unquestionable: most immigrants come to the United States seeking reunion with their families or as refugees. But in examining U.S. immigration policy and developing its recommendations, the Select Commission also asked another question: Is immigration and the acceptance of refugees in the U.S. national interest? That question was asked by many in this country when Fidel Castro pushed his own citizens out of Cuba knowing that their main destination would be the United States. Nothing about immigration — even widespread visa abuse and illegal border crossings — seems to have upset the American people more than the Cuban push-out of 1980. But these new entrants were neither immigrants nor refugees, having entered the United States without qualifying as either. Their presence brought home to most Americans the fact that U.S. immigration policy was out of control. It also brought many letters to the Select Commission calling for restrictions on U.S. immigration.

It is easy to understand the feelings which motivated these opinions, but in the light of hard-headed U.S. interests it would be a mistake to let the emotion generated by an unusual, almost bizarre episode guide national policy. While the Cuban push-out should not be permitted to happen again, the fact that it happened once should not blind us to the advantages of legally accepting a reasonable number of immigrants and refugees.

To the question: Is immigration in the U.S. national interest?, the Select Commission gives a strong but qualified yes. A strong yes because we believe there are many benefits which immigrants bring to U.S. society; a qualified yes because we believe there are limits on the ability of this country to absorb large numbers of immigrants effectively. Our work during the past 19 months has confirmed the continuing value of accepting immigrants and refugees to the United States, in addition to the humanitarian purpose served. The research findings are clear: Immigrants, refugees and their children work hard and contribute to the economic well-being of our society; strengthen our social security system and manpower capability; strengthen our ties with other nations; increase our language and cultural resources and powerfully demonstrate to the world that the United States is an open and free society.

New immigrants benefit the United States and reaffirm its deepest values. One can see them in New Orleans, where Indochinese refugees, hard at work during the day, crowd classrooms at night to learn English; in Fall River, Massachusetts, a city with more than 20 identifiable ethnic groups whose ancestral flags fly in front of City Hall and which has been restored to economic health by recent Portuguese immigrants; in Koreatown in Los Angeles, where Korean Americans have taken an inner-city slum and transformed it into a vital community; in Florida, where Cuban Americans have renewed the City of Miami, through economic ties to Latin America; in Chicago, where young Jewish immigrants from the Soviet Union work two jobs in addition to attending high school; in San Antonio, where new Mexican immigrants are taking advantage of English-literacy classes and have joined Mexican Americans with many generations of U.S. residence to create a healthy economy and to strengthen trade and cultural ties with our border neighbor; and in Denver, where, in a third grade class, students from five countries are learning the history of the United States and are learning to count in two foreign languages in addition to English, and where, in February 1980, a Vietnamese American third grader who had been in this country for only six months, identified George Washington as "the father of our country."

But even though immigration is good for this country, the Commission has rejected the arguments of many economists, ethnic groups and religious leaders for a great expansion in the number of immigrants and refugees to be accepted by the United States. Many of those in favor of expanded immigration have argued that the United States is capable of absorbing far greater numbers of immigrants than are now admitted. They contend that:

- The United States has the lowest population density of any wealthy, industrial nation in the world, with the exceptions of Canada and Australia; and

- The United States, with only six percent of the world's population, still accounts for 25 percent of the world's gross national product.

They further point out that the United States faces serious labor shortages in the decade to come, particularly of young and middle-aged workers. Greatly expanded immigration, they believe, will go a long way towards providing needed workers.

Religious leaders have presented some of these same arguments from a different perspective. They, too, note the vast resources and relatively low population density of the United States, but argue that this nation has a humanitarian responsibility to provide immigration opportunities to those seeking entry on the basis of family reunification or as refugees. They wish the United States to preserve its role as a country of large-scale immigration, despite fears about the entry of the foreign-born.

Historians, in their support of increased immigration, have cautioned against overly restrictionist tendencies. They point out that U.S. citizens have always been concerned about the arrival of immigrants, but note that immigrants have always made contributions to U.S. society. These scholars also state that the proportion of foreign-born citizens in the United States is now at an all-time low since 1850, when the government began to keep such statistics. If immigration did no harm to U.S. society when foreign-born citizens accounted for 14 to 15 percent of the population, they argue it should certainly cause no internal problems now.

The Select Commission is, however, recommending a more cautious approach. This is not the time for a large-scale expansion in legal immigration — for resident aliens or temporary workers — because the first order of priority is bringing undocumented/illegal immigration under control, while setting up a rational system for legal immigration.

The Commission is, therefore, recommending a modest increase in legal immigration sufficient to expedite the clearance of backlogs — mainly to reunify families — which have developed under the current immigration system and to introduce a new system, which we believe will be more equitable and more clearly reflect our interests as a nation.

Such a modest increase will continue to bring the benefits of immigration to the United States without exacerbating fears — not always rational — of competition with immigrants. Such an increase recognizes that immigrants create as well as take jobs and readily pay more into the public coffers than they take out, as research completed for the Select Commission shows. It also recognizes that immigrants in some locales do compete for jobs, housing and space in schools with citizens and previously entered resident aliens. In the case of refugees, there is an immediate competition with needy U.S. citizens for a variety of services which must be paid for by U.S. taxpayers. In many communities, local officials have complained about the strains which a sudden influx of refugees has placed on their capabilities to provide health services, schooling and housing.

The American people have demonstrated that they are willing to do what must be done to save a portion of the world's refugees from persecution and sometimes even from death. That is why the Select Commission has endorsed the Refugee Act of 1980, even while questioning aspects of its administration. But it is impossible for the United States to absorb even a large proportion of the 16 million refugees in this world and still give high priority to meeting the needs of its own poor, especially those in its racial and ethnic minorities. Our present refugee policy may seem unduly harsh and narrow to many, particularly when a terribly poor country such as Somalia has more than one million refugees in its care. But we must be realistic about our obligations as a society to persons in need who already live in this country.

## Undocumented/Illegal Migration

Illegal migrations of persons in search of work occur extensively throughout Europe, Latin America, as well as in Canada and the United States. Such migration to the United States is so extensive that hundreds of thousands of persons annually enter this country outside of the law. Although these migrants usually do not stay, each year tens of thousands of other aliens remain in the United States illegally after coming here originally as students or other nonimmigrant aliens. The Select Commission is well aware of the widespread dissatisfaction among U.S. citizens with an immigration policy that seems to be out of control.

Some have argued before the Select Commission that there is virtually nothing that can be done about the tidal movements of people that are propelled by economic forces. They believe this is particularly true in a country such as ours, with land and coastal borders which are easy to cross and where millions of tourists and students, having entered, find it easy to stay. Some have further testified that the United States has nothing to fear from illegal migration since immigrants who come or remain outside of the law are self-selected, hard working, highly creative persons who, even if they remain in this country, aid rather than harm U.S. society. This is a view that the Commission believes does not sufficiently consider the serious problems created by illegal migration.

One does not have to be able to quantify in detail all of the impacts of undocumented/illegal aliens in the United States to know that there are some serious adverse effects. Some U.S. citizens and resident aliens who can least afford it are hurt by competition for jobs and housing and a reduction of wages and standards at the workplace. The existence of a fugitive underground class is unhealthy for society as a whole and may contribute to ethnic tensions. In addition, widespread illegality erodes confidence in the law generally, and immigration law specifically, while being unfair to those who seek to immigrate legally.

The Select Commission's determination to enforce the law is no reflection on the character or the ability of those who desperately seek to work and provide for their families. Coming from all over the world, they represent, as immigrants invariably do, a portion of the world's most ambitious and creative men and women. But if U.S. immigration policy is to serve this nation's interests, it must be enforced effectively. This nation has a responsibility to its people — citizens and resident aliens — and failure to enforce immigration law means not living up to that responsibility.

The strong desire to regain control over U.S. immigration policy is one of several reasons for the Commission's unanimous vote to legalize a substantial portion of the undocumented/illegal aliens now in our country. Another is its acknowledgment that, in a sense, our society has participated in the creation of the problem. Many undocumented/illegal migrants were induced to come to the United States by offers of work from U.S. employers who recruited and hired them under protection of present U.S. law. A significant minority of undocumented/illegal aliens have been part of a chain of family migrants to the United States for at least two generations. Often entering for temporary work, these migrants began coming to the United States before this nation imposed a ceiling on legal immigration from the Western Hemisphere in 1968 and a 20,000 per-country visa ceiling on legal immigration for each Western Hemisphere country in 1976.

But that is not the main reason for legalizing a substantial portion of those who are here. Legalizing those who have settled in this country and who are otherwise qualified will have many positive benefits for the United States as a whole:

- Hard-working, law-abiding persons with a stake in U.S. society will come out into the open and contribute much more to it;

● No longer exploitable at the workplace, they no longer will contribute to depressing U.S. labor standards and wages;

● New and accurate information about migration routes and the smuggling of people into the United States will contribute to the targeting of enforcement resources to stop illegal migrations in the future;

● New and accurate information about the origins of migration will enable the United States to work with large sending countries in targeting aid and investment programs to deal with migration pressures at the source, in the villages and provinces of those countries;

● New and accurate information about patterns of visa abuse by those who entered as nonimmigrant aliens will help to make our visa issuance process and control at ports of entry more effective;

The recommended legalization program will help to enforce the law, however, only if other enforcement measures designed to curtail future illegal migration to the United States are instituted. That is why the Commission has linked the legalization program to the introduction of such measures. Recognizing that future migration pressures could lead to even higher levels of illegal migration to the United States, the Commission has emphasized the development of effective enforcement strategies, including a new law to penalize employers who hire undocumented/illegal aliens and new measures to control the abuse of nonimmigrant status.

No one on this Commission expects to stop illegal migration *totally* or believes that new enforcement measures can be instituted without cost. But we do believe that we can reduce illegal entries sharply, and that the social costs of not doing so may be grave. What is a serious problem today, could become a monumental crisis as migration pressures increase.

## The Reunification of Families

A better immigration system may help to reduce the pressures for illegal migration to some extent. A look at present U.S. immigration statistics reveals one relatively small but important source of illegal migration. Of the more than one million persons now registered at consular offices waiting for visas, more than 700,000 are relatives of U.S. citizens or resident aliens, including spouses and minor children of resident aliens. There is something wrong with a law that keeps out — for as long as eight years — the small child of a mother or father who has settled in the United States while a nonrelative or less close relative from another country can come in immediately. Certainly a strong incentive to enter illegally exists for persons who are separated from close family members for a long period of time.

What is basically wrong is that we have not made clear our priority to reunify the immediate relatives of U.S. residents regardless of their nationality. Among our recommendations are two which would help to do just that.

The first puts immigrants whose entry into the United States would reunify families on a separate track from other immigrants. The second puts spouses and minor children of lawful permanent resident aliens under a separate, numerically limited category without country ceilings. Eliminating country ceilings in this category, should help assure the reunification of the families of permanent resident aliens on a first-come, first-served basis within a fixed world ceiling.

## Independent Immigrants

The creation of a separate category for nonfamily immigrants — the independent category — may also somewhat reduce illegal immigration by broadening immigration opportunities. It reaffirms the importance to the United States of traditional "new seed" immigrants who come to work, save, invest and plan for their children and grandchildren, and creates an immigration channel for persons who cannot enter the United States on the basis of family reunification. It is the Commission's hope that this category will provide immigration opportunities for those persons who come from countries where immigration to the United States has not been recent or from countries that have no immigration base here.

Many other important issues have also been addressed by the Select Commission, including an upgrading of our system for administering U.S. immigration laws, the need to streamline deportation proceedings, and the importance of English-language acquisition. We have tried to address these and other issues with open minds, recognizing that few of them can be resolved easily.

That there is disagreement on some issues among Commissioners is not surprising since we represent a great variety of perspectives and since the complex issues of immigration are charged with emotion and special interest. Even though we have disagreed among ourselves in formulating some answers, we have reached consensus on a great many of the questions which faced us. Our basic concern has been the common good which must characterize good U.S. law, and we have tried to recommend policies that would be responsible, equitable, efficient and enforceable.

We have not, of course, answered every question and our answers are far from perfect, but we believe we asked the right questions and that the answers are free from the cant, hypocrisy and racism which have sometimes characterized U.S. immigration policy in years gone by. With that in mind, we hope that our recommendations, in the words of George Washington, "set a standard to which the wise and honest can repair."

# 'TO BREATHE CLEAN AIR'

## March 2, 1981

*Of the controversial and costly legislation designed to clean up the nation's polluted air, the National Commission on Air Quality (NCAQ) found in its report released March 2 that the "Clean Air Act has worked well." In introducing the study, Sen. Gary Hart, D-Colo., claimed that the quality of air is measurably better than it was in 1970 and that it is continuing to improve. "Although it is difficult to quantify this information, it is certain that if the Clean Air Act had not been enacted, our air quality would be far worse today than in 1970," Hart, the commission chairman, said as he presented its report to Congress.*

*The study, "To Breathe Clean Air," represented the two-and-a-half-year effort of the 13-member, bipartisan commission drawn from government and industry that was authorized in 1977 when the Clean Air Act was most recently revised. The report contained 433 findings and 109 recommendations on how Congress should amend the Clean Air Act, which was scheduled for revision again in 1981-82.*

### Major Findings

*Specifically, the report concluded that:*

*● The nation's air was "measurably better." In six or seven years, probably only eight metropolitan areas would fail to meet the national standards set for safe air, including Los Angeles and Ventura, Calif.; Denver; New York City; Philadelphia; San Diego; Allentown, Pa.; and Houston.*

● *Improved air quality had brought benefits worth from $4.6 billion to $51.2 billion per year, while costs of installing, maintaining and operating pollution equipment were estimated to have been $16.6 billion in 1978.*

● *Air pollution controls had added about 0.2 percent to the annual inflation rate.*

● *Costs for air pollution control were likely to rise. One estimate was that about $37 billion (in 1978 dollars) would be spent in 1987 for construction, operation and maintenance of pollution controls.*

● *The act had not been an important obstacle to energy development and "substantial increases in domestic energy production" could occur without changes being made.*

● *The law had not significantly inhibited economic growth.*

*"There is virtually no evidence ... that the Clean Air Act has actually prevented construction of new industrial facilities," said Hart. The commission did find, however, that air pollution control requirements had contributed to — but not been the sole cause of — some plant closures.*

## Environmentalist Objections

*Despite its overall support of the legislation, the commission did call for changes in the law. The most controversial was a recommendation that Congress abandon the nationwide deadlines for cleaning up dirty-air cities, or non-attainment areas. A proposed change in the pollution control program for clean-air cities, called the Prevention of Significant Deterioration Program (PSD), was almost as provocative.*

*Those two revisions would represent a "serious weakening of the Clean Air Act," charged David Hawkins, an attorney for the National Clean Air Coalition, an environmental group that had vowed to "fight hard" to protect the law. He charged that the commission "chose to cut the heart out of ... the act rather than complete the more difficult process of fine-tuning it."*

*Hart, who as NCAQ chairman had tried to get unanimous approval so that the report would carry more weight with Congress, said the recommendations reflected a "general consensus" on most issues. Yet some environmentalist commission members dissented from the report and charged that in many cases the panel went "beyond compromise," overreacted to complexities in the act and chose to eliminate basic elements rather than improve them.*

## Business Dissent

*The business community was expected to object to some recommendations, including the commission's explicit rejection of the argument that the costs of compliance should be considered in setting clean-air standards. Cost/benefit analyses had increased in popularity during the Republican administration of Ronald Reagan.*

*The commission's acid rain recommendations also were expected to evoke objections from the business community. Some evidence showed that pollution in the form of sulfur dioxide and nitrogen dioxide from autos and coal-fired electric-generating plants undergoes a chemical change into acid, after which it is washed out of the sky by rain and snow, contaminating waterways and killing fish. To combat this situation, the report called for an immediate moratorium on state efforts to relax controls on the burning of high-sulfur coal in the eastern United States. Some in the utility industry had questioned whether any human health damage had been linked to acid rain.*

*Following are excerpts from the National Commission on Air Quality report, "To Breathe Clean Air," released March 2, 1981, and excerpts from the dissenting statement of Commissioner Richard E. Ayres, in which Commissioners Annemarie F. Crocetti and John J. Sheehan joined. (Bold-face headings in brackets have been added by Congressional Quarterly to highlight the organization of the texts.):*

# Introduction

A little more than a decade ago Congress passed the Clean Air Act, the first major substantive law designed to preserve the environment. Since that time the absolute level of improvement for the most widespread air pollutants has been significant. Between 1974 and 1978 there was an 18 percent reduction in the number of days during which air quality in 23 major metropolitan areas was classified as unhealthful. And nationwide, between 1973 and 1978, average annual concentrations of carbon monoxide decreased by 33 percent, sulfur dioxide by 20 percent, and suspended particulates by 7 percent.

More significant than the level of absolute reductions, however, is the difference between current pollution levels and those that would have occurred if major control efforts had not been required during the 1970s. While it is impossible to state precisely what pollution levels would be if the Act had not been passed, it is clear that for a number of pollutants the level of emissions would now be several times as great in many areas.

## PROGNOSIS FOR THE 1980s

The prognosis for the 1980s reflects a need for the control of air pollution to be a continued national priority. During the 1980s millions of people will continue to live in areas exceeding healthful levels for ozone and suspended particulates. In at least one major urban area — Los

Angeles — the ozone problem appears to be intractable and no reasonable level of effort is likely to result in attainment of the standard in that area.

The 1980s also will present new challenges that have begun to emerge during the past few years. These problems relate to toxic pollutants, indoor air pollution, acid rain, visibility degradation, and carbon dioxide buildup. In the past, attention has been focussed on the effects on public health of six pollutants over which there has been widespread concern because they are emitted by most mobile and stationary sources of pollution. The emerging problems are related to the protection of public welfare from some of these same pollutants and the protection of the health of a smaller number of persons from the effects of more toxic and potentially more harmful pollutants.

The need for continued substantial investments comes at a time when all Americans are concerned about economic problems of a magnitude experienced only a few other times in the history of the nation. Thus, it is incumbent upon policymakers to ensure that there is not only good air quality but also an appropriate balance among all of the nation's priorities....

## ECONOMIC EFFECTS

While the public recognizes and continues to endorse the national commitment to reduce the adverse effects of air pollution, the economic effects of programs developed to respond to this public concern have become a major focus of decisionmakers responsible for developing air pollution control policy. Congress has recognized since its enactment of the Clean Air Act in 1970 that a significant investment of economic resources would be necessary to accomplish the goal of providing good air quality throughout the country. Yet, as the U.S. economy has faltered in recent years and rates of inflation have reached levels previously believed possible only for countries with greater historical economic instability, concern has heightened about the effects on the economy of controlling air pollution. Studies show that this control in recent years has cost and may continue to cost $20 billion or more per year. Although these costs have had only minor effects on national indicators such as the consumer price index, gross national product, and unemployment rate, the amounts justify careful consideration of whether the nation's economic resources are being used wisely.

The small negative economic effects of air pollution controls would be minimized further if most of the benefits of control could be reflected in the statistics used in developing national economic indicators. Some studies suggest that economic benefits may even equal or exceed costs that have been borne by the nation's consumers. Because debate will continue about the validity of various studies as a result of inadequacies in available data and methodologies for calculating benefits, there will likely not be any consensus as to the relative levels of costs and benefits of the nation's air quality programs.

Concerns about economic effects are not limited to the desirability of making investments for controlling emissions. They relate also to effects on economic growth in general, and energy development in particular, and to complexities associated with locating new major facilities. Studies conducted for the Commission and others have found that there is virtually no evidence that approvals have been denied for new and expanded facilities wishing to locate in areas both meeting and not meeting the nation's air quality standards. Projections for the future indicate also that facilities can be sited even when assumptions of high levels of energy and other growth are made. Determining whether decisions have been made by corporate policymakers, however, not to seek approvals for industrial expansion presents myriad problems because of the difficulty of assessing the numerous factors important in making substantial capital investments.

Although it appears from Commission studies that energy and other economic expansion can proceed largely as planned under federal air quality laws, the conclusions reached also find that there are few projected benefits associated with parts of the nation's prevention of significant deterioration program. These findings do not relate to the parts of the program designed to protect clean air areas of major national significance, such as national parks. In addition, Commission studies demonstrate that complexities in other programs, particularly some associated with federal-state relationships, are yielding few benefits.

While any air pollution control program will be inherently complex because of the nature of air pollution and the methods for controlling it, each program must be carefully evaluated to determine whether the benefits justify the associated costs, including those related to complexity. Obviously, such complexity has its associated cost to industry and ultimately to consumers.

The Commission particularly emphasized studies to determine whether the nation's effort to reduce its reliance on imported oil through production of domestic energy resources such as coal would be impeded by current clean air programs. With isolated exceptions of little significance through 1990 and in the Southwest through 1995 the Commission found that even high levels of projected energy development could be accommodated. However, efforts on planning for certain energy facilities, particularly oil shale projects, could occur as early as the mid-1980s. Moreover, the projected development can proceed if appropriate controls are installed and other pollution control efforts are continued without exacerbating any problems associated with pollutants which have traditionally been controlled.

Climatic changes associated with carbon dioxide buildup, and possible emissions of toxic pollutants require, however, thoughtful planning of the nation's energy programs. They also vividly demonstrate that increased energy efficiency has substantially associated benefits which go far beyond lower energy costs to the public.

## THE CLEAN AIR ACT

The structure of the Clean Air Act — as it was enacted in 1970 and modified in 1977 — provided the framework for the Commission's research activities. While the cornerstone of the Act's requirements are the provisions providing for the establishment of national ambient air quality standards to protect public health and public welfare, the Act includes specific technology requirements that also must be met regardless of whether they are necessary to meet specific air quality standards. This structure reflects a decision by Congress to combine the two general approaches available for addressing pollution problems — a goals-oriented approach and a technology-based one, rather than rely on either one alone.

The goals of the Act are embodied in the separate ambient air quality standards that are to be established for the protection of public health with an adequate margin of safety (primary standards) and for the protection of public welfare (secondary standards). Congress did not specify in the Act criteria to be taken into consideration in determining appropriate primary and secondary standards, but included a procedure for the development of criteria documents which are to delineate the basis for standards established by EPA [Environmental Protection Agency].

The Act provided also for the establishment of technology-related emission standards to control pollutants that endanger Americans and their environment. The Environmental Protection Agency is to establish national emission standards for hazardous air pollutants to protect against risks of irreversible health effects and incapacitating reversible effects. Under the Act, these standards must be set so as to ensure an ample margin of safety. In the 1977 amendments, Congress authorized EPA to set design or equipment standards for these hazardous pollutants if it is unable to determine an appropriate level for setting an emission standard for a particular pollutant.

The most well-known of the emission standards are those for automobiles. Congress declared in 1970 that those standards should lead to the reduction of the three major transportation-related pollutants by 90 percent. Since that time, there have been extensions of the deadlines to meet the standards for two of the pollutants — hydrocarbons and carbon monoxide — and a relaxation and extension of the standard for the other pollutant — nitrogen oxides. Except for provision for waivers, the ultimate level of control from these standards will be achieved on all vehicles beginning in the 1981 model year....

The Act directs that areas of the country be designated as attainment or nonattainment, depending upon whether they meet national ambient air quality standards. Attainment status determines which of two control programs apply to an area.

In areas not meeting an ambient standard, the nonattainment program requires adoption of all reasonable control measures, implementation of a permit program for new sources, and continuing progress toward meeting the standard by 1982 or, in some cases, 1987....

In areas where air quality is better than required to meet national ambient standards, the Act limits the amount of additional pollution which will be permitted. In certain areas such as larger national parks, very little additional pollution is allowed, while in other areas limitations are less stringent. In no case may air quality exceed the level set by a national ambient standard. . . .

## [CONCLUSION]

The Commission's recommendations reflect a general conclusion that the structure of the Clean Air Act is sound and needs refinement instead of fundamental changes. The changes proposed by the commission would accomplish this result by simplifying and strengthening the parts of the programs which have worked well, modifying or eliminating those which have not worked well, and adding new elements to address new problems. Taken as a whole, these recommendations would protect better the public health and welfare against air pollution; reduce unnecessary regulatory burdens; and ensure that we can meet our nation's economic, energy, and other important goals.

## Commission Findings

### [PUBLIC HEALTH STANDARDS]

### [Air Quality Standards]

1. To protect public health, government must act to control potentially harmful pollutants despite scientific uncertainty about the precise harm they cause and the levels of exposure that cause that harm. On this principle, the Act requires EPA to set national primary air quality standards to protect against pollution levels that "endanger public health, allowing an adequate margin of safety." This statutory mandate, which does not include consideration of economic factors, and the legislative history describing populations Congress intends EPA to protect, give EPA authority of a broadly precautionary nature to protect people against the adverse health effects of air pollution in a context of scientific uncertainty. . . .

6. The costs of meeting primary air quality standards are best taken into account in determining what control programs should be implemented in specific areas of the country, not in establishing a national air quality standard to protect public health. Although the level of air pollution affecting public health generally does not vary in different locations, the costs of meeting any specific standard will vary substantially, depending upon the severity of existing pollution levels, from one area to another. Thus, if a national air quality standard were based in part on the costs of complying with it, the very high costs of meeting the standard in a few severely polluted areas would probably require that the standard be set at a

less protective level than is achievable in a reasonable, economic fashion in most areas of the country. The most effective balance between the beneficial effects of good air quality on human health and the economic, social, energy, and other costs of meeting health-based standards will be achieved when conditions in particular areas can be considered in deciding when the standards should be met in the areas and what measures will be adopted to meet the standards.

7. Although not required by the Act to do so, EPA has conducted economic impact analyses as part of its process of revising the air quality standards for carbon monoxide, sulfur dioxide, ozone, and particulates. These analyses were required by an executive order issued in 1978 and superseded by an order issued February 17, 1981, that requires agencies to analyze and publish the possible economic consequences of proposed regulations that will have an estimated annual effect on the economy of at least $100 million. . . .

## [Commission Recommendations]

### NONATTAINMENT PROGRAM

. . . 47. All state implementation plans as revised in 1979 and approved by EPA should remain in effect and be implemented on the schedule specified in the plans to the extent such plans are consistent with the Commission's recommendations. States should be required to continue to fulfill those responsibilities required by EPA in 1979 and 1980 conditional approvals that are consistent with the Commission's recommendations.

48. State plan revisions should continue to be required in 1982 for all areas determined to exceed air quality standards as of December 31, 1981. The revisions should be required to include requirements for the installation of reasonably available control technology on existing sources or measures that would lead to equivalent emission reductions, except in areas that EPA determines will meet the air quality standards by December 31, 1983, and requirements for the implementation of the offset policy. Transportation control measures in ozone and carbon monoxide plan revisions should no longer be mandatory.

49. Motor vehicle inspection and maintenance programs should be required only in urban areas with populations greater than 500,000 where peak 1981 air pollution levels (using existing EPA designation guidance) are 50 percent greater than either the ozone or the carbon monoxide ambient air quality standard, instead of in all areas exceeding the ozone or carbon monoxide air quality standard by December 31, 1982.

50. Areas exceeding the ozone or carbon monoxide air quality standard but not required to implement inspection and maintenance programs should be permitted to implement inspection and maintenance programs instead of the offset policy for ozone and carbon monoxide.

51. Every 3 years, all areas exceeding air quality standards should be

required to implement additional reasonably available control technology identified by EPA or measures that would lead to equivalent reductions. States should be required to submit plan revisions that incorporate such technology requirements to EPA for review and approval.

52. The process for 3-year reviews described in the commission's recommendations should be substituted for the 1982 and 1987 deadlines for meeting air quality standards. This change does not affect approved dates of compliance for sources in state implementation plans. The states should continue to be required to meet air quality standards in all areas as expeditiously as practicable. The state should specify a date by which it intends to meet the standards. This date will not be subject to EPA and judicial review and will not be federally enforceable.

53. The Environmental Protection Agency should ensure that reasonably available control technology or offsets or other measures to achieve equivalent emission reductions are included in state plans where necessary to maintain air quality standards in areas meeting the standards.

54. As required by the Act, EPA should continue to be authorized to adopt requirements of reasonably available control technology in states not meeting air quality standards and failing to require that technology or equivalent measures.

55. The statutory system of withholding federal funds as sanctions in areas not meeting the Act's requirements for pollution controls in areas exceeding air quality standards should be replaced by a graduated system of sanctions. The sanctions should include those now mandated and authorized by the Act. EPA should be given discretionary authority to impose the sanctions based on the degree of failure to implement measures.

56. Existing sources that have been required to install equipment to control a particular pollutant should not be required during the next 10 years to install additional control equipment for that pollutant if the additional equipment would supplant the initial equipment. However, this exemption should not apply if new controls are needed to meet an air quality standard for a newly regulated pollutant or to comply with new regulations for a hazardous pollutant.

57. The Act's requirement that new sources in areas exceeding air quality standards install controls providing for the lowest achievable emission rate should be repealed and replaced by identical requirements for all new sources (in areas either violating or meeting standards), requiring best available control technology, the same type of technology now required in areas meeting air quality standards. The determination of best available control technology should be made on a case-by-case basis in accordance with the requirements under the Act's current definition of best available control technology with the following exceptions:

- A source that emits less than 500 tons of a pollutant per year and for which a new source performance standard has been established should be subject only to the new source performance standard; and

● A source that will emit 1,000 tons or more of a pollutant per year should be required to provide at least the same level of control that has been required in the same federal region for a source in the same category that emits 1,000 tons or more per year of the pollutant, unless the operator of the new source demonstrates that such previously determined control level will not provide sufficient air quality benefits to justify the incremental control over alternative best available control technology levels. In no case should emissions be allowed to exceed applicable new source performance standards. The Administrator would be authorized to modify the boundaries of a region, for the purposes of determining previously applicable best available control technology levels, to take into account regional air quality values.

58. New sources should not be required to install additional control equipment during the 10-year period after the source started operations, unless new controls are needed to meet an air quality standard for a newly regulated pollutant or to comply with new regulations for a hazardous pollutant.

59. The emissions offset policy should be revised to allow a state to require a new source in an area violating air quality standards to pay a fee instead of securing offsets, if the state develops and agrees to implement a plan to use such fees to reduce other emissions of the same pollutant. The Environmental Protection Agency should set the fees on a national basis for each pollutant, based upon the emission control costs of new source performance standards.

60. If EPA sets an air quality standard for a new pollutant, states should have 3 years to adopt and implement reasonably available control technology in areas exceeding the standard.

61. The Environmental Protection Agency should determine by December 31, 1982, which areas of the country do not meet each air quality standard based on air quality information through December 31, 1981.

62. The Environmental Protection Agency should continue to issue, and should revise every 6 years, control technique guideline documents to help states determine reasonably available control technology for categories of sources contributing significantly to violations of air quality standards.

63. By January 30, 1984, and then at least once every 3 years, EPA should review each state's progress in meeting air quality standards. The Environmental Protection Agency should use this review after consultation with state officials, to determine whether an area continues to exceed an air quality standard, and if so, to provide necessary guidance to ensure that additional reasonably available control technologies and new revisions of the state's plans are adopted.

64. By July 30, 1984, and then every 3 years, EPA and appropriate state and local agencies should develop jointly a program plan for coordinated future federal, state, and local actions. The program plan should include

additional reasonably available control technology necessary to meet and maintain standards, other necessary state procedural and administrative requirements, and an indication of state and federal funding and resource commitments. Funds for federal program grants should be made available upon completion of this program plan.

## [PREVENTION OF SIGNIFICANT DETERIORATION]

65. The preconstruction review requirements of the Act's prevention of significant deterioration (PSD) provisions should apply to all new major sources, as currently defined in the Act, and to modifications of existing major sources that increase net emissions from the source by more than *de minimis* levels. *De minimis* emission rates for nitrogen oxides, sulfur dioxide, particulate matter, and hydrocarbons should be increased to 100 tons.

66. Sources subject to preconstruction review should continue to be required to apply the best available control technology to control the emissions of any criteria or noncriteria pollutant that exceed *de minimis* levels after the application of pollution controls. The determination of best available control technology should be made on a case-by-case basis in accordance with the requirements under the Act's definitions, with the following exceptions:

- A source that emits less than 500 tons of a pollutant per year and for which a new source performance standard has been established should be subject only to the new source performance standard; and
- A source that will emit 1,000 tons or more of a pollutant per year should be required to provide at least the same level of control that has been required in the same federal region for a source in the same category that emits 1,000 tons or more per year of the pollutant, unless the operator of the new source demonstrates that such previously determined control level will not provide sufficient air quality benefits to justify the incremental control over alternative best available control technology levels. In no case should emissions be allowed to exceed applicable new source performance standards. The Administrator would be authorized to modify the boundaries of a region, for the purposes of determining previously applicable best available control technology levels, to take into account regional air quality values.

67. New sources should not be required to install additional control equipment during the 10-year period after the source started operations, unless new controls are needed to meet air quality standards for a newly regulated pollutant or to comply with new regulations for a hazardous pollutant.

68. The statutory requirement that proposed new sources submit air quality monitoring data gathered over a period of up to one calendar year

should be eliminated. Instead, the reviewing agency should be given the discretion to require preconstruction monitoring for up to one year and postconstruction monitoring data. The Environmental Protection Agency should continue to publish guidelines for state use in determining the need for actual on-site monitoring. . . .

70. The Environmental Protection Agency should be required to publish a biannual list of best available control technology determinations, regional best available control technology determinations, and other control technology (for source categories that contribute significant amounts of pollution) that has been installed on various sources where such information is available. This information should include sufficient details to make it useful to reviewing agency personnel.

71. a. The existing Class I increment system should be retained without change. In addition, the federal land manager for each Class I area should be authorized to establish a monitoring network for detecting the effects of new pollution sources on air quality within the area. The federal land manager should be authorized to establish a baseline (for determining increments) if and when the federal land manager determines that new sources are likely to affect air quality-related values within the area. EPA, in consultation with the federal land manager, should publish guidelines adopted pursuant to public notice and comment procedures applicable to EPA, describing criteria for these determinations. In the absence of a determination by the federal land manager, the baseline should be determined according to the current provisions of the Act.

b. States and Indian governing bodies also should be authorized to establish a baseline under the same conditions as federal land managers, for Class I lands within their jurisdiction other than those federal lands for which the federal land manager has direct management responsibility. The Environmental Protection Agency, in consultation with the states and Indian governing bodies, should publish guidelines adopted pursuant to public notice and comment procedures applicable to EPA, describing criteria for these determinations. In the absence of a determination by a state or Indian governing body, the baseline should be determined according to the current provisions of the Act.

72. a. Class III should be eliminated.

b. Class II should be limited to (1) those areas that cannot be redesignated as Class III under the current Act; and (2) those clean air areas which states or Indian tribes choose to designate as Class II.

c. Tracking of short-term Class II increment consumption should be eliminated, but all major new and modified sources . . . subject to PSD review should still be required to demonstrate that the new source itself will not exceed short-term increments and that emissions from the major sources and other sources in the area will not cause or contribute to violation of annual increments.

73. The current visibility protection program, which is designed to protect visibility in Class I areas and in specified "integral vista" areas adjacent to some Class I areas, should be retained.

74. Surface mining of coal should be included in the list of sources subject to the visibility provisions of the Act. Congress should consider whether other types of surface mining should be included.

## MOBILE SOURCE CONTROLS

75. The statutory gasoline and diesel automobile hydrocarbon standard of 0.41 grams per mile should be retained.

76. The statutory nitrogen oxides standard of 1.0 grams per mile should be retained for gasoline automobiles. The Act should be amended to replace the waiver provision for light diesel automobiles through the 1984 model year with a 1.5 gram per mile standard through the 1984 model year. The existing provisions for exemptions from the nitrogen oxides standard for low volume manufacturers and innovative technology on automobiles should be retained.

77. The final statutory carbon monoxide automobile standard of 3.4 grams per mile shuld be changed to 7.0 grams per mile, to be effective as soon as practicable after enactment of amendments to the Act, and remain in effect through the 1986 model year. The Environmental Protection Agency should be given authority to continue the 7.0 grams per mile standard beyond model year 1986 or establish a standard between 3.4 and 7.0 grams per mile if it is found that protection of public health can be achieved as expeditiously and effectively with a 7.0 grams per mile or an intermediate standard as with the 3.4 grams per mile standard.

78. The Environmental Protection Agency should continue to evaluate the 0.2 gram per mile particulate standard for diesel automobiles and the 0.26 gram per mile standard for light diesel trucks currently scheduled to take effect in 1985, and report to Congress within 6 months of enactment of amendments to the Act.

79. The statutory carbon monoxide and hydrocarbon standards for heavy gasoline trucks, and the carbon monoxide and hydrocarbon standards established by EPA for light trucks, should be retained. The acceptable quality level for heavy gasoline trucks weighing 8,500 pounds and over should be revised to be consistent with those that apply to automobiles.

80. The Act's provisions on nitrogen oxides emission standards for light and heavy trucks should be retained, including the existing EPA authority to relax the standards from the presumed 75 percent reduction.

81. The current provisions of Sections 202 and 206 of the Act relating to motor vehicles at high altitude should be replaced by new provisions:

a. Affirming the 1982-1983 model year automobile and light truck high altitude standards adopted by the EPA, and establishing a similar requirement of proportional reduction at high altitude for 1984 and 1985 model year light trucks;

b. Requiring manufacturers to demonstrate that model year 1984 and later automobiles and 1986 and later light trucks sold in areas at least 4,000 feet above sea level will comply with the appropriate national emissions standards; EPA should be authorized to grant waivers from this requirement for those automobiles and light trucks for which EPA determines that compliance with the requirement would be unusually expensive or impractical, subject to a limit, to be determined by Congress, on the number of vehicles for which waivers may be granted to ensure that the waivers do not affect significantly air quality in high altitude areas;

c. Either requiring or explicitly authorizing EPA, after determining the air quality and other effects of doing so, to require manufacturers to demonstrate that heavy trucks at high altitude (1) will comply with the national emission standards, or (2) will reduce emissions at high altitude by the same percentage as the appropriate national emission standards represent for emissions at sea level;

d. Allowing EPA to use any appropriate means to review and approve the manufacturers' demonstration of compliance with the high altitude requirements in (a), (b), and (c); and

e. Requiring manufacturers to provide to appropriate dealers and service facilities in high altitude areas the specifications developed by the manufacturers, under Section 215 of the Act, for performance adjustments to vehicles that have not been designed or adjusted for use in high altitude areas....

## [Dissenting Statement]

We must dissent from the Commission's report, which we feel falls short of providing an appropriate guide to Congress for its coming consideration of the Clean Air Act.

The Commission's report recommends fundamental alterations in two of the most basic programs of the Clean Air Act — the nonattainment program, designed to clean up unhealthy air, and the program to prevent deterioration of clean air. In these areas, the Commission's report has overreacted to acknowledged problems, eliminating necessary programs rather than correcting. These recommendations were adopted, and more modest alternatives rejected, by narrow margins (a tie vote in one case). Because we believe the Commission report's proposals would significantly weaken our nation's effort to cleanse dirty air and conserve clean air we cannot commend the entire report to Congress, even though we strongly agree with some of its recommendations....

### [MAJOR DISAGREEMENTS]

We turn now to the areas where we must state our strong disagreement with the Commission's report — in particular its recommendations to eliminate deadlines for achieving health standards; to eliminate requiring new plants in polluted areas to meet "lowest achievable emission rate"; to allow automatic approval of even defective state programs if delay occurs in reviewing them, regardless of the reason; and to abandon the air quality management plan designed to limit significant deterioration of clean air outside national parklands and wilderness areas.

## [DEADLINES]

The Clean Air Act recognizes a basic right of the American people to air that is fit to breathe. To secure this right, the Act created a program with three essential parts:

—National air quality standards, set at the levels needed to protect people's health,

—Deadlines for meeting those standards, and

—State planning and implementation, under federal review, of the emission control measures needed to meet the standards by the deadline.

The program has brought about important progress. As the Commission has found, in the 1970's pollution levels in the nation's dirty areas dropped substantially. Vast areas of the country which exceeded the standards in 1970 now have met them. Scores of millions more people, who live in those areas, now enjoy healthful air. More than 13,000 premature deaths have been avoided every year. And if currently programmed pollution control efforts do not falter, by the Clean Air Act's 1987 deadline for meeting the last standards, most areas now failing to attain will meet the federal standards. This will provide healthful air quality for between 15 and 70 million more people, depending upon the pollutant.

Standards and deadlines, together, are responsible for these improvements. The plain fact is that the states and EPA would have adopted and implemented far weaker emission control measures than are in place without the pressure generated by deadlines. Without a specific time for attainment, standards become just laudable goals, much too easily deferred.

To be sure, some areas — especially Los Angeles, San Diego, the New York area, Houston, and Denver — suffer such severe pollution that they are not projected to meet the Act's 1987 attainment date. These areas and others with substantial particulate problems undeniably need more time. They need the opportunity, under extended deadlines, to plan and implement the long-term emission reductions needed to reach the standards there. But while they need more time, they also need the requirement of specific dates for attainment, to be able to defend the regulatory actions and other steps they will need to take to protect people's health in a timely manner.

Seriously overreacting, however, to these areas' problems with one specific date, the Commission report recommends abolishing deadlines altogether. What is more, the Commission does not limit this proposal to just those areas with genuine difficulty meeting the existing date. Rather, the report would eliminate deadlines for *all* areas, including those currently on track, in response to the 1987 date, to attaining healthful air quality. . . .

Instead of a planning and implementation process to meet the standards by appropriate deadlines, the Commission would substitute a state and

EPA review of control requirements every three years, to see what should be done in the next three years. Supposedly, the state air pollution control agency and EPA would negotiate a set of additional control measures for reducing existing pollution which are deemed "reasonably available." This involves requiring a greater degree of emission reduction from some categories of sources that have already been subject to some requirements. It also involves placing some control requirements for the first time on types of sources that have not been controlled at all.

We believe that without deadlines, the determination of what controls are "reasonably available" would slip inevitably toward justifying status quo controls, legitimizing a failure to do more, and achieving no progress towards healthful air.

What controls are "reasonably available" is a judgment made by the states and EPA balancing the need for prompt emission control and the costs of it. Industries that would be subject to control are extremely effective at stating — and often at exaggerating — the technical difficulties and economic costs they would face. The need to attain the air quality standards by a date certain is the foil to such arguments. Without the date certain, there will be nothing concrete to limit the weight given the industries' concerns in determining what is reasonable.

Congress considered abolishing the deadlines in 1977, and wisely decided against it. Explaining that decision to the full Senate, Senator Muskie quoted with approval the opinion of EPA that deadlines are the key to progress: "If the firm statutory deadlines are nullified, every air pollution control measure imposed by EPA or a State would be held hostage to legal challenges and possible reversals on grounds of judicially-perceived 'reasonableness.' The net effect could only be further delays in ever attaining the Act's health standards.". . .

We proposed to our fellow Commissioners a workable approach to deadlines that would have both the "action-forcing" quality needed to assure attainment, and the flexibility needed in the genuine problem areas. Deadlines are essential to let citizens know if public officials are doing their jobs.

First, retain the existing 1982 and 1987 deadlines for areas that can meet them.

Second, for areas the Commission has found will not meet them, establish a process that identifies what is necessary to come into attainment, and when it can be done. States would be required to revise their State Implementation Plans within two years. The revised SIP would have to (1) specify a new date for attaining the standards, and (2) state the emission reduction measures needed to meet those deadlines, and when they will be undertaken.

Third, require EPA to review the state's deadline choices and the means indicated to attain them. EPA would disapprove a SIP only if the emission control measures specified would not, in the Agency's judgment, succeed in meeting the state's chosen deadlines. EPA would also prepare a report for Congress covering areas that projected attainment after 1987, reviewing the deadlines and measures chosen by each state, whether the measures were realistic for meeting these deadlines, and whether the deadlines could be met sooner with controls the state had decided against or overlooked.

This approach would get the most polluted areas and EPA focussing on the long-term planning needed to eventually attain the health standards even in the severe trouble spots, while maintaining means for the public to push for rapid adoption of measures that can be put in place quickly. Focussing their attention on a more realistic long-term would also remove the incentives for exaggerating what to expect from a control measure, while keeping a deadline will assure continued pressure to achieve the standards. State Implementation Plans will become both more realistic and more effective. . . .

Armed with the report prepared by EPA, Congress could judge the need for further enactments on deadlines. Congress would have a range of options. It could ratify the deadlines selected by the states. It could establish a range of attainment dates for different areas. It could set a single outside date by which all areas must meet the standards.

With this process of setting deadlines, the public would have the means to hold decisionmakers accountable for their control choices. While the Commission voted narrowly to abandon deadlines, we believe the Congress should consider the approach proposed here fully before repudiating the major device responsible for the progress achieved in the 1970s. . . .

### [PSD]

The Commission's report recommends the abandonment of the air quality management program designed to limit the pollution of clean air areas outside of our national parklands and wilderness areas.

The program Congress enacted in 1977 to protect clean air areas had as its central requirement the creation of a budget for additional pollution (called an "increment") which would limit the rate at which we spend or use up our nation's clean air resources. Congress' program established three budget levels for the country. It set a very tight budget (called Class I) for large national parks and wilderness areas, designed to restrain sharply additional pollution of those pristine areas. For the rest of the country Congress set a moderate budget (called Class II) that would allow substantial growth of well-controlled sources. To provide additional flexibility Congress set a third and larger budget (Class III) which a state could adopt for an area if it felt that the Class II budget might not provide enough room for growth.

The Commission's recommendation to drop the Class II/III program would eliminate the requirement of a moderate air pollution budget for all areas of the country outside of our national parklands and wilderness areas. Such a change would permit clean air areas in more than 90 percent of the nation to experience substantial and unnecessary pollution. This recommendation represents a major departure from a national policy of conservation of this valuable resource. We cannot support a drastic retrenchment.

The report's recommendation is not supported by its findings nor by the studies done for the Commission. The principal argument raised against the Class II/III program is that it is procedurally complex. The moderate remedy for complexity is to propose simplifying changes.... The report's recommendation chooses the extreme path of abolishing the program rather than attempting to fix it. Our nation's air resources are too important to be given away simply because the Commission did not make the effort to propose a simple and workable protection program.

The report's recommendation to eliminate Class II/III protection is by no means based on consensus. A proposal to continue Class II in a modified form failed in the Commission on a tie vote. Congress should consider this in weighing the recommendation included in the Commission's report....

# JOINT ECONOMIC REPORT

## March 2, 1981

After issuing consensus reports for the two previous years, the Joint Economic Commitee of Congress reverted in its 1981 report, released February 26, to its traditional 21-year-old practice of submitting separate Democratic and Republican prescriptions for the nation's economy.

In his introduction Sen. Roger W. Jepsen, a Republican from Iowa who became committee vice chairman in 1981, explained that in the two previous years the Republican members on the committee had supported the bipartisan effort because it "blazed a new trail in economic thought by showing ... that these outdated demand-side policies actually were a major cause of our economic problems and how a new supply-side approach ... could whip stagflation." Whereas traditional Keynsian demand-side economics held that a stimulated economy could be achieved through increased demand and consumer spending, supply-side economics purported that this could be achieved through increased saving and investment, encouraged by tax cuts.

According to Jepsen, the Democrats had "abandoned the supply-side approach" in 1981, forcing the partisan split. In his party's defense, committee Chairman Henry S. Reuss, D-Wis., maintained that the Democratic members had supported an economic program "based solidly on the supply-side recommendations" developed by the panel as a whole, but which differed significantly from the 1981 Republican JEC approach that so closely paralleled Ronald Reagan's "Program for Economic Recovery."

## Background

The U.S economy staggered into the 1980s. From 1977 through 1980, during Jimmy Carter's administration, the economy never had sustained the solid, inflation-free growth that federal economic policies sought. Instead, it lurched between slowdowns in output and sudden bursts of inflation.

The economy's faltering performance was a major, if not key, determinant of the 1980 presidential election results that turned control of the White House over to the Republicans. To combat the inflation, high interest rates and growing tax burden, Reagan and his advisers supported a supply-side economic program calling for tax cuts and reduced federal spending.

## The Republican Viewpoint

The Republican report asserted that what's "right for America" is increased economic growth, which it said can be achieved by:
- An across-the-board reduction in personal marginal income tax rates;
- Business tax reductions and accelerated depreciation allowances;
- Targeted incentives for saving and investment; and
- A reduction in government spending.

The report also called for a gradual reduction in the money supply and fewer, as well as more cost-effective, federal regulations.

The Republicans specifically addressed what they considered the two most common criticisms of the administration's supply-side theory: that gradual reductions in the money supply would increase interest rates and that across-the-board personal tax cuts would be inflationary.

According to the GOP report, inflation resulted from too great an increase in the money supply relative to the growth of goods, and "money growth must be reduced over a period of time to a level commensurate with our economy's long-run potential to expand production and maintain full employment at zero inflation." If leaders waited until inflation unwound before tightening money, they would "underwrite permanent inflation at increasingly intolerable rates."

While those on the demand side predicted personal tax cuts would stimulate spending, the committee Republicans counseled that "personal marginal tax rate cuts will impel additional work effort and production, and thereby operate to slow the rate of rise of prices."

## The Democratic Viewpoint

The Democrats claimed as the hallmark of their program "moderation in monetary and fiscal policies." They supported much of the Reagan *administration's plan, such as its calls for liberalized depreciation, for regulatory reform, and for budgetary control. But the Democrats pointed to three important differences between the Republican program and their own:*

● *If the Federal Reserve would tighten control of money, as the Republican report recommended, interest rates would remain high and discourage investment.*

● *The administration's "huge" individual income tax cuts favored the affluent, and it was not proven "that this radical tax cut will, by some trickle-down magic, produce full employment without inflation." The Democrats instead urged a moderate tax reduction and a depreciation allowance.*

● *The administration's program did not "sufficiently recognize the structural nature of our problem of investment, jobs and prices." The Democrats urged that in addition to adopting a "comprehensive strategy to stimulate jobs and investment," the president be given, if he requested it, standby authority to control wages and prices.*

*Following are excerpts from the annual report of the Joint Economic Committee, issued March 2, 1981. (Boldface headings in brackets have been added by Congressional Quarterly to highlight the organizaton of the text.):*

## [Reuss Introduction]

In his state-of-the economy address last week, President Reagan asked:

May I direct a question to those who have indicated unwillingness to accept this plan for a new beginning: an economic recovery? Have they an alternative which offers a greater chance of balancing the budget, reducing and eliminating inflation, stimulating the creation of jobs, and reducing the tax burden?

In this Report, the Joint Economic Committee Democrats present such an alternative.

This program addresses the full range of our Nation's economic difficulties. We begin, as does the Administration, with the problems of government policy: taxation, spending, regulation, and monetary policy. But we go beyond the partial answers to be found in an exclusive and narrow focus on government's role. In this Report, we address the need for fundamental structural reform throughout our economy, in the operation of government policy and in areas — such as industrial productivity, foreign energy dependence, and the wage-price spiral — which lie beyond the immediate reach of public power. We recognize that our problems are complex and deeply rooted, and that solutions require a comprehensive, cooperative approach which mobilizes the concerted efforts of labor, management, and government alike. This recognition distinguishes our program from that of the Administration. For this reason, we believe that the program we present stands the greater chance of success.

Our goal is simple: to reach full employment without inflation, as mandated by our basic Charter. We do not shrink from this responsibility. We do not consider the task to be impossible. But we recognize that there is no Aladdin's Lamp that will make our problems vanish by wishing alone. Our program will work because its components are proven and sound: investment, employment, sector-by-sector structural reform, and direct action to break the insidious spiral of inflation.

The hallmark of our program is moderation in monetary and fiscal policies, and heavy emphasis on structural reform. Structural reform is the way to escape from the macroeconomic policy trap — an unsatisfactory trade-off between intolerable inflation and intolerable unemployment — and, so to get on with economic growth, job creation, and urban and industrial revitalization. Specifically, we advocate:

(1) A monetary policy which combines continued close control over the growth of money and credit with a concerted program to bring today's high and destructive interest rates down.

(2) A tax policy of immediate relief for the lower and middle-income class groups who paid the payroll tax increases on January 1, 1981, and of liberalized business depreciation for new investment, but with a "look-before-you-leap" approach to further income tax cuts, avoiding unwise commitments to make huge tax reductions irrespective of conditions in future years.

(3) An expenditure policy which will bring control over spending and the budget, and that will do so fairly, equitably, and without destroying those programs which fight inflation and unemployment by supporting investment and creating jobs.

(4) Structural reform comprising a comprehensive strategy for investment and jobs and a program to stabilize prices, so that sensible monetary and fiscal policies will not founder or [sic] structural rigidities or wrongheaded disincentives.

(5) A firm commitment that government tax and spending actions should not increase poverty or reduce the share of income received by the middle classes.

The Administration's "Program for Economic Recovery" deserves prompt, thorough, and fair-minded consideration by the Congress. Much of it — such as to call for liberalized depreciation, for regulatory reform, for budgetary control — is exemplary. But there are important differences between the Administration's program and our own:

(1) The Administration believes that the Federal Reserve should continue to lower its monetary targets in this critical year of 1981, while we oppose such action. Interest rates are too high now, and will remain too high if the Federal Reserve continues to tighten its monetary targets even though control over inflation has not been achieved. Excessively high

interest rates will retard investment, growth, and control over Federal expenditure.

(2) The destructive fiscal facet of the Administration's program is the proposed huge individual income tax cut, amounting to more than $140 billion per year when fully effective. The tax cut favors the affluent ($30,000 for a family earning $200,000, $385 for a family earning $15,000). The assertion that this radical tax cut will, by some trickle-down magic, produce full employment without inflation is simply not proved. Instead, we urge a moderate, cost-effective tax reduction to offset the payroll tax increase, and a depreciation tax cut, followed by watchful waiting. When the budget and inflation are brought under control, the benefits should be promptly distributed to the taxpayer — but in a fair and equitable way.

(3) The Administration's program does not sufficiently recognize the structural nature of our problem of investment, jobs, and prices. Investment and job-making programs, including employment, training, economic development, and infrastructure investment programs, are repealed or drastically slashed. On the price side, there is nothing at all. The Administration utterly rejects any policy to stabilize prices, and relies instead on a wholly unproven theory that revised expectations, by themselves, will conquer inflation. We urge a comprehensive strategy to stimulate investment and jobs, based solidly on the supply-side recommendations developed in this Committee over the past two years. We urge that the President be given, if he requests it, standby authority to control wages and prices, to attack the momentum of inflation directly.

So there *is* a difference between the Administration's views and those presented in this Report. But we view this not as a stalemate, but as an opportunity for reconciliation.

The Administration says the budget must be cut. So do we, provided that the cuts are sensible and fair.

The Administration says that the growth of money and credit must be controlled. So do we, but we recommend specific action for bringing interest rates down now.

The Administration wants a vast personal income tax cut, mostly effective in the future, and we are told that, for some reason, it must be enacted now. We favor more modest tax cuts, less oriented toward the wealthy, right now, and, for the future, we favor a long, hard look before we leap.

These are not irreconcilable differences. We approach the Administration in a spirit of compromise, and we look forward to working toward a common ground.

## [Jepsen Introduction]

In the past two years, the Joint Economic Committee issued consensus reports. The Republicans on the JEC were proud to have helped forge these bipartisan reports because we believed then and believe now that their "supply-side" approach represented the best method for stopping inflation and getting our economy moving again.

This "supply-side" view was eloquently stated by the Committee Chairman, Senator Lloyd Bentsen, [D-Texas], in his introduction to the 1980 JEC Report:

> The past has been dominated by economists who focused almost exclusively on the demand side of the economy and who, as a result, were trapped into believing that there is an inevitable trade-off between unemployment and inflation. America does not have to fight inflation during the 1980's by periodically pulling up the drawbridge with recessions that doom millions of Americans to unemployment.

> The Committee's 1980 report says that steady economic growth, created by productivity gains and accompanied by a stable fiscal policy and a gradual reduction in the growth of the money supply over a period of years, can reduce inflation significantly during the 1980's without increasing unemployment. To achieve this goal, the Committee recommends a comprehensive set of policies designed to enhance the productive side, the supply side of the economy. The Committee also recommends a targeted approach to the Nation's structural economic problems and deemphasis of macro-economic fine tuning.

> The Committee recommends that fully one-half of the next tax cut be directed to enhancing saving and investment in the economy. Traditionally, tax cuts have been viewed solely as countercyclical devices designed to shore up the demand side of the economy. The Joint Economic Committee is now on record in support of the view that tax policy can and should be directed toward improving the productivity performance of the economy over the long term and need not be enacted only to counter a recession.

In its past Reports, the Joint Economic Committee blazed a new trail in economic thought by showing how the old economics has failed to solve our economic problems, that these outdated demand-side policies actually were a major cause of our economic problems and how a new supply-side approach aimed at stimulating economic growth could whip stagflation.

In this year's Report, the primary goal of the Republicans was to *build* on those consensus Reports; to improve the state of the art of supply-side economics. To accomplish this goal and to contribute substance rather than rhetoric to the national debate, the Republicans specifically addressed two major criticisms of a supply-side solution to our economic problems. To wit, that gradual reductions in the money supply will increase interest rates and, across-the-board personal marginal tax rates cuts are inflationary.

This 1981 JEC Republican Report shows that these criticisms are part myth, part ignorance and part political confusion.

We believe that the Democrats on the Joint Economic Committee have abandoned the supply-side approach which formed the basis for consensus in the past. The Democrats have chosen instead to endorse thoroughly discredited monetary policies of fine-tuning and easy money, fiscal policies to redistribute income and stimulate aggregate demand, and government allocation of credit and other scarce resources. Stagflation has been the inevitable result of these policies in the past. We cannot endorse them now.

The ten Republican members of the Joint Economic Committee have decided unanimously to issue our own Report. We cannot sign the Democrats Report. It largely affirms tried and false approaches and does not build on the 1979 and 1980 consensus Reports of this Committee. We recognize that it contains some constructive suggestions. However, on the whole, its recommendations are counter-productive, and its underlying logic is flawed.

Instead, the Republican members of the Committee have in our report built on the Committee's past consensus emphasizing saving, capital formation, slower money growth, and supply-side tax cuts. We believe that our views are right for America at this critical juncture. Let the reader judge.

## [Democratic Views]

### I. MONETARY POLICY

#### Recommendation No. 1: Long-Term Monetary Restraint

Monetary policy should be moderately restrained to reduce inflation while sustaining steady economic growth. The long-run rate of growth of money and credit is of primary importance, rather than temporary deviations from the long-run growth trajectory.

The objective of the Federal Reserve should be to bring down the long-run growth of money and credit to rates consistent with the long-run real growth potential of the economy. This means that monetary policy should adopt a posture of moderate restraint, which signals the Federal Reserve's commitment to support a national program to reduce inflation while maintaining steady growth. The Federal Reserve should make clear that noninflationary growth of money and credit must and will be achieved. Short-run deviations of money and credit from the path of long-run noninflationary growth, which are the consequence of fluctuating economic events, must not be allowed to distract either policymakers or the public from the long-run objective. The long-run money and credit targets themselves should only change in response to changes in the economy's long-run growth potential or to permanent shifts in the income velocity of money....

#### Recommendation No. 2: [Federal Reserve Should Explain Targets]

The Federal Reserve should set forth publicly each year a careful explanation of how its monetary targets have been selected. Such an explanation should relate the target to potential growth of real gross national product (GNP), to unavoidable (core) inflation, and to expected changes in the growth of velocity....

The Federal Reserve should calculate its targets each year on the basis of its long-run noninflationary money growth objective and on the state of the economy. For example, a technique could be to begin by adding to the potential growth rate of real GNP some part of the inflation rate which cannot be avoided in the forthcoming year (taken as the core rate of inflation, the underlying trend of inflation when the effects of excess demand and supply shocks have been taken out). From that value, one could substract [sic] any expected rate of increase of the velocity of money. The benchmark value derived using this option would imply a monetary policy that accommodates the economy's real growth potential and the existing core rate of inflation. If the Federal Reserve believed that a more restrained or a more stimulative policy would be called for, it should so indicate, giving its reasons....

### Recommendation No. 3: Bring Interest Rates Down

Consistent with control over the growth of money and credit, the Administration, the Federal Reserve, and the Congress should concert their actions, through the methods set forth in Recommendations 4-6, to lower interest rates....

Clearly, the general level of interest rates depends partly on the general rate of inflation. Therefore, a complete return of interest rates to historically normal levels will depend on, and must await, success against inflation. Measures to combat inflation are outlined throughout this Report.

Equally clearly, interest rates are influenced by Government's demand for credit. Measures which help to reduce the deficit, therefore, will help lower interest rates. Such measures are outlined in our chapter on fiscal policy.

### Recommendation No. 4: Do Not Tighten Targets

Since 1975, the Federal Reserve has adhered to a policy of lowering the target ranges by a small amount each year. As the Council of Economic Advisers has pointed out, the result has been erratic performance of the monetary aggregates with respect to the targets. Only in those years — 1976 and 1979 — when money demand shifted downward sharply did the growth rate of the aggregates fall within the targets. In other years — 1977, 1978, and 1980 — money demand was closer to historical levels and the targets were missed....

### Recommendation No. 6: Encourage Banks To Fight Inflation

The Administration and the Federal Reserve should encourage the banking system to develop effective methods to prevent destabilizing bursts of bank-financed lending for speculative and purely financial purposes, which make less credit available to enhance productivity and thus fight inflation.

In October, 1979, the Federal Reserve took steps to discourage bank lending for nonproductive purposes, including commodity speculation and purely financial activities, such as corporate takeovers. At that time, Chairman Volcker acknowledged that such activities compete with small business, productive capital investment, home buyers, and farmers for scarce credit resources, and can have the effect of driving up interest rates to the detriment of these productive and desirable activities.

Subsequent events, including the wave of commodity speculation in January through March, 1980, have confirmed the damage which can be done if banks fail to exercise discretion in their lending practices. Therefore, we urge the Federal Reserve to develop effective methods of persuasion to prevent destabilizing bursts of bank-financed speculative activity in the future....

## II. FISCAL POLICY

### Recommendation No. 8: Fiscal Policy: Fight Inflation and Recession

Fiscal policy should be steady and moderately restrained. This policy is necessary to reinforce the Federal Reserve's efforts to reduce inflation while supporting growth. All proposed tax and expenditure actions should be examined closely for their effects on productivity and costs....

We agree with the Administration that steps to offset the current fiscal posture of strong inflation-induced restraint are needed. But such steps should be consistent with our recommendation of steady, moderately restrained fiscal policy. Therefore, such steps should be more cautious and modest than proposed by the Administration, for two reasons.

First, the Administration is committed to increases in defense spending, over and above the significant increases proposed in the fiscal 1982 budget submitted by President Carter. That increased defense spending, if not offset by other spending cuts or absorbed by current excess capacity, will add to inflation, both by increasing the deficit and, indirectly, through the effects of military demand on the price of materiel.

Second, while Federal spending must be reduced, it is doubtful that large reductions in social spending will be achieved in time to affect expenditures significantly in fiscal 1981. Some of the cutbacks which are immediately possible — in Federal employment, and in grants to States and localities for capital projects, for example — are likely to trigger partly offsetting increases in entitlements spending — for retirement, unemployment compensation, and welfare....

### Recommendation No. 9: Liberalize Business Depreciation

Once again, we urge Congress to enact promptly a liberalization of the business depreciation allowance for new investment to increase incentives to invest, and to ensure that tax treatment does not distort business investment decisions. Prompt enactment is justified because it is the most efficient incentive to capital investment, which is especially important now in view of the entry of vast numbers of new workers into the labor pool.

We favor two changes in the tax treatment of depreciation to boost investment and productivity. First, depreciation allowances should be liberalized on new investments. Second, depreciation schedules should be reformed to remove the "non-neutrality," or bias against longer-lived investments, which affects the current system of depreciation schedules in times of high inflation.

Liberalized depreciation allowances for new business investment are needed because current allowances, which are based on historic cost, understate the real cost of replacing depreciated equipment in times of rapid inflation. Thus, depreciation allowances are smaller in real terms than Congress intended, profits are overstated, and businesses pay higher taxes and receive a lower after-tax return than they otherwise would. Liberalized depreciation allowances, constituting a move toward replacement cost depreciation would directly increase the after-tax profitability of new investment. We acknowledge the support of both the Carter and Reagan Administrations for this measure.

Depreciation schedules should also be reformed to eliminate the bias which they introduce into the composition of investment during periods of high inflation. Investment projects which yield the highest prospective returns before taxes are the most productive projects; they should, therefore, also yield the highest returns *after* taxes. Under current depreciation rules, the tax system is not "neutral" in this respect. Some projects having lower returns before taxes will be selected by companies because they have higher returns after taxes. These tax wrinkles are costly to the economy, since they result in inefficient investment patterns. In times of high inflation, nonneutrality of depreciation allowances works against long-lived investments, such as structures, and in favor of vehicles and equipment....

### Recommendation No. 10: Offset 1981 Payroll Tax Increases

An individual tax reduction designed to offset the January 1, 1981, increase in the social security payroll tax, and thus undo substantially all of the hardship imposed on the low- and middle-income groups who pay the payroll tax, should be enacted immediately.

Social security taxes will rise by $16.3 billion in 1981 as a result of a financing measures [sic] enacted in 1977. This tax falls heavily on middle income wage earners; it will increase costs and depress employment; and it may, in combination with the sizable fiscal restraint associated with income tax bracket creep, slow the economy to the point of recession or worse. There is a clear and compelling case for relief from this tax increase.

There are several different ways to effect an immediate offset of the social security payroll tax increases. One would be to roll back the payroll tax increases themselves. This has the advantage of further fighting inflation by removing the increment to employers' wage costs which the tax increases imposed, but has the disadvantage of draining revenue from the Social Security System, which might necessitate use of general revenues to maintain the fund until a more permanent solution is devised. One permanent solution which should be examined would be to extend the age of retirement gradually in later years. Another alternative would be an income tax credit to offset the payroll tax increases, which has neither the added advantage or the added disadvantage cited above. . . .

### Recommendation No. 13: Cut Spending Equitably

It is essential that spending reductions be made in a fair and equitable manner. Middle and lower income groups should not be required to carry a disproportionately great burden of budget cutbacks. Proposals to terminate or to make major reductions in Federal programs should be accompanied by economic analyses showing the effects on the living standards of different income groups and on different regions.

## III. INCOME DISTRIBUTION

### Recommendation No. 14: Do Not Worsen the Distribution of Income

The poor are threatened by proposed cutbacks in transfer programs, and the middle class has suffered a significant decline in its real income in recent years. Government tax and expenditure actions should not increase poverty or reduce the share of income going to the middle class.

## IV. STRUCTURAL REFORM

### Recommendation No. 15: [Long-Term Structural Improvement]

Even sensible monetary and fiscal policies cannot achieve full employment without inflation unless we reform our economic structure to rid it of rigidities and disincentives.

The structural rigidities and defects have proliferated in our economy as the consequence of misguided, badly designed, or dated government policies. These defects and rigidities sometimes discourage investment and jobs. Sometimes they contribute to inflation. Sometimes they do both.

We urge a comprehensive look at the ways in which government policies impede investment and promote inflation. We urge that the gamut of Federal policies be examined and, where necessary, changed to promote full employment without inflation. These include anti-competitive economic regulation, particularly in transportation and communication; cost-ineffective social regulations; inflationary trade policies; tax incentives which induce households to divert their savings to unproductive pursuits and investors to waste land, energy, credit, and other valuable resources. . . .

## IV.A. Investment and Jobs

### Recommendation No. 16: Needed: Investment and Jobs

We support the goal set out in the 1981 Economic Report of the President and by the new Administration of increasing the share of investment in GNP over the next several years. This goal is necessary to reconcile moderately restrained macroeconomic policy with a sustained push toward full employment, full production, and higher productivity growth. Components of a comprehensive investment and jobs strategy should be developed, including the actions outlined in Recommendations 17-24.

### Recommendation No. 17: Tax Incentives for Investment

Tax reduction incentives should stress the enhancement of existing and new industrial capacity and the reduction of costs of production.

Streamlining factories, modernizing equipment, and new plant and equipment investment are critical requirements for restoring economic health. The declining rate of productivity growth that has persisted throughout the 1970's and into the new decade has had a variety of causes — many of which do not readily respond to national economic policies. Whatever the range of causes, however, capital investment, particularly capital equipment that incorporates the latest scientific advances, will contribute greatly to productivity growth in American industry. To the extent American productivity improves relative to that of other industrial powers, it will also make American goods more competitive in international markets.

The current American capital stock is growing old. According to the Council of Economic Advisers, the average age of the capital stock was 7.1 years at the end of 1979. Thus, a substantial percentage of America's plant and equipment was built to take advantage of low and declining real energy prices. Everything from machine tools to factories must be redesigned to reduce the use of energy. These investments will make it possible for economic growth to proceed without sharp increases in our consumption of foreign oil.

According to recent revisions (December 1980) of the National Income and Product Accounts (NIPA), gross business fixed investment accounted for a somewhat higher percentage of GNP in the 1970's than it did in the 1960's. Yet, the diversion of investable funds to meet a faster-growing labor force, to satisfy government regulatory mandates, and to raise energy efficiency has left an inadequate residual for productivity boosting investments.

Despite the recently revised data, the Joint Economic Committee remains convinced that the 1970's was a period of inadequate investment in new plant and equipment. . . .

## Recommendation No. 21: Labor Force and Small Business

The Congress should consider ways to facilitate job creation by small businesses and to increase the proportion of Federal procurement and research and development funding that is available to small businesses, and particularly to minority-owned businesses.

Income support programs should be designed to help improve the employability of individuals by emphasizing training, education, and skill development, and should utilize small businesses, and particularly minority-owned businesses, whenever possible.

The Democrats strongly support the revitalization of small business. The share of output being produced by small businesses has been declining. Small businesses generated 43 percent of the aggregate output in 1963, 40 percent in 1972, and approximately 39 percent in 1976. This represents a decline in the share of GNP produced by small business of approximately 0.3 percent annually. During the same period, large businesses increased their share of output by 2.4 percent. In the manufacturing sector where this trend is even more pronounced, the largest 100 firms increased their share of total assets from 39.7 percent to 47.6 percent from 1950 to 1976, while the largest 200 increased their asset share from 47.7 percent to 60.0 percent during the same period. . . .

Still, more than 98 percent of commercial establishments are small businesses. While they are currently generating a decreasing share of output, they are providing an increased share of the employment growth. In the period between 1969 and 1976 small businesses accounted for approximately 87 percent of all newly generated private sector employment in the country. The largest 100 firms contributed less than 2 percent of the growth during the same period. . . . A study concluded by Data Resources, Inc., on the growth of small, extremely competitive, high-technology businesses — mainly electronic — concluded that these businesses increased their output nearly three times as fast, and generated nearly twice the employment growth as all other industrial sectors from 1969 to 1976, while their prices increased only one-sixth as fast. . . .

## Recommendation No. 24: Regional Growth

Noninflationary growth is essential to real income growth and central to the resolution of the fiscal problems of many of the Nation's cities. A strategy for investment and jobs should take advantage of the opportunities and to meet the needs of our many diverse regions. Federal policies should be examined for unintended, implicit regional, urban, or rural biases.

The single most important thing the Federal Government can do to help meet the needs of State and local governments and to foster growth in all regions of the country is to adopt policies which return the economy to a path of stable growth. If the coming decade is characterized by slow GNP growth, growing and economically stagnant States alike will suffer....

In the older industrial regions, public and private infrastructure is in place. There are large numbers of good or rehabilitatable houses, and there is an established work force. These are resources which should be maintained and developed, so as to make a revival of industrial investment profitable in the older regions. The surest way to ensure international competitiveness of basic industries is to boost the levels of private investment flowing to these major employment centers. The review called for by this Committee could include options to ensure that this rebuilding is done in a way which uses the complementary physical and human resources currently available in the older regions, and which validates existing investment in the maintenance and upgrading of those resources.

Large manufacturing industries are not the only hope for the economic revival of older cities and regions. Economic diversification is also possible, and Federal, State, and local policies should encourage it.

In the South and West, the benefits of growth have become the burdens of growth as well. Sunbelt cities are experiencing an increased demand for services, for infrastructure development, and for mass transit — demands which are often made difficult to meet by the low-density nature of much Sunbelt development. Federal policies should be alert to ways to support Sunbelt cities in their efforts to develop inefficient patterns, and to preserve the natural beauty of the region while growth proceeds.

State legislators and local officials should be aware of the benefits of structural reform in the delineation of local government boundaries which provide opportunities to increase the tax base, share adjacent resources, and attain increased self-sufficiency.

One area in which certain Sunbelt cities excel is in the geographic organization of municipal jurisdictions, which allows the Sunbelt regions to equip themselves better to deal with their problems and opportunities than most long-industrialized States. Older cities have long-frozen boundaries which State governments have not been prone to change. These boundaries allow the suburbs to be largely immune to the central city problems of decline, even as suburbs grow. In the South and West, however, many cities have succeeded in repeatedly shifting borders outward since 1945, thus combining the strengths and weaknesses of inner-city and suburban city and matching urban resources with urban needs. The Frostbelt could learn from this experience.

## IV.B. Prices

### Recommendation No. 25: Many Steps Needed for War on Inflation

Inflation is the major obstacle to sustained economic growth, lower unemployment, and increased investment. Past anti-inflation policies, from voluntary guidelines to engineered recessions, have not worked, and we doubt that anything short of a comprehensive program will work now. Inflation is a complex, deep-seated phenomenon and the war on inflation must encompass all of the measures listed in Recommendations 26 to 29. . . .

### Recommendation No. 26: Energy

Energy policy should focus on reducing the sensitivity of U.S. energy supply and price to external shocks by continuing to encourage conservation, greater domestic energy production, including the development of improved techniques for enhanced oil and unconventional gas recovery, and establishment of substantial petroleum reserves.

In the United States, during the first half of 1980, about one-fifth of the increase in the rate of inflation was caused by the direct and indirect impact of energy price increases. This year, increasing prices will raise the U.S. oil bill by about $50 billion over 1980.

The continuing exposure of U.S. energy costs to OPEC [Organization of Petroleum Exporting Countries] pricing behavior can be reduced by policies to increase the elasticity of U.S. demand for foreign oil. Significantly larger investments in conservation, domestic energy production capacity, expanded production of abundant coal, and conventional and unconventional oil and gas will create a strong incentive for the stabilization of world oil prices.

Federal energy spending is only slowly being reoriented to reflect the energy realities of the 1980's. During most of its short history, the Department of Energy acted on the assumption that electricity usage would increase at very high rates, while conventional oil supplies would remain abundant. Now, domestic oil is in short supply and electricity demand is growing much more slowly. Our continued excessive reliance on foreign oil imports requires that priority be given to Federal programs and policies which increase the efficiency of oil use and increase the supply of domestic oil and of synthetic fuels that are able to meet end-use needs now met by oil. These end uses are principally transportation and space heating.

The conservation impact of increased energy efficiency in these areas is already substantial. More fuel-efficient automobiles, improved mass transit, and better organized residential patterns have yielded large reductions in gasoline use. Dramatic further improvements — some of them from sharp departures in automotive design — are yet to come and should be encouraged. One good substitute for foreign oil is domestic oil recovered by enhanced techniques. Good alternatives to oil in transport and heating including alcohol-based fuels and solar heating and cooling.

Each time energy prices rise, billions of dollars in plant and equipment are rendered economically obsolete. It has been estimated that the capital expenditures necessary to adapt the U.S. capital stock to utilize oil efficiently when it was only $18 a barrel amounted to $364 billion in 1978

dollars. At $35 a barrel, the level of needed capital investment will be much
higher. Eventually, of course, energy users will adapt to these new high
prices, but substantial time lags with serious impacts on productivity have
resulted, as this Report addresses in Chapter IV.A. A variety of estimates
of the loss in productivity caused by increasing energy prices have
indicated that between 15 and 70 percent of the decline in the rate of
productivity growth can be accounted for by energy price increases. While
a national decision has been made to maximize conservation efforts
through the decontrol of energy prices, a complementary program of
targeted tax incentives to accelerate the replacement of obsolete equipment with more energy-efficient equipment should be considered, as well.

Finally, the Nation should develop, in concert with our allies, an explicit
national policy toward OPEC, including an adequate program of petroleum reserves. A major objective of that policy should be to promote the
same price stability in oil that is normally assumed for most goods in
international commerce.

Such a policy would require that our own government take serious steps
to reduce our vulnerability to price shocks. The most effective step that
the United States can take in protecting its economy from the shock of oil
price increases is to develop adequate reserves of petroleum and petroleum
substitutes. The importance of such reserves can be seen to some degree by
comparing the price effects of the shutdown of Iranian oil exports in the
1978-79 winter season with the price effects of the continuing Iran/Iraq
war. When the Iranian revolution virtually ended their oil production,
world oil stocks were near traditional levels. Furious bidding on spot
markets to supplement these reserves sent oil prices soaring. At the
outbreak of the Iran/Iraq war, however, oil stocks worldwide were at their
highest in history at 4.7 billion barrels. As a result, this cushion has so far
prevented a duplication of the earlier run on spot oil supplies, aided in no
small measure by slack oil demand.

In the past, decisions on the pace of filling the Strategic Petroleum
Reserve were influenced by policy pronouncements within OPEC. The
United States should now proceed to build the necessary reserves. A
domestic oil reserve can take many forms, including the Strategic Reserve,
industrial reserves, and increased reserves of natural gas which can
displace substantial amounts of oil.

### Recommendation No. 27: Regulation

We should reduce unnecessary government regulations and
paperwork, and utilize the most cost-effective techniques to meet
necessary regulatory objectives.

While it is difficult to quantify the effect of Federal Government
regulations and red tape on inflation, there is no doubt that government
regulations impose many billions of dollars of compliance costs on American businesses, which are translated directly into higher prices. We believe
that a comprehensive program to reduce inflation and improve the

productivity of the American economy must include measures to improve regulatory cost-effectiveness and to reduce the unnecessary costs of redundant, ineffective, wasteful, and conflicting regulations. Measures to sharply reduce the paperwork burden of Federal rules and regulations must be taken, as well. . . .

One approach which merits consideration is the regulatory budget. Such a budget would permit Congress to tabulate the annual cost of government regulations and limit the regulatory burden which each agency can impose on the private sector and consumers.

Enactment of a regulatory budget could make it possible for Congress and the Federal agencies to establish better priorities for the use of the Nation's resources. A regulatory budget could significantly improve the process by which regulatory agencies dictate the allocation of private resources toward important public uses. A regulatory budget would require the development of better techniques for measuring the costs and benefits of many regulatory programs.

### Recommendation No. 28: Productivity

We must increase our rate of productivity growth, which requires attention to investment, employment, infrastructure, labor force, education and training, research and development, business leadership, and improved labor-management relations. . . .

### Recommendation No. 29: Standby Wage-Price Control Authority

The Administration has disbanded the Council on Wage and Price Stability. While COWPS had lost effectiveness, the stubborn nature of the wage-price spiral may require some form of incomes policy. We are willing to support an Administration initiative for standby wage-price control authority. Such authority should only be invoked as part of a comprehensive anti-inflation strategy. . . .

President Reagan has correctly recognized the importance of short-term symbolic actions to catch the public's attention as a prelude to a full-fledged assault on inflation. His hiring freeze, regulatory freeze, abolition of the Council on Wage-Price Stability and cuts in government travel and consulting have all contributed to a public expectation that dramatic and effective action against inflation will soon be forthcoming.

We applaud the intent of the President's initial actions and share the Administration's recognition that further steps may be necessary to root out deeply ingrained inflationary expectations. The American people have a long history of unfulfilled government promises to reduce inflation from past Administrations. They base their inflationary expectations much more on the inflation they observe in the supermarket and the department store, than on government pronouncements. The new President has proposed an extensive economic program which will be fully debated by the Congress. Yet, that program, if enacted, will operate on prices indirectly and with a lag at best and, therefore, may not effectively curb inflationary expectations. We believe that the Congress must cooperate with the President in fighting inflation and should not deny the President a full range of policy options for dealing with double digit inflation, including standby wage-price control authority if requested by him. Providing such authority, however, should be contingent upon the introduction of the comprehensive and productivity-enhancing anti-inflation program discussed above. . . .

## VII. REVIEW AND OUTLOOK FOR THE ECONOMY

. . . Five policy steps were taken on March 14 [1980] following the first quarter's inflation and the resulting effects on financial markets and inflationary expectations:

(1) Budget revisions which called for a balanced budget in fiscal year 1981 were submitted to Congress.

(2) Voluntary prenotification of price increases by large firms and an increased staff for the Council on Wage and Price Stability were requested.

(3) Steps to encourage energy conservation, including a gasoline conservation fee of about 10 cents per gallon, were advocated.

(4) Structural changes to encourage productivity growth, savings, and research and development were recommended.

(5) The President authorized the Federal Reserve to institute a system of credit controls. (Details are discussed in the *Economic Report of the President*).

The effort to balance the fiscal year 1981 budget was ultimately unsuccessful; in President Reagan's February 18 message the estimated fiscal year 1981 deficit under current law is $48.8 billion. This deficit is largely a consequence of the weakness in the economy. The size of the fiscal year 1981 deficit obscures the shift toward fiscal restraint which did occur last year. This restraint can be measured by the increase in the high employment budget surplus (HES). According to the 1981 *Economic Report of the President*, the adjusted HES rose by approximately $10 billion over the four quarters of 1980.

The last of the March 14 measures had the largest impact. Total consumer installment credit outstanding, which had grown at an annual rate of 11.2 percent over the previous 6 months, fell at an 11.9 percent rate between March and June. Commercial bank loans to business and industry dropped at a 9.4 percent rate over the same period, after rising at a 12.2 percent rate over the previous 6 months. Many consumers apparently thought that they could not use their credit cards at all, and some returned them.

To date, the economic policy steps taken in March appear to have had two results. First, the sharply accelerating inflationary expectations of early 1980 appear to have been reduced. But the underlying core rate of inflation . . . appears to have been little affected by the March policy steps.

Second, the slump was undoubtedly exacerbated by the credit controls. Real consumer spending for durables fell at a 43-percent annual rate in the second quarter. Unemployment rose from 6.2-6.3 percent in the first months of the year to the 7.4- to 7.6-percent range for the last eight months. Even in hindsight, it is difficult to judge whether the March policy steps were successful; such a judgment would require comparing the gain from reduced inflationary expectations against the cost in higher unemployment and lost production. Whatever the verdict, it is clear that today we are faced with unacceptably high rates of both inflation and unemployment....

Forecasters are divided on whether or not we will experience a "W-shaped recession," with another drop in real GNP in early 1981; but this question is not really of major consequence. The important point is that almost all forecasters foresee a very sluggish recovery for the remainder of 1981 and early 1982. Due to this stagnation, unemployment is predicted to be 7.2-8.2 percent in the fourth quarter of 1981 and in the 6.1-7.6 percent range by the end of 1982. In comparison with other postwar recoveries, this would be about the weakest. For example, if the trough of the 1980 recession was in the second quarter, an unemployment rate of 7.6 percent or more six quarters after the trough, as predicted by four of these forecasters and President Reagan's February 18 report, would exceed the trough rate — this would be unprecedented, and the rate would approximately equal that six quarters after the trough of the 1973-75 recession.

There are several reasons why most forecasters foresee such a slow recovery:

(1) Real disposable income is expected to be flat, with gains in nominal income at best continuing to stay even with price increases, and social security and inflation-induced income tax rate increases.

(2) Personal consumption was 94.4 percent of disposable income in 1980 versus an average of 92.9 percent for the 1970's; this consumption ratio is unlikely to rise much higher.

(3) Continuing high interest rates will discourage purchases of homes and consumer durables, especially automobiles.

(4) Inventory investment is unlikely to show strength, although by December the total business and retail inventory-sales ratios had both fallen below the December 1979 levels; also high interest rates encourage lean inventories.

(5) Real defense spending will rise, but real Federal nondefense spending and real State and local government outlays will both decline. Overall, DRI [Data Resources Inc.] estimates that real government spending for goods and services will decrease by 0.8 percent.

(6) Real net exports in 1980 were $52.2 billion, 3.5 percent of real GNP, the highest percentage since 1947, though nominal net exports were only 1.0 percent of nominal GNP. Higher OPEC prices and recessions abroad may reduce net exports in 1981.

The main hope for a faster recovery lies with nonresidential fixed investment. This may be helped by tax incentives, but it currently amounts to only 10.5 percent of real GNP, thus even a 20 percent increase would raise real GNP by only 2 percent; further, high interest rates and low capacity utilization will continue to deter capital spending; and there are usually significant lags in the effects to policy changes in this area.

With regard to inflation, the outlook is for continued significant price increases through 1982. Factors behind this continued high inflation include the following:

(1) The momentum built up by past wage and price increases persists in the face of slack demand in labor and product markets. For example, in 1980 average hourly compensation in the nonfarm business sector rose by 10.0 percent (12.1 percent in manufacturing). In 1981, this momentum will continue. The collective bargaining calendar will be relatively light, but more than 10 million workers will receive automatic pay increases from deferred wage increases in contracts negotiated in earlier years or from cost-of-living adjustments.

(2) The recent and prospective poor rates of productivity growth mean that almost all increases in compensation are reflected in unit labor cost and passed through into higher prices. And in the longer run our recent drop in the rate of productivity growth has a multiplier effect on inflation, as the productivity-induced increase in inflation becomes part of the wage-price spiral.

(3) Food prices rose by 10 percent in 1980 and probably will continue rising at least as rapidly in 1981.

(4) Energy prices rose by 18 percent rate in 1980 and could increase nearly as fast in 1981.

(5) Restrictive monetary policy should in the long run reduce the rate of inflation. However, in the short run, the resulting high interest rates are a cost which is usually passed through in prices. In addition, the lags between monetary changes and effects seem unclear; recent and future financial innovations such as NOW accounts have further complicated matters: and the breakdown of the effects of changes in the money supply between price and real output is uncertain.

(6) A variety of government policies such as indexed programs, the increases in the minimum wage and social security tax rates, and oil price decontrol in 1981 will contribute to inflation, at least in the short run. . . .

## [Republican Views]

### SUMMARY OF RECOMMENDATIONS

The Nation's chief economic goal must be to increase economic growth.

It is through economic growth that we can best assure economic stability and opportunity for all.

The Nation's economic bills have been the result of bad economic policies, not external shocks or defects in our free enterprise system.

We propose the following economic packages to boost employment, productivity and growth and to lower inflation:

> Across-the-board reduction in personal marginal income tax rates;
>
> Business tax reductions and accelerated depreciation allowances;
>
> Targeted incentives for saving and investment; and
>
> Reduction in Federal Government spending as a percentage of gross national product.

Departures from the target path of money growth to offset credit market fluctuations, supply shocks or changes in velocity simply result in higher interest rates, worse inflation and make it more difficult to implement a rational monetary policy.

A fiscal policy that aims at reducing the tax barriers to saving and production, that causes a shift of many nontaxable assets from tax exempt into taxable venture and is accompanied by reductions in the spending and borrowing burdens of government is not inflationary.

Special incentives for personal saving are absolutely necessary, especially in times of high inflation, in order for the saving rate to at least reach its historic level.

Inflation is basically the result of too great an increase in the money supply relative to the growth of goods in the economy. Beginning immediately, we must gradually reduce the rate of growth in the money supply.

A strong dollar, stability in our balance of payments and a more competitive American economy can best be achieved by stopping inflation and increasing productivity and growth.

In an effort to facilitate world trade, we should expand our Nation's export base, reduce the tax burden on U.S. workers abroad, reconsider the application of extraterritorial anti-trust laws and increase direct investment abroad. In addition, we should strengthen the capabilities of the IMF [International Monetary Fund], including the disciplining of member nations which follow irresponsible domestic policies.

All government regulations should accomplish their statutory objectives in the most cost-effective manner. When there are alternative options for achieving a particular regulatory goal, the least costly way should be adopted unless an overriding statutory goal requires the adoption of a less cost-effective alternative.

Congress and the Executive Branch should begin immediately to develop a regulatory budget to encourage government agencies to reduce the costs of regulations and provide additional incentives for agencies to develop cost-effective regulations. A regulatory budget would supplement the annual fiscal budget to give the public, Congress and the President a more comprehensive view of the Federal Government's command over resources for public purposes.

## [I. ECONOMIC GROWTH]

As the 1980's begin, the list of national priorities is lengthening: Inflation and interest rates are too high. They must be reduced. The Nation still is too dependent for its energy upon insecure foreign sources. Energy dependence must be reduced. Unemployment, and particularly minority unemployment, remains high and has debilitating effects on the social and economic condition of the country. Unemployment must be reduced. And while the poverty rate has been cut in half since the mid-1960's, the number of persons actually in poverty has risen. Poverty must be reduced. In addition:

Events in Afghanistan, Iran, Poland, and elsewhere have driven home the need for a renewed commitment to national defense. We must find the resources to meet this commitment.

In spite of vigorous environmental, health and safety initiatives, more remains to be done. We must find the resources for orderly protection and improvement of the environment, and the health and safety of all Americans.

The Nation's infrastructure — its highways, bridges, harbors, and waterways — are in various stages of decay. The process of erosion must be reversed.

Foreign competition is not only increasingly aggressive, it is increasingly effective. This competition must be met.

The answer to these problems is faster economic growth. The economy's growth has slowed in recent years. Continued slow growth will widen the gaps that have opened in recent years between expectations and realizations, particularly for minorities. As a result, a divisive struggle for income shares, which always threatens, could occur. This would be tragic. All Americans have a far greater interest in the size of the economic pie than in any feasible distribution. More rapid economic growth will transform dreams into realities, and national priorities into achievements.

Demands upon the Nation's resources are growing. These demands will tax our ingenuity and our resolve. They will stretch to the limits the Nation's productive capacity. If they are to be satisfied, economic growth must be accelerated, resources cannot be squandered, and the productivity of America's workers must rise.

Herein lies the rub: Productivity is not rising. It is falling. In 1980, output per manhour *fell* by 0.3 percent. In 1979, productivity declined by 0.4 percent. Without increases in productivity, real standards of living cannot be raised, it will be difficult to reduce inflation, interest rates, unemployment and poverty, to become less energy dependent and more competitive internationally, to rebuild the Nation's infrastructure, clean up the environment, improve health and safety, and improve our defense capability.

No nation can tolerate declining productivity growth — let alone absolute declines in productivity — for very long. To the obvious costs of output not produced and wants unsatisfied must be added the potentially more costly effect of increased animosity among the Nation's diverse interest groups. As economic growth slows, struggles for bigger shares of a shrinking economic pie can cause inflation to accelerate, and will cause resource misallocations and still slower growth, more unsatisfied demands, increased animosity across and within income groups, and among labor, business, farmers and Government. In short, declining economic growth feeds on itself: Slow economic growth engenders even slower growth. . . .

## [Reversing the Decline of Productivity]

The way to move up to a faster growth track is clear: The monetary and fiscal policy levers must be pushed in the right direction and kept there; specifically, monetary policy should be put on "slow" and fiscal policy on "go." An anti-inflationary, pro-growth strategy must include the following initiatives:

A steady reduction in the growth rate of the money supply;

An across-the-board reduction in personal marginal tax rates;

Reduction in business tax rates and depreciation reform;

Targeted incentives for saving and investment;

A reduction of Federal Government spending as a percent of GNP;

A reduction of off-budget borrowing by the federal Government; and

A reduction in the regulatory burden on the private sector.

Inflation and interest rates will come down when and only when the Federal Reserve forgets about fine tuning, abandons any vestiges of "accommodation" by an interest rate targeting policy, and focuses instead on steady reductions in the growth rate of the money supply. It is equally imperative that we recognize that both personal and business marginal tax *rate* reductions are in order, and cut them. Business tax rate reductions are necessary to help offset rising energy and other input prices, to increase investment, risktaking and entrepreneurship, and to stimulate current output and employment. Personal marginal tax rate reductions and additional saving incentives are needed to prevent or at least slow bracket creep, to encourage work effort, saving, and a reduction of installment debt. The new personal saving, coupled with a reduction in installment debt will permit financing of additional investment (on top of that financed by new business saving).

The strategy of reduced money growth and personal and business marginal tax rate reductions is fundamentally anti-inflationary and pro-growth. Steady reductions in money growth will reduce inflation and inflationary expectations. Erosion of inflationary expectations will itself help reduce inflation. It will do so by decreasing anticipatory buying in expectation of continued high inflation. In addition, the erosion of inflationary expectations will pull down long-term interest rates relatively quickly. This will stimulate long-term investment and growth. For their part, permanent business tax rate reductions will reduce both current and future production costs, and increase the profitability of investments generally. Production and growth will increase as a result.

Business tax reductions will have desirable effects, both in the short and in the long run. In the short run — where plant and equipment is fixed — business tax reductions either slow the rate of increase, or actually reduce, costs of production. If large enough, business tax reductions can more than offset the upward pressure on costs coming from rising input prices; in particular, rising energy prices. In this event, business tax reductions would reduce costs, increase quantity willingly supplied at any given price, and thereby stimulate both current production and employment. As for the long run — where plant and equipment are not fixed — *permanent* business tax rate reductions can reduce the cost streams associated with investment projects. Given projected revenue streams, it follows that more projects will become economic, and investment will be stimulated. Thus, in both the short and long runs, rate reductions stimulate output, employment, and investment.

While business tax rate reductions will stimulate supply, personal marginal tax rate cuts will stimulate both demand and supply. Demand will rise via the positive effect of tax rate cuts on real disposable incomes. Supply will rise because of the positive effect of marginal tax rate cuts in real after-tax rates of return to personal effort and saving.

There can be no doubt that the absolute amount of saving will rise as a result of a personal marginal tax rate cut. While it has been decreasing, the saving rate is still positive. Therefore, some portion of the increase in real disposable income will be saved. Moreover, because they will increase after-tax return to saving, personal marginal tax rate cuts will impel an increase in the propensity to save out of disposable income. However, in these inflationary times, still greater incentives to save are needed. Inflation has reduced the saving rate in recent years, and there is now urgent need for additional saving to fuel faster economic growth. This need leads us to recommend additional saving incentives. These extra incentives should aim at increasing additionally the after-tax rate of return to saving and should center around steep reductions in the marginal tax rates on interest and dividend income. If these cuts are made, saving will rise to at least its historic level and will provide a major source of the financing needed to get the economy growing at a faster rate.

Whether marginal tax rate reductions induce additional work effort depends upon whether increases in real after-tax returns to effort are effective catalysts to additional effort. We believe they are. This reflects our judgment that the work ethic is not dead: Reward work better, and people will work harder, longer and smarter. Tax work, and people will substitute leisure and/or "underground" or untaxed activities.

To complement the strategy of slower money growth and reduced personal and business marginal tax rates, we commend, as absolutely necessary, an accompanying reduction in the burden of the federal Government on the private sector. When tax rate cuts are combined with reductions in Federal spending, on- and off-budget borrowing, and a rational regulatory policy — one that recognizes that whatever the benefits of regulation, its direct and indirect costs must be minimized — the heavy hand of Government will no longer prevent the economy from moving to a faster growth track.

The result of this monetary-fiscal-regulatory package will be growth in real incomes and jobs, a reduction in inflation and interest rates, an expansion of resources to clean up the environment, an increase in our competitive effectiveness, a greater ability to meet our defense needs, a declining share of GNP being commanded by Government, and the disappearance of the "zero sum society."

## II. MONETARY POLICY

A proper monetary policy is crucial to the achievement of reduced inflation and interest rates, improved living standards, and economic stability. A proper monetary policy is not difficult to define. It is one that is focused on the long run and tailors money growth so that it is "commensurate with the economy's long-run potential to increase production." . . .

The facts, in brief, are these: From 1955 to 1964, average annual money growth, measured by the percentage change in M1B from the prior year, was 1.94 percent. It jumped to 5.55 percent in the 1965 to 1974 period and to 6.62 percent from 1975 to 1980. (In essence M1B equals coin, currency and checking deposits in commercial banks (old M1) plus automated transfer service (ATS) accounts, negotiable order of withdrawal (NOW) accounts, and share drafts in all depository institutions. M1B closely measures the Nation's means of carrying out its transactions.)

In association with these long, high jumps in money growth, we have experienced rising inflation, volatile interest rates around a rising trend, lower real GNP growth, reduced productivity increases, generally higher unemployment and growing use of resources to cope with inflation rather than to improve living standards. These are the legacies of a faltering fiscal policy and overregulation. Our poor economic performance is also the result of allowing the quantity of money to grow faster and faster; not every year but, by and large, during the past 17 years.

Clearly, we must reduce money growth, and we must do it now. We cannot, as some suggest, wait until inflation unwinds before we do so. If we wait, we will underwrite permanent inflation at increasingly intolerable rates. As shown by the data assembled above, over long periods, the rate of inflation tends to match the rate of increase in the quantity of money. More important, the latter tends to lead. Measured over four-quarter periods, the rate of inflation follows in the wake of earlier money growth. In the post-Korean War period, the lag has averaged eight quarters. Reasons for the lag include regulatory delays, contractual rigidities, and rigidities involving advertized and "established" prices. . . .

The evidence warns against waiting until inflation unwinds before reducing money growth. The lesson, in short, is that if we do, it will not. Specifically, money growth must be reduced over a period of time to a level commensurate with our economy's long-run potential to expand production and maintain full employment at zero inflation. These are the goals of the Full Employment and Balanced Growth Act of 1978. They will not be achieved unless money growth is decelerated. Using M1B as our measure of money, and year on year changes as our measurement standard, one sensible guideline is 6 percent growth in 1981, 5½ percent in 1982, and 5 percent in 1983 and 4½ percent in 1984. These guidelines are meant only as an example of the gradual reduction in M1B growth which is required to stop inflation and promote economic stability, growth, and low interest rates. . . . .

In setting forth this objective for monetary policy, we reject the contention that there is some "core" or "underlying" rate of inflation which is independent of money growth. Sustained inflation is not an inertial process which converts unpleasant outside shocks into a wage-price spiral. It is not "one darn thing after the other." It is "the same thing over and over again." The recurring event . . . is excessive money growth.

## Objections Considered

It will be objected that the world is too complex and full of surprises for the Federal Reserve to adhere to a pre-set decelerating M1B growth track. It will be argued that the Fed will have to deviate from any such path (1) to keep order in credit markets, (2) to accommodate supply shocks, and (3) to compensate for changes in money demand and the velocity at which M1B circulates. We consider these objections below.

### Keeping Order in Credit Markets

Many fear that, unless the Federal Reserve keeps order in credit markets, interest rates will rise much higher than even today's historically high rates and bring on another recession. They favor resisting upward pressures on interest rates even at the cost of allowing money to grow faster than desired over the long-run. We reject this counsel. It assumes that increases in money growth will reduce interest rates generally when, in fact, history demonstrates that the opposite is true.

Historically, increases in money growth have operated directly to decrease interest rates. However, this direct effect is both short-lived and trivial. It is followed within three to six months by increases in interest rates which ultimately (in about two years) equal (in percentage terms) the increase in money growth. If the Fed were to increase M1B growth by way of trying to prevent interest rates from rising (as it unfortunately has so often in the past), it would buy at most a few months of so-called order in credit markets. We would then pay for this by living for years in a higher interest rate environment. Although it is tempting to focus on the next few months, rather than upon the long run, it is a mistake to do so.

Throughout the past 4 years, the Federal Reserve was urged repeatedly by the administration and others to increase the rate of money growth in order to reduce interest rates. Looking backward, it is clear that this advice was wrong. We should have *reduced* M1B growth ½ to 1 percent a year after 1976 (when it grew 5.56 percent) instead of increasing it to 7.53 percent in 1977 and 8.16 percent in 1978. Inflation could not have reaccelerated if we had. By accelerating money growth, the Fed avoided the higher interest rates it was trying to prevent for only a few months, but engineered a subsequent prolonged period of skyrocketing interest rates. The 90-day T-Bill rate averaged 4.93 percent in the second half of 1976 and 4.99 percent in the year as a whole. It fell to an average of 4.72 percent in the first half of 1977 and to a low of 4.54 percent in May. By July, 1977, it averaged 5.15 percent and it has climbed much higher since then.

## Supply Shocks

Supply shocks have two macroeconomic impacts. One is a temporary reduction in the growth rate of the Nation's output of goods and services; the other a temporary bulge in the general rate of inflation. Other things equal, the two must balance in the sense that total spending on *all* goods and services will be unaffected, even though spending on the particular goods and services immediately involved may rise or fall depending on the demand elasticities for these goods and services.

For example, consider the devastating supply-side shock that occurred in late 1973 and 1974 when OPEC raised the price of oil and, for a time, the Arab nations embargoed shipments of oil to the United States. We had to make do, during the embargo at least, with less oil and we had to pay higher prices for it both during and after the embargo. The price rise made a non-trivial amount of the Nation's plant and equipment permanently non-economic overnight. As a result, real GNP growth was decreased and GNP inflation increased; both, however, only temporarily. Estimates provided in a recent study by the House Subcommittee on Domestic Monetary Policy indicate that the 1973 to 1974 OPEC oil supply shock reduced real GNP growth about 4 percentage points below what it otherwise would have been in 1974 and raised GNP inflation about 3 percentage points that same year. These estimates are close enough in absolute value to be considered as balancing with respect to total spending on GNP goods and services. . . .

## The Final Objection

In the final analysis, real GNP growth is unaffected by money growth. However, in the short run, decreases in money growth will, other things the same, decrease real growth. We recognize this but reject counsel to keep money growth high in consideration of this effect. To do so would keep inflation and interest rates high and require, in time, accelerating money growth and thus higher and higher inflation and interest rates. The end result of this course of action would be a calamitous boom-bust cycle.

If we want to stop inflation and reduce interest rates, we must reduce money growth as part of the overall strategy described in Section One. There is no other way. Fortunately, the short-run decrease in real growth which reducing M1B growth will bring, other things the same, can be minimized and possibly even avoided entirely. Other things need not stay the same. In particular, new fiscal policies can be put in place which will propel economic growth upward while, at the same time, our recommended monetary policy is damping inflation. We turn now to the new fiscal policies to be put in place.

## III. FISCAL POLICY

Decelerating money growth will in time eliminate inflation. The Nation must recognize that it will take a period of years, not months, for inflation to slow substantially. Many warn that the transition to stable prices will be hard. However, the bumps can be smoothed in advance. A properly coordinated fiscal policy can make the transition from a stagnant, inflationary economy to a robust, non-inflationary economy more certain and less painful. The elements of such a fiscal policy would include:

An across-the-board reduction in personal marginal income tax rates;

Business tax and depreciation reform;

Targeted incentives for saving and investment;

A reduction in Federal Government spending as a percentage of gross national product; and

A reduction in off-budget borrowing and spending by the Federal Government.

It is unfortunate that the national debate over fiscal policy has centered around whether tax cuts, by themselves, could reverse the economy's poor performance. This is unfortunate because it has been evident for some time that tax cuts would be accompanied by reductions in government spending and borrowing. In the past, this Committee has made it clear that supply-side tax cuts must be accompanied by reductions in government spending. The last election campaign saw both candidates support reductions in the growth of taxes and government restraints on the economy. President Reagan made no secret of his plan to propose a fiscal package including major spending cuts as well as marginal tax rate cuts. The question of whether tax cuts alone could turn the economy around was never a meaningful, operational issue and today definitely is moot.

Nonetheless, there is considerable controversy about the proposal to cut marginal personal income tax rates across the board. Those opposed deny that such a cut would have significant positive impact on productivity and real growth, and assert that it would be inflationary. Their arguments require us to evaluate how across-the-board personal marginal income tax rate cuts will impact on the economy. In this evaluation it is useful to distinguish between the direct effects on markets for goods and services and the effects which some say we must expect as a result of credit market changes that will be induced by such tax cuts.

## [Effects of Reducing Marginal Tax Rates]

Our view is that across-the-board personal marginal income tax reduction will increase productivity and real growth substantially and will not increase inflation. The effect on real growth is unambiguous. It is a logical deduction from *both* demand and supply-side economics. In demand models, tax reduction increases demand which pulls up supply. In supply models, supply is increased directly. President Kennedy recognized this in his 1963 *Economic Report* when he stated, "Only when we have removed the heavy drag our fiscal system now exerts on personal and business purchasing power and on the financial incentives for *greater risk-taking and personal effort* can we expect to restore the high levels of employment and high rate of growth that we took for granted in the first decade after the war." (Our emphasis.)

However, the direct inflationary impact of across-the-board personal marginal income tax cuts cannot be determined by logical deduction from economic theory. On the demand side, personal income tax rate cuts will stimulate spending, and could thereby add to inflationary pressures. On the supply side, personal marginal tax rate cuts will impel additional work effort and production, and thereby operate to show the rate of rise of prices. The question is which of these effects dominates. It is our view that the supply effect does. In addition, we want to stress that our fiscal policy program calls for spending cuts — which may reduce demand somewhat — and special incentives for saving and investment. These incentives, which are aimed at substantially reducing the marginal tax rate on *all* savings income, will help shift individual activities toward saving and away from consumption. Consequently, we can expect an extra large part of the personal tax cut and the income it generates to be used to increase supply (saving and investment) as opposed to demand (consumption). . . .

## Spending Cuts

In a static framework, spending cuts and tax cuts have offsetting effects on the budget deficit. In a dynamic world they do not. In our view, it is not necessary to plan static spending cuts which will exactly equal the static tax cuts that are planned. The planning marginal tax rate reductions will increase real GNP more than the spending cuts will decrease it. This is because marginal tax rate reductions will increase personal effort, saving, investment, entrepreneurship and risktaking. Judicious spending cuts needs [*sic*] not decrease effort, saving, investment, entrepreneurship and risktaking; some spending cuts might, but others will actually increase them....

## IV. THE INTERNATIONAL ECONOMY

The United States operates in an open world economy. This means that steps taken by the Federal Government for domestic economic policy reasons have rapid international effects and vice versa, steps taken for international reasons have rapid domestic effects. The linkages between domestic economic policy and the international economy take place primarily through the foreign exchange markets. Exchange rate changes affect investment, trade flows and the balance of U.S. international payments. In turn, changes in trade flows and the balance of payments often impede domestic policy responses. In the past, some of these responses have been destabilizing domestically.

The international economy is a far different system from what existed a decade ago. The introduction of floating exchange rates in 1973, the sophistication of today's foreign exchange market traders, and the increased mobility of international capital have removed old constraints but placed new ones on domestic economic policy. Under the new system, domestic policy initiatives can quickly translate into a rise or a fall in the dollar exchange rate before the initiatives themselves have had a chance to take effect in the U.S. economy. Because of the new "openness" in the international economic system, domestic economic policy must be formulated taking into consideration its international effects....

### [International Policies for Domestic Growth]

The progress made in the past two years toward defining the components of a competitive trade policy, as reflected by recommendations made by the Congress, the Executive Branch and by organizations such as the President's Export Council, needs to be followed up immediately with action to ensure that the hard-fought consensus does not evaporate in a constantly shifting international competitive environment. Recent statistics provide little reason to cheer....

It is critical at this important juncture that the Federal Government improve the climate for U.S. firms' direct investment abroad and increase export of services. U.S. foreign direct investment, while providing an efficient allocation of capital, also has promoted U.S. competitiveness and served to accelerate exports to overseas manufacturing facilities. Such direct investment also serves a development function by providing needed capital and technology to the developing areas of the World....

## V. GOVERNMENT REGULATION

During the past 15 years the Federal Government has increasingly relied on regulation of the private sector to channel resources toward such public goals as a cleaner environment, safer workplaces, less hazardous consumer products and equal employment opportunities. These programs usually impose significant compliance costs on businesses which are then passed on to consumers through higher prices.

Many government regulations, particularly those affecting health, safety and the environment, have contributed significantly to the overall well-being of the vast majority of American consumers and workers. We would not turn back the clock, because many regulatory policies have produced substantial benefits for the public.

However, regulatory programs impose heavy costs and burdens on business (and ultimately consumers) and, until recently, these costs have been almost entirely ignored in setting regulatory policy. It is time we took a hard look at the cost side of this equation. . . .

## Cost Effective Regulation

Regulatory programs should attempt systematically to consider costs and benefits whenever possible. As noted, a cost-benefit test for government regulations, as desirable as it is in theory, does create some problems in practice.

However, for most regulatory programs, such computations are not necessary to reduce regulatory-imposed waste and inefficiencies. Congress, in enacting regulatory programs, generally presumes or sets a level of benefits to be achieved, just as it does with spending programs. The benefit level is not, and should not be, determined by the administering agency. Rather, the agency should be charged with achieving the congressionally mandated goals at the least cost. This eliminates the need to measure benefits and instead focuses on costs, which can be more accurately measured.

We believe that a cost-effectiveness requirement would be the simplest way of assuring that regulatory goals are achieved at the lowest possible cost and with the least waste of resources. We believe a cost-effectiveness rule would be a more effective way of controlling regulatory costs without reducing the benefits of regulatory programs than would a cost-benefit test.

## Regulatory Budget

. . . A regulatory budget would constrain the regulatory agencies to limit the compliance costs that their regulations impose. It would certainly make the agencies more conscious of those costs. But it would have other important effects as well. A regulatory budget, along with the fiscal budget, would provide a more accurate picture of the Federal Government's total impact on the economy, allowing Congress to determine how much of the Nation's output is to be devoted to public uses. It would make possible a better balance between regulatory programs and traditional government spending programs. It would enhance the protection of the public's health and safety by requiring that the Federal Government establish consistent priorities in pursuing regulatory objectives.

# REAGAN BUDGET REVISIONS
## March 10, 1981

President Reagan on March 10 presented his fiscal 1982 budget revisions to Congress. Not since Franklin D. Roosevelt had any president recommended such extensive changes in his predecessor's spending plans.

Making former President Carter's fiscal 1982 budget virtually a dead letter, the new administration cut $48.6 billion from projected spending. Moreover, the 6.1 percent rise in spending over fiscal 1981 was only about half the 11.6 percent increase shown in the Carter budget. The Reagan document forecast $695.3 billion in expenditures and $650.3 billion in receipts, anticipating a deficit for fiscal 1982 of $45 billion.

The sweeping spending reductions were part of an economic recovery program that Reagan said would increase productivity, decrease inflation and spur job-creating investment. His economic program also called for deep cumulative cuts in tax rates, a highly restrictive monetary policy and the reversal of a trend toward ever-increasing regulation.

### 'Victory of Ideas'

In a speech March 20 to the Conservative Political Action Conference, Reagan said that "our victory [in the 1980 election] was not so much a victory of politics as it was a victory of ideas, not so much a victory for any one man or party as it was a victory for a set of principles." The budget revisions were widely seen as the embodiment of those ideas and principles. The top Reagan administration officials believed in them, and they were convinced that most Americans did, too.

*But the revisions represented a sharp break with the past. They would cut back an array of social welfare programs that had largely been pushed through by Democratic administrations going back in history 50 years. Under the Reagan plan, only the Defense Department would receive greatly augmented funds. Military spending, set at $162 billion for fiscal 1981, would grow to $189 billion in fiscal 1982 and to $343 billion in fiscal 1986.*

*The president had outlined his economic program in a televised address from the White House February 5 and again in an address to a joint session of Congress, also on national television, on February 18. But for many it was Reagan's budget itself that showed most clearly his determination to reverse the growth of federal spending and the government.* (Economic message, p. 213)

## Stockman Role

*The document,* Fiscal Year 1982 Budget Revisions, *contained a short message by President Reagan, followed by 159 pages of changes in the Carter budget, which it referred to as the "January budget."*

*The extensive revisions were put together in record time under the direction of David A. Stockman, Reagan's director of the Office of Management and Budget (OMB), and a former Republican representative from Michigan. Later Stockman would become perhaps the budget's chief advocate apart from the president himself.*

*Some of the proposed cutbacks were:*
*• About $1.1 billion from Agriculture Department nutrition and commodity programs.*
*• $700 million from the Health and Human Services Department.*
*• $900 million from consolidation of the Labor Department youth training programs and the reduction of the U.S. Employment Service staff.*
*• $700 million from Veterans Administration construction programs and personnel.*

## Budget Assumptions

*The Reagan budget's projections were based on a number of economic assumptions considered optimistic by many economists outside the administration. The budget assumed that the jobless rate would drop to 7.2 percent in fiscal 1982 and to 6.6 percent in fiscal 1983, that the personal savings rate in 1981-86 would average 7 percent (the average was only 5.7 percent in 1976-80), and that the business investment share of the economy would grow from 5 percent in 1980 to 11.2 percent in 1986. Such rapid growth in business investment would be the greatest in the nation's history. The budget also assumed that the inflation rate would drop to 8.3 percent in fiscal 1982 and to 7 percent in 1983.*

*Reagan administration officials saw the success of the economic program as dependent in large part on a huge three-year, 30 percent reduction in personal income tax rates and on other tax cuts. The deep tax cuts were recommended by advocates of "supply-side" economics, who believed that the stimulated economy would grow so rapidly that it would more than offset the loss of revenue. But the supply-side theory was untested, and it remained a matter of debate.*

## Reaction

*Initially, criticism of the president's far-reaching budget recommendations appeared to have been muted by the very number and range of the program cuts. As the plan moved into Congress, however, Democratic members argued that the cuts would hurt not only the working poor but also the "truly needy," that they would spur the economy in the Sun Belt region at the expense of the old industrial cities of the East and Midwest and that they would set off a new wave of inflation.*

*On the other hand, in Congress and among the public, a strong budget-cutting mood existed. Writing in* The New York Times *April 26, Rudolph G. Penner, resident scholar at the American Enterprise Institute for Public Policy Research in Washington, D.C., and an OMB official in the Ford administration, said, "At this moment, the agreement over spending cuts is . . . astounding."*

> *Following are excerpts from Part I,* Fiscal Year 1982 Budget Revisions, *submitted to Congress March 10, 1981, including a statement by President Reagan:*

## TO THE CONGRESS OF THE UNITED STATES:

On February 18, I spoke to a Joint Session of Congress about the economic crisis facing America. I pledged then to take the action necessary to alleviate the grievous economic plight of our people. The plan I outlined will stop runaway inflation and revitalize our economy if given a chance. There is nothing but politics-as-usual standing in the way of lower inflation, increased productivity, and a return to prosperity.

Our program for economic recovery does not rely upon complex theories or elaborate Government programs. Instead, it recognizes basic economic facts of life and, as humanely as possible, it will move America back toward economic sanity. The principles are easily understood, but it will take determination to apply them. Nevertheless, if inflation and unemployment are to be curtailed, we must act.

First, we must cut the growth of Government spending.

Second, we must cut tax rates so that once again work will be rewarded and savings encouraged.

Third, we must carefully remove the tentacles of excessive Government regulation which are strangling our economy.

Fourth, while recognizing the independence of the Institution, we must work with the Federal Reserve Board to develop a monetary policy that will rationally control the money supply.

Fifth, we must move, surely and predictably, toward a balanced budget.

The budget reform plan announced on February 18 includes 83 major cuts resulting in $34.8 billion outlay savings for 1982, with greater future savings. With this message, over 200 additional reductions are proposed. An additional $13.8 billion in savings are now planned. Further, I am proposing changes in user charges and off-budget payments that will bring total fiscal savings to $55.9 billion. This compares with $49.1 billion in fiscal savings announced on February 18.

In terms of appropriations and other budget authority that will affect future spending, we are proposing elimination of $67 billion in 1982 and over $475 billion in the period 1981 to 1986.

These cuts sound like enormous sums — and they are — until one considers the overwhelming size of the total budget. Even with these cuts, the 1982 budget will total $695.3 billion, an increase of 6.1 percent over 1981.

The budget reductions we are proposing will, undoubtedly, face stiff opposition from those who are tied to maintaining the status quo. But today's status quo is nothing more than economic stagnation coupled with high inflation. Dramatic change is needed or the situation will simply get worse, resulting in even more suffering and misery, and possibly the destruction of traditional American values.

While recognizing the need for bold action, we have ensured that the impact of spending reductions will be shared widely and fairly by different groups and the various regions of the country. Also, we have, as pledged, maintained this society's basic social safety net, protecting programs for the elderly and others who rely on Government for their very existence.

Budget cuts alone, however, will not turn this economy around. Our package includes a proposal to reduce substantially the personal income tax rates levied on our people and to accelerate the recovery of business with capital investment. These rate reductions are essential to restoring strength and growth to the economy by reducing the existing tax barriers that discourage work, saving, and investment. Individuals are the ultimate source of all savings and investment. Lasting economic progress, which is our goal, depends on our success in encouraging people to involve themselves in this kind of productive behavior.

Our tax proposal will, if enacted, have an immediate impact on the economic vitality of the Nation, where even a slight improvement can produce dramatic results. For example, a 2 percent increase in economic growth will add $60 billion to our gross national product in one year alone. That $60 billion adds to the State and local tax base, to the purchasing power of the American family, and to the resources available for investment.

When considering the economic recovery package, I urge the Members of Congress to remember that last November the American people's message was loud and clear. The mandate for change, expressed by the American people, was not my mandate; it was our mandate. Together we must remember that our primary responsibility is to the Nation as a whole and that there is nothing more important than putting America's economic house in order.

The next steps are up to Congress. It has not been easy for my Administration to prepare this revised budget. I am aware that it will not be easy for the Congress to act upon it. I pledge my full cooperation. It is essential that, together, we succeed in again making this Nation a land whose expanding economy offers an opportunity for all to better themselves, a land where productive behavior is rewarded, a land where one need not fear that economic forces beyond one's control will, through inflation, destroy a lifetime of savings.

RONALD REAGAN

THE WHITE HOUSE,
March 10, 1981

## Economic and Budget Policy

On February 5, President Reagan spoke to the American people about the economic problems that we face:
— runaway inflation;
— excessive regulation;
— tax burdens that have diminished incentives to work, produce, save, and invest;
— large and increasing budget deficits; and
— uncontrolled growth of the Federal budget.

### THE ECONOMIC PLAN

The President then outlined his plan to deal with these problems. It consists of four broad parts: (1) an immediate, substantial, and sustained reduction in the growth of Federal expenditures; (2) a significant reduction in Federal tax rates over the next 3 years; (3) elimination of unnecessary Federal regulations; and (4) a slower, steady, and predictable growth of the money supply set by the independent Federal Reserve System. These four complementary policies form an integrated and comprehensive program.

This plan reflects faith in the private sector, rather than the Federal Government, as the fundamental source of economic motivation and growth. It is based on the belief that Government economic policy must again become reliable and consistent. The approach embodied in the Administration's plan is a major departure from past policies, which consisted of rapid growth of Federal spending, excessive increases in the money supply, frequent changes of direction, historically high and continually rising tax burdens, and unwarranted regulation. The plan proposes to restore State and local government responsibilities in areas of public services in which the Federal Government has, in recent years, become excessively or improperly involved.

The major features of the President's economic plan were described in his address to a joint session of the Congress and in the February 18 report, *A Program for Economic Recovery*. The present document updates that report and contains further information on the budget revisions the President is proposing, including additional changes now proposed by the Administration to achieve the 1981 and 1982 outlay targets announced on February 18....

## LESSONS OF PAST ECONOMIC EVENTS

The experience of the past decade has taught workers and businessmen alike that frequent Government tinkering with economic policy results in increased uncertainty, unpredictable interest rates, rapid price increases, steep increases in Federal budget outlays, and uncertain real returns to savings and investment. In contrast, the President's economic plan moves toward dependable stability.

For the future, budget control is essential. The excessive past rates of increase in Federal outlays have inhibited economic growth, raised the Nation's real tax burden, diverted resources from more productive private uses, and discouraged production and investment.

Borrowing to finance growing deficits has brought about a substantial reallocation of national savings from the private sector to the Federal Government. More than three-fourths of the nondefense portion of the Federal budget is for current expenditure rather than investment. The growing public sector demands on available savings, to finance current expenditures by the Government, has impeded the private sector capital formation necessary for sustained economic growth.

Sluggish growth and rising unemployment led, in a vicious circle, to additional budget spending, higher budget deficits, and still less growth. The budget became a captive of deteriorating economic forces rather than a catalyst for economic improvement. A year ago, for example, the Congress and the executive branch reached a consensus as to the need to balance the budget, and made an effort to do so. An economic recession, however, along with the explosive increase in interest rates, overwhelmed these efforts. This volatility and deterioration in the performance of the national economy increased estimated 1981 spending by $47 billion while receipts increased by less than $8 billion. The plan to balance the budget fell apart. Once again, external economic forces reversed planned policy.

This Administration's budget control plan explicitly recognizes the interaction between external economic forces and internal Federal policy changes. The surest path to a balanced budget is a coordinated program to rejuvenate economic growth and restore the value of money. If this is done, external economic forces will act to enhance the Government's internal fiscal policies rather than to undermine them.

## BUDGET RESTRAINT

Restraining the growth of Federal spending lies at the center of the program for economic recovery. In recent years, deeply embedded inflationary fears have been reinforced by numerous upward budget revisions and growing Federal deficits. During the past 2 years, Federal spending has increased from the original budget estimates by amounts totaling nearly $100 billion, and the rate of increase in Government spending has averaged 16%. The President's budget control plan is designed to create a much better economic environment. Compared to the current policy base, the plan will save $40 billion in outlays in 1982. Reduction targets of $97.0 billion in 1983 and more than $125 billion annually during 1984-1986 have been established.

During the 1981-84 period, the budget plan would reduce the rate of growth of Federal expenditures to 5.5% annually. Together with a stable monetary policy, this abrupt downward shift in spending growth is the only credible way to reduce inflationary expectations and remove the historically large inflation premium that is currently embedded in interest rates.

... [T]his Administration's proposals substantially alter the previous administration's tax and spending policies. Sharp reductions in spending growth would occur under the budget reform plan. Spending in 1982 would grow by 6.1% under the Administration's revised budget, only about half as fast as the 11.6% growth in spending proposed by the previous administration. The substantial reduction in the Government tax burden is illustrated by:

— a much slower growth rate in budget receipts during 1982 — 8.3% for the revised budget in comparison to 17.2% in the January budget; and

— almost a 2 percentage point reduction in the receipts share of GNP in 1982 — from 22.1% under the January budget to 20.4% under the Administration proposals.

In addition to budget spending reductions, off-budget outlay savings of $4.7 billion are proposed in 1982, and significantly larger reductions are proposed for later years. Some of these budget and off-budget reductions, which are partially offset by upward revisions to the base, occur in Federal lending or loan guarantee programs. Under the revised budget, direct loan obligations would be $2.6 billion lower for 1982 than under the January budget proposals, and new loan guarantee commitments would be $18.4 billion lower.

The combination of incentive-strengthening tax rate reductions and firm expenditure control will lead to a balanced budget by 1984. The President's proposals project a 1984 spending target of $770 billion, which is $120 billion below the January budget projection for that year. The 1984 outlay target share of GNP is estimated at 19.3%, 2.7 percentage points below the January budget estimate. The receipt share of GNP under President Reagan's proposals also stands at 19.3% in 1984, with the

## January Versus Revised Budget Totals

[In billions of dollars]

|  | Actual 1980 | Estimate 1981 | Estimate 1982 |
|---|---|---|---|
| **Budget Authority** | | | |
| January budget | 658.8 | 726.5 | 809.8 |
| Change | — | −16.3 | −37.5 |
| Revised budget | 658.8 | 710.1 | 772.4 |
| **Outlays** | | | |
| January budget | 579.6 | 662.7 | 739.3 |
| Change | — | −7.6 | −44.0 |
| Revised budget | 579.6 | 655.2 | 695.3 |
| **Receipts** | | | |
| January budget | 520.0 | 607.5 | 711.8 |
| Change | — | −7.2 | −61.4 |
| Revised budget | 520.0 | 600.3 | 650.3 |
| **Deficit (−)** | | | |
| January budget | −59.6 | −55.2 | −27.5 |
| Change | — | 0.3 | −17.4 |
| Revised budget | −59.6 | −54.9 | −45.0 |

Federal tax burden reduced by $152 billion from the January budget estimate.

As a result of the President's tax proposals, Federal receipts are estimated to rise by 28% between 1981 and 1984, when budget balance is first attained, and by 57% over the entire 1981-1986 period. Under the previous administration's proposals, Federal receipts would have risen by 96% over this 5-year period. But this extraordinary tax burden would inhibit investment and output growth, and thus would have triggered additional outlays for unemployment benefits and the like, resulting in higher budget deficits. However, the new policy of tax rate reduction is expected to expand the economy's productive base, lower unemployment, and reduce budget outlays. As a result, the decline in tax rates is likely to generate both strong economic improvement and impressive gains in receipts, paving the way for a balanced budget....

By holding the growth of Federal spending below the rate of growth of gross national product, the new policy achieves serious and reliable budget control. The tax share will be equal to the outlay share by 1984, at significantly lower levels than under previous policy. The reduced size of the public sector will free up the resources for a strong, rapidly growing private sector.

The reduced Federal share of GNP under the new budget plan, reinforced by monetary stability, will signal a sharp reduction in future rates of inflation, and will thus have beneficial effects on financial, labor, product, commodity, and foreign exchange markets. As inflationary expectations moderate, interest rates will decline and business confidence will improve. Long-term capital markets will recover, making possible the refinancing of corporate balance sheets. Wage and price demands will become less aggressive. Commodity prices will stop rising, and the dollar will strengthen in foreign exchange markets. Tax burdens will ease. Better fiscal policies will become the basis for economic revival.

## BUDGET REDUCTION PLAN

The expenditure plan proposed in this document is complete for 1981 and 1982. Projections of 1983 and future-year spending consistent with the specific budget reductions included in this program are also shown. However, ... further spending reductions affecting 1983 and subsequent years are also planned. These further reductions will be identified in later messages and budgets.

Because of the long lags in the Federal spending process, large reductions in spending authority do not result in corresponding immediate reductions in outlays. For example, the proposed reductions in budget authority amount to $21 billion in 1981. The resulting outlay reductions in 1981 are estimated to total less than a third of this amount.

Spending has achieved runaway momentum because criteria on which to judge the merits of spending programs have been largely absent. As a result, virtually any demand for Federal assistance, from any sector of the economy or region, has been considered valid.

The President's budget revisions represent a sharp departure from the policies of the past two decades. The January budget estimates showed Federal spending increasing at an annual rate of 13.3% over the period from 1977 to 1981. This Administration's program will reduce the rate of growth of Federal spending to only 5.5% a year over the 1981-1984 period. Restrained and steady fiscal policy will replace the excessively expansionary and erratic policies of the past and will permit sound monetary policies.

This change will benefit Americans of all income classes, regions, and ages. Similarly, as is fitting in our democracy, the impact of budget restraint will be widely shared. No group except the truly needy should be exempt. No one should expect to share the benefits of budget restraint without also sharing its costs.

Despite the limited time that this Administration has had to review the budget, the proposed revisions are extensive and detailed. This detail demonstrates clearly that the costs of the budget restraint program are shared equitably.

The proposed budget reductions were developed on the basis of a set of clear, consistent, and economically sound criteria. The Administration has applied the following nine criteria for evaluating claims for Federal support.

The first criterion is the preservation of the social safety net. The social safety net consists of those programs, mostly begun in the 1930's, that now constitute an agreed-upon core of protection for the elderly, the unemployed, and the poor, and those programs that fulfill our basic commitment to the people who fought for this country in times of war. Under the President's plan, expenditures for these programs will increase as a percentage of total Federal outlays, from 36.8% in 1981 to 40.1% in 1984.

The second criterion is the revision of entitlements to eliminate unintended benefits. This criterion applies primarily to newer Federal entitlement programs and related income security programs that have undergone rapid growth during the last 20 years. The criterion also applies to certain aspects of social safety net programs that have been added unnecessarily or have grown excessively. Outlays for new or expanded entitlements have grown from $5.6 billion in 1970 to a January budget estimate of $56.9 billion for 1982.

The third criterion is the reduction of benefits for people with middle to upper incomes. Given the current economic climate and the proposed major reductions in income taxes, these spending reductions are a matter of simple equity and common sense. This criterion directly challenges the drift toward the universalization of social benefit programs.

The fourth criterion is the recovery of allocable costs by means of user fees. The user fee principle is applicable to activities that provide direct economic benefits to a specific and known group of individuals or enterprises and where there is no need or reason for these beneficiaries to be subsidized by all taxpayers. The Administration proposes applying this criterion to certain Coast Guard expenses, inland waterways, and the air traffic control system. The scope for application of this principle extends to other areas as well.

The fifth criterion is the application of rigorous standards to economic subsidy programs. The budget reform plan proposes to eliminate grants and subsidies that were designed to alleviate specific problems of economic deterioration, but have instead made our economic problems worse by interfering with the workings of the marketplace. Significant reductions are proposed for nonproductive jobs programs, unnecessary subsidies to develop energy technologies, and a host of other subsidy programs that contribute to, rather than help solve, our national economic problems.

The sixth criterion is a stretch-out of public sector capital investment programs. Many of these projects are desirable and should be completed expeditiously under normal economic conditions. However, the present economic crisis argues for stretching out and delaying these investments in the short run.

The seventh criterion is the imposition of fiscal restraint on other programs of national interest. These programs have some merit, but given current constraints on available resources they must be curtailed or eliminated.

The eighth criterion is consolidation of many categorical grants to State and local governments into block grants. The Federal Government in

Washington has no special wisdom in dealing with many of the social and educational issues faced at the State and local level. By consolidating many of the 550 categorical grant programs, it will be possible to achieve numerous efficiencies. The health, education, and social services programs proposed for consolidations encompass 616 pages of law, 1,400 pages of regulations, over 10,000 separate grants, and approximately 88,000 grant sites. It takes over 7 million hours to fill out the reports that are required each year, and several thousand Federal employees to administer these programs.

The ninth and final criterion is the reduction of Federal overhead, personnel costs, and program waste and inefficiency. As a start, President Reagan placed a complete freeze on Federal hiring and ordered limits on the procurement of office equipment, consulting services, and travel. This is a beginning. Federal management, personnel levels, and administration are being further evaluated and tightened.

Many people will find some of the individual, specific budget reductions described in these pages difficult to accept. This is because every dollar now paid in Federal taxes or borrowed by the Federal Government in private financial markets is paid out to a recipient who has an interest in seeing this payment continued, whether the Federal Government and its taxpayers can truly afford it or not. People who plead for special treatment or exemption from the criteria outlined above threaten the rationale and validity of the entire budget reform plan. The plan is designed to share the temporary economic burden of constraining the Federal Government to its proper role, based on stated principles. One exception logically leads to many other exceptions and to erosion of the plan and of its long-term benefits for the economy and for all Americans.

The application of these criteria makes it possible to continue to finance programs that comprise the social safety net and aid the truly needy, and those — like a strengthened national defense — that are essential Federal Government responsibilities.

The benefits of the President's economic plan to the average American will be substantial. Inflation, now at double-digit rates, can be cut in half by 1986. Reduced tax burdens and increased private saving will provide funds for productive investment. As a result, the American economy should be able to produce some 13 million new jobs by 1986.

The creativity and ambition of the American people are the vital forces of economic growth. The motivation and incentive of our people — to supply new goods and services and earn additional income for their families — are the mainspring of our Nation's economy. The U.S. economy faces no insurmountable barriers to sustained growth. It confronts no permanently disabling tradeoffs between inflation and unemployment or between high interest rates and high taxes. New economic policy can revive the incentives to work and save. It can restore the willingness to invest in the private capital required to achieve a steadily rising standard of living. Most important, it can help the American people regain their faith in the future.

▼▼▼

# MORMON CHURCH ON SUCCESSION
## March 18, 1981

Discovery of an antique manuscript shed light on a question — how the church's leader was to be chosen — that had divided the two main branches of the Mormon Church for almost a century and a half. The document expressed the wish of Joseph Smith Jr., the founder and first president of the Church of Jesus Christ of Latter-day Saints, that his son Joseph III succeed him as president and that future presidents be his lineal descendants. The document, dated January 17, 1844, was in handwriting identified as that of Thomas Bullock, one of several men who served as Smith's clerk. The document was discovered by Mark William Hoffman, a collector of historical materials relating to the church, and was made public at a news conference in Salt Lake City, Utah, March 18.

The Church of Jesus Christ of Latter-day Saints, popularly called the Mormon Church, was founded in upstate New York in 1830 by Smith who claimed to have visions and to have discovered "gold plates," constituting the Book of Mormon. The Book of Mormon stressed free will and the importance of effort for man's salvation. A second Mormon scripture, Doctrine and Covenants, contained the revelations reported by Smith and predicted a second coming of Christ, who would reign from a new Jerusalem or Zion. But the Mormons had difficulty establishing Zion — finding themselves unpopular for some of their policies, including polygamy.

The Mormon Church split into several factions in 1844 after Smith and his brother Hyrum were shot to death by a mob in Carthage, Ill. Brigham Young, president of the church's senior council, known as the

*Quorum of the Twelve Apostles, assumed leadership of the church in 1847. He led the migration of most of the church membership to the valley of the Great Salt Lake, which became the center of Mormon colonization. This branch of the church, today the largest and wealthiest of all Mormon factions, selected its presidents from among the 12 apostles, basing this method on instructions given by Smith in early 1844. Church leaders said they did not plan to change the Utah church's practices in the light of the newly discovered document.*

*Emma Smith, the widow of Joseph Jr., disliked Young and abhorred his support of polygamy. She was among those who chose not to migrate to the West with Young. Those who stayed behind founded the Reorganized Church of Jesus Christ of Latter-day Saints, now headquartered in Independence, Mo. They claimed that Joseph Smith III was the correct president of the church. Currently headed by Wallace B. Smith, the Reorganization has never had a president who was not a direct descendant of the original founder, although the presidency was not seen as an absolute birthright.*

*Discovery of the document that indicated the Reorganization was following the procedure prescribed by the church founder was expected to make little difference in the government of the church. It did provide a measure of satisfaction to the Missouri-based church, where an official said, "It's wonderful, but we knew it all along."*

*Following is the text of the blessing of Joseph Smith Jr., made public by the Church of Jesus Christ of Latter-day Saints March 18, 1981:*

A blessing, given to Joseph Smith, 3rd, by his father, Joseph Smith, Jun., on Jan 17, 1844.

Blessed of the Lord is my son Joseph, who is called the third, — for the Lord knows the integrity of his heart, and loves him, because of his faith, and righteous desires. And, for this cause, has the Lord raised him up; — that the promises made to the fathers might be fulfilled, even that the anointing of the progenitor shall be upon the head of my son, and his seed after him, from generation to generation. For he shall be my successor to the Presidency of the High Priesthood: a Seer, and a Revelator, and a Prophet, unto the Church; which appointment belongeth to him by blessing, and also by right.

Verily, thus saith the Lord: if he abides in me, his days shall be lengthened upon the earth, but, if he abides not in me, I, the Lord, will receive him, in an instant, unto myself.

When he is grown, he shall be a strength to his brethren, and a comfort to his mother. Angels will minister unto him, and he will be wafted as on eagle's wings, and be as wise as serpents, even a multiplicity of blessings shall be his. Amen.

# SUPREME COURT
# ON STATUTORY RAPE
## March 23, 1981

*In a 5-4 decision the Supreme Court ruled March 23 that California's statutory rape law does not violate the right of equal protection of the law, guaranteed by the 14th Amendment. California and 10 other states permit the prosecution of a male for having sexual relations with a female under age 18 to whom he is not married. These statutes exempt the girl from criminal liability.*

*The case,* Michael M. v. Superior Court of Sonoma County, *involved two minors, Michael M., 17, and Sharon, 16. Both teenagers had been drinking and, although there was evidence of physical violence against Sharon, her participation in the sexual act was not unwilling. Michael M. argued that his conviction for statutory rape should be reversed because section 261.5 of the California Penal Code discriminates on the basis of sex.*

## Court's Opinion

*There was no majority opinion; Justice William H. Rehnquist delivered the court's opinion in which Chief Justice Warren E. Burger and Justices Lewis F. Powell Jr. and Potter Stewart joined. "We need not be medical doctors to discern that young men and young women are not similarly situated with respect to the problems and the risks of sexual intercourse," Rehnquist wrote. Only women become pregnant, and the state has an interest in preventing illegitimate pregnancies. "A criminal sanction imposed solely on males ... serves to roughly 'equalize' the deterrents on the sexes," he said. The petitioner's claim that he was a minor "is irrelevant since young men are as capable as older men of inflicting the harm sought to be prevented," he continued.*

*In a separate concurring opinion, Justice Stewart said that "The Constitution is violated when government ... invidiously classifies similarly situated people on the basis of the immutable characteristics with which they were born. Thus, detrimental racial classifications always violate the Constitution. ... By contrast, while detrimental gender classifications by government often violate the Constitution, they do not always do so, for the reason that there are differences between males and females that the Constitution necessarily recognizes."*

*Justice Harry A. Blackmun also concurred, noting that the court acknowledged the problem of teen-age pregnancy in this case, but chose to place restrictions on a minor's right to an abortion without parental notification in H. L. v. Matheson, decided the same day.*

## Dissenting Opinions

*Justice William J. Brennan Jr. wrote the dissenting opinion in which Justices Byron R. White and Thurgood Marshall joined. Brennan stated that California had not proved that "there are fewer teenage pregnancies under its gender-based statutory rape law than there would be if the law were gender-neutral." Historically, he said, the law was based on the premise that young women "were to be deemed incapable of consenting to an act of sexual intercourse."*

*In his separate dissent, Justice John Paul Stevens wrote, "Local custom and belief — rather than statutory laws ... will determine the volume of sexual activity among unmarried teenagers." If society is interested in preventing the risk-creating conduct, he said, it is irrational to exempt 50 percent of the potential violators from prosecution. Stevens felt that the law should be applied equally to males and females.*

> *Following are excerpts from the Supreme Court's 5-4 decision March 23, 1981, that a gender-based law against statutory rape does not violate the Constitution, from the concurring opinions of Justices Potter Stewart and Harry A. Blackmun, and the dissenting opinions of Justices William J. Brennan Jr. and John Paul Stevens:*

### No. 79-1344

| | |
|---|---|
| Michael M., Petitioner,<br>*v.*<br>Superior Court of Sonoma County<br>(California, Real Party in<br>Interest). | On Writ of Certiorari to the Supreme Court of California. |

[March 23, 1981]

JUSTICE REHNQUIST announced the judgment of the Court.

The question presented in this case is whether California's "statutory rape" law, § 261.5 of the California Penal Code, violates the Equal Protection Clause of the Fourteenth Amendment. Section 261.5 defines unlawful sexual intercourse as "an act of sexual intercourse accomplished with a female not the wife of the perpetrator, where the female is under the age of 18 years." The statute thus makes men alone criminally liable for the act of sexual intercourse.

In July 1978, a complaint was filed in the Municipal Court of Sonoma County, Cal., alleging that petitioner, then a 17½ year old male, had had unlawful sexual intercourse with a female under the age of 18, in violation of § 261.5. The evidence adduced at a preliminary hearing showed that at approximately midnight on June 3, 1978, petitioner and two friends approached Sharon, a 16½ year old female, and her sister as they waited at a bus stop. Petitioner and Sharon, who had already been drinking, moved away from the others and began to kiss. After being struck in the face for rebuffing petitioner's initial advances, Sharon submitted to sexual intercourse with petitioner. Prior to trial, petitioner sought to set aside the information on both state and federal constitutional grounds, asserting that § 261.5 unlawfully discriminated on the basis of gender. The trial court and the California Court of Appeal denied petitioner's request for relief and petitioner sought review in the Supreme Court of California.

The Supreme Court held that "Section 261.5 discriminates on the basis of sex because only females may be victims, and only males may violate the section." The court then subjected the classification to "strict scrutiny," stating that it must be justified by a compelling state interest. It found that the classification was "supported not by mere social convention but by the immutable physiological fact that it is the female exclusively who can become pregnant." Canvassing "the tragic human cost of illegitimate teenage pregnancies," including the large number of teenage abortions, the increased medical risk associated with teenage pregnancies, and the social consequences of teenage child bearing, the court concluded that the state has a compelling interest in preventing such pregnancies. Because males alone can "physiologically cause the result which the law properly seeks to avoid" the court further held that the gender classification was readily justified as a means of identifying offender and victim. For the reasons stated below we affirm the judgment of the California Supreme Court.

As is evident from our opinions, the Court has had some difficulty in agreeing upon the proper approach and analysis in cases involving challenges to gender-based classifications. The issues posed by such challenges range from issues of standing, see *Orr* v. *Orr* (1979), to the appropriate standard of judicial review for the substantive classification. Unlike the California Supreme Court, we have not held that gender-based classifications are "inherently suspect" and thus we do not apply so-called "strict scrutiny" to those classifications. See *Stanton* v. *Stanton* (1975). Our cases have held, however, that the traditional minimum rationality test takes on a somewhat "sharper focus" when gender-based classifications are challenged. See *Craig* v. *Boren* (1976) (POWELL, J., concurring). In *Reed* v. *Reed* (1971), for example, the Court stated that a gender-based classification will be upheld if it bears a "fair and substantial relationship" to legitimate state ends, while in *Craig* v. *Boren* the Court restated the test to require the classification to bear a "substantial relationship" to "important governmental objectives."

Underlying these decisions is the principle that a legislature may not "make overbroad generalizations based on sex which are entirely unrelated to any differences between men and women or which demean the ability or social status of the affected class." *Parham* v. *Hughes* (1979) STEWART, J. plurality). But because the Equal Protection Clause does not "demand that a statute necessarily apply equally to all persons" or require "things which are different in fact . . . to be treated in law as though they were the same," *Rinaldi* v. *Yeager* (1966), quoting *Tigner* v. *Texas* (1940), this Court has consistently upheld statutes where the gender classification is not invidious, but rather realistically reflects the fact that the sexes are not similarly situated in certain circumstances. . . . As the Court has stated, a legislature may "provide for the special problems of women." *Weinberger* v. *Wiesenfeld* (1975).

Applying those principles to this case, the fact that the California Legislature criminalized the act of illicit sexual intercourse with a minor female is a sure indication of its intent or purpose to discourage that conduct. Precisely why the legislature desired that result is of course somewhat less clear. This Court has long recognized that "inquiries into congressional motives or purposes are a hazardous matter," *United States* v. *O'Brien* (1968); *Palmer* v. *Thompson* (1970), and the search for the "actual" or "primary" purpose of a statute is likely to be elusive. . . . Here, for example, the individual legislators may have voted for the statute for a variety of reasons. Some legislators may have been concerned about preventing teenage pregnancies, others about protecting young females from physical injury or from the loss of "chastity," and still others about promoting various religious and moral attitudes towards premarital sex.

The justification for the statute offered by the State, and accepted by the Supreme Court of California, is that the legislature sought to prevent illegitimate teenage pregnancies. That finding, of course, is entitled to great deference. *Reitman* v. *Mulkey* (1967). And although our cases establish that the State's asserted reason for the enactment of a statute may be rejected, "if it could not have been a goal of the legislation," *Weinberger* v. *Wiesenfeld,* this is not such a case.

We are satisfied not only that the prevention of illegitimate pregnancy is at least one of the "purposes" of the statute, but that the State has a strong interest in preventing such pregnancy. At the risk of stating the obvious, teenage pregnancies, which have increased dramatically over the last two decades, have significant social, medical and economic consequences for both the mother and her child, and the State. Of particular concern to the State is that approximately half of all teenage pregnancies end in abortion. And of those children who are born, their illegitimacy makes them likely candidates to become wards of the State.

We need not be medical doctors to discern that young men and young women are not similarly situated with respect to the problems and the risks of sexual intercourse. Only women may become pregnant and they suffer disproportionately the profound physical, emotional, and psychological consequences of sexual activity. The statute at issue here protects women from sexual intercourse at an age when those consequences are particularly severe.

The question thus boils down to whether a State may attack the problem of sexual intercourse and teenage pregnancy directly by prohibiting a male from having sexual intercourse with a minor female. We hold that such a statute is sufficiently related to the State's objectives to pass constitutional muster.

Because virtually all of the significant harmful and inescapably identifiable consequences of teenage pregnancy fall on the young female, a legislature acts well within its authority when it elects to punish only the participant who, by nature, suffers few of the consequences of his conduct. It is hardly unreasonable for a legislature acting to protect minor females to exclude them from punishment. Moreover, the risk of pregnancy itself constitutes a substantial deterrence to young females. No similar natural sanctions deter males. A criminal sanction imposed solely on males thus serves to roughly "equalize" the deterrents on the sexes.

We are unable to accept petitioner's contention that the statute is impermissibly underinclusive and must, in order to pass judicial scrutiny, be *broadened* so as to hold the female as criminally liable as the male. It is argued that this statute is not *necessary* to deter teenage pregnancy because a gender-neutral statute, where both male and female would be subject to prosecution, would serve that goal equally well. The relevant inquiry, however, is not whether the statute is drawn as precisely as it might have been, but whether the line chosen by the California Legislature is within constitutional limitations. *Kahn* v. *Shevin* [1974].

In any event, we cannot say that a gender-neutral statute would be as effective as the statute California has chosen to enact. The State persuasively contends that a gender-neutral statute would frustrate its interest in effective enforcement. Its view is that a female is surely less likely to report violations of the statute if she herself would be subject to criminal prosecution. In an area already fraught with prosecutorial difficulties, we decline to hold that the Equal Protection Clause requires a legislature to enact a statute so broad that it may well be incapable of enforcement.

We similarly reject petitioner's argument that § 261.5 is impermissibly overbroad because it makes unlawful sexual intercourse with prepubescent females, who are, by definition, incapable of becoming pregnant. Quite apart from the fact that the statute could well be justified on the grounds that very young females are particularly susceptible to physical injury from sexual intercourse, see *Rundlett* v. *Oliver* (CA1 1979), it is ludicrous to suggest that the Constitution requires the California Legislature to limit the scope of its rape statute to older teenagers and exclude young girls.

There remains only petitioner's contention that the statute is unconstitutional as it is applied to him because he, like Sharon, was under 18 at the time of sexual intercourse. Petitioner argues that the statute is flawed because it presumes that as between two persons under 18, the male is the culpable aggressor. We find petitioner's contentions unpersuasive. Contrary to his assertions, the statute does not rest on the assumption that males are generally the aggressors. It is instead an attempt by a legislature to prevent illegitimate teenage pregnancy by providing an additional deterrent for men. The age of the man is irrelevant since young men are as capable as older men of inflicting the harm sought to be prevented.

In upholding the California statute we also recognize that this is not a case where a statute is being challenged on the grounds that it "invidiously discriminates" against females. To the contrary, the statute places a burden on males which is not shared by females. But we find nothing to suggest that men, because of past discrimination or peculiar disadvantages, are in need of the special solicitude of the courts. Nor is this a case where the gender classification is made "solely ... for administrative convenience," as in *Frontiero* v. *Richardson* (1970) or rests on "the baggage of sexual stereotypes" as in *Orr* v. *Orr* (1979). As we have held, the statute instead reasonably reflects the fact that the consequences of sexual intercourse and pregnancy fall more heavily on the female than on the male.

Accordingly, the judgment of the California Supreme Court is affirmed.

*Affirmed.*

JUSTICE STEWART, concurring.

**B**

...[W]e have recognized that in certain narrow circumstances men and women are *not* similarly situated, and in these circumstances a gender classification based on clear differences between the sexes is not invidious, and a legislative classification realistically based upon those differences is not unconstitutional. See *Parham* v. *Hughes* [1979]; *Califano* v. *Webster* [1977].... "[G]ender-based classifications are not invariably invalid. When men and women are not in fact similarly situated in the area covered by the legislation in question, the Equal Protection Clause is not violated." *Caban* v. *Mohammed* [1979] (dissenting opinion).

Applying these principles to the classification enacted by the California Legislature, it is readily apparent that § 261.5 does not violate the Equal Protection Clause. Young women and men are not similarly situated with respect to the problems and risks associated with intercourse and pregnancy, and the statute is realistically related to the legitimate state purpose of reducing those problems and risks.

## C

As the California Supreme Court's catalogue shows, the pregnant unmarried female confronts problems more numerous and more severe than any faced by her male partner. She alone endures the medical risks of pregnancy or abortion. She suffers disproportionately the social, educational, and emotional consequences of pregnancy. Recognizing this disproportion, California has attempted to protect teenage females by prohibiting males from participating in the act necessary for conception.

The fact that males and females are not similarly situated with respect to the risks of sexual intercourse applies with the same force to males under 18 as it does to older males. The risk of pregnancy is a significant deterrent for unwed young females that is not shared by unmarried males, regardless of their age. Experienced observation confirms the common-sense notion that adolescent males disregard the possibility of pregnancy far more than do adolescent females. And to the extent that § 261.5 may punish males for intercourse with prepubescent females, that punishment is justifiable because of the substantial physical risks for prepubescent females that are not shared by their male counterparts.

## D

The petitioner argues that the California Legislature could have drafted the statute differently, so that its purpose would be accomplished more precisely. "But the issue, of course, is not whether the statute could have been drafted more wisely, but whether the lines chosen by the ... [l]egislature are within constitutional limitations." *Kahn* v. *Shevin* [1974]. That other States may have decided to attack the same problems more broadly, with gender-neutral statutes, does not mean that every State is constitutionally compelled to do so.

## E

In short, the Equal Protection Clause does not mean that the physiological differences between men and women must be disregarded. While those differences must never be permitted to become a pretext for invidious discrimination, no such discrimination is presented by this case. The Constitution surely does not require a State to pretend that demonstrable differences between men and women do not really exist.

JUSTICE BLACKMUN, concurring in the judgment.
It is gratifying that the plurality recognizes that "[a]t the risk of stating the obvious, teenage pregnancies ... have increased dramatically over the

last two decades" and "have significant social, medical and economic consequences for both the mother and her child, and the State." There have been times when I have wondered whether the Court was capable of this perception, particularly when it has struggled with the different but not unrelated problems that attend abortion issues. See, for example, the opinions (and the dissenting opinions) in *Beal* v. *Doe* (1977); *Maher* v. *Roe* (1977); *Poelker* v. *Doe* (1977); *Harris* v. *McRae* (1980); *Williams* v. *Zbaraz* (1980); and today's opinion in *H. L.* v. *Matheson*.

Some might conclude that the two uses of the criminal sanction — here flatly to forbid intercourse in order to forestall teenage pregnancies, and in *Matheson* to prohibit a physician's abortion procedure except upon notice to the parents of the pregnant minor — are vastly different proscriptions. But the basic social and privacy problems are much the same. Both Utah's statute in *Matheson* and California's statute in this case are legislatively-created tools intended to achieve similar ends and addressed to the same societal concerns: the control and direction of young people's sexual activities. The plurality opinion impliedly concedes as much when it notes that "approximately half of all teenage pregnancies end in abortion," and that "those children who are born" are "likely candidates to become wards of the State."

I, however, cannot vote to strike down the California statutory rape law, for I think it is a sufficiently reasoned and constitutional effort to control the problem at its inception. For me, there is an important difference between this state action and a State's adamant and rigid refusal to face, or even to recognize, the "significant . . . consequences" — to the woman — of a forced or unwanted conception. . . .

I think too, that it is only fair, with respect to this particular petitioner, to point out that his partner, Sharon, appears not to have been an unwilling participant in at least the initial stages of the intimacies that took place the night of June 3, 1978. . . . Petitioner's and Sharon's nonacquaintance with each other before the incident: their drinking; their withdrawal from the others of the group; their foreplay, in which she willingly participated and seems to have encouraged; and the closeness of their ages (a difference of only one year and 18 days) are factors that should make this case an unattractive one to prosecute at all, and especially to prosecute as a felony, rather than as a misdemeanor charge-able under § 261.5. But the State has chosen to prosecute in that manner, and the facts, I reluctantly conclude, may fit the crime.

JUSTICE BRENNAN, with whom JUSTICE WHITE and MAR-SHALL join, dissenting.

**I**

It is disturbing to find the Court so splintered on a case that presents such a straightforward issue: whether the admittedly gender-based classification in Cal. Penal Code § 261.5 bears a sufficient relationship to the State's asserted goal of preventing teenage pregnancies to survive the "mid-level" constitutional scrutiny mandated by *Craig* v. *Boren* (1976). Applying the analytical framework provided by our precedents, I am convinced that there is only one proper resolution of this issue: the classification must be declared unconstitutional. I fear that the plurality and JUSTICES STEWART and BLACKMUN reach the opposite result by placing too much emphasis on the desirability of achieving the State's asserted statutory goal — prevention of teenage pregnancy — and not enough emphasis on the fundamental question of whether the sex-based discrimination in the California statute is *substantially* related to the achievement of that goal.

## II

After some uncertainty as to the proper framework for analyzing equal protection challenges to statutes containing gender-based classifications, this Court settled upon the proposition that a statute containing a gender-based classification cannot withstand constitutional challenge unless the classification is substantially related to the achievement of an important governmental objective. . . . This analysis applies whether the classification discriminates against males or against females. . . . The burden is on the government to prove both the importance of its asserted objective and the substantial relationship between the classification and that objective. . . . And the State cannot meet that burden without showing that a gender-neutral statute would be a less effective means of achieving that goal. . . .

The State of California vigorously asserts that the "important governmental objective" to be served by § 261.5 is the prevention of teenage pregnancy. It claims that its statute furthers this goal by deterring sexual activity by males — the class of persons it considers more responsible for causing those pregnancies. But even assuming that prevention of teenage pregnancy is an important governmental objective and that it is in fact an objective of § 261.5, California still has the burden of proving that there are fewer teenage pregnancies under its gender-based statutory rape law than there would be if the law were gender-neutral. To meet this burden, the State must show that because its statutory rape law punishes only males, and not females, it more effectively deters minor females from having sexual intercourse.

The plurality assumes that a gender-neutral statute would be less effective than § 261.5 in deterring sexual activity because a gender-neutral statute would create significant enforcement problems. The plurality thus accepts the State's assertion that

> "a female is surely less likely to report violations of the statute if she herself would be subject to criminal prosecution. In an area already fraught with prosecutorial difficulties, we decline to hold that the Equal Protection Clause requires a legislature to enact a statute so broad that it may well be incapable of enforcement."

However, a State's bare assertion that its gender-based statutory classification substantially furthers an important governmental interest is not enough to meet its burden of proof under *Craig* v. *Boren*. Rather, the State must produce evidence that will persuade the Court that its assertion is true. . . .

The State has not produced such evidence in this case. . . .

. . . Common sense . . . suggests that a gender-neutral statutory rape law is potentially a *greater* deterrent of sexual activity than a gender-based law, for the simple reason that a gender-neutral law subjects both men and women to criminal sanctions and thus arguably has a deterrent effect on twice as many potential violators. Even if fewer persons were prosecuted under the gender-neutral law, as the State suggests, it would still be true that twice as many persons would be *subject* to arrest. The State's failure to prove that a gender-neutral law would be a less effective deterrent than a gender-based law, like the State's failure to prove that a gender-neutral law would be difficult to enforce, should have led this Court to invalidate § 261.5.

### III

Until very recently, no California court or commentator had suggested that the purpose of California's statutory rape law was to protect young women from the risk of pregnancy. Indeed, the historical development of § 261.5 demonstrates that the law was initially enacted on the premise that young women, in contrast to young men, were to be deemed legally incapable of consenting to an act of sexual intercourse. Because their chastity was considered particularly previous, those young women were felt to be uniquely in need of the State's protection. In contrast, young men were assumed to be capable of making such decisions for themselves; the law therefore did not offer them any special protection.

It is perhaps because the gender classification in California's statutory rape law was initially designed to further these outmoded sexual stereotypes, rather than to reduce the incidence of teenage pregnancies, that the State has been unable to demonstrate a substantial relationship between the classification and its newly asserted goal. . . .

I would hold that § 261.5 violates the Equal Protection Clause of the Fourteenth Amendment and I would reverse the judgment of the California Supreme Court.

JUSTICE STEVENS, dissenting.

Local custom and belief — rather than statutory laws of venerable but doubtful ancestry — will determine the volume of sexual activity among unmarried teenagers. The empirical evidence cited by the plurality demonstrates the futility of the notion that a statutory prohibition will significantly affect the volume of that activity or provide a meaningful solution to the problems created by it. Nevertheless, as a matter of constitutional power, unlike my Brother BRENNAN, I would have no doubt about the validity of a state law prohibiting all unmarried teenagers from engaging in sexual intercourse. The societal interests in reducing the incidence of venereal disease and teenage pregnancy are sufficient, in my judgment, to justify a prohibition of conduct that increases the risk of those harms.

My conclusion that a nondiscriminatory prohibition would be constitutional does not help me answer the question whether a prohibition applicable to only half of the joint participants in the risk-creating conduct is also valid. It cannot be true that the validity of a total ban is an adequate justification for a selective prohibition; otherwise, the constitutional objection to discriminatory rules would be meaningless. The question in this case is whether the difference between males and females justifies this statutory discrimination based entirely on sex. . . .

If pregnancy or some other special harm is suffered by one of the two participants in the prohibited act, that special harm no doubt would constitute a legitimate mitigating factor in deciding what, if any, punishment might be appropriate in a given case. But from the standpoint of fashioning a general preventive rule — or, indeed, in determining appropriate punishment when neither party in fact has suffered any special harm — I regard a total exemption for the members of the more endangered class as utterly irrational.

In my opinion, the only acceptable justification for a general rule requiring disparate treatment of the two participants in a joint act must be a legislative judgment that one is more guilty than the other. . . .

# ATTEMPTED ASSASSINATION OF PRESIDENT REAGAN

## March 30, 1981

*Less than three months after he took office, President Reagan survived an assassination attempt, one of several against public figures during 1981. Reagan was shot in the chest at 2:25 p.m. on March 30, and three others with him also were wounded in a hail of six explosive bullets fired at close range by a lone gunman outside the Washington Hilton Hotel. The shooting occurred as the president was leaving the Hilton after addressing the national conference of the Building and Construction Trades Department, AFL-CIO.*

*John W. Hinckley Jr., 25, of Evergreen, Colo., was overpowered and arrested at the scene. Police said they took from him a six-shot, .22 caliber Roehm Model RG14 revolver, which records showed Hinckley had purchased October 13, 1980, from Randy's Pawn Shop in Dallas, Texas. On August 24, a federal grand jury indicted Hinckley on 13 counts of attempted murder and assaults in connection with the shooting.*

*Evidence found by police at Washington's Park Central Hotel, where Hinckley had stayed briefly, suggested that he may have been infatuated with teen-aged movie actress Jodie Foster and was trying to impress her by shooting Reagan.*

### Others Wounded

*Also wounded in the fusillade were Press Secretary James S. Brady, shot in the head; Secret Service agent Timothy J. McCarthy, shot in the right side; and Thomas K. Delahanty, a District of Columbia policeman, who was shot in the neck.*

*The president, Brady and McCarthy were taken to George Washington University Hospital, and Delahanty to the Washington Hospital Center. Despite the explosive bullets and the gravity of some of the wounds, each of the victims survived. President Reagan returned to the White House on April 12; Brady, who was injured most seriously, convalesced through much of 1981.*

## Shooting Recorded

*As television pool cameras routinely filmed the president's departure, a commotion occurred in the press area, shots rang out, the suspect was overwhelmed and Secret Service agents pushed the startled president into his limousine. The car sped off, leaving Brady, McCarthy and Delahanty wounded and bleeding on the rain-slicked sidewalk. Hinckley had positioned himself unnoticed among reporters covering the president.*

*At first the president's wound was not discovered, and the limousine raced for the refuge of the White House. Then, as Reagan began coughing up blood, the destination was changed and he was rushed to the hospital's emergency room. An examination quickly confirmed the wound, and in a two-hour operation an unexploded bullet was removed from his left lung.*

*Filmed accounts of the shooting were shown and reshown in the frantic news coverage of the event, which began almost immediately. The intensity of the coverage and the competitiveness among broadcasters resulted in some confusion. First reports limited the shooting to Brady, McCarthy and Delahanty, saying that the president had escaped. Later reports said that Brady had died from his wound and that the president had undergone open-heart surgery. Although the inaccurate reports were corrected quickly, millions were misled for a time.*

*The shooting raised questions about presidential succession and some immediate uncertainty in the White House. Vice President George Bush cut short a Texas speaking trip and returned to Washington, arriving at the White House at 6:59 p.m. Meanwhile, Secretary of State Alexander M. Haig Jr., who days earlier had lost a decision on crisis management to the vice president, told reporters in a 4:15 p.m. briefing, "I am in control here," while trying to provide reassurance in the moments immediately after the shooting. As he spoke, his voice trembled and his face perspired.*

*Haig's statements caused some controversy. According to the Constitution, the order of presidential succession does not go directly from the vice president to the secretary of state as Haig implied. The chain of command goes first to the Speaker of the House and then to the president pro tempore of the Senate. The secretary of state, then other Cabinet members follow.*

*President Reagan was the ninth president to suffer an assassination attempt. Abraham Lincoln, James A. Garfield, William McKinley and John F. Kennedy all died while in office from assassins' bullets.*

*1981 was marred by a rash of attacks on prominent world figures. On May 13 Pope John Paul II was shot in St. Peter's Square, on May 30 President Ziaur Rahman of Bangladesh was shot and killed in the city of Chittagong, and on October 6 President Anwar Sadat of Egypt was assassinated in Cairo. (Shooting of Pope Paul II, p. 427; Sadat assassination, p. 733)*

## *Treasury Department Report*

*A Treasury Department management review team August 19 issued a 101-page report on the performance of the Secret Service and other department agencies during and after the Reagan shooting. While stating that the Secret Service had performed well, the report called for improving some procedures and for increasing the number of agents available for protective duty. It said the incident pointed up the need for standardized procedures for guarding the president during public appearances. These procedures traditionally had been informally negotiated between the White House advance team, which wanted the maximum publicity for the president, and the Secret Service advance team, which was responsible for his safety.*

*Prepared by Treasury Department attorneys, the report also called for easing the attorney general's domestic security guidelines. These guidelines prevented the Federal Bureau of Investigation from gathering domestic intelligence unless it was related to a criminal investigation. This restriction had resulted in a "decline in the quantity and quality of intelligence" and made it more difficult to keep track of potentially dangerous people.*

*Following are the texts of the first statement to reporters March 30 at 3:37 p.m. by presidential assistant David R. Gergen confirming the attempt on President Reagan's life; of the briefing for the press by Secretary of State Alexander Haig at 4:14 p.m.; of the partial transcript of the March 30 medical briefing by Dr. Dennis O'Leary, as recorded by* The New York Times; *of the statement of Vice President George Bush at 8:20 p.m.; and of excerpts from Management Review on the Performance of the U.S. Treasury on the assassination attempt, issued August 19. (Boldface headings in brackets have been added by Congressional Quarterly to highlight the organization of the texts.):*

# GERGEN STATEMENT

Good afternoon. This is to confirm the statements made at George Washington Hospital that the President was shot once in the left side, this afternoon, as he left the hotel. His condition is stable.

A decision is now being made whether or not to operate to remove the bullet. The White House and the Vice President are in communication, and the Vice President is now en route to Washington. He is expected to arrive in the city this afternoon.

Mrs. Reagan is currently in the city with the President at the hospital.

I'd like to add two notes. We have been informed by [Assistant to the President and Chief of Staff] Jim Baker that the President walked into the hospital.

I would also like to inform you that in the building [the White House] as of the moment are the Secretary of State, the Secretary of the Treasury, the Secretary of Defense, and the Attorney General, as well as other Assistants to the President.

# HAIG BRIEFING

**SECRETARY HAIG:** I just wanted to touch upon a few matters associated with today's tragedy. First, as you know, we are in close touch with the Vice President who is returning to Washington. We have in the Situation Room all of the officials of the Cabinet who should be here and ready at this time.

We have informed our friends abroad of the situation, the President's condition as we know it, stable, now undergoing surgery. And there are absolutely no alert measures that are necessary at this time we're contemplating.

Now, if you have some questions, I'll be happy to take them.

**Q:** The Crisis Management, is that going to be put into effect when Bush arrives?

**Secretary Haig:** The Crisis Management is in effect.

**Q:** Who is making the decisions for the government right now? Who's making the decisions?

**Secretary Haig:** Constitutionally, gentlemen, you have the President, the Vice President, and the Secretary of State in that order and should the President decided [sic] he wants to transfer the helm to the Vice President, he will do so. He has not done that. As of now, I am in control here, in the White House, pending return of the Vice President and in close touch with him. If something came up, I would check with him, of course.

**Q:** What is the extent of the President's injury?

**Secretary Haig:** Well, as best we know, he's had one round enter his body, in the left side, into the left lung and there is surgery underway to remove the round now. When the President entered surgery, he was conscious. His signs were stable. And the situation is very clear.

**Q:** Did you talk with him by phone before surgery?

**Secretary Haig:** No, I did not nor was it necessary. I was in close touch with both Mr. Meese and Mr. Baker throughout and have been from —

**Q:** Mr. Secretary, approximately when did you arrive at the White House after following —

**Secretary Haig:** Very few moments after the incident, very few moments after the incident.

**Q:** And do you know what is the condition of Mr. Brady?

**Secretary Haig:** We understand that — I just saw on television what you saw and it sounds serious.

**Q:** What's the reaction of the Soviets on this? Any reaction?

**Secretary Haig:** I don't anticipate any reaction. I think you've gotten all that you need for the moment. In fact —

**Q:** Will you remain in charge here until the Vice President returns?

**Secretary Haig:** We will stay right where we are until the situation clarifies.

**Q:** How long has the President been in surgery, sir?

**Q:** When is the Vice President expected here?

**Q:** 8:00?

**Secretary Haig:** Later this afternoon.

**Q:** Do you know when the operation began on the President, about what time?

**Q:** Will he go to the hospital?

**Secretary Haig:** Was I here? Yes.

**Q:** What time?

**Secretary Haig:** What time was the — I don't know. Just it was shortly after that announcement that you heard on the —

**Q:** What time will the Vice President be back, sir?

**Q:** Early evening?

**Secretary Haig:** I'm not going to make it a habit of saying what I —

**Q:** Will you come back and talk to us soon?

**Q:** Mr. Secretary, any additional measures being taken — was this a conspiracy or was this a —

**Secretary Haig:** We have no indications of anything like that now, and we are not going to say a word on that subject until the situation clarifies itself.

**Q:** Do you anticipate from what you know of the President's condition that the Vice President will have to for a period of time take the role of acting President?

**Q:** That's a fundamentally premature question.

# DR. O'LEARY'S PRESS BRIEFING

The President is in the recovery room. He is in stable condition and he is awake. He was in no time in any serious danger. He was alert and awake with stable vital signs up until the time he underwent anesthesia.

He was in the operating room for approximately two hours. Part of that time was spent ascertaining that he did not have any blood in his abdominal cavity — indeed he did not.

It was a single bullet wound that entered slightly underneath in the left armpit. It traversed about three inches of the chest wall and then ricocheted off the seventh rib into the left lower lobe of the lung and moved about three inches into the lung substance itself.

The operative incision is about six inches in width; a relatively simple procedure. The bullet was removed and then the incision was closed.

As I say, he is stable and in good condition.

**Q:** What is the prognosis for him?

**A:** The prognosis is excellent.

**Q:** And you're saying that he will no doubt recover?

**A:** (Shakes head yes.)

**Q:** How long a time, doctor?

**A:** That is always difficult to say. The President, however, is an excellent physical specimen and we do not anticipate any problems. It is always hard to be precise as to how long he'll be hospitalized but he has a clear head and should be able to make decisions by tomorrow certainly.

**Q:** Did the bullet fragment when it hit the lungs?

**A:** The bullet was distorted and we believe it probably was distorted by virtue of impacting against the seventh rib as it redirected its path into the lung tissue.

**Q:** (Two questioners at once drown each other out.)

**A:** We do not believe there is any permanent injury. The heart area was explored. The heart was not involved at all. There were no major bleeding points in the lung and there was no involvement of the aorta, the major vessel running through the chest.

**Q:** Has the lung been reinflated?

**A:** The lung has been reinflated; he has a couple of chest tubes in.

**Q:** Can you tell us about the Secret Service agent?

**A:** Mr. McCarthy had a single bullet wound also; entered the posterior right chest and passed through the lung tissue, causing virtually no damage at all except for the passage tract; passed through the diaphragm into the dome of the liver, and passed through the liver into the lateral side of the chest, where it lodged against the end of the 11th rib.

Mr. McCarthy had — did have blood in his abdominal cavity. The same test that was performed on the President was also performed on him and it was positive. The abdominal cavity was carefully explored and the only damage was the bullet through the liver itself. And a drain was placed in this area and he is doing extremely well; has been in the intensive care unit now for about 45 minutes.

**Q:** James Brady?

**A:** Okay, Mr. Brady is still in surgery. His condition is critical. We don't have any further information at this time.

**Q:** Dr. O'Leary, how long would you anticipate that the President would remain hospitalized?

**A:** Well, that is difficult to say. It might be as long as two weeks, but that is just a guesstimate at this point in time.

**Q:** Will he remain here doctor? (Other questions are muffled.)

**A:** That's not for me to answer. The question was the amount of blood: The President required a transfusion of approximately five units of blood before surgery but none during the course of surgery.

Mr. McCarthy required no transfusion at all.

**Q:** About the D.C. policeman, please?

**A:** The D.C. policeman was taken to the Washington Hospital Center. We have no first-hand information on him.

**Q:** The Brady surgery?

**A:** Mr. Brady had — was shot in the side of the forehead. The bullet went . . .

**Q:** Which side?

**A:** I'm not certain sir. The bullet did pass through his brain and came out the other side. He obviously has some significant brain injury and he is in critical condition. But I'm sorry we have no further information at this time.

**Q:** Dr. O'Leary, who performed the operation on the President?

**A:** The operation on the President was performed by Dr. Benjamin Aaron, who's on our full-time faculty here as a cardiovascular thoracic surgeon.

**Q:** Title?

**A:** I think he's an associate professor of surgery.

**Q:** The other surgeon?

**A:** Okay, the other surgeon was Dr. Joseph Giordano, who is head of our trauma team and was in the emergency room almost simultaneously with the arrival of the President.

**Q:** Why did the operation take so long?

**A:** The length of the operation really had a lot to do with the testing to make sure that there was no bleeding into the abdominal cavity. That took about 45 minutes.

**Q:** What was that test?

**A:** It's called a peritoneal lavage.

**Q:** (Inaudible.)

**A:** Okay, that test is important — it's very simple. A small incision is made beneath the umbilicus and several liters of fluid are placed into the abdomen and then the fluid is brought back outside and looked at to determine whether there's any blood in it. That fluid can move anywhere throughout the whole abdominal cavity and if any organ has been damaged and there's any bleeding, one will find blood in the fluid that comes out.

That test was negative in the President and, as I said, positive in Mr. McCarthy.

**Q:** Doctor, in view of the President's age, is there any danger that the lung might collapse again?

**A:** Very doubtful. The President is physiologically very youthful.

**Q:** The caliber of the bullet?

**A:** The caliber of the bullet is going to be very hard to tell, in the President, because it was a really mangled bullet.

**Q:** Is there a possibility of any other complications besides the lung problem?

**A:** It's really doubtful. Again I would emphasize that he is physiologically very young. He's in good shape.

**Q:** Can you tell us where the bullet entered and at what angle? From the front from the rear? Can you give us a ...?

**A:** Well, one would assume that it probably seemed to come from a little bit top down, entering approximately here (pointing to rib), traverse down approximately three inches, striking the top of the seventh rib, laterally, and then going about three inches into the tissue of the lung itself.

**Q:** It deflected downward further from the seventh rib?

**A:** No, it's like coming down, hitting the rib, and then deflecting in to take a new path about ...

**Q:** (Inaudible.)

**A:** It was in the perinchema, in the tissue of the lung itself — contained within the lung itself.

**Q:** You said the President was conscious through much of the time. What, if anything, did he say?

**A:** Well, the surgeons said that his last remark before he underwent anaesthesia was he wanted to make sure that all of them were Republicans. They said that today everyone is a Republican.

**Q:** How narrowly did the President escape mortal injury?

**A:** That's a hard question to answer. As I stated, he was never in any serious danger. The bullet was really not very close to any vital structure.

**Q:** How far is not so close? How far from the heart?

**A:** Oh, probably several inches.

**Q:** Was that because he struck the rib — was it fortunate that...?

**A:** If it had not struck the rib it might not have entered the lung cavity.

**Q:** You mean it would've passed though his body?

**A:** It could've passed right through the chest wall, if it had not struck the rib.

**Q:** Would you say, clinically speaking, that the President is fully able to discharge the duties of his office as of now?

**A:** I would say probably not now. One has to let the effects of the anaesthesia wear off. But I think all of us feel that by tomorrow that he would be fully capable of doing that.

## BUSH STATEMENT

Well, I have a very brief statement that I would like to read. I am deeply heartened by Dr. O'Leary's report on the President's condition, that he has emerged from this experience with flying colors and with the most optimistic prospects for a complete recovery. I can reinsure [*sic*] this Nation and a watching world that the American Government is functioning fully and effectively. We've had full and complete communication throughout the day, and the officers of the Federal Government have been fulfilling their obligations with skill and with care.

I know I speak on behalf of the President and his family when I say that we are very grateful to all the many people from across this country who've expressed their concern at this act of violence. And finally, let me add our profound concern on behalf of two brave law enforcement officers who served to protect the President and then, of course, for a friend of everybody here, dedicated public servant, Jim Brady. We're going to watch their progress with all our prayers and with all our hopes.

Now, I'm going to walk over and speak briefly to Mrs. Reagan, who's returned to the Residence.

Thank you all very much.

# TREASURY DEPARTMENT REPORT

## Protective Intelligence

### PROCEDURES

The Secret Service responsibility for developing intelligence for protective purposes is assigned to the Office of Protective Research. Within that office are six divisions. The primary intelligence collection and analysis functions are assigned to the Intelligence Division and the Liaison Division. In the Washington, D.C. area, these two divisions are substantially augmented by personnel of the Washington field office intelligence squad.

### Intelligence Received Via The White House

White House personnel turn over to the Secret Service letters and telephone calls that appear threatening to the President or another official. If the matter requires further investigation a field investigation is authorized. Individuals who come to the White House complex and appear threatening to the President or others are interviewed and, if further investigation is warranted, referred to the protective intelligence squad of the Washington field office.

### Intelligence Received From the Field

Intelligence in the field is collected through field office investigations, from state and local agencies, and from the field offices of other Federal agencies. Intelligence from state and local agencies will include information elicited from or volunteered by law enforcement groups, local mental hospitals, and state and local government offices.

The degree to which the field is successful in generating intelligence is solely attributable to informal field liaison efforts aimed at either requesting information and assistance or educating local agencies to the Service's intelligence needs. These efforts are informally monitored and encouraged by the Intelligence Division at headquarters.

Secret Service Director Stuart Knight has stated on several occasions that the Freedom of Information Act and the Privacy Act have contributed to a decrease over the last several years in intelligence information received from various sources, including other law enforcement agencies and foreign countries. For example, in testimony before committees of both the House and Senate following the March 30 assassination attempt, Knight testified that foreign law enforcement organizations, as well as state and local police, are reluctant to share information with the Secret Service and other Federal agencies. This reluctance, he believes, is largely the result of the Freedom of Information Act and Privacy Act, which have led foreign and other information sources to believe that the United States government agencies cannot maintain the confidentiality of the information they receive.

The Secret Service's view is almost universally shared by other law enforcement officials. In a report entitled "Impact of the Freedom of Information and Privacy Acts on Law Enforcement Agencies," dated November 15, 1978, the Comptroller General noted that "law enforcement officials at all levels of government have stated in congressional testimony that the proliferation of access and privacy laws has been instrumental in creating a restrictive climate which affects their ability to obtain information from the public and institutions, to recruit and maintain informants, and to exchange information with other law enforcement agencies."

Law enforcement officials reported, according to the GAO Report, that the Privacy Act has had some of its most severe effects on their ability to obtain information from institutions such as hospitals, banks and telephone companies. While law enforcement agencies could previously obtain records from these institutions on an informal basis, an increasing number require the agencies to obtain a subpoena before providing the information. Secret Service officials told the GAO that since most of the threats against the President come from mentally unstable individuals, timely access to records maintained by mental institutions is critical when the President or other dignitaries travel around the country.

## Intelligence from other Federal Agencies

The Service has entered into memoranda of understanding or agreements with other Federal agencies, such as the Federal Bureau of Investigation and the Central Intelligence Agency. These agreements describe in broad, general terms the intelligence sought by the Service, and an examination of various editions of these agreements used over the past ten years shows little substantive evolution in the description of information the agencies are to furnish.

Neither the Liaison Division nor the Intelligence Division has any procedures for monitoring whether Federal agencies have internal guidelines implementing the agreements and educating their personnel as to Service intelligence needs, although the Intelligence Division itself tries to use its limited staff to perform these functions informally with respect to some agencies. Infrequently, Liaison arranges meetings with representatives of other Federal agencies in which Intelligence Division personnel can describe their intelligence requirements.

Liaison Division agents maintain informal relations with the rest of the Federal community, and will serve as a conduit for Intelligence Division requests to these agencies for specific information. Some agencies provide formal liaison contacts while others do not, forcing Liaison Division agents to establish their own contacts on an informal basis. Liaison Division agents also distribute to their Federal agency contacts boilerplate descriptions, similar to those in the formal agreements, of Service intelligence needs. How these handouts are utilized by the Federal agencies is not monitored.

In some instances Federal agencies provide the Service with intelligence in response to a direct request for specific information from the Intelligence Division, or in response to a request from the Liaison Division. At other times, these agencies, especially the FBI and the CIA, unilaterally provide intelligence they judge to be of interest to the Service. Intelligence suppliers have not been assessed or evaluated with a view to improving their performance.

Information collected and disseminated by the FBI is the most important source of Secret Service intelligence on potential domestic threats to the President, and has a significant impact on the ability of the Service to fulfill its mission. As a general matter, intelligence received from the FBI will be of two types: information about the intentions and objectives of individuals and groups, and information about what individuals and groups have actually done.

Since the Service is interested in predictive information — that is, intelligence which will enable it to assess possible threats to the President — information about intentions is a good deal more valuable to the Service than information about completed acts, from which future intentions may only be inferred.

This distinction has led the Service to become increasingly concerned in recent years about a decline in the FBI's domestic intelligence activities, and the almost exclusive emphasis which the FBI has begun to place on its role as an agency engaged in investigation for purposes of assisting prosecutorial authorities. Generally speaking, much domestic intelligence investigation may be usefully characterized as the process of discovering, through informants or otherwise, the intentions and objectives of groups. On the other hand, investigations in aid of prosecution focus principally on actions already taken — information which at best is only of marginal utility to the Service.

### [Hinckley's Nashville Arrest]

As example of the limited usefulness of law enforcement information to the Service is the arrest of John W. Hinckley at the Nashville Airport on October 9, 1980. The facts of that incident are not in dispute. Hinckley had attempted to board a commercial airliner with three pistols. Although he could have transported them lawfully in baggage checked through to his destination, he instead tried to carry them into the passenger compartment and was arrested by airport police. The fact that Hinckley has been accused of the shooting on March 30, 1981, has raised questions about whether the Service should have been on notice of the threat he posed to the President.

The arrest coincided with substantial Presidential campaign activity in Tennessee. Then-candidate Ronald Reagan had just cancelled a trip scheduled for October 8 to Memphis; President Carter was conducting a town meeting in Nashville's Grand Old Opry; and the wife of Vice President Mondale had left Nashville a day earlier. Local police officials considered the arrest routine and unrelated to President Carter's visit — a reasonable conclusion in light of the fact that the President was still speaking when Hinckley was arrested.

Nevertheless, the arrest was reported to the FBI because the attempted boarding with the pistols violated Federal as well as local law. The FBI treated the case as one that the local U.S. Attorney would automatically decline to prosecute, and did not refer it. Neither did the FBI pass the information along to the Secret Service — also not an unreasonable decision in light of the fact that there are thousands of such arrests annually in the United States and nothing in the circumstances of Hinckley's arrest to suggest that he was or would become a danger to the President. In the absence of evidence of a threat, the agreement between the Service and the FBI did not require the FBI to report Hinckley's arrest to the Service.

Even assuming, however, that the information had been passed on to the Service by the FBI, one cannot conclude that the consequences would have been different. The Service does not have the manpower to interview every person who was arrested — for example, on a weapons charge — in each city visited by the President in the course of a political campaign. Absent a stronger suggestion on the face of the data that an investigation should be undertaken, the most the Service could reasonably do with raw arrest information would be store it for later correlation with other facts. If, for example, the same person were arrested in another city the President is visiting, the coincidence might suggest that he is "stalking" the President and justify a more thorough investigation. Today, the Service's resources do not permit such data correlation.

The data processing and intelligence resources required for a system which could achieve such correlations would be massive, and even then there could be no assurance that the linking of circumstantial data to support an inference of danger would be more than mere chance. Normally, follow-up investigation would still be needed.

Limitations on resources — and indeed effective use of resources by the Service — compel the Service to concentrate its efforts on collecting, analyzing and investigating information which more directly indicates a threat to the President. This is information about the overtly or covertly expressed intentions of individuals or groups.

From the protection-oriented perspective of the Service, therefore, the decline in FBI domestic intelligence activities has caused a critical overall decline in the useful information the Service receives from the FBI. In November 1979, Secret Service Director Stuart Knight testified before the Senate Judiciary Committee that the Service was, at that time, receiving only about 40 percent of what it had previously received from the FBI, and that this reduced intelligence product had deteriorated in quality. Explaining what he meant by quality, he referred to the loss of information concerning motives and plans.

Knight repeated these statements in the aftermath of the March 30 assassination attempt, in testimony before other committees of the House and Senate, specifically attributing this loss of useful intelligence to the Attorney General's Domestic Security Guidelines. These are discussed below.

### [Attorney General's Guidelines]

On March 10, 1976, then Attorney General Edward Levi issued Domestic Security Guidelines which, in effect, prevented the FBI from engaging in domestic intelligence gathering unless it was in possession of "specific and articulable facts giving reason to believe that an individual or a group is or may be engaged in activities which (1) involve the use of force or violence and which (2) involve or will involve the violation of federal law for one or more of [certain] purposes [related to the overthrow of the government or abridgement of civil rights]."

The Domestic Security Guidelines define three stages of investigation: preliminary, limited and full. Preliminary and limited investigations are confined to determining whether a full investigation is warranted. They may be undertaken only on the reasonable belief that a violation of federal law, by way of force or violence, is involved, and they may only be carried on for short periods of time. A limited investigation allows a somewhat greater range of investigative techniques than is available in a preliminary investigation, but it must be authorized in writing by a Special Agent in Charge or FBI Headquarters. Full investigations must be authorized by FBI Headquarters based on specific and articulable facts concerning the use of force or violence in committing certain crimes.

The Guidelines limit the period during which a full investigation may be conducted to one year, extendable only if the Department of Justice gives written authority.

The Service's criticism of these Guidelines raises serious questions which cannot be ignored in any study of the Service's performance. As the March 30 incident reveals, physically surrounding the President is not sufficient protection. The President's ultimate shield must be the ability of the Secret Service to keep him out of dangerous environments. This the Service cannot do without adequate intelligence resources — information about the intentions and plans of potentially dangerous people.

Despite its importance to the Service's mission, the Service has done little to document or analyze the decline in FBI intelligence dissemination which it attributes to the Domestic Security Guidelines. Circumstantial data, however, appears to confirm the Service's view that the decline has been very substantial.

In interviews conducted for this report, FBI officials have estimated that more than 20,000 so-called domestic security cases were open shortly prior to the promulgation of the Attorney General's Domestic Security Guidelines. While some of those cases were converted into standard criminal investigations when the necessary information was developed, very few of the remainder produced criminal prosecutions. Some officials at the Bureau state that all but about 7,000 of those cases were terminated by the FBI for reasons other than the restrictions imposed by the Domestic Security Guidelines, but they nonetheless appear to accept the estimates of the number of domestic security cases which the FBI was handling before 1976.

Whatever the reason for termination of these cases, the decline in their number since publication of the Attorney General's Domestic Security Guidelines has been precipitous. According to a 1976 report by the General Accounting Office, the ten FBI field offices studied by the Comptroller General during 1974 actively investigated 19,659 domestic intelligence cases, which the report asserted to represent 35 percent of a total of 55,500 cases on "subversives and extremists" opened or reopened by the FBI during 1974....

## RECOMMENDATIONS

1. Because of the apparent effect of privacy and government information disclosure laws on the ability of the Secret Service to collect useful intelligence on a voluntary basis, consideration should be given to narrowing the scope of these laws as they relate to the release of information furnished to the Secret Service, and to protecting the right of the Secret Service to have access to information in the hands of private organizations and state and local governmental authorities.

2. The Secret Service should be given an executive mandate, perhaps in

the form of an Executive Order or proclamation, to require greater assistance from other Federal agencies in the collection of intelligence.

3. Consideration should be given to permitting the FBI to pursue domestic security investigations where no criminal predicate is available; this may be done through appropriate modifications of the Attorney General's Domestic Security Guidelines for the FBI.

4. The Secret Service has not developed indicators to help identify "dangerous" individuals and groups, either by associating and correlating intelligence that might reveal the intentions of individuals and groups from their prior activities or by using so-called "profiles." Using data in the files of its Intelligence Division, the Service should attempt to develop useful indicators to assist it in identifying "dangerous" individuals, groups, and personality types. The Service should create within the Intelligence Division a more sophisticated planning and research operation, including five to ten non-agent employees with professional training in statistical methods and behavioral sciences. This group should be responsible, on an ongoing basis, for analyzing the intelligence data base in order to identify what types of information the Intelligence Division should be looking for, and what it should be doing with it.

5. The problems with maintaining Liaison Division as an intelligence-gathering group are compounded by its location outside the Intelligence Division. Liaison Division should be restructured and placed within the Intelligence Division. The resulting Liaison Branch should become aggressively involved in soliciting intelligence from other agencies and monitoring the amount and quality of intelligence generated. This Liaison Branch should take the lead in redrafting the agreements with other agencies so that they are more useful guides to the Service's intelligence needs that draw on the information developed by the recommended planning and research operation. If a liaison unit is needed to conduct work that facilitates advances and trips, it should be staffed through a separate liaison unit that does not compete for resources directly with the intelligence liaison function.

6. The Intelligence Division planning and research operation should also work closely with Data Systems Division to better define the data systems needs of the Intelligence Division, to insure that adequate computer programming and data processing support is provided to this enterprise, and to insure that the computer is being optimally applied to routine Intelligence Division needs.

## Advance Preparations for March 30, 1981

### CONCLUSIONS

...1. The Secret Service has established procedures to govern the conduct of advance preparations for the travel of protected persons.

Special alterations in those procedures, which do not appear in the PPD Manual, govern advance preparations for trips in the Washington, D.C. area. Those procedures assign a heavier share of the responsibility to the Washington field office. In addition, there is some evidence that the routine nature of advances and heavy protective work load in the Washington area has resulted in agents devoting less attention to detail than is commonly the case in other locations.

2. While the agents conducting the advance for the President's March 30 visit to the Hilton handled their responsibilities capably, their preparations did not address certain details which are included in the standard procedures for an advance. This may be understandable, since the procedures were developed for environments outside Washington, D.C., and do not take account of the fact that trips in the capital have become routine. The problem for the Service appears to be to develop procedures for Presidential trips in Washington, D.C., which take realistic account of their routine nature and of the fact that auxiliary agencies such as the local police have established their own views of what the Secret Service should require of them.

3. The political mission of the White House staff conflicts at times with the security mission of the Secret Service; security measures taken to protect the President are often determined by give-and-take between the two groups. Without some agreement between these two groups with regard to substantive security guidelines, the level of protection provided the President will inevitably be inconsistent.

The visit to the Hilton illustrated the anomalous outcomes resulting from the absence of a substantive agreement. Inside the Hilton, elaborate security precautions were taken to safeguard the President from a pre-screened group that would be kept at a substantial distance; outside the Hilton, members of the general public, without any Secret Service pre-screening whatever, could walk to a rope barricade and stand within 15 feet of the President.

## RECOMMENDATIONS

1. The advance staff of the White House and the senior managers of the Secret Service should commit whatever time and resources are required to develop a single document, on which both groups can agree, in which they detail the balance that is to be struck among the security, scheduling, and public exposure requirements of the President. The document should be updated, at least annually, and should include specific information concerning such items as:

a. The distances between the public and the President during his entrance and exit from areas with controlled access;

b. The advisability of permitting unscreened members of the public to have advance notice of an opportunity for gaining proximity to the President;

c. The circumstances in which the President will make himself available for questions from the press;

d. The amount of information regarding Presidential visits to be released to the public;

e. The advisability of locating the press in the area of motorcade vehicles;

f. Procedures for screening, electronically or otherwise, members of the public who can get close enough to the President to threaten his security;

g. The structure and placement of PPD formations around the President and arrangements with the White House staff to avoid interference with those formations.

2. The Washington field office and the protective divisions of the Secret Service should commit whatever time and resources are required to develop detailed procedures for the conduct of advances in the Washington, D.C. area. The number of advances conducted in the Washington area, the routine and repetitive quality of these advances, and other distinguishing characteristics of Secret Service operations in the Washington, D.C., area should be taken into account in developing these procedures. These procedures should provide for the earliest possible notification to the Washington field office of proposed trips, preferably simultaneously with the notification given to the lead advance agent by the protective divisions, and a statement of the responsibilities of each member of the Washington field office advance team. In addition, the Washington field office should conduct a review of intelligence advance procedures in the Washington, D.C. area, assisted by the Intelligence Division; this review should address the categories of advance intelligence data to be collected by the Washington field office, as well as the procedures by which it is to be collected. . . .

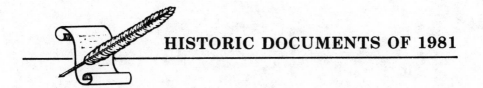

# APRIL

# PARDON OF MILLER AND FELT

## April 15, 1981

On April 15 President Ronald Reagan pardoned two former officials of the Federal Bureau of Investigation (FBI), W. Mark Felt and Edward S. Miller, who had been convicted of conspiring to violate the constitutional rights of American citizens by authorizing illegal, warrantless break-ins. The so-called "black bag jobs" were part of the Nixon administration's search during the early 1970s for members of the Weather Underground, a militant group opposed to the Vietnam War.

In his five-paragraph statement, the president granted full and unconditional pardons to the two men who, he said, had served the country with "great distinction" and whose "convictions ... grew out of their good-faith belief that their actions were necessary to preserve the security interests of our country."

Reagan recalled Jimmy Carter's unconditional pardon of Vietnam draft evaders four years earlier and said he wished to extend the nation's generosity to "two men who acted on high principle to bring an end to the terrorism that was threatening our Nation."

## Legal Proceedings

Felt, former acting associate director of the FBI, and Miller, former chief of the FBI's intelligence division, were found guilty by a jury in U.S. District Court in Washington, D.C., in November 1980. Felt was fined $5,000 and Miller $3,500, but Chief Judge William Bryant imposed no jail sentence on either man.

*Defense attorneys for Miller and Felt argued that the break-ins were necessary for national security because of links between the Weather Underground and North Vietnam, Cuba and the Palestine Liberation Organization. Felt testified that he had received general approval for warrantless break-ins in terrorism cases from L. Patrick Gray III, the FBI's director at the time. But Felt also acknowledged that Gray had not given specific approval for the break-ins in the Weather Underground investigation. Neither Gray nor Miller testified in the case.*

*Richard Nixon testified on October 29, 1980, that he approved a plan in 1970 that relaxed restraints on domestic intelligence-gathering operations and authorized federal agents to conduct break-ins. Four days later he rescinded his approval because of FBI Director J. Edgar Hoover's objection. Nixon said that rescission amounted to "neither an authorization nor a prohibition" of the use of warrantless searches. Gray became acting FBI director following Hoover's death in May 1972.*

*The prosecution argued that the searches were intended only to capture the Weathermen and had nothing to do with foreign powers, and that Felt and Miller knew they were illegal.*

*In instructing the jury, Judge Bryant appeared to invoke many of the prosecution's legal arguments. He said search warrants were required unless the break-ins were part of a foreign intelligence investigation in which each entry was approved in advance. For the break-ins to be legal, the persons whose homes had been searched had to have had a "significant connection" with a foreign power.*

## Sympathy for Felt and Miller

*Gray also was charged with conspiracy in the case, but the government dropped the charges, admitting it could not prove his role in authorizing the surreptitious entries. This prompted sympathy from some observers because Miller and Felt, as Gray's subordinates at the FBI, were being charged for crimes for which their superior was not.*

*Although the judge's instructions to the jury left little doubt about his belief that the break-ins were illegal, his sentencing was light. The convictions could have carried prison terms of up to 10 years and fines of up to $10,000 for each man.*

## Reaction to Pardons

*Neither Miller nor Felt had applied officially for a pardon, but after the pardons were announced Miller called them "a very fine thing for the present FBI" because they would eliminate any reluctance that agents might have to "do their job 100 percent."*

*But the chief prosecutor at the Felt-Miller trial, John W. Nields Jr., expressed the fear that the pardons would "send out a terrible signal — that the government can violate the Constitution and then forgive itself."*

*The legal implications of the pardons were hazy. They relieved Miller and Felt of paying the fines, but it was not clear whether the pardons also expunged the convictions from their records. In July 1981 the U.S. Court of Appeals ruled that, despite the pardons, Miller and Felt could continue with their appeal to overturn the lower court's findings. Lawyers for the two men sought the appeal to prevent the convictions from being used against them in related civil proceedings. Felt, for example, was suspended from practicing law after the conviction, and both men also were being sued in a civil case in New York stemming from the government's investigation of antiwar radicals.*

*Following is the text of President Reagan's statement, issued April 15, 1981, pardoning two former FBI agents, W. Mark Felt and Edward S. Miller:*

Pursuant to the grant of authority in article II, section 2 of the Constitution of the United States, I have granted full and unconditional pardons to W. Mark Felt and Edward S. Miller.

During their long careers, Mark Felt and Edward Miller served the Federal Bureau of Investigation and our Nation with great distinction. To punish them further — after 3 years of criminal prosecution proceedings — would not serve the ends of justice.

Their convictions in the U.S. District Court, on appeal at the time I signed the pardons, grew out of their good-faith belief that their actions were necessary to preserve the security interests of our country. The record demonstrates that they acted not with criminal intent, but in the belief that they had grants of authority reaching to the highest levels of government.

America was at war in 1972, and Messrs. Felt and Miller followed procedures they believed essential to keep the Director of the FBI, the Attorney General, and the President of the United States advised of the activities of hostile foreign powers and their collaborators in this country. They have never denied their actions, but, in fact, came forward to acknowledge them publicly in order to relieve their subordinate agents from criminal actions.

Four years ago, thousands of draft evaders and others who violated the Selective Service laws were unconditionally pardoned by my predecessor. America was generous to those who refused to serve their country in the Vietnam war. We can be no less generous to two men who acted on high principle to bring an end to the terrorism that was threatening our Nation.

# MAXIM SHOSTAKOVICH DEFECTION
## April 15, 16, 1981

*Soviet conductor Maxim Shostakovich and his son defected to the United States on April 16. They were performing with the Soviet Symphony Orchestra in Furth, West Germany, when they asked for police protection on April 11. The U.S. State Department announced April 16 that the Shostakovichs would not be given political asylum but instead would be admitted to the United States as refugees under the Refugee Act of 1980.*

*The department had said the previous day that it would grant political asylum to the Shostokovichs, but Dean E. Fischer, department spokesman, said that "Political asylum is only granted in the United States to persons who are already in the country and who demonstrate a well-founded fear of persecution if they have to return to their native country."*

*In an April interview with the West German magazine, Stern, Shostakovich said the chief reason for his defection was his humiliating treatment at the hands of Soviet cultural bureaucrats. Shostakovich said musicians were regularly examined before going abroad on questions such as the difference between capitalism and communism, or on current events, such as who were the political leaders of the country they were to visit.*

*Shostakovich's father, Dmitri, during his lifetime was the most respected court composer for the Soviet regime. However, with the 1979 publication of his memoirs, Testimony, his reputation within Russia began to change. The book declared that Dmitri's apparent loyalty to the party had been a deception.*

*Neither Maxim nor his son, also named Dmitri, had been openly involved in any political dispute with the Soviet government. But in a statement released after his defection Shostakovich said that, "I cannot continue to exist according to the old strictures ... be this endless variety of ways of abasing human dignity, the steady violation of human rights, the manifestations of explicit anti-Semitism; or the creation of conditions in which the best representatives of science and culture who disagree with these circumstances are either tossed into oblivion and hopelessly isolated ... or find themselves forced by such situations to leave their country." He cited as other examples Soviet writer Alexander I. Solzhenitsyn and cellist Mstislav Rostropovich and his wife, soprano Galina Vishnevskaya. (Historic Documents of 1978, p. 403; 1975, p. 161)*

*Maxim was the conductor of the Soviet Symphony Orchestra of the Central Television and Radio, and his son was a concert pianist with the orchestra at the time of their defection.*

*Following are excerpts from the April 15 and 16, 1981, press briefings held by State Department spokesman Dean E. Fischer on the defection of Maxim Shostakovich and his son and the statement by Shostakovich as it appeared in* The Washington Star *May 23:*

# FISCHER APRIL 15 PRESS BRIEFING

**Q:** Has the State Department decided to grant asylum to Mr. Shostakovich?

**A:** Maestro Shostakovich has been in touch with the State Department about this matter. They have asked, of course, to come to the United States. Their request is being considered processed as quickly as possible, and they are expected to arrive later this week.

**Q:** Do you see any obstacle to his being granted political asylum?

**A:** No, I do not.

**Q:** You used the plural pronoun. Who is with him?

**A:** I'm sorry. It is, as I understand it, the son [Maxim] of the composer [Dmitri] for the USSR State Symphony and his [Dmitri's] grandson.

**Q:** In other words, you expect that he will be granted political asylum when he arrives?

**A:** Yes, I don't see any obstacle to that. He is expected to arrive, as I say, later this week.

**Q:** On what sort of visa to enter the country will he arrive if the decision has not yet been made on political asylum?

**A:** This question I cannot answer.

**Q:** Did Secretary Clark [Deputy Secretary of State William P. Clark] have a role in this request?

**A:** Judge Clark spoke to the conductor of the National Symphony in this connection.

# APRIL 16 PRESS BRIEFING

**Dean Fischer:** Good afternoon. I have two announcements I would like to make.

First, the press briefing tomorrow will be at 11:30 instead of the usual hour.

The second announcement concerns something I said here yesterday on the Shostakovich defection. Yesterday I gave out the information that the Shostakovichs had been granted political asylum or were going to be granted political asylum. That is incorrect.

The Shostakovichs are being processed into the United States as refugees under the provisions of the Refugee Act of 1980. This is the same process by which thousands of other refugees who are fleeing their native country out of a well-founded fear of persecution enter the United States every year.

I'll take your questions.

**Q:** Do we still see no obstacles to their being granted political asylum?

**A:** I don't want to get into the area of political asylum.

**Q:** Is it being considered?

**A:** I can't comment on that.

**Q:** What is the element of persecution of someone who's conducting a state orchestra and someone who's a soloist with that orchestra? How are they being persecuted?

**A:** I don't have any details on that.

**David Passage:** Refugee status replaces political asylum.

**Q:** No. But you just said the Refugee Act is for those people who are fleeing their countries because of well-founded fear of persecution. I'm just wondering what sort of persecution these people were fearing.

**A:** I have no details to give you on that. I can explain, if you like, the distinction I'm drawing between political asylum and the refugee status. Do you want me to do that? That's not an answer to your question, but I don't have any details in response to it.

**Q:** What is the difference between political asylum and the refugee status?

**A:** That's what I was about to do. Political asylum is only granted in the United States to persons who are already in the country and who can demonstrate a well-founded fear of persecution if they have to return to their native country.

Refugee status is conferred under the terms of the Refugee Act of 1980 to persons who have left their homeland but are not yet in the United States.

# SHOSTAKOVICH STATEMENT

In retrospect, it seems to me that the ship of our lives, long since rudderless, has gone aground on the shores of a dismal archipelago dominated by the horribly unnatural relationship between its inhabitants — people blinded and disoriented by the total disinformation, both in the sphere of world cultural achievements and in the realm of public opinion, and by the ruling authorities. Powers that are now so deeply rooted that the only alternative is — almost unconsciously or with knowledgeable hyprocrisy — to pamper and cultivate them, sacrificing everything truly human in exchange for the possibility for side-by-side coexistence. Now I am overwhelmed by the sensation, that, even though we had almost adjusted — at the price of crippling our souls and scarring our hearts — to this more than unnatural way of life, a propitious wind has now filled the sails of fate and brought the nearly rotted wreckage of our lives onto the expanses of the world's oceans of freedom.

It is painful and frightening to look back, for I know that, following the directives and orders which rule the existence of my country, everything I have touched will be wiped out to be forgotten; all those whose lives touched mine will be harshly punished — having been caught by the grinding millstones of the "system".

I know all this — but I cannot act differently. I cannot continue to exist according to the old strictures; under laws which generate in a man constant feelings of protest at each contact with the all-encompassing reality: be this the endless variety of ways of abasing human dignity, the steady violation of human rights, the manifestations of explicit anti-Semitism; or the creation of conditions in which the best representatives of science and culture who disagree with these circumstances are either tossed into oblivion and hopelessly isolated — as happened repeatedly to my father — or find themselves forced by such situations to leave their country. Frequently they are simply expelled — like the great [Alexander] Solzhenitsyn, who wasn't afraid of the truth, or the genius [Mstislav] Rostropovich and Galina Vishnevskaya, whose names, like the names of many other of my outstanding countrymen, the authorities try to obliterate from the memory of our people. And, in the words of D. D. Shostakovich from his 13th Symphony, all this turns man into a "perpetual, mute scream...."

I want to stress that, no matter how difficult it was to leave, it would have been more difficult for me to stay — to witness the innocent spirit of my son being broken and brutalized as it collided with our reality. I want to stress that our exodus is a profundly conscious step, a sign of protest, a sign of disagreement — my spiritual legacy from my never-to-be-forgotten father, who devoted his entire life — all his creativity to the great humanitarian ideals of mankind.

In conclusion, I want to state that both my son and I voluntarily renounce the status of Soviet citizenship. Citizenship of which many honorable representatives of our motherland — from [Theodore] Chalyapin to the present days — have been deprived; their profound feelings of continued love of their country unites us, and the deep solidarity and respect we feel for them makes us kin. And, as time has shown: "forgotten they that cast the curses; remembered only those they cursed."

This step of ours is in no way an indication that we renounce our true devotion to our people. It is only an expression of a protest, within our capabilities, against the undeserved deprivations of these people, a protest against the system under which they live.

But, no matter how painful our exodus is to us, we believe in the great prophecy of Pushkin: "She will rise, the star of captivating bliss, Russia shall awake from her sleep . . . " and on the pages of history they will inscribe the names of our outstanding countrymen, those true patriots who stood and continue to stand in the forefront of the fighters for our free and happy motherland.

# COMMEMORATION OF THE HOLOCAUST

## April 30, 1981

*An emotional ceremony in the East Room of the White House marked the first annual Days of Remembrance, sponsored by the United States Holocaust Memorial Council. The April 30 event commemorated the Holocaust, the systematic destruction of more than six million Jews by the Nazis before and during World War II. In addition to speeches by President Ronald Reagan and council chairman Elie Wiesel, the day included a candle-lighting ceremony by seven survivors of the concentration camps and the recitation of Kaddish, the Hebrew prayer for the dead.*

*In an apparent contradiction to his administration's announced policy downplaying human rights in foreign affairs, Reagan said that "the persecution of people, for whatever reason — persecution of people for their religious belief — that is a matter to be on that negotiating table or the United States does not belong at that table." Later the same day, Larry Speakes, White House deputy press secretary, explained that the president had been affected emotionally and had not intended to place preconditions on negotiations with any foreign power.*

*Reagan said he was horrified to hear that some groups contend that the Holocaust never happened. In recent years groups such as the Institute for Historical Review and the Liberty Lobby had stated that the Holocaust was a Jewish myth. One Reagan nominee, Warren Richardson, withdrew his name for consideration for the post of an assistant secretary of health and human services, after his connection with the Liberty Lobby became public. Richardson had served as chief lobbyist and general counsel to the Liberty Lobby from 1969 to 1973. Reagan said that during his military service in World War II his assignment was to edit combat film. He saw the first film taken in the camps in April 1945 and remembered the horror on the faces of American servicemen who first witnessed the scene.*

*The Days of Remembrance were also observed by ceremonies at the Rayburn House Office Building and by speeches on the floor of the House of Representatives. Ten members of Congress served on the memorial council.*

## Purposes of Memorial Council

*The U.S. Holocaust Memorial Council was established as an agency within the Interior Department by Congress October 7, 1980. The purpose was to carry out the recommendations of the President's Commission on the Holocaust, which included the establishment of Days of Remembrance as an annual civic observance throughout the United States, the construction in Washington, D.C., of a permanent living memorial to the victims, the establishment of an educational foundation, and the creation of a committee of conscience responsible for providing an early warning against the threat of genocide anywhere in the world.*

*Elie Wiesel, author and teacher, served as chairman of both the council and the president's commission. Wiesel, born in 1928 in Romania, was a survivor of Auschwitz and Buchenwald where his mother, father and younger sister died. Weisel described his experiences in his first book, Night, published in 1960.*

## Other Holocaust Events

*Two other 1981 meetings were concerned with the Holocaust. A June gathering in Jerusalem brought together 5,000 concentration camp survivors and their children from 23 countries. The purpose was to pass the legacy of what the parents had suffered to the children who pledged to remember and to keep reminding the world what happened to Jews in Europe. In October the Holocaust Commission sponsored a three-day conference of survivors and servicemen who liberated the camps. Wiesel said that the conference was called in part to counteract a rising tide of revisionist history of the Holocaust. He said that in the past decade more than 100 anti-Semitic publications had appeared in more than a dozen countries claiming that the concentration camps and genocide of the Jews had never happened.*

*In an effort to shed light on the role played by the U.S. government and American Jewish groups in events in Nazi Germany, the American Commission on the Holocaust began its investigations in September 1981.*

*This group, headed by former Supreme Court Justice Arthur J. Goldberg, was not connected with the president's commission.*

*Following are the texts of remarks delivered April 30, 1981, by Elie Wiesel, chairman of the U.S. Holocaust Memorial Council, and President Reagan at the White House, and remarks by Rep. William Lehman, D-Fla., and Rep. Bill Green, R-N.Y., in the House of Representatives. (Boldface headings in brackets have been added by Congressional Quarterly to highlight the organization of the texts.):*

# REMARKS OF ELIE WIESEL

Mr. President, distinguished members of the House, of the Senate, and of the diplomatic corps, honored guests, friends. About sadness later; first some words of gratitude. We thank you, Mr. President, for joining us and for participating in this solemn assembly of remembrance. Your presence here today, Mr. President, so soon after the senseless attack upon your person, is a tribute to your understanding and concern for human values and is especially meaningful to us. We all know that your being here, Mr. President, is not a ceremonial gesture, but an expression of your sense of history and your dream of a future with hope and dignity for the American nation and for all mankind.

So, we thank you, Mr. President, and we thank our Father in heaven for having spared you. And now with your permission, Mr. President, I would like to read to you or rather to share with you some lines written first by an old Jewish poet and then by a young Jewish poet. The old Jewish poet was named Leivick and he wrote in Yiddish which was the language of the martyrs — the language of those who were killed in those days. . . .

The other poem was written by a young boy in Theresienstadt named Mottele and he wrote in that ghetto in those days of the awe and fear and sadness, he wrote a poem that reflects more than his own moods, more than his own fate, and I quote, "From tomorrow on I shall be sad. From tomorrow on, not today. What is the use of sadness, tell me? Because these evil winds begin to blow? Why should I grieve for tomorrow today? Tomorrow may be good. Tomorrow the sun may shine for us again. We shall no longer need to be sad. From tomorrow on I shall be sad. From tomorrow on, not today. No, today I will be glad. And every day, no matter how bitter it may be, I will say from tomorrow on I shall be sad, not today."

Mr. President, how does one commemorate the million Motteles and Shloimeles and Leahles and Soreles? How does one commemorate six million victims, all descendents of Abraham and Isaac and Jacob? What words does one use? What metaphors does one invoke to describe the brutal and unprecedented extinctions of a world — thousands and thousands of flourishing Jewish communities survived the fury of the Crusades, the hatred of pogroms, the afflictions of wars and the misery, the shame, the despair of religious and social oppressions only to be swept away by the Holocaust? In all their chronicles and testaments, memoirs and prayers, litanies and poems, the victims stressed one single theme over and over again — remember, remember the horror, remember. Bear witness. And that is their legacy to us, the living.

Of course, there may be some who'll be asked, "Why remember at all? Why not allow the dead to bury the dead? Is it not in man's nature to push aside memories that hurt and disturb?" The more cruel the wound, the greater the effort to cover it. The more horrifying the nightmare, the more powerful the desire to exorcise it. Why then would anyone choose to cling to unbearable recollections of emaciated corpses or violations of every human law? Maybe we have not yet learned to cope with the events, intellectually, socially, philosophically, theologically. Perhaps we never will. The more we know, the less we understand. All we can do is remember. But how does one remember? How does one remember and communicate an event filled with so much fear and darkness and mystery that it negates language and imagination? Auschwitz, Mr. President, history marks it with the burning seal. Our century, Mr. President, may well be remembered not only for the monuments it erected, or for the astonishing technological advances it made, but most of all for Treblinka and Majdanek, Belsen and Ponar, Auschwitz and Buchenwald. How is one to explain what happened? It could have been stopped or at least slowed down at various stages. One word, one statement, one move — it was not stopped. Why not?

I'm a teacher, Mr. President. And my students, young, fervent, compassionate American students, often express their puzzlement in my classroom — why the complacency? Why the tacit acquiescence? Why weren't the Hungarian Jews, for example, warned about their fate? When they arrived in Auschwitz at midnight they mistook it for a peaceful village. Why weren't the railways to Birkenau bombed by either the Allies or the Russians? And the Russians were so close.

The calculated viciousness of the executioner, the helplessness of the doomed, the passivity of the bystander — all these lie beyond our comprehension — the killers' fascination with death, the victims with hope, the survivors' testimony. A new vocabulary needs to be invented to describe the event. Can you imagine the silence preceding a selection in a death count? The feel of a man who suddenly understands that he is the last of his family — the last of the line? Imagine? No, no one can imagine that kingdom. Only those who were there know what it meant to be there — theirs was the kingdom that will forever remain forbidden and forbidding.

And yet, and yet, we must tell the tale, we must bear witness. Not to do so would mean to render meaningless the years and the lives that we, those of us who survived, received as a gift, as an offering to be shared and redeemed.

We must tell the tale, Mr. President, and we want to tell it not to divide people but, on the contrary, to bring them together, not to inflict more suffering but, on the contrary, to diminish it, not to humiliate anyone but, on the contrary, to teach others to humiliate no one. This is why we bear witness, Mr. President and friends, not for the sake of the dead. It is too late for the dead. Not even for our own sake. It may be too late for us as well.

We speak for mankind. The universality of the Jewish tragedy lies in its uniqueness. Only the memory of what was done to the Jewish people and through it to others can save the world from indifference to the ultimate dangers that threaten its very existence.

Mr. President, that the survivors have not lost their sanity, their faith in God, or in man, that they decided to build on ruins in Israel or in the United States of America, that they decided to choose generosity instead of anger, hope instead of despair, is a mystery even to us. They had every reason to give up on life and its promise. They did not. Still at times, Mr. President, they are overcome by doubt and fear. The world has not learned its lesson. Anti-Semitic groups spring up more and more and some shamelessly, viciously, deny that the Holocaust ever occurred. In our lifetime fascist groups increase their memberships and parade in the streets. Intolerance, bigotry, fanaticism, mass executions in some places, mass starvation in others, religious wars, quasi-mediaeval upheavals, and, of course, ultimately, the nuclear menace and our indifference to it. What is to be done?

Though Jewish, profoundly Jewish in nature, the Holocaust has universal implications, and I believe, we believe that the memory of what was done may shield us in the future.

Naturally, other nations were persecuted and even decimated by the Nazis and their allies and their collaborators, and we honor their memory. But the Jewish people represented a different target. For the first time in history being became a crime. Jews were destined for annihilation not because of what they said or proclaimed or did or possessed or created or destroyed, but because of who they were.

Is that why we survivors, we Jews, we human beings, are so concerned? And is that why we are so attached to a land where so many survivors have found a haven, pride and refuge and hope? Please understand us, Mr. President. We believe that the subject of the Holocaust must remain separate from politics, but if we plead so passionately for Israel's right not only to be secure but also to feel secure, it is because of Israel's nightmares which are also our nightmares.

Israel is threatened by a holy war, which means total war, which means total annihilation. Mr. President, some may say that these are words, words — yes, words. But we are a generation traumatized by experience. We take words seriously. The very idea of another Jewish catastrophe anywhere in our lifetime is quite simply unbearable to us.

Israel must never feel abandoned. Israel must never feel alone. Israel must never feel expendable, Mr. President. We plead with you because it is the dream of our dreams. It is perhaps the pain of our pain but the hope of our hopes. It is an ancient nation of 4,000 years that should not be judged in categories of one day or one incident. Only in its totality can we understand and perceive and love Israel.

We must believe so because there were times, 40 years ago, when Jewish communities felt abandoned and betrayed. In 1943 on April 16th the gallant, young commander in chief of the Warsaw Ghetto Uprising, Mordechai Anieleuits, wrote to a friend, and I quote, "We are fighting. We shall not surrender. But as our last days are approaching, remember that we have been betrayed." That is what he felt. That is what we all felt. That is what we all felt. They were betrayed then. To forget them now would mean to betray them again, and we must not allow this to happen.

In the Jewish tradition, Mr. President, when a person dies we appoint him or her as our emissary in heaven to intercede in our behalf. Could it be that they, the six million Jews, were messengers? But then, then, Mr. President and friends, whose messengers are we?

Thank you.

# REAGAN SPEECH

I feel a little unnecessary, because I don't know that anyone could say anything that would add to those words that we've just heard. It is a particular pleasure for me to be here with you today. This ceremony has meaning not only for people of the Jewish faith, those who have been persecuted, but for all who want to prevent another Holocaust.

Jeremiah wrote of the days when the Jews were carried off to Babylon and Jerusalem was destroyed. He said, "Jerusalem weeps in the night and tears run down her cheeks." Today, yes, we remember the suffering and the death of Jews and of all those others who were persecuted in World War II. We try to recapture the horror of millions sent to gas chambers and crematoria. And we commemorate the days of April in 1945 when American and Allied troops liberated the Nazi death camps.

The tragedy that ended 36 years ago was still raw in our memories, because it took place, as we've been told, in our lifetime. We share the wounds of the survivors. We recall the pain only because we must never permit it to come again. And yet, today, in spite of that experience, as an entire generation has grown to adulthood, who never knew the days of World War II, and we remember ourselves, when we were younger, how distant history seemed, anything that came before our time — and so the signs do exist: the ugly graffiti, the act of violence, the act of terrorism here and there, scattered throughout the world and not quite large enough in dimension for us to rally as we once did in that war.

## [Reagan an Eyewitness]

I'm horrified today when I know and hear that there are actually people now trying to say that the Holocaust was invented, that it never happened, that there weren't 6 million people whose lives were taken cruelly and needlessly in that event, that all of this is propaganda. Well, the old cliche that a picture's worth a thousand words — in World War II, not only do we have the survivors today to tell us at first hand, but in World War II, I was in the military and assigned to a post where every week, we obtained from every branch of the service all over the world the combat film that was taken by every branch. And we edited this into a secret report for the general staff. We, of course, had access to and saw that secret report.

And I remember April '45. I remember seeing the first film that came in when the war was still on, but our troops had come upon the first camps and had entered those camps. And you saw, unretouched — no way that it could have ever been rehearsed — what they saw, the horror they saw. I felt the pride when, in one of those camps, there was a nearby town, and the people were ordered to come and look at what had been going on, and to see them. And the reaction of horror on their faces was the greatest proof that they had not been conscious of what was happening so near to them.

And that film still, I know, must exist in the military, and there it is, living motion pictures, for anyone to see, and I won't go into the horrible scenes that we saw. But it remains with me as confirmation of our right to rekindle these memories, because we need always to guard against that kind of tyranny and inhumanity. Our spirit is strengthened by remembering, and our hope is in our strength.

## [Commitment of Free People]

There is an American poem that says humanity, with all its fears and all its hopes, depends on us. As a matter of fact, it was the Pope, at the end of World War II, when the world was so devastated, and yet, we alone remained so strong, who said, "America has a genius for great and unselfish deeds, and into the hands of America, God has placed an afflicted mankind." I think that that was a trust given to us that we should never betray. It is this responsibility as free people that we face today. It's this commitment among free people that we celebrate.

The hope of a ceremony such as this is that even a tortured past holds promise if we learn its lessons. According to Isaiah, there will be a new heaven and a new earth and the voice of weeping will be heard no more. Together, with the help of God, we can bear the burden of our nightmare. It is up to us to ensure that we never live it again.

Theodore Roosevelt said that the Presidency was a bully pulpit. Well, I, for one, intend that this bully pulpit shall be used on every occasion, where it is appropriate, to point a finger of shame at even the ugliness of graffiti, and certainly wherever it takes place in the world, the act of violence or terrorism, and that even at the negotiating table, never shall it be forgotten for a moment that wherever it is taking place in the world, the persecution of people, for whatever reason — persecution of people for their religious belief — that is a matter to be on that negotiating table, or the United States does not belong at that table.

# REMARKS OF REP. LEHMAN

Mr. Speaker, thank you for consenting to this special order today which I and my distinguished colleague from New York, Bill Green, requested to commemorate Yom Hashoa, Holocaust Remembrance Day. In accordance with the establishment of the United States Holocaust Memorial Council, which was signed into law last October, 1 week each year will be designated as the "Days of Remembrance" for the victims of the holocaust and will be marked by a national, civic commemoration and by private and public observances around the country. This week of April 26 through May 3, 1981, marks the first observance since this historic legislation was passed.

People forget, and some people deny that the holocaust happened, even in the face of undeniable evidence. Just as the Nazis tried to erase the existence, the culture, and the history of Jews, there are those today who would still try to erase even that most painful of all memories, the holocaust. Even today, continuing ignorance and bigotry compels us to keep that memory alive.

This remembrance is not only for the victims, but for the living, both present and future. We, the living, must bear the responsibility of insuring that no individual, institution, or government can ever again decide who shall have the right to live.

The holocaust has great significance for Americans. American soldiers liberated many of the camps and were the first witnesses of what the rest of the world, including our country, had ignored. Many of the survivors of the holocaust finally immigrated to the United States and became U.S. citizens, and many went to Israel, where outside threats to Jewish life still exist.

Instead of monuments, the holocaust survivors have stressed the importance of studying the lessons of the holocaust. We must teach ourselves and others, Jews and non-Jews, to understand the unique and universal implications of the annihilation of 6 million Jews, not as an accidental occurrence, but as a primary goal of the Nazis. We need to comprehend the holocaust and to apply that understanding to the present and to the future. The prevention of genocide against Jews, Armenians, or any other people, must be a constant concern. . . .

# REMARKS OF REP. GREEN

Mr. Speaker, I am proud to join my distinguished colleague Bill Lehman of Florida, in reserving this time on the floor of the House of Representatives to commemorate Yom Hashoah, the days of remembrance. I wish to thank my colleagues from both sides of the aisle for participating with us in this special order.

As a member of the United States Holocaust Memorial Council and of its predecessor Commission on the Holocaust, I am gratified that the first annual commemoration to mark these days provided in the legislation establishing the Council was held this morning. President Reagan participated in this moving event. Because the Council seeks to encourage national commemorations. I would also acknowledge the numerous events taking place in the country this week.

This Sunday May 3, at my temple, Temple Emanu-el in New York City, there will again this year be a major civil gathering there to pay tribute to those who perished in the Warsaw ghetto uprising, now 38 years ago. And in cities and towns across the Nation, in our schools and synagogues and churches and local meeting halls, people have gathered to mark this special time on our calendar. For some, it is also a time of private recollections.

As Americans of all faiths, we observe this collective remembrance so that we will never forget the unspeakably tragic and horrendous events of this darkest period in our world history. Remembering, indeed, is not easy for us to do, but it is necessary that we do it. As we acknowledge the pain and suffering of millions of innocent people, of the 6 million Jews who died because of who they were, and the other millions of innocent people who also perished, we renew our pledge to do all that we can to prevent another holocaust anywhere ever again. As we think of the cultures and traditions that were lost then, we are renewed in our efforts to gather and pass along to future generations knowledge of that period in our history. And as we remember the failure of the world's political institutions to stop the killing too many refused to admit was going on, we seek ways to hear the voices of those who speak out whenever suffering and inhumanity again occur. We should also never forget that the State of Israel was born out of the destruction of the holocaust and the hard work of its survivors. For this reason it is so special to so many.

In reflecting on the events which brought us to this time for remembrance, the totality of what occurred during the holocaust is impossible to absorb. We have heard and read the individual stories and the overall statistics, and know how immense were the numbers who endured, too few of whom survived. It is from this sense of the larger horror that each of us comes to our individual recollection and from that to our own renewed pledge to prevent there ever being another holocaust. This, I believe, is the central message of these "Days of Remembrance.". . .

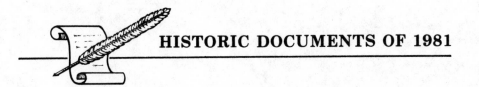
# MAY

# MAY

# FREEDOM OF INFORMATION
## May 4, 9, 1981

*Attorney General William French Smith announced May 4 new guide-lines for federal agencies responding to requests for material under the Freedom of Information Act (FOIA). Smith's memo was the opening salvo in the Reagan administration's effort to tighten the law first enacted in 1966 and amended in 1974. Late in 1981 the administration proposed legislation to close loopholes they perceived as problems. The American media responded with protests to any new restrictions on the release of information.*

*The new guidelines replaced those set out by former Attorney General Griffin B. Bell in May 1977 and reversed a previous requirement that, even if covered by one of the act's nine exemptions, material should be re-leased unless the agency could show that "demonstrable harm" could result from the release. The new directives permitted each federal agency to develop its own release policy, but Smith's memorandum emphasized that the foremost goal in administering the Freedom of Information Act was the disclosure of agency records. The memo advised agencies to remain aware of the cost of litigation that might result from a failure to comply with a legitimate request and that non-disclosure could at times serve to conceal fraud, waste or wrongdoing within federal agencies.*

### Existing Exemptions

*Under the law, agencies could withhold information only if it met conditions spelled out in nine exemptions. These included:*

*• Classified national security information.*

- *Agency internal personnel rules.*
- *Information specifically exempted by statute, such as tax returns and patent applications.*
- *Trade secrets and other confidential information obtained from businesses and other private parties.*
- *Inter- or intra-agency memorandums.*
- *Personal information, including personnel and medical files that would constitute invasion of an individual's privacy.*
- *Law enforcement information that would interfere with ongoing investigations or an individual's right to a fair trial, or would endanger a law enforcement officer.*
- *Information related to reports on financial institutions.*
- *Geological and geophysical information.*

*When an agency declined to disclose information, the person requesting the information could sue to determine whether the refusal was justified. In such cases the Justice Department served as the agency's attorney.*

## Administration's Views

*In a May 9 speech, Deputy Attorney General Edward C. Schmults outlined the administration's views of "the adverse and seemingly unanticipated consequences" of the FOIA. Speaking to the Second Circuit Judicial Conference, Schmults said the FOIA was used in unintended ways and the costs of administering the act were many times greater than expected. The original intention of the act — to cultivate an informed electorate — was thwarted by the huge volume of requests by special private interests, not by scholars or the media, normal conduits of information to the public. By far the greatest number of requests came from businesses seeking information on government regulations, lawsuits or the activities of competitors. Another problem cited by Schmults was the accidental disclosure of the names of informants in criminal cases when requested by prisoners.*

## Congressional Action

*At the end of 1981 Congress was at work on a compromise between two bills that would revise FOIA. The administration bill (S 1751, HR 4805) would further restrict the release of law enforcement and business information and would allow the agencies to charge higher fees to cover costs. The other bill (S 1730), introduced by Sen. Orrin G. Hatch, R-Utah, would give agencies fewer exemptions than the president's bill but would provide more protection for businesses seeking to protect confidential material. The Constitution Subcommittee of the Senate Judiciary Committee December 14 approved a version of S 1730 that borrowed heavily from the administration's bill and would make it easier for the Central Intelligence Agency to further restrict information.*

## Media Reaction

*Although media requests for information comprised only about 5 percent of total requests for information, media groups lobbied against both bills. Groups such as the American Newspapers Association, the Radio and Television News Directors Association, the Society of Professional Journalists and the Reporters Committee for Freedom of the Press stated that the existing law provides substantial and effective exemptions for intelligence and law enforcement files on live investigations. They also said the costs of administering FOIA, estimated at more than $50 million annually, are irrelevant in a budget in excess of $700 billion.*

*Testifying October 15, a representative of the Reporters Committee called the administration bill "a major mutilation of the public accountability of government which underlies the concept of the Act.... The Administration bill and the Hatch bill are, in most respects, an across-the-board frontal assault on public access to government information as we now know it under the Federal Freedom of Information Act. If either is passed, it will encourage inefficiencies, illegalities and cover-ups by government bureaucrats and high officials in the law enforcement community and in the government regulatory agencies because it will shut down the public information necessary to monitor these government activities."*

> *Following is the text of Attorney General William French Smith's memo advising federal departments and agencies of new guidelines for compliance with the Freedom of Information Act, released May 4, 1981, and excerpts from a speech by Deputy Attorney General Edward C. Schmults to the Second Circuit Judicial Conference, delivered May 9. (Boldface headings in brackets have been added by Congressional Quarterly to highlight the organization of the text.):*

# ATTORNEY GENERAL'S MEMORANDUM

MEMORANDUM FOR:   HEADS OF ALL FEDERAL
DEPARTMENTS AND AGENCIES

FROM   :   William French Smith
Attorney General

SUBJECT   :   *Freedom of Information Act*

The letter of the Attorney General of May 5, 1977 regarding the Freedom of Information Act is superseded by this memorandum. The Department's current policy is to defend all suits challenging an agency's decision to deny a request submitted under the FOIA unless it is determined that:

(a) The agency's denial lacks a substantial legal basis; or

(b) Defense of the agency's denial presents an unwarranted risk of adverse impact on other agencies' ability to protect important records.

As always, agencies must be guided by the principle that, subject to the specific exemptions provided by Congress, disclosure of agency records is the foremost goal in administering the Act. Accordingly, in responding to individual FOIA requests, agencies are urged to consider the public interests which favor disclosure, to weigh the potential costs of FOIA litigation, and to ensure that nondisclosure will not serve to conceal or otherwise facilitate fraud, waste or other wrongdoing by government employees.

Agencies should consult with the Department of Justice, Office of Legal Policy and Freedom of Information Committee, before final denial of an FOIA request which appears to present significant legal or policy issues. Agencies are further invited to solicit the advice of the Department of Justice on any other appropriate occasion.

The policies and procedures announced in this letter are intended to establish a cooperative relationship between the Department of Justice and other agencies in administering the FOIA.

Since experience in administering the Act has demonstrated various problems, I will be soliciting legislative proposals from your agency in the near future in a collaborative endeavor to reform the FOIA.

## SCHMULTS' SPEECH

... The Freedom of Information Act is one part of the massive network of new federal statutes enacted over the past two decades. Those new statutes address a broad spectrum of important issues — including civil rights, environmental protection, occupational safety and health, toxic substances, and wrongdoing within government. I'm sure none of us would quarrel with the basic goals of these laws. We are all proponents of equal opportunity and justice without regard to race or sex, age or handicap; of clean air and water; of safe working places; of protection against toxic substances; and of incorruptible government. Government has not proved itself very adroit or farsighted in many instances, however, when it comes to promoting those goals without adverse and seemingly unanticipated consequences. Many of the comprehensive implementing regulations are ambiguous and have fostered new problems. Many of the statutes themselves have been misused to promote not the public interest but private special interests.

The Freedom of Information Act is a perfect example of federal statutes that serve their original aims only in part and now serve other less desirable purposes. One of the highest priorities of the Reagan Administration's Justice Department is to identify those kinds of statutes and regulations with which it deals. And then to begin the process of correction and improvement.

Concerning the Freedom of Information Act itself, one basic problem and three resulting problems require correction. First, it is being used in unintended ways. Second, the unintended uses interfere unduly with important governmental activities. Third, the financial burden is dramatically greater than anticipated. And fourth, the government is too slow in responding to those requests that are within the purpose of the Act.

During the evolution of the Freedom of Information Act, proponents have repeatedly emphasized its purpose: to cultivate an informed electorate by providing the public access to government information whenever consistent with the public interest in effective government. In explaining the justification for the Act, one House Report asserted that the informational "needs of the electorate have outpaced the laws which guarantee public access to the facts in Government." A Senate Report invoked the revered words of James Madison in describing the purpose of the Act:

> "Knowledge will forever govern ignorance, and a people who mean to be their own governors must arm themselves with the power knowledge gives. A popular government without popular information or the means of acquiring it, is but a prologue to a farce or a tragedy or perhaps both."

As one supporter put it, the Act would grant the American public access to the government information necessary for "responsible citizenship."

## [Misuse of Act]

Some fourteen years of experience in administering the Act, however, have convincingly demonstrated that it is used for purposes other than those intended by the Congress. Only a tiny fraction of the requests for disclosure have come from scholars or the news media, the primary groups that could communicate government information to the electorate.

The Antitrust Division of the Department of Justice, for example, estimates that more than half of the Freedom of Information Act requests it receives are made by actual or potential litigants in private antitrust suits. The requests generally seek the fruits of the government's investigative efforts to buttress private legal claims for damages, not to reveal information to the public.

The Drug Enforcement Administration and the Federal Bureau of Investigation [FBI] have documented numerous requests by or on behalf of prisoners seeking information about cohorts in crime or about enforcement methods or sources, information of doubtful relevance to informing the electorate. The Director of the FBI, Judge William Webster, has asserted that many of those requests are instigated by inmates seeking to identify the informants who "probably" were responsible for their incarceration.

Corporations enlist the Act in their search for information that would confer a competitive advantage. One witness at a Congressional hearing complained: "The Act has increasingly become a vehicle for surveillance, at public expense, of the private affairs of commercial enterprises by the adversaries." Large corporations also employ the Act as a government-subsidized tool for informal discovery in dealing with the Government. The FDA [Food and Drug Administration], the SEC [Securities and Exchange Commission], and the FCC [Federal Communications Commission] have all reported that the predominant percentage of requests they receive come directly or indirectly from corporations they regulate.

Most striking of all, foreign agents may have actually used the Act in their search for intelligence information. Similarly, organized crime figures may have used the Act in an effort to identify government informants.

The tremendous number of requests under the Act that are clearly not within the purpose for which it was enacted have also impaired important government functions. Sponsors insisted that the Act was to strike a workable balance between the right of the public to know and the public interest in effective government. In operation, however, the Freedom of Information Act thwarts or undermines several important government functions.

The FBI, for example, is responsible for combatting foreign intelligence, terrorism, and organized crime within the United States. Targets of its investigations use requests under the Act in an attempt to discover the identity of FBI sources — as well as the scope, capabilities, techniques, and limitations of the Bureau.

## [Risk of Retaliation]

Although the FBI believes that disclosure of records under the Act has not yet lead [sic] to physical retaliation against a confidential source, the Bureau is properly alarmed about the risk. The risk of disclosure of FBI records has made private persons, nonfederal law enforcement officials, and informants reticent about providing vital information. Many informants have actually stopped cooperating with the FBI, for example, because they feared that their identities would be disclosed under the Act.

In addition to impairing law enforcement, the Act makes it more difficult for government to gather reliable information from businesses. The federal government obtains records from private enterprise in numerous capacities. Businesses have an undeniable commercial interest in maintaining the confidentiality from competitors of many of these records — for example, technical information submitted to the government in the procurement process. Nevertheless, the possibility of disclosure under the Act is real because agencies frequently lack the information or economic forecasting capacity to predict the competitive harm attributable to disclosure. Because of the insufficient safeguards against the release of sensitive commercial information, countless businessmen are loathe to make such information available to the government. Federal officials have detected a recent deterioration in the quality of information received from the business community, which they ascribe in part to the Act.

## [Costs of Administration]

The costs of administering the Freedom of Information Act are also overwhelmingly greater than expected. The Act was passed in 1967 without much attention to costs. During deliberations over amendments in 1974, the highest Congressional estimate of annual costs was $100,000. It is clear now, however, that annual costs are at least 450 times that high. The FBI alone employs approximately 300 fulltime employees to process requests, at an *annual* cost at least 100 times that total estimate.

Last, just as the majority of requests under the Freedom of Information Act serve purposes other than the one for which it was enacted, those unintended uses significantly slow the processing of requests for information that would serve the goal of better informing the electorate. Reducing the former would obviously allow us to speed up responding to the latter. In addition, other changes could conceivably help. For example, a two-tier system granting priority to requests from the media or scholars has been suggested by some. Similarly, some have suggested giving priority to requests for fewer than some specific number of pages since most of the shorter requests may be for information whose disclosure would serve the real purpose of the Act. These are only two suggestions worthy of further consideration. In the final analysis, however, something should be done if at all possible, to speed up the consideration and disclosure of information sought for purposes clearly within the intent of the Act.

Although I cannot at this time give you any details of what the Attorney General will propose to meet the kinds of problems I have outlined this evening, we intend to act and to act speedily. Just last Monday, the Attorney General issued a memorandum to all heads of federal departments and agencies seeking their further ideas and making some changes in the Justice Department's approach to litigation under the Act. Although that memorandum emphasizes the importance of disclosing requested information legally within the Act, it also alters the previous guidelines issued by the Department four years ago. Henceforward, as long as agencies act consistent with the terms of the statute's nine exemptions, the Justice Department will defend their decisions to withhold information without requiring the agency to show that demonstrable harm could result.

The Supreme Court has observed that the science of government is the science of experiment. The executive branch has served as the laboratory for the Freedom of Information Act experiment over the past 14 years. The first phases of the experiment have concluded; some undesirable results have been detected; and the time has come to make changes in the Act's formula for balancing diverse, legitimate interests. The Department will therefore propose amendments to the Act that further the commendable goals that inspired Congressional action: providing the public with information important to a healthy democracy and protecting the public interest in an effective government. . . .

# DEATH OF IRA HUNGER STRIKER
## May 5, 1981

*Carrying on a conflict that traced its origins back 800 years — when King Henry II of England began sending settlers to Ireland to extend his sovereignty — the Irish Republican Army (IRA) drew world attention in the summer of 1981 with the deaths of 10 imprisoned IRA hunger strikers.*

*The strike was begun on March 1 by Robert Sands, convicted for a firearms offense and serving a 14-year sentence in the Maze Prison near Belfast, Northern Ireland. Sands said he was seeking status from the British government as a political prisoner because he viewed himself as a soldier in a war of independence, rather than as a criminal. Sands, after the British government refused to consent to his demands, continued his strike saying, "To accept the status of criminal would be to degrade myself and to admit that the cause I believe in and cherish is wrong."*

*While in prison, Sands was elected as a member of Parliament from the predominately Catholic area of Fermanagh and South Tyrone. Irish nationals hoped his election would put added pressure on the British government to give in to Sands' demands. But British Prime Minister Margaret Thatcher held firm, saying, "There can be no compromise with murder and terrorism." Sands died on his 66th day without food.*

### Thatcher's Policy

*Sands' death set off an increase in violence between Irish Catholics and Protestants in the turbulent area in and around Belfast. But Thatcher, in a visit there three weeks after Sands' death, reiterated the government's stance toward the prisoners of H block, named for the shape of the cell block containing the striking Irish nationals. "Faced with the failure of their discredited cause, the men of violence have chosen in recent months to play what may well be their last card," she said. "They have turned their violence against themselves through the hunger strike to death. They seek to work on the most basic of human emotions — pity — as a means of creating tension and stoking the fires of bitterness and hatred."*

*American support for the strikers was expressed by five prominent Irish Democrats and other political leaders. On May 5 Sen. Edward M. Kennedy of Massachusetts addressed the Senate, calling Sands' death the "symptom of a deeper crisis." On May 6 Kennedy, Sen. Daniel Patrick Moynihan of New York, House Speaker Thomas P. O'Neill Jr. of Massachusetts and Gov. Hugh L. Carey of New York sent a telegram to Thatcher urging her to be more flexible regarding the strikers. Kennedy introduced a joint resolution, SJ Res. 89, June 10 calling for an end to the strike. Sent to the Foreign Relations Committee, the resolution was still awaiting action when the hunger strike ended in October. On August 3, 18 politicians wrote President Reagan urging his support in bringing an end to the demonstration.*

*Later, the surviving hunger strikers announced five demands: the right to wear their own clothes rather‾ than prison uniforms, special work assignments, more visits by friends and relatives, time off for good behavior and free association with other nationalist prisoners.*

## Deaths of Nine Strikers

*The British government refused to grant their demands, and on May 12 the second hunger striker, Francis Hughes, died on his 59th day without food. By October 3, when the hunger strike finally was called off, eight more prisoners, all in their mid- to late twenties, had starved to death. The strike was ended when family members began to intervene and permit forced feeding and medical attention to be given to the unconscious men to prevent their deaths.*

*When the strike ended, the Thatcher government agreed to several concessions, giving all prisoners in Northern Ireland the right to wear civilian clothes and halving the sentences of all who conformed to prison rules. These concessions did not amount to a grant of political status, according to the British government.*

*Following are excerpts from Sen. Edward M. Kennedy's speech on Sands' death to the U.S. Senate May 5; the texts of the May 6 telegram to British Prime Minister Margaret Thatcher from Kennedy, Sen. Daniel Patrick Moynihan, House Speaker Thomas P. O'Neill Jr., and Gov. Hugh L.*

*Carey; the May 7 statement by Humphrey Atkins, then secretary of state for Northern Ireland; Atkins' May 12 radio interview; Thatcher's statements in reply to the Kennedy telegram and on conditions in Maze Prison, both issued May 14; SJ Res. 89, introduced June 10 by Kennedy and excerpts from his accompanying statement; and the October 6 statement of James Prior, secretary of state for Northern Ireland, announcing the end of the hunger strike and improvements in prison conditions:*

# KENNEDY'S MAY 5 STATEMENT

... I am deeply saddened by the death of Bobby Sands, and I send my heartfelt prayers to all the members of his family.

His death is a sad day for Ireland and for all who seek peace in Northern Ireland and an end to the violence that has claimed so many lives and has scarred so many more in recent years.

At this time of heightened tension, I urge all sides in Northern Ireland to resist calls for further violence. It will only compound this latest tragedy if, out of reactions of desperation or motives of vengeance, the death of Bobby Sands sparks a new round of senseless killing and destruction.

Each new death in Northern Ireland is another death too many. More than 2,000 citizens have lost their lives in the present round of violence and terror....

If the painful end of this tragic hunger strike is to have any hopeful or lasting meaning, surely it is the lesson that too many people have died. The time has come for all those of good will on both sides of the community in Northern Ireland — the vast majority of Protestants and Catholics — to denounce the voices of bigotry, to renounce the path of terrorism and extremism, and to join together now in a new and more dedicated search for a common peaceful future....

In the distress of the moment, we must not ignore the fact that three other prisoners in Northern Ireland are nearing a critical phase in their own hunger strikes. We must not yield to terrorism. But we also must not yield to impulses of intransigence that can only fan the flames of greater terrorism.

I urge the British Government, which has clear responsibility for prison administration in Northern Ireland, to act on an urgent basis to end its posture of inflexibility, and to implement reasonable reforms capable of achieving a humanitarian settlement of the other hunger strikes, so that the tragedy of Bobby Sands is not repeated.

The death of Bobby Sands is a symptom of a deeper crisis — a crisis that will go on and on and on in Northern Ireland, until the Government of Great Britain, the Government of Ireland, and all who truly seek and end to violence care enough to speak and work for peace.

# MAY 6 TELEGRAM TO THATCHER

Minister Margaret Thatcher
10 Downing Street
London, England

Dear Prime Minister Thatcher:

We want you to know personally of our deep concern over the spectre of worsening violence and tragedy that threaten to engulf Northern Ireland after the death of Bobby Sands.

In recent months, we have praised your hopeful initiative with Prime Minister Haughey of Ireland, and we have looked forward to further progress in securing a peaceful settlement of the conflict.

Throughout these tragic years of killing and destruction in Northern Ireland, we have consistently and unequivocally condemned all violence from any source.

But we question a posture of inflexibility that must lead inevitably to more senseless violence and more needless deaths in Northern Ireland.

We urge you to act now, before additional lives are lost, to implement sensible and reasonable reforms in the administration of the Maze Prison — reforms that offer real hope of ending this violent impasse and achieving a peaceful and humanitarian settlement of the three hunger strikes that are now nearing the point of no return.

Surely it is possible to compromise on the practical issues of prison administration, without compromising in any way on the basic principle of opposition to violence. Surely leaders of Great Britain have an urgent responsiblity to do all within their power to end this tragic and unnecessary crisis.

Edward M. Kennedy                     Thomas P. O'Neill, Jr.
United States Senate                  Speaker, House of Representatives

Patrick Moynihan                      Hugh L. Carey
United States Senate                  Governor, State of New York

# ATKINS' MAY 7 STATEMENT

We have seen today the funeral of a man who took his own life, either by his own decision or on the instructions of those who felt it was useful to their cause that he should die. Whatever the reason, it was a tragedy that he should have added his name to the list of those who have died in Northern Ireland as victims of a campaign which can contribute nothing to the resolution of the historic and deep-seated problems of this Province.

And we shall shortly see — the event deserves no less publicity — the funeral of Constable Ellis, an officer of the law murdered yesterday in Belfast in the course of his duties. The dead Constable Ellis differs from the dead Mr. Sands in that his death was not of his choosing. The two bereaved families can surely not be the only two who realize there can be no worthwhile dividend from terrorism.

I regret very much the death of any person, whether policeman, soldier or citizen going about his daily business who is murdered by those who claim to be acting in pursuit of a political objective. All of us know that the claim of political justification is bogus.

I must say to you with all the seriousness at my command that we will not give way to this demand for political status. There is no question here of any lack of flexibility. We come right up against the matter of principle. Is murder any less murder because the person responsible claims he had a political motive? The answer is, No. Is robbery with violence any less a crime because the perpetrator said he had a political motive? The answer is, No. Is the kneecapping of a milkman acceptable because its perpetrators say they had a political motive? The answer is, No.

If you were to answer, 'Yes' to those questions, you would encourage murder and violence throughout the Western world, in the United Kingdom, in Europe and in the United States. This is not a matter for argument nor is it a matter for negotiation. We really must have clear in our minds that the central issue is not whether or not the Government is being flexible enough; it is about political status.

The Government's position is perfectly clear. We are not prepared to concede the principle of political status for which Robert Sands was ordered to die, nor are we prepared to do so to prevent others taking the same course.

Some people have said that if we were flexible in our administration of the prison system in Northern Ireland it would save the lives of those who wish to hold us to ransom.

There is nothing flexible about murder and bombing. There is nothing flexible about the demands. Mr. Sands and others have made it clear, all too clear, time and again, that it is political status — that is, to be recognized as a different class of prisoner — that they want.

By contrast, we have shown that we have been prepared to be flexible. We have in the past year introduced a number of changes in precisely the kind of matters — prison clothing, letters and parcels, remission — which are alleged by some to be what the hunger strikers are concerned about. We have established one of the most humane and liberal prison regimes in the Western world, which has taken serious account of the findings of the European Commission on Human Rights. And we will continue to do so.

We have shown that in our consideration of the treatment of all prisoners we are prepared to be flexible. We have proved this by the provision of civilian-type clothing to all prisoners, and (even to those who break the prison rules) the provision of the right to additional letters and visits, the granting of facilities for compassionate home leave, and in many other ways. Prisoners who have decided to end their protest and conform with prison rules have received some restoration of lost remission. All of us who are concerned with creating a more humanitarian regime are glad that the so-called 'dirty protest,' which so disgusted all who heard of it, has been ended and that those prisoners involved are now living in clean, furnished cells.

Despite all of these developments, however, the 'five demands' which constitute political status, stand.

We as a Government are concerned with the well-being of all prisoners. We have taken, as I have outlined, a number of steps to improve the conditions of those held in custody. But we are not prepared to give in to blackmail in the form of a hunger strike or of any other form of pressure.

We must and will govern in the interests of all of the people of Northern Ireland. That is the message which any Government must give to those who seek to subvert democratic government by the exercise of violence.

## ATKINS' MAY 12 INTERVIEW

**Q.** What is your reaction to the death of Hughes?

**A.** I regret it just as I regretted the death of the first hunger striker. And I regret it because it is a wasted life. Hughes has died in pursuit of an ambition which he knew he could not get. He died because he said, and repeated right up to the end, that he wanted political status — political recognition that the crimes for which he was imprisoned were in some way different. And the British Government has made it clear that it will not give that recognition.

**Q.** Who was Francis Hughes and why was he in prison?

**A.** He was convicted on six charges including murder and two charges of attempted murder. He was convicted on all six and sentenced to prison for life and for a total of 83 years on other offences. He was described, sometime ago now, as one of Ulster's most wanted men, and the judge at his trial said the offences were particularly vicious.

**Q.** Does the second death have any effect on Government policy in relation to demands by protesting prisoners for special category status or what the IRA calls 'political status'?

**A.** No it does not, because what has been made perfectly clear to us, right up to today, is that what the Provisional IRA are wanting is a recognition that the crimes they have committed, because they have a political motive, are somehow less serious than other crimes. They have demanded this all the time and have said they want to be treated differently from other prisoners. They want in effect to be able to run the prisons themselves, wear what they like, do what they like, talk to whom they like and not to anyone else, to be free of any kind of loss of remission for not obeying prison rules, in fact to run the prisons in their own way. Now this is something we cannot possibly agree to and they know it.

**Q.** Recent events in Northern Ireland have been heavily reported in the overseas media. Sometimes the publicity has been heavily biased against the British Government. What is your view of the publicity?

**A.** Well, I regret any biased publicity, whichever way it is biased and it is not for me to say whether a true picture has been presented or not. I only know that the events of the past week, the death of two hunger strikers and the funeral of Sands have received a lot of publicity. But you know there was another funeral in Belfast this afternoon. That of a young boy, Desmond Guiney aged 14. He was buried in Belfast this afternoon and he died two days ago because when he was helping his father who was delivering milk to the people of West Belfast their lorry was attacked by a gang of rioters, people rioting I suppose in support of the demands of people like Hughes. The lorry was attacked, forced off the road, overturned and Desmond Guiney was killed and his father has been unconscious since that happened. These, I think, deserve just as much publicity as the death of a hunger striker because Desmond Guiney was not involved in any way, yet he is in his grave too.

**Q.** Would you agree that the weight of international opinion is not running against the British Government despite adverse publicity?

**A.** I don't believe it is because no Government in the Western world has asked us to do anything other than we are doing. Now I am not surprised at that because what we are being asked to do by the IRA is to admit the legitimacy of violence if it is pursued by people who do not like the Government and no Government in the Western world can do this. There are other, better ways of getting a point of view across to Governments and there are other ways of making Governments in democracies change their minds. Those ways are political ways, not the ways of violence so it does not surprise me that no Government in the Western world has sided with the Provisional IRA. Other people have. I venture to think the people who have sided with the IRA are ill-informed.

**Q.** The Northern Ireland problem and the role of the police and the army in the Province seem to be misunderstood and misrepresented overseas, particularly in parts of the U.S. How would you clarify this situation for the Irish American?

**A.** I think you are right. There are people throughout the world who, for one reason or another, some good, some bad, who want to misrepresent what is happening. Surely, the only way to understand a country is to know about it. To know what is happening, to know the present situation, and that is why I hope that people will seriously study what is going on in Northern Ireland at the moment — what the British Government wants in Northern Ireland. And in a nutshell it is that the people of Northern Ireland first of all have more of a say in running their affairs than they have at the moment, and secondly should be able to give expression to what they want for the future, to which of course the British Government will pay attention. As things stand at the moment the overwhelming majority of Northern Ireland want to remain part of the U.K. And so they will. That may change. Maybe one day many years hence the majority will say they want to do something else. Then of course the British Government will pay attention to that. This is called self-determination, it is called democracy. It is the way, in the Western world we run our affairs.

**Q.** Some American politicians believe the British Government is adopting a posture of inflexibility that must lead inevitably to more death and violence in Northern Ireland. What is your answer to this?

**A.** Very simple. We are flexible about the prison regime. In fact in Northern Ireland we have one of the most liberal and one of the most advanced prison regimes in Europe. I don't know about prisons in America but certainly in Europe this is the best regime that exists and we are prepared and have been prepared all the time to take account of criticism, of comments, of suggestions of how we can improve it. But on one thing we are and will remain quite inflexible. That is the matter of principle. It is that murder is murder, crime is crime and that because the perpetrator of murder or crime claims a political motive there is no justification for treating him any differently from anybody else.

**Q.** What is your view of children being manipulated by the IRA to confront the police and the army in Northern Ireland?

**A.** This is one of the most distressing features of what is going on at the moment because a great many of those who have been in the streets in recent days and weeks have been young children from about eight years old upwards and there is no doubt in my mind that they are being encouraged to do this by more sinister people behind them. Because it is very difficult to treat a riot in the way that one would wish to, if, in fact the rioters are all children who really don't know what they are doing. One doesn't want to go for them and arrest them, one wants to tell them to go home and stay at home and I think it is quite despicable that evil men who have evil motives should use children to further their ends.

**Q.** Apart from the use of children, the IRA is using what may be described as hunger strike politics in a seemingly desperate bid to achieve special category status. Is the Government prepared to compromise or negotiate with the hunger strikers or the other Republican protestors?

**A.** On the principle of political status, that is to say treating a crime in a different way because the perpetrator claims a political motive, no, we are not prepared to compromise or negotiate. That is why I regret the death of Hughes this afternoon, as the one before. Because that is what he said — said before he started and right up to the end that he wanted political status and there is no way in which the Government is going to compromise on that principle.

**Q.** Finally, Secretary of State, how do you foresee the events of the immediate future?

**A.** I hope very much that the remaining hunger strikers will realize that there is no need for them to lose their lives. That if they do, it will be in vain and will only bring trouble and distress, and that they will give up their hunger strike. None of us wants anyone to die in Northern Ireland. There have been too many deaths already. And I don't want — no member of the Government and the vast majority of the people of Northern Ireland — don't want anyone else to die, so I hope they'll stop.

# THATCHER'S MAY 14 STATEMENTS

I am writing to thank you for your message of May 6. I welcome your clear restatement of your unequivocal condemnation of all violence in Northern Ireland. I welcome too your efforts to discourage American support for the men of violence in Northern Ireland and to promote better understanding among all the people of Ireland.

You question a 'posture of inflexibility' that must lead inevitably to more violence and death in Northern Ireland. But that is *not* the Government's posture. It is important that there should be no misunderstanding between us. I am therefore sending you with this a full account of what has happened in the Maze Prison since the protesters' complaints were investigated by an independent international body, the European Commission of Human Rights.

This full account shows that H. M. Government has in fact acted with great flexibility. We have offered a series of improvements in conditions to all prisoners — most of which the protesters have rejected. We have also facilitated visits to the hunger strikers by the European Commission of Human Rights, by members of the Dublin Parliament, by the representative of the Official Opposition here and by the personal representative of the Pope. None of these actions has had any effect upon the prisoners, whose sole purpose is to establish a political justification for their appalling record of murder and violence, which deserve the same total comdemnation in Northern Ireland as they would get in the United States.

The prisoners, and those who speak for them, claim that the protests are *not* about prison conditions, but *are* about the demand for political status. Political status would mean that the prisoners, not the prison authorities, would determine what the day-to-day regime within the prison should be. On this the Government will not compromise. It is not prepared, through the granting of political status, to legitimize criminal acts undertaken in pursuit of political ends. It is not prepared to surrender control of the prisons. It is not prepared to be coerced by protest action, in whatever form, into changes for which there is no justification on humanitarian grounds. We know from experience that to do so would not bring the protests to an end. On the contrary, yielding to coercion would provoke further coercion, and would encourage more young people to follow the path of violence.

It is the Government's profound hope that there will be no more deaths directly or indirectly due to the present hunger strike. Such deaths can serve no purpose. If political status remains the protesters' objective, then it cannot and will not be conceded. If they have other grounds for complaint against the prison regime, then further recourse to the European Commission of Human Rights remains available to them. The Government has shown that it is prepared to respond to the Commission's findings and to facilitate in any way it can the Commission's conduct of its investigations.

More widely, the Government remains committed to the search for ways in which the people of Northern Ireland can assume greater responsibility for their own affairs, Through political institutions in which all sections of the community can have confidence. It believes that the best hope for long-term peace and stability is to be found in the political process, not in violence and intimidation. And the Government remains determined to build on the unique relationship that already exists between the United Kingdom and the Republic of Ireland, to the benefit of all the peoples of these islands.

## Thatcher on Maze Prison

In 1978 the European Commission of Human Rights considered the situation at the Maze Prison in the context of an application made to the Commission by four prisoners.

The prisoners' main complaint was that their right to freedom of conscience and belief (under Article 9 of the European Convention for the Protection of Human Rights and Fundamental Freedoms) was denied them because the prison authorities sought to apply to them the normal prison regime. The Commission in their decision of June 1980 found that a right to preferential status for a certain category of prisoners was not amongst those guaranteed by the Convention or by Article 9 in particular.

The applicants also argued that the regime under which they lived amounted to inhuman and degrading treatment and punishment in breach of Article 3 of the Convention. The Commission declared that all their complaints under this Article were inadmissible [sic] on the grounds that they were manifestly ill-founded. At that stage many of the prisoners were, as you know, conducting a uniquely disgusting form of protest in which they fouled their cells with food and excreta. They had broken up furniture in their cells and had used it to damage the windows and other fittings. The European Commission recognized that these conditions were self-inflicted. The prison authorities, of course, made arrangements for the cells to be cleaned and repainted at frequent intervals.

But among their other findings the Commission emphasized the prison authorities' duty 'to keep under constant review their reaction to recalcitrant prisoners engaged in a developing and protracted protest' and commented that 'efforts should have been made by the authorities to ensure that the applicants could avail of certain facilities such as taking regular exercise in the open air with some form of clothing (other than prison clothing) and making greater use of the prison amenities under similar conditions.' It also said that 'arrangements should have been made to enable the applicants to consult outside medical specialists even though they were not prepared to wear prison uniform or underwear.'

Thus the prisoners' claim for political or special status has been investigated recently and decisively rejected by an independent authority of the highest standing: the conditions at the Maze Prison were covered as part of the Commission's investigation and no serious complaint against them was sustained, and the Commission did not, where it felt necessary, hesitate to criticize the Government and the prison authorities.

These criticisms were respected and new arrangements to satisfy them have been in force for more than a year. That is not all. During the course of 1980 the protesting prisoners were offered, whether or not they ended their protest, a range of improved conditions in connection with letters, visits, recreation, association and compassionate leave. In October last year the Government ended prison uniform as such in Northern Ireland prisons in favor of the issue of civilian-type clothing in a range of colors and styles. Of these measures, the protesting prisoners had, by the beginning of March this year, made use in some cases of the facility of additional visits to relatives in ill-health. Apart from that there has been no response.

The first hunger strike ended on December 18, 1980. Contrary to what has been alleged, no undertakings were given to the hunger strikers or the remaining protesting prisoners at that time, before it or after: what the Government had sought to do was to explain to all protesting prisoners what facilities and opportunities were available to them within the existing prison regime, which, as was also made clear to them, the Government is committed to maintaining and, as circumstances allow, improving. That explanation stands and the same facilities remain available. When the ending of the first hunger strike failed to lead to the ending of the other protests, the prison authorities, with the full backing of the Government, took the initiative to move 96 of the protesting prisoners into clean cells. When it became clear that those prisoners had stopped fouling their cells, normal cell furniture was provided.

This process completed, the next step towards a conforming regime was the issue of the civilian-type clothing. The prisoners refused this, saying that they were not prepared to wear it unless their own clothing was provided at the same time: and that they would take part in no work other than that of cleaning their own cells and receiving full-time education. (The Commission had, incidentally, said in its findings that it did not consider there to be anything inherently degrading or objectionable about the requirement to wear a prison uniform or to work.) The Government had no choice but to say it could not accept these conditions. The prisoners' response, on January 27, was to smash the furniture they had been given and to damage the fabric of their cells.

On March 2 the prisoners engaged in the 'dirty' protest at the Maze, and at Armagh, said they were ending this form of protest, but were doing so not as a step towards conformity with the prison regime but in support of the hunger strike which had then just begun. The Government, nevertheless, welcomed the prisoners' decision to end the conditions that they had imposed upon themselves: the prisoners were transferred to clean cells as quickly as the necessary arrangements could be made: and when they asked for the issue of furniture this was, notwithstanding the actions of January 27, initiated. As in January, the prison authorities responded to this scaling down of protest action by scaling down the punishment awarded, in this case by reducing by half the rate at which the protesting prisoners forfeited remission. For those prisoners who had ended protest action altogether since the previous hunger strike, the prison authorities had already, as they had undertaken, completed a review of remission and, where the prisoner concerned had by a period of conforming behavior shown that his decision to cease his protest was a firm one, restored some of the remission previously forfeited."

# KENNEDY'S JUNE 10 STATEMENT

I send to the desk a resolution on the hunger strike in Northern Ireland, and I ask that it may be referred to the Senate Committee on Foreign Relations....

The announcement this week that more prisoners will join the hunger strike is a tragic new escalation of the crisis. Now, before additional deaths and bloodshed occur, it is essential for the parties to make an urgent effort to end this lethal stalemate and to achieve a fair and humanitarian resolution of the issues in the strike.

The joint resolution we are introducing today is designed to help the parties reach that goal. It contains five significant provisions:

*First,* it condemns the violence on all sides in Northern Ireland.

*Second,* it urges the parties to explore all possible steps to end the hunger strike.

*Third,* it urges the British Government, which has clear responsibility for prison administration in Northern Ireland, to exercise greater flexibility with respect to prison procedure. Surely it is possible to achieve a reasonable compromise on issues such as clothing, prison work requirements, and to association of the prisoners, without compromising in any way on the basic principle of opposition to violence. This provision of the resolution also calls on Britain to invite the European Commission on Human Rights or other appropriate independent parties to participate in the effort to settle the strike. In the past, British has implemented recommendations of the Commission with respect to the modification of prison rules, and a similar initiative at this time by the Commission could provide the breakthrough needed to end the current strike.

*Fourth,* the resolution urges political leaders in Britain, Ireland, and Northern Ireland to seek the earliest possible negotiated settlement of the larger conflict in Northern Ireland. That settlement must be achieved with the consent of all the parties. It must recognize the rights of both the Catholic and Protestant community. And it must secure full respect for the human rights of all the people of Northern Ireland. . . .

*Fifth,* the resolution requests the President to express to the Prime Minister of Great Britain the concern of the American people for an immediate end to the hunger strike and a lasting settlement of the conflict in Northern Ireland. The United States has an important role to play in the search for peace, and the Administration should not hesitate to exercise it. . . .

# SJ RES. 89

Whereas the continuing violence in Northern Ireland has taken the lives of more than two thousand men, women, and children in the past decade;

Whereas an end to the killing and the violence in Northern Ireland can be achieved only through a political settlement with the consent of all the parties;

Whereas Congress is deeply concerned over the hunger strike in Northern Ireland and the deaths resulting from the strike;

*Resolved by the Senate and House of Representatives of the United States in Congress assembled, that —*

(1) Congress condemns the violence on all sides in Northern Ireland;

(2) Congress urges the parties to explore all possible steps to avoid further deaths in the hunger strike and achieve an immediate and humanitarian resolution of the issues in the strike;

(3) Congress urges the Government of Great Britain, in order to facilitate the resolution of the issues in the hunger strike —

(a) to exercise greater flexibility in the administration of prison rules in Northern Ireland; and

(b) to invite the European Commission on Human Rights or other appropriate independent parties to participate in the effort to settle the strike;

(4) Congress urges the political leaders in Great Britain, Northern Ireland, and the Republic of Ireland to seek the earliest possible settlement of the larger conflict in Northern Ireland through a negotiated agreement that achieves a lasting peace, that has the consent of all the parties, that recognizes the rights of both the Catholic and the Protestant community in Northern Ireland, and that secures full respect for human rights of all the people of that land; and

(5) Congress requests the President of the United States to express to the Prime Minister of Great Britain the concern of the American people for an immediate settlement of the hunger strike and a lasting settlement of the conflict in Northern Ireland.

# PRIOR'S OCTOBER 6 STATEMENT

The hunger-strike has ended by the voluntary action of the protesters. It is time to heal the deep wounds and fresh divisions caused by the strike both inside and outside the prisons, and help to bring to an end the violence which for so long has prevented the social, political and economic development of Northern Ireland.

On October 3 I said that I would be making a statement about the development of the prison system. Both my predecessor and I were always determined to be reasonable and flexible and to seek improvements where they could be made. We also made it clear that we would not act under duress. Until now, the hunger-strike made movement impossible. Now it is over. I want to play my part in seeking reconciliation and an end to violence by introducing changes along the lines set out by my predecessor on June 30 and July 8.

I must make it quite clear what I am not prepared to do. The protesters' view on work and association are not compatible with a civil prison system, especially the modern and humane system which makes the principal jails of the Province as advanced as any in the world. There is room for development here and elsewhere. But there will be no question of a political or military system of administration or any return to Special Category status.

I have decided to make the following important changes. They will apply to all prisoners in all prisons in Northern Ireland.

**Clothes.** Prisoners will in future be able to wear their own clothing at all times. To avoid any misunderstandings, the practical arrangements for this change will be set out in a leaflet which Lord Gowrie will arrange to have circulated to all prisoners tomorrow. These arrangements cover, for example, the need to ensure that clothing worn by prisoners does not resemble that of prison officers, is not tantamount to a uniform, and is not otherwise offensive or unsuitable. We also need to specify the quantities of clothing and make laundry arrangements. These are practical matters and need cause no serious problems. The change will take perhaps two or three weeks to complete. Families may bring clothes to the prisons when they have been informed of the details in the leaflets. Those who prefer to continue to wear the prison-issue civilian-style clothing will of course be able to do so.

**Remission.** At present, prisoners who have lost remission as a penalty for certain protest action may have 20 percent of that lost remission restored after three months of full conformity with prison rules. A number of prisoners have already gained from this. I am now introducing a more generous scheme for restoration of lost remission. Lord Gowrie will make full details known shortly, based on the following principles:

> (i) The new scheme will extend to all prisoners who have lost remission other than as a result of violent acts against prison officers or other prisoners;

(ii) The amount of lost remission which may be restored will be increased to a maximum of 50 percent, i.e. those who have already qualified for the earlier 20 percent restoration will gain a further 30 percent and those who newly qualify will gain the full 50 percent;

(iii) The new scheme will apply only to those prisoners who have either already completed a period of three months conformity with prison rules, or who now do so.

The new scheme applies to past behavior. It does not mean that prisoners who in the future lose remission for breaches of prison rules will have their remission restored.

On the issue of association, conforming prisoners already have many opportunities for mixing with one another at mealtimes, work, exercise, and during their periods of association each evening and at weekends. There is little immediate scope for expansion here, but I have accepted that there should be some provision for prisoners in adjacent wings of H-blocks to share association in recreation rooms and exercise areas. Before this change can be implemented new arrangements for the control and supervision of such movement and certain additional physical changes will be required. These will take some weeks.

The Government has made it clear that the development of the prison system is a continual process: in particular, that the possibility of widening the scope of work in the prisons can be examined but only within certain well-defined limits. There are obvious practical and financial limitations on what can be arranged. Here I should like to pay tribute to prison staffs, for successfully maintaining an enlightened system for conforming prisoners while coping with the great stress and strain occasioned by the protest. I am very conscious that many, indeed most, of the prisoners are young men. Even in the context of deservedly long sentences on conviction for violent crimes, many of them will, in the normal way, be released during their working lives. I do therefore want to encourage a system where the very advanced training and educational facilities available, which have much impressed me, may be freely used by all prisoners. Lord Gowrie will continue to keep a close eye on developments in this field as the new arrangements settle down.

The changes which I am announcing will take some time to work through. I hope that as they come into effect protesting prisoners will recognize the benefits of conformity with the rules, and the penalties which exist for those who break them. In order to create a breathing-space and ease the changeover in the prison system, for 28 days from yesterday no loss of remission will be imposed as a penalty for breaches of prison rules arising out of the refusal to wear clothes.

I hope that the end of the hunger-strike, together with the measures I have described above, will help end the confrontation which has caused so much tragedy and suffering inside and outside the prisons. We must never forget that while ten young men had died tragically in the Maze, many more people have died during the period of the strike as innocent victims of the violence outside. Our task is to stop the men who are causing that violence, and to turn all our energies towards creating a better future for the people of Northern Ireland. I want to get on with this task. In the spirit of reconciliation with which I have put forward my prison reforms I look for cooperation and support in this wider purpose from all the leaders of the community.

# SPACE SHUTTLE
# MISSION REPORT

## May 12, 1981

*More than 54 hours and 36 orbits after a dramatic liftoff from its launching pad at Cape Canaveral, Fla., the first space shuttle, christened Columbia, glided to a perfect landing April 14 on a dry California lake bed at Edwards Air Force Base. The flight of the hybrid vehicle, part rocket and part aircraft, was deemed "100 percent successful" by Donald Slayton, the orbital test manager for the National Aeronautics and Space Administration (NASA).*

*Nine years earlier, on January 5, 1972, President Richard Nixon declared the United States "should proceed at once" with the development of a reusable space shuttle that "would take the astronomical costs out of astronautics." Such a vehicle, he added, would "help transform the space frontier of the 1970s into familiar territory, easily accessible for human endeavor in the 1980s and 1990s." Work subsequently began on a project that would culminate in the Columbia spacecraft.*

*When launched, Columbia was attached to a 154-foot-tall fuel tank and two solid-fuel booster rockets. About two minutes after liftoff, the boosters separated from the two other components and fell by parachute into the Atlantic Ocean, where they were retrieved for reuse. The fuel tank, not reusable, separated from Columbia just before orbit was reached and plunged to destruction in the Indian Ocean. Then it was up to Columbia's two pilots, John W. Young, a civilian, and Navy Capt. Robert L. Crippen, to guide the craft in orbit and return it to Earth. Unlike any earlier spaceship, the Columbia, with its stubby wings and tail structure, was designed so that it could glide back through the atmosphere to an airplane-like landing.*

## Significance of Shuttle

*The advent of the shuttle marked the beginning of a new era in space. Besides reusability, another key to the space shuttle program was the orbiting vehicle's large cargo volume, which was about the same as that of a railroad boxcar.*

*Rich Gore wrote in* National Geographic *that "Apollo's moon-landing program, Skylab, and the missions to the planets were the age of space exploration." He continued, saying "the shuttle begins the age of space exploitation."*

*American and foreign companies would be able to buy cargo space to launch communications satellites, or to conduct industrial or scientific experiments in the weightless environment. The shuttle also had military applications; it could be used to put spy satellites in place or to send aloft the components of a manned orbital military command post.*

## Critics Decry Expense

*Despite the claimed benefits of the shuttle program, it did not escape criticism. More than $10 billion dollars had been spent on the program before the first test flight of the Columbia. This price tag undercut somewhat the reusability defense invoked by space program advocates as they justified the program against the attacks of those who believed the money should be spent on social programs. Even some scientists within the space exploration field were upset at the huge shuttle budget, as they saw proposals for planetary exploration to Mars and Venus as well as a rendezvous mission to Halley's Comet rejected or deferred by NASA due to lack of funds.*

*NASA also had to grapple with an unexpected lack of support from business. So few businesses had rented out space on future shuttles that NASA began offering "Get Away" budget deals to entice business into the space venture. Still, the level of support was disappointing.*

*Then, in June 1981, NASA announced a 30 percent cut in the shuttle budget, forcing the number of scheduled flights through fiscal year 1985 to be reduced to 30 from 48.*

## Columbia Difficulties

*Originally scheduled for March 1979, the Columbia launching was delayed by engine troubles and problems with the heat-resistant tiles attached to the vehicle's surface. During the actual takeoff April 12, 16 of the shuttle's heat-shielding silicon tiles were damaged or lost. But those tiles left unprotected a "non-critical area" that was not exposed to the greatest heat during the shuttle's fiery re-entry into the atmosphere.*

*And, in an otherwise successful pre-liftoff test on March 19, one technician died and two others were injured when they were exposed to the pure nitrogen atmosphere in an area around the engines inside the shuttle.*

## Second Flight

*The second flight of the Columbia, piloted by Air Force Col. Joe H. Engle and Navy Capt. Richard H. Truly, was launched November 12 after a delay caused when a chemical spill damaged some of the heat-shielding tiles. Soon after launch one of the three fuel cells failed, and the flight was ended several days early. Officials at NASA called the mission a success, however, because most of the scheduled tests were completed. The most significant of these experiments was the test of Columbia's 50-foot mechanical arm. Capable of handling loads up to 65,000 pounds, the arm would be used to place objects into orbit and to retrieve material from space. The flight ended November 14 with a safe landing at Edwards Air Force Base.*

*No backup vehicles for Columbia existed. But if all went according to plan NASA expected to declare the shuttle "operational" by late 1982. Originally, NASA had hoped to launch a shuttle about every two weeks, but talk of this dropped with the news of the budget cut. Still, considering the technical success of the first two test flights, observers expected the shuttle eventually to merit the description bestowed on it by former astronaut Neil Armstrong: "A space truck."*

*Following are excerpts from the mission operation report on the flight of the space shuttle Columbia, released May 12, 1981, by the National Aeronautics and Space Administration:*

## Introduction

The STS-1 mission, the first of four manned orbital flights planned for the Orbital Flight Test (OFT) phase of the Space Shuttle Program, was completed on April 14, 1981.

The Space Shuttle is the prime element of the U.S. Space Transportation System (STS) for space research and applications in future decades. The primary goal of the OFT phase of the Space Shuttle program is to demonstrate a capability for routine prelaunch, launch, orbital, entry, approach, landing, and turnaround operations. The Space Shuttle flight system for OFT consists of the Orbiter Columbia with its three main engines, an external tank and two solid rocket boosters. The Orbiter, its main engines and the retrievable booster components are reusable elements; the tank is expended on each launch.

The first OFT flight was designed to maximize crew and vehicle safety by reducing ascent and entry aerodynamic loads on the vehicle as much as possible. Each successive flight will be planned to expand the operating envelope including increased ascent and entry loads and varied launch and entry payload weight and center-of-gravity locations.

The first flight of the OFT program was designated STS-1. This STS-1 POSTFLIGHT REPORT assesses the achievement of the STS-1 mission objective and provides a detailed description of the STS-1 flight....

## STS-1 Mission Description

### GENERAL

The first flight of the Space Shuttle was completed at 10:20:58 a.m., PST [Pacific Standard Time], on April 14, 1981, with touchdown of the Orbiter Columbia. The landing was at Edwards Air Force Base (EAFB), California, 54 hours, 20 minutes, and 54.1 seconds after launch from the Kennedy Space Center (KSC), Florida....

The commander of the mission was John W. Young, and the pilot was Robert L. Crippen.

The data presented in this document are based on quick-look reports. Detailed analysis of all data is continuing, and a final evaluation report prepared by the Integrated Systems Evaluation Team will be issued by the Johnson Space Center (JSC) Space Shuttle Program Office prior to the flight readiness review for the STS-2 mission.

### Final Countdown

The STS-1 mission was launched at 7:00:03.9 a.m., EST [Eastern Standard Time], on April 12, 1981, following a scrubbed attempt on April 10. The countdown on April 10 proceeded normally until T-20 minutes (20 minutes prior to launch in the countdown sequence) when the Orbiter general purpose computers (GPC's) were scheduled for transition from the vehicle checkout mode to the vehicle flight configuration mode. The launch was held for the maximum time and scrubbed when the four primary GPC's would not provide the correct timing for the backup flight system GPC. Analysis and testing indicated the primary set of GPC's provided incorrect timing to the backup flight system at initialization and caused the launch scrub.

The problem resulted from a Primary Ascent Software System (PASS) skew during initialization. The PASS GPC's were reinitialized and dumped to verify that the timing skew problem had cleared. During the second final countdown attempt on April 12, transition of the primary set of Orbiter GPC's and the backup flight system GPC occurred normally at T-20 minutes.

The launch pad damage from the STS-1 launch was less than predicted.

All launch facilities, systems, and support equipment performed as designed.

## Ascent

The STS-1 mission was launched from Pad A of Launch Complex 39 at KSC on an azimuth of 66.96 degrees. Lift-off was achieved with both solid rocket boosters (SRB's) igniting and the Space Shuttle main engines (SSME's) operating at rated power level (100%). The SSME's were throttled down to 65% thrust level for maximum dynamic pressure control and back up to 100% thrust level at the predicted times. The maximum dynamic pressure of ascent was encountered at a GET [Ground Elapsed Time] 56 seconds. (The 00:00:00 point (hr:min:sec) of GET is SRB ignition.) The SRB separation command was initiated at 00:02:10.4 GET following SRB burnout.

Second stage flight utilized the SSME's at 100% thrust level until 3 g's [gravity] were reached, and 3 g's were maintained by SSME throttling until approximately 6 seconds before main engine cutoff (MECO) when the engines were throttled to 65% where they remained until MECO. MECO occurred at 00:08:34.4 GET, and separation from the ET [External Tank] occurred 23.7 seconds later. After separation of the ET, the Orbiter was inserted into an orbit of 133.7-n.mi. [nautical mile] apogee and 132.7-n.mi. perigee, with a 40.3-degree inclination. This orbit was achieved by two orbital maneuvering system firings (OMS-1 and OMS-2). The 86.3-second OMS-1 maneuver was initiated at 00:10:34.1 GET with the 75.0-second OMS-2 maneuver occurring at 00:44:02.1 GET at the apogee of the orbit resulting from the OMS-1 burn.

The ascent trajectory was as planned with all events up through payload bay door opening and radiator deployment occurring normally. Prior to the initial OMS burn, the chamber pressure measurements for both engines were reading off-scale high on the ground. The crew indicated proper operation of the onboard indicators. This was traced subsequently to a ground calibration problem.

Some real-time data were lost, as expected, during SRB operations because of signal attenuation due to the SRB plume. Other communications losses during orbit number one were encountered at the IOS (Indian Ocean Station) where two-way S-band lockup was not obtained, at the Yarragadee Tracking Station in western Australia where UHF [Ultrahigh Frequency] voice was intermittent, and at the Orroral Valley Tracking Station in eastern Australia where no S-band downlink voice was received. Communications subsequent to orbit one were excellent.

The main propulsion system performed normally with two apparent transducer failures and an unexpected rise in the pogo precharge pressure. Data indicated the precharge pressure exceeded 1425 psia [pounds per square inch, absolute], and this situation is being analyzed. This is not believed to be a problem since engine operation was satisfactory for the remainder of the ascent burn.

The auxiliary power units (APU's) operated as expected with no apparent problems. The hydraulic systems also operated normally, although all three water spray boiler and vent temperatures were off-scale low. Additionally, lubrication oil temperatures were higher than expected. These conditions were caused by freezing of preload water in the spray boilers. The icing in the boilers quickly thawed when the APU heat output increased.

The fuel cells, cryogenics, and electrical power distribution systems all performed satisfactorily with no anomolies. The lift-off electrical loads were about 23 kw [kilowatt], some 5 to 7 kw lower than predicted.

The structural, mechanical, and thermal systems all performed well.

## Solid Rocket Booster and External Tank Disposal

SRB Disposal — The SRB's were jettisoned after burnout (ignition + 130.4 seconds) on tumbling free-fall trajectories. Both SRB's fell within the predicted impact footprint in the Atlantic Ocean approximately 140 n.mi northeast of KSC. Splashdown occurred approximately 7 minutes, 10 seconds after lift-off. The SRB's were recovered by retrieval ships. The boosters were found floating high in the buoy position indicating good water entry. . . . One was dewatered with the nozzle plug and the other with the "barb" backup fixture. The solid rocket motor cases, frustums, and remaining items, except for 2 (of 6) SRB parachutes which were not retrieved, have been returned to KSC for inspection and processing.

ET Disposal — ET separation from the orbiter was nominal at 0:08:58.1 GET. After separation, the ET followed a ballistic trajectory, and upon its return into the atmosphere, it began to break up about 100,000 feet above the planned breakup altitude of 180,000 feet. Photography of the ET separation taken from the Orbiter indicates that the ET tumble system failed to activate. The tumble system, which is activated before separation by signals from the Orbiter to a pyrotechnic valve inside the liquid oxygen tank nose cap, is designed to prevent aerodynamic skip during reentry to ensure that tank debris will fall within a preplanned disposal area. Verbal reports from the ET tracking ship, USNS [United States Naval Ship] Arnold, positioned in the Indian Ocean were that the debris foot print was larger than expected. Tracking data are being returned from the ship on an expedited basis for evaluation.

## Onorbit

The STS-1 orbital operations phase was initiated at the completion of the OMS-2 maneuver. Day 1 of the STS-1 flight was concerned primarily with configuring the Orbiter for onorbit operation (i.e., opening payload bay doors, reconfiguring software, IMU [Inertial Measurement Unit] alinements). After opening the payload bay doors, the crew directed the onboard TV camera at the OMS pods, showing some thermal protection system (TPS) damage on both pods. . . . An assessment of the thermal and structural loads for the area of the TPS damage on the OMS pods was conducted. The assessment of the structural loads on the TPS, assuming worst case descent conditions, indicated sufficient margin existed to insure that additional damage would not occur due to the entry environment.

The DFI [Development Flight Instrumentation] PCM [Pulse-Code Modulation] recorder was noted to be in the continuous record mode about 1 hour into the flight. Attempts to place the recorder in the high sample mode were unsuccessful with the recorder apparently not responding to mode switch changes. Because of this condition, the recorder was stopped by removing power. Data review indicated that the mode switch was placed in the high sample mode at the planned time. An in-flight test showed that the recorder was not responding to mode switch changes. A procedure was developed for the crew to further troubleshoot the recorder and determine its status for entry and landing. All DFI PCM data continued to be transmitted and recorded over tracking stations.

An attempt was made to replace the DFI PCM recorder with the ascent wideband recorder; however, the crew could not remove all of the fasteners holding the panel covering the recorder and the replacement was not made. Postflight troubleshooting of the DFI PCM recorder revealed that a loose shim had jammed the tape mechanism.

Orbiter temperatures remained within acceptable limits. The flight control systems checks using one APU went as planned.

At 6:20:46.5 GET, after verification of critical vehicle systems, the first of 2 OMS maneuvers was initiated to transfer the Orbiter to a higher orbit. The OMS-3 firing was completed as planned, and at 7:05:32.5 GET, the OMS-4 maneuver was initiated raising the orbit to a 148-n.mi. apogee by a 147.9-n.mi. perigee.

The firing time for OMS-3 was 28.8 seconds and for OMS-4 was 33.1 seconds. The propellant remaining after the maneuvers was at the predicted levels, indicating satisfactory system performance.

The right OMS pitch gimbal primary channel exhibited degraded performance during gimbal checks for the maneuvers, and a fault summary message of right-OMS-pitch-gimbal-fail was noted. The data were reviewed, and the analysis concluded that the gimbal drive actuator rate did not meet specification performance requirements, and the primary was used as a backup for the deorbit maneuver.

Four reaction control system (RCS) maneuvers were performed to verify that all thrusters were operating properly.

At 40:02:39 GET, the APU-2 gas generator injector bed temperature dropped to 236°F (normal range: 350°F to 410°F), indicating the loss of gas generator heater B. The heater was switched from the B to the A system and the temperatures began increasing. Approximately 4.5 hours later, the gas generator injector bed temperatures were again decreasing. The heater was switched to the B system, but no increase was noted. It was then returned to system A, but no increase in temperature was realized, indicating loss of both heaters. It was determined through a real-time ground test that APU 2 would start satisfactorily at a bed temperature as low as

70°F. The temperature was predicted to be higher than 70°F for APU start for deorbit, however, a start override was required and was accomplished successfully.

During the flight control system checkout, the horizontal situation indicator (HSI) compass card did not respond properly. The indicator was off 5 degrees during the "low" test and did not drive at all during the repeated "high" test. A test procedure was performed by the crew and the indicator again failed to respond, with the card appearing stuck. Later, during checkout, the crew reported normal HSI function.

The Y-star tracker experienced an anomaly. Bright object protection was being provided by an interim backup circuit which senses light in the field of view and was latching the shutter closed. The crew opened the shutter via an override command for subsequent alinements.

The onorbit electrical loads were about 15 to 25kw, some 2kw lower than predicted.

## Descent and Landing

Entry preparation was accomplished according to the crew activity plan and without problems. The deorbit maneuver using both OMS engines was initiated at approximately 53:21:31.1 GET during the 36th orbit, and 31 minutes later, the Orbiter entered the communications blackout period of approximately 6-minutes duration. A nominal reentry was flown and touchdown . . . was made at 180 knots at 10:20:58 a.m., PST, on dry lake bed Runway 23 at Edwards Air Force Base, California. Total runway rollout distance from the touchdown point was 8993 feet. Postrollout operations were accomplished without incident, and ground cooling was connected about 16 minutes after landing. The flight crew egressed the Orbiter 1 hour and 8 minutes after landing. This occurred after a delay for the ground crew to clear hazardous vapors detected in the vicinity of the Orbiter side hatch.

Structural, power, and heat rejection entry loads were generally lower than predicted as were the APU, RCS, and active thermal control subsystem consumables usage. Orbiter structure backface temperatures were also lower than expected.

## Ground Operations/Turnaround

Following flight crew egress and Orbiter safing, the Columbia was towed to the Mate/Demate Device for weight and balance checks, purge of the main propulsion system, and propellant detanking. An inspection of the Orbiter was performed. The most significant discrepancies were a delamination of a section of graphite epoxy structure on the right OMS pod due to overheating and lesser overheating damage on the left OMS pod, a 1.25-inch cut through 5 of 17 plies on the inboard tire of the left main landing gear, and the loss of sleeve and bearing pieces from the uplock roller of the right main landing gear which were found on the approach path 4-miles short of the touchdown point. A detailed inspection of the thermal protection tiles revealed minor damage to approximately 400 tiles. About 200 tiles will require replacement — 100 as a result of flight damage and 100 identified prior to STS-1 as suitable for one flight. After completion of inspection activities, the tailcone assembly was installed. The tailcone is an aerodynamic fairing that attaches to the aft end of the Orbiter for ferry flight. The ferry flight departed Edwards at 10:16 a.m., PDT [Pacific Daylight Time], on April 27, 1981. Following a stop at Tinker AFB, Oklahoma, for refueling, the 747 and Orbiter remained overnight then proceeded to the Kennedy Space Center Shuttle Landing Facility, landing at 11:25 a.m., EDT [Eastern Daylight Time], on April 28. After demating from the 747 aircraft, the Columbia was towed to the Orbiter Processing Facility to begin processing for reuse in the STS-2 mission. . . .

## Payloads

The payload cargo for STS-1 was limited to development flight test instrumentation. The test instrumentation consisted of Development Flight Instrumentation, the Passive Optical Sample Assembly, and the Aerodynamic Coefficient Identification Package.

### DEVELOPMENT FLIGHT INSTRUMENTATION (DFI)

The DFI subsystem included special-purpose sensors required to monitor spacecraft conditions and performance parameters not already covered by critical operational systems. The DFI subsystem consists of transducers, signal conditioning equipment, pulse-code modulation (PCM) encoding equipment, frequency multiplex equipment, PCM recorders, analog recorders, timing equipment, and checkout equipment. About 1 hour into the flight, the PCM recorder locked into continuous recording and would not respond to mode switch changes. Because of the no-response conditions, power was removed. Prior to seat ingress for deorbit, power was restored to record data continuously through descent and landing. Power was then removed at seat egress after rollout and the recorder was removed and returned to JSC for data dump and assessment where it was determined that no data were recorded during the entry phase.

### PASSIVE OPTICAL SAMPLE ASSEMBLY (POSA)

The POSA consisted of an array of passive samples with various types of surfaces exposed to all STS-1 mission phases. The array was mounted on the DFI pallet in the Orbiter payload bay. Ground based assessments will be used to assess contamination constraints to sensitive payloads to be flown on future missions.

## AERODYNAMIC COEFFICIENT
## IDENTIFICATION PACKAGE (ACIP)

The ACIP experiment hardware consisted of a self-contained package of three linear accelerometers, three angular accelerometers, three rate gyros, and signal conditioning and PCM equipment mounted on the wing box carry through structure near the longitudinal center-of-gravity.

The ACIP instruments were used to sense vehicle motions during flight from entry initiation to touch down to provide data for postflight determination of aerodynamic coefficients, aerocoefficient derivatives and vehicle handling qualities. During ascent and onorbit operations, the ACIP was controlled by ground realtime and stored program commands. During descent, control was by stored program commands. All of the STS-1 crew activity objectives related to ACIP were accomplished.

# SHOOTING OF THE POPE

## May 13, 1981

Pope John Paul II was shot and seriously wounded in St. Peter's Square in Vatican City May 13. Two American women among the 10,000 worshipers in the square that day also were wounded. Worldwide reaction to the shooting was swift and sharp, with President Reagan, as well as others, issuing immediate statements of support for the pontiff.

Arrested on the scene was a 23-year-old Turkish citizen, Mehmet Ali Agca, who previously had been convicted of the terrorist murder of a Turkish newspaper editor. In November 1979 he escaped from a maximum security Turkish prison, leaving behind a letter that threatened the pope's life if he visited Turkey in late 1979 as planned. The pope made the trip with increased security precautions.

In the May 13 incident, the 60-year-old head of the Roman Catholic Church was shot twice, receiving wounds in the abdomen, arm and hand. He immediately underwent surgery that lasted over five hours. He spent 22 days in the hospital and returned August 5 for additional surgery. During a lengthy recuperation that ended in the fall, the pope worked on his third encyclical, "On Human Work." (Excerpts, p. 695)

## Assailant's Trial

The three-day trial of Agca, held in an Italian court, ended July 22, 1981, when he was found guilty of attempting to kill the pope and the two American women who were wounded. The judges and the jury did not *accept the defense attorney's argument that Agca was a misguided, psychopathic "religious fanatic" who could not be held accountable for his actions. Although it was never proven that Agca was part of a conspiracy aimed at the pope, Turkish military authorities reported that Agca had established links with an extreme right-wing group in Turkey, the Nationalist Action Party.*

*The sentence was life imprisonment, and the court ruled that Agca spend the first year of his sentence in solitary confinement.*

*After his initial court appearance on the first day of the trial, Agca boycotted the proceedings because he did not recognize Italy's right to try him for an act committed on the territory of Vatican City, which had the status of a separate foreign state. A 1929 treaty allowed for the transferral of trials between the Vatican and Italy.*

## Well-traveled Pope

*Ever since his election to the papacy in October 1978, the vigorous Pope John Paul II had made himself and the church visible worldwide. He was known to have an irrepressible desire to bring the church directly to the people, showing little regard for his personal safety. Although the Polish pope aroused some controversy with his conservative views on birth control and abortion, he remained personally popular throughout the world.* (Pope's journey to Far East, p. 203)

*The American reaction to the shooting, which occurred only six weeks after the attempted assassination of President Reagan, reflected incredulity and outrage. Reagan sent the following message to the pope: "I have just received the shocking news of the attack on you. All Americans join me in hopes and prayers for your speedy recovery from the injuries you have suffered in the attack. Our prayers are with you."* (Shooting of Reagan, p. 351)

*After a minute of silent prayer in the Senate, Pete V. Domenici, R-N.M., and Edward M. Kennedy, D-Mass., introduced and the Senate adopted a resolution saying that "we join now in common concern and we pause in prayer to God for the life, the health, and the recovery of John Paul II."*

> *Following are the texts of a statement by President Reagan on the papal attack, issued May 13, 1981; a statement issued by Cardinal Humberto Medeiros of Boston; a statement of evangelist Billy Graham; and the first public message delivered by Pope John Paul II, on May 17, following the shooting:*

# REAGAN STATEMENT

Pope John Paul II, a man of peace and goodness — an inspiration to the world — has been struck today by a would-be assassin's bullet. The world is horrified, and all of us grieve over this terrible act of violence.

Pope John Paul II was wounded today while doing what he had done so well and so often throughout his travels — reaching out to others, offering hope, light and the peace of God.

We are grateful that he has been spared. We pray that all of us will heed Pope John Paul's call for a "world of love, not of hate;" that we will hear his words reminding us that all men are brothers, that they must forever forsake the ways of violence and live together in peace.

The people of the United States, whose unbounded affection for Pope John Paul II was shown in our city streets a year and a half ago, join millions throughout the world in fervent prayer for his full and rapid recovery.

# STATEMENT OF CARDINAL MEDEIROS

On hearing of the assassination attempt on the life of Pope John Paul II, my immediate reaction was a mixture of shock, sickness and sadness.

Then I asked: If this man, so strong a force for goodness, justice and peace, is attacked, who then among us is safe? What a tragic example of the dwindling regard and respect for human life. But then I am reminded that when we remove God from the center of our lives the vacuum is only too easily filled with evil or madness.

I plead for prayers from every generous heart, regardless of faith, that God will restore to his people this gift which is Pope John Paul II, the servant of the servants of God.

# STATEMENT OF BILLY GRAHAM

I am deeply shocked and profoundly saddened by the senseless shooting of Pope John Paul II today. My thoughts are with him and I join the millions of Christians of all backgrounds in fervently praying for his swift, complete and permanent recovery. This event is a tragic illustration of the moral and spiritual chaos which affects our world. It also forcefully reminds us of the need for spiritual renewal in our world toward which Christians must pray and work.

Since becoming pope in October 1978, he has exerted a profound moral and spiritual influence on our world for which I am deeply grateful. His burden and his work for world peace have been far greater than most people realize. Just a few months ago it was my privilege to meet with him at the Vatican.

I was deeply impressed by his friendship, his love of people and his humble spirit. Our world needs the moral vision and courage of people like John Paul II as never before and I urge Christians everywhere to pray for the recovery of this remarkable man.

# MAY 17 MESSAGE FROM POPE

Praised be Jesus Christ!

Beloved brothers and sisters, I know that during these days and especially in this hour of the Regina Coeli you are united with me. With deep emotion I thank you for your prayers and I bless you all.

I am particularly close to the two persons wounded together with me. I pray for that brother of ours who shot me and whom I have sincerely pardoned.

United with Christ, priest and victim, I offer my sufferings for the church and for the world.

To you, Mary, I repeat: *"Totus tuus ego sum"* (I belong entirely to you).

# SUPREME COURT ON RIGHTS OF CRIMINALS

## May 18, 1981

*Nearly 15 years after its landmark Miranda decision, the Supreme Court May 18 voted 9-0 in two cases to give criminal defendants new protection against self-incrimination and to broaden their constitutional right to counsel.*

*In the first of two rulings on unrelated murder cases, Estelle v. Smith, the justices set aside the death penalty imposed on a Texas man as a result of a court-ordered interview he gave to a psychiatrist prior to his murder trial. The defendant, the court held, should have been warned in advance that the examination results might be used against him in determining his sentence and that he had a right to consult an attorney before agreeing to such an interview.*

*In the second decision, Edwards v. Arizona, the court ruled that police may not continue to interrogate a suspect once he has invoked his right to have an attorney present unless the defendant initiates the conversation.*

## Background

*The 1981 rulings were written by two longtime critics of the court's June 13, 1966, decision in Miranda v. Arizona, which held that police must advise criminal suspects of their right to remain silent and their right to have an attorney present during questioning.*

*Chief Justice Warren E. Burger, a federal appeals court judge at the time of the Miranda ruling, wrote the court's opinion in the 1981 Texas death penalty case, while Justice Byron R. White, one of the dissenters in the court's 5-4* Miranda *decision, was the author of the opinion in the second case.*

*The single most controversial criminal law ruling of the court headed by Chief Justice Earl Warren (1953-1969),* Miranda *was based upon the Fifth Amendment privilege against compelled self-incrimination and the Sixth Amendment guarantee of the right to counsel.*

*Ernest Miranda was convicted of kidnapping and rape on the basis of statements he made to police in apparent ignorance of his rights. In overturning his conviction, the court said that before questioning a suspect, police must advise him of his rights to remain silent and to have an attorney present, and must respect those rights once they are invoked. An interrogation could proceed only if the suspect's attorney were present, or if the defendant "voluntarily, knowingly and intelligently" waived his rights.*

*In May 1980 the high court defined what was, and what was not, to be considered interrogation within the scope of the* Miranda *ruling. In the case of* Rhode Island v. Innis, *the court held that the conversation between Innis and the police that indirectly persuaded the defendant to locate the murder weapon was not interrogation. (Court on 'Interrogation' in Criminal Cases, Historic Documents of 1980, p. 432)*

## Psychiatric Examination

*In* Estelle v. Smith, *the high court set aside the death penalty imposed on Ernest Benjamin Smith after his murder conviction for his role in a 1973 armed robbery during which an accomplice shot and killed a store clerk.*

*Before his trial, Smith was examined by a psychiatrist at the order of the judge to ascertain if he was competent to stand trial. After a 90-minute interview with the accused, Dr. James P. Grigson said Smith was indeed competent.*

*Following Smith's murder conviction, a separate sentencing hearing was held. Texas law requires that, before imposing a death penalty, a jury must make certain findings, including a determination that the person poses a future danger to the community. On the basis of his pretrial interview, Grigson testified that Smith would always be dangerous.*

*Known in Texas as "Dr. Death," Grigson himself was considered a controversial witness. In each of more than 70 sentencing hearings in which he had testified since 1967, Grigson claimed the defendant was a "sociopath" who was dangerous to society. In only one of those cases did the defendant escape the death sentence. Many psychiatrists shy away from making firm predictions about the future behavior of individuals, but not Grigson. Indeed, the American Psychiatric Association filed a brief in the Smith case that questioned the use of testimony such as*

Grigson's. The brief stated: "It gives the appearance of being based on expert medical judgment, when in fact no such expertise exists."

The Supreme Court ruled that the death sentence was unconstitutionally imposed because Smith had not been warned of his rights prior to his psychiatric examination. "A criminal defendant who neither initiates a psychiatric evaluation nor attempts to introduce any psychiatric evidence may not be compelled to respond to a psychiatrist if his statements can be used against him at a capital sentencing proceeding," wrote Burger.

While the court was unanimous in setting aside Smith's death sentence, Justices Potter Stewart, Lewis F. Powell Jr. and William H. Rehnquist made clear they did so only on the basis that he had been denied his right to counsel. Stewart and Powell saw no need to address the issue of a self-incrimination warning, and Rehnquist said he would not extend such a warning to this situation.

## Police Interrogation

In Edwards v. Arizona, the court overturned the murder conviction of Robert Edwards, which was based on a confession he made to police under questioning about a holdup and murder in a Tucson bar.

After his arrest, Edwards was given the standard Miranda warning about his rights. He denied involvement in the crime, and then asked for an attorney, at which point the interrogation stopped. The next morning, however, Edwards was visited in jail by two detectives, who again advised him of his rights. In the ensuing conversation, the defendant made incriminating statements which were later used to convict him.

Arizona courts upheld Edwards' conviction, finding that he had waived his right to remain silent and to have his lawyer present when he voluntarily talked with the detectives the morning after his arrest.

The Supreme Court, however, ruled that the resumption of police-initiated questioning violated Edwards' rights as set forth in Miranda. A defendant, "having expressed his desire to deal with the police only through counsel, is not subject to further interrogation by the authorities until counsel has been made available to him, unless the accused himself initiates further communication, exchanges or conversations with police," White wrote.

In separate concurring opinions, Burger, Powell and Rehnquist expressed reservations about the expansion of Miranda outlined by White, but all three stopped short of actual dissents. Burger said that "the extraordinary protections afforded a person in custody suspected of criminal conduct are not without a valid basis, but as with all 'good' things they can be carried too far." The Chief Justice had voiced similar

*thoughts in a speech to the American Bar Association earlier in the year.*
(Chief Justice on crime, p. 191)

> *Following are excerpts from two unanimous Supreme Court*
> *decisions on the right to protection against self-incrimina-*
> *tion and the right of the accused to counsel, decided May 18:*

## No. 79-1127

| | |
|---|---|
| W. J. Estelle, Jr., Director, Texas Department of Corrections, Petitioner, *v.* Ernest Benjamin Smith. | On Writ of Certiorari to the United States Court of Appeals for the Fifth Circuit. |

[May 18, 1981]

CHIEF JUSTICE BURGER delivered the opinion of the Court.

We granted certiorari to consider whether the prosecution's use of psychiatric testimony at the sentencing phase of respondent's capital murder trial to establish his future dangerousness violated his constitutional rights.

## I

### A

On December 28, 1973, respondent Ernest Benjamin Smith was indicted for murder arising from his participation in the armed robbery of a grocery store during which a clerk was fatally shot, not by Smith, but by his accomplice. In accordance with Art. 1257 (b)(2) of the Texas Penal Code (Vernon 1973) concerning the punishment for murder with malice aforethought, the State of Texas announced its intention to seek the death penalty. Thereafter, a judge of the 195th Judicial District Court of Dallas County, Texas, informally ordered the State's attorney to arrange a psychiatric examination of Smith by Dr. James P. Grigson to determine Smith's competency to stand trial.

Dr. Grigson, who interviewed Smith in jail for approximately 90 minutes, concluded that he was competent to stand trial. In a letter to the trial judge, Dr. Grigson reported his findings: "[I]t is my opinion that Ernest Benjamin Smith, Jr. is aware of the difference between right and wrong and is able to aid an attorney in his defense." This letter was filed with the court's papers in the case. Smith was then tried by a jury and convicted of murder.

In Texas, capital cases require bifurcated proceedings — a guilt phase and a penalty phase. If the defendant is found guilty, a separate proceeding before the same jury is held to fix the punishment. At the penalty phase, if the jury affirmatively answers three questions on which the State has the burden of proof beyond a reasonable doubt, the judge must impose the death sentence. One of the three critical issues to be resolved by the jury is "whether there is a probability that the defendant would commit criminal acts of violence that would constitute a continuing threat to society." In other words, the jury must assess the defendant's future dangerousness.

At the commencement of Smith's sentencing hearing, the State rested "subject to the right to reopen." Defense counsel called three lay witnesses: Smith's stepmother, his aunt, and the man who owned the gun Smith carried during the robbery. Smith's relatives testified to his good reputation and character. The owner of the pistol testified as to Smith's knowledge that it would not fire because of a mechanical defect. The State then called Dr. Grigson as a witness.

Defense counsel were aware from the trial court's file of the case that Dr. Grigson had submitted a psychiatric report in the form of a letter advising the court that Smith was competent to stand trial. This report termed Smith "a severe sociopath," but it contained no more specific reference to his future dangerousness. Before trial, defense counsel had obtained an order requiring the State to disclose the witnesses it planned to use both at the guilt stage and, if known, at the penalty stage. Subsequently, the trial court had granted a defense motion to bar the testimony during the State's case-in-chief of any witness whose name did not appear on that list. Dr. Grigson's name was not on the witness list, and defense counsel objected when he was called to the stand at the penalty phase.

In a hearing outside the presence of the jury, Dr. Grigson stated: (1) that he had not obtained permission from Smith's attorneys to examine him; (b) that he had discussed his conclusions and diagnosis with the State's attorney; and (c) that the prosecutor had requested him to testify and had told him, approximately five days before the sentencing hearing began, that his testimony probably would be needed within the week. The trial judge denied a defense motion to exclude Dr. Grigson's testimony on the ground that his name was not on the State's list of witnesses. Although no continuance was requested, the court then recessed for one hour following an acknowledgement by defense counsel that an hour was "all right."

After detailing his professional qualifications by way of foundation, Dr. Grigson testified before the jury on direct examination: (a) that Smith "is a very severe sociopath"; (b) that "he will continue his previous behavior"; (c) that his sociopathic condition will "only grow worse"; (d) that he has no "regard for another human being's property or for their life, regardless of who it may be"; (e) that "[t]here is no treatment, no medicine . . . that in any way at all modifies or changes this behavior"; (f) that he "is going to go ahead and commit other similar or same criminal acts if given the opportunity to do so"; and (g) that he "has no remorse or sorrow for what he has done." Dr. Grigson, whose testimony was based on information derived from his 90-minute "mental status examination" of Smith (*i.e.,* the examination ordered to determine Smith's competency to stand trial), was the State's only witness at the sentencing hearing.

The jury answered the three requisite questions in the affirmative, and, thus, under Texas law the death penalty for Smith was mandatory. The Texas Court of Criminal Appeals affirmed Smith's conviction and death sentence, and we denied certiorari.

## B

After unsuccessfully seeking a writ of habeas corpus in the Texas state courts, Smith petitioned for such relief in the United States District Court for the Northern District of Texas pursuant to 28 U.S.C. § 2254. The District Court vacated Smith's death sentence because it found constitutional error in the admission of Dr. Grigson's testimony at the penalty phase. The court based its holding on the failure to advise Smith of his right to remain silent at the pretrial psychiatric examination and the failure to notify defense counsel in advance of the penalty phase that Dr. Grigson would testify. The court concluded that the death penalty had been imposed on Smith in violation of his Fifth and Fourteenth Amendment rights to due process and freedom from compelled self-incrimination, his Sixth Amendment right to the effective assistance of counsel, and his Eighth Amendment right to present complete evidence of mitigating circumstances.

The United States Court of Appeals for the Fifth Circuit affirmed. The court held that Smith's death sentence could not stand because the State's "surprise" use of Dr. Grigson as a witness, the consequences of which the court described as "devastating," denied Smith due process in that his attorneys were prevented from effectively challenging the psychiatric testimony. The court went on to hold that, under the Fifth and Sixth Amendments, "Texas may not use evidence based on a psychiatric examination of the defendant unless the defendant was warned, before the examination, that he had a right to remain silent; was allowed to terminate the examination when he wished; and was assisted by counsel in deciding whether to submit to the examination." Because Smith was not accorded these rights, his death sentence was set aside. While "leav[ing] to state authorities any questions that arise about the appropriate way to proceed when the state cannot legally execute a defendant whom it has sentenced to death," the court indicated that "the same testimony from Dr. Grigson based on the same examination of Smith" could not be used against Smith at any future resentencing proceeding.

## II

## A

Of the several constitutional issues addressed by the District Court and the Court of Appeals, we turn first to whether the admission of Dr.

Grigson's testimony at the penalty phase violated respondent's Fifth Amendment privilege against compelled self-incrimination because respondent was not advised before the pretrial psychiatric examination that he had a right to remain silent and that any statement he made could be used against him at a sentencing proceeding. Our initial inquiry must be whether the Fifth Amendment privilege is applicable in the circumstances of this case.

## (1)

The State argues that respondent was not entitled to the protection of the Fifth Amendment because Dr. Grigson's testimony was used only to determine punishment after conviction, not to establish guilt. In the State's view, "incrimination is complete once guilt has been adjudicated," and, therefore, the Fifth Amendment privilege has no relevance to the penalty phase of a capital murder trial. We disagree.

The Fifth Amendment, made applicable to the states through the Fourteenth Amendment, commands that "[n]o person ... shall be compelled in any criminal case to be a witness against himself." The essence of this basic constitutional principle is "the requirement that the State which proposes to convict *and punish* an individual produce the evidence against him by the independent labor of its officers, not by the simple, cruel expedient of forcing it from his own lips." *Culombe* v. *Connecticut* (1961) (opinion announcing the judgment) (emphasis added)....

The Court has held that "the availability of the [Fifth Amendment] privilege does not turn upon the type of proceeding in which its protection is invoked, but upon the nature of the statement or admission and the exposure which it invites." *In re Gault* (1967). In this case, the ultimate penalty of death was a potential consequence of what respondent told the examining psychiatrist. Just as the Fifth Amendment prevents a criminal defendant from being made " 'the deluded instrument of his own conviction,' " *Culombe* v. *Connecticut*, it protects him as well from being made the "deluded instrument" of his own execution.

We can discern no basis to distinguish between the guilt and penalty phases of respondent's capital murder trial so far as the protection of the Fifth Amendment privilege is concerned. Given the gravity of the decision to be made at the penalty phase, the State is not relieved of the obligation to observe fundamental constitutional guarantees. See *Green* v. *Georgia* (1979); *Presnell* v. *Georgia* (1978); *Gardner* v. *Florida* (1977) (plurality opinion). Any effort by the State to compel respondent to testify against his will at the sentencing hearing clearly would contravene the Fifth Amendment. Yet the State's attempt to establish respondent's future dangerousness by relying on the unwarned statements he made to Dr. Grigson similarly infringes Fifth Amendment values.

**(2)**

The State also urges that the Fifth Amendment privilege is inapposite here because respondent's communications to Dr. Grigson were nontestimonial in nature. The State seeks support from our cases holding that the Fifth Amendment is not violated where the evidence given by a defendant is neither related to some communicative act nor used for the testimonial content of what was said.... 

However, Dr. Grigson's diagnosis, as detailed in his testimony, was not based simply on his observation of respondent. Rather, Dr. Grigson drew his conclusions largely from respondent's account of the crime during their interview, and he placed particular emphasis on what he considered to be respondent's lack of remorse. Dr. Grigson's prognosis as to future dangerousness rested on statements respondent made, and remarks he omitted, in reciting the details of the crime. The Fifth Amendment privilege, therefore, is directly involved here because the State used as evidence against respondent the substance of his disclosures during the pretrial psychiatric examination.

The fact that respondent's statements were uttered in the context of a psychiatric examination does not automatically remove them from the reach of the Fifth Amendment. The state trial judge, *sua sponte,* ordered a psychiatric evaluation of respondent for the limited, neutral purpose of determining his competency to stand trial, but the results of that inquiry were used by the State for a much broader objective that was plainly adverse to respondent. Consequently, the interview with Dr. Grigson cannot be characterized as a routine competency examination restricted to ensuring that respondent understood the charges against him and was capable of assisting in his defense. Indeed, if the application of Dr. Grigson's findings had been confined to serving that function, no Fifth Amendment issue would have arisen.

Nor was the interview analogous to a sanity examination occasioned by a defendant's plea of not guilty by reason of insanity at the time of his offense. When a defendant asserts the insanity defense and introduces supporting psychiatric testimony, his silence may deprive the State of the only effective means it has of controverting his proof on an issue that he interjected into the case. Accordingly, several courts of appeals have held that, under such circumstances, a defendant can be required to submit to a sanity examination conducted by the prosecution's psychiatrist....

Respondent, however, introduced no psychiatric evidence, nor had he indicated that he might do so. Instead, the State offered information obtained from the court-ordered competency examination as affirmative evidence to persuade the jury to return a sentence of death. Respondent's future dangerousness was a critical issue at the sentencing hearing, and one on which the State had the burden of proof beyond a reasonable doubt. To meet its burden, the State used respondent's own statements, unwittingly made without an awareness that he was assisting the State's efforts to obtain the death penalty. In these distinct circumstances, the

Court of Appeals correctly concluded that the Fifth Amendment privilege was implicated.

### (3)

In *Miranda* v. *Arizona* (1966), the Court acknowledged that "the Fifth Amendment privilege is available outside of criminal court proceedings and serves to protect persons in all settings in which their freedom of action is curtailed in any significant way from being compelled to incriminate themselves." *Miranda* held that "the prosecution may not use statements, whether exculpatory or inculpatory, stemming from custodial interrogation of the defendant unless it demonstrates the use of procedural safeguards effective to secure the privilege against self-incrimination."....

The considerations calling for the accused to be warned prior to custodial interrogation apply with no less force to the pretrial psychiatric examination at issue here.... During the psychiatric evaluation, respondent assuredly was "faced with a phase of the adversary system" and was "not in the presence of [a] person[] acting solely in his interest." Yet he [Smith] was given no indication that the compulsory examination would be used to gather evidence necessary to decide whether, if convicted, he should be sentenced to death. He was not informed that, accordingly, he had a constitutional right not to answer the questions put to him....

... We agree with the Court of Appeals that respondent's Fifth Amendment rights were violated by the admission of Dr. Grigson's testimony at the penalty phase.

A criminal defendant, who neither initiates a psychiatric evaluation nor attempts to introduce any psychiatric evidence, may not be compelled to respond to a psychiatrist if his statements can be used against him at a capital sentencing proceeding. Because respondent did not voluntarily consent to the pretrial psychiatric examination after being informed of his right to remain silent and the possible use of his statements, the State could not rely on what he said to Dr. Grigson to establish his future dangerousness....

"Volunteered statements ... are not barred by the Fifth Amendment," but under *Miranda* v. *Arizona*, we must conclude that, when faced while in custody with a court-ordered psychiatric inquiry, respondent's statements to Dr. Grigson were not "given freely and voluntarily without any compelling influences" and, as such, could be used as the State did at the penalty phase only if respondent had been apprised of his rights and had knowingly decided to waive them. These safeguards of the Fifth Amendment privilege were not afforded respondent and, thus, his death sentence cannot stand.

### B

When respondent was examined by Dr. Grigson, he already had been indicted and an attorney had been appointed to represent him. The Court of Appeals concluded that he had a Sixth Amendment right to the assistance of counsel before submitting to the pretrial psychiatric interview. We agree.

The Sixth Amendment, made applicable to the states through the Fourteenth Amendment, provides that "[i]n all criminal prosecutions, the accused shall enjoy the right ... to have the Assistance of Counsel for his defence.". . . And in *United States* v. *Wade* (1967), the Court explained:

> "It is central to [the Sixth Amendment] principle that in addition to counsel's presence at trial, the accused is guaranteed that he need not stand alone against the State at any stage of the prosecution, formal or informal, in court or out, where counsel's absence might derogate from the accused's right to a fair trial.". . .

Here, respondent's Sixth Amendment right to counsel clearly had attached when Dr. Grigson examined him at the Dallas County Jail, and their interview proved to be a "critical stage" of the aggregate proceedings against respondent. . . . Defense counsel, however, were not notified in advance that the psychiatric examination would encompass the issue of their client's future dangerousness, and respondent was denied the assistance of his attorneys in making the significant decision of whether to submit to the examination and to what end the psychiatrist's findings could be employed.

Because "[a] layman may not be aware of the precise scope, the nuances, and the boundaries of his Fifth Amendment privilege," the assertion of that right "often depends upon legal advice from someone who is trained and skilled in the subject matter." *Maness* v. *Meyers* (1975). As the Court of Appeals observed, the decision to be made regarding the proposed psychiatric evaluation is "literally a life or death matter" and is "difficult ... even for an attorney" because it requires "a knowledge of what other evidence is available, of the particular psychiatrist's biases and predilections, [and] of possible alternative strategies at the sentencing hearing." It follows logically from our precedents that a defendant should not be forced to resolve such an important issue without "the guiding hand of counsel.". . .

Therefore, in addition to Fifth Amendment considerations, the death penalty was improperly imposed on respondent because the psychiatric examination on which Dr. Grigson testified at the penalty phase proceeded in violation of respondent's Sixth Amendment right to the assistance of counsel.

### C

Our holding based on the Fifth and Sixth Amendments will not prevent the State in capital cases from proving the defendant's future dangerousness as required by statute. A defendant may request or consent to a psychiatric examination concerning future dangerousness in the hope of escaping the death penalty. In addition, a different situation arises where a defendant intends to introduce psychiatric evidence at the penalty phase. . . .

## III

Respondent's Fifth and Sixth Amendment rights were abridged by the State's introduction of Dr. Grigson's testimony at the penalty phase, and, as the Court of Appeals concluded, his death sentence must be vacated. Because respondent's underlying conviction has not been challenged and remains undisturbed, the State is free to conduct further proceedings not inconsistent with this opinion. Accordingly, the judgment of the Court of Appeals is

*Affirmed.*

No. 79-5269

Robert Edwards, Petitioner,     On Writ of Certiorari to the
*v.*     Supreme Court of Arizona.
State of Arizona.

[May 18, 1981]

JUSTICE WHITE delivered the opinion of the Court.

We granted certiorari in this case . . . limited to question one presented in the petition, which in relevant part was "whether the Fifth, Sixth, and Fourteenth Amendments require suppression of a post-arrest confession, which was obtained after Edwards had invoked his right to consult counsel before further interrogation; . . . ."

## I

On January 19, 1976, a sworn complaint was filed against Edwards in Arizona state court charging him with robbery, burglary, and first-degree murder. An arrest warrant was issued pursuant to the complaint, and Edwards was arrested at his home later that same day. At the police station, he was informed of his rights as required by *Miranda* v. *Arizona* (1966). Petitioner stated that he understood his rights, and was willing to submit to questioning. After being told that another suspect already in custody had implicated him in the crime, Edwards denied involvement and gave a taped statement presenting an alibi defense. He then sought to "make a deal." The interrogating officer told him that he wanted a statement, but that he did not have the authority to negotiate a deal. The officer provided Edwards with the number of a county attorney. Petitioner made the call, but hung up after a few moments. Edwards then said, "I want an attorney before making a deal." At that point, questioning ceased and Edwards was taken to county jail.

At 9:15 the next morning, two detectives, colleagues of the officer who had interrogated Edwards the previous night, came to the jail and asked to see Edwards. When the detention officer informed Edwards that the detectives wished to speak with him, he replied that he did not want to talk to anyone. The guard told him that "he had" to talk and then took him to meet with the detectives. The officers identified themselves, stated they wanted to talk to him, and informed him of his *Miranda* rights. Edwards was willing to talk, but he first wanted to hear the taped statement of the alleged accomplice who had implicated him. After listening to the tape for several minutes, petitioner said that he would make a statement so long as it was not tape recorded. The detectives informed him that the recording was irrelevant since they could testify in court concerning whatever he said. Edwards replied "I'll tell you anything you want to know, but I don't want it on tape." He thereupon implicated himself in the crime.

Prior to trial, Edwards moved to suppress his confession on the ground that his *Miranda* rights had been violated when the officers returned to question him after he had invoked his right to counsel. The trial court initially granted the motion to suppress, but reversed its ruling when presented with a supposedly controlling decision of a higher Arizona court. The court stated without explanation that it found Edwards' statement to be voluntary. Edwards was tried twice and convicted. Evidence concerning his confession was admitted at both trials.

On appeal, the Arizona Supreme Court held that Edwards had invoked both his right to remain silent and his right to counsel during the interrogation conducted on the night of January 19. The court then went on to determine, however, that Edwards had waived both rights during the January 20 meeting when he voluntarily gave his statement to the detectives after again being informed that he need not answer questions and that he need not answer without the advice of counsel: "The trial court's finding that the waiver and confession were voluntarily and knowingly made is upheld."

Because the use of Edward's confession against him at his trial violated his rights under the Fifth and Fourteenth Amendments as construed in *Miranda* v. *Arizona,* we reverse the judgment of the Arizona Supreme Court.

## II

In *Miranda* v. *Arizona,* the Court determined that the Fifth and Fourteenth Amendments' prohibition against compelled self-incrimination required that custodial interrogation be preceded by advice to the putative defendant that he has the right to remain silent and also the right to the presence of an attorney. The Court also indicated the procedures to be followed subsequent to the warnings. If the accused indicates that he wishes to remain silent, "the interrogation must cease." If he requests counsel, "the interrogation must cease until an attorney is present."

*Miranda* thus declared that an accused has a Fifth and Fourteenth Amendment right to have counsel present during custodial interrogation. Here, the critical facts as found by the Arizona Supreme Court are that Edwards asserted his right to counsel and his right to remain silent on January 19, but that the police, without furnishing him counsel, returned the next morning to confront him and as a result of the meeting secured incriminating oral admissions. Contrary to the holdings of the state courts, Edwards insists that having exercised his right on the 19th to have counsel present during interrogation, he did not validly waive that right on the 20th. For the following reasons, we agree.

First, the Arizona Supreme Court applied an erroneous standard for determining waiver where the accused has specifically invoked his right to counsel. It is reasonably clear under our cases that waivers of counsel must not only be voluntary, but constitute a knowing and intelligent relinquishment or abandonment of a known right or privilege, a matter which depends in each case "upon the particular facts and circumstances surrounding that case, including the background, experience and conduct of the accused." *Johnson* v. *Zerbst* (1938). See *Faretta* v. *California* (1975); *North Carolina* v. *Butler* (1979); *Brewer* v. *Williams* (1977); *Fare* v. *Michael C.* (1979).

Considering the proceedings in the state courts in the light of this standard, we note that in denying petitioner's motion to suppress, the trial court found the admission to have been "voluntary," without separately focusing on whether Edwards had knowingly and intelligently relinquished his right to counsel. The Arizona Supreme Court, in a section of its opinion entitled "Voluntariness of Waiver," stated that in Arizona, confessions are prima facie involuntary and that the State had the burden of showing by a preponderance of the evidence that the confession was freely and voluntarily made. The court stated that the issue of voluntariness should be determined based on the totality of the circumstances as it related to whether an accused's action was "knowing and intelligent and whether his will was overborne." Once the trial court determines that "the confession is voluntary, the finding will not be upset on appeal absent clear and manifest error." The court then upheld the trial court's finding that the "waiver and confession were voluntarily and knowingly made."

In referring to the necessity to find Edwards' confession knowing and intelligent, the State Supreme court cited *Schneckloth* v. *Bustamonte* (1973). Yet, it is clear that *Schneckloth* does not control the issue presented in this case. The issue in *Schneckloth* was under what conditions an individual could be found to have consented to a search and thereby waived his Fourth Amendment rights.... *Schneckloth* itself ... emphasized that the voluntariness of a consent or an admission on the one hand, and a knowing and intelligent waiver on the other, are discrete inquiries. Here, however sound the conclusion of the state courts as to the voluntariness of Edwards' admission may be, neither the trial court nor the Arizona Supreme Court undertook to focus on whether Edwards understood his right to counsel and intelligently and knowingly relinquished it.

It is thus apparent that the decision below misunderstood the requirement for finding a valid waiver of the right to counsel, once invoked.

Second, although we have held that after initially being advised of his *Miranda* rights, the accused may himself validly waive his rights and respond to interrogation, see *North Carolina* v. *Butler,* the Court has strongly indicated that additional safeguards are necessary when the accused asks for counsel; and we now hold that when an accused has invoked his right to have counsel present during custodial interrogation, a valid waiver of that right cannot be established by showing only that he responded to further police-initiated custodial interrogation even if he has been advised of his rights. We further hold that an accused, such as Edwards, having expressed his desire to deal with the police only through counsel, is not subject to further interrogation by the authorities until counsel has been made available to him, unless the accused himself initiates further communication, exchanges or conversations with the police.

*Miranda* itself indicated that the assertion of the right to counsel was a significant event and that once exercised by the accused, "the interrogation must cease until an attorney is present." Our later cases have not abandoned that view. In *Michigan* v. *Mosley* (1975), the Court noted that *Miranda* had distinguished between the procedural safeguards triggered by a request to remain silent and a request for an attorney and had required that interrogation cease until an attorney was present only if the individual stated that he wanted counsel. (WHITE, J., concurring). In *Fare* v. *Michael C.,* the Court referred to *Miranda's* "rigid rule that an accused's request for an attorney is *per se* an invocation of his Fifth Amendment rights, requiring that all interrogation cease." And just last Term, in a case where a suspect in custody had invoked his *Miranda* right to counsel, the Court again referred to the "undisputed right" under *Miranda* to remain silent and to be free of interrogation "until he had consulted with a lawyer." *Rhode Island* v. *Innis* (1980). We reconfirm these views and to lend them substance, emphasize that it is inconsistent with *Miranda* and its progeny for the authorities, at their instance, to reinterrogate an accused in custody if he has clearly asserted his right to counsel.

In concluding that the fruits of the interrogation initiated by the police on January 20 could not be used against Edwards, we do not hold or imply that Edwards was powerless to countermand his election or that the authorities could in no event use any incriminating statements made by Edwards prior to his having access to counsel. Had Edwards initiated the meeting on January 20, nothing in the Fifth and Fourteenth Amendments would prohibit the police from merely listening to his voluntary, volunteered statements and using them against him at the trial. The Fifth Amendment right identified in *Miranda* is the right to have counsel present at any custodial interrogation. Absent such interrogation, there would have been no infringement of the right that Edwards invoked and there would be no occasion to determine whether there had been a valid waiver. *Rhode Island* v. *Innis* makes this sufficiently clear.

But this is not what the facts of this case show. Here, the officers conducting the interrogation on the evening of January 19, ceased interrogation when Edwards requested counsel as he had been advised he had the right to do. The Arizona Supreme Court was of the opinion that this was a sufficient invocation of his *Miranda* rights, and we are in accord. It is also clear that without making counsel available to Edwards, the police returned to him the next day. This was not at his suggestion or request. Indeed, Edwards informed the detention officer that he did not want to talk to anyone. At the meeting, the detectives told Edwards that they wanted to talk to him and again advised him of his *Miranda* rights. Edwards stated that he would talk, but what prompted this action does not appear. He listened at his own request to part of the taped statement made by one of his alleged accomplices and then made an incriminating statement, which was used against him at his trial. We think it is clear that Edwards was subjected to custodial interrogation on January 20 within the meaning of *Rhode Island* v. *Innis* and that this occurred at the instance of the authorities. His statement, made without having had access to counsel, did not amount to a valid waiver and hence was inadmissible.

Accordingly, the holding of the Arizona Supreme Court that Edwards had waived his right to counsel was infirm and the judgment of that court is reversed.

*So ordered.*

# U.S. VOTE AGAINST INFANT FORMULA CODE

## May 21, 1981

The United States May 21 cast the sole vote against the World Health Organization (WHO) code on infant formula. WHO, an agency of the United Nations, proposed the code to curb aggressive marketing of formula in Third World countries. Proponents of the code argued that increased use of breastmilk substitutes was a direct cause of infant diarrhea, mulnutrition and death. Strong support for the code was voiced in the media and in Congress, and the negative U.S. stand drew sharp criticism. The vote took place at WHO's annual meeting in Geneva, Switzerland.

The WHO code did not advocate a ban on the sale of infant formula, but aimed at ending certain marketing methods considered unfair or unscrupulous. These included such practices as dressing sales personnel as nurses to give free samples of formula to new mothers, telling the mothers that bottle feeding was preferable to breast-feeding and giving kickbacks to health workers to promote the use of formula. Women in developing countries often did not have the education or the money to use the breastmilk substitutes correctly. If the formula was mixed with contaminated water, or the bottles were not clean or the formula was diluted with too much water, the infants suffered.

The WHO code was advisory and would not have the effect of law unless adopted by the legislature of each country endorsing it. Elliott Abrams, then assistant secretary of state for international organization affairs, writing in The Washington Post May 21, said that the administration could not support the code because its provisions were contrary to

447

*American law. The administration regarded the ban on advertising the products as a violation of the right of free speech. Abrams said the United States supported the practice of breast-feeding for all infants and regretted that WHO had not written a code the United States could endorse.*

*American manufacturers of infant formula lobbied heavily against the code, arguing that there was no persuasive evidence linking the promotion of formula with a decrease in breast-feeding. The leading American companies, Abbott Laboratories, the American Home Products Corp. and Bristol-Myers, accounted for about $150 million in annual sales of formula abroad. The Nestlé Co. of Switzerland accounted for $500 million of the $1 billion in annual sales to the Third World. Nestlé, the target of a worldwide boycott organized by activist groups, attempted to avoid publicity during the debate on the code.*

## Reaction in Congress

*Congressional reaction to the U.S. position was negative. On May 19 a delegation of more than a dozen House members attempted to meet with President Reagan to persuade him to support the code. The president refused to see them. In the House Rep. Clement J. Zablocki, D-Wis., June 16 introduced a joint resolution, H J Res 287, expressing dismay at the U.S. vote and urging support for the code. The House adopted the resolution 301-100.*

*Sen. David Durenberger, R-Minn., June 17 introduced an amendment to the State Department authorization bill, S 1193. In language somewhat milder than the House resolution, the amendment expressed the concern of the Senate and urged the United States and the breastmilk substitute industry "to support the basic aim of the Code. . . ." The amendment also voiced the concern that "the vote has subjected United States policy to widespread misinterpretation." The Senate passed the bill June 18 by a vote of 89-2. A House-Senate conference committee did not complete work in 1981 on a compromise version of the bill. But in December Congress passed the foreign aid authorization bill, S 1196, allotting $5 million to encourage the practice of breast-feeding and to further research in nutrition for infants.*

## Officials Protest

*Two officials of the Agency for International Development (AID) resigned May 18 in protest against the U.S. position. Dr. Stephen C. Joseph, the highest-ranking health professional at the agency, said that the United States "has been swayed by the self-interest arguments of the infant formula industry." Eugene Babb, the deputy assistant administra-*

*tor for food and nutrition, stated, "This is not an issue of free enterprise versus government regulation. The issue is whether or not the United States supports responsible commercial behavior of U.S. firms doing business in developing countries." Accepting the two resignations, M. Peter McPherson, AID administrator, said, "The Administration feels that it is inappropriate for an agency of the United Nations to move in the direction of regulating economic activity."*

*Another casualty of the furor created by the U.S. vote was Ernest W. Lefever, Reagan's choice for assistant secretary of state for human rights. Lefever's Ethics and Public Policy Center accepted more than $25,000 in grants from Nestlé. Critics charged that the center had helped promote the sale of formula in exchange for the financial assistance. Lefever denied the allegations. After withdrawing his name from consideration for the post, Lefever claimed in a June 10 letter to* The New York Times *that the center, in fact, had reprinted an article critical of Nestlé's policy of aggressive promotion of infant formula in the Third World. The Nestlé involvement was only one of several controversies surrounding Lefever's nomination; he withdrew his name June 5 after the Senate Foreign Relations Committee voted 13 to 4 to reject him. In November Elliott Abrams was appointed to the post.*

*Following are excerpts from the International Code of Marketing of Breastmilk Substitutes as adopted by the World Health Organization May 21 and the text of HJ Res 287, adopted by the House of Representatives June 16. (Boldface headings in brackets have been added by Congressional Quarterly to highlight the organization of the texts.):*

# INTERNATIONAL CODE OF MARKETING OF BREASTMILK SUBSTITUTES

The Member States of the World Health Organization:

Affirming the right of every child and every pregnant and lactating woman to be adequately nourished as a means of attaining and maintaining health;

Recognizing that infant malnutrition is part of the wider problems of lack of education, poverty, and social injustice;

Recognizing that the health of infants and young children cannot be isolated from the health and nutrition of women, their socioeconomic status and their roles as mothers;

Conscious that breastfeeding is an unequalled way of providing ideal food for the healthy growth and development of infants; that it forms a unique biological and emotional basis for the health of both mother and child; that the anti-infective properties of breastmilk help to protect infants against disease; and that there is an important relationship between breastfeeding and child-spacing;

Recognizing that the encouragement and protection of breastfeeding is an important part of the health, nutrition and other social measures required to promote healthy growth and development of infants and young children; and that breastfeeding is an important aspect of primary health care;

Considering that when mothers do not breastfeed, or only do so partially, there is a legitimate market for infant formula and for suitable ingredients from which to prepare it; that all these products should accordingly be made accessible to those who need them through commercial or non-commercial distribution systems; and that they should not be marketed or distributed in ways that may interfere with the protection and promotion of breastfeeding;

Recognizing further that inappropriate feeding practices lead to infant malnutrition, morbidity and mortality in all countries, and that improper practices in the marketing of breastmilk substitutes and related products can contribute to these major public health problems;

Convinced that it is important for infants to receive appropriate complementary foods, usually when the infant reaches four to six months of age, and that every effort should be made to use locally available foods; and convinced, nevertheless, that such complementary foods should not be used as breastmilk substitutes;

Appreciating that there are a number of social and economic factors affecting breastfeeding, and that, accordingly, governments should develop social support systems to protect, facilitate and encourage it, and that they should create an environment that fosters breastfeeding, provides appropriate family and community support, and protects mothers from factors that inhibit breastfeeding;

Affirming that health care systems, and the health professionals and other health workers serving in them, have an essential role to play in guiding infant feeding practices, encouraging and facilitating breastfeeding, and providing objective and consistent advice to mothers and families about the superior value of breastfeeding, or, where needed, on the proper use of infant formula, whether manufactured industrially or home-prepared;

Affirming further that educational systems and other social services should be involved in the protection and promotion of breastfeeding, and in the appropriate use of complementary foods;

Aware that families, communities, women's organizations and other nongovernmental organizations have a special role to play in the protection and promotion of breastfeeding and in ensuring the support needed by pregnant women and mothers of infants and young children, whether breastfeeding or not;

Affirming the need for governments, organizations of the United Nations system, nongovernmental organizations, experts in various related disciplines, consumer groups and industry to cooperate in activities aimed at the improvement of maternal, infant and young child health and nutrition;

Recognizing that governments should undertake a variety of health, nutrition and other social measures to promote healthy growth and development of infants and young children, and that this Code concerns only one aspect of these measures;

Considering that manufacturers and distributors of breastmilk substitutes have an important and constructive role to play in relation to infant feeding, and in the promotion of the aim of this Code and its proper implementation;

Affirming that governments are called upon to take action appropriate to their social and legislative framework and their overall development objectives to give effect to the principles and aim of this Code, including the enactment of legislation, regulations or other suitable measures;

Believing that, in the light of the foregoing considerations, and in view of the vulnerability of infants in the early months of life and the risks involved in inappropriate feeding practices, including the unnecessary and improper use of breastmilk substitutes, the marketing of breastmilk substitutes requires special treatment, which makes usual marketing practices unsuitable for these products;

THEREFORE:

The Member States hereby agree the following articles which are recommended as a basis for action.

## ARTICLE 1

### Aim of the Code

The aim of this Code is to contribute to the provision of safe and adequate nutrition for infants, by the protection and promotion of breastfeeding, and by ensuring the proper use of breastmilk substitutes, when these are necessary, on the basis of adequate information and through appropriate marketing and distribution.

## ARTICLE 2

### Scope of the Code

The Code applies to the marketing, and practices related thereto, of the following products: breastmilk substitutes, including infant formula; other milk products, foods and beverages, including bottle-fed complementary foods when marketed or otherwise represented to be suitable, with or without modification, for use as a partial or total replacement of breastmilk; feeding bottles and teats. It also applies to their quality and availability, and to information concerning their use. . . .

## ARTICLE 4

### Information and Education

4.1  Governments should have the responsibility to ensure that objective and consistent information is provided on infant and young child feeding for use by families and those involved in the field of infant and young child nutrition. This responsibility should cover either the planning, provision, design and dissemination of information, or their control.

4.2  Informational and educational materials whether written, audio, or visual, dealing with the feeding of infants and intended to reach pregnant women and mothers of infants and young children, should include clear information on all the following points: (a) the benefits and superiority of breastfeeding; (b) maternal nutrition, and the preparation for and maintenance of breastfeeding; (c) the negative effect on breastfeeding of introducing partial bottlefeeding; (d) the difficulty of reversing the decision not to breastfeed; and (e) where needed, the proper use of infant formula, whether manufactured industrially or home-prepared. When such materials contain information about the use of infant formula, they should include the social and financial implications of its use; the health hazards of inappropriate foods or feeding methods; and, in particular, the health hazards of unnecessary or improper use of infant formula and other breastmilk substitutes. Such materials should not use any pictures or text which may idealize the use of breastmilk substitutes.

4.3  Donations of informational or educational equipment or materials by manufacturers or distributors should be made only at the request and with the written approval of the appropriate government authority or within guidelines given by governments for this purpose. Such equipment or materials may bear the donating company's name or logo, but should not refer to a proprietary product that is within the scope of this Code, and should be distributed only through the health care system.

## ARTICLE 5

### The General Public and Mothers

5.1  There should be no advertising or other form of promotion to the general public of products within the scope of this Code.

5.2  Manufacturers and distributors should not provide, directly or indirectly, to pregnant women, mothers or members of their families, samples of products within the scope of this Code.

5.3  In conformity with paragraphs 1 and 2 of this Article, there should be no point-of-sale advertising, giving of samples, or any other promotion device to induce sales directly to the consumer at the retail level, such as special displays, discount coupons, premiums, special sales, loss-leaders and tie-in sales, for products within the scope of this Code. This provision should not restrict the establishment of pricing policies· and practices intended to provide products at lower prices on a long-term basis.

5.4   Manufacturers and distributors should not distribute to pregnant women or mothers of infants and young children any gifts of articles or utensils which may promote the use of breastmilk substitutes or bottle-feeding.

5.5   Marketing personnel, in their business capacity, should not seek direct or indirect contact of any kind with pregnant women or with mothers of infants and young children.

## ARTICLE 6

### Health Care Systems

6.1   The health authorities in Member States should take appropriate measures to encourage and protect breastfeeding and promote the principles of this Code, and should give appropriate information and advice to health workers in regard to their responsibilities, including the information specified in Article 4.2.

6.2   No facility of a health care system should be used for the purpose of promoting infant formula or other products within the scope of this Code. This Code does not, however, preclude the dissemination of information to health professionals as provided in Article 7.2.

6.3   Facilities of health care systems should not be used for the display of products within the scope of this Code, for placards or posters concerning such products, or for the distribution of material provided by a manufacturer or distributor other than that specified in Article 4.3.

6.4   The use by the health care system of "professional service representatives", "mothercraft nurses" or similar personnel, provided or paid for by manufacturers or distributors, should not be permitted.

6.5   Feeding with infant formula, whether manufactured or home-prepared, should be demonstrated only by health workers, or other community workers if necessary; and only to the mothers or family members who need to use it; and the information given should include a clear explanation of the hazards of improper use.

6.6   Donations or low-price sales to institutions or organizations of supplies of infant formula or other products within the scope of this Code, whether for use in the institutions or for distribution outside them, may be made. Such supplies should only be used or distributed for infants who have to be fed on breastmilk substitutes. If these supplies are distributed for use outside the institutions, this should be done only by the institutions or organizations concerned. Such donations or low-price sales should not be used by manufacturers or distributors as a sales inducement.

6.7   Where donated supplies of infant formula or other products within the scope of this Code are distributed outside an institution, the institution or organization should take steps to ensure that supplies can be continued as long as the infants concerned need them. Donors, as well as institutions or organizations concerned, should bear in mind this responsibility.

6.8 Equipment and materials, in addition to those referred to in Article 4.3, donated to a health care system may bear a company's name or logo, but should not refer to any proprietary product within the scope of this Code.

## ARTICLE 7

### Health Workers

7.1 Health workers should encourage and protect breastfeeding; and those who are concerned in particular with maternal and infant nutrition should make themselves familiar with their responsibilities under this Code, including the information specified in Article 4.2.

7.2 Information provided by manufacturers and distributors to health professionals regarding products within the scope of this Code should be restricted to scientific and factual matters, and such information should not imply or create a belief that bottle-feeding is equivalent or superior to breastfeeding. It should also include the information specified in Article 4.2.

7.3 No financial or material inducements to promote products within the scope of this Code should be offered by manufacturers or distributors to health workers or members of their families, nor should these be accepted by health workers or members of their families.

7.4 Samples of infant formula or other products within the scope of this Code, or of equipment or utensils for their preparation or use, should not be provided to health workers except when necessary for the purpose of professional evaluation or research at the institutional level. Health workers should not give samples of infant formula to pregnant women, mothers of infants and young children, or members of their families.

7.5 Manufacturers and distributors of products within the scope of this Code should disclose to the institution to which a recipient health worker is affiliated any contribution made to or on his behalf for fellowships, study tours, research grants, attendance at professional conferences, or the like. Similar disclosures should be made by the recipient.

## ARTICLE 8

### [Employees of Manufacturers]

8.1 In systems of sales incentives for marketing personnel, the volume of sales of products within the scope of this Code should not be included in the calculation of bonuses, nor should quotas be set specifically for sales of these products. This should not be understood to prevent the payment of bonuses based on the overall sales by a company of other products marketed by it.

8.2 Personnel employed in marketing products within the scope of this Code should not, as part of their job responsibilities, perform educational functions in relation to pregnant women or mothers of infants and young children. This should not be understood as preventing such personnel from being used for other functions by the health care system at the request and with the written approval of the appropriate authority of the government concerned.

## ARTICLE 9

### Labelling

9.1 Labels should be designed to provide the necessary information about the appropriate use of the product, and so as not to discourage breastfeeding.

9.2 Manufacturers and distributors of infant formula should ensure that each container has a clear, conspicuous, and easily readable and understandable message printed on it, or on a label which cannot readily become separated from it, in an appropriate language, which includes all the following points: (a) the words "Important Notice" or their equivalent; (b) a statement of the superiority of breastfeeding; (c) a statement that the product should be used only on the advice of a health worker as to the need for its use and the proper method of use; (d) instructions for appropriate preparation, and a warning against the health hazards of inappropriate preparation. Neither the container nor the label should have pictures of infants, nor should they have other pictures or text which may idealize the use of infant formula. They may, however, have graphics for easy identification of the product as a breastmilk substitute and for illustrating methods of preparation. The terms "humanized", "maternalized" or similar terms should not be used. Inserts giving additional information about the product and its proper use, subject to the above conditions, may be included in the package or retail unit. When labels give instructions for modifying a product into infant formula, the above should apply.

9.3 Food products within the scope of this Code, marketed for infant feeding, which do not meet all the requirements of an infant formula, but which can be modified to do so, should carry on the label a warning that the unmodified product should not be the sole source of nourishment of an infant. Since sweetened condensed milk is not suitable for infant feeding, nor for use as a main ingredient of infant formula, its label should not contain purported instructions on how to modify it for that purpose.

9.4 The label of food products within the scope of this Code should also state all the following points: (a) the ingredients used; (b) the composition/analysis of the product; (c) the storage conditions required; and (d) the batch number and the date before which the product is to be consumed, taking into account the climatic and storage conditions of the country concerned.

## ARTICLE 10

### Quality

10.1   The quality of products is an essential element for the protection of the health of infants and therefore should be of a high recognized standard.

10.2   Food products within the scope of this Code should, when sold or otherwise distributed, meet applicable standards recommended by the Codex Alimentarius Commission and also the Codex Code of Hygienic Practices for Foods for Infants and Children.

## ARTICLE 11

### Implementation and Monitoring

11.1   Governments should take action to give effect to the principles and aim of this Code, as appropriate to their social and legislative framework, including the adoption of national legislation, regulations or other suitable measures. For this purpose, governments should seek, when necessary, the cooperation of WHO, UNICEF and other agencies of the United Nations system. National policies and measures, including laws and regulations, which are adopted to give effect to the principles and aim of this Code should be publicly stated, and should apply on the same basis to all those involved in the manufacture and marketing of products within the scope of this Code.

11.2   Monitoring the application of this Code lies with governments acting individually, and collectively through the World Health Organization as provided in paragraphs 6 and 7 of this Article. The manufacturers and distributors of products within the scope of this Code, and appropriate nongovernmental organizations, professional groups, and consumer organizations should collaborate with governments to this end.

11.3   Independently of any other measures taken for implementation of this Code, manufacturers and distributors of products within the scope of this Code should regard themselves responsible for monitoring their marketing practices according to the principles and aim of this Code, and for taking steps to ensure that their conduct at every level conforms to them.

11.4   Nongovernmental organizations, professional groups, institutions, and individuals concerned should have the responsibility of drawing the attention of manufacturers or distributors to activities which are incompatible with the principles and aim of this Code, so that appropriate action can be taken. The appropriate governmental authority should also be informed.

11.5 Manufacturers and primary distributors of products within the scope of this Code should apprise each member of their marketing personnel of the Code and of their responsibilities under it.

11.6 In accordance with Article 62 of the Constitution of the World Health Organization, Member States shall communicate annually to the Director-General information on action taken to give effect to the principles and aim of this Code.

11.7 The Director-General shall report in even years to the World Health Assembly on the status of implementation of the Code; and shall, on request, provide technical support to Member States preparing national legislation or regulations, or taking other appropriate measures in implementation and furtherance of the principles and aim of this Code.

# H J RES 287

Whereas there is overwhelming scientific evidence that breastfeeding has substantial advantages for infant health and growth, that it offers an uncontaminated food supply, an early transfer of antibodies protective against infections [sic] diseases, and a naturally evolved and tested nutritional source, and that it is an important factor in bonding between mother and child;

Whereas numerous studies, in a wide variety of developed and developing countries, over a long period of time, have shown that artificial infant feeding is associated with higher rates of illness and death and, in poor communities, with lessened growth and nutrition;

Whereas the problem of unrefrigerated infant formula prepared with polluted water and placed in inadequately cleaned bottles is further complicated by flies and heat in tropical climates;

Whereas one hundred million of the one hundred and twenty-five million children in the world below the age of one are born in developing countries;

Whereas ten million of these one hundred million children will probably not live until their first birthday;

Whereas diarrhea and other infectious diseases, when combined with the problems of malnutrition, account for more than half of these deaths;

Whereas the use of infant formula rather than breastfeeding is estimated to account for up to a million of these deaths per year; and

Whereas at a recent meeting of the World Health Organization, the United States was the only country, in a one hundred and eighteen to one vote, to vote against a voluntary code to encourage breastfeeding and to curb inappropriate marketing and advertising of infant formula, particularly in the Third World: Now, therefore, be it

*Resolved by the Senate and House of Representatives of the United States of America in Congress assembled,* That the Congress—

(1) expresses its dismay at the negative vote cast by the United States on May 21, 1981, at the Thirty-fourth World Health Assembly of the World Health Organization on the "International Code of Marketing of Breastmilk Substitutes";

(2) urges the administration to notify promptly the World Health Organization that the Government of the United States will cooperate fully with other nations in implementation of the code;

(3) urges the United States infant formula industry to abide by the guidelines of that code, particularly with respect to exports and the activities of subsidiaries in developing countries; and

(4) reaffirms the dedication of the United States to the protection of the lives of all the world's children and the support of the United States for efforts to improve world health.

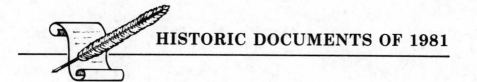
# June

# CIA ON INTERNATIONAL TERRORISM

## June 15, 1981

*Industrialized democracies and symbols of Western power continued in 1980 to be the objects of global terrorism, according to a study released June 15, 1981, by the Central Intelligence Agency's National Foreign Assessment Center. The annual report,* Patterns of International Terrorism: 1980, *also noted that more casualties resulted from international terrorism in 1980 than in any year since 1968, when the CIA began its analysis of terrorism statistics, and that assassinations and other terrorist attacks meant to injure or kill — rather than merely threaten or arouse fear — had increased over previous years.*

## Administration's Terrorism Policy

*In his presidential campaign Ronald Reagan had espoused a foreign policy that emphasized a hard-line approach toward the Soviet Union. To deter the Soviets from achieving their "Marxist dream of one communist world," Reagan advocated increasing America's military strength.*

*The intricate negotiations for the release of the American hostages held by terrorists in Iran for more than a year concluded just as Reagan was to be inaugurated on January 20, 1981. When Reagan greeted the returnees at the White House the following week, he declared, "Let terrorists be aware that when the rules of international behavior are violated, our policy will be one of swift and effective retribution." (Iranian release of U.S. hostages, p. 145)*

*Early in his administration, Reagan made it clear he planned to downgrade substantially former President Jimmy Carter's emphasis on human rights and that he instead would stress support for nations struggling against "international terrorism" instigated by communists.*

*Alexander M. Haig, Jr., in his first press conference as secretary of state January 28, reiterated the new administration's tough stance on terrorism. He caused a stir by accusing the Soviet Union of "training, funding, and equipping international terrorists." Haig offered no concrete evidence to support his assertions.*

## Draft Report

*It was into this political environment that the report prepared by CIA analysts was issued. A draft version of the report was rejected earlier by William J. Casey, Reagan's choice as CIA director. Statistics in the report going back to 1968 were revised to include "threats" as well as actual acts of politically motivated violence.*

*Casey's aides claimed the report had been poorly prepared and that it was not unusual for a study to be circulated and returned for revisions. But certain analysts complained that Casey wished the report to justify the administration's rigid foreign policy and to substantiate Haig's claims about the Soviets.*

*The final report stated that the Soviets supported revolutionary violence, which "frequently entails acts of international terrorism." The Soviets also maintained close relationships with a number of governments and organizations, for example Libya and the Palestine Liberation Organization (PLO), that directly supported purely terrorist groups. But the report stopped short of accusing the Soviets of actually training and supporting terrorists themselves.*

## Libya

*The final report was much more specific in its allegations directed against Libya. It said the Muammar Qaddafi government's support for terrorism included financing terrorist operations, procuring weapons and training guerrilla fighters. A month earlier the Reagan administration had expelled Libyan diplomats, partly in protest of the terrorist issue.*

*Citing a "general pattern of unacceptable conduct," which included "support for international terrorism," the United States May 6 ordered Libya to close its diplomatic mission in Washington, D.C. Calling for the withdrawal of all personnel within five days, the order fell just short of a formal break in diplomatic relations between the two countries. This order came only two weeks after police charged that a Libyan man studying in the United States had been shot in October 1980 by an American mercenary recruited by the Libyan government.*

## Other Findings

*Other major findings of the report included:*

● *In 1980 almost twice as many assassinations and assassination attempts occurred as in any previous year.*

● *During the two previous years, the Iraqi government reduced its support for most terrorist groups, but it conducted terrorist attacks against Iranian diplomats in Europe and the Middle East.*

● *Syria backed radical elements of the PLO, including the Popular Front for the Liberation of Palestine (PFLP), which was heavily involved in international terrorism.*

● *Iran was consumed with domestic difficulties in 1980 and was not actively supporting additional terrorist activities, although at that time the American hostages were still being held in Tehran.*

● *Cuba directly supported guerrilla groups, many of which were engaged in terrorist operations.*

● *The Provisional Irish Republican Army, which had conducted over the years more international terrorist attacks than any other single terrorist group, was not so active in 1980 as in previous years.*

● *Palestinian terrorist actions in 1980 did not reach the levels experienced during the 1970s.*

## Combating Terrorism

*The Reagan administration began taking steps to combat terrorism in 1981. In comparison with its early pronouncements on the subject, however, the actions appeared modest. The administration called for increasing security at American embassies, improving crisis management and constructing safe havens where embassy staffs could resist an attack long enough to destroy secret documents. Also, training courses on terrorism for diplomats were being offered.*

*The steps the government could take to combat terrorism were tempered by political realities. With Libya, for example, the United States needed to balance its disapproval of Qaddafi's tactics against the U.S. need for Libyan oil.*

*Following are excerpts from the Central Intelligence Agency's National Foreign Assessment Center annual report, entitled* Patterns of International Terrorism: 1980, *issued June 15, 1981. (Boldface headings in brackets have been added by Congressional Quarterly to highlight the organization of the text.):*

## [Definitions]

### TERRORISM

The threat or use of violence for political purposes by individuals or groups, whether acting for, or in opposition to, established governmental authority, when such actions are intended to shock or intimidate a target group wider than the immediate victims.

### INTERNATIONAL TERRORISM

Terrorism conducted with the support of a foreign government or organization and/or directed against foreign nationals, institutions, or governments. Terrorism has involved groups seeking to overthrow specific regimes (for example, Yugoslavia and El Salvador), to rectify national or group grievances (for example, the Palestinians), or to undermine international order as an end in itself (for example, the Japanese Red Army)....

## Overview

International terrorism resulted in more casualties in 1980 than in any year since the analysis of statistics related to terrorism began in 1968. The total number of events last year was also high — second only to 1978.

Established patterns of striking at targets in industrialized democracies and attacking symbols of Western power continued into 1980. Americans remained the primary targets of international terrorism, with nearly two out of every five incidents involving US citizens or property.

Terrorist events aimed at causing casualties, especially assassinations, increased over previous years. Over 30 percent of the attacks in 1980 resulted in at least one casualty.

Last year marked the first year that a large number of deadly terrorist attacks were carried out by national governments. The Libyan Government's assassination campaign against dissidents living in Europe and the exchange of terrorist attacks on diplomats in the Middle East were the most noteworthy examples of government-sponsored terrorism.

There was a sharp increase in right-wing terrorist activity in Europe. The attacks at the Munich Oktoberfest and at the railroad station in Bologna, Italy, rank among the worst terrorist incidents ever recorded.

On the positive side, incidents involving hostages and barricade incidents were more successfully countered in 1980, as governments became better equipped to deal with such situations. Two prominent hostage-takings — the Iranian Embassy in London and a skyjacking in Turkey — were countered successfully by military force, and another two in Latin America were resolved by careful negotiations.

## TRENDS

Both the number of international terrorist casualties ... and incidents ... were higher in 1980 than in 1979. Although there were fewer victims killed than in 1979 and fewer wounded than in 1974, there were more total casualties in 1980 than during any previous year since our data base was begun in 1968.

The number of terrorist incidents apparently aimed at causing casualties — most notably assassination attempts — increased dramatically in 1980. Assassinations and attempted assassinations have increased steadily since 1975; in 1980 almost twice as many such incidents took place as in any previous year. The high number of assassinations in 1980 is due, in part, to well-planned assassination campaigns by:

• The Muslim Brotherhood against the Soviet military in Syria.

• The Libyan Government against expatriates residing in Europe.

• Iran and Iraq, each targeting the other's diplomats in Europe and the Middle East.

• The Armenian terrorists against Turkish diplomats worldwide.

As has been noted in our previous surveys, however, most terrorist incidents do not cause casualties, and only one-fourth of all attacks between 1968 and 1980 resulted in death or personal injury.

Terrorists continue to prefer to conduct their operations in the industrialized democracies. Over 30 percent of the incidents took place in Western Europe alone, both by indigenous organizations against foreign targets and by foreign-based groups. About 20 percent of the incidents occurred in Latin America and another 20 percent in the Middle East.

There were 278 attacks on Americans in 1980 — the second highest of any year since 1968 — and 34 of these incidents caused casualties. Ten Americans, including six in El Salvador, two in Turkey, one in the Philippines, and one on the West Bank, were killed in international terrorist attacks, and 94 Americans were wounded. Damage to US property was recorded in 97 incidents (34 percent).

... Thirty-three percent of all attacks against Americans occurred in Latin America and 20 percent occurred in the Middle East. Attacks against Americans in 1980 were recorded in at least 51 countries; most of the attacks occurred in El Salvador, Turkey, the Philippines, West Germany, and Colombia.

Between 1968 and 1980, US and Canadian nationals were the most victimized; West Europeans were the second most frequent targets. US businessmen and diplomats — especially individuals who are symbols of Western power and wealth — are still the primary targets, with at least 38 percent of all events involving US citizens or property. Although businessmen have been the most frequent victims in past years, they were second only to US diplomats in 1980. One hundred and twelve attacks were directed against US diplomats — more than in any previous year. Most of these attacks occurred in Latin America, with one-quarter resulting in

465

damage to US property. About 30 percent of these incidents were telephone or letter threats received at US embassies or consulates. While these threats resulted in no direct damage or casualties, each was disruptive. They caused increased security efforts, personnel alerts, and absorbed time in searching for bombs or evacuating buildings.

Other countries whose nationals have been prominent victims are Israel, the United Kingdom, West Germany, France, Turkey and the Soviet Union. In 1980, the pattern of victims was somewhat different than in previous years. The US remained the primary target, but the order of the other major victims was different. The installations and citizens of the USSR were the second most frequent target followed by those of Turkey, Iraq, France, Iran, and Israel. . . .

The categories of attacks in 1980 were similar to previous years. Bombings were still the most favored operation. The most noteworthy change was the dramatic rise in the number of assassinations and skyjackings. The security precautions designed to make smuggling of traditional weapons on board airliners more difficult failed to deter skyjacking in 1980. Skyjackers effectively used threats, hoaxes, or nonmetallic weapons, with the result that skyjackings increased for the second consecutive year.

## [EVENTS WITH DEATHS OR INJURIES]

Analyses of the incidents that caused casualties highlight the dangers and broad psychological impact of international terrorism. They provoke a response from governments, attention from the world media, and almost always involve a well-trained and experienced terrorist organization.

Our records show 1,435 terrorist incidents between 1968 and 1980 that caused at least one casualty. The number of such attacks has generally increased each year since 1968. . . . In 1980, there were 213 of these incidents — far more than any in previous years. Bombings and assassinations accounted for over 65 percent of all incidents with casualties. Each of the other categories of attacks — kidnapings, barricade and hostage situations, and skyjackings — accounted for only a small portion of the casualties. Most of the attacks with casualties occurred in Western Europe and the Middle East. US citizens remained the most victimized of any nationality, but the percentage of events with US victims dropped from 38 percent for all incidents to 28 percent of all incidents with casualties. Citizens of the United Kingdom and Israel were also prominent victims of events with casualties. . . .

The overall pattern of international terrorist attacks in 1980 involving casualties is generally similar to previous years — that is, assassinations with small arms accounted for over 40 percent, and explosive bombings for 35 percent of the total incidents. Most of the attacks occurred in the Middle East and Western Europe. The most active groups in the attacks with casualties in 1980 were Iranian Government operations, Armenian terrorist groups, and the Muslim Brotherhood in Syria. The order of the most victimized nationalities was slightly different from that of previous years; the most numerous victims were Americans, Israelis, Soviets, Turks, Iraqis, and Libyans, in that order. In 1979 the most victimized nationalities were Americans, British, and French. In 1978, the US and British were the main victims.

## STATE-SPONSORED INTERNATIONAL TERRORISM

Nations support terrorist groups or engage in terrorist activity for a variety of reasons, ranging from the need to carry out their own policies in foreign countries to the desire to establish or strengthen regional or global influence.

Despite increased state support for international conventions and agreements designed to reduce international terrorism, a number of Third World nations are unwilling to back sanctions against states that support international terrorist groups or engage directly in international terrorist attacks.

Our files contain records of almost a hundred terrorist attacks conducted directly by national governments. They occurred in every year since 1972, but the majority of them took place in 1980. Almost half were assassinations or attempted assassinations. These state-sponsored attacks were more lethal than other terrorist incidents, with over 42 percent of them resulting in casualties. At least 33 victims were injured and another 40 killed in these 100 events. Most of them occurred in the Middle East, were carried out by Middle East nations, and were directed against citizens of other Middle East countries. They were almost always directed against diplomats.

**Soviet Union.** The Soviets are deeply engaged in support of revolutionary violence, which is a fundamental element of Leninist ideology. Such violence frequently entails acts of international terrorism. The ostensible position of the Soviets that they oppose terrorism while supporting so-called national liberation movements is further compromised by Moscow's close relationship with and aid to a number of governments and organizations which are direct supporters of purely terrorist groups. In the Middle East, for example, the Soviets sell large quantities of arms to Libya — knowing that Libya is a major supporter of terrorist groups — and they back a number of Palestinian groups that have conducted terrorist operations. In Latin America, Moscow relies heavily on Cuba — which provides guerrilla and terrorist groups with training, arms, sanctuary, and advice — to advance Soviet interests. In other parts of the world, particularly Africa, the Soviets have long supported guerrilla movements and national liberation organizations that occasionally engage in terrorism.

**Libya.** The government of Colonel Qadhafi is the most prominent state sponsor of and participant in international terrorism. Despite Qadhafi's repeated public pronouncements that he does not support terrorist groups, there has been a clear and consistent pattern of Libyan aid to almost every major international terrorist group, from the Provisional Irish Republican Army (PIRA) to the Popular Front for the Liberation of Palestine (PFLP).

One of Qadhafi's stated policies is to silence the Libyan students suspected of opposition activity and Libyan expatriates who have criticized his regime. Early in 1980, he warned Libyan exiles that they should return home, or they would be punished in place. During the remainder of the year. Qadhafi's assassination teams carried out his threats. Our records list 14 attacks by Libyan assassination teams in Europe and the United States. They occurred in seven countries and resulted in 11 Libyan exiles murdered and one wounded. The murder on 19 April 1980 of a well-known Libyan businessman in Rome and the assassination on 25 April last year of a Libyan lawyer in London are two examples of this assassination campaign.

Libya's support for terrorism includes financing for terrorist operations, weapons procurement and supply, the use of training camps and Libyan advisers for guerrilla training, and the use of Libyan diplomatic facilities abroad as support bases for terrorist operations. Libya has trained terrorists from Latin America, Western Europe, the Middle East, and East Asia. Qadhafi's major goals involve the Middle East and Africa, particularly the destruction of Israel, the advancement of the Palestinian cause, and the overthrow of conservative and moderate Arab states. Most of his efforts, therefore, are directed toward aiding Middle Eastern terrorism. His second concern is to be recognized as a champion of national liberation movements, especially those of an Islamic cast.

**South Yemen.** The Government of the People's Democratic Republic of Yemen provides camps and other training facilities for a number of international terrorist groups. The PFLP maintains a major terrorist training camp there, and members of many different terrorist groups have all benefited from the PFLP training facilities....

Our records from 1968 to 1980 suggest that the Government of South Yemen has not participated directly in international terrorist attacks and show that South Yemeni citizens have been involved in only a few incidents since 1968.

**Iraq.** During the past two years, the Iraqi Government has reduced its support for most terrorist groups. During the mid-1970s various West European terrorist groups reportedly received Iraqi aid, including training and logistical support. Iraq also provides assistance to some radical Palestinian organizations, including the Arab Liberation Front (ALF).

In 1980, the Iraqi Government conducted terrorist attacks against Iranian diplomats in Europe and the Middle East. These attacks resulted in the deaths of several Iranian diplomats.

**Syria.** As a major supporter of the Palestine Liberation Organization (PLO), Syria has played an increasingly important role in Palestinian activities. It has backed radical elements within the PLO, including the PFLP, the PFLP-General Command, and the Democratic Front for the

Liberation of Palestine. The Syrian Government also created Sa'iqa, whose Eagles of the Palestinian Revolution have been involved in terrorist attacks. . . .

**Iran.** Despite its radical, anti-Western policies, the Tehran government is not presently an active supporter of groups practicing international terrorism. Many groups currently seek Iranian support, but internal political upheavals, socioeconomic problems, and the war with Iraq now seem to be Tehran's main preoccupations.

In 1980, however, the Iranian Government itself initiated numerous acts of international terrorism. Our records list international terrorist attacks carried out by Iranian nationals last year — at least half of which were directly carried out by Iranian Government officials. These attacks occurred in Europe, the Middle East, and the United States. They included armed attacks on Iraqi diplomatic facilities and assassinations of Iraqi citizens. Most prominently, the taking of the US hostages in Tehran was a clear act of international terrorism, violating all norms of diplomatic behavior; this incident clearly was approved by the Iranian Government.

**Cuba.** Havana openly advocates armed revolution as the only means for leftist forces to gain power in Latin America, and the Cubans have played an important role in facilitating the movement of men and weapons into the region. Havana provides direct support in the form of training, arms, safe havens, and advice to a wide variety of guerrilla groups. Many of these groups engage in terrorist operations.

## RIGHT-WING TERRORISM

Most right-wing terrorism falls in the category of domestic violence and is not dealt with in this paper. When the attacks cross international boundaries or involve foreign victims such as the Bologna or Munich bombings, however, they are included in the records on international terrorism.

Right-wing terrorism is difficult to categorize and analyze, because it is perpetrated anonymously by groups with few or no articulated goals. Very little information is available on the type and frequency of the attacks, the group structure, or the personalities involved. Unlike publicity-seeking left-wing terrorist groups who tend to select targets that provide the greatest political impact, right-wing groups tend to be motivated by desire to terrorize or destroy specific enemies. These groups seldom indulge in such spectacular incidents as hostage-taking or hijackings; instead, they most often conduct assassinations and bombings. Some of the bombing attacks, however, have resulted in mass casualties and thus generated intense publicity.

The bombing of the train station in Bologna, Italy, and the explosion during Munich's Oktoberfest produced more casualties than any previous terrorist attacks in Western Europe.

## OUTLOOK

Although individual terrorist attacks rely heavily upon the element of surprise, general patterns of terrorist behavior are more predictable. There will be exceptions, but we expect certain trends evident in 1980 to carry over into 1981:

• The increase in casualties and casualty-producing incidents — particularly in light of the dramatic rise of assassinations — is especially significant. Although, mass casualty operations have been rare, terrorists may now believe that some casualities are necessary to generate the amount of publicity formerly evoked by less bloody operations.

• The vast majority of incidents will continue to be simple in conception and implementation, posing little risk to the perpetrators. Although added security precautions at sensitive facilities and paramilitary rescue squads may deter spectacular confrontational attacks, these measures clearly cannot protect all potential targets from simple hit-and-run operations.

• Regional patterns of victimization and location of operations are likely to remain virtually unchanged. Representatives of affluent countries, particularly US Government officials and business executives, will continue to be attractive targets. Latin America and the Middle East again are likely to be the main trouble spots.

• West German terrorists, having suffered reversals during the past three years, are likely to feel greater pressure to engage in operations in order to remind their domestic and international sympathizers that they remain revolutionary leaders.

• Most terrorist activity by right-wing groups will remain domestic in nature and thus will not be reflected in our statistics. Because rightist groups are often willing to engage in mass-casuality attacks, however, and because their operations are often effective, their activities will pose a significant danger to public order in many countries. We expect right-wing terrorist activity to increase in 1981.

• 1980 marked the first time a large number of terrorist assassinations were directly sponsored by governments. These attacks proved to be an efficient, low-cost method of achieving limited goals. Some Third World nations, especially Middle Eastern countries, are likely to continue this practice. Most notably, Iran and Iraq probably will continue their war of terrorism, and Syria is also likely to engage in terrorist attacks.

• The Palestinian groups continue to have a terrorist capability. Some rejectionist groups may seek to embarrass PLO leader Arafat and the moderate elements of the PLO by renewing their terrorist attacks against Western democracies. If progress is not made on resolving the Palestinian problem, Arafat will find it increasingly difficult to restrain extremist Palestinian groups from conducting international terrorist attacks.

• The Armenian Secret Army's assassination campaign against Turkish diplomats is likely to continue next year at an even greater pace. In addition to the Turks, Armenian terrorists may include Western, especially US, diplomats among their targets.

● International terrorism is a tactic of leftist insurgents in El Salvador and will continue to be a factor affecting political stability in El Salvador as well as Guatemala and, perhaps, Honduras.

● On the positive side, hostage situations were more successfully opposed in 1980, as more governments became better able to deal with hostage-takings. Improved training and equipment will probably enable governments to be even more effective in dealing with hostage situations in the future.

● The development and implementation of more effective international countermeasures will continue to be impeded by differing perspectives among nations, and by a reluctance on the part of many states to commit themselves to a course of action that might invite retribution — either by terrorist groups or by states sympathetic to the terrorists' cause.

# Appendix A
## Major International Terrorist Groups

... Groups such as the Provisional Irish Republican Army (PIRA) and the Basque Fatherland and Liberty Movement (ETA) primarily conduct operations against domestic targets, but they are also active in the international arena. The PIRA has conducted more international terrorist attacks than any other single terrorist group. They routinely attack the British military in Europe. The ETA has not been as active internationally as the PIRA, but they conducted a campaign of terrorism against French nationals in the Basque area of Spain. Some of the attacks described in this section are not included in the statistical totals in this paper because they did not involve more than one nation, but they do provide insight into the activities of these major groups.

### WESTERN EUROPE

Although PIRA was not as active in 1980 as in previous years, the group was able to attack symbols of the British Government and the Crown. The PIRA assassinated a British Army colonel and attempted to kill two other British soldiers stationed in Bielefeld, West Germany. The PIRA also tried to increase pressure on the British by attempting a mass casualty attack. They exploded a bomb on a crowded commuter train as it passed through a tunnel near Belfast, but three people were killed and 10 to 15 were injured.

Attempting to expand their tactics beyond violence, seven PIRA members in Northern Ireland's Maze Prison conducted a two-month hunger strike which captured the headlines in British newspapers. After weeks of negotiations, the British Government refused to grant political status to the prisoners, the PIRA's major demand. As several prisoners neared death, however, the British issued a statement proposing improvements in prison conditions. Perhaps realizing it was the best they could hope to achieve, the PIRA leaders called a halt to the strike. Although the hunger strike received a great deal of attention, it failed to bring about a change in the status of PIRA prisoners and apparently did little else to affect British policy in Northern Ireland. . . .

On 30 April, five armed men seized the Iranian Embassy in London. After capturing 26 hostages, they demanded the release of 91 prisoners and autonomy for an Arab province in Iran. They also demanded an aircraft to fly them to an undisclosed location. The terrorists released seven of the hostages and allowed two deadlines to pass without carrying out their threats. On 5 May, however, the terrorists killed two hostages, precipitating the British Government's decision to mount an assault on the Embassy. The Army's antiterrorist commandos stormed the building and rescued the remaining hostages, killing three terrorists and capturing two others. This successful operation was viewed as a major accomplishment by governments that have invested in costly training and elaborate contingency planning for antiterrorist strike forces.

On the European continent, the ETA, the Marxist-Leninist-oriented Basque separatist organization, assassinated dozens of police and military officers. . . .

Mainly because of the government's efficient countermeasures, West German terrorists of both the left and right carried out only a few international terrorist attacks during the year. The one major exception and one of the bloodiest attacks recorded in West German history was the bombing by right-wing terrorists at the Munich Oktoberfest. The explosive device could have killed hundreds of people had it not exploded prematurely while being emplaced in a crowded area. Instead, only 12 people were killed and another 200 injured. The terrorist handling the bomb was killed.

In Italy, both leftist and rightist terrorism continued in 1980, almost completely confined to domestic violence. The Red Brigades, although somewhat hampered by government actions, attacked symbols of the Italian establishment, including executives, a prominent newspaperman, a doctor from the prison system, and many policemen and civil servants. . . .

Although right-wing terrorism in Italy has been overshadowed by that of far-leftist groups for the past few years, it has continued to be active; the Italian Government credits almost one-half of all casualties from terrorism in Italy to right-wing groups. One of these groups — the neofascist Revolutionary Armed Nuclei — first claimed and then denied responsibility for the most lethal incident in 1980, a bomb attack at the Bologna railroad station on 2 August. Holiday travelers crowded the station and the explosion killed over 80 people and injured at least 200. . . .

Despite the imposition of martial law in all of Turkey's 67 provinces during the latter part of the year, the Secret Army for the Liberation of Armenia, the Dev Yol, and the Marxist-Leninist Armed Propaganda Unit (MLAPU) succeeded in generating mass publicity with a series of international terrorist attacks that caused the deaths of two US servicemen. The

Armenian terrorists appeared well trained, well equipped, and efficient as they conducted an assassination campaign against Turkish diplomats worldwide. These attacks occurred in Switzerland, Italy, Greece, France, the United States, and Australia. The Armenians also exploded bombs at Turkish facilities in Europe, the Middle East, and the United States.

The Dev Yol conducted numerous attacks in Turkey against both Turkish and US personnel and facilities. In November, they assassinated a US Air Force sergeant at his home in Adana, Turkey.

The MLAPU assassinated a US Navy chief petty officer and an El Al airport manager and carried out numerous attacks against Turkish and American facilities in Turkey.

## MIDDLE EAST

The US diplomatic hostages continued to be held by Iran through 1980. This operation differed from previous embassy seizures in several significant ways. In Tehran, the captors had the support of the government, which defied all rules of customary and codified international legal practice.

In Syria, the Muslim Brotherhood (MB) conducted an active and lethal assassination campaign against Soviet military advisers during the first part of 1980. The MB is a Muslim fundamentalist group that attacked Soviet targets to express a general dislike of the Soviet Union and the Assad regime and specific opposition to the Soviet invasion of Afghanistan.

Palestinian terrorist actions in 1980 did not reach the level experienced during the 1970s. The Iran-Iraq war divided the Arab world, diverting attention from the Palestinian issue and greatly complicating the PLO's attempts at diplomacy. The Syrian and Libyan Governments, along with many rejectionist Palestinian groups, attempted to pressure Arafat into curtailing his diplomacy and keeping his distance from moderate Arab states.

Fatah, the largest group in the PLO, while presumably waiting for the results of Arafat's diplomatic initiatives, restricted its international terrorist attacks to Middle East countries. Fatah also continued to train groups that often use terrorism and maintained contacts with supporters abroad.

Other Palestinian groups met with mixed success. The Palestinian Front for the Liberation of Palestine-General Command and the Black June Organization continued operations against Israel and carried out attacks in other Middle East countries, especially Lebanon. The PFLP was relatively inactive after its leader, George Habbash, was incapacitated following surgery in September.

## LATIN AMERICA

In Colombia the 19th of April Movement (M-19) conducted one of the most publicized terrorist attacks of 1980. On 27 February, armed members of M-19 shot their way into the Dominican Republic Embassy in Bogota.

They timed the attack to coincide with a diplomatic reception. After taking 57 people hostage, including the ambassadors of 11 countries, the terrorists demanded the release of 311 prisoners, a $50 million ransom, and safe passage out of the country. During the course of the protracted negotiations, the terrorists freed a majority of hostages and vastly scaled down their demands. They finally accepted safe passage to Cuba and a $2 million private ransom. The entire incident lasted 61 days and illustrated the success of careful, patient negotiation by responsible governments in a hostage situation.

In El Salvador, at least 10,000 people were reported killed by left- and right-wing groups as the nation's domestic strife spread. El Salvador also ranks high among countries affected by international terrorism. The primary targets of attacks in El Salvador included embassies and private facilities from other Central American countries, the United States, and Israel. Several diplomats and business officials were also assassinated....  The [Panamanian] embassy [in San Salvador] seizure ended with the safe release of the hostages. In addition the U.S. Embassy was seriously damaged by a People's Revolutionary Army (ERP) rocket attack on 16 September 1980.

In Guatemala, international terrorist attacks followed a similar pattern. Leftist terrorist groups attacked facilities of a few foreign countries and kidnaped foreign nationals....

## Appendix B
## Antiterrorist Measures

### REGIONAL COOPERATION

In 1980, cooperation in combating terrorism was a topic of discussion among European countries. In November, the North Atlantic Assembly adopted a resolution on terrorism that urged member governments and parliaments of the North Atlantic Alliance to exchange information on terrorist-related groups.... In December, the 15 NATO foreign ministers adopted a Declaration on Terrorism and the US hostages in Iran. That declaration vigorously condemned terrorist acts as particularly odious, regardless of their cause or objectives....

### UNITED NATIONS

During 1980, four nations ratified the General Assembly's convention against the taking of hostages. The convention, which had been in various UN committees for three years, was adopted by consensus in December 1979. It calls for states to prosecute or extradite hostage-takers without exception. Language on the rights of national liberation movements, the right of asylum, and the Geneva conventions and protocols on the law of war was included, thereby insuring greater support for the final document. Forty states have signed the convention, which will come into effect when it is ratified by 18 more states.

In December, the General Assembly also adopted a consensus resolution sponsored by the Nordic countries calling for effective measures to enhance the protection, security, and safety of diplomatic and consular missions. The resolution reaffirmed the need for all states to ensure the security of diplomatic missions and to prohibit on their territories illegal activities directed against such offices. . . .

# COURT ON DOUBLE CELLING
# OF PRISONERS
## June 15, 1981

*By an 8-1 vote the Supreme Court decided June 15 that placing two prisoners in a cell intended for one does not, by itself, violate the Constitution's Eighth Amendment stricture against cruel and unusual punishment. The decision reversed the rulings of two lower courts and noted that the relatively new prison at issue in the case, the Southern Ohio Correctional Facility (SOCF), was considered a model facility by penal experts.*

*Writing for a five-member majority, Justice Lewis F. Powell Jr. said that prison conditions "must not involve the wanton and unnecessary infliction of pain, nor may they be grossly disproportionate to the severity of the crime warranting imprisonment." Deprivations of basic human needs "could be cruel and unusual," but conditions that are "harsh and restrictive" are not unconstitutional unless they can also be said to violate contemporary standards of decency. Justice Powell added, "To the extent that such conditions are restrictive and even harsh, they are part of the penalty that criminal offenders pay for their offenses against society."*

*The case, Rhodes v. Chapman, was initiated by two inmates of SOCF. The prison, built in the early 1970s, consisted of 1,620 cells, each measuring 63 square feet. A minimum of 60 square feet per person was considered the acceptable standard by the American Public Health Association, the Justice Department and other experts. At the time of the trial, 1,400 of the facility's 2,300 inmates were sharing cells, but three quarters of the prison population had the option of spending most of their waking hours in the institution's day rooms, work places, schools, library or gymnasiums. It was not alleged that the size of the prison population had led to deprivations of food, medical care or sanitation. Although prison jobs and educational opportunities were curtailed due to the increased numbers of prisoners, this kind of deprivation was not considered punishment by any of the courts involved in the case.*

*Justice Powell was joined in his opinion by Chief Justice Warren E. Burger and Justices William H. Rehnquist, Potter Stewart and Byron R. White.*

## Necessity of Judicial Review

*Justice William J. Brennan Jr. filed a concurring opinion in which Justices Harry A. Blackmun and John Paul Stevens joined. Brennan emphasized that the decision "should in no way be construed as a retreat from careful judicial scrutiny of prison conditions...." He pointed out that, although this was the first time the Supreme Court had ruled on what prison conditions constitute cruel and unusual punishment, the question had been addressed repeatedly by lower courts. In at least 24 states, individual prisons or whole prison systems had been found unconstitutional under the Eighth and Fourteenth Amendments. Brennan stated that judicial intervention was indispensable if constitutional dictates and basic humanitarian considerations were to be observed in prisons.*

*Brennan said that overcrowding and cramped living conditions were the most common problem in prison administration. According to National Institute of Justice statistics, two thirds of all inmates in federal, state and local correctional facilities were housed in cells or dormitories providing less than the minimum standard. "Public apathy and the political powerlessness of inmates have contributed to the perverse neglect of the prisons," he said. Even conscientious prison officials could do little if the state legislatures were unwilling to spend tax money to improve the facilities. Under these circumstances, he said, the courts were in "the strongest position to insist that unconstitutional conditions be remedied, even at significant financial cost."*

## Dissenting Opinion

*Justice Thurgood Marshall dissented on the grounds that conditions at the Ohio prison ran counter to the state's policies for prison administration. "No one argued at the trial and no one has contended here that double celling was a legislative policy judgment," he said. He stated that he saw no reason to reverse the conclusions of two courts that the overcrowding, if permitted to continue, would cause deterioration in the prisoners' mental and physical health. He further stated that "too often state governments are insensitive to the requirements of the Eighth Amendment, as evidenced by the repeated need for federal intervention to protect the rights of inmates."*

*Following are excerpts from the majority opinions of Justices Lewis F. Powell Jr. and William J. Brennan Jr. that the double celling of prisoners was not unconstitutional and the dissenting opinion of Justice Thurgood Marshall:*

No. 80-332

| James A. Rhodes et al., Petitioners, *v.* Kelly Chapman et al. | On Writ of Certiorari to the United States Court of Appeals for the Sixth Circuit. |

[June 15, 1981]

JUSTICE POWELL delivered the opinion of the Court.

The question presented is whether the housing of two inmates in a single cell at the Southern Ohio Correctional Facility is cruel and unusual punishment prohibited by the Eighth and Fourteenth Amendments.

I

Respondents Kelly Chapman and Richard Jaworski are inmates at the Southern Ohio Correctional Facility (SOCF), a maximum-security state prison in Lucasville, Ohio. They were housed in the same cell when they brought this action in the District Court for the Southern District of Ohio on behalf of themselves and all inmates similarly situated at SOCF. Asserting a cause of action under 42 U.S.C. § 1983, they contended that "double celling" at SOCF violated the Constitution. The gravamen of their complaint was that double celling confined cellmates too closely. It also was blamed for overcrowding at SOCF, said to have overwhelmed the prisons facilities and staff. As relief, respondents sought an injunction barring petitioners, who are Ohio officials responsible for the administration of SOCF, from housing more than one inmate in a cell, except as a temporary measure.

The District Court made extensive findings of fact about SOCF on the basis of evidence presented at trial and the court's own observations during an inspection that it conducted without advance notice. These findings describe the physical plant, inmate population, and effects of double celling. Neither party contends that these findings are erroneous.

SOCF was built in the early 1970's. In addition to 1620 cells, it has gymnasiums, workshops, school rooms, "day rooms," two chapels, a hospital ward, commissary, barber shop, and library. Outdoors, SOCF has a recreation field, visitation area, and garden. The District Court described this physical plant as "unquestionably a top-flight, first-class facility."

Each cell at SOCF measures approximately 63 square feet. Each contains a bed measuring 36 by 80 inches, a cabinet-type night stand, a wall-mounted sink with hot and cold running water, and a toilet that the inmate can flush from inside the cell. Cells housing two inmates have a two-tiered bunk bed. Every cell has a heating and air circulation vent near the ceiling, and 960 of the cells have a window that inmates can open and close. All of the cells have a cabinet, shelf, and radio built into one of the walls, and in all of the cells one wall consists of bars through which the inmates can be seen.

The "day rooms" are located adjacent to the cell blocks and are open to inmates between 6:30 a.m. and 9:30 p.m. According to the District Court, "[t]he day rooms are in a sense part of the cells and they are designed to furnish that type of recreation or occupation which an ordinary citizen would seek in his living room or den." Each day room contains a wall-mounted television, card tables, and chairs. Inmates can pass between their cells and the day rooms during a 10-minute period each hour, on the hour, when the doors to the day rooms and cells are opened.

As to the inmate population, the District Court found that SOCF began receiving inmates in late 1972 and double celling them in 1975 because of an increase in Ohio's state-wide prison population. At the time of trial, SOCF housed 2,300 inmates, 67% of whom were serving life or other long-term sentences for first-degree felonies. Approximately 1,400 inmates were double celled. Of these, about 75% had the choice of spending much of their waking hours outside their cells, in the day rooms, school, workshops, library, visits, meals, or showers. The other double celled inmates spent more time locked in their cells because of a restrictive classification.

The remaining findings by the District Court addressed respondents' allegations that overcrowding created by double celling overwhelmed SOCF's facilities and staff. The food was "adequate in every respect," and respondents adduced no evidence "whatsoever that prisoners have been underfed or that food facilities have been taxed by the prison population." The air ventilation system was adequate, the cells were substantially free of offensive odor, the temperature in the cell blocks was well controlled, and the noise in the cell blocks was not excessive. Double celling had not reduced significantly the availability of space in the dayrooms or visitation facilities, nor had it rendered inadequate the resources of the library or school rooms. Although there were isolated incidents of failure to provide medical or dental care, there was no evidence of indifference by the SOCF staff to inmates' medical or dental needs. As to violence, the court found that the number of acts of violence at SOCF had increased with the prison population, but only in proportion to the increase in population. Respondents failed to produce evidence establishing that double celling itself caused greater violence, and the ratio of guards to inmates at SOCF satisfied the standard of acceptability offered by respondents' expert witness. Finally, the court did find that the SOCF administration, faced with more inmates than jobs, had "water[ed] down" jobs by assigning more inmates to each job than necessary and by reducing the number of hours that each inmate worked; it also found that SOCF had not increased its staff of psychiatrists and social workers since double celling had begun.

Despite these generally favorable findings, the District Court concluded that double celling at SOCF was cruel and unusual punishment. The court rested its conclusion on five considerations. One, inmates at SOCF are serving long terms of imprisonment. In the court's view, that fact "can only accent[uate] the problems of close confinement and overcrowding." Two, SOCF housed 38% more inmates at the time of trial than its "design capacity." In reference to this the court asserted, "Overcrowding necessarily involves excess limitation of general movement as well as physical and mental injury from long exposure." Three, the court accepted as contemporary standards of decency several studies recommending that each person in an institution have at least 50-55 square feet of living quarters. In contrast, double celled inmates at SOCF share 63 square feet. Four, the court asserted that "[a]t best a prisoner who is double celled will spend most of his time in the cell with his cellmate." Five, SOCF has made double celling a practice; it is not a temporary condition.

On appeal to the Court of Appeals for the Sixth Circuit, petitioners argued that the District Court's conclusion must be read, in light of its findings, as holding that double celling is *per se* unconstitutional. The Court of Appeals disagreed; it viewed the District Court's opinion as holding only that double celling is cruel and unusual punishment under the circumstances at SOCF. It affirmed, without further opinion, on the ground that the District Court's findings were not clearly erroneous, its conclusions of law were "permissible from the findings," and its remedy was a reasonable response to the violations found.

We granted the petition for certiorari because of the importance of the question to prison administration. We now reverse.

## II

We consider here for the first time the limitation that the Eighth Amendment, which is applicable to the States through the Fourteenth Amendment, *Robinson* v. *California,* (1962), imposes upon the conditions in which a State may confine those convicted of crimes. It is unquestioned that "[c]onfinement in a prison ... is a form of punishment subject to scrutiny under the Eighth Amendment standards." *Hutto* v. *Finney* (1978).... But until this case, we have not considered a disputed contention that the conditions of commitment at a particular prison constituted cruel and unusual punishment. Nor have we had an occasion to consider specifically the principles relevant to assessing claims that conditions of confinement violate the Eighth Amendment. We look, first, to the Eighth

Amendment precedents for the general principles that are relevant to a State's authority to impose punishments for criminal conduct.

## A

The Eighth Amendment, in only three words, imposes the constitutional limitation upon punishments: they cannot be "cruel and unusual." The Court has interpreted these words "in a flexible and dynamic manner," *Gregg* v. *Georgia* (1976) (joint opinion), and has extended the Amendment's reach beyond the barbarous physical punishments at issue in the Court's earliest cases. See *Wilkerson* v. *Utah* (1879); *In re Kremmler* (1890). Today the Eighth Amendment prohibits punishments which, although not physically barbarous, "involve the unnecessary and wanton infliction of pain," *Gregg* v. *Georgia,* or are grossly disproportionate to the severity of the crime, *Coker* v. *Georgia* (1977) (plurality opinion); *Weems* v. *United States* (1910). Among "unnecessary and wanton" inflictions of pain are those that are "totally without penological justification." *Gregg* v. *Georgia; Estelle* v. *Gamble* (1976).

No static "test" can exist by which courts determine whether conditions of confinement are cruel and unusual, for the Eighth Amendment "must draw its meaning from the evolving standards of decency that mark the progress of a maturing society." *Trop* v. *Dulles* (1957) (plurality opinion). The Court has held, however, that "Eighth Amendment judgments should neither be nor appear to be merely the subjective views" of judges. *Rummel* v. *Estelle* (1980). To be sure, "the Constitution contemplates that in the end [a court's] own judgment will be brought to bear on the question of the acceptability" of a given punishment. *Coker* v. *Georgia* (plurality opinion); *Gregg* v. *Georgia* (joint opinion). But such " 'judgment[s] should be informed by objective factors to the maximum extent possible.' " *Rummel* v. *Estelle,* quoting *Coker* v. *Georgia* (plurality opinion). For example, when the question was whether capital punishment for certain crimes violated contemporary values, the Court looked for "objective indicia" derived from history, the action of state legislatures, and the sentencing by juries. . . . Our conclusion in *Estelle* v. *Gamble* that deliberate indifference to an inmates medical needs is cruel and unusual punishment rested on the fact, recognized by the common law and state legislatures, that "[a]n inmate must rely on prison authorities to treat his medical needs; if the authorities fail to do so, those needs will not be met."

These principles apply when the conditions of confinement compose the punishment at issue. Conditions must not involve the wanton and unnecessary infliction of pain, nor may they be grossly disproportionate to the severity of the crime warranting imprisonment. In *Estelle* v. *Gamble* we held that the denial of medical care is cruel and unusual because, in the worst case, it can result in physical torture, and, even in less serious cases, it can result in pain without any penological purpose. In *Hutto* the conditions of confinement in two Arkansas prisons constituted cruel and unusual punishment because they resulted in unquestioned and serious deprivations of basic human needs. Conditions other than those in *Gamble* and *Hutto,* alone or in combination, may deprive inmates of the minimal civilized measure of life's necessities. Such conditions could be cruel and unusual under the contemporary standard of decency that we recognized in *Gamble.* But conditions that cannot be said to be cruel and unusual under contemporary standards are not unconstitutional. To the extent that such conditions are restrictive and even harsh, they are part of the penalty that criminal offenders pay for their offenses against society.

**B**

In view of the District Court's findings of fact, its conclusion that double celling at SOCF constitutes cruel and unusual punishment is insupport-able. Virtually every one of the court's findings tends to *refute* respon-dents' claim. The double celling made necessary by the unanticipated increase in prison population did not lead to deprivations of essential food, medical care, or sanitation. Nor did it increase violence among inmates or create other conditions intolerable for prison confinement. Although job and educational opportunities diminished marginally as a result of double celling, limited work hours and delay before receiving education do not inflict pain, much less unnecessary and wanton pain; deprivations of this kind simply are not punishments. We would have to wrench the Eighth Amendment from its language and history to hold that delay of these desirable aids to rehabilitation violates the Constitution.

The five considerations on which the District Court relied also are insufficient to support its constitutional conclusion. The court relied on the long terms of imprisonment served by inmates at SOCF; the fact that SOCF housed 38% more inmates than its "design capacity"; the recom-mendation of several studies that each inmate have at least 50-55 square feet of living quarters; the suggestion that double celled inmates spend most of their time in their cells with their cellmates; and the fact that double celling at SOCF was not a temporary condition. These general considerations fall far short in themselves of proving cruel and unusual punishment, for there is no evidence that double celling under these circumstances either inflicts unnecessary or wanton pain or is grossly disproportionate to the severity of crimes warranting imprisonment. At most, these considerations amount to a theory that double celling inflicts pain. Perhaps they reflect an aspiration toward an ideal environment for long-term confinement. But the Constitution does not mandate comfort-able prisons, and prisons of SOCF's type, which house persons convicted of serious crimes, cannot be free of discomfort. Thus, these considerations properly are weighed by the legislature and prison administration rather than a court. There being no constitutional violation, the District Court had no authority to consider whether double celling in light of these considerations was the best response to the increase in Ohio's state-wide prison population.

## III

This court must proceed cautiously in making an Eighth Amendment judgment because, unless we reverse it, "[a] decision that a given punishment is impermissible under the Eighth Amendment cannot be reversed short of a constitutional amendment," and thus "[r]evisions cannot be made in the light of further experience." *Gregg* v. *Georgia*. In assessing claims that conditions of confinement are cruel and unusual, courts must bear in mind that their inquiries "spring from constitutional requirements and that judicial answers to them must reflect that fact rather than a court's idea of how best to operate a detention facility." *Bell* v. *Wolfish* [1979].

Courts certainly have a responsibility to scrutinize claims of cruel and unusual confinement, and conditions in a number of prisons, especially older ones, have just been described as "deplorable" and "sordid." *Bell* v. *Wolfish*. When conditions of confinement amount to cruel and unusual punishment, "federal courts will discharge their duty to protect constitutional rights." *Procunier* v. *Martinez* (1974).... In discharging this oversight responsibility, however, courts cannot assume that state legislatures and prison officials are insensitive to the requirements of the Constitution or to the perplexing sociological problems of how best to achieve the goals of the penal function in the criminal justice system: to punish justly, to deter future crime, and to return imprisoned persons to society with an improved chance of being useful, law-abiding citizens.

In this case, the question before us is whether the conditions of confinement at SOCF are cruel and unusual. As we find that they are not, the judgment of the Court of Appeals is reversed.

*It is so ordered.*

JUSTICE BRENNAN, with whom JUSTICE BLACKMUN and JUSTICE STEVENS join, concurring in the judgment.

Today's decision reaffirms that "[c]ourts do have a responsibility to scrutinize claims of cruel and unusual confinement." With that I agree. I also agree that the District Court's findings in this case do not support a judgment that the practice of double-celling in the Southern Ohio Correctional Facility is in violation of the Eighth Amendment. I write separately, however, to emphasize that today's decision should in no way be construed as a retreat from careful judicial scrutiny of prison conditions, and to discuss the factors courts should consider in undertaking such scrutiny.

## I

Although this Court has never before considered what prison conditions constitute "cruel and unusual punishment" within the meaning of the Eighth Amendment, such questions have been addressed repeatedly by the lower courts. In fact, individual prisons or entire prison systems in at least

24 States have been declared unconstitutional under the Eighth and Fourteenth Amendments, with litigation underway in many others. Thus, the lower courts have learned from repeated investigation and bitter experience that judicial intervention is *indispensable* if constitutional dictates — not to mention considerations of basic humanity — are to be observed in the prisons.

No one familiar with litigation in this area could suggest that the courts have been overeager to usurp the task of running prisons, which, as the Court today properly notes, is entrusted in the first instance to the "legislature and prison administration rather than a court." And certainly, no one could suppose that the courts have ordered creation of "comfortable prisons," on the model of country clubs. To the contrary, "the soul-chilling inhumanity of conditions in American prisons has been thrust upon the judicial conscience." *Inmates of Suffolk County Jail* v. *Eisenstadt* (Mass. 1973).

Judicial opinions in this area do not make pleasant reading. For example, in *Pugh* v. *Locke* (1978), Judge Frank Johnson described in gruesome detail the conditions then prevailing in the Alabama penal system. The institutions were "horrendouly overcrowded," to the point where some inmates were forced to sleep on mattresses spread on floors in hallways and next to urinals. The physical facilities were "dilapidat[ed]" and "filthy," the cells infested with roaches, flies, mosquitoes, and other vermin. Sanitation facilities were limited and in ill repair, emitting an "overpowering odor"; in one instance over 200 men were forced to share one toilet. Inmates were not provided with toothpaste, toothbrush, shampoo, shaving cream, razors, combs, or other such necessities. Food was "unappetizing and unwholesome," poorly prepared and often infested with insects, and served without reasonable utensils. There were no meaningful vocational, educational, recreational or work programs. A United States health officer described the prisons as "wholly unfit for human habitation according to virtually every criterion used for evaluation by public health inspectors." Perhaps the worst of all was the "rampant violence" within the prison. Weaker inmates were "repeatedly victimized" by the stronger; robbery, rape, extortion, theft, and assault were "everyday occurrences among the general inmate population." Faced with this record, the court — not surprisingly — found that the conditions of confinement constituted cruel and unusual punishment, and issued a comprehensive remedial order affecting virtually every aspect of prison administration. . . .

Overcrowding and cramped living conditions are particularly pressing problems in many prisons. Out of 82 court orders in effect concerning conditions of confinement in federal and state correctional facilities as of March 31, 1978, 26 involved the issue of overcrowding. Two-thirds of all inmates in federal, state, and local correctional facilities were confined in cells or dormitories providing less than 60 square feet per person — the minimal standard deemed acceptable by the American Public Health Association, the Justice Department, and other authorities.

The problems of administering prisons within constitutional standards are indeed "complex and intractable," but at their core is a lack of resources allocated to prisons. Confinement of prisoners is unquestionably an expensive proposition: the average direct current expenditure at adult institutions in 1977 was $5,461 per inmate; the average cost of constructing space for an additional prisoner is estimated at $25,000 to $50,000. Oftentimes, funding for prisons has been dramatically below that required to comply with basic constitutional standards. For example, to bring the Louisiana prison system into compliance required a supplemental appropriation of $18,431,622 for a single year's operating expenditures, and of $105,605,000 for capital outlays.

Over the last decade, correctional resources, never ample, have lagged behind burgeoning prison populations. In *Ruiz* v. *Estelle* (SD Tex. 1980), for example, the court stated that an "unprecedented upsurge" in the number of inmates has "undercut any realistic expectation" of eliminating double- and triple-celling, despite construction of a new $43 million unit. The number of inmates in federal and state correctional facilities has risen 42% since 1975, and last year grew at its fastest rate in 3 years. A major infusion of money would be required merely to keep pace with prison populations.

Public apathy and the political powerlessness of inmates have contributed to the pervasive neglect of the prisons. Chief Judge Henley observed that the people of Arkansas "knew little or nothing about their penal system" prior to the *Holt* litigation, despite "sporadic and sensational" exposes. *Holt* v. *Sarver* (ED Ark. 1970). Prison inmates are "voteless, politically unpopular, and socially threatening." Thus, the suffering of prisoners, even if known, generally "moves the community in only the most severe and exceptional cases." As a result even conscientious prison officials are "[c]aught in the middle," as state legislatures refuse "to spend sufficient tax dollars to bring conditions in outdated prisons up to minimally acceptable standards." *Johnson* v. *Levine* (CA4 1978). After extensive exposure to this process, Judge Pettine came to view the "barbaric physical conditions" of Rhode Island's prison system as "the ugly and shocking outward manifestations of a deeper dysfunction, an attitude of cynicism, hopelessness, predatory selfishness, and callous indifference that appears to infect, to one degree or another, almost everyone who comes in contact with the [prison]." *Palmigiano* v. *Garrahy* (CA1 1979).

Under these circumstances, the courts have emerged as a critical force behind efforts to ameliorate inhumane conditions. Insulated as they are from political pressures, and charged with the duty of enforcing the Constitution, courts are in the strongest position to insist that unconstitutional conditions be remedied, even at significant financial cost....

Progress toward constitutional conditions of confinement in the Nation's prisons has been slow and uneven, despite judicial pressure. Nevertheless, it is clear that judicial intervention has been responsible, not only for remedying some of the worst abuses by direct order, but for "forcing the legislative branch of government to reevaluate correction policies and to appropriate funds for upgrading penal systems.". . .

[Section II Omitted]

## III

. . . Virtually the only serious complaint of the inmates at the Southern Ohio Correctional Facility is that 1,280 of the 1,620 cells are used to house two inmates.

I have not the slightest doubt that 63 square feet of cell space is not enough for two men. I understand that every major study of living space in prisons has so concluded. That prisoners are housed under such conditions is an unmistakeable signal to the legislators and officials of Ohio: either more prison facilities should be built or expanded, or fewer persons should be incarcerated in prisons. Even so, the findings of the District Court do not support a conclusion that the conditions at the Southern Ohio Correctional Facility — cramped though they are — constitute cruel and unusual punishment.

The "touchstone" of the Eighth Amendment inquiry is "the effect upon the imprisoned." The findings of the District Court leave no doubt that the prisoners are adequately sheltered, fed, and protected, and that opportunities for education, work, and rehabilitative assistance are available. One need only compare the District Court's description of conditions at the Southern Ohio Correctional Facility with descriptions of other major state and federal facilities . . . to realize that this prison, crowded though it is, is one of the better, more humane large prisons in the Nation.

The consequence of the District Court's order might well be to make life worse for many Ohio inmates, at least in the short run. As a result of the order, some prisoners have been transferred to the Columbus Correctional Facility, a deteriorating prison nearly 150 years old, itself the subject of litigation over conditions of confinement and under a preliminary order enjoining racially segregative and punitive practices. . . .

The District Court may well be correct *in the abstract* that prison overcrowding and double-celling such as existed at the Southern Ohio Correctional Facility generally results in serious harm to the inmates. But cases are not decided in the abstract. A court is under the obligation to examine the *actual effect* of challenged conditions upon the well-being of the prisoners. The District Court in this case was unable to identify any actual signs that the double-celling at the Southern Ohio Correctional Facility has seriously harmed the inmates there; indeed, the Court's findings of fact suggest that crowding at the prison has not reached the point of causing serious injury. Since I cannot conclude that the totality of conditions at the facility offends constitutional norms, and am of the view that double-celling in itself is not *per se* impermissible, I concur in the judgment of the Court.

487

JUSTICE MARSHALL, dissenting.

From reading the Court's opinion in this case, one would surely conclude that the Southern Ohio Correctional Facility (SOCF) is a safe, spacious prison that happens to include many two-inmate cells because the State has determined that that is the best way to run the prison. But the facility described by the majority is not the one involved in this case. SOCF is overcrowded, unhealthful, and dangerous. None of those conditions results from a considered policy judgment on the part of the State. Until the Court's opinion today, absolutely no one — certainly not the "state legislatures" or "prison officials" to whom the majority suggests . . . that we defer in analyzing constitutional questions — had suggested that forcing long-term inmates to share tiny cells designed to hold only one individual might be a good thing. On the contrary, as the District Court noted, "everybody" is in agreement that double celling is undesirable. No one argued at trial and no one has contended here that double celling was a legislative policy judgment. No one has asserted that prison officials imposed it as a disciplinary or a security matter. And no one has claimed that the practice has anything whatsoever to do with "punish[ing] justly," "deter[ring] future crime," or "return[ing] imprisoned persons to society with an improved chance of being useful, law-abiding citizens." The evidence and the District Court's findings clearly demonstrate that the *only* reason double celling was imposed on inmates at the SOCF was that more individuals were sent there than the prison was ever designed to hold.

I do not dispute that the state legislature indeed made policy judgments when it built SOCF. It decided that Ohio needed a maximum security prison that would house some 1600 inmates. In keeping with prevailing expert opinion, the legislature made the further judgments that each inmate would have his own cell and that each cell would have approximately 63 square feet of floor space. But because of prison overcrowding, hundreds of the cells are shared, or "doubled," which is hardly what the legislature intended.

In a doubled cell, each inmate has only some 30-35 square feet of floor space. Most of the windows in the Supreme Court building are larger than that. The conclusion of every expert who testified at trial and of every serious study of which I am aware is that a long-term inmate must have to himself, at the very least, 50 square feet of floor space — an area smaller than that occupied by a good-sized automobile — in order to avoid serious mental, emotional, and physical deterioration. The District Court found that as a fact. Even petitioners, in their brief in this Court, concede that double celling as practiced at SOCF is "less than desirable."

The Eighth Amendment "embodies 'broad and idealistic concepts of dignity, civilized standards, humanity, and decency,'" against which conditions of confinement must be judged. *Estelle* v. *Gamble* (1976), quoting *Jackson* v. *Bishop* (CA8 1968). Thus the State cannot impose punishment that violates "the evolving standards of decency that mark the progress of a maturing society." *Trop* v. *Dulles* (1957) (plurality opinion). For me, the legislative judgment and the consistent conclusions by those who have studied the problem provide considerable evidence that those standards condemn imprisonment in conditions so crowded that serious harm will result. The record amply demonstrates that those conditions are present here. It is surely not disputed that SOCF is severely overcrowded. The prison is operating at 38% above its design capacity. It is also significant that some two-thirds of the inmates at SOCF are serving lengthy or life sentences, for, as we have said elsewhere, "the length of confinement cannot be ignored in deciding whether the confinement meets constitutional standards." *Hutto* v. *Finney* (1978). Nor is double celling a short-term response to a temporary problem. The trial court found, and it is not contested, that double celling, if not enjoined, will continue for the forseeable future. The trial court also found that most of the double-celled inmates spend most of their time in their cells.

It is simply not true, as the majority asserts, that "there is no evidence that double celling under these circumstances either inflicts unnecessary or wanton pain or is grossly disproportionate to the severity of crimes warranting imprisonment." The District Court concluded from the record before it that long exposure to these conditions will *"necessarily"* involve "excess limitation of general movement as well as physical and mental injury..." (emphasis added). And of course, of all the judges who have been involved in this case, the trial judge is the only one who has actually visited the prison. That is simply an additional reason to give in this case the deference we have always accorded to the careful conclusions of the finder of fact. There is not a shred of evidence to suggest that anyone who has given the matter serious thought has ever approved, as the majority does today, conditions of confinement such as those present at SOCF. I see no reason to set aside the concurrent conclusions of two courts that the overcrowding and double celling here in issue are sufficiently severe that they will, if left unchecked, cause deterioration in respondents' mental and physical health. These conditions in my view go well beyond temporary standards of decency and therefore violate the Eighth and Fourteenth Amendments. I would affirm the judgment of the Court of Appeals.

If the majority did not more than state its disagreement with the courts below over the proper reading of the record, I would end my opinion here. But the Court goes further, adding some unfortunate dicta that may be read as a warning to federal courts against interference with a State's operation of its prisons. If taken too literally, the majority's admonitions might eviscerate the federal courts' traditional role of preventing a State from imposing cruel and unusual punishment through its conditions of confinement.

The majority concedes that federal courts "certainly have a responsibility to scrutinize claims of cruel and unusual confinement," but adds an apparent caveat:

"In discharging this oversight responsibility, however, courts cannot assume that state legislatures and prison officials are insensitive to the requirements of the Constitution or to the perplexing sociological problems of how best to achieve the goals of the penal function in the criminal justice system: to punish justly, to deter future crime, and to return imprisoned persons to society with an improved chance of being useful, law-abiding citizens."

As I suggested at the outset, none of this has anything to do with this case, because no one contends that the State had those goals in mind when it permitted SOCF to become overcrowded. This dictum, moreover, takes far too limited a view of the proper role of a federal court in an Eighth Amendment proceeding and, I add with some regret, far too sanguine a view of the motivations of state legislators and prison officials. Too often, state governments truly are "insensitive to the requirements of the Eighth Amendment," as is evidenced by the repeated need for federal intervention to protect the rights of inmates. See, *e. g., Hutto* v. *Finney* (1978) (lengthy periods of punitive isolation); *Estelle* v. *Gamble* (1976) (failure to treat inmate's medical needs); *Battle* v. *Anderson* (CA10 1977) (severe overcrowding); *Gates* v. *Collier* (CA5 1974) (overcrowding and poor housing conditions); *Holt* v. *Sarver* (CA8 1971) (unsafe conditions and inmate abuse); *Pugh* v. *Locke* (1978) (constant fear of violence and physical harm)....

A society must punish those who transgress its rules. When the offense is severe, the punishment should be of proportionate severity. But the punishment must always be administered within the limitations set down by the Constitution. With the rising crime rates of recent years, there has been an alarming tendency toward a simplistic penological philosophy that if we lock the prison doors and throw away the keys, our streets will somehow be safe. In the current climate, it is unrealistic to expect legislators to care whether the prisons are overcrowded or harmful to inmate health. It is at that point — when conditions are deplorable and the political process offers no redress — that the federal courts are required by the Constitution to play a role. I believe that this vital duty was properly discharged by the District Court and the Court of Appeals in this case. The majority today takes a step toward abandoning that role altogether. I dissent.

# COURT ON WORKER HEALTH
## June 17, 1981

*By a 5-3 vote the Supreme Court June 17 ruled that the regulations protecting textile workers from exposure to toxic substances must be upheld without regard to the balance between costs and benefits. Ruling on two cases,* American Textile Manufacturers Institute v. Donovan *and* National Cotton Council v. Donovan, *the court found that Congress had struck that balance itself when it enacted the 1970 Occupational Safety and Health Act. The law required the Occupational Safety and Health Administration (OSHA) to set standards that would assure "to the extent feasible" that no worker "will suffer material impairment of health" from exposure to a hazardous substance throughout his working life.*

*The cotton dust standards had been upheld by the U.S. Court of Appeals for the District of Columbia. Those appealing the decision to the Supreme Court in one case were 12 individual cotton textile manufacturers and the American Textile Manufacturers Institute Inc., a trade association representing approximately 175 companies. In the other case the appeal was brought by the National Cotton Council of America, a non-profit corporation that promotes the consumption of cotton products.*

*The standards challenged by industry were aimed at protecting textile workers from the effects of byssinosis or "brown lung," and other respiratory diseases. The 1978 standards required the manufacturers to install ventilators to clean cotton dust from the air and to provide masks equipped with respirators for workers. The standards lowered the permissible level of cotton dust in the air from 1,000 micrograms per cubic* meter of air to 200 micrograms for the most hazardous areas of the mills. That level was said to be the equivalent of a grain of salt in a box of air measuring a cubic meter. The textile industry argued that the cost of implementing the 1978 OSHA regulations, estimated at more than $665 million, would force some smaller companies out of business.

## Majority Opinion

Writing for the majority, Justice William J. Brennan Jr. stated, "Any standard based on a balancing of costs and benefits by the Secretary that strikes a different balance than that struck by Congress would be inconsistent with the command set forth in § 6 (b)(5). Thus, cost-benefit analysis by OSHA is not required by the statute because feasibility analysis is." Justices Byron R. White, Thurgood Marshall, Harry A. Blackmun and John Paul Stevens joined in the majority opinion.

Justices William H. Rehnquist, Potter Stewart and Chief Justice Warren E. Burger dissented. Stewart stated that OSHA had not presented substantial evidence to justify the cost of the standard and that "feasibility" could not, therefore, be determined. Rehnquist, with whom Burger joined, said the "feasibility" test was no standard at all, but simply served to mask an unconstitutional delegation of legislative power to the executive branch. Justice Lewis F. Powell Jr. took no part in the decision of the cases.

## Effect on Reagan Policy

Two days after he was sworn in on January 20, President Reagan appointed the Task Force on Regulatory Relief, chaired by Vice President George Bush. The task force was authorized to review regulatory proposals by government agencies, assess regulations already on the books, oversee the development of legislation and recommend regulatory reforms. The Supreme Court decisions dealt a blow to the Reagan policy, announced by Executive Order 12291, that required federal agencies to subject regulations to cost-benefit analysis. The court heard arguments in the case January 21, the day after President Reagan took office. Two months later, in a highly unusual move, the administration asked the court not to rule on the cases, but that request was ignored.

Following are excerpts from the Supreme Court's decision June 17, 1981, upholding the cotton dust standard promulgated by the Occupational Safety and Health Administration and from the dissenting opinions of Justices Potter Stewart and William H. Rehnquist:

No. 79-1429

American Textile
Manufacturers
Institute, Inc., et al,
Petitioners,
*v.*
Raymond J. Donovan,
Secretary of Labor,
United States
Department of Labor, et al.

On Writ of Certiorari to the
United States Court of Appeals
for the District of Columbia
Circuit.

[June 17, 1981]*

JUSTICE BRENNAN delivered the opinion of the Court. [JUSTICE POWELL took no part in the decision of these cases.]

Congress enacted the Occupational Safety and Health Act of 1970 (the Act) "to assure so far as possible every working man and woman in the Nation safe and healthful working conditions. . . ." The Act authorizes the Secretary of Labor to establish, after notice and opportunity to comment, mandatory nationwide standards governing health and safety in the workplace. In 1978, the Secretary, acting through the Occupational Safety and Health Administration (OSHA), promulgated a standard limiting occupational exposure to cotton dust, an airborne particle byproduct of the preparation and manufacture of cotton products, exposure to which induces a "constellation of respiratory effects" known as "byssinosis." This disease was one of the expressly recognized health hazards that led to passage of the Occupational Safety and Health Act of 1970.

Petitioners in these consolidated cases, representing the interests of the cotton industry, challenged the validity of the "Cotton Dust Standard" in the Court of Appeals for the District of Columbia Circuit pursuant to § 6 (f) of the Act. They contend in this Court, as they did below, that the Act requires OSHA to demonstrate that its Standard reflects a reasonable relationship between the costs and benefits associated with the Standard. Respondents, the Secretary of Labor and two labor organizations [Industrial Union Department, AFL-CIO, and Amalgamated Clothing & Textile Workers Union, AFL-CIO], counter that Congress balanced the costs and benefits in the Act itself, and that the Act should therefore be construed not to require OSHA to do so. They interpret the Act as mandating that OSHA enact the most protective standard possible to eliminate a significant risk of material health impairment, subject to the constraints of

---

*Together with No. 79-1583, *National Cotton Council of America* v. *Donovan, Secretary of Labor, et al.,* also on certiorari to the same court.

economic and technological feasibility. The Court of Appeals held that the Act did not require OSHA to compare costs and benefits. We granted certiorari (1980) to resolve this important question, which was presented but not decided in last Term's *Industrial Union Department* v. *American Petroleum Institute* (1980), and to decide other issues related to the Cotton Dust Standard.

## I

Byssinosis, known in its more severe manifestations as "brown lung" disease, is a serious and potentially disabling respiratory disease primarily caused by the inhalation of cotton dust. Byssinosis is a "continuum ... disease," that has been categorized into four grades. In its least serious form, byssinosis produces both subjective symptoms, such as chest tightness, shortness of breath, coughing, and wheezing, and objective indications of loss of pulmonary functions. In its most serious form, byssinosis is a chronic and irreversible obstructive pulmonary disease, clinically similar to chronic bronchitis or emphysema, and can be severely disabling. At worst, as is true of other respiratory diseases including bronchitis, emphysema, and asthma, byssinosis can create an additional strain on cardiovascular functions and can contribute to death from heart failure.... One authority has described the increasing seriousness of byssinosis as follows:

> "In the first few years of exposure [to cotton dust], symptoms occur on Monday, or other days after absence from the work environment; later, symptoms occur on other days of the week; and eventually, symptoms are continuous, even in the absence of dust exposure." A. Bouhuys, Byssinosis in the United States.

While there is some uncertainty over the manner in which the disease progresses from its least serious to its disabling grades, it is likely that prolonged exposure contributes to the progression. It also appears that a worker may suddenly contract a severe grade without experiencing milder grades of the disease.

Estimates indicate that at least 35,000 employed and retired cotton mill workers, or 1 in 12 such workers, suffers from the most disabling form of byssinosis. The Senate Report accompanying the Act cited estimates that 100,000 active and retired workers suffer from some grade of the disease. One study found that over 25% of a sample of active cotton preparation and yarn manufacturing workers suffer at least some form of the disease at a dust exposure level common prior to adoption of the current Standard. Other studies confirm these general findings on the prevalence of byssinosis.

Not until the early 1960's was byssinosis recognized in the United States as a distinct occupational hazard associated with cotton mills. In 1966, the American Conference of Governmental Industrial Hygienists (ACGIH), a private organization, recommended that exposure to total cotton dust be limited to a "threshold limit value" of 1,000 micrograms per cubic meter of air (1000 $\mu$g/m³) averaged over an 8-hour workday. The United States Government first regulated exposure to cotton dust in 1968, when the Secretary of Labor, pursuant to the Walsh-Healey Act promulgated airborne contaminant threshold limit values, applicable to public contractors, that included the 1000 $\mu$g/m³ limit for total cotton dust. Following passage of the Act in 1970, the 1000 $\mu$g/m³ standard was adopted as an "established Federal standard" under § 6 (a) of the Act, a provision designed to guarantee immediate protection of workers for the period between enactment of the statute and promulgation of permanent standards.

In 1974, ACGIH, adopting a new measurement unit of respirable rather than total dust, lowered its previous exposure limit recommendation to 200 $\mu$g/m³ measured by a vertical elutriator, a device that measures cotton dust particles 15 microns or less in diameter. That same year, the Director of the National Institute for Occupational Safety and Health (NIOSH), pursuant to the Act, submitted to the Secretary of Labor a recommendation for a cotton dust standard with a permissible exposure limit (PEL) that "should be set at the lowest level feasible, but in no case at an environmental concentration as high as 0.2 mg lint-free cotton dust/cu. m.," or 200 $\mu$g/m³ of lint-free respirable dust. Several months later, OSHA published an Advance Notice of Proposed Rulemaking, requesting comments from interested parties on the NIOSH recommendation and other related matters. Soon thereafter, the Textile Worker's Union of America, joined by the North Carolina Public Interest Research Group, petitioned the Secretary, urging a more stringent PEL of 100 $\mu$g/m³.

On December 28, 1976, OSHA published a proposal to replace the existing Federal standard on cotton dust with a new permanent standard, pursuant to § 6 (b)(5) of the Act. The proposed standard contained a PEL of 200 $\mu$g/m³ of vertical elutriated lint-free respirable cotton dust for all segments of the cotton industry. It also suggested an implementation strategy for achieving the PEL that relied on respirators for the short-term and engineering controls for the long-term. OSHA invited interested parties to submit written comments within a 90-day period.

Following the comment period, OSHA conducted three hearings in Washington, D.C., Greenville, Miss., and Lubbock, Tex. that lasted over 14 days. Public participation was widespread, involving representatives from industry and the workforce, scientists, economists, industrial hygienists, and many others. By the time the informal rule-making procedure had terminated, OSHA had received 263 comments and 109 notices of intent to appear at the hearings. The voluminous record, composed of a transcript of written and oral testimony, exhibits, and post-hearing comments and briefs, totaled some 105,000 pages. OSHA issued its final Cotton Dust Standard — the one challenged in the instant case — on June 23, 1978. Along with an accompanying statement of findings and reasons, the Standard occupied 69 pages of the Federal Register.

The Cotton Dust Standard promulgated by OSHA establishes mandatory PELs over an 8-hour period of 200 $\mu$g/m$^3$ for yarn manufacturing, 750 $\mu$g/m$^3$ for slashing and weaving operations, and 500 $\mu$g/m$^3$ for all other processes in the cotton industry. These levels represent a relaxation of the proposed PEL of 200 $\mu$g/m$^3$ for all segments of the cotton industry.

OSHA chose an implementation strategy for the Standard that depended primarily on a mix of engineering controls, such as installation of ventilation systems, and work practice controls, such as special floor sweeping procedures. Full compliance with the PELs is required within 4 years, except to the extent that employers can establish that the engineering and work practice controls are infeasible. During this compliance period, and at certain other times, the Standard requires employers to provide respirators to employees. Other requirements include monitoring of cotton dust exposure, medical surveillance of all employees, annual medical examinations, employee education and training programs, and the posting of warning signs. A specific provision also under challenge in the instant case requires employers to transfer employees unable to wear respirators to another position, if available, having a dust level at or below the Standard's PELs, with "no loss of earnings or other employment rights or benefits as a result of the transfer."

On the basis of the evidence in the record as a whole, the Secretary determined that exposure to cotton dust represents a "significant health hazard to employees," and that "the prevalence of byssinosis should be significantly reduced" by the adoption of the Standard's PELs. In assessing the health risks from cotton dust and the risk reduction obtained from lowered exposure, OSHA relied particularly on data showing a strong linear relationship between the prevalence of byssinosis and the concentration of lint-free respirable cotton dust. Even at the 200 $\mu$g/m$^3$ PEL, OSHA found that the prevalence of at least Grade ½ byssinosis would be 13% of all employees in the yarn manufacturing sector.

In enacting the Cotton Dust Standard, OSHA interpreted the Act to require adoption of the most stringent standard to protect against material health impairment, bounded only by technological and economic feasibility. OSHA therefore rejected the industry's alternative proposal for a PEL of 500 $\mu$g/m$^3$ in yarn manufacturing, a proposal which would produce a 25% prevalence of at least Grade ½ byssinosis. The agency expressly found the Standard to be both technologically and economically feasible based on the evidence in the record as a whole. Although recognizing that permitted levels of exposure to cotton dust would still cause some byssinosis, OSHA nevertheless rejected the union proposal for a 100 $\mu$g/m$^3$ PEL because it was not within the "technological capabilities of the industry." Similarly, OSHA set PELS for some segments of the cotton industry at 500 $\mu$g/m$^3$ in part because of limitations of technological feasibility. Finally, the Secretary found that "engineering dust controls in weaving may not be feasible even with massive expenditures by the industry," and for that and other reasons adopted a less stringent PEL of 750 $\mu$g/m$^3$ for weaving and slashing.

The Court of Appeals upheld the Standard in all major respects. The court rejected the industry's claim that OSHA failed to consider its proposed alternative or give sufficient reasons for failing to adopt it. The court also held that the Standard was "reasonably necessary and appropriate" within the meaning of § 3 (8) of the Act, because of the risk of material health impairment caused by exposure to cotton dust. Rejecting the industry position that OSHA must demonstrate that the benefits of the Standard are proportionate to its costs, the court instead agreed with OSHA's interpretation that the Standard must protect employees against material health impairment subject only to the limits of technological and economic feasibility. The court held that "Congress itself struck the balance between costs and benefits in the mandate to the agency" under § 6 (b)(5) of the Act and that OSHA is powerless to circumvent that judgment by adopting less than the most protective feasible standard. Finally, the court held that the agency's determination of technological and economic feasibility was supported by substantial evidence in the record as a whole.

We affirm in part, and vacate in part.

## II

The principal question presented in this case is whether the Occupational Safety and Health Act requires the Secretary, in promulgating a standard pursuant to § 6 (b)(5) of the Act to determine that the costs of the standard bear a reasonable relationship to its benefits. Relying on §§ 6 (b)(5) and 3 (8) of the Act, petitioners urge not only that OSHA must show that a standard addresses a significant risk of material health impairment, see *Industrial Union Department* v. *American Petroleum Institute* (plurality opinion), but also that OSHA must demonstrate that the reduction in risk of material health impairment is significant in light of the costs of attaining that reduction. Respondents on the other hand contend that the Act requires OSHA to promulgate standards that eliminate or reduce such risks "to the extent such protection is technologically and economically feasible." To resolve this debate, we must turn to the language, structure, and legislative history of the Occupational Safety and Health Act.

### A

The starting point of our analysis is the language of the statute itself. *Steadman* v. *SEC* (1981); *Reiter* v. *Sonotone Corp.* (1979). Section 6 (b)(5) of the Act, (emphasis added), provides:

"The Secretary, in promulgating standards dealing with toxic materials or harmful physical agents under this subsection, shall set the standard which most adequately assures, *to the extent feasible,* on the basis of the best available evidence, that no employee will suffer material impairment of health or functional capacity even if such employee has regular exposure to the hazard dealt with by such standard for the period of his working life."

Although their interpretations differ, all parties agree that the phrase "to the extent feasible" contains the critical language in § 6 (b)(5) for purposes of this case.

The plain meaning of the word "feasible" supports respondents' interpretation of the statute. According to Webster's Third New International Dictionary of the English Language, "feasible" means "capable of being done, executed, or effected.". . . Thus, § 6 (b)(5) directs the Secretary to issue the standard that "most adequately assures . . . that no employee will suffer material impairment of health," limited only by the extent to which this is "capable of being done." In effect then, as the Court of Appeals held, Congress itself defined the basic relationship between costs and benefits, by placing the "benefit" of worker health above all other considerations save those making attainment of this "benefit" unachievable. Any standard based on a balancing of costs and benefits by the Secretary that strikes a different balance than that struck by Congress would be inconsistent with the command set forth in § 6 (b)(5). Thus, cost-benefit analysis by OSHA is not required by the statute because feasibility analysis is. See *Industrial Union Department* v. *American Petroleum Institute,* (MARSHALL, J., dissenting).

When Congress has intended that an agency engage in cost-benefit analysis, it has clearly indicated such intent on the face of the statute. One early example is the Flood Control Act of 1936.

"[T]he Federal Government should improve or participate in the improvement of navigable waters or their tributaries, including watersheds thereof, for flood-control purposes if the *benefits to whomsoever they may accrue are in excess of the estimated costs,* and if the lives and social security of people are otherwise adversely affected."

A more recent example is the Outer Continental Shelf Lands Act Amendments of 1978, providing that offshore drilling operations shall use:

"the best available and safest technologies which the Secretary determines to be economically *feasible,* wherever failure of equipment would have a significant effect on safety, health, or the environment, except where the Secretary determines that the *incremental benefits are clearly insufficient to justify the incremental costs of using such technologies.*"

These and other statutes demonstrate that Congress uses specific language when intending that an agency engage in cost-benefits analysis. See

*Industrial Union Department* v. *American Petroleum Institute,* (MAR-
SHALL, J., dissenting). Certainly in light of its ordinary meaning, the
word "feasible" cannot be construed to articulate such congressional
intent. We therefore reject the argument that Congress required cost-
benefit analysis in § 6 (b)(5)....

[Section B Omitted]

## C

The legislative history of the Act, while concededly not crystal clear,
provides general support for respondents' interpretation of the Act. The
congressional reports and debates certainly confirm that Congress meant
"feasible" and nothing else in using that term. Congress was concerned
that the Act might be thought to require achievement of absolute safety,
an impossible standard, and therefore insisted that health and safety goals
be capable of economic and technological accomplishment. Perhaps most
telling is the absence of any indication whatsoever that Congress intended
OSHA to conduct its own cost-benefit analysis before promulgating a toxic
material or harmful physical agent standard. The legislative history
demonstrates conclusively that Congress was fully aware that the Act
would impose real and substantial costs of compliance on industry, and
believed that such costs were part of the cost of doing business....

...Nowhere is there any indication that Congress contemplated a
different balancing by OSHA of the benefits of worker health and safety
against the costs of achieving them. Indeed Congress thought that the
*financial costs* of health and safety problems in the workplace were as
large or larger than the *financial costs* of eliminating these problems. In its
statement of findings and declaration of purpose encompassed in the Act
itself, Congress announced that "personal injuries and illnesses arising out
of work situations impose a substantial burden upon, and are a hindrance
to, interstate commerce in terms of lost production, wage loss, medical
expenses, and disability compensation payment." The Senate was well
aware of the magnitude of these costs:

> "[T]he economic impact of industrial deaths and disability is
> staggering. Over $1.5 billion is wasted in lost wages, and the annual
> loss to the Gross National Product is estimated to be over $8 billion.
> Vast resources that could be available for productive use are
> siphoned off to pay workmen's compensation benefits and medical
> expenses." S. Rep. No. 91-1281.

Senator Eagleton [Thomas F. Eagleton, D-Mo.] summarized, "Whether
we, as individuals, are motivated by simple humanity or by simple
economics, we can no longer permit profits to be dependent upon an
unsafe or unhealthy worksite." Legis. Hist. 1150-1151.

## III

[Section A Omitted]

## B

After estimating the cost of compliance with the Cotton Dust Standard, OSHA analyzed whether it was "economically feasible" for the cotton industry to bear this cost. OSHA concluded that it was, finding that "although some marginal employers may shut down rather than comply, the industry as a whole will not be threatened by the capital requirements of the regulation." ... In reaching this conclusion on the Standard's economic impact, OSHA made specific findings with respect to employment, energy consumption, capital financing availability, and profitability. To support its findings, the agency relied primarily on RTI's [Research Triangle Institute, OSHA-contracted group that prepared a financial analysis of the standard] comprehensive investigation of the Standard's economic impact.

RTI evaluated the likely economic impact on the cotton industry and the United States economy of OSHA's original proposed standard, an across-the-board 200 $\mu$g/m$^3$ PEL. RTI had estimated a total compliance cost of \$2.7 billion for a 200 $\mu$g/m$^3$ PEL, and used this estimate in assessing the economic impact of such a standard. ... OSHA estimated total compliance costs of \$656.5 million for the final Cotton Dust Standard, a Standard less stringent than the across-the-board 200 $\mu$g/m$^3$ PEL of the proposed standard. Therefore, the agency found that the economic impact of its Standard would be "much less severe" than that suggested by RTI for a 200 $\mu$g/m$^3$ PEL estimate of \$2.7 billion. Nevertheless, it is instructive to review RTI's conclusions with respect to the economic impact of a \$2.7 billion cost estimate. RTI found:

> "Implementation of the proposed [200 $\mu$g/m$^3$] standard will require adjustments within the cotton textile industry that will take time to work themselves out and that may be difficult for many firms. In time, however, prices may be expected to rise and markets to adjust so that revenues will cover costs. Although the impact on any one firm cannot be specified in advance, nothing in the RTI study indicates that the cotton textile industry as a whole will be seriously threatened by the impact of the proposed standard for control of cotton dust exposure.". . .

The Court of Appeals found that the agency "explained the economic impact it projected for the textile industry," and that OSHA has "substantial support in the record for its ... findings of economic feasibility for the textile industry." On the basis of the whole record, we cannot conclude that the Court of Appeals "misapprehended or grossly misapplied" the substantial evidence test.

## IV

The final Cotton Dust Standard places heavy reliance on the use of respirators to protect employees from exposure to cotton dust, particularly during the 4-year interim period necessary to install and implement feasible engineering controls. One part of the respirator provision requires the employer to give employees unable to wear a respirator the opportunity to transfer to another position, if available, where the dust level meets the standard's PEL. When such a transfer occurs, the employer must guarantee that the employee suffers no loss of earnings or other employment rights or benefits. Petitioners do not object to the transfer provision, but challenge OSHA's authority under the Act to require employers to guarantee employees' wage and employment benefits following the transfer. The Court of Appeals held that OSHA has such authority. We hold that, whether or not OSHA has this underlying authority, the agency has failed to make the necessary determination or statement of reasons that its wage guarantee requirement is related to the achievement of a safe and healthful work environment. . . .

## V

When Congress passed the Occupational Safety and Health Act in 1970, it chose to place pre-eminent value on assuring employees a safe and healthful working environment, limited only by the feasibility of achieving such an environment. We must measure the validity of the Secretary's actions against the requirements of that Act. For "[t]he judicial function does not extend to substantive revision of regulatory policy. That function lies elsewhere — in Congressional and Executive oversight or amendatory legislation." *Industrial Union Department* v. *American Petroleum Institute* (BURGER, C. J., concurring); see *Tennessee Valley Authority* v. *Hill*, (1978).

Accordingly, the judgment of the Court of Appeals is affirmed in all respects except to the extent of its approval of the Secretary's application of the wage guarantee provision of the Cotton Dust Standard. To that extent, the judgment of the Court of Appeals is vacated and the case remanded with directions to remand to the Secretary for further proceedings consistent with this opinion.

JUSTICE STEWART, dissenting.

Section 6 (b)(5) of the Occupational Safety and Health Act provides:

> "The Secretary, in promulgating standards dealing with toxic materials or harmful physical agents under this subsection, shall set the standard which most adequately assures, *to the extent feasible*, on the basis of the best available evidence, that no employee will suffer material impairment of health or functional capacity even if

such employee has regular exposure to the hazard dealt with by such standard for the period of his working life.

(emphasis added). Everybody agrees that under this statutory provision the Cotton Dust Standard must at least be *economically* feasible, and everybody would also agree, I suppose, that in order to determine whether or not something is economically feasible, one must have a fairly clear idea of how much it is going to cost. Because I believe that OSHA failed to justify its estimate of the cost of the Cotton Dust Standard on the basis of substantial evidence, I would reverse the judgment before us without reaching the question whether the Act requires that a standard, beyond being economically feasible, must meet the demands of a cost-benefit examination.

The simple truth about OSHA's assessment of the cost of the Cotton Dust Standard is that the agency never relied on any study or report purporting to predict the cost to industry of the Standard finally adopted by the agency. OSHA did have before it one cost analysis, that of the Research Triangle Institute, which attempted to predict the cost of the final Standard. However, as recognized by the Court, the agency flatly rejected that prediction as a gross over-estimate. The only other estimate OSHA had, the Hocutt-Thomas [Hovan Hocutt and Arthur Thomas, employees of dust control equipment manufacturers] estimate prepared by industry researchers, was not designed to predict the cost of the final OSHA Standard. Rather, it assumed a far less stringent and inevitably far less costly standard for all phases of cotton production except roving. The agency examined the Hocutt-Thomas study, and concluded that it too was an over-estimate of the costs of the less stringent standard it was addressing. I am willing to defer to OSHA's determination that the Hocutt-Thomas study was such an over-estimate, conceding that such subtle financial and technical matters lie within the discretion and skill of the agency. But in a remarkable non sequitur, the agency decided that because the Hocutt-Thomas study was an over-estimate of the cost of a less stringent standard, it could be treated as a reliable estimate for the more costly final Standard actually promulgated, never rationally explaining how it came to this happy conclusion. This is not substantial evidence. It is unsupported speculation.

Of course, as the Court notes, this Court will reexamine a Court of Appeals' review of a question of substantial evidence "only in what ought to be the rare instance when the standard appears to have been misapprehended or grossly misapplied." *Universal Camera Corp.* v. *NLRB* [1951]. But I think this is one of those rare instances where an agency has categorically misconceived the nature of the evidence necessary to support a regulation, and where the Court of Appeals has failed to correct the agency's error. Of course, broad generalizations about the meaning of "substantial evidence" have limited value in deciding particular cases. But within the confines of a single statute, where the agency and reviewing courts have identified certain specific factual matters to be proved, we can establish practical general criteria for comprehending "substantial evidence."

Unlike the Court, I think it clear to the point of being obvious that, as a matter of law, OSHA's prediction of the cost of the Cotton Dust Standard lacks a basis in substantial evidence, since the agency did not rely on even a single estimate of the cost of the actual Standard it promulgated. Accordingly, I respectfully dissent.

JUSTICE REHNQUIST, with whom THE CHIEF JUSTICE joins, dissenting.

A year ago I stated my belief that Congress in enacting § 6 (b)(5) of the Occupational Safety and Health Act of 1970 unconstitutionally delegated to the Executive Branch the authority to make the "hard policy choices" properly the task of the legislature. *Industrial Union Department* v. *American Petroleum Institute* (1980) (concurring opinion). Because I continue to believe that the Act exceeds Congress' power to delegate legislative authority to nonelected officials, see *Hampton & Co.* v. *United States* (1928) and *Panama Oil Refining Co.* v. *Ryan* (1935), I dissent.

I will repeat only a little of what I said last Term. Section 6 (b)(5) provides in pertinent part:

> "The Secretary, in promulgating standards dealing with toxic materials or harmful physical agents under this subsection, shall set the standard which most adequately assures, *to the extent feasible,* on the basis of the best available evidence, that no employee will suffer material impairment of health or functional capacity even if such employee has regular exposure to the hazard dealt with by such standard for the period of his working life." (Emphasis added.)

As the Court correctly observes, the phrase "to the extent feasible" contains the critical language for the purpose of this case. We are presented with a remarkable range of interpretations of that language. Petitioners contend that the statute *requires* the Secretary to demonstrate that the benefits of its "Cotton Dust Standard," in terms of reducing health risks, bears a reasonable relationship to its costs. Respondents, including the Secretary of Labor at least until his postargument motion, counter that Congress itself balanced costs and benefits when it enacted the statute, and that the statute *prohibits* the Secretary from engaging in a cost-benefit type balancing. Their view is that the Act merely requires Secretary to promulgate standards that eliminate or reduce such risks "to the extent technologically or economically feasible." As I read the Court's opinion, it takes a different position. It concludes that, at least as to the "Cotton Dust Standard," the Act does not require the Secretary to engage in a cost-benefit analysis, which suggests of course that the Act *permits* the Secretary to undertake such an analysis if he so chooses.

Throughout its opinion, the Court refers to § 6 (b)(5) as adopting a "feasibility standard" or a "feasibility requirement." But as I attempted to point out last Term in *Industrial Union Department* v. *American*

*Petroleum Institute,* the "feasibility standard" is no standard at all. Quite the contrary, I argued there that the insertion into § 6 (b)(5) of the words "to the extent feasible" rendered what had been a clear, if somewhat unrealistic, statute into one so vague and precatory as to be an unconstitutional delegation of legislative authority to the Executive Branch. Prior to the inclusion of the "feasibility" language, § 6 (b)(5) simply required the Secretary to "set the standard which most adequately assures, on the basis of the best available professional evidence, that no employee will suffer any impairment of health. . . ." Legislative History, Occupational Safety and Health Act of 1970, 92d Cong. 943 (hereinafter Legis. Hist.) Had that statute been enacted, it would undoubtedly support the result the Court reaches in this case and it would not have created an excessive delegation problem. The Secretary of Labor would quite clearly have been authorized to set exposure standards without regard to any kind of cost-benefit analysis.

But Congress did not enact the statute. . . . Congress simply said that the Secretary should set standards "to the extent feasible." Last year, JUSTICE POWELL reflected that "one might wish that Congress had spoken with greater clarity." *American Petroleum Institute,* (POWELL, J., concurring). I am convinced that the reason that Congress did not speak with greater "clarity" was because it could not. The words "to the extent feasible" were used to mask a fundamental policy disagreement in Congress. I have no doubt that if Congress had been required to choose whether to mandate, permit, or prohibit the Secretary from engaging in a cost-benefit analysis, there would have been no bill for the President to sign.

The Court seems to argue that Congress *did* make a policy choice when it enacted the "feasibility" language. Its view is that Congress required the Secretary to engage in something called "feasibility analysis." But those words mean nothing at all. They are a "legislative mirage, appearing to some members [of Congress] but not to others, and assuming any form desired by the beholder." *American Petroleum Institute.* Even the Court does not settle on a meaning. It first suggests that the language requires the Secretary to do what is "capable of being done." But, if that is all the language means, it is merely precatory and "no more than an admonition to the Secretary to do his duty. . . ." Legis. Hist. 367 (remarks of Sen. Dominick) [Peter H. Dominick, R-Colo.]. The Court then seems to adopt the Secretary's view that feasibility means "technological and economic feasibility." But there is nothing in the words of § 6 (b)(5), or their legislative history, to suggest why they should be so limited. One wonders why the "requirement" of § 6 (b)(5) could not include considerations of administrative or even political feasibility. As even the Court recognizes, when Congress has wanted to limit the concept of feasibility to technological and economic feasibility, it has said so. Thus the words "to the extent feasible" provide no meaningful guidance to those who will administer the law.

In believing that § 6 (b)(5) amounts to an unconstitutional delegation of legislative authority to the Executive Branch, I do not mean to suggest that Congress, in enacting a statute, must resolve all ambiguities or must "fill in all of the blanks." Even the neophyte student of government realizes that legislation is the art of compromise, and that an important, controversial bill is seldom enacted by Congress in the form in which it is first introduced. It is not unusual for the various factions supporting or opposing a proposal to accept some departure from the language they would prefer and to adopt substitute language agreeable to all. But that sort of compromise is a far cry from this case, where Congress simply abdicated its responsibility for the making of a fundamental and most difficult policy choice — whether and to what extent "the statistical possibility of future deaths should ... be disregarded in light of the economic costs of preventing those deaths." *American Petroleum Institute*. That is a "quintessential legislative" choice and must be made by the elected representatives of the people, not by nonelected officials in the Executive Branch. As stated last Term:

> "In drafting § 6 (b)(5), Congress was faced with a clear, if difficult, choice between balancing statistical lives and industrial resources or authorizing the Secretary to elevate human life above all concerns save massive dislocation in an affected industry. That Congress recognized the difficulty of that choice is clear.... That Congress chose, intentionally or unintentionally, to pass this difficult choice on to the Secretary is evident from the special quality of the standard it selected."

In sum, the Court is quite correct in asserting that the phrase "to the extent feasible" is the critical language for the purposes of this case. But that language is critical, not because it establishes a general standard by which those charged with administering the statute may be guided, but because it has precisely the opposite effect: in failing to agree on whether the Secretary should be either mandated, permitted or prohibited from undertaking a cost-benefit analysis. Congress simply left the crucial policy choices in the hands of the Secretary of Labor. As I stated at greater length last Term, I believe that in so doing Congress unconstitutionally delegated its legislative responsibility to the Executive Branch.

# U. N. CONDEMNATION
# OF ISRAELI RAID ON IRAQ

## June 19, 1981

The United Nations Security Council June 19 unanimously passed a resolution condemning the June 7 Israeli bombing of an Iraqi nuclear power plant. The Israelis had flown eight American-made F-16 fighter planes, accompanied by six F-15's, 1,200 miles through Jordan and Saudi Arabia and bombed the Osirak nuclear power plant near Baghdad, Iraq. According to reconnaisance photographs, all of the bombs were direct hits. The raid took two minutes.

The attack destroyed the $275 million French-built plant that, according to Israeli spokesmen, was scheduled to produce material from which nuclear bombs could be made to use against their country. The reactor previously had been damaged in September 1980 in an Iranian air raid.

Claiming that the destruction of the reactor was necessary before it began normal operations, the Israeli government said that if it had not acted when it did, "We would have been compelled to passively observe the process of the production of atomic bombs in Iraq, whose ruling tyrant would not hesitate to launch them against Israeli cities, the centers of its populations." Iraq has never formally recognized Israel's existence and both countries viewed each other as enemies.

Twenty Arab countries and the Palestine Liberation Organization convened June 12 in emergency session in Baghdad to condemn Israel's raid on the nuclear reactor center. The Iraqis contended that the plant was designed for peaceful purposes and that Israel destroyed it because it feared the emergence of advanced technology in the Arab world.

## American Reaction

*The United States' reaction to the raid was swift disapproval. The Reagan administration, despite the government's traditional support of Israel, saw the use of American-made planes in the attack as a violation of the Arms Control Export Act under which the fighters were sold. Secretary of State Alexander M. Haig Jr., reporting to Congress on the matter, said, "We will make clear the seriousness with which we view the obligations of foreign countries to observe scrupulously the terms and conditions under which the United States furnishes defense articles and defense services."*

*The Arms Export Control Act, as amended in 1976 by Congress, obliges the administration to report to Congress promptly when it has information that a violation of an arms supply agreement "may have occurred."*

*President Reagan announced June 11 that four planes of the type used in the raid would not be turned over to Israel as scheduled, but would be held pending resolution of whether the attack constituted an offensive action. The United States finally agreed to give Israel the planes on August 17, after a 10-week delay.*

## U.N. Resolution

*International reaction to the raid was centered in the United Nations Security Council where the U.S. delegation, led by Jeane J. Kirkpatrick, initiated efforts to pass the resolution condemning the act. Kirkpatrick said in an address before the Council that, "The danger of war and anarchy in this vital strategic region threatens global peace and presents this council with a grave challenge... Nonetheless, we believe the means Israel chose to quiet its fears about the purposes of Iraq's nuclear program have hurt, and not helped, the peace and security of the area."*

*Israel's ambassador to the United Nations, Yehuda Z. Blum, said during debate June 12, "... Israel was exercising its inherent and natural right of self-defense, as understood in general international law." The resolution strongly condemned the attack by Israel, calling it a "clear violation of the Charter of the United Nations and the norms of international conduct." Israel did not have a seat on the Security Counsel and thus could not vote on the resolution.*

*Despite the U.N. condemnation Israeli officials continued to defend their action. They were supported in their views by several members of Congress, including Sen. Alan Cranston, D-Calif., a member of the Senate Foreign Relations Committee, who said the attack was necessary to preserve stability in the troubled Middle East.*

*Following are excerpts from the June 12 statement by Yehuda Z. Blum, Israeli ambassador to the United Nations; excerpts from the statement by Jeane J. Kirkpatrick, U.S. ambassador to the United Nations, and Security Council Resolution 487, condemning the Israeli raid on Iraq, both June 19, 1981. (Boldface headings in brackets have been added by Congressional Quarterly to highlight the organization of the texts.):*

# STATEMENT OF ISRAELI AMBASSADOR

... Mr. President, on Sunday, June 7, 1981, the Israeli Air Force carried out an operation against the Iraqi atomic reactor called "Osiraq." That reactor was in its final stages of construction near Baghdad. The pilots' mission was to destroy it. They executed their mission successfully.

In destroying Osiraq, Israel performed an elementary act of self-preservation, both morally and legally. In so doing, Israel was exercising its inherent right of self-defense as understood in general international law and as preserved in Article 51 of the United Nations Charter.

A threat of nuclear obliteration was being developed against Israel by Iraq, one of Israel's most implacable enemies. Israel tried to have that threat halted by diplomatic means. Our efforts bore no fruit. Ultimately we were left with no choice. We were obliged to remove that mortal danger. We did it cleanly and effectively. The Middle East has become a safer place. We trust the international community has also been given pause to make the world a safer place.

These facts and the potentials for a safer world are widely recognized. Several states in the Middle East and beyond are sleeping more easily today in the knowledge that Saddam Hussein's nuclear arms potential has been smashed.

But all this will not preclude a hypocritical parade here in the Security Council. Nothing will prevent numerous members of the United Nations from the usual ganging up on Israel for reasons of spite and expediency. Nothing will stop them from hurling abuse at us, even though they know in their hearts that it is Israel that has relieved them of an awesome menace. Their cant and crocodile tears will do this Organization no credit. The sham and charade will not add to the stature of this Council. And pontification will not further the cause of peace.

Israel has long believed in a different, more constructive approach. We advocate the establishment of a nuclear-weapon-free zone in the Middle East, grounded in a multi-lateral treaty, reached through direct negotiations by all the States concerned. This is the moment for the Security Council to lend its support to Israel's proposal. . . .

## [Iraq's Attitude Toward Israel]

Mr. President, ever since the establishment of the State of Israel over 33 years ago, Iraq has been conspiring to destroy it. Iraq joined several other Arab states which attacked Israel the day after it became independent in 1948. But while other Arab states — Egypt, Lebanon, Jordan and Syria — signed Armistice Agreements with Israel in 1949, Iraq adamantly refused to do so. Instead, it fomented and supported the unrelenting Arab belligerency and terrorism against Israel. It also took part in the Arab wars against Israel in 1967 and 1973. And it has doggedly rejected any international measure or instrument which might imply even the most indirect recognition of Israel and its right to exist.

On October 22, 1973, when this Council called for a ceasefire in the Yom Kippur War, the Baghdad Government announced.

> Iraq does not consider itself a party to any resolution, procedure or measure in armistice or cease-fire agreements on negotiations or peace with Israel, now or in the near future.

In June, 1977, the then President of Iraq, Ahmad Hasan al-Bakr, asserted that, and I quote:

> Efforts ... must be consolidated ... to support the liquidation of the racist Zionist entity so as to build a democratic society.

More recently, the Iraqi Ambassador in New Delhi had the following to say at a press conference reported by the Middle East News Agency on October 24, 1978:

> Iraq does not accept the existence of a Zionist state in Palestine ... the only solution is war.

And only last year, during the Seventh Emergency Special Session of the General Assembly, the Representative of Iraq found it necessary to re-state his Government's opposition to the very existence of my country.

In sum, Iraq declares itself to have been in a state of war with Israel since 1948. Hence, it has rejected all United Nations efforts to seek a peaceful settlement of the Arab-Israel dispute. It has publicly rejected Security Council Resolutions 242 and 338.

## [Iraq's National Charter]

Iraq has missed no opportunity to make it clear that it would not abide by international law in respect to Israel and that it reserves its freedom of action with regard to Israel. This perverse doctrine found expression in the so-called "National Charter" of Iraq proclaimed by its President, Saddam Hussein, in February of last year and circulated as document A/35/110-S 13816, at the request of the Permanent Representative of Iraq.

The principles allegedly underlying that Charter were said to include *inter alia* the non-use of force and peaceful settlement of disputes. Yet they were specifically excluded with regard to my country on the grounds that it is and I quote, "a deformed entity [which is] ... not considered a State." That same Charter commit[t]ed Iraq in no uncertain terms to all-out warfare against Israel, and enjoined other Arab states to participate in that war, using and I quote again, "all means and techniques."

In a letter to the Secretary General of March 11, 1981, circulated both as a document of the General Assembly and of this Council (A/35/131 S 13838), I drew attention to the fact that this undisguised denial by one Member State of the right of another Member State to exist is in flagrant violation of the purposes and principles of the United Nations Charter. I observed that it was a matter for surprise that a document so violently opposed to everything that the United Nations stands for should be circulated at all as a document of this Council, whose primary responsibility is the maintenance of international peace and security. The United Nations, and this Council in particular, were unmoved.

Not by accident has Iraq taken a lead among those Arab states which reject out of hand any solution of the Arab-Israel dispute by peaceful means. To translate its words into deeds, Iraq has used its petro-dollars to develop a sophisticated technological and military infrastructure. It sees itself as the leader and linch-pin of the so-called Eastern Front which the Arab rejectionist States established in Baghdad in 1978 against Israel. Despite its involvement in a war of aggression against Iran, Iraq has continued to indicate its willingness to send men and material to take part in any military hostilities which the rejectionist Arab States may initiate against Israel.

## [Nuclear Armament]

Over and beyond the development of its conventional forces, Iraq has in recent years entered the nuclear armaments field methodically and purposefully, while at the same time piously appending its signature to international instruments specifically prohibiting it from doing so.

As far back as September 8, 1975, Saddam Hussein was quoted by the Lebanese weekly, *al-Usbu al-Arabi,* as saying that the acquisition of nuclear technology by his country was the first Arab attempt towards nuclear armament. By way of comment on reports that Iraq would be the first Arab country to acquire an atomic bomb, the Iraqi oil minister at the time was reported on November 30, 1976, in the Kuwaiti paper *al-Qabas* to have declared a week earlier that all Arab States should participate in a project to produce an atomic bomb. And according to the *International Herald Tribune* of June 27, 1980, Na'im Haddad, a senior member of Iraq's Revolutionary Command Council, stated at the meeting of the Arab League in 1977, that "the Arabs must get an atom bomb."

In brief, this Council is now confronted with an absurd situation. Iraq claims to be at war with Israel. Indeed it prepares for atomic war. And yet it complains to the Security Council when Israel, in self-defense, acts to avert nuclear disaster.

I would like to remind the representative of Iraq that a state cannot invoke in its favour benefits deriving from certain provisions of international law without being prepared at the same time also to abide by the duties flowing from international law. Arab states including Iraq seek to impose on Israel duties stemming from the international law of peace while simultaneously claiming for themselves the privileges of the international law of war.

Mr. President, in recent years, Iraq has been the most active Arab State in the nuclear field. Its activities indicated beyond any shadow of doubt that its goal has been the acquisition of a military nuclear option....

During 1980 the supplier dispatched to Iraq the first shipment of the enriched uranium ... containing 12 kilograms. This shipment enabled Iraq to put into operation a smaller nuclear reactor provided by the same supplier. Israel learned from unimpeachable sources that, following the delivery, expected soon, of two additional shipments of weapons-grade uranium weighing about 24 kilograms, Isiraq would be completed, and put into operation within the next few weeks and not later than the beginning of September 1981. 36 kilograms of weapons-grade uranium in Iraq's possession would enable it to make a nuclear bomb....

In order to build up the reserves of uranium needed to attain self-sufficiency, Iraq has operated in four parallel directions:

a. It has bought weapons-grade enriched uranium on the international black market.

b. It has acquired uranium through bilateral deals.

c. It has obtained enrichment facilities, and

d. It has begun an intensive search for uranium on its own territory.

Iraq already possesses aircraft capable of delivering nuclear warheads. In addit[i]on, it is involved in the development of a new surface-to-surface missile with an effective range of up to 3,000 kilometres, also capable of delivering a nuclear warhead.

Mr. President, unlike Israel, Iraq for well-known reasons has not embarked on its large-scale nuclear program for reasons of pure research, despite its protestations to the contrary. And again, unlike Israel, Iraq has certainly not embarked upon its nuclear program because it faces an energy crisis. It is blessed with abundant supplies of natural oil. And when not engaged in foreign adventures against one of its neighbors, it is normally one of the largest oil suppliers in OPEC.

No amount of bluster can hide one simple, basic fact: Iraq's nuclear program has, beyond a shadow of doubt, just one aim — to acquire nuclear weapons and delivery systems for them....

Mr. President, the combination of an Osiris reactor, and about 80 kilograms of weapons-grade nuclear fuel, together with laboratories for the production of plutonium would have enabled Iraq to acquire a nuclear weapons capability by the mid-1980s. To produce nuclear weapons, Iraq could have opted for one of two paths:

a. The production of three to four nuclear explosive devices on the enriched uranium path, by using the fuel supplied for operating Osiraq or,

b. The use of plutonium produced by Osiraq and the reprocessing laboratory for the production of one plutonium bomb a year.

Further cause for anxiety was given by the delivery of weapons-grade nuclear material without proper provision for the return of the fuel rods after use.

Any lingering doubts about Iraq's intentions to acquire nuclear weapons to be used against Israel were removed just two days ago by the Iraqi Minister of Information. According to yesterday's *New York Times,* Latif Jassem wrote in the state-run newspaper *al-Jumhuriva,* on June 10, 1981 that the Israel attack on Osiraq last Sunday showed that Israel knew that "its real and decisive danger," came from Iraq.

In plain terms, Iraq was creating a mortal danger to the people and State of Israel. It had embarked on ramified programs to acquire nuclear weapons. It had acquired the necessary facilities and fuel. Osiraq was about to go critical in a matter of weeks.

## [Israel's Concern]

Mr. President, over the last few years, Israel has followed Iraq's nuclear development program with growing concern. We have repeatedly expressed our demand both publicly and through diplomatic channels that nuclear assistance to Iraq be terminated. On various occasions, Israel representatives drew the attention of the United Nations General Assembly and of its First Committee to the frantic efforts being made by Iraq and its supporters to establish a nuclear axis aimed against Israel. The Government of Israel has repeatedly urged the European countries involved to stop assisting Iraq's systematic drive to attain a military nuclear capability, stressing the grave implications of such aid to Iraq for all concerned. We also urged other friendly governments to use their influence in that direction. All these public and diplomatic efforts by Israel went unheeded while, at the same time, the pace of Iraq's nuclear development increased.

I should add that Israel was not alone in its apprehensions. Several neighbors of Iraq and other states in the Middle East also expressed their deep concern to Iraq's suppliers over Iraq's nuclear ambitions — but to no avail. . . .

Mr. President, the Government of Israel, like any other government, has the elementary duty to protect the lives of its citizens. In destroying Osiraq last Sunday, Israel was exercising its inherent and natural right of self-defense, as understood in general international law and well within the meaning of Article 51 of the United Nations Charter. . . .

The decision taken by my Government in the exercise of its right to self-defense, after the usual international procedures and avenues had proved futile, was one of the most agonizing we have ever had to take. We sought to act in a manner which would minimize the danger to all concerned, including a large segment of Iraq's population. We waited until the eleventh hour after the diplomatic clock had run out, hoping against hope that Iraq's nuclear arms project would be brought to a halt. Our Air Force was only called in when, as I have said, we learned on the basis of completely reliable information, that there was less than a month to go before Osiraq might have become critical. Our Air Force's operation was consciously launched on a Sunday, and timed for late in the day, on the assumption that the workers on the site, including foreign experts employed at the reactor, would have left. That assumption proved correct, and the loss in human life, which we sincerely regret, was minimal.

I should add that these same considerations worked in the opposite direction as regards Iraq's other nuclear facilities, and constrained Israel from taking action against the smaller Western supplied research reactor as well as a small Soviet research reactor. Both of those facilities are operational, and if attacked, could release substantial amounts of radiation. . . .

Mr. President, Iraq has unashamedly used the United Nations as an instrument to divert international attention from its nuclear weapons program. By way of a smokescreen, it launched an attack on Israel which came to be known as the "Iraqi Initiative," at the Tenth Special Session of the General Assembly in 1978 devoted to disarmament. Despite its manipulation of that Special Session and of the First Committee of the General Assembly ever since, in its unremitting campaign against Israel, nothing can or could camouflage its own nuclear weapons program.

## [Nuclear-Weapon-Free Zone]

By contrast, Israel has long been committed to the concept that the most effective way to prevent the spread of nuclear weapons to the Middle East would be the creation of a nuclear-weapon-free zone in the region, modelled on the Tlatelolco Treaty which is based on an initiative of the Latin American countries and on direct negotiations among them.

Israel has repeatedly given expression to this idea. Since 1974, Israel has proposed it annually in the General Assembly and in other international forums. At the 35th Session of the General Assembly in 1980 Israel submitted a draft resolution on this subject (A/C.1/35/L.8.), which spelled out in precise terms our proposal for the establishment of a nuclear-weapon-free zone in the Middle East. To our great regret this proposal was rejected out of hand by a number of Arab states, first and foremost by Iraq, whose representative even challenged Israel's right to sit on the First Committee. The Iraqi position could only mean that Iraq rejects any possibility of creating a nuclear-weapon-free zone in the Middle East. . . .

Mr. President, the Security Council now has a clear-cut choice before it. It can either resign itself to the perpetuation of the well established pattern of one-sided denunciations of my country which can only serve as a cover and encouragement for those who entertain destructive designs against it. Alternatively, the Council can address itself seriously to the perils and challenges that confront us all. . . .

Israel has always held the conviction that no international conflict can be solved by the use of force.

By the same token it must also be clear that the selfish pursuit of narrow interests, economic and other, can only exacerbate international tensions.

For its part, Israel will not allow itself to be the victim of such a cynical approach. We are an ancient people. We are imbued with an indomitable will to live. That will has been forged in a crucible of 3,000 years of suffering. We have survived the most terrible of tests. We have reestablished our national independence. We are firmly rooted in our own land. We have the means and the determination to defend ourselves. And we are resolved to do so.

For 30 years and more the world has watched with equanimity the unrestrained and unending aggression of Iraq and others against my country. Iraq and its supporters, both in the Arab world and beyond, have been encouraged by the apathy and appeasement of the international community and by their ability to manipulate this world organization for their bellicose ends and lawless policies.

The time has surely come for the United Nations in general, and this Council in particular, to persuade Iraq and its supporters that international conflicts cannot be solved by plotting the demise of a sovereign state. The only way to solve any conflict is to negotiate its peaceful resolution — for peace and peace alone will ensure the rights of all the states involved and guarantee their well-being and security.

Thank you Mr. President.

# KIRKPATRICK'S REMARKS

. . . The issue before the Security Council in the past week — Israel's attack upon the Iraqi nuclear reactor — raises profound and troubling questions that will be with us long after the conclusion of these meetings. The Middle East, as one prominent American observed last week, "provides combustible matter for international conflagration akin to the Balkans prior to World War I," a circumstance made all the more dangerous today by the possibility that nuclear weapons could be employed in a future conflict.

The area that stretches from Southwest Asia across the Fertile Crescent and Persian Gulf to the Atlantic Ocean, is, as we all know, torn not only by tension and division but also by deeply rooted, tenacious hostilities that erupt repeatedly into violence. In the past 2 years alone, one country in the area, Afghanistan, has been brutally invaded and occupied but not pacified. Afghan freedom fighters continue their determined struggle for their country's independence. Iraq and Iran are locked in a bitter war. And with shocking violence, Libya, whose principal exports to the world are oil and terror, invaded and now occupies Chad. Lebanon has its territory and its sovereignty violated almost routinely by neighboring nations. Other governments in the area have, during the same brief period, been the object of violent attacks and terrorism. Now comes Israel's destruction of the Iraqi nuclear facility. Each of these acts of violence undermines the stability and well-being of the area. Each gravely jeopardizes the peace and security of the entire area. The danger of war and anarchy in this vital strategic region threatens global peace and presents this Council with a grave challenge.

## [U.S. Commitment]

My government's commitment to a just and enduring peace in the Middle East is well-known. We have given our full support to efforts by the Secretary General to resolve the war between Iran and Iraq. Our abhorrence of the Soviet Union's invasion and continued occupation of Afghanistan — against the will of the entire Afghan people — requires no elaboration on this occasion. For weeks, our special representative Philip Habib has been in the area conducting talks which we still hope may help to end the hostilities in Lebanon and head off a conflict between Israel and Syria. Not least, we have been engaged in intensive efforts to assist in the implementation of the Egyptian-Israeli treaty, efforts that have already strengthened the forces for peace in the Middle East and will, we believe, lead ultimately to a comprehensive peace settlement of the Arab-Israeli conflict in accordance with Resolutions 242 and 338 of the Security Council.

As in the past, U.S. policies in the Middle East aim above all at making the independence and freedom of people in the area more secure and their daily lives less dangerous. We seek the security of all the nations and peoples of the region.

• The security of all nations to know that a neighbor is not seeking technology for purposes of destruction.

• The security of all people to know they can live their lives in the absence of fear of attack and do not daily see their existence threatened or questioned.

• The security of all people displaced by war, violence, and terrorism.

The instability that has become the hallmark and history of the Middle East may serve the interests of some on this Council; it does not serve our interests; it does not serve the interests of our friends, be they Israeli or Arab.

We believe, to the contrary, that the peace and security of all the nations in the region are bound up with the peace and security of the area.

It is precisely because of my government's deep involvement in efforts to promote peace in the Middle East that we were shocked by the Israeli air strike on the Iraqi nuclear facility and promptly condemned this action, which we believe both reflected and exacerbated deeper antagonisms in the region which, if not ameliorated, will continue to lead to outbreaks of violence.

However, although my government has condemned Israel's act, we know it is necessary to take into account the context of this action as well as its consequences. The truth demands nothing less. As my President, Ronald Reagan, asserted in his press conference:

> ... I do think that one has to recognize that Israel had reason for concern in view of the past history of Iraq, which has never signed a cease-fire or recognized Israel as a nation, has never joined in any peace effort for that ... it does not even recognize the existence of Israel as a country.

With respect to Israel's attack on the Iraqi nuclear reactor, President Reagan said: "... Israel might have sincerely believed it was a defensive move."

## [Israel Reprimanded]

The strength of U.S. ties and commitment to Israel is well known to the members of this Council. Israel is an important and valued ally. The warmth of the human relationship between our peoples is widely understood. Nothing has happened that in any way alters the strength of our commitment or the warmth of our feelings. We in the Reagan Administration are proud to call Israel a friend and ally.

Nonetheless we believe the means Israel chose to quiet its fears about the purposes of Iraq's nuclear program have hurt and not helped the peace and security of the area. In my government's view, diplomatic means available to Israel had not been exhausted, and the Israeli action has damaged the regional confidence that is essential for the peace process to go forward. All of us with an interest in peace, freedom, and national independence have a high stake in that process. Israel's stake is highest of all.

My government is committed to working with the Security Council to remove the obstacles to peace. We made clear from the outset that the United States will support reasonable actions by this body which might be likely to contribute to the pacification of the region. We also made clear that my government would approve no decision that harmed Israel's basic interests, was unfairly punitive, or created new obstacles to a just and lasting peace.

The United States has long been deeply concerned about the dangers of nuclear proliferation. We believe that all nations should adhere to the Nonproliferation Treaty. It is well known that we support the International Atomic Energy Agency (IAEA) and will cooperate in any reasonable effort to strengthen it.

We desire to emphasize, however, that security from nuclear attack and annihilation will depend ultimately less on treaties signed than on the construction of stable regional order. Yes, Israel should be condemned; yes, the IAEA should be strengthened and respected by all nations. And yes, too, Israel's neighbors should recognize its right to exist and enter into negotiations with it to resolve their differences.

The challenge before this Council was to exercise at least the same degree of restraint and wisdom that we demand of the parties directly involved in Middle East tensions. Inflammatory charges, such as the Soviet statement that the United States somehow encouraged the raid or that we knew of the raid beforehand, are false and malicious. One can speculate about whose interest is served by such innuendo. Certainly the spirit of truth, restraint, or peace is not served by such innuendo. Certainly the process of peace is not forwarded.

Throughout the negotiations of the last days, my government had sought only to move us closer to the day when genuine peace between Israel and its Arab neighbors will become a reality. We have searched for a reasonable outcome of the negotiations in the Security Council, one which would protect the vital interests of all parties, and damage the vital interests of none, which would ameliorate rather than exacerbate the dangerous passions and division of the area. In that search we were aided by the cooperative spirit, restrained positions, and good faith of the Iraqi Foreign Minister Sa'dun Hammadi. We sincerely believe the results will move that turbulent area a bit closer to the time when all the states in the region have the opportunity to turn their energies and resources from war to peace, from armaments to development, from anxiety and fear to confidence and well-being.

# SECURITY COUNCIL RESOLUTION

*The Security Council,*

*Having considered* the agenda contained in document S/Agenda/2280,

*Having noted* the contents of the telegram dated 8 June 1981 from the Foreign Minister of Iraq (S/14509),

*Having heard* the statements made to the Council on the subject at its 2280th through 2288th meetings;

*Taking note* of the statement made by the Director-General of the International Atomic Energy Agency (IAEA) to the Agency's Board of Governors on the subject on 9 June 1981, and his statement to the Council at its 2288th meeting on 19 June 1981,

*Further taking note* of the resolution adopted by the Board of Governors of the IAEA on 12 June 1981 on the "military attack on the Iraq nuclear research centre and its implications for the Agency" (S/14532),

*Fully aware* of the fact that Iraq has been a party to the Treaty on Non-Proliferation of Nuclear Weapons since it came into force in 1970, that in accordance with that Treaty Iraq has accepted IAEA safeguards on all its nuclear activities, and that the Agency has testified that these safeguards have been satisfactorily applied to date,

*Noting furthermore* that Israel has not adhered to the non-proliferation Treaty,

*Deeply concerned* about the danger to international peace and security created by the premeditated Israeli air attack on Iraqi nuclear installations on 7 June 1981, which could at any time explode the situation in the area, with grave consequences for the vital interests of all States,

*Considering* that, under the terms of Article 2, paragraph 4, of the Charter of the United Nations: "All Members shall refrain in their international relations from the threat or use of force against the territorial integrity or political independence of any State, or in any other manner inconsistent with the Purposes of the United Nations",

1. *Strongly condemns* the military attack by Israel in clear violation of the Charter of the United Nations and the norms of international conduct;
2. *Calls upon* Israel to refrain in the future from any such acts or threats thereof;
3. *Further considers* that the said attack constitutes a serious threat to the entire IAEA safeguards régime which is the foundation of the non-proliferation Treaty;
4. *Fully recognizes* the inalienable sovereign right of Iraq, and all other states, especially the developing countries, to establish programmes of technological and nuclear development to develop their economy and industry for peaceful purposes in accordance with their present and future needs and consistent with the internationally accepted objectives of preventing nuclear-weapons proliferation;
5. *Calls upon* Israel urgently to place its nuclear facilities under IAEA safeguards;
6. *Considers that* Iraq is entitled to appropriate redress for the destruction it has suffered, responsibility for which has been acknowledged by Israel;
7. *Requests* the Secretary-General to keep the Security Council regularly informed of the implementation of this resolution.

# COURT ON ALL-MALE DRAFT
## June 25, 1981

*Deferring to the wishes of Congress, the Supreme Court ruled in*
*Rostker v. Goldberg June 25 that the government may exclude women*
*from the military draft and registration for it. Because women are barred*
*from combat duty by law and by military policy, they are not "similarly*
*situated" with men for purposes of draft registration, the court said.*

*"The fact that Congress and the executive have decided that women*
*should not serve in combat fully justifies Congress in not authorizing*
*their registration, since the purpose of registration is to develop a pool of*
*potential combat troops," declared Justice William H. Rehnquist, writing*
*for the court's 6-3 majority. Although the case before the court involved*
*registration only, the justices indicated clearly that their decision ap-*
*plied to actual conscription as well.*

*Joining Rehnquist in the majority decision were Chief Justice Warren*
*E. Burger and Justices Potter Stewart, Harry A. Blackmun, Lewis F.*
*Powell Jr. and John Paul Stevens. Justices William J. Brennan Jr.,*
*Byron R. White and Thurgood Marshall dissented.*

### Power of Congress

*Central to the decision was a conservative view of the high court's role*
*in reviewing decisions made by Congress in the exercise of its constitu-*
*tional responsibility to raise and regulate the armed forces. "... Perhaps*
*in no other area has the Court accorded Congress greater deference," the*
*justices noted. "Not only is the scope of Congress' constitutional power in*

*this area broad, but the lack of competence on the part of the courts is marked."*

*The majority said that deference to congressional judgment does not entail abdication of the court's responsibility to assess the constitutionality of legislative actions. But in the draft case, the court said, "we must be particularly careful not to substitute our judgment of what is desirable for that of Congress, or our own evaluation of the evidence for a reasonable evaluation by the legislative branch."*

*The court noted that Congress fully considered President Carter's request that women as well as men be required to register for the draft. The decision to exclude women was not an "accidental byproduct" of the traditional view of women but rather a considered judgment, the justices said.*

*Rehnquist's opinion specifically cited arguments that the Senate Armed Services Committee developed at some length in its June 20, 1980, report on the fiscal 1981 defense authorization bill:*

> *In the committee's view, the starting point for any discussion of the appropriateness of registering women for the draft is the proper role of women in combat. . . . The policy precluding the use of women in combat is, in the committee's view, the most important reason for not including women in a registration system.*

*Rehnquist said that Congress had every right, in shaping registration for the draft, "to focus on the question of military need rather than 'equity.'"*

## The Dissent

*Marshall and White wrote separate dissenting opinions; Brennan signed both. Marshall called the majority decision "inconsistent with the Constitution's guarantee of equal protection of the laws." He said that "even in the area of military affairs, deference to congressional judgments cannot be allowed to shade into an abdication of this court's ultimate responsibility to decide constitutional questions."*

*An all-male draft registration, Marshall said, "categorically excludes women from a fundamental civic obligation." With its decision, he said, "the court today places its imprimatur on one of the most potent remaining public expressions of ancient canards about the proper role of women."*

*In a separate dissent, White questioned the need to restrict the draft to individuals who could fill combat positions. He said there was no evidence Congress had concluded that all military posts must be filled by combat-ready men, and thus there was inadequate justification for requiring only men to register.*

## Background

There had been no actual draft since 1973, and registration was suspended in 1975. President Jimmy Carter reinstituted registration in 1980 in response to the Soviet invasion of Afghanistan. In providing funds for the start-up of registration, Congress considered but rejected the notion of requiring women to sign up, voting just enough funds to register young men.

The validity of the Selective Service Act of 1948 was cast in doubt July 18, 1980, when a three-judge federal panel in Philadelphia ruled the act unconstitutional because it did not provide for the registration of women. The 1948 law gave the president the authority to register men only.

The judges enjoined the U.S. government from going ahead with the sign-up. But Supreme Court Justice Brennan, who had jurisdiction over appeals from the judicial district that included Philadelphia, stayed the injunction. Brennan's order allowed registration to proceed pending a review of the Philadelphia ruling by the full Supreme Court.

The Philadelphia judges issued their ruling in a case brought by the American Civil Liberties Union (ACLU) on behalf of a group of University of Pennsylvania students in 1971. The students argued that the Vietnam War draft discriminated against men. Their case, moot since the end of the Vietnam draft, was revived when President Carter signed Proclamation 4771 July 2, 1980, reinstating registration.

The Philadelphia panel held that a law registering only men violated their right to equal protection of the laws and "unconstitutionally discriminates between males and females." Congressional proponents of male-only registration had argued that women were not needed by the military to meet the manpower problems the sign-up was designed to help alleviate: rapid mobilization of combat troops in time of war. But the Philadelphia judges said "women do serve a useful role in the military" and "the complete exclusion of women from the pool of registrants does not serve 'important governmental objectives.'"

## Implications

The Supreme Court's decision had political as well as legal implications that were likely to extend beyond the confines of the ruling itself. The court's decision allowed policy makers in Congress and the White House to consider the possibility of reviving the draft free of the controversial prospect that the Constitution might require the inclusion of women. President Reagan early in 1982 announced his intention to enforce the law requiring young men to register.

Opponents of the Equal Rights Amendment (ERA) to the Constitution said that the ruling aided their cause by making clear that women were

*not liable for compulsory military service under the Constitution as it
existed at the time of the ruling.*

> *Following are excerpts from the Supreme Court's June 25
> decision in* Rostker v. Goldberg, *upholding Congress' exclu-
> sion of women from draft registration, and from the dissent-
> ing opinion of Justice Marshall:*

No. 80-251

| | |
|---|---|
| Bernard Rostker, Director of Selective Service, Appellant, *v.* Robert L. Goldberg et al. | On Appeal from the United States District Court for the Eastern District of Pennsylvania. |

[June 25, 1981]

JUSTICE REHNQUIST delivered the opinion of the Court.

The question presented is whether the Military Selective Service Act, 50
U.S.C. App. § 451 *et seq.,* violates the Fifth Amendment to the United
States Constitution in authorizing the President to require the registration
of males and not females.

I

Congress is given the power under the Constitution "To raise and
support Armies," "To provide and maintain a Navy," and "To make Rules
for the Government and Regulation of the land and naval Forces."
Pursuant to this grant of authority Congress has enacted the Military
Selective Service Act, 50 U. S. C. App. § 451 *et seq.* ("the MSSA" or "the
Act"). Section 3 of the Act empowers the President, by proclamation, to
require the registration of "every male citizen" and male resident aliens
between the ages of 18 and 26. The purpose of this registration is to
facilitate any eventual conscription: pursuant to § 4 (a) of the Act, those
persons required to register under § 3 are liable for training and service in
the Armed Forces. The MSSA registration provision serves no other
purpose beyond providing a pool for subsequent induction.

Registration for the draft under § 3 was discontinued in 1975. Presidential Proclamation No. 4360 (April 7, 1975). In early 1980, President Carter
determined that it was necessary to reactivate the draft registration
process. The immediate impetus for this decision was the Soviet armed
invasion of Afghanistan. According to the Administration's witnesses
before the Senate Armed Services Committee, the resulting crisis in
Southwestern Asia convinced the President that the "time has come" "to
use his present authority to require registration ... as a necessary step to
preserving or enhancing our national security interests." The Selective
Service System had been inactive, however, and funds were needed before
reactivating registration. The President therefore recommended that

funds be transferred from the Department of Defense to the separate Selective Service System. He also recommended that Congress take action to amend the MSSA to permit the registration and conscription of women as well as men.

Congress agreed that it was necessary to reactivate the registration process, and allocated funds for that purpose in a joint resolution which passed the House on April 22 and the Senate on June 12 [1980]. The resolution did not allocate all the funds originally requested by the President, but only those necessary to register males. Although Congress considered the question at great length, it declined to amend the MSSA to permit the registration of women.

On July 2, 1980, the President, by proclamation, ordered the registration of specified groups of young men pursuant to the authority conferred by § 3 of the Act. Registration was to commence on July 21, 1980.

These events of last year breathed new life into a lawsuit which had been essentially dormant in the lower courts for nearly a decade. It began in 1971 when several men subject to registration for the draft and subsequent induction into the Armed Services filed a complaint in the United States District Court for the Eastern District of Pennsylvania challenging the MSSA on several grounds. A three-judge district court was convened in 1974 to consider the claim of unlawful gender-based discrimination which is now before us. On July 1, 1974, the court declined to dismiss the case as moot, reasoning that although authority to induct registrants had lapsed, plaintiffs were still under certain affirmative obligations in connection with registration. Nothing more happened in the case for five years. Then, on June 6, 1979, the court clerk, acting pursuant to a local rule governing inactive cases, proposed that the case be dismissed. Additional discovery thereupon ensued, and defendants moved to dismiss on various justiciability grounds. The court denied the motion to dismiss, ruling that it did not have before it an adequate record on the operation of the Selective Service System and what action would be necessary to reactivate it. On July 1, 1980, the court certified a plaintiff class of "all male persons who are registered or subject to registration under 50 U.S.C. App. § 453 or are liable for training and service in the armed forces of the United States under 50 U.S.C. App § 454, 456 (h) and 467 (c)."

On Friday, July 18, 1980, three days before registration was to commence, the District Court issued an opinion finding that the Act violated the Due Process Clause of the Fifth Amendment and permanently enjoined the Government from requiring registration under the Act. The court initially determined that the plaintiffs had standing and that the case was ripe, determinations which are not challenged here by the Government. Turning to the merits, the court rejected plaintiffs' suggestions that the equal protection claim should be tested under "strict scrutiny," and also rejected defendants' argument that the deference due Congress in the area of military affairs required application of the traditional "minimum scrutiny" test. Applying the "important government interest" test articulated in *Craig* v. *Boren* (1967), the court struck down the MSSA. The court stressed that it was not deciding whether or to what extent women should serve in combat, but only the issue of registration, and felt that this "should dispel any concern that we are injecting ourselves in an inappropriate manner in military affairs." The court then proceeded to examine the testimony and hearing evidence presented to Congress by representatives of the military and the Executive Branch, and concluded on the basis of this testimony that "military opinion, backed by extensive study, is that the availability of women registrants would materially increase flexibility, not hamper it." It rejected Congress' contrary determination in part because of what it viewed as Congress' "inconsistent positions" in declining to register women yet spending funds to recruit them and expand their opportunities in the military.

The United States immediately filed a notice of appeal and the next day, Saturday, July 19, 1980, JUSTICE BRENNAN, acting in his capacity as Circuit Justice for the Third Circuit, stayed the District Court's order enjoining commencement of registration. Registration began the next Monday. On December 1, 1980, we noted probable jurisdiction.

## II

Whenever called upon to judge the constitutionality of an Act of Congress — "the gravest and most delicate duty that this Court is called upon to perform," *Blodgett* v. *Holden* (1927) (Holmes, J.) — the Court accords "great weight to the decisions of Congress." *CBS, Inc.* v. *Democratic National Committee* (1973). The Congress is a coequal branch of government whose members take the same oath we do to uphold the Constitution of the United States. As Justice Frankfurter noted in *Joint Anti-Fascist Refugee Committee* v. *McGrath* (1951) (concurring opinion), we must have "due regard to the fact that this Court is not exercising a primary judgment but is sitting in judgment upon those who also have taken the oath to observe the Constitution and who have the responsibility for carrying on government." The customary deference accorded the judgments of Congress is certainly appropriate when, as here, Congress specifically considered the question of the Act's constitutionality.

This is not, however, merely a case involving the customary deference accorded congressional decisions. The case arises in the context of Congress' authority over national defense and military affairs, and perhaps in no other area has the Court accorded Congress greater deference. In rejecting the registration of women, Congress explicitly relied upon its constitutional powers under Art. I, § 8, cls. 12-14. The "specific findings" section of the Report of the Senate Armed Services Committee, later adopted by both Houses of Congress, began by stating:

"Article I, section 8 of the Constitution commits exclusively to the Congress the powers to raise and support armies, provide and maintain a Navy, and make rules for Government and regulation of the land and naval forces, and pursuant to these powers it lies within the discretion of the Congress to determine the occasions for expansion of our Armed Forces, and the means best suited to such expansion should it prove necessary."

This Court has consistently recognized Congress' "broad constitutional power" to raise and regulate armies and navies, *Schlesinger* v. *Ballard* (1975). As the Court noted in considering a challenge to the selective service laws, "The constitutional power of Congress to raise and support armies and to make all laws necessary and proper to that end is broad and sweeping." *United States* v. *O'Brien* (1968). See *Lichter* v. *United States* (1948).

Not only is the scope of Congress' constitutional power in this area broad, but the lack of competence on the part of the courts is marked. In *Gilligan* v. *Morgan* (1973), the Court noted:

> "It is difficult to conceive of an area of governmental activity in which the courts have less competence. The complex, subtle, and professional decisions as to the composition, training, equipping, and control of a military force are essentially professional military judgments, subject always to civilian control of the Legislative and Executive branches."

See also *Orloff* v. *Willoughby* (1953)....

In *Schlesinger* v. *Ballard* (1975), the Court considered a due process challenge, brought by males, to the navy policy of according females a longer period than males in which to attain promotions necessary to continued service. The Court distinguished previous gender-based discriminations held unlawful in *Reed* v. *Reed* (1971) and *Frontiero* v. *Richardson* (1973). In those cases, the classifications were based on "overbroad generalizations." In the case before it, however, the Court noted:

> "the different treatment of men and women naval officers ... reflects, not archaic and overbroad generalizations, but, instead, the demonstrable fact that male and female line officers in the Navy are not similarly situated with respect to opportunities for professional service. Appellee has not challenged the current restrictions on women officers' participation in combat and in most sea duty."

In light of the combat restrictions, women did not have the same opportunities for promotion as men, and therefore it was not unconstitutional for Congress to distinguish between them.

None of this is to say that Congress is free to disregard the Constitution when it acts in the area of military affairs. In that area as any other Congress remains subject to the limitations of the Due Process Clause ... but the tests and limitations to be applied may differ because of the military context. We of course do not abdicate our ultimate responsibility to decide the constitutional question, but simply recognize that the

Constitution itself requires such deference to congressional choice. See *CBS, Inc.* v. *Democratic National Committee*. In deciding the question before us we must be particularly careful not to substitute our judgment of what is desirable for that of Congress, or our own evaluation of evidence for a reasonable evaluation by the Legislative Branch. . . .

The Solicitor General argues . . . that this Court should scrutinize the MSSA only to determine if the distinction drawn between men and women bears a rational relation to some legitimate government purpose, see *United States Railroad Retirement Board* v. *Fritz* (1980), and should not examine the Act under the heightened scrutiny with which we have approached gender-based discrimination, see *Michael M.* v. *Superior Court of Sonoma County* (1981); *Craig* v. *Boren; Reed* v. *Reed*. We do not think that the substantive guarantee of due process or certainty in the law will be advanced by any further "refinement" in the applicable tests as suggested by the Government. Announced degrees of "deference" to legislative judgments, just as levels of "scrutiny" which this Court announces that it applies to particular classifications made by a legislative body, may all too readily become facile abstractions used to justify a result. In this case the courts are called upon to decide whether Congress, acting under an explicit constitutional grant of authority, has by that action transgressed an explicit guarantee of individual rights which limits the authority so conferred. Simply labelling the legislative decision "military" on the one hand or "gender-based" on the other does not automatically guide a court to the correct constitutional result.

No one could deny that under the test of *Craig* v. *Boren*, the Government's interest in raising and supporting armies is an "important governmental interest." Congress and its committees carefully considered and debated two alternative means of furthering that interest: the first was to register only males for potential conscription, and the other was to register both sexes. Congress chose the former alternative. When that decision is challenged on equal protection ground, the question a court must decide is not which alternative it would have chosen, had it been the primary decisionmaker, but whether that chosen by Congress denies equal protection of the laws.

Nor can it be denied that the imposing number of cases from this Court previously cited suggest that judicial deference to such congressional exercise of authority is at its apogee when legislative action under the congressional authority to raise and support armies and make rules and regulations for their governance is challenged. As previously noted, . . . deference does not mean abdication. The reconciliation between the deference due Congress and our own constitutional responsibility is perhaps best instanced in *Schlesinger* v. *Ballard* where we stated:

> "This Court has recognized that 'it is the primary business of armies and navies to fight or be ready to fight wars should the occasion arise.' . . . The responsibility for determining how best our Armed Forces shall attend to that business rests with Congress, see U.S.

Const., Art. I, § 8, cls. 12-14, and with the President. See U.S. Const., Art. II, § 2, cl. 1. We cannot say that, in exercising its broad constitutional power here, Congress has violated the Due Process Clause of the Fifth Amendment." . . .

*Schlesinger* v. *Ballard* did not purport to apply a different equal protection test because of the military context, but did stress the deference due congressional choices among alternatives in exercising the congressional authority to raise and support armies and make rules for their governance. In light of the floor debate and the report of the Senate Armed Services Committee hereinafter discussed, it is apparent that Congress was fully aware not merely of the many facts and figures presented to it by witnesses who testified before its committees, but of the current thinking as to the place of women in the Armed Services. In such a case, we cannot ignore Congress' broad authority conferred by the Constitution to raise and support armies when we are urged to declare unconstitutional its studied choice of one alternative in preference to another for furthering that goal.

## III

This case is quite different from several of the gender-based discrimination cases we have considered in that, despite appellees' assertions, Congress did not act "unthinkingly" or "reflexively and not for any considered reason." The question of registering women for the draft not only received considerable national attention and was the subject of wide-ranging public debate, but also was extensively considered by Congress in hearings, floor debate, and in committee. Hearings held by both Houses of Congress in response to the President's request for authorization to register women adduced extensive testimony and evidence concerning the issue. These hearings built on other hearings held the previous year addressed to the same question.

The House declined to provide for the registration of women when it passed the Joint Resolution allocating funds for the Selective Service System. When the Senate considered the Joint Resolution, it defeated, after extensive debate, an amendment which in effect would have authorized the registration of women. As noted earlier, Congress in H. R. J. Res. 521 only authorized funds sufficient to cover the registration of males. The Report of the Senate Committee on Appropriations on H. R. J. Res. 521 noted that the amount authorized was below the President's request "due to the Committee's decision not to provide $8,500,000 to register women," and that "The amount recommended by the Committee would allow for registration of young men only."

While proposals to register women were being rejected in the course of transferring funds to register males, committees in both Houses which had conducted hearings on the issue were also rejecting the registration of women. The House Subcommittee on Military Personnel of the House Armed Services Committee tabled a bill which would have amended the

MSSA to authorize registration of women, H. R. 6569, on March 6, 1980. The Senate Armed Services Committee rejected a proposal to register women, S. 2440, as it had one year before and adopted specific findings supporting its action. These findings were stressed in debate in the Senate on Joint Resolution 521. They were later specifically endorsed by House and Senate conferees considering the Fiscal Year 1981 Defense Authorization Bill. Later both Houses adopted the findings by passing the Report. The Senate Report, therefore, is considerably more significant than a typical report of a single House, and its findings are in effect findings of the entire Congress.

The foregoing clearly establishes that the decision to exempt women from registration was not the "accidental byproduct of a traditional way of thinking about women." *Califano* v. *Webster* (1977) (quoting *Califano* v. *Goldfarb* (1977) (STEVENS, J., concurring)). In *Michael M.* (plurality), we rejected a similar argument because of action by the California Legislature considering and rejecting proposals to make a statute challenged on discrimination grounds gender-neutral. The cause for rejecting the argument is considerably stronger here. The issue was considered at great length, and Congress clearly expressed its purpose and intent....

For the same reasons we reject appellees' argument that we must consider the constitutionality of the MSSA solely on the basis of the views expressed by Congress in 1948, when the MSSA was first enacted in its modern form. Contrary to the suggestions of appellees and various *amici,* reliance on the legislative history of Joint Resolution 521 and the activity of the various committees of the 96th Congress considering the registration of women does not violate sound principles that appropriations legislation should not be considered as modifying substantive legislation. Congress did not change the MSSA in 1980, but it did thoroughly reconsider the question of exempting women from its provisions, and its basis for doing so. The 1980 legislative history is, therefore, highly relevant in assessing the constitutional validity of the exemption.

The MSSA established a plan for maintaining "adequate armed strength ... to ensure the security of [the] nation." Registration is the first step "in a united and continuous process designed to raise an army speedily and efficiently," *Falbo* v. *United States* (1944), see *United States* v. *Nugent* (1953), and Congress provided for the reactivation of registration in order to "provide the means for the early delivery of inductees in an emergency." ... [O]nly those registered may be drafted, and registration serves no purpose beyond providing a pool for the draft. Any assessment of the congressional purpose and its chosen means must therefore consider the registration scheme as a prelude to a draft in a time of national emergency. Any other approach would not be testing the Act in light of the purpose Congress sought to achieve.

Congress determined that any future draft, which would be facilitated by the registration scheme, would be characterized by a need for combat troops.... The purpose of registration, therefore, was to prepare for a draft *of combat troops.*

Women as a group, however, unlike men as a group, are not eligible for combat. The restrictions on the participation of women in combat in the Navy and Air Force are statutory. Under 10 U.S.C. § 6015 "women may not be assigned to duty on vessels or in aircraft that are engaged in combat missions," and under 10 U.S.C. § 8549 female members of the Air Force "may not be assigned to duty in aircraft engaged in combat missions." The Army and Marine Corps preclude the use of women in combat as a matter of established policy. Congress specifically recognized and endorsed the exclusion of women from combat in exempting women from registration.... The President expressed his intent to continue the current military policy precluding women from combat, and appellees present their argument concerning registration against the background of such restrictions on the use of women in combat. Consistent with the approach of this Court in *Schlesinger* v. *Ballard,* we must examine appellees' constitutional claim concerning registration with these combat restrictions firmly in mind....

The District Court stressed that the military need for women was irrelevant to the issue of their registration. As that court put it: "Congress could not constitutionally require registration under MSSA of only black citizens or only white citizens, or single out any political or religious group simply because those groups contained sufficient persons to fill the needs of the Selective Service System." This reasoning is beside the point. The reason women are exempt from registration is not because military needs can be met by drafting men. This is not a case of Congress arbitrarily choosing to burden one of two similarly situated groups, such as would be the case with an all-black or all-white, or an all-Catholic or all-Lutheran, or an all-Republican or all-Democratic registration. Men and women, because of the combat restrictions on women, are simply not similarly situated for purposes of a draft or registration for a draft.

Congress' decision to authorize the registration of only men, therefore, does not violate the Due Process Clause. The exemption of women from registration is not only sufficiently but closely related to Congress' purpose in authorizing registration.... The fact that Congress and the Executive have decided that women should not serve in combat fully justifies Congress in not authorizing their registration, since the purpose of registration is to develop a pool of potential combat troops. As was the case in *Schlesinger* v. *Ballard,* "the gender classification is not invidious, but rather realistically reflects the fact that the sexes are not similarly situated" in this case. *Michael M.* (plurality). The Constitution requires that Congress treat similarly situated persons similarly, not that it engage in gestures of superficial equality....

Congress also concluded that whatever the need for women for noncombat roles during mobilization, whether 80,000 or less, it could be met by volunteers....

Most significantly, Congress determined that staffing non-combat positions with women during a mobilization would be positively detrimental to the important goal of military flexibility.

"There are other military reasons that preclude very large numbers of women from serving. Military flexibility requires that a commander be able to move units or ships quickly. Units or ships not located at the front or not previously scheduled for the front nevertheless must be able to move into action if necessary. In peace and war, significant rotation of personnel is necessary. We should not divide the military into two groups — one in permanent combat and one in permanent support. Large numbers of non-combat positions must be available to which combat troops can return for duty before being redeployed." ...

In sum, Congress carefully evaluated the testimony that 80,000 women conscripts could be usefully employed in the event of a draft and rejected it in the permissible exercise of its constitutional responsibility. The District Court was quite wrong in undertaking an independent evaluation of this evidence, rather than adopting an appropriately deferential examination of *Congress'* evaluation of that evidence.

In light of the foregoing we conclude that Congress acted well within its constitutional authority when it authorized the registration of men, and not women, under the Military Selective Service Act. The decision of the District Court holding otherwise is accordingly

*Reversed.*

JUSTICE MARSHALL, with whom JUSTICE BRENNAN joins, dissenting.

The Court today places its imprimatur on one of the most potent remaining public expressions of "ancient canards about the proper role of women," *Phillips* v. *Martin Marietta Corp.,* (1971) (MARSHALL, J., concurring). It upholds a statute that requires males but not females to register for the draft, and which thereby categorically excludes women from a fundamental civic obligation. Because I believe the Court's decision is inconsistent with the Constitution's guarantee of equal protection of the laws, I dissent.

**I**

**A**

The background to this litigation is set out in the opinion of the Court, and I will not repeat that discussion here. It bears emphasis, however, that the only question presented by this case is whether the exclusion of women from registration under the Military Selective Service Act, 50 U.S.C. App. § 451 *et seq.,* (MSSA) contravenes the equal protection component of the Due Process Clause of the Fifth Amendment. Although the purpose of registration is to assist preparations for drafting civilians into the military, *we are not asked to rule on the constitutionality of a statute governing conscription.* With the advent of the All-Volunteer Armed Forces, the MSSA was specifically amended to preclude conscription as of July 1,

1973, and reactivation of the draft would therefore require a legislative amendment. Consequently, we are not called upon to decide whether either men or women can be drafted at all, whether they must be drafted in equal numbers, in what order they should be drafted, or once inducted, how they are to be trained for their respective functions. In addition, this case does not involve a challenge to the statutes or policies that prohibit female members of the Armed Forces from serving in combat. It is with this understanding that I turn to the task at hand.

## B

By now it should be clear that statutes like the MSSA, which discriminate on the basis of gender, must be examined under the "heightened" scrutiny mandated by *Craig* v. *Boren* (1976). Under this test, a gender-based classification cannot withstand constitutional challenge unless the classification is substantially related to the achievement of an important governmental objective. *Kirchberg* v. *Feenstra* (1981); *Wengler* v. *Druggist Mutual Ins. Co.* (1980); *Califano* v. *Westcott* (1979); *Orr* v. *Orr* (1979); *Craig* v. *Boren.* This test applies whether the classification discriminates against males or females. *Caban* v. *Mohammed* (1979); *Orr* v. *Orr; Craig* v. *Boren.* The party defending the challenged classification carries the burden of demonstrating both the importance of the governmental objective it serves and the substantial relationship between the discriminatory means and the asserted end. . . . Consequently, before we can sustain the MSSA, the Government must demonstrate that the gender-based classification it employs bears "a close and substantial relationship to [the achievement of] important governmental objectives." *Personnel Administrator of Massachusetts* v. *Feeney* (1979).

## C

The MSSA states that "an adequate armed strength must be achieved and maintained to insure the security of this Nation." I agree with the majority that "none could deny that ... the Government's interest in raising and supporting armies is an 'important governmental interest.'" Consequently, the first part of the *Craig* v. *Boren,* test is satisfied. But the question remains whether the discriminatory means employed itself substantially serves the statutory end. In concluding that it does, the Court correctly notes that Congress enacted (and reactivated) the MSSA pursuant to its constitutional authority to raise and maintain armies. The majority also notes that "the Court accords 'great weight to the decisions of Congress,'" quoting *CBS, Inc.* v. *Democratic National Committee* (1973), and that the Court has accorded particular deference to decisions arising in the context of Congress' authority over military affairs. I have no particular quarrel with these sentiments in the majority opinion. I simply add that even in the area of military affairs, deference to congressional judgments cannot be allowed to shade into an abdication of this Court's ultimate responsibility to decide constitutional questions. As the Court has pointed out,

> "the phrase 'war power' cannot be invoked as a talismanic incantation to support any exercise of congressional power which can be brought within its ambit. '[E]ven the war power does not remove constitutional limitations safeguarding essential liberties.' " *United States* v. *Robel* (1967), quoting *Home Bldg. & Loan Assn.* v. *Blaisdell* (1934).

See *United States* v. *Cohen Grocery Co.* (1921); *Hamilton* v. *Kentucky Distilleries & Warehouse Co.* (1919); *Ex parte Milligan* (1866).

One such "safeguar[d] of essential liberties" is the Fifth Amendment's guarantee of equal protection of the laws. When, as here, a federal law that classifies on the basis of gender is challenged as violating this constitutional guarantee, it is ultimately for this Court, not Congress, to decide whether there exists the constitutionally required "close and substantial relationship" between the discriminatory means employed and the asserted governmental objective. See *Powell* v. *McCormack* (1969); *Baker* v. *Carr* (1962). In my judgment there simply is no basis for concluding in this case that excluding women from registration is substantially related to the achievement of a concededly important governmental interest in maintaining an effective defense. . . .

## II

### A

The Government does not defend the exclusion of women from registration on the ground that preventing women from serving in the military is substantially related to the effectiveness of the Armed Forces. Indeed, the successful experience of women serving in all branches of the Armed Services would belie any such claim. Some 150,000 women volunteers are presently on active service in the military, and their number is expected to increase to over 250,000 by 1985. At the congressional hearings, representatives of both the Department of Defense and the Armed Services testified that the participation of women in the All-Volunteer Armed Forces has contributed substantially to military effectiveness. Congress has never disagreed with the judgment of the military experts that women have made significant contributions to the effectiveness of the military. . . . The justification for the MSSA's gender-based discrimination must therefore be found in considerations that are peculiar to the objectives of registration.

The most authoritative discussion of Congress' reasons for declining to require registration of women is contained in the report prepared by the Senate Armed Services Committee on the Fiscal Year 1981 Defense Authorization Bill. The Report's findings were endorsed by the House-

Senate Conferees on the Authorization Bill. Both Houses of Congress subsequently adopted the finding by passing the Conference Report. As the majority notes, the Report's "findings are in effect findings of the entire Congress." The Senate Report sets out the objectives Congress sought to accomplish by excluding women from registration and this Court may appropriately look to the Report in evaluating the justification for the discrimination.

## B

According to the Senate Report, "[t]he policy precluding the use of women in combat is ... the most important reason for not including women in a registration system." In reaffirming the combat restrictions, the Report declared:

> "Registering women for assignment to combat or assigning women to combat positions in peacetime then would leave the actual performance of sexually mixed units as an experiment to be conducted in war with unknown risk — a risk that the committee finds militarily unwarranted and dangerous. Moreover, the committee feels that any attempt to assign women to combat positions could affect the national resolve at the time of mobilization, a time of great strain on all aspects of the Nation's resources."

Had appellees raised a constitutional challenge to the prohibition against assignment of women to combat, this discussion in the Senate Report might well provide persuasive reasons for upholding the restrictions. But the validity of the combat restrictions is not an issue we need decide in this case. Moreover, since the combat restrictions on women have already been accomplished through statutes and policies that remain in force whether or not women are required to register or drafted, including women in registration and draft plans will not result in their being assigned to combat roles. Thus, even assuming that precluding the use of women in combat is an important governmental interest in its own right, there can be no suggestion that the exclusion of women from registration and a draft is substantially related to the achievement of this goal.

The Court's opinion offers a different though related explanation of the relationship between the combat restrictions and Congress' decision not to require registration of women. The majority states that "Congress ... clearly linked the need for renewed registration with its views of the character of a subsequent draft." The Court also states that "Congress determined that any future draft, which would be facilitated by the registration scheme, would be characterized by a need for combat troops." The Court then reasons that since women are not eligible for assignment to combat, Congress' decision to exclude them from registration is not unconstitutional discrimination inasmuch as "[m]en and women, because of the combat restrictions on women, are simply not similarly situated for purposes of a draft or registration for a draft." There is a certain logic to this reasoning, but the Court's approach is fundamentally flawed.

In the first place, although the Court purports to apply the *Craig* v. *Boren* test, the "similarly situated" analysis the Court employs is in fact significantly different from the *Craig* v. *Boren* approach.... The Court essentially reasons that the gender classification employed by the MSSA is constitutionally permissible because nondiscrimination is not necessary to achieve the purpose of registration to prepare for a draft of combat troops. In other words, the majority concludes that women may be excluded from registration because they will not be needed in the event of a draft.

This analysis, however, focuses on the wrong question. The relevant inquiry under the *Craig* v. *Boren* test is not whether a *gender-neutral* classification would substantially advance important governmental interests. Rather, the question is whether the gender-based classification is itself substantially related to the achievement of the asserted governmental interest. Thus, the Government's task in this case is to demonstrate that excluding women from registration substantially furthers the goal of preparing for a draft of combat troops. Or to put it another way, the Government must show that registering women would substantially impede its efforts to prepare for such a draft. Under our precedents, the Government cannot meet this burden without showing that a gender neutral statute would be a less effective means of attaining this end. See *Wengler* v. *Druggists Mutual Ins. Co.* As the Court explained in *Orr* v. *Orr* (emphasis added):

> "Legislative classifications which distribute benefits and burdens on the basis of gender *carry the inherent risk of reinforcing sexual stereotypes about the 'proper place' of women and their need for special protection....* Where, as here, the [Government's] ... purposes are as well served by a gender-neutral classification as one that gender classifies and therefore carries with it the baggage of sexual stereotypes, the [Government] cannot be permitted to classify on the basis of sexual stereotypes."

In this case, the Government makes no claim that preparing for a draft of combat troops cannot be accomplished just as effectively by *registering* both men and women but *drafting* only men if only men turn out to be needed. Nor can the Government argue that this alternative entails the additional cost and administrative inconvenience of registering women. This Court has repeatedly stated that the administrative convenience of employing a gender classification is not an adequate constitutional justification under the *Craig* v. *Boren* test. See, e.g., *Craig* v. *Boren*; *Frontiero* v. *Richardson* (1973).

The fact that registering women in no way obstructs the governmental interest in preparing for a draft of combat troops points up a second flaw in the Court's analysis. The Court essentially reduces the question of the constitutionality of male-only *registration* to the validity of a hypothetical program for *conscripting* only men. The Court posits a draft in which *all* conscripts are either assigned to those specific combat posts presently closed to women or must be available for rotation into such positions. By so doing, the Court is able to conclude that registering women would be no more than a "gestur[e] of superficial equality," since women are necessarily ineligible for every position to be filled in its hypothetical draft. If it could indeed be guaranteed in advance that conscription would be reimposed by Congress only in circumstances where, and in a form under which, all conscripts would have to be trained for and assigned to combat or combat rotation positions from which women are categorically excluded, then it could be argued that registration of women would be pointless.

But of course, no such guarantee is possible. Certainly, nothing about the MSSA limits Congress to reinstituting the draft only in such circumstances. For example, Congress may decide that the All-Volunteer Armed Forces are inadequate to meet the Nation's defense needs even in times of peace and reinstitute peacetime conscription. In that event, the hypothetical draft the Court relied on to sustain the MSSA's gender-based classification would presumably be of little relevance, and the Court could then be forced to declare the male-only registration program unconstitutional. This difficulty comes about because both Congress and the Court have lost sight of the important distinction between *registration* and *conscription*. Registration provides "an inventory of what the available strength is within the military qualified pool in this country." Conscription supplies the military with the personnel needed to respond to a particular exigency. The fact that registration is a first step in the conscription process does not mean that a registration law expressly discriminating between men and women may be justified by a valid conscription program which would, in retrospect, make the current discrimination appear functionally related to the program that emerged.

But even addressing the Court's reasoning on its own terms, its analysis is flawed because the entire argument rests on a premise that is demonstrably false. As noted, the majority simply assumes that registration prepares for a draft in which *every* draftee must be available for assignment to combat. But the majority's draft scenario finds no support in either the testimony before Congress, or more importantly, in the findings of the Senate Report. Indeed, the scenario appears to exist only in the Court's imagination, for even the Government represents only that "in the event of mobilization, *approximately two-thirds* of the demand on the induction system would be for *combat skills*." For my part, rather than join the Court in imagining hypothetical drafts, I prefer to examine the findings in the Senate Report and the testimony presented to Congress.

## C

Nothing in the Senate Report supports the Court's intimation that women must be excluded from registration because combat eligibility is a prerequisite *for all* the positions that would need to be filled in the event of a draft. The Senate Report concluded only that "[i]f mobilization were to be ordered in a wartime scenario, the *primary* manpower need would be for combat replacements." This conclusion was in keeping with the testimony presented at the congressional hearings. The Department of Defense indicated that in the event of a mobilization requiring reinstitution of the draft, the primary manpower requirement would be for combat troops and support personnel who can readily be deployed into combat. But the Department indicated that conscripts would also be needed to staff a variety of support positions having no prerequisite of combat eligibility, and which therefore could be filled by women....

The Defense Department also concluded that there are no military reasons that would justify excluding women from registration. The Department's position was described to Congress in these terms:

"Our conclusion is that there are good reasons for registering [women]. Our conclusion is *even more strongly that there are not good reasons for refusing to register them.*" (emphasis added).

All four Service Chiefs agreed that there are no military reasons for refusing to register women, and uniformly advocated requiring registration of women....

... [T]he Department of Defense acknowledged that amending the MSSA to authorize registration and induction of women did not necessarily mean that women would be drafted in the same number as men....

This review of the findings contained in the Senate Report and the testimony presented at the congressional hearings demonstrates that there is no basis for the Court's representation that women are ineligible for *all* the positions that would need to be filled in the event of a draft. Testimony about personnel requirements in the event of a draft established that women could fill at least 80,000 of the 650,000 positions for which conscripts would be inducted. Thus, with respect to these 80,000 or more positions, the statutes and policies barring women from combat do not provide a reason for distinguishing between male and female potential conscripts; the two groups are, in the majority's parlance, "similarly situated." As such, the combat restrictions cannot by themselves supply the constitutionally required justification for the MSSA's gender-based classification. Since the classification precludes women from being drafted to fill positions for which they would be qualified and useful, the Government must demonstrate that excluding women from those positions is substantially related to the achievement of an important governmental objective.

### III

The Government argues, however, that the "consistent testimony before Congress was to the effect that there is *no military need* to draft women."

And the Government points to a statement in the Senate Report that "[b]oth the civilian and military leadership agreed that there was no military need to draft women.... The argument for registration and induction of women ... is not based on military necessity, but on considerations of equity." In accepting the Government's contention, the Court asserts that the President's decision to seek authority to register women was based on "equity," and concludes that "Congress was certainly entitled, in the exercise of its constitutional powers to raise and regulate armies and navies, to focus on the question of military need rather than 'equity.'" In my view, a more careful examination of the concepts of "equity" and "military need" is required....

... [T]here is no "military need" to draft women in the sense that a war could be waged without their participation. This fact is, however, irrelevant to resolving the constitutional issue. As previously noted, it is not appellees' burden to prove that registration of women substantially furthers the objectives of the MSSA. Rather, because eligibility for combat is not a requirement for some of the positions to be filled in the event of a draft, it is incumbent on the Government to show that excluding women from a draft to fill those positions substantially furthers an important governmental objective.

It may be, however, that the Senate Report's allusion to "military need" is meant to convey Congress' expectation that women volunteers will make it unnecessary to draft any women. The majority apparently accepts this meaning when it states: "Congress also concluded that whatever the need for women for noncombat roles during mobilization, whether 80,000 or less, it could be met by volunteers." But since the purpose of registration is to protect against unanticipated shortages of volunteers, it is difficult to see how excluding women from registration can be justified by conjectures about the expected number of female volunteers. I fail to see why the exclusion of a pool of persons who would be conscripted only *if needed* can be justified by reference to the current supply of volunteers. In any event, the Defense Department's best estimate is that in the event of a mobilization requiring reinstitution of the draft, there will not be enough women volunteers to fill the positions for which women would be eligible. The Department told Congress:

> "If we had a mobilziation, our present best projection is that we could use women in some 80,000 of the jobs we would be *inducting* people for" (emphasis added).

Thus, however the "military need" statement in the Senate Report is understood, it does not provide the constitutionally required justification for the total exclusion of women from registration and draft plans.

[Sections IV and V Omitted]

## VI

After reviewing the discussion and findings contained in the Senate Report, the most I am able to say of the Report is that it demonstrates that drafting *very large numbers* of women would frustrate the achievement of a number of important governmental objectives that relate to the ultimate goal of maintaining "an adequate armed strength . . . to insure the security of this Nation." Or to put it another way, the Senate Report establishes that induction of a large number of men but only a limited number of women, as determined by the military's personnel requirements, would be substantially related to important governmental interests. But the discussion and findings in the Senate Report do not enable the Government to carry its burden of demonstrating that *completely* excluding women from the draft by excluding them from registration substantially furthers important governmental objectives.

In concluding that the Government has carried its burden in this case, the Court adopts "an appropriately deferential examination of *Congress'* evaluation of [the] evidence," (emphasis in the original). The majority then proceeds to supplement Congress' actual findings with those the Court apparently believes Congress could (and should) have made. Beyond that, the Court substitutes hollow shibboleths about "deference to legislative decisions" for constitutional analysis. It is as if the majority has lost sight of the fact that "it is the responsibility of this Court to act as the ultimate interpreter of the Constitution." *Powell* v. *McCormack.* See *Baker* v. *Carr.* Congressional enactments in the area of military affairs must, like all other laws, be *judged* by the standards of the Constitution. For the Constitution is the supreme law of the land and *all* legislation must conform to the principles it lay down. As the Court has pointed out, "the phrase 'war power' cannot be invoked as a talismanic incantation to support any exercise of congressional power which can be brought within its ambit." *United States* v. *Robel.*

Furthermore, "[w]hen it appears that an Act of Congress conflicts with [a constitutional] provisio[n], we have no choice but to enforce the paramount commands of the Constitution. We are sworn to do no less. We cannot push back the limits of the Constitution merely to accommodate challenged legislation." *Trop* v. *Dulles* (1958) (plurality opinion). In some 106 instances since this Court was established it has determined that congressional action exceeded the bounds of the Constitution. I believe the same is true of this statute. In an attempt to avoid its constitutional obligation, the Court today "pushes back the limits of the Constitution" to accommodate an Act of Congress.

I would affirm the judgment of the District Court.

# COURT ON REVOCATION
# OF PASSPORTS
## June 29, 1981

*The Supreme Court, in a 7-2 decision handed down June 29, upheld the action of former Secretary of State Cyrus R. Vance in revoking the passport of a one-time CIA officer who had worked to expose the agency's operations and its agents around the world.*

*Two lower federal courts had held that the passport revocation on national security grounds exceeded Vance's powers because Congress had never specifically authorized such an action.*

*While the former CIA officer, Philip Agee, was widely viewed in the press and elsewhere as deserving little sympathy, the court's ruling provoked an outcry from those who saw it as infringing on the right of Americans to foreign travel and even to dissent. The arguments that the court marshaled in support of its ruling especially came under fire. Critics saw the court in* Haig v. Agee *as, in effect, creating new law.*

*Chief Justice Warren E. Burger wrote the court's opinion. Justice Harry A. Blackmun filed a concurring opinion; Justice William J. Brennan Jr. wrote a dissenting opinion that was joined by Justice Thurgood Marshall.*

## Background

*The limits to the power of the executive branch in regulating foreign travel by Americans had never been explicitly defined by Congress. In revoking Agee's passport, Secretary of State Vance relied on a 1966 State*

*Department regulation authorizing the denial of a passport to anyone whose actions the secretary believed "are causing or are likely to cause serious damage to the national security or the foreign policy of the United States."*

*Agee had served in the CIA from 1957 to 1968. After leaving the agency, he embarked on a "campaign to fight the ... CIA wherever it is operating." He wrote a book,* Inside the Company: A C.I.A. Diary, *in which he claimed he was exposing the names of hundreds of covert American agents. Expelled from Britain, France and the Netherlands, Agee recently had been residing in West Germany.*

*U.S. officials asserted that Agee's publications could result in the death or injury of U.S. agents, and, indeed, several deaths of intelligence officials had been linked in some way to his purported disclosures.*

## Opinion and Dissent

*The lower courts had held that Vance's action exceeded his power under the Passport Act of 1926. In reversing, the Supreme Court's majority held that "[a]lthough the Act does not in express terms authorize the Secretary to revoke a passport or deny a passport application, neither does it expressly limit those powers." The court ruled that Vance could revoke Agee's passport because the "policy" of denying passports had been "sufficiently substantial and consistent to compel the conclusion that Congress has approved it."*

*In his dissent, Brennan argued that because the 1966 State Department regulation had been applied only once before, in 1970, there had been no consistent "practice" (as contrasted to "policy") in the matter. Congressional consent could be inferred, he wrote, only from consistent practice.*

## Agee Reaction

*Although Agee's precise reasons for his anti-CIA campaign remained unknown, he did offer some insight into his motivation in an article in* The New York Times *on July 27. He wrote, "I used my passport to travel around making trouble for the country's saboteurs, infiltrators, and subversives. Like nothing else, the sneaky spooks hated being put on the map, exposed, and ridiculed the world over. Denuded of cover, they squealed and shrieked until finally they found some friends at the Supreme Court."*

*Following are excerpts from the majority ruling of the Supreme Court in* Haig v. Agee, *and from the dissenting opinion of Associate Justice William J. Brennan Jr., June 29, 1981:*

Alexander M. Haig, Jr., Secretary of State of the United States, Petitioner,
*v.*
Philip Agee.

On Writ of Certiorari to the United States Court of Appeals for the District of Columbia Circuit.

[June 29, 1981]

CHIEF JUSTICE BURGER delivered the opinion of the Court.

The question presented is whether the President, acting through the Secretary of State, has authority to revoke a passport on the ground that the holder's activities in foreign countries are causing or are likely to cause serious damage to the national security or foreign policy of the United States.

# I

## A

Philip Agee, an American citizen, currently resides in West Germany. From 1957 to 1968, he was employed by the Central Intelligence Agency. He held key positions in the division of the Agency that is responsible for covert intelligence gathering in foreign countries. In the course of his duties at the Agency, Agee received training in clandestine operations, including the methods used to protect the identities of intelligence employees and sources of the United States overseas. He served in undercover assignments abroad and came to know many Government employees and other persons supplying information to the United States. The relationships of many of these people to our Government are highly confidential; many are still engaged in intelligence gathering.

In 1974, Agee called a press conference in London to announce his "campaign to fight the United States CIA wherever it is operating." He declared his intent "to expose CIA officers and agents and to take the measures necessary to drive them out of the countries where they are operating." Since 1974, Agee has, by his own assertion, devoted consistent effort to that program, and he has traveled extensively in other countries in order to carry it out. To identify CIA personnel in a particular country, Agee goes to the target country and consults sources in local diplomatic circles whom he knows from his prior service in the United States Government. He recruits collaborators and trains them in clandestine techniques designed to expose the "cover" of CIA employees and sources. Agee and his collaborators have repeatedly and publicly identified individuals and organizations located in foreign countries as undercover CIA agents, employees, or sources. The record reveals that the identifications divulge classified information, violate Agee's express contract not to make any public statements about Agency matters without prior clearance by the Agency, have prejudiced the ability of the United States to obtain intelligence, and have been followed by episodes of violence against the persons and organizations identified.

In December 1979, the Secretary of State revoked Agee's passport and delivered an explanatory notice to Agee in West Germany. The notice states in part:

"The Department's action is predicated upon a determination made by the Secretary under the provisions of [22 C.F.R.] Section 51.70 (b) (4) that your activities abroad are causing or are likely to cause serious damage to the national security or the foreign policy of the United States. The reasons for the Secretary's determination are, in summary, as follows: Since the early 1970's it has been your stated intention to conduct a continuous campaign to disrupt the intelligence operations of the United States. In carrying out that campaign you have traveled in various countries (including, among others, Mexico, the United Kingdom, Denmark, Jamaica, Cuba, and Germany), and your activities in those countries have caused serious damage to the national security and foreign policy of the United States. Your stated intention to continue such activities threatens additional damage of the same kind."

The notice also advised Agee of his right to an administrative hearing and offered to hold such a hearing in West Germany on 5 days' notice.

Agee at once filed suit against the Secretary. He alleged that the regulation invoked by the Secretary, 22 CFR § 51.70 (b) (4) (1980), has not been authorized by Congress and is invalid; that the regulation is impermissibly overbroad; that the revocation prior to a hearing violated his Fifth Amendment right to procedural due process; and that the revocation violated a Fifth Amendment liberty interest in a right to travel and a First Amendment right to criticize government policies. He sought declaratory and injunctive relief, and he moved for summary judgment on the question of the authority to promulgate the regulation and on the constitutional claims. For purposes of that motion, Agee conceded the Government's factual averments and its claim that his activities were causing or were likely to cause serious damage to the national security or foreign policy of the United States. The District Court held that the regulation exceeded the statutory powers of the Secretary under the Passport Act of 1926, 22 U.S.C. § 211a, granted summary judgment for Agee, and ordered the Secretary to restore his passport. *Agee* v. *Vance*, (D. C. 1980).

**B**

A divided panel of the Court of Appeals affirmed. *Agee* v. *Muskie* (1980). It held that the Secretary was required to show that Congress had authorized the regulation either by an express delegation or by implied approval of a "substantial and consistent" administrative practice, *Zemel*

v. *Rusk* (1965). The court found no express statutory authority for the revocation. It perceived only one other case of actual passport revocation under the regulation since it was promulgated and only five other instances prior to that in which passports were actually denied "even arguably for national security or foreign policy reasons." The Court of Appeals took note of the Secretary's reliance on "a series of statutes, regulations, proclamations, executive orders, and advisory opinions dating back to 1856," but declined to consider those authorities, reasoning that "the criterion for establishing congressional assent by inaction is the actual imposition of sanctions and not the mere assertion of power." The Court of Appeals held that it was not sufficient that "Agee's conduct may be considered by some to border on treason," since "[w]e are bound by the law as we find it." The court also regarded it as material that most of the Government's authorities dealt with powers of the Executive Branch "during time of war or national emergency" or with respect to persons "engaged in criminal conduct."

We granted certiorari (1980), and stayed the judgment of the Court of Appeals until our disposition of the case on the grant of certiorari.

The principal question before us is whether the statute authorizes the action of the Secretary pursuant to the policy announced by the challenged regulation.

## A

### 1

Although the historical background that we develop later is important, we begin with the language of the statute. See, *e.g.*, *Universities Research Assn., Inc.* v. *Coutu* (1981); *Zemel*. The Passport Act of 1926 provides in pertinent part:

> "The Secretary of State may grant and issue passports, and cause passports to be granted, issued, and verified in foreign countries by diplomatic representatives of the United States ... under such rules as the President shall designate and prescribe for and on behalf of the United States, and no other person shall grant, issue, or verify such passports."

This language is unchanged since its original enactment in 1926.

The Passport Act does not in so many words confer upon the Secretary a power to revoke a passport. Nor, for that matter, does it expressly authorize denials of passport applications. Neither, however, does any statute expressly limit those powers. It is beyond dispute that the Secretary has the power to deny a passport for reasons not specified in the statutes. For example, in *Kent* v. *Dulles* (1958), the Court recognized congressional acquiescence in Executive policies of refusing passports to applicants "participating in illegal conduct, trying to escape the toils of the law, promoting passport frauds, or otherwise engaging in conduct which would violate the laws of the United States." In *Zemel,* the Court held that "the weightiest considerations of national security" authorized the Secretary to restrict travel to Cuba at the time of the Cuban missile crisis. Agee concedes that if the Secretary may deny a passport application for a certain reason, he may revoke a passport on the same ground.

### 2

Particularly in light of the "broad rule-making authority granted in the [1926] Act," . . . a consistent administrative construction of that statute must be followed by the courts "unless there are compelling indications that it is wrong." *E. I. du Pont de Nemours & Co.* v. *Collins* (1977), quoting *Red Lion Broadcasting Co.* v. *FCC* (1969). . . . This is especially so in the areas of foreign policy and national security, where congressional silence is not to be equated with congressional disapproval. In *United States* v. *Curtiss-Wright Export Corp.* (1936), the volatile nature of problems confronting the Executive in foreign policy and national defense was underscored:

> "In this vast external realm, with its important, complicated, delicate, and manifold problems, the President alone has the power to speak or listen as a representative of the nation. . . ."

Matters intimately related to foreign policy and national security are rarely proper subjects for judicial intervention. In *Harisiades* v. *Shaughnessy* (1952), the Court observed that matters relating "to the conduct of foreign relations . . . are so exclusively entrusted to the political branches of government as to be largely immune from judicial inquiry or interference. . . ."

### B

### 1

A passport is, in a sense, a letter of introduction in which the issuing sovereign vouches for the bearer and requests other sovereigns to aid the bearer. Very early, the Court observed:

> "[A passport] is a document, which, from its nature and object, is addressed to foreign powers; purporting only to be a request, that the bearer of it may pass safely and freely; and is to be considered rather in the character of a political document, by which the bearer is recognized, in foreign countries, as an American citizen; and which, by usage and the law of nations, is received as evidence of the fact." *Urtetiqui* v. *D'Arcy* (1835).

With the enactment of travel control legislation making a passport generally a requirement for travel abroad, a passport took on certain added characteristics. Most important for present purposes, the only means by which an American can lawfully leave the country or return to it — absent a Presidentially granted exception — is with a passport. As a travel control document, a passport is both proof of identity and proof of allegiance to the United States. Even under a travel control statute, however, a passport remains in a sense a document by which the Government vouches for the bearer and for his conduct. . . .

The first Passport Act, adopted in 1856, provided that the Secretary of State "shall be authorized to grant and issue passports . . . under such rules as the President shall designate and prescribe for and on behalf of the United States . . . ." This broad and permissive language worked no change in the power of the Executive to issue passports; nor was it intended to do so. The Act was passed to centralize passport authority in the Federal Government and specifically in the Secretary of State. . . .

The President and the Secretary of State consistently construed the 1856 Act to preserve their authority to withhold passports on national security and foreign policy grounds. . . .

In 1903, President Theodore Roosevelt promulgated a rule providing that "[t]he Secretary of State has the right in his discretion to refuse to issue a passport, and will exercise this right towards anyone who, he has reason to believe, desires a passport to further an unlawful or improper purpose." Subsequent Executive Orders issued between 1907 and 1917 cast no doubt on this position. This policy was enforced in peacetime years to deny passports to citizens whose conduct abroad was "likely to embarrass the United States" or who were "disturbing, or endeavoring to disturb, the relations of this country with the representatives of foreign countries."

By enactment of the first travel control statute in 1918, Congress made clear its expectation that the Executive would curtail or prevent international travel by American citizens if it was contrary to the national security. . . . The 1918 statute left the power to make exceptions exclusively in the hands of the Executive, without articulating specific standards. Unless the Secretary had power to apply national security criteria in passport decisions, the purpose of the Travel Control Act would plainly have been frustrated.

Against this background, and while the 1918 provisions were still in effect, Congress enacted the Passport Act of 1926. The legislative history of the statute is sparse. However, Congress used language which is identical in pertinent part to that in the 1856 statute as amended, and the legislative history clearly shows congressional awareness of the Executive policy. There is no evidence of any intent to repudiate the longstanding administrative construction. Absent such evidence, we conclude that Congress, in 1926, adopted the longstanding administrative construction of the 1856 statute. See *Lorillard* v. *Pons* (1978).

The Executive construed the 1926 Act to work no change in prior practice and specifically interpreted it to authorize denial of a passport on grounds of national security or foreign policy. Indeed, by an unbroken line of Executive Orders, regulations, instructions to consular officials, and notices to passport holders, the President and the Department of State left no doubt that likelihood of damage to national security or foreign policy of the United States was the single most important criterion in passport decisions. The regulations are instructive. The 1952 version authorized denial of passports to citizens engaged in activities which would violate laws designed to protect the security of the United States "[i]n order to promote the national interest by assuring that the conduct of foreign relations shall be free from unlawful interference.". . .

This history of administrative construction was repeatedly communicated to Congress, not only by routine promulgation of Executive Orders and regulations, but also by specific presentations, including 1957 and 1966 reports by the Department of State explaining the 1956 regulation and a 1960 Senate Staff Report which concluded that "the authority to issue or withhold passports has, by precedent and law, been vested in the Secretary of State as a part of his responsibility to protect American citizens traveling abroad, and what he considered to be the best interests of the Nation."

In 1966, the Secretary of State promulgated the regulations at issue in this case. Closely paralleling the 1956 regulation, these provisions authorize revocation of a passport where "the Secretary determines that the national's activities abroad are causing or are likely to cause serious damage to the national security or the foreign policy of the United States."

## 2

*Zemel* recognized that congressional acquiescence may sometimes be found from nothing more than silence in the face of an administrative policy. [S]ee *Udall* v. *Tallman* (1965); *Norwegian Nitrogen Co.* v. *United States* (1933); *Costanzo* v. *Tillinghast* (1932). Here, however, the inference of congressional approval "is supported by more than mere congressional inaction." *Zemel.* Twelve years after the promulgation of the regulations at issue and 22 years after promulgation of the similar 1956 regulation, Congress enacted the statute making it unlawful to travel abroad without a passport even in peacetime. Simultaneously, Congress amended the Passport Act of 1926 to provide that "[u]nless authorized by law," in the absence of war, armed hostilities, or imminent danger to travelers, a passport may not be geographically restricted. . . .

The 1978 amendments are weighty evidence of congressional approval of the Secretary's interpretation, particularly that in the 1966 regulations. Despite the longstanding and officially promulgated view that the Executive had the power to withhold passports for reasons of national security and foreign policy, Congress in 1978, "though it once again enacted legislation relating to passports, left completely untouched the broad rule-making authority granted in the earlier Act. . . ."

## 3

Agee argues that the only way the Executive can establish implicit congressional approval is by proof of longstanding and consistent *enforcement* of the claimed power: that is, by showing that many passports were revoked on national security and foreign policy grounds. For this proposition, he relies on *Kent*.

A necessary premise for Agee's contention is that there were frequent occasions for revocation and that the claimed Executive power was exercised in only a few of those cases. However, if there were no occasions — or few — to call the Secretary's authority into play, the absence of frequent instances of enforcement is wholly irrelevant. The exercise of a power emerges only in relation to a factual situation, and the continued validity of the power is not diluted simply because there is no need to use it.

The history is clear that there have been few situations involving substantial likelihood of serious damage to the national security or foreign policy of the United States as a result of a passport holder's activities abroad, and that in the cases which have arisen, the Secretary has consistently exercised his power to withhold passports. Perhaps the most notable example of enforcement of the administrative policy, which surely could not have escaped the attention of Congress, was the 1948 denial of a passport to a Member of Congress who sought to go abroad to support a movement in Greece to overthrow the existing government. Another example was the 1954 revocation of a passport held by a man who was supplying arms to groups abroad whose interests were contrary to positions taken by the United States. In 1970, the Secretary revoked passports of two persons who sought to travel to the site of an international airplane hijacking. . . .

The Secretary has construed and applied his regulations consistently, and it would be anomalous to fault the Government because there were so few occasions to exercise the announced policy and practice. Although a pattern of actual enforcement is one indicator of Executive policy, it suffices that the Executive has "openly asserted" the power at issue. . . .

Agee also contends that the statements of Executive policy are entitled to diminished weight because many of them concern the powers of the Executive in wartime. However, the statute provides no support for this argument. History eloquently attests that grave problems of national security and foreign policy are by no means limited to times of formally declared war.

**4**

Relying on the statement of the Court in *Kent* that "illegal conduct" and problems of allegiance were "so far as relevant here, . . . the only [grounds] which it could fairly be argued were adopted by Congress in light of prior administrative practice," Agee argues that this enumeration was exclusive and is controlling here. This is not correct.

The *Kent* Court had no occasion to consider whether the Executive had the power to revoke the passport of an individual whose *conduct* is damaging the national security and foreign policy of the United States. *Kent* involved denials of passports solely on the basis of political beliefs entitled to First Amendment protection. See *Aptheker* v. *Secretary of State* (1964). Although finding it unnecessary to reach the merits of that constitutional problem, the *Kent* Court emphasized the fact that "[w]e deal with *beliefs*, with *associations*, with *ideological* matters." ([E]mphasis supplied). In particular, the Court noted that the applicants were

"being denied their freedom of movement solely because of their refusal to be subjected to inquiry into their beliefs and associations. They do not seek to escape the law nor to violate it. They may or may not be Communists. But assuming they are, the only law which Congress has passed expressly curtailing the movement of Communists across our borders has not yet become effective. It would therefore be strange to infer that pending the effectiveness of that law, the Secretary has been silently granted by Congress the larger, more pervasive power to curtail in his discretion the free movement of citizens in order to satisfy himself about their beliefs or associations."

The protection accorded beliefs standing alone is very different from the protection accorded conduct. Thus, in *Aptheker* v. *Secretary of State,* the Court held that a statute which, like the policy at issue in *Kent,* denied passports to Communists solely on the basis of political beliefs unconstitutionally "establishes an irrebuttable presumption that individuals who are members of the specified organizations will, if given passports, engage in activities inimical to the security of the United States." The Court recognized that the legitimacy of the objective of safeguarding our national security is "obvious and unarguable." The Court explained that the statute at issue was not the least restrictive alternative available: "The prohibition against travel is supported only by a tenuous relationship between the bare fact of organizational membership and the activity Congress sought to proscribe."

Beliefs and speech are only part of Agee's "campaign to fight the United States CIA." In that sense, this case contrasts markedly with the facts in *Kent* and *Aptheker.* No presumptions, rebuttable or otherwise, are involved, for Agee's conduct in foreign countries presents a serious danger to American officials abroad and serious danger to the national security.

We hold that the policy announced in the challenged regulations is "sufficiently substantial and consistent" to compel the conclusion that Congress has approved it....

### III

Agee also attacks the Secretary's action on three constitutional grounds: first, that the revocation of his passport impermissibly burdens his freedom to travel; second, that the action was intended to penalize his exercise of free speech and deter his criticism of government policies and practices; and third, that failure to accord him a prerevocation hearing violated his Fifth Amendment right to procedural due process.

In light of the express language of the passport regulations, which permits their application only in cases involving likelihood of "serious damage" to national security or foreign policy, these claims are without merit.

Revocation of a passport undeniably curtails travel, but the freedom to travel abroad with a "letter of introduction" in the form of a passport issued by the sovereign is subordinate to national security and foreign policy considerations; as such, it is subject to reasonable governmental regulation. The Court has made it plain that the *freedom* to travel outside the United States must be distinguished from the *right* to travel within the United States. This was underscored in *Califano* v. *Aznavorian* (1978):

> "Aznavorian urged that the freedom of international travel is basically equivalent to the constitutional right to interstate travel, recognized by this Court for over 100 years.... But this Court has often pointed out the crucial difference between the freedom to travel internationally and the right of interstate travel.
>
> " 'The constitutional right of interstate travel is virtually unqualified, *United States* v. *Guest* (1966); *Griffin* v. *Breckenridge* (1971). By contrast the "right" of international travel has been considered to be no more than an aspect of the "liberty" protected by the Due Process Clause of the Fifth Amendment....' "

It is "obvious' and unarguable" that no governmental interest is more compelling than the security of the Nation.... Protection of the foreign policy of the United States is a governmental interest of great importance, since foreign policy and national security considerations cannot neatly be compartmentalized.

Measures to protect the secrecy of our Government's foreign intelligence operations plainly serve these interests. Thus, in *Snepp* v. *United States* (1980), we held that "[t]he Government has a compelling interest in protecting both the secrecy of information so important to our national security and the appearance of confidentiality so essential to the effective operation of our foreign intelligence service...."

Not only has Agee jeopardized the security of the United States, but he has endangered the interests of countries other than the United States — thereby creating serious problems for American foreign relations and foreign policy. Restricting Agee's foreign travel, although perhaps not certain to prevent all of Agee's harmful activities, is the only avenue open to the Government to limit these activities.

Assuming *arguendo* that First Amendment protections reach beyond our national boundaries, Agee's First Amendment claim has no foundation. The revocation of Agee's passport rests in part on the content of his speech: specifically, his repeated disclosures of intelligence operations and names of intelligence personnel. Long ago, however, this Court recognized that "No one would question but that a government might prevent actual obstruction to its recruiting service or the publication of the sailing dates of transports or the number and location of troops." *Near* v. *Minnesota* (1931)... Agee's disclosures, among other things, have the declared purpose of obstructing intelligence operations and the recruiting of intelligence personnel. They are clearly not protected by the Constitution. The mere fact that Agee is also engaged in criticism of the Government does not render his conduct beyond the reach of the law.

To the extent the revocation of his passport operates to inhibit Agee, "it is an inhibition of *action*," rather than of speech. *Zemel,* (emphasis supplied). Agee is as free to criticize the United States Government as he was when he held a passport — always subject, of course, to express limits on certain rights by virtue of his contract with the Government. See *Snepp* v. *United States.*

On this record, the Government is not required to hold a prerevocation hearing. In *Cole* v. *Young* [1956], we held that federal employees who hold "sensitive" positions "where they could bring about any discernible effects on the Nation's security" may be suspended without a presuspension hearing. For the same reasons, when there is a substantial likelihood of "serious damage" to national security or foreign policy as a result of a passport holder's activities in foreign countries, the Government may take action to ensure that the holder may not exploit the sponsorship of his travels by the United States. "[W]hile the Constitution protects against invasions of individual rights, it is not a suicide pact." *Kennedy* v. *Mendoza-Martinez* (1963). The Constitution's due process guarantees call for no more than what has been accorded here: a statement of reasons and an opportunity for a prompt postrevocation hearing.

We reverse the judgment of the Court of Appeals and remand for further proceedings consistent with this opinion.

*Reversed and remanded.*

JUSTICE BRENNAN, with whom JUSTICE MARSHALL joins, dissenting.

Today the Court purports to rely on prior decisions of this Court to support the revocation of a passport by the Secretary of State. Because I believe that such reliance is fundamentally misplaced, and that the Court instead has departed from the express holding of those decisions, I dissent.

## [Section I Omitted]

## II

This is not a complicated case. The Court has twice articulated the proper mode of analysis for determining whether Congress has delegated to the Executive Branch the authority to deny a passport under the

Passport Act of 1926. *Zemel* v. *Rusk* (1965); *Kent* v. *Dulles* (1958). The analysis is hardly confusing, and I expect that had the Court faithfully applied it, today's judgment would affirm the decision below. . . .

As in *Kent* and *Zemel*, there is no dispute here that the Passport Act of 1926 does not *expressly* authorize the Secretary to revoke Agee's passport. Therefore, the sole remaining inquiry is whether there exists "with regard to the sort of passport [revocation] involved [here], an administrative *practice* sufficiently substantial and consistent to warrant the conclusion that Congress had implicitly approved it." *Zemel* v. *Rusk* (emphasis added). The Court today, citing to this same page in *Zemel*, applies a test markedly different from that of *Zemel* and *Kent* and in fact expressly disavowed by the latter. The Court states: "We hold that the *policy* announced in the challenged regulations is 'sufficiently substantial and consistent' to compel the conclusion that Congress has approved it. See *Zemel*." ([E]mphasis added.) The Court also observes that "a consistent administrative *construction* of [the Passport Act] must be followed by the courts 'unless there are compelling indications that it is wrong.' "

But clearly neither *Zemel* nor *Kent* holds that a longstanding Executive *policy* or *construction* is sufficient proof that Congress has implicitly authorized the Secretary's action. The cases hold that an administrative *practice* must be demonstrated; in fact *Kent* unequivocally states that mere *construction* by the Executive — no matter how longstanding and consistent — is *not* sufficient. The passage in *Kent* is worthy of full quotation:

> "Under the 1926 Act and its predecessor a large body of precedents grew up which repeat over and again that the issuance of passports is 'a discretionary act' on the part of the Secretary of State. The scholars, the courts, the Chief Executive, and the Attorneys General, all so said. This long-continued *executive construction* should be enough, it is said, to warrant the inference that Congress adopted it. . . . But the key to that problem, as we shall see, is in the manner in which the Secretary's discretion was *exercised, not in the bare fact that he had discretion.*" ([E]mphasis added).

The court's requirement in *Kent* of evidence of the Executive's *exercise* of discretion as opposed to its possession of discretion may best be understood as a preference for the strongest proof that Congress knew of and acquiesced in that authority. The presence of sensitive constitutional questions in the passport revocation context cautions against applying the normal rule that administrative constructions in cases of statutory construction are to be given great weight. *Udall* v. *Tallman* (1965). Only when Congress had maintained its silence in the face of a consistent and substantial pattern of actual passport denials or revocations — where the parties will presumably object loudly, perhaps through legal action, to the Secretary's exercise of discretion — can this Court be sure that Congress is aware of the Secretary's actions and has implicitly approved that exercise of discretion. Moreover, broad statements by the Executive Branch relating to its discretion in the passport area lack the precision of definition that would follow from concrete applications of that discretion in specific cases. Although Congress might register general approval of the Executive's overall policy, it still might disapprove of the Executive's pattern of applying that broad rule in specific categories of cases.

Not only does the Court ignore the *Kent-Zemel* requirement that Executive discretion be supported by a consistent administrative practice, but it also relies on the very Executive construction and policy deemed irrelevant in *Kent*. Thus, noting that "[t]he President and the Secretary of State consistently construed the 1856 [Passport] Act to preserve their authority to withhold passports on national security and foreign policy grounds," the Court reaches out to hold that "Congress, in 1926, adopted the longstanding administrative construction of the 1856 statute." The Court quotes from 1869 and 1901 opinions of the Attorneys General. But *Kent* expressly cited both of these opinions as examples of Executive constructions *not* relevant to the determination whether Congress had implicitly approved the Secretary's exercise of authority. The Court similarly relies on four Executive Orders issued between 1907 and 1917 to buttress its position, even though *Kent* expressly cited the same four Orders as examples of Executive constructions inapposite to the proper inquiry. Where the Court in *Kent* discounted the constructions of the Act made by "[t]he scholars, the courts, the Chief Executive, and the Attorneys General," today's Court decides this case on the basis of constructions evident from "an unbroken line of Executive Orders, regulations, instructions to consular officials, and notices to passport holders.". . .

The Court's reliance on material expressly abjured in *Kent* becomes understandable only when one appreciates the paucity of recorded administrative practice — the only evidence upon which *Kent* and *Zemel* permit reliance — with respect to passport denials or revocations based on foreign policy or national security considerations relating to an individual. The Court itself identifies only three occasions over the past 33 years when the Secretary has revoked passports for such reasons. And only one of these cases involved a revocation pursuant to the regulations challenged in this case. Yet, in 1979 alone, there were 7,835,000 Americans traveling abroad. . . .

In light of this record, the Court, somewhat defensively, comments: "The Secretary has construed and applied his regulations consistently, and it would be anomalous to fault the Government because there were so few occasions to exercise the announced policy and practice. . . . It would turn *Kent* on its head to say that simply because we have had only a few situations involving conduct such as that in this record, the Executive lacks the authority to deal with the problem when it is encountered." Of course, no one is "faulting" the Government because there are only few occasions when it has seen fit to deny or revoke passports for foreign policy or national security reasons. The point that *Kent* and *Zemel* make, and that today's opinion should make, is that the Executive's authority to revoke passports touches an area fraught with important Constitutional rights, and that the Court should therefore "construe narrowly all delegated powers that curtail or dilute them." *Kent* v. *Dulles*. The presumption is that Congress must expressly delegate authority to the Secretary to deny or revoke passports for foreign policy or national security reasons before he may exercise such authority. To overcome the presumption against an implied delegation, the Government must show "an administrative practice sufficiently substantial and consistent." *Zemel* v. *Rusk*. Only in this way can the Court satisfy itself that Congress has implicitly approved such exercise of authority by the Secretary.

## III

I suspect that this case is a prime example of the adage that "bad facts make bad law." Philip Agee is hardly a model representative of our Nation. And the Executive Branch has attempted to use one of the only means at its disposal, revocation of a passport, to stop respondent's damaging statements. But just as the Constitution protects both popular and unpopular speech, it likewise protects both popular and unpopular travelers. And it is important to remember that this decision applies not only to Philip Agee, whose activities could be perceived as harming the national security, but also to other citizens who may merely disagree with Government foreign policy and express their views.

The Constitution allocates the lawmaking function to Congress, and I fear that today's decision has handed over too much of that function to the Executive. In permitting the Secretary to stop this unpopular traveler and critic of the CIA, the Court professes to rely on, but in fact departs from, the two precedents in the passport regulation area, *Zemel* and *Kent*. Of course it is always easier to fit oneself within the safe haven of *stare decisis* than boldly to overrule precedents of several decades' standing. Because I find myself unable to reconcile those cases with the decision in this case, however, and because I disagree with the Court's *sub silentio* overruling of those cases, I dissent.

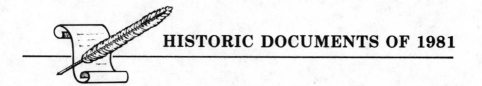

# July

# COURT ON IRANIAN CLAIMS
## July 2, 1981

*Moving quickly to meet a deadline set in U.S.-Iranian negotiations over the release of 52 American hostages, the Supreme Court July 2 unanimously ruled that President Carter had acted within his authority in agreeing to nullify legal claims against Iran. The court also decided, 7-2, that Carter's action in freezing Iran's assets in the United States had not violated the constitutional prohibition against taking property without compensation.*

*In the broadest sense, the rulings reaffirmed the authority of a president to take extraordinary actions in dealing with a foreign government at a time of crisis. Had the court not upheld the hostage agreement, many observers believed, the ability of a president to negotiate with another country with credibility might have been severely damaged.*

*On the other hand, Justice William H. Rehnquist, writing for the court, stressed that the justices were dealing narrowly in the case, Dames & Moore v. Regan et al. "We do not decide," he wrote, "that the President possesses plenary power to settle claims, even as against foreign government entities. . . ." Rehnquist also said, "Crucial to our decision . . . is the conclusion that Congress has implicitly approved the practice of claim settlement by executive agreement."*

### Hostage Accord

*The U.S.-Iranian hostage agreement was negotiated under intense pressure in the closing weeks and days of the Carter administration. In the agreement with the revolutionary Khomeini government, Carter pledged to block legal claims against Iran. Private claims were to be adjudicated by an Iranian-U.S. tribunal.*

*When agreement was finally reached, the hostages, former officials and employees of the U.S. Embassy in Tehran were flown from Iran. Their freedom was achieved only minutes after Ronald Reagan was inaugurated as president. (Release of hostages, p. 145)*

## Court Ruling

*Dames & Moore, a Los Angeles engineering firm, had filed one of more than 2,000 claims by U.S. business firms against Iran. Its lawyers argued before the court that the president lacked the constitutional power to cancel court orders involving the claims, that U.S. firms would have no redress if the Iranian-U.S. tribunal ruled against them, and that Carter's freezing of Iran's assets was an unconstitutional "taking" of property.*

*But the court said that presidents had settled claims of Americans against foreign governments with the implicit approval of Congress almost since the founding of the country. It indicated, moreover, that an American firm whose claims were not settled by the Iranian-U.S. tribunal could sue in the U.S. Court of Claims. Justices Lewis F. Powell Jr. and John Paul Stevens disagreed separately with their colleagues with respect to the freezing of Iranian assets, asserting that it was premature to rule on that aspect of the case.*

## Reaction

*News reports quoted Lloyd Cutler, White House counsel in the Carter administration, as saying that the ruling "strengthened the ability of the presidency and the U.S. government to conduct foreign policy in these very difficult times."*

*Editorial opinion generally praised the action by the court. For example, the Buffalo Evening News said, "No president should be given a blank check even in the conduct of foreign affairs. But given all the unusual aspects of this case, few are likely to quarrel with the Supreme Court's refusal to set aside the hostage accord."*

*Following are excerpts from the ruling of the Supreme Court in Dames & Moore v. Regan, upholding the U.S.-Iranian hostage agreement, a brief concurring opinion by Justice Stevens, and an opinion by Justice Powell, concurring and dissenting in part:*

No. 80-2078

| | |
|---|---|
| Dames & Moore, Petitioner, *v.* Donald T. Regan, Secretary of the Treasury, et al. | On Writ of Certiorari to the United States Court of Appeals for the Ninth Circuit. |

[July 2, 1981]

JUSTICE REHNQUIST delivered the opinion of the Court.

The questions presented by this case touch fundamentally upon the manner in which our Republic is to be governed. Throughout the nearly two centuries of our Nation's existence under the Constitution, this subject has generated considerable debate. We have had the benefit of commentators such as John Jay, Alexander Hamilton, and James Madison writing in The Federalist Papers at the Nation's very inception, the benefit of astute foreign observers of our system such as Alexis deTocqueville and James Bryce writing during the first century of the Nation's existence, and the benefit of many other treaties as well as more than 400 volumes of reports of decisions of this Court. As these writings reveal it is doubtless both futile and perhaps dangerous to find any epigrammatical explanation of how this country has been governed. Indeed, as Justice Jackson noted, "[a] judge . . . may be surprised at the poverty of really useful and unambiguous authority applicable to concrete problems of executive power as they actually present themselves." *Youngstown Sheet & Tube Co.* v. *Sawyer* (1952) (concurring opinion).

Our decision today will not dramatically alter this situation, for the Framers "did not make the judiciary the overseer of our government." We are confined to a resolution of the dispute presented to us. That dispute involves various Executive Orders and regulations by which the President nullified attachments and liens on Iranian assets in the United States, directed that these assets be transferred to Iran, and suspended claims against Iran that may be presented to an International Claims Tribunal. This action was taken in an effort to comply with an Executive Agreement between the United States and Iran. We granted certiorari before judgment in this case, and set an expedited briefing and argument schedule, because lower courts had reached conflicting conclusions on the validity of the President's actions and, as the Solicitor General informed us, unless the Government acted by July 19, 1981, Iran could consider the United States to be in breach of the Executive Agreement.

But before turning to the facts and law which we believe determine the result in this case, we stress that the expeditious treatment of the issues involved by all of the courts which have considered the President's actions makes us acutely aware of the necessity to rest decision on the narrowest possible ground capable of deciding the case. *Ashwander* v. *TVA* (1936) (Brandeis, J., concurring). This does not mean that reasoned analysis may give way to judicial fiat. It does mean that the statement of Justice Jackson — that we decide difficult cases presented to us by virtue of our commissions, not our competence — is especially true here. We attempt to lay down no general "guide-lines" covering other situations not involved here, and attempt to confine the opinion only to the very questions necessary to decision of the case.

Perhaps it is because it is so difficult to reconcile the foregoing definition of Art. III judicial power with the broad range of vitally important day-to-day questions regularly decided by Congress or the Executive, without either challenge or interference by the Judiciary, that the decisions of the Court in this area have been rare, episodic, and afford little precedential value for subsequent cases. The tensions present in any exercise of executive power under the tri-partite system of Federal Government established by the Constitution have been reflected in opinions by Members of this Court more than once. The Court stated in *United States* v. *Curtiss-Wright Export Corp.* (1926):

'[W]e are here dealing not alone with an authority vested in the President by an exertion of legislative power, but with such an authority plus the very delicate, plenary and exclusive power of the President as the sole organ of the federal government in the field of international relations — a power which does not require as a basis for its exercise an act of Congress, but which, of course, like every other governmental power, must be exercised in subordination to the applicable provisions of the Constitution."

And yet 16 years later, Justice Jackson in his concurring opinion in *Youngstown,* which both parties agree brings together as much combination of analysis and common sense as there is in this area, focused not on the "plenary and exclusive power of the President" but rather responded to a claim of virtually unlimited powers for the Executive by noting:

"The example of such unlimited executive power that must have most impressed the forefathers was the prerogative exercised by George III, and the description of its evils in the Declaration of Independence leads me to doubt that they were creating their new Executive in his image."

As we now turn to the factual and legal issues in this case, we freely confess that we are obviously deciding only one more episode in the never-ending tension between the President exercising the executive authority in a world that presents each day some new challenge with which he must deal and the Constitution under which we all live and which no one disputes embodies some sort of system of checks and balances.

I

On November 4, 1979, the American Embassy in Tehran was seized and our diplomatic personnel were captured and held hostage. In response to that crisis, President Carter, acting pursuant to the International Emergency Economic Powers Act (hereinafter "IEEPA"), declared a national emergency on November 14, 1979, and blocked the removal or transfer of "all property and interests in property of the Government of Iran, its instrumentalities and controlled entities and the Central Bank of Iran which are or become subject to the jurisdiction of the United States. . . ." Executive Order No. 42170. President Carter authorized the Secretary of the Treasury to promulgate regulations carrying out the blocking order. On November 15, 1979, the Treasury Department's Office of Foreign Assets Control issued a regulation providing that "[u]nless licensed or authorized . . . any attachment, judgment, decree, lien, execution, garnishment, or other judicial process is null and void with respect to any property in which on or since [November 14, 1979] there existed an interest of Iran." The regulations also made clear that any licenses or authorizations granted could be "amended, modified, or revoked at any time."

On November 26, 1979, the President granted a general license authorizing certain judicial procedings against Iran but which did not allow the "entry of any judgment or of any decree or order of similar or analogous effect. . . ." On December 19, 1979, a clarifying regulation was issued stating that "the general authorization for judicial proceedings . . . includes prejudgment attachment."

On December 19, 1979, petitioner Dames & Moore filed suit in the United States District Court for the Central District of California against the Government of Iran, the Atomic Energy Organization of Iran, and a number of Iranian banks. In its complaint, petitioner alleged that its wholly owned subsidiary, Dames & Moore International, S.R.L. was a party to a written contract with the Atomic Energy Organization, and that the subsidiary's entire interest in the contract had been assigned to petitioner. Under the contract, the subsidiary was to conduct site studies for a proposed nuclear power plant in Iran. As provided in the terms of the contract, the Atomic Energy Organization terminated the agreement for its own convenience on June 30, 1979. Petitioner contended, however, that it was owed $3,436,694.30 plus interest for services performed under the contract prior to the date of termination. The District Court issued orders of attachment directed against property of the defendants, and the property of certain Iranian banks was then attached to secure any judgment that might be entered against them.

On January 20, 1981, the Americans held hostage were released by Iran pursuant to an Agreement entered into the day before and embodied in two Declarations of the Democratic and Popular Republic of Algeria. The Agreement stated that "it is the purpose of [the United States and Iran] . . . to terminate all litigation as between the Government of each party and the nationals of the other, and to bring about the settlement and termination of all such claims through binding arbitration." In furtherance of this goal, the Agreement called for the establishment of an Iran-United States Claims Tribunal which would arbitrate any claims not settled within 6 months. Awards of the Claims Tribunal are to be "final and binding" and "enforceable . . . in the courts of any nation in accordance with its law." Under the Agreement, the United States is obligated:

> "to terminate all legal proceedings in United States courts involving claims of United States persons and institutions against Iran and its state enterprises, to nullify all attachments and judgments obtained therein, to prohibit all further litigation based on such claims, and to bring about the termination of such claims through binding arbitration."

In addition, the United States must "act to bring about the transfer" by July 19, 1981, of all Iranian assets held in this country by American banks. One billion dollars of these assets will be deposited in a security account in the Bank of England, to the account of the Algerian Central Bank, and used to satisfy awards rendered against Iran by the Claims Tribunal.

On January 19, 1981, President Carter issued a series of Executive Orders implementing the terms of the Agreement. Executive Order Nos. 12276-12285. These orders revoked all licenses permitting the exercise of "any right, power, or privilege" with regard to Iranian funds, securities, or deposits; "nullified" all non-Iranian interests in such assets acquired subsequent to the blocking order of November 14, 1979; and required those banks holding Iranian assets to transfer them "to the Federal Reserve Bank of New York, to be held or transferred as directed by the Secretary of the Treasury." Executive Order No. 12279.

On February 24, 1981, President Reagan issued an Executive Order in which he "ratified" the January 19th Executive Orders. Executive Order No. 12294. Moreover, he "suspended" all "claims which may be presented to the ... Tribunal" and provided that such claims "shall have no legal effect in any action now pending in any court of the United States." The suspension of any particular claim terminates if the Claims Tribunal determines that it has no jurisdiction over that claim; claims are discharged for all purposes when the Claims Tribunal either awards some recovery and that amount is paid, or determines that no recovery is due.

Meanwhile, on January 27, 1981, petitioner moved for summary judgment in the District Court against the Government of Iran and the Atomic Energy Organization, but not against the Iranian banks. The District Court granted petitioner's motion and awarded petitioner the amount claimed under the contract plus interest. Thereafter, petitioner attempted to execute the judgment by obtaining writs of garnishment and execution in state court in the State of Washington, and a sheriff's sale of Iranian property in Washington was noticed to satisfy the judgment. However, by order of May 28, 1981, as amended by order of June 8, the District Court stayed execution of its judgment pending appeal by the Government of Iran and the Atomic Energy Organization. The District Court also ordered that all prejudgment attachments obtained against the Iranian defendants be vacated and that further proceedings against the bank defendants be stayed in light of the Executive Orders discussed above.

On April 28, 1981, petitioner filed this action in the District Court for declaratory and injunctive relief against the United States and the Secretary of the Treasury, seeking to prevent enforcement of the Executive Orders and Treasury Department regulations implementing the Agreement with Iran. In its complaint, petitioner alleged that the actions of the President and the Secretary of the Treasury implementing the Agreement with Iran were beyond their statutory and constitutional powers and, in any event, were unconstitutional to the extent they adversely affect petitioner's final judgment against the government of Iran and the Atomic Energy Organization, its execution of that judgment in the State of Washington, its prejudgment attachments, and its ability to continue to litigate against the Iranian banks. On May 28, 1981, the District Court denied petitioners motion for a preliminary injunction and dismissed petitioner's complaint for failure to state a claim upon which relief could be granted. Prior to the District Court's ruling, the United States Courts of Appeals for the First and the District of Columbia Circuits upheld the President's authority to issue the Executive Orders and regulations challenged by petitioner. . . .

On June 3, 1981, petitioner filed a notice of appeal from the District Court's order, and the appeal was docketed in the United States Court of Appeals for the Ninth Circuit. On June 4, the Treasury Department amended its regulations to mandate "the transfer of bank deposits and certain other financial assets of Iran in the United States to the Federal Reserve Bank of New York by noon, June 19." The District Court, however, entered an injunction pending appeal prohibiting the United States from requiring the transfer of Iranian property that is subject to "any writ of attachment, garnishment, judgment, levy, or other judicial lien" issued by any court in favor of petitioner. Arguing that this is a case of "imperative public importance," petitioner then sought a writ of certiorari before judgment. Because the issues presented here are of great significance and demand prompt resolution, we granted the petition for the writ, adopted an expedited briefing schedule, and set the case for oral argument on June 24, 1981.

## II

The parties and the lower courts confronted with the instant questions have all agreed that much relevant analysis is contained in *Youngstown Sheet & Tube Co.* v. *Sawyer* (1952). Justice Black's opinion for the Court in that case, involving the validity of President Truman's effort to seize the country's steel mills in the wake of a nationwide strike, recognized that "[t]he President's power, if any, to issue the order must stem either from an act of Congress or from the Constitution itself." Justice Jackson's concurring opinion elaborated in a general way the consequences of different types of interaction between the two democratic branches in assessing presidential authority to act in any given case. When the President acts pursuant to an express or implied authorization from Congress, he exercises not only his powers but also those delegated by Congress. In such a case the executive action "would be supported by the strongest of presumptions and the widest latitude of judicial interpretation, and the burden of persuasion would rest heavily upon any who might attack it." When the President acts in the absence of congressional authorization he may enter "a zone of twilight in which he and Congress may have concurrent authority, or in which its distribution is uncertain." In such a case the analysis becomes more complicated, and the validity of the President's action, at least so far as separation of powers principles are concerned, hinges on a consideration of all the circumstances which might shed light on the views of the Legislative Branch toward such action, including "congressional inertia, indifference or quiescence." Finally, when the President acts in contravention of the will of Congress, "his power is at its lowest ebb," and the Court can sustain his actions "only by disabling the Congress from acting upon the subject."

Although we have in the past and do today find Justice Jackson's classification of executive actions into three general categories analytically useful, we should be mindful of Justice Holmes' admonition, quoted by Justice Frankfurter in *Youngstown* (concurring opinion), that "The great ordinances of the Constitution do not establish and divide fields of black and white." *Springer* v. *Philippine Islands* (1928) (dissenting opinion). Justice Jackson himself recognized that his three categories represented "a somewhat over-simplified grouping," and it is doubtless the case that executive action in any particular instance falls, not neatly in one of three pigeon-holes, but rather at some point along a spectrum running from explicit congressional authorization to explicit congressional prohibition. This is particularly true as respects cases such as the one before us, involving responses to international crises the nature of which Congress can hardly have been expected to anticipate in any detail.

### III

In nullifying post-November 14, 1979, attachments and directing those persons holding blocked Iranian funds and securities to transfer them to the Federal Reserve Bank of New York for ultimate transfer to Iran, President Carter cited five sources of express or inherent power. The Government, however, has principally relied on § 1702 of the IEEPA as authorization for these actions. Section 1702 (a) (1) provides in part:

"At the times and to the extent specified in section 1701 of this title, the President may, under such regulations as he may prescribe, by means of instructions, licenses, or otherwise —

"(A) investigate, regulate, or prohibit —

"(i) any transactions in foreign exchange,

"(ii) transfers of credit or payments between, by, through, or to any banking institution, to the extent that such transfers or payments involve any interest of any foreign country or a national thereof,

"(iii) the importing or exporting of currency or securities, and

"(B) investigate, regulate, direct and compel, nullify, void, prevent

or prohibit, any acquisition, holding, withholding, use, transfer, withdrawal, transportation, importation or exportation of, or dealing in, or
exercising any right, power or privilege with respect to, or transactions
involving, any property in which any foreign country or a national
thereof has any interest;

"by any person, or with respect to any property, subject to the
jurisdiction of the United States."

The Government contends that the acts of "nullifying" the attachments
and ordering the "transfer" of the frozen assets are specifically authorized
by the plain language of the above statute. The two Courts of Appeals that
have considered the issue agreed with this contention. . . .

Petitioner contends that we should ignore the plain language of this
statute because an examination of its legislative history as well as the
history of § 5 (b) of the Trading With the Enemy Act (hereinafter
"TWEA") from which the pertinent language of § 1702 is directly drawn,
reveals that the statute was not intended to give the President such
extensive power over the assets of a foreign state during times of national
emergency. According to petitioner, once the President instituted the
November 14, 1979, blocking order, § 1702 authorized him "only to
continue the freeze or to discontinue controls."

We do not agree and refuse to read out of § 1702 all meaning to the
words "transfer," "compel," or "nullify." Nothing in the legislative history
of either § 1702 or § 5 (b) of the TWEA requires such a result. To the
contrary, we think both the legislative history and cases interpreting the
TWEA fully sustain the broad authority of the Executive when acting
under this congressional grant of power. See, *e.g., Orvis* v. *Brownell* (1953).
Although Congress intended to limit the President's emergency power in
peacetime, we do not think the changes brought about by the enactment of
the IEEPA in any way affected the authority of the President to take the
specific actions taken here. We likewise note that by the time petitioner instituted this action, the President had already entered the freeze order.
Petitioner proceeded against the blocked assets only after the Treasury
Department had issued revocable licenses authorizing such proceedings
and attachments. The Treasury regulations provided that "unless licensed" any attachment is null and void and all licenses "may be amended,
modified, or revoked at any time." As such, the attachments obtained by
petitioner were specifically made subordinate to further actions which the
President might take under the IEEPA. Petitioner was on notice of the
contingent nature of its interest in the frozen assets.

This Court has previously recognized that the congressional purpose in
authorizing blocking orders is "to put control of foreign assets in the hands
of the President. . . ." *Propper* v. *Clark* (1949). Such orders permit the
President to maintain the foreign assets at his disposal for use in
negotiating the resolution of a declared national emergency. The frozen
assets serve as a "bargaining chip" to be used by the President when
dealing with a hostile country. Accordingly, it is difficult to accept
petitioner's argument because the practical effect of it is to allow individ-

ual claimants throughout the country to minimize or wholly eliminate this "bargaining chip" through attachments, garnishments or similar encumbrances on property. Neither the purpose the statute was enacted to serve nor its plain language supports such a result.

Because the President's action in nullifying the attachments and ordering the transfer of the assets was taken pursuant to specific congressional authorization, it is "supported by the strongest of presumptions and the widest latitude of judicial interpretation, and the burden of persuasion would rest heavily upon any who might attack it." *Youngstown* (Jackson, J., concurring). Under the circumstances of this case, we cannot say that petitioner has sustained that heavy burden. A contrary ruling would mean that the Federal Government as a whole lacked the power exercised by the President and that we are not prepared to say.

## IV

Although we have concluded that the IEEPA constitutes specific congressional authorization to the President to nullify the attachments and order the transfer of Iranian assets, there remains the question of the President's authority to suspend claims pending in American courts. Such claims have, of course, an existence apart from the attachments which accompanied them. In terminating these claims through Executive Order No. 12294, the President purported to act under authority of both the IEEPA and 22 U.S.C. § 1732, the so-called "Hostage Act."

We conclude that although the IEEPA authorized the nullification of the attachments, it cannot be read to authorize the suspension of the claims. The claims of American citizens against Iran are not in themselves transactions involving Iranian property or efforts to exercise any rights with respect to such property. An *in personam* lawsuit, although it might eventually be reduced to judgment and that judgment might be executed upon, is an effort to establish liability and fix damages and does not focus on any particular property within the jurisdiction. The terms of the IEEPA therefore do not authorize the President to suspend claims in American courts. This is the view of all the courts which have considered the question. . . .

The Hostage Act, passed in 1868, provides:

"Whenever it is made known to the President that any citizen of the United States has been unjustly deprived of his liberty by or under the authority of any foreign government, it shall be the duty of the President forthwith to demand of that government the reasons of such imprisonment; and if it appears to be wrongful and in violation of the rights of American citizenship, the President shall forthwith demand the release of such citizen, and if the release so demanded is unreasonably delayed or refused, the President shall use such means, not amounting to acts of war, as he may think necessary and proper to obtain or effectuate the release; and all the facts and proceedings relative thereto shall as soon as practicable be communicated by the President to Congress."

We are reluctant to conclude that this provision constitutes specific authorization to the President to suspend claims in American courts. Although the broad language of the Hostage Act suggests it may cover this case, there are several difficulties with such a view. The legislative history indicates that the Act was passed in response to a situation unlike the recent Iranian crisis. . . .

Concluding that neither the IEEPA nor the Hostage Act constitutes specific authorization of the President's action suspending claims, however, is not to say that these statutory provisions are entirely irrelevant to the question of the validity of the President's action. We think both statutes highly relevant in the looser sense of indicating congressional acceptance of a broad scope for executive action in circumstances such as those presented in this case. As noted above in Part III, the IEEPA delegates broad authority to the President to act in times of national emergency with respect to property of a foreign country. The Hostage Act similarly indicates congressional willingness that the President have broad discretion when responding to the hostile acts of foreign sovereigns. . . .

Although we have declined to conclude that the IEEPA or the Hostage Act directly authorizes the President's suspension of claims for the reasons noted, we cannot ignore the general tenor of Congress' legislation in this area in trying to determine whether the President is acting alone or at least with the acceptance of Congress. As we have noted, Congress cannot anticipate and legislate with regard to every possible action the President may find it necessary to take or every possible situation in which he might act. Such failure of Congress specifically to delegate authority does not, "especially . . . in the areas of foreign policy and national security," imply "congressional disapproval" of action taken by the Executive. *Haig* v. *Agee* (1981). On the contrary, the enactment of legislation closely related to the question of the President's authority in a particular case which evinces legislative intent to accord the President broad discretion may be considered to "invite" "measures on independent presidential responsibility." *Youngstown* (Jackson, J., concurring). At least this is so where there is no contrary indication of legislative intent and when, as here, there is a history of congressional acquiescence in conduct of the sort engaged in by the President. It is to that history which we now turn.

Not infrequently in affairs between nations, outstanding claims by nationals of one country against the government of another country are "sources of friction" between the two sovereigns. *United States* v. *Pink* (1942). To resolve these difficulties, nations have often entered into agreements settling the claims of their respective nationals. As one treatise writer puts it, international agreements settling claims by nationals of one state against the government of another "are established international practice reflecting traditional international theory." L. Henkin, Foreign Affairs and the Constitution 262 (1972). Consistent with that principle, the United States has repeatedly exercised its sovereign authority to settle the claims of its nationals against foreign countries. Though those settlements have sometimes been made by treaty, there has also been a longstanding practice of settling such claims by executive agreement without the advice and consent of the Senate. Under such agreements, the President has agreed to renounce or extinguish claims of United States nationals against foreign governments in return for lump sum payments or the establishment of arbitration procedures. To be sure, many of these settlements were encouraged by the United States claimants themselves, since a claimant's only hope of obtaining any payment at all might lie in having his government negotiate a diplomatic settlement on his behalf. But it is also undisputed that the "United States has sometimes disposed of the claims of citizens without their consent, or even without consultation with them, usually without exclusive regard for their interests, as distinguished from those of the nation as a whole." Henkin, *supra*, at 263. It is clear that the practice of settling claims continues today. Since 1952, the President has entered into at least 10 binding settlements with foreign nations, including an $80 million settlement with the People's Republic of China.

Crucial to our decision today is the conclusion that Congress has implicitly approved the practice of claim settlement by executive agreement. This is best demonstrated by Congress' enactment of the International Claims Settlement Act of 1949. The Act had two purposes: (1) to allocate to United States nationals funds received in the course of an executive claims settlement with Yugoslavia, and (2) to provide a procedure whereby funds resulting from future settlements could be distributed. To achieve these ends Congress created the International Claims Commission, now the Foreign Claims Settlement Commission, and gave it jurisdiction to make final and binding decisions with respect to claims by United States nationals against settlement funds. By creating a procedure to implement future settlement agreements, Congress placed its stamp of approval on such agreements. . . .

In addition to congressional acquiescence in the President's power to settle claims, prior cases of this Court have also recognized that the President does have some measure of power to enter into executive agreements without obtaining the advice and consent of the Senate. . . .

In light of all the foregoing — the inferences to be drawn from the character of the legislation Congress has enacted in the area, such as the IEEPA and the Hostage Act, and from the history of acquiescence in executive claims settlement — we conclude that the President was authorized to suspend pending claims pursuant to Executive Order No. 12294. As Justice Frankfurter pointed out in *Youngstown*, "a systematic, unbroken executive practice, long pursued to the knowledge of Congress and never before questioned . . . may be treated as a gloss on 'Executive Power' vested in the President by § 1 of Art. II." Past practice does not, by itself, create power, but "long-continued practice, known to and acquiesced in by Congress, would raise a presumption that the [action] has been [taken] in pursuance of its consent. . . ." *United States* v. *Midwest Oil Co.* (1915). See *Haig* v. *Agee*. Such practice is present here and such a presumption is also appropriate. In light of the fact that Congress may be considered to have consented to the President's action in suspending claims, we cannot say that action exceeded the President's powers.

Our conclusion is buttressed by the fact that the means chosen by the President to settle the claims of American nationals provided an alternate forum, the Claims Tribunal, which is capable of providing meaningful relief. The Solicitor General also suggests that the provision of the Claims Tribunal will actually *enhance* the opportunity for claimants to recover their claims, in that the Agreement removes a number of jurisdictional and procedural impediments faced by claimants in United States courts. Although being overly sanguine about the chances of United States claimants before the Claims Tribunal would require a degree of naivete which should not be demanded even of judges, the Solicitor General's point cannot be discounted. Moreover, it is important to remember that we have already held that the President has the *statutory* authority to nullify attachments and to transfer the assets out of the country. The President's power to do so does not depend on his provision of a forum whereby claimants can recover on those claims. The fact that the President has provided such a forum here means that the claimants are receiving something in return for the suspension of their claims, namely, access to an international tribunal before which they may well recover something on their claims. Because there does appear to be a real "settlement" here, this case is more easily analogized to the more traditional claim settlement cases of the past.

Just as importantly, Congress has not disapproved of the action taken here. Though Congress has held hearings on the Iranian Agreement itself, Congress has not enacted legislation, or even passed a resolution, indicating its displeasure with the Agreement. Quite the contrary, the relevant Senate Committee has stated that the establishment of the Tribunal is "of vital importance to the United States." We are thus clearly not confronted with a situation in which Congress has in some way resisted the exercise of presidential authority.

Finally, we re-emphasize the narrowness of our decision. We do not decide that the President possesses plenary power to settle claims, even as against foreign governmental entities. As the Court of Appeals for the First Circuit stressed, "the sheer magnitude of such a power, considered against the background of the diversity and complexity of modern international trade, cautions against any broader construction of authority than is necessary." *Chas. T. Main Int'l., Inc.* v. *Khuzestan Water & Power Authority* [CA1 1981]. But where, as here, the settlement of claims has been determined to be a necessary incident to the resolution of a major foreign policy dispute between our country and another, and where, as here, we can conclude that Congress acquiesced in the President's action, we are not prepared to say that the President lacks the power to settle such claims.

## V

We do not think it appropriate at the present time to address petitioner's contention that the suspension of claims, if authorized, would constitute a taking of property in violation of the Fifth Amendment to the United States Constitution in the absence of just compensation. Both petitioner and the Government concede that the question whether the suspension of the claims constitutes a taking is not ripe for review....

It has been contended that the "treaty exception" to the jurisdiction of the Court of Claims might preclude the Court of Claims from exercising jurisdiction over any takings claim the petitioner might bring. At oral argument, however, the Government conceded that § 1502 would not act as a bar to petitioner's action in the Court of Claims. We agree. Accordingly, to the extent petitioner believes it has suffered an unconstitutional taking by the suspension of the claims, we see no jurisdictional obstacle to an appropriate action in the United States Court of Claims under the Tucker Act.

The judgment of the District Court is accordingly affirmed, and the mandate shall issue forthwith.

JUSTICE STEVENS, concurring.

In my judgment the possibility that requiring this petitioner to prosecute its claim in another forum will constitute an unconstitutional "taking" is so remote that I would not address the jurisdictional question considered in Part V of the Court's opinion. However, I join the remainder of the opinion.

JUSTICE POWELL, concurring and dissenting in part.

I join the Court's opinion except its decision that the nullification of the attachments did not effect a taking of property interests giving rise to claims for just compensation. The nullification of attachments presents a separate question from whether the suspension and proposed settlement of claims against Iran may constitute a taking. I would leave both "taking" claims open for resolution on a case-by-case basis in actions before the Court of Claims. The facts of the hundreds of claims pending against Iran are not known to this Court and may differ from the facts in this case. I therefore dissent from the Court's decision with respect to attachments. The decision may well be erroneous, and it certainly is premature with respect to many claims.

I agree with the Court's opinion with respect to the suspension and settlement of claims against Iran and its instrumentalities. The opinion makes clear that some claims may not be adjudicated by the Claims Tribunal, and that others may not be paid in full. The Court holds that parties whose valid claims are not adjudicated or not fully paid may bring a "taking" claim against the United States in the Court of Claims, the jurisdiction of which this Court acknowledges. The Government must pay just compensation when it furthers the Nation's foreign policy goals by using as "bargaining chips" claims lawfully held by a relatively few persons and subject to the jurisdiction of our courts. The extraordinary powers of the President and Congress upon which our decision rests cannot, in the circumstances of this case, displace the Just Compensation Clause of the Constitution.

# FIRST WOMAN APPOINTED TO SUPREME COURT

## July 7, 1981

*In a historic action, President Reagan on July 7 nominated the first woman to the Supreme Court of the United States. After four hours of speeches September 21 on the nomination, the U.S. Senate unanimously confirmed the president's choice, Sandra Day O'Connor.*

*The senators' time was billed as a "debate," but the comments were strictly one-sided: all effusively praised the nominee. The final vote tally was 99-0 and the new justice was sworn in September 25.*

*She replaced Potter Stewart, a moderate-to-conservative justice and frequent swing vote on the court, who retired July 3, 1981, after nearly 23 years of service. At a news conference June 19, the day after his retirement was announced, Stewart, 66, said he wanted to leave the court while he still was in good health and able to enjoy the added time with his family.*

*Much speculation had surrounded the question of Reagan's choice to fill a vacancy on the high court, which, in recent years, had handed down many decisions by 5-4 margins. Court observers speculated that the panel's newest member could significantly influence the closely divided court. Adding to the speculation was Reagan's promise, made while campaigning, to consider naming a woman to the court.*

### Judicial Restraint

*From what was known about her philosophy as a superior court judge in Arizona, it appeared that O'Connor would fit in comfortably with the court as it functioned under Chief Justice Warren E. Burger. She was inclined to defer to the legislative and executive branches on most questions, practicing what had come to be known as "judicial restraint." Such restraint was highly valued by Reagan.*

*"Judicial activism," the practice of making social policy through judicial decisions, came under scrutiny by the Reagan administration in 1981. Of judicial activism, O'Connor said that the Constitution, through Articles I, II and III, "requires the federal courts scrupulously to avoid making law or engaging in general supervision of executive functions."* (Attorney general on judicial activism, p. 803)

## A Unifying Voice?

*Unlike the other justices serving at the time of her appointment, O'Connor, a former majority leader of the Arizona state Senate, brought to the court some solid political experience.*

*In a court lacking both philosophic "glue" and charismatic leadership, O'Connor's political background and the skills associated with it were expected to give her unusual influence for a new justice. She joined the court at a time when it was sharply divided on a number of critical issues — First Amendment rights, search and seizure questions, official immunity, abortion and equal rights.*

*The court's need for a persuasive unifying voice was never more evident than in three decisions made at the end of the spring 1981 term. Two of those decisions dealt with police searches of automobiles. In one, the court permitted the search of a jacket found in a car, while in the other the justices barred the search of two wrapped packages found in a car. These decisions prompted Justice Lewis F. Powell Jr. to lament that the state of the law was "intolerably confusing."*

*In the third decision, announced on the last day of the term, the court voted 6-3 to invalidate a San Diego billboard ban. Four members voted against the ban for one reason while two others voted against it for another. The three dissenters also wrote separate opinions, with Justice William H. Rehnquist, O'Connor's law school classmate, calling the court's entire discussion of the case a "Tower of Babel."*

*The court also had been equivocal on two highly sensitive issues: abortion and sex discrimination. Although the court had not backed away from the 1973* Roe v. Wade *case legalizing abortion, it had upheld a number of legislative restrictions on abortion. In the 1970s the court struck down various state and federal laws because they discriminated unfairly between the sexes. But in 1981 the court upheld a congressional decision to exclude women from the military draft.* (Court on all-male draft, p. 521)

It was expected that O'Connor would play a decisive role in cases coming before the court in these areas because the justice she replaced, Stewart, had cast the deciding vote to uphold congressional restrictions on public funding of abortion and to strike down a minority quota system in medical school admissions.

During three days of confirmation hearings before the Senate Judiciary Committee, O'Connor was asked repeatedly about her views on abortion. To the obvious frustration of some senators, she refused to comment specifically on Roe v. Wade. She stated that abortion was "repugnant" to her personally, but continued to say that her personal views would not be a factor in any case she decided.

In response to questioning by Edward M. Kennedy, D-Mass., O'Connor said she always had been concerned about discrimination against women, and that she believed in "vigorous enforcement" of civil rights laws.

## No-Nonsense Jurist

Sandra Day O'Connor had excelled both academically and professionally. She graduated magna cum laude from Stanford University in 1950 and was third in her Stanford law school class of 1952. Two slots ahead of her in first place was William H. Rehnquist, named to the Supreme Court by President Nixon in 1971.

After moving from California to Arizona with her husband, John Jay O'Connor III, O'Connor spent six years in private law practice and then served as assistant state attorney general from 1965 through 1968. She was temporarily appointed to fill a slot in the Arizona Senate in 1969 and then won election to two full terms. She was elected majority leader in 1973.

O'Connor left the Legislature in 1974 to run for superior court judge and remained in that post until Gov. Bruce Babbitt, a Democrat, appointed her to the Arizona Court of Appeals in 1979.

As a state trial and appellate judge, O'Connor was known as a serious student of the law who kept her courtroom running smoothly and displayed little patience with unprepared lawyers. Such attributes were expected to prove useful on the Supreme Court, where justices frequently engage in lively and pointed exchanges with attorneys arguing cases before them.

"She's pretty much known as an iron lady," said one Phoenix lawyer who recalled that O'Connor "jumped on me with both feet" when he fumbled in trying to answer her questions during a trial. "The best I ever got from her," the lawyer said, "was a cold politeness, and I was pretty happy I could get her to there. . . . In terms of her ability," he added, "she is a very bright lady. She knows a lot of law."

*Another Phoenix lawyer, William P. Mahoney, a former ambassador
under presidents John F. Kennedy and Lyndon B. Johnson, characterized O'Connor as "fair, objective and open-minded.... She runs a tight
court. You get the feeling she's all business. She's not a winger — left or
right," Mahoney added.*

*Following are the text of President Reagan's announcement
July 7, 1981, of the nomination of Sandra Day O'Connor to
the Supreme Court and excerpts from her testimony before
the Senate Judiciary Committee, September 9, 10 and 11.
(Boldface headings in brackets have been added by Congressional Quarterly to highlight the organization of the text.):*

# REAGAN ANNOUNCEMENT

... As President of the United States, I have the honor and the privilege
to pick thousands of appointees for positions in Federal Government. Each
is important and deserves a great deal of care for each individual called
upon to make his or her contribution, often at personal sacrifice, to
shaping the policy of the Nation. Thus each has an obligation to you, in
varying degrees, has an impact on your life.

In addition, as President, I have the privilege to make a certain number
of nominations which have a more lasting influence on our lives, for they
are the lifetime appointments of those men and women called upon to
serve in the judiciary in our Federal district courts and courts of appeals.
These individuals dispense justice and provide for us these most cherished
guarantees of protections of our criminal and civil laws. But, without
doubt, the most awesome appointment is a guarantee to us of so many
things, because it is a President — as a President, I can make an
appointment to the United States Supreme Court.

Those who sit in the Supreme Court interpret the laws of our land and
truly do leave their footprints on the sands of time. Long after the policies
of Presidents and Senators and Congressmen of any given era may have
passed from public memory, they'll be remembered.

After very careful review and consideration, I have made the decision as
to my nominee to fill the vacancy on the United States Supreme Court created by the resignation of Justice [Potter] Stewart. Since I am aware of the
great amount of speculation about this appointment, I want to share this
very important decision with you as soon as possible.

Needless to say, most of the speculation has centered on the question of
whether I would consider a woman to fill this first vacancy. As the press
has accurately pointed out, during my campaign for the Presidency I made
a commitment that one of my first appointments to the Supreme Court
vacancy would be the most qualified woman that I could possibly find.

Now, this is not to say that I would appoint a woman merely to do so.
That would not be fair to women nor to future generations of all

Americans whose lives are so deeply affected by decisions of the Court. Rather I pledged to appoint a woman who meets the very high standards that I demand of all court appointees. I have identified such a person.

So today, I'm pleased to announce that upon completion of all the necessary checks by the Federal Bureau of Investigation, I will send to the Senate the nomination of Judge Sandra Day O'Connor of Arizona Court of Appeals for confirmation as an Associate Justice of the United States Supreme Court.

She is truly a person for all seasons, possessing those unique qualities of temperament, fairness, intellectual capacity, and devotion to the public good which have characterized the 101 brethren who have preceded her. I commend her to you, and I urge the Senate's swift bipartisan confirmation so that as soon as possible she may take her seat on the Court and her place in history.

# O'CONNOR HEARINGS

**The Chairman** [Strom Thurmond, R-S.C.]: Judge O'Connor, the time has now come for you to testify. Will you stand and be sworn?

Riase your right hand.

Do you swear that the evidence you give in this hearing shall be the truth, the whole truth, and nothing but the truth, so help you God?

**Judge O'Connor:** I do.

**The Chairman:** Judge O'Connor, we will now give you the opportunity to present an opening statement if you care to do so.

## [Testimony of Sandra Day O'Connor]

**Judge O'Connor:** Thank you, Mr. Chairman. I would like to do so, with your leave and permission.

Mr. Chairman and members of the Senate Judiciary Committee, I would like to begin my brief opening remarks by expressing my gratitude to the President for nominating me to be an Associate Justice of the U.S. Supreme Court, and my appreciation and thanks to you and to all members of this committee for your courtesy and for the privilege of meeting with you.

As the first woman to be nominated as a Supreme Court Justice, I am particularly honored, and I happily share the honor with millions of American women of yesterday and of today whose abilities and whose conduct have given me this opportunity for service. As a citizen and as a lawyer and as a judge, I have from afar always regarded the Court with the reverence and with the respect to which it is so clearly entitled because of the function it serves. It is the institution which is charged with the final responsibility of insuring that basic constitutional doctrines will always be honored and enforced. It is the body to which all Americans look for the ultimate protection of their rights. It is to the U.S. Supreme Court that we all turn when we seek that which we want most from our Government: equal justice under the law.

If confirmed by the Senate, I will apply all my abilities to insure that our Government is preserved; that justice under our Constitution and the laws of this land will always be the foundation of that Government.

I want to make only one substantive statement to you at this time. My experience as a State court judge and as a State legislator has given me a greater appreciation of the important role the States play in our federal system, and also a greater appreciation of the separate and distinct roles of the three branches of government at both the State and the Federal levels. Those experiences have strengthened my view that the proper role of the judiciary is one of interpreting and applying the law, not making it.

## [Future Votes]

If confirmed, I face an awesome responsibility ahead. So, too, does this committee face a heavy responsibility with respect to my nomination. I hope to be as helpful to you as possible in responding to your questions on my background and my beliefs and my views. There is, however, a limitation on my responses which I am compelled to recognize. I do not believe that as a nominee I can tell you how I might vote on a particular issue which may come before the Court, or endorse or criticize specific Supreme Court decisions presenting issues which may well come before the Court again. To do so would mean that I have prejudged the matter or have morally committed myself to a certain position. Such a statement by me as to how I might resolve a particular issue or what I might do in a future Court action might make it necessary for me to disqualify myself on the matter. This would result in my inability to do my sworn duty; namely, to decide cases that come before the Court. Finally, neither you nor I know today the precise way in which any issue will present itself in the future, or what the facts or arguments may be at that time, or how the statute being interpreted may read. Until those crucial factors become known, I suggest that none of us really know how we would resolve any particular issue. At the very least, we would reserve judgment at that time....

I would now be happy to respond to your questions.

## [Experience in Government]

**The Chairman:** Judge O'Connor, you have been nominated to serve on the highest court in our country. What experience qualifies you to be a Justice of the U.S. Supreme Court?

**Judge O'Connor:** Mr. Chairman, I suppose I can say that nothing in my experience has adequately prepared me for this appearance before the distinguished committee or for the extent of the media attention to the nomination. However, I hope that if I am confirmed by the Senate, and when the marble doors of the Supreme Court close following that procedure, that my experience in all three branches of State government will provide some very useful background for assuming the awesome responsibility of an Associate Justice of the U.S. Supreme Court.

My experience as an assistant attorney general in the executive branch of State government and my experience as a State legislator in the Arizona State Senate and as senate majority leader of that body, my experience as a trial court judge in the Superior Court of Maricopa County and my experience as a judge in the Arizona Court of Appeals in the appellate process, have given me a greater appreciation for the concept and the reality of the checks and balances of the three branches of government. I appreciate those very keenly.

My experience in State government has also given me a greater appreciation, as I have indicated, for the strengths and the needs of our federal system of government, which envisions, of course, an important role for the States in that process.

My experience on the trial court bench dealing with the realities of criminal felony cases and with domestic relations cases and with general civil litigation has taught me how our system of justice works at its most basic level.

I hope and I trust that those experiences are valuable ones in relation to the work of the U.S. Supreme Court as the final arbiter of Federal and constitutional law as it is applied in both the State and the Federal courts throughout the Nation.

## [Roles of the Three Branches]

**The Chairman:** Judge O'Connor, the phrase "judicial activism" refers to the practice of the judicial branch substituting its own policy preferences for those of elected Representatives. Would you comment on this practice in the Federal courts and state your views on the proper role of the Supreme Court in our system of government?

**Judge O'Connor:** Mr. Chairman, I have of course made some written comments about this in the committee's questionnaire, and in addition to those comments I would like to say that I believe in the doctrine and philosophy of the separation of powers. It is part of the genius of our system.

The balance of powers concept and the checks and balances provided by each of the three branches of Government in relation to each other is really crucial to our system. In order for the system to work, it seems to me that each branch of Government has a great responsibility in striving to carry out its own role and not to usurp the role of the other branches of Government.

Certainly each branch has a very significant role in upholding the Constitution. It is not just the judicial branch of Government that has work to do in upholding the Constitution. It is indeed the Congress and the executive branch as well.

It is the role and function, it seems to me, of the legislative branch to determine public policy; and it is the role and function of the judicial branch, in my view, to interpret the enactments of the legislative branch and to apply them, and insofar as possible to determine any challenges to the constitutionality of those legislative enactments.

In carrying out the judicial function, I believe in the exercise of judicial restraint. For example, cases should be decided on grounds other than constitutional grounds where that is possible. In general, Mr. Chairman, I believe in the importance of the limited role of Government generally, and in the institutional restraints on the judiciary in particular.

## [Philosophy on Abortion]

**The Chairman:** Judge O'Connor, there has been much discussion regarding your views on the subject of abortion. Would you discuss your philosophy on abortion, both personal and judicial, and explain your actions as a State senator in Arizona on certain specific matters: First, your 1970 committee vote in favor of House bill No. 20, which would have repealed Arizona's felony statutes on abortion. Then I have three other instances I will inquire about.

**Judge O'Connor:** Very well. May I preface my response by saying that the personal views and philosophies, in my view, of a Supreme Court Justice and indeed any judge should be set aside insofar as it is possible to do that in resolving matters that come before the Court.

Issues that come before the Court should be resolved based on the facts of that particular case or matter and on the law applicable to those facts, and any constitutional principles applicable to those facts. They should not be based on the personal views and ideology of the judge with regard to that particular matter or issue.

Now, having explained that, I would like to say that my own view in the area of abortion is that I am opposed to it as a matter of birth control or otherwise. The subject of abortion is a valid one, in my view, for legislative action subject to any constitutional restraints or limitations.

I think a great deal has been written about my vote in a Senate Judiciary Committee in 1970 on a bill called House bill No. 20, which would have repealed Arizona's abortion statutes. Now in reviewing that, I would like to state first of all that that vote occurred some 11 years ago, to be exact, and was one which was not easily recalled by me, Mr. Chairman. In fact, the committee records when I looked them up did not reflect my vote nor that of other members, with one exception.

It was necessary for me, then, to eventually take time to look at news media accounts and determine from a contemporary article a reflection of the vote on that particular occasion. The bill did not go to the floor of the Senate for a vote; it was held in the Senate Caucus and the committee vote was a vote which would have taken it out of that committee with a recommendation to the full Senate.

The bill is one which concerned a repeal of Arizona's then statutes which made it a felony, punishable by from 2 to 5 years in prison, for anyone providing any substance or means to procure a miscarriage unless it was necessary to save the life of the mother. It would have, for example, subjected anyone who assisted a young woman who, for instance, was a rape victim in securing a D. & C. [dilatation and curettage] procedure within hours or even days of that rape.

At that time I believed that some change in Arizona statutes was appropriate, and had a bill been presented to me that was less sweeping than House bill No. 20, I would have supported that. It was not, and the news accounts reflect that I supported the committee action in putting the bill out of committee, where it then died in the caucus.

I would say that my own knowledge and awareness of the issues and concerns that many people have about the question of abortion has increased since those days. It was not the subject of a great deal of public attention or concern at the time it came before the committee in 1970. I would not have voted, I think, Mr. Chairman, for a simple repealer thereafter.

## [Family Planning Services Bill]

**The Chairman:** Now the second instance was your cosponsorship in 1973 of Senate bill No. 1190, which would have provided family planning services, including surgical procedures, even for minors without parental consent.

**Judge O'Connor:** Senate bill No. 1190 in 1973 was a bill in which the prime sponsor was from the city of Tucson, and it had nine other cosigners on the bill. I was one of those cosigners.

I viewed the bill as a bill which did not deal with abortion but which would have established as a State policy in Arizona, a policy of encouraging the availability of contraceptive information to people generally. The bill at the time, I think, was rather loosely drafted, and I can understand why some might read it and say, "What does this mean?"

That did not particularly concern me at the time because I knew that the bill would go through the committee process and be amended substantially before we would see it again. That was a rather typical practice, at least in the Arizona legislature. Indeed, the bill was assigned to a public health and welfare committee where it was amended in a number of respects.

It did not provide for any surgical procedure for an abortion, as has been reported inaccurately by some. The only reference in the bill to a surgical procedure was the following. It was one that said:

A physician may perform appropriate surgical procedures for the prevention of conception upon any adult who requests such procedure in writing.

That particular provision, I believe, was subsequently amended out in committee but, be that as it may, it was in the bill on introduction.

Mr. Chairman, I supported the availability of contraceptive information to the public generally. Arizona had a statute or statutes on the books at that time, in 1973, which did restrict rather dramatically the availability of information about contraception to the public generally. It seemed to me that perhaps the best way to avoid having people who were seeking abortions was to enable people not to bcome pregnant unwittingly or without the intention of doing so.

## [Constitutional Amendments]

**The Chairman:** The third instance, your 1974 vote against House Concurrent Memorial No. 2002, which urged Congress to pass a constitutional amendment against abortion.

**Judge O'Connor:** Mr. Chairman, as you perhaps recall, the *Rowe* [sic] v. *Wade* decision was handed down in 1973. I would like to mention that in the year following that decision, when concerns began to be expressed, I requested the preparation in 1973 of Senate bill No. 1333 which gave hospitals and physicians and employees the right not to participate in or contribute to any abortion proceeding if they chose not to do so and objected, notwithstanding their employment. That bill did pass the State Senate and became law.

The following year, in 1974, less than a year following the *Rowe* [sic] v. *Wade* decision, a House Memorial was introduced in the Arizona House of Representatives. It would have urged Congress to amend the Constitution to provide that the word person in the 5th and 14th amendments applies to the unborn at every stage of development, except in an emergency when there is a reasonable medical certainty that continuation of the pregnancy would cause the death of the mother. The amendment was further amended in the Senate Judiciary Committee.

I did not support the memorial at that time, either in committee or in the caucus.

**The Chairman:** Excuse me. My time is up, but you are right in the midst of your question. We will finish abortion, one more instance, and we will give the other members the same additional time, if you will proceed.

**Judge O'Connor:** I voted against it, Mr. Chairman, because I was not sure at that time that we had given the proper amount of reflection or consideration to what action, if any, was appropriate by way of a constitutional amendment in connection with the *Rowe* [sic] v. *Wade* decision.

It seems to me, at least, that amendments to the Constitution are very serious matters and should be undertaken after a great deal of study and thought, and not hastily. I think a tremendous amount of work needs to go into the text and the concept being expressed in any proposed amendment. I did not feel at that time that that kind of consideration had been given to the measure. I understand that the Congress is still wrestling with that issue after some years from that date, which was in 1974.

Thank you, Mr. Chairman.

## [Nongermane Amendments]

**The Chairman:** Now the last instance is concerning a vote in 1974 against a successful amendment to a stadium construction bill which limited the availability of abortions.

**Judge O'Connor:** Also in 1974, which was an active year in the Arizona Legislature with regard to the issue of abortion, the Senate had originated a bill that allowed the University of Arizona to issue bonds to expand its football stadium. That bill passed the State Senate and went to the House of Representatives.

In the House it was amended to add a nongermane rider which would have prohibited the performance of abortions in any facility under the jurisdiction of the Arizona Board of Regents. When the measure returned to the Senate, at that time I was the Senate majority leader and I was very concerned because the whole subject had become one that was controversial within our own membership.

I was concerned as majority leader that we not encourage a practice of the addition of nongermane riders to Senate bills which we had passed without that kind of a provision. Indeed, Arizona's constitution has a provision which prohibits the putting together of bills or measures or riders dealing with more than one subject. I did oppose the addition by the House of the nongermane rider when it came back.

It might be of interest, though, to know, Mr. Chairman, that also in 1974 there was another Senate bill which would have provided for a medical assistance program for the medically needy. That was Senate bill No. 1165. It contained a provision that no benefits would be provided for abortions except when deemed medically necessary to save the life of the mother, or where the pregnancy had resulted from rape, incest, or criminal action. I supported that bill together with that provision and the measure did pass and become law.

**The Chairman:** Thank you. My time is up. We will now call upon Senator Biden [Joseph R. Biden Jr., D-Del.].

**Senator Biden:** Thank you, Mr. Chairman.

## Judicial Activism

Judge, it is somewhat in vogue these days to talk about judicial activism and judicial intervention, usurpation of legislative responsibility and authority, et cetera.

When those terms are used, and they are — although the chairman did define his meaning of judicial activism — I suspect you would get different definitions of judicial activism from different members of the committee and the academic and judicial professions. One of the things I would just like to point out as this questioning proceeds is that judicial activism is a two-edged sword.

There is the instance where the judiciary determines that although there is no law that the Congress or a State legislature has passed on a particular issue, that there in fact should be one, and the judge decides to take it upon himself or herself to, through the process of a judicial decision, in effect institute a legislative practice.

There is also the circumstance where there are laws on the books that the judiciary has, in a very creative vein, in varying jurisdictions and on the Federal bench, constructed rationales for avoiding. However, today when we talk about judicial activism what comes to mind in almost everyone's mind is the Warren Court and liberal activists.

You are about to be confronted, I would humbly submit, by what I would characterize as conservative activists who do not believe they are being activists; who do not believe that they are in fact suggesting that judges should usurp the power of the Congress; who do not believe that they are suggesting that there should be a usurpation of legislative authority when in fact, I would respectfully submit, you will soon find that that is exactly what they are suggesting.

For example, in your William & Mary Law Review article you discussed the role of the State courts relative to the Federal courts and you believe, if I can oversimplify it, that Federal courts should give more credence, in effect, to State court decisions interpreting the Federal Constitution. You seem somewhat worried about the expansion by the Congress of litigation in the Federal courts under 42 United States Code, section 1983, the civil rights statute.

Then you go on to say, "Unless Congress decides to limit the availability of relief under that statute . . . ," and you go from there. I am wondering whether or not you would consider yourself as a judicial activist if on the Court you followed through with your belief — as I understand the article — that there is in fact too wide an expansion of access to the Federal courts under the civil rights statute, whether or not you would implement that belief, absent the amendment by Congress of the civil rights statute to which you referred. Would you be an activist in that circumstance, if you limited access to the Federal courts under the civil rights statutes absent a congressional change in the law?

## [Proper Role of Judiciary]

**Judge O'Connor:** Senator Biden, as a judge I would not feel that it was my role or function to in effect amend the statute to achieve a goal which I may feel is desirable in the sense or terms of public policy.

**Senator Biden:** Right.

**Judge O'Connor:** I would not feel that that was my appropriate function. If I have suggested that Congress might want to consider doing something, then I would feel that it is indeed Congress which should make that decision and I would not feel free as a judge to, in effect, expand or restrict a particular statute to reflect my own views of what the goals of sound public policy should be.

**Senator Biden:** I thank you for that answer because I fear that — although it probably would be clarified in subsequent questioning — my fear as this hearing began was that we would confuse the substantive issue of judicial activism, usurpation which should be addressed, and which I think has occurred in many instances, with a rigid view of an ideological disposition of a particular judge. A conservative judge can be a judicial activist. A conservative can be a judicial activist, just as a liberal judge could be a judicial activist.

In trying to examine the criteria which should be used in terms of fulfilling our responsibility as U.S. Senators in this committee under the Constitution, performing our role of advice and consent, a professor at the University of Virginia Law School summarized what he considered to be some of the criteria. Let me just cite to you what his criteria are:

He says first, the professional qualifications are integrity, professional competence, judicial temperament and legal, intellectual and professional credentials. Second, he mentions the nominee being a public person, one whose experience and outlook enables her to mediate between tradition and change and preserve the best of the social law and social heritage while accommodating law for the change in need and change in perception. Third, she would in some ways provide a mirror of the American people to whom people with submerged aspirations and suppressed rights can look with confidence and hope.

In a general sense, do you agree with those criteria as set out?

**Judge O'Connor:** Senator, I agree that it is important for the American people to have confidence in the judiciary. It appears to me that at times in recent decades some of that confidence has been lacking. I think it is important that we have people on the bench at all levels whom the public generally can respect and accept and who are regarded as being ultimately fair in their determination of the issues to come before the courts. For that reason, judicial selection is a terribly important function at the Federal as well as the State levels.

**Senator Biden:** Judge, in response to the questionnaire you stated — and I think you essentially restated it to the chairman a moment ago — that judges are "required to avoid substituting their own view of what is desirable in a particular case for that of the legislature, the branch of government appropriately charged with making decisions of public policy."

I assume from that you do not mean to suggest that you as a Supreme Court judge would shrink from declaring unconstitutional a law passed by the Congress that you felt did not comport with the Constitution.

**Judge O'Connor:** Senator, that is the underlying obligation of the U.S. Supreme Court. If indeed the case presents that issue, if there are no other grounds or means for resolving it other than the constitutional issue, then the Court is faced squarely with making that decision.

I am sure that such a decision, namely to invalidate an enactment of this body, is never one undertaken by the Court lightly. It is not anything that I believe any member of that Court would want to do unless the constitutional requirements were such that it was necessary, in their view. I think there have been only, perhaps, 100 instances in our Nation's history, indeed, when the Court has invalidated particular Acts of Congress.

**Senator Biden:** There have been many more instances where they have invalidated acts of State legislatures.

**Judge O'Connor:** Yes, that is true.

## [School Desegregation Decision]

**Senator Biden:** The second concern I have with your view of what constitutes activism on the Court and of what your role as a Supreme Court Justice would be is that it seems, from the comments by many of my colleagues on both sides of the aisle over the past several years and the comments in the press, that the Supreme Court should not have a right to change public policy absent a statutory dictate to do so.

I wonder whether or not there are not times when the Supreme Court would find it appropriate — in spite of the fact that there have been no intervening legislative actions — to reverse a decision, a public policy decision, that it had 5, 10, 20, or 100 years previously confirmed as being in line with the Constitution.

A case in point: In 1954, after about 60 years and with no major intervening Federal statute, to the best of my knowledge, the Supreme Court said in *Brown* v. *The Board of Education of Topeka* that the "separate but equal" doctrine adopted in the *Plessy* v. *Ferguson* case has no place in the field of public education.

Here is a case where, as I understand it, there was no intervening statutory requirement suggesting that "separate but equal" be disbanded, and where the Court up to that very moment — with a single exception involving a law student and where that law student could sit, to the best of my knowledge — where the Court had up to that time held consistently that "separate but equal" was equal and did comport with the constitutional guarantees of the 14th amendment, then decided that that is no longer right.

They changed social policy; a fundamental change in the view of civil rights and civil liberties in this country was initiated by a court. It was not initiated by a court, it was brought by plaintiffs, but the action of changing the policy was almost totally at the hands of the Supreme Court of the United States.

I wonder, first, whether or not you would characterize that as judicial activism and if so, was it right? If not, if it was not judicial activism, how would you characterize it, in order for me to have a better perception of what your view of the role of the Court is under what circumstances, so that you do not get caught up in the self-proclaimed definitions of what is activism and what is not that are being bandied about by me and others in the U.S. Senate and many of the legal scholars writing on this subject?

**Judge O'Connor:** The *Brown* v. *Board of Education* cases in 1954 involved a determination, as I understand it, by the Supreme Court that its previous interpretation of the meaning of the 14th amendment, insofar as the equal protection clause was concerned, had been erroneously decided previously in *Plessy* v. *Ferguson* so many years before.

I do not know that the Court believed that it was engaged in judicial activism in the sense of attempting to change social or public policy but rather I assume that it believed it was exercising its constitutional function to determine the meaning, if you will, of the Constitution and in this instance an amendment to the Constitution. That, I assume, is the basis upon which the case was decided.

Some have characterized it as you have stated, as judicial activism. The plain fact of the matter is that it was a virtually unanimous decision, as I recall, by Justices who became convinced on the basis of their research into the history of the 14th amendment that indeed separate facilities were inherently unequal in the field of public education. For that reason it rendered the decision that it did.

This has occurred in other instances throughout the Court's history. I am sure many examples come to mind, and I think by actual count they may approach about 150 instances in which the Court has reversed itself on some constitutional doctrine over the years, or in some instances doctrine or holdings that were not those of constitutional dimension.

**Senator Biden:** If I can interrupt you just for a moment, I think you are making the distinction with a difference, and I think it is an important distinction to be made. I just want to make sure that I understand what you are saying, and that is that, as I understand what you are saying, social changes — the postulates that Roscoe Pound spoke of — those societal changes that occur regarding social mores must in some way, at some point, be reflected in the law. If they are not, the law will no longer reflect the view of the people.

It seems as though we should understand that when in fact the legislative bodies of this country have failed in their responsibilities — as they did in the civil rights area — to react to the change, the change in the mores of the times, and see to it that this is reflected in the law, on those rare occasions it is proper for the Court to step in.

As Judge Colin Sites of the third circuit said, "It is understandably difficult to maintain rigid judicial restraint when presented with a citizen's grievance crying out for redress after prolonged inaction for inappropriate reasons by other branches of Government."

**Judge O'Connor:** Well, Senator, with all due respect I do not believe that it is the function of the judiciary to step in and change the law because the times have changed or the social mores have changed, and I did not intend to suggest that by my answer but rather to indicate that I believe that on occasion the Court has reached changed results interpreting a given provison of the Constitution based on its research of what the true meaning of that provision is — based on the intent of the framers, its research on the history of that particular provision. I was not intending to suggest that those changes were being made because some other branch had failed to make the change as a matter of social policy. . . .

# OTTAWA ECONOMIC SUMMIT
## July 19-21, 1981

*Freed temporarily from the common problem of rising world oil prices, the leaders and heads of state of the seven largest non-communist nations faced in 1981 at their seventh annual economic summit meeting a series of divergent problems and sometimes conflicting remedies. The result was that while all hands welcomed the mutual exchange of views, they could agree only in the broadest terms "to revitalize the economies of the industrial democracies." They remained far from any consensus on how to do it.*

*In diplomatically general terms, the conferees agreed to attack the twin problems of inflation and unemployment, to continue support for free trade policies, to help improve the economies of the world's poorer nations and to remain sensitive to the international implications of domestic economic policies. The agreements were contained in a 2,000-word communiqué issued at the summit's end on July 21 in Ottawa. Although the primary subject of the conference was economics, the participants also issued statements on global political problems and terrorism.*

*Taking part were President Reagan, Canadian Prime Minister Pierre Elliott Trudeau, French President François Mitterrand, West German Chancellor Helmut Schmidt, Japanese Prime Minister Zenko Suzuki, British Prime Minister Margaret Thatcher, Italian Prime Minister Giovanni Spadolini and President of the European Community Gaston Thorn. The first day and a half of the conference, which began July 19, were held in a luxurious log resort hotel in Montebello, Quebec, about 40*

*miles from Ottawa. The final day was held in Ottawa in the Opera House
at the National Arts Center.*

*The talks were private, and elaborate security precautions were in
evidence, including scuba divers in the Ottawa River at Montebello. News
briefings were available periodically on the views of each participating
nation, with the Americans seeming to stage the most exhaustive and
prominent affairs. Thus most news about the summit emerged through
these briefings. In addition, each of the leaders spoke publicly July 21 at
concluding ceremonies at the Opera House.*

### Economic Differences

*Evidence of the nations' divergent economic problems was clear. In the
United States, for example, controlling inflation was a major goal and
slowing monetary growth became a central tool, although its use produced record high interest rates. But in Europe expanding employment
was a major goal, and high interest rates were seen as an important
obstacle. Further, the dollar was gaining against European currencies, in
part because of high U.S. interest rates; and the dollar's strength made
imports from United States more expensive and forced higher payments
for oil, because it was priced in dollars. Concern with U.S. interest rates
thus was a major issue at the summit, one on which President Reagan refused to concede.*

*But the president did change his mind on the issue of North-South
negotiations and agreed "to participate in preparations for a mutually
acceptable process of global negotiations in circumstances offering the
prospect of meaningful progress." One outcome was the October 21-23
conference in Cancún, Mexico. (Mexican summit, see p. 769)*

*Overall, concessions were few from any of the participants, and the
final communiqué was marked most, perhaps, by artful language that
concealed many still-unresolved important problems.*

> *Following are the texts of the chairman's summary of
> political issues, July 20, 1981; the statement on terrorism,
> July 20; and excerpts from the concluding joint communi-
> qué, issued July 21. (Boldface headings in brackets have
> been added by Congressional Quarterly to highlight the
> organization of the texts.):*

# SUMMARY OF POLITICAL ISSUES

1. Our discussion of international affairs confirmed our unity of view on
the main issues that confront us all. We are determined to face them
together in a spirit of solidarity, cooperation and responsibility.

2. We all view with concern the continuing threats to international security and stability. Lasting peace can only be built on respect for the freedom and dignity of nations and individuals. We appeal to all governments to exercise restraint and responsibility in international affairs and to refrain from exploiting crises and tensions.

3. In the Middle East, we remain convinced that a solution must be found to the Arab-Israeli dispute. We all deplore the escalation of tension and continuing acts of violence now occurring in the region. We are deeply distressed by the scale of destruction, particularly in Lebanon, and the heavy civilian loss of life on both sides. We call on all states and parties to exercise restraint, in particular to avoid retaliation which only results in escalation; and to forego acts which could lead, in the current tense situation in the area, to further bloodshed and war.

4. We are particularly concerned, in this respect, by the tragic fate of the Lebanese people. We support the efforts now in progress to permit Lebanon to achieve a genuine national reconciliation, internal security and peace with its neighbours.

## [Soviet Military Power]

5. In East-West Relations, we are seriously concerned about the continuing build-up of Soviet military power. Our concern is heightened by Soviet actions which are incompatible with the exercise of restraint and responsibility in international affairs. We ourselves, therefore, need a strong defense capability. We will be firm in insisting on a balance of military capabilities and on political restraint. We are prepared for dialogue and cooperation to the extent that the Soviet Union makes this possible. We are convinced of the importance of working towards balanced and verifiable arms control and disarmament agreements in pursuit of undiminished security at lower levels of armament and expenditure.

6. We welcome the fact that, at the Madrid Conference on Security and Cooperation in Europe, Western countries have just taken another major initiative aimed at defining the area to be covered by the measures the proposed European Disarmament Conference would negotiate. Equally important, they have proposed a number of human rights provisions that would give new hope for individuals deprived of their freedom. We believe that Soviet acceptance of these initiatives would enable a balanced conclusion of the Madrid meeting and a substantial reduction of tension in Europe.

## [Afghanistan and Kampuchea]

7. As regards Afghanistan, about which we publicly stated our firm and unanimous position at last year's Venice Summit, we note that the

situation remains unchanged. Therefore, with the overwhelming majority of nations, we continue to condemn the Soviet military occupation of Afghanistan. We support international efforts to achieve the complete withdrawal of Soviet troops and to restore to the Afghan people, who are fighting a war of liberation, their right to determine their own future. We note with approval the constructive proposal of the European Council for an international conference to bring about this result and call upon the Soviet Union to accept it. We are grateful for the report given us by Foreign Secretary Carrington on his recent visit to Moscow, and his discussions there, on behalf of the Ten, on the international conference proposal.

8. Believing as we do that the Kampuchean people are entitled to self-determination, we welcome and support the Declaration of the International Conference on Kampuchea.

9. Together with other states and regional organizations, we are resolved to do what is necessary to enhance regional security and to ensure a peace built on the independence and dignity of sovereign nations. All peoples should be free to chart their own course without fear of outside intervention. To that end, we shall continue to promote peaceful resolution of disputes and to address underlying social and economic problems. We reaffirm our conviction that respect for independence and genuine non-alignment are important for international peace and security.

## [Refugees]

10. Recalling the statement on refugees adopted at the Venice Summit, we are seriously concerned over the growing plight of refugees throughout the World. We reaffirm our support for international relief efforts and our appeal to all governments to refrain from actions which can lead to massive flows of refugees.

# STATEMENT ON TERRORISM

1. The Heads of State and Government, seriously concerned about the active support given to international terrorism through the supply of money and arms to terrorist groups, and about the sanctuary and training offered terrorists, as well as the continuation of acts of violence and terrorism such as aircraft hijacking, hostage-taking and attacks against diplomatic and consular personnel and premises, reaffirm their determination vigorously to combat such flagrant violations of international law. Emphasizing that all countries are threatened by acts of terrorism in disregard of fundamental human rights, they resolve to strengthen and broaden action within the international community to prevent and punish such acts.

2. The Heads of State and Government view with particular concern the recent hijacking incidents which threaten the safety of international civil aviation. They recall and reaffirm the principles set forth in the 1978 Bonn Declaration and note that there are several hijackings which have not been resolved by certain states in conformity with their obligations under international law. They call upon the governments concerned to discharge their obligations promptly and thereby contribute to the safety of international civil aviation.

3. The Heads of State and Government are convinced that, in the case of the hijacking of a Pakistan International Airlines aircraft in March, the conduct of the Babrak Karmal government of Afghanistan, both during the incident and subsequently in giving refuge to the hijackers, was and is in flagrant breach of its international obligations under the Hague Convention to which Afghanistan is a party, and constitutes a serious threat to air safety. Consequently the Heads of State and Government propose to suspend all flights to and from Afghanistan in implementation of the Bonn Declaration unless Afghanistan immediately takes steps to comply with its obligations. Furthermore, they call upon all states which share their concern for air safety to take appropriate action to persuade Afghanistan to honour its obligations.

4. Recalling the Venice Statement on the Taking of Diplomatic Hostages, the Heads of State and Government approve continued cooperation in the event of attacks on diplomatic and consular establishments or personnel of any of their governments. They undertake that in the event of such incidents, their governments will immediately consult on an appropriate response. Moreover, they resolve that any state which directly aids and abets the commission of terrorist acts condemned in the Venice Statement, should face a prompt international response. It was agreed to exchange information on terrorist threats and activities, and to explore cooperative measures for dealing with and countering acts of terrorism, for promoting more effective implementation of existing anti-terrorist conventions, and for securing wider adherence to them.

# CONCLUDING DECLARATION

1. We have met at a time of rapid change and great challenge to world economic progress and peace. Our meeting has served to reinforce the strength of our common bonds. We are conscious that economic issues reflect and affect the broader political purposes we share. In a world of interdependence, we reaffirm our common objectives and our recognition of the need to take into account the effects on others of policies we pursue. We are confident in our joint determination and ability to tackle our problems in a spirit of shared responsibility, both among ourselves and with our partners throughout the world.

## The Economy

2. The primary challenge we addressed at this meeting was the need to revitalize the economies of the industrial democracies, to meet the needs of our own people and strengthen world prosperity.

3. Since the Venice Summit the average rate of inflation in our countries has fallen, although in four of them inflation remains in double figures. In many countries unemployment has risen sharply and is still rising. There is a prospect of moderate economic growth in the coming year but at present it promises little early relief from unemployment. The large payments deficits originating in the 1979-80 oil price increase have so far been financed without imposing intolerable adjustment burdens but are likely to persist for some time. Interest rates have reached record levels in many countries and, if long sustained at these levels, would threaten productive investment.

4. The fight to bring down inflation and reduce unemployment must be our highest priority and these linked problems must be tackled at the same time. We must continue to reduce inflation if we are to secure the higher investment and sustainable growth on which the durable recovery of employment depends. The balanced use of a range of policy instruments is required. We must involve our peoples in a greater appreciation of the need for change: change in expectations about growth and earnings, change in management and labour relations and practices, change in the pattern of industry, change in the direction and scale of investment, and change in energy use and supply.

5. We need in most countries urgently to reduce public borrowing; where our circumstances permit or we are able to make changes within the limits of our budgets, we will increase support for productive investment and innovation. We must also accept the role of the market in our economies. . . .

6. We see low and stable monetary growth as essential to reducing inflation. Interest rates have to play their part in achieving this and are likely to remain high where fears of inflation remain strong. But we are fully aware that levels and movements of interest rates in one country can make stabilization policies more difficult in other countries by influencing their exchange rates and their economies. For these reasons, most of us need also to rely on containment of budgetary deficits, by means of restraint in government expenditures as necessary. It is also highly desirable to minimize volatility of interest rates and exchange rates; greater stability in foreign exchange and financial markets is important for the sound development of the world economy.

7. In a world of strong capital flows and large deficits it is in the interests of all that the financial soundness of the international banking system and the international financial institutions be fully maintained. We welcome the recently expanded role of the IMF in financing payments deficits on terms which encourage needed adjustment. . . .

## Relations With Developing Countries

9. We support the stability, independence and genuine non-alignment of developing countries and reaffirm our commitment to cooperate with them in a spirit of mutual interest, respect and benefit, recognizing the reality of our interdependence. . . .

11. We look forward to constructive and substantive discussions with them, and believe the Cancun Summit offers an early opportunity to address our common problems anew.

12. We reaffirm our willingness to explore all avenues of consultation and cooperation with developing countries in whatever forums may be appropriate. . . .

13. While growth has been strong in most middle income developing countries, we are deeply conscious of the serious economic problems in many developing countries, and the grim poverty faced especially by the poorer among them. We remain ready to support the developing countries in the efforts they make to promote their economic and social development within the framework of their own social values and traditions. These efforts are vital to their success.

14. We are committed to maintaining substantial and, in many cases, growing levels of Official Development Assistance and will seek to increase public understanding of its importance. We will direct the major portion of our aid to poorer countries, and will participate actively in the United Nations Conference on the Least Developed Countries.

15. We point out that the strengthening of our own economies, increasing access to our markets, and removing impediments to capital flows contribute larger amounts of needed resources and technology and thereby complement official aid. The flow of private capital will be further encouraged in so far as the developing countries themselves provide assurances for the protection and security of investments.

16. The Soviet Union and its partners, whose contributions are meagre, should make more development assistance available, and take a greater share of exports of developing countries, while respecting their independence and non-alignment. . . .

18. We attach high priority to the resolution of the problems created for the non-oil developing countries by the damaging effects on them of high cost of energy imports following the two oil price shocks. We call on the surplus oil-exporting countries to broaden their valuable efforts to finance development in non-oil developing countries, expecially in the field of energy. . . .

19. We recognize the importance of accelerated food production in the developing world and of greater world food security, and the need for developing countries to pursue sound agricultural and food policies; we will examine ways to make increased resources available for these purposes. . . .

20. We are deeply concerned about the implications of world population growth. Many developing countries are taking action to deal with that

problem, in ways sensitive to human values and dignity; and to develop human resources, including technical and managerial capabilities. We recognize the importance of these issues and will place greater emphasis on international efforts in these areas.

## Trade

21. We reaffirm our strong commitment to maintaining liberal trade policies and to the effective operation of an open multilateral trading system as embodied in the GATT [General Agreement on Tariffs and Trade].

22. We will work together to strengthen this system in the interest of all trading countries, recognizing that this will involve structural adaptation to changes in the world economy.

23. We will implement the agreements reached in the Multilateral Trade Negotiations and invite other countries, particularly developing countries, to join in these mutually beneficial trading arrangements.

24. We will continue to resist protectionist pressures, since we recognize that any protectionist measure, whether in the form of overt or hidden trade restrictions or in the form of subsidies to prop up declining industries, not only undermines the dynamism of our economies but also, over time, aggravates inflation and unemployment....

27. We endorse efforts to reach agreement by the end of this year on reducing subsidy elements in official export credit schemes.

## Energy

28. We are confident that, with perseverance, the energy goals we set at Venice for the decade can be achieved, enabling us to break the link between economic growth and oil consumption through structural change in our energy economies.

29. Recognizing that our countries are still vulnerable and energy supply remains a potential constraint to a revival of economic growth, we will accelerate the development and use of all our energy sources, both conventional and new, and continue to promote energy savings and the replacement of oil by other fuels....

31. Our capacity to deal with short-term oil market problems should be improved, particularly through the holding of adequate levels of stocks.

32. In most of our countries progress in constructing new nuclear facilities is slow. We intend in each of our countries to encourage greater public acceptance of nuclear energy, and respond to public concerns about safety, health, nuclear waste management and non-proliferation. We will further our efforts in the development of advanced technologies, ...

33. We will take steps to realize the potential for the economic production, trade and use of coal and will do everything in our power to ensure that its increased use does not damage the environment.

34. We also intend to see to it that we develop to the fullest possible extent sources of renewable energy such as solar, geothermal and biomass energy. . . .

## East-West Economic Relations

36. We also reviewed the significance of East-West economic relations for our political and security interests. We recognized that there is a complex balance of political and economic interests and risks in these relations. We concluded that consultations and, where appropriate, coordination are necessary to ensure that, in the field of East-West relations, our economic policies continue to be compatible with our political and security objectives.

37. We will undertake to consult to improve the present system of controls on trade in strategic goods and related technology with the U.S.S.R.

## Conclusion

38. We are convinced that our democratic, free societies are equal to the challenges we face. We will move forward together and with all countries ready to work with us in a spirit of cooperation and harmony. We have agreed to meet again next year and have accepted the invitation of the President of the French Republic to hold this meeting in France. We intend to maintain close and continuing consultation and cooperation with each other.

# ROYAL WEDDING
## July 29, 1981

In a fairy tale setting, the future king of England, Charles Philip Arthur George, prince of Wales, was married to Lady Diana Spencer on July 29. More than 700 million television viewers around the world witnessed the wedding in St. Paul's Cathedral in London, England.

The ceremony was a masterpiece of British pomp and circumstance. The bride and groom arrived for the 11 a.m. service in horse-drawn carriages and afterwards waved to a crowd of thousands from the traditional viewing balcony at Buckingham Palace.

The 20-year-old bride, a member of Britain's aristocracy, was born at Park House, in Sandringham, on the queen's royal estate. Her family boasted an impeccable lineage, directly descended from the Stuart kings. Lady Diana's father, Earl Spencer, was equerry to King George VI and later to Prince Charles' mother, Queen Elizabeth II, whom Diana had called "Aunt Lilibet" since childhood.

Prince Charles, heir apparent to the throne, had been romantically linked to several women following his graduation from Cambridge University. At 32, his age at his marriage, he had emerged from his royal upbringing with a personality quite his own. Described as having his father's bluff heartiness, tempered by his mother's kindness and devotion to duty, the prince was known for his penchant for outdoor activities including polo, skiing, flying and windsurfing.

The wedding, for many Britons, symbolized the continuity of the monarchy in the face of the nation's economic decline and political *turmoil. Many heads of state were among those attending. Nancy Reagan, the president's wife, led the U.S. delegation. Publicity preceding the ceremony generated scores of "wedding souvenirs," including ashtrays with Charles' and Diana's pictures painted on them and special issue coins commemorating the event. Thousands of tourists visited London for the occasion, and many camped out overnight to assure a good view of the bride and groom as they left St. Paul's for Buckingham Palace after the ceremony.*

*In November, the royal couple announced that the princess was expecting a baby in June 1982.*

> *Following is the text of the address of the Archbishop of Canterbury, Dr. Robert Runcie, at St. Paul's Cathedral during the wedding of Prince Charles and Lady Diana Spencer, July 29, 1981:*

Here is the stuff of which fairy tales are made: the Prince and Princess on their wedding day. But fairy tales usually end at this point with the simple phrase: "They lived happily ever after." This may be because fairy stories regard marriage as an anti-climax after the romance of courtship.

This is not the Christian view. Our faith sees the wedding day not as the place of arrival but the place where the adventure really begins.

There is an ancient tradition that *every* bride and groom on their wedding day are regarded as a royal couple. To this day in the marriage ceremonies of the Eastern Orthodox Church crowns are held over the man and woman to express the conviction that as husband and wife they are Kings and Queens of Creation.

As it says of human-kind in the Bible: "Thou crownedst him with glory and honour, and didst set him over the work of thy hands."

On a wedding day it is made clear that God does not intend us to be puppets but chooses to work though us, and especially through our marriages, to create the future of his world.

Marriage is first of all a new creation for the partners themselves. As husband and wife live out their vows, loving and cherishing one another, sharing life's splendours and miseries, achievements and setbacks, they will be transformed in the process. A good marriage is a life, as the poet Edwin Muir says:

> Where each asks from each
> What each most wants to give
> And each awakes in each
> What else would never be.

But any marriage which is turned in upon itself, in which the bride and groom simply gaze obsessively at one another goes sour after a time.

A marriage which really works is one which works for others. Marriage has both a private face and a public importance. If we solved all our economic problems and failed to build loving families, it would profit us nothing, because the family is the place where the future is created good and full of love — or deformed.

Those who are married live happily ever after the wedding day if they persevere in the real adventure which is the royal task of creating each other and creating a more loving world.

That is true of every man and woman undertaking marriage. It must be specially true of this marriage in which are placed so many hopes.

Much of the world is in the grip of hopelessness. Many people seem to have surrendered to fatalism about the so-called inevitability of life: cruelty, injustice, poverty, bigotry and war. Some have accepted a cynical view of marriage itself.

But all couples on their wedding day are "Royal Couples" and stand for the truth that we help to shape this world, and are not just its victims. All of us are given the power to make the future more in God's image and to be "king and queens" of love.

This is our prayer for Charles and Diana. May the burdens we lay on them be matched by the love with which we support them in the years to come. And however long they live may they always know that when they pledged themselves to each other before the altar of God they were surrounded and supported not by mere spectators but by the sincere affection and the active prayer of millions of friends.

Thanks be to God.

▼▼▼

# REAGAN IMMIGRATION POLICY
## July 30, 1981

*Attorney General William French Smith presented the Reagan administration's long-awaited immigration policy in testimony July 30 before the House and Senate immigration subcommittees.*

*The administration's proposed legislative package was the result of recommendations made by the President's Task Force on Immigration and Refugee Policy, formed in March and chaired by Smith. Several of the proposals were similar to recommendations made by the bipartisan Select Commission on Immigration and Refugee Policy in its March report. (Report on immigration, p. 265)*

*The massive Cuban boatlift of 1980 and the continuing flow of Mexican and Haitian immigrants made clear to the United States the need for more effective and enforceable immigration policies. (Cuban boatlift, Historic Documents of 1980, p. 337)*

*The package Smith presented to Congress contained eight basic proposals:*
- *Increased enforcement of existing immigration and fair labor standard laws.*
- *A new law imposing penalties against employers who knowingly hire illegal immigrants.*
- *An experimental temporary worker program for as many as 50,000 Mexican nationals annually.*
- *Limited legal status for qualifying illegal aliens currently living in the United States.*
- *International cooperation, especially within the Western Hemi-*

605

sphere, to enforce immigration laws and discourage illegal entry.

• A seven-point plan to deal with mass migrations, such as those by Cuban and Haitian refugees.

• Reform of the 1965 amendments to the Immigration and Nationality Act to increase to 40,000 from 20,000 the number of immigrants permitted annually from Mexico and Canada and to facilitate entry of "independent" or non-family immigrants bringing needed skills to the United States.

• Continuation of financial assistance and social service benefits for refugees.

## Haitian Refugees

In 1981 one immigration matter of particular concern to the Reagan administration was the continuing arrival in Florida of undocumented aliens from Haiti. The administration was determined, Smith said in his testimony, not to permit another crisis like the Cuban boatlift.

As the influx continued at a rate of approximately 1,000 Haitians a month, Reagan September 29 issued a proclamation in which he declared, "These arrivals have severely strained the law enforcement resources of the Immigration and Naturalization Service and have threatened the welfare and safety of communities" in the Southeastern states. In an executive order accompanying the proclamation, the president authorized the Coast Guard to interdict outside U.S. territorial waters and turn back ships that were suspected of carrying illegal immigrants.

Under an agreement with the Haitian government, a Coast Guard cutter took up position in international waters off the coast of Haiti. Coast Guard personnel were instructed to board suspect vessels, examine documents and question those aboard to determine their status. Political refugees would be accepted in the United States; those leaving their homeland for economic reasons were to be returned.

Meanwhile, the process of separating political refugees from economic ones among those Haitians already in the United States moved sluggishly through a tangle of court proceedings and a tremendous number of applications for asylum.

The measures outlined in Reagan's executive order were controversial. Critics deplored the "nautical kangaroo courts" or "walrus courts"; the National Association for the Advancement of Colored People called the interdiction policy "a barbaric assault on human freedom." Opponents also maintained that Haitians returned to their country would be punished for their attempts to flee.

Reagan officials defended the measures as "appropriate and necessary." They declared that the Haitian government had promised no punitive actions against returnees and that the International Red Cross *and the American Embassy in Haiti would monitor the situation there.*

*As the controversy continued, some refugees still managed to make their way to the United States. On October 26 the news media reported the drownings of 33 Haitians after their small boat capsized just one mile offshore from Miami. In a parallel story, the Coast Guard intercepted another leaky vessel and returned its passengers to Haiti.*

## Congressional Action

*Congress did not act upon the administration's immigration proposals in 1981, though a measure with narrow provisions to reduce the number of private immigration bills and to increase the efficiency of the Immigration and Naturalization Service became law on December 29 (HR 4327, PL 97-116). According to Alan Simpson, R-Wyo., chairman of the Senate Subcommittee on Immigration and Refugee Policy, more comprehensive immigration legislation was expected in 1982.*

> *Following are excerpts from the July 30, 1981, testimony of Attorney General William French Smith before the Senate Subcommittee on Immigration and Refugee Policy and the House Subcommittee on Immigration, Refugees and International Law, and from President Reagan's Proclamation and Executive Order 12324 of September 29, 1981, calling for interdiction of illegal aliens. (Boldface headings in brackets have been added by Congressional Quarterly to highlight the organization of the texts.):*

# SMITH TESTIMONY

## [Introduction]

... [T]his Administration is committed to a major overhauling and strengthening of this nation's immigration and refugee policies. This morning, the President proposed that kind of a major change.

The history of America has been in large part the history of immigrants. Our nation has been overwhelmingly enriched by the fifty million immigrants who have come here since the first colonists. For nearly our first century and one-half as a nation, the Congress recognized our need for new arrivals by imposing no quantitative restrictions on immigration. Since 1921, however, the government and our people have recognized the need to control the numbers of immigrants and the process by which they enter our country.

In recent years our policies intended to effect that necessary control of our borders have failed. Last year, the number of immigrants legally and illegally entering the United States reached a total possibly greater than any year in our history, including the era of unrestricted immigration.

We have lost control of our borders. We have pursued unrealistic policies. We have failed to enforce our laws effectively.

No great nation — and especially a great democratic nation — can long countenance ineffective and unenforced laws. That is especially true when the unsettling results are so apparent to our people.

We must more effectively deter illegal immigration to the United States — whether across our expansive borders or by sea. The proposals announced this morning by the President would have that result. They represent a comprehensive and integrated approach. They recognize the realities we face and the fact that no policy will be enforceable if it ignores the true facts. Those basic facts are:

- the presence of from three to six million illegal aliens in this country;
- the continuing growth of their numbers by from one-quarter to one-half million each year.

The overriding purpose of the President's proposal is to make our laws and policies more realistic — and then to enforce those laws effectively. He believes that we must modestly expand the opportunities for legal employment to reflect the reality of America's attractiveness to much of the world. He believes that we must squarely recognize the existence of a hidden class of illegal aliens who work and live within our society but are beyond its sanctions and protections. And he believes we must develop new enforcement techniques that would allow us to enforce fully laws and policies that reflect those realities.

The proposals announced today are the result of wide consultations both within this country and internationally. They are the result of many months work by the President's Task Force on Immigration and Refugee Policy, which I had the privilege of chairing. They represent the Administration's best ideas on how to regain control of our national borders without closing the doors to this unique land of opportunity.

The President this morning stated the essential purposes of a workable immigration policy.

> We must ensure adequate legal authority to establish control over immigration; to enable us, when sudden influxes of foreigners occur, to decide to whom we grant the status of refugee or asylee; to improve our border control; to expedite (consistent with fair procedures and our Constitution) return of those coming here illegally; to strengthen enforcement of our fair labor standards and law; and to penalize those who would knowingly encourage violations of our laws. The steps we take to further these objectives, however, must also be consistent with our values of individual privacy and freedom.

The Administration's policy proposals will fulfill these purposes. They may be divided, for discussion, into four areas: Illegal immigration; Mass arrivals of undocumented aliens; Legal immigrant and refugee admissions; and Benefits for refugees and persons granted asylum.

## Illegal Immigration

Illegal immigration to the United States has increased drastically in recent years, to a point where it likely equals or exceeds legal admissions. In 1964, approximately 50,000 illegal aliens were apprehended in the United States. By 1979, the number of apprehensions had risen to more than 1 million. Although estimates vary considerably, most fix the illegal alien population of the U.S. at between three and six million, perhaps one half of whom are Mexican nationals; and the illegal population grows by 250,000 to 500,000 persons each year.

While illegal immigrants once were concentrated in agricultural employment in the southwestern states, they now reside in all regions of the country. Only 15% of the illegals are estimated to work in agriculture; 50% are employed in service industries; and 30% are in blue collar jobs.

The American people correctly perceive this as a major national problem. In a recent poll, nine of ten Americans said they favored "an all out effort" to stop illegal immigration. Americans justifiably want their government to take steps to bring immigration within effective regulation.

The Administration proposes five related initiatives to curtail illegal immigration: (1) increased enforcement of existing immigration and fair labor standard laws; (2) a law imposing penalties against employers who knowingly hire illegal aliens; (3) a new experimental temporary worker program for up to 50,000 Mexican nationals annually; (4) legal status for qualifying illegal aliens currently residing in the United States; and (5) international cooperation within the western hemisphere to enforce immigration laws and discourage illegal migration.

Together, the five elements of the President's strategy should reduce substantially illegal immigration by expanding opportunities to work lawfully in the United States — through the experimental temporary worker program and legalization — and by prohibiting employment of those outside of these programs.

### [INCREASED ENFORCEMENT]

The first element is a long-needed strengthening of enforcement of existing legal authorities. We will communicate to you and the Appropriations Committee our support for the addition to the President's FY 1982 budget for INS [Immigration and Naturalization Service] of $40 million in Fiscal Year 1982 to provide for more effective interior and border enforcement and $35 million to detain those who come here illegally pending their exclusion. Those funds will provide the INS with 564 additional positions, including 236 more Border Patrol. The additional funds will also provide for the operations of helicopters and other needed equipment; an expanded program of vehicle seizure in smuggling cases; an improved Nonimmigrant Document Control System; and improved control of alien records. We expect that the additional funds for border and area control operations should result in substantially increased apprehensions annually. . . .

Expanded compliance visits by officers of the Wage and Hour Division of the Department of Labor will discourage employment of illegal aliens, as well as others, in violation of the Fair Labor Standards Act. Additional funding and resource requirements are currently under review. We will seek an additional $6 million for this purpose in FY 1982, which would permit us to identify significantly increased numbers of workers employed in violation of fair labor standards.

## [ILLEGAL HIRING]

Second, the Administration will propose that it be made unlawful to hire illegal aliens. We cannot depend solely upon deterrence or interception at the border. The availability of employment in this country at relatively high wages without regard to legal status will continue to "pull" illegal migration. We cannot seal the border, and efforts to apprehend and deport illegal aliens in the interior is a costly and, at best, partial solution. The only credible enforcement measure remaining is a prohibition on hiring illegal aliens. The Administration will therefore propose legislation prohibiting employers of four or more employees from knowingly hiring illegal aliens. Civil fines of $500 to $1000 would be assessed for each illegal alien hired. The Department of Justice would be authorized to seek injunctions against employers who follow a "pattern or practice" of hiring illegal aliens.

The Administration is opposed to the creation of a national identity card. But, to make employer sanctions a workable deterrent, the Administration recognizes the need for a means of compliance with the law that would provide an employer with a good faith defense if he examines documentary proof of eligibility to work. Acceptable proof of eligibility to work would be (a) documentation issued by the INS, such as a permanent resident alien card or temporary worker visa; or any two of the following: (b) birth certificate, (c) driver's license, (d) Social Security card, and (e) registration certificate issued by the Selective Service System. In addition, the new hire and the employer would sign a form certifying, respectively, that (i) the new hire is eligible to work in the United States, and (ii) the employer has examined the specified identifiers and has no reason to believe the employee is not eligible to work. . . .

We believe that this new law can and will be enforced without discrimination and without burdensome regulation. Since employers may rely on existing documents and will not be required to make judgments about the authenticity of the documents, they would have no occasion to make subjective and possibly discriminatory judgments about persons who may appear to be foreign. We believe, too, that a system which relies on existing forms of documentation will effectively screen out illegal aliens, who will not ordinarily have the necessary documents.

## [EXPERIMENTAL PROGRAM]

Third, the Administration will seek legislation to establish an experimental temporary worker program for Mexican nationals. The hiring of some illegal aliens may be attributed to an insufficient supply of American workers for certain categories of jobs in some localities. Historically, many of these jobs have been filled by foreign workers employed in the United States on a temporary basis — frequently without having been legally admitted for that purpose. Where American workers have in fact not been available to fill these jobs, the presence of foreign workers has been enormously beneficial both to the United States and to Mexico.

Under our proposal, during a two-year trial period, up to 50,000 workers would be admitted annually for stays of from 9 to 12 months. The program would be targeted to specific areas and categories of jobs. Certain job categories would be excluded from this program in States where it was certified that there was an adequate supply of American workers. The Department of Labor would allocate the national ceiling among affected States.

Workers would be free to change employers during their stay here. Normal wage and working standards laws would apply to them, and employers would be required to pay Social Security taxes and unemployment insurance contributions. Workers would not be permitted to bring in spouses and children; would not have access to welfare or food stamps assistance, or be eligible for unemployment compensation.

During the trial period, the program would be evaluated for its impact on American workers, the feasibility of enforcing the program's restrictions, and the benefits to the United States and Mexico.

## [LEGAL STATUS]

Fourth, we must find some practical way of dealing with the illegal aliens now residing in the United States. We have neither the resources, the capability, nor the motivation to uproot and deport millions of illegal aliens, many of whom have become, in effect, members of the community. By granting limited legal status to the productive and law-abiding members of this shadow population, we will recognize reality and devote our enforcement resources to deterring future illegal arrivals. Our purpose is to deter illegal immigration and to prevent the recurrence of the circumstances we are now facing.

We therefore propose to permit illegal aliens, who were present in the United States prior to January 1, 1980, and are not otherwise excludable, to apply for the new status of "renewable term temporary resident." The status would be renewable after every three years, and after a total of ten years continuous residence, those residents would be eligible to apply for permanent resident status if they were not otherwise excludable, and could demonstrate English language capability.

These temporary residents would pay Social Security, income, and other taxes; but would be ineligible for welfare, federally assisted housing, food stamps or unemployment compensation. They would not be able to bring in spouses and children, but could leave the country for visits to their homeland without losing their status unless they interrupted their continuous residence for a substantial period of time.

We intend the proposed enhanced enforcement measures to precede the implementation of this legalization program to assure that illegal immigration is curtailed in the future. Those aliens who do not qualify for legalization or choose not to apply would either leave the country or be subject to deportation if apprehended.

## [INTERNATIONAL COOPERATION]

Finally, the Administration recognizes that the causes of illegal immigration are international in scope and require international solutions. Accordingly, we plan to pursue negotiations with Mexico on two important matters. First, we will explore joint measures to prevent third country nationals crossing Mexico to enter the United States illegally; and second, we will seek increased cooperation in regulating immigration in the border areas, emphasizing measures directed against alien smuggling.

In addition, Secretary of State [Alexander] Haig has already met with the Foreign Ministers of Mexico, Venezuela and Canada to consider a hemispheric development plan. Further discussions are scheduled regarding the establishment of development projects that would alleviate the factors encouraging illegal migration within the hemisphere.

## Mass Arrivals of Illegal Aliens

Mass migrations of undocumented aliens to the United States are a recent phenomenon. They are also a phenomenon for which the nation was woefully ill-prepared, and the consequences of our unreadiness have been disasterous.

The 1980 Mariel boatlift brought a wave of 125,000 Cubans to the beaches of south Florida. Among those persons were criminals and mentally ill, some of whom were forcibly expelled by Castro. Most of the Cubans have been resettled through the efforts of public and private agencies. But 1800 criminals remain in a federal penitentiary in Atlanta, and nearly 1,000 mentally ill and maladjusted remain at Fort Chaffee, Arkansas. Cuba has thus far refused to accept back these persons, notwithstanding its obligations to do so under international law.

There is also a continuing migration to Florida of undocumented aliens from Haiti and elsewhere. Although the Government of Haiti is willing to accept the return of Haitians deported by the United States, exclusion proceedings have been blocked by time-consuming judicial challenges to INS proceedings. To be sure, the foreign policy character of the Cuban and

Haitian migrations differs, but the domestic impact on our local communities and on the administration of our immigration laws is the same.

The Administration is determined not to permit another Mariel. In addition, we must act to curtail the ongoing arrivals of undocumented aliens to our shores in violation of our laws. Finally, we must deal with the recent legacy of those Cubans and Haitians who are already here.

## [SEVEN-PART PROGRAM]

To provide adequate legal authorities to deal with future migration situations, the Administration has developed a seven-part program.

1. We will seek legislation (a) to prohibit bringing undocumented aliens to the United States; and (b) to strengthen existing legal authority for the interdiction, seizure, and forfeiture of vessels used in violation of our laws.

2. We will seek legislation to authorize the President to direct the Coast Guard to interdict unregistered vessels and to assist foreign governments that request such assistance to interdict on the high seas their flag vessels, which are suspected of attempting to violate U.S. law.

3. We will request increased resources for the development of additional permanent facilities in which to detain temporarily illegal aliens upon arrival pending exclusion or granting of asylum. . . .

4. We will propose legislation to reform and expedite exclusion proceedings. Applications for asylum would be heard before newly established asylum officers within INS, with discretionary review by the Attorney General.

5. We will propose legislation to provide the President with special authority, in a Presidentially declared emergency, to prohibit U.S. residents and U.S. registered vessels from traveling to designated foreign countries for the suspected purpose of transporting illegal aliens to the U.S. . . .

6. We will pursue international measures to secure the return to Cuba of those Cubans (currently detained at Fort Chaffee, Arkansas, the Atlanta Federal Penitentiary, and certain other facilities) who would be excludable under U.S. laws; to seek additional resettlement opportunities for Haitians in other Western Hemisphere countries; and to increase cooperation with the Government of Haiti in restraining illegal migration of its nationals to the U.S.

7. We will submit legislation to repeal the Cuban Refugee Adjustment Act of 1966, but to permit Cubans and Haitians who were in the country and known to INS before January 1, 1981, to apply for a "renewable term entrant" status. . . .

The existence of these new legal authorities, and our commitment to their use, if necessary, should avert another Mariel. To assure immediate and effective government action in such an event, the Administration has prepared a contingency plan detailing the responsibilities of relevant government agencies.

## [EXCLUSION AND DETENTION]

Other representatives of the Administration will be pleased to discuss these proposed authorities in detail. I wish, however, briefly to explain two elemental changes of current practice embodied in the proposed policy: the reform of exclusion proceedings, and the necessity of detaining illegal aliens pending exclusion.

In the past, the United States has always screened and processed prospective immigrants, including refugees, overseas. Thus, those individuals actually arriving on our shores have been adjudged eligible for admission prior to arrival. Applications for asylum by persons already in the United States have been relatively few and the cases generally clear-cut. As recently as Fiscal Year 1978 fewer than 3,800 asylum applications were received. But in Fiscal Year 1980, 19,485 applications for asylum were received, and the number of pending applications will reach 60,000 during the current fiscal year, not including the approximately 140,000 applications filed by Cubans and Haitians.

In the face of these circumstances, our policies and procedures for dealing with asylum applicants, which have been generous and deliberate, have crumbled under the burden of overwhelming numbers. Our procedures should be adequate to secure the national interest. The procedural reforms we propose are fair. Moreover, they are the only rational and workable way to preserve the framework that Congress has established to govern the inspection and admission of persons seeking asylum.

Second, the Administration will seek additional resources for the construction of permanent facilities in which to house undocumented aliens temporarily until their eligibility for admission can be determined. By treating those who arrive by sea in the same way we have long treated those who arrive over our land borders, our policy will be evenhanded, and we can avoid the severe community disruptions that result from large-scale migrations.

## Legal Immigration

The basic legal framework governing immigrant admissions to the United States was established by the 1965 amendments to the Immigration and Nationality Act. These amendments retained the policy of numerically restricting certain preference categories of immigration. For the first time in our history, immigration from Western Hemisphere countries was limited, to 120,000 annually. Annual per country ceilings of 20,000 were extended to the Western Hemisphere in 1976.

With regard to refugee admissions, the Congress first dealt comprehensively with the question only recently. In the Refugee Act of 1980, Congress prescribed a uniform definition of "refugee" without geographic or ideological limitation, and established a process for the annual determination of refugee admissions by the President, after consultations with Congress.

The Administration believes that these authorities in general provide a sensible and workable structure for legal immigration. There are, however, two aspects of the present system that need reform: (1) the exisitng unrealistic limitations on immigration from Mexico and Canada, and (2) the procedures required to certify need for the labor of non-family immigrants.

Imposition of country ceilings of 20,000 annually, in conjunction with the new preference system and labor certification requirements added by the 1965 amendments, resulted in a drastic reduction in immigration from Canada and Mexico. President Reagan has recognized that the ceiling on immigration from our two closest neighbors should be increased. The Administration will therefore submit legislation to create separate annual ceilings for numerically restricted immigration from Mexico and Canada raising the totals from the present 20,000 to 40,000 for each country. The unused portion of either country's allotment would be available to citizens of the other nation. The numerically restricted immigration from other countries of the world would be adjusted so as not to be affected by this change.

The proposed change recognizes the special relationship the United States has with its closest neighbors, the fact of common borders, and the need to find realistic alternatives to illegal immigration.

The Administration also will submit legislation to streamline the procedures for admitting "independent" or non-family immigrants with needed skills. Instead of the time-consuming and costly process of individual labor certification, the Department of Labor would anually publish a list of occupations for which adequate domestic workers were not available. Foreign workers in these occupations with a verified job offer would apply to the consular offices overseas for visas. This procedure would continue to provide protection for American workers while simplifying the procedure for both employers and prospective immigrants.

## Refugee and Asylee Benefits

The Refugee Act of 1980 established financial assistance and social service benefits for refugees and those seeking and receiving asylum. Many require assistance during a period of adjustment. Since they are admitted as a matter of national policy, the federal government has assumed a special responsibility for them. Assistance is provided through grants to voluntary agencies and on a reimbursable basis to States and localities which fund local social service programs.

The Administration has reviewed these programs to assess the fairness of the present pattern of funding and to find ways to encourage self-sufficiency and to accomplish savings.

To assure effective and efficient use of refugee benefit funding, the Administration will continue the present categorical programs for FY 1982 and 1983, but the level of cash assistance payments will be reduced to those refugees who do not qualify for the normal welfare programs. It is believed that prudent economies can be achieved without imposing hardships on recipients. In addition, the Department of Health and Human Services (HHS) will explore possible options for impact aid for those localities disproportionately affected by refugee admissions. . . .

## Conclusion

The dilemmas of immigration and refugee policy require the prompt attention of the Congress and the diligent efforts of the Executive Branch in order to regain control of our borders. . . .

I believe that the proposals the President has offered are in keeping with our modern and historic appeal to the citizens of other lands. Yet they are also fair and realistic in their consideration for the citizens of this land. Only a realistic policy of the type outlined by the President can fully provide for the well-being of our people while welcoming from throughout the world others who truly do desire to contribute to this nation's continuing experiment in liberty. . . .

# SEPTEMBER 29 PROCLAMATION

The ongoing migration of persons to the United States in violation of our laws is a serious national problem detrimental to the interests of the United States. A particularly difficult aspect of the problem is the continuing illegal migration by sea of large numbers of undocumented aliens into the southeastern United States. These arrivals have severely strained the law enforcement resources of the Immigration and Naturalization Service and have threatened the welfare and safety of communities in that region.

As a result of our discussions with the Governments of affected foreign countries and with agencies of the Executive Branch of our Government, I have determined that new and effective measures to curtail these unlawful arrivals are necessary. In this regard, I have determined that international cooperation to intercept vessels trafficking in illegal migrants is a necessary and proper means of insuring the effective enforcement of our laws.

**Now, Therefore, I, Ronald Reagan,** President of the United States of America, by the authority vested in me by the Constitution and the statutes of the United States, including Sections 212 (f) and 215 (a) (1) of the Immigration and Nationality Act, as amended (8 U.S.C. 1182 (f) and 1185 (a) (1)), in order to protect the sovereignty of the United States, and in accordance with cooperative arrangements with certain foreign governments, and having found that the entry of undocumented aliens, arriving at the borders of the United States from the high seas, is detrimental to the interests of the United States, do proclaim that:

The entry of undocumented aliens from the high seas is hereby suspended and shall be prevented by the interdiction of certain vessels carrying such aliens.

**In Witness Whereof,** I have hereunto set my hand this twenty-ninth day of September, in the year of our Lord nineteen hundred and eighty-one, and of the Independence of the United States of America the two hundred and sixth.

Ronald Reagan

# EXECUTIVE ORDER 12324

By the authority vested in me as President by the Constitution and statutes of the United States of America, including sections 212 (f) and 215 (a) (1) of the Immigration and Nationality Act, as amended (8 U.S.C. 1182 (f) and 1185 (a) (1)), in view of the continuing problem of migrants coming to the United States, by sea, without necessary entry documents, and in order to carry out the suspension and interdiction of such entry which have concurrently been proclaimed, it is hereby ordered as follows:

*Section 1.* The Secretary of State shall undertake to enter into, on behalf of the United States, cooperative arrangements with appropriate foreign governments for the purpose of preventing illegal migration to the United States by sea.

*Sec. 2.* (a) The Secretary of the Department in which the Coast Guard is operating shall issue appropriate instructions to the Coast Guard in order to enforce the suspension of the entry of undocumented aliens and the interdiction of any defined vessel carrying such aliens.

(b) Those instructions shall apply to any of the following defined vessels:

(1) Vessels of the United States, meaning any vessel documented under the laws of the United States, or numbered as provided by the Federal Boat Safety Act of 1971, as amended (46 U.S.C. 1451 *et seq.*), or owned in whole or in part by the United States, a citizen of the United States, or a corporation incorporated under the laws of the United States or any State, Territory, District, Commonwealth, or possession thereof, unless the vessel has been granted nationality by a foreign nation in accord with Article 5 of the Convention on the High Seas of 1958 (U.S. TIAS 5200; 13 UST 2312).

(2) Vessels without nationality or vessels assimilated to vessels without nationality in accordance with paragraph (2) of Article 6 of the Convention on the High Seas of 1958 (U.S. TIAS 5200; 13 UST 2312).

(3) Vessels of foreign nations with whom we have arrangements authorizing the United States to stop and board such vessels.

(c) Those instructions to the Coast Guard shall include appropriate directives providing for the Coast Guard:

(1) To stop and board defined vessels, when there is reason to believe that such vessels are engaged in the irregular transportation of persons or violations of United States law or the law of a country with which the United States has an arrangement authorizing such action.

(2) To make inquiries of those on board, examine documents and take such actions as are necessary to establish the registry, condition and

destination of the vessel and the status of those on board the vessel.

(3) To return the vessel and its passengers to the country from which it came, when there is reason to believe that an offense is being committed against the United States immigration laws, or appropriate laws of a foreign country with which we have an arrangement to assist; provided, however, that no person who is a refugee will be returned without his consent.

(d) These actions, pursuant to this Section, are authorized to be undertaken only outside the territorial waters of the United States.

*Sec. 3.* The Attorney General shall, in consultation with the Secretary of State and the Secretary of the Department in which the Coast Guard is operating, take whatever steps are necessary to ensure the fair enforcement of our laws relating to immigration (including effective implementation of this Executive Order) and the strict observance of our international obligations concerning those who genuinely flee persecution in their homeland.

Ronald Reagan

The White House,
September 29, 1981

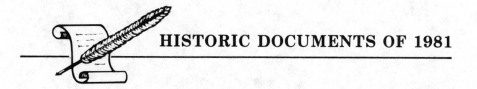

# August

# AIR CONTROLLERS STRIKE
## August 3, 1981

*On August 3 more than 11,500 members of the Professional Air Traffic Controllers Organization (PATCO) went on a nationwide strike. Stating that their jobs were unusually stressful, the controllers demanded higher wages, a shorter work week and increased retirement benefits.*

*The strike came after five months of negotiations between the union and the government that left PATCO frustrated over its inability to negotiate its demands. Yet despite warnings that the strike would seriously cripple air transportation, President Reagan refused to give in to the controllers' requests. Calling a news conference four hours after the strike was announced, Reagan cited a 1955 law that made strikes by federal employees illegal; he gave the strikers 48 hours to return to their jobs or be fired.*

*The law Reagan referred to said that "An individual may not accept or hold a position in the Government of the United States" if he "participates in a strike" against the government. "It is for this reason," Reagan said, "that I must tell those who fail to report for duty this morning that they are in violation of the law, and if they do not report for work within 48 hours, they have forfeited their jobs and will be terminated."*

## 1970 Agreement

*The controllers' union had been on especially weak ground because it formally agreed with the airlines after a work stoppage in 1970 that it would not strike again and was still subject to a court order enforcing that agreement.*

*Robert E. Poli, PATCO president, said his members would hold fast to their demands, and virtually all of the strikers refused to give in to Reagan's ultimatum. On August 7 the administration dispatched dismissal notices to more than 12,000 striking controllers. Approximately 2,500 supervisors and 4,000 regular controllers who had not joined the strike or were not members of the controllers organization moved in to take over the strikers' positions. Up to 700 military air controllers were called in to aid the substitute controllers.*

## Airline Losses

*Commercial flights were reduced from a national average of 14,000 a day to 8,000, costing the airlines an estimated $9 million a day. Three days after the strike began the airlines estimated nearly $29 million in net losses. Airports reported a reduction of 25 percent of flights because of the strike.*

*Ignoring claims that the airways would be less safe without the controllers and that his response to the strike was too harsh, Reagan steadfastly maintained that he would not rehire any of the fired controllers. "Our obligation is to those several thousand that are in there working," Reagan said in an August 13 exchange with reporters.*

*The strike dragged on for two months. The Federal Aviation Administration assured travelers that reduced flight schedules and greater "separation" distances between planes were helping to keep the flying public safe.*

## Union Decertified

*On October 22 the Federal Labor Relations Authority decertified PATCO as the official union of air traffic controllers, taking away the union's status as the exclusive bargaining agent for the controllers.*

*Union members agreed on October 28 to go back to work without their demands being met, if the president would rehire them. Under pressure to enhance relations with organized labor, the president December 9 rescinded his three-year ban on federal employment for dismissed controllers. But he refused to lift his ban on rehiring them in their old jobs or anywhere in the Federal Aviation Administration.*

*Altogether more than 10,000 air traffic controllers had been laid off since the strike began August 3.*

*Following are the texts of a statement by President Reagan on the strike by the air controllers' union and a news conference by Reagan, the attorney general and the secretary of transportion, held August 3, 1981, and Reagan's December 9 memo.* (Boldface hearings in brackets have been added by Congressional Quarterly to highlight the organization of the text.):

# AUGUST 3 NEWS CONFERENCE

**Reagan:** This morning at 7 a.m. the union representing those who man America's air traffic control facilities called a strike. This was the culmination of 7 months of negotiations between the Federal Aviation Administration and the union. At one point in these negotiations agreement was reached and signed by both sides, granting a $40 million increase in salaries and benefits. This is twice what other Government employees can expect. It was granted in recognition of the difficulties inherent in the work these people perform. Now, however, the union demands are 17 times what had been agreed to — $681 million. This would impose a tax burden on their fellow citizens which is unacceptable.

I would like to thank the supervisors and controllers who are on the job today, helping to get the Nation's air system operating safely. In the New York area, for example, four supervisors were scheduled to report for work, and 17 additionally volunteered. At National Airport a traffic controller told a newsperson he had resigned from the union and reported to work because, "How can I ask my kids to obey the law if I don't?" This is a great tribute to America.

Let me make one thing plain. I respect the right of workers in the private sector to strike. Indeed, as president of my own union, I led the first strike ever called by that union. I guess I'm maybe the first one to ever hold this office who is a lifetime member of an AFL-CIO union. But we cannot compare labor-management relations in the private sector with government. Government cannot close down the assembly line. It has to provide without interruption the protective services which are government's reason for being.

## [Violation of Oath]

It was in recognition of this that the Congress passed a law forbidding strikes by Government employees against the public safety. Let me read the solemn oath taken by each of these employees, a sworn affidavit when they accepted their jobs: "I am not participating in any strike against the Government of the United States or any agency thereof, and I will not so participate while an employee of the Government of the United States or any agency thereof."

It is for this reason that I must tell those who fail to report for duty this morning they are in violation of the law, and if they do not report for work within 48 hours, they have forfeited their jobs and will be terminated.

**Q:** Mr. President, are you going to order any union members who violate the law to go to jail?

**Reagan:** Well, I have some people around here, and maybe I should refer that question to the Attorney General.

**Q:** Do you think that they should go to jail, Mr. President, anybody who violates the law?

**Reagan:** I told you what I think should be done. They're terminated.

**Smith:** Well, as the President has said, striking under these circumstances constitutes a violation of the law, and we intend to initiate in appropriate cases criminal proceedings against those who have violated the law.

**Q:** How quickly will you initiate criminal proceedings, Mr. Attorney General?

**Smith:** We will initiate those proceedings as soon as we can.

**Q:** Today?

**Smith:** The process will be underway probably by noon today.

**Q:** Are you going to try and fine the union $1 million per day?

**Smith:** Well, that's the prerogative of the court. In the event that any individuals are found guilty of contempt of a court order, the penalty for that, of course, is imposed by the court.

## [Union Demands]

**Q:** How much more is the Government prepared to offer the union?

**Lewis:** We think we had a very satisfactory offer on the table. It's twice what other Government employees are going to get — 11.4 percent. Their demands were so unreasonable there was no spot to negotiate, when you're talking to somebody 17 times away from where you presently are. We do not plan to increase our offer to the union.

**Q:** Under no circumstances?

**Lewis:** As far as I'm concerned, under no circumstances.

**Reagan:** Will you continue to meet with them?

**Lewis:** We will not meet with the union as long as they're on strike. When they're off of strike, and assuming that they are not decertified, we will meet with the union and try to negotiate a satisfactory contract.

## [Air Service and Safety]

**Q:** Do you have any idea how it's going at the airports around the country?

**Lewis:** Relatively, it's going quite well. We're operating somewhat in excess of 50-percent capacity. We could increase that. We have determined, until we feel we're in total control of the system, that we will not increase that. Also, as you probably know, we have some rather severe weather in the Midwest, and our first priority is safety.

## [Decertification of Union]

**Q:** What can you tell us about possible decertification of the union and impoundment of its strike funds?

**Lewis:** There has been a court action to impound the strike fund of $3.5 million. We are going before the National Labor Relations Authority this morning and ask for decertification of the union.

**Q:** When you say that you're not going to increase your offer, are you referring to the original offer or the last offer which you've made? Is that still valid?

**Lewis:** The last offer we made in present value was exactly the same as the first offer. Mr. Poli asked me about 11 o'clock last evening if he could phase the increase in over a period of time. For that reason, we phased it in over a longer period of time. It would have given him a larger increase in terms of where he would be when the next negotiations started, but in present value it was the $40 million originally on the table.

**Q:** Mr. Attorney General, in seeking criminal action against the union leaders, will you seek to put them in jail if they do not order these people back to work?

**Smith:** Well, we will seek whatever penalty is appropriate under the circumstances in each individual case.

**Q:** Do you think that is an appropriate circumstance?

**Smith:** It is certainly one of the penalties that is provided for in the law, and in appropriate cases, we could very well seek that penalty.

**Q:** What's appropriate?

**Smith:** Well, that depends on the fact of each case.

**Q:** What makes the difference?

## [Amount of Fine Against Union]

**Q:** Can I go back to my "fine" question? How much would you like to see the union fined every day?

**Smith:** Well, there's no way to answer that question. We would just have to wait until we get into court, see what the circumstances are, and determine what position we would take in the various cases under the facts as they develop.

**Q:** But you won't go to court and ask the court for a specific amount?

**Smith:** Well, I'm sure we will when we reach that point, but there's no way to pick a figure now.

**Q:** Mr. President, will you delay your trip to California or cancel it if the strike is still on later this week?

**Reagan:** If any situation should arise that would require my presence here, naturally I will do that. So that will be a decision that awaits what's going to happen. May I just — because I have to be back in there for another appointment — may I just say one thing on top of this? With all this talk of penalties and everything else, I hope that you'll emphasize, again, the possibility of termination, because I believe that there are a great many of those people, and they're fine people, who have been swept up in this and probably have not really considered the result — the fact that they had taken an oath, the fact that this is now in violation of the law as that one supervisor referred to with regard to his children. And I am hoping that they will in a sense remove themselves from the lawbreaker situation by returning to their posts.

I have no way to know whether this had been conveyed to them by their union leaders who had been informed that this would be the result of a strike.

## [Deadline]

**Q:** Your deadline is 7 o'clock Wednesday morning for them to return to work?

**Reagan:** 48 hours.

**Lewis:** It's 11 o'clock Wednesday morning.

**Q:** Mr. President, why have you taken such strong action as your first action? Why not some lesser action at this point?

**Reagan:** What lesser action can there be? The law is very explicit. They are violating the law. And as I say, we called this to the attention of their leadership. Whether this was conveyed to the membership before they voted to strike, I don't know. But this is one of the reasons why there can be no further negotiation while this situation continues. You can't sit and negotiate with a union that's in violation of the law.

**Lewis:** And their oath.

**Reagan:** And their oath.

**Q:** Are you more likely to proceed in the criminal direction toward the leadership than the rank-and-file, Mr. President?

**Reagan:** Well, that again is not for me to answer.

## [Military Air Controllers]

**Q:** Mr. Secretary, what can you tell us about the possible use of military air controllers — how many, how quickly can they get on the job?

**Lewis:** In answer to the previous question, we will move both civil and criminal, probably more civil than criminal, and we now have papers in the U.S. Attorney's offices, under the Attorney General, in about 20 locations around the country where would be involved two or three principle [sic] people.

As far as the military personnel are concerned, they are going to fundamentally be backup to the supervisory personnel. We had 150 on the job, supposedly, about a half-hour ago. We're going to increase that to somewhere between 700 and 850.

## [New Hires]

**Q:** Mr. Secretary, are you ready to hire other people should these other people not return?

**Lewis:** Yes, we will, and we hope we do not reach that point. Again, as the President said, we're hoping these people come back to work. They do a fine job. If that does not take place, we have a training school, as you know. We will be advertising. We have a number of applicants right now. There's a waiting list in terms of people that want to be controllers, and we'll start retraining and reorganize the entire FAA traffic controller group.

**Q:** Just to clarify, is your deadline 7 a.m. Wednesday or 11 o'clock?

**Lewis:** It's 11 a.m. Wednesday. The President said 48 hours, and that would be 48 hours.

**Q:** If you actually fire these people, won't it put your air traffic control system in a hole for years to come, since you can't just cook up a controller in — [inaudible].

**Lewis:** That obviously depends on how many return to work. Right now we're able to operate the system. In some areas, we've been very gratified by the support we've received. In other areas, we've been disappointed. And until I see the numbers, there's no way I can answer that question.

## [Terms of Negotiation]

**Q:** Mr. Lewis, did you tell the union leadership when you were talking to them that their members would be fired if they went out on strike?

**Lewis:** I told Mr. [Robert E.] Poli yesterday that the President gave me three instructions in terms of the firmness of the negotiations: One is there would be no amnesty, the second, there would be no negotiations during the strike, and third is that if they went on strike, these people would no longer be Government employees.

**Q:** Mr. Secretary, you said no negotiations. What about informal meetings of any kind with Mr. Poli?

**Lewis:** We will have no meetings until the strike is terminated with the union.

**Q:** Have you served Poli at this point? Has he been served by the Attorney General?

**Smith:** In the civil action that was filed this morning, the service was made on the attorney for the union, and the court has determined that that was appropriate service on all of the officers of the union.

**Q:** My previous question about whether you're going to take a harder line on the leadership than rank-and-file in terms of any criminal prosecution, can you give us an answer on that?

**Smith:** No, I can't answer that except to say that each case will be investigated on its own merits, and action will be taken as appropriate in each of those cases.

**Q:** Mr. Lewis, do you know how many applications for controller jobs you have on file now?

**Lewis:** I do not know. I'm going to check when I get back. I am aware there's a waiting list, and I do not have the figure. If you care to have that, you can call our office and we'll tell you. Also, we'll be advertising and recruiting people for this job if necessary.

**Q:** Mr. Secretary, how long are you prepared to hold out if there's a partial but not complete strike?

**Lewis:** I think the President made it very clear that as of 48 hours from now, if the people are not back on the job, they will not be Government employees at any time in the future.

**Q:** How long are you prepared to run the air controller system — *[inaudible]*.

**Lewis:** Four years, if we have to.

**Q:** How long does it take to train a new controller, from the waiting list?

**Lewis:** It varies; it depends on the type of center they're going to be in. For someone to start in the system and work through the more minor office types of control situations till they get to, let's say a Chicago, or a Washington National, it takes about 3 years. So in this case, what we'll have to do if some of the major metropolitan areas are shut down or a considerable portion is shut down, we'll be bringing people in from other areas that are qualified and then start bringing people through the training schools in the smaller cities and smaller airports.

**Q:** Mr. Secretary, have you definitely made your final offer to the union?

**Lewis:** Yes, we have.

# REAGAN DECEMBER 9 MEMO

*Memorandum for the Director of the Office of Personnel Management Subject:* Federal Employment of Discharged Air Traffic Controllers

The Office of Personnel Management has established the position that the former air traffic controllers who were discharged for participating in a strike against the Government initiated on August 3, 1981 shall be debarred from federal employment for a period of three years. Upon deliberation I have concluded that such individuals, despite their strike participation, should be permitted to apply for federal employment outside the scope of their former employing agency.

Therefore, pursuant to my authority to regulate federal employment, I have determined that the Office of Personnel Management should permit federal agencies to receive applications for employment from these individuals and process them according to established civil service procedures. Your office should perform suitability determinations with respect to all such applicants according to established standards and procedures under 5 CFR, Part 731.

After reviewing reports from the Secretary of Transportation and the Administrator of the Federal Aviation Administration, I have further determined that it would be detrimental to the efficiency of operations at the Federal Aviation Administration and to the safe and effective performance of our national air traffic control system to permit the discharged air traffic controllers to return to employment with that agency. Therefore, these former federal employees should not be deemed suitable for employment with the Federal Aviation Administration.

I direct you to process their applications for reemployment with the federal government accordingly.

# SAUDI PEACE PLAN

## August 7, 1981

*As the Senate confirmed the controversial sale of AWACS (airborne warning and control system) planes to Saudi Arabia, the Reagan administration shifted into partial support for an earlier Saudi peace plan for the Middle East, drawing new attention to the previously little-noticed proposal, and setting off an intense round of Arab-Israeli debate. Even so, the Saudis' plan appeared doomed when unresolved differences among other Arab countries scuttled a key meeting of the Arab League called to consider the plan.*

*Interest in the Saudi plan centered on the seventh of its eight points, which declared, "That all states in the region should be able to live in peace," phrasing that was widely interpreted to suggest recognition of Israel's right to exist. The plan was announced by Saudi Crown Prince Fahd on August 7 in an interview broadcast over state radio. In other points the plan called for Israel to withdraw from all occupied lands, including East Jerusalem, and for the establishment of a Palestinian state, with East Jerusalem as its capital.*

*Much of the Saudis' plan echoed moderate Arab positions at the time of the 1978 Camp David accords between Prime Minister Menachem Begin of Israel and Egyptian President Anwar al-Sadat. Since then, American policy had supported the accords, which led to the Israeli-Egyptian peace treaty of 1979 and continuing negotiations for a self-governing Palestinian authority as an interim step in resolving the status of the occupied West Bank and Gaza. (Camp David accords, Historic Documents of 1978, p. 605; peace treaty, Historic Documents of 1979, p.*

223) *In keeping with the Camp David accords, initial American reaction to the Saudi peace plan was noncommittal. The State Department in August called it "largely a restatement of previously known Saudi Government positions and of principals outlined in United Nations Security Council Resolutions 242, 338, and other U.N. resolutions relating to the Arab-Israeli conflict."*

## Saudis as Peacekeepers

*In the weeks following disclosure of the peace plan, other events were moving swiftly. The United States reportedly had been impressed by Saudi help in reducing other Middle East tensions in Lebanon, and administration lobbyists began suggesting the pending AWACS sale could increase the Saudis' peacekeeping role in the area. Palestinian autonomy talks between the Israelis and Egyptians, under the Camp David agreements, were progressing poorly, supporting views that the Camp David process needed modification. And finally the assassination of President Sadat by Moslem fundamentalists raised immediate doubts about Egypt's continuing role in the peace process and its stability as an American ally in the area. (Sadat assassination, p. 733)*

## Reagan Comment on Peace Plan

*Then on October 28, as the Senate confimed the AWACS sale, President Reagan talked with reporters in the Oval Office. Responding to questions, he said, "The Saudis have shown by their own introduction of a peace proposal that they are willing to discuss peace in the Middle East. . . . We couldn't agree with all the points, nor could the Israelis, but it was the first time that they had recognized Israel as a nation, and it's a beginning point for negotiations." There was no mention of the Camp David accords. Later, in a November 10 news conference, the president reaffirmed U.S. commitment to the Camp David process, while repeating his view of the Saudi plan as "a hopeful sign." Other administration officials confirmed the president's views.*

## Reaction

*Reaction to the administration's new position on the Saudi plan was swift, strong and mixed. The most pointed came from the Israelis. Ambassador Ephraim Evron told Secretary of State Alexander M. Haig Jr. on October 30 that Israel totally rejected the plan. Prime Minister Begin called the proposal "a plan on how to liquidate Israel," and dispatched a "truth squad" from the Israeli Parliament to publicize Israel's position. But Moshe Arens, the leader of the truth squad, told reporters after meeting with Secretary Haig on November 11, that the Saudis had "gone a little way in our direction," though they still had "a*

*long way to go to become part of the Mideast peace process." Reporters
were stunned at the contrast between Arens' remarks and Begin's; Arens
later said he had been quoted "not in the spirit in which I intended."*

## Dissension in the Arab League

*The Saudis sought to arrange support for the plan in time for a
November 25 meeting of the Arab League in Fez, Morocco; but their
efforts, which gained some supporters, deeply divided the Arab world and
the various Palestinian groups. The most divisive issue, ironically, was
also the one that had attracted first American and then European
Economic Community support — implied recognition of Israel. The point
was unacceptable to Arab hardliners, and the Saudis failed to win
support from Syria, Libya and Iraq, although Palestine Liberation
Organization Chairman Yasir Arafat was a strong supporter.*

*The Arab League meeting could have considered the plan as a basis for
unified negotiations with Israel. Instead, the meeting among heads of
state, already crippled by a boycott of dissatisfied hardliners, ended in
disarray after only four hours. The incident left in doubt the future role
of the Saudis as a moderate voice in the area. The Saudi peace plan
appeared doomed, at least for the present.*

> *Following are excerpts from the radio interview with Saudi
> Prince Fahd, broadcast August 7, 1981. (Boldface headings
> in brackets have been added by Congressional Quarterly to
> highlight the organization of the text.):*

**Q.** News agencies have extensively reported that Saudi Arabia played a
part in bringing about the cease-fire in Lebanon? What is the truth about
the Saudi role?

**A.** I will not be revealing a secret if I say that Saudi Arabia played a part
in the cease-fire which came into effect in Lebanon recently. Ever since the
situation begin to dangerously deteriorate following the savage Israeli raid
on Beirut, the king directed that there was a need to make moves on
various levels in order to protect the lives of innocent civilians — old
people, women and children who were falling victim to the Israeli military
machine, which deliberately bombed, killing and wreaking destruction
both in Beirut and in southern Lebanon.

This was the principal reason why his majesty the king and Saudi Arabia
made a move. In addition, we believe that any aggression on an Arab
country is an attack on us. On the orders of his majesty the king, we
contacted Washington and expressed our extreme concern at the deterioration in the situation. We asked Washington to put pressure on Israel
before the situation exploded. The cease-fire agreement was concluded
after intensive, urgent efforts. We notified all Arab parties directly
involved in the dispute of what had taken place. In this connection I wish

to affirm that the cease-fire had been dictated by certain humanitarian circumstances at a given, crucial moment in time, bearing in mind that this does not mean that the Palestinian people should cease their march toward gaining their rights and that our national commitment to the issue of Palestine and our organic relation with the struggle of its people imposed on us to move to save the innocent souls which were harvested by the Israel aircraft. And I take the opportunity to praise the rare heroism shown by Palestinian and Lebanese fighters over those 15 days with their limited capabilities and their unlimited faith, they oppose the aircraft and missiles of the Israeli enemy. To Yasir 'Arafat I send in the name of the kingdom, king, people and government, greetings of appreciation and admiration, to him and to the Palestinian and Lebanese people, for their steadfastness and determination to confront and fight Israeli barbarism.

## [Criticism of U.S. Policies]

**Q.** Does this mean that you are satisfied with the U.S. response to the kingdom's efforts.

**A.** The U.S. Government responded to us quickly and effectively, and we appreciate this. But here we rightly talk about one aspect of our relations with the U.S., which concerns a certain circumstance. We continue to be dissatisfied with the overall U.S. policy in the Middle East, especially as concerns the Palestine problem and the rights of its peoples. And I confirmed to the U.S. that there was no dispute between us and any U.S. administration other than that which concerns the national rights of the Palestinian people. This dispute is not to be scorned, because it is connected with the security of our region and its stability; and subsequently it is related to U.S. interests. I do not understand how successive U.S. administrations continue to expose their relations, and subsequently their interests with the Arab nation, to danger by supporting Israel politically, financially and militarily while the latter continues to occupy the whole of Palestine — in addition to other Arab lands — to build settlements, expropriate land and kill the innocent with American weapons it had agreed not to use for aggression. The U.S. should halt this support in order to safeguard world peace, which threatens to explode. What increases our sorrow is that the U.S. Government continues to adhere to the Camp David accords, whose failure has been proven. We continue to hope that the Reagan administration will accept the uselessness of the Camp David agreements as a framework for just and comprehensive peace in the Middle East and will initiate a drastic change in U.S. policy which would lead to the withdrawal of Israel from the Arab territories occupied in 1967 and the establishment of an independent Palestinian state. Any attempt which does not seek to force Israel to withdraw and does not seek the establishment of a Palestinian state shall lead to more unrest, killing and destruction, as is happening in Lebanon today.

Now we fear that time will pass without the current American administration embarking on a new serious move that is drastically different from Camp David. Then we shall hear the enduring excuse that Congressional elections are nearing, which will be followed 2 years later by the presidential elections, and subsequently there is a need to await the results, and so on for 30 years. Following the recent events in Lebanon, the international and Western press, especially the Americans, expressed the opinion that the U.S. Government should recognize the PLO. It is a fact that any comprehensive peace in the region should be based on reality and fact and not illusions that lead to unfavorable consequences, as happened in Angola, Ethiopia and Afghanistan. The time has come for the U.S. Government to be less biased toward Israel and more equitable toward the Arabs.

## [Eight-point Plan]

**Q.** It appears from the analysis made by Your Highness that the setting up of an independent Palestinian state is the basic condition for any comprehensive, settlement in the Middle East. Does Your Highness have a practical vision of such a settlement or the way in which it could be reached?

**A.** Naturally I cannot go into detail now, but there are a number of principles which may be taken as guidelines toward a just settlement; they are principles which the United Nations has taken and reiterated many times in the last few years. They are:

First, that Israel should withdraw from all Arab territory occupied in 1967, including Arab Jerusalem.

Second, that Israeli settlements built on Arab land after 1967 should be dismantled.

Third, a guarantee of freedom of worship for all religions in the holy places.

Fourth, an affirmation of the right of the Palestinian people to return to their homes and to compensate those who do not wish to return.

Fifth, that the West Bank and the Gaza Strip should have a transitional period, under the auspices of the United Nations, for a period not exceeding several months.

Sixth, that an independent Palestinian state should be set up with [East] Jerusalem as its capital.

Seven, that all states in the region should be able to live in peace.

Eight, that the United Nations or member states of the United Nations should guarantee to execute these principles.

As I have said, the principles I have mentioned are not of my own making; I did not invent them — they are General Assembly decisions. They may be summed up in one principle, to emanate from the Security

Council, and to provide a framework for a comprehensive and just settlement.

I wish to reaffirm that the principles of a just comprehensive solution have become familiar and do not require great effort:

1. An end to unlimited American support for Israel.

2. An end to Israeli arrogance, whose ugliest facet is embodied in Begin's government. This condition will be automatically fulfilled if the first condition is fulfilled.

3. A recognition that, as Yasir 'Arafat says, the Palestinian figure is the basic figure in the Middle Eastern equation.

Talking about the responsibility of the U.S. in the Arab-Israeli dispute does not absolve the countries of Western Europe from their responsibilities. This applies particularly to Britain, which is now chairman of the EEC, and which bears a great responsibility for what happened to the Palestinians during its mandate. The interests of Western Europe in the Arab region is no less important or vital than those of the U.S. We have heard a great deal about European moves and a European initiative, but so far we have not seen anything definite. In my view a European move should be in two directions: Toward the Middle East on the one hand and toward the United States on the other, as the United States is the main partner in NATO and the leader of the free world.

## [Relations with Iraq]

**Q.** What is your view, Your Highness, on the continuing Iraqi-Iranian war and the Israeli attack on the Iraqi nuclear reactor?

**A.** Iraq is a fraternal Arab country and a founding member of the Arab League. Our pan-Arab commitment to safeguard Iraq's strength and invincibility do not require any underlining because we are linked to Iraq at the pan-Arab level, organically and fatefully. Iraq's strength is not only a strength for us but also a strength for the Arab nation, which cannot do without Iraq's capabilities and energies in the confrontation with the Israeli enemy. We hope that the Muslim leaders will succeed in their good offices endeavors to bring the Iraqi-Iranian war to an end.

Israel's attack on the Iraqi nuclear reactor is absolute proof of the fact that Israel is afraid of Iraq's capabilities and energies. Is it possible or logical that the Arabs would permit Israel to continue to impose its will on them by the force of arms? This is a question which I ask before it is too late to the allies, friends and enemies who are responsible for this Israeli rampaging which must be stopped.

## [Peace in Lebanon]

**Q.** Are you optimistic, Your Highness, about a solution to the Lebanese problem being in sight?

**A.** In the Kingdom we are concerned very much about strengthening security and stability in Lebanon and consolidating Lebanese legality. The Kingdom has been making its effort via the Arab followup committee to bring about a national accord. The committee has made appreciably good strides until now.

It has some tasks before it which we hope we will succeed in realizing. I have not the slightest doubt that the sister country Syria is earnest in aiding Lebanon to rise up from its fall, because a relaxation of the situation in Lebanon is reflected positively on the entire area. Lebanese relaxation may be a beginning for an Arab relaxation.

## [AWACS Sale]

**Q.** Your Highness, do you expect the U.S. Congress, after its summer recess, to agree to the sale of AWACS to the kingdom?

**A.** In the kingdom we are astonished at the uproar which has accompanied the deal of the AWACS to the kingdom. This is without doubt the work of the Zionist factions which have been applying pressure inside and outside Congress. I previously announced that the purchase of the AWACS is a sovereign act. One does not need to be dilligent [*sic*] to exercise sovereignty. Buying these planes is part of our plan to build a modern army which can defend our country. No power can prevent us from completing the building of our army. Israel and its supporters inside the United States have been trying to punish us as a result of our stand on the Camp David agreements. Our stand on the Camp David agreements is a question of principle and there is no way of going back on it. If Congress is not going to agree to sell us the planes this will not be the end. The gates of the world are open to us. We can obtain what we want in accordance with our needs.

# REAGAN BUDGET AND TAX PACKAGE SIGNED
## August 13, 1981

On August 13, 1981, President Ronald Reagan signed into law a historic package of tax and budget reductions that drastically changed the course of government spending. The signing of the new legislation was the culmination of a polished lobbying effort by Reagan to reduce the size of the federal government and to provide incentives for increased savings and investment, themes he had supported repeatedly during his 1980 election campaign. Not since the mid-1960s when Lyndon B. Johnson won a series of victories for his domestic social programs known as the Great Society had a president demonstrated such impressive political support for a major departure in public policy.

The economic package cut government spending in fiscal year 1982 by $35.2 billion and overhauled the entire network of government sponsored social programs. An accompanying tax cut plan, the Economic Recovery Tax Act of 1981, enacted a three-year, 30 percent cut in individual income tax rates and faster depreciation write-offs for business investments. The bill put an estimated $749 billion — more money than the federal government was expected to spend in fiscal 1982 — back in the hands of business and individual taxpayers over a five-year period.

## Economic Theory Applied

President Reagan's solution to the economic problems facing the nation was a largely untested theory called supply-side economics. Supply-siders held that by returning taxes to businesses and workers and by *restricting the growth of government, Americans would have more incentive to work harder and to save more. Increased savings would lead to more investment, higher productivity and a decline in inflation, they said.*

*To achieve his goals, President Reagan March 10 submitted a fiscal 1982 budget to Congress that would have reduced federal spending by $48.6 billion and cut taxes by $53.9 billion.* (Reagan budget, p. 325)

*Reagan's plan immediately was attacked as unworkable and risky. Many economists warned that the large-scale tax cuts could trigger an increase in spending rather than savings that would push inflation even higher. Democrats in Congress also claimed that the president's proposals were inequitable. They said the tax cuts would benefit primarily the well-to-do and that the new budget tore gaping holes in the "safety net" of social programs aiding the poor.*

## Budget Cuts

*Congress gave the president most of the budget cuts he requested. To make such massive cuts, it relied heavily on an arcane legislative process known as reconciliation. The mechanism was set up as a way for Congress to bring government spending in line with an agreed-upon limit on total yearly spending, after assessing expected revenues over the year and making decisions on the size of the budget deficit or surplus.*

*Under the reconciliation process contained in the Congressional Budget and Impoundment Control Act of 1974, Congress could instruct its legislative and appropriations committees to recommend changes in programs already on the books that would allow funding of those programs to be reduced or revenues increased by specified amounts. It would then be the task of the Senate and House Budget committees to combine those reconciliation recommendations into a single bill and take them to the floor of each chamber for approval.*

*Little more than two months after Reagan had introduced his budget, Congress passed its fiscal 1982 non-binding budget resolution May 21. The resolution called for $770.9 billion in budget authority, $695.45 billion in outlays, $657.8 billion in revenues and a $37.65 billion deficit. It also included instructions requiring 14 Senate committees and 15 House committees to make $36 billion in fiscal 1982 spending cuts in programs already on the books.*

*House and Senate budget committees met in July and reported their reconciliation packages. The House bill called for $37.7 billion in fiscal 1982 cuts; the Senate package included $39.5 billion in fiscal 1982 savings. The Senate quickly approved its reconciliation package.*

*The House, by a vote of 217-211 voted on June 26 to substitute "Gramm-Latta II" — a Republican-designed alternative to the Senate* *package — that cut a new total of $37.3 billion in fiscal 1982 federal spending. On July 15 more than 250 House and Senate conferees, meeting in 58 sub-conferences, began to work out the differences between the House and Senate reconciliation packages. By late July they reached final agreement on budget cuts. On July 31 the House, by voice vote, and the Senate, by an 80-14 vote, adopted the conference report on the reconciliation bill and sent it to President Reagan for his signature.*

*Programs cut under the new budget included public service jobs created under the Comprehensive Employment and Training Act (CETA). Cash benefit programs ranging from food stamps to cost of living adjustments for federal retirees were curtailed by reducing benefits and increasing eligibility requirements in years to come.*

*The legislation also provided for block grants to the states that would consolidate dozens of specific programs for health, education, social services, home energy assistance and community and economic development. The objective was to allow the states to decide how to spend funds that were previously designated for specific purposes by the federal government.*

*Several programs, however, escaped the budget ax. Those included the Legal Services Corporation, the Economic Development Administration and the Appalachian Regional Commission. Congress also refused to place an administration requested "cap" on federal contributions to the states for Medicaid or to create some of the block grants Reagan wanted. The president had called for consolidation of 84 health, education and social service categorical aid programs into six block grants.*

## Tax Reduction

*Reagan officials consistently painted the tax reduction legislation as a far more difficult concept to sell than the budget cuts. And the tax bill signed into law August 13 reflected the wide range of concessions Reagan made to ensure enactment of his revolutionary tax cut policies.*

*But none of the many changes and add-ons to the legislation did damage to the heart of the Reagan supply-side plan — across-the-board reductions in individual income taxes and faster write-offs for capital investment to spur productivity.*

*The form of the package changed substantially. Reagan had originally wanted a "clean" bill with other popular tax plans saved for a second tax measure later in the year. But, bowing to the realities of politics, the president reshaped the package several times, giving in on some details but standing firm on the central theme. By doing so, Reagan forced Democrats, intent on passing their own alternative tax plan, to move closer and closer to the administration position.*

*The final agreement was the product of an all-night session July 31 during which House and Senate conferees worked out the differences between the two versions of the tax cut bill passed earlier that week. The Senate gave its final approval to the measure August 3 by a vote of 67-8. The House cleared the package the following day on a 282-95 vote.*

## Opposition to Reagan

*On September 24, 1981, Reagan returned to Congress and asked for $2.6 billion in additional fiscal 1982 entitlement cuts, $3 billion in increased taxes and $10.4 billion in cuts in fiscal 1982 appropriations bills. This time Congress balked. Many legislators felt that the effects of the first round of cuts were still too uncertain to ask for more. Passage of Reagan's program had not broken the "cycle of negative expectations" about inflation that the president had predicted. The president was forced to withdraw his tax increase and entitlement cut requests.*

*And Congress refused to cut appropriations as much as Reagan had requested, prompting the president to issue the first veto of his term on November 23. Reagan refused to sign a continuing appropriations resolution that provided funding for most of the federal government. The veto resulted in a stop-payment shutdown of the government and thousands of government workers went home on a one-day furlough.* (Brief government shutdown, p. 831)

*Congress' reluctance to enact any more of Reagan's economic program was accompanied by a downturn in the economy that promised to be as severe if not worse than the recession of 1974-75. By the end of the year inflation had fallen. Interest rates had begun to decline but they were still beyond the reach of most individuals and businesses. And unemployment in December reached 8.9 percent; the number of adult men without jobs — 8 percent — set a post World War II record.*

*The gloomy economic forecasts throughout the fall forced the president to admit on November 6 that he probably would not be able to balance the budget by 1984 — as he had pledged throughout his election campaign.*

*The president's problems with the economy seemed to be complicated further by the appearance of a magazine article in which David Stockman, director of the Office of Management and Budget, expressed his skepticism about supply-side economics. The December issue of* The Atlantic *quoted Stockman as saying that the main objective of the supply-side theory was to reduce the top income tax bracket from 70 to 50 percent — a goal that clearly favored the well-to-do. In theory, the benefits of supply-side economics were expected eventually to "trickle down" through the economy to reach everyone else. "It's kind of hard to sell 'trickle down,' " Stockman said, "so the supply-side formula was the only way to get a tax policy that was really 'trickle down,' "*

*Following are President Reagan's remarks on signing HR 4242 and HR 3982 into law, and excerpts from a question-and-answer session with reporters, August 13, 1981, at Rancho del Cielo, his residence outside Santa Barbara, California:*

**Reagan:** Good morning.

**Reporter:** Typical California weather.

**A.** Yes, since this is the first day of this kind of weather, of fog, since we've been here, I shall refrain from saying that you're all responsible — [*laughter*] — for bringing it up with you. The Sun has been shining brightly here.

These bills that I'm about to sign — not every page — this is the budget bill, and this is the tax program — but I think they represent a turnaround of almost a half a century of a course this country's been on and mark an end to the excessive growth in government bureaucracy, government spending, government taxing.

And we're indebted for all of this — I can't speak too highly of the leadership, Republican leadership in the Congress and of those Democrats who so courageously joined in and made both of these truly bipartisan programs. But I think in reality, the real credit goes to the people of the United States who finally made it plain that they wanted a change and made it clear in Congress and spoke with a more authoritative voice than some of the special-interest groups that they wanted these changes in government.

This represents $130 billion in savings over the next 3 years. This represents $750 billion in tax cuts over the next 5 years. And this is only the beginning, because from here on now we are going to have to implement all of these, and it's going to be a job to make this whole turnaround work. It's going to be the number one priority — or continue to be the number one priority of our administration.

And again, I express my gratitude to the Congress, the 97th Congress, and to the administration, the people who worked so hard to make these come about.

And, Joe [Joseph W. Canzeri, deputy assistant to the president], I guess it is traditional that I have to use a lot of pens in these signatures.

[*At this point the president began signing H.R. 4242.*]

Oops, one letter too many. I'll have to catch up here someplace.

**Q.** One letter a pen, Mr. President?

**A.** That's the way it works out. There's a number that we have to have. Just think, if my name had had three more letters in it, we'd —

**Q.** Who gets the pens?

**A.** Some of those people that helped.

There. That is the tax program.

[*The president began signing H.R. 3982.*]

I figured how to do it, Joe, on this one to come out even — on the "n" —
I'll make one part of the "n," and then the other part.

They are signed, and now all we have to do is implement them.

If you have any questions, perhaps, on any of the features of this, fire
away.

**Q.** How about another subject, Mr. President? [*Laughter*]

**A.** You mean in the face of all of this, you want to change the subject?
Does someone have a question on the subject, first?

## The Nation's Economy

**Q.** Yeah, I do. Mr. President, the Wall Street Journal carried a story
yesterday that the revenue projections which you will be getting are going
to be lower than your administration previously thought, and that means
we're headed for a more severe economic downturn with higher interest
rates. Are you ready to revise your own projections about the economy
downward? Are we headed for a recession?

**A.** I don't know whether you'd call it a recession or not, but they're not
saying anything that we haven't said over and over again. Our own
projections have been that for the next several months this soft and soggy
economy is going to continue and that we shouldn't be fooled by these last
couple of months of seeming upturn, that this means a continued climb.
We think that we are in a soggy economy and it's going to go on.

Remember that it won't be until October that any of this will begin to be
implemented. This is the budget that begins for the year in October. The
tax programs, of course, won't be into effect until then either. And what
we're counting on is when these and these begin to take effect that we will
see the results when people begin to have the more money in their pockets
from their earnings and when the lowered expenditures of government
begin taking effect.

But, no, we're not differing with that. We've said, ourselves, to watch for
a sagging economy for the next few months....

## Federal Spending

**Q.** Back on the budget, many Governors, particularly Democratic Governors, say it's a shell game, that you've got to help them on the so-called
safety net more, or they're not going to be able to take up the slack.

**A.** Well, some Governors did say that and yet I noticed that the whole
Governors conference did support and vote for a resolution of continued
cooperation with us in these packages.

Now, it is true, we were not able to get all that we wanted in the line of
real block grants and autonomy for local and State government. You know,
one level of government — they even have that conflict between local and
State government, that each level is a little reluctant to give up autonomy
and authority. We're going to continue to work with the Congress and work

with the States and local government representatives to give them the autonomy they can have to make these programs work.

It is true we did not get all that we had wanted in that regard.

**Q.** I gather, sir, it's not autonomy so much as money that they need.

**A.** Well, the difference is — and what our reductions were based on is that the block grant, giving them the flexibility at that level to use this as they saw fit, setting the priorities, really would result in a savings, and our reductions were based on those estimated savings in unnecessary administrative overhead, direction, and restrictions that caused unnecessary spending at the local level. And as a Governor I can testify that that was true, that in many of the categorical grant programs we could see how much more efficiently they could have been run without the redtape imposed by the Federal Government. . . .

## Federal Deficits

**Q.** Mr. President, back on the budget for a minute. Given the so-called soggy conditions, it seems that you're going to have greater deficits over the next few years, less revenues, more deficits. What are those deficits now? How much more in budget cuts are you going to have to make over the next couple of years, and will you still be able to balance the budget in '84?

**A.** Well, this has always been our goal and will continue to be our goal. But remember that we always said that there were further budget cuts for the coming years, for '83 and '84. These are the ones that go into effect in '82.

**Q.** How much more, though?

**A.** Well, we know, of course, that we will have a sizable deficit for '81. There was nothing we could do about that. And, as you know, the Government has been operating in '81 without a budget, just on appropriations, and we have tried to limit once we got into management what we could, but the die was already cast as to the amount of this deficit.

Now, the possibility of increased deficits in the coming years over our previous figures are due in part to not getting totally what we have asked for in the budget cuts, but also that the tax package finally came out with additional reductions. As I say, those have possibly called for some reductions simply to recognize the realities of these two packages now, but we are going to continue to work on this and work for more budget cuts. And it just means that we're going to have to try to get more additional cuts than we might have had to get before.

I'm not sure that we might not have been, however, too conservative in our estimates on the tax program, because, remember, our tax proposals were based on the belief that the cut in tax rates would not mean a comparable cut in tax revenues, that the stimulant to the economy would be such that the Government might find itself getting additional revenues, as it did last year in the cut of the capital gains tax.

## Interest Rates

**Q.** Mr. President, are you still confident that high interest rates will come down toward the end of the year?

**A.** Yes. I noticed this morning's report in the paper, about a headline that said, "Interest Rates Up." But then when you read the story, you found that that was simply in the bond market in New York and was reflecting bond buyers' competition for the limited amount of capital that was there for investment. That's part of what's in that tax program, is to make less limited that amount of money that's available for capital investment. . . .

## Defense Spending

**Q.** Mr. President, in view of your hard line against the Soviets, are you going to be willing to make a substantial scale-down in your defense spending plans, if that's necessary?

**A.** That would depend on the negotiating table and how willing they were to actually discuss arms reductions. You will recall that the previous President tried to introduce that once, and our Secretary of State was on his way home in 24 hours from Moscow, because they wouldn't even hear of a reduction. But they are the ones, with all of the talk that's going on, the Soviet Union has been engaged in the greatest military buildup in the history of man, and it cannot be described as necessary for their defense. It is plainly a buildup that is offensive in nature.

**Q.** Then it'll lead to war.

**A.** What?

**Q.** You said earlier you didn't think it would lead to war, but you're describing something that inevitably has —

**A.** Well, no, not if they could achieve such a superiority by conning everyone else into being quiescent, that they could then say, "Look at the difference in our relative strengths. Now, here's what we want." That is what I mean by an ultimatum, "Surrender or die." And I think maybe they see that plan losing some of its potency now with our own plans. . . .

# REPORT ON VIOLENT CRIME
## August 17, 1981

*A Reagan administration advisory group presented its final report to Attorney General William French Smith on August 17, recommending that the federal government spend $2 billion over four years to assist the states in building new prisons and that national handgun control laws be strengthened. The report also called for changes in the federal bail law to permit the imprisoning of assertedly dangerous defendants before they came to trial, an easing of the federal rule excluding from criminal trials evidence that might have been obtained illegally, and an "unequivocal commitment to combating domestic drug traffic."*

*The report was issued at a time of heightened public concern over a rise in the number of violent crimes. Less than a month after the report was published, the Federal Bureau of Investigation reported that serious crimes had risen 9 percent over the previous year. But observers considered highly uncertain the extent to which the group's 64 recommendations would be endorsed by the Reagan administration.*

*The advisory group, the Attorney General's Task Force on Violent Crime, issued its report after four months of hearings in cities across the country. The cochairmen of the bipartisan, eight-member group were Griffin B. Bell, a former attorney general, and Gov. James R. Thompson of Illinois.*

### Prisons and Guns

*The recommendation considered most important by task force members, a federal contribution of $2 billion to the states for construction of* *correctional facilities, was also deemed by observers the most unlikely to receive early administration support. Under the proposal, states would contribute 25 percent of the cost of the facilities, and abandoned military bases would be considered as sites. But the recommendation was seen as running counter to the Reagan administration's philosophy of budgetary restraint.*

*Similarly, the recommendation for strengthening of federal gun control laws was seen by observers as politically difficult for the administration. The proposal would require persons to report the theft or loss of a handgun, make handgun buyers wait for checks of records and ban the importation into the country of unassembled gun parts. However, President Reagan had said in his campaign that he opposed gun control laws, and similar proposals had been opposed earlier by the National Rifle Association, a powerful lobby.*

## Civil Liberties Issues

*Civil libertarians and others were quick to criticize the task force's recommendations proposing changes in the Bail Reform Act of 1966. In an editorial,* The New York Times *said that the 1966 law "was a memorable reform. It told Federal judges to follow what was widely considered to be a constitutional principle: that the only question at a bail hearing is whether the defendant, if released, will show up for trial."*

*The task force report recommended that "[e]vidence should not be excluded from a criminal proceeding if it has been obtained by an officer acting in the reasonable, good faith belief that it was in conformity to the Fourth Amendment to the Constitution." Civil libertarians said that such measures would encourage police misconduct and weaken the constitutional presumption of innocence.*

## Reagan Speech

*Reagan in an address September 28 to the International Association of Chiefs of Police in New Orleans presented a personal philosophy based on "the absolute truths" of human nature. "Two of these truths," he said, "are that men are basically good but prone to evil; and society has a right to be protected from them." While the speech touched on some of the proposals in the task force report, it made no mention of the $2 billion spending proposal to help the states expand their prison capacity.*

> *Following are excerpts from the* Final Report *of the Attorney General's Task Force on Violent Crime, issued August 17, 1981, and from President Reagan's September 28 speech to the International Association of Chiefs of Police. (Boldface headings in brackets have been added by Congressional Quarterly to highlight the organization of the texts.):*

# FINAL REPORT

## Federal Law and Its Enforcement

### NARCOTICS

### Recommendation 16

The Attorney General should support the implementation of a clear, coherent, and consistent enforcement policy with regard to narcotics and dangerous drugs, reflecting an unequivocal commitment to combatting international and domestic drug traffic and including—

a. A foreign policy to accomplish the interdiction and eradication of illicit drugs wherever cultivated, processed, or transported; including the responsible use of herbicides domestically and internationally.

b. A border policy designed to effectively detect and intercept the illegal importation of narcotics, including the use of military assistance.

c. A legislative program, consistent with recommendations set forth elsewhere in this report, to reform the criminal justice process to enhance the ability to prosecute drug-related cases.

### Commentary

Throughout the course of our hearings, a recurrent theme has been the importance of more effectively combatting narcotics traffic. From Washington to Los Angeles, from Detroit to Miami, we have heard officials and scholars stress the connection between drugs and violent crime. Certain drugs directly cause physical harm and irrational and violent behavior. Other drugs cause addiction which, according to evidence presented to us, is directly related to a staggering amount of crime, much of it violent. Finally, drug trafficking itself, as demonstrated by so-called "cocaine cowboys," is often an extremely violent criminal activity.

We recommend a clear and coherent national enforcement policy with regard to narcotics and dangerous drugs. This policy must be characterized by a commitment to reducing the supply of — and demand for — illegal drugs, and it must be executed consistently.

The seriousness of the drug problem and of the national policy required to combat it must be reflected in the criminal justice system. Many general problems, such as insufficient bail, the suppression of truthful evidence, and the imposition of inconsistent and inadequate sentences, are particularly pronounced in drug cases. Accordingly, the recommendations set forth in Chapter 2 of this report are especially applicable to narcotics cases so that society will be better able to detect, apprehend, detain for trial, convict, and meaningfully sentence drug traffickers.

But the narcotics problem is broader than the criminal justice system. Fully 90 percent of the illegal drugs consumed in the United States come from abroad. Of all the aspects of this nation's violent crime problem, the international nature of drug trafficking most uniquely requires the powers and resources of the federal government. Plainly, state and local authorities are neither equipped nor empowered to conduct foreign relations or control access to this country by land, sea, and air.

So the national drug enforcement strategy must also be reflected in our foreign policy. The Administration must assure that United States diplomatic and economic assistance initiatives overseas are geared, whenever possible, toward the detection, interdiction, and eradication of illicit drugs before they complete (or even commence) their course to this country. Authorities agree that crop destruction is the most (and perhaps only) effective way to significantly disrupt drug traffic. This effort must not be crippled by unnecessary regulations. To this end, we recommend that the Administration assure that restrictions such as the present ban on the use of paraquat be removed unless based on an established and not speculative health risk. In this regard, we note that the Attorney General of Florida testified that 61,000 pounds of paraquat were used last year on his state's agricultural crops.

Nor can the national enforcement policy ignore the significant domestic marijuana crop. Failure to treat this phenomenon with the same seriousness (and the same methods) as we do foreign crops would betray an ambivalence about fighting drugs and would seriously weaken our efforts to persuade foreign governments to suppress drug cultivation.

The national enforcement policy must also find consistent application at our borders. The use of otherwise available military resources to detect and, if necessary, interdict drug smugglers must be authorized. To the extent that the Posse Comitatus Act prevents the military from providing such assistance, the Act should be amended. Inspection programs must be thorough, even if they require that citizens returning to this country be slightly inconvenienced by delays.

The application of scarce federal resources must be selective. The federal effort must be directed at those parts of the drug problem that state and local authorities cannot address. That is why we focus so strongly on international and border control efforts.

A final point is one often made during our hearings — the need for effective coordination. This need is recognized in all areas of law enforcement but is paramount in drug enforcement. Given the magnitude and worldwide scope of drug traffic and the multitude of federal, state, and local agencies with concurrent or overlapping jurisdiction, we recommend that the Attorney General and the Administration assure that the implementation of a national drug enforcement strategy be effectively coordinated at all levels of government. It is particularly important that the federal authorities closely coordinate with state and local law enforcement agencies that have the primary responsibility to investigate drug-related violent crime.

## GUNS

### Recommendation 17

The Attorney General should support or propose legislation to require a mandatory sentence for the use of a firearm in the commission of a federal felony.

### Recommendation 18

The Attorney General should support or propose legislation to amend the Gun Control Act of 1968 to strengthen its ability to meet two of its major purposes: allowing the trace of firearms used during the commission of an offense and prohibiting dangerous individuals from acquiring firearms. Specifically, the Act should be amended to provide the following:

a. That, on a prospective basis, individuals be required to report the theft or loss of a handgun to their local law enforcement agency.

b. That a waiting period be required for the purchase of a handgun to allow for a mandatory records check to ensure that the purchaser is not in one of the categories of persons who are proscribed by existing federal law from possessing a handgun.

### Recommendation 19

Title I of the Gun Control Act of 1968 prohibits the importation of certain categories of handguns. However, the Act does not prohibit the importation of unassembled parts of these guns, thereby permitting the circumvention of the intended purpose of this title of the Act. It is therefore recommended that the Act be amended to prohibit the importation of unassembled parts of handguns which would be prohibited if assembled.

### Recommendation 20

The Attorney General should support or propose legislation to authorize the Bureau of Alcohol, Tobacco and Firearms to classify semi-automatic weapons that are easily converted into fully automatic weapons as Title II weapons under the Gun Control Act of 1968.

### Recommendation 21

The Attorney General should direct the United States Attorneys to develop agreements with state and local prosecutors for increased federal prosecutions of convicted felons apprehended in the possession of a firearm. This proposal would enable federal prosecutions to be brought against felons apprehended in the possession of a firearm under the 1968

Gun Control Act and the Dangerous Special Offender provisions of the Organized Crime Control Act of 1970. Federal penalties under these statutes often are greater than state penalties applicable to firearms possession. Because these cases are matters over which state and local law enforcement has primary jurisdiction, they should be brought in close coordination with state and local prosecutors. The appropriate federal role is to initiate prosecutions in order to bring federal prosecutorial resources and more severe penalties to bear on the most serious offenders in a locality who are apprehended with firearms in their possession.

### Recommendation 22

The Attorney General should direct the National Institute of Justice to establish, as a high priority, research and development of methods of detecting and apprehending persons unlawfully carrying guns.

### Commentary

In the United States in 1978, firearms were used in 307,000 offenses of murder, robbery, and aggravated assault reported to the police; they were present in about one-tenth of all violent victimizations occurring in 1980. In 1978, 77.8 percent of firearm murders involved a handgun. Every year approximately 10,000 Americans are murdered by criminals using handguns. Crimes committed by individuals using handguns represent a serious problem of violence in our nation. Proffered solutions to this problem are myriad, ranging from the practical to the impossible. Positions taken are often highly emotionally charged. Additionally, there is no lack of social science data — of varying quality — to support diametrically opposed views.

However, the plethora of contradictory state gun laws has made their enforcement ineffective, indicating the need for a federal strategy that would provide consistency and uniformity across state boundaries. In addition, federal gun laws have failed in several ways to achieve their intended purposes due to either a lack of adequate enforcement mechanisms or unintended loopholes in existing law.

Despite the problems inherent in examining the issue of guns, it is possible to set forth sensible criteria for the recommendations we are making in this area. First, they should be politically feasible. Second, they should balance the importance of preserving legitimate reasons for owning guns and the costs associated with that ownership. Finally, and most importantly, it should be possible to make at least a prima facie case for the effectiveness of these recommendations in reducing violent crime.

We believe that individuals must be deterred from using handguns in the commission of a crime. We believe that the cost to an individual of committing a crime with a handgun should be made greater than the benefit. This cost, in part, should be manifested in the sentence that is meted out to those convicted of such acts. . . .

We recommend legislation to require a mandatory sentence for those convicted of the use of a firearm in the commission of a federal felony. This proposal, supported as it is by the public and the police, would provide an effective deterrent to crimes of this sort. To be effective, the mandatory sentence should be severe enough to have the necessary deterrent force. Further, the power to impose this sentence should not be vitiated by any opportunities on the part of prosecutors to circumvent it through the use of plea bargaining, charge reduction, or other methods.

Several purposes of the existing federal gun laws have not been fulfilled effectively. The 1968 Gun Control Act banned, with some exceptions, the importation of handguns (including so-called "Saturday Night Specials") into the United States. . . . However, a loophole allowed the importation of handgun parts which could then be assembled into handguns and sold. We believe that the 1968 Gun Control Act is still worthy of support and that its intent should be carried out by closing this loophole. Therefore, we recommend that the Act be amended to prohibit the importation of unassembled parts of handguns which would be prohibited if assembled.

Another purpose of the Act and of the Omnibus Crime Control and Safe Streets Act, designed to reduce violent crime, is directed at preventing the possession of handguns by proscribed groups of people. However, it has not had its desired effect. Under those Acts certain categories of individuals are ineligible to receive firearms that have been shipped in interstate commerce. These include:

Fugitives from justice

Persons under federal or state felony indictment

Persons convicted of a federal or state felony

Persons ineligible by state or local law to possess a firearm

Minors, under 18 years of age for rifles and shotguns, and under 21 years of age for handguns

Adjudicated mental defectives or persons committed to a mental institution

Unlawful users of or addicts to any depressant, stimulant, or narcotic drug

Felons

Persons dishonorably discharged from the United States Armed Forces

Mental incompetents

Former United States citizens

Illegal aliens.

There is, at present, no effective method to verify a purchaser's eligibility. The dealer must know or have reason to believe that the purchaser is ineligible to receive a firearm in order to make a transaction unlawful. However, this is very difficult to prove. A person purchasing a firearm from a federally licensed dealer is required to sign a form on which he affirms by sworn statement that he is not proscribed from purchasing a firearm. This signature relieves the dealer from any liability for illegal transfer, as long as he requests and examines a form of purchaser identification, other than a social security card, that verifies the purchaser's name, age, and place of residence.

Since drug addicts, felons, mental defectives, and the like are not the best risk for "the honor system," a waiting period between the time of signing the presently required form and delivery of the handgun to the purchaser to verify the purchaser's eligibility is sensible and necessary to effectuate the purposes of the Acts. Dealers should be required to contact law enforcement authorities and verify a purchaser's eligibility, or prospective purchasers should be required to apply for a permit to purchase a handgun at their local police departments, where their eligibility is checked. Such a requirement may also provide a "cooling off" period for individuals who might otherwise purchase and use a handgun in the heat of passion. . . .

We recommend that a waiting period be required for the purchase of a handgun to allow for a mandatory records check to ensure that the purchaser is not proscribed by the Gun Control Act of 1968 or Title VII of the 1968 Omnibus Crime Control and Safe Streets Act from owning a handgun. In order for this waiting period to be effective there should be adequate record check methods available. By making this recommendation, we are endorsing the concept of a waiting period without specifying the actual mechanism that should be employed. That task should be left to those who frame the legislation requiring such a waiting period. We do not believe that this proposal broadens the limitations on handgun ownership contained in existing law; it simply enables the intent of the law to be fulfilled — an intent that has wide public support. Handguns should be kept out of the hands of the wrong people.

## [Lost or Stolen Guns]

Not all handguns that are used in crimes arrive in the hands of perpetrators directly from a firearms dealer. Many of these guns have been resold, given away, lost, or stolen. . . . A number of proposals have been made to ameliorate this situation and improve the national firearms trace capability.

We recommend that individuals be required to report to their local law enforcement officials the loss or theft of any handgun. The police would then enter this information into the National Crime Information Center (NCIC) (this information is routinely entered into the NCIC now by local police departments *when* it is reported to them).

We do not believe it is necessary for individuals to report the resale or gift of a handgun to another individual.... Nor do we believe it necessary to have any kind of national registry of handguns to which dealers would report sales and resales of handguns. Such a registry would be too cumbersome, given the 2 million handguns sold by dealers each year and the many additional transactions between private citizens. In addition, expert testimony before us indicates that the records currently kept by manufacturers and dealers, if enhanced by reporting of thefts and losses to the NCIC, would provide an adequate trace capability....

## [Greater Use of Federal Statutes]

Federal laws prohibit convicted felons, among other types of individuals, from acquiring firearms. They also contain increased penalties for persons using a firearm in the course of a variety of federal crimes. In some states, these federal firearm laws are significantly more severe than comparable state statutes. In addition, in many federal districts the federal court dockets are not as crowded as county and city court calendars.

For the federal government to contribute more effectively to the reduction of violent crime, U.S. Attorneys should bring more prosecutions under these federal statutes. This will enable the more severe federal sanctions to be applied to the violent offenders who present a great threat to the community, but who face more limited state sanctions. To accomplish this goal, the U.S. Attorneys should develop a working agreement with state and local prosecutors to establish a mechanism for bringing to the attention of the U.S. Attorneys those persons apprehended by state and local authorities in possession of firearms in violation of federal laws. Where the firearm involved was used in the course of a serious felony, the state laws for the principal offense (e.g., homicide, robbery, rape, etc.) may be entirely adequate. However, where a previously convicted felon has committed a relatively minor offense, or has committed no provable offense other than acquisition of a firearm, the U.S. Attorney should review the case for possible federal prosecution. By working together with state and local prosecutors on these firearms violations, the U.S. Attorneys will be able to bring the federal firearms penalties to bear on those violent offenders who persist in violating the law, as evidenced by unlawful firearms possession....

## THE FREEDOM OF INFORMATION ACT

### Recommendation 31

The Attorney General should order a comprehensive review of all legislation, guidelines, and regulations that may serve to impede the effective performance of federal law enforcement and prosecutorial activities and take whatever appropriate action is necessary within the constitutional framework.

## Recommendation 32

The Attorney General should seek amendments to the Freedom of Information Act to correct those aspects that impede criminal investigation and prosecution and to establish a more rational balance among individual privacy considerations, openness in government, and the government's responsibility to protect citizens from criminal activity.

## Commentary

One concern raised by witnesses before the Task Force was the extent to which federal legislation, regulations, and guidelines, however well intended, serve to impede unnecessarily the effective enforcement of law. Within the 120 days allotted for our effort, we were unable to examine all legislation, regulations, and guidelines that may affect law enforcement, but we recommend that the Attorney General order such a comprehensive review.

The Freedom of Information Act (FOIA) was singled out by several witnesses before us as having shown negative consequences for effective law enforcement. Upon examination, we found that it is currently being used in ways that were unforeseen and unintended when it was enacted into law in 1966. When President Johnson signed into law the FOIA, he commented:

> This legislation springs from one of our most essential principles: a democracy works best when the people have all the information that the security of the Nation permits. No one should be able to pull curtains of secrecy around decisions which can be revealed without injury to the public interest.

Today, 15 years later, it is clear that the proportion of requests under the FOIA related to performing this vital function of informing the public may be very small. In recent congressional testimony, the Department of Justice reported that only 7 percent of 30,000 FOIA requests received annually come from the media or other researchers. Many requests come from persons who are obviously seeking information for improper personal advantage, including convicted offenders, organized crime figures, drug traffickers, and persons in litigation with the United States who are attempting to use the FOIA to circumvent the rules of discovery contained in the rules of criminal or civil procedure. Because requesters do not have to give a reason for the request, it is unknown precisely how great this type of abuse may be; however, the Federal Bureau of Investigation (FBI) reports that 11 percent of its requests are from prisoners and the Drug Enforcement Administration (DEA) reports that 40 percent of its requests are from prisoners and another 20 percent are from persons who are not in prison but are known by DEA to be connected with criminal drug activities.

Most observers agree that the FOIA has had beneficial consequences, including restoring public confidence in government and necessitating that law enforcement agencies scrutinize their need for collecting and maintaining criminal intelligence information. . . . [T]here is near universal agreement in the law enforcement community that, while the FOIA has had many laudable effects, in many cases it has served to protect the criminally inclined and is in need of modification to restore the delicate balance between openness in government and the government's responsibility to protect citizens from crime. . . .

In support of their conclusions that the FOIA now needs modification, witnesses . . . offered the following examples of how it has affected the ability of federal, state, and local governments to combat crime:

- Decreases in the number of informants have been reported; it is believed by many that potential informants do not come forward out of fear of disclosure through FOIA requests from persons they had helped convict. Even though their informant identities are exempt from disclosure, informants fear that they will become known through agency error or release of ancillary information on details of the informant's role in the investigation.

- In some federal agencies, a considerable number of FOIA requests come from incarcerated offenders, presumably trying to identify informants or from organized crime figures and drug dealers seeking to find out what the government knows about them and their criminal activity.

- It is suspected that some individuals (particularly offenders) are using the FOIA to slow court processing or as a "nuisance device" to harass federal agencies.

- Requests have been received for personnel rosters and investigative and training manuals of investigative agencies presumably to learn the investigation identities and the techniques the federal government uses to capture offenders.

- When an FOIA request is for material in an active investigation file, the government can deny the request but must explain why, alerting the requester that he or she is under investigation. . . .

- International law enforcement cooperation has been affected as some foreign agencies are reluctant to share with the United States information that might be disclosed under the FOIA.

- Current estimates indicate that it costs the federal government $45 million a year to administer the FOIA, the bulk of the cost being associated with salaries. The FBI alone employs approximately 300 persons to work on FOIA matters, at an annual cost of $11.5 million. . . .

The Department of Justice is currently studying the FOIA. On May 4, 1981, Attorney General William French Smith announced ". . . the commencement of a comprehensive review of the Act to assess the need for legislative reform.". . .

In making this recommendation, we know that some observers, particularly among the media, are concerned that modifications to the FOIA will impede their access, and that of researchers and the general public, to government information. This concern was expressed by several witnesses in recent testimony before congressional committees. We believe it important to stress that what we are recommending is modification that would limit access by persons seeking to use the Act for improper personal advantage, while preserving those provisions that operate in accord with original congressional intent. Drafting such modifications will not be simple, and it is important that drafters of such language avoid the simplistic approach of protecting legitimately confidential information by excepting it along with a large body of information that should be available to the public. . . .

## Criminal Procedure

### BAIL

### Recommendation 38

The Attorney General should support or propose legislation to amend the Bail Reform Act that would accomplish the following:

a. Permit courts to deny bail to persons who are found by clear and convincing evidence to present a danger to particular persons or the community.

b. Deny bail to a person accused of a serious crime who had previously, while in a pretrial release status, committed a serious crime for which he was convicted.

c. Codify existing case law defining the authority of the courts to detain defendants as to whom no conditions of release are adequate to assure appearance at trial.

d. Abandon, in the case of serious crimes, the current standard presumptively favoring release of convicted persons awaiting imposition or execution of sentence or appealing their convictions.

e. Provide the government with the right to appeal release decisions analogous to the appellate rights now afforded to defendants.

f. Require defendants to refrain from criminal activity as a mandatory condition of release.

g. Make the penalties for bail jumping more closely proportionate to the penalties for the offense with which the defendant was originally charged.

### Commentary

Federal bail practices are for the most part now governed by the Bail Reform Act of 1966. . . . The primary purpose of the Act was to deemphasize the use of money bonds in the federal courts, a practice which was perceived as resulting in disproportionate and unnecessary pretrial incarceration of poor defendants, and to provide a range of alternative forms of release. These goals of the Act . . . are ones which are worthy of support.

However, 15 years of experience with the Act have demonstrated that, in some respects, it does not provide for appropriate release decisions.

Increasingly, the Act has come under criticism as too liberally allowing release and as providing too little flexibility to judges in making appropriate release decisions regarding defendants who pose serious risks of flight or danger to the community.

*Denying bail to persons who are found by clear and convincing evidence to be dangerous.* Under the present provisions of the Bail Reform Act, the only issue that may be considered by the court in making a pretrial release decision is the likelihood that the defendant will appear for trial if released. Consideration of the danger the defendant may pose to particular individuals or to the community is not permitted. Although a defendant seeking release may pose a significant risk to the safety of others, the courts are now without authority to deny release on the ground that the defendant will likely commit dangerous or violent acts while on bail.

The concept of permitting consideration of dangerousness in the pretrial release decision has been widely supported. It is incorporated in the release provisions of the District of Columbia Code which was passed by Congress in 1970 and has been endorsed in the American Bar Association (ABA) Standards Relating to the Administration of Justice and by the National Conference of Commissioners on Uniform State Laws. In addition, in his annual address to the ABA in February of this year, the Chief Justice stressed the need to provide for greater flexibility in our bail laws to permit judges, in making determinations, to give adequate consideration to the issue of a defendant's dangerousness.

The wide and growing support for permitting consideration of a defendant's dangerousness in the pretrial release decision is simply a recognition that the courts must have authority to make responsible decisions regarding defendants who pose significant dangers to the community. The state of current federal law, which deprives the courts of this authority, is in our view no longer tolerable.

To provide an adequate means for dealing with dangerous defendants who are seeking release pending trial, the Bail Reform Act must be amended. It is obvious that there are defendants as to whom no conditions of release will reasonably assure the safety of particular persons or the community. With respect to such defendants, the courts must be given the authority to deny bail.

The Act currently makes no provision for denial of bail on the ground of dangerousness. This does not mean, however, that there are no situations in which pretrial detention may be ordered. For example, it is recognized that a defendant who has threatened witnesses may be ordered detained and, in some circumstances, detention may be ordered for defendants who appear likely to flee regardless of what release conditions are imposed. Furthermore, there is a widespread practice of detailing particularly dangerous defendants by the setting of high money bonds to assure appearance.

Amending the Act to permit the denial of bail to defendants who pose a serious danger to community safety would not only constitute a sound policy, but also would represent a more honest way of dealing with the issue of potential misconduct by those released pending trial. It is widely believed that under the present system, despite the lack of statutory authority to consider dangerousness in the release decision, many courts nonetheless do detain dangerous defendants (even though they pose little or no risk of flight) by requiring the posting of high money bonds — a phenomenon which has cast doubt on the fairness of federal release practices. . . .

*Offenders who have committed a serious crime while previously on pretrial release.* A person who has been convicted of a serious offense committed while on pretrial release has established beyond a reasonable doubt, first, that he is dangerous and, second, that he cannot be trusted to conform to the requirement of the law while on release. He should therefore be presumed to be dangerous and ineligible for release. Such a provision might be a strong deterrent to criminal conduct by those who are in a release status. A possible additional provision would be to limit the period of time during which a person would be ineligible for bail to a set period of time, such as 10 years.

*Denial of bail to assure appearance.* The Bail Reform Act should be amended to give the courts clear statutory authority to order the detention of defendants who pose such a risk of flight that no conditions of release will assure their appearance. Such an amendment would not be a departure from current law but rather a codification of case law which has recognized the authority of judges to deny release to defendants where there is a substantial likelihood that, if released, they will flee the jurisdiction to avoid prosecution.

Despite the fact that there is case law recognizing the authority to deny release based on a severe risk of flight, many judges continue to be reluctant to exercise this power in light of the absence of any such authority in controlling federal bail statutes. However, as has been the case with extremely dangerous defendants, a practice has developed of requiring extraordinarily high money bonds as a means of accomplishing the detention of defendants who pose serious risks of flight.

The courts should not be required to resort to this practice, but instead should have clear statutory authority to address the problem of flight to avoid prosecution honestly and order detention where it is the only means of assuring appearance. . . .

*Post-conviction release.* One of the most disturbing aspects of the Bail Reform Act is its standard governing release after conviction. This standard . . . presumptively favors the release of convicted persons who are awaiting imposition or execution of sentence or who are appealing their convictions. . . .

In our view, there are compelling reasons for abandoning the present standard which presumptively favors release of convicted persons. First, conviction, in which the defendant's guilt is established beyond a reasonable doubt, is presumptively correct at law. Therefore, while a statutory presumption in favor of release prior to an adjudication of guilt may be appropriate, it is not appropriate after conviction. Second, the adoption of a liberal release policy for convicted persons, particularly during the pendency of lengthy appeals, undermines the deterrent effect of conviction and erodes the community's confidence in the criminal justice system by permitting convicted criminals to remain free even though their guilt has been established beyond a reasonable doubt. . . .

*Government appeal of release decisions.* Under current law, defendants have an opportunity to move for reduction of bond and to seek reconsideration and appellate review of release decisions. The government, however, has no opportunity to obtain review of the conditions of release or the release decision itself. Faced with what it believes to be an improper release decision, the government is powerless to seek review of an often hastily made decision which will permit a defendant to flee the jurisdiction or to return to the community to resume his criminal activity. It is simply a matter of fairness and sound policy to provide the government with the same right to appeal release decisions as is given defendants.

*Mandatory condition of release that the defendant not commit another crime.* We believe that whenever a defendant is ordered released the court should be required to impose a condition that the defendant not commit another crime while on release. This mandatory release condition was included in S. 1722, the Criminal Code revision bill approved by the Senate Judiciary Committee in the past Congress. . . .

*Penalties for bail jumping should be proportionate to the severity of the penalties applicable to the offense charged.* Under current law, the maximum penalty for the offense of bail jumping . . . is 5 years imprisonment if the offense charged was a felony and imprisonment of up to 1 year if the offense with which the defendant was charged when he was released was a misdemeanor. While the prospect of a 5-year penalty for bail jumping may dissuade a defendant charged with an offense punishable by 5 or 10 years imprisonment from fleeing, it may be ineffective in the case of a defendant facing 20 years or life imprisonment who will be tempted to go into hiding until the government's case becomes stale or witnesses are unavailable and then surface at a later time to face only the limited liability for bail jumping. . . .

## EXCLUSIONARY RULE

### Recommendation 40

The fundamental and legitimate purpose of the exclusionary rule — to deter illegal police conduct and promote respect for the rule of law by preventing illegally obtained evidence from being used in a criminal trial — has been eroded by the action of the courts barring evidence of the truth, however important, if there is any investigative error, however unintended or trivial. We believe that any remedy for the violation of a constitutional right should be proportional to the magnitude of the violation. In general, evidence should not be excluded from a criminal proceeding if it has been obtained by an officer acting in the reasonable, good faith belief that it was in conformity to the Fourth Amendment to the Constitution. A showing that evidence was obtained pursuant to and within the scope of a warrant constitutes prima facie evidence of such a good faith belief. We recommend that the Attorney General instruct United States Attorneys and the Solicitor General to urge this rule in appropriate court proceedings, or support federal legislation establishing this rule, or both. If this rule can be established, it will restore the confidence of the public and of law enforcement officers in the integrity of criminal proceedings and the value of constitutional guarantees.

## Commentary

The purpose of the exclusionary rule, as applied to search and seizure issues, "is to deter — to compel respect for the constitutional guaranty in the only effectively available way — by removing the incentive to disregard it." *Mapp v. Ohio* ... (1961). Application of the rule has been carried to the point where it is applied to situations where police officers make reasonable, good faith efforts to comply with the law, but unwittingly fail to do so. In such circumstances, the rule necessarily fails in its deterrent purpose.

For example, an officer may in good faith rely on a duly authorized search or arrest warrant or on a statute that is later found to be unconstitutional; or an officer may make a reasonable interpretation of a statute which a court later determines to be inconsistent with the legislative intent; or an officer may reasonably and in good faith conclude that a particular set of facts and circumstances gives rise to probable cause, but a court later concludes otherwise. In such circumstances, we do not comprehend how the deterrent purpose of the exclusionary rule is served by exclusion of the evidence seized.

The example cited above in which an officer relies on a duly authorized search or arrest warrant is a particularly compelling example of good faith. A warrant is a judicial mandate to an officer to conduct a search or make an arrest, and the officer has a sworn duty to carry out its provisions. Accordingly, we believe that there should be a rule which states that evidence obtained pursuant to and within the scope of a warrant is prima facie the result of good faith on the part of the officer seizing the evidence. This is not to say that good faith is limited to this example, or even that this is the only case in which a prima facie rule of evidence should operate. The ultimate issue under this proposal would be whether a police officer was acting in good faith at the time that he conducted a search and seized certain evidence. The showing of good faith would be determined from all of the facts and circumstances of the search....

The present application of the exclusionary rule not only depresses police morale and allows criminals to go free when constables unwittingly blunder, but it diminishes public respect for the courts and our judicial process.

If the rule is redefined to limit its application to circumstances in which an officer did not act either reasonably, or in good faith, or both, it will have an important purpose that will be served by its application. Moreover, it will gain the support of the public and the respect of responsible law enforcement officials.

The Attorney General therefore should support legislatively and in court the position that evidence obtained in the course of a reasonable, good faith search should not be excluded from criminal trials.

The following statutory language would accomplish this purpose:

> Except as specifically provided by statute, evidence which is obtained as a result of a search or seizure and which is otherwise admissible shall not be excluded in a criminal proceeding brought by the United States unless:
>
> (1) the defendant makes a timely objection to the introduction of the evidence;
>
> (2) the defendant establishes by a preponderance of the evidence that the search or seizure was in violation of the Fourth Amendment to the Constitution of the United States; and,
>
> (3) the prosecution fails to show by a preponderance of the evidence that the search or seizure was undertaken in a reasonable, good faith belief that it was in conformity with the Fourth Amendment to the Constitution of the United States. A showing that evidence was obtained pursuant to and within the scope of a warrant constitutes prima facie evidence of such a good faith belief.

To achieve the objective of this recommendation, the Attorney General should either urge this rule in appropriate court proceedings, or support federal legislation that would establish this rule, or both. While the final decision on this issue would be within the province of the Supreme Court, it may be some time before an appropriate case is accepted for decision. Meanwhile, it might well be appropriate for Congress to consider this issue in the form of proposed legislation. However, we wish to leave to the Attorney General the decision as to the best method of accomplishing this objective....

## Federalism in Criminal Justice

### ASSISTING STATE AND LOCAL CORRECTIONS

#### Recommendation 57

The Attorney General should support or propose legislation to amend the Vocational Education Act and other applicable statutes to facilitate state and local correctional agencies' ability to gain access to existing funds for the establishment of vocational and educational programs within correctional institutions.

## Commentary

The problem of available space in state prisons to keep dangerous criminals off the street is one of the most important violent crime issues in the nation. Almost all states are in a crisis situation. As has been continuously documented in public testimony and reports, many states are experiencing alarming rates of violent crime. The higher crime rate has produced a higher prosecution and conviction rate, which, combined with the public's demand (frequently via statute) for harsher, longer sentences for the perpetrators of these crimes, has resulted in correctional systems facing unprecedented increases in populations, which they are not prepared to accommodate. One state correctional administrator recently commented that based on that state's current incarceration rate, one 400-bed prison per month could be filled. The crisis for many metropolitan jails is of similar proportion, with one sheriff testifying before his state legislature that he has 300 inmates sleeping on the floor of the county jail.

Between 1978 and 1981, the number of state prisoners increased from 268,189 to 329,122, according to the Bureau of Justice Statistics. Thus, state systems have over the past few years had to accommodate an increase of 60,000 beds. With 39 states involved in litigation or under court order relating to conditions of confinement in state prisons, jails were forced to take 6,000 state prisoners in 1980 as a means of easing overcrowding. However, they too are crowded and face lawsuits similar to those filed by inmates in state institutions. In response to this crisis, by July 1980, state correctional agencies had begun new construction of more than 60 institutions or additions at a projected cost in excess of $700 million.

The problem of overcrowding goes beyond corrections. It leads to a circumvention of the overall public and criminal justice system's intent to deal with the violent offender in a manner consistent with the gravity of the offense. Thus, a substantial number of defendants who should be incarcerated might receive probation instead simply because the judges are aware that there is currently no space available for them in prison. Such action may then have the unintended consequence of endangering the community. Clearly, judges must feel free to use incarceration as a sentencing option; it therefore becomes imperative to better understand the range of issues related to overcrowding and carefully assess proposed means of coping with this problem.

. . . [W]e acknowledged the current overpopulation problem in corrections, and now must consider the extent to which the federal government can provide assistance in alleviating crowding. The overriding concern remains the safety of the community, which is secured by ensuring that those offenders, i.e., serious, violent offenders, who need to be incapacitated are incarcerated.

More than two-thirds of the states have proposed to build or have under construction at least one major correctional facility. Some states have found the process so costly that they cannot complete their efforts or have vacant facilities because they cannot afford staffing and operation. . . .

The cost of building a maximum security facility is over $70,000 per bed in many jurisdictions as diverse as California, Minnesota, or Rhode Island. Alaska reported a staggering $130,000 for the average cost of prison construction per cell. . . . Whatever the figures, it is clear that the financial burden on the states and counties to renovate or construct correctional institutions is extraordinary.

It therefore becomes particularly important to ensure that any decision to build be one that carefully considers the makeup of the inmate population and the security requirements of the correctional system. It has been suggested by national corrections leaders, for example, that perhaps only 15 to 20 percent of inmates in state prisons require costly, maximum security institutions, though 70 percent of the facilities fall into the high security category. A rational classification system to decide what type of confinement is necessary for a given prisoner is of critical importance in freeing up maximum security space and containing costs.

*Direct federal assistance for prison construction.* Given the fact that 43 percent of prisoners are being housed in facilities built before 1925, 70 percent of prison cells fall short of federal standards for square footage, and over one-half of the state correctional systems have one or more institutions declared to be unconstitutional by federal courts, we are of the opinion that assistance leading to the replacement or renovation of outmoded or substandard correctional facilities is essential. In fact, the Criminal Justice Committee of the National Governors' Association has called federal assistance for capital construction the number-one criminal justice priority. We agree. Clearly, a federal role in this area is necessary; and, in light of the enormity of such an undertaking, we have given special consideration to a number of issues.

### [Federal Construction Assistance]

The provision of assistance in building or renovating correctional facilities need not necessarily mean that the total capacity of institutions be increased; but rather that there be the most appropriate use of available space. Even if more violent or serious offenders are confined, the number of high security bedspaces need not necessarily rise, as offenders in need of a less secure environment could be moved from maximum to medium security facilities. With resource limitations at all levels of government, any federal grant program should be confined to those criminal justice areas exhibiting greatest need. If this means construction and renovation of detention and corrections facilities, the focus should be on those for the most serious offenders, in maximum security facilities, which are typically the oldest and most in need of replacement or repair. . . .

Federal requirements should not operate so that they have the unintended effect of keeping jurisdictions from responding to their own needs;

and federal dollars need not be so great that jurisdictions merely apply without considering the extent of their actual problem. Thus, the application process should not be so complicated that states are reluctant to take advantage of the assistance, but neither should there be no strings attached, thereby condoning possible inadequately designed facilities both in terms of inmate and staff needs and the needs of the community. Therefore, for purposes of demonstrating this balance and a commitment to accepted standards of correctional planning and practice, we recommend the federal contribution to the proposed construction effort be limited to 75 percent of that effort. In addition, we believe that the federal support program should be limited in time and level of expenditure; there is no need to create a long-term federal operation with states receiving grants for a number of years. We deem an initial 4-year authorization and appropriation to be sufficient. Given differing needs and costs in the various states, we believe that the immediate objectives of the construction program can be met with a $2 billion appropriation. . . .

### [Private Sector Management]

Another proposal that we considered was the involvement of the private sector in the management of prisons. Private contractors have been heavily involved in corrections over the past decade in areas such as provision of direct program and health services, development of prison industry and community work projects, and the operation of community-based programs such as halfway houses, pre-release centers, and drug treatment facilities. However, the private sector has not been involved in the management of medium or maximum security penal institutions.

A variety of concerns have been raised as to the feasibility of such an endeavor. Some of the questions include—

• Whether the responsibility, and concomitant liabilities, for providing a secure and safe environment for violent offenders can be properly delegated from the public to the private sector.

• How the carrying out of statutory and judicial intentions can be assured.

• Whether it would be cost-effective to have to develop a new, highly trained cadre of individuals who understand management in a prison setting.

• How public employee unions and employment generally would be affected.

In addition to these and other concerns, the experience of using the private sector in running community-based programs leaves some cost questions unanswered, at least in terms of potential cost-benefit relative to secure residential facilities. It is not clear that the conventional wisdom is correct that private sector management of correctional facilities would be less expensive than public sector management; we believe this requires further study. . . .

*Use of surplus federal property.* In addition to direct financial assistance, there exists another significant opportunity for federal involvement in easing state and local correctional facility overcrowding. Section 203k(1) of the Federal Property and Administrative Services Act of 1949, as amended, provides for conveyances of property and buildings by the General Services Administration (GSA) to states and local jurisdictions at up to 100-percent discount or with no monetary consideration where such properties are to be used as educational or medical facilities, public parks, historical monuments, wildlife refuges, or public airports. . . .

We recommend an amendment to the Act, permitting a similar arrangement to enable the Administrator of GSA to make property available to the states at no cost for correctional purposes, with criteria for transfer being developed by the Department of Justice. . . .

In addition to amending the Act to permit these no-cost conveyances, due to the immediacy of the need for adequate bedspace for corrections, we believe that Congress should give requests for such use of surplus property priority over other requests for the same property. . . .

*Vocational education and training.* In addition to considering overcrowding vis-a-vis the inmates' physical environment, we recognize, as the Chief Justice has suggested, that with the emphasis on incarcerating more violent offenders, perhaps for longer periods of time, there is a responsibility to provide practical experiences for inmates that will result in their being productive both while incarcerated and upon leaving the institution and returning to society. While a large expansion of vocational and educational training for inmates could prove quite expensive, it is possible, through legislative amendment, to make available substantial resources for this purpose. . . .

The Department of Education and the Department of Justice have been working on strategies to assist corrections in obtaining monies for educational and vocational programs. We believe these efforts should be enhanced and that the appropriate statutes be amended to specifically designate correctional agencies as qualifying recipients of funds for educating inmates. Some guidelines might be included calling, as an example, for states to require certification of correctional education staff, thus encouraging a higher level of available training. . . .

# REAGAN SPEECH ON CRIME

. . . In discussing . . . sophisticated crimes, we see again the emergence of the problem of career criminals — those who make a conscious decision to pursue illicit professions, a decision based on a belief that crime does pay. I believe the emergence of this problem of career criminals has seriously undermined the notion that criminals are simply products of poverty or underprivileged backgrounds.

At the very same time that crime rates have steadily risen, our Nation has made unparalleled progress in raising the standard of living and improving the quality of life. It's obvious that prosperity doesn't decrease crime, just as it's obvious that deprivation and want don't necessarily increase crime. The truth is that today's criminals for the most part are not desperate people seeking bread for their families; crime is the way they've chosen to live. . . .

. . . There is an arrogance to the criminal mind, a belief in its own superiority over the rest of humanity. The slang of organized crime is instructive here. It isn't surprising that some of these criminals habitually refer to themselves as "wise guys," and the honest people are "working stiffs." They do really believe that they're better than the rest of us, that the world owes them a living, and that those of us who lead normal lives and earn an honest living are a little slow on the uptake. . . .

I would suggest the time has come to look reality in the face. American society is mired in excess litigation. Our courts today are loaded with suits and motions of every conceivable type. Yet, as our system of justice has become weighed down with lawsuits of every nature and description, as the courts have become the arbiters of all kinds of disputes they were never intended to handle, our legal system has failed to carry out its most important function — the protection of the innocent and the punishment of the guilty.

It's time for honest talk, for plain talk. There has been a breakdown in the criminal justice system in America. It just plain isn't working. All too often, repeat offenders, habitual law-breakers, career criminals, call them what you will, are robbing, raping, and beating with impunity and . . . quite literally getting away with murder. The people are sickened and outraged. They demand that we put a stop to it.

What is especially disturbing about our failure to deal with crime is the erosion it has caused in public confidence in our judicial system. In one recent poll, 70 percent of the people said they had little or no confidence in the ability of our courts to sentence and convict criminals. . . .

This decline in public confidence in our courts and in the legal profession remains a threat to one of our most important traditions, traditions as Americans: the heritage of our independent judiciary, free from public or political influence, and a legal profession with a reputation for high, unassailable ethics. . . .

. . . Controlling crime in American society is not simply a question of more money, more police, more courts, more prosecutors; it's ultimately a moral dilemma, one that calls for a moral or, if you will, a spiritual solution. In dealing with crime, new programs may help; more law-and-order rhetoric may be justified; the studies and surveys may still be needed; the blue ribbon panels may keep investigating. But in the end, the war on crime will only be won when an attitude of mind and a change of heart takes place in America, when certain truths take hold again and plant their roots deep in our national consciousness, truths like: Right and wrong matters; Individuals are responsible for their actions; Retribution should be swift and sure for those who prey on the innocent.

We must understand that basic moral principles lie at the heart of our criminal justice system, that our system of law acts as the collective moral voice of society. There's nothing wrong with these values, nor should we be hesitant or feel guilty about punishing those who violate the elementary rules of civilized existence. Theft is not a form of political or cultural expression; it is theft, and it is wrong. Murder is not forbidden as a matter of subjective opinion; it is objectively evil, and we must prohibit it. And no one but the thief and murderer benefits when we think and act otherwise.

Again, let me point to something that I hadn't included in my remarks but I am reminded of — the whole problem of capital punishment. Well, I had an answer to that on my desk for several years while I was Governor. It was a list of the names of 12 criminals, 12 murderers, who had all been sentenced to prison, who had all served their terms or been paroled, and released. And at the time the list was on my desk, their total number of victims was 34, not 12. I think capital punishment in the beginning might have reduced that figure considerably.

A tendency to downplay the permanent moral values has helped make crime the enormous problem that it is today, one that this administration has . . . made one of its top domestic priorities. But it has occurred to me that the root causes of our other major domestic problem, the growth of government and the decay of the economy, can be traced to many of the same sources of the crime problem. This is because the same utopian presumptions about human nature that hinder the swift administration of justice have also helped fuel the expansion of government.

Many of the social thinkers of the 1950's and '60's who discussed crime only in the context of disadvantaged childhoods and poverty-stricken neighborhoods were the same people who thought that massive government spending could wipe away our social ills. The underlying premise in both cases was a belief that there was nothing permanent or absolute about any man's nature, that he was a product of his material environment, and that by changing that environment — with government as the chief vehicle of change through educational, health, housing, and other programs — we could permanently change man and usher in a great new era.

Well, we've learned the price of too much government: runaway inflation, soaring unemployment, impossible interest rates. We've learned that Federal subsidies and government bureaucrats not only fail to solve social problems but frequently make them worse.

It's time, too, that we acknowledge the solution to the crime problem will not be found in the social worker's files, the psychiatrist's notes, or the bureaucrat's budgets. It's a problem of the human heart, and it's there we must look for the answer. We can begin by acknowledging some of those permanent things, those absolute truths I mentioned before. Two of those truths are that men are basically good but prone to evil, and society has a right to be protected from them.

The massive expansion of government is related to the crime problem in another, less obvious way. Government interference in our lives tends to discourage creativity and enterprise, to weaken the private economic sector, and preempt those mitigating institutions like family, neighborhood, church, and school — organizations that act as both a buffer and a bridge between the individual and the naked power of the state. . . .

. . . Only our deep moral values and our strong social institutions can hold back that jungle and restrain the darker impulses of human nature.

In order to return to this sense of self-imposed discipline, this concept of basic civility, we need to strengthen those private social institutions that nurture them. Our recent emphasis on voluntarism, the mobilization of private groups to deal with our social ills, is designed to foster this spirit of individual generosity and our sense of communal values. For this reason, we have moved to cut away many of the Federal intrusions of the private sector that were pre-empting the prerogatives of our private and independent institutions. That's why we've been willing to make some hard decisions in Washington about the growth of government. We've laid out a program for economic recovery. We'll stand by that program and see it through. We are determined to put an end to the fiscal joyride in Washington, determined to bring America back to prosperity and stability. . . .

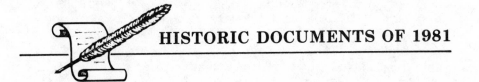

# September

# SENATE REPORT ON WILLIAMS
## September 3, 1981

*Though he persisted in claiming his innocence, Sen. Harrison A. Williams Jr., D-N.J., first was convicted in May 1981 on a nine-count federal indictment in the Abscam political corruption probe, and then was recommended for expulsion from the Senate by the Select Committee on Ethics, which said in its September 3 report that "only the most severe sanction is appropriate for such an abuse of the public trust."*

*The two actions proceeded through much of 1981, with court action dominating the process and the Senate cautious about prejudging the courts' next step. The Senate leadership December 1 deferred floor action on the committee's recommendation to "the earliest days" of the next session. Williams was sentenced to three years in prison and fined $50,000 on February 16, 1982. On March 11 Williams resigned from the Senate. By then it had become clear that his colleagues would have voted to expel him. Williams planned to appeal his conviction.*

*The actions grew out of Williams' involvement with the Abscam investigation in which undercover FBI agents masqueraded as businessmen and wealthy Arabs in an effort to catch members of Congress and other public officials committing criminal acts. Six House members and one senator, Williams, were indicted in the effort; each was found guilty. One House member, Michael "Ozzie" Myers, D-Pa., was expelled; the others either resigned, were defeated or chose not to run for re-election.* (Expulsion of Myers, Historic Documents of 1980, p. 899)

*During Williams' trial, prosecutors argued that the senator had accepted a hidden interest in a Virginia titanium mine in return for a promise to use his influence in obtaining government contracts to purchase titanium from the mine. Prosecutors further charged that Williams had promised to use his influence to help an undercover FBI agent, posing as an Arab, gain permanent U.S. residency. After a five-week trial in federal district court in Brooklyn, N.Y., Williams was found guilty of bribery, conspiracy, receipt of an unlawful gratuity, accepting outside compensation for the performance of official duties and interstate travel in aid of a racketeering enterprise. He was the first senator to be convicted of a felony while in office since 1920, when Truman H. Newberry, R-Mich. (1919-22), was convicted of irregular campaign practices.*

*The Senate Ethics Committee held three days of hearings on the case, July 14, 15 and 28. Much of the evidence, as at the trial, consisted of audio and video tape recordings that had been made by the government in the course of its undercover operation. On August 24 the committee voted unanimously to recommend expulsion. If expelled, Williams would have been the first senator to face such action since the Civil War.*

*Throughout the process, the senator maintained his innocence. "I tell this committee, under oath," he said at one point, "that while I may have been guilty of errors in judgment, while I may have crossed over the line which divides appropriate service to constituents from excessive boasting and posturing, I never engaged in any illegal conduct; I never corrupted my office and I never intended to do anything that would bring dishonor to the Senate." He further maintained that he was entrapped by overzealous government agents. Williams was a 22-year veteran of the Senate and, as chairman for 10 years of the Labor Committee, had helped enact a succession of key social programs.*

*In its report the committee rejected Williams' assertions and found him in violation of multiple federal criminal statutes, Senate rules and the Senate Code of Conduct. "Based on the evidence before it," the report concluded, "the Committee unanimously finds that Senator Williams' conduct was ethically repugnant to the point of warranting his expulsion from the United States Senate."*

> *Following are excerpts from Parts IV and V of the report of the Senate Select Committee on Ethics on the investigation of Sen. Harrison A. Williams Jr., D-N.J., released September 3, 1981. (Boldface headings in brackets have been added by Congressional Quarterly to highlight the organization of the text.):*

# IV. Findings of the Committee

Based on the evidence before it, the Committee unanimously finds that Senator Williams' conduct was ethically repugnant to the point of warranting his expulsion from the United States Senate. More particularly, the

Committee has determined that there is clear and convincing evidence to support the following findings.

The Committee finds that Senator Williams represented to the Shiek [*sic*] he would use his influence as a United States Senator to help the titanium venture obtain government contracts. Senator Williams initially made these representations in order to elicit a commitment from the Sheik for a $100 million loan. The Senator subsequently reaffirmed these representations in connection with the proposed sale of the venture for a substantial profit and continuing interest in the ongoing enterprise.

The Committee further finds that Senator Williams actually intended to use his influence to attempt to obtain government contracts after the loan was in place and the mine was under development. The Senator had a direct interest in the success of the venture, as did his friends, and on two separate occasions he indicated he was eager to provide for his own financial security upon retiring from the Senate. In light of this motive, and the substantial amount of time and attention devoted by Senator Williams to the details of these transactions, it is simply not possible to give credence to the Senator's explanation that he viewed the venture as a "pipedream" and "pie-in-the-sky" but nonetheless participated in these transactions because he felt bound to do so out of consideration for friends. Moreover, this explanation that he "boasted" to the Sheik because he was urged to do so at the "coaching" session is contrary to the Senator's own testimony at trial, that he basically ignored the coaching and did most of his talking to the Sheik his own way.

Acceptance of Senator Williams' explanation would necessarily require the conclusion that he knowingly and intentionally followed a "script" or "scenario" written for him by others for the admitted purpose of inducing the Sheik to make a $100 million loan to the titanium venture in which he and his friends had an interest. And if the Committee were to believe that Senator Williams in fact had no intention of using his position or influence to help obtain government contracts for the titanium venture, there would still be no alternative but to conclude that the Senator was a willing participant in a scheme to defraud a foreign citizen into investing money in that venture on the false understanding that a United States Senator was committed to using his influence, position, power and relationships to help it succeed. While the Committee disbelieves this explanation, it must nonetheless be observed that this kind of trading on official position would still represent, at a minimum, a fundamental violation of the standards for ethical conduct by Members of the Senate.

## [INTENTION TO CONCEAL]

The Committee finds in addition that Senator Williams intended to conceal his interest in the mining venture. On several occasions, the Senator discussed ways in which his interest would be hidden, and it is evident from those discussions that he and his associates viewed the possible use of a blind trust as a mere device by which disclosure requirements might be evaded in the future, in order to cover up the conflict inherent in the Senator's having an interest in the venture on the one hand, and his using his position to further it on the other.

The Committee also finds that — immediately after Senator Williams rejected the Sheik's offer of a cash bribe — the Senator pledged to the Sheik his total support for a private immigration bill which he agreed to introduce on the Sheik's behalf. This pledge was made by Senator Williams as an additional inducement to the Sheik for the promise of a loan.

## [UNANIMOUS CONCLUSIONS]

In light of these factual findings based upon the evidence before it, the Committee has unanimously concluded as follows:

A. With respect to violations as noticed in the Committee's letter and Resolution of May 5, 1981, the Committee concludes:

(1) Senator Williams violated the federal criminal statutes of conspiracy, bribery, receiving an illegal gratuity, conflict of interest and interstate travel in aid of a racketeering enterprise; all as found by the jury on May 1, 1981 in the United States District Court for the Eastern District of New York.

(2) Senator Williams violated the Senate Code of Conduct by violating the conflict of interest requirements of Rule 37 and by committing acts in violation of 18 U.S.C. § § 201 and 203. Moreover, he agreed to conceal his interest in what he believed to be a valuable business enterprise for the purpose and with the intent of circumventing the public financial disclosure requirements of Senate Rule 34.

(3) Senator Williams engaged in improper conduct which reflected adversely upon the Senate, as contemplated in Section 2 (a) (1) of S. Res. 338, 12 amended.

B. With respect to violations as specified in the Committee's Resolution of July 7, 1981 and the attachment thereto, the Committee concludes:

(1) Senator Williams committed multiple violations of the following Federal statutes: Bribery; Receiving an Illegal Gratuity; Conflict of Interest; Interstate Travel in Aid of a Racketeering Enterprise; and Conspiracy; all as found by a jury in the United States District Court for the Eastern District of New York on May 1, 1981, which returned a verdict of guilty on each of nine counts of an indictment.

(2) Senator Williams attempted to obtain a loan of money for a business enterprise in which he had a financial interest, or expected to have a financial interest, by making representations that he would use his official position in the United States Senate to assist the enterprise in obtaining government contracts, in conflict with his duties as a

United States Senator and in violation of Rule 37 of the Senate Code of Conduct.

(3) Senator Williams agreed to receive a loan of money for a business enterprise in which he had a financial interest, or expected to have a financial interest, in return for representations that he would use his official position in the United States Senate to assist the enterprise in obtaining government contracts, in conflict with his duties as a United States Senator and in violation of Rule 37 of the Senate Code of Conduct.

(4) Senator Williams received shares of stock in three corporations which he expected would own and operate the aforesaid business enterprise, in return for representations that he would use his official position in the United States Senate to assist the enterprise in obtaining government contracts, in conflict with his duties as a United States Senator and in violation of Rule 37 of the Senate Code of Conduct.

(5) Senator Williams agreed to receive a share of the proceeds from the sale of the aforesaid business venture, together with an equity interest in the ongoing venture, in return for representations that he would use his official position in the United States Senate to assist the ongoing venture in obtaining government contracts, in conflict with his duties as a United States Senator and in violation of Rule 37 of the Senate Code of Conduct.

(6) Senator Williams attempted to obtain a loan of money for the aforesaid business venture, and to obtain a share of the proceeds from the sale of that venture, by making representations that he would use his official position in the United States Senate to introduce and aid the progress of legislation which would assist an individual in immigrating to the United States, in conflict with his duties as a United States Senator and in violation of Rule 37 of the Senate Code of Conduct.

(7) Senator Williams agreed to receive a loan of money for the aforesaid business venture, and to receive a share of the proceeds from the sale of that venture, together with an equity interest in the ongoing venture, in return for representations that he would use his official position in the United States Senate to introduce and aid the progress of legislation which would assist an individual in immigrating to the United States, in conflict with his duties as a United States Senator and in violation of Rule 37 of the Senate Code of Conduct.

(8) Senator Williams agreed to conceal his ownership interest in the aforesaid business venture, as well as his share of profits to be received upon sale of the venture, and his equity interest in the ongoing venture, with intent to conceal a conflict of interest (Senate Code of Conduct Rule 37), and to circumvent the public financial disclosure requirements of Senate Rule 34.

(9) Senator Williams improperly failed to report to law enforcement authorities an offer of a bribe, made to him on January 15, 1980.

(10) Senator Williams did not answer truthfully and fully the ques-

tions propounded to him on February 2, 1980 by a Special Agent of the
Federal Bureau of Investigation, concerning his activities and involvement with the business enterprise about which he was questioned.

## V. Recommendation of Expulsion

The Committee has concluded that over a period of some ten months
Senator Williams made promises and representations to FBI undercover
personnel that he would use his position, power, influence and relationships to foster the success of a business venture in which he had a financial
interest, in exchange for the promise of a loan to that venture. That
misconduct, which showed a fundamental disregard for the integrity of the
Senate and the honor of its Members, was in violation of law and Senate
Rule 37, and in derogation of the standards of ethical conduct the public
and his peers have a right to expect from a Member. That misconduct, as
evidenced by the Senator's own words and acts, tends to bring the Senate
into dishonor and disrepute, and only the most severe sanction is appropriate for such an abuse of the public trust. On August 24, 1981, the
Committee therefore unanimously agreed to recommend that Senator
Williams be expelled from the United State Senate.

Accordingly, the Committee hereby recommends that the Senate agree
to the following Resolution:

*Resolved,* That the conduct of Senator Harrison A. Williams, Jr., of
New Jersey in connection with his agreement to use his official position
to further a business venture in which he and others had a financial
interest was in violation of the laws of the United States and the
Standing Rules of the Senate, was ethically repugnant, and tends to
bring the Senate into dishonor and disrepute; and that therefore,
pursuant to Article 1, Section 5, Clause 2 of the United States Constitution, Senator Harrison A. Williams, Jr. be, and hereby is, expelled from
the United States Senate.

In reaching this decision to recommend expulsion, the Committee is
mindful that there are still pending before Judge [George C.] Pratt certain
"due process" motions in Senator Williams' case. . . . The Committee's
unanimous recommendation of expulsion reflects its strong conviction that
its own determination of this matter, and that of the Senate, must be made
independently of the jury's verdict, Judge Pratt's rulings on the due
process motions, and, indeed, any action which any court may take with regard to Senator Williams' criminal case.

However, as stated in its Resolution of August 24, 1981, the Committee
recognizes that matters could arise out of the decision on the due process
motions, expected to be rendered by Judge Pratt next month, which some
Members of the Senate may feel would be in mitigation of the sanction recommended by this Committee. Therefore, while adhering to its view that
under the Constitution the Senate's resolution of this matter is unaffected

by the outcome of the criminal proceedings against Senator Williams, the Committee further recommends that the Senate proceed expeditiously to final disposition of the foregoing Resolution only when Judge Pratt has ruled on the aforesaid motions. Especially in light of the extensive record in this matter, with which all Members must now become familiar, this recommendation should not result in any significant delay of that disposition.

# STATE DEPARTMENT
# ON CHEMICAL WARFARE
## September 13, 14, November 11, 1981

*In a speech to the Berlin Press Association September 13, Secretary of State Alexander M. Haig Jr. stated that the United States had "physical evidence" that toxic chemical weapons had been used in Southeast Asia. Haig implied that the Soviet Union and its allies were using the lethal chemicals.*

*Haig's speech, designed to strengthen Western European morale and confidence in NATO, defended western values and pointed out weaknesses and dangers of the communist bloc. As critics in Europe and at home decried a growing militancy and U.S. arms buildup, Haig warned of "the danger of adopting a double standard toward international behavior." He declared, "[A]t the very time when the United States is being accused of delay on arms control, others appear to be violating one of the oldest arms control agreements — that prohibiting the use of toxins."*

*Haig did not go into detail about the physical evidence supporting his charge, but promised a fuller statement from the U.S. government the next day.*

## Physical Evidence

*On September 14 Walter J. Stoessel Jr., under secretary of state for political affairs, followed up Haig's charge with a statement on the use of chemical warfare agents in Southeast Asia and Afghanistan.*

*The United States had obtained a leaf and stem sample in March from Cambodia near the Thai border. Analysis of the sample revealed high levels of three lethal mycotoxins. Although mycotoxins are poisons produced naturally by fungi, the United States declared that the levels of the toxins were 20 times higher than would occur naturally. Furthermore, the government contended, the mycotoxins identified were not indigenous to Southeast Asia.*

*The new leaf and stem evidence, along with continuing reports from eyewitnesses of toxic gas attacks, led the U.S. government to its "preliminary" conclusion that the Soviet Union and its allies were using mycotoxins in chemical warfare in Laos, Cambodia and Afghanistan.*

## Background

*The issue of chemical warfare in these countries was not a new one; reports of its use dated to 1976. The United States had been gathering testimony from doctors, refugees, journalists and others and had issued a compendium of their statements in June 1980. The State Department released an update to the compendium in March 1981 that contained several descriptions of "yellow rain" attacks and the aftereffects on people, animals and vegetation. This yellow gas, settling on the ground in the form of powder, reportedly was responsible for several thousand deaths. The United States believed that the previously unidentified chemicals in "yellow rain" were the mycotoxin agents.*

*The use of toxins violates the 1925 Geneva Protocol, the 1972 Biological Weapons Convention and accepted precepts of international law. In December 1980, responding to U.S. pressure, the United Nations established an impartial team to investigate reports of chemical warfare in Southeast Asia. The team visited three refugee camps in Thailand, but with no guarantee of safety, did not visit sites in Cambodia, Laos and Afghanistan where attacks allegedly took place. In its December 1981 report, the group was "unable to reach a final conclusion" on chemical weapons use without trips to the sites. No guarantee existed that such visits would be possible.*

## Smoking Gun

*The physical evidence statements by Haig and Stoessel sparked debate on the chemical warfare issue. Some scientists disputed the government's claim that the mycotoxins were not indigenous to Southeast Asia. Others questioned the methods and reliability of the sample analysis.*

*On November 10 Richard Burt, the State Department's director of politico-military affairs, testified before the Senate Foreign Relations Subcommittee on Arms Control that the United States had new evidence to support its claims of "yellow rain" attacks. Samples of contaminated water and yellow powder taken from rocks in Cambodia contained lethal amounts of mycotoxins. "We now have the smoking gun," Burt stated, and he cited several reasons for linking the Soviets to the new biological weapons.*

*By the end of 1981, the issue remained unresolved. The United States continued to make charges and gather reports; the Soviets denied the accusations; and other countries hesitated to get involved.*

*Following are excerpts from Secretary of State Alexander M. Haig Jr.'s speech to the Berlin Press Association on September 13, 1981; a September 14, 1981, statement on chemical warfare by Walter J. Stoessel Jr., under secretary of state for political affairs; and testimony by Richard Burt, the State Department's director of politico-military affairs, before the Senate Foreign Relations Subcommittee on Arms Control, Oceans, International Operations and Environment on November 10, 1981.*(Boldface headings in brackets have been added by Congressional Quarterly to highlight the organization of the texts.):

# HAIG'S WEST BERLIN ADDRESS

... I detect a growing double standard in the West toward appropriate norms of international behavior: One is a supercritical standard applied to those who cherish diversity, tolerate dissent, and seek peaceful change. Another is a more tolerant standard applied to those who abhor diversity, suppress dissent, and promote violent change.

● The Soviet Union has occupied Afghanistan since 1979. The Afghans' religion, culture, and national life are in danger of destruction. One-fifth of the entire nation has been exiled. The people of Afghanistan cherish their freedom. They are not going to give up their struggle. But why are the voices of conscience among us which cry out against this aggression so muted?

● Vietnam, which inspired such widespread concern in the West not long ago, has enslaved its southern populations, has seized Kampuchea, and now threatens the peace of Southeast Asia.

● Libya, a country which finances terror and assassinations in countries far from its borders, has invaded and occupied its neighbor Chad and calls it "unification."

Where are the demonstrations against these outrages? The phrase "national liberation" has been used to justify international terror and violence. Can a nation be liberated when its people are deprived of liberty? Can a nation be free when its independence is subordinate to the will of a foreign power? Can a people be uplifted when innocent civilians are the targets of terror?

Despite its professions of peace and good will, the Soviet Union has engaged in an enormous military buildup beyond all requirements of self-defense. It has, as well, armed and encouraged its proxies to promote violent change that serves its strategic objectives. All of this has occurred despite continuing efforts by the West for arms control and a relaxation of tensions. Where are the protests against such Soviet actions?

## [Self-criticism by Democracies]

Democracies invariably expect more of themselves than of their adversaries. Our openness, our free press, our democratic institutions subject our actions to a relentless criticism that they do not experience.

This is a source of strength and health for democracies. But when it paralyzes essential efforts to defend freedom, as it did in the 1930s, not only freedom, but peace too, is endangered. It is Soviet tanks, not NATO's defense against those tanks, that threaten the peace of Europe. It is the rapid expansion of Soviet nuclear weaponry in the European theater that has forced NATO to respond. We have made clear that we are equally prepared to respond in a positive way to Soviet restraint. We would welcome the reduction of armaments on both sides. But the hopes for such reductions will be doomed if our people succumb to a double standard that falsely blames the troubled state of the world not on aggression but on the effort to defend against it.

When democracies become too feeble or too fearful to resist aggressive dictatorships, then who is there to defend democracy? To us here today, children of the 20th century, this is more than a rhetorical question. Are we going to be blind again?

Once more, terror and intimidation are being used to silence those who speak out; once more attacks on synagogues and churches have become the instrument of perverted political causes; once more a totalitarian regime is invoking the slogans of self-determination to advance its imperial ambitions. And at the very time when the United States is being accused of delay on arms control, others appear to be violating one of the oldest arms control agreements — that prohibiting the use of toxins.

## [Lethal Chemical Weapons]

For some time now, the international community has been alarmed by continuing reports that the Soviet Union and its allies have been using lethal chemical weapons in Laos, Kampuchea, and Afghanistan. As a result of this deep international concern, last fall the United Nations established an impartial group of medical and technical experts to investigate the matter. In spite of this international attention and action, however, reports of this unlawful and inhuman activity have continued. Moreover, we now have physical evidence from Southeast Asia which has been analyzed and found to contain abnormally high levels of three potent mycotoxins — poisonous substances not indigenous to the region and which are highly toxic to man and animals.

The use in war of such toxins is prohibited by the 1925 Geneva protocol and related rules of customary international law; their very manufacture for such purposes is strictly forbidden by the 1975 biological weapons convention. We are, therefore, taking steps to insure that this evidence is called to the attention of states and that it is provided to both the Secretary General of the United Nations and to the group of experts investigating this problem under his auspices. Tomorrow, in my capital, the United States will have more to say on this subject....

# STOESSEL'S STATEMENT

Yesterday in Berlin Secretary Haig recalled that the United States, along with many other members of the world community, has been for some time concerned over reports of use of lethal chemical weapons in Afghanistan and Southeast Asia.

He announced that the United States Government now had physical evidence from Southeast Asia found to contain three potent toxic agents.

As Secretary Haig promised, we are taking steps to provide this information to the world community through the United Nations, its member governments, and through the representatives of the national and international press here today.

Reports of the use of chemical warfare agents in Southeast Asia date back to 1976. The U.S. has publicly expressed its concern about these events on numerous occasions over these years. We have privately and formally expressed our concern to the Soviet, Vietnamese and Laotian Governments, only to be told that our concerns are unfounded.

In June of 1980, we prepared a 125-page compendium of reports of chemical weapons use, and we used that compendium as a basis for supporting the December 1980 U.N. Resolution to establish an impartial international investigation into reports of chemical weapon use. We followed that up with an update to the compendium in March of 1981.

After earlier unsuccessful attempts to obtain physical evidence of chemical weapons use, we have recently uncovered significant though preliminary information to demonstrate clearly that our concerns were entirely justified.

## [Presence of Mycotoxins]

Specifically, we believe we have obtained good evidence that rather than a traditional lethal chemical agent, three potent and lethal mycotoxins of the trichothecene group have been used. A mycotoxin is a poison typically produced in nature by living organisms.

Analysis of a leaf and stem sample from Kampuchea has revealed high levels of lethal mycotoxins of the trichothecene group. The levels detected were up to 20 times greater than any recorded natural outbreak.

Since normal background levels of these toxins are essentially undetectable, the high levels found are considered to be abnormal, and it is highly unlikely that such levels could have occurred in a natural intoxication. In point of fact, these mycotoxins do not occur naturally in Southeast Asia.

The possession and use of toxins is a violation of both the 1925 Geneva Protocol and the 1972 Biological Weapons Convention, as well as the rules of customary international law of armed conflict.

Over the past several years a number of medical doctors working on this problem have visited Southeast Asia. They visited the borders in question, interviewed and examined refugees, reviewed medical records including public health data, and spoke directly with eyewitnesses to events in both Laos and Kampuchea.

Detailed analysis of this and other information leads us to conclude that mycotoxins, not traditional chemical warfare agents, produced the bizarre effects which cause reported deaths.

The test results we have recently obtained, together with the information provided by the physicians who have visited Southeast Asia, represent strong and compelling but nonetheless preliminary evidence that the lethal agents used are mycotoxins.

## [Possibility of Other Agents]

I want to caution you that there are certainly other agents being used that we have not yet identified. Incapacitating and riot control agents as well as other possible lethal agents may be involved.

We are attempting to obtain additional information from Laos and Kampuchea in an effort to obtain corroborative evidence. We are sharing this information with the United Nations group of experts investigating chemical weapons use, as well as our friends and allies throughout the world.

The United States believes that in the light of this new information, increased effort must be made to visit the regions where chemical attacks are being reported. We have, therefore, urged the Secretary General's group of experts to take steps immediately to visit refugee camps and the areas of reported attacks in Kampuchea and the other regions in question to obtain testimony firsthand from eyewitnesses and victims of attacks, medical personnel, official [sic] of refugee organizations, and any other evidence available.

We have also urged that the utmost effort be made to contact and obtain testimony from the many victims and eyewitnesses who have departed the refugee camps and started new lives elsewhere....

# BURT'S TESTIMONY

I am pleased to appear before you today ... to bring you up to date on our latest findings. . . .

... [T]here is no subject of greater urgency than that we are here to discuss today. Over the past 5 years and perhaps longer, weapons outlawed by mankind, weapons successfully banned from the battlefields of the industrialized world for over five decades, have been used against unsophisticated and defenseless people in campaigns of mounting extermination which are being conducted in Laos, Kampuchea, and more recently in Afghanistan.

Reports of the use of lethal chemical weapons in Southeast Asia began to appear in 1976, although the initial attacks may, in fact, predate that by several years. The sites of these first attacks were in remote highlands of Laos, 6 weeks by jungle track from the nearest neutral territory. The targets were the villages of the highland tribes, such as the Hmong, traditionally resistant to the lowland Pathet Lao. The victims were the inhabitants of these villages — men, women, and children, particularly the children, who proved least able to resist the lethal effects of the poisons being employed against them.

In succeeding years the attacks multiplied and spread, first to Kampuchea and then to Afghanistan. Reports were necessarily fragmentary, incomplete, and episodic. The sources were the victims themselves or the refugee workers, doctors, nurses, and journalists who had spoken with those who survived the long trek from the deserted villages, the poisoned wells, and the deadly fruit of their homeland to safe havens in Thailand.

As information accumulated, it was clear to the U.S. Government that something important and sinister was occurring, but it was not clear precisely what. Repeated stories from rural peoples in widely separated regions, in different countries, all correlated with each other. This made it impossible to discount these reports as self-serving inventions by dissident elements in conflict with the local regime. Yet while, over time, we felt compelled to credit these reports as true, we remained puzzled by them for two reasons.

**First,** because analysis of samples taken from the areas of attack — samples of vegetation, clothing, and human tissue — had shown no detectable traces of any known chemical agent;

**Second,** because the extent and sequence of the signs and symptoms reported were also inconsistent with the effects of any known chemical agent or combination of such agents.

## [State Department Action]

In 1979, despite these remaining gaps in our evidence, the State Department, with the support of other agencies, began to take several important steps.

• We set up an interagency committee to coordinate the government's work on chemical weapons use and worked with the intelligence community to devote greater resources to the development and analysis of information on the subject.

• We began to brief other governments on this issue and to encourage them to develop and share with us their own information on these attacks.

• We began to express our concerns publicly and to seek wider international action.

As a result of these steps, we succeeded last fall in securing a favorable vote in the U.N. General Assembly — over the vehement opposition of the U.S.S.R., Vietnam, and their allies — mandating a U.N. investigation of reports of chemical weapons use.

A second result of these steps was the decision, by a group of U.S. Government scientists and experts on the U.S. interagency committee on chemical weapons use, to take a fresh look at reporting on chemical weapons use from the beginning and, in particular, to reexamine the pattern of the attacks and the resultant symptoms.

## Pattern of Attacks and Symptoms

Many of the reported attacks, particularly in Laos, did follow a pattern — not an invariable pattern but one with consistent elements from report to report. These attacks were conducted by low, slow-flying aircraft, sometimes identified as an AN-2 — a Soviet biplane used as a crop duster in the U.S.S.R. The plane would release a cloud, often described as yellow, sometimes orange, red, or other tints. The cloud would descend upon a village or upon people in the neighboring rice paddies. The cloud seemed to be made up of small particles which would make sounds, when falling on rooftops or vegetation, similar to that made by rain. It came to be called, by its victims, the "yellow rain."

For those directly exposed to this yellow rain, its effect was quick and dramatic. They would experience an early onset of violent itching, vomiting, dizziness, and distorted vision. Within a short time they would vomit blood-tinged material, then large quantities of bright red blood. Within an hour they would die, apparently of shock and the massive loss of blood from the stomach.

Those on the periphery of the attack, or under shelter, or those who returned to the village after an attack and ate contaminated food, would experience similar symptoms over a longer period, accompanied by bloody diarrhea. These people, too, would often die — after a week or two of agony — of dehydration.

These symptoms in this order cannot be explained by positing the use of any known chemical agent, either of the blistering type, such as the mustard gas of World War I, or of the more modern nerve agents. Similar symptoms, however, have been reported in natural outbreaks of toxin poisoning of a certain type, specifically trichothecene toxins. Toxins are biologically produced chemical substances, poisons which appear in nature, on grain for instance. In some locales these pose serious hazards to public health.

The U.S. Government scientists and experts on the chemicals weapons use committee combined their hypothesis of trichothecene poisoning based upon the symptomalogy [sic] of reported chemical weapons attacks with a review of the literature which revealed that the Soviet Union had a long experience in the field of trichothecene toxicology, and had done much research, including research into the massive production of trichothecene toxins. Some such research had, in fact, been done in Soviet institutes under military control and with connections to the Soviet chemical weapons program. We concluded, therefore, that we should begin to look for evidence of possible toxin use. As a first step in this direction, we started to reanalyze samples already tested for other chemical agents for the presence of toxins.

So far I have been citing evidence mainly from Southeast Asia and particularly Laos, where the yellow rain attacks were first reported and where they have been conducted most systematically. In Kampuchea growing reports in recent years suggest that a wide range of chemical warfare agents are in use, including "yellow rain." Cyanide, for instance, has been discovered in wells. Vietnamese soldiers have been captured poisoning the wells of refugee camps on the Thai border.

### [AFGHANISTAN]

In Afghanistan, too, the evidence of chemical weapons use has been rising. We are today in much the same position — in terms of our ability to establish a pattern of such use and to identify specific agents being employed in Afghanistan — as we were in 1979 regarding Southeast Asia. We have numerous eyewitness reports — of victims, of journalists — we have sensitive intelligence of technical and human origin, and we have testimony of those who have fought on the Soviet side. Based upon this information, we are certain that chemical weapons are being used in Afghanistan. These include irritants, new and as yet unidentified incapacitants, and familiar lethal agents, including nerve gas. A number of former Afghan military officers, trained in the Soviet Union in chemical warfare, have identified lethal agents brought into Afghanistan, have pinpointed the sites where these are stored, and have specified when they have been used. These reports are corroborated by reports from refugees and victims of these same attacks.

## Physical Evidence in Southeast Asia

We do not, as yet, have physical evidence of chemical warfare in Afghanistan; in Southeast Asia we do. The first set of samples we subjected to test for trichothecene toxins was taken from a village in

Kampuchea. It was collected within a day of an attack on the village which killed people in the same brutal manner I have described. The results of that analysis, as you are already aware, showed that:

● The leaf and stem in question contained levels of trichothecene mycotoxins 20 times higher than that found in natural outbreaks;

● The trichothecene mycotoxins found do not occur naturally in the combination identified in Southeast Asia;

● In parts of the world where these mycotoxins do appear naturally, they do so in combination with certain other toxins which were not present in this sample;

● The effect of these trichothecene mycotoxins on man and animals is the symptomatology I have described. These toxins produce all the symptoms I have mentioned, and they are not known to produce any symptoms not reported. The fit, in other words, was perfect.

### [MYSTERY SOLVED]

Others ... are better qualified to discuss the technical process of analysis and to interpret the results for you. The significance of this discovery, however, can be simply stated. We had solved the mystery. We had fitted together the jigsaw puzzle which had bedeviled us for 5 years. We now knew what was causing the bizarre and brutal deaths of Laotian and Kampuchean villagers. We had ascertained that a completely new class of weapons had been developed and was in use.

In the past few weeks we have completed analysis of further samples from both Kampuchea and Laos. The results have confirmed our earlier findings and reinforce the conclusions we have drawn from them. One of these new samples was of water, taken from the same Kampuchean village at the same time as the set of leaves and stems, which was first analyzed positively for trichothecenes. The other two samples are from sites of separate attacks in Laos, one of which was provided to us for analysis by Congressman Jim Leach [of Iowa].

All three of these samples reveal very high quantities of trichothecene mycotoxins, quantities even higher than in the first samples of yellow powder from Laos were scraped from rocks, not naturally a medium for high levels of toxins. One of the Laos samples, for example, contained 150 parts per million of $T^2$ toxin. This is almost 50 times higher than the level of $T^2$ in the original sample from Kampuchea. The water sample from Kampuchea contained 66 parts per million of deoxynivalenol.

In addition to samples collected from sites of reported attacks, we have also obtained samples of background soil and vegetation of the same species as originally tested from near the same area in Kampuchea. These were tested by the same analytical technique and found to be free of any trichothecenes, thus further confirming the absence of natural occurrence of these toxins in that region. . . .

## ['THE SMOKING GUN']

Ever since the U.S. Government began to voice its concerns over reports of chemical weapons use, critics have demanded that we produce the smoking gun. The testimony of victims, of witnesses, or refugee military officers who had engaged in chemical warfare activities, and the technical intelligence was not enough. Those who did not believe said they would not believe — unless we produced a smoking gun, physical proof.

We now have the smoking gun. We now have four separate pieces of physical evidence. We may soon have more as, I regret to say, chemical attacks have been reported in Laos and Kampuchea within the last month. We are taking every step to make this evidence widely available in order that others can form their own conclusions. There will always be those who will not believe. We are persuaded, however, that any person, any government, any journalist who approaches this issue with an open mind, who travels to the borders of conflict and seeks out victims and those who have treated them, that anyone who conducts his own inquiry, will come to the same conclusions we have.

## [UNIDENTIFIED CHEMICAL AGENTS]

Having answered one question which bedeviled us for 5 years, we have opened up a new set of unanswered questions. Toxins are one type of chemical weapons in use in Southeast Asia. But there are other chemical warfare agents in use there and in Afghanistan, which we have yet to identify. The trichothecene mycotoxins we have discovered are a highly lethal mixture. But we are not certain that this is the only type of toxins in use, and we are not certain precisely why this combination has been chosen or what other combinations we may yet discover.

We are also addressing ourselves to the question of why toxins have been developed and used as a weapon, when other lethal chemical warfare agents are available, off the shelf, so to speak.

There seem a variety of factors that make toxin weapons particularly effective against the rural, defenseless peoples of nations like Laos and Kampuchea. The violence of the death — with victims experiencing severe vomiting, diarrhea, extreme irritation of the eyes and skin and respiratory system, and often dying rapidly; the ease in which the powder can be carefully applied to a limited area; and the survival rate of those on the periphery, who can report what they have seen, all contribute to making this type of weapon suitable for driving people from their homes and villages and insuring that they stay away. The limited protection needed by those who must handle this material — gloves and a simple face mask, as opposed to a complete protective suit, and the simple method of delivery, such as crop-dusting aircraft — contributes to its attractiveness as an effective weapon of terror. Finally, the difficulty in detecting and identifying the toxins contributes to its attractiveness. It has, after all, taken the

U.S. Government, with all the technical resources at its disposal, 5 years and many thousands of man-hours to discover the true nature of "yellow rain."

## Issue of Responsibility

I have so far addressed the question of chemical weapons use but not the issue of who is responsible for their use. The Soviet Union is, of course, directly involved in the fighting in Afghanistan and thus in the use of chemical weapons in that country. In Laos and Kampuchea, on the other hand, these weapons would seem to be employed by indigenous forces — the Vietnamese, Laotians, and Kampucheans. Nonetheless, the links to the Soviet Union are strong.

• The Soviets are providing extensive military assistance and advice in Laos, Kampuchea, and to the Vietnamese forces fighting there. The Soviets certainly know what is happening and are in a position to stop it if they chose.

• The Soviets are advising and controlling chemical warfare activity in Southeast Asia. Soviet chemical experts have inspected a number of chemical weapons storage facilities there. Both lethal and nonlethal chemicals are believed to be stored at these sites and are transported between storage facilities and ordinance camps or field use areas as needed.

• There exists, in so far as we are aware, no facilities in Southeast Asia capable of producing the mold and extracting the mycotoxins in the quantities in which they are being used.

• Such facilities do exist in the Soviet Union, including microbiological plants under military control and with heavy military guard.

• The Soviets have resisted every effort to mount an impartial investigation of chemical weapons use in Southeast Asia and Afghanistan.

For over 2 years we have sought, and failed to receive, from the Soviet Union an explanation of the anthrax outbreak at Sverdlovsk. We have also raised with the Soviet Union our concerns regarding chemical weapons use in Afghanistan and Southeast Asia. More recently, we have raised these issues again in the context of new information on the use of toxins. We have still not received a substantive response.

The use of toxins as warfare agents in Southeast Asia has grave implications for present and future arms control arrangements. As biologically produced chemical substances, toxins fall within the prohibitions of both the 1925 Geneva Protocol, forbidding the use of chemical weapons in warfare, and the 1972 Biological Weapons Convention, which forbids the production, stockpiling, or transfer of toxin weapons. These agreements, signed by both the Soviet Union and Vietnam, and the customary international law, which has developed out of the former, are being flagrantly violated.

A common feature of the Geneva Protocol and the Biological Weapons Convention is that neither contains any provisions for verification and neither contains adequate mechanisms for resolving issues of compliance. It is too early to determine the full consequences of the use of chemical and toxin warfare agents for future arms control arrangements. There should be no doubt, however, that the U.S. Government will insist that any future arms control agreements contain whatever provisions are needed to permit verification and to insure that questions of compliance are dealt with seriously. The day the United States signs unverifiable arms control agreements is over. Let us hope that the day when others urge us to do so in the cause of relaxed tensions or increased international goodwill is over as well. For nothing increases tension or poisons goodwill more than the lack of compliance with agreements concluded.

## U.S. Steps

Let me next turn to the steps we have taken as a result of the new information on toxin use. As I have noted we have raised this issue again with the Soviet Union, to no effect. We have raised the issue with Vietnam and Laos, also without effect. We have made our evidence available to the United Nations and to all its member countries. We have sent our experts to a number of European capitals and to New York, where they met with the U.N. experts. We have indicated our hope that the U.N. experts continue their inquiry and travel at least to all of those countries neighboring the scenes of conflict — they have just visited Thailand, and Pakistan has offered an invitation as well — to interview refugees and other sources. We have also encouraged other nations and other private organizations, including journalists, to mount their own inquiries into what is going on in Southeast Asia and Afghanistan.

Our objective is to stop these attacks. We will keep this issue before the world community and on the international agenda as long as we need to do so. For the present, we believe priority should be given to the U.N. inquiry. A vote in the General Assembly on whether to extend the mandate for that investigation will be taken in the next 6 weeks. It is very important that this be done.

We are also reviewing other means to focus world opinion on this issue. If we are to succeed, we must make sure this is not simply perceived as a U.S.-Soviet contest from which others can disengage. This means we must insure our evidence is made as widely available as possible, while avoiding any appearance of engaging in a propaganda campaign. For if our efforts are to have any utility, others must take this information as seriously as we.

There is reason they should. For over 50 years, as I have said, chemical weapons have been successfully banned from the battlefields of the industrialized world. This success is due, I expect, as much to the deterrent effect of possible retaliation as to respect for the sanctity of international law. What is going on today in Afghanistan and Southeast Asia is not an East-West issue. It is an issue of universal import with particular consequences for those countries least prepared to defend against the use of chemical and biological agents. It is our task to put our information at the disposal of the world community. It is the response of the world community — not just that of the U.S. Government, its friends, and allies — which will, in the end, determine whether these attacks continue and proliferate or are halted forever.

# PAPAL ENCYCLICAL ON WORK
## September 15, 1981

*Pope John Paul II, the leader of the Roman Catholic Church, issued the third encyclical of his pontificate September 15. Entitled* Laborem Exercens *in Latin and* On Human Work *in English, the circular letter to all Roman Catholic bishops re-examined the church's basic social doctrine in light of the contemporary technological revolution. Both earlier encyclicals dealt essentially with the subject of God and social justice. (Historic Documents of 1980, p. 967)*

Laborem Exercens *reflected the Polish pope's scholarly background as well as his pastoral concern for the modern Christian. By the end, the pontiff had surrounded his social critique with a theology — deriving from the biblical mandate that man "subdue the earth" — that holds that work contributes not only to earthly progress and welfare but also to the development of God's kingdom.*

*Fearing the degradation and dehumanization of workers, the pope maintained that man should be central to any consideration of work. He called special attention to the dignity and rights of workers at a time when technical, economic and political developments could overshadow these human considerations as they had during the industrial revolution of the 19th century. "...[T]he value of human work is not primarily the kind of work being done, but the fact that the one who is doing it is a person," the pope said.*

*In the encyclical the pope discussed just remuneration for work, the rights of labor unions, the rights and responsibilities of management as well as the roles of women, multinational corporations, handicapped workers and farmers.*

## Communism and Capitalism

*Pope John Paul II was the first pontiff from a country behind the so-called Iron Curtain separating the Soviet bloc countries from the Western world. During his early tenure as pope, John Paul II had focused special attention on Catholics living within the Soviet bloc and had been openly concerned with the struggles in Poland between the Solidarity labor union and the ruling communist government.* (Polish workers' demands, Historic Documents of 1980, p. 793)

*The encyclical itself was couched in general terms without references to specific political situations. And in his balanced critique of Marxist and capitalist economic systems, the pope demonstrated his remarkable diplomatic capabilities.*

*He asserted the priority of labor over capital and, while restating the church's belief in the right to private property, argued that this right was not absolute but "subordinate to the right to common use." He pointed to the potential dehumanization inherent in capitalism due to the reduction of man to an instrument of production to gain profit and in Marxism due to the "excessive bureaucratic centralization," which exploited the worker as if he were a cog in the wheel.*

*The pope cited labor unions as necessary protectors of worker rights and endorsed the use of strikes. But he also warned that strikes should not be abused, especially for political purposes. Although he acknowledged that the struggle for worker rights would touch the political arena, he maintained unions did not have the "character of political parties struggling for power." These comments came when Solidarity continued to be accused by Communist parties in Eastern Europe of seeking political power, but before martial law was instituted in Poland on December 13, 1981.* (Martial law in Poland, p. 881)

*The comments calling for the disassociation of unions and political parties recalled the pope's 1980 request that members of the clergy not hold public office. Democratic Rep. Robert F. Drinan of Massachusetts, a Jesuit priest and one of the most liberal members of the U.S. House of Representatives, announced on May 5 that he would comply with the pope's request and not seek a sixth term in November 1980.* (Drinan order, Historic Documents of 1980, p. 411)

## Women and the Family

*The pope defended the right of women to work free of the fear of sex discrimination on the job. But at the same time he maintained that society should ensure a woman's economic right to stay at home and fulfill her "irreplaceable role" as mother. The pope suggested that society should pay each head of household a family wage — enough to support a family without the other spouse working — or that other social measures such as family allowances or grants to mothers devoting themselves exclusively to raising children should be incorporated into the economics of the society. "Experience confirms that there must be a social re-evaluation of the mother's role," the pope asserted.*

## Background

*The pope had hoped to issue this latest encyclical on May 15, the 90th anniversary of Pope Leo XIII's 1891 social encyclical* Rerum Novarum *(Of New Things), which is considered the basic document of Roman Catholic social doctrine. But the May 13 attempt on his life in St. Peter's Square had prevented him from fulfilling his initial intention.* (Shooting of the pope, p. 427)

*Following are excerpts from Pope John Paul II's encyclical,* Laborem Exercens, *issued September 15, 1981. (Boldface headings in brackets have been added by Congressional Quarterly to highlight the organization of the text.):*

## [Preface]

Through work man must earn his daily bread and contribute to the continual advance of science and technology and, above all, to elevating unceasingly the cultural and moral level of the society within which he lives in community with those who belong to the same family. And work means any activity by man, whether manual or intellectual, whatever its nature or circumstances; it means any human activity that can and must be recognized as work, in the midst of all the many activities of which man is capable and to which he is predisposed by his very nature, by virtue of humanity itself. Man is made to be in the visible universe an image and likeness of God himself, and he is placed in it in order to subdue the earth. From the beginning therefore he is called to work. Work is one of the characteristics that distinguish man from the rest of creatures, whose activity for sustaining their lives cannot be called work. Only man is capable of work, and only man works, at the same time by work occupying his existence on earth. Thus work bears a particular mark of man and of humanity, the mark of a person operating within a community of persons. And this mark decides its interior characteristics; in a sense it constitutes its very nature.

## Introduction

### 1. HUMAN WORK ON THE 90th ANNIVERSARY
### OF RERUM NOVARUM

Since May 15 of the present year was the 90th anniversary of the publication by the great pope of the "social question," Leo XIII, of the decisively important encyclical which begins with the words *rerum novarum* [of new things], I wish to devote this document to human work and, even more, to man in the vast context of the reality of work. . . .

. . . Man's life is built up every day from work, from work it derives its specific dignity, but at the same time work contains the unceasing measure of human toil and suffering and also of the harm and injustice which penetrate deeply into social life within individual nations and on the international level. While it is true that man eats the bread produced by the work of his hands — and this means not only the daily bread by which his body keeps alive but also the bread of science and progress, civilization and culture — it is also a perennial truth that he eats this bread by "the sweat of his face," that is to say, not only by personal effort and toil, but also in the midst of many tensions, conflicts and crises, which in relationship with the reality of work disturb the life of individual societies and also of all humanity.

We are celebrating the 90th anniversary of the encyclical *Rerum Novarum* on the eve of new developments in technological, economic and political conditions which, according to many experts, will influence the world of work and production no less than the industrial revolution of the last century. There are many factors of a general nature: the widespread introduction of automation into many spheres of production, the increase in the cost of energy and raw materials, the growing realization that the heritage of nature is limited and that it is being intolerably polluted, and the emergence on the political scene of peoples who, after centuries of subjection, are demanding their rightful place among the nations and in international decision making. These new conditions and demands will require a reordering and adjustment of the structures of the modern economy and of the distribution of work. . . .

It is not for the church to analyze scientifically the consequences that these changes may have on human society. But the church considers it her task always to call attention to the dignity and rights of those who work, to condemn situations in which that dignity and those rights are violated, and to help to guide the above-mentioned changes so as to ensure authentic progress by man and society.

### 2. IN THE ORGANIC DEVELOPMENT OF THE
### CHURCH'S SOCIAL ACTION AND TEACHING

It is certainly true that work as a human issue is at the very center of the "social question" to which, for almost a hundred years since the publication of the above-mentioned encyclical, the church's teaching and the many undertakings connected with her apostolic mission have been especially directed. The present reflections on work are not intended to follow a different line, but rather to be in organic connection with the whole tradition of this teaching and activity. At the same time, however, I am making them, according to the indication in the Gospel, in order to bring out from the heritage of the Gospel "what is new and what is old." Certainly work is part of "what is old" — as old as man and his life on earth. Nevertheless, the general situation of man in the modern world, studied and analyzed in its various aspects of geography, culture and civilization, calls for the discovery of the new meanings of human work. It likewise calls for the formulation of the new tasks that in this sector face each individual, the family, each country, the whole human race and finally the church herself.

During the years that separate us from the publication of the encyclical *Rerum Novarum*, the social question has not ceased to engage the church's attention. . . .

. . . The disproportionate distribution of wealth and poverty and the existence of some countries and continents that are developed and of others that are not call for a leveling out and for a search for ways to ensure just development for all. This is the direction of the teaching in John XXIII's encyclical *Mater et Magistra,* in the pastoral constitution *Gaudium et Spes* of the Second Vatican Council and in Paul VI's encyclical *Populorum Progressio.* . . .

## Work and Man

### 4. IN THE BOOK OF GENESIS

The church is convinced that work is a fundamental dimension of man's existence on earth. She is confirmed in this conviction by considering the whole heritage of the many sciences devoted to man: anthropology, paleontology, history, sociology, psychology, and so on; they all seem to bear witness to this reality in an irrefutable way. But the source of the church's conviction is above all the revealed word of God, and therefore what is a conviction of the intellect is also a conviction of faith. The reason is that the church — and it is worthwhile stating it at this point — believes in man: She thinks of man and addresses herself to him not only in the light of historical experience, not only with the aid of the many methods of scientific knowledge, but in the first place in the light of the revealed word of the living God. Relating herself to man, she seeks to express the eternal designs and transcendent destiny which the living God, the creator and redeemer, has linked with him.

The church finds in the very first pages of the Book of Genesis the source of her conviction that work is a fundamental dimension of human existence on earth. An analysis of these texts makes us aware that they express — sometimes in an archaic way of manifesting thought — the fundamental truths about man, in the context of the mystery of creation itself. These truths are decisive for man from the very beginning, and at the same time they trace out the main lines of his earthly existence, both in the state of original justice and also after the breaking, caused by sin, of the creator's original covenant with creation in man. When man, who had been created "in the image of God . . . male and female," hears the words: "Be fruitful and multiply, and fill the earth and subdue it," even though these words do not refer directly and explicitly to work, beyond any doubt they indirectly indicate it as an activity for man to carry out in the world. Indeed, they show its very deepest essence. Man is the image of God partly through the mandate received from his creator to subdue, to dominate, the earth. In carrying out this mandate, man, every human being, reflects the very action of the creator of the universe. . . .

. . . As man, through his work, becomes more and more the master of the earth, and as he confirms his dominion over the visible world, again through his work, he nevertheless remains in every case and at every phase of this process within the Creator's original ordering. And this ordering remains necessarily and indissolubly linked with the fact that man was created, as male and female, "in the image of God." This process is, at the same time, universal: It embraces all human beings, every generation, every phase of economic and cultural development, and at the same time it is a process that takes place within each human being, in each conscious human subject. Each and every individual is at the same time embraced by it. Each and every individual, to the proper extent and in an incalculable number of ways, takes part in the giant process whereby man "subdues the earth" through his work.

## 5. WORK IN THE OBJECTIVE SENSE: TECHNOLOGY

This universality and, at the same time, this multiplicity of the process of "subduing the earth" throw light upon human work, because man's dominion over the earth is achieved in and by means of work. There thus emerges the meaning of work in an objective sense, which finds expression in the various epochs of culture and civilization. Man dominates the earth by the very fact of domesticating animals, rearing them and obtaining from them the food and clothing he needs, and by the fact of being able to extract various natural resources from the earth and the seas. But man "subdues the earth" much more when he begins to cultivate it and then to transform its products, adapting them to his own use. Thus agriculture constitutes through human work a primary field of economic activity and an indispensable factor of production. Industry in its turn will always consist in linking the earth's riches — whether nature's living resources, or the products of agriculture, or the mineral or chemical resources — with man's work, whether physical or intellectual. This is also in a sense true in the sphere of what are called service industries and also in the sphere of research, pure or applied. . . .

While it may seem that in the industrial process it is the machine that "works" and man merely supervises it, making it function and keeping it going in various ways, it is also true that for this very reason industrial development provides grounds for reproposing in new ways the question of human work. Both the original industrialization that gave rise to what is called the worker question and the subsequent industrial and post-industrial changes show in an eloquent manner that, even in the age of ever more mechanized "work," the proper subject of work continues to be man.

The development of industry and of the various sectors connected with it, even the most modern electronics technology, especially in the fields of miniaturization, communications and telecommunications and so forth, shows how vast is the role of technology, that ally of work that human thought has produced in the interaction between the subject and object of work (in the widest sense of the word). Understood in this case not as a capacity or aptitude for work, but rather as a whole set of instruments which man uses in his work, technology is undoubtedly man's ally. . . . However it is also a fact that in some instances technology can cease to be man's ally and become almost his enemy, as when the mechanization of work "supplants" him, taking away all personal satisfaction and the incentive to creativity and responsibility, when it deprives many workers of their previous employment or when, through exalting the machine, it reduces man to the status of its slave. . . .

## 6. WORK IN THE SUBJECTIVE SENSE: MAN AS THE SUBJECT OF WORK

In order to continue our analysis of work, an analysis linked with the word of the Bible telling man that he is to subdue the earth, we must concentrate our attention on work in the subjective sense, much more than we did on the objective significance. . . . If the words of the Book of Genesis to which we refer in this analysis of ours speak of work in the objective sense in an indirect way, they also speak only indirectly of the subject of work; but what they say is very eloquent and is full of great significance.

Man has to subdue the earth and dominate it, because as the "image of God" he is a person, that is to say, a subjective being capable of acting in a planned and rational way, capable of deciding about himself and with a tendency to self-realization. As a person, man is therefore the subject of work. As a person he works, he performs various actions belonging to the work process; independently of their objective content, these actions must all serve to realize his humanity, to fulfill the calling to be a person that is his by reason of his very humanity. . . .

And so this "dominion" spoken of in the biblical text being meditated upon here refers not only to the objective dimension of work, but at the same time introduces us to an understanding of its subjective dimension. Understood as a process whereby man and the human race subdue the earth, work corresponds to this basic biblical concept only when throughout the process man manifests himself and confirms himself as the one who "dominates." This dominion, in a certain sense, refers to the subjective dimension even more than to the objective one: This dimension conditions the very ethical value of its own, which clearly and directly remains linked to the fact that the one who carries it out is a person, a conscious and free subject, that is to say, a subject that decides about himself. . . .

The ancient world introduced its own typical differentiation of people into classes according to the type of work done. Work which demanded from the worker the exercise of physical strength, the work of muscles and hands, was considered unworthy of free men and was therefore given to slaves. By broadening certain aspects that already belonged to the Old Testament, Christianity brought about a fundamental change of ideas in this field, taking the whole content of the gospel message as its point of departure, especially the fact that the one who, while being God, became like us in all things devoted most of the years of his life on earth to manual work at the carpenter's bench. This circumstance constitutes in itself the most eloquent "gospel of work," showing that the basis for determining the value of human work is not primarily the kind of work being done, but the fact that the one who is doing it is a person. The sources of the dignity of work are to be sought primarily in the subjective dimension, not in the objective one.

Such a concept practically does away with the very basis of the ancient differentiation of people into classes according to the kind of work done. This does not mean that from the objective point of view human work cannot and must not be rated and qualified in any way. It only means that the primary basis of the value of work is man himself, who is its subject. This leads immediately to a very important conclusion of an ethical nature: However true it may be that man is destined for work and called to it, in the first place work is "for man" and not man "for work." Through this conclusion one rightly comes to recognize the pre-eminence of the subjective meaning of work over the objective one. . . .

## 7. A THREAT TO THE RIGHT ORDER OF VALUES

It is precisely these fundamental affirmations about work that always emerged from the wealth of Christian truth, especially from the very message of the "gospel of work," thus creating the basis for a new way of thinking, judging and acting. In the modern period, from the beginning of the industrial age, the Christian truth about work had to oppose the various trends of materialistic and economistic thought.

For certain supporters of such ideas, work was understood and treated as a sort of "merchandise" that the worker — especially the industrial worker — sells to the employer, who at the same time is the possessor of the capital, that is to say, of all the working tools and means that make production possible. This way of looking at work was widespread especially in the first half of the 19th century. Since then explicit expressions of this sort have almost disappeared and have given way to more human ways of thinking about work and evaluating it. The interaction between the worker and the tools and means of production has given rise to the development of various forms of capitalism — parallel with various forms of collectivism — into which other socioeconomic elements have entered as a consequence of new concrete circumstances, of the activity of workers' associations and public authorities, and of the emergence of large transnational enterprises. Nevertheless, the danger of treating work as a special kind of "merchandise" or as an impersonal "force" needed for production (the expression "work force" is in fact in common use) always exists, especially when the whole way of looking at the question of economics is marked by the premises of materialistic economism. . . .

## 8. WORKER SOLIDARITY

. . . [V]arious ideological or power systems and new relationships which have arisen at various levels of society have allowed flagrant injustices to persist or have created new ones. On the world level, the development of civilization and of communications has made possible a more complete diagnosis of the living and working conditions of man globally, but it has also revealed other forms of injustice much more extensive than those which in the last century stimulated unity between workers for particular solidarity in the working world. This is true in countries which have completed a certain process of industrial revolution. It is also true in countries where the main working milieu continues to be agriculture or other similar occupations. . . .

. . . [T]here must be continued study of the subject of work and of the subject's living conditions. In order to achieve social justice in the various parts of the world, in the various countries and in the relationships between them, there is a need for ever new movements of solidarity of the workers and with the workers. This solidarity must be present whenever it is called for by the social degrading of the subject of work, by exploitation of the workers and by the growing areas of poverty and even hunger. The church is firmly committed to this cause for she considers it her mission, her service, a proof of her fidelity to Christ, so that she can truly be the "church of the poor." And the "poor" appear under various forms; they appear in various places and at various times; in many cases they appear as a result of the violation of the dignity of human work: either because the opportunities for human work are limited as a result of the scourge of unemployment or because a low value is put on work and the rights that flow from it, especially the right to a just wage and to the personal security of the worker and his or her family.

## 9. WORK AND PERSONAL DIGNITY

Remaining within the context of man as the subject of work, it is now appropriate to touch upon, at least in a summary way, certain problems that more closely define the dignity of human work in that they make it possible to characterize more fully its specific moral value. In doing this we must always keep in mind the biblical calling to "subdue the earth," in which is expressed the will of the Creator that work should enable man to achieve that "dominion" in the visible world that is proper to him.

God's fundamental and original intention with regard to man, whom he created in his image and after his likeness, was not withdrawn or canceled out even when man, having broken the original convenant with God, heard the words: "In the sweat of your face you shall eat bread." These words refer to the sometimes heavy toil that from then onward has accompanied human work; but they do not alter the fact that work is the means whereby man achieves that "dominion" which is proper to him over the visible world, by "subjecting" the earth. Toil is something that is universally known, for it is universally experienced. It is familiar to those doing physical work under sometimes exceptionally laborious conditions. It is familiar not only to agricultural workers, who spend long days working the land, which sometimes "bears thorns and thistles," but also to those who work in mines and quarries, to steelworkers at their blast furnaces, to those who work in builders' yards and in construction work, often in danger of injury or death. It is also familiar to those at an intellectual workbench; to scientists; to those who bear the burden of grave responsibility for decisions that will have a vast impact on society. It is familiar to doctors and nurses, who spend days and nights at their patients' bedside. It is familiar to women, who sometimes without proper recognition on the part of society and even of their own families bear the daily burden and responsibility for their homes and the upbringing of their children. It is familiar to all workers and, since work is a universal calling, it is familiar to everyone. . . .

. . . Work is a good thing for man — a good thing for his humanity — because through work man not only transforms nature, adapting it to his own needs, but he also achieves fulfillment as a human being and indeed in a sense becomes "more a human being."

Without this consideration it is impossible to understand the meaning of the virtue of industriousness, and more particularly it is impossible to understand why industriousness should be a virtue: For virtue, as a moral habit, is something whereby man becomes good as man. This fact in no way alters our justifiable anxiety that in work, whereby matter gains in nobility, man himself should not experience a lowering of his own dignity. Again, it is well known that it is possible to use work in various ways against man, that it is possible to punish man with the system of forced labor in concentration camps, that work can be made into a means for oppressing man, and that in various ways it is possible to exploit human labor, that is to say, the worker. All this pleads in favor of the moral obligation to link industriousness as a virtue with the social order of work, which will enable man to become in work "more a human being" and not be degraded by it not only because of the wearing out of his physical strength (which, at least up to a certain point, is inevitable), but especially through damage to the dignity and subjectivity that are proper to him.

## 10. WORK AND SOCIETY: FAMILY AND NATION

Having thus confirmed the personal dimension of human work, we must go on to the second sphere of values which is necessarily linked to work. Work constitutes a foundation for the formation of family life, which is a natural right and something that man is called to. These two spheres of values — one linked to work and the other consequent on the family nature of human life — must be properly united and must properly permeate each other. In a way, work is a condition for making it possible to found a family, since the family requires the means of subsistence which man normally gains through work. Work and industriousness also influence the whole process of education in the family, for the very reason that everyone "becomes a human being" through, among other things, work, and becoming a human being is precisely the main purpose of the whole process of education. Obviously, two aspects of work in a sense come into play here: the one making family life and its upkeep possible, and the other making possible the achievement of the purposes of the family, especially education. . . .

# [Conflict Between Labor and Capital]
## 11. DIMENSIONS OF THE CONFLICT

. . . [T]he issue of work has of course been posed on the basis of the great conflict that in the age of and together with industrial development emerged between "capital" and "labor," that is to say between the small but highly influential group of entrepreneurs, owners or holders of the means of production, and the broader multitude of people who lacked these means and who shared in the process of production solely by their labor. The conflict originated in the fact that the workers put their powers at the disposal of the entrepreneurs and these, following the principle of maximum profit, tried to establish the lowest possible wages for the work done by the employees. In addition there were other elements of exploitation connected with the lack of safety at work and of safeguards regarding the health and living conditions of the workers and their families.

This conflict, interpreted by some as a socioeconomic class conflict, found expression in the ideological conflict between liberalism, understood as the ideology of capitalism, and Marxism, understood as the ideology of scientific socialism and communism, which professes to act as the spokesman for the working class and the worldwide proletariat. Thus the real conflict between labor and capital was transformed into a systematic class struggle conducted not only by ideological means, but also and chiefly by political means. . . .

## 12. THE PRIORITY OF LABOR

The structure of the present-day situation is deeply marked by many conflicts caused by man, and the technological means produced by human work play a primary role in it. We should also consider here the prospect of worldwide catastrophe in the case of a nuclear war, which would have almost unimaginable possibilities of destruction. In view of this situation we must first of all recall a principle that has always been taught by the church: the principle of the priority of labor over capital. This principle directly concerns the process of production: In this process labor is always a primary efficient cause, while capital, the whole collection of means of production, remains a mere instrument or instrumental cause. This principle is an evident truth that emerges from the whole of man's historical experience. . . .

. . . All the means of production, from the most primitive to the ultramodern ones — it is man that has gradually developed them: man's experience and intellect. In this way there have appeared not only the simplest instruments for cultivating the earth, but also through adequate progress in science and technology the more modern and complex ones: machines, factories, laboratories and computers. Thus everything that is at the service of work, everything that in the present state of technology constitutes its ever more highly perfected "instrument," is the result of work.

This gigantic and powerful instrument — the whole collection of means of production that in a sense are considered synonymous with "capital" — is the result of work and bears the signs of human labor. At the present stage of technological advance, when man, who is the subject of work, wishes to make use of this collection of modern instruments, the means of production, he must first assimilate cognitively the result of the work of the people who invented those instruments, who planned them, built them and perfected them, and who continue to do so. Capacity for work — that is to say, for sharing efficiently in the modern production process — demands greater and greater preparation and, before all else, proper training. Obviously it remains clear that every human being sharing in the production process, even if he or she is only doing the kind of work for which no special training or qualifications are required, is the real efficient subject in this production process, while the whole collection of instruments, no matter how perfect they may be in themselves, are only a mere instrument subordinate to human labor. . . .

## 13. ECONOMISM AND MATERIALISM

In the light of the above truth we see clearly, first of all, that capital cannot be separated from labor; in no way can labor be opposed to capital or capital to labor, and still less can the actual people behind these concepts be opposed to each other. . . .

Opposition between labor and capital does not spring from the structure of the production process or from the structure of the economic process. In general the latter process demonstrates that labor and what we are accustomed to call capital are intermingled; it shows that they are inseparably linked.... In working, man also "enters into the labor of others." Guided both by our intelligence and by the faith that draws light from the work of God, we have no difficulty in accepting this image of the sphere and process of man's labor. It is a consistent image, one that is humanistic as well as theological. In it man is the master of the creatures placed at his disposal in the visible world....

This consistent image, in which the principle of the primacy of person over things is strictly preserved, was broken up in human thought.... The break occurred in such a way that labor was separated from capital and set in opposition to it, and capital was set in opposition to labor, as though they were two impersonal forces, two production factors juxtaposed in the same "economistic" perspective. This way of stating the issue contained a fundamental error, what we can call the error of economism, that of considering human labor solely according to its economic purpose....

Obviously the antinomy between labor and capital under consideration here ... did not originate merely in the philosophy and economic theories of the 18th century; rather it originated in the whole of the economic and social practice of that time, the time of the birth and rapid development of industrialization, in which what was mainly seen was the possibility of vastly increasing material wealth, means, while the end, that is to say man, who should be served by the means, was ignored. It was this practical error that struck a blow first and foremost against human labor, against the working man.... The same error, which is now part of history and which was connected with the period of primitive capitalism and liberalism, can nevertheless be repeated in other circumstances of time and place if people's thinking starts from the same theoretical or practical premises. The only chance there seems to be for radically overcoming this error is through adequate changes both in theory and in practice, changes in line with the definite conviction of the primacy of the person over things and of human labor over capital as a whole collection of means of production.

## 14. WORK AND OWNERSHIP

The historical process briefly presented here has certainly gone beyond its initial phase, but it is still taking place and indeed is spreading in the relationships between nations and continents. It needs to be specified further from another point of view. It is obvious that when we speak of opposition between labor and capital, we are not dealing only with abstract concepts or "impersonal forces" operating in economic production. Behind both concepts there are people, living, actual people: On the one side are those who do the work without being the owners of the means of production, and on the other side those who act as entrepreneurs and who own these means or represent the owners. Thus the issue of ownership or property enters from the beginning into the whole of this difficult historical process. The encyclical *Rerum Novarum,* which has the social question as its theme, stresses this issue also, recalling and confirming the church's teaching on ownership, on the right to private property even when it is a question of the means of production. The encyclical *Mater et Magistra* did the same.

The above principle, as it was then stated and as it is still taught by the church, diverges radically from the program of collectivism as proclaimed by Marxism and put into practice in various countries in the decades following the time of Leo XIII's encyclical. At the same time it differs from the program of capitalism practiced by liberalism and by the political systems inspired by it. In the latter case, the difference consists in the way the right to ownership or property is understood. Christian tradition has never upheld this right as absolute and untouchable. On the contrary, it has always understood this right within the broader context of the right common to all to use the goods of the whole of creation: The right to private property is subordinated to the right to common use, to the fact that goods are meant for everyone.

Furthermore, in the church's teaching, ownership has never been understood in a way that could constitute grounds for social conflict in labor. . . . [P]roperty is acquired first of all through work in order that it may serve work. This concerns in a special way ownership of the means of production. Isolating these means as a separate property in order to set it up in the form of "capital" in opposition to "labor" — and even to practice exploitation of labor — is contrary to the very nature of these means and their possession. They cannot be possessed against labor, they cannot even be possessed for possession's sake, because the only legitimate title to their possession — whether in the form of private ownership or in the form of public or collective ownership — is that they should serve labor and thus by serving labor that they should make possible the achievement of the first principle of this order, namely the universal destination of goods and the right to common use of them. From this point of view, therefore, in consideration of human labor and of common access to the goods meant for man, one cannot exclude the socialization, in suitable conditions, of certain means of production. . . .

In the present document, which has human work as its main theme, it is right to confirm all the effort with which the church's teaching has striven and continues to strive always to ensure the priority of work and thereby man's character as a subject in social life and especially in the dynamic structure of the whole economic process. From this point of view the position of "rigid" capitalism continues to remain unacceptable, namely the position that defends the exclusive right to private ownership of the means of production as an untouchable "dogma" of economic life. The principle of respect for work demands that this right should undergo a constructive revision both in theory and in practice. . . .

... [W]hile the position of "rigid" capitalism must undergo continual revision in order to be reformed from the point of view of human rights, both human rights in the widest sense and those linked with man's work, it must be stated that from the same point of view these many deeply desired reforms cannot be achieved by an *a priori* elimination of private ownership of the means of production. For it must be noted that merely taking these means of production (capital) out of the hands of their private owners is not enought to ensure their satisfactory socialization. They cease to be the property of a certain social group, namely the private owners, and become the property of organized society, coming under the administration and direct control of another group of people, namely those who, though not owning them, from the fact of exercising power in society manage them on the level of the whole national or the local economy.

This group in authority may carry out its task satisfactorily from the point of view of the priority of labor; but it may also carry it out badly by claiming for itself a monopoly of the means of production and not refraining even from offending basic human rights. Thus, merely converting the means of production into state property in the collectivist systems is by no means equivalent to "socializing" that property. We can speak of socializing only when the subject character of society is ensured, that is to say, when on the basis of his work each person is fully entitled to consider himself a part owner of the great workbench at which he is working with everyone else....

## 15. THE "PERSONALIST" ARGUMENT

... [T]he person who works desires not only due remuneration for his work; he also wishes that within the production process provision be made for him to be able to know that in his work, even on something that is owned in common, he is working "for himself." This awareness is extinguished within him in a system of excessive bureaucratic centralization, which makes the worker feel that he is just a cog in a huge machine moved from above, that he is for more reasons than one a mere production instrument rather than a true subject of work with an initiative of his own. The church's teaching has always expressed the strong and deep conviction that man's work concerns not only the economy but also, and especially, personal values....

## Rights of Workers

### 16. WITHIN THE BROAD CONTEXT
### OF HUMAN RIGHTS

While work, in all its many senses, is an obligation, that is to say a duty, it is also a source of rights on the part of the worker. These rights must be examined in the broad context of human rights as a whole, which are connatural with man and many of which are proclaimed by various international organizations and increasingly guaranteed by the individual states for their citizens. Respect for this broad range of human rights constitutes the fundamental condition for peace in the modern world: peace both within individual countries and societies and in international relations, as the church's magisterium has several times noted, especially since the encyclical *Pacem in Terris*. The human rights that flow from work are part of the broader context of those fundamental rights of the person.

However, within this context they have a specific character corresponding to the specific nature of human work as outlined above. It is in keeping with this character that we must view them. Work is, as has been said, an obligation, that is to say, a duty, on the part of man. . . .

For when we speak of the obligation of work and of the rights of the worker that correspond to this obligation, we think in the first place of the relationship between the employer, direct or indirect, and the worker. . . .

Since the direct employer is the person or institution with whom the worker enters directly into a work contract in accordance with definite conditions, we must understand as the indirect employer many different factors, other than the direct employer, that exercise a determining influence on the shaping both of the work contract and consequently of just or unjust relationships in the field of human labor.

## 17. DIRECT AND INDIRECT EMPLOYER

The concept of indirect employer includes both persons and institutions of various kinds and also collective labor contracts and the principles of conduct which are laid down by these persons and institutions and which determine the whole socioeconomic system or are its result. The concept of "indirect employer" thus refers to many different elements. The responsibility of the indirect employer differs from that of the direct employer — the term itself indicates that the responsibility is less direct — but it remains a true responsibility: The indirect employer substantially determines one or other facet of the labor relationship, thus conditioning the conduct of the direct employer when the latter determines in concrete terms the actual work contract and labor relations. This is not to absolve the direct employer from his own responsibility, but only to draw attention to the whole network of influences that condition his conduct. When it is a question of establishing an ethically correct labor policy, all these influences must be kept in mind. A policy is correct when the objective rights of the worker are fully respected.

The concept of indirect employer is applicable to every society and in the first place to the state. For it is the state that must conduct a just labor policy. However, it is common knowledge that in the present system of economic relations in the world there are numerous links between individual states, links that find expression, for instance, in the import and export process, that is to say, in the mutual exchange of economic goods, whether raw materials, semimanufactured goods or finished industrial products. These links also create mutual dependence, and as a result it would be difficult to speak in the case of any state, even the economically most powerful, of complete self-sufficiency or autarky.

Such a system of mutual dependence is in itself normal. However it can easily become an occasion for various forms of exploitation or injustice and as a result influence the labor policy of individual states; and finally it can influence the individual worker who is the proper subject of labor. For instance the highly industrialized countries, and even more the businesses that direct on a large scale the means of industrial production (the companies referred to as multinational or transnational), fix the highest possible prices for their products, while trying at the same time to fix the lowest possible prices for raw materials or semimanufactured goods. This is one of the causes of an ever increasing disproportion between national incomes. The gap between most of the richest countries and the poorest ones is not diminishing or being stabilized, but is increasing more and more to the detriment, obviously, of the poor countries. . . .

. . . The attainment of the worker's rights cannot however be doomed to be merely a result of economic systems which on a larger or smaller scale are guided chiefly by the criterion of maximum profit. On the contrary, it is respect for the objective rights of the worker — every kind of worker: manual or intellectual, industrial or agricultural, etc. — that must constitute the adequate and fundamental criterion for shaping the whole economy, both on the level of the individual society and state and within the whole of the world economic policy and of the systems of international relationships that derive from it. . . .

## 18. THE EMPLOYMENT ISSUE

. . . In order to meet the danger of unemployment and to ensure employment for all, the agents defined here as "indirect employer" must make provision for overall planning with regard to the different kinds of work by which not only the economic life, but also the cultural life of a given society is shaped; they must also give attention to organizing that work in a correct and rational way. In the final analysis this overall concern weighs on the shoulders of the state, but it cannot mean one-sided centralization by the public authorities. Instead, what is in question is a just and rational coordination, within the framework of which the initiative of individuals, free groups and local work centers and complexes must be safguarded, keeping in mind what has been said above with regard to the subject character of human labor. . . .

Rational planning and the proper organization of human labor in keeping with individual societies and states should also facilitate the discovery of the right proportions between the different kinds of employment: work on the land, in industry, in the various services, white-collar work and scientific or artistic work, in accordance with the capacities of individuals and for the common good of each society and of the whole of mankind. The organization of human life in accordance with the many possibilities of labor should be matched by a suitable system of instruction and education aimed first of all at developing mature human beings, but also aimed at preparing people specifically for assuming to good advantage an appropriate place in the vast and socially differentiated world of work.

As we view the whole human family throughout the world, we cannot fail to be struck by a disconcerting fact of immense proportions: the fact that while conspicuous natural resources remain unused there are huge numbers of people who are unemployed or underemployed and countless multitudes of people suffering from hunger. This is a fact that without any doubt demonstrates that both within the individual political communities and in their relationships on the continental and world levels there is something wrong with the organization of work and employment, precisely at the most critical and socially most important points. . . .

## 19. [WAGES]

. . . [T]here is no more important way for securing a just relationship between the worker and the employer than that constituted by remuneration for work. Whether the work is done in a system of private ownership of the means of production or in a system where ownership has undergone a certain "socialization," the relationship between the employer (first and foremost the direct employer) and the worker is resolved on the basis of the wage, that is, through just remuneration of the work done. . . .

. . . [W]ages . . . are still a practical means whereby the vast majority of people can have access to those goods which are intended for common use: both the goods of nature and manufactured goods. Both kinds of goods become accessible to the worker through the wage which he receives as remuneration for his work. Hence in every case a just wage is the concrete means of verifying the justice of the whole socioeconomic system and, in any case, of checking that it is functioning justly. It is not the only means of checking, but it is a particularly important one and in a sense the key means.

This means of checking concerns above all the family. Just remuneration for the work of an adult who is responsible for a family means remuneration which will suffice for establishing and properly maintaining a family and for providing security for its future. Such remuneration can be given either through what is called a family wage — that is, a single salary given to the head of the family for his work, sufficient for the needs of the family without the other spouse having to take up gainful employment outside the home — or through other social measures such as family allowances or grants to mothers devoting themselves exclusively to their families. These grants should correspond to the actual needs, that is, to the number of dependents for as long as they are not in a position to assume proper responsibility for their own lives.

Experience confirms that there must be a social re-evaluation of the mother's role, of the toil connected with it and of the need that children have for care, love and affection in order that they may develop into responsible, morally and religiously mature and psychologically stable persons. It will redound to the credit of society to make it possible for a mother — without inhibiting her freedom, without psychological or practical discrimination, and without penalizing her as compared with other women — to devote herself to taking care of her children and educating them in accordance with their needs, which vary with age. Having to abandon these tasks in order to take up paid work outside the home is wrong from the point of view of the good of society and of the family when it contradicts or hinders these primary goals of the mission of a mother.

In this context it should be emphasized that on a more general level the whole labor process must be organized and adapted in such a way as to respect the requirements of the person and his or her forms of life, above all life in the home, taking into account the individual's age and sex.... The true advancement of women requires that labor should be structured in such a way that women do not have to pay for their advancement by abandoning what is specific to them and at the expense of the family, in which women as mothers have an irreplaceable role.

Besides wages, various social benefits intended to ensure the life and health of workers and their families play a part here....

## 20. IMPORTANCE OF UNIONS

All these rights, together with the need for the workers themselves to secure them, give rise to yet another right: the right of association, that is, to form associations for the purpose of defending the vital interests of those employed in the various professions. These associations are called labor or trade unions....

Catholic social teaching does not hold that unions are no more than a reflection of the "class" structure of society and that they are a mouthpiece for a class struggle which inevitably governs social life. They are indeed a mouthpiece for the struggle for social justice, for the just rights of working people in accordance with their individual professions. However, this struggle should be seen as a normal endeavor "for" the just good: In the present case, for the good which corresponds to the needs and merits of working people associated by profession; but it is not a struggle "against" others. Even if in controversial questions the struggle takes on a character of opposition toward others, this is because it aims at the good of social justice, not for the sake of "struggle" or in order to eliminate the opponent. It is characteristic of work that it first and foremost unites people. In this consists its social power: the power to build a community. In the final analysis, both those who work and those who manage the means of production or who own them must in some way be united in this community. In the light of this fundamental structure of all work — in the light of the fact that, in the final analysis, labor and capital are indispensable components of the process of production in any social system — it is clear that even if it is because of their work needs that people unite to secure their rights, their union remains a constructive factor of social order and solidarity, and it is impossible to ignore it. . . .

. . . [U]nion activity undoubtedly enters the field of politics, understood as prudent concern for the common good. However, the role of unions is not to "play politics" in the sense that the expression is commonly understood today. Unions do not have the character of political parties struggling for power; they should not be subjected to the decision of political parties or have too close links with them. In fact, in such a situation they easily lose contact with their specific role, which is to secure the just rights of workers within the framework of the common good of the whole of society; instead they become an instrument used for other purposes. . . .

One method used by unions in pursuing the just rights of their members is the strike or work stoppage, as a kind of ultimatum to the competent bodies, especially the employers. This method is recognized by Catholic social teaching as legitimate in the proper conditions and within just limits. In this connection workers should be assured the right to strike, without being subjected to personal penal sanctions for taking part in a strike. While admitting that it is a legitimate means, we must at the same time emphasize that a strike remains, in a sense, an extreme means. It must not be abused; it must not be abused especially for "political" purposes. . . .

## 21. DIGNITY OF AGRICULTURAL WORK

All that has been said thus far on the dignity of work, on the objective and subjective dimension of human work, can be directly applied to the question of agricultural work and to the situation of the person who cultivates the earth by toiling in the fields. . . .

Agricultural work involves considerable difficulties, including unremitting and sometimes exhausting physical effort and a lack of appreciation on the part of society, to the point of making agricultural people feel that they are social outcasts and of speeding up the phenomenon of their mass exodus from the countryside to the cities and unfortunately to still more dehumanizing living conditions. Added to this are the lack of adequate professional training and of proper equipment, the spread of a certain individualism and also objectively unjust situations. In certain developing countries, millions of people are forced to cultivate the land belonging to others and are exploited by the big landowners, without any hope of ever being able to gain possession of even a small piece of land of their own. . . .

In many situations radical and urgent changes are therefore needed in order to restore to agriculture — and to rural people — its just value as the basis for a healthy economy, within the social community's development as a whole. . . .

## 22. THE DISABLED PERSON AND WORK

Recently national communities and international organizations have turned their attention to another question connected with work, one full of implications: the question of disabled people....

The various bodies involved in the world of labor, both the direct and the indirect employer, should, ... by means of effective and appropriate measures, foster the right of disabled people to professional training and work so that they can be given a productive activity suited to them....

## 23. WORK AND THE EMIGRATION QUESTION

Finally, we must say at least a few words on the subject of emigration in search of work. This is an age-old phenomenon which nevertheless continues to be repeated and is still today very widespread as a result of the complexities of modern life. Man has the right to leave his native land for various motives — and also the right to return — in order to seek better conditions of life in another country. This fact is certainly not without difficulties of various kinds....

The most important thing is that the person working away from his native land, whether as a permanent emigrant or as a seasonal worker, should not be placed at a disadvantage in comparison with the other workers in that society in the matter of working rights. Emigration in search of work must in no way become an opportunity for financial or social exploitation. As regards the work relationship, the same criteria should be applied to immigrant workers as to all other workers in the society concerned. The value of work should be measured by the same standard and not according to the difference in nationality, religion or race....

# DEFENSE REPORT
# ON SOVIET POWER
## September 29, 1981

*Emphasizing the Reagan administration's contention that the Soviet Union was engaged in a drive for military superiority, the Defense Department September 29 issued a solemn though lavishly illustrated report on Soviet armed strength. While the 99-page booklet met a rather mixed reaction in both the United States and Western Europe, it was praised by officials of the North Atlantic Treaty Organization (NATO) and of Britain's ruling Conservative Party.*

*In the United States, the handsomely produced report raised questions as to its domestic purpose. Secretary of Defense Caspar W. Weinberger denied at a press conference that the booklet was timed to buttress administration proposals for an expanded military budget or its plans for the mobile MX missile system and a new manned bomber.*

*The report, "Soviet Military Power," contained numerous artist's renditions of Soviet weapons, maps, photographs, charts and tables. One of the most striking of the illustrations was an outline of the Nizhniy Tagil tank plant in the Ural Mountains superimposed on a map of Washington, D.C. The dimensions of the tank plant were shown as extending about two miles from the Lincoln Memorial to the U.S. Capitol.*

## Background

*The booklet was published at a time of increasing opposition in Europe to the deployment of U.S. nuclear weapons on European soil. Concern*

717

*that Europe might find itself a battleground in an exchange between the two superpowers had led to large demonstrations in European cities, a growing peace movement in West Germany and the advocacy of unilateral nuclear disarmament within Britain's Labor Party. Overriding specific anxieties was a feeling on the part of many Europeans that, for the first time, Soviet and American leaders were starting to believe that a limited nuclear war could be winnable.*

*Some of the opposition to nuclear weapons among Europeans was focused on the planned deployment, in 1983, of American cruise and Sherman missiles. Spotlighting the Soviet Union's buildup, the booklet reported that the Soviets had deployed, largely in Europe, 250 SS-20 medium range missiles that would be superior to NATO weapons until the cruise and Sherman missiles could be emplaced.*

## New Information

*The booklet provided two pieces of information that previously had been military secrets. A map included an assessment of the deployment and state of readiness of the Soviet Union's 180 combat divisions. Then, too, the booklet disclosed that the Soviets were believed to have surpassed the United States in developing such "directed energy weapons" as lasers and in exploiting space for military purposes.*

## Reaction

*News reports said that leaders of the NATO governments were generally pleased with the report. John Nott, Britain's defense minister, was quoted as saying that the booklet made clear that the United Kingdom must maintain its nuclear capablity.* The New York Times *reported that Nott said that "[a]ny talk of unilateral disarmament is dangerous nonsense, threatening the very safety of the realm."*

*A number of American analysts pointed out that the report did not attempt to provide a systematic comparison of Soviet and U.S. armed forces. Moreover, some analysts said that though the production of Soviet arms had recently increased, much of the increase could be attributed to sales to foreign countries in exchange for hard currency badly needed by the Soviet Union.*

*Tass, the press agency of the Soviet government, called the booklet "Washington's new propagandistic trick."*

> *Following are excerpts from the report, "Soviet Military Power," published by the Department of Defense on September 29, 1981:*

# Preface

The Soviet Armed Forces today number more than 4.8 million men. For the past quarter century, we have witnessed the continuing growth of Soviet military power at a pace that shows no signs of slackening in the future.

All elements of the Soviet Armed Forces — the Strategic Rocket Forces, the Ground Forces of the Army, the Air Forces, the Navy and the Air Defense Forces — continue to modernize with an unending flow of new weapons systems, tanks, missiles, ships, artillery and aircraft. The Soviet defense budget continues to grow to fund this force buildup, to fund the projection of Soviet power far from Soviet shores and to fund Soviet use of proxy forces to support revolutionary factions and conflict in an increasing threat to international stability.

To comprehend the threat to Western strategic interests posed by the growth and power projection of the Soviet Armed Forces it is useful to consider in detail the composition, organization and doctrine of these forces, their ideological underpinning, and their steady acquisition of new, increasingly capable conventional, theater nuclear and strategic nuclear weapons systems. It is equally important to examine the USSR's industrial base, military resource allocations, and continuing quest for military/technological superiority which contribute to the effectiveness of its armed forces and proxy forces, and which support the Soviets' position as a world leader in arms exports.

The facts are stark:

- The Soviet Ground Forces have grown to more than 180 divisions — motorized rifle divisions, tank divisions and airborne divisions — stationed in Eastern Europe, in the USSR, in Mongolia, and in combat in Afghanistan. Soviet Ground Forces have achieved the capacity for extended intensive combat in the Central Region of Europe.

- The Soviets have fielded 50,000 tanks and 20,000 artillery pieces. The Soviet divisions are being equipped with the newer, faster, better armored T-64 and T-72 tanks. Some artillery units, organic to each division, include new, heavy mobile artillery, multiple rocket launchers and self-propelled, armored 122-mm and 152-mm guns.

- More than 5,200 helicopters are available to the Soviet Armed Forces, including increasing numbers of Mi-8 and Mi-24 helicopter gunships used in direct support of ground forces on the battlefield.

- More than 3,500 Soviet and Warsaw Pact tactical bombers and fighter aircraft are located in Eastern Europe alone. In each of the last eight years, the Soviets have produced more than 1,000 fighter aircraft.

- Against Western Europe, China and Japan, the Soviets are adding constantly to deliverable nuclear warheads, with the number of launchers growing, with some 250 mobile, SS-20 Intermediate Range Ballistic Missile launchers in the field, and with three nuclear warheads on each SS-20 missile.

● The Soviets continue to give high priority to the modernization of their Intercontinental Ballistic Missile (ICBM) force and their Submarine Launched Ballistic Missile (SLBM) force stressing increased accuracy and greater warhead throwweight. The Soviet intercontinental strategic arsenal includes 7,000 nuclear warheads, with 1,398 ICBM launchers, 950 SLBM launchers and 156 long-range bombers. This does not include some 150 nuclear-capable BACKFIRE bombers.

● The Soviets have eight classes of submarines and eight classes of major surface warships, including nuclear-powered cruisers and new aircraft carriers, presently under construction. This growing naval force emerging from large, modern shipyards is designed to support sustained operations in remote areas in order to project Soviet power around the world

● The Soviet Air Defense Forces man 10,000 surface-to-air missile launchers at 1,000 fixed missile sites across the Soviet Union.

● The growth of the Soviet Armed Forces is made possible by the USSR's military production base which continues to grow at the expense of all other components of the Soviet economy. There are 135 major military industrial plants now operating in the Soviet Union with over 40 million square meters in floor space, a 34 percent increase since 1970. In 1980, these plants produced more than 150 different types of weapons systems for Soviet forces and for export to client states and developing countries.

● Today, the Soviets have more than 85,000 men fighting in Afghanistan. Soviet naval forces are deployed in the major oceans of the world. The USSR is gaining increased access to military facilities and is supporting proxy conflicts in Africa, Southwest Asia, Southeast Asia and the Western hemisphere.

There is nothing hypothetical about the Soviet military machine. Its expansion, modernization, and contribution to projection of power beyond Soviet boundaries are obvious.

A clear understanding of Soviet Armed Forces, their doctrine, their capabilities, their strengths and their weaknesses is essential to the shaping and maintenance of effective U.S. and Allied Armed Forces.

The greatest defense forces in the world are those of free people in free nations well informed as to the challenge they face, firmly united in their resolve to provide fully for the common defense, thereby deterring aggression and safeguarding the security of the world's democracies.

Caspar W. Weinberger
Secretary of Defense

## II Military Resource Allocation

In 1980, the first of the Soviets' TYPHOON-Class 25,000-ton strategic ballistic missile submarines was launched from a newly completed construction hall at the Severodvinsk Shipyard on the White Sea. Earlier in the year the same shipyard launched the first of the extremely large OSCAR-Class guided missile nuclear submarines, a submarine capable of firing 24 long-range, antiship cruise missiles while remaining submerged.

In 1980, some 2,400 kilometers southeast of Severodvinsk, the mammoth Nizhniy Tagil Railroad Car and Tank Plant, an industrial facility covering 827,000 square meters of floor space, manufactured 2,500 T-72 tanks.

To support the continuing growth and modernization of the armed forces, the Soviet Union over the past quarter century has increased military expenditures in real terms, devoting an average of 12-to-14 percent of its Gross National Product each year to the Soviet military. The estimated dollar costs of Soviet military investment exceeded comparable US spending by 70 percent in 1979. The defense sector is the first priority of Soviet industrial production.

The Soviet and non-Soviet Warsaw Pact military industrial base is by far the world's largest in number of facilities and physical size. The Soviet Union alone produces more weapons systems in greater quantities than any other country.

The Soviet military industry has grown steadily and consistently over the past 20-to-25 years. Its physical growth and the commitment of large quantities of financial and human resources is its most dynamic aspect, but its cyclical production is its most important. Production plants remain at work. As old weapons programs are phased out, new ones are begun, leaving no down times or long periods of layoffs and inactivity. The cyclical process, the continuing facility growth and the high rates of production keep the arms industry in a high state of readiness to meet any contingency and any demand for new weapons. The military production industry includes 135 major final assembly plants involved in producing weapons as end products. Over 3,500 individual factories and related installations provide support to these final assembly plants.

Construction at the Severodvinsk Naval Shipyard illustrates the growth of Soviet facilities over time. Over the past decade seven classes of submarines have been produced, and during this time, floor space has increased by several hundred thousand square meters, or approximately three-quarters again the yard's size ten years earlier. The new large construction hall used to assemble the TYPHOON and OSCAR submarines accounted for about 25 percent of this increase. Moreover, Severodvinsk is only one of five Soviet yards producing submarines.

In the aerospace industry, even though there has been significant construction in recent years including a number of new large final assembly buildings at established plants, the Soviets have revealed that they are constructing a wholly new, large aircraft plant at Ulyanovsk. This plant, when completed, will be well-suited for the fabrication and assembly of large aircraft — transports or bombers — underscoring the Soviets' continuing drive to improve further their industrial base. Qualitative improvements in production technology, which typically accompany new and more sophisticated aircraft, have paralleled the physical growth of the industry.

The Army's sector of Soviet military industry is traditionally large to support the growing Ground Forces. Army industrial floorspace has expanded by over ten percent in the late 1970s. All segments of the Army's industrial base have been expanded despite their already massive size. For instance, a major Soviet tank producer which was already nearly five times as large as the US manufacturers, has again been expanded.

The Soviet Union and Warsaw Pact need all of these facilities for the large number of major weapons and support systems currently in production — more than 150 in all. . . .

The most important aspect of aircraft production is the sustained high rates of fighter aircraft production. Helicopter production shows a decline at midpoint, but then a gradual buildup probably indicating a phase-out/phase-in of a new system, or increased orders for helicopters.

Missile production shows the wide range of missiles in production. Every class of missiles, from Surface-to-Air to ICBMs, is produced in significant quantities.

Naval ship construction demonstrates the USSR's capability to sustain high rates throughout. Moreover, the number of auxiliary ships produced in Eastern Europe has freed Soviet building ways for other projects.

Soviet Army materiel production shows a jump in the output of tanks and other armored vehicles in 1979 and 1980. The production of self-propelled artillery, however, exhibits a steady decline since 1977. This probably represents the phasing out of production of an old weapon and the introduction of a new one. Such transition is fairly common in Soviet production practices. The evolutionary introduction of new systems continues. Overall, Soviet Ground Forces materiel production has increased over the past five years.

An even greater increase is evident when Soviet Ground Forces materiel production is combined with that of the Warsaw Pact allies. . . .

## IV Soviet Theater Forces

Over the past 15 years the Soviets have steadily expanded and upgraded their military forces designated for theater operations with particular attention directed toward the European theater. During this period, the Soviet objective for this modernization has been the conversion of the Red Army from a balanced offensive-defensive force to one geared to fast-paced offensive operations. A key aim appears to have been the provision in peacetime of a standing Army at the leading edge of the potential battlefield such that it could begin operations with minimal mobilization and, thereby, with little warning.

The forces are highly mobile, and they are organized and supplied for a rapid initial push from a peacetime posture. At the outset of a war, the Soviets plan to move quickly slicing through NATO forces in the Central

Region and driving to the English Channel, while concurrently securing the northern and southern flanks. During the initial operations, necessary additional forces would be mobilized and moved to the battlefield. All of this the Soviets aim to accomplish before the full weight of NATO reinforcements could be brought to bear. The Soviets have given priority attention to all elements of their Armed Forces with a role to play in the sweep across Europe. Modernization and upgrading is underway in each of the following elements of Soviet Theater Forces:

> Long Range Missile and Air Forces
> Ground Forces
> Frontal Aviation
> Military Transport Aviation
> Special Purpose Forces
> Navy....

## TACTICAL NUCLEAR WEAPONS

The Soviets have deployed large numbers of tactical nuclear delivery systems, and we believe they have stockpiled reloads for these systems. The Soviets rely on dual-capable systems for most of their shorter-range theater nuclear delivery capability and have adapted some of their 203-mm and 240-mm artillery pieces deployed in the USSR to fire nuclear projectiles. Towed 203-mm and 240-mm weapons are being replaced with self-propelled models. Their medium-range launchers are capable of firing nuclear, conventional, or chemical munitions, and consist of the FROG (and its SS-21 replacement), the SCUD B (and its SS-X-23 replacement), and the SS-12/SCALEBOARD (and its SS-22 replacement). An increase in the number of nuclear-capable systems combined with modernization of these systems give the Warsaw Pact improved nuclear options. A *Front* normally has tactical rockets, such as the free-rocket-over-ground (FROG), and the operational-tactical missiles (SCUDs) to complement nuclear-capable artillery, aviation and other longer-range missiles.

The follow-on to the FROG, the SS-21, has improved accuracy and range. Initial operational capability for the SS-21 was attained in 1976; however, only a few have been deployed.

Until recently, the West relied extensively upon the qualitative superiority of its forces to offset the numerical superiority of the USSR and its allies. That margin of quality is rapidly diminishing in the face of a massive Soviet effort to modernize its forces and those of its Warsaw Pact allies. Modern tanks, armored fighting vehicles, artillery, rocket launchers, antiaircraft artillery, surface-to-air and surface-to-surface missiles, and other weapons now being fielded in large quantities are the direct result of an intensive, multi-year Soviet investment program. This program is expected to continue in spite of predicted Soviet economic problems. The Soviet advantage in tanks, presently about three to one in the European theater alone, will grow throughout the decade....

## CHEMICAL WARFARE

The armed forces of the Soviet Union in particular and the Warsaw Pact forces in general are better equipped, structured and trained than any other military force in the world to conduct offensive and defensive chemical warfare operations. Their capabilities are steadily improving.

The Soviets have deployed a variety of modern agents and multiple delivery systems, and have the tactical doctrine for large-scale employment of chemical weapons. A significant portion of all Soviet delivery systems — including missile and rocket systems, aerial bombs and artillery — are chemical-weapon capable. Warsaw Pact forces are well-trained, organized and equipped for offensive CW operations.

In Soviet military doctrine, toxic chemicals are associated primarily with theater warfare. The basic principle is to achieve surprise by using massive quantities of chemical agents against unprotected troops or against equipment or on terrain to deny its use.

A large chemical warfare organization is organic to the Soviet service structure. Throughout the Warsaw Pact each combat unit down to regimental level has a sizable contingent for chemical defense. Chemical specialists are also assigned at the company level. All Warsaw Pact combat and combat support forces are well equipped and realistically trained to insure their survivability and to increase their operational effectiveness in toxic environments....

## THE SOVIET NAVY

Over the last two decades the Soviet Navy has been transformed from a basically coastal defense force into ocean-going force designed to extend the military capability of the USSR well out to sea and to perform the functions of tactical, theater and strategic naval power in waters distant from the Soviet Union. The Soviets have a larger array of general purpose submarines, surface warships and combat naval aircraft than any other nation. The submarines, about 70 of which carry antiship cruise missiles, constitute the most serious threat to US and Allied naval forces and the worldwide sea lines of communication upon which we and our Allies depend. In the mid-1960s the Soviets had 260 major surface warships and amphibious ships. Today they have 362.

In the European theater, Soviet naval forces would have a variety of key missions. These would include securing vital areas of the sea and strategic passages such as the waters north of the Greenland/Iceland/United Kingdom Gap, the Gap itself, the Baltic Sea, the Gulf of Finland, the passages on either side of Denmark, the Bosporus and Dardenelles and the Mediterranean Sea. Additionally, the Soviet Navy would seek to interdict the sea lanes to Europe, and would mount operations on the high seas against NATO carrier task forces, other surface warships and submarines.

The largest Soviet surface warship is the KIEV-Class aircraft carrier. At present, two KIEVs are deployed and two more are under construction. The KIEVs are armed with antiship cruise missiles, antisubmarine and over-the-horizon target acquisition helicopters, anti-aircraft missiles, anti-submarine rockets and missiles, believed to be nuclear-capable, and the FORGER vertical- and short-takeoff and landing (VSTOL) jet aircraft.

The principal surface warships which the Soviets are building today have greater range, firepower and electronics capabilities than in the past. The modern ships of the Soviet Navy are among the fastest and most heavily armed in the world.

Present surface warship building programs include about 12 hulls under construction in four new classes of large warships, including a 23,000-ton nuclear-powered cruiser as well as the continued construction of KIEV-Class carriers and destroyer and frigate classes. The Soviet Navy has led the world in the use of cruise missiles in naval warfare. Since the installation of the SS-N-1 cruise missile on the KILDIN and KRUPNYY classes of destroyers in the late 1950s, the Soviets have extensively developed and deployed this type of weapon. Today the Soviet Navy has some 20 cruisers, carriers, and destroyers, about 70 submarines and 300 land-based aircraft armed with anti-ship cruise missiles. . . .

## SUBMARINES

The Soviet Navy currently operates some 377 submarines, including 180 nuclear-powered submarines compared to some 115 in the U.S. Navy.

*Attack Submarines.* The Soviet Navy operates about 220 attack submarines. Most are diesel-electric powered and many are of recent construction. About 60 of the torpedo attack submarines are nuclear powered, being of the NOVEMBER, ECHO, VICTOR, and ALFA Classes. The last is believed to be the fastest submarine in service today in any Navy. An improved VICTOR Class is now in production and the small, ALFA Class, which combines deep-diving capabilities with its high speed, may well be in series production. The Soviet Navy continues to build diesel-powered submarines, the FOXTROT Class, for overseas sales, i.e., India, Libya and Cuba, and the new TANGO Class for use by the Soviet Navy. The prime weapons of these attack submarines are antisubmarine and antiship torpedoes; however, mines also can be carried. The newer submarines have rocket-delivered ASW weapons as well.

*Cruise Missile Submarines:* Even while ambitious surface combatant construction programs were underway, the Soviets continued to turn out submarines at virtually the same pace they have maintained through the 1970s. One new class introduced in 1980, the OSCAR, is an extremely large SSGN capable of launching up to 24 long-range, antiship cruise missiles while remaining submerged. The missile fired by the OSCAR is probably a submarine variant of the same new antiship cruise missile first deployed aboard KIROV. This missile has an estimated range of over 450 kilometers. The Soviets began their submarine cruise missile programs in the 1950s converting existing submarines to fire the long-range SS-N-3 missile. Then, newer submarines designed to carry the SS-N-3 joined the Soviet fleet, the diesel-powered JULIETT Class and the nuclear-powered ECHO I and II Classes.

After producing about 50 submarines of the JULIETT and ECHO Classes, the Soviets completed the first CHARLIE I Class SSGN in 1968 with the improved CHARLIE II following several years later. These nuclear-powered submarines can fire eight antiship cruise missiles while remaining submerged at a range of up to 100 kilometers from the intended target. Soviet cruise missile submarines also carry ASW and antiship torpedoes.

The Soviet Navy's cruise missile submarines and their missile-armed bombers form the greatest threat to Allied naval surface forces operating on the high seas. This is especially so when within range of Soviet air bases where the Soviets can launch coordinated attacks using not only reconnaissance aircraft to provide target data for submarine-launched missiles, but also their extensive force of naval and air force missile-equipped bombers. . . .

## V Soviet Strategic Forces

Over the past 20 years, the Soviet Union has devoted substantial resources to the development and deployment of intercontinental ballistic missile (ICBM) and submarine launched ballistic missile (SLBM) forces. Fewer resources have been allocated to bomber forces, although new weapons systems — primarily the BACKFIRE bomber — have been deployed.

Under Brezhnev, the Soviet missile forces have moved from a position of clear inferiority in the early-to-middle 1960s to one in which they are generally recognized as equal or superior in certain measures to those of the West. In 1964, the Soviets had only a few operational SLBMs, many of which had to be launched from surfaced submarines. While the USSR had more ICBMs than SLBMs, the number was significantly fewer than US ICBMs. Moreover, the majority of Soviet ICBMs were inaccurate systems housed in launchers that were clustered together and unhardened, making them vulnerable to attack. The USSR then embarked on high-priority development and deployment programs first focused on increasing single-silo ICBM deployment to a level greater than that of the United States. A similar buildup of SLBM launchers on modern, nuclear-powered ballistic missile submarines (SSBNs) was underway by the late 1960s. These massive 1960s ICBM and SLBM deployment programs, largely centered on the SS-9 and SS-11 ICBMs and the SS-N-6/YANKEE SLBM/SSBN weapons systems, provided the foundation from which subsequent strategic nuclear modernization programs were to grow. . . .

## SOVIET MIRVed ICBMs

*SS-17:* Since it first became operational in 1975, the SS-17 has been deployed in 150 converted SS-11 silos. Both single and multiple re-entry vehicle (RV) versions of the SS-17 have been developed, but few if any of the single RV versions are deployed. The maximum range of the SS-17 is believed to be about 10,000 kilometers. Although much more accurate than its predecessor, the SS-11, the SS-17 is not as accurate as the SS-18 and SS-19 ICBMs.

The SS-17 employs a cold-launch technique which delays main engine ignition until the missile has exited its hardened silo. This technique minimizes launch damage to the silo and is consistent with the notion of building in the capability to reload and refire missiles during a protracted nuclear conflict.

*SS-18:* The SS-18, the largest of the current Soviet ICBMs, is similar in dimensions to the SS-9, which it replaced, and is about twice the size of the proposed US MX missile. Like the SS-17, the SS-18 also uses a cold-launch technique. Both single and MIRVed versions of the SS-18 have been tested. The MIRVed versions carry eight or ten reentry vehicles. Each warhead of the ten RV variants has a better than 50 percent chance of destroying a MINUTEMAN silo. When used in pairs against a single target, the warheads are even more destructive. The single RV versions of the SS-18, with their large destructive power and accuracy, are capable of destroying any known fixed target with high probability.

*SS-19:* The SS-19 ICBM became operational in 1974. It uses a hot-launch technique with engine ignition occurring while the missile is in its silo. The SS-19 is estimated to have three-to-four times the payload carrying capacity of the SS-11, and the missile is much larger in volume, comparable in size to the proposed US MX. There are both single and multiple RV versions of the SS-19. The MIRVed version, which makes up most of the SS-19 force, is believed capable of delivering six RVs to a range of about 9,000 kilometers. . . .

## ICBM PRODUCTION

Four major Soviet design bureaus specialize in strategic missiles development. These bureaus are supported by activities at main assembly plants, at hundreds of component production plants, at test ranges, and at launch complexes. The Soviet missile development program shows no signs of slackening. We expect improvements leading to new missiles and to the modification of existing missile systems. These improvements are expected to continue the trend towards greater capabilities against such hardened military structures as ICBM silos. As the accuracy of future Soviet missiles increases, it will be feasible for the Soviets to reduce the size of individual RVs and thereby to increase the number of MIRVs carried on each missile, assuming no external constraint such as that imposed by arms limitations.

It is anticipated that the Soviets will develop solid-propellant ICBMs to supplement or replace some of the current liquid propellant systems. The SS-16, a small ICBM about the same size as the MINUTEMAN, is a solid-propellant ICBM which was developed by the Soviets in the early 1970s for mobile deployment. The system was never deployed. Future solid-propellant ICBM development and deployment could give the Soviets additional flexibility in handling and in basing their missile forces. Future missiles are expected to include upgraded versions of the present systems as well as new missiles....

## VI Quest for Technological Superiority

The Soviets have often stated their goal of superiority in science and technology. The present, growing Soviet military capability reflects the achievements of a technological base that has grown steadily since the late 1950s, despite the fact that the Soviets have nothing comparable to the commercial technology base in the Western World.

The recent increase in the level of deployed Soviet military technology is significant, because the West has customarily relied on its now eroding technological superiority to offset the Soviet Union's historical quantitative advantage in deployed weapons. Even the United States' lead in basic military technology is presently being challenged.

During the 1970s, the Soviets have dramatically reduced the US lead in virtually every important basic technology. The United States is losing its lead in key technologies, including electro-optical sensors, guidance and navigation, hydro-acoustics, optics and propulsion. In many areas where the United States continues to lead the Soviets, their technology has achieved a level of adequacy with respect to present military requirements.

Over the past ten years, the Soviet Union is estimated to have taken the lead in the development of directed energy weapons such as high-power lasers and possibly radio frequency devices. The USSR is also thought to have enlarged its lead in electrical power sources for such directed energy weapons, as well as its more customary lead in chemical explosives....

### SPACE PROGRAMS

The Soviets have a vigorous and constantly expanding military space program. In the past ten years they have been launching spacecraft at over 75 per year, at the rate of four-to-five times that of the United States. The annual payload weight placed into orbit by the Soviets is even more impressive — 660,000 pounds — ten times that of the United States. Some, but by no means all, of this differential can be accounted for by long-life US satellites using miniaturized high technology components. Such an activity rate is expensive to underwrite, yet the Soviets are willing to expend resources on space hardware at an approximate eight percent per year growth rate in constant dollars.

We estimate that 70 percent of Soviet space systems serve a purely military role, another 15 percent serve dual military/civil roles, and the remaining 15 percent are purely civil. The Soviet military satellites perform a wide variety of reconnaissance and collection missions. Military R & D experiments are performed onboard Soviet manned space stations, and the Soviets continue to develop and test an ASAT antisatellite co-orbital interceptor....

## VIII The Challenge

The Soviets begin the 1980s with strategic nuclear, theater nuclear and conventional armed forces and supporting elements that in both absolute and relative terms are substantially more capable than they were at the beginning of the 1970s.

The Soviet leadership, the key members of which have shepherded these forces for over 20 years, places great stock both in the international political influence and in the reality of military power that the forces underwrite in concert with other less visible means in the struggle with the West. In developing and deploying their strategic nuclear forces, the Soviets have subscribed neither to Western notions of strategic sufficiency nor to the concept of assured destruction. Instead, while they believe that nuclear war and its debilitating results must be avoided, they see the development of superior capabilities wedded to a strategy designed to achieve military victory and a dominant postwar position as the only rational approach to nuclear forces. The Soviet Union now exceeds the United States in the number of strategic nuclear vehicles. Soviet SS-20 theater nuclear forces are being deployed in increasing numbers against Western Europe and Asia.

As a result of a decade of missile force modernization and expansion, the Soviets have improved the reliability, payload and accuracy of their ballistic missiles allowing an improved hard-target kill capability. All evidence indicates that the Soviets will continue their steady effort to improve the quality of their land-based missile force, striving for higher reliability, faster response time and greater accuracy.

In the last ten years, the Soviets have introduced four classes of new ballistic missile submarines. The long-range missiles of the DELTA-Class SSBNs can reach the United States while still in Soviet ports. The Soviets now have over 30 operational DELTAs. The SS-N-18, a missile installed in the DELTA III, has a range of about 7,500 kilometers and a post-boost vehicle capable of dispensing MIRVs. The TYPHOON SSBN, twice the size of the DELTA, has been launched and will be deployed in the 1980s.

Throughout the past decade, the Soviets have maintained their heavy-bomber strike force and have developed and deployed the BACKFIRE bomber capable of both theater and intercontinental delivery. Evidence would indicate that the Soviets are in the process of developing a new long-range bomber, and possibly a strategic cruise missile carrier.

In the tactical ballistic missile field the 40-mile FROG and 500-mile SCALEBOARD short-range ballistic missile systems were replaced by or augmented with the newly developed SS-21 and SS-22 SRBM systems. Soviet tactical missile systems of the next decade can be expected to incorporate new technology to make them lighter and more mobile, more accurate and more responsive.

During the 1970s, new generations of Soviet infantry weapons — assault rifles, antitank grenade launchers and multiple rocket launchers with greater range and lethality — were introduced. Heavily armed helicopter gunships now number in the thousands.

Over the past ten years the Soviets have expanded their ground forces to more than 180 divisions. The Soviets today have superior ground forces in Europe. They have a substantial advantage both in number of troops and quantity of armored assault vehicles. . . .

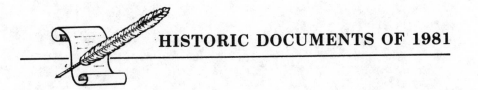

# October

# SADAT ASSASSINATION
## October 6, 1981

*The assassination of Egyptian President Anwar al-Sadat on October 6 brought to a tragic end the remarkable odyssey of a statesman who had steered Egypt through perhaps the most abrupt change in policy in modern Middle East history.*

*Egypt had been the foremost enemy of the Jewish state of Israel, formally established in 1948 after the partition of Palestine. Under the flamboyant and charismatic leadership of Gamal Abdel Nasser, Egypt between 1954 and 1970 had waged four wars against the nation it considered to be the usurper of Arab and Islamic rights. Nasser tried to forge a consensus among Arab nations for a "holy war" against Israel, enlisting Soviet support for that endeavor. But the Russian connection was uneasy and ephemeral. Most Egyptians were uncomfortable with the relationship and wary of foreign interference in the country's internal and regional affairs.*

*Nasser's plan for a grand design of Arab nations to wage war against Israel never materialized. He died of a heart attack in September 1970 and was succeeded by a relative unknown in Egypt and the West — Anwar al-Sadat — who, in the space of eight years, turned Egypt's foreign policy around 180 degrees, forging an alliance with the United States and a peace with Israel.*

### Sadat's Presidency

*Few foreign observers expected Sadat to be much more than an interim*

733

*president of the most powerful Arab nation or to leave a significant imprint on Egyptian and Middle East history. They were soon proved wrong. On October 6, 1973, Egyptian forces crossed the Suez Canal and marched into the Sinai — an area occupied by Israel since the Arabs' humiliating defeat in the June 1967 Six-Day War. The Israelis, caught unaware while observing the holy day of Yom Kippur, suffered substantial military losses. Although Israel eventually succeeded in turning back its Arab enemies, the Egyptians viewed their initial effort as an indication that Israel's forces were no longer invincible.*

*The 1973 war marked a turning point in the Middle East. In contrast to the 1967 war — when Israel seized, besides the Sinai, Jordan's West Bank and Syria's Golan Heights — the fourth Arab-Israeli war provided Egypt and the other Arab nations with a psychological victory. Sadat's troops established the first Egyptian presence in the Sinai since 1967. The war gave the Egyptian president the national and international prestige to risk better relations with the United States and a peace with Israel at the expense of friction with the Soviet Union and the Arab world. These policies may have been responsible for Sadat's death at the hands of Egyptian Moslem extremists while he was reviewing, ironically, a parade commemorating the 1973 war.*

*It was a combination of external and internal events that jeopardized the Sadat regime. He was an extremely popular leader in the West, especially in the United States. But many persons outside Egypt underestimated the price Sadat paid in his own country for his daring foreign policy initiatives and his failure to solve his country's severe economic problems. His alliance with the United States, his peace with Israel and his disavowal of Nasser's pan-Arab socialism in favor of encouraging foreign — primarily Western — investment were at odds with the Islamic fundamentalist movement that had become a strong force in the Middle East, including Egypt.*

## Reaction to Sadat's Death

*Sadat's isolation in the Arab world was at no time more apparent than in death. Palestinians and Arab hardliners — primarily the Libyans, Syrians, Iraqis and members of the Palestine Liberation Organization (PLO) — took to the streets to rejoice at the death of one whom they considered to be a traitor to the Arab cause. Those demonstrations of joy, shocking to the Western world, were vivid reminders that Arabs had indeed come to view Sadat very differently than did many outside the region. For the Palestinians, Sadat's persistent willingness to negotiate with the Israeli government of Menachem Begin was ample proof of Egypt's "betrayal" of their cause.*

### *Election of Mubarak*

*Following the assassination, Vice President Hosni Mubarak, Sadat's closest adviser, was quickly nominated by the Egyptian parliament as the official National Democratic Party candidate and was elected president exactly one week after Sadat's death. Mubarak was not well known in the West, although U.S. officials considered him energetic, practical and able. He was a participant, along with Nasser and Sadat, in the 1952 coup that overthrew King Farouk. He then rose through the ranks of the military to become commander in chief of the air force. He was appointed vice president by Sadat in 1975. In that capacity he presided over cabinet sessions in Sadat's absence and often acted as his representative in meetings with foreign leaders, including those with U.S. and Israeli officials and members of the Saudi Arabian royal family. He also participated in the Egyptian-Israeli peace talks. It was inconceivable that Sadat would have trusted a man who did not share his views on foreign and domestic issues.*

*Although Mubarak immediately reaffirmed Egypt's commitment to the peace treaty with Israel, it appeared that the new leadership's first priority would be to deal with Egypt's domestic problems. Most observers felt Mubarak would have to appeal to other political groups and accommodate both right-wing and left-wing opposition. And almost certainly he would have to pay more attention to Islamic and Arab sensitivities than did his predecessor.*

*Following are the texts of Egyptian Vice President Hosni Mubarak's announcement of the assassination of President Anwar al-Sadat and the announcement by the Interior Ministry of the imposition of certain restrictions, both October 6, 1981; excerpts from the People's Assembly speech of Deputy Prime Minister Fu'ad Muhyi ad-Din October 7; the October 9 statement from the Defense Ministry on the assassination; and excerpts from an interview with Mubarak by* Al-Ahram, *dated October 22 (Boldface headings in brackets have been added by Congressional Quarterly to highlight the organization of the texts.):*

# MUBARAK ANNOUNCEMENT

In the name of God, the compassionate, the merciful:
To the righteous soul will be said: O (thou) soul, in (complete) rest and satisfaction: come back thou to thy lord, well pleased (thyself), and well-pleasing unto him: Enter thou, then, among my devotees! [Koranic verse] Everything is true which the almighty God says!

I am at a loss for words, and while full of emotion, I announce to the Egyptian nation, to the Arab and Islamic peoples and to the whole world the death of the struggling leader and hero, Anwar as-Sadat.

The leader, to whose love millions of hearts were attached, has been martyred! The hero of war and of peace has been martyred! The man, who had given his nation since his youth his blood, sweat and life has been martyred! The struggler, who had not ceased struggling for a split second for the sake of great principles, sublime values and immortal standards, has been martyred! The leader, who has freed the will of his homeland and who has given his nation an unparalled [sic] glory, was martyred while he was standing aloof, looking at his greatest achievements on the day of the great glory, the glory of October — the symbol of strength and the base of peace!

God almighty has so willed that the leader should be martyred on a day which, in itself, symbolizes the leader. God almighty has also willed that the field in which he fell a martyr should be among his soldiers and heroes and among the millions of sons of the people, while these millions were celebrating with pride the anniversary of the great 10 Ramadan, the anniversary of the day on which dignity and greatness were restored for the Arab nation. This victory was bestowed only by God. It was achieved through the will of the people, through the thinking and decision of the leader and commander, and through the heroism of the armed forces.

## [Future of Egypt]

A sinful and treacherous hand has assassinated the leader. Although we have lost the leader and commander, we derive our consolation from the fact that the whole Egyptian people — in their millions throughout the country, its cities and countryside alike — are now being torn apart by sorrow and pain. The Egyptian people declare that we will proceed on the path charted by the leader and that we will follow your course without deviation, the course of peace, out of our belief that this is the path of righteousness, justice and freedom!

We will proceed on the leader's path, the path of democracy and prosperity.

We tell the leader, while he is with his lord: The people who have believed in your leadership will proceed forward, guided by the beacon of the principles and values which you have entrenched, believing in democracy and the supremacy of the law, and seeking to achieve development and prosperity.

We tell the leader, may God rest his soul: We stand in one united, solid and coherent front around all the banners you have raised.

Oh great people of Egypt, oh peoples of our Arab nation: The calamities of history have accustomed us to reconcile ourselves to the fact that great leaders disappear from the scene of history who, through their struggle, write history's events and chart its course.

We also grew accustomed to dress our wounds, to overcome our pain, to be patient and to believe in the will of God almighty, and to continue the procession with determination and persistence!

Oh great people of Egypt, I announce in the name of the soul of the late great and in the name of the people and their constitutional institutions and armed forces that we will adhere to all the international charters and treaties and commitments signed by Egypt. We will not stop pushing the wheel of peace in fulfillment of the message of the commander and leader.

We will also remember him with all pride when his hope will be achieved; that is, when our flags will be raised all over Sinai, and when comprehensive peace will be achieved on the two sides of the borders in the whole region.

Rest assured, our great leader, Egypt will continue to exist as the state of the institutions, of the supremacy of the law, of stability, of security and peace and of prosperity. The desert will be cultivated and the edifice will rise high and the good and green revolution will be completed! Egypt will continue to raise its head. It will remain immune thanks to the strong arms of its sons and to its army. Egypt will remain dignified through its principles, strong through its authenticity and proud of its history and ancient civilization.

Oh leader and commander: Your people will remember you forever as an epitome of overwhelming heroism of surging dignity and pride, of perspicacity and sound viewpoints and of wisdom and good example. Your people will remember you as an example of nobleness and faithfulness, of ethics and values, of authenticity and sacrifice and redemption. Your people will remember you as an epitome of Egypt's grandeur and glory!

Oh great people, since our Constitution stipulates in Article 84 that when the post of the president of the republic becomes vacant, the presidency is assumed temporarily by the People's Assembly speaker. The People's Assembly announces the vacancy of the post of the president of the republic and a president is chosen within a period not exceeding 60 days. Therefore, the post of the president has been temporarily assumed by Dr. Sufi Hasan Abu Talib, speaker of the People's Assembly.

The People's Assembly has also been summoned for an extraordinary session to be held at noon tomorrow, 7 October 1981, to declare the post of the president of the republic vacant and to begin to take the constitutional measures required for electing the president of the republic.

Oh great people, our leader has fallen in the field of struggle. The best honor we can render him and his noble memory is to cling steadfastly to God's rope, all of us and without allowing our ranks to be divided. We can also honor the leader by continuing to struggle so that Egypt will always be lofty, strong and steadfast, proud and amply dignified!

May God have mercy on the soul of the great and believing leader. May he give the leader abode in paradise with the martyrs and the truthful. May God endow his family, the Egyptian people and Arabism, the Islamic world and the whole world with patience at the loss of a hero of peace and a hero who ranks among the makes [sic] of history.

Long may Egypt live and long may its great people live! Peace be with you.

# GATHERINGS, MARCHES BANNED

With great sadness and sorrow, the Interior Ministry announces that the loss of the departed leader Muhammad Anwar as-Sadat defies all comment and that it is greater than all statements. When realizing the depth of sadness, pain and sorrow of the great, noble and loyal people of Egypt, the Ministry is at the same time fully confident of the vigilance of the masses and their appreciation of the delicacy of the situation through which our dear Egypt is passing and how the enemies lie in wait for it, particularly in such a circumstance. Therefore, the decision to proclaim the state of emergency was issued to defend the homeland and the citizens from any tampering aimed at exploiting this event to disturb the security of the masses and the stability of their internal front.

Whereas the state of emergency bans all gatherings and marches, regardless of their aim or type, instructions have been issued to the police organs to fully implement this. The Ministry urges the citizens to fully abide by this to cut the road before any tamperers. Let us believe in the destiny of the creator who has no lord above him and let us rise with our feelings over the pain in a framework of self-control and the vigilant appreciation of the national interests, which require the maximum degrees of security and stability. We will thus be loyal to the soul of the leader. We implore God to safeguard Egypt from every evil, protect its people and march and compensate it.

# AD-DIN ASSEMBLY SPEECH

In the name of God the compassionate merciful. The medals on his chest were numerous and so we imagined that there was no more room for new medals: The medal of the rule of law, the medal of October, the medal of peace, the medal of liberating the Egyptian will, the medal of justice, the medal of development, and the medal of the 23 July and 15 May Revolutions. We thought that there was no more room for a new medal — that is until yesterday. But he had kept on his chest room for the most sublime medal of all the shining medals, that of a martyr, which he added to his other glorious and lasting medals. He did not die. How could the one who loved Egypt so much die, the one who devoted all his life, all his childhood, youth and manhood to Egypt? It is as fate decreed that he should achieve his most cherished aspiration and so his blood was mixed with Egypt's soil at the moment of his martyrdom. The millions went with him to every place and moved toward him. The millions came to see him from every location. He lived for the sake of Egypt as a revolutionary young man; he was imprisoned, detained and persecuted. How many others have sacrificed as much as Anwar as-Sadat did in his youth? How many of us here in the hall were imprisoned and detained in their youth as

Anwar as-Sadat was imprisoned and detained and his family and children were displaced? How many of us did and sacrificed as much as he did and never retreated, hesitated, or weakened as he never did? He did not retreat one single step in the face of the onslaught of colonialism. As-Sadat never retreated. He remained courageous, standing on his legs challenging and resisting. Even at the moment of his martyrdom yesterday he was killed standing on his own legs. He refused to sit down or to lie down; while those around him pulled him down he remained standing on his own legs and always defiant. This was his nature and instinct. This was the last lesson from Anwar as-Sadat. No more lessons after today, no speeches and no guidance. But he has left constitutional institutes, a mature people, loyal disciples, and noble companions who are capable of carrying on with the march and achieving the hopes and aspirations. He has placed his trust and hopes in you. This was the last lesson and the difficult test for every member of the People's Assembly, the Consultative Council, the government, the party and in every other place.

He often talked to us about 25 April 1982 and how we will celebrate the final withdrawal from the Sinai.... We will celebrate this withdrawal on schedule but the hero will be absent. We will all feel that right has been upheld. We will continue the march. The withdrawal will be completed and we will build Egypt as As-Sadat wanted it. May God bestow mercy upon the president as much as he has given his country, the Arab nation and the whole world....

# DEFENSE MINISTRY STATEMENT

The annual armed forces celebrations marking the anniversary of their victory in the 6 October war included the holding of a big military parade at the parades grounds in An-Nasr City. Symbolic units of the main branches of the armed forces participated in the parade. A few days before the parade, these units assembled in the open air areas near the stadium to prepare for the parade and carry out the necessary rehearsals.

One of the small units, which it was decided would participate in the parade this year, was under the command of first lieutenant named Khalid Ahmad Shawqi al-Islambuli. He is the brother of one of those who were recently arrested and who belonged to the Society of Repudiation and Renunciation [Takfir].

Blinded by black hatred, the aforesaid officer exploited these circumstances and agreed with three misled youths to participate in committing the crime. He provided them with the opportunity of riding with the crew members of the car allocated to him wearing military uniforms. He gave leave to three soldiers who were among the original members of the crew on the morning of the parade, claiming that they were sick. He replaced them with the reservist forces for the parade to complete the crew. It was natural that his partners should get the weapons allocated to the original members of the crew.

In view of the fact that the existing instructions forbid the armed forces participating in military parades from carrying any ammunition to avoid any mistakes, the traitors managed to obtain a quantity of bullets and four offensive and defensive handgrenades ... from sources outside the armed forces.

Just before the unit moved to participate in the military parade column, First Lieutenant Khalid secretly distributed the ammunition and grenades among his partners and kept some for himself.

When the car reached the main reviewing stand, First Lieutenant Khalid ordered the driver to stop. He was sitting next to the driver and he threatened to kill him if he disobeyed. When the driver hesitated, the aforesaid officer pulled the handbrake and the car stopped. He alighted first and was followed by the three others who were riding in the back and who had their weapons with them.

At first everyone thought that the car had developed trouble and that these individuals were going to try to push it forward. However, the traitorous criminals began hurling their bombs and shooting in the direction of the main reviewing stand. The firing continued despite the fact that the president's special guards exchanged fire with them. When the criminals tried to escape, they were arrested after being wounded.

The president and some of those who were in the main reviewing stand were wounded. His excellency was immediately moved by a helicopter to the armed forces hospital in Al-Ma'adi' where his pure soul departed.

The military prosecution is continuing its investigation of the criminals. The public interest dictates that no other information be disclosed now about the perpetrators of the incident.

## INTERVIEW WITH MUBARAK

**Q:** You had previously said that you would not combine the posts of president of the republic and prime minister and that you will make changes in some leading posts. What made you change your mind?

**A:** In my opinion, there is no urgent need for a general, comprehensive change now. A short while ago, we carried out a limited Cabinet reshuffle. I consulted with the late President Anwar as-Sadat on this reshuffle. When I effect a change, there will have to be objective reasons for it. If we take into consideration the surprise of the assassination and the delicate phase we are passing through, then it can be said that we will continue the march. All officials, led by the ministers, are discharging their duties efficiently in light of the directives included in my speech to the People's Assembly.

As for my post as prime minister, while I do not wish to combine the posts of president and prime minister, this will however continue for a while until the circumstances are ripe for the appointment of a prime minister who will assume his full responsibilities and who will be in charge of the executive side.

**Q:** What about the posts of vice president and party leader?

**A:** I am thinking about the question of the party leadership, and I will make a decision on it in the near future. As for choosing a vice president, the importance of the position requires that I give it deep thought so my choice will be sound and enable the highest degree of continuity and commitment.

**Q:** What are the policy lines that you deem it necessary to underscore in the coming phase of domestic work?

**A:** The first priority goes to assurance of security and stability. Security and stability not only because they constitute the main basis of our constructive work to alleviate the sufferings of the masses and achieve development and prosperity for which we are working hard but because they constitute an urgent popular demand; because the masses, appalled by the recent developments and the incidents of violence and terrorism, insist that stability should receive first priority; because they realize that without security and stability the wheel of production will stop and confusion will prevail in the country. The role of the masses here is not merely a role of requesting this but the important role of positive contribution and participation with the government in consolidating security and stability. The aim of the terrorist plan was to seek to carry out a Khomeyni-style revolution that would destroy. The aim was to strike at the leaderships, stop economic progress and abolish liberties. It has been proved that the terrorists were going to carry out repeated waves of terrorism that would have set the social progress we have achieved back many years.

**Q:** Without prejudicing the investigation, does the picture that has taken shape appear very ugly to Your Excellency?

**A:** The picture is indeed extremely ugly, but, thanks be to God, the late President Anwar as-Sadat had made the decision, on which a referendum was held, and it was possible to arrest some of the leaders of the terrorist groups. If it were not for this, the terrorist groups would have succeeded in fulfilling their reactionary designs, and this would have made handling the situation extremely difficult. It would have meant taking massive repressive measures that would not be good to take because they would affect the atmosphere of democracy.

**Q:** If you do not mind postponing discussion of this point a little, I would like to ask you if, as Your Excellency said, security, safety and stability get first priority, what gets second and third priorities?

**A:** The second priority goes to continuing ... to provide housing and food for the people. This is a vital matter and we must do our utmost to accomplish this because it means meeting the basic legitimate needs of the people. We will also give top priority to the services which affect the vast masses. This is our commitment and it stems from our ideology which says development above all means satisfying the basic needs of the vast base of the masses who are working hard with honor and commitment to increase production and boost all forms of progress in society. . . .

**Q:** Directing the economic resolutions and turning the economic openness into production openness and consequently taking into consideration the social cost factor in the openness — taking into consideration the increase in the gap in incomes of the various classes — how would you help the junior officials and persons with limited income and how do we make them benefit from the economic development taking place in society?

**A:** This is a very important question vis-a-vis the economic decisions. We are proceeding along the right path. We have achieved some sort of balance in the payments balance and in the state's budget. We are determined to go ahead with ending the deficit, which leads to the printing of the banknotes, and the inflation, which leads to a rise in the prices and which badly affects the purchase power and standard of living of the people with limited income. However, to maintain this balance, we must increase local production. We cannot continue to depend on imports, because this would disturb the balance of payments and cause inflation and eventually it would lead to a deficit in the budget. This was the vicious circle in which we found ourselves in the past years.

When I speak about the increase in production, I mean increase in the public sector and the private sector as well. Therefore, it is necessary to turn the openness into a production openness. . . . We must embark on production projects and set aside the consumer projects now. For example, we have sufficient gas projects or projects that produce luxury goods. We could reduce them. We want production projects which would benefit the overwhelming majority of the people. We want ready-made clothes and popularly priced refrigerators. I welcome anything which can be produced and be within the means of the man in the street.

I have actually discovered that there are a number of production projects which have been submitted to the investment organization for consideration. I have given my instructions to the ministers concerned to consider these important projects quickly. There is no sense and no justification at all in suspending projects that produce ready-made clothes or food commodities for the people and save us millions of dollars in imports. There is no sense in suspending projects serving housing such as those producing clay and sand bricks to stop agricultural land erosion. I have instructed the ministries to give clear reasons for their rejection of any projects submitted to the investment authority. . . .

**Q:** Once again, we go back to the crime of the assassination. Has it transpired that foreign quarters were behind it?

**A:** Until now the investigation has not revealed that foreign quarters were behind this crime, despite all Sa'd ad-Din ash-Shadhili's claims of responsibility. It is possible for Ash-Shadhili, who has betrayed his country, to betray any regime for which he works. Nor do I want to talk about Ash-Shadhili, because the Egyptian Armed Forces know a great many things about his stances. Other quarters have claimed responsibility for the assassination. As is clear, their objective is clear; they are trying to exploit the obnoxious incident in a cheap way to make mercenary-style profit from the rejectionist states. However, and when it comes to the frail statements which were issued by Ash-Shadhili and his ilk, these statements have been answered by the Egyptian people. Indeed so, because the noble Egyptian people have unanimously determined to continue with the procession and to fill the vacuum within the framework of a scrupulous adherence to constitutional legitimacy. The Egyptian people's determination has enabled the transition of power to take place within a complete democratic framework — as the whole world has unanimously agreed.

**Q:** Since the first moment Your Excellency acceded to power, you have won the support of all the citizens and their appreciation. The reason is that you have emphasized several principal matters; namely, keeping our hands clean, ending corruption, observing discipline in actions and work and increasing production. What are the measures which will be taken to implement these principles through binding rules to be applied to officials of the state's administrative and governmental organs, particularly in the wake of your first meeting with the Cabinet and with the governors?

**A:** There are laws which govern the basic principles which I emphasized in my speech. Therefore, these laws will be implemented to the letter. We will not be lenient with anyone who will commit mistakes; we will not tolerate any kind of indiscipline and deviation and we will not let any trader with the people's livelihood escape from retribution. Nor will there be any room for favoritism. In my speeches to the ministers and to the governors I affirmed that all the citizens stand equal before the law. There will be neither nepotism nor friendship, and neither of these will excuse anyone or allow him to violate the law. Anybody who practices any kind of favoritism will be brought severely to task. Nor will we be lenient with such a person under any circumstances. My speech included all these principles — and I mean every word I said in it. The law will be applied without exception and the phenomena of bribery and of corruption in the government will be combatted. We fear no one and we are apprehensive of no one. Let all the citizens rest assured that our specific and definite policy is that all citizens are equal before the law. . . .

**Q:** The terrorist groups have tried to exploit the purity of the Egyptian youths. What is your policy for a sound national and religious orientation of the youths?

**A:** Devoting attention to the Egyptian youths is one of my major preoccupations. This is because the youths of our country represent an enormous proportion of the Egyptian people. I have admired the articles and the inquiries which you have published in AL-AHRAM and which have dealt accurately with the quality of the problems faced by the youths at this juncture. I am thinking of forming a committee to study this subject as a prelude to the formation of an organ which will work full time to carry out this enormous process. The Egyptian youths need our positive efforts to spare them the uncertainty they might confront. In this respect, the state's responsibility for filling the youths' free time is fundamental. We have set up athletic complexes in As-Salam City — and this is a basic matter which must be taken into account when new cities are planned. Furthermore, it is imperative to expand in the same direction the basis of the services extended in the existing cities.

I want to focus my attention on formulating a plan for the cultural, athletic, social and religious care of youths. A group of enlightened intellectuals should contribute to the laying down of this plan. Furthermore, this plan will furnish the scientific means for confronting social trends of extremism.

**Q:** As Your Excellency has affirmed, seeking to achieve security and stability for the people requires firmness as well as speaking to the people frankly about all the facts. Does Your Excellency believe that the state of emergency law might help achieve security and stability?

**A:** When we proclaimed a state of emergency, our purpose was, in fact, to achieve security for the citizens and for the country. We will never use this law for political or any other objectives — absolutely not. It was necessary to declare a state of emergency to realize stability to confront anarchy and terrorism.

We made announcements about this objective in the wake of the criminal assassination. We will never be lax in implementing the law. I think that this process of achieving security and stability will require several months. If stability occurs expeditiously, and if we wait a while longer to ascertain the restoration of normalcy, then we will rescind the emergency law. However, if we rescind this law, some subversive elements might think that it is possible for them to rock stability again. I expect that, with help from the citizens and with the various organs discharging their duty, stability will be achieved.

We do not want to apply the emergency law just for the sake of applying it. The reason is that we want to see a return to normal life. We also want to tackle the problems which we are facing through a dialogue with our political parties, on condition that achievement of the public interest is the major objective of us all.

**Q:** The public would like to know your stance, views and method on the future of democracy?

**A:** Democracy in Egypt is unavoidable. It will continue and become stronger. At present, however, all the parties must stand together and rise above their differences to serve the general national interests. All must abandon the sterile party and personal views under the present circumstances through which we are passing and which require the highest standard of national vigilance and patriotic unity, because if this does not happen and if the stage is left for the terrorist groups alone, then democracy itself would be in danger. The parties wouldn't have the opportunity to continue to exist and exercise their role in the practice of democracy which we want to stretch and expand to increase popular participation in the management of the country's affairs. Therefore, I expect the political parties to rise above the party differences under the current delicate circumstances through which we are passing, promote the general national interests and help the consolidation of the foundations of security and stability.

Without such a cooperation between the majority and the opposition, the road will be open for the adoption of violent measures against anyone who plays with fire. It will not be lenient with any organization or party that jeopardizes the citizens' security and safety. There will be no hesitation in adopting this method as long as the question is connected with stability in our country. Stability is the sublime aim, and I appeal to our parties to work for its achievement. Let us all agree on the establishment of security and safety and on serving the country's general interests. . . .

**Q:** Concerning the relations with the Arab world, what are the general principles of our policy in this regard?

**A:** There is a general principle which must be fully understood. This principle is that we must not enter into propaganda outbiddings . . . with anyone. Our method must not be one of reaction. There are some newspapers and radios which attack us, but we will never embark on vituperations of this kind. It is our view that we watch what will happen in the Arab world. We will attack nobody and will wait until every side reconsiders its policies. If a state decides on a rapprochement with Egypt, then we will welcome this rapprochement and will act positively to strengthen it. However, we will not answer any vituperations, particularly by the rejectionist states. Yasir 'Arafat, for example, attacks us, but we will not answer him. Syria is also attacking us, and we will not answer it. This is not a weakness on our part, but we prefer not to enter into political outbiddings. It was also the opinion of President as-Sadat, God bless his soul, not to answer, but he decided to answer when their excesses became intolerable.

However, we will not answer this time. In the next few months, we will try to learn what the rejectionist states precisely want. There is no problem between us and the Arab states, but they were the ones to sever their relations with us. The Palestinian question was and will remain one of our primary questions for which we have made and continue to make sacrifices. We have not sold it as they claim. Anyhow, I am convinced that not all the Arab states reject the line we are following. We will have to wait and see, and I hope that all our Arab brothers will reconsider their calculations.

**Q:** Especially that our line has been clearly announced since the beginning?

**A:** Our line is clear, and I said this is my speech. Our international commitments remain valid. We are committed to Camp David and to our treaty with Israel and there will be no going back on this. We will retrieve our territory in April. The peace process is continuing. Our policy toward Israel before and after the withdrawal will not change at all, because this is a political line which we have adopted. It is not possible to change this line because we have committed ourselves to it and we honor our commitments.

We will continue the autonomy discussions and will exert our utmost efforts with Israel and the United States. We have not monopolized the efforts to settle the Palestinian question. Anyone who has a solution to the Palestinian problem, let him present it. We do not claim to be responsible for the Palestinian question and we do not speak in the name of the Palestinians. However, we contribute as much as we can to place the Palestinians at the beginning of the road. It is their right to handle their question by themselves and resolve it the way they want. If they ask us for help, then we will not hesitate in giving this help....

# SAKHAROV HUNGER STRIKE
## October 9, 1981

*Soviet physicist and human rights activist Andrei D. Sakharov an-
nounced October 9 that he and his wife Yelena G. Bonner would begin a
hunger strike on November 22 to demand that the authorities allow their
daughter-in-law to emigrate from the Soviet Union. Sakharov's stepson
Aleksei Semyonov and Yelizaveta Alekseyeva had been married by proxy
during the summer of 1981 in Montana. Semyonov, a graduate student at
Brandeis University in Waltham, Mass., left the Soviet Union in 1978
under pressure from the authorities. Sakharov felt the refusal to grant
Alekseyeva an exit visa was in direct violation of the Helsinki Accord and
was an action intended to punish him for his outspoken stand on
individual freedom and justice.*

*A distinguished nuclear physicist, Sakharov was considered to be the
father of the Soviet hydrogen bomb. He had been a top scientist in the
Soviet nuclear weapons program for two decades until the 1970s. In
recognition of his work he received the Stalin Prize and the Order of
Socialist Labor three times, the highest civilian honor in the Soviet
Union. In 1953, at the age of 32, he was elected a full member of the Soviet Academy of Sciences, the youngest man to have achieved that
distinction.*

## Punishment for Dissent

*But like many scientists involved with weapons development from both
the East and West, Sakharov began to question the ethical issues*

*involved with nuclear weapons and testing. He unsuccessfully appealed to Premier Nikita Khrushchev in the early 1960s to halt large-scale nuclear testing. He increasingly protested Soviet policies and the lack of intellectual freedom. Following the 1968 publication of his manifesto,* Progress, Coexistence, and Intellectual Freedom, *he was discharged from the weapons program, lost his security clearance and was stripped of many honors. His manifesto called for, among other things, an end to the arms race and the gradual convergence of the American and Soviet political systems to meet the problems of the world. From that time, Sakharov developed into a leading moral force in the Soviet human rights movement. He won the Nobel Peace Prize in 1975 in recognition of his efforts.*

*Soviet authorities penalized Sakharov and fellow dissidents for their activities. Scientists Anatoly B. Shcharansky and Yuri F. Orlov, members of the Helsinki Watch Group that monitors human rights violations, were serving long terms in Soviet labor camps. The group was formed following the 1975 signing of the Helsinki Accord by 35 nations, including the Soviet Union. The accord recognized the existence of certain fundamental human rights, including the right to travel and to free associations. As a result of activist pressure, Soviet authorities conducted a massive crackdown on all forms of dissension, sending hundreds of people to prison. After publicly condemning the Soviet invasion of Afghanistan, Sakharov was banished in January 1980 to Gorky, a city 250 miles east of Moscow. In Gorky, which was closed to foreigners, Sakharov and his wife lived in near total isolation. A team of KGB personnel monitored their every move and harassed them in their daily activities. (Historic Documents of 1980, p. 103)*

*Alekseyeva, who served as Sakharov's go-between since his banishment, became the subject of constant harassment for her association with Sakharov and Bonner and was refused permission to emigrate. Sakharov, working on her behalf, appealed directly to President Leonid I. Brezhnev and to fellow members of the Soviet scientific community to intercede. As a last resort, Sakharov and Bonner notified the authorities of their intention to fast until their demands were met. Sakharov wrote his "foreign colleagues" in the West outlining his reasons and beliefs for undertaking the hunger strike.*

## Response to Soviet Stance

*American response to the Soviet authorities' position was significant. President Reagan sent a message to Brezhnev, and 25 prominent American scientists, including 18 Nobel laureates, also sent a letter to the Soviet leader in attempts to persuade him to permit Alekseyeva's emigration. The scientists' letter, published December 1 in* The New York Times, *said, "What possible harm to the Soviet Union could result from this young woman's emigration. We appeal to the Soviet authorities to let her go."*

*The U.S. Senate November 24 adopted a resolution condemning the Sakharovs' "villainous harassment." After 13 days without food, the Sakharovs were forcibly taken to separate hospitals in Gorky where they continued to refuse nourishment. There was growing concern over Sakharov's fragile health.*

*On December 8 Sakharov and Bonner were told that Alekseyeva would be granted permission to leave the Soviet Union and they ended their hunger strike. The government's reversal showed a rare deference to international opinion, and it was seen as an even more unusual reaction to the threats of a political dissident. After visiting Sakharov and Bonner and being assured of their immediate safety, Alekseyeva left for the United States on December 19, 1981. A recuperating Bonner said their success in winning the visa "showed they can do nothing against our truth."*

*Following are the texts of Andrei Sakharov's "Letter to My Foreign Colleagues," dated October 9, 1981, and S Res 246, adopted by the Senate November 24:*

# SAKHAROV LETTER

I am aware of the interest you are taking in my plight and I am deeply grateful for it.

On November 22*, I and my wife Elena Bonner, having despaired to break through the KGB-built wall by any other means, are forced to begin hunger-strike demanding that our daughter-in-law Liza Alekseyeva be allowed to leave the USSR to join our son.

I repeatedly wrote on this matter, now I am telling about it in more detail in the letter to my colleagues, which is enclosed.

## A Letter To My Foreign Colleagues

I have written frequently about my son Alyosha and his wife Liza Alekseyeva. After Alyosha's forced emigration three and a half years ago, Liza became the hostage of my public activity. Violating their own international obligations, the Soviet authorities are not giving her permission to emigrate; they are persecuting her, threatening her with arrest, attempting to deprive her of hope and drive her to despair. In June, 1981, Alyosha and Liza affirmed their fidelity to each other by entering into marriage by proxy in accordance with the laws of the USA (the state of Montana). Although the Soviet authorities do not acknowledge the validity

---

*"November 16" in the original, but later the date was changed.

of such marriage*, it is, in any case, yet another affirmation of Alyosha and Liza's deep desire to be together. According to the Helsinki Accord and other international documents signed by the USSR, such a desire is sufficient grounds for Liza to receive permission to emigrate.

I feel a direct responsibility for Liza and Alyosha's difficult fate and cannot take a calm attitude toward their years of suffering. That suffering has been entirely caused by their nearness to me, their confidence in me when I insisted that Alyosha emigrate thinking that Liza would be able to join him later on. I am ready to take responsibility for my own public and publicistic activities in accordance with the laws of the state and I demand an open trial. To use my son and his wife for revenge and to put pressure on me is unworthy, illegal, and intolerable. There can be no question of any contact with my Soviet colleagues nor of any scientific work while this tragedy of my loved ones continues. It is precisely in this matter that I need help most of all and where, at the same time, such help has the best chance of being meaningful.

Twice I have addressed requests for intervention to the Chairman of the Presidium of the Supreme Soviet, Leonid Brezhnev. In July, 1980 I sent him a telegram and in May, 1981 a letter. Neither my telegram nor my letter was answered. I assume that neither of my requests reached Brezhnev nor even his office but were blocked by the KGB which thought that, having deprived me of my three Hero of Socialist Labor and other awards, the Presidium of the Supreme Soviet of the USSR had, in that fashion, sanctioned any other illegal actions against me. It is precisely for that reason that I am asking my foreign friends to request the officials of their countries, upon contact with Brezhnev and other high-level Soviet leaders, to bring this problem to their attention and to work toward its resolution — this is the only method of breaking the KGB blockade. Unfortunately, I still have no evidence of any efforts in that direction.

A year ago I addressed a request to the President of the Academy of Sciences of the USSR A. Alexandrov and its Vice President E. Velikhov to defend me against hostage-taking, but I received no answer from them just as my repeated letters and telegrams to Velikhov received no answer.

In February, 1981 I wrote to Academician Ya. Zeldovich with whom I was connected by long years of co-work and by, I thought, friendly relations, and to Academician Yu. Khariton, the head of the Institute where I had worked for 18 years. In June, 1981 I addressed the same request for help in Liza's case to Academician P. Kapitsa and to Academician B. Kadomtsev who is working in controlled fusion. Ya. Zeldovich answered with a letter in which he categorically refused to help me,

---

*In fact, there is nothing in the Soviet law that may prevent the authorities from recognizing a proxy marriage. Moreover, according to the Soviet Matrimonial Code (article 32) "marriages between Soviet citizens and foreigners when contracted outside the USSR provided that the formal requirements established by law of the place of such contract are met are recognized as authentic (legal) in the USSR."

referring (I am convinced, without basis) to the shakiness of his own position supposedly revealed by his "not being allowed further than Hungary.*" Zeldovich, an academician, like myself a three-time recipient of the Hero of Socialist Labor award, had (as I did) access to secret information but he was not involved in public or human rights activities. I did not ask him or the other academicians for public actions, only some quiet words. Academicians Yu. Khariton, P. Kapitsa, B. Kadomtsev sent absolutely no replies to my letters. Zeldovich's answer and the position of other Soviet scientists has been a bitter disappointment to me, not only on the personal level but as a manifestation of a pernicious abandoning of responsibility and of the possibility of influencing events (I am not only speaking in connection with myself) and, at the same time, this was not done from considerations of principle but because of shamefully petty reasons.

I feel a wall of misunderstanding, indifference, and passivity around me. The tragedy of Liza and Alyosha continues and perhaps — if nothing changes — will last even longer. In this extreme position, after long and painful reflection, my wife, Elena Bonner, a veteran wounded in the Second World War, and I have made the decision to begin a hunger strike on November 22 to demand that Liza be given permission to emigrate from the USSR. In communicating this decision I hope that you will understand the motives behind this step we are taking, its inner necessity for us in this tragic situation. In the past I have been on hunger strike in support of prisoners of conscience in the USSR**. I consider the defense of our children just as rightful as the defense of other victims of injustice, but in this case it is precisely me and my public activities which have been the cause of human suffering. I also think that this step is a continuation of my many years of speaking out in defense of the right to freely choose one's country of residence, the lack of which in our country leads to many tragedies.

I am counting on your help!

# S RES. 246

Whereas Andrei Dimitriyevich Sakharov has worked tirelessly and courageously for many years to secure basic human freedoms for citizens and residents of the Soviet Union, particularly those rights and freedoms proclaimed and guaranteed by the Final Act of the Conference on Security and Cooperation in Europe, signed at Helsinki, August 1, 1975;

Whereas Andrei Sakharov was awarded the 1975 Nobel Prize for Peace for his love of truth and strong belief in the inviolability of human beings,

---

*Position that a person is holding in the Soviet hierarchy is frequently described in terms of where he is allowed to travel: only inside the country, to Eastern Europe (Hungary, for example), or to "capitalist countries".

**Dr. Sakharov was on hunger-strike in 1973 during President Nixon's visit to Moscow demanding release of V. Bukovsky and other prisoners of conscience.

his courageous defense of the human spirit, and for his role as conscience of mankind;

Whereas Andrei Sakharov has been an eloquent and outspoken champion of dissidents in the Soviet Union who have sought to have their government abide by its formal commitments to protect human rights, and who have suffered at the hands of the Soviet state in consequence;

Whereas Andrei Sakharov has been subjected to villainous harassment, punishment, loss of his livelihood, and acts of physical violence by agents of the Soviet state in retaliation for his activities in defense of human rights;

Whereas the harassment and persecution of Andrei Sakharov by the Soviet state has been aggravated by the refusal of Soviet authorities to allow Yelizaveta Alekseyeva, his stepson's fiancé [sic], to join her intended husband, Aleksei Semyonov, in the United States, in flagrant violation of the Helsinki accords signed by the Soviet Union;

Whereas Andrei Sakharov and his wife Yelena Bonner have announced their intention to commence a hunger strike on Sunday, November 22, 1981, in protest of this refusal by Soviet authorities because in Doctor Sakharov's words, they have found the "exploitation of the fates" of Mr. Semyonov and Miss Alekseyeva "for revenge and pressure against me to be mean, illegal, and intolerable";

Whereas the American people share the outrage of Doctor Sakharov and his wife at this illegal refusal of Soviet authorities to allow Miss Alekseyeva to emigrate; and

Whereas the Government of the Soviet Union is responsible and accountable for the fate of Andrei Sakharov and his wife, Yelena; Now, therefore, be it

*Resolved,* That it is the sense of the Senate that the Congress associates itself fully and completely with the hunger strike protest by Andrei Sakharov and urges the Government of the Soviet Union to abide by its commitments and to permit Yelizaveta Alekseyeva to emigrate.

Sec. 2. The Secretary of State is requested to transmit to the Government of the Soviet Union a copy of this resolution.

# 'PROJECT TRUTH'
## October 15, 1981

*"Project Truth" was introduced by the United States International Communication Agency (ICA) director, Charles Z. Wick, as an effort to counter Soviet propaganda. The project was to include the monthly publication of a "Soviet Propaganda Alert," designed to brief the staff of agency posts abroad on Soviet propaganda activities. The second component of the project, "Dateline America," provided ready answers to the propaganda. Legislation passed in 1947 and 1973 prohibited the distribution of this type of propaganda in the United States, but excerpts from the first alert were read into the* Congressional Record *October 26 and 27 by Rep. Robert H. Michel, R-Ill. Michel said the publication "serves an excellent purpose since it makes us aware of Soviet propaganda devices." But critics of the project expressed concerns that the communications agency would become a propaganda tool of the U.S. government.*

### Soviet 'Disinformation'

*"Project Truth" was created in response to Reagan administration pressure to acknowledge and neutralize Soviet propaganda activities directed against the United States. According to ICA officials the project was intended to provide a rapid and accurate reply service to agency posts abroad to counter propaganda about U.S. activities. Examples of Soviet-initiated "disinformation," defined as the use of false or distorted information to another country's disadvantage, had been released by the State Department October 8. These cases included reports, allegedly originating from Moscow, that linked the U.S. with the seizure of the*

*Grand Mosque in Mecca in 1979 and implicated the Central Intelligence Agency (CIA) with the death of Panama's General Omar Torrijos in August 1981. The State Department later added to its list of Soviet disinformation a forged letter from President Reagan to King Juan Carlos of Spain that contained slurs directed toward certain groups in Spain and other countries. It was speculated that this letter was intended to influence the Spanish parliament's vote on Spain's member-ship in the North Atlantic Treaty Organization (NATO).*

*To minimize the effects of Soviet propaganda, "Project Truth" and its publication, "Soviet Propaganda Alert," intended to reflect a policy of "know your enemy." The publication characterized the themes and techniques used by the Soviets to discredit the United States, including claims that the United States was not seriously interested in arms control and, with its allies, was responsible for most of the terrorist activities in the world. Wick announced that the agency would work closely with the State and Defense departments and the CIA to gather "evidence" for the project.*

## Controversial Policy

*This new undertaking raised serious questions about the agency's independence, especially of the agency's largest operation, the Voice of America (VOA), and of its credibility abroad. Since its inception during World War II, the VOA had withstood White House attempts to direct policy and had continued to broadcast a diverse program of entertain-ment, news and commentary. The medium itself had been the message. There had been, however, increasing pressure to use the VOA more aggressively to promote U.S. policies and interest.*

*Responding to charges that the VOA would become a propaganda tool, its director, James B. Conkling, insisted that the agency would adhere to its charter and remain a non-politicized, non-propaganda organization. In an apparent contradiction to this philosophy, however, Conkling appointed Philip Nicolaides to serve as the VOA coordinator for com-mentary and news analysis. In a September 21 memo Nicolaides had urged that the VOA "reverse the tendency toward mush that flowered in the previous administration" and act as a propaganda agency. Conkling ignored a petition circulated among VOA employees asking him to cancel Nicolaides' appointment; he insisted that he and Nicolaides would abide by their oaths to honor the VOA's charter. Despite this assurance the controversy about the VOA's independence continued. On December 21 Bernard H. Kamenske, news division director, resigned after 26 years with the agency. Kamenske was credited with framing the 1976 charter that sought to guarantee newsroom independence from interference by management.*

*Following is the text of "Soviet Propaganda Alert" No. 1, released by the United States International Communica-*

*tion Agency October 15, 1981.* (Boldface headings in brackets have been added by Congressional Quarterly to highlight the organization of the text.):

# I. [Soviet Propaganda Characteristics]

## A. SOVIET EXTERNAL PROPAGANDA*

Soviet external propaganda has two main purposes:
- To represent the Soviet Union as dedicated to peace and detente, and
- To show the Soviet Union as a just, fair, progressive society, worthy of admiration if not emulation.

For these purposes, Soviet propagandists follow several basic principles. The first of these is a *systematic denigration of the U.S., its culture, political system, and belief structures.* By showing that the U.S. — the acknowledged representative of all things Western — is a doomed, decadent, inherently evil society which opposes all progressive change, Soviet propagandists hope to persuade target audiences that it is not a fit model for their own countries.

The Soviet Union presents itself as the *only* alternative to the U.S. as a system of social organization. *It portrays itself as the near-perfect society.* Armed with an ideology that maintains that the Soviet form of society is the inevitable next step in human development, Soviet propagandists draw invidious comparisons between almost every aspect of American and Soviet life.

Another key feature of Soviet propaganda is the argument that while the U.S. and the West are doomed in historical terms, *the U.S. is all the more dangerous because it will defend its way of life to the end, taking the rest of the world with it to destruction if need be.*

By contrast, *the Soviet Union arms only to defend itself and its allies.* It does this reluctantly because its main goal is to perfect the social, cultural, and economic lives of its citizens; and armaments are a drain on that process.

From these basic principles flow the whole litany of Soviet propaganda and, for that matter, foreign policy:
- Support for "national liberation" movements is justified in terms of putting them on the road to the higher plane of existence enjoyed by the Soviet Union.
- The foreign and domestic policies of Western countries are criticized because they are dedicated to the preservation of the status quo and are opposed to progressive change.

---

* In the Soviet lexicon, the word "propaganda" does not carry the negative connotation that it does in the West.

- Western military measures are portrayed as inherently aggressive because they are directed against the Soviet Union and the progressive principles for which it stands.
- Anti-imperialism (anti-Americanism) is claimed to be good because it represents a movement against the *ancien regime* and toward historical progress. The methods used in the anti-imperialist struggle are sometimes harsh but are justified by the ends.
- The Soviet Union is the natural ally of Third World countries and all others who have freed themselves from imperialism (i.e., Eastern Europe).

## B. SOVIET PROPAGANDA TECHNIQUES

Soviet propagandists employ a vast array of techniques, crude and sophisticated. As well as simply being very good at what they do, Soviet propagandists are not restrained by truth, honesty, and morality; rather, they are guided by a new morality, defined by Lenin as that which serves the good of the Party. Their ideology rationalizes the use of falsehood and deception by promising that the end — the perfect society — justifies all means and that shrinking from the use of all available means constitutes betrayal of the cause.

Soviet propagandists use selective information, half-truths, distortions, and innuendo, as well as outright lies. Many Soviet propagandists (such as Radio Moscow's Vladimir Pozner) have an excellent understanding of the American psyche and take advantage of American feelings about fair play to justify their own actions or call those of the West into question.

A favorite Soviet propaganda technique is *indirection:* an item from a Western or other non-Soviet source is cited in support of the Soviet position on an issue, the item sometimes having been planted by the Soviets. Ironically, the Soviets tend to think sources from the bourgeois West will have the greatest credibility, even among their own population. An alternative form of indirection is the inaccurate citation of a foreign source or the portrayal of the source as broadly representative of the larger society when it is not (i.e., frequent citations from the U.S. Communist Party newspaper, *Daily Worker*).

*Disinformation* is another technique. It is impossible to tell how widespread the practice is because good disinformation is usually not detected. One form of disinformation is the "revelation" of false information (such as a forged U.S. document), preferably in a foreign source that cannot be directly associated with the Soviet Union. Another disinformation technique is to draw attention to past covert actions by U.S. intelligence agencies and then to imply that the attempted assassination of the Pope or the bombings in Iran are similar types of activities. From here it is a short step to the suggestion that the U.S. could have been involved.

A most effective technique is *imputing false motives* to U.S. policy. The Soviets are quick to exploit any opening offered by a U.S. action by pointing out adverse consequences or offensive features to the countries affected. Thus, any U.S. action which can be interpreted to support Israel is portrayed as being anti-Arab in nature. U.S. attempts to achieve "balance" in situations such as the recent South African incursion into ·Angola are dismissed as hypocrisy.

Another technique is *to debase the meaning of words.* Soviet propaganda has succeeded in appropriating the word "socialist" as a synonym for the word "communist," and propagandists seldom refer to themselves or their East European allies as communist countries. In so doing, they acquire at least semantic legitimacy with groups and countries that consider themselves to be socialist but not communist. Perhaps the term most debased is "anti-Soviet": virtually every development in the world is seen as either pro- or anti-Soviet and whatever is not clearly "pro" is immediately labeled "anti." There is also the example of the application of "national liberation movement" to groups which seek the violent over-throw of governments unfriendly or neutral toward the Soviet Union.

*Diversion* is a technique used to blunt attacks on the USSR. When the USSR is criticized, Soviet propaganda responds with a barrage of countercharges, trying to turn the accusation made against the USSR against the accusers themselves. For example, Western charges of Soviet experimentation with biological warfare, arising in connection with the Sverdlovsk anthrax incident, were answered by a Soviet propaganda blitz on *Western* development of biological weapons. Soviet propagandists often concoct even the most absurd accusations in the belief that even these will help distract attention from the charges against the USSR.

This is not to say that everything that Soviet propagandists create is untrue or that Soviets necessarily disbelieve their own arguments even if they appear to be untrue in Western eyes. Because their ideology dictates the "correct" interpretation of most facts, Soviets may often read a vastly different meaning into a situation or action than would their Western counterparts. Over the years, Soviet ideologists have developed an array of philosophical rationalizations that make all Western actions appear to be threatening or malevolent regardless of their objective intent, while all Soviet actions are laudable, no matter how they might appear to the outside observer.

## II. [Current Soviet Propaganda Themes]

This list of current propaganda themes and variations is not exhaustive. Soviet propagandists adjust quickly to changing situations, developing variations on general and constant themes in the Soviet repertoire to suit the needs of the moment. Thus, a general theme (e.g.: "The U.S. is a threat to peace") can be refined to apply to an unlimited range of geographic and situational requirements.

The themes are organized according to their geographic concerns — global, regional, or country-specific — and within these categories according to whether they involve military-strategic matters or seek to contrast the Soviet Union with the United States.

## A. GLOBAL THEMES: MILITARY-STRATEGIC

The aggressiveness of the U.S. as contrasted with the peace-loving nature of the USSR is one of the dominant themes of Soviet propaganda. It encompasses many sub-themes, some of which are discussed below.

According to Soviet propaganda, *the U.S. is escalating the arms race, provoking conflict, and trying to counter every aspect of Soviet influence in the world in its efforts to regain the military-strategic superiority it once possessed.* Aggressive behavior by the U.S. stems largely from its inability and/or unwillingness to adjust to the new "correlation of forces" in the world (the decline of the Western capitalism and the rise of socialism). U.S. frustration at no longer being "number one" is expressed in violence, directed primarily at its chief rival, the Soviet Union.

*The USSR,* on the other hand, has always been and *continues to be dedicated to the struggle for peace. Its military might is intended only to defend itself and other peoples who want and deserve help in defending themselves.* In recent months, the so-called Brezhnev "peace offensive" has been cited repeatedly as testimony to the peace-loving nature of Soviet policy.

While Soviet propaganda always represents U.S. military-strategic aggressiveness as a real and dangerous threat, it also indicates that U.S. actions will ultimately prove futile. For as Marxism-Leninism teaches, the capitalist/imperialist world is doomed, despite its desperate efforts to survive, and socialism — with the USSR its leading representative — is the future. Nonetheless, the forces of socialism cannot wait passively for the collapse of the capitalist world; they must actively counter its "last gasps" of harmful activity.

### Sub-Themes

1. *The U.S. seeks military superiority over the Soviet Union.* The U.S. has lost the military preeminence in the world it enjoyed after World War II when only it possessed nuclear weapons. The U.S. wishes to regain its former position in order to blackmail the Soviet Union and its allies, to force its will upon other countries, and to resist forces of change and progress, especially in the Third World.

2. *The U.S. is not seriously interested in arms control negotiations.* The U.S. strives to create an international atmosphere which is counterproductive to arms talks, it has failed to respond to any of the sincere Soviet initiatives in the sphere of arms control, and it has blocked ongoing efforts such as the MBFR [Mutual and Balanced Force Reduction] talks. Although the American failure to ratify SALT II is no longer a major emphasis, it is still regularly referred to in the context of more general criticisms of U.S. arms control behavior.

3. *The U.S. is introducing sinister new weapons such as the neutron weapon, the Pershing II, the MX, chemical and biological weapons.* In its drive to regain superiority, the U.S. is developing and deploying new weapons systems which endanger the alleged parity that Soviet propagandists maintain now exists between the two countries. The U.S. is willing to use any weapon, including chemical and biological devices which most other countries have outlawed. The U.S. is also developing the space shuttle mainly for military use and is working on killer satellites, particle-beam weapons, and laser applications.

4. *The U.S. is forcing its allies to accept its weapons and to increase their own arms expenditures.* The U.S. blackmails its allies into accepting the placement of weapons (e.g. Pershing II's). Its allies resist because they recognize that the U.S. is trying to export a future war, that is, to ensure that it is not fought on U.S. soil. There is a growing split between the U.S. and its allies.

5. *The U.S. seeks to forge an anti-Soviet alliance with such countries as China, Japan, Pakistan, and Turkey.* The U.S. wants bases for its troops or the right to stockpile military supplies on the soil of other countries. The U.S. uses economic aid, military assistance, weapons sales, or simple blackmail to gain concessions.

6. *The U.S. engages in psychological warfare against the Soviet Union.* It spreads untruths about the USSR through its propaganda activities — especially radio: VOA [Voice of America], RFE [Radio Free Europe], and RL [Radio Liberty] — and foments anti-Soviet hysteria and war mentality. These activities are in violation of basic international agreements such as CSCE [Conference on Security and Cooperation in Europe].

7. *The U.S. wages economic warfare against the USSR.* The U.S. is trying to provoke a costly new round of the arms race that will strain, exhaust and ultimately destroy the Soviet economy. It also uses economic weapons such as the grain embargo to force the Soviet Union to accede to its will. Soviet propagandists always strongly emphasize that the Soviet economy will never be ruined by a forced arms race. Although the Soviet leadership would much prefer to use Soviet resources for improving the people's living conditions, the USSR is certainly capable of keeping pace with U.S. military strength and is determined to do this, even if sacrifices are necessary in other sectors of the economy.

8. *The U.S. grossly interferes in the internal affairs of other countries.* The U.S. seeks to manipulate the domestic political process of other countries, including its allies. It attempts to guarantee that these countries' domestic and foreign policies will be subordinate or at least complementary to its own. The U.S. is willing to use all methods to this end, including propaganda, blackmail, bribery, and assassination. In the case of countries that seek to free themselves of U.S. or colonial domination, the U.S. assists repressive regimes in putting these movements down or sponsors counterrevolutionary activities which will restore the status quo.

9. *The U.S. faces vast resistance to its aggressive plans.* The world public opposes the aggressive plans of the U.S. and its allies. Large-scale resistance is seen in almost all countries. Pacifism and neutralism are growing, especially in those countries most threatened by U.S. plans. Even within the U.S., there is a major split between the Government and the people over defense policy.

10. *The U.S. and allies are responsible for international terrorism.* The U.S., Israel and some of the NATO allies are behind terrorist activity in the world. There is a tradition of terrorism associated with right-wing extremists in the West and the U.S. is a violent, unstable society which spawns terrorist activity.

11. *The CIA [Central Intelligence Agency] is behind much of the unrest in the world.* In its efforts to carry out its policies, the U.S. resorts to all available means. Along with military, economic, and psychological weapons, the U.S. employs the CIA to subvert other countries and to bring their policies in line with its own. It attempts to control other governments through its agents or to destabilize those countries it cannot control. The CIA has unlimited funds and will employ any means to achieve its ends.

12. *The Soviet Union seeks only peace and detente.* Soviet policy is peace-loving and defensive. The USSR has often sought to reach agreement with the U.S. and its allies to reduce tensions, disarm, and engage in peaceful economic and social intercourse. The Soviet Union respects the independence and sovereignty of other countries and does not interfere in their internal affairs. The world public recognizes and appreciates this policy, and regards the Soviet Union as the greatest force for peace on the planet.

13. *The Soviet Union arms only to defend itself and its allies.* The USSR is forced to respond to U.S. and Western threats by building its own forces. These forces are purely defensive, but can be used to defend the gains of socialism and national liberation movements such as in Afghanistan.

14. *The U.S. cannot succeed in gaining military superiority.* The Soviet people are willing to make whatever sacrifices are necessary to provide adequate defense. In spite of the U.S.'s superior resources, it will never be allowed to regain military superiority.

## B. GLOBAL THEMES: U.S. AND USSR
## AS COMPETING SOCIAL MODELS

The propaganda themes listed in this section are meant by the Soviets to show that *the U.S. is an unattractive, vicious, exploitative society which has outlived its time. The Soviet Union is portrayed as the society which has found the answers to the challenges of modern society.* While the Soviet Union is acknowledged to have some problems, these are of a temporary nature and will fade as the society develops.

The Soviets are especially defensive about social and economic comparisons with the U.S. and other Western countries. They react immediately to charges from Western officials which call into question the quality of life in the Soviet Union or challenge the idea that the USSR constitutes a model for future society.

### Sub-Themes

1. *The U.S. slanders the Soviet Union.* U.S. policy is pervasively anti-Soviet. "Bourgeois falsifiers" in the West carry on a relentless campaign of anti-Soviet slander. They slur the Soviet way of life, Soviet reality, nationality relations, foreign policy, economic system, etc. Western "secret services" and their "mouthpieces" and "voices" are in the forefront of this campaign of anti-Sovietism.

2. *The neocolonialist U.S. and its allies are not friends of the Third World.* The U.S. holds up the American system as a model for Third World countries but in fact it is not a fit model. Imitating it means continuing in a mode of colonial-style oppression and injustice. The U.S. supports tyrannical regimes (e.g. Chile, South Africa) if they are pro-West and anti-Soviet, and it opposes national liberation movements. It has no genuine concern for the welfare of the Third World peoples; its main concern is access to resources. American exploitation of Third World takes many forms — economic, cultural, political. For example, U.S. corporations extract profit from the Third World while exploiting their resources; the CIA manipulates foreign regimes by "dirty tricks"; U.S. museums and private collectors steal Latin American artifacts.

3. *The Soviet Union is the natural ally of Third World countries.* Its dedication to the interests of the common people is manifested in its support of national liberation movements. The USSR generously extends opportunities to Third World students to study in the USSR. It unstintingly gives economic assistance for peaceful purposes and sends Soviet technicians and specialists of all kinds to Third World countries to work jointly with the indigenous population on construction and other projects.

4. *The U.S. is an insecure, unstable, inhumane society in a permanent state of crisis.* Its most striking features are:
- High unemployment (especially among blacks).
- Racial discrimination.
- Abject poverty juxtaposed with excessive wealth concentrated in the topmost elite.
- Widespread demoralization as well as material deprivation among the poor, the unemployed, and the otherwise disadvantagd.
- High cost of education, medical care, etc. (access and quality depend upon ability to pay).
- Rampant crime and antisocial behavior (decadence, drugs, and pornography).

- Neglect of and lack of respect for the elderly.
- Widespread worker dissatisfaction (as evidenced by strikes).
- Political prisoners.
- Lack of genuine democracy.

*Note:* While usually less prominent and extensive than propaganda on international issues, propaganda on U.S. internal affairs is nonetheless a staple feature of the Soviet media. Themes are longstanding and change little over time, although treatment and tone vary. Commentary is usually tied to some news event or development in the U.S. which illustrates negative aspects of American society. Soviets do not need to make up stories or "disinformation" although they are not above it. All they must do is give one-sided coverage of issues, drawing from Western press articles and data that show American society in an unfavorable light.

By contrast, Soviet propagandists portray the USSR as having solved or nearly solved most of its problems. Because economic rights (jobs, wages, pensions) are considered to be basic human rights in the Soviet Union, the system is shown to be more humane and dedicated to the welfare of the masses. Social relations are based on equality, antisocial behavior is an aberration, and the people regard the system as fair and just.

5. *The U.S. violates fundamental human rights while accusing others of doing so.* The U.S. hypocritically attacks the Soviet Union for alleged human rights violations, while it is the U.S. that is violating fundamental human rights. The U.S. is interested in human rights only as an issue with which to attack the Soviet Union.

6. *Soviets who fall prey to Western propaganda tend to be unsuccessful and miserable when they emigrate.* Soviet emigres miss their homeland intolerably, regret their decision to emigrate, and are desperate to return to USSR. Their reasons for being disenchanted with life in the West tend to be both economic and "spiritual": difficulty of getting a job commensurate with one's education and experience; unsatisfactory living conditions; feeling out of place in a cold, uncaring, dog-eat-dog, every-man-for-himself capitalist society.

## C. REGIONAL AND COUNTRY THEMES

Many of the global themes previously described appear in Soviet propaganda directed at or concerning specific regions and countries. This section sets out the main lines of propaganda about a few countries and areas.

1. *Poland.* Soviet propaganda accuses outsiders — especially the West and particularly the U.S. — of interfering in internal Polish affairs, stirring up trouble through its radio propaganda (VOA and RFE), and supporting antisocialist elements. Various Polish organizations and individuals have been criticized, but favorite targets are Solidarity, the Committee for the Defense of the Workers (KOR), and groups which allegedly seek to separate Poland from the socialist community or restore capitalism. FRG [West Germany] interference and revanchism is also a recurrent theme.

2. *Afghanistan.* Major emphasis is on the humanitarian, economic, and otherwise peaceful aid rendered by the Soviet Union to Afghanistan. Outsiders, especially the U.S. together with the PRC [Peoples' Republic of China] and Pakistan, are charged with interfering in Afghan affairs and in the Persian Gulf, supporting and encouraging the "bandits" (insurgents) and generally provoking discord and chaos. The CIA is accused of being behind "bandit" activity.

3. *Iran.* The Iranian people are said to have overthrown the oppressive, U.S.-backed regime of the Shah. The U.S. is still trying to regain its previous dominance and is behind attempts to overthrow the revolutionary regime. The U.S. (through the CIA) is responsible for the rash of assassinations of Iranian leaders.

4. *China.* China is accused of taking an uncooperative and hostile stance toward the Soviet Union. It is depicted as conspiring with the U.S. on military and political adventures which threaten the USSR and its allies and endanger peace — for example, in Afghanistan. The point is made, however, that the USSR remains ready to have normal relations with the PRC.

5. *Japan.* Japan is ganging up with China and the U.S. against the Soviet Union. It is making outrageous claims on Soviet territory (the disputed Northern Territories).

6. *Cuba.* Cuba and the USSR are loyal allies. Cuba is the bastion of progressivism and freedom in Latin America. Latin Americans elsewhere seek to follow its example, but are often discouraged or prevented from this by the U.S. (through the CIA) together with its allies. Since Castro took power, the U.S. "special services" have been plotting and conniving against him. The U.S. constantly threatens and provokes Cuba.

7. *El Salvador.* The U.S. is propping up an oppressive, unpopular regime. It has promoted falsehoods about the situation there, bolstered with forged and falsified (by the CIA) documents. The U.S. has made false claims about Soviet clandestine involvement in El Salvador in order to distract attention from its own activities.

8. *South Africa.* South Africa is a racist renegade state which suppresses its national liberation movement with the support if not the assistance of the U.S. Its recent attack on Angola is evidence of its lawless, aggressive nature, and the UN veto is evidence of U.S. support.

9. *Middle East.* The main propaganda target is Israel, which is depicted as the prime military and political threat in the region. Zionism is condemned as a pernicious force and is equated with anti-imperialism [*sic*]. Egypt is another favorite target of Soviet propaganda, with personal attacks often made on President Sadat. The U.S. is criticized for efforts to reach a "separate deal" with Israel and Egypt which is doomed to fail. The U.S. is also charged with general aggressiveness in this area. This is contrasted to the "peace, friendship and cooperation" offered by Soviet Middle East policy. Steadfast Soviet support for the PLO's [Palestine Liberation Organization] cause is reiterated.

10. *Western Europe.* NATO countries are often lumped in with the U.S.

in propaganda on military/strategic themes. On TNF [Theater Nuclear Forces], the U.S. and "some NATO leaders" are the villains, while the European people are generally described as peace-loving. All manifestations of opposition to neutron weapon and other weapons receive heavy play. Disagreements or conflicts between the U.S. and its European allies receive heavy and unbalanced attention from Soviet propagandists. A constant theme is that the U.S. exploits Europe in its (U.S.) anti-Soviet policies and uses heavy pressure in countering European resistance to U.S. domination. Another theme, used mostly in connection with the FRG is the "resurgent neo-Fascism, neo-Nazism" in the West.

## III. A Case Study:
## The Anti-Neutron Weapon Campaign

This section describes a Soviet propaganda campaign on a specific issue to show how propaganda themes and techniques fit together in a concrete situation. The anti-neutron weapon campaign is a major effort, is current, and is typical of Soviet propaganda activity.

The Soviets have mounted an intensive worldwide propaganda offensive against the neutron weapon (ERW) [Enhanced Radiation Weapon] in response to the recent U.S. announcement of plans to put ERW into production. The campaign began immediately after the U.S. announcement on August 6, and it has quickly grown into one of the biggest Soviet propaganda efforts in recent memory.

The Soviets' current themes and techniques are largely reminiscent of those used in their 1977-78 anti-neutron weapon campaign. Some themes, however, are given new or different emphasis, in line with present circumstances.

### ERW IN THE CONTEXT
### OF GENERAL PROPAGANDA THEMES

In addition to targeting the ERW issue directly, Soviet propaganda frequently treats it as one of many elements constituting the most important "general trends" in U.S. nuclear-strategic policy. ERW is almost always brought up in the context of discussions of these broader themes, several of which are listed below:

● The U.S. is initiating a costly new spiral of the arms race. The neutron weapon decision is an obvious component of this. The U.S. hopes to achieve military superiority over the USSR but this is a futile effort. Escalating the arms race can only lead to an ever more dangerous world situation and the peoples of both countries will suffer because the resources needed for butter will go for guns.

● The U.S. is seeking to destabilize the world situation and to take advantage of that instability to intervene in other countries in order to further its own interests. The neutron weapon is linked to other U.S.

military programs and plans geared to this goal. The neutron weapon decision, for example, is tied to U.S. preparations for nuclear aggression in the Persian Gulf-Indian Ocean area; the creation of the "Rapid Deployment Force," in combination with ERW and other things, assumes a "particularly sinister character."

## MAJOR THEMES ON ERW

Most of the Soviet propaganda on ERW interweaves a variety of general (e.g., "The U.S. is not serious about arms control negotiations") and specific themes. The specific themes include:

● The neutron weapon is a new type of weapon, distinct from other weapons; its introduction will significantly disturb the present military parity between the USSR and the U.S.

● By blurring the line between conventional and nuclear-strategic weaponry, the neutron weapon lowers the threshold for nuclear war and makes nuclear war more "thinkable."

● The neutron weapon is a particularly "monstrous" and "barbaric" weapon. That it is designed expressly to destroy living things while leaving inanimate objects and property intact is a clear and horrifying reflection of capitalist/imperialist priorities.

● The U.S. is making "nuclear hostages" of the Western Europeans. In the event of nuclear war, Europeans would become the first victims and many countries would cease to exist.

● It is common knowledge that despite the present U.S. decision to store the weapons on American territory, the neutron weapon is intended primarily for use in Western Europe and deployment of the weapon on European soil can be expected before too long. The U.S. failed to consult with its allies on this decision — although it affects them directly and it continues to "trample callously" on their concerns. The U.S. thus seeks to impose its will on Western Europe regardless of strong opposition at a popular — and even to some extent official — level.

● Worldwide opposition to U.S. introduction of the neutron weapon has been and continues to be fierce. Manifestation of anti-neutron weapon sentiment has been greatest in Europe, but is occurring elsewhere, too, including in the United States. Popular demonstrations have taken place, prominent figures have spoken out, letter-writing campaigns have been conducted, committees have been formed, and other activities against the neutron weapon have been undertaken.

● The neutron weapon decision "complicates" and "puts off" the question of LRTNF [Long Range Theater Nuclear Forces] talks, thus intensifying the overall problem of European security.

● The U.S. argument that the neutron weapon is a defensive, anti-tank weapon, intended to offset Soviet tank strength in Europe, is nonsense. The weapon can be used offensively, for example, to clear the way for invading troops.

• Although the USSR opposes the production of any new types of weapons, it will respond with a "proper counterbalance" to the neutron weapon if the U.S. does not reconsider its decision to produce the weapon. The USSR is prepared to acquire a neutron weapon or whatever is necessary to defend against the American threat.

## TRENDS IN SOVIET ERW PROPAGANDA

Slight shifts in emphases on several themes have been noted recently. Thus far, Soviet propagandists have been concentrating heavily on what the neutron weapon means for Europe. While anti-neutron weapons propaganda is not directed exclusively to a European audience, this is nonetheless the group on which it has a primary and immediate impact.

Now in mid-September [1981] it appears that the Soviets are increasingly stressing the possible opportunities for use of neutron weapons in the Third World — opportunities, they suggest, which the Pentagon is pondering. According to Soviet propagandists, the neutron weapon can be used wherever the U.S. perceives a "sphere of vital interest" — which, it is noted, appears to be anywhere and everywhere. The Persian Gulf is mentioned as one of the most likely locations for U.S. use of the neutron weapons.

Anti-ERW propaganda dealing with the European context has not been decreased, but perhaps an attempt is being made to broaden the appeal of the Soviet campaign and make *everyone* feel more threatened by ERW and thus inclined to protest against it.

There has also been a shift of emphasis away from the theme of "the neutron weapon as an offensive weapon for clearing the way for invading troops." Stress is increasingly being placed on the argument that radiation contamination hazard from the weapon is much longer lasting and more intense than U.S. officials contend. If the Soviets want to play up the latter theme (as they evidently do), they cannot simultaneously charge that the weapon could be used to quickly clear the way for troops to move into or through an area.

There is no indication of a perceptible reduction in the intensity or quantity of anti-ERW propaganda generated by the mass media of the USSR and Soviet bloc countries. Their rhetoric also continues to be harsh.

## TECHNIQUES

The techniques used in the anti-ERW campaign are no different from those commonly used in any Soviet external propaganda activity. Different themes are played up for different audiences, or one theme is treated in a sophisticated or simple manner. Thus a Radio Moscow English broadcast targetted to North America is likely to emphasize the cost of ERW and other weapons to the American public, commenting that it would be better for ordinary American citizens if arms expenditures rather than social programs were cut. Broadcasts to Western Europe, on the other hand, stress U.S. "victimization" of Western Europe and European opposition to ERW.

Various approaches used in the anti-neutron weapon campaign include the following:

• TASS statements and official statements issued by top Soviet officials giving the Soviet position on ERW. As these constitute "news," they are generally reported widely in foreign media.

• Statements issued by prominent Soviet figures in fields such as medicine, science, religion (e.g. the Patriarch of Moscow, the head of the USSR Academy of Sciences). These usually condemn ERW on "humanitarian" grounds.

• Testimony by military experts (Soviet or non-Soviet) on the military characteristics of ERW. This material is often intended to refute American information on the subject. For example, an expert may discuss (in fairly technical terms) how the longterm ERW radiation hazard is much greater than U.S. specialists have disclosed.

• Citation or reproduction of articles, speeches, reports, etc., appearing in non-Soviet, especially Western, mass media which support Soviet anti-ERW themes. References to Western sources to support Soviet positions is very common in Soviet external and internal propaganda. The Soviets may use foreign-originated material to suggest things they prefer not to state directly themselves or consider more credible to audiences if presented in non-Soviet sources. To give one example of Soviet use of foreign media items: Publicity was given to a secret ACDA [Arms Control and Disarmament Agency] study supposedly unearthed by Jack Anderson that "revealed attempts to reassure the U.S. leadership by emphasizing what would remain intact after the use of nuclear weapons." This, according to the Soviets, provided "futher convincing evidence" that the U.S. is preparing for nuclear war.

• Personal attacks on U.S. officials considered responsible for the ERW decision — Secretary [of Defense Caspar W.] Weinberger and Counselor [to the President Edwin] Meese, for example. Their worldview in general and their motives for promoting particular policies are impugned.

# MEXICAN SUMMIT MEETING
## October 22-23, 1981

On October 22 and 23, leaders of 14 developing and eight industrialized nations met in Cancún, Mexico, to discuss the problems of world poverty. The participating developing countries had outlined five areas they wanted to focus on in the conference: cooperation and development; world agriculture and food security; energy; international trade; and monetary and financial questions. No decisions for action had been expected to emerge from the conference and none did. Many of the leaders hoped that the talks would give impetus to global negotiations between industrialized and poor countries at the United Nations on development problems.

The developing countries and some of the industrialized nations had been pushing for negotiations on world economic problems for several years. Those countries hoped to bring about the creation of an organization, such as the United Nations General Assembly, where each member would have a single vote to guide decisions on the world's economy. The United States, Great Britain and West Germany opposed such a body because it could overrule agencies such as the World Bank and the International Monetary Fund, whose decisions were controlled by the industrialized nations.

### Limits on Bureaucracy

President Reagan participated in all four of the general sessions at Cancún and held additional informal sessions with leaders of undevel-

*oped countries. On October 23 Reagan said the United States would approve global negotiations only under certain conditions. "If there are those who by global negotiations mean some gigantic new international bureaucracy to be in charge, that we would be opposed to," the president said. "If global negotiations means that we continue negotiations as to how all of us can help resolve these problems, we're perfectly willing to."*

*The United States also continued to oppose the creation of an energy affiliate for the World Bank. The proposed agency would finance exploration, development and marketing of energy alternatives in developing nations. The U.S. government believed such an affiliate would undercut private enterprise.*

*Private enterprise was at the heart of the Reagan administration's proposals for ending world poverty. A week before the Cancún conference, Reagan had outlined his approach in a speech before the World Affairs Council of Philadelphia. The president said that the United States record of providing food and other aid to developing countries far outshone the Soviet Union's record. He said this demonstrated that the free enterprise system, accompanied by free trade and investment, were the best ways to help developing countries. Despite the lack of definite progress on most substantive issues, Reagan and his aides said they felt that Reagan had won a personal and diplomatic victory in meeting with the world leaders.*

## Origin of Mexican Conference

*The Cancún conference had its beginnings in 1980 when a committee of world leaders led by former West German Chancellor Willy Brandt issued a report endorsing much of the Third World's requests for more economic development aid and a greater voice in operations of the international banks. The committee suggested holding the informal meetings, which were chaired by Mexican President José López Portillo and Canadian Prime Minister Pierre Elliott Trudeau. Other countries taking part were Great Britain, France, Japan, Sweden, West Germany, Austria, China, India, Venezuela, Saudi Arabia, Algeria, Tanzania, the Philippines, Guyana, Nigeria, Yugoslavia, Brazil, Bangladesh and the Ivory Coast. The Soviet Union declined an invitation to attend, claiming that world poverty was the fault of the capitalist countries.*

*The meeting itself took place at a resort hotel off the Yucatan coast of Mexico, where the atmosphere was one of informality and spontaneity. The hotel was reachable by only one road or by boat, limiting public access and assuring better security for the world leaders. Almost 2,000 journalists and 1,500 delegates attended the event.*

*Following are the text of President Reagan's October 22, 1981, statement at the first plenary session of the interna-*

*tional meeting on cooperation and development and excerpts from the summary issued by the co-chairmen, President José López Portillo of Mexico and Prime Minister Pierre Elliott Trudeau of Canada, October 23 at Cancún, Mexico.* (Boldface headings in brackets have been added by Congressional Quarterly to highlight the organization of the text.):

# REAGAN'S OCTOBER 22 STATEMENT

I am honored to be with all of you on this historic occasion.

In many ways, this summit is not ours alone. It belongs to the millions who look to us for help and for hope. If they could speak to us today, I believe they might tell us that words are cheap, that cooperative action is needed — and needed now. In their name, let us join together and move forward. Let us meet the challenge of charting a strategic course for global economic growth and development for all nations.

Each of us comes to Cancun from a different domestic setting, where our major responsibilities are found. My own government has devoted much of the past year to developing a plan of action to strengthen our economy. For years, our government has overspent, overtaxed, and overregulated, causing our growth rates to decline and our inflation and interest rates to rise. We have taken bold measures to correct these problems, and we are confident they will succeed — not tomorrow, nor next week, but over the months and years ahead.

We believe restoring sound economic policies at home represents one of the most important contributions the U.S. can make to greater growth and development abroad. The actions we are taking will renew confidence in the dollar, strengthen our demand for imports, hold down inflation, reduce interest rates and the cost of borrowing, and increase resources for foreign investment.

## [Diversity of Economic Problems]

I have also had a chance to study and discuss with various leaders the domestic problems you face. I know how diverse and serious they are. For the poorest countries, more food and energy are urgently needed, while raising productivity through education, better health and nutrition, and the acquisition of basic facilities such as roads and ports represent longer-term goals.

Middle-income countries need foreign capital, technical assistance, and the development of basic skills to improve their economic climate and credit worthiness in international capital markets. The more advanced developing nations, which already benefit from the international economy, need increasing access to markets to sustain their development.

And across the income spectrum, many among you who are oil importers face acute financial difficulties from the large debt burdens resulting from the oil price shocks of the 1970's. High interest rates are exacerbating these problems, such that debt servicing and energy costs are making excessive claims on your foreign exchange earnings.

We recognize that each nation's approach to development should reflect its own cultural, political, and economic heritage. That is the way it should be. The great thing about our international system is that it respects diversity and promotes creativity. Certain economic factors, of course, apply across cultural and political lines. We are mutually interdependent, but, above all, we are individually responsible.

We must respect both diversity and economic realities when discussing grand ideas. As I said last week in Philadelphia, we do not seek an ideological debate; we seek to build upon what we already know will work.

## [Freedom Key to Growth]

History demonstrates that time and again, in place after place, economic growth and human progress make their greatest strides in countries that encourage economic freedom.

Government has an important role in helping develop a country's economic foundation. But the critical test is whether government is genuinely working to liberate individuals by creating incentives to work, save, invest, and succeed.

Individual farmers, laborers, owners, traders, and managers — they are the heart and soul of development. Trust them. Because whenever they are allowed to create and build, wherever they are given a personal stake in deciding economic policies and benefiting from their success, then societies become more dynamic, prosperous, progressive, and free.

With sound understanding of our domestic freedom and responsibilities, we can construct effective international cooperation. Without it, no amount of international good will and action can produce prosperity.

## [International Economic Institutions]

In examining our collective experience with development, let us remember that international economic institutions have also done much to improve the world economy. Under their auspices, the benefits of international commerce have flowed increasingly to all countries. From 1950 to 1980, GNP [Gross National Product] per capita in 60 middle-income countries increased twice as fast as in the industrial countries when real purchasing power is taken into account.

Despite the mid-seventies recession, we were able to liberalize the international trading system under the leadership of the GATT [General Agreement on Tariffs and Trade]. This created new trading opportunities for a number of developed and developing countries.

The IMF [International Monetary Fund] remains the centerpiece of the international financial system. It has adjusted its programs and increased its resources to deal with the major pressures and problems of our era. The World Bank and other multilateral development banks have dramatically increased their resources and their overall support for development.

Much remains to be done to help low-income countries develop domestic markets and strengthen their exports. We recognize that. But we are just as convinced that the way to do this is not to weaken the very system that has served us well, but to continue working together to make it better.

## [Role of United States]

I am puzzled by suspicions that the U.S. might ignore the developing world. The contribution America has made to development — and will continue to make — is enormous.

We have provided $57 billion to the developing countries, in the last decade — $43 billion in development assistance and $14 billion in contributions to the multilateral development banks. Each year, the U.S. provides more food assistance to developing nations than all other nations combined. Last year, we extended almost twice as much official development assistance as any other nation.

Even more significant is the U.S. contribution in trade. Far too little world attention has been given to the importance of trade as a key to development.

The U.S. absorbs about one-half of all manufactured goods that non-OPEC [Organization of Oil Producing Countries] developing countries export to the industrialized world, even though our market is only one-third the total industrialized world market. Last year alone, we imported $60 billion worth of goods from non-OPEC developing countries. That is more than twice the official development assistance from all OECD [Organization for Economic Cooperation and Development] countries. Our trade and capital markets are among the most open in the world.

The range and breadth of America's commitment extend far beyond concessional assistance. We believe in promoting development by maximizing every asset we have.

As the world's largest single market, we can be a powerful conductor for economic progress and well-being. We come to Cancun offering our hand in friendship as your partner in prosperity. Together, we can identify the roadblocks to development and decide the best ways to stimulate greater growth everywhere we can. We have yet to unleash the full potential for growth in a world of open markets.

The U.S. is here to listen and learn. And when we leave Cancun, our search for progress will continue. The dialog will go on. The bonds of our common resolve will not disappear with our jet trails.

## [Commitment at Ottawa Summit]

We are prepared to carry out the commitment in the Ottawa Summit Declaration to conduct a more formal dialog — bilaterally, with regional groups, in the United Nations, and in specialized international agencies. We take seriously the commitment at Ottawa "to participate in preparations for a mutually acceptable process of global negotiations in circumstances offering the prospects of meaningful progress."

It is our view that "circumstances offering the prospect of meaningful progress" are future talks based upon four essential understandings among the participants:

— The talks should have a practical orientation toward identifying, on a case by case basis, specific potential for or obstacles to development which cooperative efforts may enhance or remove. We will suggest an agenda composed of trade liberalization, energy and food resource development, and improvement in the investment climate.

— The talks should respect the competence, functions, and powers of the specialized international agencies upon which we all depend, with the understanding that the decisions reached by these agencies within respective areas of competence are final. We should not seek to create new institutions.

— The general orientation of the talks must be toward sustaining or achieving greater levels of mutually beneficial international growth and development, taking into account domestic economic policies.

— The talks should take place in an atmosphere of cooperative spirit, similar to that which has brought us together in Cancun, rather than one in which views become polarized and chances for agreement are needlessly sacrificed.

If these understandings are accepted, then the U.S. would be willing to engage in a new preparatory process to see what may be achieved. I suggest that officials of our governments informally confer in the months ahead as to appropriate procedures.

## [Substantive Suggestions]

But our main purpose in coming to Cancun is to focus on specific questions of substance, not procedural matters. In this spirit, we bring a positive program of action for development, concentrated around these principles:

— stimulating international trade by opening up markets, both within individual countries and among countries;

— tailoring particular development strategies to the specific needs and potential of individual countries and regions;

— guiding our assistance toward the development of self-sustaining productive activities, particularly in food and energy;

— improving the climate for private capital flows, particularly private investment; and

— creating a political atmosphere in which practical solutions can move forward, rather than founder on a reef of misguided policies that restrain and interfere with the international marketplace or foster inflation.

In our conversations, we will be elaborating on the specifics of this program. The program deals not in flashy new gimmicks, but in substantive fundamentals with a track record of success. It rests on a coherent view of what's essential to development — namely political freedom and economic opportunity.

Yes, we believe in freedom. We know it works. It's just as exciting, successful, and revolutionary today as it was 200 years ago.

I want to thank our hosts for arranging this historic opportunity. Let us join together and proceed together. Economic development is an exercise in mutual cooperation for the common good. We can and must grasp this opportunity for our people and together take a step for mankind.

# SUMMARY BY CO-CHAIRMEN

... We strongly believe that the very fact that 22 leaders from some of the world's most influential yet diverse countries were prepared to come to Cancún and discuss these issues clearly demonstrated the importance and gravity that they attached to them. The North/South relationship was seen as one of the most serious challenges to be faced in the coming decade, ranking with and linked to the maintenance of world peace, as a priority for the attention of all governments.

The spirit which prevailed among us as we addressed these fundamental issues was extremely constructive and positive. It was clear from the outset that we were not here — indeed we could not be here — to take decisions on behalf of the rest of the world. Our task was rather to bring our voices to bear at the highest level on the fundamental issues, to identify the major problems and to try to evaluate and promote possible solutions.... We believe that together we succeeded in creating a spirit of genuine confidence and trust amongst ourselves.

Our task now will be to ensure that we build upon this trust and understanding, carry this momentum forward into the future and translate thought into action and progress with the aim of revitalizing the world economy and accelerating the development of developing countries. It is in this light that Heads of State and Government were clearly determined to attack the problems on an urgent basis in the international institutions existing for this purpose, and to continue to give their personal attention to this process.

Obviously there were differences of view expressed. Among 22 very diverse nations it could not be expected that interests would be identical or approaches necessarily the same. But what struck us most forcefully were the many areas of shared priorities and of common ground....

## [Interdependence Acknowledged]

All participants recognized the importance of interdependence in terms of the functioning of their economies, reflected in the fact that the economic prosperity of any country or group of countries increasingly depends on the existence of conditions for growth and stability in other nations. They all appreciated that many of the economic problems which beset them individually could only be solved through joint action among states and that in this sense there was a high degree of mutual self-interest involved in promoting closer international cooperation. There was a strongly shared view that in the global community the problems of economic disparities among nations needed to be seen as the reponsibility of all and therefore required concerted action. The view was expressed that, in an increasingly integrated world economy, no country or group can evade their responsibilities. In this respect, regret was voiced about the absence of the Soviet Union from the Meeting.

At the same time the importance of strengthening and increasing the effectiveness of cooperation among developing countries was seen as an element of growing significance in international relations. Many participants regretted the amount of resources devoted to armaments which could be better employed for developmental purposes.

It was recognized that many of the problems were deep and complex and not subject to quick or simplistic solutions. With a long and difficult period ahead, leaders committed themselves to working together to try to build an international economic order in which all states would be able to realize their potential with equal opportunities, and the developing countries in particular would be able to grow and develop according to their own values.

The Heads of State and Government confirmed the desirability of supporting at the United Nations, with a sense of urgency, a consensus to launch Global Negotiations on a basis to be mutually agreed and in circumstances offering the prospect of meaningful progress. Some countries insisted that the competence of the specialized agencies should not be affected.

## [Major Challenges]

With respect to substance we focussed on what we viewed as the major issues and the challenges facing the world economy under the headings of: food security and agricultural development; commodities, trade and industrialization, energy; and monetary and financial issues. Throughout the Meeting the discussion was pragmatic and direct, touching both on broad approaches and frequently on specific details. These discussions make clear the political will of all participants at Cancún to more forward and to take action.

## [FOOD SECURITY AND AGRICULTURE]

Discussions on this topic indicated several general areas of understanding and shared viewpoints regarding the following principal question:

—Persistent and widespresd manifestations of hunger are entirely incompatible with the level of development attained by the world economy and, in particular, with existing food production capacity. Within as brief a period as possible, hunger must be eradicated....

— Sustained and long-term internal effort on the part of the developing countries to attain increasing self-sufficiency in food production is the basic element in obtaining a real answer to the problem of hunger. Nevertheless, this effort requires timely and sufficient international technical and financial support....

— First, developing countries should define and put into operation ... national food strategies covering the entire cycle of food production, productivity, distribution and consumption, that include effective action for rural development, by means of increasing incomes of food producers, which, paradoxically, are the ones most affected by hunger.

— Food aid should be seen as a temporary tool in emergency situations. ... [F]ood aid should not be used as a permanent replacement for the necessary development of the required food production in developing countries themselves.

— The rate of population growth in some countries leads to increases in food demand that are difficult to meet. The experience of a certain number of countries has shown that development of a population policy aids in solving some of the most acute aspects of the food problem.

— The workings of international agricultural and food organizations operating within the framework of the United Nations need to be reviewed in order to avoid duplication of work, to use available resources more effectively and to improve their general efficency....

## COMMODITIES, TRADE AND INDUSTRIALIZATION

Participants addressed a range of problems under this item.

— Noting the slow progress in implementing the UNCTAD [United Nations Conference on Trade and Development] Integrated Program for Commodities, particularly in the negotiation of new commodity agreements, they agreed on the need to complete procedures for bringing the Common Fund into operation. Because earnings from commodity exports are of fundamental importance to the economic growth and stability of developing countries, a range of possible approaches was suggested including more intensive efforts to negotiate effective international agreements to stabilize commodity prices....

— The need to improve the Generalized System of Preferences for developing countries was also recognized, as well as the need for continued efforts on the part of governments to resist protectionist pressures....

— A number of participants referred to the importance of industrialization of developing countries and the contribution which increased trade could make to this objective. Restructuring of developed country industries was identified as being relevant to this objective. . . .

## ENERGY

— It was recognized that energy is one of the key problem areas of the 1980s that must be tackled seriously and urgently. The problem was characterized more as a global one than as purely a North-South issue.

— In order to ensure an orderly transition from the era of hydro-carbons to the era of diversified energy sources, the proposal for a World Energy Plan as a framework providing an overall approach covering this complex process was recalled and interest expressed in it.

— The potential contribution of regional energy cooperation schemes was also pointed out in the discussion.

— It was also recognized that energy conservation must be pursued by major oil-consuming countries. Development of new and renewable sources of energy also required emphasis, as was agreed at the recent Nairobi Conference.

— Emphasized in the discussion was the serious problem developing countries face in meeting their large energy import bills which for many represent a good part of their limited foreign exchange earnings.

— The need for increased energy investment, from both private and official sources, in developing countries was stressed. . . .

## MONETARY AND FINANCIAL ISSUES

— Participants reviewed the financial difficulties being experienced by developing countries with regard to their balance of payments deficits, their debt service burden and their development financing needs.

— They discussed conditions of access by developing countries to the various sources of financing and the role of the relevant multilateral institutions, in particular the International Monetary Fund and the World Bank. . . .

# MEMO ON HUMAN RIGHTS
## October 27, 1981

*The Reagan administration's human rights policy was defined by Deputy Secretary of State William P. Clark in a State Department memorandum October 27, following months of domestic and foreign criticism of the United States' apparent lack of commitment. Approved by Secretary of State Alexander M. Haig Jr., the memorandum emphasized that the United States could not hope to counter Soviet influence around the world without a foreign policy that actively defended and promoted political freedom and civil liberties.*

*The Reagan administration had been criticized for its reluctance to make a forceful human rights commitment. Skeptical of the effectiveness of President Carter's highly visible human rights campaign, Reagan had preferred the practice of "quiet diplomacy." This approach called for encouraging other nations to comply rather than publicly reproaching human rights offenders. Haig echoed this philosophy during his confirmation hearings when he announced the administration's intention of no longer holding authoritarian allies of the United States accountable for their human rights activities. "The assurances of basic human liberties will not be improved by replacing friendly governments which incompletely satisfy our standards of democracy with hostile ones that are even less benign," he said.*

### Controversial Appointment

*The growing human rights debate severely tested administration policy during the confirmation hearings of Ernest W. Lefever for assistant secretary of state for human rights and humanitarian affairs. Lefever and other critics of President Carter's policy, including President Reagan, said that it was necessary to offer support and friendship to potentially friendly regimes, even human rights violators, to help further specific United States interests. Supporters of Lefever's nomination criticized Carter policy decisions that they said ignored abuses in economically vital nations such as Saudi Arabia and other members of OPEC (the Organization of Petroleum Exporting Countries). Rep. Henry J. Hyde, R-Ill., said, "It has been accurately stated that when America develops a car that runs on bananas and not gasoline, we will crack down hard on human rights in the OPEC countries and be far more tolerant of abuses in Central and South America." Lefever's nomination ran into opposition because of his alleged connection with the Nestlé Co. of Switzerland. The Lefever nomination was eventually withdrawn after it was defeated in a Senate Foreign Relations Committee vote. (U.S. vote on infant formula code, p. 447)*

## Place of Human Rights

*The memorandum reflected an apparent shift of administration policy. It suggested that once again the issue of human rights was to have a conspicuous place in U.S. foreign policy. Elliot Abrams, sworn in December 10 as assistant secretary of state for human rights and humanitarian affairs, was to be the human rights spokesman for not only the State Department, but the entire government, including the Pentagon. He was also designated to guide human rights policy for the International Communication Agency (ICA) and U.S. representatives abroad.*

*The central thesis of the Clark memorandum was that the global threat of communism compelled this human rights stand because it "conveys what is ultimately at issue in our contest with the Soviet bloc." To persuade other nations to resist communism or even a passive neutralism, the United States must, said the memo, actively encourage the practice of political and civil freedoms.*

*The statement called for an even-handed approach to countries violating human rights, including friendly nations, but noted that efforts to improve conditions should be acknowledged to encourage further progress. It also emphasized that, in weighing possible retaliatory actions, the United States would balance the human rights violations of a country against other considerations, including U.S. economic and defense interests.*

*The memo also called for turning the annual report, "Country Reports on Human Rights Practices," into a closer reflection of the stated policy goals. The memo called attention to the possible confusion of human liberty with human needs, such as employment and housing, which might imply that governments had equal control over both. The State Department was required by law to prepare the report on human rights conditions in countries that received foreign aid from the United States. The report also included assessments of conditions in all other foreign countries that were members of the United Nations. Preparation of the report was one of the responsibilities of the assistant secretary of state for human rights and humanitarian affairs.* (Human rights report, p. 179)

*Following is the text of the State Department memorandum on human rights policy, prepared by Deputy Secretary of State William P. Clark and Richard T. Kennedy, under secretary of state for management, dated October 27, 1981.* (Boldface headings in brackets have been added by Congressional Quarterly to highlight the organization of the text.):

MEMORANDUM FOR THE SECRETARY:

FROM:      The Deputy Secretary [and]
           Richard T. Kennedy

SUBJECT:   Appointment of Elliott Abrams to Human Rights Bureau and Reinvigoration of Human Rights Policy

This memorandum proposes the appointment of Assistant Secretary Elliott Abrams to head the Human Rights Bureau, and suggests how that announcement might best be handled. It also discusses reinvigoration of the bureau and outlines what we think should be the heart of our human rights policy.

## Human Rights Policy

"Americans don't fight and die for a second car or fancy refrigerator. They will fight for ideas, for the idea of freedom." (Representative Millicent Fenwick.)

*Human rights is at the core of our foreign policy* because it is central to what America is and stands for. "Human rights" is not something we tack on to our foreign policy but is its very purpose: the defense and promotion of freedom in the world. This is *not* merely a rhetorical point: *We will never maintain wide public support for our foreign policy unless we can relate it to American ideals and to the defense of freedom.* Congressional belief that we have no consistent human rights policy threatens to disrupt important foreign policy initiatives. Human rights has been one of the main avenues for domestic attack on the Administration's foreign policy.

### [EAST—WEST RELATIONS]

"Human Rights" — meaning political rights and civil liberties — conveys what is ultimately at issue in our contest with the Soviet bloc. The

781

fundamental distinction is our respective attitudes toward freedom. *Our ability to resist the Soviets around the world depends in part on our ability to draw this distinction and to persuade others of it.*

*Neutralism* abroad and a sagging domestic spirit partially are caused by fear of Soviet military might and our perceived inability or lack of desire to resist it. Perhaps even a more significant cause lies in the notion of "relativism" — why arm, and why fight, if the two superpowers are morally equal? *Our human rights policy must be at the center of our response. Our audience is not only at home but in Western Europe and Japan and among electorates elsewhere.* We must continue to draw the central distinction in international politics between free nations and those that are not free. *To fail at this will ultimately mean failure in staving off movement toward neutralism in many parts of the West.* That is why a credible U.S. policy in this area is so vitally important. Overall U.S. foreign policy, based on a strong human rights policy, will be perceived as a positive force for freedom and decency.

## IMPLEMENTATION

We recommend a two-track policy, positive as well as negative, to guide our rhetoric and our policy choices. *On the positive track we should take the offensive:*

● Expounding our beliefs and affirmatively opposing the U.S.S.R. in the U.N., C.S.C.E [Conference on Security and Cooperation in Europe] and other bodies.

● Hitting hard at abuses of freedom and decency.

● Reinforcing international moral and legal standards, including strong responses to outrages against diplomats and acts of terrorism.

● Maintaining our reputation as a reliable partner for our friends so as to maximize the influence of our quiet diplomacy.

On the *negative track, we must reconsider our relations in light of serious abuses.* However, the human rights element in making decisions affecting bilateral relations must be balanced against U.S. economic, security, and other interests. We must take into account the pressures a regime faces and the nature of its enemies. This policy must be applied evenhandedly. *If a nation, friendly or not, abridges freedom, we should acknowledge it, stating that we regret and oppose it.* However, our response or retaliatory actions should result from a balancing of all pertinent interests. *Human rights is not advanced by replacing a bad regime with a worse one,* or a corrupt dictator with a zealous Communist politburo.

In practice, we must, for instance, abstain from supporting or vote against friendly countries in the M.D.B.'s [multilateral development banks] on human rights grounds if their conduct merits it. We should, however, motivate improvement in human rights by voting "yes" when there has been substantial progress. In highly controversial areas such as crime control equipment, we should not issue licenses in questionable cases. The cost for such a decision would be minimal — this equipment is readily available from other sources. Thus, our decision will not damage another nation's security. On the other hand, failure to make such a decision would undercut our human rights policy.

## DEALING WITH THE SOVIETS

*We must also be prepared to give human rights considerations serious weight in our dealings with the Soviet Union.* The Soviets are a special case, for they are the major threat to liberty in the world. Human rights *must* be central to our assault against them, if we are to rally Americans and foreigners to resist Soviet blandishments or fight Soviet aggression. We must raise human rights issues in our discussions with the Soviets. In forums such as the UN, we must address the Soviets' abuses of freedom and liberty. With Soviet or Soviet-sponsored invasions in Afghanistan and Kampuchea under attack in the UN, with Poles demanding political freedom, now is the time to press the issue of Soviet human rights violations.

Any significant improvement in U.S.-Soviet relations *must* include demonstrable Soviet movement toward greater freedom. We may want to use the means of quiet diplomacy but we must not neglect the goal. For example, this Administration might possibly seek the repeal of the Jackson-Vanik Amendment. Abrams has made clear that he could only support such an effort in the context of the sort of agreement reached between Jackson [Sen. Henry M. Jackson, D-Wash.] and Kissinger [former Secretary of State Henry A. Kissinger] in 1975. To seek repeal without such an agreement would, in his view, make a mockery of our human rights policy by condoning the actions of a major human rights offender.

## COSTS OF IMPLEMENTATION

*A human rights policy means trouble,* for it means hard choices which may adversely affect certain bilateral relations. At the very least, we will have to speak honestly about our friends' human rights violations and justify any decision wherein other considerations (economic, military, etc.) are determinative. There is no escaping this without destroying the credibility of our policy, for otherwise we would be simply coddling friends and criticizing foes. Despite the costs of such a human rights policy, *it is essential.* While we need a military response to the Soviets to reassure our friends and allies, we also need an ideological response. Our struggle is for political liberty. We seek to improve human rights performance whenever we reasonably can. We desire to demonstrate, by acting to defend liberty and identifying its enemies, that the difference between East and West is the crucial political distinction of our times.

# Reinvigorating the HA Bureau

We recommend that the stated human rights policy be implemented through these proposals:

1. *Appoint Elliott Abrams as Assistant Secretary* [for Human Rights and Humanitarian Affairs]. Abrams has run IO [International Organization Affairs] well and has proven he can administer a bureau. His status and track record as an Assistant Secretary will help at confirmation hearings, as will his former association with Senators Jackson and Moynihan [Sen. Daniel Patrick Moynihan, D-N.Y.]. At IO, Abrams has overseen the UN Human Rights Commission and has become familiar with human rights issues. Abrams must be afforded the opportunity to appoint three new DASs [deputy assistant secretaries] and make other personnel changes, if he finds it necessary. We have promised him our help in implementing personnel changes as fast as possible and in persuading FSOs [foreign service officers] to join this bureau. To have HA successfully wage the "battle of ideas," internal restructuring may be necessary, as may be addition of a *Public Affairs Office* to the bureau. We have told Abrams we will look sympathetically at reasonable requests for specific new positions.

We attach draft statements by you and the President announcing Abrams' appointment. This indication of high level support will help launch our new policy successful [*sic*]: We believe it essential that you or the President give a major human rights address to an appropriate audience within a few months.

2. *Name of the Bureau.* We propose the name of the HA Bureau remain as it is, so that we not create needless controversy which might even harm our nominee and undercut our policy. However, we should move away from "human rights" as a term, and begin to speak of "individual rights," "political rights" and "civil liberties." We can move on a name change at another time.

3. *Policy Management.* A new Assistant Secretary will need credibility before Congress and the public in stating, when necessary, that human rights issues have been raised at the highest levels. He should therefore be able to raise particularly crucial issues with you. The usual reporting relationship will be to the Deputy Secretary.

In addition, as to interagency coordination, Judge Clark [William P. Clark] should be named to head the Interagency Group on Human Rights and Foreign Assistance, for this will lend additional credibility to our policy. HA should be designated the lead agency on human rights not only for the Department but also for the government, with a specific role providing policy guidance on human rights issues to ICA [International Communication Agency] and to all U.S. representatives to international organizations such as the UN and the MDBs. HA should also be able, with proper approval, to involve other governmental agencies in implementing human rights policies — for example, by using Defense Attachés in some cases as part of our "quiet diplomacy."

4. *Integration of HA into the Department.* The Assistant Secretary must be able to fully integrate the bureau into the work of the Department. Thus he must be permitted to participate in preparation for bilaterals, so that he has the opportunity to argue for placing human rights matters on the agenda, and he must have full access to records of bilaterals, in order to monitor pressure and progress on human rights issues. In addition, HA should have access to intelligence information, and have ability to task the intelligence community. Exposure of human rights violations — such as photos of Vietnamese prison camps — could, for instance, be an extremely valuable foreign policy tool.

5. *Country Reports.* We propose that Country Reports be turned to our policy goals. Our reports should (a) be objective; (b) weigh not only the concerned government's conduct, but also its human rights record and orientation of opposition within the country; (c) look not only at individual cases of human rights violations but also at long term structural questions, so as to give perspective to discussions of communist versus noncommunist dictatorships; and (d) avoid describing human needs (jobs, housing) as "rights," which both confuses the issue of liberty with that of wealth and implies that government has an equally central role in both.

▼▼▼

# SENATE APPROVAL OF AWACS SALE TO SAUDI ARABIA

## October 28, 1981

*On October 28 President Reagan narrowly won his first major foreign policy test in Congress when the Senate refused by a dramatic 48-52 vote to disapprove the sale of five AWACS (advanced warning and control system) airplanes and other air defense equipment to Saudi Arabia.*

*The AWACS radar surveillance planes, designed to provide early warning of air attacks, also were equipped with advanced computer systems to guide F-15 fighter planes and their missiles to their targets.*

*The $8.5 billion arms package also included tanker planes, fuel tanks and highly sophisticated AIM-9L air-to-air missiles for 60 F-15 fighter planes that Congress agreed to sell the Saudis in 1978 after a similar fight with the Carter administration.*

*Israel strongly opposed the AWACS sale, viewing it as a threat to Israeli air superiority in the region. The American Jewish community campaigned strongly against it, and many members of Congress joined in opposition to the sale. Many feared that the Saudis might not be able to prevent the AWACS secrets from falling into unfriendly hands.*

### Senate Vote

*The debate and subsequent vote on the sale drew national attention because it became a test of Reagan's personal powers of persuasion. Fifty senators — one fewer than the majority needed to block the sale — had cosponsored the resolution of disapproval. The House had voted 301-111*

787

*on October 14 to disapprove the sale. Since disapproval required action by both houses of Congress, Reagan concentrated his efforts on the Republican-dominated Senate. In the end, Reagan won by persuading seven first-term GOP senators among those cosponsors to switch their positions.*

*Reagan won the issue after he put his personal prestige on the line, arguing that a congressional veto would impair his ability to conduct foreign policy. Saudi Arabia had presented the arms sale as a test of U.S.-Saudi relations; Reagan emphasized that point by saying the AWACS sale had become the most visible symbol of his efforts to promote a Mideast strategic consensus against the Soviet Union.*

## U.S.-Israeli Relations

*The sale left a bitter taste in the mouths of some of Israel's closest supporters in Congress, and it contributed to a deterioration of relations between the United States and Israel. This decline was exacerbated by Israel's December 14 annexation of the Golan Heights, formerly held by Syria. Israel's action led to the cancellation of a memorandum of understanding on strategic cooperation for the Middle East between the United States and Israel.* (Israeli annexation of the Golan Heights, p. 899)

> *Following are excerpts from remarks to the Senate by Minority Leader Robert C. Byrd, D-W.Va., October 21, 1981; the text of President Reagan's letter to Senate Majority Leader Howard H. Baker Jr., R-Tenn.; excerpts from Reagan's remarks to the press and a statement by Israeli Ambassador Ephraim Evron, all October 28.* (Boldface headings in brackets have been added by Congressional Quarterly to highlight the organization of the texts.):

# SEN. BYRD'S SPEECH

... In my view, there is only one issue involved in a matter of this importance, and that is whether or not it will serve the interests of the United States.

The overarching question which should guide our discussion is this: What is the best course for America to steer toward a lasting peace in the Middle East? That must be the top priority; for, without peace, other long-term goals in that region will never be achieved.

It is apparent at the outset that the proposed sale of sophisticated aircraft and the associated equipment and weaponry is but a subsidiary piece of what must be a broader policy determination by this Government. And it is precisely because a coherent policy framework for the United States in the Middle East has not yet been developed by this administration, that the decision on AWACS has been so difficult for me and many of my colleagues. In deciding the merits of this relatively narrow question — the sale some 4 years hence of 5 AWACS aircraft as well as enhancements for fighter planes already agreed to — we have had to extend ourselves into presumptions, hypothetical scenarios, and guesswork about the sale's impact on the deeper currents running in the politics of the Middle East.

These calculations unfortunately lack the perspective which a larger policy framework would lend to them. The crying need today is for action on the larger issues which are burning for resolution in that tragic region.

From the outset, the issue of AWACS sales to Saudi Arabia unfortunately has been politicized, affording little opportunity to weigh the merits of the case. Issues peripheral to the debate have come to dominate the headlines, obscuring deep concerns that I, and many of my colleagues, have regarding the sale.

## [AWACS Not a Threat to Israel]

For example, some have expressed concern that the AWACS technology could be used to give the Saudis a capability of offensive action against Israel.

However, the administration has addressed this issue in some detail, and I am generally satisfied that the assurances we have received from the Saudis, as well as the continued close cooperation in the use and maintenance of the aircraft and our complete commitment to Israel's security, minimize this danger.

The existence of a Saudi AWACS will not significantly alter the balance of air forces vis-a-vis the Israelis. Even if the Saudis were to attempt to use AWACS in a war against Israel, according to a staff study by the Senate Committee on Foreign Relations, they would probably not succeed, and the costs to the Saudis would be very high. . . .

It should also be observed that earlier this year the Saudis used their influence, through quiet diplomacy, to help secure a reduction in tensions in Lebanon. Indeed, our envoy in the Lebanese situation, Mr. Philip Habib, has stated that the Saudi influence in the Lebanese situation was essential to the cease-fire agreement in the country.

Another hypothetical situation put forward by some analysts is a possible Saudi attempt to link up with Syrian and Jordanian command centers in a coordinated attack. The Saudis have agreed, however, according to the administration, that no Saudi AWACS-gathered information will be shared with third countries or parties without prior mutual consent of the United States. . . .

I think it is important to underscore, forcefully, the following points. The vote on this issue is not a test of the United States-Saudi relationship, as some would have it, or a test of the United States-Israeli relationship, as others would have it. This is not a test between the Prime Minister of Israel and the President of the United States as to who will call the shots in our foreign policy. These are peripheral issues which obscure and obfuscate the fundamental concerns which Congress must address in arriving at a decision on this matter.

## [Need for Middle East Policy]

The real issue is that the Congress of the United States is being called upon to acquiesce in a major foreign policy decision impacting upon a vital, but highly volatile, region of the world. We are being called upon to make such a decision in the absence of a clearly defined or workable policy for the Middle East on the part of the administration.

In attempting to arrive at a prudent decision on this matter, all we are given by the administration is some vague notion that it is important for the U.S. to forge a "strategic consensus" in that region. It is upon this fragile reed alone that the administration predicates its foreign policy in the Middle East. Somehow, in the absence of addressing directly the potentially explosive Arab-Israeli issues, the administration hopes to bring the adversaries in the region together in some loose strategic alliance to counter the threat of the Soviet Union and her proxies.

However, the Middle East peace process must be brought back to the forefront of our policy, and significant progress demonstrated for any strategic consensus on the Soviet threat to be viable. At present, in light of the assassination of President Sadat, I do not know where events will lead us in the Middle East, but I am deeply concerned.

Mr. President, I have no idea what the administration is doing relative to the Middle East. In the absence of a coherent policy, the administration has reacted with a series of ad hoc and ill-conceived responses to events rooted primarily in the Arab-Israeli dispute and not the Soviet threat. As a consequence, these responses have been contradictory and have served to undermine our fundamental goal in the region — and that fundamental goal is the promotion of peace and stability

The administration's actions toward Mr. Begin have, in my judgment, already given him too little incentive to pursue Camp David. To his credit, Mr. Begin has committed his government to complete the total withdrawal of Israeli forces from the Sinai scheduled for next April. But much more is to be expected of Mr. Begin. Mr. Begin has been given a large historic opportunity — it is to replace Mr. Sadat as the key architect of peace at this juncture. Surely no one is more aware of this than Mr. Begin himself. He is capable of exhibiting great political courage in this matter, and the circumstances demand nothing less.

## [Arab-Israeli Dispute]

The central issue for American policy in the Middle East is the Arab-Israeli dispute, and not the Soviet threat to the region. This is not to say that there is not a Soviet threat. Soviet influences, direct and indirect, are a primary and destructive force throughout the region.

The Soviets, through their proxies and clients in the Yemens, Ethiopia, Libya, Iraq, Syria, and elsewhere, are promoting instabilities which could be a primary cause of a major war there. The American answer can only partly be the arming of our friends, for this does nothing to resolve the central irritation — which is the Arab-Israel dispute. We must take immediate action to settle the issues in that dispute, including the breathing of new life into the Camp David peace process as well as broadening that process to include a resolution of the Palestinian question. The fundamental questions of the status of the West Bank and Jerusalem, the future of the Palestinians, and the right of Israel to live in recognized, secure borders are the paramount issues, and they will not go away.

The administration has expended most of its time and capital to date in attempting to build an anti-Soviet strategic consensus among our friends — including the Israelis, Egyptians, Saudis, the Gulf States, and Jordan. Yet, such a consensus would only be viable if the Arab-Israeli issues are resolved. In resolving them, a strategic consensus would become viable. If there is no progress in resolving them, it would seem impossible to develop such a regional consensus.

The Egyptians and Israelis took the initiative to reopen the autonomy talks on the West Bank and Gaza which were called for in the Camp David accords. The United States did not throw its prestige and creativity into those talks. It should have done so....

## [Three Policy Principles]

Mr. President, there are three fundamental principles upon which our policy toward the Middle East should be based.

First, our commitment to the security of Israel is, and always should be, unwavering and uncompromising.

Second, in light of the importance of Persian Gulf oil to the industrial health of the West, and in recognition of the strategic geography of the Persian Gulf, it is important this this region be secured against any threat.

And third, we should immediately begin refocusing on the Arab-Israeli peace process since it is the major obstacle to the administration's ability to forge a strategic consensus in response to the Soviet threat and represents the most immediate threat to stability in the region.

## [Three Concerns]

Within this framework, I would like to address three of the principal concerns I have regarding this sale.

First, we are transferring highly sophisticated technology which, if compromised, could be of significant benefit to the Soviet AWACS program. This should be as much an issue of sovereignty for the United States as it is for Saudi Arabia.

Second, we are launching an ever-escalating round of sophisticated weapons transfers to a highly volatile region of the world in which the primary focus of concern for the countries in the region remains the Arab-Israeli conflict, not the Soviet threat....

And third, we have all but abandoned the Camp David process, leaving the future of the Egypt-Israeli peace treaty uncertain at best....

## [Arms Race in Middle East]

I am concerned that in light of the irresolution of the Palestinian issue, we will be precipitating another escalation in the arms race in the Middle East. Will we be faced with annual litmus tests? We hear that the Saudis "consider this as the litmus test." Well, are we going to be faced with annual litmus tests on the part of the Saudis and the Israelis?

What will be the next test? More F-15's and F-16's for Israel to counter the perceived threat posed by the Saudis? In the case of the Saudis, will we be confronted in the coming years with an AWACS enhancement with top-of-the-line equipment available to make jamming impossible — more missiles, planes and other armaments to deal with whom they perceive to be the primary threat in the region — Israel?

As long as the Arab-Israeli dispute is pushed into the background, this sale does not make any sense. Rather than contributing to stability in the region, I fear it will only raise the threshold of tension. I am concerned that we are fast approaching the point where we are handing over grenades to potential adversaries in the region with the pins already pulled.

## [Israel's Resolve]

As demonstrated by the raid on the Iraqi nuclear reactor, the Israelis have made it very clear that they will strike any perceived or potential threat to their security. If the level of tension should reach a crisis point, such as direct armed conflict with Syria, I think any strategic planner would have to calculate that the Saudi Air Force and AWACS would be one of the first targets....

I would now like to turn to my final area of concern. The administration reasons that once this package is approved, then we can begin focusing our attention on resolving the Arab-Israeli dispute. This is like putting the cart before the horse. As events this year in the Middle East have demonstrated, this is a very risky path down which to proceed. The track record has not been good on such intractable problems as the West Bank or the future status of Jerusalem.

My concern is what happens if the administration is wrong. What if there is no further progress on a comprehensive peace in the Middle East? Where will that leave Jordan, one of our closest allies in the Arab world for the past 25 years, whose King was [sic] given up on any prospects for meaningful negotiations on the West Bank? Will more weapons be the answer as one country continues to play us, the United States, off against another? How will we then extricate ourselves from demands for more and more sophisticated weapons and yet preserve stability in the region? It is time for some creative thinking to take place as to how we get the peace talks back on track. . . .

# REAGAN LETTER TO BAKER

On October 1, 1981, I formally notified the Congress of our intention to sell AWACS aircraft and F-15 enhancement items to Saudi Arabia. This sale will enhance our vital national security interests by contributing directly to the stability and security of the critical area from the Persian Gulf through the Middle East to North Africa. It will improve significantly the capability of Saudi Arabia and the United States to defend the oilfields and facilities on which the security of the Free World depends, and it will pose no realistic threat to Israel.

When this proposed sale was first announced last spring, the Congress expressed concerns about certain aspects of the sale. After analyzing these concerns in detail, we entered into a series of discussions with the Government of Saudi Arabia over the summer.

The Government of Saudi Arabia has agreed, and I am convinced welcomes the fact, that the United States will have an important, long-term role and will maintain direct involvement in the development of the Saudi air defense system, including the AWACS. We also have reached agreement with the Saudi Government on a number of specific arrangements that go well beyond their firm agreement to abide fully by all the standard terms of the normal Letter of Offer and Acceptance as required by the Arms Export Control Act.

Transfer of the AWACS will take place only on terms and conditions consistent with the Act and only after the Congress has received in writing a Presidential certification, containing agreements with Saudi Arabia, that the following conditions have been met:

## 1. Security of Technology

A. That a detailed plan for the security of equipment, technology, information, and supporting documentation has been agreed to by the United States and Saudi Arabia and is in place; and

B. The security provisions are no less stringent than measures employed by the U.S. for protection and control of its equipment of like kind outside the continental U.S.; and

C. The U.S. has the right of continual on-site inspection and surveillance by U.S. personnel of security arrangements for all operations during the useful life of the AWACS. It is further provided that security arrangements will be supplemented by additional U.S. personnel if it is deemed necessary by the two parties;

D. Saudi Arabia will not permit citizens of third nations either to perform maintenance on the AWACS or to modify any such equipment without prior, explicit mutual consent of the two governments; and

E. Computer software, as designated by the U.S. Government, will remain the property of the USG.

## 2. Access to Information

That Saudi Arabia has agreed to share with the United States continuously and completely the information that it acquires from use of the AWACS.

## 3. Control Over Third-Country Participation

A. That Saudi Arabia has agreed not to share access to AWACS equipment, technology, documentation, or any information developed from such equipment or technology with any nation other than the U.S. without the prior, explicit mutual consent of both governments; and

B. There are in place adequate and effective procedures requiring the screening and security clearance of citizens of Saudi Arabia and that only cleared Saudi citizens and cleared U.S. nationals will have access to AWACS equipment, technology, or documentation, or information derived therefrom, without the prior, explicit mutual consent of the two governments.

## 4. AWACS Flight Operations

That the Saudi AWACS will be operated solely within the boundaries of Saudi Arabia, except with the prior, explicit mutual consent of the two governments, and solely for defensive purposes as defined by the United States, in order to maintain security and regional stability.

## 5. Command Structure

That agreements as they concern organizational command and control structure for the operation of AWACS are of such a nature to guarantee that the commitments above will be honored.

## 6. Regional Peace and Security

That the sale contributes directly to the stability and security of the area, enhances the atmosphere and prospects for progress toward peace, and that initiatives toward the peaceful resolution of disputes in the region have either been successfully completed or that significant progress toward that goal has been accomplished with the substantial assistance of Saudi Arabia.

The agreements we have reached with Saudi Arabia on security of technology, access to information, control over third-country participation, and AWACS flight operations will be incorporated into the U.S./Saudi General Security of Military Information Agreement, the Letters of Offer and Acceptance (the government-to-government sales contracts), and related documents. These documents will stipulate that the sale will be cancelled and that no equipment or services will be delivered in the event any of the agreements is breached. I will not authorize U.S. approval of any of these contracts and agreements until I am satisfied that they incorporate fully the provisions that satisfy the concerns that you and I share. I do not foresee any need for changes in these arrangements, but should circumstances arise that might require such changes, they would be made only with Congressional participation.

## [U.S. ROLE IN AWACS PROGRAM]

I believe it is important to look beyond these agreements to their practical consequences, and to the implications of U.S. security assistance and training requested by Saudi Arabia. For example, the agreement we have reached with the Saudi Government to protect the security of equipment also affects the nature, extent, and duration of the U.S. role in the AWACS program. Since skilled Saudi personnel available for this program will remain in short supply, the U.S./Saudi agreement that third-country nationals will not be permitted to operate or maintain the Saudi AWACS will, in practice, extend U.S. involvement in Saudi AWACS operations and activities well into the 1990s. U.S. military and contractor personnel will be required to provide extensive operational training for Saudi AWACS aircrews; it will be 1990 at the earliest before the eight Saudi crews needed to operate all five AWACS aircraft will be trained, and replacement and refresher training of individual Saudi crew members will require USAF Technical Assistance Field Teams during the 1990s. Critical AWACS maintenance, logistics, and support functions, particularly radar and computer software support, will, of necessity, be performed by U.S. personnel in Saudi Arabia and in the United States, for the life of the AWACS.

The Saudi agreement not to share AWACS-gathered information with third countries also has significant practical consequences. This agreement, combined with the standard requirement that U.S.-supplied equipment be used solely for defensive purposes, as well as the agreed-to Saudi AWACS configuration, precludes any possibility that Saudi AWACS could contribute to coordinated operations with other countries' armed forces against any nation in the region without our consent and cooperation.

## [AREA OF OPERATION]

Concerning the agreement to operate AWACS only inside the Kingdom, it should also be noted that the Saudi Air Force will be trained to operate the AWACS in accordance with standard USAF AWACS doctrine and procedures, which call for AWACS to remain at all times a "safe distance" behind sensitive political borders — normally 100 to 150 nautical miles — to ensure AWACS security and survivability. Given the physical location of the oilfields AWACS is to defend, the vulnerability of AWACS should it operate near sensitive borders, and the history of Saudi observance of U.S. Air Force tactical doctrine, we are confident that the Saudis will adopt these practices.

### [IMPROVED COOPERATION]

In a broader sense, by enhancing the perception of the United States as a reliable security partner, we improve the prospects for closer cooperation between ourselves and the Saudi Government in working toward our common goal of a just and lasting peace in the region. Since assuming the responsibilities of the Presidency, I have been impressed by the increasingly constructive policy of Saudi Arabia in advancing the prospects for peace and stability in the Middle East. The Saudi Government's critical contribution to securing a ceasefire in Lebanon is a striking example. I am persuaded that this growing Saudi influence is vital to the eventual settlement of the differences that continue to divide Israel and most of the Arab world.

### [SECURITY OF ISRAEL]

I am confident that the Saudi AWACS will pose no realistic threat to Israel. I remain fully committed to protecting Israel's security and to preserving Israel's ability to defend against any combination of potentially hostile forces in the region. We will continue to make available to Israel the military equipment it requires to defend its land and people, with due consideration to the presence of AWACS in Saudi Arabia. We have also embarked on a program of closer security cooperation with Israel. This proposed sale to Saudi Arabia neither casts doubt on our commitment, nor compromises Israeli security.

It is my view that the agreements we have reached with the Government of Saudi Arabia take account of the concerns raised by the Congress. I am persuaded, as I believe the Congress will be, that the proposed Saudi air defense enhancement package makes an invaluable contribution to the national security interests of the United States, by improving both our strategic posture and the prospects for peace in the Middle East. I look forward to continuing to work with you toward these vital goals.

Sincerely,

Ronald Reagan

# REAGAN PRESS CONFERENCE

I want to express my gratitude to the members of the United States Senate for their approval of the sale of the AWACS defense system to

Saudi Arabia. Today I think we've seen the upper chamber at its best. The United States Senate has acted with statesmanship, with foresight, and with courage.

I can't fully express my gratitude to Senator Baker and the other Senate leaders, Democrats as well as Republicans, who played such a crucial role in this decision.

Today's action by the Senate will not only strengthen Saudi-American relations but will also protect our economic lifeline to the Middle East, win favor among moderate Arab nations, and most important, continue the difficult but steady progress toward peace and stability in the Middle East.

We've acted in concert to demonstrate that the United States is indeed a reliable security partner. Our friends should realize that steadfastness to purpose is a hallmark of American foreign policy, while those who would create instability in this region should note that the forces of moderation have our unequivocal support in deterring aggression.

This vote alone doesn't mean that our security problems in that part of the world have been completely solved. This package is but a part of our overall regional security strategy. Our strategy seeks to enhance the capacity of friendly states to defend themselves and to improve our own ability to project our own forces into the region should deterrence fail. We'll continue to pursue efforts in both areas.

Our support for the security of Israel is, of course, undiminished by today's vote. The United States will maintain its unshakeable commitment to the security and welfare of the State of Israel, recognizing that a strong Israel is essential to our basic goals in that area.

Much work still remains ahead. I trust that all of us who disagreed openly and vigorously in recent days can now put aside our honest differences and work together for common goals — friendship, security, and peace at last in the cradle of our civilization. Because of actions like to-day's by the Senate, the cause of peace is again on the march in the Middle East. For this, all of us can be grateful.

**Q.** When did you know that you had won?

**A.** When they came in and handed me the votes.

**Q.** Didn't you know earlier today that you could count it up?

**A.** A little while ago, this afternoon, I felt the count was — that at least we were going to be assured of a tie. And that would have been a victory, because it required a majority vote to stop this.

**Q.** Do you think this will be an inducement to get the Saudis into the Middle East peace process now?

**A.** Yes, I do. I think that, as a matter of fact, the Saudis have shown by their own introduction of a peace proposal that they are willing to discuss pease in the Middle East.

**Q.** With Egypt and Isreal?

**A.** Yes, they submitted a plan. We couldn't agree with all the points, nor could the Israelis, but it was the first time that they had recognized Israel as a nation, and it's a beginning point for negotiations. . . .

**Q.** What aspect of what you told the Senators did you think was the convincing aspect, and what final thing do you think turned the tide in the last few days?

**A.** Well, contrary to some of the things that have been said, there have been no deals made. None were offered. I talked strictly on the merits of the proposal. And basically I tried to point out, in every instance, the progress that has been made so far in the Middle East towards stability and peace and the part that was played in that by Saudi Arabia and Prince Fahd, beginning with the cease-fire in Lebanon, in which they played a major role. And I simply played on that; that this, I felt, was essential for the security of Israel, for the entire Middle East, and for ourselves on the world scene....

## EVRON STATEMENT

The unique and close friendship between the U.S. and Israel transcends any temporary disagreements between us.

Our two countries have the same basic objectives, namely: We both seek peace with security for Israel and her neighbors and we share commitments to the implementation of the Camp David accords. Israel also shares the U.S. concern with regard to the interests of the free world.

Only a strong and secure Israel makes peace and stability in the area achievable. President Reagan, whose friendship for Israel is deeply appreciated by its people, has committed the U.S. to maintaining the military strength and qualitative edge of Israel's defense capability. We trust that in view of the massive flow of sophisticated weaponry to Arab countries hostile to Israel, this commitment will be acted upon.

# OPEC PRICE CUT
## October 29, 1981

*At one time considered an invincible economic cartel, the Organization of Petroleum Exporting Countries (OPEC) bowed in 1981 to supply and demand, the traditional economic forces that it once so successfully had exploited. Reacting to declining world oil demand, increased production in other countries and use of alternative energy sources, the 13-member organization announced two price cuts during the year.*

*Representatives of the OPEC nations met four times during 1981. For most of the year OPEC was plagued with an internal split over pricing policy, which also had divided the cartel during 1980. Market prices for crude oil varied from $32 in Saudi Arabia to $41 in the more militant countries of Libya and Nigeria. The moderate Saudis, concerned over the impact of continued price hikes on Western economies and future oil demand, wanted a unified price of $34 a barrel. The OPEC nations charging higher prices balked.* (Historic Documents of 1980, p. 995)

*Two meetings, a regularly scheduled session in May and a special conclave in August, failed to produce a compromise, and some Western analysts said that OPEC might be near collapse. But on October 29, at an emergency meeting in Geneva, the attending oil ministers accepted the Saudi position, setting the price of a barrel of crude oil at $34 through at least the end of 1982 for the cartel's 13 members: Algeria, Ecuador, Gabon, Indonesia, Iran, Iraq, Kuwait, Libya, Nigeria, Qatar, Saudi Arabia, United Arab Emirates and Venezuela.*

### Increased Production by Saudis

*In an apparent effort to force lower prices, the Saudis deliberately had increased production in the latter part of 1980 and into 1981, thus maintaining the oversupply of oil already clogging world markets. After the October meeting Saudi Arabia scaled back production to 8.5 million barrels daily from 10.5 million. Sheik Ahmed Zaki Yamani, the Saudi oil minister, said his country's output was likely to stay at that level unless "market situations force it down."*

*In a regularly scheduled meeting held December 9-12, 1981, in Abu Dhabi, United Arab Emirates, OPEC announced its second price cut, to take effect January 1, 1982. Unlike the earlier cut in the base price, the second reductions were in the so-called differentials that allowed OPEC members to add to or subtract from the base price for oil, to reflect quality and market proximity. The cut averaged out to less than half a cent a gallon on all OPEC oil.*

## Oil Glut

*By 1981 the world appeared to have developed a means to limit OPEC's oil power. As early as 1973, the group's price hikes contributed to the economic recession and high inflation that had plagued so many countries, including the United States. The price of oil continued to increase throughout the decade — by more than 150 percent in 1979-80. Finally, world demand for oil began to slip.*

*Total U.S. oil consumption dropped by about 8 percent in 1980 to 16.9 million barrels per day (bpd), and this trend continued in 1981. In 1979 consumption had averaged 18.4 million barrels daily; in 1978, 18.8 million. The International Energy Agency in Paris estimated oil consumption in the non-communist world in the second quarter of 1981 would average 46.1 million bpd, compared to 49.4 million bpd in 1980. Countries also began to look elsewhere — to Mexico, the North Sea, Angola, Canada, Malaysia and other areas — for their oil supplies.*

*By April 1981 U.S. oil imports had fallen by 23 percent from the previous April, the lowest average monthly level since 1973. And imports for the month represented only 35 percent of U.S. domestic consumption compared to 45 percent for all of 1979.*

*Meanwhile, oil production by OPEC members in 1981 declined to 20 million bpd — the lowest average daily rate since 1960 — from 31 million bpd in 1979. Between 1973 and 1980 the OPEC share of total world oil production declined to 43.6 percent from 55 percent, with the Middle East members of OPEC slipping from 41.1 percent in 1973 to 33.6 percent in 1980.*

*Throughout 1981 economists were talking about an oil "glut" of between 1 and 3 million barrels daily, although few would predict how long the oversupply would last.*

*Following are excerpts from the communiqué issued October 29, 1981, at the conclusion of the OPEC ministerial meeting*

*in Geneva, Switzerland, as published by* The New York
Times:

The 61st (extraordinary) meeting of the conference of the Organization
of Petroleum Exporting Countries was held in Geneva, Switzerland, on
Oct. 29, 1981. The president of the 60th meeting of the conference, H. E.
Dr. Subroto, Minister of Mines and Energy of Indonesia and head of its
delegation, presided over the meeting.

The conference, after examining the prevailing conditions in the oil
market, and recognizing the necessity to adopt a unified pricing system for
OPEC crudes in order to create the right conditions for stability in that
market, has resolved to set the official price of the marker crude —
Arabian light 34 degrees API F.O.B. Ras Tanura — at $34 per barrel,
effective not later than Nov. 1, 1981, and to abide by that price until the
end of 1982.

The conference has also agreed to a set of value differentials for the
pricing of all other OPEC crudes in accordance with their respective
qualities and geographical locations.

The conference is aware that this decision will have an evident positive
effect over the economy of the world through an organization of the oil
market which, in turn, will contribute also to the consolidation of OPEC as
the main hydrocarbon supplier to the international market, thus maintaining its relevance as an energy source.

In compliance with its decision taken at the 60th meeting of the
conference in May 1981, the conference has decided that the ministerial
committee on long-term strategy will continue its work and report to the
conference in its next ordinary meeting, to be held in Abu Dhabi, United
Arab Emirates, in December this year.

The conference expressed its sincere gratitude to the Federal Government of Switzerland and the Republic of Canton of Geneva for their warm
hospitality and the excellent arrangements made for the meeting.

# ATTORNEY GENERAL ON JUDICIAL ACTIVISM
## October 29, 1981

*In a speech October 29 Attorney General William French Smith outlined the Justice Department's plans to reduce policy making by federal courts. Smith delivered his remarks to the Federal Legal Council, a group of top lawyers in federal departments and agencies.*

*Smith criticized the extent to which federal courts have engaged in judicial policy making, and he stated that the Justice Department would "attempt to reverse this unhealthy flow of power from the state and federal legislatures to federal courts." This philosophy of reducing the role of federal courts was in keeping with President Reagan's plan to return as much government responsibility to the states as possible; Smith made it clear that the Justice Department intended "to play an active role in effecting the principles upon which Ronald Reagan campaigned."*

*Because federal judges are appointed to the bench for life, they are not as susceptible to prevailing political forces as are elected officials. Yet "basic changes in public sentiment can still portend judicial philosophy," Smith declared, and noting a "groundswell of conservatism" in the country, he concluded the time was right to try to limit judicial activism.*

## Three Areas of Concern

*Smith focused on three areas of judicial decision making that particularly concerned the administration: justiciability, equal protection and mandatory injunctions. Applying justiciability to determine whether a court should actually hear a case would limit the kinds of cases brought to court. Federal courts should apply these doctrines more stringently, Smith argued, so as not to overstep their proper bounds into areas better handled by the legislative branch.*

*Similarly, federal courts should not employ the law of equal protection expansively, Smith stated, nor should they make decisions that are constitutionally assigned to the other branches of government. Smith also criticized the courts' use of their remedial powers — especially mandatory injunctions — by which they instruct the parties before them on the actions they must take. Federal courts should spend their time adjudicating rather than administrating, he maintained.*

*Perhaps by design, the particular doctrines that Smith addressed pertain to the three primary components of any case: the court's power to hear the case, the court's decision on the merits of the case, and the remedy the court prescribes if a violation is found. Clearly the administration believed greater judicial restraint was needed at the most fundamental levels.*

## Separation of Powers

*In attacking the "intrusions upon the legislative domain" by federal courts, Smith mentioned several areas in which he believed they had violated the constitutional concept of separation of powers. These areas included environmental protection, abortion rights, school busing, employment quotas, rights of aliens, prison systems and public housing. All were controversial social issues, and Smith was careful not to attack specific decisions. Instead he chastized the courts more generally for becoming administrators in situations for which they did not have proper resources or expertise.*

*Smith did imply, however, that because the administration believed judicial remedies had failed in cases of school busing and employment quotas, the Justice Department would not bring such suits to court during the Reagan administration.*

## Defense of Justice Department

*Turning from criticism of the courts, Smith addressed criticism of his own department. As if to answer complaints by conservatives that the Reagan Justice Department was still enforcing liberal laws of the previous administration, Smith explained that it was the Justice Department's duty to enforce the laws on the books — "even those with which the administration does not agree." "If we were to do less," Smith declared, "we would ourselves be guilty of the same kind of transgressions that I have pledged we would combat on the part of the Judiciary."*

*Smith's speech drew criticism from some public interest groups who accused him of urging the courts to follow the conservative 1980 election results. The attorney general rejected these charges, defending his remarks as commentary on the proper role of federal courts.*

*Following are excerpts from Attorney General William French Smith's speech to the Federal Legal Council October 29, 1981.* (Boldface headings in brackets have been added by Congressional Quarterly to highlight the organization of the text.):

. . . [C]onsistent with the Constitution and the laws of the United States, the Department of Justice intends to play an active role in effecting the principles upon which Ronald Reagan campaigned.

Already, there have been many significant changes. We have proposed a comprehensive crime package of more than 150 administrative and legislative initiatives that would help to redress the imbalance between the forces of law and the forces of lawlessness. We have proposed a new approach to immigration and refugee policy designed to reassert control over our own borders. We have brought the Government's antitrust policies back to the real economic world by focusing upon truly anticompetitive activities rather than outmoded and exotic theories. We have firmly enforced the law that forbids federal employees from striking. We have opposed the distortion of the meaning of equal protection by courts that mandate counterproductive busing and quotas. We have helped to select appointees to the federal bench who understand the meaning of judicial restraint.

## ['Groundswell of Conservatism']

As significant as all these changes are, however, they represent only a beginning. Today, I will discuss the next stage in this process. We intend, in a comprehensive way, to identify those principles that we will urge upon the federal courts. And we intend to identify the cases in which to make our arguments — all the way to the Supreme Court. We believe that the groundswell of conservatism evidenced by the 1980 election makes this an especially appropriate time to urge upon the courts more principled bases that would diminish judicial activism. History teaches us that the courts are not unaffected by major public change in political attitudes. As the great jurist Benjamin Cardozo once wrote: "The great tides and currents which engulf the rest of men do not turn aside in their course and pass the judges by." . . .

Federal judges . . . remain free from direct popular control. Nevertheless, basic changes in public sentiment can still portend changing judicial philosophy. Various doubts about past conclusions have already been expressed in Supreme Court opinions, concurrences, and dissents — which makes the next few years inviting ones to urge modifications upon that Court and other federal courts.

We intend to do exactly that. Solicitor General Rex Lee is already working with our Assistant Attorneys General to identify those key areas in which the courts might be convinced to desist from actual policy-making. In some areas, what we consider errors of the past might be corrected. In other areas, past trends might at least be halted and new approaches substituted. Today, I want to outline some of those areas upon which we are focusing.

## [Judicial Policy Making]

It is clear that between *Allgeyer* v. *Louisiana* in 1897 and *Nebbia* v. *New York* in 1934 the Supreme Court engaged in — and fostered — judicial policy-making under the guise of substantive due process. During this period, the Court weighted the balance in favor of individual interests against the decisions of state and federal legislatures. Using the due process clauses, unelected judges substituted their own policy preferences for the determinations of the public's elected representatives.

In recent decades, at the behest of private litigants and even the Executive Branch itself, federal courts have engaged in a similar kind of judicial policy-making. In the future, the Justice Department will focus upon the doctrines that have led to the courts' activism. We will attempt to reverse this unhealthy flow of power from state and federal legislatures to federal courts — and the concomitant flow of power from state and local governments to the federal level.

Three areas of judicial policy-making are of particular concern. First, the erosion of restraint in considerations of justiciability. Second, some of the standards by which state and federal statutes have been declared unconstitutional — and, in particular, some of the analysis of so-called "fundamental rights" and "suspect classifications." And third, the extravagant use of mandatory injunctions and remedial decrees.

## [Justiciability]

Article III of the Constitution limits the jurisdiction of the federal courts to the consideration of cases or controversies properly brought before them. Nevertheless, in recent years, a weakening of the courts' resolve to abide by the case or controversy requirement has allowed them greater power of review over government action. Often, the federal government itself has in the past moved courts to show less deference to the boundaries of justiciability — in particular, in environmental litigation. The Justice Department will henceforth show a more responsible concern for such questions. We will assert the doctrine in those situations that involve any of its four elements — standing, ripeness, mootness, and presence of a political question. Vindicating the principle of justiciability would help return the courts to a more principled deference to the actions of the elected branches.

Like the concept of judicial restraint itself, the constitutional requirement of justiciability limits the permissible reach of the courts irrespective of the desirability of reaching the underlying legal issues involved. The doctrine of justiciability therefore limits the possibility of judicial encroachment upon the responsibilities of the other branches or the states — even in those situations when the other branches or level of government has chosen not to act. Some responsibilities are entrusted solely to nonjudicial processes. In those instances, we intend to urge the judicial forebearance envisioned by the Constitution.

## ['Fundamental' Rights]

Just as courts have sometimes overstepped the proper bounds of justiciability, their analyses of equal protection issues have often trespassed upon responsibilities our constitutional system entrusted to legislatures. Through their determination of so-called "fundamental rights" and "suspect classifications," courts have sometimes succeeded in weighting the balance against proper legislative action.

In the 1942 case of *Skinner* v. *Oklahoma*, the Supreme Court first emphasized the concept of fundamental rights that invites courts to undertake a stricter scrutiny of the inherently legislative task of line-drawing. In the nearly forty years since then, the number of rights labeled "fundamental" by the courts has multiplied. They now include the first amendment rights and the right to vote in most elections — rights mentioned in the Constitution. In addition, however, they include rights that — though deemed fundamental — were held to be only implied by the Constitution. The latter group — which has become a real base for expanding federal court activity — includes the right to marry, the right to procreate, the right of interstate travel, and the right of sexual privacy that, among other things, may have spawned a right — with certain limitations — to have an abortion.

We do not disagree with the results in all of these cases. We do, however, believe that the application of these principles has led to some constitutionally dubious and unwise intrusions upon the legislative domain. The very arbitrariness with which some rights have been discerned and preferred, while others have not, reveals a process of subjective judicial policy-making as opposed to reasoned legal interpretation.

At the very least, this multiplication of implied constitutional rights — and the unbounded strict scrutiny they produce — has gone far enough. We will resist expansion. And, in some cases, we will seek to modify the use of these categories as a touchstone that almost inevitably results in the invalidation of legislative determinations. We will seek to modify especially the application of a strict scrutiny to issues whose very nature requires the resources of a legislature to resolve.

## [Suspect Classifications]

We shall also contest any expansion of the list of suspect classifications, which, once established by a court, almost inevitably result in the overturning of legislative judgments. Thus far, the Supreme Court has employed a strict-scrutiny test when legislative classifications turn upon race, national origin, or, in many instances, alienage. In addition, when classifications are based upon sex or legitimacy, the Court has on occasion conceived and applied a middle test somewhere between the special strict-scrutiny test and the normal rational-basis test.

Already, some limitations have been forged in the Supreme Court to temper these analyses of suspect and quasi-suspect classifications — for example, in the case of alienage. The Department of Justice will encourage further refinement in these areas — in particular, by resisting increase in the number of suspect or quasi-suspect classifications and by tempering the strictness of the analysis applied to classifications based upon alienage. Throughout, as with the so-called fundamental rights, we shall be guided by the principle that legislatures, rather than courts, are better suited both constitutionally and practically to make certain kinds of complex policy determinations. We shall, however, remain vigilant to the Civil War Amendments' *explicit* concern over classifications based on race.

## [Use of Judicial Power]

The extent to which the federal courts have inappropriately entered legislative terrain can be seen most clearly — and felt — in their use of mandatory injunctions and attempts to fashion inequitable remedies for perceived violations. Throughout history, the equitable powers of courts have normally reached only those situations a court can effectively remedy. Implicit within that historical limitation is the recognition that some kinds of remedial efforts require resources and expertise beyond those of a federal court — even one aided by special masters.

Nevertheless, federal courts have attempted to restructure entire school systems in desegregation cases — and to maintain continuing review over basic administrative decisions. They have asserted similar control over entire prison systems and public housing projects. They have restructured the employment criteria to be used by American business and government — even to the extent of mandating numerical results based upon race or gender. No area seems immune from judicial administration. At least one federal judge had even attempted to administer a local sewer system.

In the area of equitable remedies, it seems clear that federal courts have gone far beyond their abilities. In so doing, they have forced major reallocations of governmental resources — often with no concern for budgetary limits and the dislocations that inevitably result from the limited judicial perspective.

In many of these cases, the Department will also seek to ensure better responses to the problems at issue by the more appropriate levels and branches of government. We have already begun that process in the case of busing and quotas, both of which have largely failed as judicial remedies.

Thus far, I have discussed some of those things that the Department of Justice *will do* to further the goals of this Administration. Through legislation and litigation, we will attempt to effect the goals I have outlined. There are, however, some things that we *cannot — and will not — do*.

## [Role of Executive Branch]

Throughout my remarks today, I have emphasized the importance of judicial restraint to the constitutional principle of separation of powers. The Constitution confides certain powers in the Legislative Branch and not in the Judicial Branch. In a similar fashion, the Constitution delineates the proper domain of the Executive and Legislative functions. The Constitution directs the President to ensure the faithful execution of the laws, which forms the basis of the Attorney General's litigating authority for the government as a whole. That constitutional command also requires the Executive Branch to defend measures duly enacted by the Congress — even those with which the Administration does not agree.

Statutes with which we disagree are nevertheless the law of the land. As such, they must be defended against attack in the courts. They must also be fully enforced by the Executive Branch when their validity and meaning are clear. Some have suggested that this Administration intends to do less. Other have suggested that this Administration should do less.

In fact, the Department of Justice intends to do exactly what the Constitution requires — to enforce the laws duly and constitutionally enacted by the Congress. If we were to do less, we would ourselves be guilty of the same kind of transgressions that I have pledged we would combat on the part of the Judiciary. Under the Constitution, the Executive cannot unilaterally alter the clear enactments of Congress any more than the courts can. When it disagrees with a law, the Executive Branch can urge and support changes by the Congress. In the case of laws that are clearly and indefensibly unconstitutional, the Executive can refuse to enforce them and urge invalidation by the Courts. When reasonable defenses are available, we will defend a statute that does not intrude upon the powers of the Executive Branch. That is our responsibility under the Constitution irrespective of our views on substantive policy. In the case of ambiguous laws, the Executive can in good faith urge and pursue those interpretations that seem most consistent with the intentions of the Congress, the policies of the Administration, and the other laws of the land. The Executive can do all of these things, but it can constitutionally do no more....

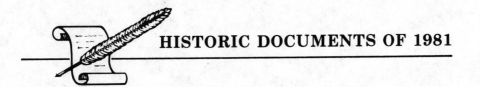

# November

# NEW CANADIAN CONSTITUTION
## November 5, 1981

*Canada's federal government November 5 reached a long-sought agreement with leaders of nine of the 10 provinces on a new constitution that would sever virtually all remaining ties to the British Crown. Pierre Elliott Trudeau, Canada's prime minister, hailed the historic accord, declaring, "Canada becomes, in the technical and legal sense, an independent country."*

*But the fact that the holdout province was Quebec, with five million French-speaking residents in a country of only 24 million, cast a long shadow over the future of Canada's nationhood. Quebec's premier, René Lévesque, and other provincial nationalists bitterly opposed a provision guaranteeing the right of English- and French-speaking minorities throughout Canada to be educated in their own language.*

### British North America Act

*The agreement struck by Trudeau and the provincial premiers called for the transformation of the British North American Act of 1867, which established the Canadian federation, into a strictly Canadian constitution with the addition of a bill of rights and an amending procedure. For 114 years, changes in the old constitution required the approval of the British Parliament.*

*While the November 5 accord was achieved at the price of significant compromises by the Trudeau government, it did represent the culmination of attempts at constitutional reform ranging over half a century.*

813

*Moreover, when the new constitution was sent to the Canadian Parliament, it was adopted by the House of Commons December 2 by a vote of 246-24 and by the Senate December 8 by a vote of 59 to 23. (Quebec separatist vote, Historic Documents of 1980, p. 401)*

*The document was to be presented early in 1982 to the British Parliament, which was seen as certain to approve it. While the new constitution would transfer all political powers to Canada, it would retain the British monarch as head of state.*

## Victory's Price

*To obtain the support of nine of the 10 provincial leaders, Trudeau, of French and Scottish ancestry and himself a Quebecer, was forced to make far-reaching compromises on the constitutional reforms. Outstanding among them were an amending procedure that would allow dissenting provinces to nullify the application of amendments in their jurisdictions and the elimination of a clause guaranteeing Eskimos, Indians and other native groups the treaty rights they had obtained from the British Crown.*

*Because of the compromises, Trudeau, an ardent federalist who had long hoped to make adoption of a new constitution the crowning event of his career, was accused by the influential* Toronto Star *of having "broken faith with all Canadians and with his own most cherished beliefs."*

## Quebec and Native Rights

*Promoting the peaceful coexistence of both Canada's French- and English-speaking citizens had long been one of the thorniest problems of the federal government in Ottawa. Quebec voters in May 1980 had rejected Premier Lévesque's goal of eventual independence for the province. Yet guarantees on education in the new constitution were viewed by many in the province as a threat to Quebec's political powers.*

*The elimination from the constitution of guarantees of land and other rights to Canada's aboriginal peoples was demanded, according to press reports, by several provincial leaders worried about long litigation and costly land settlements.*

*Following are excerpts from Canada's new constitution agreed to by the federal government and the premiers of nine of the 10 provinces on November 5, 1981:*

## Part I

### CANADIAN CHARTER OF RIGHTS AND FREEDOMS

Whereas Canada is founded upon principles that recognize the supremacy of God and the rule of law:

## Guarantee of Rights and Freedoms

1. The *Canadian Charter of Rights and Freedoms* guarantees the rights and freedoms set out in it subject only to such reasonable limits prescribed by law as can be demonstrably justified in a free and democratic society.

## Fundamental Freedoms

2. Everyone has the following fundamental freedoms:

    (a) freedom of conscience and religion;
    (b) freedom of thought, belief, opinion and expression, including freedom of the press and other media of communication;
    (c) freedom of peaceful assembly; and
    (d) freedom of association.

## Democratic Rights

3. Every citizen of Canada has the right to vote in an election of members of the House of Commons or of a legislative assembly and to be qualified for membership therein.

4. (1) No House of Commons and no legislative assembly shall continue for longer than five years from the date fixed for the return of the writs at a general election of its members.

(2) In time of real or apprehended war, invasion or insurrection, a House of Commons may be continued by Parliament and a legislative assembly may be continued by the legislature beyond five years if such continuation is not opposed by the votes of more than one-third of the members of the House of Commons or the legislative assembly, as the case may be.

5. There shall be a sitting of Parliament and of each legislature at least once every twelve months.

## Mobility Rights

6. (1) Every citizen of Canada has the right to enter, remain in and leave Canada.

(2) Every citizen of Canada and every person who has the status of a permanent resident of Canada has the right

    (a) to move to and take up residence in any province; and
    (b) to pursue the gaining of a livelihood in any province.

(3) The rights specified in subsection (2) are subject to

    (a) any laws or practices of general application in force in a province other than those that discriminate among persons primarily on the basis of province of present or previous residence; and

815

(b) any laws providing for reasonable residency requirements as a qualification for the receipt of publicly provided social services.

(4) Subsections (2) and (3) do not preclude any law, program or activity that has as its object the amelioration in a province of conditions of individuals in that province who are socially or economically disadvantaged if the rate of employment in that province is below the rate of employment in Canada.

## Legal Rights

7. Everyone has the right to life, liberty and security of the person and the right not to be deprived thereof except in accordance with the principles of fundamental justice.

8. Everyone has the right to be secure against unreasonable search or seizure.

9. Everyone has the right not to be arbitrarily detained or imprisoned.

10. Everyone has the right on arrest or detention

(a) to be informed promptly of the reasons therefor;

(b) to retain and instruct counsel without delay and to be informed of that right; and

(c) to have the validity of the detention determined by ways of *habeas corpus* and to be released if the detention is not lawful.

11. Any person charged with an offence has the right

(a) to be informed without unreasonable delay of the specific offence;

(b) to be tried within a reasonable time;

(c) not to be compelled to be a witness in proceedings against that person in respect of the offence;

(d) to be presumed innocent until proven guilty according to law in a fair and public hearing by an independent and impartial tribunal;

(e) not to be denied reasonable bail without just cause;

(f) except in the case of an offence under military law tried before a military tribunal, to the benefit of trial by jury where the maximum punishment for the offence is imprisonment for five years or a more severe punishment;

(g) not to be found guilty on account of any act or omission unless, at the time of the act or omission, it constituted an offence under Canadian or international law or was criminal according to the general principles of law recognized by the community of nations;

(h) if finally acquitted of the offence, not to be tried for it again and, if finally found guilty and punished for the offence, not to be tried or punished for it again; and

(i) if found guilty of the offence and if the punishment for the offence has been varied between the time of commission and the time of sentencing, to the benefit of the lesser punishment.

12. Everyone has the right not to be subjected to any cruel and unusual treatment or punishment.

13. A witness who testified in any proceedings has the right not to have any incriminating evidence so given used to incriminate that witness in any other proceedings, except in a prosecution for perjury or for the giving of contradictory evidence.

14. A party or witness in any proceedings who does not understand or speak the language in which the proceedings are conducted or who is deaf has the right to the assistance of an interpreter.

## Equality Rights

15. (1) Every individual is equal before and under the law and has the right to the equal protection and equal benefit of the law without discrimination and, in particular, without discrimination based on race, national or ethnic origin, colour, religion, sex, age or mental or physical disability.

(2) Subsection (1) does not preclude any law, program or activity that has as its object the amelioration of conditions of disadvantaged individuals or groups including those that are disadvantaged because of race, national or ethnic origin, colour, religion, sex, age or mental or physical disability.

## Official Languages of Canada

16. (1) English and French are the official languages of Canada and have equality of status and equal rights and privileges as to their use in all institutions of the Parliament and government of Canada.

(2) English and French are the official languages of New Brunswick and have equality of status and equal rights and privileges as to their use in all institutions of the legislature and government of New Brunswick.

(3) Nothing in this Chapter limits the authority of Parliament or a legislature to advance the equality of status or use of English and French.

17. (1) Everyone has the right to use English or French in any debates and other proceedings of Parliament.

(2) Everyone has the right to use English or French in any debates and other proceedings of the legislature of New Brunswick.

18. (1) The statutes, records and journals of Parliament shall be printed and published in English and French and both language versions are equally authoritative.

(2) The statutes, records and journals of the legislature of New Brunswick shall be printed and published in English and French and both language versions are equally authoritative.

19. (1) Either English or French may be used by any person in, or in any pleading in or process issuing from, any court established by Parliament.

(2) Either English or French may be used by any person in, or in any pleading in or process issuing from, any court of New Brunswick.

20. (1) Any member of the public in Canada has the right to communicate with, and to receive available services from, any head or central office of an institution of the Parliament or government of Canada in English or French, and has the same right with respect to any other office of any such institution where

(a) there is a significant demand for communications with and services from that office in such language; or

(b) due to the nature of the office, it is reasonable that communications with and services from that office be available in both English and French.

(2) Any member of the public in New Brunswick has the right to communicate with, and to receive available services from, any office of an institution of the legislature or government of New Brunswick in English or French.

21. Nothing in sections 16 to 20 abrogates or derogates from any right, privilege or obligation with respect to the English and French languages, or either of them, that exists or is continued by virtue of any other provision of the Constitution of Canada.

22. Nothing in Sections 16 to 20 abrogates or derogates from any legal or customary right or privilege acquired or enjoyed either before or after the coming into force of this Charter with respect to any language that is not English or French.

## Minority Language Educational Rights

23. (1) Citizens of Canada

(a) whose first language learned and still understood is that of the English or French linguistic minority population of the province in which they reside, or

(b) who have received their primary school instruction in Canada in English or French and reside in a province where the language in which they received that instruction is the language of the English or French linguistic minority population of the province,

have the right to have their children receive primary and secondary school instruction in that language in that province.

(2) Citizens of Canada of whom any child has received or is receiving primary or secondary school instruction in English or French in Canada, have the right to have all their children receive primary and secondary school instruction in the same language.

(3) The right of citizens of Canada under subsections (1) and (2) to have their children receive primary and secondary school instruction in the language of the English or French linguistic minority population of a province

(a) applies wherever in the province the number of children of citizens who have such a right is sufficient to warrant the provision to them out of public funds of minority language instruction; and

(b) includes, where the number of those children so warrants, the right to have them receive that instruction in minority language educational facilities provided out of public funds.

## Enforcement

24. (1) Anyone whose rights or freedoms, as guaranteed by this Charter, have been infringed or denied may apply to a court of competent jurisdiction to obtain such remedy as the court considers appropriate and just in the circumstances.

(2) Where, in proceedings under subsection (1), a court concludes that evidence was obtained in a manner that infringed or denied any rights or freedoms guaranteed by this Charter, the evidence shall be excluded if it is established that, having regard to all the circumstances, the admission of it in the proceedings would bring the administration of justice into disrepute.

## General

25. The guarantee in this Charter of certain rights and freedoms shall not be construed so as to abrogate or derogate from any aboriginal, treaty or other rights or freedoms that pertain to the aboriginal peoples of Canada including

(a) any rights or freedoms that have been recognized by the Royal Proclamation of October 7, 1763; and

(b) any rights or freedoms that may be acquired by the aboriginal peoples of Canada by way of land claims settlement.

26. The guarantee in this Charter of certain rights and freedoms shall not be construed as denying the existence of any other rights or freedoms that exist in Canada.

27. This Charter shall be interpreted in a manner consistent with the preservation and enhancement of the multicultural heritage of Canadians.

28. Notwithstanding anything in this Charter, except section 33, the rights and freedoms referred to in it are guaranteed equally to male and female persons.

29. Nothing in this Charter abrogates or derogates from any rights or privileges guaranteed by or under the Constitution of Canada in respect of denominational, separate or dissentient schools.

30. A reference in this Charter to a province or to the legislative assembly or legislature of a province shall be deemed to include a reference to the Yukon Territory and the Northwest Territories, or to the appropriate legislative authority thereof, as the case may be.

31. Nothing in this Charter extends the legislative powers of any body or authority.

### Application of Charter

32. (1) This Charter applies

(a) to the Parliament and government of Canada in respect of all matters within the authority of Parliament including all matters relating to the Yukon Territory and Northwest Territories; and

(b) to the legislature and government of each province in respect of all matters within the authority of the legislature of each province.

(2) Notwithstanding subsection (1), section 15 shall not have effect until three years after this section comes into force.

33. (1) Parliament or the legislature of a province may expressly declare in an Act of Parliament or of the legislature, as the case may be, that the Act or a provision thereof shall operate notwithstanding a provision included in section 2 or sections 7 to 15 of this Charter, or section 28 of this Charter in its application to discrimination based on sex referred to in section 15.

(2) An Act or a provision of an Act in respect of which a declaration made under this section is in effect shall have such operation as it would have but for the provision of this Charter referred to in the declaration.

(3) A declaration made under subsection (1) shall cease to have effect five years after it comes into force or on such earlier date as may be specified in the declaration.

(4) Parliament or a legislature of a province may re-enact a declaration made under subsection (1).

(5) Subsection (3) applies in respect of a re-enactment made under subsection (4).

### Citation

34. This Part may be cited as the *Canadian Charter of Rights and Freedoms.*

[Parts II and III Omitted]

## Part IV

### PROCEDURE FOR AMENDING
### CONSTITUTION OF CANADA

37. (1) An amendment to the Constitution of Canada may be made by proclamation issued by the Governor General under the Great Seal of Canada where so authorized by

(a) resolutions of the Senate and House of Commons; and

(b) resolutions of the legislative assemblies of at least two-thirds of the provinces that have, in the aggregate, according to the then latest general census, at least fifty percent of the population of all the provinces.

(2) An amendment made under subsection (1) that derogates from the legislative powers, the proprietary rights or any other rights or privileges of the legislature or government of a province shall require a resolution supported by a majority of the members of each of the Senate, the House of Commons and the legislative assemblies required under subsection (1).

(3) An amendment referred to in subsection (2) shall not have effect in a province the legislative assembly of which has expressed its dissent thereto by resolution supported by a majority of its members prior to the issue of the proclamation to which the amendment relates unless that legislative assembly, subsequently, by resolution supported by a majority of its members, revokes its dissent and authorizes the amendment.

(4) A resolution of dissent made for the purposes of subsection (3) may be revoked at any time before or after the issue of the proclamation to which it relates:

38. (1) A proclamation shall not be issued under subsection 37(1) before the expiration of one year from the adoption of the resolution initiating the amendment procedure thereunder, unless the legislative assembly of each province has previously adopted a resolution of assent or dissent.

(2) A proclamation shall not be issued under subsection 37(1) after the expiration of three years from the adoption of the resolution initiating the amendment procedure thereunder.

39. Where an amendment is made under subsection 37(1) that transfers provincial legislative powers relating to education or other cultural matters from provincial legislatures to Parliament, Canada shall provide reasonable compensation to any province to which the amendment does not apply. . . .

47. The Queen's Privy Council for Canada shall advise the Governor General to issue a proclamation under this Part forthwith on the adoption of the resolutions required for an amendment made by proclamation under this Part.

48. A constitutional conference composed of the Prime Minister of Canada and the first ministers of the provinces shall be convened by the Prime Minister of Canada within fifteen years after this Part comes into force to review the provisions of this Part.

[Part V Omitted]

## Part VI
### GENERAL

51. (1) The Constitution of Canada is the supreme law of Canada, and any law that is inconsistent with the provisions of the Constitution is, to the extent of the inconsistency, of no force or effect.

(2) The Constitution of Canada includes

(a) the *Canada Act*, including this Act;

(b) the Acts and orders referred to in Schedule I; and

(c) any amendment to any Act or order referred to in paragraph (a) or (b).

(3) Amendments to the Constitution of Canada shall be made only in accordance with the authority contained in the Constitution of Canada. . . .

56. The English and French versions of this Act are equally authoritative.

57. Subject to section 58, this Act shall come into force on a day to be fixed by proclamation issued by the Queen or the Governor General under the Great Seal of Canada. . . .

59. This Act may be cited as the *Constitution Act, 1981,* and the Constitution Acts 1867 to 1975 (No. 2) and this Act may be cited together as the *Constitution Acts, 1867 to 1981.*

# REAGAN ON NUCLEAR ARMS IN EUROPE
## November 18, 1981

*In a speech before the National Press Club November 18, President Reagan offered to cancel plans to deploy new American intermediate-range missiles in Western Europe if the Soviet Union would dismantle similar forces already aimed at Europe. The offer, he said, had been made in a "simple, straightforward, yet historic message" to Soviet President Leonid Brezhnev.*

*Reagan said his so-called "zero option" proposal would be made at the U.S.-Soviet nuclear talks scheduled to begin November 30 in Geneva. Specifically, the proposal called on the Russians to remove new multiple-warhead SS-20 and older, single-warhead SS-4 and SS-5 missiles from Soviet Europe. In exchange, the United States would choose not to deploy over 500 single-warhead cruise and Pershing II missiles in Western Europe in 1983. This plan for American deployment had been endorsed by the North Atlantic Treaty Organization in 1979.*

*"This would be an historic step," Reagan said in his speech, which was broadcast live on national television. "With Soviet agreement, we could together substantially reduce the dread threat of nuclear war which hangs over the people of Europe. This, like the first footstep on the moon, would be a giant step for mankind."*

*Reagan also proposed that the United States and the Soviet Union begin strategic arms talks "as soon as possible next year." He said the aim of the talks should be "truly substantial reductions in our strategic arsenals," as opposed to limits of the kind negotiated in the 1970s under the two SALT (Strategic Arms Limitation Talks) treaties.*

*"To symbolize this fundamental change in direction," Reagan said, "we will call these negotiations START — Strategic Arms Reduction Talks."*

## European Concern

*Billed as Reagan's first major foreign policy speech, the Press Club address followed statements by the president that had triggered anti-nuclear protests in Europe. At an October 17 meeting with newspaper editors, Reagan had been asked if there could be a limited exchange of nuclear weapons between the United States and the Soviet Union.*

*"I don't honestly know," the president had answered — but then continued: "I could see where you could have the exchange of tactical weapons against troops in the field without it bringing either one of the major powers to pushing the button." This remark caused a storm of protest among Europeans who fear the United States and the Soviet Union could use Western Europe as a nuclear battleground.*

*In his Press Club speech, Reagan alluded to the anti-nuclear movement, saying that because Europe's "new generation" was not present at the creation of the Atlantic Alliance, "many of them do not fully understand its roots in defending freedom and rebuilding a war torn continent."*

*"Some young people question why we need weapons — particularly nuclear weapons — to deter war and assure peaceful development," Reagan said, adding: "I understand their concerns. Their questions deserve to be answered."*

## Soviet Reaction

*The official Soviet government press agency Tass reacted to the Reagan speech by taking issue with the president's numbers on medium-range missiles. The agency said that Reagan's claim that the Soviets had a six to one advantage in such missiles was a "groundless allegation based on absolutely fantastic figures."*

*The Tass position affirmed the view taken by Brezhnev in an interview with the West German magazine* Der Spiegel, *published November 2. Revealing normally secret details about Soviet missile deployment, the Soviet president argued at that time that an "approximate parity" exists between Soviet and Western medium-range missiles in Europe.*

*Following are excerpts from President Reagan's speech on arms reduction and nuclear weapons, delivered November 18, 1981, at the National Press Club in Washington, D.C.* (Boldface headings in brackets have been added by Congressional Quarterly to highlight the organization of the text.):

... Back in April while in the hospital I had, as you can readily understand, a lot of time for reflection. And one day I decided to send a personal, handwritten letter to Soviet President Leonid Brezhnev reminding him that we had met about 10 years ago in San Clemente, California, as he and President Nixon were concluding a series of meetings that had brought hope to all the world. Never had peace and goodwill seemed closer at hand. ...

Twice in my lifetime, I have seen the peoples of Europe plunged into the tragedy of war. Twice in my lifetime, Europe has suffered destruction and military occupation in wars that statesmen proved powerless to prevent, soldiers unable to contain, and ordinary citizens unable to escape. And twice in my lifetime, young Americans have bled their lives into the soil of those battlefields not to enrich or enlarge our domain, but to restore the peace and independence of our friends and Allies.

All of us who lived through those troubled times share a common resolve that they must never come again. And most of us share a common appreciation of the Atlantic Alliance that has made a peaceful, free, and prosperous Western Europe in the post-war era possible.

But today, a new generation is emerging on both sides of the Atlantic. Its members were not present at the creation of the North Atlantic Alliance. Many of them don't fully understand its roots in defending freedom and rebuilding a war-torn continent. Some young people question why we need weapons, particularly nuclear weapons, to deter war and to assure peaceful development. They fear that the accumulation of weapons itself may lead to conflagration. Some even propose unilateral disarmament.

I understand their concerns. Their questions deserve to be answered. But we have an obligation to answer their questions on the basis of judgment and reason and experience. Our policies have resulted in the longest European peace in this century. Wouldn't a rash departure from these policies, as some now suggest, endanger that peace?

## [Atlantic Alliance]

From its founding, the Atlantic Alliance has preserved the peace through unity, deterrence and dialog. First, we and our Allies have stood united by the firm commitment that an attack upon any one of us would be considered an attack upon us all. Second, we and our Allies have deterred aggression by maintaining forces strong enough to insure that any aggressor would lose more from an attack than he could possibly gain. And third, we and our Allies have engaged the Soviets in a dialog about mutual restraint and arms limitations, hoping to reduce the risk of war and the burden of armaments and to lower the barriers that divide East from West.

These three elements of our policy have preserved the peace in Europe for more than a third of a century. They can preserve it for generations to come, so long as we pursue them with sufficient will and vigor.

Today, I wish to reaffirm America's commitment to the Atlantic Alliance and our resolve to sustain the peace. And from my conversations with allied leaders, I know that they also remain true to this tried and proven course.

## [Soviet Military Buildup]

NATO's policy of peace is based on restraint and balance. No NATO weapons, conventional or nuclear, will ever be used in Europe except in response to attack. NATO's defense plans have been responsible and restrained. The Allies remain strong, united, and resolute. But the momentum of the continuing Soviet military buildup threatens both the conventional and the nuclear balance.

Consider the facts. Over the past decade, the United States reduced the size of its Armed Forces and decreased its military spending. The Soviets steadily increased the number of men under arms. They now number more than double those of the United States. Over the same period, the Soviets expanded their real military spending by about one-third. The Soviet Union increased its inventory of tanks to some 50,000, compared to our 11,000. Historically a land power, they transformed their navy from a coastal defense force to an open ocean fleet, while the United States, a sea power with trans-oceanic alliances, cut its fleet in half.

During a period when NATO deployed no new intermediate-range nuclear missiles and actually withdrew 1,000 nuclear warheads, the Soviet Union deployed more than 750 nuclear warheads on the new SS-20 missiles alone.

Our response to this relentless buildup of Soviet military power has been restrained but firm. We have made decisions to strengthen all three legs of the strategic triad: sea-, land-, and air-based. We have proposed a defense program in the United States for the next 5 years which will remedy the neglect of the past decade and restore the eroding balance on which our security depends.

## [Threat to Western Europe]

I would like to discuss more specifically the growing threat to Western Europe which is posed by the continuing deployment of certain Soviet intermediate-range nuclear missiles. The Soviet Union has three different type such missile systems: the SS-20, the SS-4, and the SS-5, all with a range capable of reaching virtually all of Western Europe. There are other Soviet weapons systems which also represent a major threat.

Now, the only answer to these systems is a comparable threat to Soviet threats, to Soviet targets; in other words, a deterrent preventing the use of these Soviet weapons by the counter-threat of a like response against their own territory. At present, however, there is no equivalent deterrent to these Soviet intermediate missiles. And the Soviets continue to add one new SS-20 a week.

To counter this, the Allies agreed in 1979, as part of a two-track decision, to deploy as a deterrent land-based cruise missiles and Pershing II missiles capable of reaching targets in the Soviet Union. These missiles are to be deployed in several countries of Western Europe. This relatively limited force in no way serves as a substitute for the much larger strategic umbrella spread over our NATO allies. Rather, it provides a vital link between conventional shorter-range nuclear forces in Europe and intercontinental forces in the United States.

Deployment of these systems will demonstrate to the Soviet Union that this link cannot be broken. Deterring war depends on the perceived ability of our forces to perform effectively. The more effective our forces are, the less likely it is that we'll have to use them. So, we and our allies are proceeding to modernize NATO's nuclear forces of intermediate range to meet increased Soviet deployments of nuclear systems threatening Western Europe.

## [Proposals Sent to Brezhnev]

Let me turn now to our hopes for arms control negotiations. There's a tendency to make this entire subject overly complex. I want to be clear and concise. I told you of the letter I wrote to President Brezhnev last April. Well, I've just sent another message to the Soviet leadership. It's a simple, straightforward, yet historic message. The United States proposes the mutual reduction of conventional intermediate-range nuclear and strategic forces. Specifically, I have proposed a four-point agenda to achieve this objective in my letter to President Brezhnev.

The first and most important point concerns the Geneva negotiations. As part of the 1979 two-track decision, NATO made a commitment to seek arms control negotiations with the Soviet Union on intermediate range nuclear forces. The United States has been preparing for these negotiations through close consultation with our NATO partners.

We're now ready to set forth our proposal. I have informed President Brezhnev that when our delegation travels to the negotiations on intermediate range, land-based nuclear missiles in Geneva on the 30th of this month, my representatives will present the following proposal: The United States is prepared to cancel its deployment of Pershing II and ground launch cruise missiles if the Soviets will dismantle their SS-20, SS-4 and SS-5 missiles. This would be an historic step. With Soviet agreement, we could together substantially reduce the dread threat of nuclear war which hangs over the people of Europe. This, like the first footstep on the moon would be a giant step for mankind.

Now, we intend to negotiate in good faith and go to Geneva willing to listen to and consider the proposals of our Soviet counterparts, but let me call to your attention the background against which our proposal is made.

During the past 6 years while the United States deployed no new intermediate-range missiles and withdrew 1,000 nuclear warheads from

Europe, the Soviet Union deployed 750 warheads on mobile, accurate ballistic missiles. They now have 1,100 warheads on the SS-20s, SS-4s and 5s. And the United States has no comparable missiles. Indeed, the United States dismantled the last such missile in Europe over 15 years ago.

As we look to the future of the negotiations, it's also important to address certain Soviet claims, which left unrefuted could become critical barriers to world progress and arms control.

## [Soviet Advantage]

The Soviets assert that a balance of intermediate range nuclear forces already exists. That assertion is wrong. By any objective measure ... the Soviet Union has developed an increasing overwhelming advantage. They now enjoy a superiority on the order of six to one....

Now, Soviet spokesmen have suggested that moving their SS-20s beyond the Ural Mountains will remove the threat to Europe. ... [T]he SS-20s, even if deployed behind the Urals, will have a range that puts almost all of Western Europe — the great cities — Rome, Athens, Paris, London, Brussels, Amsterdam, Berlin, and so many more, all of Scandinavia, all of the Middle East, all of northern Africa, all within range of these missiles which incidentally, are mobile and can be moved on shorter notice....

## [Strategic Weapons]

The second proposal that I've made to President Brezhnev concerns strategic weapons. The United States proposes to open negotiations on strategic arms as soon as possible next year.

I have instructed Secretary Haig to discuss the timing of such meetings with Soviet representatives. Substance, however, is far more important than timing. As our proposal for the Geneva talks this month illustrates, we can make proposals for genuinely serious reductions, but only if we take the time to prepare carefully.

The United States has been preparing carefully for resumption of strategic arms negotiations because we don't want a repetition of past disappointments. We don't want an arms control process that sends hopes soaring only to end in dashed expectations.

Now, I have informed President Brezhnev that we will seek to negotiate substantial reductions in nuclear arms which would result in levels that are equal and verifiable. Our approach to verification will be to emphasize openness and creativity, rather than the secrecy and suspicion which have undermined confidence in arms control in the past.

While we can hope to benefit from work done over the past decade in strategic arms negotiations, let us agree to do more than simply begin where these previous efforts left off. We can and should attempt major qualitative and quantitative progress. Only such progress can fulfill the hopes of our own people and the rest of the world. And let us see how far we can go in achieving truly substantial reductions in our strategic arsenals.

To symbolize this fundamental change in direction, we will call these negotiations START — Strategic Arms Reduction Talks.

## [Conventional Forces in Europe]

The third proposal I've made to the Soviet Union is that we act to achieve equality at lower levels of conventional forces in Europe. The defense needs of the Soviet Union hardly call for maintaining more combat divisions in East Germany today than were in the whole Allied invasion force that landed in Normandy on D-Day. The Soviet Union could make no more convincing contribution to peace in Europe, and in the world, than by agreeing to reduce its conventional forces significantly and constrain the potential for sudden aggression.

## [Conference on Disarmament]

Finally, I have pointed out to President Brezhnev that to maintain peace we must reduce the risks of surprise attack and the chance of war arising out of uncertainty or miscalculation.

I am renewing our proposal for a conference to develop effective measures that would reduce these dangers. At the current Madrid meeting of the Conference on Security and Cooperation in Europe, we're laying the foundation for a Western-proposed conference on disarmament in Europe. This conference would discuss new measures to enhance stability and security in Europe. Agreement in this conference is within reach. I urge the Soviet Union to join us and many other nations who are ready to launch this important enterprise.

All of these proposals are based on the same fair-minded principles — substantial, militarily significant reductions in forces, equal ceilings for similar types of forces, and adequate provisions for verification.

My administration, our country, and I are committed to achieving arms reductions agreements based on these principles. Today I have outlined the kinds of bold, equitable proposals which the world expects of us. But we cannot reduce arms unilaterally. Success can only come if the Soviet Union will share our commitment, if it will demonstrate that its often-repeated professions of concern for peace will be matched by positive action.

Preservation of peace in Europe and the pursuit of arms reductions talks are of fundamental importance. But we must also help to bring peace and security to regions now torn by conflict, external intervention, and war.

# [Peace and Economic Growth]

The American concept of peace goes well beyond the absence of war. We foresee a flowering of economic growth and individual liberty in a world at peace.

At the economic summit conference in Cancun, I met with the leaders of 21 nations and sketched out our approach to global economic growth. We want to eliminate the barriers to trade and investment which hinder these critical incentives to growth, and we're working to develop new programs to help the poorest nations achieve self-sustaining growth.

And terms like "peace" and "security," we have to say, have little meaning for the oppressed and the destitute. They also mean little to the individual whose state has stripped him of human freedom and dignity. Wherever there is oppression, we must strive for the peace and security of individuals as well as states. We must recognize that progress and the pursuit of liberty is a necessary complement to military security. Nowhere has this fundamental truth been more boldly and clearly stated than in the Helsinki Accords of 1975. These accords have not yet been translated into living reality.

Today I've announced an agenda that can help to achieve peace, security, and freedom across the globe. In particular, I have made an important offer to forego entirely deployment of new American missiles in Europe if the Soviet Union is prepared to respond on an equal footing.

There is no reason why people in any part of the world should have to live in permanent fear of war or its spectre. I believe the time has come for all nations to act in a responsible spirit that doesn't threaten other states. I believe the time is right to move forward on arms control and the resolution of critical regional disputes at the conference table. Nothing will have a higher priority for me and for the American people over the coming months and years.

Addressing the United Nations 20 years ago, another American President described the goal that we still pursue today. He said, "If we all can persevere, if we can look beyond our shores and ambitions, then surely the age will dawn in which the strong are just and the weak secure and the peace preserved."

He didn't live to see that goal achieved. I invite all nations to join with America today in the quest for such a world. . . .

# BRIEF GOVERNMENT SHUTDOWN
## November 23, 1981

A large part of the federal government closed down for a few hours November 23 after President Reagan vetoed a continuing appropriations bill that he characterized as "budget-busting." Later the same day Congress approved an emergency three-week spending measure that Reagan signed. "Unessential" government workers numbering between 200,000 and 400,000, who had been sent home on furlough, returned to work November 24.

The partial shutdown of the government was the first in U.S. history of such scope. Some of the lapses in traditional services during the hiatus were dramatic. The Washington Monument and the Statue of Liberty, for example, were closed. But such vital federal services as the maintenance of the armed services and the disbursement of Social Security checks continued unabated.

A debate raged as to which branch of the government, the executive or the legislative, should shoulder the criticism for the crisis. Reagan told a national television audience that his veto had been necessary in his fight against "excessive government spending." However, Sen. Robert C. Byrd, D-W.Va., the Senate minority leader, called the confrontation "a manufactured shoot-out at the OK Corral."

## Scope of Shutdown

Technically, appropriations for most of the government ran out at midnight, Friday, November 20. The president's order setting the shutdown in motion was predicated on an 111-year-old law, the Antideficiency Act, which prohibited the government from spending money before it was appropriated by Congress.

During the hiatus, callers to the White House were told by a tape-recorded message that "the White House is involved in an orderly phasedown. . . . No one is here to answer your call." In downtown New York, some confusion resulted when offices in the 40-story Jacob K. Javits Federal Building were closed. Top administration officials, including Vice President George Bush, canceled speeches, trips or congressional testimony.

All of the numerous essential government services ranging from treating patients at Veterans Administration hospitals to feeding the animals at the National Zoo went on as usual. A spokesman for the Office of Management and Budget told reporters that there was neither any need to make a count of workers furloughed nor any way to calculate the shutdown's cost.

## Legislative Actions

Since the beginning of the fiscal year, October 1, Congress had passed only one of the 13 regular appropriations bills required to keep government departments running. In the absence of such legislation, it had provided funding authority by continuing resolution. Thus the stage was set for the dramatic confrontation November 23.

When the money ran out, early in the weekend, Congress worked almost around the clock, including unusual Sunday sessions, to achieve agreement on a spending bill the president would approve. But Reagan vetoed the compromise measure Congress believed he would sign, saying it provided "less than one-fourth of the savings I requested."

The immediate deadlock was broken when Congress late November 23 passed a three-week extension of funding authority. Reagan signed the emergency measure at 6:40 p.m., and government operations and services resumed the next morning.

The confrontation's real end came December 15 when Reagan signed new temporary legislation extending funding for most programs through March 31, 1982, or until regular fiscal 1982 appropriations bills were enacted. The president said the measure he signed would produce "substantial savings for the taxpayers."

Following is the text of President Reagan's November 23, 1981, veto message, returning H.J. Res. 357, the continuing appropriations bill, to the House of Representatives:

*To the House of Representatives:*

I am returning to the Congress without my signature H.J. Res. 357, the Continuing Resolution providing appropriations for Fiscal Year 1982.

This Resolution presented me with a difficult choice:

—Either to sign a budget-busting appropriations bill that would finance the entire Government at levels well above my recommendations, and thus set back our efforts to halt the excessive Government spending that has fueled inflation and high interest rates, and destroyed investments for new jobs;

—Or, to hold the line on spending with a veto, but risk interruption of Government activities and services.

I have chosen the latter. The failure to provide a reasonable Resolution means that some citizens may be inconvenienced and that there is a possibility of some temporary hardship. Nevertheless, a far greater threat to all Americans is the sustained hardship they will suffer by continuing the past budget-busting policies of big spending and big deficits.

When reports came to us in September that spending and the deficit for Fiscal Year 1982 were rising, we took action to stem the tide.

On September 24, I asked for a reduction of 12 percent in the appropriations for nearly all non-defense discretionary programs and a modest reduction in our planned program to strengthen the national defense. The 12 percent cut would have saved $8.5 billion — a significant contribution to reducing the deficit, but a modest sum in a budget which will total more than $700 billion.

By refusing to make even this small saving to protect the American people against over-spending, the Congress has paved the way for higher interest rates and inflation, and a continued loss of investment, jobs and economic growth. At the same time, the Continuing Resolution fails to provide sufficient security assistance to allow America to meet its obligations.

The practice of loading the budget with unnecessary spending — and then waiting until after the eleventh hour to pass a Continuing Resolution on the assumption that it was safe from a Presidential veto — has gone on much too long. It is one of the principal reasons why the growth of Government spending is still not under control.

For much of the past fiscal year, most of the domestic budget was funded in this manner — through a Continuing Resolution, without regular appropriations bills subject to Presidential approval or disapproval. These so-called stop-gap resolutions are actually budget-busters that can last for an entire year and create the kind of economic mess we inherited last year.

A few days ago I offered to meet the Congress half-way. But the Continuing Resolution the Congress has now passed provides less than one quarter of the savings I requested. This represents neither fair compromise nor responsible budget policy.

In the hours ahead the Congress has the opportunity to reconsider, and I urgently request that it do so. In the meantime, we are making every effort to avoid unnecessary dislocations and personal hardship. I can give assurance that:

—Social Security and most other benefit checks will be paid on schedule.

—The national security will be protected.

—Government activities essential to the protection of life and property, such as the treatment of patients in veterans hospitals, air traffic control and the functioning of the Nation's banks, will also continue.

But in order to prevent unnecessary inconvenience and hardship as Thanksgiving approaches, I must urge the Congress to act promptly and responsibly.

Ronald Reagan

The White House,
November 23, 1981.

# SATURN SCIENCE SUMMARY
## November 25, 1981

*The color photographs and other data transmitted to Earth by Voyager I in November 1980 and Voyager II in August 1981 provided scientists with more information about the planet Saturn than had been gathered in all recorded history.*

*"The extended, close-range observations provided high-resolution data far different from the picture assembled during several centuries of Earth-bound studies," according to the Saturn Science Summary of the Voyager missions, issued by the National Aeronautics and Space Administration (NASA) November 25.*

## The Rings

*Photographs taken by Voyager I had revealed unexpected gaps in the A-, B- and C-rings of Saturn, the report stated. Scientists had hypothesized at first that the gaps "might be created by tiny satellites orbiting with the rings and sweeping out bands of particles," it said.*

*But the photographs taken by Voyager II, which were of higher resolution, "showed no sign of satellites down to about five to nine kilometers (three to six miles)." Another experiment showed that gaps in the B-ring actually appeared to be the result of "variations in density of ring material, probably caused by traveling density waves or other, stationary forms of waves."*

*Voyager I's most surprising discovery had been the thin, outer F-ring, which appeared in photographs to be composed of twisted or braided strands. Voyager II, which was reprogrammed to photograph the F-ring in more detail, discovered further that the brightest of the F-ring strands was subdivided into at least ten strands. According to the NASA report, "the twists in the F-ring are believed to originate in gravitational perturbations," caused by two nearby satellites.*

*Both Voyager I and II also measured sporadic discharges of electricity in the form of radio waves. Scientists were still unsure where these discharges came from, the NASA report stated, although it was possible they originated in the rings.*

## Satellite Observation

*As a result of Voyager I's reconnaissance, scientists discovered that Saturn has at least 17 moons or satellites. At the time the NASA report was issued, "no new satellites [had] yet been identified in Voyager II data, but charged-particle shadowing effects ... show evidence for ... possibly an 18th satellite, in the same orbit as Mimas."* (Flight of Voyager I, Historic Documents of 1980, p. 989.)

*Voyager II photographs also revealed an enormous crater on the satellite Tethys. Measuring 250 miles wide and ten miles deep — one-third the diameter of Tethys — it was the largest crater in the moon system of Saturn. Other craters were also found on the satellites of Mimas, Dione and Rhea.*

*After it finished its flight near Saturn, Voyager I began a long trip into the far reaches of outer space. But Voyager II's trajectory was supposed to carry it to Uranus in 1986 and Neptune in 1989. If the spacecraft's instruments continued to function, scientists hoped to gain increased knowledge about these two far-distant planets.*

*Following is the text of the Saturn Science Summary of the the findings of the Voyager II space flight, released by the National Aeronautics and Space Administration November 25, 1981.* (Boldface headings in brackets have been added by Congressional Quarterly to highlight the organization of the text.):

The Voyager 1 and 2 Saturn encounters occurred nine months apart, in November 1980 and August 1981. As Voyager 1 is heading out of the solar system, Voyager 2 is enroute to a January 1986 Uranus encounter and an August 1989 Neptune encounter.

The two encounters increased our knowledge and altered our understanding of Saturn. The extended, close-range observations provided high-resolution data far different from the picture assembled during several centuries of Earth-based studies.

Here is a summary of the scientific findings of the two Voyagers at Saturn:

## Saturn

Saturn is composed almost entirely of hydrogen and helium. Voyager 1 found that about 11 percent of the mass of Saturn's atmosphere is helium, while almost all the rest is hydrogen.

It appears that subdued contrasts and color differences on Saturn are primarily a result either of more horizontal mixing or less production of localized colors in Saturn's atmosphere than in Jupiter's. While Voyager 1 saw only a few markings, Voyager 2 saw many: Long-lived ovals, tilted features in east-west shear zones and others similar to, but smaller than, the features on Jupiter. One white oval was 7,000 by 5,000 kilometers (4,000 by 3,000 miles) with 100 meter-per-second (200 mile-per-hour) circumferential winds.

Winds blow at extremely high speeds on Saturn. Near the equator, the Voyagers measured winds about 500 meters per second (1,100 miles an hour). The winds blow primarily in an easterly direction. The strongest winds are found near the equator, and velocity falls off uniformly at higher latitudes. At latitudes greater than 35°, the winds alternate eastward and westward as the latitude increases. The marked dominance of eastward jet streams indicates that winds are not confined to the cloud layer, but must extend inward at least 2,000 kilometers. Furthermore, measurements by Voyager 2 showing a striking north-south symmetry lead some scientists to suggest that the winds may extend from north to south clear through the interior of the planet.

When Voyager 2 flew behind Saturn its radio beam penetrated Saturn's atmosphere, measuring the upper-atmosphere temperature and density. Minimum temperatures of about 82° Kelvin (−312° Fahrenheit) were measured at the 70-millibar level (surface pressure on Earth is about 1,000 millibars). The temperature increased to 143° Kelvin (−202° Fahrenheit) at the deepest levels probed — about 1,200 millibars. Temperatures near the north pole were about 10° Celsius (18° Fahrenheit) colder at the 100 millibar level than temperatures at mid-latitudes. Scientists believe the difference may be a seasonal effect.

The Voyagers found aurora-like ultraviolet emissions of hydrogen at mid-latitudes in Saturn's atmosphere, and auroras at polar latitudes (above 65 degrees). Scientists suggest the high-latitude auroral activity leads to formation of complex hydrocarbon molecules that are carried toward the equator. The mid-latitude auroras, which occur only in sunlit regions, remain a puzzle; bombardment by electrons and ions, known to cause auroras on Earth, occurs primarily at high latitudes.

Both Voyagers measured the rotation rate of Saturn — the length of the day — at 10 hours, 39 minutes, 24 seconds.

## The Rings

Perhaps the greatest surprises and the most perplexing puzzles the two Voyagers found are in the rings.

Voyager 1 found a great deal of unexpected structure in the classical A-, B-, and C-rings. One suggestion was that the structure might be unresolved ringlets and gaps. Ring photos by Voyager 1 were of lower resolution than those of Voyager 2, and scientists at first believed that gaps might be created by tiny satellites orbiting within the rings and sweeping out bands of particles. One such large gap was detected at the inner edge of the Cassini Division.

Voyager 2 measurements provided the data scientists need to understand the structure. Higher-resolution photos of the inner edge of the Cassini Division showed no sign of satellites down to about five to nine kilometers (three to six miles). No systematic searches were conducted in any other ring gaps.

Voyager 2's photopolarimeter provided more surprises. The instrument measured changes in starlight from Delta Scorpii as the spacecraft flew above the rings and the starlight passed through them. The photopolarimeter could resolve structure smaller than 300 meters (1,000 feet).

The star-occultation experiment showed that few clear gaps exist anywhere in the rings. The structure in the B-ring, instead, appears to be variations in density of ring material, probably caused by traveling density waves or other, stationary, forms of waves. Density waves are formed by the gravitational effects of Saturn's satellites. They propagate outward from positions where the ring particles orbit Saturn in harmony with the satellites. (Those resonant points are locations where a particle would orbit Saturn in one-half or one-third the time required by a satellite, such as Mimas.) For example, at the 2:1 resonant point with the satellite 1980S1, a series of outward-propagating density waves has characteristics that indicate there are about 60 grams of material per square centimeter of ring area and that the velocity of the particles relative to one another is about one millimeter per second. The small-scale structure of the rings may therefore be largely transitory, although larger-scale features, such as the Cassini and Encke Divisions, appear to be more permanent.

The edges of the rings where the few gaps exist are so sharp that the ring must be less than about 200 meters (650 feet) thick there.

In almost every case where clear gaps do appear in the rings, eccentric ringlets are found. All seem to show variations in brightness. In some cases the differences are due to clumping or kinking, and in others to nearly complete absence of ring material. Some scientists believe the only plausible explanation for the clear regions and kinky ringlets within them is the presence of nearby undetected moonlets.

Two separate, discontinuous ringlets were found in the A-ring gap, about 73,000 kilometers (45,000 miles) from Saturn's cloud tops. At high resolution, at least one of those ringlets has multiple strands.

## [F-RING STRANDS]

Saturn's F-ring was discovered by Pioneer 11 in 1979. Photos of that ring taken by Voyager 1 showed three separate strands that appear twisted or braided. Voyager 2 found five separate strands in a region that had no apparent braiding, but did reveal apparent braiding in another region. The photopolarimeter found that the brightest of the F-ring strands was subdivided into at least 10 strands. The twists in the F-ring are believed to originate in gravitational perturbations caused by the two shepherding satellites, 1980S26 and 1980S27. Clumps of material in the F-ring appear fairly uniformly distributed around the ring every 9,000 kilometers (5,600 miles), a spacing that coincides with the relative motion of F-ring particles and the shepherding satellites in one orbital period. By analogy, scientists believe similar mechanisms might be operating for irregular ringlets that exist in gaps in the main ring system.

## [B-RING SPOKES]

The spokes found in the B-ring appear only at radial distances between 43,000 kilometers (27,000 miles) and 57,000 kilometers (35,000 miles) above Saturn's clouds. Some spokes, those that are narrow and have a radial alignment, may be recently formed. The broader, less radial spokes appear to have formed earlier than the narrow examples and seem to follow Kepplerian orbits: Individual areas rotate at speeds governed by distances from the center of the planet. In some cases, scientists believe they see evidence that new spokes are reprinted over older ones. Formation of the spokes is not restricted to regions near the planet's shadow. As both spacecraft approached Saturn, the spokes appeared dark against a bright ring background. As the Voyagers departed, the spokes appeared brighter than the surrounding ring areas, indicating they backscatter the reflected sunlight more efficiently.

Spokes are also visible at high phase angles in light reflected from Saturn on the unilluminated underside of the rings. That suggests, scientists say, that charging of the small particles by photoionization alone may not be responsible for levitating them above the bulk of the ring material.

## [IRREGULAR ORBITS]

Another challenge scientists face in understanding the rings is that even general dimensions do not seem to remain true at all positions around Saturn: The distance of the B-ring's outer edge, near a 2:1 resonance with Mimas, varies by at least 140 kilometers (87 miles). Furthermore, the elliptical shape of the outer edge does not follow a Kepplerian orbit, since Saturn is at the center of the ellipse, rather than at one focus. Although the gravitational effects of Mimas are most likely responsible for the elliptical shape, present theory predicts a somewhat smaller magnitude than was observed.

Voyager 1 measured radio waves that originate in sporadic electric discharges. The source of those discharges is still unknown; it is possible that they originate in the rings; Voyager 2 measured similar discharges, but at a rate only 10 percent that of Voyager 1, and with a different polarization.

## Titan

Titan is the largest of Saturn's satellites. It is the second largest satellite in the solar system, and the only one known to have a dense atmosphere.

It may turn out to be the most interesting body, from a terrestrial perspective, in the solar system.

For almost two decades, space scientists have searched for clues to the primeval Earth. The chemistry going on in Titan's atmosphere may be similar to that which occurred in the Earth's atmosphere several billion years ago.

Because of its thick opaque atmosphere, astronomers believed Titan was the largest satellite in the solar system. Their measurements were necessarily limited to measurements at the cloud tops. Voyagers 1's close approach and diametric radio occultation show Titan's surface diameter is only 5,150 kilometers (3,200 miles) — slightly smaller than Ganymede, Jupiter's largest satellite. Both are larger than Mercury. Titan's density appears to be about twice that of water ice; it may be composed of nearly equal amounts of rock and ice.

## [SURFACE HIDDEN]

Titan's surface cannot be seen in any Voyager photos; it is hidden by a dense, optically thick photochemical haze whose main layer is about 50 kilometers (30 miles) thicker in the southern hemisphere than in the northern. Several distinct, detached haze layers can be seen above the visibly opaque haze layer. Those haze layers merge with the main layer over the north pole of Titan, forming what scientists first thought was a darkened hood. The hood was found, under the better viewing conditions of Voyager 2, to be a dark ring around the pole. The southern hemisphere is slightly brighter than the northern, possibly the result of seasonal effects. When the Voyagers flew past, the season on Titan was the equivalent of April on Earth, or early spring in the northern hemisphere and early fall in the south.

## [ATMOSPHERE OF TITAN]

The atmospheric pressure near Titan's surface is about 1.6 bars, 60 percent greater than Earth's. The atmosphere is mostly nitrogen, also the major constituent of Earth's atmosphere.

The surface temperature appears to be about 95° Kelvin (−288 degrees Fahrenheit), only 4°K above the triple-point temperature of methane. Methane, therefore, quite possibly plays the same role on Titan as water does on Earth — as rain, snow and vapor: Rivers and lakes of methane under a nitrogen sky. Clouds may drop liquid-methane rain or snow. Titan's methane, through continuing photochemistry, is converted to ethane, acetylene, ethylene, and (when combined with nitrogen) hydrogen cyanide. The last is an especially important molecule, since it is a building block of amino acids. Titan's low temperature undoubtedly inhibits more complex organic chemistry.

Titan has no intrinsic magnetic field; therefore it has no electrically conducting and convecting liquid core. Its interaction with Saturn's magnetosphere creates a magnetic wake behind the satellite. The big satellite also serves as a source for both neutral and charged hydrogen atoms in Saturn's magnetosphere.

## New Satellites

Before the first spacecraft encounter, Saturn was believed to have 10 satellites. Saturn is now known to have at least 17 satellites. Three of those were discovered by Voyager 1. No new satellites have yet been identified in Voyager 2 data, but charged-particle shadowing effects seen by the cosmic-ray instrument on Voyager 2 show evidence for material, possibly an 18th satellite, in the same orbit as Mimas. A shadow of what may be the same material has been reported in Pioneer 11 data.

The innermost satellite, 1980S28, orbits near the outer edge of the A-ring and is about 30 kilometers (20 miles) in diameter. It was discovered by Voyager 1.

The next satellite outward, 1980S27, shepherds the inner edge of the F-ring and is about 100 kilometers (60 miles) in diameter. Next is 1980S26, outer shepherd of the F-ring, about 90 kilometers (50 miles) in diameter. Both shepherds were found by Voyager 1.

Next are 1980S1 and 1980S3 (the coorbitals) that share approximately the same orbit — 91,100 kilometers (56,600 miles) above the clouds. As they near each other, the satellites trade orbits (the outer orbit is about 50 kilometers farther from Saturn that the inner). 1980S1 is about 190 kilometers (120 miles) in diameter, and 1980S3 is about 120 kilometers (70 miles) in diameter. Both were discovered from ground-based observations.

Another new satellite, 1980S6, shares the orbit of Dione, about 60 degrees ahead of its larger companion. It is about 30 kilometers (20 miles) in diameter, and was discovered in ground-based photographs.

Two more new satellites are called the Tethys Trojans because they circle Saturn in the same orbit as Tethys, about 60 degrees ahead of and behind that body. They are 1980S13 (the leading Trojan) and 1980S25 (the trailing Trojan). Both were found in 1981 among ground-based observations made in 1980, and are comparable in size to 1980S6.

## Other Satellites

Mimas, Enceladus, Tethys, Dione and Rhea are approximately spherical in shape and appear to be composed mostly of water ice. Enceladus reflects almost 100 percent of the sunlight that strikes it. All five satellites represent a size of satellite not previously explored.

Mimas, Tethys, Dione and Rhea are all cratered; Enceladus appears to have by far the most active surface of any satellite in the system. At least five types of surface-terrain units have been identified. Although craters can be seen across portions of its surface, the lack of craters in other areas implies an age less than a few hundred million years for the youngest regions on the surface. It seems likely that portions of the surface are still undergoing change, since there are areas that are covered by ridged plains with no evidence of cratering down to the limit of resolution of the Voyager 2 cameras (2 kilometers or 1.2 miles). Other areas are criss-crossed by a pattern of linear faults. It is unlikely that a body so small could contain enough radioactive material for the modification to be produced internally. A more likely source of heating appears to be tidal interaction with Dione (like Jupiter's Io). For Enceladus' present orbit, however, current theories of tidal heating do not predict generation of sufficient energy to explain all the heating that must have occurred. Because it reflects so much sunlight, Enceladus current surface temperature is only 72° Kelvin (−330° Fahrenheit).

### [TETHYS]

Photos of Tethys taken by Voyager 2 show an enormous impact crater nearly one-third the diameter of Tethys, larger than Mimas. The crater appears to have formed when Tethys was relatively fluid, since the surface recovered, after the impact, almost its original shape. A gigantic fracture covers three-fourths of Tethy's circumference. Scientists believe the fissure can be explained if Tethys was once fluid and its crust hardened before the interior. Freezing and consequent expansion of the interior could cause a surface fracture about the size of the one observed, although the expansion would not be expected to cause only one large crack. The canyon has been named Ithaca Chiasma. Tethys' current surface temperature is about 86° Kelvin (−305° Fahrenheit).

### [MIMAS AND HYPERION]

Photos of Mimas also showed a huge crater. The crater is about one-third the diameter of Mimas. The Mimas crater has greater surface relief, implying that Mimas was much more rigid at the time of the event that caused the crater.

Hyperion shows no evidence of internal activity. Its irregular shape and evidence of bombardment by meteoritic material make it appear to be the oldest surface in the Saturn system.

## [IAPETUS AND PHOEBE]

Iapetus has long been known to have large differences in surface brightness. Brightness of the surface material on the trailing side has been measured at 50 percent, while the leading side material reflects only 5 percent of the sunlight that strikes it. Most of the dark material is distributed in a pattern directly centered on the leading surface, causing conjecture that the material was swept up as it spiralled inward, presumably from Phoebe. The trailing face of Iapetus, however, has several craters with dark floors. That implies that the dark material originated in the satellite's interior. It is possible that the dark material came both from Phoebe and from Iapetus' interior.

Phoebe was photographed by Voyager 2 after the spacecraft passed Saturn. Phoebe orbits in a retrograde direction (opposite to the direction of the other satellites' orbits) in a plane much closer to the ecliptic than to Saturn's equatorial plane. Voyager 2 found that Phoebe is roughly circular in shape, and reflects about 6 percent of the sunlight. It is also quite red in color. Phoebe rotates on its axis about once in nine hours. Thus, unlike the other Saturnian satellites, it does not always show the same face to the planet. If, as scientists believe, Phoebe is a captured asteriod with its composition unmodified since its formation in the outer solar system, it is the first such object that has been photographed.

## [DIONE AND RHEA]

Both Dione and Rhea have bright, wispy streaks that stand out against an already-bright surface. The streaks are probably the results of ice that evolved from the interior along fractures in the crust.

# The Magnetosphere

The size of Saturn's magnetosphere is determined by external pressure of the solar wind. When Voyager 2 entered the magnetosphere, the solar-wind pressure was high and the magnetosphere extended only 19 Saturn radii (1.1 million kilometers or 712,000 miles) in the Sun's direction. Several hours later, however, the solar-wind pressure dropped and Saturn's magnetosphere ballooned outward over a six-hour period. It apparently remained inflated for at least three days, since it was 70 percent larger when Voyager 2 crossed the magnetic boundary on the outbound leg.

Unlike all the other planets whose magnetic fields have been measured, Saturn's field is tipped only about one degree relative to the rotation poles. That rare alignment was first measured by Pioneer 11 in 1979 and was later confirmed by Voyager 1.

Several distinct regions have been identified within Saturn's magnetosphere. Inside about 400,000 kilometers (250,000 miles) there is a torus of $H^+$ and $O^+$ ions, probably originating from water ice sputtered from the surfaces of Dione and Tethys. (Those ions are positively charged atoms of hydrogen and oxygen that have lost one electron.) Strong plasma-wave emissions appear to be associated with the inner torus.

At the outer regions of the inner torus some ions have been accelerated to high velocities. In terms of temperatures, such velocities correspond to 400 million to 500 million° Kelvin.

Outside the inner torus is a thick sheet of plasma that extends out to about 1 million kilometers (620,000 miles). The source for material in the outer plasma sheet is probably Saturn's ionosphere, Titan's atmosphere, and the neutral hydrogen torus that surrounds Titan between 500,000 kilometers (300,000 miles) and 1.5 million kilometers (1 million miles).

Radio emissions from Saturn had changed between the encounters of Voyager 1 and 2. Voyager 2 detected Jupiter's magnetotail as it approached Saturn in the winter and early spring of 1981. Soon afterward, when Saturn was believed to be bathed in the Jovian magnetotail, the ringed planet's kilometric radio emissions were also undetectable.

During portions of Voyager 2's Saturn encounter, kilometric radio emissions again were not detected. The observations are consistent with effects caused by Jupiter's magnetotail, although Voyager scientists say they have no direct evidence that the shutdown of Saturn's natural radio signals was caused by Jupiter's magnetotail.

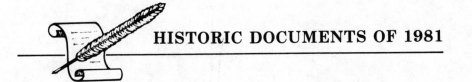

# December

# RICHARD V. ALLEN INVESTIGATION
## December 1, 1981

*In a statement issued December 1, the Justice Department announced it had found no evidence of criminal wrongdoing on the part of presidential national security adviser Richard V. Allen in his receipt of cash from a Japanese women's magazine.*

*The Federal Bureau of Investigation (FBI) had begun an inquiry in September when $1,000 in cash was found in a safe in an office Allen used in the Old Executive Office Building. The presidential adviser had been given the money after arranging an interview for the magazine with Nancy Reagan, the day after President Reagan's inauguration.*

*After reviewing the FBI's report, which included interviews with 36 persons in both the United States and Japan, the Justice Department concluded that Allen had meant to give the money to the government but "through oversight" never officially reported it. "The $1,000 received by Allen was intended as an honorarium for Mrs. Reagan," the department statement read. ". . . [T]he magazine records are consistent on that point. There is no evidence that the cash was intended for Allen." The report also found that "Allen did not intend to keep the money for his personal use." (Federal laws prohibit U.S. officials from accepting anything of value for performance of their official duties.)*

### Gifts and Financial Disclosure

*While exonerating Allen on his receipt of the cash, the Justice Department stated it would continue its investigation into charges that*

*Allen had received wrist watches from two Japanese and that he had filed an incomplete financial disclosure statement with the White House a year earlier.*

*The watches had been given to Allen by his friends, Tamotsu and Chizuko Takase, when he was trying to arrange the magazine interview with Mrs. Reagan. Mrs. Takase acted as interpreter for the Japanese journalists who did the interview.*

*Questions also had been raised about the sale of Allen's consulting firm, Potomac International Corp., to Peter D. Hannaford, a former aide to Reagan before he became president. Allen had just begun receiving monthly payments from Hannaford, who purchased the business on an installment plan, at the time of the inauguration. Hannaford still retained some of Allen's Japanese clients.*

*Allen did not reveal detailed information on the sale when he filed his financial disclosure statement with the White House in February 1981. Nor did he list clients who paid him more than $5,000 a year.*

*Attorney General William French Smith announced December 23 that Allen had not acted illegally with regard to the watches and the financial disclosure issue. It would not be necessary, he said, to appoint a special prosecutor for an independent inquiry.*

## White House Politics

*Allen had taken paid leave from his White House post November 29, two days before the Justice Department released its first statement on its investigation. Following Smith's announcement on December 23, Allen stated his intention to return to his job, saying he felt vindicated.*

*But throughout the investigation the White House had maintained that Allen was not guaranteed his job, regardless of the outcome of the inquiry. Indeed, reports had circulated that, irrespective of the Japanese affair, Reagan aides were unhappy with Allen's performance as national security adviser. At the beginning of 1982, the president requested that Allen resign, even though a White House inquiry also had cleared him of any wrongdoing. On January 4, Reagan appointed Deputy Secretary of State William P. Clark to replace Allen.*

> Following are excerpts from the Justice Department report on the investigation of Richard V. Allen, released December 1, 1981. (Boldface headings in brackets have been added by Congressional Quarterly to highlight the organization of the text.):

On September 21, 1981, Edwin Meese, III, Counselor to the President, after having been told of this matter by White House employees, turned over copies of documents to the Attorney General that were found in a safe in an office used by Allen in the Old Executive Office Building. The documents consisted of a larger outer envelope bearing Oriental characters; a smaller inner envelope with $10,000 written on it containing ten $100 bills; a piece of paper resembling a receipt with Oriental writing, including the figure $10,000; a business card of a Japanese Chamber of Commerce official and a faxgram dated January 14, 1981 from that official to Allen. No explanation or criminal allegation was furnished with the documents.

## Summary of Investigation

Through interviews of 36 individuals in the United States and Japan* and analysis of documentary evidence and forensic examinations, the investigation has yielded a complete, coherent and materially uncontradicted account of how the cash came to be found in the safe. On January 21, 1981, an envelope containing ten $100 bills was intercepted by Allen when Japanese journalists attempted to hand it to Mrs. Reagan as an honorarium for a brief interview Mrs. Reagan had given to the journalists. Allen gave the envelope to his secretary with instructions to turn it over to the appropriate officials. The secretary placed the envelope in a safe and, through oversight, the cash was never officially reported or turned over to the appropriate officials. The envelope was discovered on September 15, 1981 in a safe in an office used by Allen in the Old Executive Office Building by individuals moving into the office.

### ARRANGING THE INTERVIEW

Sometime in December 1980, Kamisaka Fuyoko, a writer for a Japanese women's magazine called "Shufu No Tomo" (translated: "Friends of the Housewife" or "The Housewife's Friend," hereinafter referred to as "The Magazine") discussed with Mrs. Takase Chizuko in Japan the possibility of interviewing Nancy Reagan for The Magazine. Mrs. Takase knew Allen through her husband's business and personal relationship with him and she undertook to arrange such an interview. Mrs. Takase telephoned Allen and sought his help in arranging the interview. Allen in a memorandum dated December 8, 1980 wrote to Charles Tyson, then a scheduling official for the transition team, passing on Mrs. Takase's request and stating that he supported the request if time for a short interview could be arranged. Allen recalls referring the request for an interview to Peter Hannaford, who at that time was in the process of taking over Allen's private consulting business, Potomac International Corporation. Mrs. Takase

---

*The FBI is not permitted to conduct interviews in Japan. Thus all interviews in Japan had to be conducted by the Japanese National Police Agency.

states that she called Allen on January 15, 1981 prior to departing Japan and that Allen told her that there was almost no possibility of obtaining an interview because of the Reagans' busy schedule.

Mrs. Takase, Mrs. Kamisaka and Kimoto Yoshiko, an editor of The Magazine, departed Tokyo for Washington, D.C. on January 15, 1981, in hopes of obtaining an interview with Mrs. Reagan. Prior to departing, they discussed the subject of an honorarium for Mrs. Reagan and decided on $1,000, which was withdrawn from The Magazine's accounting section in Japan. Mrs. Kimoto placed the $1,000 in a "ceremonial pouch" (the envelope) in Washington, D.C. prior to the interview. None of the women knew who wrote $10,000 on the envelope or the receipt form, but each stated that only $1,000 was put in the envelope. Accounting records obtained from The Magazine indicate that $1,000 was vouchered and dispensed for the honorarium. The records also indicate that a total of $10,000 in cash was disbursed by the accounting office to the women to cover their expenses for the trip.

Upon arriving in Washington on January 16, 1981, the three women went to Hannaford's office where they told Hannaford that they were still seeking a response to their interview request. Shortly thereafter, Hannaford called Mrs. Reagan's Chief of Staff to request an interview of Mrs. Reagan for the three women. Hannaford did not contact Allen regarding the request. Neither Hannaford nor Potomac International Corporation received any compensation from The Magazine for the assistance provided. Mrs. Reagan's Chief of Staff had only a faint recollection regarding the request, but believes that he passed on Hannaford's request to Mrs. Reagan. Both Mr. and Mrs. Takase contacted Allen regarding the interview during the three-day period before the Inauguration. There is no indication that Allen provided any assistance during that time period.

On January 20, Mrs. Takase received a phone call from the transition office informing her that an interview might be possible and she should stand ready. The following day, on January 21, the women received a message from the transition office to come to the White House at 5:45 p.m.

## THE INTERVIEW

White House records and interviews indicate that Mrs. Reagan met with the three Japanese women for between five and ten minutes at around 6:00 p.m. in the living quarters of the White House. In addition to Mrs. Reagan and Allen at least five others were present. In the course of the session, Mrs. Kamisaka presented Mrs. Reagan with a lacquer box that she had purchased in Japan. The box was immediately turned over by Mrs. Reagan to the Government through appropriate White House channels.

Allen states that one of the women also attempted to present Mrs. Reagan with an envelope and some news clippings. Allen stepped in and took possession of the envelope and the clippings before they could be passed to Mrs. Reagan. One of the women asked Allen to sign a receipt but he refused "since he had not accepted it for himself." Allen stated that he did not return the envelope to the women because he thought it would offend them. Allen did not recall from which of the women he took the envelope; Mrs. Kamisaka believes it was Mrs. Takase, Mrs. Kimoto recalls that she gave the envelope to Mrs. Takase at the end of the interview but did not see what Mrs. Takase did with it, and Mrs. Takase cannot recall who had the envelope.

## STORAGE OF THE ENVELOPE

Allen states that after the interview he returned to his office where he opened the envelope while sitting at his desk. He recalled that it contained ten $100 bills. In his first interview, Allen said he recalled seeing the receipt, but in a later interview he said that he had not seen the receipt or a notation showing $10,000. In any event, he immediately turned the envelope over to his secretary, advising her that the money should be turned over to the appropriate officials. His secretary placed the envelope in a four-drawer safe in her office located next to Allen's former office in the Old Executive Office Building. Allen did not thereafter see the envelope. Peter Hannaford, Secretary of the Navy John Lehman, and Allen's wife have all told the FBI that they recall Allen telling them sometime shortly after January 21 about the incident, including the fact that he had intercepted an envelope containing cash that one of the women had attempted to hand to Mrs. Reagan.

## [RESPONSIBILITY OF SECRETARY]

Allen told the FBI that he should have made sure the envelope was turned over in the proper manner; however, due to the confusion of moving into the White House, his secretary did not get around to cataloguing the money and properly disposing of it. Allen's secretary corroborated these facts and has told the FBI that she wanted to accept full responsibility for the money since it was her responsibility to dispose of it properly.

In February, Allen's secretary moved to new office space in the West Wing of the White House. At about the same time, another National Security Council secretary also moved out of the Old Executive Office Building office previously occupied by Allen's secretary. In the process of moving, she checked the safe in the office to make sure it was empty. In one of the drawers she discovered a gift package and an envelope with Oriental writing. She opened the envelope and observed ten $100 bills. She immediately summoned yet another National Security Council secretary to the office and showed her the envelope. The second secretary remembers seeing ten or eleven $100 bills.

The second secretary then notified Allen's secretary that they had found an envelope with $1,000 in the safe. She was instructed by Allen's secretary to notify an assistant to Allen, who was occupying Allen's former office. She gave the envelope and packages to the assistant who says he received the envelope from her, opened it and counted ten $100 bills. On his own initiative the assistant put the envelope and packages in the two-drawer safe in Allen's former office "for safekeeping." He left the National Security Council in March 1981 with the envelope still in the safe and without notifying Allen of what he had done with the envelope. The envelope was next discovered in the two-drawer safe on September 15.

## DISCOVERY OF THE ENVELOPE

On September 15, 1981, three military officers on special detail to the White House were moving into Allen's former office in the Old Executive Office Building when they opened a two-drawer safe they had presumed was empty. In the safe were several gift-wrapped packages, the receipt form and the envelope containing $1,000. The $1,000 was observed by two of the officers and a secretary. The secretary turned the envelope and packages over to Barbara Diering, the head of the Administrative Office of the National Security Council. While in Diering's office, the items were inspected by Jerry Jennings, the Chief of Security for the National Security Council staff. A business card of a Japanese Chamber of Commerce official was taped to one of the packages. In an effort to locate any related documents which might bear on the envelope, Jennings found in another office a faxgram from the Japanese Chamber of Commerce official to Allen, requesting assistance in obtaining an audience with Ronald Reagan. Jennings mistakenly believed that this faxgram was related to the envelope because of the proximity of the envelope containing the ten $100 bills to the gift box which had the business card attached.* On September 21, Jennings turned over to Meese the envelope, the faxgram and the business card. Later the same day, Meese turned over copies of the documents to the Attorney General.

---

*Jennings believed that the business card was somehow related to the envelope because it was attached to a box proximate to the envelope when he inspected the items in Diering's office. The individuals who opened the safe, however, stated that the envelope fell out from among the packages when they removed them from the safe. They did not know where the envelope had been placed among the boxes and when the envelope and boxes were given to Diering, no effort was made to duplicate the original position of the envelope. Jennings' assumption that the envelope's position among the boxes had some significance when he later inspected them was thus incorrect. The faxgram and business card are wholly irrelevant to the envelope.

The gift boxes were opened and inspected by the FBI with Allen's permission. They contained gifts of nominal value. Allen does not remember precisely when he received the various gifts, but he says they will all be properly catalogued. None of the gifts has any relationship to the envelope or The Magazine interview.

## Analysis

### FACTS

The facts uncovered in the investigation of this matter involving the envelope containing $1,000 are consistent on all material points. These points are:

(1) The $1,000 received by Allen was intended as an honorarium for Mrs. Reagan. Each of the three Japanese women and The Magazine records are consistent on that point. There is no evidence that the cash was intended for Allen.

(2) Allen did not intend to keep the money for his personal use. Both Allen and his secretary agree on Allen's expressed intent to turn the money over through proper channels. The fact that Allen wholly parted with dominion and control over the money, left the envelope in a safe accessible to others, and told several people, including the present Secretary of the Navy, about the cash, is inconsistent with an intent to keep the money for personal use. There is no evidence to indicate Allen intended to keep the money for himself.

(3) There was only $1,000 in the envelope turned over to Allen. Although the receipt and envelope contain the figure $10,000, all the evidence indicates that only $1,000 was given to Allen. The three women and The Magazine's records indicate $1,000 was given and everyone who saw the envelope and money, a total of eight people, observed only $1,000 with one exception and that person recalled observing ten or eleven $100 bills.

### RELEVANT CRIMINAL STATUTES

The bribery statute, 18 U.S.C. 201 (c), requires that Allen receive something of value in return for being influenced in the performance of an official act. In this matter, the money was not given to Allen for anything he had done; rather, it was intended as an honorarium for Mrs. Reagan and simply intercepted by Allen. It was neither given nor received to benefit Allen or to influence him in any way. Indeed, he was not even aware of the contents of the envelope until after the meeting was completed.

For the same reason, the gratuity statute, 18 U.S.C. 201 (g), is inapplicable. That statute proscribes the receipt of something of value by a public official "for himself for or because of any official act performed or to be performed by him." In this instance, Allen was not given the $1,000 for himself and it was not intended by Allen or the women to thank Allen for anything.

18 U.S.C. 209 proscribes receipt of compensation by an official for his services as an official from sources other than the Government. Again, there is no evidence that the money was either given to or received by Allen with an intent to compensate him. Similarly, 18 U.S.C. 203, proscribing compensation to a Government official for services in relation

to a Government proceeding, is inapplicable because the money was not intended to compensate Allen for anything.

In sum, when the uncontradicted facts are analyzed in the context of possibly applicable criminal laws, it is clear that there was no criminal violation by Allen regarding the $1,000....

# SENATE REPORT ON CASEY
## December 1, 1981

*In a brief six-page report, issued December 1, the Senate Select Committee on Intelligence criticized William J. Casey, director of the Central Intelligence Agency (CIA), for providing the committee with inadequate information on his business activities. The committee asserted, however, that "no basis" had been found "for concluding that Mr. Casey is unfit to hold office as Director of Central Intelligence." Casey, appointed to the top CIA job by President Reagan, was a former chairman of the Securities and Exchange Commission.*

*The committee's three-month investigation of Casey's affairs had been spurred by questions raised in the press regarding his choice of CIA deputy director, a securities civil case in which he was involved and allegations that he had omitted information from congressional questionnaires and other forms at the time of his appointment.*

### Dissenting Senator

*One member of the 15-member Senate committee, Sen. Joseph R. Biden, D-Del., dissented strongly and unexpectedly from the report. Biden said that he had "come to the conclusion that ... Casey had displayed a consistent pattern of omissions, misstatements, and contradictions in his dealings with this and other committees of Congress." Although all of the other committee members voted for the report, Sen. Patrick J. Leahy, D-Vt., called the finding of "not unfit to serve" a "determination ... best made by the president."*

## Background

*Casey had been criticized several months earlier for his appointment of Max Hugel, first as special assistant and then as CIA deputy director for operations. A* Washington Post *story July 14 reported that Hugel had been accused by two former business associates of illegal or improper stock trading practices. The same day the story appeared in the newspaper, Hugel resigned.*

*Questions had also been raised by a securities case involving a farming business, Multiponics Inc., in which Casey had been a partner. A civil suit brought in 1974 contained allegations of misrepresentations in a Multiponics stock-offering circular. However, a federal judge on November 10, reversing a previous ruling that Casey had knowingly "misrepresented or omitted facts" to private investors, called "persuasive" Casey's denial that he had been aware of any omissions or misrepresentations in the circular.*

## Committee Report

*The Senate committee report disposed of the issues of the Multiponics stock offering and Casey's hiring of Hugel in a few lines. It agreed with the decision of the judge in the securities case that Casey had "no active role" in the preparation of the circulars. With reference to the Hugel appointment, it merely said that Casey had "volunteered" in a hearing that his appointment of Hugel had been a mistake for which he took full responsibility. "The committee concurs," the report said succinctly.*

## Omissions

*The report chastized Casey for having been "at minimum inattentive to detail, particularly with regard to filling out two forms required by the Office of Government Ethics" and the Senate committee itself.*

*Among the omissions from forms cited in the report were "at least nine investments" and "personal debts and contingent liabilities." The report also said that Casey had failed to list 70 legal clients he had represented, four civil suits in which he had been involved and corporations and foundations on which he served. It said that "[a]mong the clients not disclosed" were two foreign governments and an oil company.*

## Casey Response

*Casey issued a statement December 2, asserting, "I am pleased that the . . . committee, after an exhaustive investigation, has reported nothing which reflects on the integrity, the business practices and the ethical standards in which I have always taken pride."*

*Following are excerpts from the December 1, 1981, report of
the Senate Select Committee on Intelligence on the Casey
inquiry:*

# I. Background

William J. Casey was confirmed by the United States Senate, 95-0, on
January 28, 1981, as Director of Central Intelligence. One week before,
Max Hugel was named by Mr. Casey to be his special assistant at the
Central Intelligence Agency (CIA). On May 11, Mr. Hugel was named CIA
Deputy Director for Operations. The Washington Post, on July 14,
reported Mr. Hugel was accused by two former business associates of
illegal or improper stock trading practices. The publicity regarding Mr.
Hugel resulted in press reports questioning Mr. Casey's judgment in
selecting the Deputy Director for Operations, and noting Mr. Casey's
possible civil liability in a securities case, *Maiden* v. *Biehl*. . . .

# II. Scope of the Inquiry

From July 29, 1981 through October 31, 1981, thirteen staff members,
including the Minority Staff Director and Minority Counsel, worked on
the investigation with Special Counsel. On July 31, Senator Barry Goldwater appointed Deputy Special Counsel and on September 9, 1981,
Senator Daniel Patrick Moynihan appointed Minority Special Counsel for
the inquiry.

Two hundred and thirty-nine documents were received in response to
Committee requests, totalling approximately 10,500 pages. These documents included voluminous court records and opinions, transcripts, previous Congressional hearings at which Mr. Casey testified, reports and
financial records of financial transactions and business ventures of Mr.
Casey, his Central Intelligency [*sic*] Agency and Federal Bureau of
Investigation background checks, and the forms submitted for the Office
of Government Ethics and the Senate Select Committee on Intelligence.
Additionally, two staff members traveled to New Orleans to read approximately 1,500 pages of the bankruptcy case and the trustee's civil action,
and to review more than 26,000 pages of related proceedings to find
relevant portions. Three trips were made to New York to interview
witnesses and review other documents. A total of over 70 persons were
interviewed by phone, and more than 40 were personally interviewed.

The specific areas of inquiry derived from allegations contained in press
reports, from individual citizens contacting the Committee or from questions arising after the staff reviewed documents. These areas were organized into four main categories: (1) Mr. Casey's private dealings; (2) Mr.
Casey's activities while in previous government service and/or beneficiary

of a blind trust (April 1971-January 1976); (3) Mr. Casey's forms filed with the Office of Government Ethics and Senate Select Committee on Intelligence; and (4) Mr. Casey's appointments of Mr. Hugel.

## III. Findings

The Committee's inquiry into these categories showed that Mr. Casey was at minimum inattentive to detail, particularly with regard to filling out two forms required by the Office of Government Ethics and the Senate Select Commitlee on Intelligence.

The written responses by Mr. Casey to this Committee's questionnaire, filed on January 2, 1981, were deficient in several respects. The original answers omitted at least nine investments valued at more than a quarter of a million dollars, personal debts and contingent liabilities of nearly five hundred thousand dollars, a number of corporations or foundations on whose board Mr. Casey served, four civil law suits in which he was involved in the last five years, and more than seventy clients he had represented in private practice in the last five years. Among the clients not disclosed to the Committee were two foreign governments, the Republic of Korea and the Republic of Indonesia, and an oil company controlled by the latter, Pertamina of Indonesia.

Mr. Casey's representation of Indonesia in 1976 raised a question whether he should have registered under the Foreign Agents Registration Act. The question was not resolved by the Committee because it is a technical one involving whether there was an attempt to influence or persuade agency officials, and if so, whether an exemption applied because his representation was in the course of an established agency proceeding.

The large amount of information which Mr. Casey omitted from his initial disclosure forms to the Select Committee and the Office of Government Ethics considerably lengthened the Committee's inquiry. The Committee is concerned that this pattern suggests an insufficient appreciation of the obligation to provide complete and accurate information to the oversight committees of the Congress. In view of the duty of the Director of Central Intelligence to keep the Select Committee "fully and currently informed of all intelligence activities. . . ." (National Security Act of 1947, as amended, Section 501 (a)), the Committee is concerned that Mr. Casey understand the importance it places on this obligation.

A primary concern of the Committee was the appointment of Mr. Hugel as Deputy Director for Operations. Mr. Casey volunteered in the July 29, 1981 hearing that this appointment was a "mistake" for which he takes "full responsibility." The Committee concurs.

The Committee thoroughly explored Mr. Hugel's background investigation by the CIA and could not find any evidence that Mr. Hugel's background investigation was treated differently from that of other appointees. Mr. Hugel was interviewed by Special Counsel in the presence of the Committee Chairman and Vice Chairman. Mr. Hugel's responses were circumscribed, but nothing emerged to disprove Mr. Casey's under-standing of how the Hugel appointment came about.

With respect to *Maiden* v. *Biehl,* in which Mr. Casey is a defendant, the available evidence indicates that Mr. Casey had no active role in the preparation or legal review of the offering circular which the plaintiffs claim was false and misleading. Any civil liability in the case would derive, therefore, from his membership on the board of directors and, hence, would be a matter of legal rather than moral responsibility. . . .

## V. Conclusion

Having reviewed the facts obtained in the course of its four-month investigation, the Committee reaffirms its July 29, 1981 statement that no basis has been found for concluding that Mr. Casey is unfit to hold office as Director of Central Intelligence. . . .

# EXECUTIVE ORDER
# ON INTELLIGENCE AGENCIES
## December 4, 1981

*Seeking to "remove the aura of suspicion and mistrust that can hobble our nation's intelligence efforts," President Reagan December 4 issued Executive Order 12333 expanding the information-gathering authority of the Central Intelligence Agency (CIA) and other intelligence organizations. The order, which had the force of law, loosened restrictions that President Carter had imposed on U.S. intelligence agencies.*

*Specifically, the Reagan order permitted the CIA and other agencies besides the Federal Bureau of Investigation (FBI) to collect "significant foreign intelligence" within the United States, provided the effort was not aimed at monitoring domestic activities of American citizens and corporations.*

*In addition, the order allowed the CIA to conduct domestic or foreign operations approved by the president, if they were undertaken to further "national foreign policy objectives abroad" and "not intended to influence United States political processes, public opinion, policies, or media." Carter had prohibited domestic covert operations.*

## Criticism from Congress

*Members of Congress had criticized three earlier drafts of the order for going too far in easing the Carter safeguards. Members of the House and Senate Intelligence committees had been concerned that Reagan would not adequately limit CIA operations within the United States.*

*After the final order was issued, some members still had reservations. Sen. Daniel Patrick Moynihan, D-N.Y., said there still were "a very few provisions" that could "pose problems" if they were "misinterpreted or stretched beyond the legitimate intent of their authors."*

*The White House had accepted 15 of the 18 major changes to earlier drafts that had been proposed by the Senate Intelligence Committee. Deleted, for example, was a provision that would have allowed the CIA to infiltrate domestic organizations without a court warrant.*

*In a separate executive order, also issued December 4, Reagan continued the Intelligence Oversight Board begun by Carter and recommissioned the 19-member Foreign Intelligence Advisory Board, which Carter had disbanded. Composed of three private citizens appointed by the president, the Oversight Board was authorized to inform the president of any "intelligence activities" that any member believed was "in violation of the Constitution or laws of the United States, executive orders or presidential directives."*

## Increase in Soviet Spies

*In a speech to the World Affairs Council in Los Angeles December 18, Attorney General William French Smith explained that the Reagan orders were necessary to help counter a "dramatic" increase in Soviet spies in the United States and the growing threat of international terrorist groups.*

*"At one time," he said, "the FBI could match suspected hostile intelligence agents in the United States on a one-to-one basis. Now the number of hostile agents has grown so much that our FBI counterintelligence agents are greatly outnumbered."*

*According to Smith, Soviet spies were living in the United States as students, scientists, businessmen, refugees and newsmen. "About one-third of the Soviet bloc personnel in the United States assigned to embassies, consulates and the U.N. or other international organizations are believed to be full-time intelligence officers," he said.*

*Calling the threat of international terrorism the "most serious of all," Smith emphasized that the White House was "firmly committed to revitalizing the United States intelligence effort."*

*Following are the text of President Reagan's announcement of his directives on intelligence agency activities and excerpts from Executive Order 12333, both December 4, 1981.* (Boldface headings in brackets have been added by Congressional Quarterly to highlight the organization of the texts.):

# REAGAN STATEMENT

Today I am issuing two Executive orders, one to govern the activities of our intelligence agencies and one to reestablish the Intelligence Oversight Board, which works to ensure that our intelligence activities are lawful. These orders are designed to provide America's intelligence community with clearer, more positive guidance and to remove the aura of suspicion and mistrust that can hobble our Nation's intelligence efforts.

This action is consistent with my promise in the campaign to revitalize America's intelligence system. The American people are well aware that the security of their country — and in an age of terrorism, their personal safety as well — is tied to the strength and efficiency of our intelligence-gathering organizations.

These orders have been carefully drafted — in consultation with the intelligence committees of both Houses of the Congress — to maintain the legal protection of all American citizens. They also give our intelligence professionals clear guidelines within which to do their difficult and essential job. Contrary to a distorted image that emerged during the last decade, there is no inherent conflict between the intelligence community and the rights of our citizens. Indeed, the purpose of the intelligence community is the protection of our people.

This is not to say mistakes were never made and that vigilance against abuse is unnecessary. But an approach that emphasizes suspicion and mistrust of our own intelligence efforts can undermine this Nation's ability to confront the increasing challenge of espionage and terrorism. This is particularly true in a world in which our adversaries pay no heed to the concerns for individual rights and freedoms that are so important to Americans and their Government. As we move into the 1980's, we need to free ourselves from the negative attitudes of the past and look to meeting the needs of the country.

## [Guarantee of Rights]

To those who view this change of direction with suspicion, let me assure you that while I occupy this office, no intelligence agency of the United States, or any other agency for that matter, will be given the authority to violate the rights and liberties guaranteed to all Americans by our Constitution and laws. The provisions of these Executive orders make this abundantly clear.

Most Americans realize that intelligence is a good and necessary profession to which high caliber men and women dedicate their lives. We respect them for their honorable and often perilous service to our Nation and the cause of freedom. For all our technological advances, the gathering of information and its analysis depend finally on human judgment; and good judgment depends on the experience, integrity, and professionalism of those who serve us in the intelligence community.

Let us never forget that good intelligence saves American lives and protects our freedom. The loyalty and selflessness of our intelligence community during hard times are testimony to its commitment to the principles on which our country is based. I have faith in our intelligence professionals and expect each and every one of them to live up to the ideals and standards set by these Executive orders.

These orders charge our intelligence agencies to be vigorous, innovative, and responsible in the collection of accurate and timely information — information essential for the conduct of our foreign policy and crucial to our national safety. The country needs this service and is willing to allocate the resources necessary to do the job right.

## [Truthful Analysis]

It is not enough, of course, simply to collect information. Thoughtful analysis is vital to sound decisionmaking. The goal of our intelligence analysts can be nothing short of the truth, even when that truth is unpleasant or unpopular. I have asked for honest, objective analysis, and I shall expect nothing less. When there is disagreement, as there often is, on the difficult questions of our time, I expect those honest differences of view to be fully expressed.

These orders stipulate that special attention be given to detecting and countering the espionage and other threats that are directed by hostile intelligence services against us at home and abroad. These hostile services respect none of the liberties and rights of privacy that these orders protect. Certainly the same can be said of international terrorists, who present another important area of concern and responsibility for our intelligence professionals.

I want to stress that the primary job of the CIA [Central Intelligence Agency] is to conduct intelligence activities overseas and to deal with certain foreign persons who come into this country. The FBI [Federal Bureau of Investigation] takes primary responsibility for security activities within the United States, directed against hostile foreigners and those Americans who seek to do damage to our national security.

These orders do not alter this basic division of labor; they reaffirm it. They also encourage the fullest possible cooperation among the CIA, the FBI, and other agencies of the intelligence community as they seek to deal with fundamental challenges to our national security — challenges that respect neither national boundaries nor citizenship.

As these Executive orders are issued, I again want to express my respect and admiration for the men and women of our intelligence community: They run the risks; they bear the tensions; they serve in silence. They cannot fully be thanked in public, but I want them to know that their job is vital and that the American people, and their President, are profoundly grateful for what they do.

# EXECUTIVE ORDER 12333

[Part 1 Omitted]

## Part 2 Conduct of Intelligence Activities

2.1 *Need.* Accurate and timely information about the capabilities, intentions and activities of foreign powers, organizations, or persons and their agents is essential to informed decision-making in the areas of national defense and foreign relations. Collection of such information is a priority objective and will be pursued in a vigorous, innovative and responsible manner that is consistent with the Constitution and applicable law and respectful of the principles upon which the United States was founded.

2.2 *Purpose.* This Order is intended to enhance human and technical collection techniques, especially those undertaken abroad, and the acquisition of significant foreign intelligence, as well as the detection and countering of international terrorist activities and espionage conducted by foreign powers. Set forth below are certain general principles that, in addition to and consistent with applicable laws, are intended to achieve the proper balance between the acquisition of essential information and protection of individual interests. Nothing in this Order shall be construed to apply to or interfere with any authorized civil or criminal law enforcement responsibility of any department or agency.

2.3 *Collection of Information.* Agencies within the Intelligence Community are authorized to collect, retain or disseminate information concerning United States persons only in accordance with procedures established by the head of the agency concerned and approved by the Attorney General, consistent with the authorities provided by Part I of this Order. Those procedures shall permit collection, retention and dissemination of the following types of information.

(a) Information that is publicly available or collected with the consent of the person concerned;

(b) Information constituting foreign intelligence or counterintelligence, including such information concerning corporations or other commercial organizations. Collection within the United States of foreign intelligence not otherwise obtainable shall be undertaken by the FBI or, when significant foreign intelligence is sought, by other authorized agencies of the Intelligence Community, provided that no foreign intelligence collection by such agencies may be undertaken for the purpose of acquiring information concerning the domestic activities of United States persons;

(c) Information obtained in the course of a lawful foreign intelligence, counterintelligence, international narcotics or international terrorism investigation;

(d) Information needed to protect the safety of any persons or organizations, including those who are targets, victims or hostages of international terrorists organizations;

(e) Information needed to protect foreign intelligence or counterintelligence sources or methods from unauthorized disclosure. Collection within the United States shall be undertaken by the FBI except that other agencies of the Intelligence Community may also collect such information concerning present or former employees, present or former intelligence agency contractors or their present or former employees, or applicants for any such employment or contracting;

(f) Information concerning persons who are reasonably believed to be potential sources or contacts for the purpose of determining their suitability or credibility;

(g) Information arising out of a lawful personnel, physical or communications security investigation;

(h) Information acquired by overhead reconnaissance not directed at specific United States persons;

(i) Incidentally obtained information that may indicate involvement in activities that may violate federal, state, local or foreign laws; and

(j) Information necessary for administrative purposes.

In addition, agencies within the Intelligence Community may disseminate information, other than information derived from signals intelligence, to each appropriate agency within the Intelligence Community for purposes of allowing the recipient agency to determine whether the information is relevant to its responsibilities and can be retained by it.

2.4 *Collection Techniques.* Agencies within the Intelligence Community shall use the least intrusive collection techniques feasible within the United States or directed against United States persons abroad. Agencies are not authorized to use such techniques as electronic surveillance, unconsented physical search, mail surveillance, physical surveillance, or monitoring devices unless they are in accordance with procedures established by the head of the agency concerned and approved by the Attorney General. Such procedures shall protect constitutional and other legal rights and limit use of such information to lawful governmental purposes. . . .

2.5 *Attorney General Approval.* The Attorney General hereby is delegated the power to approve the use for intelligence purposes, within the United States or against a United States person abroad, of any technique for which a warrant would be required if undertaken for law enforcement purposes, provided that such techniques shall not be undertaken unless the Attorney General has determined in each case that there is probable cause to believe that the technique is directed against a foreign power or an agent of a foreign power. Electronic surveillance, as defined in the Foreign Intelligence Surveillance Act of 1978, shall be conducted in accordance with that Act, as well as this Order.

2.6 *Assistance to Law Enforcement Authorities*. Agencies within the Intelligence Community are authorized to:

(a) Cooperate with appropriate law enforcement agencies for the purpose of protecting the employees, information, property and facilities of any agency within the Intelligence Community;

(b) Unless otherwise precluded by law or this Order, participate in law enforcement activities to investigate or prevent clandestine intelligence activities by foreign powers, or international terrorist or narcotics activities;

(c) Provide specialized equipment, technical knowledge, or assistance of expert personnel for use by any department or agency, or, when lives are endangered, to support local law enforcement agencies. Provision of assistance by expert personnel shall be approved in each case by the General Counsel of the providing agency; and

(d) Render any other assistance and cooperation to law enforcement authorities not precluded by applicable law.

2.7 *Contracting*. Agencies within the Intelligence Community are authorized to enter into contracts or arrangements for the provision of goods or services with private companies or institutions in the United States and need not reveal the sponsorship of such contracts or arrangements for authorized intelligence purposes. Contracts or arrangements with academic institutions may be undertaken only with the consent of appropriate officials of the institution.

2.8 *Consistency With Other Laws*. Nothing in this Order shall be construed to authorize any activity in violation of the Constitution or statutes of the United States.

2.9 *Undisclosed Participation in Organizations Within the United States*. No one acting on behalf of agencies within the Intelligence Community may join or otherwise participate in any organization in the United States on behalf of any agency within the Intelligence Community without disclosing his intelligence affiliation to appropriate officials of the organization, except in accordance with procedures established by the head of the agency concerned and approved by the Attorney General. Such participation shall be authorized only if it is essential to achieving lawful purposes as determined by the agency head or designee. No such participation may be undertaken for the purpose of influencing the activity of the organization or its members except in cases where:

(a) The participation is undertaken on behalf of the FBI in the course of a lawful investigation; or

(b) The organization concerned is composed primarily of individuals who are not United States persons and is reasonably believed to be acting on behalf of a foreign power.

2.10 *Human Experimentation*. No agency within the Intelligence Community shall sponsor, contract for or conduct research on human subjects except in accordance with guidelines issued by the Department of Health and Human Services. The subject's informed consent shall be documented as required by those guidelines.

2.11 *Prohibition on Assassination.* No person employed by or acting on behalf of the United States Government shall engage in, or conspire to engage in, assassination.

2.12. *Indirect Participation.* No agency of the Intelligence Community shall participate in or request any person to undertake activities forbidden by this Order. . . .

# COURT ON FREE SPEECH
## December 8, 1981

*Basing its decision on the First Amendment right of free speech and association, the Supreme Court voted 8-1 December 8 that student religious organizations have the same right as other student groups to use state university buildings for their regular meetings.*

*The case had attracted wide attention because it came at a time of revived political interest in the issue of church-state relations. Several religious organizations had filed briefs with the court.*

## Background

*From 1973 to 1977 officials at the University of Missouri had allowed an evangelical student group called Cornerstone to meet regularly in buildings on the Kansas City campus. They had been allowed to meet despite a university rule prohibiting the use of university buildings or grounds for religious worship.*

*In 1977, however, officials refused to let the group meet on campus, citing the university rule. Cornerstone sued, arguing that the rule violated its members' First Amendment right of free speech and exercise of religion.*

*The university countered that its rule was necessary to preserve the separation of church and state as required by the First Amendment ban on the state establishment of religion. The Missouri state constitution had a similar ban.*

*The university won a district court ruling, but the students won in the court of appeals. The university appealed to the Supreme Court, which ruled for the students.*

## Majority Opinion

*Writing for the majority, Justice Lewis F. Powell Jr. argued that once a university creates a forum that is generally open for use by student groups, it may not deny access to certain groups simply because they wish to talk about a particular subject, namely religion.*

*"The university's argument misconceives the nature of this case,"* *Powell wrote. "The question is not whether the creation of a religious forum would violate the Establishment Clause. The university has opened its facilities for use by student groups, and the question is whether it can now exclude groups because of the content of their speech."*

*Powell argued that if the government discriminates against a certain form of speech protected by the First Amendment, it "must show that its regulation is necessary to serve a compelling state interest and that it is narrowly drawn to achieve that end." He further noted that "an open forum in a public university does not confer any imprimatur of state approval on religious sects or practices."*

## Dissenting Opinion

*As the only dissenter in the 8-1 decision, Justice Byron R. White wrote: "I believe the states to be a good deal freer to formulate policies that affect religion in divergent ways than does the majority." He said he would uphold the university position, arguing that the Constitution leaves some room "for state policies that may have some beneficial effect on religion [and for those] . . . that may incidentally burden religion."*

*In White's view, the majority appeared to endorse the idea that because "religious worship uses speech, it is protected by the free speech clause of the First Amendment." If, he argued, the First Amendment prohibits a state from treating verbal acts of worship any differently from other verbal acts, the court would need to reconsider a number of its major rulings on church-state issues. Specifically, he referred to court decisions in 1962 and 1963 that outlawed the use of state-prescribed prayer in public schools.*

*Following are excerpts from the Supreme Court's December 8 decision in* Widmar v. Vincent *upholding the right of a student religious group to use university facilities and from the dissenting opinion:*

No. 80-689

| Gary E. Widmar, et al., Petitioners *v.* Clark Vincent et al. | On Writ of Certiorari to the United States Court of Appeals for the Eighth Circuit |

[December 8, 1981]

JUSTICE POWELL delivered the opinion of the court.

This case presents the question whether a state university, which makes its facilities generally available for the activities of registered student groups, may close its facilities to a registered student group desiring to use the facilities for religious worship and religious discussion.

## I

It is the stated policy of the University of Missouri at Kansas City to encourage the activities of student organizations. The University officially recognizes over 100 student groups. It routinely provides University facilities for the meetings of registered organizations. Students pay an activity fee of $41 per semester (1978-1979) to help defray the costs to the University.

From 1973 until 1977 a registered religious group named Cornerstone regularly sought and received permission to conduct its meetings in University facilities. In 1977, however, the University informed the group that it could no longer meet in University buildings. The exclusion was based on a regulation, adopted by the Board of Curators in 1972, that prohibits the use of University buildings or grounds "for purposes of religious worship or religious teaching."

Eleven University students, all members of Cornerstone, brought suit to challenge the regulation in Federal District Court for the Western District of Missouri. They alleged that the University's discrimination against religious activity and discussion violated their rights to free exercise of religion, equal protection, and freedom of speech under the First and Fourteenth Amendments to the Constitution of the United States.

Upon cross motions for summary judgment, the District Court upheld the challenged regulation. *Chess* v. *Widmar* (WD Mo. 1979). It found the regulation not only justified, but required, by the Establishment Clause of the Federal Constitution. Under *Tilton* v. *Richardson* (1971), the court reasoned, the State could not provide facilities for religious use without giving prohibited support to an institution of religion. The District Court rejected the argument that the University could not discriminate against religious speech on the basis of its content. It found religious speech entitled to less protection than other types of expression.

871

The Court of Appeals for the Eighth Circuit reversed. *Chess* v. *Widmar* (CA8 1980). Rejecting the analysis of the District Court, it viewed the University regulation as a content-based discrimination against religious speech, for which it could find no compelling justification. The Court held that the Establishment Clause does not bar a policy of equal access, in which facilities are open to groups and speakers of all kinds. According to the Court of Appeals, the "primary effect" of such a policy would not be to advance religion, but rather to further the neutral purpose of developing students' " 'social and cultural awareness as well as [their] intellectual curiosity.' " ( . . . University bulletin's description of the student activities program. . .).

We now affirm.

## II

Through its policy of accommodating their meetings, the University has created a forum generally open for use by student groups. Having done so, the University has assumed an obligation to justify its discriminations and exclusions under applicable constitutional norms. The Constitution forbids a State to enforce certain exclusions from a forum generally open to the public, even if it was not required to create the forum in the first place. See *e.g., City of Madison Joint School District* v. *Wisconsin Public Employment Relations Comm'n.* (1976) (although a State may conduct business in private session, "where the State has opened a forum for direct citizen involvement," exclusions bear a heavy burden of justification); *Southeastern Promotions, Ltd.* v. *Conrad* (1975) (because municipal theater was a public forum, city could not exclude a production without satisfying constitutional safeguards applicable to prior restraints).

The University's institutional mission, which it describes as providing a *"secular* education" to its students, does not exempt its actions from constitutional scrutiny. With respect to persons entitled to be there, our cases leave no doubt that the First Amendment rights of speech and association extend to the campuses of state universities. See, *e.g., Healy* v. *James* (1972); *Tinker* v. *Des Moines Independent School District* (1969); *Shelton* v. *Tucker* (1960).

Here the University of Missouri has discriminated against student groups and speakers based on their desire to use a generally open forum to engage in religious worship and discussion. These are forms of speech and association protected by the First Amendment. See, *e.g., Heffron* v. *International Soc'y for Krishna Consciousness* (1981); *Niemotko* v. *Maryland* (1951); *Saia* v. *New York* (1948). In order to justify discriminatory exclusion from a public forum based on the religious content of a group's intended speech, the University must therefore satisfy the standard of review appropriate to content-based exclusions. It must show that its regulation is necessary to serve a compelling state interest and that it is narrowly drawn to achieve that end. See *Carey* v. *Brown* (1980).

## III

In this case the University claims a compelling interest in maintaining strict separation of church and State. It derives this interest from the "Establishment Clauses" of both the Federal and Missouri Constitutions.

### A

The University first argues that it cannot offer its facilities to religious groups and speakers on the terms available to other groups without violating the Establishment Clause of the Constitution of the United States. We agree that the interest of the University in complying with its constitutional obligations may be characterized as compelling. It does not follow, however, that an "equal access" policy would be incompatible with this Court's Establishment Clause cases. Those cases hold that a policy will not offend the Establishment Clause if it can pass a three-pronged test: "First, the [governmental policy] must have a secular legislative purpose; second, its principal or primary effect must be one that neither advances nor inhibits religion. . . ; finally, the [policy] must not foster 'an excessive government entanglement with religion.' " *Lemon* v. *Kurtzman* (1971). See *Committee for Public Education* v. *Regan* (1980); *Roemer* v. *Maryland Public Works Bd.* (1976).

In this case two prongs of the test are clearly met. Both the District Court and the Court of Appeals held that an open-forum policy, including nondiscrimination against religious speech, would have a secular purpose and would avoid entanglement with religion. But the District Court concluded, and the University argues here, that allowing religious groups to share the limited public forum would have the "primary effect" of advancing religion.

The University's argument misconceives the nature of this case. The question is not whether the creation of a religious forum would violate the Establishment Clause. The University has opened its facilities for use by student groups, and the question is whether it can now exclude groups because of the content of their speech. See *Healy* v. *James* (1972). In this context we are unpersuaded that the primary effect of the public forum, open to all forms of discourse, would be to advance religion.

We are not oblivious to the range of an open forum's likely effects. It is possible — perhaps even foreseeable — that religious groups will benefit from access to University facilities. But this Court has explained that a religious organization's enjoyment of merely "incidental" benefits does not violate the prohibition against the "primary advancement" of religion. *Committee for Public Education* v. *Nyquist* (1973); see, *e.g., Roemer* v. *Maryland Public Works Bd.* (1976); *Hunt* v. *McNair* (1972); *McGowan* v. *Maryland* (1961).

We are satisfied that any religious benefits of an open forum at UMKC would be "incidental" within the meaning of our cases. Two factors are especially relevant.

First, an open forum in a public university does not confer any imprimatur of State approval on religious sects or practices. As the Court of Appeals quite aptly stated, such a policy "would no more commit the University . . . to religious goals," than it is "now committed to the goals of the Students for a Democratic Society, the Young Socialist Alliance," or any other group eligible to use its facilities. *Chess* v. *Widmar.*

Second, the forum is available to a broad class of non-religious as well as religious speakers; there are over 100 recognized student groups at UMKC. The provision of benefits to so broad a spectrum of groups is an important index of secular effect. See, *e.g. Wolman* v. *Walter* (1977); *Committee for Public Education* v. *Nyquist,* (1973). If the Establishment Clause barred the extension of general benefits to religious groups, "a church could not be protected by the police and fire departments, or have its public sidewalk kept in repair." *Roemer* v. *Maryland Public Works Bd.* (1976) (plurality opinion); quoted in *Committee for Public Education* v. *Regan* (1980). At least in the absence of empirical evidence that religious groups will dominate UMKC's open forum, we agree with the Court of Appeals that the advancement of religion would not be the forum's "primary effect."

## B

Arguing that the State of Missouri has gone further than the Federal Constitution in proscribing indirect State support for religion, the University claims a compelling interest in complying with the applicable provisions of the Missouri Constitution.

The Missouri courts have not ruled whether a general policy of accommodating student groups, applied equally to those wishing to gather to engage in religious and non-religious speech, would offend the State Constitution. We need not, however, determine how the Missouri courts would decide this issue. It is also unnecessary for us to decide whether, under the Supremacy Clause, a state interest, derived from its own constitution, could ever outweigh free speech interests protected by the First Amendment. We limit our holding to the case before us.

On one hand, respondents' First Amendment rights are entitled to special constitutional solicitude. Our cases have required the most exacting scrutiny in cases in which a State undertakes to regulate speech on the basis of its content. See, *e.g., Carey* v. *Brown* (1980); *Police Dept.* v. *Mosley* (1972). On the other hand, the State interest asserted here — in achieving greater separation of church and State than is already ensured under the Establishment Clause of the Federal Constitution — is limited by the Free Exercise Clause and in this case by the Free Speech Clause as well. In this constitutional context, we are unable to recognize the State's interest as sufficiently "compelling" to justify content-based discrimination against respondents' religious speech.

## IV

Our holding in this case in no way undermines the capacity of the University to establish reasonable time, place, and manner regulations. Nor do we question the right of the University to make academic judgments as to how best to allocate scarce resources or "to determine for itself on academic grounds who may teach, what may be taught, how it shall be taught, and who may be admitted to study." *Sweezy* v. *New Hampshire* (1957) (Frankfurter, J., concurring in the judgment); see *Regents of the Univ. of Cal.* v. *Bakke* (1978) (opinion of POWELL, J., announcing the judgment of the Court). Finally, we affirm the continuing validity of cases, *e.g.*, *Healy* v. *James* (1972), that recognize a University's right to exclude even First Amendment activities that violate reasonable campus rules or substantially interfere with the opportunity of other students to obtain an education.

The basis for our decision is narrow. Having created a forum generally open to student groups, the University seeks to enforce a content-based exclusion of religious speech. Its exclusionary policy violates the fundamental principle that a state regulation of speech should be content-neutral, and the University is unable to justify this violation under applicable constitutional standards.

For this reason, the decision of the Court of Appeals is,

*Affirmed.*

JUSTICE STEVENS, concurring in the judgment.

As the Court recognizes, every university must "make academic judgments as to how best to allocate scarce resources." The Court appears to hold, however, that those judgments must "serve a compelling state interest" whenever they are based, even in part, on the content of speech. This conclusion apparently flows from the Court's suggestion that a student activities program — from which the public may be excluded — must be managed as though it were a "public forum." In my opinion, the use of the terms "compelling state interest" and "public forum" to analyze the question presented in this case may needlessly undermine the academic freedom of public universities.

Today most major colleges and universities are operated by public authority. Nevertheless, their facilities are not open to the public in the same way that streets and parks are. University facilities — private or public — are maintained primarily for the benefit of the student body and the faculty. In performing their learning and teaching missions, the managers of a university routinely make countless decisions based on the content of communicative materials. They select books for inclusion in the library, they hire professors on the basis of their academic philosophies, they select courses for inclusion in the curriculum, and they reward scholars for what they have written. In addition, in encouraging students to participate in extracurricular activities, they necessarily make decisions concerning the content of those activities.

Because every university's resources are limited, an educational institution must routinely make decisions concerning the use of the time and space that is available for extracurricular activities. In my judgment, it is both necessary and appropriate for those decisions to evaluate the content of a proposed student activity. I should think it obvious, for example, that if two groups of 25 students requested the use of a room at a particular time — one to view Mickey Mouse cartoons and the other to rehearse an amateur performance of Hamlet — the First Amendment would not require that the room be reserved for the group that submitted its application first. Nor do I see why a university should have to establish a "compelling state interest" to defend its decision to permit one group to use the facility and not the other. In my opinion, a university should be allowed to decide for itself whether a program that illuminates the genius of Walt Disney should be given precedence over one that may duplicate material adequately covered in the classroom. Judgments of this kind should be made by academicians, not by federal judges, and their standards for decision should not be encumbered with ambiguous phrases like "compelling state interest."

Thus, I do not subscribe to the view that a public university has no greater interest in the content of student activities than the police chief has in the content of a soap box oration on Capitol Hill. A university legitimately may regard some subjects as more relevant to its educational mission than others. But the university, like the police officer, may not allow its agreement or disagreement with the viewpoint of a particular speaker to determine whether access to a forum will be granted. If a state university is to deny recognition to a student organization — or is to give it a lesser right to use school facilities than other student groups — it must have a valid reason for doing so. *Healy* v. *James* [1972].

In this case I agree with the Court that the University has not established a sufficient justification for its refusal to allow the Cornerstone group to engage in religious worship on the campus. The primary reason advanced for the discriminatory treatment is the University's fear of violating the Establishment Clause. But since the record discloses no danger that the University will appear to sponsor any particular religion, and since student participation in the Cornerstone meetings is entirely voluntary, the Court properly concludes that the University's fear is groundless. With that justification put to one side, the University has not met the burden that is imposed on it by *Healy*.

Nor does the University's reliance on the Establishment Clause of the Missouri State Constitution provide a sufficient justification for the discriminatory treatment in this case. As I have said, I believe that the University may exercise a measure of control over the agenda for student use of school facilities, preferring some subjects over others, without needing to identify so-called "compelling state interests." Quite obviously, however, the University could not allow a group of Republicans or Presbyterians to meet while denying Democrats or Mormons the same privilege. It seems apparent that the policy under attack would allow groups of young philosophers to meet to discuss their skepticism that a Supreme Being exists, or a group of political scientists to meet to debate the accuracy of the view that religion is the "opium of the people." If school facilities may be used to discuss anti-clerical doctrine, it seems to me that comparable use by a group desiring to express a belief in God must also be permitted. The fact that their expression of faith includes ceremonial conduct is not, in my opinion, a sufficient reason for suppressing their discussion entirely.

Accordingly, although I do not endorse the Court's reasoning, I concur in its judgment.

JUSTICE WHITE, dissenting.

In affirming the decision of the Court of Appeals, the majority rejects petitioners' argument that the Establishment Clause of the Constitution prohibits the use of university buildings for religious purposes. A state university may permit its property to be used for purely religious services without violating the First and Fourteenth Amendments. With this I agree. See *Committee for Public Education* v. *Nyquist* (1973) (WHITE, J., dissenting); *Lemon* v. *Kurtzman* (1971) (Opinion of WHITE, J.). The Establishment Clause, however, sets limits only on what the State may do with respect to religious organizations; it does not establish what the State is *required* to do. I have long argued that Establishment Clause limits on state action which incidentally aids religion are not as strict as the Court has held. The step from the permissible to the necessary, however, is a long one. In my view, just as there is room under the Religion Clauses for state policies that may have some beneficial effect on religion, there is also room for state policies that may incidentally burden religion. In other words, I believe the states to be a good deal freer to formulate policies that affect religion in divergent ways than does the majority. See *Sherbert* v. *Verner* (1963) (Harlan, J., dissenting). The majority's position will inevitably lead to those contradictions and tensions between the Establishment and Free Exercise Clauses warned against by Justice Stewart in *Sherbert* v. *Verner*.

The university regulation at issue here provides in pertinent part:

> "No University buildings or grounds (except chapels as herein provided) may be used for purposes of religious worship or religious teaching by either student or nonstudent groups. Student congregations of local churches or of recognized denominations or sects, although not technically recognized campus groups, may use the facilities ... under the same regulations that apply to recognized campus organizations, provided that no University facilities may be used for purposes of religious worship or religious teaching."

Although there may be instances in which it would be difficult to determine whether a religious group used university facilities for "worship" or "religious teaching," rather than for secular ends, this is not such a case. The regulation was applied to respondents' religious group, Cornerstone, only after the group explicitly informed the University that it

877

sought access to the facilities for the purpose of offering prayer, singing hymns, reading scripture, and teaching biblical principles. Cornerstone described their meetings as follows: "Although these meetings would not appear to a casual observer to correspond precisely to a traditional worship service, there is no doubt that worship is an important part of the general atmosphere." The issue here is only whether the University regulation as applied and interpreted in this case is impermissible under the federal Constitution. If it is impermissible, it is because it runs afoul of either the Free Speech or the Free Exercise Clause of the First Amendment.

A large part of respondents' argument, accepted by the court below and accepted by the majority, is founded on the proposition that because religious worship uses speech, it is protected by the Free Speech Clause of the First Amendment. Not only is it protected, they argue, but religious worship *qua* speech is not different from any other variety of protected speech as a matter of constitutional principle. I believe that this proposition is plainly wrong. Were it right, the Religion Clauses would be emptied of any independent meaning in circumstances in which religious practice took the form of speech.

Although the majority describes this argument as "novel," I believe it to be clearly supported by our previous cases. Just last term, the Court found it sufficiently obvious that the Establishment Clause prohibited a state from posting a copy of the Ten Commandments on the classroom wall that a statute requiring such a posting was summarily struck down. *Stone* v. *Graham* (1980). That case necessarily presumed that the state could not ignore the religious content of the written message, nor was it permitted to treat that content as it would, or must treat, other — secular — messages under the First Amendment's protection of speech. Similarly, the Court's decisions prohibiting prayer in the public schools rest on a content-based distinction between varieties of speech: as a speech act, apart from its content, a prayer is indistinguishable from a biology lesson. See *School District of Abington Township* v. *Schempp* (1963); *Engel* v. *Vitale* (1962). Operation of the Free Exercise Clause is equally dependent, in certain circumstances, on recognition of a content-based distinction between religious and secular speech. Thus, in *Torcaso* v. *Watkins* (1961), the Court struck down, as violative of the Free Exercise Clause, a state requirement that made a declaration of belief in God a condition of state employment. A declaration is again a speech act, but it was the content of the speech that brought the case within the scope of the Free Exercise Clause.

If the majority were right that no distinction may be drawn between verbal acts of worship and other verbal acts, all of these cases would have to be reconsidered. Although I agree that the line may be difficult to draw in many cases, surely the majority cannot seriously suggest that no line may ever be drawn. If that were the case, the majority would have to uphold the University's right to offer a class entitled "Sunday Mass." Under the majority's view, such a class would be — as a matter of constitutional principle — indistinguishable from a class entitled "The History of the Catholic Church."

There may be instances in which a state's attempt to disentangle itself from religious worship would intrude upon secular speech about religion. In such a case, the state's action would be subject to challenge under the Free Speech Clause of the First Amendment. This is not such a case. This case involves religious worship only; the fact that that worship is accomplished through speech does not add anything to respondents' argument. That argument must rely upon the claim that the state's action impermissibly interferes with the free exercise of respondents' religious practices. Although this is a close question, I conclude that it does not....

...[R]esolution of this case is best achieved by returning to first principles. This requires an assessment of the burden on respondents' ability freely to exercise their religious beliefs and practices and of the state's interest in enforcing its regulation.

Respondents complain that compliance with the regulation would require them to meet "about a block and a half" from campus under conditions less comfortable than those previously available on campus. I view this burden on free exercise as minimal. Because the burden is minimal, the state need do no more than demonstrate that the regulation furthers some permissible state end. The state's interest in avoiding claims that it is financing or otherwise supporting religious worship — in maintaining a definitive separation between church and state — is such an end. That the state truly does mean to act toward this end is amply supported by the treatment of religion in the state constitution. Thus, I believe the interest of the state is sufficiently strong to justify the imposition of the minimal burden on respondents' ability freely to exercise their religious beliefs.

On these facts, therefore, I cannot find that the application of the regulation to prevent Cornerstone from holding religious worship services in university facilities violates the First and Fourteenth Amendments. I would not hold as the majority does that if a university permits students and others to use its property for secular purposes, it must also furnish facilities to religious groups for the purposes of worship and the practice of their religion. Accordingly, I would reverse the judgment of the Court of Appeals.

# MARTIAL LAW IN POLAND
## December 13, 1981

*In the face of mounting labor unrest and challenges to its authority, the Polish government December 13 declared a state of emergency and issued a decree of martial law curtailing civil rights and suspending operations of the independent trade union federation Solidarity. The 6 a.m. pronouncement by Gen. Wojciech Jaruzelski, the Communist Party leader and premier of Poland, followed a midnight raid on Solidarity headquarters, the coordinated arrests of union activists and former Communist Party leaders, a communications blackout, and reports of tank and troop movements within the beleaguered country.*

*Jaruzelski insisted the apparently well-planned crackdown was temporary and was taken to save the country from civil war. "The anti-state subversive action of the forces hostile to socialism had pushed the community to the brink of civil war," he said. "Anarchy, arbitrariness, and chaos were ruining the economy, rendering the country powerless and endangering the sovereignty and biological existence of the nation."*

*Throughout 1981 Western observers had watched the unfolding events in Poland with anxious eyes. Countless warnings against Soviet intervention came from the U.S. government, especially after Warsaw Pact countries staged military maneuvers in and around Poland. While President Reagan blamed the Soviets for Poland's troubles, the Soviet Union countered that the country's problems were internal and that the Reagan administration's rhetoric was reviving the Cold War.*

## *Overnight Changes*

Some observers pointed to the difference between the tone of Jaruzelski's speech, which was relatively moderate and appealed to national sentiment, and the harsh terms of the actual decrees, numbering as many as 61, outlining the "norms of public order" during martial law.

Personal identity papers had to be carried at all times, and a nationwide curfew was imposed from 10 p.m. to 6 a.m. All demonstrations and gatherings, except church services, were banned. Civil liberties safeguarded under the Polish constitution were suspended and censorship of mail was legalized. The six-day work week was reinstated; adults were told they might be required to do volunteer work for the state.

Only government-sponsored news was reported, and private printing presses were confiscated; public and private telephone and telex lines linking Poland to the outside world were cut off. These activities created a virtual news vacuum within and outside the country.

According to reports reaching the West, thousands of people were rounded up and interned, including Solidarity leader Lech Walesa, many union activists and sympathizers, intellectuals, journalists, academicians and students. Jaruzelski announced that several former government officials, including Edward Gierek, the party chief ousted in September 1980, also had been arrested. The government held Gierek and other government officials "responsible personally for pushing the country into crisis" by their policies during the 1970s.

Some observers maintained the arrests of Communist Party leaders, along with the Solidarity activists, were designed to add credence to the government stand that martial law was imposed to prevent economic collapse, rather than to wipe out the powers gained by the independent union federation.

## *1981 Power Struggles*

The harsh move apparently was triggered by Solidarity's December 12 threat to call for a national referendum on setting up a non-communist government if its demands were not met. Solidarity had planned to present the government with requests for free elections, joint government-union management of the economy and union access to the government-controlled media.

But Solidarity's threat to the Polish government had been increasing gradually ever since August 1980 when, for the first time in an Eastern-bloc country, the government agreed to permit workers to form labor unions free of government domination. Amidst continuing worker strikes and economic decline throughout 1981, Solidarity continued to consolidate its power. The first month of 1981 saw workers strike to gain the *long-sought five-day work week. That goal finally was secured January 31, despite government objections that productivity levels already were dangerously low.* (Historic Documents of 1980, p. 793)

*As the independent union's power grew, so did Communist Party reaction against it. Strategically located between the Soviet Union and East Germany and the most populated Eastern-bloc country, Poland presented a considerable problem for the Soviet Union. Moscow feared that the liberalizing tendencies would threaten the Warsaw government and serve as an example to workers in other Soviet satellites, perhaps even in the Soviet Union itself. The primacy of the Communist Party would be eroded and rival centers of power — labor, intellectuals, religious organizations — would encourage the kind of political pluralism anathema to Moscow.*

*Also of grave concern to the Soviets was the Polish economy. Partly due to the wildcat strikes, industrial production in Poland continued to drop in 1981 — falling 11.4 percent in August compared with the same period in 1980. Poland's coal production alone plummeted 23 percent from the same month the year before. Traditionally, Poland was one of the world's leading coal exporters. Capital investment for August was down 20 percent, wages were up almost 27 percent. Food supplies dropped 38 percent, meat 29 percent, vodka 26 percent. During most of 1981 Poland also was beset by negotiations with its Western creditors over its staggering foreign debts, which could have forced the economy into bankruptcy if called due.*

*Throughout 1981 the Communist Party was in disagreement over how to handle the labor unrest and the shaky economy. By the time martial law was imposed, several government officials had been deposed in favor of General Jaruzelski, who held supreme power as first secretary of the party, commander of the armed forces, premier and defense minister. Solidarity, too, witnessed its own power struggles as an increasingly radical faction within the trade union federation, advocating the direct politicization of the union, challenged the more moderate members, led by Walesa, who were working toward compromise with the government. But the struggle for power that culminated in martial law was between the country's controlling communist government and the workers' union, which by this time was composed of at least 60 percent of the country's 17 million workers.*

## Reactions

*Reaction from Washington to the introduction of military rule in Poland was immediate but, according to some critics, too vague. Secretary of State Alexander M. Haig Jr., stating the United States was "seriously concerned" about Poland, warned the Soviet Union December 13 not to interfere. All U.S. economic aid, including food, to Poland was suspended the following day. The Soviets, also on December 14, called martial law in Poland "an internal matter," advising the United States not to meddle.*

*Poland's ambassador to Washington, Romuald Spasowski, announced December 20 that he had asked for and been granted political asylum in the United States. In an emotional appeal to the American and Polish peoples, Spasowski described his defection as "my expression of solidarity" with Lech Walesa. After Spasowski's defection, the Polish government portrayed its former, most senior diplomat as a traitor and a mentally unbalanced individual.*

*In an address televised from the White House December 23, Reagan declared that the Soviets deserved a major share of the blame for the crisis, but he restricted his sanctions at that time to Poland. His proposed actions included:*

* *Continuing the suspension of U.S. government-sponsored shipments of food into Poland until "absolute assurances" were received that the distribution of these products would be monitored and guaranteed by independent agencies.*
* *Withdrawal of the right of Poland's fishing fleet to operate in American waters.*
* *Ending Export-Import Bank credit insurance to Poland, which was expected to end private lending to Poland.*
* *Suspending Poland's civil aviation in the U.S.*

## Sanctions Against Soviets

*Speculation arose that the lack of allied support for the U.S. stance, especially concerning Soviet involvement in the crisis, explained the restriction of the sanctions to Poland. But on December 29 Reagan again placed much of the blame for the Polish situation on the Soviet government and extended similar sanctions to the Soviet Union. These included:*

* *Suspension of new export licenses for high-technology items, including oil and natural gas equipment that would have been used to build a pipeline from Siberia to Western Europe.*
* *Postponing talks on a maritime pact and on a long-term grain agreement.*
* *Restricting Soviet access to U.S. ports and withdrawing Soviet air service privileges.*
* *Shutting down a Soviet office that arranged purchases of non-agricultural products in the United States.*
* *Vowing to review all existing energy, science and technology agreements between Washington and Moscow.*

*But Reagan refrained from wielding what many observers considered his strongest economic weapon. He did not impose a flat embargo on grain sales to the Soviet Union, perhaps to avoid conflict with American farmers still smarting from the Carter-imposed grain embargo after the Soviet invasion of Afghanistan in late 1979.*

## The Polish Debt

*Reagan also did not declare Poland's overdue debts to the U.S. government in default, a move that would have severely strained the economy of Poland, and possibly of the Soviet Union. But declaring a default also could have hurt the economies of Western creditor nations, including the United States, West Germany, France and Britain. The total Polish debt in the West was estimated at around $27 billion.*

*In April 1981 Poland worked to secure an agreement with representatives of its Western creditor governments to reschedule, or postpone, about $2.5 billion in official interest and principal debt falling due in 1981. Later in the year, a stricter agreement on the rescheduling of about $3 billion of Polish debt due during 1981 was reached between Poland and its Western commercial creditors. Both these agreements were designed to prevent the collapse of a Polish economy teetering on the brink of bankruptcy.*

## Response of Pope John Paul II

*Polish-born Pope John Paul II appealed December 13 to his countrymen, more than 90 percent of whom were Roman Catholics, to "peacefully build a peaceful future." "Polish blood must not be spilled," the Pope declared in his native tongue to some 30,000 pilgrims in St. Peter's Square in the Vatican.*

*Throughout the year, the Roman Catholic Church served as a moderating influence, urging the workers not to challenge the primacy of the Communist Party, lest the Soviet Union step in. But the Church appeared to maintain a critical balance between strong support of the workers' rights and a recognition that Poland was indeed part of the Soviet sphere of influence. (Papal encyclical on work, p. 695.)*

*Following are the texts of Polish Premier Gen. Wojciech Jaruzelski's speech announcing the imposition of martial law in Poland, December 13, 1981; the speech of the Polish ambassador to the United States, Romuald Spasowski, announcing his defection, December 20, as it appeared in* The New York Times; *and excerpts from President Reagan's December 23 address to the nation on the situation in Poland. (Boldface headings in brackets have been added by Congressional Quarterly to highlight the organization of the texts.):*

# GEN. JARUZELSKI'S SPEECH

Citizens of the Polish People's Republic,

I address you today as a soldier and as chief of the Polish government on matters of the supreme importance.

Our country has found itself at the precipice.

The achievement of many generations, the Polish house raised from ashes is being ruined. The state structures are ceasing to operate. Ever new blows are being dealt daily to the dying economy. The living conditions are becoming an increasingly heavy burden for the people.

The lines of merciless division run across every works enterprise, across many Polish homes. The atmosphere of unending conflicts, disagreements and hatred is sowing mental devastation, and mutilating the tradition of tolerance. Strikes, strike readiness, protest actions have become the norm. Even school children are being drawn into it. Last night sit-ins were staged in many public buildings. Calls are being issued for physical showdown with "the red", with people who hold different views. Cases of terrorism, threats and moral lynches, as well as those of direct violence are multiplying.

The wave of impudent offences, assaults and break-ins has spread wide across the country. Fortunes running into millions of zlotys of sharks of the economic underground are growing. Chaos and demoralization have assumed disastrous dimensions. The nation has reached the limits of mental endurance. Many people are becoming desperate.

Not days but hours are bringing national catastrophe closer.

Honesty demands to ask the question of whether it had to come to this. Assuming the office of the Chairman of the Council of Ministers I believed that we shall be able to raise ourselves. Have we done everything to halt the spiral of crisis?

## [Reforms and Opposition]

History will judge our actions. We have not been free from mistakes. We are drawing conclusions from them. Above all, however, the past months have been a busy time for the government which had to cope with enormous difficulties. Unfortunately, the national economy was made into an arena of political struggle. The deliberate torpedoeing [sic] of government undertakings has caused that the results are incomparable to the efforts made, to our intentions. We cannot be denied good will, the sense of measure and patience. Perhaps there was too much of it sometimes. One cannot fail to see respect for social agreements shown by the government. We went even further. The initiative of the Great National Accord has won the support of millions of Poles. It created a chance for the deepening of the system of people's rule, of the expansion of the scope of reforms.

These hopes have now failed.

The leadership of Solidarność was missing at the common table. The words uttered in Radom, the debates in Gdańsk unveiled to the end of the true intentions of its leading circles. These intentions are conformed on a mass scale by everyday practice, intensified aggressiveness of extremists, open striving towards complete dismantling of the socialist Polish statehood.

How much longer can one wait for sobering down? How long the hand extended to agreement is to meet a clenched fist? I speak this with a heavy heart, with enormous bitterness. It could have been different in our country. It should have been different.

Further continuation of the present state would inevitably lead to catastrophe, to complete chaos, to poverty and famine. The severe winter could multiply losses and claim many victims, especially among the weakest, whom we are most anxious to protect.

## [Necessity for Action]

In this situation, inaction would be a crime towards the nation. We must say, enough.

It is necessary to prevent, to block the road to confrontation, which has been openly forecast by Solidarność leaders. We must announce this precisely today when the date is known of imminent mass political demonstrations, including such in the centre of Warsaw, to be convened in connection with the December events. That tragedy cannot be repeated. We must not, we have no right to permit that the announced demonstrations become the spark which could ignite the whole country. The nation's instinct of self-preservation must be allowed to speak. Adventurists must have their arms tied before they could push the motherland into a precipice of fratricidal struggle.

Very great is the burden of responsibility which falls on me at this dramatic moment of Polish history. It is my duty to shoulder this responsibility — at stake is the future of Poland for which my generation had fought at all fronts of war and to which it gave the best years of life.

I announce that today the Military Council of National Redemption has been constituted.

## [Declaration of Martial Law]

The Council of State, in conformity with the provisions of the constitution, proclaimed at midnight tonight martial law in the whole country.

I wish for all to understand the motives and objectives of our action. We are not heading toward a military coup, toward military dictatorship. The nation has enough strength, enough wisdom to develop an efficient democratic system of socialist government. In this system the armed forces will be able to stay where is their rightful place — in the barracks. None of the Polish problems can be solved by force in the longer run.

The Military Council of Nation [sic] Redemption does not replace the constitutional organs of authority. Its sole aim is to protect legal order in the state, to create executive guarantees to make it possible to restore order and discipline. This is the last road to make possible the beginning of overcoming the crisis in the country, to save the state from disintegration.

The Country's Defence Committee has appointed plenipotentiary-military commissars at all levels of state administration and in certain economic units. The Plenipotentiary-Commissars have the right to supervise the activity of state administration organs — from the ministries to rural communities.

Proclamation of the Military Council of National Redemption and the decrees published today define in detail the norms of public order for the duration of martial law.

The Military Council will be dissolved once the rule of law is reestablished in the country, conditions are created for normal functioning of civil administration and the representative bodies. As the situation normalises, internal restrictions in public life will be reduced or lifted.

Let no one count on weakness or hesitation.

## [Solidarity Members Interned]

In the name of national interest, preventive internment has been applied to a group of persons threatening the state security. In that group are extremist Solidarność activists and illegal anti-state organisations.

On orders of the Military Council, several dozen persons who bear personal responsibility for the fact that through their activities during the 1970s they brought about a severe crisis of the state or abused official position for personal advantages have also been interned. Among them are Edward Gierek, Piotr Jaroszewicz, Zdzislaw Grudzień, Jerzy Lukaszewicz, Jan Szydlak, Tadeusz Wrzasczyk, and others. The full list will be published.

We shall consistently cleanse Polish life from evil, no matter where it may occur.

The Military Council will ensure conditions for radical sharpening of struggle against delinquency. The activity of criminal gangs will be considered by courts according to summary jurisdiction procedure.

Persons who engage in large-scale speculation, who draw illegal income and who violate norms of social relationship will be prosecuted and punished with full severity. Wealth accumulated illegally will be confiscated.

Persons holding managerial posts who are guilty of the dereliction of duty, wastefulness and particularism, abuse of office and soullness [sic] attitude to problems of the citizens will be dismissed from posts in a disciplinary course on request of plenipotentiary-military commissars.

It is necessary to restore respect for man's work, ensure respect for law and order. It is necessary to guarantee personal security to every one who wants to live in peace and work peacefully.

Provisions of a special decree envisage pardoning and remittal of certain offences and encroachments against the interests of the state committed before December 13 this year. We are not seeking revenge. He who without bad will let himself be carried away by emotions, submitted to false inspiration, can take advantage of that chance.

## [Role of Military]

Citizens,
The Polish soldier has served his homeland faithfuly. Always in the first line, in every social need. Also today, he will discharge his duty with honor.

Our soldier has clean hands. He does not know pursuing private interests, but only tough service. He has no other aim but the good of the nation.

Recourse to the assistance of the army can and does only have a temporary extraordinary character. The army will not replace the normal mechanisms of socialist democracy. But democracy can only be introduced and developed in a strong state in which law is respected. Anarchy is contradiction and the enemy of democracy.

We are only a drop in the stream of the Polish history. It is made up not of glorious pages alone. It also contains dark pages: liberum veto, pursuit of private advantages and quarrels. The result was downfall and defeat. This tragic circle must be broken one day. We cannot afford another repetition of history.

We desire a great Poland — great by her achievements, culture, forms of social life and her standing in Europe. The only road to this goal is socialism, accepted by the society, constantly enriched by the experience of life. This is the Poland we shall build. This Poland we shall defend.

## [Role of Party]

In this task, party members have a special role to fulfil. In spite of mistakes made and bitter setbacks, the party is still the active and creative force in the process of historic transformations. To effectively perform its leading mission and fruitfully cooperate with allied forces, the party must be supported by honest, modest and courageous people. People who in every environment will earn the name of champions for social justice, for the good of the country. This is its prospect.

We shall cleanse the eternally living sources of our ideology from deformities and distortions. We shall protect the universal values of socialism and constantly enrich it with national elements and traditions. On this road, socialist ideals will be closer to the majority of the nation, to non-party working people, to the younger generation and, also, to the healthy, especially the working class-stream, of Solidarność which, by its own strength, and its own interest, will separate from it the prophets of confrontation and counter-revolution.

This is how we conceive of the idea of national accord. We uphold this idea. We respect the multitude of viewpoints. We appreciate the patriotic stance of the church. There exists the supreme aim, the love of the motherland, the necessity to strengthen the independence won with such effort, respect for one's own state which unites all thinking responsible Poles. This is the most solid foundation of genuine agreement.

## [Socialist Renewal]

Just as there is no retreat from socialism, there is also no return to wrong methods and practices from before August 1980. The steps taken today are designed to preserve the basic premises of socialist renewal. All important reforms will be continued in conditions of order, businesslike discussions and discipline. This also applies to economic reform.

I will not make promises. Before us is a difficult period. It is necessary, today, to recognize the tough realities, to understand the necessity of sacrifices to ensure a better tomorrow.

One thing that I want to achieve is peace. This is the basic condition from which a better future should begin. We are a sovereign country. Therefore, we must overcome this crisis with our own strength. With our own hands we must avert the threat. History would not forgive the present generation if it wasted this chance.

We must put an end to further degradation to which the international position of our state is being subjected. A country of 36 million inhabitants in the heart of Europe cannot remain endlessly in the humiliating role of suppliant. We cannot fail to notice that derisory opinions about a "Republic which stands by anarchy" have reappeared. It is necessary to do all to ensure that such opinions be consigned to the lumber-room of history.

## [Appeal to Allies]

In this difficult moment I address our socialist allies and friends. We highly appreciate their confidence and constant assistance. The Polish-Soviet alliance is and will remain the cornerstone of the Polish reason of state, the guarantee of the inviolability of our frontiers. Poland is and will remain the lasting link of the Warsaw treaty, the unfailing member of the socialist community of nations.

I also address our partners in other countries with whom we wish to develop good and friendly relations.

I address the whole world opinion. I appeal for understanding for the exceptional conditions which occurred in Poland, for emergency measures which have become necessary. Our actions endanger nobody. Their only objective is to remove internal threats and thereby to prevent dangers to peace and international cooperation. We intend to keep the concluded treaties and agreements. We wish that the word "Poland" may always evoke respect and sympathy in Europe and the world.

## [Appeal to Citizens]

Fellow Countrymen, Brothers and Sisters,

I address you all as a soldier who well remembers the atrocities of war. May not a single drop of Polish blood be spilt in this harassed country which had sustained so many defeats, so much suffering. By common effort let us avert the spectre of civil war. Let us not build barricades where a bridge is needed.

I address you, brothers, farmers: do not let your fellow-countrymen to inalienable right to strike for such a period which will be indispensable for overcoming the severest difficulties. We must do everything to ensure that the fruits of your hard work will not be wasted.

I address you, brothers farmers: do not let your fellow-countrymen to starve. Do take care of the Polish soil to ensure that it may feed us.

I address you, citizens of the older generation: do save from oblivion the truth of the war years, of the difficult time of reconstruction. Hand it down to your sons and your grandchildren. Pass on to them your ardent patriotism, your readiness to make sacrifices for the good of your homeland.

I address you, Polish mothers, wives and sisters: do take every care to ensure that no more tears are shed in Polish families.

I address you, young Polish women and men: do show civic maturity and deep reflection on your own future, on the future of the motherland.

I address you, teachers, creators of science and culture, engineers, doctors, and journalists: may at this dangerous turn in our history reason prevail over inflamed emotions and intellectual interpretation of patriotism over the illusive myths.

I address you, my comrades in arms, soldiers of the Polish army, in active service and reservists: be faithful to the path which you have pledged to the motherland for better and for worse. The destiny of the country depends on your posture today.

I address you, functionaries of the People's militia and the security service: protect the state against the enemy and the working people against lawlessness and violence.

I address all Polish citizens — the hour of a difficult trial has struck. We must live up to this trial and prove that "we deserve Poland".

Fellow Countrymen,

In front of the entire Polish nation and in front of the whole world I wish to repeat the immortal words: Poland has not died as long as we live.

# POLISH AMBASSADOR'S STATEMENT

Ladies and Gentlemen. I am the Ambassador of Poland to Washington. I am the most senior Polish diplomat and this is my fifth ambassadorial post. I am also for the second time posted in Washington as Ambassador. I wish to talk to you on recent events in my country.

A week ago a state of war has been imposed upon Poland, state of war against the Polish people.

Under the umbrella of the military, specially trained units and security police began an unprecedented reign of terror. Factories have been stormed where workers defended themselves. Solidarity members have been arrested in their offices and at night at home.

All communication lines have been cut off to isolate the country and to confuse the world. Death penalty has been introduced for not reporting to work. With unique precision, the police undertook all visible steps to extinguish every ember of freedom trying to eliminate independently minded people.

The professors from the Academy of Science have been put to prison. The activity of religious and Catholic organizations has been forbidden. The cruel night of darkness and silence was spread over my country.

Now, thousand of best sons and daughters of the Polish nation are faced with the ordeals of imprisonment. In prison, in camps, in the open air without shelter, without enough food, without heating in freezing temperatures, my brothers, old and young, men and women, face brute force and are exposed to enormous sufferings. There are even indications that some are being transported to camps in neighboring countries.

## [Not Internal Issue]

This carefully orchestrated and directed crackdown is not an internal Polish issue. This is the most flagrant and brutal violation of human rights which makes a mockery of the Polish signature put under the Final Act of the Helsinki accord.

I, ladies and gentlemen, cannot be silent. I shall not have any association, not speaking about representation, with the authorities responsible for this brutality and inhumanity.

I have decided this the moment I learned that Lech Walesa, the most beloved leader of Solidarity, is arrested and kept by force. This, what I am doing now, is my expression of solidarity with him.

## [Asylum Granted]

I have decided to make this statement to stand up openly and to say that I will do everything possible to assist the Polish people in their hour of need. I have asked the Government of the United States to give shelter and political asylum to me and to my family. Both have been granted and I wish to express my thanks to the President of the United States and to the Secretary of State and to many of my friends in the Administration for allowing us to stay in your country.

I turn now to you Americans who are listening to me and watching me. Now at this very moment when you sit in front of your TV sets, evil forces crash on Poland and its deeply patriotic and religious people. Think about those Poles. Try to imagine their loss when you listen every day to the news. Remember, they are best sons and daughters of my country — those workers, those students, those intellectuals.

A new chapter of Poland's struggles for independence and human dignity has opened a week ago. We will never give up.

## [Need for Dialogue]

The only solution to the tragedy is a political solution by dialogue. Nobody can put in prison 36 million people and make them slaves in the very center of Europe. Violence and suppression will only aggravate the situation and history proves that they are bound finally to collapse.

The road to peace is the only road. The Catholic Church in Poland represents a great moral force — the souls of the Polish nation. The Solidarity has close to 10 million people. It is natural that through the three-party talks, the church, the Solidarity and the authorities, a real effort should be made to find accommodation and peace. That is, in my mind, the only road to follow.

Whatever the future will be, don't be silent, Americans. To defend freedom is in your tradition. Show your solidarity, show your support and humanitarian assistance to those who are in such need at this hour.

I wish to say also goodbye to the many ambassadors and their wives, my colleagues in Washington. Thank you for your understanding. I will not forget your friendship, me with my wife will not forget the warmth many of you have shown to us.

I wish to thank also wholeheartedly all my American friends for their cooperation. Thank you for your assistance and understanding my country.

## [Salute to People of Poland]

Let me turn now to the people of Poland. All Poles abroad salute you. We will never stop struggling until Poland be Poland and you experience that dignity which should be a part of every human being, so help us God.

Let me turn now to the Polish-Americans. The Polish people have confidence in your strong bonds with the country of your forefathers. Let everybody know that in your heart and mind, you are with the people of Warsaw, of Gdansk, Cracow and Poznan, with the heroic workers of the shipyards and with the brave miners in Silesia.

Let me turn now to the Polish diplomats in foreign missions outside Poland. Be Polish and true to yourself. Remember this is the hour. Do whatever your conscience dictates you to do in order to assist our brothers and sisters in Poland.

There is only one morality in the human family, the morality of people who live according to the principles of truth and justice. This is — it is this morality which shall prevail.

Long live Poland and thank you for your attention.

# REAGAN'S CHRISTMAS MESSAGE

... As I speak to you tonight, the fate of a proud and ancient nation hangs in the balance. For a thousand years, Christmas has been celebrated in Poland, a land of deep religious faith, but this Christmas brings little joy to the courageous Polish people. They have been betrayed by their own government.

The men who rule them and their totalitarian allies fear the very freedom that the Polish people cherish. They have answered the stirrings of liberty with brute force, killings, mass arrests, and the setting up of concentration camps. Lech Walesa and other Solidarity leaders are imprisoned, their fate unknown. Factories, mines, universities and homes have been assaulted.

The Polish Government has trampled underfoot solemn commitments to the UN Charter and the Helsinki accords. It has even broken the Gdansk agreement of August 1980, by which the Polish Government recognized the basic right of its people to form free trade unions and to strike.

## [Soviet Involvement]

The tragic events now occurring in Poland, almost 2 years to the day after the Soviet invasion of Afghanistan, have been precipitated by public and secret pressure from the Soviet Union. It is not coincidence that Soviet Marshal Kulikov, chief of the Warsaw Pact forces, and other senior Red Army officers were in Poland while these outrages were being initiated. And it is no coincidence that the martial law proclamations imposed in December by the Polish Government were being printed in the Soviet Union in September.

The target of this depression [repression] is the Solidarity Movement, but in attacking Solidarity its enemies attack an entire people. Ten million of Poland's 36 million citizens are members of Solidarity. Taken together with their families, they account for the overwhelming majority of the Polish nation. By persecuting Solidarity, the Polish Government wages war against its own people.

I urge the Polish Government and its allies to consider the consequences of their actions. How can they possibly justify using naked force to crush a people who ask for nothing more than the right to lead their own lives in freedom and dignity? Brute force may intimidate, but it cannot form the basis of an enduring society, and the ailing Polish economy cannot be rebuilt with terror tactics.

## [Aid for Poland]

Poland needs cooperation between its government and its people, not military oppression. If the Polish Government will honor the commitments it has made to basic human rights in documents like the Gdansk agreement, we in America will gladly do our share to help the shattered Polish economy, just as we helped the countries of Europe after both World Wars.

It's ironic that we offered, and Poland expressed interest in accepting, our help after World War II. The Soviet Union intervened then and refused to allow such help to Poland. But if the forces of tyranny in Poland, and those who incite them from without, do not relent, they should prepare themselves for serious consequences. Already, throughout the Free World, citizens have publicly demonstrated their support for the Polish people. Our Government, and those of our Allies have expressed moral revulsion at the police state tactics of Poland's oppressors. The Church has also spoken out in spite of threats and intimidation. But our reaction cannot stop there.

## [U.S. Actions]

I want emphatically to state tonight that if the outrages in Poland do not cease, we cannot and will not conduct "business as usual" with the perpetrators and those who aid and abet them. Make no mistake, their crime will cost them dearly in their future dealings with America and free peoples everywhere. I do not make this statement lightly, or without serious reflection.

We have been measured and deliberate in our reaction to the tragic events in Poland. We have not acted in haste, and the steps I will outline tonight and others we may take in the days ahead are firm, just and reasonable.

In order to aid the suffering Polish people during this critical period, we will continue the shipment of food through private humanitarian channels, but only so long as we know that the Polish people themselves receive the food. The neighboring country of Austria has opened her doors to refugees from Poland. I have therefore directed that American assistance, including supplies of basic foodstuffs, be offered to aid the Austrians in providing for these refugees.

But to underscore our fundamental opposition to the repressive actions taken by the Polish Government against its own people, the administration has suspended all Government-sponsored shipments of agricultural and dairy products to the Polish Government. This suspension will remain in force until absolute assurances are received that distribution of these products is monitored and guaranteed by independent agencies. We must be sure that every bit of food provided by America goes to the Polish people, not to their oppressors.

The United States is taking immediate action to suspend major elements of our economic relationships with the Polish Government. We have halted the renewal of the Export-Import Bank's line of export credit insurance to the Polish Government. We will suspend Polish civil aviation privileges in the United States. We are suspending the right of Poland's fishing fleet to operate in American waters. And we're proposing to our allies the further restriction of high-technology exports to Poland.

These actions are not directed against the Polish people. They are a warning to the Government of Poland that free men cannot and will not stand idly by in the face of brutal repression. To underscore this point, I've written a letter to General [Wojciech] Jaruzelski, head of the Polish Government. In it, I outlined the steps we are taking and warned of the serious consequences if the Polish Government continues to use violence against its populace. I have urged him to free those in arbitrary detention, to lift martial law, and to restore the internationally recognized rights of the Polish people to free speech and association.

The Soviet Union, through its threats and pressures, deserves a major share of blame for the developments in Poland. So, I have also sent a letter to President [Leonid] Brezhnev urging him to permit the restoration of basic rights in Poland as provided for in the Helsinki Final Act. In it, I informed him that if this repression continues, the United States will have no choice but to take further concrete political and economic measures affecting our relationship.

When 19th-century Polish patriots rose against foreign oppressors, their rallying cry was, "For our freedom and yours." Well, that motto still rings true in our time. There is a spirit of solidarity abroad in the world tonight that no physical force can crush. It crosses national boundaries and enters into the hearts of men and women everywhere. In factories, farms and schools, in cities and towns around the globe, we the people of the free world stand as one with our Polish brothers and sisters. Their cause is ours, and our prayers and hopes go out to them this Christmas.

## [Asylum for Polish Ambassador]

Yesterday, I met in this very room with Romuald Spasowski, the distinguished former Polish Ambassador who has sought asylum in our country in protest of the suppression of his native land. He told me that one of the ways the Polish people have demonstrated their solidarity in the face of martial law is by placing lighted candles in their windows to show that the light of liberty still glows in their hearts.

Ambassador Spasowski requested that on Christmas Eve a lighted candle will burn in the White House window as a small but certain beacon of our solidarity with the Polish people. I urge all of you to do the same tomorrow night, on Christmas Eve, as a personal statement of your commitment to the steps we're taking to support the brave people of Poland in their time of troubles.

Once, earlier in this century, an evil influence threatened that the lights were going out all over the world. Let the light of millions of candles in American homes give notice that the light of freedom is not going to be extinguished. We are blessed with a freedom and abundance denied to so many. Let those candles remind us that these blessings bring with them a solemn obligation, an obligation to the God who guides us, an obligation to the heritage of liberty and dignity handed down to us by our forefathers and an obligation to the children of the world, whose future will be shaped by the way we live our lives today....

# ISRAELI ANNEXATION OF GOLAN HEIGHTS
## December 14, 1981

*In a surprise political move December 14, Israeli Prime Minister Menachem Begin asked the Knesset, the Israeli parliament, to approve legislation annexing the Golan Heights. The measure, approved by a vote of 63 to 21, provided that "the law, jurisdiction and administration of the State shall apply to the Golan Heights." Israel had occupied the former Syrian territory since the 1967 Six-Day War. The annexation brought swift reaction from the United Nations Security Council and from the United States, Israel's strongest ally.*

## Security Council Action

*Declaring the Golan Heights annexation "null and void," the U.N. Security Council December 17 voted unanimously in favor of a resolution condemning the action as "without international legal effect," and threatening to take "appropriate measures" if it were not rescinded. The Security Council vote came after two days of bargaining between American and Syrian diplomats over the text of the resolution. Seeking to avoid a U.S. veto, the Syrian delegates agreed to several changes in wording.*

*In particular, the United States had sought to include a reference to Security Council Resolution 338, approved following the 1973 war in the Middle East. That resolution contained a reference to the right of every Middle Eastern state to live within secure boundaries — a reference Syria objected to because it implied a recognition of the right of Israel to exist. A compromise was reached when the United States accepted the*

*Syrian proposal that the phrase "relevant Security Council resolutions" be substituted for the 338 resolution.*

*A second compromise involved replacing the word "appropriate" for "necessary" in the section that described the kind of "measures" the council might consider if Israel refused to reverse the annexation. The United States had wanted to avoid any mention of future action by the council.*

## Diplomatic Fallout

*The day following the U.N. vote, on December 18, the Reagan administration further expressed its disapproval of Israel's action by indefinitely suspending a military cooperation agreement it had signed with Israel three weeks earlier on November 30. The memorandum of understanding, which provided for joint military exercises and the possible pre-positioning of forces, had been designed "to enhance Strategic Cooperation to deter all threats from the Soviet Union" in the Mideast region.*

*In a statement issued by State Department spokesman Dean Fischer, the administration announced that the strategic cooperation agreement "obliged each party to take into consideration in its decisions the implications for the broad policy concerns of the other. We do not believe that spirit was upheld in the case of Israel's decision on the Golan."*

*According to U.S. government officials, the purpose of the suspension was to alert Israel that the United States would not tolerate such unilateral action and to avert major Israeli military operations in southern Lebanon.*

*"The Israeli action was taken with no advance notice to us or discussion with us," Fischer's statement read. "We are particularly disappointed that the Government of Israel took this action just as we were facing a serious political crisis in Poland...."*

## Israeli Reaction

*On December 29, Israeli Prime Minister Menachem Begin reacted to the American suspension of the strategic accord with anger. "There is no power on earth that will bring about ... repeal," of the Golan Heights annexation law, he said in a statement to U.S. Ambassador Samuel W. Lewis. "The people of Israel have lived 3,700 years without a memorandum of understanding with America and will continue to live without it another 3,700 years. In our eyes, it [the U.S. action] is a cancellation of the memorandum."*

*Begin's statement, which was endorsed by the full Israeli cabinet, was characterized by The New York Times as "perhaps the harshest statement ever made by an Israeli Prime Minister about the United States."*

*Specifically, Begin accused the United States of treating Israel like a "vassal state" and vowed: "You will not frighten us with punishments. He who threatens us will find us deaf to his threats."*

*Begin also raised the issue of anti-Semitism in the United States. Referring to charges that an anti-Semitic campaign was waged in the U.S. Senate in connection with the sale of AWACS planes to Saudi Arabia, the prime minister said: "No one will frighten the large and free Jewish community of the United States. No one will succeed in deterring them with anti-Semitic propaganda."*

*On January 20, 1982, the Security Council attempted to adopt a resolution instituting sanctions against Israel, but that move was vetoed by the United States.*

*Following are excerpts from the speech of Israeli Prime Minister Menachem Begin to the Knesset, December 14, 1981; the text of Security Council Resolution 497, adopted December 17; excerpts from Begin's December 20 remarks to U.S. Ambassador Samuel W. Lewis; and the text of the memorandum of understanding between the United States and Israel on strategic cooperation, signed November 30. (Boldface headings in brackets have been added by Congressional Quarterly to highlight the organization of the texts.):*

# BEGIN'S KNESSET SPEECH

... Mr. Chairman,

I herewith call upon the Knesset, regardless of party or faction — whether it supports the Government or is opposed to its course — to act, at this session, to enact the Golan Heights Law, as follows:

Golan Heights Law - 5742/1981

1. "The law, jurisdiction and administration of the State shall apply to the Golan Heights, as described in the appendix.

2. This law shall become valid on the day of its passage in the Knesset.

3. The Minister of the Interior shall be charged with the implementation of this law, and he is entitled to enact regulations for its implementation."

Mr. Chairman, Ladies and Gentlemen, Members of the Knesset, there can be, in our country or beyond its borders, no serious person, who has studied the history of the Land of Israel, who would attempt to deny that, for many generations, the Golan Heights were an integral part of the Land of Israel.

By rights, therefore, the northern border of the Land of Israel — which both in the Balfour Declaration and in the international mandate, is referred to as Palestine — ought to include the Golan Heights. There were, moreover, efforts by the Zionist movement, at the time, to determine the border in this manner. However, two colonialist powers that divided a large part of the world between them, following the Great War known today as the First World War, decided otherwise and fixed the border of the Land of Israel approximately ten meters east of the Sea of Galilee. This fact merely serves as proof of the arbitrariness of colonial rulers in an era that has passed, never to return. We are not bound by this arbitrariness, and I am certain that the overwhelming majority of the Knesset and of the nation will support me in asserting that, from the historical point of view, the Golan Heights were and will remain an integral part of the Land of Israel.

## [Syrian Domination of the Heights]

Following the renewal of our independence, the Syrians dominated the Heights — and they demonstrated to us what they were capable of doing to the civilian population living in the kibbutzim, the moshavim and the towns in the valley below. The Syrians turned the lives of these tens of thousands of civilians into hell. Spurred on by their deep and abiding hatred, they would open fire, from the heights on our towns and villages, instituting a reign of blood and terror throughout the area, their targets were man, woman and child — and the attacks took their toll in killed and wounded. In those days, which can under no circumstances be forgotten, it was said that the children being born were "children of the shelters."

Indeed, our children in the thousands were to be found in the shelters, at times, not for a day or a week but for months on end without seeing the light of day. At every alert — and there were many such alerts — they ran for their lives, to the shelters. Is it conceivable that Israel could ever agree to a possible renewal of this situation? No wonder that in this matter of the Golan Heights there is a universal, or nearly universal, national consensus in Israel, and noted statesmen in other countries have publicly or privately expressed their view that Israel cannot leave the Golan Heights or hand them over to the Syrians.

## [Israeli Government Policy]

The Government, in presenting itself to the Tenth Knesset and requesting its confidence, asserted, in paragraph 11 of its basic policy guidelines, as follows:

"Israel will not descend from the Golan Heights and will not remove a single settlement that has been established on the Heights.

The Government will decide upon the suitable timing of the application of the law, jurisdiction and administration of the State to the Golan Heights."

I herewith serve notice upon the Knesset that the Government of Israel decided today, unanimously, that the law, jurisdiction and administration of the State shall be applied, without delay, to the Golan Heights....

## [Requests for Negotiations]

What we are concerned with today is not only the historical aspect, not only the security aspect, which means ensuring the lives of our citizens, but also the moral-political aspect. How often we called upon the Syrian rulers to open negotiations with us for a peace treaty. On several occasions I issued such calls from the rostrum of the Knesset. Again and again, I said that I invite President Assad to Jerusalem, or, alternatively, I am prepared to go to Damascus in order to engage there in negotiations aimed at arriving at a peace settlement between us. The Syrians rejected our outstretched hand with the total denial of the right of our existence as the Jewish State. Can anyone really believe that we are going to wait for an unlimited period of time for a sign from the Syrians that they are prepared to talk with us about peace and good-neighborly relations? On 17 Tevet 5741, December 24, 1980 — in other words, almost exactly one year ago — the Minister of Justice stated from the rostrum of the Knesset:

"There exists a framework agreement for peace in the Middle East — namely, the Camp David Agreement — and Syria will have to face up to the question whether it wants peace negotiations or whether it wants to continue the state of war. Insofar as Israel is concerned, the option of negotiations between us and Syria is open. But Syria must understand that Israel will not be able to wait indefinitely, and there will come a time when Israel will have to adopt an unequivocal decision on the subject of the sovereignty over the Golan Heights."

## [Syrian Stance]

We all know today where Syria stands — not in the past, but in the present — from the moral-political point of view. At the Arab Summit Conference at Fez, Syria's Foreign Minister Haddam, in rejecting the plan put forward by Prince Fahd, declared that the Arabs should not submit any kind of plan. They should, rather, "wait a hundred years or more, until Israel will be weakened, and then we will act...."

In their essence, of course, these words are absurd. Israel's defensive military strength will not be diminished. The development and maintenance of this strength has been the concern of all of our past governments and of the present government, as these will be the concern of future governments, regardless of their political composition, because for us this is a matter of life or death. But the aim, or design, of the enemy has been clarified beyond any doubt, by the statement of the Syrian Foreign Minister: he expects us to be weakened, and then the Arabs will act.

You need not suppose, however, Ladies and Gentlemen, Members of the Knesset, that these things were said for the ears of the Arab leaders alone. Yesterday, the ruler of Syria, President Assad, came along and confirmed Haddam's statement, almost in full. Here is what President Assad said, as reported by the Kuwaiti newspaper, *Ar-Rai Al-Aam:*

"He will not recognize Israel even if the Palestinians will deign to do so. He rejected the Saudi 'Peace Plan' on the grounds that it served as an opening for Arab recognition of Israel and the Arabs so long as the strategic balance plays into Israel's hands. He called upon the Arab states to persist in their rejectionist stand until they attained the power necessary to impose peace conditions on Israel in the spirit of the Arab demands."

## [Syria and Terrorism]

It is also clear to all where Syria stands in the international arena. Libya, which supports international terror and also practices it, planned to carry out such criminal acts within the United States. The United States reacted by taking steps to safeguard the lives of its citizens. In this context, Syria says that it will stand up with all the strength it can muster, against the United States of America and in favour of the aggressor, Libya.

Meanwhile, Syria is extending its domination in Lebanon, ignoring the repeated demands of the local population, and of international elements, to evacuate a land that does not belong to it — a land that was beautiful, tranquil and peaceloving until the Syrians, together with the murderous terrorists, took over the country — because of its strategic importance in the event that Syria should make war upon Israel.

These, Mr. Chairman, are the reasons — of history, security, as well as political and moral reasons — why I have the honor, in the name of the Government, to submit the Golan Heights Law and to propose that it be sent to the Foreign Affairs and Security Committee, to be prepared for its second reading, and to adopt it in all its three readings.

# SECURITY COUNCIL RESOLUTION 497

*The Security Council,*

*Having considered* the letter of 14 December 1981 from the Permanent Representative of the Syrian Arab Republic contained in document S/14791,

*Reaffirming* that the acquisition of territory by force is inadmissible, in accordance with the United Nations Charter, the principles of international law, and relevant Security Council resolutions,

1. *Decides* that the Israeli decision to impose its laws, jurisdiction and administration in the occupied Syrian Golan Heights is null and void and without international legal effect;

2. *Demands* that Israel, the occupying Power, should rescind forthwith its decision;

3. *Determines* that all the provisions of the Geneva Convention Relative to the Protection of Civilian Persons in Time of War of 12 August 1949 continue to apply to the Syrian territory occupied by Israel since June 1967;

4. *Requests* the Secretary-General to report to the Security Council on the implementation of this resolution within two weeks and decides that in the event of non-compliance by Israel, the Security Council would meet urgently, and not later than 5 January 1982, to consider taking appropriate measures in accordance with the Charter of the United Nations.

# BEGIN STATEMENT
# TO AMERICAN AMBASSADOR

During the last six months the U.S. Government "punished" Israel thrice. On June 7 we destroyed the atomic bomb producing plant, Osirak, near Baghdad. I do not want to come back to the question who gave us ultimately the information that potentially that plant may have a capability of producing atomic bombs. We didn't have any doubt whatsoever about it. Therefore, our act of destroying the atomic reactor was to us an act of salvation; an act of national self-defense in the highest sense of the term. We saved the lives of hundreds of thousands of our citizens, including tens of thousands of children. Nevertheless, you announced that you are "punishing" us and you breached a written and signed contract which included delivery dates of F-16 aircrafts.

Not long passed and we, in self-defense, after there was a massacre among our people — three men killed, one of them a survivor of Auschwitz, and 29 wounded — bombed the headquarters of the PLO in Beirut. You have no moral right to lecture us on civilian casualties. We have read the history of the Second World War and we know what happened to civilians when you carried out military operations against the enemy. We also read the history of the Vietnam War and your term, "body counts."

We wrack our brains to avoid civilian casualties, but sometimes it is unavoidable as happened in the bombing of the PLO headquarters. We sometimes put at risk the lives of our soldiers in order to avoid civilian casualties. Nevertheless, you "punished" us and you suspended the delivery of the F-15's.

## [Golan Heights Law]

A week ago, on the recommendation of the Government, the Knesset adopted by a two-thirds overwhelming majority in all three readings, the

Golan Law. And again you declare that you are "punishing" Israel. What kind of talk is that, "punishing" Israel? Are we a vassal state? A banana republic? Are we boys of 14-years old, that if they don't behave they have their knuckles smacked? I will tell you of whom this Government is composed. It is composed of men who fought, risked their lives and suffered. You cannot and will not frighten us with "punishments" and threats. Threats will fall on deaf ears. We are willing only to hear reasoning. You have no right to "punish" Israel and I protest the use of this term.

## [Memorandum of Understanding]

You announced that you are suspending the deliberations on the Memorandum of Understanding on Strategic Cooperation and that your return to the talks that were already fixed in advance would be resumed conditional on progress of the Autonomy talks and the situation in Lebanon. You are trying to make Israel hostage to the Memorandum of Understanding. I understand from that announcement that the American Government renounces the Memorandum of Understanding. No Sword of Damocles will be hung over our heads. We register the fact that you have renounced the Memorandum of Understanding. The people of Israel have lived for 3,700 years without a Memorandum of Understanding with America and will continue to live without it for another 3,700 years. As we see it, by your announcement, this is the renunciation of the Memorandum of Understanding.

We shall not agree that you demand of us to permit the Arabs of Jerusalem to participate in the elections of the administrative council and to threaten us that if we do not agree you will suspend the Memorandum of Understanding.

You have imposed upon us pecuniary sanctions and in the process you have broken the word of the President. When the Secretary of State Haig was here he read out from a paper the words of the President that the U.S. will buy from Israel military and other hardware for $200 million. Now you say, it will not be so. This is breaking the word of the President. Is this done? Is it proper? You have cancelled another one hundred million dollars. What do you want to do? Hit us in the pocket?

## [Anti-Semitism]

In 1946 there lived in this very house a British general whose name was Barker. Today I live in this house. When we fought against him you called us terrorists and we continued the fight. After we blew up his headquarters in the sequestered part of the King David [Hotel], Barker said: "You can punish that race only by hitting at its pocket," and he issued an order to his British troops that all the Jewish coffee-shops be out of bounds. To hit us in our pockets? That is the philosophy of Barker. Now I understand why the effort in the Senate to achieve a majority for the arms deal with Saudi Arabia was accompanied by an ugly anti-Semitic campaign. First there was a slogan: "Begin or Reagan," the inference being that to oppose the deal with Saudi Arabia you support a foreign Prime Minister and are disloyal to the President of the United States, and thus such Senators as Jackson, Kennedy, Moynihan, Packwood and, of course, Senator Boschwitz, are disloyal citizens. But then another slogan was heard: "We will not allow the Jews to determine the foreign policy of the United States." What is the meaning of this slogan? The Greek minority in the United States did much to determine the resolution in the Senate forbidding the delivery of arms for Turkey after Turkey had invaded Cyprus. Nobody will frighten the great and free Jewish community in the United States. Nobody will succeed in intimidating them by anti-Semitic propaganda. They will stand by us; this is the land of their forefathers — they have the right and duty to support it.

There are those who say that the law adopted by the Knesset has to be rescinded. The word "rescind," is a concept from the time of the Inquisition. Our forefathers went to the stake rather than rescind their faith. We are not going to the stake. Thank God, we have enough strength to defend our independence and defend our rights. If it would depend on me, I would say don't rescind the law. It depends on the Knesset and it is my conviction that on this earth there is no man who can influence the Knesset to annul the law which was adopted by a two-thirds majority. Mr. Weinberger said, and later Mr. Haig, that the passage of the law damages Resolution 242. One who says that has not read the resolution or perhaps has forgot it or did not understand it. The soul of 242 is a negotiation to determine secure and recognized boundaries. Syria declares that it will not conduct negotiations with us, does not recognize us and will not recognize us and, with that, deprived 242 of its very soul. How, then, could we damage 242? As for the future, please tell the Secretary of State that the Golan Law shall remain in force. There is no force in the world that can bring about its abrogation. As for the charge that we surprised you, the truth is we didn't want to embarrass you. We knew your difficulty. You come to Riyadh and Damascus. It was President Reagan who said that Mr. Begin was right, for had he approached the United States beforehand with regard to the Law, the United States would have said, no. We did not want you to say, no, and then apply the Law to the Golan Heights. Our intention was not to embarrass you. . . .

# MEMORANDUM OF UNDERSTANDING

## Preamble

This Memorandum of Understanding reaffirms the common bonds of friendship between the United States and Israel and builds on the mutual security relationship that exists between the two nations. The Parties recognize the need to enhance Strategic Cooperation to deter all threats from the Soviet Union to the region. Noting the long-standing and fruitful cooperation for mutual security that has developed between the two countries, the Parties have decided to establish a framework for continued consultation and cooperation to enhance their national security by deterring such threats to the whole region.

The Parties have reached the following agreements in order to achieve the above aims.

## Article I

United States-Israeli Strategic Cooperation, as set forth in this Memorandum, is designed against the threat to peace and security of the region caused by the Soviet Union or Soviet-controlled forces from outside the region introduced into the region. It has the following broad purposes:

a. To enable the Parties to act cooperatively and in a timely manner to deal with the above mentioned threat.

b. To provide each other with military assistance for operations of their forces in the area that may be required to cope with this threat.

c. The Strategic Cooperation between the Parties is not directed at any State or group of States within the region. It is intended solely for defensive purposes against the above mentioned threat.

## Article II

1. The fields in which Strategic Cooperation will be carried out to prevent the above mentioned threat from endangering the security of the region include:

a. Military cooperation between the Parties, as may be agreed by the Parties.

b. Joint military exercises, including naval and air exercises in the Eastern Mediterranean Sea, as agreed upon by the Parties.

c. Cooperation for the establishment and maintenance of joint readiness activities, as agreed upon by the Parties.

d. Other areas within the basic scope and purpose of this agreement, as may be jointly agreed.

2. Details of activities with these fields of cooperation shall be worked out by the Parties in accordance with the provisions of Article III below. The cooperation will include, as appropriate, planning, preparations, and exercises.

## Article III

1. The Secretary of Defense and the Minister of Defense shall establish a Coordination Council to further the purposes of this Memorandum:

a. To coordinate and provide guidance to Joint Working Groups;

b. To monitor the implementation of cooperation in the fields agreed upon by the Parties with the scope of this agreement;

c. To hold periodic meetings, in Israel and the United States, for the purposes of discussing and resolving outstanding issues and to further the objectives set forth in this Memorandum. Special meetings can be held at the request of either Party. The Secretary of Defense and Minister of Defense will chair these meetings whenever possible.

2. Joint Working Groups will address the following issues:

a. Military cooperation between the Parties, including joint US-Israeli exercises in the Eastern Mediterranean Sea.

b. Cooperation for the establishment of joint readiness activities including access to maintenance facilities and other infrastructure, consistent with the basic purposes of this agreement.

c. Cooperation in reseach and development, building on past cooperation in this area.

d. Cooperation in defense trade.

e. Other fields within the basic scope and purpose of this agreement, such as questions of prepositioning, as agreed upon by the Coordinating Council.

3. The future agenda for the work of the Joint Working Groups, their composition, and procedures for reporting to the Coordinating Council shall be agreed upon by the Parties.

## Article IV

This Memorandum shall enter into force upon exchange of notification that required procedures have been completed by each Party. If either Party considers it necessary to terminate this Memorandum of Understanding, it may do so by notifying the other Party six months in advance of the effective date of termination.

## Article V

Nothing in the Memorandum shall be considered as derogating from previous agreements and understandings between the Parties.

## Article VI

The Parties share the understanding that nothing in this Memorandum is intended to or shall in any way prejudice the rights and obligations which devolve or may devolve upon either government under the Charter of the United Nations or under International Law. The Parties reaffirm their faith in the purposes and principles of the Charter of the United Nations and their aspiration to live in peace with all countries in the region.

# UNICEF REPORT ON CHILDREN
## December 18, 1981

*Seventeen million of the world's children died in 1981 at a rate of one every two seconds, according to a United Nations Children's Fund (UNICEF) report issued December 18. On a daily basis, 40,000 lost their lives. Most of these deaths were caused by malnutrition and childhood diseases.*

*Titled "The State of the World's Children 1981-82," the report stated that "a child's life was worth less than $100 in 1981." If such an amount had been spent on each of the poorest 500 million mothers and young children in the world, it said, the "basics of life" could have been brought to them.*

*Of the 17 million children who died in 1981, less than ten percent were immunized against the six most common childhood diseases. According to the report, the cost of immunizing all of the Third World's infants against the diseases worked out to approximately five dollars per child. "The cost of not doing so," it stated, "works out at approximately five million deaths a year."*

*According to the report, more than three-fourths of the 1981 infant deaths occurred in Africa and South Asia. Malnutrition was the primary cause. In 1981, for the tenth successive year, nations south of the Sahara saw a decrease in food production per person.*

### Gloomy Forecast

*The UNICEF report foresaw little change for 1982. Predicting that 17 million of the 125 million children born in 1982 would die before their fifth birthday, it stated "there is every reason to suggest that times are getting darker for the world's poorest children."*

*Acknowledging that the economic resources available for improving infant health care are not increasing, the UNICEF report concluded that the "only possible response is to seek to increase the ratio between resources and results." It suggested that one way to get "more development per dollar" was to use paraprofessional workers who would work directly in underdeveloped communities. They would treat simpler illnesses and refer the more difficult cases to clinics or hospitals.*

## People Participation

*The report also suggested the use of more "people participation." It described how, in the African country of Malawi, a water-scarce region now has a piped water supply because 150,000 villagers themselves dug the trenches and laid the pipes. Because of such local involvement, costs were kept to only three dollars per person.*

*According to the report, over three-fourths of UNICEF staff members were living and working in developing countries. This was in keeping with the agency's "decentralized strategy of participation in development." During 1981 the agency helped train over 115,000 health workers and 90,000 teachers. It also helped equip almost 43,000 health centers and 88,000 primary schools.*

*Following are excerpts from "The State of the World's Children 1981-82," issued December 18 by the United Nations Children's Fund (UNICEF). (Boldface headings in brackets have been added by Congressional Quarterly to highlight the organization of the text.):*

## Children in Dark Times

### A YEAR OF SILENT EMERGENCY

Far from being priceless, a child's life was worth less than $100 in 1981. Wisely spent on each of the poorest 500 million mothers and young children in the world, such a sum could have bought improved diets and easier pregnancies, elementary education and basic health care, safer sanitation and more water. In other words, it could have brought the basics of life. And at the same time as meeting the most pressing human need in the world today, it could have helped to slow down population growth and accelerate economic growth in the world of tomorrow. In short, meeting the needs of all the world's children was both the greatest of humanitarian challenges and the best of investment opportunities.

In practice, it proved too high a price for the world community to pay. And so, every two seconds of 1981, a child paid that price with its life.

About those 17 million who died during the year, there is little more to be said. Whoever they once were, whatever religion they were growing up in, whatever language they were beginning to speak, and whatever potential their lives held, they were simply failed by the world into which they were born.

Not ten per cent of them were immunized against the six most common and dangerous diseases of childhood. The cost of so immunizing all of the Third World's infants works out at approximately $5 per child. The cost of not doing so works out at approximately five million deaths a year.

For the children of 1982, the facts of life on earth will not be significantly different. Of the 125 million who will be born, 17 million will again be dead before their fifth birthday. And between 1981 and 1982, although there is no trend so pronounced as to break through the inevitable imprecision of available figures, there is every reason to suggest that times are getting darker for the world's poorest children.

To the extent that this annual decimation of the world's newborn is a reprisal for the failings of economic development, the immediate future holds little hope of a reprieve....

This has been ... another year of 'silent emergency': of 40,000 children quietly dying each day; of 100 million children quietly going to sleep hungry at night; of ten million children quietly becoming disabled in mind or body; of 200 million 6-11 year olds quietly watching other children go to school; of one-fifth of the world's people quietly struggling for life itself. But it has also been a year in which economic trends indicate that progress against such poverty is not only slowing down in many nations, but being thrown into reverse. Only two years ago, the World Bank reported that the total number of people living in absolute poverty was 780 million. Optimistically, said the Bank at that time, that number would fall to 720 million by the end of the 1980s. Pessimistically, it would rise to 800 million during the decade.

Yet a more recent United Nations study has now concluded that 'the world economy is experiencing greater instability and a more severe disruption of steady growth than at any time since the end of the Second World War ... unless specific steps are taken, the consequence of this adverse external environment will be to increase the numbers of the absolute poor to one billion before the end of the Third Development Decade'.

It was a conclusion accepted by the heads of all United Nations agencies, including the World Bank itself. And, in all probability, it means that, in many countries, more children will die next year than this.

## [SOCIAL GOALS AND SLOW PROGRESS]

Last year, in this report UNICEF asserted that by the year 2000 the number of infant deaths in low-income countries could be reduced to 50 per 1,000 or less, that average life expectancy could be raised to 60 years or more, and that every child should have at least the four years of primary education necessary to acquire literacy. The report noted that although idealistic in the context of past experience, these goals are realistic in the sense that the principal obstacle standing in the way of their realization is the absence of the will and commitment to achieve them. . . .

To reach such goals, progress towards them would in fact have to be two or three times as fast over the next 20 years as it has been over the last 20. But in many nations today, the rate of development as measured by all three of the chosen indicators is already slowing down.

The Third World's infant mortality rate — that sensitive indicator of the well-being of mothers and children — fell by a steady four or five points a year in the 1960s. For the past five years, it has barely flickered. Average life expectancy, which increased by seven or eight months a year in the 1960s and early 1970s, is now increasing by only two or three months a year. School enrollment rates, which again rose by a regular four or five per cent a year up to the mid-1970s, now seems to have reached a plateau.

With the developing world's infant mortality still ten times higher than in the industrialized world, with its life expectancy still 15 years less, and with a third of its 6-11 year olds still out of school, this deceleration of progress cannot be explained by the approach of any natural limits. Rather it is a sign that development itself is in some nations becalmed and in others actually drifting backwards.

In short, the optimism of the 1960s which gave ground to the realism of the 1970s has now receded even further to make room for the doubt and pessimism which seems to be settling into the 1980s. It is a process of disillusionment both aggravated and symbolised by the decline in the share of the rich world's wealth which has been invested in aid. In 1965, when the United Nations first called upon the donor countries to increase the level of their aid to 0.7 per cent of their GNPs [Gross National Product], the actual level stood at 0.49 per cent. Today, despite the efforts of a handful of nations who have met that target, the average level rests at 0.37 per cent. . . .

### [MEETING CHILDREN'S NEEDS]

The realism or naivety of any goal is almost always as much a question of priorities as of possibilities. And it is not the possibility of achieving primary health care and primary education for the great majority of children which is in question. It is its priority.

Such goals could be achieved, for example, for less than the industrialized world spends on alcoholic drinks each year. Similarly, the broader goals of meeting the basic human needs of the overwhelming majority of men, women and children on earth could be realized by devoting as much each year to the task of achieving them as is now devoted every six weeks to the task of maintaining and increasing the world's military capacity.

However uncomfortable such comparisons may be, they are necessary to put into perspective the accusation that the goal of making significant improvements in the lives of the world's children by the end of this century is 'naive', and to put in its place a decision about priorities.

In dark times, children need priority. And while there will always be emotion behind that statement, it is also an appeal to reason.

More specifically, it is an appeal to two reasons — one of which is timeless and one of which is particular to this, the last quarter of the twentieth century.

Ninety per cent of the growth of the human brain and 50 per cent of the growth of the human body occurs in the first five years of the human life. The corresponding susceptibility of those years should alone argue that priority be given — in family affairs and in world affairs — to the needs of the young.

In the acquisition of their needs, and in the defence of their rights, children themselves are relatively powerless. They have neither physical strength, nor economic sanction. They have no unions, and no votes.

Usually it is the parents who are empowered to protect and provide. But if parents are deprived of that power, then the responsibility falls to the community of which the child is part. . . .

## THE LARGEST GENERATION

This timeless concern is today sharpened to a particular edge by specific changes in the growth and structure of world population.

After a rapid increase in the rate of population growth — caused by relatively sudden successes in controlling certain diseases, epidemics and famines which meant that more infants survived to have children of their own — fertility rates have now begun to fall in almost every region of the world. The beginning of this decline is as unprecedented as was the surging increase which preceded it. Taken together, both forces now have a special bearing on the state of the world's children.

One effect is that 40 per cent of the developing world's people are under the age of 15 and about to enter their child-bearing years. As birth rates fall, the numbers of children as a proportion of the total population will also fall. But in our time, the Third World's ratio of younger to older . . . is at its height. In Germany or the USSR, for example, there are now two people of working age for every one who is too young or too old to work. In Bangladesh, Mexico or Nigeria, the ratio is one to one.

The result is a temporary but powerful extra strain on the Third World's capacity to provide for its children. In education, for example, those of primary school age now amount to 25 per cent of the population. In the industrialized world, the corresponding figure is only 15 per cent.

The decline in fertility which is just beginning to become visible will in time lower that proportion. But meanwhile the capacity of the Third World to provide essential services for the young is stretched to the limit

— and beyond — by quantitative pressures on low-income countries which leave little room for the qualitative improvements which are required to improve the well-being of the world's children.

When these internal pressures coincide, as is now happening, with external economic pressures resulting from world-wide recession, then the welfare of the largest generation of children in history is further squeezed.

As nutrition, health, education and the normalcies of childhood are usually preconditions of successful parenthood, it is vital to both this generation and the next that the children of today be protected against the present economic weather.

The welfare of children — and future parents — is not the only issue at stake. For the question of whether or not improvements in the lives of the young are brought about in the 1980s is also crucial to the slowing down of population growth itself.

Acceptance of family planning and a decline in birth rates is closely connected with such changes as the improvement of health care, the decline of infant mortality, and the spread of education (especially for girls). A setback in progress towards these social goals is, therefore, likely to also be a setback in the trend towards lower population growth — so increasing the numbers of children in future generations at the same time as decreasing their parents capacity to provide for them.

Conversely, the stepping-up of national and international efforts to meet such needs would have the opposite effects of both improving life for the children of today, investing in their capacity as the parents of tomorrow, and creating the conditions necessary for a further slow-down in population growth itself. . . .

The commonly held view that reducing infant mortality only stores up more births and more trouble for the future is . . . a mistaken one. Meeting basic human needs is not only necessary to prevent human suffering in the present, but also to reduce the growth of population itself, thereby avoiding more human suffering in the future. Whether today's world population of 4.5 billion eventually stabilises at 10-11 billion or 13-14 billion sometime round the end of the next century depends heavily on what happens to birth rates in the last two decades of this century. . . .

## [More Benefits Per Dollar]

The plea for priority for children — and for resources — has been made. But if another 'realism' dictates that the resources available nationally and internationally for meeting the needs of children are to remain close to present levels then the only possible response is to seek to increase the ratio between resources and results. Somehow, ways must be found to get more development per dollar.

Learning from experience, better use of available knowledge, wisdom, research, and most important of all, the *will* — these are the qualities which can convert additions to economic resources into multipliers of human benefits. And, in an increasing number of cases, social improvement programmes are coming to be seen not as an inevitable drain on national budgets, nor even as just cost-effective welfare expenditures, but as productive investments in themselves. . . .

In 1981, the ratification of the WHO/UNICEF 'International Code of Marketing of Breastmilk Substitutes' by the World Health Assembly represents one of the greatest opportunities of recent times to effect a change which would combine improvement in human life with reductions in economic costs. The improvement for infants can be illustrated in a single fact — because of the nutritional and immunological properties of mother's milk, those who are breastfed for less than six months, or not at all, are five to ten times more likely to die in the second six months of life than those who are breastfed for more than six months. But for a Third World currently spending $1 billion a year on infant formula products, and for low-income families spending $3.50 out of a weekly wage of $15 to buy it for their children, the switch from the promotion of bottlefeeding to the promotion of breastfeeding could also mean a very significant economic saving.

The scope for such combinations of social programs and economic gain is clearly far from exhausted. It cannot make economic sense for one third of all children's hospital beds in the developing world to be occupied by children suffering from cheaply preventable diarrhoeal diseases. It is neither socially nor economically acceptable to have 500,000 children a year being affected by poliomyelitis when 20,000 shots of vaccine cost less than $1,000. Nor is it either humane or sensible to have allowed over 500 children to lose their eyesight every day during 1981 when Vitamin A tablets costing only a few cents could have prevented it.

Meeting the most basic needs of the majority of the world's children is a less direct and self-contained task than these examples imply. But in the wider arenas of nutrition, health care and education, ways have to be found of using human wit and wisdom as much as money itself in bringing about improvements in the lives of the world's children.

Such breakthroughs rarely happen by accident. They happen by an interaction between the experience of the past, the opportunities of the present, and increased priority to the needs of children and low-income families. It is that interaction which UNICEF seeks to catalyse. And it is to that experience, and to those opportunities that this report now turns.

### [RECRUITING PARAPROFESSIONALS]

In the task of providing basic services to meet the greatest needs of the greatest numbers, past experience suggests that an army of paraprofessional development workers — backed by more specialized government services and stimulating the people's own involvement in the creation of those services — is probably the only way forward for the 1980s.

From one point of view, the use of paraprofessionals is an economic necessity. To train, equip and install a fully qualified medical doctor in every Third World community (even if such doctors were prepared to serve there, which the majority are not) is an impossibility for the foreseeable future. . . .

In the Third World, paraprofessionals chosen for training by and from the communities which they will serve are likely to be more knowledgeable about local skills and resources, more sensitive to local culture and tradition, and more at home with, and acceptable to, those whom they will serve.

In this way, paraprofessional development workers can blur the alienating distinction between experts and people and help to involve rather than exclude the poor from the process of change.

## [COMMUNITY PARTICIPATION]

If the potential importance of paraprofessional development workers is one of the 'legs' of a strategy of 'more development per dollar', then the concept of people's participation is the other. Indeed without the organized participation of the poor, no community development project has more than the dimmest hope of lasting success. . . .

Of equal importance is individual participation. A mother who knows the benefits of breastfeeding or of boiling contaminated water before drinking, for example, greatly reduces the need for subsequent and costly curative measures.

But the necessity of people's participation can sometimes obscure the fact that being involved in the decisions and processes which affect one's own life is an end as well as a means and that people's participation therefore has a double valency with the development process. As Denis Goulet has observed: 'Development is not a cluster of benefits "given" to people in need but rather a process by which a populace acquires greater mastery over its own destiny.'. . .

Paraprofessionals and people's participation therefore represent virtue as well as necessity. But as an approach to development, there are those who accuse it of making the former out of the latter.

It might, for example, be said that primary health care workers are merely the lowest and cheapest rung in a 'delivery system' directed from the top downwards and designed to provide a second-class service to the poor in order to contain the problem of poverty and so avoid change in the society of which that poverty is a part.

In some instances, this is undoubtedly true. It is still the case that, across the Third World as a whole, 80 per cent of health budgets are being spent on doctors and hospitals for the urban few whilst primary health care workers are packed off to look after the rural many. In such cases, the concept of people's participation, similarly, is usually just a fancy name for making the poor responsible for their poverty.

In other cases, the pattern of paraprofessionals and people's participation in the provision of basic services is seen not as an end but as a beginning, not as a minimum service but as the maximum which can be achieved at any particular time and at any particular place, not as a separate health service for the poor but a means by which the existing health services — including doctors and hospitals — can be geared to the needs of the poor....

## [ONE PLUS ONE EQUALS THREE]

One of the most obvious lessons of the development effort is that prevention is almost always more cost-effective than cure. And concern for the prevention of illness means that primary health care is inseparable from such issues as agriculture, housing, sanitation, water supply, education, female emancipation, or the questions of work and wages which are the basis of an adequate diet and a healthy people....

A cat's cradle of ... synergisms links almost every aspect of development: female literacy catalyses family planning programmes; less frequent pregnancies improves maternal and child health; improved health makes the most of pre-school or primary education; education can increase incomes and agricultural productivity; better incomes or better food reduces infant mortality; fewer child deaths tend to lead to fewer births; smaller families improve maternal health; healthy mothers have healthier babies; healthier babies demand more attention; stimulation helps mental growth; more alert children do better at school ... and so it continues in an endless pattern of either mutually reinforcing or mutually retarding relationships which can minimize or multiply the benefits of any given input.

For such synergisms to work positively, and so increase the ratio between results and resources, the integration of services is obviously necessary. And that brings us right back to the broad range of the primary health or community development worker's concerns.

Far from the village, separate government departments for agriculture, health, education and employment may make their separate services available. But the community development worker living with the problem of underdevelopment at village or community level has no temptation to see nutrition, health, education and poverty as separate issues....

## [Investing in Children]

At the community level, paraprofessionals and people involvement are the most important ways in which the 1980s can extract more development per dollar and improve the lives of the world's children even within the financial constraints of the years to come. But implemented in isolation from changes in national and international priorities, they are unlikely to fulfill more than a fraction of their potential or to be the beginning of the end for absolute poverty. For a broader and ever more powerful synergism also exists between improvements in health, nutrition, education, and improvements in social and economic development — in productivity by and for the poor majority.

But as the budget of the Third World's governments — and the aid flows they are likely to receive from the industrialized world — are also severely affected by world recession, ways must also be found at the national and international level of making every dollar go further.

## [NEW ECONOMICS]

Again, the lessons of the development effort in recent years point to one outstanding way in which this might be done. In summary, that lesson is that the creation of productive employment opportunities by and for the poor, and of social services designed to meet their needs, will not only alleviate poverty now but will actually help to accelerate economic growth itself.

The implicit proposal — a direct rather than indirect attack on absolute poverty through the provision of services and employment opportunities designed to meet the needs of the poor majority — ran counter to contemporary economic wisdom. Such approaches it was said were inefficient and would lead to decreases in investment and to a slowing down of the very growth which made the expansion of such services possible.

But as the 1960s became the '70s, it was clear that the persistence of poverty represented not only a continuing human tragedy but also an undermining of the process of growth itself.

Labour is as important as capital in the process of increased production. And a malnourished, unhealthy and illiterate population was therefore a serious constraint on productivity. From this point of view, social services which build up 'human capital' are not consumption but investment. Humanitarian concern thereby acquired economic respectability. Says former World Bank President Robert McNamara: 'Human development — education and training, better health and nutrition, and fertility reduction — are shown to be important not only in alleviating poverty directly but also in increasing the incomes of the poor and GNP growth as well.' . . .

In theory, then, the approach of trying to meet basic needs — for food, health-care, education and jobs — represents increased value for development expenditure.

In practice, comparisons across different developing countries also show that economic growth in those countries with high life expectancy and literacy rates grew faster in the 1960s and '70s than those where health and education services lagged behind. Many of those countries and regions which achieved sustained per capita growth in GNP of 6% or more during the 1960s and 1970s — such as Japan, Singapore, Taiwan, Hong Kong, Romania or South Korea — made a greater than usual effort, and with greater than usual effectiveness, to advance the well-being of low-income families and their children. . . .

In 30 developing countries surveyed by the World Bank, primary education was found to be the most productive investment opportunity available — able, in time, to yield a hard economic return of approximately

24 per cent. In the same study, the productivity of farmers with four years of primary education was found to be 13 per cent higher than that of farmers who had never attended school. . . .

### [CHANGING PRIORITIES]

Almost all of these ways of achieving more benefits for children and mothers per dollar — whether they be broad strategies of switching emphasis to human development or more detailed plans to build 50 health centres rather than one hospital — require changes in priorities. And such changes are not easy in view of established interests in existing patterns.

For they are strategies which contribute to and depend upon the greater priority to low-income families implied by a 'basic needs first' approach to development. . . .

But while there can be little doubt that switching priority to the majority of children and mothers renders more efficient the process of using available resources to improve the quality of life, such decisions are ultimately political.

The political will required to invest in the poor majority is perhaps the scarcest resource of all in the struggle for world development. . . .

# FEDERAL JUDGE ON ERA RATIFYING PROCEDURE

## December 23, 1981

A federal district judge in Idaho on December 23 dealt the proposed Equal Rights Amendment (ERA) to the U.S. Constitution a severe setback by ruling against its supporters on two key procedural questions. Judge Marion J. Callister ruled that Congress had acted illegally in 1979 when it extended a deadline for ratification and that states could rescind their earlier votes approving the proposal.

The ruling was greeted with dismay by backers of the ERA who were working to obtain the approval of the amendment by three-fourths of the states before a new June 30, 1982, deadline. Since five states had reversed their earlier approval, the ERA was, immediately after Judge Callister's ruling, eight states short of ratification.

The outlook for the ERA improved slightly on January 25, 1982, however, when the U.S. Supreme Court agreed to hear an appeal of the Idaho decision and stayed enforcement of Judge Callister's ruling pending the appeal.

## Background

The proposed amendment would bar discrimination based on sex by government officials and agencies and by institutions that received federal aid. Congress approved the ERA by the necessary two-thirds majorities in the House and Senate on March 22, 1972. At the same time, Congress set a seven-year time limit for ratification.

During the next six years, 35 states approved the proposed amendment which, if ratified, would become the 27th Amendment. In 1978, with time running out, the ERA's supporters persuaded Congress to extend the ratifying period by 39 months. That time, however, the Senate and the House acted on simple majority votes.

The Idaho lawsuit was brought by the states of Idaho and Arizona. Viewed as a major test of the ERA, the suit posed two challenges. First, it asked that the extension by Congress of the original deadline be overturned as unconstitutional, and, second, it sought a ruling on whether states could legally rescind their earlier votes for ratification.

The defense by the U.S. Justice Department was joined by the National Organization of Women (NOW), which had long spearheaded the drive for ratification.

## Mormon Judge

Months before his decision, Judge Callister himself had become an issue in the case. At the time the suit reached his court, he was one of about 150 regional representatives of the Church of Jesus Christ of Latter-day Saints. The church, widely known as the Mormon Church, had strongly opposed the ERA on the ground that it would undermine family life.

Because of the important office that Judge Callister held in his church's organization, the U.S. Justice Department had filed a motion asking him to disqualify himself. In the motion, the Justice Department asserted that the "appearance of impartiality is as important as the fact of impartiality." But Callister refused, saying that, even if he served in the very highest councils of his church, it would not affect his legal judgment on the bench. Later, the church relieved the judge of his position in its hierarchy.

## Ruling

Judge Callister ruled against the ERA's supporters on both issues raised in the lawsuit. He wrote, "Congress may by a two-thirds vote of both houses set a reasonable time limit for the states to act in order for the ratification to be effective. When this time is set, it is binding on Congress and the states and it cannot be changed by Congress thereafter." He also ruled that "... Idaho's rescission of its ratification ... effectively nullified its prior ratification.... This same is true for any other state." If the ruling were upheld by the Supreme Court the end of the road for the ERA would have come on March 29, 1979, the first deadline.

## Reaction

*Eleanor Smeal, the president of NOW, decried the ruling, declaring that Judge Callister was biased. "The will of the people is being stepped on by a single federal judge," she was quoted in the press as saying. On the other hand, Phyllis Schlafly, leader of an organization opposing ratification, termed Callister's ruling "a great victory for constitutional integrity and fairness."*

*Following are excerpts from U.S. District Judge Marion J. Callister's ruling December 23, 1981, in* Idaho vs. Freeman, *on two questions involving the ratification procedure for the proposed Equal Rights Amendment (ERA). (Boldface headings in brackets have been added by Congressional Quarterly to highlight the organization of the text.):*

# In the United States District Court for the District of Idaho

THE STATE OF IDAHO, et al,
      Plaintiffs,
and
CLAUDE L. OLIVER, etc., et al,
      Plaintiff-Intervenors,
-vs-
REAR ADMIRAL ROLAND G. FREEMAN,
III, Administrator of General Services
Administration,
      Defendant,
and
NATIONAL ORGANIZATION FOR
  WOMEN, et al,
      Defendant-Intervenors.

Civil No. 79-1097
MEMORANDUM DECISION

[December 23, 1981]

# I. Introduction

This matter comes before the Court on defendant's motion to dismiss and the parties' cross-motions for summary judgment. In an extensive stipulation filed with the Court, all the material facts in this case have been agreed to by the parties. This proceeding calls into question the validity of Idaho's act of rescinding its prior ratification of the proposed "Equal Rights Amendment" to the Constitution of the United States, and the constitutionality of Congress' act in extending the time period in which ratifications may be received. The plaintiffs bringing this suit consisting of the State of Idaho, the leadership of the Idaho State Legislature, and individual legislators of that body; the State of Arizona, legislative leadership of both houses and individual legislators from the Arizona legislature. These plaintiffs are joined by the plaintiff-intervenors, legislators from the State of Washington. They seek from this Court a declaration that, as a matter of federal constitutional law, Idaho's act of rescinding its prior ratification is valid and effective; that Congress' extension of the seven-year time limitation in which to present ratifications is unconstitutional in that it violates the grant of power given Congress under article V of the Constitution, and that the running of the seven-year time limitation tolls and terminates any ratifications enacted by the states to that point. Furthermore, the plaintiffs seek a mandatory injunction directing the defendant, the Administrator of General Services Administration, Rear Admiral Rowland G. Freeman III, to remove the name of the State of Idaho from all official records which would indicate that Idaho has adopted the proposed twenty-seventh amendment and return its prior ratification documents. Finally, the plaintiffs petition for an order enjoining the Administrator of General Services Administration from taking further account of any purported ratifications after the expiration of the original ratification period.

On May 13 and 14, 1981, oral argument was presented by the defendant, represented by the Department of Justice, and defendant-intervenors, the National Organization for Women, on their motions to dismiss or in the alternative for summary judgment; plaintiffs and plaintiff-intervenors' cross-motion for summary judgment was also considered at that time. These motions present the Court with essentially questions of first impression necessitating consideration of the premises of one of the pivotal provisions of the United States Constitution, the article V amending clause. In addition, the Court is confronted with the perennially perplexing problem of the legitimate relationship of the courts with the coordinate branches, particularly the Congress, in determining whether the questions presented here are proper for judicial resolution. After careful consideration of the difficult issues presented, it appears that the weight of constitutional precedent dictates that the defendant and defendant-intervenors' motion to dismiss or in the alternative for summary judgment should be dismissed and plaintiffs' motion for summary judgment should be granted in accordance with the principles discussed below.

## II. Background

In March of 1972 Congress passed a resolution proposing the "Equal Rights Amendment," as the twenty-seventh amendment to the Constitution of the United States, and submitted it for ratification to the legislatures of the states:

## JOINT RESOLUTION

Proposing an amendment to the Constitution of the United States relative to equal rights for men and women.

*Resolved by the Senate and House of Representatives of the United States of America in Congress assembled (two-thirds of each House concurring therein),* That the following article is proposed as an amendment to the Constitution of the United States, which shall be valid to all intents and purposes as part of the Constitution when ratified by the legislatures of three-fourths of the several States within seven years from the date of its submission by the Congress:

## ARTICLE —

SECTION 1. Equality of rights under the law shall not be denied or abridged by the United States or by any State on account of sex.

SEC. 2. The Congress shall have the power to enforce, by appropriate legislation, the provisions of this article.

SEC. 3. This amendment shall take effect two years after the date of ratification.

H.J.Res 208, 86 Stat. 1523 (1972). From the advent of the amendment and until 1978, 35 of the requisite 38 state legislatures took action ratifying the amendment and sent official certifications of their actions to the General Services Administrator pursuant to 1 U.S.C. § 106 (b). But, in that same time period five states, Nebraska, Tennessee, Idaho, Kentucky, and South Dakota, while initially assenting to ratification, passed resolutions of rescission withdrawing their prior consent. The original seven-year ratification restriction set in the resolution proposing the "Equal Rights Amendment" would have expired on March 22, 1979, had not Congress taken action to extend the time period.

On October 6, 1978, an extension resolution, House Joint Resolution 638, was presented to Congress for consideration. It read:

Joint Resolution
Extending the deadline for the ratification
of the Equal Rights Amendment.

*Resolved by the Senate and House of Representatives of the United States of America in Congress assembled,* That notwithstanding any provision of House Joint Resolution 208 of the Ninety-second Congress, second session, to the contrary, the article of amendment proposed to the States in such joint resolution shall be valid to all intents and purposes as part of the Constitution when ratified by the legislature of three-fourths of the several States not later than June 30, 1982.

While a majority of both Houses favored the extension resolution, proponents of the measure could not generate a two-thirds concurrence as had been the case when the original time period had been enacted. Therefore, the House acting by a vote of 253 to 189 and the Senate acting by a vote of

927

60 to 36 enacted the extension resolution by a simple majority. The resolution was later signed by the President.

The State of Idaho, which requires a super-majority, two-thirds, of the legislature to act in adopting an amendment, took action the first year the Equal Rights Amendment was proposed. The Idaho House of Representatives adopted Senate Joint Resolution No. 133 on March 24, 1972, by a vote of 31 to 4 and later that day the Senate passed it by a vote of 39 to 5....

In February of 1977 the state legislature of Idaho took action to rescind its prior ratification of the proposed Equal Rights Amendment. On February 4, 1977, House Concurrent Resolution 10 was introduced and passed by the House by a vote of 44 to 26. On February 8, 1977, the Senate passed HCR 10 by a vote of 18 to 17. Thus, by a simple majority Idaho declared its prior ratification "rescinded, voided, repealed, with[drawn], recalled and disaffirmed...." The Secretary of the State of Idaho certified Idaho's rescission to the Acting Administrator of the General Services Administration. The certification was duly received and noted but questioned as to its validity. The State of Idaho and legislators then brought this action to declare its validity and compel the proper entry of Idaho's action of rescission, including the return of the prior certificate of ratification....

## III. The Issues

As indicated earlier the issues presented in this litigation are ones of first impression. A number of prominent Supreme Court cases have dealt with interpretations of the amendment clause, article V of the federal Constitution, but none have made direct holding on any of the questions considered here. While the areas that the Court is asked to address deal ostensibly with an interpretation of the fundamental nature of the process of amending the Constitution, at the threshold, however, are questions of justiciability that would preclude consideration of any of the substantive issues if they are found applicable. First, the Court must consider if the proper parties are before the Court and whether the issues raised are "ripe" for adjudication. If these hurdles are overcome, the Court must then consider whether the questions proffered are not properly "political questions" and thus better left to the legislative or executive branch. Only if these preliminary questions are found not to bar this Court's jurisdiction is it proper for the Court to address what have been denoted the merits of the case, which are: first, whether or not a rescission of a prior ratification is a proper exercise of the state's power under article V to act on a proposed amendment. A subsidiary issue to this inquiry is that if a rescission is a proper exercise of the state's authority, is Idaho's resolution of rescission procedurally flawed. Second, is it a proper exercise of congressional authority under Article V to alter a previously proposed time limitation for ratification; if so, must Congress act by two-thirds majority or would a simple majority suffice. Third, assuming the propriety of the congressional extension of the ratification period, how does the extension affect a state which has supposedly enacted its ratification conditioned upon the original time limitation placed on the amendment. Finally, a question is raised with regard to the propriety of the mandatory injunctive relief requested by the plaintiff.

## IV. Justiciability

[Sections A and B Omitted]

### C. POLITICAL QUESTION

Defendant maintains that if the questions presented in the instant case are determined to be otherwise justiciable, the case is barred from consideration by this Court because it presents a non-justiciable "political question." The case law in the federal courts uniformly holds that a cause of action presenting a "political question" will not be adjudicated by the courts. . . .

The careful balance between the participants in the amendment process is critical to understand in order to assess the full scope of authority each has been assigned. For such an understanding it is necessary to probe the deliberations of the founding fathers in their drafting of article V, as well as their experiences under local state charters, constitutions, and, the Constitution's predecessor, the Articles of Confederation.

It appears that the founding fathers were well schooled in the concept of the amendability of governing laws. Most, if not all, of the original states had constitutions or charters which provided for orderly change, by amendment, pursuant to specific procedures. When the Articles of Confederation were drafted provision was made for amendments of error, but concern was expressed at the same time that the ability to amend would augment the power of the national government to the detriment of the autonomy of the states. . . . The Articles of Confederation reflected this fear of a strong national government by emphasizing both the autonomy of the states and the delegated limited authority to the national government. . . .

. . . As a subsidiary matter of detail, Congress has the power, pursuant to its authority to designate the mode of ratification, to set a reasonable time period in which ratification may take place. . . .

. . . It is important to note that Congress' part in determining whether or not a consensus has been reached in a reasonable contemporaneous time period is not one where they must initially or ultimately determine the actual existence of consent or consensus, for that determination Congress must look to the expressions of the states in their role of representing the people locally. Rather, the congressional determination is one of timing, i.e., whether the concepts which gave rise to the amendment continue in full force and effect during the period in which the states act in ratifying.

This role of orchestrating the expressions of the states which Congress has under its power to propose the mode of ratification is appropriate for two related reasons. First, in its role as a national legislature the Congress is best suited to act in accumulating the states' expressions of consent to formulate a broad picture of local consensus. Second, Congress, it would appear, is also best suited, because of the basic nature of the question, to determine whether or not the expressions of consent are sufficiently contemporaneous in time with each other and with the proposal of the amendment. For example, at the time of the Constitutional Convention the founding fathers saw the necessity of an amending clause as being predicated on the need for a process to meet and solve unanticipated constitutional crises. As such it was anticipated that the need for changing the Constitution would not arise in a theoretical vacuum but be brought about by socio-political economic forces which would serve as the impetus for the move to amend. An amendment, therefore, would be a reasoned response to the particular pressures and a specific solution to them. It follows that as long as the socio-political, economic pressures continue, and the proposed amendment remains responsive to those pressures, it can be said that the amendment is still viable, and any state's action in ratifying would be considered "contemporaneous" with all other actions on the amendment. If, however, a change occurs in the socio-political economic milieu, or in the proposed amendment's ability to respond, then the amendment cannot be said to be viable nor would a state's act in ratifying the amendment be "contemporaneous" with the spirit of the proposal or with other states which ratified soon after the amendment was proposed.... Therefore, since the essential inquiry regarding the contemporaneousness of the consensus is one in which the socio-political economic underpinnings are monitored, it would appear such an exercise is clearly best suited to the capabilities of Congress.

The states, on the other hand, have complete and exclusive power over the process of determining actual consent. They determine whether or not sufficient local consensus exists and the process by which that consensus is determined. It is this allocation of exclusive control over the actual process of ratification, or determination of actual consensus, that creates the "barrier to national encroachment" that the founding fathers saw as a necessity....

## 2. Lack of Judicially Manageable Standard

A number of important cases have dealt with the parameters of this formulation of the political question doctrine. *Goldwater v. Carter* (1979); *Dyer v. Blair* (N.D. Ill. E.D., 1974); *Powell v. McCormack* (1969); *Baker v. Carr* (1962); *Coleman v. Miller* (1939). More importantly several of these cases have dealt with this standard in the context of article V disputes. *Dyer v. Blair* and *Coleman v. Miller*. From a review of these cases in light of the questions before this Court, it appears well settled that these issues are not barred from consideration by the Court for a lack of a judicially manageable standard. . . .

At the outset it should be noted that little has been written on the parameters of this formulation of the political question barrier. Thus key provisions have yet to be clarified: for example, what is meant by "an unusual need" to adhere to a decision made by a political branch. It is unclear whether an "unusual need" is manifest by considerations that go beyond the traditional notions of separation of powers, or whether it is merely a reiteration of that basic requirement. Aside from the problem of a lack of guidance as to the application of the formulation the whole approach has been severely criticized. This criticism is based on the argument that "it seems an unusual approach for the body recognized as having the power to review acts of Congress to adopt and rely on an act of Congress as precedent. . . ." This argument is even more persuasive when one considers that presumably Congress' own determination would have no binding effect on any subsequent Congress.

In the application of this prudential consideration calling for deference to a decision made by a political branch, one unequivocal factor necessary before the Court can take cognizance of this limitation on its jurisdiction is that there must be a clear, definitive decision in existence that the courts can defer to. In *Coleman v. Miller* apparently one of the first times this prudential consideration was given application, the court found that the question of the effectiveness of a ratification after a prior rejection was a political question based on the fact that "the political departments of the Government dealt with the effect of both previous rejection and of attempted withdrawal and determined that both were ineffectual in the presence of an actual ratification." In reaching this conclusion, the court drew upon the history of the ratification of the thirteenth, fourteenth, and fifteenth amendments. . . .

If the question of the effectiveness of a ratification after a rejection and the effect of a rescission on a prior ratification are treated similarly as "political questions," it would, in effect, mean that Congress would have control over ultimately assessing whether or not there is continued local consent. For example, if Congress could refuse to recognize a state's rescission, it would mean that Congress would supplant the expression of the people's representative with its own assessment of consent by holding that the prior expression of consent is still valid. Such a broad interpretation of congressional powers would destroy the balance created in article V and remove the state's power to create a barrier to encroachment by the national government. Therefore, while it might be conceded that the effectiveness of a ratification in light of a prior rejection is proper for resolution by a political arm of government, the question of the effect of a rescission in light of a prior ratification does not bring into play the same type of considerations, and thus, because the questions posed by a rescission are not proper for consideration by the political branch, they should be treated differently. . . .

From the Court's review of all the ramifications of the "political question" doctrine, there does not appear to be any compelling reasons for it to withhold its jurisdiction with regard to the questions presented. Furthermore, the Court is persuaded that both the questions of the efficacy of a rescission and the proper procedure for establishing a time period for ratification are the type of questions that must be interpreted with the kind of consistency that is characteristic of judicial rather than political decision making. Whatever the outcome of these questions as they relate to the powers vested by article V, they must be interpreted consistently for each amendment that may be proposed. The Court will now turn to a consideration of how these questions should be resolved.

## D. RESCISSION

In addressing the question of whether or not a rescission of a prior ratification is a proper exercise of the state's authority under article V to act on proposed amendments, it must be noted that whatever authority the states have is derived solely from the Constitution itself. The critical portion of article V that the Court must examine provides that an amendment becomes part of the Constitution "when ratified by the Legislatures of three fourths of the several States, or by Conventions. . . ." With reference to the phrase "when ratified," commentators and courts have explored a variety of interpretations to what can best be termed "subsequent acts," i.e., the subsequent act of ratifying after a rejection or rescinding after a ratification. Three separate approaches have been postulated which are important to review in this Court's consideration of the question of the state's power to rescind.

The first approach to be considered contends that whatever action is initially taken by the state, whether rejection or ratification, exhausts the state's power under article V making any subsequent act to reverse the prior action a nullity. This approach was argued in *Wise v. Chandler* (1937) before the highest state court of Kentucky and was defended on the grounds that the power of a state legislature to ratify cannot be any greater than its alternative, the state convention. . . .

The second approach postulated would condone only the act of ratification, and the negative expressions of rejection or rescission would be treated as a nullity. This approach was relied upon by the State Supreme Court of Kansas in adjudicating the issues in *Coleman v. Miller* (1937). This approach is premised on a literal reading of article V which speaks only of ratification. The argument follows that because the article does not confer upon the states the specific power to reject or rescind, but only to ratify, any of these negative acts cannot be recognized. Advocates of this position argue that greater efficiency would be given to the amendment process and lead to less confusion in that only positive acts would be counted towards final ratification. The United States Supreme Court had an opportunity to consider this approach when it reviewed the decision of the Kansas court. From the Supreme Court's opinion in the *Coleman* matter it appears that this approach found little approval. In the "Opinion of the Court" Justice Hughes wrote that they found "no reason for disturbing the decision of the Supreme Court of Kansas . . . its judgment is affirmed *but upon the grounds stated in this opinion." Coleman* (emphasis added). Thus they rejected the approach of the Kansas court and chose to base their decision on other criteria.

A third approach which has received support is that both the subsequent acts of ratification after a rejection and rescission after ratification should be recognized. Of course, one clear limitation is evident which is that any subsequent rescission after a prior ratification could not come after three-fourths of the states had ratified, for at that point the amendment automatically becomes part of the Constitution and a state cannot withdraw its consent thereafter. This approach is grounded on the argument that it is illogical to impute more finality to ratification than to rejection, especially since the act of ratification itself has no binding effect until concurred in by the requisite three-fourths majority. Furthermore, this view is justified on the grounds that not allowing a withdrawal of approval might make an overly cautious legislature hesitant to act, or bind an overly zealous legislature to a position which upon mature reflection it does not support. . . .

Considering that an amendment cannot become part of the Constitution until a proper consensus of the people has been reached and it is the exclusive role of the states to determine what the local sentiment is, it logically follows that the subsequent act of rescission would promote the democratic ideal by giving a truer picture of the people's will as of the time three-fourths of the states have acted in affirming the amendment. To allow a situation where either the first act of a state is irrevocable or where a rejection can be changed by a ratification, but not permit rescission, would permit an amendment to be ratified by a technicality — where clearly one is not intended — and not because there is really a considered consensus supporting the amendment which is the avowed purpose of the amendment procedure. Furthermore, an irrevocable ratification prior to the time that three-fourths have acted would completely disassociate the democratic notion of a considered consensus from the ratification procedure and create the very real possibility that an amendment could become part of the Constitution when the people have not been unified in their consent. . . .

It seems clear from the statements of the founding fathers and from most courts in considering the amendment process that a ratification is linked to that great wellspring of legitimate constitutional power — the will of the people. The founding fathers were careful to make sure the Constitution was ratified by the consent of the people, and it follows that any amendment must again draw from that wellspring by securing a contemporaneous consensus before it can become a part of that original document. The states are the entity embodied with the power to speak for the people during the period in which the amendment is pending. To make a state's ratification binding with no right to rescind would give ratification a technical significance which would be clearly inappropriate considering that the Constitution through article V gives technical significance to a state's ratification at only one time — when three-fourths of the states have acted to ratify. Until the technical three-fourths has been reached, a rescission of a prior ratification is clearly a proper exercise of a state's power granted by the article V phrase "when ratified" especially when that act would give a truer picture of local sentiment regarding the proposed amendment.

Recognizing the validity of a state's power to rescind its prior ratification, the defendant challenges Idaho's rescission resolution arguing that it is procedurally faulty. Defendant maintains that in passing the House Concurrent Resolution 10, Idaho violated its own rules by adopting the resolution by less than the two-thirds majority used to ratify. Without ellucidating [sic] on the defendant's contentions, the Court would indicate that under the holding of *Dyer v. Blair,* the "State legislatures . . . have the power and the discretion to determine for themselves how they should discharge the responsibilities committed to them by the federal government. . . . Moreover . . . there is no federal objection to the state legislatures' independent determination of their own voting requirements." Thus, the states have complete discretion over the procedural requirements regarding the requisite majorities to act under its article V powers. This would be true whether the state is exercising its affirmative power of ratification or the negative function of rescission. . . . Therefore, at this juncture it is not proper for the Court to review the procedure of the rescission solution since proper certification has been made by the state to the national government.

## E. EXTENSION

The question of whether it is a proper exercise of congressional authority under article V to alter a previously proposed time limitation for ratification, and if so by what majority, presents for the Court a question of constitutional interpretation of congressional authority, and an inquiry into the procedural aspects of exercising that power. Thus, the Court's inquiry is two-fold: First, does Congress under its power to "propose" the "Mode of Ratification" have the power to change its proposal once it has been made and sent to the states; second, if the initial proposal can be subsequently changed, may Congress act by less than a two-thirds majority. One related question that has been raised that should be dealt with at this time is whether or not a state's ratification resolution specifically acknowledging the ratification period set by Congress is impaired if the original time period is extended or whether it is a "conditional" ratification arguably prohibited by the amendment process.

To begin with, the actions of Congress in relation to a proposed amendment must be properly characterized in order to approach the questions presented. First, it must be recognized that Congress' power to participate in the amendment process stems solely from article V. . . . Thus Congress, outside of the authority granted by article V, has no power to act with regard to an amendment, i.e., it does not retain any of its traditional authority vested in it by article I. The power of Congress to set a time period in which ratification must be completed is derived from their function of setting the mode of ratification. *See Dillon v. Gloss* (1921). The defendant in this action attempts to create a substance/procedure dycotomy [*sic*] by contending that since the time restriction in this instance is part of the proposing resolution it is proper for reconsideration where if the time period were part of the amendment itself it would not be. The argument follows that a change of a substantive aspect of an amendment is clearly improper once it has been submitted to the states, but a change in the proposing resolution, on the other hand, does not change the essential nature of the amendment and thus is a matter of detail which Congress can change at will. The Supreme Court in *Dillon v. Gloss* had an opportunity to address this substance/procedure dycotomy [*sic*] when the eighteenth amendment was challenged on the grounds that the seven-year ratification period called for in Section 3 of that amendment was unconstitutional. While the *Dillon* court indicated that "[a]n examination of article V discloses that it is intended to invest Congress with a wide range of power in proposing amendments," the court did not recognize the setting of the time limitation as being a function of Congress' power to propose amendments but instead indicated that

> [w]hether a definite period for ratification should be fixed so that all may know what it is and speculation on what is a reasonable time may be avoided, is, in our opinion, a matter of detail which Congress may determine as an *incident of its power to designate the mode of ratification.* (emphasis added)

The court did not recognize a substance/procedure dycotomy [*sic*] and thus any authority to limit the time period for consideration must flow from the Congress' power to set the mode of ratification. Accordingly, the Court's attention is drawn to a consideration of Congress' power to set and change the time period for ratification under its power to set the mode of ratification.

The United States Supreme Court in *United States v. Sprague* (1931) recognized that Congress has absolute discretion within its power to propose the mode of ratification to establish which of the two local entities will act as the spokesman for the people. The Supreme Court in the *Dillon* and *Coleman* cases found that as a "subsidiary matter of detail" to this congressional prerogative, Congress must also determine whether or not the local expressions of consent are "sufficiently contemporaneous in that number of States to reflect the will of the people in all sections at relatively the same period. . . ." The court in *Dillon* further clarified the scope of

Congress' power by indicating that while Congress is not compelled to make a determination of a reasonable time period in advance of the actions of the requisite number of states, it is not precluded from doing so. The *Dillon* court held that Congress may fix a reasonable time in advance "so that all may know what it is and speculation ... be avoided.".... Thus the inference that can be drawn from *Dillon* and *Coleman* is that within Congress' role of determining a reasonably contemporaneous consensus, or in other words, determining whether the socio/political economic forces giving rise to the amendment remain alive and unchanged during the period in which the states act in giving their assent to the proposal, Congress may exercise its function in one of two ways: first, it can leave the question of a reasonable time open until the requisite number of states have acted and thus continually monitor the viability of the amendment; second, where it appears to Congress that the socio/political, economic factors giving rise to the amendment are such that they are unlikely to change for an indefinite period of time, and rather than have the proposed amendment pending perpetually, Congress can set an arbitrary yet reasonable time period in order to establish a termination point for consideration and thus promote prompt action on the amendment by the states.

It, therefore, appears compelling that in order to fulfill the purposes for fixing a time limitation for ratification as outlined in *Dillon* — "so all may know and speculation ... be avoided" — the congressional determination of a reasonable period once made and proposed to the states cannot be altered. If Congress determines that a particular amendment requires ongoing assessment as to its viability or monitoring of the time period, it can do so, not by defeating the certainty implied by the *Dillon* case, but by not setting a time period at the outset and reserving the question until three-fourths of the states have acted.

The Court's conclusion that Congress cannot change the ratification period once it is set also finds support from the form in which it is presented to the states. While the setting of a time period for ratification has been described as a "subsidiary matter of detail," pursuant to Congress' power to propose the mode of ratification, if the Congress chooses to fix a time period by making it part of its proposal to the states, that determination of a time period becomes an integral part of the proposed mode of ratification. Once the proposal has been formulated and sent to the states, the time period could not be changed any more than the entity designated to ratify could be changed from the state legislature to a state convention or vice versa. Once the proposal is made, Congress is not at liberty to change it.

In any event, while the general power of Congress to change its prior proposal may be argued, it is more than clear that in this instance Congress' promulgation of the extension resolution was in violation of the constitutional requirement that Congress act by two-thirds of both Houses when exercising its article V powers....

One final observation. Reviewing several of the most recent resolutions proposing amendments to the Constitution and referring particularly to the resolution proposing the Equal Rights Amendment, the mode of ratification has been proposed by the approval of two-thirds of both Houses of Congress, thus indicating by general practice that this is the appropriate measure of approval.

Therefore, the Court is persuaded that the congressional act of extending the time period for ratification was an improper exercise of Congress' authority under article V. While Congress is not required to set a time period in advance of the requisite number of states acting to ratify, if it chooses to do so to remove uncertainty regarding the question, it cannot thereafter remove that certainty by changing the time period. In addition, since it is clear that Congress must act by a two-thirds concurrence of both Houses when acting pursuant to its authority under article V, and because the extension resolution was enacted by only a simple majority, the extension resolution is an unconstitutional exercise of congressional authority under article V. . . .

## [Summary]

In summary, the Idaho plaintiffs have standing to bring this action. The matter is ripe for determination and the Court has jurisdiction and properly should determine the issues presented.

The clear purpose of article V of the United States Constitution is to provide that an amendment properly proposed by Congress should become effective when three-fourths of the states, at the same time and within a contemporaneous period, approve the amendment by ratification through their state legislatures.

To allow an amendment to become effective at any time without the contemporaneous approval of three-fourths of the states would be a clear violation of article V of the Constitution. It follows, therefore, that a rescission of a prior ratification must be recognized if it occurs prior to unrescinded ratification by three-fourths of the states. Congress has no power to determine the validity or invalidity of a properly certified ratification or rescission.

Congress, when acting as an amending body under article V, may, by two-thirds vote of both Houses, propose an amendment and the mode of ratification. Congress has no power to propose either an amendment or a mode of ratification except by a two-thirds vote of both Houses.

As part of the mode of ratification, Congress may by a two-thirds vote of both Houses set a reasonable time limit for the states to act in order for the ratification to be effective. When this time is set, it is binding on Congress and the states and it cannot be changed by Congress thereafter.

Accordingly, the Court declares that Idaho's rescission of its ratification of the twenty-seventh amendment effectively nullified its prior ratification and Idaho may not be counted as a ratifying state. The same is true for any other state which has properly certified its action of rescission to the Administrator of the General Services [Administration].

The Court further declares that the majority action of Congress in attempting to extend the period for ratification of the twenty-seventh amendment is void and of no effect.

In view of the Court's declarations, it appears that the injunctive relief sought by plaintiffs is unnecessary and the same is denied.

DATED this 23rd day of December, 1981.

MARION J. CALLISTER
UNITED STATES DISTRICT COURT

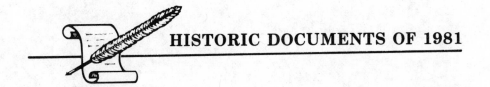

# CUMULATIVE INDEX, 1977-81

# CUMULATIVE INDEX, 1977-81

## A

# D

## F

# H

# U

# X, Y, Z